Who's Who

in

Verdi

Jonathan Lewsey

Ashgate

Aldershot • Burlington USA • Singapore • Sydney

Published by
Ashgate Publishing Limited
Gower House
Croft Road
Aldershot
Hants GU11 3HR
England

Ashgate Publishing Company
131 Main Street
Burlington, VT 05401-5600 USA

Ashgate website: http://www.ashgate.com

British Library Cataloguing-in-Publication Data

Lewsey, Jonathan
  Who's who in Verdi
  1. Verdi, Giuseppe, 1813–1901 – Criticism and interpretation
  2. Operas – Librettos
  I. Title
  782.1'092

Library of Congress Cataloging-in-Publication Data

Lewsey, Jonathan.
  Who's who in Verdi / Jonathan Lewsey.
    p. cm.
  Includes bibliographical references and discography.
    1. Verdi, Giuseppe, 1813–1901. Operas. 2. Operas – Stories, plots, etc. 3. Operas – Characters. I. Title.

ML410.V4 L38 2001
782.1'0269'092–dc21

00-061801

ISBN 1 85928 440 X (cased)
ISBN 1 85928 441 8 (paperback)

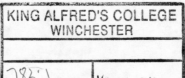
Printed on acid-free paper

Typeset in Sabon by J.L. & G.A. Wheatley Design, Aldershot, Hants
Printed and bound in Great Britain by MPG Books Ltd, Bodmin, Cornwall

Contents

Contents

Preface

This book is more a tribute to Verdi's librettists than to Verdi himself, for it concentrates exclusively on the dramatic content of the operas, making virtually no reference to the music. This is entirely intentional. There are ample books available which give comprehensive musical exegesis, notably those of Charles Osborne and Julian Budden. Both authors have published exemplary studies of Verdi's operas with copious reference to, and examples from, the music and with appropriate biographical information. If you turn to the *New Grove Dictionary of Opera* you will find that the plot summaries are peppered with allusions to musical structure and harmonic nuance. This is admirable if you are musically literate and are already familiar with the plot outlines but makes about as much sense to the uninitiated as Egyptian hieroglyphics.

In a letter which Verdi wrote to his librettist, Francesco Piave, the composer makes clear his position with regard to the libretti he set. Verdi was writing to defend his determination that the character of Triboletto (to become Rigoletto) should, against the censor's wishes, remain a hunchback in his opera: 'It was precisely because of these original and characteristic traits that I chose the subject, and if they are cut out I shall not be able to write the music. If I am told that my music will do just as well for this drama as for the other, I must answer that I do not understand such reasoning. *I tell you frankly that my music, whether good or bad, is never fortuitous* [my italics], and that I always try to give it a distinct character'.

In other words it is the precise nature of the scenario that stimulates Verdi to write the music. Change that scenario in any particular and the music will change accordingly. For some this may sound too obvious to be even worth stating. But it is my experience that it cannot be stated often enough. The opera composer is a very different sort of animal from the instrumental composer. Verdi, like Wagner, devoted himself almost exclusively to the medium of opera. As with Wagner it is clear that it was Verdi's unique sensibility as a dramatist that not only contributed to but actually constituted his musical genius. The words of the libretti Verdi set cannot therefore be dismissed as merely an irritating adjunct to the glories of the music he composed for they, and the situations they invoke, are not just an integral part of the musical design, but entirely responsible for it. If we truly want to understand the music we must understand the drama behind the music; not just at a superficial level – scanning through the details of the plot five minutes before the curtain rises in the theatre – but through understanding precisely what motivates each character at any given moment.

The facts of a plot are easily laid down. A character's motivation is not always so easy to pin down, particularly if the original source has been severely truncated in order to satisfy the exigencies of the operatic stage. Nevertheless I early determined to take each libretto on its individual merits and not to be tempted into lengthy digressions on where libretto and source converge or diverge. Excellent source books already abound. When it comes to psychological motivation there is always an abundance of possible interpretations. The conclusions that I come to about individual characters are unashamedly subjective, and if they do no more than stimulate thought and debate – or even violent dissent – I shall rest content.

Many of Verdi's libretti have been condemned as having no literary merit, of being banal, inept even. Yet the fact remains that they elicited a wealth of great music from the composer. The libretto which has traditionally come in for the most criticism is that of *Il Trovatore*. And yet this is the work which the Italian conductor, Gianandrea Gavazzeni, referred to as 'the Italian St Matthew Passion'. It is undeniably a great opera. How we judge a work of art depends on the criteria we employ when apprehending it. Often critics and commentators will, wittingly or not, judge a libretto by the light of the classical unities, which remain as instinctive in dramatic art as does the golden mean in figurative painting. Clearly by these lights the vast majority of operatic libretti will fall short in the same way as the novels of Dostoevsky will fall short if expected to conform to the elegant coherence of a novel by Jane Austen. But Dostoevsky's aims were a whole universe away from those of Jane Austen.

A librettist's aims are simple: to stimulate a composer's inspiration. He must, by definition, play second fiddle. If a librettist presents a composer with a polished work of art there is going to be nothing that the composer may add. Wagner and Mussorgsky solved the problem by writing their own libretti (as has Sir Michael Tippett in more recent times). There are many who might argue that it would have been better if they hadn't, or at least that someone better qualified should have been called in to prune away the unessentials. But the words that they wrote are the words that stimulated their genius. Verdi may not have written his own libretti but he took an entirely proactive stance towards their creation, as can be seen from even a cursory glimpse at his correspondence with his librettists. He knew what he wanted and he usually got it.

The libretti of Solera are considered to be inferior to those of Piave, Cammarano etc. and yet they supplied Verdi with broad and trenchant themes with a high moral content that were ideally suited to Verdi's specific genius. In this respect I cannot do better than quote Andrew Porter in an essay included in the libretto accompanying the Philips recording of *I Lombardi*:

> 'And yet . . . our view of the theatre, and of the diverse techniques by which theatrical experiences may be constructed, has changed so much that today – after the teachings of Artaud, of Brecht, of Piscator – (Solera's) libretto of *I Lombardi* is less likely to be despised. . . . *I Lombardi* could be fitted without strain into the programme of Artaud's First Manifesto, as "a romantic melodrama in which the improbability will become an active and concrete element of poetry" '.

The librettist must necessarily paint with a very broad stroke, otherwise the composer has no room for manoeuvre. Libretti which do not allow such leeway –

for example those that Hugo van Hofmansthal wrote for Richard Strauss – create almost insuperable problems for their composers. Opera is not discursive. It is by its nature didactic. The purpose of a book such as this is to try and uncover the subtext which the librettist is compelled by necessity to keep to a minimum. But if studied carefully enough the subtext will be found. It is my contention that it is from this very subtext, rather than from the didactic word itself, that the composer's true motivation and inspiration will be found.

It is a truism of contemporary post-Stanislavsky acting that a character must have an existence before and after the action of the drama. Without an awareness of that existence the actor cannot hope to give a veristic portrayal of that character. It used to be the case until very recently that opera was chiefly about spectacle and great singing. This is no longer the case. Nowadays directors are attempting to bring a degree of naturalism hitherto unthought-of to opera. Increasingly successful directors of opera are coming from the straight theatre. Sometimes they are almost musically illiterate (which must surely be a cause of frustration to the conductors with whom they collaborate); but above all the likes of Patrice Chereau, Peter Hall and Elisha Moshinsky will understand the dynamics of drama. The aim of this book, which complements my **Who's Who and What's What in Wagner**, is to assist not just audiences but also directors and singers in approaching opera in the only way which would seem to make sense – as music *drama*.

Introduction
Colin Wilson

In 'Opera Nights', Ernest Newman commented: 'Never what one could call the sunniest of men, Verdi became decidedly gloomy in his last years. As he looked back on his life, he said in 1895, he could see little more than an immense number of notes, and unfortunately he had his doubts whether the notes were worth very much'.

The gloom was not, of course, due entirely to doubts about his music. It was a matter of temperament. The problem was that he had always been a workaholic, who could never persuade himself that it was time to relax. At the age of 28, after one resounding failure, he had decided to give up composing and return to teaching music. And even at that age, he had been working hard for eighteen years, since his appointment as organist in his village church at the age of 10. This was why Verdi lacked the *dolce far niente* of the Italian temperament. Like most men of genius, he was entirely without the capacity for sweet idleness.

The truth is that, when we consider his life objectively, Verdi had little to complain about. His career was certainly less beset with obstacles than that of Wagner, who was born in the same year, 1813. Verdi became famous at the age of 29 with *Nabucco*, and never looked back. And while it is true that Wagner also achieved his first success at the age of 29 with *Rienzi*, he spent most of the next twenty years looking back, and at the age of 40 was forced to flee abroad to avoid imprisonment for debt.

Yet it is still possible to understand why the ageing Verdi doubted the value of his own music. Wagner's success was based on his determination, and his determination was based upon his certainty that he was Europe's musical saviour. One of Bernard Shaw's earliest books was called 'The Perfect Wagnerite', and sprang out of his conviction that Wagner was an important philosopher and social thinker as well as a great composer. Shaw could never have written a book called 'The Perfect Verdi-ite', because in that sense, Verdi had 'nothing to say'. Or rather, what Verdi 'had to say' is to be found in his music, and nowhere else. The tremendous force of Verdi's music sprang out of the strength of his personality. Francis Toye on Puccini has commented that Puccini was not a great composer because he was not a great man. Whether that is true or not, it is certainly true that Verdi was a great composer because he *was* a great man. The plots of some of the operas may be absurd; but the music in which he set them often has the force of a whirlwind. Listening to *Rigoletto* or *Trovatore* or *Otello*, you could believe that the man who created them was a magician who could, like Prospero, conjure up tempests.

I was first subjected to this force in my mid-teens, when I attended a performance of *Otello* in my home town. The place was called the Little Theatre, and the orchestra pit was so small that it could scarcely contain the players. Moreover, I was a Wagnerite; I loved the *Flying Dutchman* overture and the prelude to Act 3 of *Lohengrin* and the *Liebestod* from *Tristan und Isolde* and the 'Ride of the Valkyrie'. But with that storm at the beginning of *Otello* I was completely carried away, and listened to the rest of the opera in a state of awe and delight. As Dr Johnson said of William Law, Verdi quite 'overmastered me'.

It was not until my first book *The Outsider* came out (when I was 24) that I could finally afford a gramophone and long-playing records. (The LP had only been invented a few years earlier.) Among the first opera records I ever bought were *Otello* (with Ramon Vinay as the Moor), *Il Trovatore* with Del Monaco, and *La Traviata* with Tebaldi. Then I discovered *Aida* with Callas. I had never heard this opera before (except the march from Act 1), and I found it as overwhelming as *Tristan*.

At this time, the Italian record company Cetra was issuing an enormous number of operas taken from live performances, often with bangs, thumps and coughs, and poor quality recording; nevertheless, I bought them indiscriminately – 'Cav' and 'Pag' and Montemezzi and Zandonai – and, of course, all the Verdi I could find, including rarely performed works like *Luisa Miller* and *Un Giorno di Regno*, the fiasco that led Verdi to consider abandoning opera. Some of these, like *La Battaglia di Legnano* and *I Due Foscari*, I have played only once. But there they all are, still sitting on my Verdi shelf, next to the dog's basket.

When Jonathan Lewsey asked me to write this Introduction, I admitted to him that my enthusiasm for opera had diminished over the years. There was a time when – as a musical editor once told me – I had one of the largest opera collections in England. I bought new opera sets in the hope that one day I would have time to play them (and in many cases have not succeeded). I loved nothing so much as spending evenings with music-loving guests, comparing ancient recordings of Caruso and Tamagno and Edouard de Reszke with the latest stereo versions of the same arias or ensembles. (The full story of my love affair with opera is told in my book on music, *Brandy of the Damned*.)

Alas, I failed to realize that life is simply not long enough to play hundreds of new records (I estimate my collection at between twenty and thirty thousand) and read ten or so new books a week, as well as pursuing the career of a full-time writer. And since the advent of the compact disc, I have bought few new operas, and often failed to play even those.

But since I had agreed to write this Introduction, I crawled on all fours near the dog's basket and selected a few records that I had not played in years. These included a two-disc set entitled 'Verdi and Toscanini', consisting mainly of tracks taken from NBC broadcasts of the 1940s.

As soon as I put it on, I was swept away by the old magic. The first track, 'Va pensiero' from *Nabucco*, has never been a favourite of mine; it owed its immense popularity to its patriotic associations, the audience identifying themselves with the Hebrew slaves of the chorus, and the Babylonians with the Austrians. I find the tune somewhat sugary. But Toscanini conducts it with a force and freshness that is irresistible. It was as if I was hearing it for the first time. The same was true of the Act 3 trio from *I Lombardi*, the quartet from *Rigoletto*, and of the overtures from *I Vespri Siciliani*, *La Forza del Destino* and *Luisa Miller*. The only tracks about which I had my doubts were the 'Balabili' dances from Act 3 of *Otello*, which were written for the Paris production and are completely undistinguished, and a curious work called 'Hymn of the Nations', composed in 1862 for the International Exhibition in Paris, which sounds like an electrifying piece of Verdi grand opera which has somehow been inserted into the wrong composition. The finale of Toscanini's version, with the Internationale and Star Spangled Banner, makes the bathos complete.

And this, of course, is the essential problem. Verdi could sustain an absurd plot with magnificent music, but in a patriotic hymn it sounds all wrong. You feel that, in writing 'The Hymn of the Nations', he displays a puzzling lack of judgement, and that this lack of judgement springs from the fact that, unlike Beethoven or Wagner, he felt he had nothing in particular to say, and was merely fulfilling a commission and trying to please the public. Beethoven once declared that his music was an 'entrance into the higher worlds of knowledge'. Verdi would have felt absurd making any such claim; he regarded himself as simply a workmanlike composer, which explains why, at the end of his life, he could feel that he had simply produced an enormous number of notes. He was wrong, of course, but in trying to explain why he was wrong, we are forced to conclude that Verdi was, like Mozart, an example of pure musical genius, whose greatness was so much a part of himself that he was totally unselfconscious about it. How otherwise could the son of a village innkeeper, with no musical background, soar so effortlessly to the level of musical greatness displayed in *Nabucco* and *Ernani*? It is true that this greatness is mixed with crudities and vulgarities; but then, as Francis Toye comments, these vulgarities are 'a by-product of the vitality and passion without which there can be no great art'. It is because Verdi had more vitality than Donizetti or Bellini, more even than Rossini, that his music makes such an impact.

Looking at Verdi's early career, one has to conclude that he was born with some freak musical gene. He was not, like Mozart or Bach or Scarlatti, an offspring of a musical family. He simply had that deep, instinctive love for music that almost seems to suggest reincarnation. Toye describes how, as a child, he used to stand in ecstasy as he listened to an old wandering violinist who played to his father's customers. At the age of seven, when serving the priest at mass, he heard for the first time the sound of the organ, and was so overwhelmed that the priest had to ask him three times for water, and finally gave him a push that sent him down the steps.

It was after this that his father bought him an old spinet that had to be repaired by a local workman. He kept it until the end of his life. The child began to take lessons from the local organist of Le Roncole. And in three years, by the age of 10, Verdi replaced him. The salary, less than two pounds a year, was supplemented by fees for weddings and funerals. Soon after he had become organist, his father arranged for him to go to study in the nearby town of Busseto – not music, but to read and write. Verdi stayed with a poor cobbler, and walked on Sundays and feastdays to Roncole, three miles away, to play the organ.

Soon he was virtually adopted by an old friend of his father, Antonio Barezzi, a prosperous grocer of Busetto. Barezzi loved music, and was the president of the local Philharmonic Society. A murder close to the house of the cobbler made Barezzi decide to take the boy into his own home. Verdi lost no time in falling in love with Barezzi's pretty daughter Margherita. He played duets with her, and studied music and Latin, and copied parts for the Philharmonic Society, and read books from the public library, and continued to walk once or twice a week to Roncole, and composed overtures and marches and a Te Deum – it is hard to imagine how he found time to fall in love. He later told a friend 'My youth was hard'.

At the age of 18, Verdi received a form of scholarship that enabled him to move to Milan. Then came a serious setback. The local Conservatory turned him down, partly on the grounds that he was too old. But at that point, Verdi had a remarkable piece of luck. The local Philharmonic Society was rehearsing Haydn's 'Creation', and at the request of his music teacher, Verdi was allowed to attend the rehearsals. Nobody even glanced at the skinny youth, who looked and dressed like a peasant. But one day, through some misunderstanding, all three regular conductors failed to show up, and as impatience grew, the choirmaster asked Verdi if he would play the piano.

Verdi later described how he noticed little ironic smiles from the well-dressed ladies and gentlemen as he sat down. But it was soon clear that Verdi was not only a technically brilliant pianist, but had a deep feeling for the music. He was so carried away that he began to conduct with one hand while he played with the other. At the end, he found himself surrounded by admirers, including two Counts. And soon Verdi was asked to take all the rehearsals. The performance of the 'Creation' was such a success that it had to be repeated in the presence of the Archduke and Archduchess.

Soon after, Count Renato Borromeo asked Verdi to compose a cantata for the marriage of one of his family. This was a success, and the choirmaster suggested that Verdi should write an opera. He handed him the libretto of *Oberto, Conte di Bonifacio*, written by a local dramatist. It was an absurd piece of work, but, like so many of Verdi's later operas, contained the seeds of the kind of drama that could thrill Italian audiences. Count Oberto's daughter Leonora has been seduced by the philandering Riccardo, who has then deserted her to become engaged to the lovely Cunizia. Count Oberto was so upset at Leonora's loss of virginity that he cast her off.

This kind of tangled situation could be guaranteed to keep an audience on the edge of their seats. By one of those amazing coincidences that are the lifeblood of Grand Opera, Count Oberto and his dishonoured daughter both turn up in the town where the villain is about to become betrothed. Father and daughter declare a truce in order to inform Cunizia that her lover is a scoundrel. Cunizia says that in that case, she will renounce Riccardo, provided he will marry Leonora, who is still in love with him. But just as it looks as if they are working out a sensible solution, which would ruin the opera, Oberto and Riccardo fight a duel, and Oberto is killed. In an agony of remorse, Riccardo decides to leave Italy. And Leonora, who has lost her lover and her father, resolves to die.

Verdi did not turn *Oberto* into a masterpiece (although many later operas demonstrate that you can make a silk purse out of a sow's ear), but it has the sheer vitality that characterizes all his best music. With its enormous energy, it deserved the modest success it achieved. Its young composer obviously knew how to express intense emotions in soaring melodic lines.

But much was to happen before *Oberto* reached the stage. Verdi's old music teacher, Ferdinando Provesi, died in Busseto, and there was talk of giving the organist's post to Verdi. But Verdi was much disliked by the ecclesiastical authorities, and they chose their own candidate, a man called Ferrari. The result was a dispute that divided the town. Verdi was less concerned than he might have been because Barezzi had given his blessing to marriage with Margherita.

They married when Verdi was 23 and Margherita 18 (although another biographer states that he was only five months her senior). A daughter, Virginia, was born in the following year, but died a year and a half later. By that time, the Verdis also had a son, Icilio, and in February 1839, they decided to move to Milan.

Life there was difficult, and they lived in relative poverty. Verdi was considering a retreat back to Busseto when Massini, the man who had commissioned *Oberto*, persuaded La Scala to accept it. The publisher Ricordi bought the rights – thus laying the basis of his own fortune by establishing a lifelong relationship with Verdi – and the opera was finally presented in November 1839, when Verdi had just turned 26. It failed to make him famous, but was enough of a success to establish his name as a composer of promise. The impresario Merelli, who had produced it, immediately offered Verdi a contract for three more operas.

Then everything went wrong. Merelli wanted Verdi to write a comic opera – *Un Giorno di Regno* (King for a Day) – and he complied, but with deep reluctance. He was not in a comic mood; his son had died just before the first performance of *Oberto*, and Verdi was soon struck down by angina, probably due to stress. Then Margherita became ill, and in June 1840 she died of encephalitis. Verdi felt his life had come to an end, yet was obliged to go on working on his detested comic opera.

This was presented in September 1840, and was predictably a failure. Francis Toye calls it a 'hodge-podge'. And Verdi himself was so shattered that he persuaded Merelli to tear up his contract, and decided to return to teaching music.

And at this point, in a manner that might have been devised by a Hollywood script writer, Verdi's fortunes took a turn for the better. Walking through a glass arcade one evening a few months later, he bumped into Merelli, who told him that the composer Nicolai had turned down the libretto of an opera about Nebuchadnezzar. They strolled into La Scala, and Merelli persuaded Verdi to take the libretto home with him. Back at his lodgings, Verdi threw it on the table, and it fell open at a page showing *Va Pensiero*, the chorus of Hebrew slaves. In a Hollywood film he would promptly have sat down at the piano and composed it, but, this being real life, he merely turned back to the beginning of the libretto and read it straight through. And finally, at Merelli's insistence, he began to write *Nabucco*. It came slowly and painfully at first, then began to flow.

Verdi knew his Bible, and this was why *Nabucco* appealed to him. It demanded the kind of seriousness that he was ready to bring to it. And he must certainly have been aware that the Italian public would recognize the underlying patriotic message. He wrote fast, and there is evidence that he knew it was going to be a success. When he delivered it to Merelli, months ahead of time, and demanded that it should be produced in the following season, the impresario said that was impossible; he already had three new operas to launch. Verdi lost his temper and wrote Merelli an angry letter – then instantly regretted it, convinced that he had ruined his career. But Merelli only sent for him, gave him a lecture, and agreed to produce *Nabucco* with costumes out of stock.

And so, on March 22, 1842, the 29-year old Verdi became famous. His reception could not have been more rapturous if he had been a general who had driven the Austrians out of Italy. *Va Pensiero* had to be repeated. Within days, everyone was humming it. Reviews were uniformly favourable. And although Verdi himself chose to grumble about his success, recalling bitterly the catcalls after *Un Giorno di Regno*, he had no doubt that his life had changed permanently. He was showered with invitations, many of which he accepted. (In later life, he refused all invitations, except from old friends.) Toye says that top hats, ties and sauces were named after him.

Now all he had to do was produce a worthy successor. When he was presented with another libretto by Solero, who had written *Nabucco*, the prospects looked remote. As the reader can see by turning to Jonathan Lewsey's account on pages 281–8, *I Lombardi* deserves a high place as one of the most preposterous plots in all grand opera, with a virtuous brother who fails to recognize his wicked brother when they meet, and a Moslem hero who is converted to Christianity on his deathbed and becomes an angel. But all this is unimportant compared to the power of the music. The audience certainly felt so on that opening night.

Solero had once again shrewdly chosen a subject that could be interpreted as a political protest against the Austrians: the crusaders (Italians, of course) winning back Jerusalem. The chief of police ensured its success by summoning the composer, the librettist and the impresario to his office to explain themselves – Verdi refused to go, which is just as well, since his temper would certainly have guaranteed the banning of the opera. As it was, Merelli described *I Lombardi* as a masterpiece, and asked the chief of police (an Italian) if he was prepared to suppress a great Italian opera. The plea worked, and permission was given.

As the rumour of the attempted suppression spread all over Milan, so the crowds gathered, until even by mid-afternoon they surrounded the theatre. The audience, realizing that they were witnessing another patriotic demonstration, called for frequent encores and cheered themselves hoarse.

Now, at last, the Italian public had no doubt it had found a worthy successor to Rossini, Bellini and Donizetti. Verdi's admirers wanted battle cries and marching tunes, and he was glad to oblige.

Incredibly, his next opera was an even greater success. Victor Hugo's *Hernani* had been the great dramatic triumph of 1830, when his Shakespearean conception of drama had won the day in opposition to French classicism. The hero, Hernani, is an outlaw who is determined to win Elvira from her aging guardian, Don Ruy Gomez, who intends to marry her himself. It is full of heroics, highflown sentiments and absurd vows – exactly the material for a Verdi opera. At the same time, Hugo's fame as a liberal was sure to provoke the censor. The first performance of *Ernani* in Venice was by no means as noisy a triumph as *Nabucco* and *I Lombardi*, but it soon carried Verdi's name all over Europe.

It is worth mentioning two typical stories about *Ernani*, which tell us a great deal about Verdi's character. Ernani's promise to commit suicide is represented by a horn call, and the director of La Fenice felt that a hunting horn was too coarse an instrument for his theatre. He and Verdi head-butted one another until Verdi's superior will prevailed, and La Fenice echoed to the sound of the horn.

Moreover, the prima donna was dissatisfied with the trio that ended the opera, and demanded instead an aria for herself. Verdi's librettist Piave hastened to comply, but Verdi was inflexible. The disaffected lady might have ruined his chances of success by performing badly, but fortunately, vanity or artistic conscience prevailed, and the opera triumphed. Verdi and his leading lady virtually ceased to speak to one another. But when she sang the part again at Bologna, she had conceded that Verdi was right, and the two were reconciled.

This iron will can be seen throughout Verdi's career. It meant that he was never spoiled by success, and never deeply discouraged by failure. He was indifferent even to the stupidity of music critics, such as London's two leading pundits, Chorley and Davison, who maintained for years that Verdi was incapable of writing a melody. It was a younger generation of critics, like Bernard Shaw and Ernest Newman, who were enraptured by his genius.

Verdi's strength of character also meant that he was not afraid of striking out in a new direction, as when he abandoned the sham-heroics of *Il Corsaro* and *La Battaglia di Legnano* for the gentler lyricism of *Luisa Miller* (based on a Schiller play), or in the 'intimate' *La Traviata*, which provoked laughter and hisses at its first performance, (although a year later, restaged in Venice, it became as popular as its two predecessors *Rigoletto* and *Il Trovatore*).

And so, as Vincent Sheean notes in 'Orpheus at Eighty', Verdi's career was a series of triumphs such as few composers have enjoyed. He outlived Wagner (whom he admired) by almost two decades, and in those final years wrote three works that many regard as his greatest: the Manzoni Requiem, *Otello* and *Falstaff*. In spite of Chorley and Davison, few people would dispute that he was the greatest melodist of the nineteenth century. Then why is it that a touch of their condescending attitude can still be found in England?

The first and most obvious reason is that, *pace* Francis Toye, so much of Verdi's early music *is* vulgar and noisy. Then there is the implausible and fantastic nature of some of the plots – the kind of thing that led Dr Johnson to describe opera as an absurd and irrational entertainment.

Above all, though, there is the curious fact that, in spite of his unsurpassed musical intelligence, Verdi seems to have devoted so little thought to what makes an operatic masterpiece. It seems to have been pure chance that, in his final years, he was presented with the two finest libretti (by Boito) that he ever set. Verdi simply lacked Wagner's recognition that a really great opera needs a unity of words and music – even though Salvator Cammarano, the librettist of *Luisa Miller*, said as much in a letter to Verdi: 'If I were not afraid to be branded a Utopian, I should be tempted to say that for an opera to obtain the maximum of perfection, the same mind should be responsible for both the text and the music.' This was obviously impossible for Verdi, since he was no poet or playwright, but it seems surprising that he should not have taken Cammarano's words to heart, and attempted to forge a far closer link between himself and his librettist, instead of accepting whatever was put in front of him.

Of course, Verdi often spent a great deal of time wrangling with his librettists and demanding changes; but he seldom penetrated to the essential weaknesses of the text. Provided there were opportunities for heroics, Verdi was content.

So it was fortunate that he was able to gain the services of Arigo Boito, himself a composer of distinction, in those final two operas. How this came about is interesting. In 1862, when he was only 20, Boito had written the words for Verdi's 'Hymn of the Nations', after meeting Verdi in Paris. But he then became a Wagnerite, and concluded that Verdi's type of opera was too old fashioned. Boito's own remarkable *Mefistofele* was a 'sensational failure' at La Scala in 1869; although the music is not Wagnerian in flavour, much of it is for chorus, and the Wagnerian influence is clear. (In its revised version it was a considerable success, and still holds the stage.)

But Boito had ears to hear, and when he heard *Aida* and the Manzoni Requiem, he knew this was great music, whether it obeyed the Wagnerian rules or not. He was completely converted. Verdi, knowing Boito's opinion of him, remained hostile when his publisher Ricordi raised Boito's name in connection with a possible libretto of *Otello*. At all events, the two men were brought together, and Verdi, recognizing his need for a good librettist, was courteous. He would have preferred 'King Lear', but when he saw Boito's libretto, instantly recognized its worth. And so 'the chocolate venture' (as Verdi called it, no doubt intending a racist comment on Otello's colour) went ahead, and produced the greatest masterpiece of Verdi's career. It seems the supreme irony that many critics described it as Wagnerian.

Posterity is certainly in Boito's debt for persuading Verdi – at 74 – even to consider writing another opera. Everyone, including Verdi himself, considered *Otello* his swan song, the perfect close to his incredible career. Nevertheless, he agreed to toy with *Falstaff* almost in a spirit of amateurism, giving no commitment that it would ever be finished. Verdi felt like scaling no more mountains. If his other operas were paintings, this was to be a water colour, a mere sketch, perhaps to be presented privately at his home, Sant'Agata. But a lifetime of mastery came to his aid, and enabled him to produce one of the few comic operas worthy to be mentioned in the same breath as 'The Marriage of Figaro'. I found Jonathan Lewsey's tribute, both to the opera and the man, one of the most perceptive pages in this book.

It should now be clear to the reader that I find something profoundly satisfying not only about Verdi's music, but about his career. The lives of many great composers – Mozart, Beethoven, Schubert, Berlioz, Wagner – are so much less satisfying than their music. Yeats once said:

> The intellect of man is forced to choose
> Perfection of the life or of the work.

Yet I have always felt that this should not be so. And the life of Verdi provides me with an excellent illustration of my own view.

Like his own Falstaff, he leaves behind a sense of well-being. And this springs from the fact that, melancholic or not, Verdi was not simply a successful composer, but a successful human being.

A

Abdallo (*Nabucco*). Devoted elderly retainer of the king of Babylon.

Even when his master suffers total eclipse and is reduced to insanity and ignominy, Abdallo remains faithful to his king. He is the retainer every king needs to bolster his sense of his own importance. Only through the likes of Abdallo can kings retain their thrones.

It is Abdallo who is there in **Nabucco**'s greatest hour of need. When his daughter's mortal peril brings the king back to his senses, and he clamours at the door of his prison to be released, it is Abdallo who is there to release him (Act 4 Scene 1). Abdallo has rallied an entourage of staunch supporters against the day when the king regains his sanity. For it never occurs to Abdallo that the king will *not* regain his sanity. Such an eventuality would be unthinkable, for Abdallo's entire *raison d'être* is bound up in the life of his king. Abdallo serves the king as the king should properly serve God. Abdallo does not question Nabucco's assumption of the godhead himself, for as far as he is concerned Nabucco *is* God. He recognizes no greater authority.

When Abdallo thinks Nabucco is dead his allegiance passes immediately to **Fenena** Act 2 Scene 2). Through long life he has learned the wisdom of opportunism. It is possible that Abdallo knows the truth about **Abigaille**'s origins. If anybody would know it would be Abdallo. Even if he doesn't he may recognize instinctively that it is Fenena who is her father's true successor. The joy of discovering his master to be still alive (Act 2 Scene 2) is quickly succeeded by dismay at the dramatic loss of Nabucco's sanity. Thereafter Abdallo remains utterly loyal to his master. While Abigaille treats her father with barely concealed contempt, Abdallo never ceases to treat him with the respect and deference due to his king.

It must be torture to leave Nabucco alone with Abigaille (Act 3 Scene 1). He will probably attempt to eavesdrop on the interview. He needs to know what transpires if he is to protect his master. Having released his master he is at first reluctant to allow Nabucco to go forth in case his 'sick mind may be affronted'. When he realizes that Nabucco's mind is restored to perfect sanity he is overjoyed and gladly returns the sword to the king and, together with the soldiers, celebrates the fact that: 'The traitors shall fall...like locusts to the ground!' and the sun shall 'shine upon Assyria once again!'

At the close of the opera Abdallo joins Nabucco in announcing his faith in the one God, great Jehovah. Pure apocryphal nonsense, of course: an ageing retainer like Abdallo would hardly be likely to change the habits of a lifetime and forsake the age-old tradition of his homeland. The only possible justification for the interpreter of the role can be that Abdallo, automatically and without quibble, will do exactly what is required of him by his master, even if that means leaping into the lions' den or, as in this case, adopting the Hebrew religion.

Abigaille (*Nabucco*). Ostensibly the daughter of **Nabucco**, but in reality the daughter of slaves.

Abigaille is one of the most compelling of all Verdi's heroines, albeit one of the most one-dimensional (her closest operatic relative is surely Elettra in Mozart's *Idomeneo*). Verdi never again achieved the mythic grandeur touched upon in *Nabucco*, where all the characters are possessed of singular, archetypal stature; none more so than the main protagonist and his adoptive daughter.

The turning point in Abigaille's life comes between Acts 1 and 2 when she learns that she is not, as she has always assumed, the elder legitimate daughter of Nabucco, but the daughter of slaves. This is a severe shock to Abigaille who is already suffering from the fact that her love for the Hebrew prince, **Ismaele**, is not returned, the latter being in love with her sister (her predicament parallels that of **di Luna** [*Il Trovatore*], **Pagano** [*I Lombardi*] and **Francesco** [*I Masnadieri*]). Abigaille has always been accustomed to receiving preferential treatment over her younger sister, **Fenena**, and has felt secure in the knowledge that one day she will inherit her father's kingdom. Deprived of even the security that knowledge confers, the paranoia at the root of her nature gains ascendancy. Now she sees her sole mission in life as being to prevent her father from divulging the truth about her origins, and to succeed to the throne regardless of her illegitimacy. A woman scorned in love is one thing, but a woman scorned in love, rejected by her father and deprived of her inheritance is a recipe for psychosis.

Yet Verdi ensures that we never lose sympathy for Abigaille's plight. There is genuine pathos and regret in her aria, *Anch'io dischiuso un giorno* (Act 2 Scene 1) where she remembers a time when she too once opened her heart to happiness and felt compassion for the suffering of others. She longs for a day when she might be able to 'return to that enchantment'. In the meantime, like Lady Macbeth, she makes a conscious decision to forestall within herself the 'milk of human kindness'. The fact that Fenena betrays her country by converting to Judaism and releasing the Hebrew slaves plays into Abigaille's hands, giving her the political justification she needs to warrant her personal vendetta. In the cabaletta to her aria, *Salgo già del trono aurato*' (Act 2 Scene 1), fired by the support of the priests and soothsayers, who have already spread the rumour that Nabucco has fallen in battle, she exults in the notion that one day 'Royal princessess will come hither to beg favours of the humble slave'.

When her father is struck down (Act 2 Conclusion), Abigaille has all the proof she needs that destiny has given her the Babylonian throne. She takes especial pleasure in gaining her father's signature to what is effectively Fenena's death warrant (Act 3 Scene 1). For Nabucco has suddenly become as much her enemy as surely as are the Hebrews – in her mind at any rate. Anything that comes between herself and her objective is to be despatched without remorse. Abigaille, by her own admission, has become as narcissistic as an infant. But it is the narcissism of self-hate. It gives her

no happiness. It is a matter of necessity, essential to the survival of her all too fragile ego. When her bid for ascendancy crumbles it is almost a relief to her. For this is the real cause of Abigaille's persona; the battle that rages within herself. It is in this respect that comparisons may be drawn with Elettra in Mozart's *Idomeneo*. Elettra, however, rages on to the end. Abigaille accedes to the imperatives of her instinctive humanity and relinquishes her insanity with the same determination that her father has demonstrated when escaping from the prison of *his* insanity (Abigaille and her 'father' clash so disastrously because they have so much in common. She is right in feeling herself truly to be Nabucco's heir).

When all her hopes of ascendancy have crumbled and she takes poison Abigaille tacitly acknowledges how far she has fallen. When, at the close of the opera, she pleads with her father on behalf of Fenena and Ismaele and then herself prays to the one God, Jehovah, for redemption she demonstrates the compassionate nature which she has so ruthlessly and disastrously attempted to excise within herself.

Acciano (*I Lombardi*). Tyrant of Antioch, father to **Oronte**.
Acciano appears in only one scene (Act 2 Scene 1) when he receives the ambassadors in the hall of his palace. When the curtain rises he is in the process of advising the ambassadors of the advance upon Antioch of the Crusaders. Acciano warns the ambassadors that, 'strong and cruel, they exult in rape and robbery; everywhere they leave a trail of havoc and ruin'. No doubt the Christians would refer in exactly the same way to the Arabs. It is refreshing in an opera to have the opportunity, if only briefly, of seeing matters from an alternative perspective. The ambassadors swear to see the 'infidels' overthrown and the scene ends.

Acciano is not seen again, for shortly after his palace is invaded by the Crusaders and he is one of the first to be slain. Whether or not he realizes in his death throes that his son has survived we cannot know since the affray happens offstage.

Adhemar de Monteil (*Jerusalem*). Papal Legate.

The Papal Legate has no equivalent in *I Lombardi*. He is on hand at the conclusion of Act 1 in the **Count of Toulouse's** palace to pronounce anathema on **Gaston**, who has just been accused of instigating the Count's murder.

The Papal Legate is again on hand, in Act 3 Scene 2 in the public square in Ramla, to inform the crowd that Gaston, who has recently been discovered still alive in Palestine by the Crusaders, is to be dishonoured and executed under the walls of Jerusalem. The Papal Legate in common with everybody else, with the exception of **Hélène**, is under a total misapprehension concerning Gaston, who is innocent of the crime of which he is accused.

Adorno, Gabriele (*Boccanegra*). See **Gabriele**

Ahasuerus (*Stiffelio*).

The Ahasuerians are an invention of Souvestre and Bourgeois, the authors of *Le Pasteur, ou L'Evangile et le foyer*, the play from which Piave fashioned the libretto for *Stiffelio*. There is no historical evidence for such a sect.

Ahasuerus, otherwise known as 'the Wandering Jew', is the central figure in a medieval legend and he entered Western consciousness with the force of an archetype. The character of Kundry, in Wagner's *Parsifal*, is loosely based on the legend, as is the title role in Wagner's earlier opera, *Der Fliegende Holländer*. Ahasuerus was condemned to wander the earth until Judgement Day for the crime of having either spurned or insulted Christ when on the road to Calvary. He thus represents a prime symbol for the Original Sin that afflicts all humankind. The Ahasuerians presumably embrace the fact of Original Sin and devote their lives to atonement in order to be worthy eventually of salvation.

'Some feign that he is Enoch: others dream
He was pre-Adamite, and has survived
Cycles of generation and of ruin.
The sage, in truth, by dreadful abstinence,
And conquering penance of the mutinous flesh,
Deep contemplation and unwearied study,
In years outstretched beyond the date of man,
May have attained to sovereignty and science
Over those strong and secret things and thoughts
Which others fear and know not'.

Shelley.

AIDA

Opera in 4 Acts. Libretto translated by Antonio Ghislanzoni from the French prose of Camille du Locle (1868), plot by Augustus Mariette Bey.

First performance: 24 December 1871 at the Cairo Opera House.

Cast:
The King of Egypt (bass)
Amneris: his daughter (mezzo-soprano)
Aida: her slave (soprano)
Radames: Captain of the Guards (tenor)
Amonasro: King of Ethiopia (baritone)
Ramfis: High Priest (bass)
A messenger (tenor)

Time: The age of the Pharaohs
Place: Memphis and Thebes

Synopsis

Act 1 Scene 1   A hall in the Royal Palace of Memphis. To the left and right are colonnades decorated with statues and flowery shrubs. At the rear there is a great door, beyond which can be seen temples, the palaces of Memphis and the Pyramids.

Ramfis tells Radames of a rumour that the Ethiopians are once again on the defensive, threatening Thebes and the valley of the Nile. Radames wishes to know if Ramfis has consulted **Isis** as to who shall lead the Egyptian troops. Ramfis makes it as clear as he can, without actually stating it, that Radames has been elected for the honour.

He departs to inform the King of Isis's decree. Radames expresses the fervent hope that he may indeed be the warrior chosen to lead the Egyptians. His most pressing motivation is the desire to impress and woo the Ethiopian slave girl, Aida. He sings rhapsodically of his love for her (*Celeste Aida*).

Amneris enters. She immediately notices the joy which radiates from Radames's face. She desperately hopes that his joy may be occasioned by his love for her, although she suspects that Radames may be in love with another. Radames tells a half-truth. He is dreaming of being given the honour of leading the Egyptian legions into battle. He is concerned that Amneris may already have realized that he is in love with one of her slave girls.

At this moment Aida enters and the tender glances which Radames throws in her direction betrays his secret. Aida is in tears. She claims to be consumed with fear on behalf of her country, herself and her mistress. Amneris is not deceived, and seethes with rage at the slave who has so obviously poached her beloved from her.

The King enters preceded by his guard and followed by Ramfis, ministers, priests, officers and others. He announces that a messenger has arrived from Ethiopia bearing grave tidings. The messenger is brought in and relates how the Ethiopians have already invaded Egypt, ravaging the land, apparently unopposed, and even now are advancing on Thebes. They are led by a fierce, relentless warrior, Amonasro, Aida's father, though nobody but Aida knows this. All join the King in calling for war and death to defeat the Ethiopians.

The King announces that Isis has already named the Egyptian's leader: Radames. Radames is overjoyed. Aida is consumed with anxiety, for the battle will be fought between her father and her lover. The King commands Radames to go to the Temple of the Vulcan,[1] there to put on sacred arms and

journey forth to victory. Amneris presents Radames with a banner to carry into battle and exhorts him to return victorious. All depart variously, leaving Aida to echo Amneris's final words (*Ritorna vincitor!*).

Left alone Aida is torn by conflicting emotions. Victory for Radames will mean defeat for her father. How to reconcile the rival claims of her loyalties? She longs to be reunited with her father and yet cannot wish harm on her lover; 'my mind is lost in bitter night and is in such cruel anguish I wish to die', she declares. She prays to the gods to have pity on her.

Act 1 Scene 2 Interior of the Temple of Vulcan at Memphis. A mysterious light shines down from above. There is a low row of columns disappearing into the distance. There are statues of various gods. In the middle is the altar, decorated with sacred symbols and standing on scaffolding covered with tapestries. Incense rises from censers, swinging on gold tripods. Priests and priestesses. Ramfis is at the foot of the altar.

A priestess is invoking mighty Phtha,[2] the life-giving spirit of the world. She is echoed by Ramfis and the other priests. Then Radames is brought into the temple. He carries no weapons. As he goes to the altar the priestesses perform the sacred dance; the priests, meanwhile, place a silver veil over Radames's head. Ramfis then reminds

---

[1] In Roman mythology Vulcan was the son of Jupiter and Juno. Vulcan was the god of fire and destruction (which is presumably why Ramfis and

the priests invoke Phtha from within his temple prior to Radames going to war against the Ethiopians). Since the action of the opera is supposed to take place at the very peak of Egyptian civilization a whole millennium before Egypt was conquered by Rome (30 BC) the presence of a temple of Vulcan is an anomaly.

[2] Phtha. The patron god of Memphis. In Memphite theology Phtha created the world, through heart and tongue. He was generally revered as patron god of artisans, craftsmen and artists. As with the triumvirate of Isis, Osiris and Horas, Phtha belongs to a triumvirate consisting of himself, his consort, Sekhmet, and his son, Nefertum. The name Egypt derives from Hut-ka-Phtha, which means 'the mansion of Phtha'. Worship of Phtha was pronounced in the period of Memphis's rise to ascendancy c2686–2081 BC. The action of the opera takes place c1230 BC by which time an increasingly complex mélange of deities was being propitiated by the Egyptians.

Radames that he holds in his hands the destiny of Egypt. 'May the sacred sword, tempered by the gods, become in your hands blazing terror and a death for the enemy', he exhorts (*Morta diletto ai Numi*). The priests join Ramfis's exhortation. Then Radames joins them in praying to Phtha to give his protection to their undertaking. While Radames is being invested with the sacred arms the priests and priestesses resume the sacred hymn and the mystic dance.

Act 2 Scene 1   A room in the apartments of Amneris. Amneris is surrounded by slave girls who are dressing her for the victory celebrations. Incense is burning. Youthful Moorish slaves dance around her, waving large feather fans. They express the hope that Radames may return home to the mingled songs of love and glory. Amneris is daydreaming of the moment she will be reunited with Radames. Once the Moorish slaves have concluded their dance Amneris dismisses all her attendants. She has sent for Aida for she is determined to discover whether her slave is in love with Radames.

Aida enters (*Fu la sorte dell'armi a' tuoi funesta*). Amneris tells her, with 'feigned tenderness', that the war has turned against the Ethiopians. She presses Aida to confide in her if there is anyone amongst the Egyptian soldiers that she loves. She then lets slip that Radames has been killed on the battlefield. Aida is distraught and cannot hide her feelings. Now Amneris has the proof that she has been looking for. Having witnessed Aida's obvious distress Amneris tells her that in fact Radames is alive. Now she can have no doubt as to her slave's love for Radames, for Aida's distress turns immediately to ecstatic joy. Amneris reminds Aida that her rival in love is a Pharaoh's daughter. Momentarily Aida forgets her station and is about to reveal that she also is a princess (being daughter of the Ethiopian King). She stops herself short. Such a disclosure would fatally compromise her position at the Egyptian court. She pleads with Amneris to show some compassion, but Amneris is not disposed to be compassionate. She is furious: 'I am the master of your fate and my heart rages with

hate and vengeance', she declares before departing, leaving Aida alone to pray to the gods to take pity on her suffering.

Act 2 Scene 2   A gate in the city of Thebes. There is a group of palm trees in the foreground. To the right is the Temple of Ammon[3] and to the left a throne, covered with a purple baldaquin. To the rear is a triumphal gate. The stage is crowded with people. The King enters, followed by ministers, priests, captains, standard-bearers, slaves carrying huge feather fans. Amneris enters next, accompanied by Aida and slave girls. The King takes his place on the throne and Amneris takes her place on his left.

The people sing in praise of their King and give thanks for the victory which has been vouchsafed them. The Egyptian troops, following the trumpeters, pass before the King. Then come chariots, ensigns, sacred vessels and statues of the gods. Dancing girls carry treasure won from the enemy. Finally Radames enters, borne on a litter covered with a baldaquin, carried by twelve captains.

All sing in praise of the conquering hero. The King descends from his throne and embraces Radames, inviting him to accept from his daughter's hand the triumphal wreath. He tells Radames that he may now ask of him whatever he desires. Nothing shall be denied him. Radames asks that before he reply the Ethiopian prisoners should be brought in. The prisoners enter, escorted by guards. The last of them is Amonasro, dressed as an officer. Aida immediately recognizes her father. In a hurried aside Amonasro warns Aida not to betray him. She has already revealed that he is her father (Amneris has taken note of the fact) but at

---

[3]   Ammon is the Greek form of the name of the god, Amun (also transliterated to Amen and Amon). Amun was originally a local god of Thebes. When Thebes became the central powerbase in the New Kingdom (c1580 BC) Amun became the supreme state god and was worshipped throughout Egypt. As patron of the Pharaohs he was given the qualities of the Sun god, Re, and known as Amun-Re. As with most Egyptian gods he was part of a triad which included his consort, Mut and their son, Khons – known as the Theban Triad.

all costs she must not reveal that he is the Ethiopian King.

Summoned by the King, Amonasro proudly describes how he and his compatriots fought for their King and country. 'If love of our country is a crime then we are all guilty and ready to die', he declares. He turns to the King and pleads for mercy. The King is disposed to be merciful but Ramfis and the priests insist that the gods have destined them to die. They should be executed forthwith. Meanwhile Radames notices the grief in Aida's eyes, which makes her all the more beautiful to him. Amneris, noticing Radames's glance fixed on Aida, seethes with rage and longs for vengeance. The slave girls and prisoners all implore the King to be merciful while the priests continue to call for their immediate execution.

Finally Radames turns to the King and reminds him that he swore to give him what he might choose to ask for. He now asks the King that the Ethiopians be granted life and freedom. The priests are infuriated. Ramfis makes an impassioned speech pointing out that the Ethiopians will be eager for revenge. They are highly dangerous. He advocates that Aida and her father should be retained by the Egyptian state. The King sees the sense of this (although he is still ignorant of the fact that Amonasro is the Ethiopian King). Otherwise the Ethiopians will be released and in addition Radames shall be granted the hand in marriage of his daughter, Amneris. Amneris is, of course, delighted. 'Let the slave try to steal my love if she dare', she mutters to herself. Ramfis and the priests, meanwhile, mollified by the king's compromise, determine to pray that 'the fates may forever be auspicious to our nation'.

Aida is in despair; 'for him, glory and the throne; for me oblivion and the tears of hopeless love', she laments. Amonasro manages to murmur a word of comfort to his daughter. He has already observed the true cause of Aida's discomfiture, her love for Radames. He tells her to be brave and wait patiently, 'for the day of vengeance is already dawning'. Radames meanwhile is himself

thunderstruck: 'Ah no, the throne of Egypt is not worth Aida's heart', he reflects.

Act 3 The banks of the Nile. Granite rocks are interspersed with palm trees. The temple of Isis is at the summit of the rocks, half hidden by the palms. It is a clear, starry night, with a bright moon. A chorus from within the temple is heard, beseeching Isis, the goddess, 'who dost awaken the chaste fire in human hearts' to 'succour us in thy mercy'. A boat draws up at the river bank. Amneris, Ramfis, and a group of veiled women and guards alight. Ramfis addresses Amneris, inviting her to attend the temple of Isis and beseech the goddess's favour on the eve of her wedding. Amneris replies that she will indeed pray that Radames shall give her his whole heart. They enter the temple.

Aida enters furtively. She is veiled. She knows that Radames will soon arrive. She fears he may be going to take a last farewell of her, in which case she is resolved to drown herself in the Nile. She laments the fact that she will never again see her beloved fatherland (O patria mia). She remembers with searing poignancy the beloved contours of her homeland.

Amonasro suddenly appears (A te grave cagion m'adduce). Aida is taken aback. Amonasro loses no time in addressing the matter which concerns him. He has observed his daughter and is well aware of her passion for Radames. He is also aware that Radames returns her love and that Aida is at this very moment awaiting him. Her rival in love is the princess of a hated race, their deadly enemy. He tells Aida that if she wishes to she can defeat her rival and obtain for herself, 'fatherland, throne and love'. He has clearly been eavesdropping on his daughter's lament and now echoes her fond memories of home. He reminds Aida how pitiless the Egyptians have been towards her people and homeland, how they defiled their altars, temples and homes, carried their young girls off into slavery, murdered mothers, old men and children. All this is by way of preparing his daughter for the main purpose of his visit.

The Ethiopians are preparing for battle and are determined to conquer. Only one thing is lacking. They need to know the route that the Egyptians will be taking so that they may prepare an ambush. The only person who can find this out is Aida. She must extract the crucial information from Radames. Aida is appalled and initially refuses, but Amonasro is not to be denied. With ferocious intensity he rounds on Aida: 'Arise then, soldiers of Egypt! Sack and burn our cities! Spread terror, rape and death!' He disowns his daughter, evoking for Aida a nightmare vision of waves of blood flowing over the anguished cities and the shades of the dead arising out of the black smoke, pointing accusingly at Aida and chorusing: 'because of you our country dies'. So that Aida should be in no doubt he conjures a picture of Aida's mother cursing her daughter. By now terror-struck, Aida pleads with her father to have pity on her. But Amonasro, who has worked himself into a towering rage, violently re-pulses her: 'You are not my daughter. You are a slave of the Pharaohs', he spits at her. Aida can resist no longer. Totally overcome she begs him not to revile her and assures him that she will prove herself worthy of her country. 'Remember that a whole people, conquered and suffering, can rise again through you!' Amonasro reminds her. Having assured her that he will be listening to every word of her exchange with Radames, who is now approaching, he conceals himself amongst the surrounding palm trees.

Radames enters (*Pur ti riveggo*). He is overjoyed to see Aida, but she repulses him, reminding him that 'the rites of another love' await him. Radames is insistent that she is the only one whom he loves. Aida warns him against perjuring himself. Radames is bewildered. Why does she suddenly doubt his love? Aida changes her line of attack. Perhaps he does love her; but how is he going to escape the wiles of Amneris, the King's command, the people's will, and the wrath of the priesthood? Radames reveals his plan. He will win a glorious victory against the Ethiopians, and then claim Aida's hand as part of his victor's wreath.

Radames is being hopelessly naïve. Aida's immediate reaction is; 'and do you not fear Amneris's wrath? Her vengeance, like a thousand bolts will strike me, my father and my people'. 'I shall defend you', Radames rejoins. It would be in vain, of course. There is only one hope for them, and that is to flee. Will Radames not flee with her back to her homeland where they can live in peace together amid 'the virgin forests, fragrant with sweet flowers', oblivious to the rest of the world. It is an alluring picture she paints, but Radames is disturbed at the proposal to abandon his fatherland, where he first 'plucked the flower of glory'. Sensing his hesitation Aida assumes that he cannot really love her. Imperiously she tells him to leave forthwith and go to Amneris, who awaits him. When Radames exclaims, 'No, never!' she rejoins: 'Never, you say? Then the headsman's axe will fall on me, on my father—'. (Aida has learnt something from her father's bullying tactics.)

This is too much for Radames. He capitulates. Let them flee to the never-ending desert, he declares. There 'the stars will shine upon us with a purer, brighter light!' Radames is not specific about where that desert might be. Aida is quite clear. It will be 'the happy land of my fathers'. Radames is beyond caring. All he wants is to be united with Aida. He has dropped his guard completely, and it is now that Aida asks the crucial question. When they make their escape how are they to avoid the Egyptian legions? (It must not be forgotten that throughout this scene Aida is keenly aware of her father eavesdropping.) Radames, un-suspecting, tells her that the route by which his men will be marching will be free until the morrow. And that route is? Aida coaxes. The pass of Napata, Radames tells her. At which Amonasro leaps forward and triumphantly declares, 'My men will be there!'

Radames is appalled. He demands to know who has overheard them. Amonasro unhesitatingly declares himself: 'Aida's father, the King of the Ethiopians'. Radames already knows that Amonasro is Aida's father, but he had no idea he was the Ethiopian King. He is immediately aware of the treachery of which he is guilty and of which he has been a victim. (*Tu, Amonasro! Tu, il Re?*) He is consumed with dread and imagines he must be in the clutches of a nightmare. One thought obsesses him: he has betrayed his country and is dishonoured. Amonasro and Aida attempt to pacify him. Amonasro assures him he is not guilty. It was rather the will of fate. He must realize this is a futile argument with a proud warrior such as Radames. Father and daughter try to persuade him to flee with them forthwith, beyond the Nile. But it is too late.

Amneris, Ramfis, the priests and guards, alerted by the commotion, emerge from the temple. Amonasro, seeing Amneris, flings himself upon the princess with dagger drawn. At all costs he will not allow his plans to be defeated. Radames does not hesitate. He springs upon Amonasro and disarms him. Now he urges Amonasro and Aida to make their escape, since by now they are hopelessly outnumbered. Aida and Amonasro do as he bids them, pursued by guards. Radames despairingly surrenders himself to Ramfis: 'Sacerdote, io resto a te' ('Priest, I am in your hands').

Act 4 Scene 1   A hall in the King's palace. To the left is a great door leading to the underground judgement chamber. To the right a hallway leads to Radames's cell.

Amneris is standing sadly in front of the gate. She is torn asunder by conflicting emotions (*L'abborrita rivale a me sfuggia*). On the one hand the knowledge that Radames intended to flee with Aida, who has apparently managed to escape, has filled her with bitter fury. On the other hand she cannot deny the fact that she still loves him. 'O if only he might love me!' she exclaims. Her sole desire now is to save him. But how? She summons the guards to bring Radames to her. The guards duly exit and return with Radames.

Amneris tells Radames that the priests, even now, are in council and are deciding his fate. She pleads with him to try to convince the priests of his innocence. She, meanwhile, will plead with the King on his behalf. But Radames has no intention of

being conciliatory for Amneris's sake. He announces that he will not defend himself: 'I feel myself neither traitorous nor guilty', he says. 'My incautious words revealed the secret, it is true. But both my thoughts and my honour remain unstained by guilt'. This is a perfectly reasonable defence. But unfortunately it is not the sort of argument likely to stand up in a court of law, and especially not before Ramfis and his implacable priesthood. Radames refuses point-blank even to attempt to defend himself. He knows he will die, but he is prepared for it. For now, 'the source of all joy [i.e. Aida] is dry, every hope is gone'.

Amneris becomes exasperated. He cannot die, he must live. She needs him to live. She reminds him that she knows only too well the anguish of disprized love. She would give up all for him, she claims, courts, thrones and life itself. However she becomes enraged when Radames refers to Aida. She commands him not to speak of her. But it is all Radames wants to speak of. He assumes Aida must be dead. Amneris disabuses him. Amonasro was indeed killed, but not Aida who made her escape. She disappeared and nothing is known of her, Amneris tells him. Radames prays that Aida may make it safely home and will never know the fate that has befallen him.

Amneris declares that she will save Radames, but on one condition: he must never see Aida again. Staunchly Radames refuses even to discuss it. Amneris becomes increasingly desperate. 'Madman, you insist on dying?' Radames concurs that indeed he does. Out of patience Amneris declares that he has succeeded in perverting her love into hatred. She swears revenge and Radames is returned to his prison. Left alone Amneris collapses into a chair. She is desolate. She realises that without Radames's co-operation she cannot hope to save him. She blames herself for having given Radames over to the priests. She curses her jealousy which has brought about his death and eternal mourning for her.

At this moment the priests pass the hall on their way to Radames's prison. The sight of these implacable ministers of justice is too much for Amneris and she covers her face with her hands. Ramfis and the priests are heard intoning their prayers from within the prison. Then Radames, surrounded by guards, crosses the scene and goes down into the vault. Shortly after Ramfis's voice is heard, challenging Radames to defend himself. Radames remains silent. Amneris desperately pleads with the gods to have pity. Finally Ramfis declares Radames's sentence: he shall die a traitor's death. Beneath the altar of the offended god he shall be buried alive.

The priests return from the vault and Amneris accosts them, assuring them that it is they who commit a crime in sentencing an innocent man. The priests ignore her protestations, coldly stating, 'He is a traitor! He shall die', even when Amneris implores them for the sake of her love for him. As they leave she curses them, calling upon Heaven's vengeance to strike them down.

Act 4 Scene 2 Interior of the temple of Vulcan and Radames's tomb. The stage is divided into two levels. The upper part represents the interior of the Temple of Vulcan, resplendent with gold and light. The lower level is a vault. Rows of arches disappear into the darkness. Huge statues of Osiris, with crossed hands, hold up the pillars of the vault.

Radames is seated on the steps on which he has descended into the vault. Above, two priests are replacing the large stone which seals the vault. In spite of his hideous predicament all Radames can think of is Aida. 'Where are you?' he wonders (*La fatal pietra*).

Suddenly he hears a sigh and then, almost immediately, beholds Aida herself. He thinks he must be dreaming. But he is not dreaming. Seeing the priests digging the tomb Aida anticipated its purpose, and concealed herself within, in order to await her beloved and die with him. Radames is overwhelmed at this proof of her enduring love. He is also dismayed, for he feels a sense of his own culpability. 'I, in loving you, have killed you. You are too lovely to die'.

Aida is already delirious. Presumably she has been concealed for some time in the tomb. She experiences a vision of the angel of death with shining wings approaching to bear them both up to Heaven where, 'every sorrow ends and the joy of immortal love begins'. From above are heard the hymns of the priests and priestesses invoking the gods. Radames desperately tries to move the stone which seals the vault, but to no avail. He goes to Aida and the two sing a sad farewell to Earth, 'dream of joy which vanished into sorrow'.

Amneris enters the Temple above, dressed in mourning, and prostrates herself on the stone which seals the vault. The extent of her real devotion to Radames now becomes poignantly clear as she prays for peace for her beloved. Radames and Aida, oblivious to her proximity, continue their farewell. Finally Aida sinks, dying in Radames's arms as the curtain falls.

Not since *Nabucco* had Verdi's pen addressed such a monolithic drama as *Aida*. The gods are different, as are the lineaments and the relationships. But the impact is similarly direct, enhanced by the huge advance in technique and musical subtlety that a lifetime of operatic composing had vouchsafed its composer. Where *Aida* differs from *Nabucco* is in the fact that the main substance of the story concerns the intimate personal relationships of the three main protagonists. In *Nabucco* the central issue is the battle of its chief protagonist, Nabucco, with the God of the Hebrews.

Verdi never revisited such a mythic tale as that of *Nabucco*. He quickly appreciated that his strength lay in the vibrant portrayal of the human-all-to-human, and not the transcendental. (Where *Nabucco* falls down, principally, is in the banality of much of the music associated with Nabucco's transcendental battle. The music is most successful where elucidating the inner psychological struggles of the characters as individuals.) While the religion of Isis and Osiris ostensibly plays a considerable part in *Aida,* it yet remains in the background, more in the manner of scene-painting than active engagement. Otherwise the opera retains the formula that

Verdi had discovered worked best for him; namely the vivid portrayal of personal interactions against a backdrop of political intrigue.

Of all Verdi's operas *Aida* is the one in which he most clearly addresses the 'Romeo and Juliet' motif. Thus the central pair of lovers are from opposing camps, Aida being Ethiopian and Radames Egyptian. Each must decide to what extent they are willing to sacrifice their loyalty to King and country to the service of their love. Ultimately their love wins, but only at the cost of their lives. The message would appear to be pessimistic: mixed marriages do not work. But that would be to take too simplistic a view. Ultimately the lovers are defeated not by political considerations, but by Amneris's jealousy. During the course of the opera Radames earns the right to select Aida as his bride. The King is so indebted to him that it is conceivable that he could have been persuaded to forego his plan that Radames should marry his daughter. If Aida's rival had been just another Ethiopian slave there might have been no problem for the lovers. But the fact that Amneris is the Egyptian King's daughter, and Aida her personal slave, immeasurably complicates the issue. This is the nub of the drama, made blisteringly clear in the final scene, where Amneris places herself on top of the stone which seals the entrance to Radames's tomb. She it is who has sealed it, and she knows it. It gives her no happiness. She has allowed her jealousy to override all other feelings she may have. Too late she realizes that Radames means more to her than just a punch-bag for her passion.

Aida does not respond well to the 'kitchen-sink' school of production or exegesis, the school that loves to reduce an heroic drama to a mundane level. Yes, the passions of the three lovers could be portrayed in a suburban setting, but it would make a nonsense of the score which is directly in the Meyerbeerian Grand Opera tradition. These characters need a vast arena in which to work out their destinies. The love of Radames and Aida is the love by which empires stand or fall, the love of Antony and Cleopatra, of Paris and Helen, if for no other reason than that they are willing to make the ultimate sacrifice in its service. Like the deaths of Romeo and Juliet, those of Aida and Radames are emblematic of that element of irrationality in human nature which will always transcend all petty divisiveness.

The real tragedy lies in the fact that Aida's sacrifice will never be known. Whatever the implications, this is no grand statement on her part. Finally, it is a purely private matter, the desire to make a commitment beyond that she owes to King, father and country. A private tragedy in a supremely public arena is as good a summary as any of this most popular of Verdi's operas.

Aida (*Aida*). Slave of Amneris.
Aida, slave to a princess, is herself a princess. Incipient in her make-up she contains all the hauteur and disdain which characterizes Amneris herself. Yet her nature has been refined by adversity and suffering. Her enslavement and the helplessness of her predicament means that she cannot give vent to her natural hauteur. She must learn humility in order to survive. This she does, but what she cannot do is forget her origins. Born a princess, the prerogatives and privileges of royalty are instinctive to her. She could never contemplate marrying a humble peasant. She must marry a successful man, a radiant man, a hero. Deprived of any possibility of finding a worthy Ethiopian her eyes alight on the most worthy Egyptian: **Radames**. He is the only man fit for a princess. But how to attain him when he is an enemy warrior and she merely a slave?

The fact that Aida is specifically assigned to Amneris, the King's daughter, makes it easier for her. As Amneris is herself in love with Radames the latter is often invited to the princess's apartments. It is not long before Radames becomes aware of the young and beautiful slave. For Radames, Aida represents everything Amneris can never be, by virtue of the fact that everything in Amneris's life has been given. She expects, she demands and she receives. There is no conquest. There is therefore no possibility of fulfilment for Radames because he will never receive anything back from Amneris. Her love is adamantine and reflects only the power and voracious appetites of her own ego. Aida, on the other hand, exudes patience, nobility and suffering. She needs rescuing. This is a far more alluring challenge to a young warrior than the wilful expectations of the princess.

None of this is explicated in the opera, but something similar must form the background of the liaison which develops between the two. It has all the force of that which is forbidden, one of the most powerful forces known to man. Aida and Radames need each other, because ostensibly they cannot have each other. Of course Radames could take his pick of any one of the Ethiopian slaves and have his way with her, much as a Turkish Pasha might select a girl from his Harem. But such a transaction has not been the trigger for the passion which exists between Aida and Radames. Their love is founded on an equal need in them each to be rescued: Radames from the clutches of Amneris and Aida from her slavery.

For Aida her love is a misery from the beginning because she knows that it must involve the sacrifice of her loyalty to her homeland. She must become a traitor in order to love. This motive recurs throughout world literature, and no more so than in the operatic literature. Why is this the case? Because all motives concerning love involve betrayal: betrayal of the homeland that is synonymous with the mother and the father. In the son's case the betrayal will be of the mother; in the daughter's it will be of the father. It is perhaps the most primordial psychological syndrome there is.

In the world's great love stories this syndrome is represented more often than not as the conflict between love and duty. Duty is the daughter of stasis. If all human beings were perennially dutiful they would never leave home. They would remain locked in the vice-like grip of father and/or mother and the greater father and/or mother, that is, the homeland and nationalistic pride that too often falls over into chauvinism, which in itself is just another way of denoting the terror of being forcibly propelled out of the all too comfortable gridlock of stasis.

It is in this gridlock that Amneris is trapped. Had Aida not been captured and exiled into slavery she would have become like Amneris: a spoilt dissatisfied princess who is shunned because she exudes the horror of being enslaved to her past.

'Some are born great, some achieve greatness, and some have greatness thrust upon them' (Shakespeare's *Twelfth Night*, Act 2 Scene 5). The same could be said of freedom and all its attendant dilemmas and horrors. Aida has freedom thrust upon her, paradoxically at the moment when she is thrown into slavery. It is a tribute to her spirit that she knows how to capitalise on it. She cannot escape the penalties of conscience, the conscience that binds her to the past. In the anguish of her dilemma she comes close to denying past, present and future: 'The sacred words *father* and *lover* – I can no longer speak them, nor remember. For each, in my fear and confusion, I should like to pray, to weep. But my prayer changes to cursing – tears, for me, are a crime; so too my sighs. My mind is lost in a bitter night, and in such cruel anguish I wish to die' (Act 1 Scene 1: *Ritorna vincitor!*). This is no mere rhetoric. This is a clear explication of how she feels. There appears absolutely no way out of the conundrum in which she finds herself. It is almost a relief when Amneris unveils her secret. For a split second she almost revels in the fact that she is, or rather she knows herself to be, a worthy adversary for Amneris. When Amneris haughtily pronounces, 'I am your rival, I, daughter of the Pharaohs' (Act 2 Scene 1), Aida, in that moment, forgets her station: *Mia rivale! Ebben sia pure, Anch'io son tal . . .* ('My rival! Then so be it, for I too am . . .'). In other words, I am equally worthy to love Radames for I too am a princess. She saves herself from certain death when she stops short of revealing her unique vulnerability. However great the dilemma, however great the anguish, she does not want to die through loss of self-control in the midst of a spiteful wrangle.

Aida's predicament is exacerbated by the sudden advent, in the midst of her anguish, of her father. When she sees him, her father and her King, the embodiment of all that has given her previous life vitality and meaning, trudging into Thebes amidst the Ethiopian slaves, she knows with total certainty where her loyalty lies. She must save her father. In the excess of her emotions she betrays her father, but not her King and royal lineage. She thus spares him his life by default. It befalls Radames to spare her father's life in actuality, by exercising his victor's prerogative, and pleading with the King to grant the Ethiopians their freedom. Radames does not know that Aida's father is **Amonasro**, King of the Ethiopians. His argument proves this, for he observes to the Egyptian King that the Ethiopian King is dead. Thus the Ethiopians must be considered powerless. Paradoxically it is **Ramfis**, the High Priest, who insists that Aida and her father should remain as hostages. The prospect brings little joy to Aida.

When Radames is granted Amneris's hand in marriage Aida is desolate: 'What hope, now, is left to me? For him, glory and the throne, for me oblivion and the tears of a hopeless love'. Aida's destiny has reached its crossroads. For now she is confronted in succession by the demands of father and homeland, followed hard on the heels by her lover and potential redeemer (Act 3). The call of father and homeland is imperious, and ultimately unanswerable. That she betrays Radames, that she blatantly manipulates him into revealing state secrets is unquestionable. But what is the end result? The same result that materializes from all such betrayal: nobody wins. Her father is killed, her lover is doomed and she has lost both past and future.

From her own point of view Aida has no option but to sacrifice herself to the future that might have been. When she conceals herself in her lover's tomb she fulfils her destiny in the only way left to her (Act 4). Her loyalty to her father has been proved misguided. She has only assisted him in achieving his own demise. She can only

appreciate this when it is too late to save him. It may be too late to save her lover, but it is not too late to join him.

Verdi's *Aida* can be seen as an Italian *Tristan und Isolde*. It fulfils the same function in Verdi's oeuvre as *Tristan* did in Wagner's. It marks a culmination. It also marks a decadence which is never again matched. Not for nothing did Thomas Mann use the music of *Aida* (Radames and Aida's duet, Act 4) in his novel, 'The Magic Mountain',[4] as paradigmatic of the sickness at the heart of Romanticism. The conclusion of *Aida* would seem to suggest that the only true consummation of love lies in death. It is the supreme illogicality, yet irrefutable.

Un Alcade (*La forza del destino*). See Mayor of Hornachuelos

Alfredo (*La Traviata*)

Alfredo is the prototype of the obsessed operatic lover. At first glance it might seem that he belongs to the same stable as Pinkerton in Puccini's *Madame Butterfly*. He is capable of behaving in a similarly 'caddish' fashion, and yet his behaviour at the conclusion of Act 2 is justifiable, if inexcusable. Pinkerton's behaviour is simply inexcusable.

Alfredo epitomizes the kind of lover whose first priority is never to conquer. Rather he allows himself to be conquered. He is not mother-obsessed, like Manrico (*Il Trovatore*), therefore he is not capable of the heroics and histrionics that characterize Manrico. Such heroics always stem from the need to escape the domination (or the absence) of a mother and the need to assert something incontrovertibly by which the individual cannot fail to be acknowledged and congratulated.

Alfredo suffers rather from a father complex. **Germont** has sought at every turn to impose on his son the moral codes by which he himself has lived and the expectations that he has for his son. These expectations will include respectable marriage,

---

[4] Thomas Mann: *The Magic Mountain*. See Chapter 8, 'The Fullness of Harmony'. Pub. Penguin.

respectable occupation, respectable income, respectable reputation. But Alfredo needs to find what he himself is before he can begin to fulfil the prescriptions laid out for him by his father. Because his father has so clearly achieved respectable marriage, occupation, income and reputation these will be the last things to which Alfredo will aspire. When the opera opens Alfredo is the typical playboy son of a successful father. By the close he has gone beyond his self-obsession. **Violetta** has taught him that behaving like a spoilt brat is not the way to conquer life or, for that matter, death.

Alfredo sees Violetta and, like a thousand-and-one other men, is immediately enchanted by this essence of femininity, elegance, poise and beauty. It becomes all the more irresistible because of the keen awareness that underneath the elegance and poise lurks a sexual volcano. Where Alfredo differs from other men is that he is acutely aware that all the elegance, poise and humour is a mask which conceals a soul that is sick and suffocating. He sees this because he needs to see it. He needs Violetta desperately for his own survival because, above all, he needs to escape from his own narcissism. The best way to achieve this is to devote himself to redeeming another from her narcissism. Consumption, as portrayed by the Romantics, is a narcissistic illness. Puccini's Mimi (*La Bohême*) is dying of an inability to relate to life; she is totally absorbed in her own sensations. These lead her to great ecstasies, extreme emotions and hysteria. But these waste away her vitality, because the energy these extremities of emotion consume goes nowhere. There is no objective focus for the vast resources of energy that the individual contains within, so the emotions end up consuming themselves.

The courtesan, or prostitute, is narcissistic by definition. How can she be anything else? Whatever the ostensible reason the choice of prostitution, however dressed up, indicates a direct denial of self. Alfredo intuitively recognizes all this about Violetta and identifies with it. He is in danger of consuming himself. Intimidated by his father, he has no identity of his own. If he can redeem Violetta there is a slim possibility that he might be able to redeem himself. So he woos Violetta like a medieval troubador. (Verdi himself invites the parallel by having Alfredo's offstage serenade to Violetta, at the conclusion of Act 1, remarkably similar in tone and cadence to Manrico's serenade in *Il Trovatore*.) Violetta is charmed and exhilarated for it is a call from the deep. It invites her to a new type of existence and consciousness. Hitherto she has strenuously avoided the depths for fear of drowning. But now monsters from the deep are struggling to the surface and threatening to strangle her. Alfredo's summons come from the same depths but contain an altogether sweeter allure. Rather than asphyxiating her these voices offer a promise of redemption.

Alfredo knows right away that Violetta (knows she) needs him as much as he needs her. Who else of her acquaintances and lovers would have sat patiently by her bedside throughout the recent crisis of her illness? In elementary mathematics two minuses make a plus and certainly this is the case with Violetta and Alfredo. Each saves the other from him/her self. Each needs to live through the other. If they each live only through the other then they can do without the rest of the world. They represent a self-contained unit unto themselves. Thus their life in the country is truly an idyll. Neither gives any thought for the morrow, living only for the moment and for each other. Violetta forgets about her illness; indeed her illness temporarily forgets about her, while Alfredo can forget about his father and the chronic sense of insufficiency that has dogged him all his life. Suddenly he feels necessary.

But the world cannot be kept at bay indefinitely (Act 2 Scene 1). When Alfredo learns that Violetta is planning to sell all her worldly goods and give him the proceeds in order that he may pay off the debts accrued in sustaining their idyll, he is appalled. The sense of worthlessness that has recently been in such blissful abeyance returns with a vengeance. He is wounded where it most hurts, in the place of honour and worldly responsibility, that is, where his father 'lives'.

13

To compound his misery his father unexpectedly arrives amidst the ruins of his idyll as though to underline further his sense of inadequacy. He can barely bring himself to acknowledge his father, let alone speak to him. If he makes the connection between his father's sudden appearance and Violetta's disappearance he does not acknowledge the fact. It would seem to him a dreary inevitability anyway. What does Alfredo read when he opens the letter Violetta has left him? He does not read it aloud in the opera, but in the play it is read in its entirety:

'By the time you read this I shall already be the mistress of another man. So all is over between us. Go back to your father, my dear, and to your sister, a pure young girl who knows nothing of your troubles, who will soon help you to forget what you have been made to suffer by the fallen creature they call Margherite Gautier. You were good enough to love her for a while and it is to you that she owes the only happy moments in a life which she hopes will not last long now'.

The letter is a monumental shock, not simply because of the inherent loss to himself, but because it invalidates his one attempt at heroism: to save Violetta. It also leaves him back where he started, a prey to father and family, and if he has learnt anything at all it is that this is *not* what he wants. His father's presence only underlines the horror of Violetta's proposal. The 'spoilt brat' reasserts itself.

What galls Alfredo more than anything is that it all boils down to money. Suddenly he is made aware that the idyll has been entirely supported by Violetta's money and that he has no more self-determination than he had at the outset. Violetta has decided that their relationship is at an end, and therefore there is nothing further to discuss. His sense of outrage is complete.

The only way Alfredo can redeem some vestige of pride is to make money through gambling (Act 2 Scene 2). Unlike Violetta he has never had to earn his living. He has always been dependent on his father but he will not turn to his father now to extricate him from his present difficulties. Gambling is the recourse of the desperate. Either you win or you lose. There is no halfway. Losing corroborates the sense of worthlessness. Winning vindicates and empowers the ego. Alfredo wins, and it would have been better for him had he lost. The ease with which he wins serves to confirm for him how utterly worthless money in itself is. It comes and goes but has absolutely no bearing on what really matters: his self-esteem and his love. His winning also serves to confirm to him that he is right, that morally he is justified in his cause. He is empowered to wreak vengeance on the woman he loves in the worst possible way he can think of, by publicly humiliating her. By throwing the money at her he emphasizes its utter worthlessness and also, by association, *her* worthlessness. How can she choose to renounce their love for the sake of money? It is incomprehensible to him. In his anger and resentment he is convinced that Violetta must have been worthless from the start.[5] However he is immediately stricken with remorse because he knows full well how grossly unfair he has been. He knows that the Violetta he loves does not care deeply about money any more than he does. It is only the courtesan who needs the means to support the luxurious living and entertainment which will bolster her self-esteem.

Alfredo's anger now turns on the man who has taken her from him: the Baron **Douphol**. He challenges the Baron to a duel and wounds him but then, bewildered, he flees abroad. The pivotal moment of the evolution in Alfredo's consciousness comes when he receives the letter from his father giving him the true facts and begging him to return. Suddenly the enemy is no longer the enemy. Suddenly he finds he can love Violetta with impunity. It is this which gives to the final scene of *La Traviata* its almost unbearable poignancy (Act 3).

---

[5] Alfredo's outburst in Act 2 prefigures the scene in *Otello*, where Otello publicly humiliates Desdemona. The motive of jealousy is never far from Verdi's preoccupations.

Reunited with Violetta as an individual and, most importantly, in the presence of his father, the two worlds which have so often seemed completely at odds have finally coalesced. He may love Violetta and yet may still retain his father's affection. That it is too late and Violetta dies in his arms is not Alfredo's fault. But it is his fate. With Violetta dead he is alone, facing the world and must somehow account to his father without allowing himself to be overpowered. At this point we move beyond the confines of Verdi's opera.

Mistress Alice Ford (*Falstaff*)

Alice Ford is the true object of **Falstaff's** attentions. He woos **Meg** because he knows she has money, and money is what motivates him above all. But with Alice he is enamoured not just of her money, but also of her person. That Alice is already a mother and wife probably appeals to Falstaff who needs both, a mother to look after him and a wife to revitalize his ailing sense of potency. But Alice has still a lively sense of fun and is very much the cheer-leader of the 'Merry Wives'. She is something of an exhibitionist and enjoys hugely regaling her friends with the letter she has received from Falstaff. Initially a part of her must be flattered. But when she realizes that her friend Meg has received precisely the same letter amusement turns to outrage. She must conclude, as does Meg, that she has been the victim of a ruthless chancer.

But Alice is not one to mope. She relishes the thought of exacting revenge: 'You'll see that if I start tricking that fat lump, I'll make him turn faster that any reel'. In spite of herself Alice is in awe of her husband. She knows his temper and jealous nature. She knows that she plays a dangerous game in stringing Falstaff along, but she cannot just ignore the man's impertinence. She receives considerable encouragement from her daughter, **Nannetta**, who finds it all hysterically funny. The rendezvous at her home is Alice's idea: 'First, bring him to us, we'll flatter him ... and then we'll turn him inside out ... we'll roast him at the fire ... what fun!' There is something undeniably sadistic about the determination of the 'Merry Wives' to make Falstaff suffer. But then wounded vanity is a powerful goad.

Alice is content to let **Mistress Quickly** be her ambassador and especially to have the sprightly old woman at her side when it comes to fulfilling the rendezvous. Alice could never have carried through her plan without the support of Meg and Quickly. When it comes to the moment of Falstaff's arrival (Act 2 Scene 2), Alice demonstrates a similar aptitude for marshalling the troops as her husband demonstrates later in the scene, ordering her companions to their posts. She must inevitably be nervous when Falstaff enters, not knowing what to expect from him. When she declares 'I despise the false god of gold', it is in response to Falstaff's promises of bedecking her in fine jewellery. But one inevitably reflects (and no doubt Falstaff in his straightened circumstances does too) that it is easy for her to despise gold when married to one of the wealthiest merchants in town.

When Falstaff starts to press his suit, Alice becomes alarmed. The thought of his monstrous girth on top of her is hardly alluring. One must assume that the agreed signal for Mistress Quickly to enter was Alice's cry of 'Per carita!' ('for pity's sake!'), for at that moment Quickly comes running in with the information that Mistress Meg wishes to see Alice. Falstaff must hide himself.

Meg duly arrives. All is going to plan; but then the unexpected happens. Mistress Quickly returns in a genuine state of agitation, because Alice's husband is now truly on his way, accompanied by a posse of henchmen, in a towering rage and baying for blood. Now Alice is genuinely concerned, for this is not how she wanted to play the scene. She had always intended to tell her husband, but she wanted to tell him in her own time, and only when Falstaff had been well and truly punished. (She is, of course, unaware that Bardolfo and Pistola have already briefed Ford who has confirmed for himself Falstaff's intentions [Act 2 Scene 1].) Now she is forced into the position of a guilty adulteress. Certainly her husband treats her as such.

15

Alice is outraged at her husband's behaviour. How dare he accuse her of adultery without a shred of evidence to prove her guilt! 'He is insane', she splutters. Her only thought now is the necessity of removing Falstaff from the house as quickly as possible. It was never originally planned to eject Falstaff out of the window in the dirty linen basket. It is Falstaff himself who, in his desperation to escape, suggests that the basket might be a suitable means of escape. It is in fact an extremely perilous means of escape. Falstaff could well have been killed, but there is no time to think. When Alice tells her servants to empty the basket near the bulrushes, 'in front of that bunch of washer-women', she is presumably motivated by the thought that thereby Falstaff's fall will be cushioned, and there will also be witnesses to assist him out of the water.

The moment Falstaff has been evicted Alice loses no time in apprising her husband of the true state of affairs. From now on the gulling of Falstaff is as much her husband's doing as her own. Nevertheless Alice feels considerably aggrieved with her husband, and she lets him know it. She falls in happily with Quickly's plans for scotching Ford's plot to marry Nannetta off to Caius. She certainly does not want Doctor Caius for a son-in-law.

If Windsor possessed an amateur dramatic society in the late 16th century it is certain that Alice would be one of its leading lights. She so obviously enjoys masterminding the masquerade with which the opera concludes. First, she casts the production, thereafter she stage manages it. She will surely have her hands full with the band of elves and imps, all played by children. She has no qualms about goading them into tormenting the prone body of Falstaff, whose cries for help are pitiful. She then ensures that the elves set up the lighting for the dual wedding so that there can be no possible doubt, when the wedding veils are raised, as to who is married to whom. This is the moment of her revenge on her husband for having so doubted her integrity.

After the wedding, when Falstaff rhetorically asks 'now which one is the dupe?' it is Alice who lines up Falstaff, Ford and Caius, and declares loudly 'all three of them'. She forces her husband to regard the 'sweet, eager love' of Nannetta and Fenton. There was no doubt a time when Alice and Ford were themselves similarly besotted. It is always a matter of regret, to encroaching age, to be deprived of the passion and simplicity of youth. Unlike her husband Alice has not forgotten what it was to be young and in love, and she will not countenance her daughter's young life being wrecked through marriage to an old pedant like Doctor Caius. As far as she concerned Caius deserves his 'marriage' to Bardolfo, for having been so vain as to think he could possess Nannetta in the first place. And as for her husband, she still has much to forgive him for. But then the action of the opera has proved that Alice is not one to let grudges fester. If she still harbours resentment against her husband he'll soon know about it.

Alvaro (*Alzira*). Governor of Peru and father of **Gusmano**.

Alvaro plays a crucial part in underpinning Voltaire's chief concern in his play, namely to exemplify the virtues of compassion and forgiveness. Because Alvaro is saved from a hideous death at the hands of the Incas by none other than the Inca prince, **Zamoro**, he relinquishes his worldly power in favour of his son and devotes his remaining energies to promoting the cause of peace and reconciliation between the Spanish and the Incas. Since Alvaro was himself originally the prime figurehead of Spanish aggression against the Peruvian natives his conversion has something of a Paulian eloquence and his advocacy is consequently all the more potent. He encourages his son's marriage to an Inca girl but when his son threatens to kill **Alzira's** true love, Zamoro, he is the first to plead for mercy on Zamoro's behalf.

At the end of the opera, when Gusmano has been mortally wounded, Alvaro gives his dying son his benediction, ecstatic that Gusmano has finally embraced the Christian ethic of forgiveness and compassion. The fact that Alvaro shows not a sign of bitterness towards Zamoro for murdering his son may exemplify the Christian virtues, but from the point of view of dramatic verisimilitude beggars belief.

Don Alvaro (*La forza del destino*)

The audience must wait until Act 3 Scene 1 of the opera to discover something of Alvaro's background. Up until then his character has been very sketchily suggested. His aria (*La vita è un inferno all'infelice*) redresses the balance. It is justifiably a favourite with operatic tenors. Apart from its plangent melody it establishes Alvaro as a passionate yet honourable hero who never wittingly perpetrated a cowardly or dishonourable act, but seems nevertheless to be pursued by a malignant fate.

In the aria Alvaro describes how his father, in the hope of freeing his native land, Peru, from its foreign masters, the Spanish, sought an alliance with the last of the Incas. Presumably this entailed taking an Inca wife. Alvaro was born in a prison. His parents, who dreamed of a throne, were instead executed. Exiled and nameless, Alvaro all his life has sought a resting place. **Leonora** has represented his last hope of that. By this stage of the opera he believes Leonora to be dead.

In the play, from which Piave and Verdi took their libretto, the populace discuss Don Alvaro in the opening scene. He has apparently recently arrived from the Americas and is, reputedly, fabulously wealthy, something which is never emphasized in the opera. He is half Inca. This is revealed in Alvaro's Act 3 aria, but is also implicit in his lyrical outpouring in Act 1 Scene 1: 'And when the sun, God of India, lord of my royal race inundates the world with its splendour he will shine on our wedded joy'.

Alvaro is given, and fashions for himself, an extraordinary destiny. Born into dispossessed royalty he is an exile all his life. In view of his enormous wealth he could, had he so chosen, have settled into a life of contented domesticity. But Alvaro is driven by demons. When he meets Leonora he

imagines he has found the resting place that his beleaguered soul has always sought.

Alvaro encourages Leonora to elope with him because her family is not willing to accept an Inca into their midst. Alvaro's very first entrance through the window of Leonora's room immediately establishes his illegitimate status. When the lovers' attempt at elopement goes disastrously wrong Alvaro longs for only one thing: death. To which end he joins the army and, because he is careless for his own safety, he establishes a reputation for heroism. Just at the moment he seems to have faced death, his life is saved, in spite of himself, and he is challenged by **Don Carlo** to a duel. So overjoyed is he when he learns that Leonora is still alive that for a few moments he forgets his death-longing and desperately hopes that Carlo will let bygones be bygones and that they may join in searching for Leonora.

But Carlo is wholly entrenched in his desire to wreak vengeance. Alvaro must fight him. If Alvaro had hoped to be slain he is disappointed and from this point on can see only one recourse. Since destiny will not allow him to avoid living out the full term of his existence he must do what he has hitherto always sought to evade: namely accede to his destiny and deliver himself into the hands of Almighty God.

However he may wish otherwise he cannot spare Leonora her fate. His intentions have never been dishonourable; his only fault lies in contravening the laws of a rigidly hierarchical society that will always put honour and duty before love and spontaneity. He has become a murderer and a seducer, in spite of himself. Something of the fate of Orestes[6] hovers over Alvaro's head. He has followed the dictates of his own superior will only to find himself hopelessly compromised. In the moment that he is confronted by the enraged

---

6 In Greek mythology Orestes was the son of Agamemnon and Klytemnestra. His father was murdered by his mother and her lover, Aegisthus. He avenged his father's death by murdering Klytemnestra and Aegisthus. He was then tormented by the Erinyes (the Furies) until rescued finally by the goddess, Athena.

Carlo he accepts that he can do nothing to change the course of destiny. He has only one option and that is to submit. He sees the passion that consumes Carlo for what it is: ultimately self-defeating. Carlo is little more than a robot, reacting to the pressures of a society that allows no room for expression of personal conscience.

Assuming the identity of Father Rafaele Alvaro gains admittance to the monastery of Our Lady of the Angels where, if **Melitone**'s remarks are anything to go by, he is held in some awe for his fierce devotion and asceticism. Five years pass. Alvaro must assume he will end his days in the quiet sanctity of the Cloister. If so, he has reckoned without Don Carlo's maniacal persistence. For Carlo tracks Alvaro to the monastery and challenges him to resume their interrupted duel (*Invano Alvaro*: Act 4 Scene 1). Alvaro tries valiantly to uphold the indifference to worldly passions proper to a monk, but to no avail. It is deeply humiliating to him – and this is underlined by Verdi's music – that he betrays his monkish vows to the extent of allowing Carlo to goad him into resuming their long-interrupted duel. This failing would seem to indicate that five years of retreat from the world and dedication to God have done nothing to obviate within himself the sin of pride.

This is only confirmed in the original St Petersburg version of the opera where, in the concluding scene, Alvaro hurls derision on Padre **Guardiano** and invites the earth to open so that Hell may swallow him before committing the most grievous sin of his life so far: suicide. In this version Alvaro becomes only the latest casualty in a long line of Romantic anti-heroes in Verdi's operas: characters who cannot under any circumstances come to terms with their existence and therefore seek to end it. The most obvious of these are Carlo (*I Masnadieri*) and Corrado (*Il Corsaro*). Verdi had by this stage in his career grown beyond such adolescent histrionics. He wanted something more for his hero. Hence the revised ending in which Alvaro's failure to rebuff Carlo's taunts becomes but a lapse, albeit a heinous one,

on his road to spiritual fulfilment. The ending of *La forza del destino* proffers the hope that there may be a reality beyond the passion-driven hysteria to which human existence is so prone. Alvaro must learn to surmount what has hitherto made of his life a nightmare, namely his search for redemption within the world beyond himself. As is the case with Stiffelio in the conclusion of the earlier opera, Alvaro is forced to acknowledge that redemption is entirely dependent upon the willingness to accede to a compassionate ethos that refuses to kow-tow before the hegemony of passion. It is not that readily palatable to the Mediterranean temperament. Verdi was to continue to explore and explicate the tragedies that must inevitably result from the absence of such a compassionate ethos.

It is eloquent testimony to the rootlessness of Alvaro's existence that all that is of any value to him is contained in one small valise, and even this he must surrender in his dying moments to the scrutiny of a stranger who turns out to be his sworn enemy. It would seem that it is Alvaro's destiny that nothing of this Earth shall remain sacred for him. The moment he relinquishes the key to his valise he relinquishes his autonomy. Prostrate on an operating table he is more helpless than he has ever been. He has no choice but to surrender himself. He makes Carlo swear to respect the sanctity of his letters, which are apparently bound in a package within the valise, but perversely omits to remember that the valise also contains a portrait of Leonora. His omission in this respect is as eloquent as anything he has either said or done. It is as though, like Leonora in Act 1 Scene 1, he is subconsciously willing a fatal resolution to the misery of his life.

Finally there is one scene in the opera in which Alvaro does not even appear and yet provides perhaps the most eloquent commentary on his plight; that is Act 3 Scene 3 in the military encampment where the soldiers gather under the tutelage of **Preziosilla** and haggle with **Trabucco**. What is the point of this scene if not to highlight the absurdity of Alvaro's plight, ostracized and condemned by a society that is principally peopled by sheep? If they are not fighting wars over a piece of land, a religious principle, a glass of wine or a lover, they are succumbing to the panaceas peddled by fortune-tellers and the temptations of drink and venality. The scene, in spite of its riotous cheerfulness which superficially acts as a dramatic sop to the previous scene, is an indictment of the very world which has beleaguered Alvaro. It would seem to confirm that in withdrawing from it to the cloister Alvaro is pursuing the only sensible course of action open to a man of his passionate sensibility.

ALZIRA

Lyric Tragedy in a Prologue and two Acts. Libretto by Salvatore Cammarano, after Voltaire's tragedy *Alzire, ou Les Américains* (1730).

First performance: 12 August 1845 at the Teatro San Carlo, Naples.

Cast:
Alvaro: Governor of Peru (bass)
Gusmano: his son (baritone)
Ovando: Spanish Duke (tenor)
Zamoro: chief of a Peruvian tribe (tenor)
Ataliba: chief of another Peruvian tribe (bass)
Alzira: Ataliba's daughter (soprano)
Zuma: her sister (mezzo-soprano)
Otumbo: Peruvian warrior (tenor)

Time: mid-16th century
Place: Peru

Synopsis
Prologue **The Prisoner**. A vast plain, irrigated by the Rima river. The Eastern sky is filled with majestic clouds, glowing in the light of the rising sun. Otumbo enters at the head of a tribe of Indians, dragging the aged Spanish Governor, Alvaro, in chains. The Indians tie Alvaro to a tree and sing with relish of the torture they are about to inflict on him in revenge for the death of their many compatriots, who have been slain by the invading Spanish forces (*Muoia, muoia*). Alvaro prays that the Indians may be pardoned by God, to whom he now turns in his last extremity. Meanwhile the Indians, shouting in exultation, rush at him, some with darts, others with spears and burning torches. It seems that nothing now can save Alvaro. But at this critical moment the Indians are interrupted by the arrival of Zamoro, who is sighted by Otumbo, disembarking from a canoe.

The Indians are astounded and delighted to find Zamoro still alive, for reports have been circulating of his death. They throw themselves at his feet. Zamoro ignores them and makes straight for Alvaro. He stands staring at the old man and appears to be moved to compassion. He turns to his compatriots and demands that they turn Alvaro over to him, declaring that he will not allow the joy of his return home to be tainted with blood. The Indians have no objection, no doubt assuming that Zamoro will scalp him on their behalf. But this is not Zamoro's intention. He releases the old man and tells him to return to his people and relate to they, 'who call us savages, how a savage gave you your life'. At a sign from Zamoro Alvaro leaves, escorted by several tribesmen. The other Indians make no comment on this uncharacteristic act of compassion towards an enemy. They are too overwhelmed with joy at having Zamoro restored to them.

Zamoro now relates how he has been horribly tortured by the Spaniard, Gusmano (*Un Inca ... eccesso orrible*) and given over to the executioners. By some miracle he survived and now is consumed by thoughts of revenge on the one hand, and joy at the prospect of being reunited with his betrothed, Alzira on the other. He is, however, in for a shock. Alzira and her father are held prisoner by Spanish forces in Lima.

Zamoro immediately determines to rescue Alzira. The Indians are dubious as to how this may be done. Zamoro tells them how, on his recent journey, he made contact with many other Indian tribes, and how the assembled forces will soon join them and finally confound the Spanish. The Indians are overjoyed at this revelation and sing lustily of their longing for revenge.

Act 1 **Vita per Vita** (Life for Life). Scene 1. A square in Lima. The Spanish militia assembles to the sounds of lively military instruments. The officers gather in a group. They have just received word from Spain, from their king, commanding them to take up arms and fly: 'to conquer new palms and new kingdoms'.

Alvaro, Gusmano, Ataliba and other officers enter. Alvaro addresses his forces, informing them of his decision to resign as Governor and hand over the reins to his son, Gusmano. The soldiers affirm their loyalty and Gusmano announces that his first act is to proclaim peace between the Spanish and the Inca. He reports that the Inca 'has bowed down before the venerated ruler of the Spanish monarchy'. Ataliba confirms his allegiance and Gusmano decrees that from henceforth the gates of the city shall be open to all who come. He reminds Ataliba of his promise of Alzira's hand in marriage: 'a precious pledge to render our peace more solemn'. Ataliba fears that his daughter will not be ready as yet for marriage since she harbours a terrible sadness in her heart. Gusmano concedes that he will have to be patient. He knows that Alzira is in love with Zamoro, whom he has himself defeated in battle and whom he now believes to be dead (*Eterna la memoria*). However, Alvaro urges Gusmano to prosecute his suit forthwith, for 'love gives rise to love'. Gusmano is easily persuaded. He demands that Ataliba use his paternal influence to bring Alzira round. Ataliba, conscious that the peace treaty depends on this alliance, tells Gusmano to rely on him to achieve Alzira's compliance. He departs. Gusmano reflects that in spite of all the worldly glory he has achieved, it is as nought without Alzira's love (*Quanto un mortal può chiedere*). Alvaro and the chorus join in, hoping that Alzira will soon grant her love to him.

Act 1 Scene 2 Ataliba's apartment in the Governor's palace. Zuma enters, silently, followed by other young Indian girls. Raising a curtain, beyond which Alzira can be seen reclining on a couch, Zuma comments on her mistress's sorrow that has kept her awake all night. Only now, as day breaks, does Alzira find repose. The other girls all pray that sleep may bring peace to her oppressed soul. Alzira is heard murmuring Zamoro's name. Then suddenly she rises up and rushes about calling frantically. Zuma rushes to her side. Coming to, Alzira describes her dream (*Da Gusmano, su fragil barca*). She was fleeing from Gusmano, but a terrible cloud arose and covered the sky and sea. Vainly she called for help. Her boat was about to be swallowed up by the sea when: 'in the arms of a wandering spirit I am raised above the cloud'. The spirit is her beloved Zamoro. She is now convinced that Zamoro has achieved his true destiny and has been transfigured into an 'immortal star'. Her only ambition now is to ascend herself to this star and 'be united with him and live a life of eternal love' (*Nell'astro che più fulgido*). The maidens try to console her.

Ataliba enters and dismisses the maidens. Ataliba has come to assert his paternal authority and convince his daughter that she must honour the promise that he has made for her to marry Gusmano. Alzira is incredulous. She recapitulates all Gusmano's crimes against the Incas, not least that he deprived her beloved Zamoro of 'life and kingdom'. Ataliba urges her to consider the lot of their oppressed people: 'deprived of their rulers and their gods'. Their only remaining hope is Gusmano's love for Alzira. Alzira continues to object until finally Ataliba pronounces: 'when the father commands the daughter obeys'. He leaves. Alzira is in despair. She would rather die then marry Gusmano.

Zuma enters with the news that a member of the tribe craves an audience with her. Zuma exits and shortly after Zamoro himself enters. It takes some time for Alzira to believe that she is not confronted by a ghost. Zamoro confirms that reports of his death were false. The two sing rhapsodically of their joy at being reunited. Then Zamoro challenges Alzira with the news he has heard that she is betrothed to Gusmano. He is quickly persuaded that such an eventuality is unthinkable to Alzira. The two confirm their eternal love (*Risorge ne' tuoi lumi*).

Gusmano and Ataliba enter followed by Spanish officers and soldiers, Zuma and Indian maidens. Gusmano is outraged to see Alzira in the arms of Zamoro. Both he and Ataliba have difficulty comprehending the fact that Zamoro is still alive. Incredulity quickly turns to wrath and Gusmano orders Zamoro to be arrested. Now Ataliba is outraged. Gusmano justifies himself by claiming Zamoro is a traitor. Zamoro answers that he has come to claim Alzira as his bride. But Gusmano refuses to listen, desperate as he is not to lose Alzira. He orders that Zamoro be taken straight to a place of execution. Alzira flings herself between the soldiers and Zamoro. Zamoro defiantly turns on Gusmano, telling him that he had hoped to meet him in honourable battle: 'you call yourself a warrior? You are a hangman, not a warrior' (*Teco sperai combattere*). Gusmano takes no notice and commands his soldiers to carry Zamoro off to the block. At this crucial moment Alvaro enters.

Alvaro immediately recognizes Zamoro as the man who but recently saved his life and orders that he be granted a pardon. Gusmano is severely compromised. When Alvaro, his own father, goes on his knees before him and begs him to be merciful towards Zamoro (*Nella polve, genuflesso*), he has little choice but to comply. In an aside he gives vent to his anguish at the thought of losing Alzira. However, he is saved from having to make a resolution by one of his officers, Ovando, who enters and announces that: 'a hostile throng' has just crossed the river Rima and is threatening the city. Apparently the crowd is demanding that Zamoro be surrendered to them. Gusmano sees a way out of the imbroglio which will save him from too much loss of face. He orders that Zamoro be released; he will meet him on the field of battle (*Trema, trema . . . a ritorti fra l'armi*). Shouting invective at his enemy he and the other warriors brandish their swords angrily and depart from the opposite side of the stage to Zamoro and Ataliba. The women hold Alzira back as she attempts to follow her beloved.

Act 2   **La Vendetta di un Selvaggio** (The revenge of the savage). Scene 1. Inside the fortifications at Lima. Groups of Spanish soldiers are imbibing cheerfully and noisily. Meanwhile a number of Indian prisoners in chains, among them Zamoro, are seen crossing the front of the stage, guarded by Spanish soldiers. The soldiers clink their tankards and sing of their recent victory.

Gusmano enters and addresses the soldiers, telling them that on the morrow the spoils that they have culled from the enemy will be divided amongst them. The soldiers hail their hero. Ovando enters bearing the sentence on Zamoro, recently passed by a military tribunal and which now only requires Gusmano's signature. Gusmano reads the document aloud, just as Alzira is entering.

Frantically Alzira pleads with Gusmano for mercy. Gusmano dismisses Ovando and the soldiers and then tells Alzira that the price of Zamoro's life is her hand in marriage. Alzira's desperate pleas not to exact such a heavy price only fuel Gusmano's jealousy (*Il pianto . . . l'angoscia*). Only when he is on the point of putting his signature to Zamoro's death warrant does Alzira agree to his condition.

Ovando enters and Gusmano relays the news that Alzira is shortly to be his wife. He despatches Ovando with instructions to illuminate the city with bridal torches. Left alone with Alzira Gusmano appears oblivious to his intended bride's obvious despair (*Colma di gioia ho l'anima*). He is consumed by desire: 'a love such as a savage could never understand'.

Act 2 Scene 2.   A gloomy cave, barely lit by moonlight. Otumbo enters cautiously and strikes a golden shield which hangs suspended. The remainder of the routed Indians emerge from the recesses of the cavern where they have been hiding. Otumbo tells them that he has been able to put some of the fabled Inca gold ('which has brought us such misfortune') to good use, for he has bought off the Spanish soldiers guarding Zamoro. Zamoro should be able to effect his escape and will be joining them shortly.

Zamoro enters. He is disguised in the uniform of a Spanish soldier. On his entrance all prostrate themselves. He signals to them to rise, then slowly looks around. His features display great sadness and also shame as he becomes aware of the Spanish uniform that he wears. Otumbo and the Indians attempt to revive his spirits by reminding him that their hopes all rest with him. Zamoro can only think of his lost love, Alzira (*Irne lungi ancor dorrei*). He cannot bear to contemplate exile without her. Otumbo urges him to make good his escape and 'forget a faithless woman'. It suddenly becomes clear that Zamoro does not realize the deal that Ataliba has made with Gusmano. Otumbo enlightens him with a half-truth to the effect that Alzira intends marrying Gusmano. He does not elucidate the reason that Alzira has agreed to this. With a savage cry Zamoro tears at his hair in anguish whilst a 'convulsive tremor assails his entire body'. When he has recovered his composure his only thought is for vengeance (*Non di codarde lagrime*). Ignoring the pleas of Otumbo and the other Indians he determines to return to the city, 'in search of vengeance and death'.

Act 2 Scene 3   The Great Hall of the Governor's residence. Beyond the balcony can be seen the illuminated city of Lima. A platform has been erected in the middle of the Hall. Around the platform are crowds of Spanish soldiers with Alzira's maidens to one side. The women rejoice in the auspicious marriage alliance that will unite the two warring factions and bring peace at last (*Tergi del pianto America*).

Gusmano, Alzira, Alvaro, Ataliba, Ovando and Zuma all enter and ascend the platform. Gusmano addresses the Assembly, proudly introducing his new wife-to-be. Alzira is clearly distraught. Gusmano remains oblivious. He is in triumphant mood, exulting in his victory over the Indians as much as having finally won the bride of his desire (*E dolce la tromba*). He extends his hand to Alzira, requiring her to accompany him to the Temple for the wedding ceremony. But before he is able to clasp her hand a

soldier hurls himself upon him and plunges a dagger into his breast.

It is, of course, Zamoro, disguised as a Spanish soldier and who, true to his vow, has come to exact his revenge. Zuma and the women recognize him and suddenly: 'a hundred swords flash above his head'. Zamoro invites them to strike him dead and calls on Gusmano to: 'learn from me ... how to die'. He has fulfilled his mission in slaying Gusmano.

With his dying breath Gusmano reveals what is, in effect, a complete *volte face* (which prefigures Riccardo's act of clemency at the conclusion of *Un ballo in maschera*). He describes how the voice of God has spoken to him and inspired him to forgiveness (*I numi tuoi*). He confesses that he knows that Alzira belongs to Zamoro and expresses the wish that 'they may live their days together in love and that Zamoro may bless him who forgave you'. Alzira and Zamoro are overwhelmed. They conclude that Gusmano's God must be a great God indeed. All are overcome with emotion. As his final act Gusmano seeks, and receives, his father's blessing. Alvaro can say no more than the one word, 'Figlio' ('Son'). But 'contained within it are a thousand blessings'. Gusmano expires as the curtain falls.

The tale of *Alzira* is derived from Voltaire's play, *Alzire*. Voltaire was first and foremost a writer of ideas. It was never his primary objective to create believable drama. All his writings, whether novels or plays, were essentially polemical, vehicles with which to expound his philosophy. Just as in *Candide* he confounds the Enlightenment dictum (originating with Leibniz) that 'all is for the best in this the best of all possible worlds', so in *Alzire* his aim was principally to illustrate the arrogance and hypocrisy of Westerners who would redeem and enlighten the Savages in order to demonstrate that the true Christian virtues of compassion and forgiveness were not necessarily the sole province of those initiated into the Christian Church.

It cannot be said that Verdi and Cammarano greatly helped to humanize the story. The action remains stilted in the extreme. Yet the underlying message is such that Verdi could identify with it. His all-embracing humanity always responded to themes that centre around the need for compassion and that inveigle the individual in different moral dilemmas. Verdi's characters do not, on the whole, soliloquize. If they do it is more rhetoric than poetry. The emotions they express are, on the whole, straightforward. Their struggles are not so much with themselves as with each other and with an intransigent world.

The drama of *Alzira* works towards the moment when Gusmano promises his forgiveness to his arch enemy, Zamoro. From a psychological viewpoint this is nonsense. Nothing in Gusmano's character has given any indication that he would suddenly exhibit such a profound sea-change. It is only philosophically – from the vantage point of 18th century humanism – that the denouement of the opera makes sense. Confronted with death Gusmano suddenly realizes the absurdity of his petty feud, or vendetta, against Zamoro and magnanimously gives him back his girl. For the first time in the drama he exemplifies a truly Christian spirit. Unfortunately opera is not the medium for preaching, any more than is straight theatre. It is a medium for presenting dramatic conflicts and dialectics, and finding a way to resolve them satisfactorily. In a world in which all human beings exemplify the Christian ethic there would be no need for opera. Thomas Mann, an inveterate moralist, saw opera as actively pernicious in its overt appeal to the passions and senses. The best course for those of like mind is not to attend opera!

Moralists such as Voltaire should never attempt to write for the theatre since theatre relies on achieving a dialectic. A dialectic does not necessarily have a harmonious conclusion. The moralist will always attempt to confer one. Certainly this is the case in *Alzira*. When Zamoro stabs Gusmano one might expect a word of protest from Gusmano's father, Alvaro, who witnesses the apparently unprovoked attack and is responsible for the

fact that Zamoro is still alive. But because Zamoro has saved Alvaro's life and because it is Voltaire's aim to demonstrate the superiority of Christian forgiveness over all other passions, Alvaro remains calmly aside and only intervenes to grant Gusmano his benediction before his son dies. This is very fine, highly commendable even, but dramatic nonsense.

Alzira (*Alzira*). Daughter to **Ataliba** and the heroine of the opera which bears her name. Alzira is certainly the focus for much of the dramatic argument, though hers is not the leading role. Like **Elvira** (*Ernani*) Alzira is dramatically overshadowed by the men who compete with each other for her affections. This in itself is a tribute to her strength of character.

Alzira has been taken prisoner with her father and sister by the Spanish. She is thus separated from her compatriots and most especially from her beloved **Zamoro**, whom she believes to be dead. Her first appearance (Act 1 Scene 2) confirms that she is a highly-strung girl with a vivid imagination. She awakens from a nightmare and then recounts her dream in vivid detail for the benefit of her sister, **Zuma**, and her handmaidens. Her dream is a straightforward metaphor for her situation and her desire to be redeemed from it; she is adrift on an ocean 'but a terrible cloud arises that covers both sky and sea'. She is on the verge of drowning when she is suddenly raised above the cloud where she discovers her beloved: 'the Universe in that moment seemed to me clothed in love'. Alzira imagines that Zamoro has been transformed into 'an immortal spark' (that is, a star) that shines on her. His is the brightest star in the sky. Her only desire now is to be reunited with him.

When Alzira learns from Ataliba that she is to be married to **Gusmano** she vehemently protests. She sees it as a gross betrayal by her father who had previously promised to see her united with Zamoro. The insult is compounded because it is Gusmano who is responsible for taking from Zamoro 'both life and kingdom'. It is impossible for Alzira, in her overwrought state, to understand the political considerations which motivate her father: principally the well-being of his people. It is that same motivation which causes him to utter the stern injunction, 'when the father commands the daughter obeys' as he departs. Alzira is in despair, but her despair is short-lived for shortly afterwards Zamoro himself enters her apartment and the two are joyfully reunited. Alzira desperately tries to defend her beloved when Gusmano attempts to have him arrested and dragged straight to his execution. Nobody takes too much notice of her. Her only consolation is her abiding love for Zamoro and the knowledge that whatever happens Zamoro returns her love in equal measure.

When the Incas have been defeated in battle and Zamoro is again imprisoned, awaiting execution, Alzira pleads with Gusmano to exercise mercy. Gusmano is receptive, but only on one condition: that she marry him. If she will agree to this then Zamoro will be released. It is an impossible condition, for Alzira knows full well that Zamoro would rather die than see her married to his arch enemy. Alzira succinctly summarizes her predicament when she declares in her soliloquy: 'through too much love I am guilty of infidelity'. Her only thought is to save her beloved.

Alzira indicates the true and utterly selfless nature of her love for Zamoro (in stark contrast to Gusmano, who is entirely self-obsessed) and puts her lover's survival above all other consideration, so sacrificing any hope of happiness for herself. In Voltaire's moralistic scheme she, an Indian savage, exemplifies a truly Christian love such as the Christian, Gusmano, can have no conception of.

Her selflessness also underlines a moral implicit in the destinies of all the other main protagonists; namely that the first lesson of our humanity is to renounce that which one most desires. Only thus in this life can one truly achieve one's ends. There is always a higher good beyond that after which the individual strives. By sacrificing her happiness in the short term Alzira, in order to preserve

Zamoro's life, ensures the eventual realization of her dearest wish.

She cannot, of course, know this. But then Voltaire's philosophy, in common with that of all the Enlightenment *philosophes*, rarely attempted to adapt itself to the vagaries of life. Rather it preferred to posit an ideal, golden age to which all apparent vagaries were ultimately pointing. Certainly the tale of *Alzira* dramatically illustrates this dubious thesis.

When Gusmano, on his death bed, exonerates Zamoro and blesses his and Alzira's union Alzira is astounded. In that moment, and only then, does she cease to be a pawn in a political chess game and is granted a chance of fulfilment as an individual. She joins with Zamoro in praising Gusmano's clemency as being divinely inspired. Alzira is a woman caught up in a chauvinistic world where a woman's feelings are very low on the list of priorities. But by her passionate and uncompromising dedication to her love she manages to shame the men who fight over her into finally ceasing to worry about their own agendas and acknowledge her needs as being of intrinsic value. Her victory is not insignificant.

Amalia (*I Masnadieri*). Count **Massimiliano**'s niece.

The character of Amalia belongs firmly in the tradition of Verdi's 'strong women'. She has a mind of her own, loves her man, in spite of all his faults, and will endure almost anything in order to serve that love. Betrothed to **Carlo**, who has already been sent into exile when the action of the opera commences, she feels herself to be an exile at the Court. However, she bears Massimiliano, Carlo's father, no rancour for having banished her lover. She knows perfectly well that Carlo's delinquency gave Massimiliano no choice and that it has caused him as much suffering as it has her. One must presume that it is partly that very independence of spirit that attracted Amalia to Carlo in the first place.

In her soliloquy (Act 1 Scene 3) she remembers the embraces of her love in extraordinarily vivid and erotic terms: 'In his arms a whirlpool of intoxication engulfed us; heart beat on heart like two voices in unison. Soul was merged with soul, united in the self same fire, and Earth and Heaven seemed fused in that embrace'. It is language almost worthy of Tristan and Isolde. Her love for Carlo is a transcendent passion. It completes her in a way that nothing else in her life can.

The genuine nobility of Amalia's spirit is nowhere better indicated than in the scene with Massimiliano which follows her soliloquy. She is genuinely distressed that Massimiliano suffers so much from Carlo's absence. Their shared grief unites them with a powerful bond, since they are the only two at Court who do miss Carlo; certainly **Francesco** does not.

When Francesco and **Arminio** bring the news that Carlo is dead it is the darkest moment of this young girl's life, not least because Francesco reports that Carlo's dying words have been to release Amalia from her bond and to grant Francesco the right to take her as his bride. This is an appalling shock to Amalia for it seems to indicate that Carlo never really loved her. Her grief is compounded by the apparent death from shock of Massimiliano. However, thanks to the stricken conscience of the family steward, **Arminio**, she does not have to suffer long under the misapprehension that her beloved Carlo and her father (for thus she addresses Massimiliano) are dead. Arminio tells her that both are still alive (Act 2 Scene 1), although he does not elaborate. She has no way of knowing what has befallen either of them but she is simply overjoyed to know that they are alive. She never seems to doubt that Arminio tells the truth.

It is with this certainty in her heart that she is able to contend with the vulgar suit of Francesco who, after a brief attempt at romantic wooing, quickly reveals the baseness of his intentions, namely to make Amalia his 'concubine and slave'. Amalia demonstrates her true mettle when, pretending to embrace Francesco, she grabs his dagger and wards him off. Aware that there is no

longer any place for her at the Court and that her life will be made an unspeakable misery by Francesco's lechery, she flees. She has nowhere to go to; her flight is a launch into the unknown. She carries with her only the knowledge that the one person who means everything to her is still alive. As will materialize later she does not appear to have absorbed the fact that Massimiliano is still alive.

Amalia is an intelligent young woman and must have reasoned with herself that if Carlo were still alive and Francesco has spread it about that he is dead, he must have told Carlo some lie to ensure that he never returns. Whatever the truth, of one thing Amalia is sure, he must need her help. Some deep subliminal instinct must lead her to the place where she fortuitously runs into Carlo (either that or one must dismiss the coincidence as just another operatic absurdity) (Act 3 Scene 1). When confronted with her lover she does not at first recognize his 'sun-drenched features'. Presumably he is quite different from the pallid neurotic she last saw on the eve of his banishment. When it dawns on her that it really is Carlo before her, she is overwhelmed and spontaneously throws herself into his arms. She is no longer inhibited by the constraints of life at Court. What she does not realize is that Carlo belongs with the band of robbers that she knows to be in the vicinity. Carlo is in no hurry to enlighten her. An interesting feature of this scene is that Amalia clearly does not recollect that Arminio told her that her uncle, Massimiliano, is still alive. She makes no mention of the fact and even tells Carlo how, with his father buried, Francesco has threatened her life and honour.

Soon after their ecstatic reunion Carlo must make some excuse to leave Amalia alone for a while. He needs to make contact with his fellow brigands and explain matters to them. Amalia can have no inkling of the torment that Carlo undergoes. Maybe she falls, exhausted from the exertions of her escape from the castle and her joy at being reunited with her lover. At any rate, before Carlo returns she encounters some of the bandits who, starved of women's company as they are, are as overjoyed to come across her as she was to come across her beloved Carlo. When she is dragged in by the bandits they describe her as 'stupendo bottino!' (stupendous booty!) (Act 4 Scene 2). Luckily for her both her lover and her uncle are present. But Carlo is no longer the same man she has but recently been reunited with, however. He appears to be raving, even at one moment invoking the bandits to kill not only her but her uncle and himself. For a brief span she must be dumbfounded by his behaviour, ignorant as she is of his moral dilemma. When he reveals the truth her horror is short-lived. Again she throws herself into his arms. 'Angel or demon, I will not leave you', she declares. For a few moments the couple are carried away by the bliss of their unassailable love, but then the robbers call Carlo back to an awareness of his responsibility to them. Carlo needs little prompting. The impossibility of his dilemma strikes home and, seeing no other recourse, he stabs Amalia before surrendering himself.

Amalia has no time to review her options. She is given no chance to make her own resolution. Her life is taken suddenly and remorselessly. Carlo would no doubt say in his defence that she would have wished it no other way. He may well have been right.

Amelia (*Un ballo in maschera*). Renato's wife.

Amelia is first and foremost wife and mother, and only thereafter lover. This is her tragedy, that she cannot accept the transition from the role of lover to that of wife and mother. Being married to a righteous man is not necessarily the stuff of which romantic dreams are made. Renato unquestionably loves Amelia deeply, and she him; but it is a love which is built on a mutual dependency of need. The satisfaction of that need leads inevitably to the propagation of a new one and, in Amelia's case, that is to escape the stultification of a respectable marriage. But it is not just that. It is also to be avenged.

It is made abundantly clear early on in the opera that Renato's deepest reverence is for his master, **Riccardo**. It is in essence the reverence for that which he is not. Where Renato is tradition-bound, stable and unimaginative, Riccardo is impulsive, inspirational and unpredictable, while at the same time, paradoxically, being the figurehead for the same social order which deplores all these qualities. Thus Renato takes Amelia for granted because it is an unspoken law of his universe that the woman should be the very bedrock on which the social order is built. Amelia's rebellion is the rebellion of one who refuses to fulfil a predetermined role; who is determined above all to live. Her revenge is against a life of stultification.

All Renato's libido is directed towards his hero, Riccardo. How could he have time for Amelia when he is so obsessed with preserving the life of the one to whom he has bound himself? Why should Amelia not commit herself to the same icon? Since Riccardo is the source of all happiness and worth in the world it is entirely natural that she should find herself in love with him, and loved by him. How can it be wrong since her husband is so besotted? From this perspective Amelia's love for Riccardo can be seen as only another way for her to conform as she has conformed all her life; and yet this is taking the need to conform one step too far. For by living out her love for Riccardo she oversteps the limit of what would be possible or conceivable for Renato. For Renato there can be no logical resolution to his love and need for Riccardo. It is an end in itself, rooted in his own pathological insecurity. To be confronted with the fact that his wife has taken that irrevocable, inconceivable step and lived out on a personal level that which would be impossible for him is intolerable.

For Amelia the whole affair has about it an air of inevitability, so that even when she is forced by her own tormented conscience to visit **Ulrica** in her cavern (Act 1 Scene 2) to seek a way of eradicating her love she manages, consciously or otherwise, to arrive at the sorceress's cavern at the same instant that Riccardo happens to be there. The affair must run its course until it achieves its objective, namely the life and death confrontation with her husband. Whose life is it to be? Amelia has moulded herself into the lineaments of her husband's needs irrespective of her own. She has watched him devote his every waking moment to the propitiation of an arrogant, if benevolent, despot. She needs now to usurp him. She needs to know that her life is not merely an adjunct, that her husband's enslavement is not in itself a necessity, an existential imperative. It is entirely apposite that Ulrica decrees that Amelia shall only find a panacea at a gallows hill at midnight. She must, in other words, die to her old self which has hitherto taken everything on trust. She must galvanize herself out of her lethargy. She must understand why it is that she so needs to kill the love that causes her such torment. Only by administering the most intensive shock will Amelia understand. Alone at midnight in 'the ghostly field where crime and death are joined together' (Act 2) Amelia is suddenly confronted by the most primeval fear: that she herself might die. She knows that this is what she must do, but every fibre of her being mitigates against it. She has a cruel dilemma, for her love for Riccardo and her very existence have become synonymous. If she loses one she will lose the other. She does not want to die, but she does not wish to go on living a lie. Her life with Renato is a lie. Her life with Riccardo is barely a possibility.

In the extremity of her suffering Amelia falls to her knees to ask for guidance and it is at this moment that Riccardo appears and momentarily succeeds in resolving the dilemma. In his arms she knows beyond any doubt what it is she wants. She may have difficulty admitting it to him, but eventually the strength of her own convictions compels her to admit it; and when she does so it is as though a volcano, long simmering, has suddenly erupted. Verdi's music makes this paradigmatically clear as she finally declares her love in an augmentation of phrasing that has few parallels in all Verdi. In that moment we realize that Amelia has no choice. She is answering a summons from the depths of her being, a summons which will not be ignored.

Only in this moment can the excess of her suffering become clear and the extent to which Riccardo has become for her the embodiment of her salvation.

It is typical of Amelia's destiny that Renato should be close at hand to rescue her from herself and her predicament. For Renato's obsession with protecting Riccardo, by now has become, did he but know it, synonymous with protecting his wife. Given into her husband's care by Riccardo, who must always look after himself first and foremost, she enjoys a few moments of anonymity, a few moments in which she belongs to neither one, neither her husband nor her lover. But in the moment that her veil falls off she must take responsibility for the vagaries of her soul. Once again she is confronted by death, but this time it is not to be a self-imposed abandonment of herself to that which she needs; rather it is an act of atonement, and one which deep down she knows is not necessary. Her plea to Renato (*Morrò, ma prima in grazia*) is a plea to him to think not just of the present of his own wounded pride, but of the future that they have made between them – before their lives and their marriage became an impossibility. Renato must take some responsibility for a situation that, in truth, he has brought upon himself. For years he has surrendered his potency as a man to Riccardo. Now, in discovering Riccardo to have cuckolded him, he is brought up short, and confronted finally with his own insufficiency. Suddenly he is made aware of all that he has lost. He can no longer hide away from the fact, nor can he ever forgive Riccardo.

There is only one person who can determine Riccardo's fate, and that is Amelia. Renato must be allowed the vicarious pleasure of witnessing his wife decree who shall kill Riccardo, even though he must know that it is tantamount to murdering not only Riccardo, but his wife, himself and their marriage. Riccardo is the one common denominator that they have. That it is Amelia who decrees that Renato shall be the one to execute vengeance is, for Renato, sweet justice.

Amelia knows that she must warn Riccardo, but what she has not reckoned upon is that Riccardo is not interested in self-preservation. For his love for life is entirely identified with his potency as ruler and the freedom for self-determination that he reckons an inalienable right. Because the forces that move the protagonists are largely unconscious, Riccardo, Amelia and Renato all remain sublimely oblivious to the true agenda that their tragedy delineates. It is not just another sordid little domestic feud – it is a fight for survival of three dispossessed human beings. The only winner in the long run will be Riccardo who gets what he has always longed for: abnegation of responsibility in death. Amelia must live to fight another day, deprived of her lover and married to a man who no longer has a focus for his need to hero worship; a man who inevitably will place the blame for his dispossession squarely at her feet.

Amelia Grimaldi (real name Maria Boccanegra) (*Boccanegra*). Daughter of Simon **Boccanegra** and Maria, the deceased daughter of Fiesco, after whom she was named.

Since she was born out of wedlock, the daughter of a mixed liaison between Plebeian and Patrician (as treacherous a union as between white and black in the Southern States of America in the early years of the 20th century), she was handed over to a foster mother, an old woman who died. Thence she was taken to a convent and brought up as an orphan by the nuns. But as fate would have it, soon after her arrival at the cloister the real Amelia Grimaldi, who was being cared for by the nuns in the convent, died. When the Grimaldi family was exiled the unknown child was given the name of Amelia Grimaldi and left in the care of 'Andrea' (Fiesco) in Genoa in the hope that this would prevent the Grimaldi fortune being confiscated by the Doge. The orphan, Maria, was brought up as Amelia in her stead.

In Amelia lives the spirit of her mother, or rather she brings the spirit of her mother into the main body of the opera. It is Maria

(Amelia's mother) who hovers over the Prologue in her dying moments. She is the focus of all Boccanegra and Fiesco's thoughts. Boccanegra's only thought is to be reunited with the beloved from whom he has been separated for so long, the more so since their daughter has disappeared. Fiesco desperately desires possession of the child, for her mother is dying. With Maria's death the desire to find the daughter becomes an obsession with Fiesco which is only assuaged when he becomes Amelia's guardian. Amelia is well aware of her background and the reasons for the charade. She is only grateful to have found a home and a guardian who has brought her up as if she were his own daughter.

She does not realize, however, that Fiesco is her grandfather. All she knows of her mother is a likeness given to her by Giovanna (her foster mother) on her death-bed. She knows nothing of her true father. Amelia loves 'Andrea' but she lives, as her opening soliloquy (*Come in quest'ora bruna*) proves, with a sense of oppression never far from the surface. The memory of the pain of her sudden abandonment, and feeling of somehow being a trespasser in the world, haunts her. Her recently discovered love for **Gabriele Adorno** has given her hope for the future. Because she lives in exile, as it were from herself, and is keenly aware of all that disturbs and agitates those around her, she is acutely aware that the two people that matter to her most, Gabriele and Andrea, are placing themselves in great danger by plotting the overthrow of the Doge and the reinstatement of the Patricians. Politics mean nothing to her, but loss does.

When she discovers her long lost father she experiences a colossal sense of arriving, of homecoming (Act 1 Scene 1). The chasm in her life is filled. As if to confirm her newfound security, Boccanegra peremptorily dismisses **Paolo's** unwanted suit. Yet her bliss is to be short lived, for all too soon it becomes apparent that her lover and her guardian are plotting the murder of her father. Thus when she enters the council chamber in the Doge's palace (Act 1 Scene 2) it is in time to witness

Gabriele on the verge of stabbing Boccanegra. She has no hesitation in interposing herself between the two men she loves most. If Gabriele is to kill Boccanegra he must kill her first.

Amelia is not afraid of clearly identifying Paolo as the instigator of her abduction. With the Doge as her father, what does she have to fear? She is more concerned to pacify her beloved guardian, Andrea (Fiesco), who is so outraged by Boccanegra's eloquent speech (*Fratricidi! Plebe! Patrizi!*) that he is visibly trembling.

When Amelia next meets Gabriele (Act 2) it is to be reviled by her lover who has allowed Paolo to convince him that Amelia is in the palace simply in order to satisfy the old man (Boccanegra's) 'lustful pleasure'. It seems incomprehensible that Amelia does not tell Gabriele forthwith that she is Boccanegra's daughter. What are her reasons for concealing this? Probably fear that she will lose Gabriele's love once he knows. Her confrontation with Gabriele is interrupted by the arrival of Boccanegra himself. Amelia realizes that Gabriele cannot be discovered in the palace and urges him to conceal himself. Meanwhile she fears to leave him alone with her father and hovers in the vicinity once Boccanegra has dismissed her. It is as well that she does, for her worst fears are confirmed when Gabriele, for the second time in the opera, attempts to murder Boccanegra. Again Amelia interposes herself between father and lover. It is an archetypal situation. The truth is that it is impossible for the two to be equally propitiated. If one receives satisfaction the other cannot avoid suffering loss. The exclusivity of the father–daughter relationship is a major theme in Verdi's operas.

Amelia has to work hard to convince her father to spare Gabriele's life. However the situation is reversed when Boccanegra inadvertently reveals that Amelia is his daughter by referring to her as such. Gabriele is dumbfounded. So appalled is he at what he has almost perpetrated that he begs for justice, even if that should mean his own execution. For the second time in the opera Amelia prays to the spirit of her mother to intercede on Gabriele's behalf and move Boccanegra's heart to compassion. The three protagonists have little time to reflect for sounds of insurrection are heard from the street below. It would seem that Amelia's prayer is answered for Gabriele now declares his intention never to fight against Boccanegra again but to sue for peace between the rival factions. In return Boccanegra promises Gabriele Amelia's hand in marriage. It is a moment of inexpressible relief for Amelia, second only to the moment when she discovered her long-lost father.

Amelia suffers grievously at the loss of her father so soon after discovering him (Act 3). Fervently she prays that her love will 'vanquish the chill of death', but it cannot and does not. She can only bow in resignation before Fiesco's declaration that all mortal happiness is false enchantment. It can be small consolation to her that Boccanegra's dying wish is that she should approach his death-bed to take a last farewell. With Gabriele she kneels next to the corpse as the curtain falls.

An exile all her life it is Boccanegra's privilege to effect Amelia's rehabilitation with his own demise. The daughter of a Plebian, now married to a Patrician, Amelia's life will embody the principle for which her father strove so passionately – that is an end to sectarian strife. Inevitably history will sooner rather than later revert to the strife without which it would cease to move forward. But Amelia's personal destiny will have been to effect a small, though significant, respite. Her love for her father, her love for Gabriele, her love for the memory of her progenitor, her love for Fiesco represent a nexus which slowly, but inevitably, achieves the rapprochement her father, with his blistering passions, could only dream of.

Amneris (*Aida*). Daughter of the **King** of Egypt.

At the outset Amneris appears to be a fairly average, bad-tempered operatic princess. Yet she undeniably finds transcendence of her origins through the suffering she brings upon herself.

What is Amneris's love for **Radames**? Is it just the love of a spoilt princess for Egypt's most eligible bachelor? Or is it built on some deeper foundation? At first it would seem to be the former and it could be argued that her increasing desperation as the opera progresses is the result of her hankering after the trophy which eludes her. This thesis is valid up until the final scene when her very real distress, as she grieves at the door of Radames's tomb, suggests a far deeper passion than had hitherto appeared to be the case.

From the beginning Amneris is aware that her love is not returned and she soon becomes aware that her rival is none other than her own slave, **Aida**. This inevitably exacerbates her anger and despair. Above all, at this stage of her odyssey, she fears the world's derision. The scene in her apartments at the opening of Act 2 makes clear her narcissism. Partly it is a narcissism thrust upon her by her station in life. How can an Egyptian princess, whose every whim is catered for, not be narcissistic? In the scene with Aida which ensues she displays an unattractive tendency to gloat over her slave's discomfiture (*Fu la sorte dell'armi*). She appears to enjoy deceiving Aida into believing Radames to be dead and revelling in the power that she holds over her slave. She is, in reality, miserable. The degree to which she taunts and torments Aida is in direct proportion to her misery, for she already knows that Radames loves Aida, merely from having observed them together in the opening scene of the opera.

Having ascertained that Aida is in love with Radames in equal measure, Amneris can have no further doubt that the couple are lovers and that her own position is correspondingly hopeless. All she has to hold onto is the knowledge that she is the King's daughter and that she thereby holds over both Aida and Radames the power of life or death. Amneris's only moment of hope comes when her father announces before the entire court and populace that he intends granting Radames his daughter's hand in marriage (Act 2 Scene 2). But Amneris must know that this is a hollow victory. She commands her slaves to do her every whim, but she cannot command the hearts of Radames and Aida.

It is to seek the god's blessing for her marriage to Radames that Amneris goes to the temple of **Isis** to pray that he may love her as passionately as she loves him (Act 3). But at this critical moment she actually finds herself witnessing Radames not only betraying her love for him, but the State itself, synonymous for Amneris with her father. In that moment all restraint deserts her. But as soon as she hands Radames over to the priests she bitterly regrets her rashness. Her despair, at the end of the opera, is entirely due to awareness that she is solely responsible for having secured Radames's downfall. Nevertheless, her interview with Radames, prior to the priests' judgement (Act 4 Scene 1) is in good faith. She certainly intends to try and save him, although she must know the case is hopeless. All that she can do thereafter is to pray that her beloved's soul may find peace. (This in itself is a remarkable transformation in her awareness. For the first time she forgets herself and her own feelings and concentrates her attention solely on the well-being of the other.) What Amneris will never know is that Aida has concealed herself in Radames's tomb, thereby excluding her for all time from the thoughts of either.

Finally, Amneris's destiny is the one truly tragic destiny in the opera. For she is a victim of fate from the beginning, a fate that makes her the daughter of a Pharaoh, that makes her love a man who can never love her, and ultimately cheats her of all hopes of happiness. When the curtain falls one has no fears for Aida and Radames. They have each other. It is Amneris, left behind, to grieve and reflect through a life burdened thereafter with all the weighty affairs of State, who must engage our sympathies.

Amonasro (*Aida*). The Ethiopian King and Aida's father.

At first glance Amonasro would appear to be the least sympathetic of all Verdi's father figures. He seems to have no thought for his daughter's welfare. As far as he is concerned she has only one function, and that is to serve the cause of Ethiopian independence and sovereignty. Since Ethiopia is in the process of being enslaved by Egypt one can hardly blame him if he is less than sympathetic to his daughter's plight.

When Amonasro is taken prisoner after being defeated in battle by **Radames**, it is imperative that his identity remains concealed from the Egyptians. It would mean certain death were the Egyptians to know who he is. He is therefore dismayed that Aida betrays him to the extent of revealing that he is her father (Act 2 Scene 2). When the Egyptian **King** calls on him to identify himself he declares that he has witnessed his King 'in the dust at my feet ... dead of his wounds'. He makes a passionate plea to the King: 'If love of one's country is a crime, then we are all guilty and ready to die'. He pleads with him to show mercy to the captives, a plea which is then taken up and echoed by all the Ethiopians.

Thereafter Amonasro must simply wait upon events. But he does not waste the opportunity to observe the Egyptian court, and he quickly realizes that his daughter and the Egyptian General are involved with each other. Since he has heard the King announce that Radames shall be granted **Amneris**'s hand in marriage Amonasro cannot fail to appreciate the potentially explosive nature of the situation. Nevertheless it gives him hope that he may be able to redeem his own and his country's apparently hopeless predicament. He determines that Aida must extract from Radames the vital information that could turn the situation around. He knows that it will not be easy. He is fortunate that he has not been imprisoned but is allowed the freedom to roam as he pleases. Thus he is able to follow his daughter to her rendezvous with Radames on the banks of the Nile and assail her before Radames arrives (Act 3).

Knowing that both their lives depend on him successfully convincing Aida to glean the information he so desperately needs, he shows no compunction in bullying her into submission. When it looks as though Aida

will resist his attempts at persuasion he resorts to invoking her deceased mother (who presumably has been killed by the Egyptians): 'A horrid spectre rises in the shadows before us ... it lifts its bony arms ... It is your mother ... see her ... she is cursing you!' Then, for good measure, he declares that Aida is no longer his daughter, but merely 'a slave to the Pharaohs'. This is too much for Aida and her resistance collapses.

As Amonasro eavesdrops on his daughter's conversation with Radames his faith in his daughter's loyalty must surely be restored. Inexorably Aida leads Radames to the point of divulging the crucial information, namely which route the Egyptian army will be taking as it goes to meet the Ethiopian insurgents. When Radames becomes hysterical, realizing that he has betrayed his country, albeit inadvertently, Amonasro joins his daughter in attempting to pacify him. It might be thought that Amonasro should have remained concealed and then Radames need never have known that he has betrayed his country. In fact Amonasro has no option but to reveal himself. For were Radames to elope with Aida the troops would not be led by him and could well be diverted to another route, thus confounding Amonasro's plans. Somehow Radames must be persuaded to join the Ethiopians. That it will prove no easy task to persuade him is immediately apparent.

As it turns out Amonasro does not even have the opportunity to make the attempt. For Amneris suddenly appears with an entourage of Egyptian priests and guards. Amonasro is appalled. He knows that this is the end of any hope of escape, and thus any hope for his country; which is why he hurls himself upon Amneris with the full intention of killing her. Radames cannot allow this to happen. He throws himself between Amonasro and Amneris, but he does at least then urge Amonasro and Aida to flee. They need little persuading and make off with the Egyptian guards in hot pursuit. At the opening of Act 4 it is soon revealed by Amneris that Amonasro has been killed but that Aida has escaped. No doubt Amonasro holds off the pursuing guards in an effort to ensure his daughter's escape. All along Amonasro's one motivation has been the safety of his people and of his daughter.

In common with the majority of Verdi's father figures Amonasro has been widowed. His daughter is all the family left to him. He is forced to bully her to ensure she assists in their mutual escape from captivity. But ultimately he sacrifices his life in order that she may live. His sacrifice is not in vain. For thus he enables Aida finally to make her own choice and to give her life in the service of her love for Radames, for whose destiny she is ultimately responsible.

Ancella (*Boccanegra*). Amelia's maidservant.
Operatic managements cannot have thanked Verdi for this extravagance. Amelia's maidservant only has one line in which she announces to her mistress the arrival of a messenger from the Doge (Act 1 Scene 1). Presumably she returns to usher the visitor into Amelia's apartments. Thereafter in the opera Amelia is only seen within the Doge's palace. It is unlikely her servant accompanies her.

'Andrea' (*Boccanegra*). See **Fiesco**

Anna (*Nabucco*). Sister of the High Pontiff, **Zaccaria**.
Anna's role is chiefly to act as handmaiden to her exalted brother.

Act 1 Anna is on stage to witness **Nabucco's** desecration of the Temple and to join her brother and the assembled Hebrews in praying for divine intervention.

Act 2 Scene 2 She intervenes to prevent the Hebrews lynching **Ismaele** and disabuses them of the notion that Ismaele has betrayed them, since **Fenena** has converted to Judaism.

At the conclusion of the opera Anna is again on stage to celebrate the divine justice of Jehovah.

One has to question whether the role is strictly necessary since at no point does she actually further the action. She is really a spokeswoman for the Hebrew virgins, who are on stage at the opening of the opera and are invoked by the Levites to pray for salvation as Nabucco threatens outside the Temple. She is probably a considerable age. Her presence helps to soften the otherwise unrelentingly stern and patriarchal presence of Zaccaria.

Annina (*La Traviata*). Violetta's maid.
The role of a courtesan's maid is as demanding as that of a lady's maid, and more. Above all it demands discretion. She must be utterly trustworthy. She is more of a confidante than domestic servant and she must be prepared to be broadminded.

Annina merely tolerates the men in her mistress's life. In her scene with **Alfredo** (Act 2 Scene 1) she can barely conceal her contempt for him. While Alfredo has been taking his leisure Violetta has been worrying herself sick about the mounting debts. Annina has returned from Paris, whence she was despatched by Violetta to sell her mistress's assets in order to settle their debts and finance their continued existence in the country. What sort of a man would wait to learn of impending bankruptcy from his mistress's maid, she wonders? Her demeanour is scornful as she tells Alfredo what has been transpiring. When Alfredo finally realizes the true picture he rushes off in pursuit of Violetta, whilst Annina no doubt reflects that he is acting a little late in the day. It is quite likely that the sojourn in the country, with Alfredo and Violetta having no time for anybody but each other, has become irksome to Annina.

When she reads the name of **Baron Douphol** on the letter that Violetta gives her to deliver personally she is surprised. Whether she is shocked or delighted is left to the interpreter to decide. Life in Paris is undoubtedly more entertaining for a young servant girl. But at the same time Annina must by now realize that Violetta's happiness is entirely wrapped up in Alfredo and the arrangement with Douphol is purely one of financial convenience. She therefore cannot help but be concerned for her mistress. Any misgivings she might have are amply borne out by events.

Annina does not witness Alfredo's outburst at **Flora**'s party, but she will surely hear about it from Violetta herself. (One can imagine a scene similar to that of Desdemona and Emilia (Act 3 *Otello*).) From that moment Violetta's health declines rapidly and Annina is powerless to do anything about it. Maybe she attempts to console her mistress (as Suzuki does Butterfly in Puccini's opera). But nothing she can say will bring any consolation. As Violetta's health declines she has no further possibility of pursuing her profession. Inevitably they fall into straightened circumstances. It is a tribute to Annina that she stays with her mistress, even after she must be aware that Violetta is dying and she will soon be without a job. As Violetta's condition worsens she loses her ability to deal with her finances and Annina is forced to take responsibility for what little remains. We can be certain that she will be efficient. Violetta becomes increasingly dependent upon Annina for all her needs. The strain of nursing a terminally ill patient becomes evident in Act 3 where Violetta is continually summoning Annina to bring her water, open the curtains, etc. Annina is forced by Violetta to reveal the true state of their financial situation: only twenty louis remains. Violetta wants to give half of these to the poor.

Annina can only be delighted when Alfredo turns up for she knows that he is the only person who might conceivably effect a recovery. But he is far too late. Annina knows it and can only stand by and watch as Violetta expires in the arms of the only man she has ever truly loved.

Three Apparitions (Tre Apparizione) (*Macbeth*)
Act 3 Scene 1   The first apparition warns **Macbeth** against **Macduff**. The second apparition tells Macbeth: 'no man of woman born shall harm you'. The third apparition tells him he will be 'glorious and invincible' until he sees Birnam wood set in motion against him.

All three of these prophecies will be borne out. Macduff will kill Macbeth at the conclusion. Macduff was born by Caesarean section, so technically answers the description of 'no man of woman born'. Finally the assault on Macbeth's castle was achieved by the Scottish army camouflaging itself with branches cut from the trees of Birnam wood. It does appear to the sentries on guard at Macbeth's castle that Birnam wood is actually moving when the army advances.

Un Araldo (a herald). See **Herald**

Un Araldo Reale (*Don Carlo*). See **Herald**

La Contessa d'Aremberg (*Don Carlo*).
Elisabeth's favoured companion who accompanies her mistress to Spain when the latter becomes the consort of the Spanish King (**Philip**).

In Act 1 the Countess enters with di **Lerma** and other ladies-in-waiting who come to apprise Elisabeth of the fact that she is shortly to become the Spanish Queen. She cannot fail to notice the distress the news causes her mistress.

At the opening of Act 2 Scene 2 the Countess will be waiting with the other ladies of the Court outside the cloister of San Yuste. When the Queen emerges she should remain in attendance, but in common with the rest of the Court tactfully leaves Elisabeth alone with **Don Carlo**. This is in direct contravention of the King's express orders that the Queen is never to be left unattended, least of all with his son.

When Philip enters and finds Elisabeth unattended he demands to know who should have been in attendance. The Countess confesses it was she and is forthwith banished from the Court. 'At daybreak you will return to France', Philip tells her. The Countess bursts into tears. Elisabeth is grief-stricken and says a passionate farewell to the last remaining friend she has in the Spanish Court. She gives the Countess a ring, as a 'last token of her regard' and exhorts her not to reveal to those at home how miserable she truly is.

The Countess is undoubtedly distraught at leaving Elisabeth but may well be relieved to return to her homeland.

Arminio (*I Masnadieri*). Steward to the Count of Moor's family.

I Masnadieri is first and foremost a family drama since it concerns a family torn asunder by rivalries and hatred. The family steward, who is answerable to every one of the leading protagonists, is thus in an unenviable position. Inevitably he suffers from confused loyalties.

Initially it would appear that Arminio serves **Francesco**. He aids the latter in his bid to rid himself of his favoured elder brother, **Carlo**. Arminio is required by Francesco to disguise himself in order to fool the Count into believing that he is a soldier, fresh from the battle of Prague, who has just witnessed Carlo's death. The fact that he succeeds (Act 1 Scene 3) in hoodwinking **Massimiliano** is no mean feat, considering the old man must be all too familiar with his steward's features. It could be argued that Massimiliano suffers from failing faculties, but this would be to ignore the fact that **Amalia** is also present and fails to recognize him. However, it causes Arminio little joy that he is not recognized. He is tormented thereafter by conscience and shortly after seeks out Amalia (Act 2 Scene 1) and in spite of the latter's impatience insists on relaying the fact that both Carlo and Massimiliano are still alive. He does not, however, wait for a response but flees forthwith.

Later in the opera (Act 3 Scene 2) Arminio is discovered bringing meagre rations to help sustain his erstwhile master, Massimiliano, in the latter's helpless imprisonment. Arminio has taken pity on Massimiliano and taken food to the captive old man, since he knows of Francesco's intention to leave his father to starve to death. In so doing he risks his own safety. When he is apprehended by Carlo it would appear that he mistakes Carlo for Francesco, for he begs for mercy and then splutters: 'I did not have the heart'. This could mean that he had not the heart to leave Massimiliano to starve to death, but more probably implies that he has been ordered to murder the old man so Francesco need have no more worries on account of his father.

In Act 4 Scene 1 Arminio is summoned by Francesco. In this scene it becomes clear that Arminio is far more than just a servant to Francesco. He is friend and confidante, in fact Francesco's only friend and link to the real world, for Francesco has alienated himself from all his family. But it is a role that Arminio is finding increasingly hard to tolerate. As Francesco tells his dream of the last Day of Judgement Arminio may well gain the impression that his master is insane. As Francesco relays the final line of his dream, 'Accursed one, the Son of God, did not suffer for thee', Arminio flees the scene in horror. He returns shortly in even greater distress for he comes to report that the castle is being attacked by 'A furious troop of horsemen' (that is, Carlo's bandits).

Later (Act 4 Scene 2) the bandits report back to Carlo that they have been unable to capture Francesco who would appear to have fled. Perhaps Arminio has fled with them, though all indications seem to contradict such an assumption. If he did flee he may well flee the family that has caused him so much anguish. One could hardly blame him.

AROLDO

Opera in 4 Acts. Libretto by Francesco Maria Piave, based on his *Stiffelio* libretto.

First performance: 16 August 1857 at the Teatro Nuovo, Rimini.

Cast:
Aroldo: Saxon knight (tenor)
Mina: his wife (soprano)
Egberto: Mina's father and an elderly knight (baritone)
Godvino: a knight (tenor)
Briano: a holy man (bass)
Enrico: cousin of Mina (tenor)
Elena: cousin of Mina (mezzo-soprano)

Time: c1200
Place: England and Scotland

Synopsis
Note: It will be seen that in many particulars the synopsis of *Aroldo* is identical to that of *Stiffelio*, but there are sufficient points of divergence to warrant a separate synopsis.

Act 1. Scene 1   A parlour in Egberto's dwelling. There is a large window from which can be seen the battlements of the castle. There are doors on each side, table with writing materials, chairs, etc. The stage is empty. From the right can be heard sounds, indicating the conclusion of a banquet.

The guests raise their glasses in honour of Aroldo who has returned from Palestine where his feats of valour have earned him fame and glory (*Tocchiamo! A gaudio insolito*). 'The hero who could vanquish the infidel Saracen deserves to rest calmly on the bosom of his wife!' they sing.

Mina enters in agitation. She has just absented herself from the banquet thrown by her father (Egberto) to honour the return of her husband, Aroldo. Mina is tormented by remorse concerning her infidelity to Aroldo in his absence. She calls on God to recognize her anguish and repentance (*Salvami tu, gran Dio*).

Aroldo and Briano enter. Aroldo wants to know why Mina is so distracted. Mina makes out it is the culmination of her anxiety over the perils her husband has endured in recent months. Aroldo tells her that had it not been for Briano, she might have been grieving over her husband's death, for Briano found him wounded at Ascalona and saved his life. Together they had visited the 'sacred places'. They swore on the Holy Tomb to 'live and fight united'. Mina is eager to know if Briano will remain with them as their protecting angel. To which Briano replies, 'May the hand of the Lord protect him forever from guilt and remorse' and then exits.

Aroldo tells Mina how his love for her has been the one thing which has sustained him through all his trials (*Sotto il sol di Siria ardente*). This only exacerbates Mina's sense of guilt and worthlessness. She bursts into tears. Aroldo is perplexed and begs her to unburden herself. He reminds her that today is their wedding anniversary. Invoking the memory of his deceased mother he takes her hand and immediately notices that her wedding ring is missing. He is dismayed; the more so when he can obtain no explanation from Mina. He reminds her that his mother

had given the ring to him with her dying breath. Its loss would be catastrophic to them. At this moment a horn is heard and Briano enters. Aroldo's men have arrived. He and Briano go off to meet them, Aroldo promising to return soon.

Mina collapses into a chair, burying her head in her hands. She knows she has only a temporary respite before she must provide an explanation. Egberto enters, unseen, from the left. He suspects his daughter's affair with Godvino and has decided to resolve the matter once and for all. Meanwhile Mina has decided to write a letter to Aroldo, confessing all. As she starts writing her father approaches and seizes the letter, thinking Mina is writing to Godvino. When Egberto reads what is clearly the opening of a confession he is horrified. He orders his daughter not to confess her guilt to her husband, for he knows this would mean 'despair and death' for Aroldo. Mina tells him she cannot deceive her husband any longer. Egberto accuses her of cowardice in addition to infamy (*Dite che il fallo a tergere*), for would it not be far more difficult to hold her counsel and be consumed with remorse than to blurt out her guilt? Mina at first refuses to countenance the possibility of living a lie. Egberto commands her to obey but Mina stands firm. Eventually Egberto resorts to blackmail. Must he have to stifle his rage and shame and continue to call she, whom he despises, his daughter? Mina is in tears. She was 'dragged into the mire of sin unwillingly', she tells her father, and has already suffered the torments of her guilt. Still her father insists. When he tells her that it is her duty as Aroldo's wife to obey his injunction, Mina capitulates. Egberto now commands her to return with him to the banquet. They exit together, Mina reflecting that beneath her smiles there will be an 'atrocious tempest' in her soul.

Act 1 Scene 2   A hall brightly lit for festivities. A closed book with a lock and key lies on a table. Ladies and Knights cross the stage, greeting each other as they pass.

Godvino enters cautiously from the right. He goes to the book and takes a letter out of his pocket. He takes the key to unlock the book, keeping his back towards the right of the stage, from where Briano now enters, unseen. Godvino puts the letter inside the book, observed by Briano, who is perplexed as to who he is and what he is doing. As Godvino mingles with the newly-arrived guests the chorus sings of the joys of returning home safely from 'ferocious battlefields' and the pleasures of recounting 'dangerous adventures' to their loved ones.

Enrico enters, dressed similarly to Godvino, followed by Aroldo, Mina on her father's arm, Elena, squires, pages, etc. Enrico extends his hand to Briano, receiving only a cold bow in response. Briano thinks he has recognized the strange character he observed at the table. His suspicions are (he thinks) confirmed when Enrico goes to the table and picks up the book. Finding it locked Enrico puts it down and disappears amongst the guests. Briano takes Aroldo to one side. He points to the book and tells Aroldo that his honour 'depends on it'. When he further reveals that a note has been hidden in the book and indicates Enrico, Aroldo's worst suspicions are confirmed.

But before he has a chance to take action Aroldo finds himself surrounded by guests, all singing in praise of 'he who has brought so much honour to Kent' (*Per te della croce possente guerriero*). Egberto asks him to relate the heroic deeds of King Richard in Palestine. Pressed by Enrico, Aroldo appears to oblige, but instead of recounting Richard's deeds of heroism he tells a story about a man who was so deceitful that he laid a trap to ruin the honour of a friend by placing a letter in a book (*Vi fu in Palestina*). He then picks up the book that Godvino has left for Mina. When Elena lets slip the fact that Mina has the key to unlock the book Aroldo commands his wife to surrender it. Mina is reluctant so Aroldo forces the lock himself. A note falls out. But before Aroldo can read it Egberto snatches it from him. Aroldo demands to have the letter back but Egberto refuses even to discuss the matter, invoking his old age as immunity from Aroldo's blandishments. The latter erupts in fury.

Mina interposes herself between her husband and her father and Aroldo is prevented from doing injury to the old man. Egberto whispers to Godvino that he will meet him in the cemetery where he will find 'a choice of weapons'. Briano and the rest of the guests bewail the turn of events which threatens to spoil the evening's enjoyment.

Act 2   The old cemetery in the castle of Kent. In the centre is a cross with steps. To the right a door of the church, lit from within and reached by a great stairway. To the left, towards the rear, can be seen the castle. The moon shines on the tombs, some shaded by cypress trees. One tomb, that belonging to Mina's mother, is of recent construction.

Mina is wandering, distraught, in the grounds of her father's castle and has strayed into the cemetery. She imagines her crime is inscribed on every one of the tombstones. She stumbles on her mother's tomb and prays that she should come to her assistance and intervene for her daughter at the throne of God (*Ah, dagli scanni eterei*).

Godvino enters. Mina is appalled and implores him to leave. When Godvino reiterates his love for her she upbraids him and requests that he return her ring, which was the pledge of a 'guilty love'. She imagines the angry ghost of her mother remonstrating from the depths of her tomb and she repeatedly begs Godvino to flee. But Godvino is not to be deflected. Mina is on the verge of threatening to tell Aroldo everything when her father appears carrying two swords. He commands Mina to leave. Realizing her father will brook no opposition, Mina exits.

Throwing down his cloak, Egberto presents Godvino with a choice of swords. Godvino puts it to Egberto that it will hardly be a fair fight, Egberto being an old man. Egberto is insulted and accuses him of cowardice. Godvino refuses to pay any attention, until Egberto taunts him with the fact that he is a bastard who does not know who his father is. At this Godvino demands a sword. They fight but are interrupted by the arrival of Aroldo from the church. Aroldo is dismayed to find them fighting on sanctified ground, so Egberto invites Godvino to continue the duel somewhere else. Aroldo says he will only follow and, when Egberto tries to pull rank, declares that he speaks now in the name of the Lord. He steps between the two men and appeals to them to put down their swords. Egberto refuses but Aroldo manages to persuade Godvino, as the younger man, to disarm himself. He then shakes Godvino's hand. Egberto is outraged and tells Godvino: 'you shake the hand of the man you betrayed'.

Egberto immediately regrets his rashness for Aroldo demands an explanation. Vainly Egberto tells Godvino to leave. It is too late anyway; for now Mina enters and, to Egberto's dismay, pleads with Aroldo to show mercy. Thus she makes clear her culpability. For the first time Aroldo realizes that it is Godvino who has been his wife's lover. As Aroldo imprecates against his wife Egberto warns Godvino that he holds him responsible for his daughter's misery; his crime will not go unavenged. Godvino indicates his willingness to resume their duel. Egberto tells Aroldo that it is not Mina whom he should punish, hoping thus to precipitate Godvino's despatch. But Godvino does not wish to fight Aroldo.

Sounds of singing can be heard from the church and Briano enters. He chastises Aroldo for ignoring the pious praying of the congregation within the church and urges him to become his 'normal self again'. Against all his natural instincts, which long only for vengeance, Aroldo is prevailed upon by Briano to remember his vows as a Crusader knight. He kneels in prayer as the congregation prays for mercy from the Almighty. But his pleas for mercy stick in his throat. There can be no mercy for the great wrong Mina has done him. Briano invokes the Cross and once again Aroldo's passion is tempered. This time he falls in a faint as the curtain falls on Act 2.

Act 3 An antechamber in Egberto's house. Various doors lead off. There is a table with writing materials. Egberto enters thoughtfully with a letter. It is from Mina. It appears she is trying to follow Godvino into exile. He is outraged that he has been unable

to avenge Mina's honour and throws his sword aside in disgust. 'What use is life without honour?' He is about to poison himself, but the thought of leaving everything he values – Aroldo and his daughter chief amongst them – is too much for him. To his own dismay he finds that he is weeping. The dishonour that his daughter has brought upon him has removed his entire *raison d'être* (*Mina pensai che un angelo*). He determines to follow through his suicide. He scribbles a last farewell to Aroldo and is about to take the poison when Briano's voice interrupts him.

Briano has entered the old man's chambers in search of Aroldo, for he wishes to tell him of Godvino's imminent return. He assures Egberto that Godvino will be arriving shortly. Egberto is overjoyed by this news (*Oh, gioia inesprimibile*), for the only thing that matters to him now is to have the opportunity of wreaking vengeance and thereby regain his honour. He leaves, but remains within earshot of the scene which ensues.

Aroldo enters, followed immediately by Godvino. Confronted with Aroldo Godvino fully expects to die. But Aroldo has decided to divorce Mina and requires only to know of him whether he will look after Mina in the years to come. Having failed to elicit a response from Godvino, who cannot believe that Mina will ever be free, Aroldo tells Godvino to witness his interview with Mina. Jorg is despatched to fetch Mina. Aroldo tells Godvino that he wishes to know whether Godvino would prefer 'freedom laden with guilt, or to go forward with the woman (he) ruined'. He commands Godvino to wait in an adjoining room.

When Mina arrives Aroldo announces their separation. Mina does not immediately grasp his meaning, assuming that he is leaving on a journey. Aroldo disabuses her. He will henceforth pursue his own path while she may be united with her lover to her enduring dishonour. He gives her the divorce document which he has already signed and requests her to sign it. Mina is devastated. Aroldo assumes her tears are merely an act of appeasement and coldly rebuffs her. Mina, outraged that Aroldo should consider her so calculating, demands the divorce document, signs it and returns it to him. She requests that he now listens to what she has to say. Aroldo makes to leave but Mina restrains him and, falling on her knees, requires him to judge her as if in the presence of God. She admits her guilt openly but insists that Aroldo is the man she loves. She tells him that Godvino has betrayed her.

At this moment Egberto enters from the left, carrying a bloody sword. Briano enters from the right. Egberto says simply, 'he is there no more', indicating that he has slain Godvino. In answer to the shocked enquiries as to his meaning Egberto continues that it was, 'an expiation. He who could reveal the dishonour is dead'. He exits. Briano urges Aroldo to repair to the church. Aroldo is only too eager to escape from these 'evil walls' which God has cursed (*Ah, si, voliamo al tempio*). Briano leads him out and as the curtain falls Mina collapses in a faint, fearing that for her there will be no forgiveness.

Act 4 A deep valley in Scotland near to Loch Lomond which can be seen in the distance. To the left and right are forest-clad mountains. Nearby is a grove of pines, close to a modest house. It is sunset. In the distance can be heard approaching sounds of bagpipes and horns. Voices of shepherds, women and hunters are heard coming down from the mountains onto the stage. All are rejoicing at the end of a successful day (see **Chorus**). They disperse. Aroldo and Briano enter from a hilltop and descend towards the house. They are both dressed in hermit's attire.

Aroldo looks towards the departing folk and muses on the contrast between their happy singing and his own tormented heart. It is clear that his love for Mina and despair over her loss is as great as ever. A bell is heard tolling from a nearby village. It is Evensong. Briano and Aroldo kneel to pray then enter the house (*Angiol di Dio*).

Night falls. A storm is brewing. The wind whips up the surface of the lake. From all around mountaineers and women enter. Voices are heard shouting, 'to the lake'. The

storm breaks out. Lightning and thunder fill the air. The mountaineers rush onstage, some to the hilltops, others to the shore. They have spotted a boat in trouble. A group of men throw a rope and, with difficulty, they manage to pull the boat ashore. It is half shattered, its sails in shreds. As the wind eases the two occupants step forth. It is Mina and Egberto. The villagers tell them to knock on the door of the hermits who will be able to give them shelter.

Mina is on the point of collapse and her father urges her to be patient a little longer while he investigates the house. He bids Mina wait for him and goes to knock on the door. Aroldo calls out from inside and Egberto asks for shelter. Aroldo comes to the door and Mina instantly recognizes his voice. She throws herself at Aroldo who, shocked, immediately begs her to leave (*Ah da me fuggi*). All that he holds dear, his family, his country, he has lost because of her. He fears that her presence now may only tempt him to curse her.

Egberto attempts to explain their presence in Scotland. Having revealed his crime so brazenly Egberto has been forced to flee his home. Mina has accompanied him into exile and they have taken refuge in Scotland. He begs Aroldo that even if he cannot accept Mina as his wife to respect her as Egberto's daughter. Mina tries to calm her father and suggests they leave, but before doing so she must speak one last word to Aroldo. As Briano emerges from the house Mina begs Aroldo not to deprive her of the hope that one day he will find it in his heart to forgive her so that she will be able to die happy when the time comes (*Allora che gli anni avran domo il core*). Aroldo is much moved by her predicament and Briano reminds him of the incident of the adulteress: 'The Just One said ... "let he who has not sinned cast the first stone". And the woman arose, forgiven'. Aroldo weeps. Mina's hopes rise as she witnesses Aroldo's tears and they fall into each other's arms as Aroldo tells Mina she has his forgiveness. All proclaim that 'the law of divine love triumphs' as the curtain falls.

In the character studies for *Aroldo* will be found extensive comparisons between *Aroldo* and its progenitor, *Stiffelio*. This has to be the main interest in *Aroldo* since it does not stand alone with anything like the dramatic cohesiveness of the earlier work. In this respect it is almost unique amongst the many instances of revision and re-writing that Verdi was forced to undertake throughout his career. Often these revisions were either undertaken in deference to the censor or in respect of specific performing exigencies. Verdi was a craftsman first and genius second. Thus in the cases of *Don Carlo, La forza del destino* and *Simon Boccanegra*, there can be no question that Verdi dramatically improved on the originals. In the cases of *Rigoletto, La Traviata* and *Un ballo in maschera*, where the revisions were in response to the censor's stipulations, the works were not materially affected.

In *Aroldo*, however, there is only loss, in spite of the gain of a whole extra act of Verdi's music.[7] The extra Act is made necessary by the change of locale and general profile of the work. But it is by way of a compromise solution which in no way enhances the original whole.

Aroldo (*Aroldo*). English Crusading knight, married to **Mina**.
From being an Ahasuerian preacher in *Stiffelio* the hero of *Aroldo* becomes just another of those Crusading knights so favoured by Romantic opera composers (see *I Lombardi* and *La battaglia di Legnano*). Aroldo is God-fearing but he is not a priest. The central tussle within Aroldo remains that between his love for his wife and the jealousy provoked by her infidelity on the one hand,

and on the other the dictates of the Christian ethos of compassion and forgiveness that he has always hitherto made the centre of his life. But the plot has lost the eloquence and dramatic verisimilitude that pertains in *Stiffelio* where all our sympathies are engaged by the dedicated priest whose faith is suddenly put to the utmost test.

In *Aroldo* the hero has no forewarning of the catastrophe that is about to befall him, as he does in *Stiffelio*. For in *Stiffelio* the boatman, Walter, tells Stiffelio, on his return to the castle before he has even encountered his wife, how he has witnessed a young man making a precipitate exit from one of the castle windows early one morning and how, in his haste, he has dropped a notecase. Walter gives the notecase to Stiffelio to do with as he will. Stiffelio regales the entire company with this story, thus forewarning **Lina** and her lover, but then declares that he does not wish to be a party to somebody else's guilty secret and forthwith burns the notecase. Stiffelio would not be human were he not to give some thought as to who the young man might be and whose bedroom he was departing from. But the thought of Lina being unfaithful to him is too unspeakable to contemplate.

In *Aroldo* the first inkling that Aroldo has that something is amiss with his marriage comes when he notices Mina's distraction at their first meeting. He asks her, 'Why so sad?' (Act 1 Scene 1). Thereafter their colloquy follows much the same path as that of Stiffelio and Lina. Instead of being hailed as a devout man of God, Aroldo is hailed as a mighty warrior of the Cross. Otherwise the remainder of the Act is almost identical to the conclusion of Act 1 of *Stiffelio*.

It is interesting to note how the confrontation with Mina/Lina at the conclusion of Act 1 of each opera prefigures that of **Philip II** (**Filippo**) and **Elisabeth** in Act 4 of *Don Carlo*. Both men seek to humiliate their women; both men will not take 'no' for an answer. They break the lock on the offending receptacle and the evidence of guilt is then clearly revealed to them. But in Aroldo/Stiffelio's case it is snatched away by the

---

[7]   The additional Act to *Aroldo* exhibits probably the weakest music Verdi ever composed. There is a strangely unaccustomed and total absence of inspiration. The action limps along and the music follows as though nobody concerned can really quite believe where they find themselves – composer, characters, singers, orchestra, conductor. Thankfully *Stiffelio* is now finding its rightful place in the repertoire and *Aroldo* can be consigned to the libraries and desks of musicologists where it belongs.

father-in-law before they have a chance to take possession of the incriminating evidence. Egberto's intervention only delays the evil moment which occurs for Aroldo (as for Stiffelio) outside the church and is precipitated by none other than Egberto himself (Act 2). The truth is no less painful for Aroldo than for Stiffelio. The only difference between the two is that it is more difficult to believe Aroldo's collapse at the foot of the Cross than it is to empathize with Stiffelio's (Act 2). With Aroldo it seems more like a display of histrionics than genuine contrition.

It is quite a different matter for a husband to have his wife at his feet insisting that he judge her than for a priest to have a wife demanding that he forget that once they were man and wife and to act for her in his professional capacity as a father confessor (Act 3). This is the central difference between the two operas and between the characters of Stiffelio and Aroldo. Aroldo has no conflict between his duty as a man and as a husband, whereas for Stiffelio it is this that defines his whole predicament.

Aroldo's flight to Scotland only succeeds in weakening his character further by comparison with Stiffelio. We cannot help feeling that it is the action of a guilt-ridden and hysterical man. When we meet Aroldo in Act 4 he is deploring the happiness of the shepherds and hunters who are celebrating the close of day. Aroldo has been accompanied on his flight by his spiritual confessor, **Briano**. It is clear throughout the opera that Aroldo's spiritual life is entirely bound up in his confessor. The relationship of Stiffelio to **Jorg** in the earlier opera is very different. There Jorg is also a father-confessor, but it is clear throughout that Stiffelio takes responsibility for his own spiritual destiny. Aroldo, on the other hand, refers to Briano for everything. Thus Briano is more of a spiritual crutch than a mentor. One senses that Aroldo has only survived the trials that life has thrown at him by virtue of the fact that Briano has always been at his side to provide succour. Indeed he almost admits as much.

At the conclusion of the opera it is Briano who brings about a solution to Aroldo's dilemma by reminding him of Christ's injunction: 'Let he who has not sinned cast the first stone'. In *Stiffelio* the impulse to forgive comes entirely from within Stiffelio himself. The only prompting that Jorg gives is to incite him to open the Holy Book. Inevitably his act of forgiveness has thereby far greater eloquence and power.
(See also **Stiffelio**.)

Arrigo (*La Battaglia di Legnano*). A Veronese warrior.
Arrigo's consuming need is to dedicate himself – to his country, to his lover, to his mother. All he wishes in return is equal dedication. In his mother and in his country he is not disappointed, but in his lover he is cruelly disappointed. This central lack renders, in his eyes, all that he has given to and received from the other parties as nought.

Arrigo is a brave man who has distinguished himself in battle and would go through it all again if he felt that the reward would be the woman whom he loves. It is a well-worn operatic cliché, but it is justifiable. Ever since the age of chivalry, and no doubt ever since history began, the hero has needed his muse; the *raison d'être* for his heroics. Without it he is useless. It is accepted as perfectly normal that the poet should have his muse, but it is equally true of the soldier, the businessman, the navvy. Without a muse, without a representation of the feminine (Graves' White Goddess), there is no point to the struggle with the intractable world. It is something of which the Romantics were acutely conscious, none more so than Verdi. He may not have overtly depicted lovesick loons, as did Puccini and all the adherents to the *veristic* ethos, but he did repeatedly revisit the theme of the embattled hero, the outsider, struggling with an inflexible world, against all the odds, with the sole object of winning the bride of his desires.

In *Il Trovatore* Verdi was to elaborate on a psychological complex, particularly germane when reviewing the case of Arrigo: namely that of a hero's relationship with his mother, and the way in which that relationship conflicts with, or is usurped by, and complements the relationship with the lover. Both Arrigo and Manrico have difficulties escaping the all-powerful domination of their respective mothers. In Manrico's case he has never actually succeeded in making the break, but throughout the opera is depicted as being in the throes of making his first bid for freedom. In the case of Arrigo he has already made the break; or he imagines he has. He imagines throughout his campaigns on behalf of Italian independence that **Lida** awaits him. He is seriously wounded and taken prisoner of war and thereafter is nursed back to health by his mother. As soon as he is well he travels to Milan to claim his bride, only to discover she is already married, and to his best friend at that. His sense of betrayal is absolute.

It is unlikely that up to this moment Arrigo has questioned anything in his life. He has made his plans and fulfilled them while under the succour of his mother, then he has fallen in love, his love has been returned, they have sworn an oath to be true to each other forever. And then the bombshell. The woman he loves, and who professes to love him, has agendas of her own. She is still as hopelessly in thrall to her father as he is to his mother. Her father's dying wish has been that she should marry **Rolando**, so she has married Rolando. But Arrigo is not interested in Lida's agendas or, as he sees it, feeble excuses. She has betrayed him and rendered him impotent and helpless, without recourse. The only recourse he has is to turn his back on life, utterly, and return to the bliss of unconsciousness: to the womb.

When Lida goes in search of Arrigo, having failed to get a response to her letter, she discovers him writing a letter of farewell to his mother (Act 3 Scene 3). The gesture could not be more eloquent. From Arrigo's perspective it has all been a confidence trick. There has been no sense to any of his endeavours. When he set out in life it was to please and appease the mother (there is never once a mention of his father). Thereafter he sought to woo a lover and in the process transferred his need to love, be loved by and appease his

mother, onto his lover. When Lida fails him it is not just lover, but mother as well that he loses. Consigned to the outer darkness and reviled by his best friend, he is only too happy to sign on with the Knights of Death. Mother and lover have by necessity become synonymous with the Motherland (they always were). By sacrificing himself he can restore the balance of his psyche, as is indicated in the final pages of the opera, when he has reconciled himself with Lida, with Rolando and above all with his country.

La Battaglia di Legnano may not be one of Verdi's greatest early operas[8] (though there are many incidental felicities), but it is an essential step on the journey which was to lead to masterworks such as *Il Trovatore, I Vespri Siciliani* and *Don Carlo*. The character of Arrigo anticipates in many telling ways the heroes of those three works.

Arrigo (*I Vespri Siciliani*). Sicilian patriot, son of **Monforte**, the French governor. In love with the Duchess **Elena**.

When the opera opens Arrigo is on trial. His crimes are not specified, though it later becomes clear that he has been implicated in the alleged plot hatched against the French by Elena's brother, Duke Federigo, who has recently been executed. Arrigo has unaccountably been acquitted and released; unaccountably because Monforte is not renowned for his leniency. But then Arrigo is not aware that Monforte has recently discovered that he is Arrigo's father – the result of an illicit liaison with a Sicilian woman. When Arrigo first enters (Act 1) not even the audience is aware of these facts. It is therefore necessary to take Arrigo at his word, namely that he has been the victim of a miscarriage in justice and that his acquittal is not because of, but in spite of, the intervention of Monforte.

It is immediately apparent that Arrigo is a hot-blooded young man with no inclination to kow-tow to the French governor. The first confrontation of the two men is remarkable for the fact that neither Arrigo nor the audience

---

[8] It is, in fact, 13th in the canon.

realizes its full import. Only Monforte knows that he addresses his son. His probing questions encourage Arrigo to talk about himself and his early life. Arrigo reveals that he was adopted by Duke Federigo, a long-standing enemy of Monforte and brother to Elena, with whom Arrigo is in love. Arrigo has only fond memories of his time serving the Duke and has no compunction about making his devotion plain. It becomes clear that the insurrection for which he has recently been on trial was instigated by Federigo, which fact makes Arrigo's outspokenness all the more daring. But Monforte cannot help admiring the young man's audacity, and is even moved to offer Arrigo the opportunity of joining the French forces. It is an absurd suggestion which Arrigo is quick to rebuff. When Monforte issues an injunction against Arrigo ever entering the house of Elena, Arrigo's immediate reaction is to rush off to beg admittance of the Duchess. It is the typical perversity of arrogant youth.

Arrigo's love for the Duchess Elena is partly built on the mutual passion that they have for the restoration of Sicily's independence. Initially he is uncertain whether his love is even returned. He is acutely conscious that he is hardly an eligible suitor, being well below Elena in social station. He is merely a lowly soldier, whereas Elena belongs to the nobility. But Arrigo needs a muse, and Elena is happy to supply it. Every hero needs a muse to spur him on to further heroics. For are not all heroics an absurdity by definition? Elena underlines her awareness of the nature of their relationship when she tells Arrigo that she returns his love on condition that he avenge her brother's death (Act 2). Arrigo is only too happy to comply. He desperately needs Elena's love. Without it he is rootless and his destiny has no focus.

When arrested by Monforte Arrigo is ready to accept that his end is truly nigh. How can it be otherwise when he has so recently escaped French justice? He must assume that Monforte is going to reverse the decision of the judges to acquit him at his recent trial. He is therefore perplexed when he finds himself being treated by the French with 'the greatest respect'. When Monforte reveals the truth, namely that he is Arrigo's father, Arrigo is appalled (Act 3 Scene 1). Suddenly he knows that his life has become an impossibility. All his friends, companions from his youth, the woman he loves, the man he reveres as though he were a father (**Procida**) have suddenly become his sworn enemies and there is nothing he can do about it. His predicament gives new meaning to the well-worn adage that we can choose our friends but not our families. Monforte does not have the imagination to appreciate the true nature of the dilemma he presents to his son. If he did he would not be surprised by the vehemence of Arrigo's refusal when he demands that Arrigo publicly acknowledge him as his father. For if Arrigo were to do this it would represent a political defeat for him as much as a personal tragedy.

It says a great deal for Elena that she comprehends the true extent of her lover's predicament and gives herself to Arrigo in spite of the fact that it alienates her from the whole resistance movement and all that has defined her life to date, principally her loyalty and need to avenge her brother's death. It says equally much for Arrigo's strength of personality and the passion which informs his every word and deed that Elena is convinced of the necessity of the sacrifice she makes. (Paradoxically in giving herself to Arrigo Elena achieves her dearest wish to avenge her brother's death, quite literally: for it is in the very moment that her hand is joined with that of Arrigo's (Act 5) that the massacre of the French by the Sicilians commences.)

Arrigo's personality invites many comparisons with that of Manrico in *Il Trovatore*. Like Manrico he is mother-obsessed (see Act 3 Scene 1 *I Vespri Siciliani*) and it is this same obsession that sends him out into the world and subsequently fuels the passion with which he seeks to serve the Sicilian cause. In the same way that Elena must avenge her brother, Arrigo needs to justify his mother's love by avenging her. Arrigo and Elena's relationship is defined by a central absence in each of their lives. Arrigo is brother and lover to Elena and she is mother and lover to him. Their need for each other is built on the possibility of assuaging the agonizing sense of alienation each carries around within. Only in the light of this psychological mechanism does Arrigo's public acknowledgement of Monforte and Elena's apparent *volte face* at the conclusion become comprehensible. Neither has to search any longer for that which they lack. Each finds a perfect embodiment in the other. Thoughts of vengeance become irrelevant.

Unfortunately for them this is not the case in the political sphere, and never can be, where they must still endure. Sicily is not appeased, even if they are. Thus Arrigo must take the consequences of his betrayal of Sicily. He will not join in the fighting at the conclusion. How could he? He may very well die with his father. The resolution of his personal need has placed him leagues beyond Procida's chauvinistic call to nationalistic patriotism. Beyond the call but not the arm. Such is the basis of all romantic love tragedies.

Arvino (*I Lombardi*). Son of Folco, the Governor of Rhodes.

When the fates allot a man's destiny they may decree that he shall be granted grace, success and worldly accomplishment but they will demand a price. Certainly the price Arvino has to pay for his worldly ascendancy is to be given a brother, **Pagano**, who bitterly resents everything that he has achieved for himself or been given. Pagano is especially jealous of Arvino's wife, **Viclinda**. As the narrative of the opera will make clear Arvino's curse will eventually be revealed as a blessing, but it will be a long and arduous journey.

Arvino has undoubtedly been the favoured son, the one destined to take on the father's mantle. Because he is favoured he will inevitably be the object of envy. He will always be in a difficult position with regard to the rest of the world and his family. In Arvino's case it is his brother he has to look out for. Who knows the history behind Pagano's obsession with Arvino's chosen bride? Did

Pagano's attempt on Arvino's life come out of the blue, apparently without motivation, or had Pagano's accumulated rancour been clear for all to see. Whatever the case one thing is certain; Pagano's obsessive 'love' for Viclinda is symptomatic of a far deeper neurosis and it is something Arvino and Viclinda have to confront.

It is a measure of Arvino's generosity of spirit that he is prepared to forgive Pagano's attempted murder of him and embrace him back into the family. But as soon as Pagano has returned Arvino is aware that his brother is still seething with rage: 'My whole soul was upon my lips, but suddenly an icy grip seized my heart; in those looks there is fury, for sure; a dreadful suspicion awakes within me' (Act 1 Scene 1). His suspicion will be all too justified as events turn out. For even as they speak Pagano is plotting revenge. Suspecting danger Arvino encourages his wife to stay in her apartment but not to go to bed for, whether it is his imagination or not he cannot be sure, he thinks he has heard 'the sound of many feet' (Act 1 Scene 2). Arvino retires to his quarters but is shortly disturbed by Viclinda's cries for help. He discovers Pagano about to abduct his wife but, worse, he finds that Pagano has murdered their father, thinking that it was Arvino himself. Arvino's first reaction is to kill Pagano but he is prevented by his daughter, **Giselda**. It is probably only out of respect for his wife and daughter that he does not kill Pagano.

Thereafter Arvino tries to put all thought of his brother out of his mind. But by an extraordinary twist of fate (or the librettist's opportunism) one of the first persons he encounters, when he finally reaches the Holy Land on Crusade, albeit unwittingly, is his brother (Act 2 Scene 2). He has not been seeking him out. He has heard by chance that in the neighbourhood of Antioch there resides a hermit with a reputation for extraordinary holiness. Nobody knows his name or that he is in any way related to Arvino. Arvino does not recognize his brother because Pagano meets him with the visor on his helmet lowered. Irony of ironies, Arvino has come to the hermit because his family has been torn asunder and he believes the hermit's prayers might assist him to retrieve his daughter.

Pagano is able to give the reassurance Arvino seeks and leads him forthwith to the palace of **Acciano** in Antioch. There the Crusaders meet violent opposition. It is not actually specified, but it would seem that Arvino himself kills Acciano (the only justification for this assertion being that **Sofia** precedes Arvino into the harem and exclaims, 'I saw the raging beast who killed them' [Act 2 Scene 3]). Arvino enters and Giselda, appalled, covers her face with her hands. Whether Arvino actually wielded the blows that felled Acciano, and apparently **Oronte** as well, is immaterial. What matters is that as far as Giselda is concerned her father is responsible for their deaths. What Arvino does not know is that his daughter has fallen in love with the tyrant's son, Oronte. Did he but know this Giselda's outburst might be more explicable to him. Since he does not know this, her tirade against the impious bloodshed perpetrated by the Crusaders, is not just insane, it is, as far as he is concerned, blasphemous. It offends against everything that Arvino has ever thought, everything that he has attempted in his life. Thus he, in his turn, becomes irrational, draws his dagger and is on the verge of murdering his own daughter. He is only prevented by the intervention of his brother (did he but know it), who joins Sofia and the guards in restraining him. What Arvino cannot accept is that deep down he knows that his daughter is right. This is intolerable for him. He can only push it out of his mind and assume that Giselda has lost her reason.

When Arvino receives word that Pagano has been spotted prowling around the Crusaders' camp (Act 3 Scene 2), the past must surely come back on him. His first thought is, 'I can correct heaven's error in not punishing him'. Arvino has learnt nothing from all the miseries that have befallen his family. He still sees bloodshed as the inevitable recourse and natural solution to all problems. He rushes off to find Pagano in order to exact retribution. He does not succeed in finding him, for by the time he next appears he is preparing an assault on Jerusalem with the Crusaders and Pagano is still alive.

Arvino is at least reconciled with his daughter, whose vision of Oronte (Act 4 Scene 1) has reawakened her dedication to the Crusaders' cause. The hermit (Pagano) is amongst the Crusaders preparing to launch their attack on Jerusalem. Indeed they view the holy man's presence as crucial to the success of their mission, since he provides a spiritual focus. It is this, more than anything, that reunites the brothers. That Pagano risks life and limb and genuinely exudes spiritual authority is reason enough for Arvino. Arvino is not a philosopher, he is a soldier. At the end, when Pagano is dying of his wounds sustained in battle, Arvino is forced to realize the extent of his brother's repentance and sacrifice.

Assassin (Sicario) (*Macbeth*)

Appears (Act 2 Scene 3) in the banquet scene to report to **Macbeth** on **Banquo's** murder and **Fleance's** escape. He must quail somewhat at having to report the failure to murder Fleance. Macbeth remarks that there is blood on his face and is consequently anxious that his guests should not see him. The assassin is hastily dismissed.

Ataliba (*Alzira*). Alzira's father.

Ataliba is chief of a Peruvian tribe of Incas. When the opera commences he has been taken prisoner, together with his daughter, by the Spanish. His prospects look bleak since his countrymen hold the Spanish Governor of Peru, **Alvaro**, and would surely have killed him had it not been for the intervention of **Zamoro**. However, when Alvaro returns and reports how his life has been spared by a compassionate Inca and urges a treaty to be signed between the two parties, Ataliba is saved from a gruesome death. He is naturally in favour of a peace treaty, not only because it will ensure that his own life is spared, but because he knows it will save an incalculable number of other lives from his tribe. Part of Voltaire's message in *Alzire* is that age brings wisdom. The whole endeavour for peace, whilst initiated by Zamoro in the first place, is carried through with unstinting determination by the two elder statesmen, Ataliba and Alvaro, who throughout have to contend with the vagaries of headstrong youth and wilful passion.

Ataliba is not insensitive to the fact that his daughter is a crucial part of the peace negotiations. He knows that Alzira is still in mourning for Zamoro, who is believed to be dead, but he is certain that his daughter will understand the political necessity of undertaking marriage to **Gusmano**. He attempts to convince Gusmano that he should allow Alzira time before pressing her into marriage in order that she may mourn the loss of her former love (Act 1 Scene 1). But Gusmano is impatient. Ataliba, realizing that the whole peace process relies on Alzira's cooperation, promises to exert his influence on her.

The scene that ensues (Act 1 Scene 2) belongs to the large number of father/daughter confrontations that proliferate in Verdi's scores. Ataliba is chieftain first and father second. When he realizes that his daughter is not disposed to be cooperative he has no choice but to remind her of her duty to her people. He leaves her to ponder her options. When he returns to find her in the arms of Zamoro he must realize that he has a near-impossible task ahead of him. However he is dismayed by Gusmano's impetuosity and strives to restrain the latter's desire to see Zamoro executed forthwith.

Ataliba is probably relieved by news of the proximity of the Inca hordes since it forces a conclusion to his dilemma. But he deplores the prospect of more loss of life on both sides in the impending battle. Nevertheless he does nothing to avert it. Probably it would be beyond his capability anyway. For Ataliba is chieftain of just one of many tribes. It is unlikely that he would be able to influence the entire assembled forces. Besides, Gusmano and Zamoro are determined to meet each other on the battlefield. As it is, it turns out badly for the Incas who are defeated. From the point of view of their future under Spanish rule it would have been better for the Incas had the battle never been fought. Once Gusmano has defeated Zamoro there is no gainsaying his decree: he will marry Alzira and Zamoro must die. Ataliba is powerless to do anything other than be a bystander. At the conclusion of the opera Ataliba is naturally overjoyed by Gusmano's final act of forgiveness and blessing on Alzira and Zamoro's union.

Attendant to Lady Macbeth[9] (Dama) (*Macbeth*)

Lady Macbeth's attendant is the first to realize her mistress's deranged state of mind as revealed in her sleep-walking. She summons the **Doctor** to witness the queen's nocturnal ramblings (Act 4 Scene 2). Lady Macbeth is beyond the ministrations of a doctor. Shortly after it is the Attendant who announces to **Macbeth** that the queen is dead (Act 4 Scene 3).

The Attendant can hardly fail to be aware of her mistress's obsessive character. She is present throughout the banquet scene and is thus witness to Macbeth's deranged behaviour as he experiences his vision of **Banquo's** ghost. The Macbeth castle cannot be a happy place to work in. Her mistress's sleep-walking must confirm her worst fears.

ATTILA

Opera in a Prologue and 3 Acts. Libretto by Temistocle Solera, based on the play, *Attila, König der Hunnen* (1808), by Zacharias Werner.

First performance: 17 March 1846 at the Teatro la Fenice, Venice.

Cast:
Attila: King of the Huns (bass)
Ezio: Roman General (baritone)
Odabella: daughter of the Lord of Aquileia (soprano)
Foresto: Aquileian knight (tenor)
Uldino: a young Breton, Attila's slave (tenor)
Leo: an old Roman (bass)

---

9   In Shakespeare's play Lady Macbeth's attendant is referred to as a 'Gentlewoman'.

Time: AD 452
Place: Italy

Synopsis

Attila has invaded Italy and razed the town of Aquileia (see **Attila**).

Prologue Scene 1 The main square of Aquileia. Night is drawing to a close, the stage is lit by torches. The scene reveals a pathetic pile of ruins after a terrible four-day fire. Flames still occasionally flare up. Crowds of Huns, Herulians and Ostrogoths sing in praise of Odin and their leader, Attila (*Urli, rapine, gemiti*). They exhibit an almost religious veneration for the Hun, who grants them such a glorious orgy of 'shouts, pillage, groans, blood, rape, devastation, massacre and fire'. Attila approaches and all prostrate themselves in readiness.

Attila arrives in a chariot drawn by slaves. He is attended by captains, kings, etc. Dismounting from his chariot he orders his subjects to rise from the dust, gather around him and sing the victor's hymn as befits true heroes. He seats himself on a throne of lances and shields. The company resumes its eulogizing.

Uldino enters, accompanied by Odabella and a group of Aquileian women. Attila, descending from his throne, asks who has dared to spare the lives of the Aquilean maidens against his strict orders. Uldino, who is responsible for receiving the women in order to further his own vendetta against the Hun, explains to the incredulous company that the women are, in fact, remarkable warriors. Attila is scornful. Odabella vehemently defends the honour of Italian women who don their armour and fight like men in the thick of the battlefield, while the Hun women remain on the sidelines, 'wailing and weeping' (*Allor che i forti corrono*). Attila is impressed by Odabella's incontestable valour and offers to grant her whatever favour she desires from him. Odabella demands the return of her sword. Attila, without hesitation, gives her his sword. In an exultant aside Odabella vows to wreak vengeance on the Hun with his own sword (*Da te questo or m'è concesso*). Attila, meanwhile, cannot deny the fact that he is suddenly overcome

with emotion in the presence of this extraordinary woman.

The Huns resume the eulogizing of their great kin. Odabella and the women exit. Attila tells Uldino to bring before him the envoy from Rome. Uldino exits and Attila urges his men to restrain themselves for they must listen to what the envoy has to say. However, Attila continues ominously, 'he shall have our answer afterwards in the Capitol'.

Ezio enters, accompanied by Roman officers. Attila hails Ezio as 'a worthy adversary ... the shield and boast of Rome!' Ezio requires that he be allowed to speak alone with Attila and Attila orders his retainers to leave.

Alone with Ezio Attila takes the Roman envoy's hand and expresses the hope that he does not come suing for peace. Ezio replies that the Emperor in the East is old and feeble, the ruler in the West but a young boy (*Tardo per gli anni*). If Attila will join forces with him he will deliver 'the whole world' into his hands. 'You may have the universe [that is, Italy] but let Italy [that is, Rome] remain mine', Ezio proposes. Attila is not impressed. He has no intention of consorting with a traitor: 'Where the bravest hero is a traitor false to his oath, there the people are lost and the very air is tainted; there the god is impotent, there the king a craven'. Realizing that Attila will never accept his proposition, Ezio attempts to retrieve some dignity by resuming his official mantle as ambassador to Rome: 'So now I bring you the will of imperial Caesar ...', he commences. But Attila cuts his rhetoric short. 'In vain! Who now can restrain the onslaught of the consuming wave?' he declares. He then accuses Ezio of pride (the very same cardinal sin which he so paradigmatically illustrates) (*Vanitosi! Che abbietti e dormenti*). He concludes, 'I will scatter to the winds the guilty ashes of your proud cities'. Ezio is scornful. He has already defeated Attila on the field of Châlon. What will be different next time they meet? Attila will be at the head of a similar rabble whilst Ezio will command the same army of superior warriors.

Prologue Scene 2   A mudflat in the Adriatic lagoons. (Eventually this was to become the site for the city of Venice). Scattered around are a few huts, raised on piles. An altar of stones, in the foreground, dedicated to San Giacomo. Further away is a cabin attached to a wooden shed (later to become the belfry of San Giacomo). It is just before dawn. The sky is stormy but clears through the scene until the sun shines brilliantly in a bright blue sky. The slow tolling of bells greets the morning.

Hermits emerge from the huts and approach the altar. They sing in praise of the Lord who has seen fit to spare them the worst of the storm that has been raging. 'The Creator be praised!', they exclaim as they kneel in prayer.

Small boats approach from which Foresto alights, together with Aquilean men, women and children. The hermits comment that the people must be escaping from the fury of the Hun. Foresto decrees that each of the Aquileans should erect a hut in this 'magical place between sea and sky'. The Aquileans sing in praise of Foresto, their 'shield and salvation'. Foresto gives vent to his fears for his beloved Odabella, who has been taken prisoner by the Barbarians (*Ella in poter del barbaro!*). It would be easier to bear, he exclaims, if she were dead. At least he would have the certainty, one day, of joining her in immortality. The Aquileans try to encourage him to have faith: 'Now that the tempest has ceased at last, the sun will shine more brightly', they tell him. Foresto's thoughts turn to his homeland, from which he has been so cruelly divorced, now become 'a ruin, a desert, a desolation, over which silence and despondency reign' (*Cara patria*). These thoughts, however, revive his anger and determination to remedy the ills perpetrated by the Huns. He resolves that he shall see his homeland rise like a phoenix from the ashes. This in turn inspires his people to take courage.

Act 1 Scene 1   A forest near Attila's camp. It is night. The moonlight shines on a stream. Odabella, discovering herself alone, realizes that she can at last give vent to the grief that

assails her. She thinks first of her Father, and then of Foresto (*Oh nel fuggente nuvolo*). She longs to be reunited with the two most important people in her life.

Odabella is startled by the sound of footsteps. They are the footsteps of her beloved Foresto who enters, dressed as a Barbarian. Overjoyed to see him she throws herself into his arms and is astonished when she is repulsed by him. Foresto tells her how he has observed her carousing with the Huns (*Si, quell'io son, ravvisami*). He inevitably assumes that she has gone over to the enemy. Only when Odabella tells him to recall the Apocryphal story of Judith and Holophernes,[10] 'who saved Israel', is Foresto appeased. For Judith feigned love for an enemy in order to secure the enemy's demise. Foresto takes little convincing. He throws himself at Odabella's feet. Odabella declares that she would prefer it if he threw himself upon her bosom... Together the lovers sing of the rapture of being reunited: 'One hope, one single vow, revives us and consoles us' (*Oh t'inebria nell'amplesso*).

Act 1 Scene 2   Attila's tent. Uldino is stretched out asleep on the ground, covered by a tiger skin. To the left, in the background, behind a half-lowered curtain can be seen Attila. He sleeps restlessly on a low Oriental couch, also covered with tiger skins. Attila starts in his sleep and calls to Uldino, who is immediately at his side. Attila has had a dream which he now describes in vivid terms for the benefit of his servant (*Mentre gonfiarsi l'anima*): 'As my soul seemed to swell with pride before Rome, a huge old man appeared who seized me by the hair... My senses were dazed, my hand froze upon my sword; he smiled in my face and thus commanded me: "Thou art appointed as scourge only against mankind. Withdraw! The path now is barred; this is the territory

---

10   See the book of Judith in The Apocrypha. Judith was an attractive Jewish widow who saved the city of Bethulia from siege by pretending to give herself to the general of the besieging Assyrian army, Holophernes. Once in his tent she succeeded in incapacitating Holophernes with drink and flattery before beheading him.

of the gods!'". Attila is seriously disturbed by his dream. Uldino dissembles horror. Attila quickly remembers himself and orders Uldino to summon the Druids, the captains and the kings. He has determined to pay no heed to his dream, but to wage war on Rome.

Left alone Attila utters defiance at the ghostly vision that has so disturbed his sleep. He has no intention of calling a halt to his campaign; rather he is only strengthened in his resolve that finally 'the world shall know me as avenger'.

Uldino returns, accompanied by Druids, captains and kings. The assembly demands to hear Attila's command. Attila announces that he has resolved that they should go to war immediately. 'Odin... calls you to glory', he exhorts them. The assembled company is only too happy to hear these fighting words. Trumpets are sounded, quickly succeeded by a 'religious harmony' of voices in the distance. Attila is perplexed. 'This is not the echo of my trumpets', he declares. His mind is clearly still a prey to the visions recently visited upon him.

Act 1 Scene 3   Attila's camp. From the hall in the background a group of maidens and children, clad in white and carrying palms, is seen advancing in procession, preceded by Leo (a Roman bishop, later to become Pope Leo I) and six elders. The scene is filled with Attila's armed troops. Among the crowd appear Foresto, with lowered visor, and Odabella.

Attila is at first uncertain as to who is advancing. However when he sets eyes on Leo he immediately recognizes the old man from his vision. His worst fears are confirmed when Leo portentously utters the very words that Attila has heard him utter in his dream. He is overcome with superstitious dread and flings himself on the ground, declaring, 'Here man withdraws; before the gods the king prostrates himself' (*No! ... non è sogno*). His followers are all bewildered. They have never seen their king thus. Leo, Odabella, Foresto and the maidens exult in the obvious efficacy of their faith.

Act 2 Scene 1   Ezio's camp. In the distance can be seen the great city of Rome, with its seven hills. Ezio is alone. He emerges from his tent clutching an unfurled parchment. He is clearly annoyed. The parchment is a missive from Rome, announcing a truce with the Huns and recalling him. Ezio chafes against the orders from above. 'Why should a valiant veteran warrior always submit like some sort of servile concubine to the whims of a poor-spirited coward?' he fulminates. Ezio dreams of seeing Rome return to its former glory: 'Who can now recognize Rome in this abject corpse?' he muses (*Dagli immortali vertici*).

A party of Attila's slaves presents itself, preceded by some Roman soldiers. The slaves give Ezio Attila's greetings and relay their master's request that Ezio and his captains should attend him. Ezio agrees to attend.

The slaves leave, all except one. It is Foresto in disguise. Foresto loses no time in telling Ezio that the Barbarian heathen will die that very day. He tells Ezio that it is up to him to complete the work, which Foresto will initiate, by having his troops at the ready to put the Huns to rout. Ezio needs no persuading. He readily agrees and Foresto hurries away.

Ezio has no compunction about disregarding his orders from Rome. In any case he envisages a hero's death for himself. 'All Italy will mourn the last of the Romans', he declares.

Act 2 Scene 2   Attila's camp as in Act 1. It is prepared for a solemn feast. The night is brilliantly lit by a hundred flames springing from specially prepared oak branches. Huns, Ostrogoths, Herulians, etc. fill the stage. Attila seats himself, followed by Druids, priestesses, captains and kings. Odabella is near him, dressed as an Amazon. The assembly declares its intention of feasting until morning, 'on limbs and severed heads', among other delicacies. Trumpets announce the arrival of Roman officers, preceded by Uldino.

Ezio enters with his followers, including Foresto now dressed in warrior's attire. Attila welcomes Ezio and invites him and his followers to join the banquet as the seal on their truce. Ezio utters some hollow words of flattery. Meanwhile some Druids approach Attila and, in an undertone, warn him against trusting the foreigners. They have apparently observed many ill omens. Attila refuses to listen to them, calling instead on the priestesses to strike up their lyres as a signal to commence the festivities. All sit down. The priestesses begin their song. It is not the sort of song Attila had hoped for but rather, echoing the Druids' fears, full of foreboding including, '... the wind whistles, the thunder roars, only the note of the trumpet sounds forth'.

At this moment a sudden strong gust of wind extinguishes a large number of the torches. All rise in an 'instinctive movement of terror'. A gloomy silence falls on the assembly. Foresto has run towards Odabella, while Ezio approaches Attila. Ezio makes one last appeal to Attila to fight with him and 'not disdain the hand of an old warrior'. Attila refuses even to discuss it, though he is secretly appalled by the superstitious dread which threatens to overcome him. Meanwhile Foresto tells Odabella that shortly Attila will be offered a poisoned chalice by none other than his servant, Uldino. Odabella, however, has her own agenda. She dreams of the moment when she may plunge Attila's sword into his breast. Uldino reflects to himself that his moment of revenge approaches (this is the first time we learn that Uldino is himself a dispossessed and discontented enemy of Attila). In this moment it suddenly becomes clear that Attila is entirely surrounded by enemies.

The sky has cleared. All heave a sigh of relief. Attila orders the torches to be re-lit, and the festivities to resume. He commands Uldino to bring him 'the loving cup', at which Odabella becomes greatly agitated. She knows that Uldino has poisoned Attila's goblet and she does not want to be cheated of the opportunity to despatch Attila herself. As Attila is about to drink she suddenly lurches forward and prevents him from drinking the poison. Attila immediately demands to know who is responsible for the outrage. Foresto steps into the breach. Attila recognizes him as an old enemy and draws his sword. Foresto is scornful. It is all too easy for Attila to fell him in his own camp, surrounded by his own warriors. Attila, who is feeling highly vulnerable, is stunned by the younger man's reproach.

Odabella now comes forward. Since it was she who revealed the crime and saved Attila she claims the prerogative of punishing the miscreant. Attila is pleased by her audacity and concedes that her's shall be the privilege. In return for her loyalty he declares that Odabella shall become his wife. He asks of his warriors a single day's respite to celebrate his nuptials and then 'the avenging scourge shall sound again'. He tells Ezio to report to Rome that the truce is in shreds. Foresto rails against Odabella, who he imagines guilty of the rankest treachery, whilst Odabella pleads with him to believe that she has her reasons. He will have proof the next day that she is not the traitress that he believes her to be. Ezio is perplexed as to who revealed the plot to murder Attila. Uldino is similarly puzzled although mightily obliged to Foresto for having taken the blame for his crime. Attila's followers emphasize that they need to see the traitors punished. 'We will no more be the scorn... of their gods', they declare.

Act 3 The wood, as in Act 1. It divides Attila's camp from Ezio's. It is morning. Foresto is alone. He has come to meet Uldino who has promised to tell him the hour of Odabella's wedding to Attila. He is seething with fury. Uldino arrives and announces that the procession accompanying Odabella to Attila's tent is even now on its way. Foresto is aghast. He tells Uldino to give the signal to Ezio and his troops to make their assault. Uldino exits.

Alone again Foresto rails against his fruitless love. He cannot begin to comprehend what motivates Odabella (*Che no avrebbe il misero*). He has obviously forgotten Odabella's injunction to recall the story of Judith.

Ezio enters in great haste from the direction of the Roman camp. He and his warriors have grown impatient for the signal. Together Foresto and Ezio confirm that none of the Barbarians shall escape with their lives. In the distance is heard a chorus singing in praise of Odabella and inviting her to enter Attila's tent. Foresto's jealousy is inflamed to fever-pitch, but Ezio urges him to restrain his fury.

Odabella, dressed in Amazon costume, enters in terror. She has apparently been visited by a vision of the wrathful ghost of her father. Ezio realizes that they must commence their assault immediately or be discovered. He orders the signal to be given. Seeing Foresto, Odabella begs him to believe that she loves only him (*Te sol, te sol quest'anima*). But Foresto does not believe her. Ezio is impatient to launch the assault.

Attila enters and goes straight to Odabella. He demands to know why she flees from him. Then he becomes aware of the presence of Foresto, Ezio and their soldiers. He realizes that some plot must be afoot and is incensed. He swears vengeance. Odabella is unimpressed. She tells Attila that the shade of her father, murdered by him, haunts her. She hurls the crown from her head. 'Cursed be the embrace which would have made me bride to the king', she concludes. Foresto by now does not know what to think. All he knows is that he must find some way to ameliorate the anguish which consumes him. Ezio reminds Attila of the unappeased blood that has been spilt by Attila's forces in their various assaults against the Romans. Meanwhile from offstage come sounds that indicate that the Roman assault on Attila's camp has commenced. It is the moment the Romans have been waiting for. Foresto makes to run Attila through with his sword but is prevented by Odabella's intervention. She stabs Attila with the sword he gave her, crying 'Father!... Ah father, I sacrifice him to you'. Attila's dying words echo those of Julius Caesar: 'E tu pure, Odabella?' ('And you also, Odabella?') As he dies Roman soldiers run in from all directions. All join together in affirming: 'God, the people and the King are fully avenged!'

At a superficial level the story of *Attila* is simply a re-working of the biblical story of Judith and Holophernes. The parallel with Odabella's enterprise does not need underlining. This story provides a theme which has been revisited throughout the ages, whereby a woman uses her charms to seduce an enemy purely in order to exact retribution for some previous wrong.

The opera also reads both as a rehearsal for and a revival of various stock situations which recur throughout Verdi's oeuvre; viz. the plight of the refugee (the Scottish in *Macbeth*, Hebrews in *Nabucco*); the misapprehension that the loved one is a traitor (*I Vespri Siciliano*), a man or woman's obsessive search for revenge (de **Silva** in *Ernani*), the haunted desolation of power (**Jacopo Foscari** and **Boccanegra**), to name only the most obvious. Which is not to say that *Attila* does not in itself dramatically cohere. It is indeed one of Verdi's most powerful early dramas, immediately preceding the first clarion call of his genius, *Macbeth*. It shares with that work an atmosphere that is predominantly dark and oppressive. There are very few chinks of light. The scene on the mudflats (Act 1 Scene 2) is the possible exception, principally because Attila himself is not present.

As with so many of Verdi's memorable creations an air of dark fatality surrounds Attila from first to last. He is a leader of men, in decline. His sin of hubris is by no means unique but his defiance of fate is only matched by that of **Nabucco**. As with Nabucco it is the attribute which most lends Attila stature, not to say a certain grandeur. Attila receives the clearest possible warning not to approach Rome and ignores it. When he is struck down at the gates of Rome he assumes, not unnaturally, that he has paid the price for his hubris. His dream has been vindicated and he can rest easy. But dreams, be they ever so specific, usually have a double meaning lurking somewhere.

An ambiguity surrounds Ezio's moral stance. Primarily he is in revolt against the decadence and corruption that is rife at the Roman court to which he is answerable. This leads him to contemplate allying himself with Rome's enemies. He can justify this to himself, but in the eyes of Attila, whose life is guided by a rigid code of honour (in Werner's conception at any rate), Ezio's treachery is inexcusable from any standpoint. For a despot it must inevitably be an article of faith that those who serve remain unswervingly loyal to the leader, whatever the circumstances. Attila's disgust at Ezio's treachery is the disgust of a man of principle confronted by the opportunism of an unprincipled adventurer. But, blinded by his own vanity, Attila fails to appreciate that Ezio could prove to be a dangerous adversary.

The name of Attila will be associated for all time with barbaric cruelty and butchery. Attila's followers live up to their reputation, but Attila himself (as portrayed in Werner's play), transcends these expectations. He is a doomed man from the start and yet he has no more to reproach himself with than did the average Roman emperor. The fact that Attila himself provides Odabella with the weapon with which to kill him only emphasizes the fatalism that underpins his bravado. It is the hero's first prerogative to will the time and manner of his own death, which in effect is what Attila does when he surrenders his sword. At least, with Attila, what you see is what you get. All the other characters in the opera are involved in subterfuge of some sort, thus preventing them from truly relating to each other. It is a paradox that the enemies of tyranny are often compelled to behave in an ignoble fashion that would be considered unworthy even by the standards of the moral bankruptcy of those they seek to displace.

Attila (*Attila*). King of the Huns.

'King of a thousand forests, the minister and prophet of Odin; his sword is a blood-red comet, his voice the thunder of heaven. Battle is launched from his eyes in the din of a hundred tempests; against the links of his stout armour swords break as against a rock.' (Thus the Huns celebrate their leader at the opening of the opera.)

The historical Attila (c406–53) was a descendant of the Mongols who had been driven out of Northern China. He dedicated himself to taking revenge on a world that had so dispossessed his ancestors by leading a spectacular campaign of slaughter, rape, pillage and conquest that led him ultimately to the gates of Rome. Attila requested the hand in marriage of the Emperor Valentinian's sister. When Valentinian refused Attila declared war. But instead of continuing his invasion of Italy he concentrated his assault on Gaul, thereafter marauding in France. His triumphal progress was finally halted at Châlon, mentioned in the opera.

Attila then remembered his true aims and led his army into Italy. Valentinian was forced to bribe him not to ransack Rome. Attila died shortly afterwards. Some sources relate that he suffered a seizure in the process of taking a young virgin's maidenhood.

Verdi/Solera's Attila is based solely on the character as portrayed in Zacharias Werner's play, *Attila, König der Hunnen*. Werner's portrayal is an average romanticization of a savage Barbarian who yet demonstrates a strong moralistic bent. Attila is one of those monolithic characters like Nabucco, so suited to Solera/Verdi's peculiar combined talent. He is guilty of the sin of hubris, of overreaching himself, not merely taking issue with Man but with the gods themselves. Therefore he must be punished.

It is possible to empathize with his predicament, for Attila has an essential nobility of soul. He knows what he is up against and he knows that it is not given him to grasp that which is beyond his control. He also knows that he cannot be false to his basic nature or change the way he is. He has always had a philosophy of 'smash and grab', a philosophy deeply ingrained in the Barbarian temperament. It has its roots in necessity and is what feeds the essential sense of empowerment with which Attila fuels his life. Indeed life without that sense of empowerment is of no interest to him. It is with the greatest dismay that he realizes he is losing it (end of Act 2) when, subsequent to the portents of ill-omen, he reflects to himself: 'Oh fury, I no longer feel Attila's heart within me'. It is at this moment that Attila 'dies'. When **Odabella** plunges his own sword into his breast she only dispenses with the husk of a man who has already ceased to be (Act 3).

Attila's integrity is never in doubt. When **Ezio** offers to desert Rome (Prologue Scene 1) for an alliance with Attila the latter's immediate response is to lecture Ezio on his lack of integrity: 'Where the bravest hero is a traitor false to his oath, there the people are lost and the very air is tainted; there the god is impotent, there the king a craven'. He sees in Ezio the very sin that will prove to be his own downfall: pride. When he experiences the vision of Bishop **Leo** warning him that he is appointed only as a scourge against mankind and not against the gods Attila is paralysed with terror (Act 1 Scene 2). But he is quickly embarrassed by his own fear and declares his willingness to confront the ghost in the next life. Thus it is that the need to impress his hegemony on his fellow human beings causes him at this critical moment to ignore his better instincts. Meanwhile the world shall experience his lust for vengeance.

Attila will not have to wait for the next life to meet Bishop Leo. He will be confronted by him very shortly at the very moment he prepares to sack Rome when Leo utters the very same words that Attila heard him utter in his dream (Act 1 Scene 3). The great warrior is totally unnerved. It is almost certainly the first such evidence of supernatural power that he has witnessed and it leaves him prostrate.

The prospect of their leader prostrate in the dust is something Attila's followers never thought to see, least of all in response to the imprecations of a doddery old bishop. For the first time Attila acknowledges that he is answerable to a force greater than himself. He ceases to be aware of his surroundings or of his warriors. He is only aware of himself as a miserable pawn in a chess game. He takes the hint and calls a truce. But it is too late.

Attila cannot know that he is surrounded by individuals – **Foresto**, Odabella, **Uldino**, Ezio – all of whom are consumed with the same obsession as has always consumed him: lust for revenge. But what for Attila has begun as a generalized resentment against

the world is, for each of the other protagonists, a matter of personal grievance. The combined force of their individual resentments is too much even for Attila. He senses his encroaching impotence and he fights it as he has always fought. It is the only response he knows. Obstacles are there to be surmounted or ignored, never kow-towed to. He ignores the warnings of the Druid priests but cannot fail to acknowledge the air of doom that settles over his banquet when a sudden violent gust of wind blows out all the torches (Act 2 Scene 2). Vainly he brags: 'my festivities thrive on squalls and tempests'. When Odabella saves him from drinking from the poisoned cup offered him by Uldino, he must assume that he has discovered the source of his oppression and assume he can now relax in the arms of his new and devoted bride. He tells Ezio to let it be known in Rome that he has 'torn aside the veil of dreams'.

The poignancy of Attila's ending lies in the fact that it is only with his dying breath that he realizes that all along he has been 'nursing a viper to his breast'. How could he possibly know that Odabella only saved his life in order to be able to kill him herself? That it is his own sword which runs him through is poetic justice; an indulgence of Werner. As with all conquering heroes Attila has fallen a victim to the fact that he has outlived his usefulness which is identified with the need to conquer. Something he can never be expected to appreciate is that there must always be a clearly defined limit as to what can be conquered or acquired, and that he has long since overstepped the limit.

Azucena (*Il Trovatore*). A Vizcayan gypsy woman.

Verdi originally intended that *Il Trovatore* should be entitled 'The Gypsy's Revenge'. There can be no question that for Verdi the principal character of the opera remained Azucena. Indeed Verdi gave as much thought to the character of Azucena as he did to that of Lady Macbeth in the earlier opera. When Cammarano submitted his first draft Verdi was dismayed at the way in which his librettist had watered down Azucena's role. He wrote to Cammarano: 'Azucena does not retain her strange and novel character. It seems to me that the two great passions of this woman, filial love and maternal love, no longer retain all the power ... I do not want her to be mad at the end'. Later in the letter he specifies: 'Do not make her mad. Overwhelmed by care, grief, terror, sleeplessness; she is incapable of constructive utterance; her senses are oppressed but she is not mad'.

It is essential to preserve throughout the opera an awareness of the two ruling passions of this woman: her love for **Manrico** and her ferocious thirst to avenge her mother. Once Manrico is dead her need for revenge finds expression in her exultant cry aimed directly at **di Luna** at the conclusion: 'Cielo! ... egl'era tuo fratello ... Sei vendicata, o madre!' ('Heaven! ... He was your brother! ... Mother, you are avenged!') The protective embrace of the mother and the ravening rage and blood lust of the avenging daughter – Verdi was justified in emphasizing the dichotomy at the heart of the character, for it is this which singles her out from the generality of Verdi's heroines. Lady Macbeth is broken by conscience – Violetta is brought low by her fatal disease. But Azucena is the only fully rounded portrait of a mother to appear in Verdi. (Indeed it is extremely rare in opera to find a mother given a major role. Kundry, in Wagner's *Parsifal*, seeks to emulate the mother in order to achieve the seduction of Parsifal. Britten gives a caricature of the overbearing mother in *Albert Herring*. The only other comparable portrayals that come to mind are those of Kabanicha in Janacek's *Katya* Kababova and Kostelnicka in *Jenufa*.)

Verdi had a particular penchant for introducing his heroines – or anti-heroines – with a substantial aria. *Strida la vampa!* (Act 2 Scene 1) must surely take the prize as being one of the most arresting and testing. Azucena relates the events surrounding her mother's execution as a witch. The gypsies do not appear to have heard the tale before. They comment, 'Your song is a sad one!' But it is always present in Azucena's mind, revolving over and over like a mantra. She is particularly haunted by her mother's dying words to her: 'Mi vendica!' ('Avenge me!') This phrase becomes a dramatic and musical *leitmotiv* throughout the opera.

When Manrico questions her about her tale Azucena is genuinely incredulous that he does not know the details. So obsessed is she herself that she cannot conceive that he does not know. She does not appear to realize that she has never told him. She now recapitulates the tale in all its horrific details: *Condotta ell'era in ceppi*. She describes how her mother was dragged to the stake, crying 'Avenge me! Avenge me!' and how she (Azucena) managed to steal the Count's son, and how, in a moment of delirium, she took the child, as she thought, and threw him into the pyre, only to realize, when she came to her senses, that she had in fact thrown her own son into the flames (see **Synopsis**).[11]

Azucena, like Lady Macbeth, has deliberately attempted to obliterate in herself the 'milk of human kindness', and in so doing has induced in herself a fateful blindness. As all such negative rage must, it ultimately turns on its progenitor. Possessed of only one thought – to avenge her mother – Azucena is as insensitive to any perspective other than her own, as is di Luna. A large part of Azucena's obsessive love for Manrico is rooted in her awareness that he is her best hope of achieving vengeance. She nearly confounds her own best hope when she tells Manrico, in an excess of passion, the truth

---

[11] Commentators have enjoyed pointing out the absurdity of this plot configuration. In fact it is no more absurd than many of the great operatic scenarios. In our post-Freudian and Jungian world, a world that is no longer constrained by purely literal interpretation of the text, that rather is willing to seek for the archetypes lurking below the surface, it is possible to view *Il Trovatore* (as indeed a great many other supposedly absurd libretti), as offering many fascinating insights. When all is said and done *Il Trovatore* is about a mother who, wittingly or not, murders her own son in order to be avenged on the man who murdered her mother. It is about deep primal urges that cannot be glibly interpreted or explained. Hence its perennial fascination and appeal.

about his origins; namely that he is not her son but the elder di Luna's. Such a drastic revelation is too much for Manrico's fragile psyche. He accepts almost without question Azucena's explanation that it was a slip of the tongue (a Freudian slip if ever there was one), yet he cannot help but recall how, when he had di Luna at his mercy, he was unable to kill him as he wished. He cannot explain this, other than to say: 'A cry came down from Heaven that said to me: "Do not strike!"' It is perceived by Manrico as a divine revelation. Nowadays it would be seen as unconscious awareness of the true identity of his victim. Either way the result is the same. For Azucena, who has no blood connection and is only concerned to see justice done, it is incomprehensible. She makes Manrico swear not to pass up the opportunity again should it present itself.

Azucena appears to be oblivious to the fact that Manrico is in love with di Luna's own beloved – **Leonora**. If she did know this she might well bless their union as being in itself a sweet vengeance. But it is not something that Azucena can bring herself even to acknowledge, so passionate is her attachment to her adopted son. The reasons for this are manifold: her guilt over the murder of her own baby; guilt at the thought that she had actually intended to murder Manrico; desperation to see justice done by her mother through Manrico; and above all, the need to give the sort of mother-love which she no doubt enjoyed from her own mother, and which she effectively excised in herself when she threw her child into the flames.

When Azucena next appears she is being dragged before the Count in chains (Act 3 Scene 1). She is genuinely terrified; she knows who di Luna is but he does not at first recognize her. Azucena has followed in pursuit of Manrico: 'the ingrate left and forgot me. Abandoned, I wander about, hunting for that son who cost my heart horrible pangs. The love I feel for him no other mother on Earth has felt!' It does not matter that Manrico is not actually her son, for she has ritually taken over the role of Mother. It could be said that in saving his

life she has become responsible for his re-birth.

When she is recognized by **Ferrando** as the gypsy responsible for stealing the Count's younger son Azucena forgets herself and calls on Manrico to come to her aid. She is not prepared to suffer an ignominious end without him. Above all it is imperative for her that before she dies she effects her revenge. She has never felt more helpless than she is now. She eloquently describes her enforced restraint as a 'long drawn-out death'. For Azucena this is no mere hyperbole. She has only just proudly proclaimed: 'It is the gypsy's custom to move her wandering steps without a plan – the sky is her roof and the world is her country'. But more than this her chains invoke her mother's fate – which has haunted her all her life. In a moment of profound self-appraisal she warns di Luna that 'God protects the helpless and God will punish you!' Azucena's obsessive assumption of the role of the Mother must be inextricably bound up in the fact that she has herself been responsible for the murder of her own son. How can she forgive herself this sin? In that moment she failed both in her duty to avenge her mother and in her duty *as* a mother. God protected the helpless baby boy that she intended to fling into the flames, yet punished her by taking from her her own son.

In the final scene of the opera (Act 4 Scene 2) Azucena is half delirious. She is tended by her loving 'son'. This in itself is enough to bring her a measure of peace as she contemplates her end. Yet still she must relive the horror of her mother having been burnt at the stake. The very words: 'Il rogo' ('The stake') reverberate incessantly in her mind. At this juncture only Manrico can succeed in soothing her.

Azucena has known little peace in her life and now, as her end approaches, she has a vision of what life could have been, should have been and now never will be (*Ai nostri monti*). From the constraints of captivity any freedom seems like unspeakable bliss. For Azucena peace is entirely identified with being with her son. No other peace would mean anything to her. The scene is an extraordinary reversal of the traditional cradle scene where a child is lulled to sleep by his mother or nurse. The mother has become the anguished child needing consolation and succour. Azucena requires a great sacrifice of Manrico. Had she lived to see him wed to Leonora it is doubtful whether she could have tolerated it. She falls unconscious and remains so throughout her son's passionate exchanges with Leonora. When she comes to it is to see her son being dragged off to his execution. Di Luna takes her to the window. Manrico's execution takes place within seconds. Only after it has happened does Azucena tell di Luna the truth; namely that Manrico was his brother.

She has fulfilled her destiny to avenge her mother.

B

UN BALLO IN MASCHERA

Opera in 3 Acts. Libretto by Antonio Somma, based on Eugène Scribe's libretto, *Gustave III* (1833), itself based on fact.

First performance: 17 February 1859 at the Teatro Apollo, Rome.

Cast:

Amelia: Renato's wife (soprano)
A judge (tenor)
Oscar: a page (soprano)
Renato: a creole, Riccardo's secretary (baritone)
Riccardo: Count of Warwick and Governor of Boston (tenor)
Samuel: enemy of the Count (bass)
Amelia's servant (tenor)
Silvano: a sailor (bass)
Tom: another conspirator (bass)
Ulrica: a black fortune-teller (contralto)

Time: late 17th century.
Place: in and around Boston.
Historical Background The libretto of *Un Ballo in Maschera* was based on the events surrounding the assassination of Gustavus III of Sweden at a masked ball in 1792. Because the censors would not allow the depiction of a ruling monarch being murdered on stage Verdi and Somma moved the events to colonial America. Thus King Gustave became Riccardo in the opera and his murderer, Johan Jacob Anckarström, Renato.[12]

Synopsis

Act 1 Scene 1   A drawing room in the Governor's mansion. To the rear a door leading to the Governor's apartments. It is morning. In the foreground are deputies, officers, townsfolk, gentlemen and Samuel, Tom and their henchmen. All are waiting for Riccardo.

The officers and gentlemen express the sycophantic wish that Riccardo's 'noble heart' should rest. He is shielded in this dwelling by 'the love of a virgin world'. However, Samuel, Tom and their henchmen mutter darkly of their hatred for the Governor and of the need for those who died for Riccardo to be avenged. Oscar enters from Riccardo's rooms and announces his Lordship. Riccardo enters and greets the assembly, graciously accepting petitions from the deputies. He reassures them that they can rely on him since: 'power has no beauty unless it dries its subjects' tears and strives for uncorrupted glory'. Oscar bids Riccardo read the list of invitations to the ball that is planned for the following evening. Riccardo's only concern is that Oscar should not have omitted to include 'any beauty'. Oscar hands him the list and Riccardo's eye immediately alights on the name of Amelia, with whom he is apparently infatuated. He reflects (*La rivedrà nell'estasi*) how, when night falls, Amelia's presence outshines even the

---

12   The transference of the action of *Un Ballo in Maschera* from Sweden to Boston hardly makes for credibility. In fact, considering the Italian names of the protagonists it might have been better had the opera been set in Mantua, like *Rigoletto* (Riccardo invites many comparisons with the Duke of Mantua) but there were political reasons why this could not be – see Appendix A. Having said which, the libretto of *Un Ballo in Maschera* is one of the finest Verdi set before the Boito libretti. While not adhering totally to classical unity, the action has a cohesiveness and logic rare in Verdi's operas before *Otello* and *Falstaff*.

brightest star. Oscar joins the officers and gentlemen in their deferential expressions of faith in Riccardo's magnanimity, while Samuel and Tom reflect that the time to execute their revenge is not yet ripe and that they should leave the enemy's house. Riccardo dismisses Oscar and the others. Oscar, last to leave, meets Renato at the door and tells him that he may now seek an audience.

Renato notes how sad Riccardo seems, little realizing that the cause of Riccardo's melancholy is his own wife, Amelia. Riccardo starts guiltily when he sees Renato approaching. When Renato declares that he knows what oppresses Riccardo, the latter is alarmed, thinking his secret liaison must have been discovered. He is hugely relieved when he realizes that Renato has discovered not his wife's infidelity, but a conspiracy against Riccardo's life. Riccardo is sublimely indifferent to the danger to his life and refuses even to listen to the names of the conspirators. 'What does it matter?' he says, 'I despise them'. Renato tries to point out that upon Riccardo's fate rests the fate of many thousands of other lives. It is his duty to ensure the conspiracy is stillborn (*Te perduto*).

Oscar re-enters and announces the Judge, who enters carrying sheaves of paper for Riccardo to sign. First there is an indictment against a Negro seeress called Ulrica. Riccardo asks Oscar his opinion of the seeress. Oscar gives a spirited defence (*Volta la terrea*), which is hardly a defence at all, since he relates that she has a pact with Lucifer. But Oscar is deliberately appealing to Riccardo's sense of the outrageous. His appeal is successful. Riccardo ignores the remonstrations of the Judge and orders Oscar to summon everyone back into his presence. He then invites the company to a rendezvous at Ulrica's house that very evening. Renato is alarmed at the prospect of Riccardo putting himself at such risk. Riccardo remains indifferent to his friend's counsel and declares that they should meet at 3 am at the 'oracle's cavern'. Samuel and Tom, meanwhile, realize (as Renato knew they would) that this could be an ideal

opportunity to assassinate the Governor. The rest of the Court revels at the prospect of some harmless fun at the seeress' expense.

Act 1 Scene 2   The Seeress' cavern. To the left is a fireplace in which a fire is burning. The magic cauldron is smoking on its tripod. A door leads to a dark recess on the same side; on the other side is a winding staircase hiding a secret door. To the rear is the main entrance with a big window beside. In the middle is a rough table. At the back townsfolk mingle. Ulrica is seated at the table. Nearby a youth and a girl are having their fortunes told.

The women and children appear blithely unconcerned that Ulrica may be in league with the devil. All that does concern them is that they learn what the future holds for them. Ulrica, 'as if inspired', summons the 'King of the Depths' to make haste and enlighten her (*Re dell'abisso*). Riccardo, disguised as a fisherman, enters and searches unsuccessfully for members of his court. To Riccardo's amusement the townswomen crudely tell him to keep back. Meanwhile Ulrica's invocation has been successful and she has been granted an apparition of her titular god. Now nothing is hidden from her. She can see the future clearly. She calls for silence.

Silvano enters, breaking his way through the crowd. He is a sailor in the Count's service who has served for fifteen years and now seeks to know if his loyalty is going to be rewarded. He gives Ulrica his hand and is told that he can be 'of good cheer', for soon he will be granted 'gold and rank'. Silvano assumes the seeress is joking. But Ulrica is quite serious. Riccardo, meanwhile, has scribbled a commission for Silvano which he then conceals in the sailor's pocket. Silvano reaches inside his pocket for money to pay Ulrica but his hand alights on the parchment. Taking it out he reads it aloud. It hails him as 'officer'. The sailor is dumbfounded. The townsfolk sing the praises of the 'immortal Sybyl who brings riches and pleasures to all'.

A knock is heard at the secret door. Ulrica goes and opens it to admit one of Amelia's servants, whom Riccardo immediately recognizes. The servant whispers to Ulrica, (but is overheard by Riccardo), advising the witch that her mistress requests a private audience. Ulrica tells the servant to bring his mistress to her. The servant leaves. Riccardo conceals himself in an adjacent room while Ulrica dismisses the townsfolk on the pretext of needing to consult Satan in private. All exit as Amelia enters, observed only by Riccardo. Questioned by Ulrica as to the reason for her visit Amelia reveals that she comes in the hope that Ulrica may be able to bring some peace to her troubled heart. She is consumed by an illicit passion. Riccardo is overjoyed at this proof of Amelia's love for him. Ulrica tells Amelia she can help, but only if Amelia is willing to pick a herb that can be found growing exclusively at the foot of a nearby gallows. It must be picked at midnight. Amelia is horrified, but Ulrica is insistent. Riccardo avers that she shall not be alone for he will follow her.

Meanwhile the townsfolk who are waiting outside are growing impatient and are knocking at the door. Ulrica dismisses Amelia, who leaves by the secret door. She then opens the main door. Samuel, Tom and their fellow conspirators enter, followed by Riccardo's entourage, Oscar, gentlemen and officers, all in bizarre disguises. Riccardo joins them. The company calls on Ulrica to 'mount her tripod', and pronounce her prophecy. Oscar loudly asks where his lordship is. Riccardo hastily silences him. He turns to Ulrica and demands that she reveal his fate (*Di' tu se fedele*). He pretends that he is separated from his beloved by his passion for the sea. Ulrica upbraids him: 'Whoever you are, your mad words can change to sobs one day. For he who violates the hidden realm must wash away his guilt with tears, and he who insolently challenges his fate must pay for his sin in his fate itself'. Undeterred, Riccardo advances and proffers Ulrica his palm. Ulrica immediately detects that it is 'the hand of a great man, living under the sign of Mars'. Then suddenly she lets his hand drop and tells him to leave forthwith and ask no more. But Riccardo is insistent. So Ulrica tells him what she has

seen: namely that he will die soon, but not 'on the field of honour', as Riccardo might hope, but at the hands of a 'friend'. All present are horrified. Riccardo refuses to be perturbed (*È scherzo od è follia*).

Ulrica, meanwhile, confronts Samuel and Tom and demands to know what they are concealing. The conspirators realize that she has penetrated their secret and are acutely uncomfortable. Then Riccardo demands that she repeat the prophecy and reveal who his killer will be. Ulrica declares it will be, 'the first to touch (his) hand today'. Riccardo offers his hand to all his companions, inviting any one of them to take it. None dare to. At this moment Renato appears at the door. Riccardo goes to greet him and shakes his hand. All refuse to believe that Renato could be about to murder Riccardo and assume that the seeress has made a mistake. Samuel and Tom breathe sighs of relief that suspicion has thus been diverted from them. Renato addresses Riccardo by name, thus unmasking the Governor.

Riccardo teasingly points out that Ulrica's oracle did not reveal to her his identity, nor the fact that this very day she was to have been exiled. However he is disposed to be magnanimous and throws her a purse instead. Ulrica attempts to reiterate her warning but Riccardo does not wish to hear any more. He has enjoyed his fun and Ulrica wisely decides to hold her peace. She reflects to herself, however, that Riccardo already has 'a foot in the grave'.

Meanwhile a chorus can be heard in the distance. It is Silvano returning with a crowd of townsfolk to pay homage to their lord. Riccardo reflects, as the people offer their love and blessings, that he cannot begin to harbour suspicions when 'a thousand hearts exult in dying for me'. Samuel and Tom are forced to acknowledge that the 'servile multitude' makes it impossible for them to carry out their plan that night. Renato philosophizes, 'Evil fortune forever hovers even over the grandest triumph, in which a hypocritical fate conceals an evil end'.

Act 2 At the foot of a rocky hill in a deserted field near Boston. On the left are two columns, white in the moonlight. Amelia appears on the hillside. She kneels in prayer, then rises to her feet and slowly descends. She is in a highly overwrought state as she searches for the herb which she imagines will cure her of her love (*Ecco l'orrido campo ove s'accoppia*). Everything, even the sound of her own footsteps, fills her with terror. As she moves on in search of the herb she reflects sadly 'once love is dead, what then is left?' Something within her persists in restraining her from taking the drastic step she has entered upon. Her agitation is increased by the sound of a bell striking midnight. Thoroughly overwrought, she imagines she sees a head, rising up 'from beneath the earth'. It sighs, and in its eyes, 'anger flashes. It stares at me – silent, terrible!' She falls to her knees and prays for strength.

It is at this moment that Riccardo appears (*Teco io sto*). His advent only increases Amelia's agitation. She begs him to leave, but Riccardo has no intention of leaving. Instead he confirms his undying love for her. As she begs him to take pity on her he tries to reassure her, but she points out that she belongs to his dearest friend, Renato. Riccardo upbraids her for so cruelly reminding him of the fact, which obviously disturbs even his light-hearted conscience. He describes in vivid terms the anguish which has assailed him as he has battled with his conscience and prayed to Heaven for guidance (*Non sai tu che se l'anima mia*). But finally he knows that the only thing which can bring him repose is that his love for Amelia be returned. Amelia's resolve begins to waver. She pleads with Riccardo to leave, but with less conviction. Riccardo begs for only one word from her; 'T'amo' ('I love you'). Amelia needs no more persuading. She admits that she loves him and begs that he should help protect her from her troubled heart. Riccardo does not wish to protect her from her own feelings, however. He is exultant in the knowledge that his love is returned: 'Oh, let remorse and friendship be destroyed within my breast; let all be dead, all except my love', he says (*O, qual soave brivido*). He begs her to repeat her

declaration of love. Amelia is forced to admit that in spite of the fact that she has come to this 'melancholy' place with the express intention of killing her love and, if necessary, herself, she is unable to do so. The moonlight grows ever brighter and with it Amelia's conviction of where her true destiny lies. In one of the most transcendent moments in all Verdi she reiterates her love. Distilled into the phrase is all the desperation and pathos of the knowledge that choosing this love is tantamount to choosing death. It is something over which she has no volition and is both a moment of supreme choice and also supreme acquiescence. Riccardo is ecstatic. The two are still celebrating their love when they are suddenly interrupted by the arrival of Renato himself.

Amelia lowers her veil in fright. Renato goes up to Riccardo and tells him that he has come to save him from an ambush. Apparently the conspirators are hiding nearby. Renato managed to circumnavigate them by wrapping himself in a cloak so as to look like one of them. As he was passing he heard one of them call out: 'It is Riccardo with an unknown beauty!' Renato covers Riccardo with his cloak and tells him to make his escape. Amelia makes to leave with Riccardo, but Renato detains her. Still not recognizing his wife he tells her that her presence at Riccardo's side would only expose them both to danger. He goes to check if the way is clear and Amelia takes the opportunity to urge Riccardo to escape alone. But Riccardo will not hear of leaving Amelia alone with her husband. Finally Amelia threatens to remove her veil if Riccardo does not leave forthwith.

Renato has now returned and there is no time to prevaricate further. Riccardo makes Renato swear that he will accompany Amelia to the gates of the town without speaking to or looking at his charge. Renato agrees. Amelia, meanwhile, is convinced that the conspirators are closing in to effect their ambush, a suspicion corroborated by Renato who urges Riccardo to flee. Riccardo is suddenly struck by the impossibility of his position. He is outraged that his life is in danger, but realizes that he is powerless to do anything about it. Were he not guilty of having betrayed his staunchest friend then he could take a stand and brazen it out, but since he is himself guilty he must flee and abandon Amelia to her fate. Muttering a prayer that the Lord may protect her he departs.

Renato instructs Amelia to follow him. He notices her agitation and tries to reassure her. Samuel, Tom and their men enter from above. Renato tells Amelia to lean against him. She is naturally reluctant, but has little choice. By now Samuel has caught sight of Amelia's white veil. Renato challenges the conspirators. Samuel immediately realizes that it is not Riccardo they are about to assail and, recognizing Renato, remarks ironically: 'We waited in vain for a beautiful woman's smile'. He demands to see 'this goddess's face'. By now several more conspirators have arrived.

The moon is now shining brightly. Tom advances on Amelia and attempts to pull her veil off. Renato draws his sword and the conspirators fall upon him. Amelia attempts to go to his assistance and as she does so her veil falls. Renato is thunderstruck, as are all the conspirators who immediately recognize her. Samuel and Tom are hugely amused at this turn of events and fall to making ribald remarks at Renato's expense. Renato's immediate thought is to be avenged on Riccardo. He loses no time in requesting a meeting with Samuel and Tom the next morning. The conspirators are at first reluctant, assuming that Renato wants 'satisfaction' from them. Renato reassures them that this is not what he has in mind and they agree to meet him. The conspirators disperse in different directions, reflecting on the amusing change of events.

Renato coldly addresses his wife. He has sworn to accompany her to the gate of the town and he will be true to his word. Amelia pleads with him to have pity on her, but Renato is not disposed to converse. One can imagine the couple trudging to the gates of the town in stony silence as the curtain falls on Act 2.

Act 3 Scene 1   The library of Renato's house. To one side a mantel, on which are two bronze vases. Opposite are bookshelves. On the rear wall is a full-length portrait of Riccardo. There is a table in the centre.

Renato and Amelia enter. Renato lays down his sword and closes the door. He tells his wife that for such an offence tears are useless. There can be no excuse for what she has done: 'Blood must flow and you must die!' he concludes. Frantically Amelia implores him to believe that she has not dishonoured him. But Renato is beyond her reach. He takes up his sword. In desperation Amelia manages to check him by begging him to allow her to see her beloved only child once more before she dies (*Morrò, ma prima in grazia*). In spite of himself Renato is moved to compassion. Without looking at her he points to the door and tells her to go to her son. 'In the darkness and the silence, there, hide your blushes and my shame', he bids her. Amelia goes out.

Alone, Renato reflects that it is not Amelia that he should be slaying, but the one who has brought so much shame on him, that is, Riccardo. Gazing at the portrait of Riccardo he vows revenge before collapsing into a grief-stricken reverie on the loss of his beautiful wife, concluding that, 'now only hate and death live in my widowed heart!' (*Eri tu*).

Samuel and Tom enter. Renato loses no time in confronting them with his mission. He reveals that he knows that they are plotting to murder Riccardo. He lays papers before them which apparently contain proof of the plans. They immediately assume that Renato intends to inform Riccardo. But Renato disabuses them: 'I want a part in it', he says. The conspirators are initially incredulous, but quickly realize that Renato is in earnest. Renato's only stipulation is that he himself should be the one to do the deed. However Samuel and Tom also each have potent reasons to be the one to wield the knife. So Renato decrees they should draw lots. He takes a case from the mantelpiece and places it on the table. Samuel writes their names on three pieces of paper and places them in the vase.

At this moment Amelia enters. Apparently Oscar has just arrived bearing an invitation from Riccardo. Renato, outraged, tells her that Oscar can wait. But then, in a flash of inspiration, he bids her stay since 'it seems heaven has sent you'. He tells Samuel and Tom not to fear: 'she knows nothing... on the contrary, she will bring us luck'. He hands the vase to Amelia and informs her that there are three names in it and she must choose one. Oblivious to the reason for the lottery Amelia yet intuits that she is being made a 'partner in a murder'. With trembling hands she draws a slip from the vase and gives it to her husband, who passes it to Samuel. Samuel reads the name: 'Renato'. Renato is exultant. Amelia by now realizes the full import of what she has been a party to. Renato instructs that Oscar be admitted.

Oscar enters and tells Amelia that she is invited with her husband to a masked ball that evening. Amelia peremptorily declines but Renato, having gleaned that Riccardo will be attending, realizes that fate has played into his hands. In his imagination he can already see Riccardo, 'lifeless among the dancers, staining the floor with his blood'. Amelia's only thought is to wonder how she might manage to warn Riccardo without betraying her husband. Perhaps Ulrica can do it, she reflects. Samuel and Tom are as enthusiastic as Renato to take advantage of the ball. They resolve that they will all wear blue costumes with a red sash tied in a knot to the left. Their password will be 'Morte!' ('death!'). Oblivious to the conspiracy unfolding Oscar rhapsodizes on the anticipated brilliance of the party, the music and the guests that will grace the mansion that evening.

Act 3 Scene 2 A luxurious room in Riccardo's home. There is a table with writing materials. At the back is a great curtain separating the study from the ballroom. Riccardo is sitting writing at his desk. His conscience has got the better of him and he is arranging to send Renato and Amelia to England (*Ma se m'è forza perderti*). However he is having difficulty in following his resolution through. Eventually he picks up his pen,

signs the document and conceals it in his shirt front. 'Ah, I have signed my sacrifice!' he reflects. He is suddenly overwhelmed by the realization that this may be 'the last hour of our love'. Dance music is heard. He catches sight of Amelia and wonders whether to take a last opportunity to speak with her. But he decides against it.

Oscar enters with a letter which he gives to Riccardo, telling him that it is from 'an unknown lady', with instructions to deliver it secretly. Riccardo reads the letter which warns him against attending the ball since an attempt will be made on his life. As has been clearly established by this point in the opera Riccardo cares nothing for his personal safety. He instructs Oscar to prepare himself to accompany him to the ball. As Oscar exits Riccardo expresses his joy at the thought of seeing Amelia once more.

Act 3 Scene 3 A spacious, richly hung ballroom. Guests crowd the room. Most are wearing masks. Some are in costume, others in evening dress without masks. Everyone is mingling, some trying to escape being unmasked, but all revelling in gaiety and high spirits. The guests sing a hedonistic chorus. Samuel, Tom and their men, dressed in their costumes of blue dominoes and red sashes, appear. Renato, dressed in similar attire, comes slowly forward. Samuel approaches him and they exchange their password, 'Morte!' Renato is convinced that Riccardo will not come.

Meanwhile Oscar is observing them. As the conspirators disperse among the crowd Oscar follows Renato and takes pleasure in letting him know that he has recognized him. Renato is in no mood for jesting. He pulls off Oscar's mask and demands to know why he is downstairs while his lordship is asleep upstairs. It is a deliberate attempt to discover Riccardo's whereabouts. 'He is here', Oscar tells Renato. But he refuses to divulge which of the maskers is Riccardo. Renato realizes that he must restrain himself.

Oscar launches into a teasing song (*Saper vorreste*). He has been instructed not to reveal how Riccardo is disguised and he will keep his word. Oscar and Renato are temporarily separated by maskers and groups of dancers, but Renato catches up with the page. Finally he convinces Oscar that it is important that he speaks with Riccardo. (It should be remembered that neither Riccardo nor Oscar know that Renato has found out about his wife's affair so have no reason to be suspicious of Renato's intentions.) Oscar divulges Riccardo's disguise and then disappears into the throng. Renato catches sight of one of his men across the room and leaves.

Soon the movement of the dance brings Riccardo to the front. He is dressed in a black costume with a pink ribbon, as described by Oscar. He is lost in thought. Amelia is behind him, dressed in a white costume. She addresses Riccardo, disguising her voice. She asks him why he is here and tells him to leave, for he is 'surrounded by death'. She urges him to flee. Riccardo presses her to reveal her identity. Amelia breaks down and, in her own voice, declares, 'For your life I would sacrifice my own'. She confesses her love anew and begs Riccardo to make his escape while he still can. Riccardo refuses even to discuss it: 'I have nothing save you in my soul, and the rest of the world is forgotten', he says. He tells her that he wants to save her and to this end has decided to send her and Renato to England. He takes his leave of her, but after a few steps returns for one final farewell. It will indeed prove to be his final farewell, for Renato leaps between the couple and stabs Riccardo. Amelia screams for help. Oscar runs to Riccardo's side, quickly followed by other guests. He identifies Renato as the murderer. All surround Renato and tear off his mask. Astonished they cry for vengeance on the traitor. Riccardo, with his dying breath, tells them to let Renato be. Drawing the despatch, which he has earlier signed, from his shirt he motions Renato to approach. He swears that Amelia is pure and declares that in spite of his love for her, he would never have offended either her heart or Renato's name. He was about to post them both to England. Declaring that he is still ruler, he absolves everyone of guilt. To general dismay, not least

Renato who is consumed with remorse, Riccardo dies and the curtain falls.

The ambience of a court, however or wherever constituted, where the principal concern can never be for the fulfilment of the individual's needs but must be the preservation of the hierarchy, is inevitably hidebound, superficial and frivolous. Thus the prince, king, governor, boss (the nomenclature is of no consequence), is no more free than the lowliest servant. He/she must fulfil his/her preordained role. The character of Riccardo, based on that of Gustavus III of Sweden, is constrained to obey certain fixed, immutable laws by which he has been granted the privilege of his office in the first place. It is essential that any such individual be gifted with a singular lack of imagination. Occasionally Nature will be unkind. Occasionally a prince will be born who is more suited to being a creative artist than a prince. Gustavus III was such a prince, as is his fictional counterpart. Riccardo needs constant diversity of stimulation. His needs can only be appeased by contravening the inevitable boundaries dictated by his office.

The difference between the Duke of Mantua (in *Rigoletto*) and Riccardo is that the former is a despot, albeit a benevolent one, while Riccardo is ostensibly the figurehead within a State struggling towards democracy. Certainly this was the case with the Swedish king. The despot is answerable to no-one; the governor in a burgeoning republic is answerable to everyone. Riccardo's appetites and energies are no less than those of the Duke of Mantua, but his freedom to indulge them is considerably more circumscribed. Historically the despot is more vulnerable than the democratically elected prince, though this is not necessarily borne out in practice as is evidenced by Riccardo's eclipse. At the conclusion of *Rigoletto* the Duke waltzes off happily into the sunset, despite all Rigoletto's efforts to dispose of him. (It is part of Verdi's message that justice is only rarely seen to he done, let alone actually instigated.) The Duke appears to be untouchable, while Rigoletto's life is blighted. In *Un Ballo in Maschera* Riccardo is not immune from the malignancy of fate, although it is not so much that he is victimized from without; rather he accedes to the pressure from within.

Unlike the Duke Riccardo is not, by nature, a philanderer (although one might have that impression on his first entrance). He does, however, have the same lively imagination and restless disposition. But whereas with the Duke his restlessness is assuaged with numerous erotic escapades, Riccardo, more sensitive, more intelligent by far, needs somehow to sublimate his inherent eroticism. All his craving for a creative outlet finds expression in his passion for his best friend's wife. What does this say about him? Only that the search is more important to him than the attainment. Riccardo would take no pleasure in notching up a catalogue of conquests, as does Don Giovanni, as related by Leporello in Mozart's opera. He would quickly become bored. More stimulating to Riccardo is the art of masquerade and play-acting. He needs to escape the prison of his own personality and the one thing inimical to that escape is the notion of commitment. He convinces himself that he wants to commit himself to Amelia, but he must know from the outset (as he finally acknowledges at the opening of Act 3) that it is an impossibility.

Riccardo's whole life, as evidenced in the action of Verdi's opera, is one long game of Russian roulette. The problem with the sort of incessant risk-taking in which he indulges is that sooner or later a price is demanded. Ultimately there is only one escape from the miseries or tedium of the present, and that is in death. Most people will welcome the security that their place in the hierarchical structure of society offers, not least for the sense of legitimacy that it confers and the reassuring sense of owning a meaningful portion of an enduring, well structured universe. Riccardo does not appreciate such consolations. He is in love with contingency because he knows only too well that that is all there is. When he visits Ulrica, the seeress, it is with no real con-viction that she will have any meaningful contribution to make to his understanding of existence.

In the event his conscience is badly assaulted by her prediction that Renato will be responsible for his death. So affected is he by this that he makes no comment on the matter whatsoever. As is usually the case when we do not wish to acknowledge something of crucial significance he dismisses the suggestion and apparently gives it no further thought. But then only he, and Amelia, know the true justification that Renato could have for murdering him.

The whole *raison d'être* for a seeress, or oracle, is to place the day-to-day eventualities of life in a wider perspective: to bring into the light that which is hidden and cannot otherwise be articulated. From the moment that Ulrica predicts his death at the hands of his staunchest ally and friend, Riccardo knows that he is living on borrowed time. But this is not news to him. He has always known it and he welcomes it. He has always been impatient with the strictures imposed by a bourgeois ethos. He has no desire to continue living a lie, and that is what his life amounts to. He loves what he cannot have and loathes what is given him. His death is not a tragedy, for it was determined at the outset by his evident inability to reconcile himself with his pre-ordained station in life.

Riccardo refuses to be constrained by the pronouncements of the judiciary, allows himself to be ruled by the infantile recommendations of a mere boy, and all the time languishes for the love of the least attainable woman in his entourage. *Un Ballo in Maschera* is one of Verdi's most rewarding operas because it succeeds by unfolding, without hysteria, but with steady inevitability, a dilemma which is at the centre of all Verdi's work: the conflict that arises between the needs of the individual and the inexorable requirements of the society in which that individual has his being.

Banquo (*Macbeth*). A general.
There is no historical evidence that Banquo ever existed, let alone fathered the Stuart

lineage. He appears in Holinshed's *Chronicles*, Shakespeare's source for his play, which in turn was derived principally from the semi-mythical history of Hector Boece. In Holinshed Banquo assists Macbeth in the murder of Duncan, but Shakespeare's sound dramatic instinct made Banquo simply a victim rather than an accomplice to the Macbeths' villainy.

Where **Macbeth** is a tormented existentialist, Banquo is a pillar of rectitude and honour. Where Macbeth has hitched his destiny to the sterility that is the defining feature of his own and his wife's ego-centredness, Banquo gives his life for the sake of the future. In his dying moments he urges his son to escape so that the witches' prophecy may be fulfilled and he may, though deprived of any chance of kingship himself, become father to a line of kings (Act 2 Scene 2). Macbeth's ego-centricity ensures that his renown will become defamation. He will be condemned by history to the one thing he has always dreaded: obscurity. Banquo, on the other hand, will prevail down the centuries.

Banquo is perceptive. He intuits from the start the peril in which he stands. When the witches first hail Macbeth king of Scotland he notices that, far from exulting, Macbeth quakes (Act 1 Scene 1). In other words he is already subject to a guilty conscience. Shortly after this he observes how the 'hope of a kingly throne puffs him up with pride'. Unlike Macbeth Banquo never has any doubt that the prophecies come from Hell and he wisely observes: 'often the evil spirit of Hell speaks truths in order to ensnare us; then later they abandon us, accursed, above the pits it has prepared for us'. Macbeth's attempts to convince himself that he will not 'lift a grasping hand to attain the crown' seem hollow by comparison with Banquo's burning conviction.

From this moment on Banquo is besieged by misgivings. Prior to the discovery of Duncan's murder he expresses his sense of oppression with vivid naturalistic imagery which provides a stark contrast with Macbeth's obsessive solipsism: 'Oh what a rough night. In the pitchy air wailing voices, strange screams of death were heard; the bird of ill-omen made dismal clamour and the earth was felt to shake'. This is an adaptation of a speech given by Lennox in Shakespeare's play (Act 2 Scene 3).

It is given to Banquo to announce to the court the murder of their king. Banquo can have no doubts as to who has perpetrated the crime. From this moment he knows that his own life is in danger. For not only is he the only one privy to Macbeth's innermost thoughts when the witches delivered their prophecy but he also represents the one obstacle standing between Macbeth and the possibility of propagating an enduring lineage. Paradoxically it will be Banquo's death, rather than his life, which will ensure Macbeth's downfall, for it is from that moment that Macbeth's star is eclipsed.

It matters not whether one believes that Banquo's spirit actually returns to haunt Macbeth or whether one conceives Macbeth's behaviour as indicative of the feverish workings of an unhealthy conscience. The fact remains that in the banquet scene Macbeth's guilt is graphically unveiled. Banquo will die not knowing whether or not his son will escape the cut-throats (Act 2 Scene 1). But at least he has the comfort of knowing the odds are in his favour, whereas for Macbeth, childless and riddled with guilt, the future is bleak.

Barbarigo (*I Due Foscari*). A Senator and member of the Junta.

Barbarigo's role is ambiguous, yet pivotal. As a member of the Junta he is responsible for seeing that justice is done and is instrumental in securing Jacopo's continued exile. At the same time he is moved to compassion by the miscreant's fate. On his appearance at the opening of the opera he is in company with **Loredano** and is thus inevitably identified as the latter's associate. He is once again in the company of Loredano at the opening of Act 3 on the piazzetta of St Marco watching the commencement of the regatta. Loredano clearly considers Barbarigo his confidante for he vents his spleen onto the **Foscari** and the 'rabble' who care not whether they be ruled by Foscari or Malipiero.

It is Barbarigo who informs the Doge, **Francesco**, that he has received a letter from one Erizzo who has confessed to the murder of Donatao (see **Synopsis**), thus exonerating Francesco's son, **Jacopo** (Act 3 Scene 2). This news brings great relief to the old man even though, as it turns out, the news has arrived too late: Jacopo has died of a broken heart. It is clear that Barbarigo, in stark contrast to Loredano, takes no pleasure in the relentless persecution of the Foscari. Indeed when **Lucrezia** brings her two small sons to plead at the Doge's throne for mercy on her husband's behalf, Barbarigo is moved to intercede with Loredano: 'let these tears, Loredano, speak to your heart! Let these tender infants disarm your dreadful fury; at least give way to pity for the unhappy pair' (Act 2 Scene 2). His plea falls on deaf ears.

At the conclusion of the opera when, having robbed Francesco of his office, Loredano is inclined to gloat, Barbarigo again intercedes, exhorting Loredano to respect the old man's grief. For has not Francesco not only been deprived of office, but also of his only sole remaining son? When the bell tolls announcing Malipiero's accession to the Doge's throne, before Francesco has barely relinquished the office, Barbarigo joins the other Senators in deploring the old man's fate. This would seem to indicate that in spite of being responsible for Jacopo's sentence and Francesco's departure from office he, and many of the others, are far from happy at their resolution. They may even have voted against the majority.

But it is the majority that must always win and ultimately Loredano has ensured the majority are with him. Politically Barbarigo is impotent; as a human being he is none the worse for being so.

Federico Barbarossa (*La Battaglia di Legnano*).

Barbarossa is an historical figure. There were in fact two Barbarossas: Frederick I (1123–1190) and his grandson Frederick II (1194–1250). The Barbarossa that appears in Verdi's opera was Frederick I, who was king of Germany and Italy from 1152–1190, and Holy Roman Emperor from 1155–1190. The historical king died of drowning crossing a river when on Crusade in Asia Minor. Thus when the Second **Consul** reports that **Arrigo** has succeeded in either wounding or killing the Emperor, having hurled him from his saddle, it is safe to assume that the emperor is merely wounded. The date of the action of the opera is 1176 so Frederick still had fourteen years to live. The historical Barbarossa eventually signed a peace treaty with the Lombards at the Peace of Constance in 1183 by which he agreed to a severe limitation of his powers in Italy. He had already agreed to recognize Pope Alexander III in 1177. But we do not turn to opera to learn the facts of history, rather we turn for illumination concerning the universal human predicament and how to come to terms with the fact of our existence.

Barbarossa appears only in Act 2 when **Arrigo** and **Rolando** have travelled to Como as envoys of the Lombard League to plead with the city of Como to put aside its enmity with Milan and join them in their efforts to rebuff the Germans. Como is not receptive to their appeal and the reason becomes quickly apparent when Barbarossa appears and it is clear the Lombards have been preempted. There is nothing sympathetic about Barbarossa. He clearly enjoys the discomfiture of the Italians and enjoys his display of might when he reveals the hills surrounding Como to be inundated with his troops. Rolando's and Arrigo's defiant exclamation that the 'mercenary swords of your robber bands shall not conquer a people that is rising to freedom, nor shall Italy's great destiny be changed by them' receives a response from Barbarossa that is to the point. 'I am Italy's destiny!' he declares, 'Soon it will all be beneath my yoke! And Milan, twice destroyed, shall inspire the rebellious with terror!' It is the archetypal challenge of the tyrant whose only passion is to conquer and control. It rang many concordant bells in the minds of the first Italian audiences, particularly as Legnano was at that time still under Austrian occupation.

When the opera was first performed (1849) the Republican movement still had a long way to go before establishing itself. It should be remembered that *La Battaglia di Legnano* was premiered only months after not only Italy, but all of Europe, had been convulsed with revolutions. The spectacular success of the opera was more to do with the political message it purveyed than with the intrinsic qualities of Verdi's score. The figure of Barbarossa provided a powerful focus for the republican detestation of all external aggression and tyranny

Bardolfo (*Falstaff*). Follower of **Falstaff**.
Bardolfo's most distinctive feature is his enormous, rubicund nose, of which he is as proud as Falstaff is of his belly. 'Do you see this meteor?' he asks **Doctor Caius** in the opening scene of the opera, 'It goes to rest every night as red as this'. Where **Pistola** has a choleric temperament, however, Bardolfo shares more of his master's serene good nature. He describes himself to **Master Ford** as a 'simple soldier' (Act 1 Scene 2), content to have food and drink for his belly. Hence his opportunism. He deserts Falstaff as soon as it becomes clear that the latter no longer has the means to pay him.

Naturally enough he seeks employment with Ford, whom he can straightaway make his debtor by revealing Falstaff's plans for the seduction of Ford's wife, **Alice**. Indisputably it gives him pleasure to betray Falstaff, for whom he has that mixture of affection and contempt which is an inevitable part of any servant's attitude to his master. Once having decamped, Bardolfo can give vent to all the accumulated spleen of years (thirty, if Falstaff is to believed: 'I've been soaking that purple fungus of yours for thirty years now', Act 1 Scene 1). The ostensible reason he gives for having left Falstaff's service is that his sense of honour is offended by Falstaff's latest commission: the delivery of love letters to Alice and **Meg**. But this is only an excuse, an excuse nevertheless that

has a dramatic effect on Falstaff, to whom the very word 'honour' is obnoxious (*L'Onore! Ladri!*).

At the opening of Act 2 Bardolfo and Pistola return to beg forgiveness of Falstaff. They do it in mock-heroic style, 'beating their breasts' in sign of repentance. It is probably a scene which has been enacted many times previously. Falstaff's response is to the point: 'Man goes back to his vices like a cat to the milk'. Being a soldier and a man of action (when not too drunk to move himself) Bardolfo enjoys every minute of the search of Ford's house (Act 2 Scene 2). He will feel totally at home as Ford assumes the mantle of a military general, organizing and commanding his 'soldiers' as though on military campaign.

In Act 3 Scene 2 Bardolfo takes especial pleasure in joining in the physical abuse of Falstaff. It is no doubt an opportunity he has been long anticipating. Unfortunately, while Bardolofo is hurling verbal and physical abuse at Falstaff, his chronic halitosis betrays him, revealing his identity to the stricken knight. Falstaff can take consolation in the fact that Bardolfo soon has outstanding problems of his own. For now Mistress Quickly takes Bardolfo aside and offers him an alternative disguise (since his cowl has just fallen off), namely a bridal veil. All unsuspecting Bardolfo accepts the white veil with which to mask himself. When he reappears dressed as the Fairy Queen he is holding hands with Doctor Caius, to whom Ford now proceeds to marry him. Bardolfo is literally speechless when it is revealed to whom he is married. Presumably he is not too perturbed, taking it in the spirit of Midsummer madness which characterizes all that transpires in the final scene. Caius, on the other hand, who takes everything seriously, is horrified. Bardolfo will have no trouble joining in the final choruses and asserting that 'The whole world is a jest; man was born a great jester'. It is more or less the philosophy he has adopted all his life.

Bardolfo fares better in Verdi's opera than he does in Shakespeare's plays, where his part is not particularly memorable. Verdi's characterization ensures that we do not forget the little man with the huge rubicund nose who ends up married to Doctor Caius. In *Henry V* the Boy describes Bardolfo as 'a thief, a coward'. He is accused of stealing a sacramental vessel from a French Church and is sentenced to death. Sad to relate Bardolfo is executed for his crime.

Baron Douphol (*La Traviata*). See **Douphol**

The Baron (*Un giorno di regno*). See **Baron Kelbar**

LA BATTAGLIA DI LEGNANO

Opera in 4 Acts. Libretto by Salvatore Cammarano, after Joseph Méry's drama, *La Battaille de Toulouse* (1828).

First performance: 27 January 1849 at the Teatro Argentina, Rome.

Cast:
Federico Barbarossa (bass)
First Milanese Consul (Primo Console di Milano) (bass)
Second Milanese Consul (Secondo Console di Milano) (bass)
Mayor of Como (Il Podestà di Como) (bass)
Rolando: a leading Milanese warrior (baritone)
Lida: his wife (soprano)
Arrigo: Veronese warrior (tenor)
Marcovaldo: German prisoner (baritone)
Imelda: servant to Lida (mezzo-soprano)
A Herald (Un araldo) (tenor)
Arrigo's Esquire (Uno scudiero di Arrigo) (tenor)

Time: 1176
Place: Milan and Como
Historical Background The Lombard League takes its name from the region of central northern Italy, Lombardy, which in turn was named after the tribe of Lombards who settled there in the 6th century. By the 12th century the cities of Lombardy, including Milan, had become economically and politically powerful and they formed the Lombard League in order to present a united front against the aggression of Frederick I

(Barbarossa), whom they succeeded in defeating at the battle of Legnano in 1176. The Lombard League can be seen as a precursor of the Risorgimento in the 19th century which finally saw the emergence of a united Italy. It certainly served well the nationalistic agendas of composer and librettist to remind the Italian people of the benefits of unity, a message which was warmly acknowledged and embraced at the opera's first performance.

Synopsis
Act 1: 'He is alive!'[13] An area in rebuilt Milan, close to the city walls. From one part of the city soldiers from Piacenza cross the stage, followed by platoons from Verona, Brescia, Novara and Vercelli (cities belonging to the Lombard League). The streets and balconies are filled with people. The houses are decked with bunting and garlands of all colours and hues. The troops are showered with flowers from above. Arrigo is among the Veronese warriors. The people sing in praise of the Lombard League: 'And may a shiver freeze the bones of fierce Barbarossa'.

Arrigo, meanwhile, is ecstatic to be back in Milano, 'first among the Lombard cities'. 'I greet you; I who like you have risen from the grave', he exclaims. For Arrigo has only recently recovered from life-threatening wounds received in battle. He has been nursed back to health by his mother (*La pia materna mano*). But all the time his only thoughts have been for his beloved Lida whom he assumes to be awaiting his return to Milan.

Voices are heard in the distance. As they draw nearer they can be heard singing in praise of Italy: 'strong and united by the sword and the spirit'. Amongst the men Arrigo spies his old friend, Rolando, whom he now hails. Rolando is amazed to see Arrigo still alive; he had assumed that Arrigo had perished from his wounds. Arrigo describes to his friend how he was first taken

---

[13] Refers to Arrigo. Imelda bears news to her mistress that Arrigo did not die of his battle wounds.

prisoner of war and then nursed back to health by his mother in his native Verona. Rolando describes the intense grief he has suffered, believing Arrigo to have died in the midst of the 'flames of Susa'. His only consolation has been the kisses of his infant son (*Ah! m'abbraccia, d'esultanza*). The two friends embrace enthusiastically.

The Oath   The sound of trumpets is heard, announcing the arrival of the two Consuls. They proceed to exhort the soldiers to stand firm in their determination to defend Milan. All swear to evict the savage hordes (that is, the Germans) from their beloved country. All leave in procession, led by the Consuls. Arrigo is escorted by Rolando.

Act 1 Scene 2   A shady spot amidst groups of trees near the water-filled moat surrounding the ramparts which dominate the background. Lida, followed by her women, comes forward. She is deep in thought. She sits in the shade, still in reflective mood, gazing at the sky. The women wonder why Lida is so sad when all are celebrating the return of the Italian warriors. Lida answers by assuring them that she also loves her country but that, 'where joy and laughter abound, there is no place for me'. Both her parents and brothers are dead. 'My only heritage is grief, weeping my only comfort', she declares. Her eyes fill with tears. The women group themselves at the back of the stage to allow her to give full rein to her grief. She proceeds to do so in eloquent fashion (*Quante volte come un dono*). The only thing which prevents her from killing herself is the fact that she now has a son and she knows that even to wish for death would be a sin.

To Lida's great consternation Marcovaldo now enters. Marcovaldo is a German prisoner who has unwisely been given free rein of the castle by Rolando. He shamelessly abuses his freedom by lusting after Lida. When Marcovaldo presses his suit Lida is furious. To her great relief they are interrupted almost immediately by the arrival of Imelda with news that Lida's husband, Rolando, is returning home; more than that, he is returning in the company of Arrigo.

Imelda clearly knows that this news will cheer her mistress. Lida is overwhelmed for she had assumed, as had her husband, that Arrigo had perished at Susa.

Marcovaldo is not slow to notice the blush that inflames Lida's cheek at the mention of Arrigo's name. Lida reflects to herself that she cannot restrain 'the heart-throbs of love' that she feels at the very thought of Arrigo (*A frenarti, o cor, nel petto*). She prays that the 'life of sorrow' that she endures may be sufficient chastisement for her sins. Meanwhile Imelda and the women observe that Lida has been granted a brief respite from her sorrow and Marcovaldo resolves to watch Lida for signs that will disclose the 'secrets of her heart'.

Rolando enters with Arrigo. Both Lida and Arrigo are overcome. Rolando is initially oblivious, having no knowledge of the erstwhile liaison between his wife and his best friend. He quickly becomes aware, however, that Arrigo seems distraught. Arrigo shrugs it off as, 'a relic of my wounds', but Marcovaldo is not deceived. Perhaps Rolando is subliminally aware that something is afoot for he proceeds to recall how Arrigo was once a guest in the house of Lida's father. He is just assuring Arrigo that he is welcome in his house when he is interrupted by the arrival of a herald. Rolando dismisses Marcovaldo and the women.

The herald brings news that the League's spies have reported 'a mighty army of imperial troops' on the march. The Consuls have ordered a meeting of the captains and senators. Rolando exits hastily, followed by the herald. Lida and Arrigo are left alone. Lida appears rooted to the spot. Arrigo springs to her side and seizes her roughly by the arm. He is appalled to find Lida married to another man, let alone his best friend (*È ver? Sei d'altri*). 'Is it true? You are another's and you swore to be mine for ever!' he cries. He demands an explanation. Lida lamely tries to defend herself. It was falsely reported he had been killed, she says. Her father was dying and required her to marry Rolando. Her avowal that she is miserable in her marriage falls on deaf ears.

Arrigo is derisory. He reminds Lida that she gave her solemn word 'at the feet of the Almighty' that she would remain faithful to him. Lida is beside herself but Arrigo is remorseless. He declares that his only recourse now is to die in defence of his country. He is oblivious to Lida's pleas to kill her: 'better death at your feet than so dreadful an existence!' she laments. Arrigo repulses her and exits quickly, leaving Lida to retire in 'the utmost desolation of grief'.

Act 2 'Barbarossa'. A magnificent room in the town hall of Como. At the rear an open gallery with closed shutters. The chief officers and magistrates are assembling. It is already common knowledge that Milan 'stoops' to a treaty with Como but, as the councillors point out, it is 'too late and in vain'. There is clearly no love lost between the two cities. The citizens of Como have not forgotten the 'mortal injuries' dealt them by the Milanese.

The Mayor announces messengers from the Lombard League. All seat themselves and the messengers, Rolando and Arrigo, are brought in. Rolando relates how a new horde of barbarians is threatening Holy Italy. He makes a plea for the ancient hostilities between their two cities to be put aside that they may unite to deflect a common enemy. When the Mayor invokes the pact that Como has made with the German emperor, Federico Barbarossa, Arrigo loses all restraint. He denounces the pact and brazenly challenges the assembly. Rolando, equally incensed, seconds his friend's challenge. Together they make an impassioned plea: 'Let not history call you murderers of your brothers!'

Suddenly Barbarossa himself appears. All are taken aback and Arrigo and Rolando are appalled. Barbarossa taunts them: 'Why do the words die on your rash lips?' He assures the Italians that their fate is sealed. The clash of military instruments is heard drawing ever nearer. Barbarossa's troops are approaching. At a sign from him the doors of the gallery are opened. Through them can be seen the surrounding hills, swarming with German troops. 'Now let Milan hear the announcement of her downfall!', Barbarossa declares

and signals to the envoy to leave. Rolando and Arrigo remain arrogantly defiant. Barbarossa's arrogance becomes increasingly inflated. The act concludes with all calling for 'War to the death!'

Act 3 'Infamy'. Scene 1 Subterranean vaults in the basilica of San Ambrogio in Milan. Here and there fresh graves. To the rear stairs giving access from above. A low-burning torch casts a feeble light.

The Knights of Death (Cavalieri della Morte) descend silently and singly. Each of them wears a sash slung diagonally across one shoulder. A figure of a human skull adorns each sash. The so-called Knights of Death are formed from a specially selected corps of fighters taken from the Lombard League. Their mission is to fight to the death, if necessary, in defence of their country. Arrigo has come to enlist.

The knights command Arrigo to repeat the words of the 'holy and forbidding oath'. Arrigo confirms his solidarity and utter dedication unto death, if necessary, to the cause of Italian independence. The knights are agreed that Arrigo is a worthy new recruit. They address the eldest amongst them. He commands Arrigo to kneel at the foot of a grave and then binds him with his sash. The knights cross their swords over Arrigo's head, then raise him to his feet. All embrace him. Finally, when Arrigo has also unsheathed his sword, the knights pronounce their oath in a single voice (*Giuriam d'Italia por fine ai danni*). They swear to achieve the liberation of Italy and to give their lives if necessary in the process. Any found wanting in dedication shall be execrated for all time. All exit.

Act 3 Scene 2 Apartments in Rolando's castle. Lida comes quickly forward. She appears pale and unsteady. She is pursued by Imelda who desperately tries to elicit from her mistress whither she is hurrying. Imelda has observed Lida scribbling a note which she then concealed in her bosom. Realizing there is no point in denying the fact, Lida confesses that the note, 'like an adder ... pierces my breast ... and its poison seeks out the most secret fibres of my heart!' She invites

Imelda to denounce her, but then distractedly wonders to whom her sin should be denounced. All she longs for is death. She throws herself into a chair in a paroxysm of grief, then rises, looks about her, stares at Imelda, bursts into tears and throws herself into her maid's arms. Imelda has already guessed that the cause of Lida's suffering is the sudden reappearance of Arrigo. She persuades Lida to give her the note so that she may deliver it.

Rolando enters. Imelda hastily conceals Lida's letter. Rolando announces that he has come to take leave of his wife and son prior to departing for battle. He despatches Imelda to fetch his child. When Imelda returns she places the boy in Rolando's arms and departs. Rolando tells Lida that should he die in battle it is incumbent upon her to ensure that their son learns the meaning of virtue. Lida is barely coherent. Rolando now makes the little boy kneel down. Then, raising his eyes to heaven, he stretches his right hand over the child's head. He invokes the Lord's blessing on him before handing the child to his wife. Mother and son leave.

Arrigo enters. He is not wearing the black sash. Rolando, who has apparently summoned him, goes to his friend and leads him to the front of the stage. Having checked that no one is eavesdropping, he passionately confides in his friend that he is fearful he might die in the forthcoming battle thereby leaving a widow and a son unprotected in the world. He beseeches Arrigo to take responsibility for them should the worst happen (*Se al nuovo di pugnando*). Arrigo is overcome with guilt and remorse but cannot refuse his friend's request. Placing his right hand in Rolando's he overcomes his reluctance and swears solidarity with his friend. The two men embrace in farewell. Arrigo exits, 'sobbing and in haste'. Rolando leaves in the opposite direction.

He is just reaching the threshold when he hears his name called in a low voice. It is Marcovaldo, come to apprise Rolando of his suspicions regarding Lida and Arrigo's liaison. Rolando is at first outraged by the suggestion. He would undoubtedly have

'slain the messenger' had he been armed. Luckily for Marcovaldo he is not wearing his dagger. Marcovaldo hastily produces evidence of his accusation, the letter that Lida has sent to Arrigo (he has apparently bribed Imelda into giving it to him). Rolando reads the note aloud, his voice shaking with fury. In the note Lida confides in Arrigo that she has learnt of the oath he has sworn with the 'knights of death'. She implores Arrigo to agree to a meeting before the battle, for the sake of their 'ancient love'. Rolando rushes off swearing revenge (*Ahi scellerate alme d'inferno*).

Act 3 Scene 3 A room, high up in a tower. On one side an iron door, to the rear a balcony over the moat by the ramparts. Arrigo's sash is on the back of a chair.

Arrigo is taking the night air. He comes into the room, sits at a little table and prepares to write a farewell letter to his mother. Lida comes forward silently. She gazes fixedly at the letter and quickly apprehends its import. She upbraids Arrigo for his selfishness in willing his own death. Arrigo's only answer is, 'You have ceased to love me. I cannot live'.

This elicits from Lida a confession that she does love him. Nevertheless she is adamant that they must shun each other, he for the sake of his mother and she for the sake of her son. She wonders why she has not received a reply to her letter. Arrigo is just protesting that he never received it when there is a violent knocking at the door. Rolando's voice is heard calling Arrigo's name. Lida and Arrigo remain rooted to the spot, 'as though thunderstruck'. Then Arrigo, pulling himself together, urges Lida to hide on the balcony. Lida rushes out and Arrigo bolts the shutters after her.

Rolando enters. He glances around, clearly suspecting Lida's presence. He tells Arrigo that he has heard that he has taken a vow with the 'warriors of death'. His tone is heavily sarcastic. 'doubtless kind consideration counselled you ... to keep this from your friend', he says. He has come to speed Arrigo on his way. Arrigo objects that it is still night. 'You are mistaken', Rolando replies; 'already the dawn appears'. He flings open the shutters, thus revealing his wife on the balcony. She is shaking with terror. Rolando silences her attempts at an explanation. Lida falls on her knees at her husband's feet. Rolando is derisory (*Ah! d'un consorte, o perfidi*). 'You have made a fearful mockery of a husband', he storms and then tells Lida she is no longer his wife. Arrigo attempts to plead on Lida's behalf, which incenses Rolando further. He grasps the hilt of his dagger. In a melodramatic gesture Arrigo bares his chest to receive Rolando's knife. Rolando seems on the point of stabbing him when Lida intervenes. Rolando stops short.

He has decided on a new course of action. To kill Arrigo now would be too easy an end for his treacherous friend. 'You shall have worse torture than a hundred deaths!' he tells Arrigo (*Vendetta d'un momento*). Trumpets are heard from the streets below. The Lombard army is assembling and the trumpets are summoning its officers. 'Let your punishment be dishonour!' Rolando declares as he sweeps out of the room, bolting the door behind him. Panic-stricken, Arrigo throws himself at the door and desperately tries to open it.

Thus Arrigo is prevented from joining the troops and thus his fate is sealed, since he will be in direct contravention of the oath he took with the Knights of Death. His mind goes over all the insults that will be hurled at him, principally accusations of cowardice. Meanwhile Lida collapses in a chair. Beside himself Arrigo rushes to the window and throws himself from the balcony. Lida faints as the curtain falls.

Act 4 'To die for the Fatherland'. A square in Milan with the porch of a church in view. Women, old men and children mingle on the streets and in the church porch. Lida is present in the company of Imelda. All are on their knees, listening to psalms being sung within the church.

Lida has just ascertained from Imelda that Arrigo has survived his fall from the balcony. He apparently landed in the moat and was thereafter observed rejoining his troops. Lida

is overjoyed. She prays for the safe return of both Arrigo and her husband.

Voices are heard proclaiming victory. All rise to their feet. The second consul enters with senators, followed by a crowd of citizens. The consul confirms that the enemy has been defeated at the battle of Legnano. The emperor Barbarossa has been wounded, or slain, by none other than Arrigo. The consul enters the church with the senators. The citizens embrace one another with kisses and tears of joy. Meanwhile a number of platoons are seen passing in the distance on their return from the battlefield. The air resounds with the joyful clamour of military instruments and the festive pealing of bells. Lida and Imelda declare: 'No one who is not a Lombard could possibly understand this joy!'

At that moment funeral trumpets are heard, heralding the arrival of a wounded knight, escorted by a squadron of the Knights of Death. It is Arrigo, mortally wounded and supported by the Knights. The Milanese captains follow, among them Rolando, who advances silently and with bowed head. Arrigo asks to be put down on the steps of the church. The knights duly lay him down.

Seeing Rolando Arrigo asks his friend to take his hand, just once, before death overtakes him. Rolando silent and unsure, moves towards Arrigo. Arrigo throws himself on Rolando's neck. The knights withdraw a short distance. Arrigo swears, 'by Italy's salvation' that Lida's heart is pure. Lida, meanwhile, pleads with Rolando to put aside his bitterness and allow himself to be reunited with his friend. Rolando, overcome with emotion, relents. He embraces Lida and holds out his right hand to Arrigo.

The first consul enters, followed by soldiers and the triumphal chariot. Spying the flag that flies from the chariot Arrigo requests that the knights bring it to him. He kisses the banner and falls back dead amidst general lamentation. The curtain falls.

Few of Verdi's operas can have a more blatantly political agenda than *La Battaglia di Legnano* which was composed in 1848, the year of revolutions in Europe. The work was aimed specifically at both reflecting and encouraging a mood of patriotic fervour. This it succeeded in doing, becoming, as Verdi intended it should, a popular rallying call for the advocates of Mazzini's and Garibaldi's *Risorgimento*. But it would be a mistake thereby to dismiss the opera as just another tub-thumping pot-boiler. In fact the work contains the threads of various themes which were to establish themselves as of particular significance in Verdi's concerns: viz. the close friendship of two men under threat from external sources; a wife's illicit passion for another man; a father's anguish and the need to relinquish control of his offspring, all within the context of the ongoing battle to safeguard the human right of liberty against the forces of reaction and oppression.

The chief dramatic interest lies in the love triangle between Arrigo, Rolando and Rolando's wife, Lida. The pathos in the story stems from the fact that nobody is to blame that there is a triangle in the first place. The three protagonists are, as is so often the case in Verdi's operas, the victims of circumstance. The circumstances are not notably outlandish, either. It is the sort of triangle that can all too easily develop amongst close friends. As in *La forza del destino* the origin of the triangle lies in Lida's original inability to assert her independence from her father. She has married Rolando principally because her father told her to. Her true love has remained with Arrigo, to whom she has vowed to be true eternally.

When Lida first appears in the opera (Act 1 Scene 2) she is lamenting the deaths of both her parents and her brother. She is also lamenting the death of Arrigo, who is believed to have died in battle. But she cannot admit this to her maidservants. The problem for Lida is that she cannot commit herself to the present or, for that matter, to the future. She has a husband who loves her. She has a son whom she loves. Yet still she lives in the past. This is a major theme in many of Verdi's operas: the conflict between the reactionary desire to preserve the status quo which is

always at odds with the heroic. Sometimes, as with Medora (*Il Corsaro*), this tendency is identified with the feminine. It is the exception rather than the rule. Verdi's most memorable heroines are those who succeed in fighting for their corner: Gulnara (*Il Corsaro*), Abigaille (*Nabucco*), Giselda (*I Lombardi*), Aida, even Gilda (*Rigoletto*). Verdi was not principally concerned with archetypes, as Wagner was. In myth it is traditionally the feminine that seeks to preserve the status quo. In Verdi it is more often the father-figure who seeks to inhibit the natural forward thrust of life. More often than not it is the daughter who rebels and allies herself with some anarchic spirit whose values are at total odds with those of her father.

In *La Battaglia di Legnano* it is Rolando who truly represents the forces of reaction. For Lida, her husband is synonymous with her father, since he was her father's choice of husband for her rather than her own. How can she ever love him with the spontaneity of passion which the young and idealistic Arrigo awakened in her? Arrigo seeks above all to transcend the boundaries of what is prescribed in life, but as with so many of Verdi's heroes he first has to break away from the mother. It is made abundantly clear in the opera that to a certain extent he is still tied to his mother's apron strings. Herein lies the true impossibility of Arrigo and Lida's passion. Neither of them has succeeded in truly individuating. Psychologists may well argue that this is a problem faced by all couples: how to find and extend the common ground which is not circumscribed by the inherited parental mandate. But at least Arrigo and Lida still have something against which to fight. There is still a dynamic which makes sense of their lives. Rolando's efforts are all directed at preserving and maintaining that which he has already obtained. The only truly creative possibility in his life resides in his son.

These are the tensions out of which great dramas are made and ultimately by which life itself is engendered and sustained. Verdi is not passing judgement, merely observing and elaborating syndromes endemic in all human lives. The very universality of the themes he elucidates and to which he gives such vibrant expression is indicative of his indisputable genius.

Cavaliere Belfiore, posing as Stanislaus King of Poland (*Un giorno di regno*).
It is not every day that an ordinary soldier has the opportunity to play at being the King, but that is the peculiar honour that befalls Belfiore. The honour could not have befallen him at a more inconvenient time, for the woman he loves, the **Marchesa di Poggio**, is just about to be married off by her uncle to an old bore Count **Ivrea**, military commander of Brest.

As it turns out, Belfiore is the perfect man for the job. He turns the situation to his advantage and uses his sudden access to special powers to manipulate events to his own, and his friends', advantage. Belfiore is, above all, an opportunist. He enjoys to the full his new-found status and gives himself wholeheartedly to the masquerade.

On his first entrance (Act 1 Scene 1) Belfiore, in an aside, wishes that his Parisian companions could see him now: 'You who consider me totally mad, come here and decide if anyone is as wise as I', he comments; 'the most knavish officer of the entire regiment suddenly assumes the guise of philosopher and knight'. The most interesting facet of *Un giorno di regno* is the way in which it illustrates the importance of the self-image.[14] Belfiore's self-image changes

and expands through the 'greatness' that is suddenly thrust upon him. Which is not to suggest he had any problem with his self-image before assuming his peculiar role. Having become a 'King', however, he immediately gains in stature; for he quickly learns to believe what he sees in the mirror and, more importantly, what he sees in the mirror of other people's eyes. This is what truly perplexes the Marchioness: the 'King' is so obviously regal, something with which she cannot equate the man she thought she knew and knows she loves.

Belfiore discovers himself by default. It is more than probable that up to this moment in time he has been almost entirely self-centred. (An average rank and file soldier must, by definition, be self-centred for the majority of his time is spent subjugating himself; whatever time that is left to him must, by necessity, be employed in his own needs.) Suddenly Belfiore, with virtually no preparation or warning, must learn how to give commands, not just respond to them. It is a huge volte-face. (The real challenge for him will come at the moment when he returns to his normal existence as a rank and file soldier. How will he reconcile his newly-found potency with his menial role in the army?)

When Belfiore comes to stay with the Baron **Kelbar**, he has no idea that a double wedding is to take place, and furthermore that one of the brides is the girl to whom he thought he was engaged. This news is a shock for him. He almost forgets his disguise. In a panic he determines to write to the court

---

[14] There is a story by the Brazilian writer, Machado de Assis (1839–1908), called 'The Looking Glass' which tackles the importance of the self-image head-on.

A young man, who has achieved local celebrity by rising to the rank of Second Lieutenant in the army, goes to stay with his aunt who lives on an isolated farm. The aunt is inordinately proud of her nephew and lavishes excessive praise on him, insisting that all her servants address him as 'Segnor Lieutenant'. Unfortunately, when she is called away the servants take the opportunity to quit the farm. The soldier therefore finds himself utterly bereft of company, and of the adulation to which he is by now accustomed. He becomes a prey to acute depression and anxiety. When he

thinks he is in danger of losing his reason he suddenly has an idea. He takes his lieutenant's uniform out of the cupboard, puts it on and parades in front of the mirror. By this simple expedient he finds he feels immeasurably better and thereafter repeats the exercise each day until his aunt returns. [I am indebted to Colin Wilson who cites Machado's story in *New Pathways in Psychology* (Gollancz) and *The Craft of the Novel* (Gollancz). Mr Wilson has made an intensive study of the psychological significance of the self-image. See also his novel *The Personality Surgeon* (NEL 1987). For another, amusing, exploration of the theme of masquerade see *Confessions of Felix Krull* (Thomas Mann. Minerva)].

requesting that he be relieved of his duties, because if he 'reigns any longer (he) will lose his love'. This, of course, is farcical. The notion that his love life will be considered more important than the safety of the monarch is hardly likely to be taken seriously.

Belfiore enjoys dispensing royal favours and, during his interview with **Edoardo** (Act 1 Scene 1), he reflects to himself 'when my court goes up in smoke his plea will not have been in vain; if only to ridicule that insane old man, I shall know how to rule for one day at least'. He has been presented with the perfect opportunity to cock a snook at the privileged aristocracy whom he normally must serve.

Belfiore empathizes with Edoardo because he can see his former self in the young man and wants to help him out of the impasse his life has reached. Edoardo feels himself always at the mercy of forces greater than himself; such is the lot of a soldier (as Belfiore knows only too well), and such is the lot of youth. Suddenly Belfiore has discovered that life does not necessarily have to be like that. It is possible to take charge of your destiny.

Along with the pleasure of helping the young and needy, goes the pleasure of trouncing the elderly and complacent. Belfiore particularly enjoys causing the **Treasurer**, who is hoping to win **Giulietta**, grave discomfiture. Knowing that the Treasurer is motivated chiefly by money and position Belfiore offers him a fictitious post in the cabinet, in addition to a fictitious Princess with a fictitious fortune (see **Synopsis**, Act 1 Scene 3). The Treasurer falls headlong into the trap. As a final insult Belfiore urges him to settle on Edoardo one of his castles and five thousand crowns per annum thereby ensuring that the Baron has no reason for refusing to allow Giulietta to marry Edoardo (Act 2 Scene 1). Whether or not the Treasurer stands by his obligations once the 'King' is revealed not to be the King the opera does not relate.

All the time Belfiore is devoting himself to rectifying injustice he is keenly aware that he himself is behaving less than fairly towards the Marchioness. This is the most difficult aspect of his 'kingship' that he must endure. As the opera progresses he becomes increasingly concerned that the Marchioness might actually follow through her threat to marry Count Ivrea. But he is powerless to remedy the situation until he is relieved of his duties of kingship. In spite of this Belfiore enjoys hugely the farcical confrontation with the Marchioness (Act 2 Scene 2) where the Marchioness is well aware that Belfiore is not the King, and Belfiore knows perfectly well that the Marchioness knows, but neither can admit the fact. The Marchioness gives Belfiore many opportunities to 'come clean', but Belfiore knows that it could be construed as treason were he to divulge the truth. Thus his relief when a letter finally arrives relieving him of his duty, which is becoming increasingly onerous, is immense (Act 2 Scene 3).

Belfiore demonstrates his true generosity when, having received the letter from the court, he does not immediately throw his regal status out of the window, but first ensures that the Baron gives permission for Edoardo and Giulietta to be married. Having ensured this, which has been the chief triumph of his 'reign', he can set about reconciling himself with the Marchioness.

Bethune (*I Vespri Siciliano*). Officer in the French army occupying Sicily.

Bethune is directly answerable to **Monforte** where **Roberto** and **Tebaldo** are directly answerable to him. Unlike the rank and file, represented by Roberto and Tebaldo, Bethune can take a more detached view of the French occupation of Sicily. At the opening of the opera he warns the soldiers 'the Sicilian man is jealous and the hearts of his women are proud'. Prophetic words, as it turns out. He also reveals that he knows the history of the Duchess **Elena**. He knows that she mourns her brother, who was apparently executed by the French for having an affair with a Swabian girl, 'fatal fondness that his blood paid for'. It is clear that Bethune is uncomfortable about the justice meted out by France, though he is not willing to go so far as **Vaudimont** and admit that an injustice was committed in the case of Elena's brother (Act 1 Scene 1).

Bethune is mostly at Monforte's side and is despatched by the latter to invite **Arrigo** to attend the palace. He then carries out his orders to arrest Arrigo should the latter be unwilling to accompany him. It is unlikely Bethune knows Arrigo is Monforte's son. Monforte's attitude to the Sicilian must be puzzling, to say the least, particularly since once Arrigo is safely secured in the castle Monforte instructs that the prisoner is to be treated with the greatest respect.

Bethune is not present when **Procida** incites his soldiers to carry off the Sicilian brides-to-be (Act 2). It is doubtful whether Bethune would have countenanced such behaviour. Had he been present to prevent this outrage he could well have averted the tragedy of the final denouement. As it is he is too preoccupied with prosecuting Monforte's desperate attempts at a reconciliation with Arrigo. He must realize the justification for Monforte's faith in Arrigo when the latter averts the Sicilians' attempted assassination of his master (Act 3 Scene 2). When Monforte orders the executions of Procida and Elena (Act 4) Bethune protests. He knows the populace is already in revolt. However Bethune is too good an officer to persist in questioning his orders.

One must assume he will perish in the final massacre.

SIMON BOCCANEGRA

Opera in three Acts with Prologue. Libretto by Francesco Maria Piave (with additions by Giuseppe Montanelli) after Antonio Garcia Gutiérrez's play of the same title.

First performance: Teatro la Fenice, 12 March 1857. Revised version with considerable additions and alterations by Boito: Teatro alla Scala, Milan, 24 March 1881.

Cast:
Prologue:
Simon Boccanegra: a corsair in the service of the Genoese Republic (baritone)
Jacopo Fiesco: a Genoese nobleman (bass)

Paolo Albiani: a Genoese goldsmith (bass)
Pietro: a Genoese popular leader (baritone)

Main Opera:
Simon Boccanegra: first Doge of Genoa (baritone)
Maria Boccanegra: his daughter, under the name of **Amelia** Grimaldi (soprano)
Jacopo Fiesco: under the name of Andrea (bass)
Gabriele Adorno: a Genoese gentleman (tenor)
Paolo Albiani: the Doge's favourite courtier (bass)
Pietro: a courtier (baritone)
A Captain of the Crossbowmen: (tenor)
Ancella: Amelia's maidservant (mezzo-soprano)

Time: middle of the 14th century. Between the Prologue and Act 1 there is a lapse of 25 years.
Place: Genoa.
Background to the Opera The action of the opera takes place in Genoa in the 14th century against a background of political feuding between the Patricians and the Plebeians. Fiesco, Gabriele Adorno and the outlawed Grimaldi family are Patricians. Boccanegra, Paolo and Pietro are Plebeians. The situation is further complicated by the rivalry between the Guelf and Ghibelline parties within the Patricians themselves. The bitter strife between the rival factions is aggravated by the fact that Boccanegra, a pirate-adventurer, has been involved in an illicit love affair with Fiesco's daughter, Maria, who has borne him a daughter. In order to avoid public scandal the child has been brought up away from their world on an island near Pisa by an old woman.

Meanwhile Amelia Grimaldi, the only daughter of the wealthy Patrician Grimaldi family, (who do not appear in the opera) has been put into a convent for her safety. There she dies. Coincidentally, at the time of her death, an orphan arrives at the same convent. This is, in fact, Boccanegra's daughter, Maria, named after her mother. Since the Grimaldis are living in exile and warding off persistent attempts by the Doge to rob them of their wealth it is essential that knowledge of the heiress's death be kept from him. The orphan is therefore adopted and brought up as Amelia Grimaldi. Fiesco has been appointed guardian to the child, but as a Patrician he is forced to go underground. He assumes the name of Andrea, by which name he is known to all the characters in the main part of Verdi's opera. For most of the opera neither he, nor the orphan, who has grown up bearing the name of Amelia, nor anybody else, is aware that the child is in fact his own granddaughter.

Synopsis

Prologue A square in Genoa. In the background can be seen the church of San Lorenzo; to the right stands the Palace of the Fieschi from which a large balcony overlooks the square; in an alcove next to the balcony is an image of the Virgin Mary, in front of which burns a lamp. Other houses are to the left. Several streets lead into the square. It is night.

Paolo and Pietro are discussing the forthcoming election of a Doge. They agree to favour Boccanegra who, like themselves, is a Plebeian and a popular hero for having rid the seas of the threat from African pirates. Pietro departs in order to rally the people's support for Boccanegra and Paolo, left alone, gives vent to his hatred of the Patricians.

Boccanegra enters. Paolo immediately proposes that Boccanegra should stand for election, but Boccanegra is reluctant. Paolo points to the Fieschi palace and remarks that Maria (Boccanegra's lost love) languishes there. If Boccanegra were to become Doge he would be in a stronger position to marry Maria for, as Paolo points out, 'who could deny her to the Doge?' It is with this consideration in mind, rather than any overweening ambition, that Boccanegra agrees to Paolo's suggestion that he stand for election as Doge. He leaves in a distracted frame of mind, and Paolo retires into the shadows.

Pietro enters, followed by sailors and workmen. He proposes to the crowd that

they vote for a Plebeian in the forthcoming election. Paolo steps forward and proposes Boccanegra as a candidate. The people are anxious as to the reaction of the powerful Fieschi. Paolo reassures them that the Fieschi will keep silent as they have problems of their own. He tells them about the ailing Maria imprisoned in the palace, and of the ghostly light 'like a tormented soul' that is to be seen passing across the palace windows at night. As he speaks a light appears in one of the windows; the people cross themselves in superstitious dread and disperse.

The stage is now deserted. Fiesco emerges from the palace. From his opening words it is immediately clear that Maria has died (*A te l'estremo addio*). He bids farewell to the 'proud palace, cold tomb of my angel'. He curses his daughter's seducer, whom he blames for her premature demise. Turning to the Holy Shrine he even imprecates against the callousness of the Virgin in allowing his daughter to be so abused; but immediately begs forgiveness for his blasphemy. In his soliloquy (*Il lacerato spirito*) he reflects that 'the tortured soul of a sad father was doomed to infamy and sorrow', and he prays that his daughter may intercede for him in Heaven.

At this moment sounds of weeping are heard from within the palace. The women are lamenting Maria's death whilst monks are heard intoning the Miserere. A sorrowful procession of people emerges from the palace, crosses the square and disappears. Boccanegra returns. In stark contrast to the grief around him (he is as yet oblivious of Maria's death) he is in a buoyant mood for, aware that he is everybody's favoured candidate for the Doge's office, he can now envisage a time when he will be able to gain Fiesco's consent to his marriage to Maria (*Suona ogni labbro il mio nome*).

But Boccanegra's elation is short-lived for he is now accosted by Fiesco, who informs him that he has only just been invoking on Boccanegra's head the avenging wrath of heaven. Throwing himself on the ground at Fiesco's feet Boccanegra begs for mercy. He reminds Fiesco of his recent triumphs at sea, but Fiesco is implacable. In desperation

Boccanegra bares his chest and invites Fiesco to stab him to death. Fiesco views these histrionics as indicative of Boccanegra's ill-breeding and tells Boccanegra there is only one way in which he can be appeased, namely that Boccanegra surrenders into his care the grandchild he has been granted through Boccanegra's illicit union with his daughter.

Boccanegra now has no option but to reveal to the old man the painful truth – that he does not know where his daughter is. He tells Fiesco how, after the birth of his daughter she was given to an aged woman to bring up. The woman lived on the 'shores of a hostile land ... hidden from the world'. One night Boccanegra landed on the shore to visit his daughter, but found the old woman dead and his daughter beside herself. For three days the child cried, then she 'disappeared and was seen no more'. Fiesco may well doubt the veracity of this account which is not, in fact, very convincing. He declares that if Boccanegra cannot satisfy his wish then there can be no peace between them. Haughtily he turns his back on him and, ignoring the latter's pleas, moves away, leaving Boccanegra alone and distraught.

Boccanegra now gives vent to his rage and frustration at the 'implacable race of Fieschi!' How, he wonders, could such a beauty as his beloved Maria have been born to such a 'nest of vipers'? He determines he must see Maria and goes to the door of the palace where he knocks three times. He is puzzled to find the doors open and observes that there is total silence within the palace. He enters in trepidation. He does not hear Fiesco's exhortation from behind him, 'Go in and embrace a cold corpse!'

Moments later Boccanegra reappears on the balcony. He is exceedingly perplexed for he has found the palace entirely deserted. He takes the lamp from the Holy Shrine and goes back inside. Soon after his voice is heard desperately calling the name of his beloved Maria. Triumphantly Fiesco declares, 'the hour of your punishment is at hand!' Boccanegra staggers out of the palace. He imagines he inhabits a nightmare from which

he will soon awaken. In the distance voices are heard joyfully calling his name, in stark contrast to his own anguished cries. 'Voices from Hell!' he exclaims.

Pietro and Paolo enter with sailors and people carrying torches. They announce that the people acclaim Boccanegra as their new Doge. Boccanegra is appalled as, for quite different reasons, is Fiesco. The curtain falls on the Prologue as the populace raises its torches high and shouts: 'Long live Simon'. The bells of the city ring out in wild celebration.

Act 1   Twenty-five years have passed. Scene 1   The gardens of the Grimaldi palace, outside the city of Genoa. To the left stands the palace, in the background the sea. Dawn is breaking.

Amelia (in reality Boccanegra's daughter and Fiesco's granddaughter, Maria) is looking towards the horizon. She sings (*Come in quest'ora bruna*) of the beauty of the dawn. Yet the sky and the sea remind her of the 'dark cruel night' when her foster mother died and she was left alone in the world. The grandeur of the Grimaldi palace can never eradicate from her memory the recollection of her humble beginnings. Now she is impatient for her lover who 'dries my tears each day/as the dawn dries the dew from the flowers'. Her lover is Gabriele Adorno who, it soon materializes, is in league with Amelia's guardian, 'Andrea' (Fiesco) in a plot to overthrow the Doge (Boccanegra). Amelia is aware of her lover's potentially treasonous involvement and is concerned.

Gabriele is heard singing a serenade in the distance. Soon he enters. Amelia, overjoyed as she is to see him, loses no time in telling him that she knows his secret. She has observed him plotting with 'Andrea', Lorenzin, and others and is concerned about the danger to which he is exposing himself. She pleads with him to give up futile plans of political glory and concentrate on their love for each other (*Vieni a mirar la cerula*). Gabriele more or less tells her not to bother herself with things that do not concern her. Suddenly Amelia notices the figure of a man lurking in the shadows. Apparently this figure is to be seen in the same place each day. Gabriele wonders if it may be a rival for Amelia's affections, though this suggestion probably hides a deeper concern as to the intruder's true identity.

A servant enters and announces a messenger from the Doge. Gabriele makes to leave, not wishing to come face to face with Boccanegra, but Amelia requests that he remain. Pietro enters and bows to Amelia. He tells her that the Doge is returning from a hunt in Savona and seeks hospitality in the Grimaldi palace. Amelia assures him that the Doge is welcome. She already knows that Boccanegra comes to seek her hand for one of his favourites. She urges Gabriele to lose no time in finding Fiesco and making preparations for their own marriage in order to forestall the Doge's plans. She goes into the palace.

As Gabriele is departing he meets Fiesco who is returning to the palace. Fiesco does not need to be told what Gabriele wants from him; he is well aware that Gabriele and Amelia are lovers and welcomes the liaison. He could not wish for a worthier suitor for his ward than the scion of the Adorno family who happens also to be a fellow conspirator against the upstart Plebeian Doge. However he feels honour-bound to make known to Gabriele the truth about Amelia's lowly origins and relates the facts concerning her upbringing. Gabriele is not in the slightest bit deterred. He declares anew his love for Amelia. Fiesco is overjoyed and affectionately embraces Gabriele (*Vieni a me, ti benedico*).

Sounds of trumpets are heard announcing the imminent arrival of the Doge. Both men hasten away, fearful of being discovered in the Grimaldi palace by Boccanegra, who now enters with Paolo and attendants. Boccanegra tells Paolo that since 'events are pressing' they must leave within the hour. He dismisses Paolo and the attendants as Amelia approaches. As Paolo withdraws he cannot refrain from expressing his wonderment at Amelia's beauty; thus the audience is left in no doubt as to the identity of Amelia's suitor.

Boccanegra addresses Amelia formally, and without prevarication presents her with a parchment on which she discovers a pardon for her exiled brothers (the Grimaldis). He tells her that her brothers owe their pardon to her. Why, he wonders, does she hide such beauty as hers 'in this hermitage' (*Dinne, perchè in quest'eremo*). One senses that Boccanegra is himself attracted to Amelia, although at this juncture he cannot guess the true reason for the attraction. When he commences his suit on behalf of Paolo Amelia impetuously interrupts him and blurts out that she is indeed in love with someone 'who ardently returns my love' ... And it is not the 'villain who, desirous of me, reaches for the wealth of the Grimaldi'. In order to scotch any further suggestion that she should marry Paolo, Amelia now tells Boccanegra the truth about her origins, that she is not in fact a Grimaldi, that she was orphaned as a child and brought up in Pisa by a poor old woman.

The mention of Pisa immediately alerts Boccanegra. He listens intently as Amelia describes her humble origins. So graphic is her account he can have little doubt as to the girl's true identity. Overcome with emotion he asks if anybody ever visited her. 'A sailor', comes the reply. 'And was the name of the woman whom fate snatched from you Giovanna?' 'Yes it was'. Boccanegra produces a locket containing a likeness of Amelia's mother, Maria. Amelia has just described how, before she died, the old woman gave her such a likeness and she now produces this locket. She instantly recognizes that the picture that Boccanegra shows her is the same as the one she possesses. Boccanegra exclaims 'Maria!' – Amelia's true name – and then blurts out: 'You are my daughter!' and begs her to embrace him (*Figlia! A tal nome palpito*). Amelia embraces her father, assuring him that they shall never again be parted.

Boccanegra leads his new-found daughter towards the palace as Paolo enters, anxious to know whether his suit (by proxy) is successful. Boccanegra's reply is to the point: 'Abandon all hope!' For explanation he merely says, 'It is my will', before following Amelia into the palace. Paolo is incensed. 'Have your forgotten that you owe me your throne?' he mutters after Boccanegra's receding back.

Pietro enters and Paolo tells him that since he is denied Amelia, he intends to kidnap her. Pietro will find Amelia, he informs him, alone on the beach every night (thus confirming that it has been Paolo's shadowy figure that Amelia has noticed lurking in her vicinity every night). Paolo peremptorily orders Pietro to bring her to his ship, but then revises his instructions telling Pietro to take her instead to Lorenzin's house. Paolo wants to ensure that there is no risk of himself being implicated. He further tells Pietro that if Lorenzin makes any objection he need only mention that Paolo knows of Lorenzin and Gabriele's plot to overthrow the Doge. Pietro assures him that it shall be done.

Act 1 Scene 2 The Council Chamber of the Doge's palace. The Doge is seated on the throne. On one side of the Chamber sit twelve Councillors of the People and on the other side sit twelve Noble Councillors. Seated apart are four maritime consuls and the Constables. Pietro and Paolo are seated amongst the back rows of the Commoners.

Boccanegra addresses the assembly. He relates how the King of Tartary offers tokens of peace and rich gifts, and announces that the Black Sea is now open to 'our Ligurian ships'. He asks for, and receives, the Councillors' consent that he accept the King of Tartary's suit. He now proceeds to a message received from Francesco Petrarch[15] (the renowned poet) imploring Genoa to come to some sort of peaceful settlement with Venice. Paolo curtly interposes: 'Let him look to his rhymes, the singer of the blonde Avignonese!' Paolo is not alone in treating Petrarch's message with scorn; all the Councillors chorus: 'War on Venice!' This is precisely what Boccanegra wants to put

an end to. He points out that their two kingdoms (known in the 14th century as Adria and Liguria) have a common fatherland. The Councillors' response to this is immediate: 'Our Fatherland is Genoa!' It will be no easy task to persuade them otherwise.

A distant tumult is heard. Paolo runs to the window and tells the assembly that the commotion is coming from the square of the Fieschi. The assembly breaks into uproar. Boccanegra rushes to the window. Pietro points out to him that it is Gabriele Adorno who leads the uprising. While Boccanegra is preoccupied with absorbing this fresh turn of events, Pietro advises Paolo to flee, for he has quickly appreciated that something must have gone awry with the abduction of Amelia. Boccanegra is, however, too quick-witted for them. Observing Paolo's imminent departure he orders the maritime consuls to guard the doors. 'He who flees is a traitor!' he declares. Paolo stops in his tracks. Shouts of 'Death to the Patricians!' are heard from below. The Noble Councillors prepare to defend themselves with their swords. Boccanegra is outraged when the Plebeian Councillors also draw their swords with cries of 'Evviva!' for is not Boccanegra himself a Plebeian? Their treachery goads him into action. As the crowd shouts 'Death to the Doge!' he rises 'with haughty arrogance' and commands the herald to open the palace doors and tell the crowd that he has heard their threats, that he is not afraid and that he is awaiting them. He then orders the Councillors to put up their swords. They all obey. Moments later a trumpet is heard, followed by silence as the Herald delivers Boccanegra's message. It is a crucial moment, the fulcrum of the whole scene, and of Boccanegra's political career. He has gambled and, as the shouts of 'Long live the Doge!' shortly proclaim, won.

The people burst into the Council Chamber shouting for vengeance: 'Give us the blood of the foul murderer!' For a split second it is unclear to whom they refer. Then Gabriele Adorno owns to the fact that he has killed Lorenzin. He quickly justifies

---

[15] Francesco Petrarch (1304–1374). Italian lyric poet who devoted much of his life to composing Sonnets in praise of his Muse, Laura, who was a married woman and refused to become his mistress.

himself; he has killed Lorenzin because the latter had abducted Amelia. The people do not believe him. Gabriele reveals that in his dying moments Lorenzin revealed that 'a man of power had urged him to the crime'. For a moment Pietro fears that Paolo will be discovered, but Gabriele declares that Lorenzin died before revealing the name. Gabriele makes it clear that he has no doubt as to the identity of the villain, namely Boccanegra himself. Boccanegra attempts to have Gabriele arrested, but the latter wrenches himself free and hurls himself at Boccanegra. At this critical moment Amelia enters and throws herself between the two men. The guards seize Gabriele and disarm him.

Boccanegra commands the guards not to harm Gabriele. His anger has abated at the sight of his newly-discovered daughter and he asks Amelia to describe how she was abducted and how she was able to escape. Amelia relates how she was walking alone by the sea and was seized by three 'ruffians'. She fainted and when she came to she found herself Lorenzin's prisoner. She threatened her captor that the Doge would hear of her abduction, at which Lorenzin apparently let her go. She is just about to unveil Paolo as the true instigator of the crime when the Plebeians and Patricians, each anticipating that the criminal will be from the opposing faction, break out in uproar. Amelia is terrified, and Boccanegra is impelled to put a stop to what threatens to become a full-scale riot. With passionate intensity he addresses the assembly (*Fratricidi! Plebe! Patrizi!*) and implores the rival factions to put aside their differences (see **Boccanegra**). The crowd is subdued. Amelia silences Fiesco who has been holding himself aloof and now threatens to give vent to his rage. Pietro urges Paolo to take flight, but Paolo refuses. 'The serpent within me swells with poison', he mutters.

Gabriele surrenders his sword to Boccanegra, who refuses it, telling him that he shall remain a prisoner only so long as the plot remains undiscovered. Then Boccanegra, 'with terrible force', calls on Paolo. Paolo comes forward out of the crowd. He is shaking with fear. 'With great majesty and increasing violence' Boccanegra addresses him. 'In you is vested the people's trust. The people's honour depends upon your loyalty. I need your assistance. There is within these walls a villain who hears me and who quails. Already my hand reaches out for him. I know his name ... He trembles. You, in the sight of God and in my sight are witness. May he be accursed!' He then commands Paolo to repeat the malediction after him. Aware that he has been discovered and shaking with terror Paolo has no option but to oblige. He repeats the curse. The malediction is echoed by the entire assembly.

This conclusion to Act 1 is surely one of the most dramatic moments in all Verdi. It owes more than a little to the dramatic genius of Boito who was entirely responsible for the Council Chamber scene, added for the wholesale revision of the opera in 1881. It can easily be seen how this unique collaboration of two musico-dramatic geniuses was here flexing its muscles for the impending much greater challenges of *Otello* and *Falstaff*. Boccanegra's closing speech has within it the invincible force of Shakespearean tragedy.

Act 2   The Doge's quarters in the palace in Genoa. Doors at each end. From a balcony the city can be seen. On a table there stands a carafe and a goblet. Night is falling. Boccanegra has unveiled the plot against him. 'Andrea' (Fiesco) and Gabriele are condemned to death and Paolo is disgraced. As the curtain rises Paolo is instructing Pietro to bring the prisoners, Gabriele and Andrea to him. He gives Pietro a key which gives access to a secret passage from the dungeons. Pietro exits.

Left alone Paolo gives vent to his rage and frustration (*Me stesso ho maledetto!*). Aware, since Boccanegra so spectacularly humiliated him, that he is now despised and rejected by the Senate and by the Genoese he now has only one objective: to be avenged. He takes a phial from his pocket and pours the contents into the goblet on the table. 'Let Death make her choice', he mutters to himself. The choice lies between poison and the dagger, for Paolo has already decided to try and provoke either Fiesco or Gabriele into murdering Boccanegra.

The two prisoners are led in by Pietro who withdraws. Paolo comments that he knows Fiesco hates Boccanegra as much as he does and asks whether it was Fiesco who incited the Guelfs to insurrection. When Fiesco admits that it was Paolo tells him it was in vain; the Doge plans a 'new slaughter'. He then points out to Fiesco that he is already under sentence of death. What has he to lose now by murdering Boccanegra? Fiesco scornfully refuses even to discuss the matter, and Paolo dismisses him back to his dungeon.

Gabriele is about to follow, but is prevented by Paolo. At first Gabriele is equally dismissive of Paolo's incitement to murder. But then Paolo succeeds in convincing him that Amelia is 'marked out for the old man's lustful pleasure'. He reminds Gabriele that his options are limited – either he murders Boccanegra or he will himself die in captivity. Paolo leaves him to contemplate his options.

Gabriele immediately explodes with fury and resentment against his imagined rival. 'You killed my father (this is the first we learn of Gabriele's true motivation for desiring Boccanegra's downfall) and now you steal my beloved!' Even a fatal blow to Boccanegra could not satisfy Gabriele's desire for vengeance. His fury soon exhausts itself and he is suddenly overcome with self-pity and pity for his beloved. He prays that Amelia may be restored to him, but only, he remarks ominously, if her honour remains intact (*Cielo, pietoso, rendila*). If the latter is not the case then he never wishes to see her again.

Amelia enters. Gabriele is immediately suspicious. Her presence in the palace would seem to confirm Paolo's insinuation. He accuses her of being faithless. Amelia admits to loving Boccanegra but insists that her love is pure – perversely she refuses to reveal that Boccanegra is her father. (Perhaps she fears that if Gabriele were to discover her true relation to Boccanegra he would stop loving her. What she fails to appreciate is that her reticence is putting her father's life in grave danger.) Gabriele pleads with her (*Parla, in tuo cor virgineo*).

A trumpet is heard heralding the imminent arrival of the Doge. Amelia urges Gabriele to hide but he refuses. He has already resolved that he will murder Boccanegra. However he allows Amelia to lead him to concealment on the balcony. Boccanegra enters reading a letter.

Finding his daughter so obviously distraught he wants to know what troubles her. Tearfully Amelia reveals that she is in love with Gabriele. Since at that very moment Boccanegra has been reading a list of conspirators, amongst whom is Gabriele's name, he is displeased by the revelation. Amelia, however, confesses her love in such passionate terms that Boccanegra is forced to concede that if Gabriele repents he will consider granting him a pardon. Having relented thus far he demands to be left alone. Amelia tries to persuade her father to allow her to remain, knowing as she does that Gabriele is concealed on the balcony, but Boccanegra is insistent. Amelia withdraws but remains close at hand, fearing for her father's safety.

Alone, Boccanegra wearily reflects: 'Must the traitors once more test your mercy? … yet punishment could be interpreted as fear'. He is thirsty and, fatally, pours himself a goblet of water from the poisoned carafe. The water tastes bitter. Boccanegra ascribes the bitterness to his own debilitated state. He collapses into a chair, overwhelmed by the urge to sleep.

Gabriele approaches the sleeping old man. Thoughts of the vengeance he owes his father confirm his resolution. He draws a dagger and is about to stab Boccanegra when Amelia comes forward and, for the second time in the opera, flings herself between her father and her lover. Gabriele is infuriated by Amelia's interference and also perplexed by her insistence that her love for Boccanegra is 'holy'. Boccanegra comes to as Amelia beseeches Gabriele to put away his dagger. He bares his chest and invites Gabriele to strike him. All he wants to know before he dies is who admitted Gabriele into the palace, for Boccanegra knows that Gabriele should be incarcerated in one of the palace dungeons. In spite of being threatened with torture Gabriele refuses to disclose who admitted him.

Boccanegra is well aware of what prompts Gabriele's aggression towards him. 'You have avenged your father', he tells Gabriele. 'You have stolen from me a sweet treasure, my daughter ...' (*Ah, quel padre tu ben vendicasti*). Having finally learned the true relationship between Amelia and Boccanegra Gabriele is suddenly contrite. He invites Boccanegra to exact just retribution for his crime, but Boccanegra craves only peace and that his tomb might be the 'altar of Italian friendship'. As though to prompt his resolution a mob is heard outside the palace calling all men of Liguria to arms. Boccanegra taunts Gabriele by suggesting he should go and join them, but the latter confirms that he will never again fight against Boccanegra. In which case, Boccanegra tells him, he can take a message of peace to the mob, 'and may tomorrow's sun not shine on fraternal massacres!' Boccanegra confirms that Gabriele's loyalty will be rewarded with Amelia's hand in marriage. The two former enemies confirm their solidarity by drawing their swords and calling, 'To arms!' as the curtain falls.

Act 3   Interior of the Ducal Palace. At the back are large openings through which Genoa can be seen illuminated for a celebration. Behind Genoa lies the sea. Fiesco is on stage with a captain of the bowmen. Paolo enters, surrounded by guards. Shouts are heard of 'Long live the Doge', confirming that Boccanegra and Gabriele have been successful in quelling the insurrection. The captain gives Fiesco his sword back, telling him he is now free. 'And what of the Guelfs?' Fiesco asks. The captain is to the point: 'Defeated!' he says. 'Then it is a sad freedom', remarks Fiesco. Paolo is brought in. He is en route to his execution. He is defiant and takes obvious pleasure in revealing to Fiesco that he has poisoned Boccanegra, who even now will be succumbing to the effects. Fiesco is outraged. He may have felt a life-time

enmity towards Boccanegra but he is fundamentally a man of honour and is disgusted by Paolo's underhand treachery.

A chorus is heard offstage celebrating the nuptials of Amelia and Gabriele. Paolo boasts that it was he who abducted Amelia. This is news to Fiesco who, for the first time in the opera, loses his haughty self-restraint and draws his sword. Paolo urges him to strike, thus hoping that he may cheat the gallows, but Fiesco restrains himself. The guards drag Paolo away. Fiesco sees Boccanegra approaching and stands to one side. He has determined that the time has come to meet his long-time adversary face to face.

Boccanegra enters, preceded by the captain and a trumpeter. The captain makes a public proclamation to the effect that the Doge commands that all torches should be extinguished: 'let not the heroic dead be offended by the shouts of victory'. He exits, followed by the trumpeter.

Boccanegra is already feverish from the poison (*M'ardon le tempia!*). The sea breezes are a relief. He views the sea with intense nostalgia – if only he could have died a dignified death at sea, he thinks aloud. Fiesco comes forward. 'It would have been better for you if you had', he says dourly. Boccanegra is disorientated and does not yet recognize Fiesco. He calls for the guards. Fiesco tells him the 'paid assassins are not here' and although Boccanegra will kill him he must first hear him out. With apocalyptic metaphors he addresses Boccanegra: 'The rays of your star are eclipsed', he tells him. 'Conqueror, among the restless shades of your murdered victims you shall perish' (*Delle faci festanti*). As if to corroborate his speech the lights of the city and of the port start to go out. Something familiar in the voice addressing him disturbs Boccanegra: But it cannot be ... Fiesco is surely dead? 'Thus do the dead greet you!' Fiesco rejoins. All the pent-up anger of years now erupts from Fiesco as he declares his sole ambition to be avenged.

Far from being perplexed by the old man's vehemence Boccanegra is overjoyed at the opportunity for reconciliation. Moreover, he feels that Fiesco is the one person who can effect a peace between the warring factions in Genoa. He reminds Fiesco that he once offered him forgiveness if he were to surrender into Fiesco's care his daughter by Maria. Now he tells Fiesco that Amelia Grimaldi, the girl that Fiesco has been caring for, is none other than that very same daughter who bears the name of her deceased mother. Fiesco is overwhelmed by the revelation. He is overcome with emotion and breaks down, weeping. In a heart-rending solo he tells Boccanegra: 'I feel a terrible reproof even in your pity'. But Boccanegra does not seek to reprove, nor even to gloat over the old man's misery. He wants only amity between them. He asks to be allowed to embrace Maria's father, and tells Fiesco that his pardon will be balm to his soul. Sadly Fiesco tells Boccanegra of Paolo's treachery but Boccanegra does not need to be told. He already feels the poison working within him. Both men bewail the cruelty of fate.

Amelia enters with Gabriele and an entourage of senators, ladies and pages bearing torches. The young lovers are preparing to celebrate their nuptials. Amelia is astounded to see Fiesco in her father's presence. Boccanegra, knowing that time is short, loses no time in telling Amelia that Fiesco is in fact her grandfather. The two, who have unknowingly shared their lives for so long, embrace with deep emotion. Then Boccanegra reveals that he is dying. Falling at his feet Amelia and Gabriele are incredulous. Boccanegra rises and, placing his hands on their respective heads, blesses their union concluding: 'for their sake let flowers spring forth from the thorns of my martyrdom' (*Gran Dio, li benedici*).

The dark message which has predominated throughout the opera is enunciated by Fiesco: 'All mortal happiness is false enchantment: the human heart is a spring of never-ending tears'. The assembled company echoes the sentiment.

Boccanegra's last wish is that the Doge's crown should be given to Gabriele. Fiesco goes to the balcony, surrounded by senators and pages, who raise their torches, and addresses the populace below: 'People of Genoa! In Gabriele Adorno hail now your Doge!' Voices are heard objecting that Simon Boccanegra is the Doge. Fiesco pronounces him dead and urges the people to pray for Boccanegra's soul. All kneel and the opera closes with the slow and sombre tolling of a death-knell.

In spite of Fiesco's morbid declaration that all mortal happiness is 'false enchantment; the human heart is a spring of never ending tears' (sentiments echoed by the chorus: 'Yes it is true. Man weeps eternally. Nature wraps herself in a mantle of sorrow'), paradoxically by the end of the opera all the main protagonists have achieved that after which they have striven. Gabriele achieves the hand in marriage of Amelia, in addition to political glory and the reinstatement of the Patricians in the Doge's seat; Amelia achieves reunion with her long-lost father and also recognition from her grandfather, together with the secure knowledge that her love for Gabriele is returned in equal measure; Boccanegra achieves a truce with Fiesco and dies in the knowledge that his lifetime's aim of peace in Genoa and amity between the warring factions has a far greater possibility of achieving fruition than when he first came to office.

Fiesco's doom-laden pronouncement is more a Nietzschian acknowledgement of 'eternal recurrence': that it is rarely given to any one individual to achieve personal fulfilment and happiness; that personal fulfilment is more often than not to be sacrificed to the greater good, however that may be conceived. The individuals in the opera may achieve their ends, but in each case the price is high – in some cases exorbitantly high – and the road to that achievement has been excessively difficult; 'a spring of never-ending tears'.

With Boccanegra's death Amelia loses her father while Fiesco loses the man whose destiny has been the guiding force in the passage of his own tortured life. The message would seem to be that only through loss is there any possibility of reconciliation.

Boccanegra gives expression to this insight in one of the most striking images in the text, an insight which could equally well be transcribed meaningfully to any one of the main protagonists, viz. 'For their sake let flowers spring forth from the thorns of my martyrdom'. The only point of human existence is the meaning that can, and must, be distilled from even the most intense suffering.

Simon Boccanegra (*Boccanegra*). First Doge of Genoa.

The character of Simon Boccanegra has its origins in an historical figure, Simon Boccanegra, who was the first Doge of Genoa, elected in 1339 and given the title of Perpetual Doge. The office of Doge originated in Venice where it had been established for several hundred years before the Genoese established a similar system. Just as in the opera the historical Simon Boccanegra had to contend with constant feuding between the Patrician and Plebeian factions, as well as with bickering amongst the Guelph and Ghibelline parties within the Patricians themselves. He was also poisoned, at a banquet in 1363, so the time scale of the opera matches the actual historical time scale.

Boccanegra is referred to as 'that pirate Doge' by **Gabriele Adorno** (Act 1 Scene 2). He has accepted nomination for the office of Doge with great reluctance and in the knowledge that he will have to contend with bitter enmity from the powerful Patrician factions. The irony in Verdi's opera is that he accepts the position solely so as to gain the good graces of **Fiesco** and the hand in marriage of Fiesco's daughter, Maria.

When the opera opens (Prologue) Boccanegra is a young man. He has led an adventurous life and achieved renown sufficient for him to be a popular choice for the people's Doge. In the course of the Prologue we learn of his love for Maria and of Fiesco's fierce opposition to the affair. We also learn that he has fathered a daughter by Maria and that his daughter has disappeared. By the conclusion of the Prologue Maria has died and Boccanegra is left marooned in a hostile environment with an awesome responsibility to shoulder.

The main body of the opera takes place twenty-five years later. Boccanegra is now an elderly man (by fourteenth-century standards). The strain of relentless public duties and a loveless existence has taken its toll. The discovery of his long-lost daughter at this late stage of his life is a boon he could never have envisaged in his wildest imaginings. From the moment that he learns of **Amelia**'s true identity he becomes first and foremost a doting father and secondly a Doge. All his actions thereafter must be seen in this light. Amelia fills a huge yawning chasm in his life and when she begs him not to give her to the scheming and untrustworthy **Paolo** he complies without a thought to the consequences. It is this, more than anything, which precipitates his downfall.

In the Council Chamber scene (Act 1 Scene 2) Boccanegra shows himself in sympathy with the poet Petrarch in a desire for conciliation and peace. Nevertheless he is still capable of imposing his will and commanding the submission of even the most brazen of his court; witness the brutal humiliation of Paolo at the end of the scene. The extremity of this is, however, no mere histrionic gesture to confirm his sovereignty. It is motivated by the discovery that Paolo has been responsible for abducting his beloved daughter. Indeed all Boccanegra's most passionate utterances are motivated by thoughts of his daughter. When Gabriele attempts to assassinate him Boccanegra's pride is at first outraged but on seeing Amelia's grief his thoughts are only to console her. (At this stage he does not know that Gabriele is Amelia's lover.) The inevitable rage he must feel towards his would-be assassin is displaced onto the whole Genoese nation when he erupts into his tirade (*Fratricidi! Plebe! Patrizi!* – see **Synopsis**). It is an impassioned plea to the Genoese to abandon their futile internecine struggles. 'I weep for you, for the peaceful Genovese slopes where the olive tree buds in vain; I weep for your flowers whose gaiety is a lie and I cry Peace! And I cry Love!' The Councillors are so taken aback by the intensity of Boccanegra's appeal that they immediately subside.

Boccanegra's imprecations against Paolo give him the same moral authority in the eyes of his court as is possessed by the Grand Inquisitor in *Don Carlo*. But this is not the righteous fury of a despot or religious fundamentalist, but of an aggrieved and outraged father. It is unlikely that Boccanegra has ever previously demonstrated such passion. It should be remembered that the curse that Boccanegra requires Paolo to pronounce upon himself is no mere figure of speech. It is an awesome condemnation which for Paolo, and for those present, would have had an all too practical and immediate significance.

Boccanegra's death comes hard on the heels of his discovery that Amelia is desperately in love with a young man, Gabriele. The fact that that young man has just tried to assassinate him only compounds the shock and underlines his own redundancy. For in the space of hours Boccanegra must undergo the full odyssey required of a father, first to gain a child who is irrefutably a reflection of his own image of ideal femininity, and then to renounce that image in favour of another, younger, and equally irrefutably, more eligible man. Through the course of his life Boccanegra has seen enough of the chronic effect upon a human life of refusing to relinquish (see **Fiesco**). He knows he has no option but to let go. He is even prepared to pardon Gabriele's (unpardonable) offence of treason. It is, however, fiercely painful for him and he needs now time to himself, hence his insistence that Amelia leave him (Act 2). 'Here I must wait the dawn', he says. Like Sachs, in Wagner's *Die Meistersinger* (Act 3), Boccanegra will burn the midnight oil in order to reconcile himself to the inevitable. Such vigils have, down the ages, been a favoured way of seeking enlightenment. There will be no enlightenment for Boccanegra, but there will be reconciliation.

The fact that Gabriele compounds his guilt by attempting a second time to murder him (and is again pardoned) underlines the poignancy of Boccanegra's predicament. It is only at this late stage in the opera that we learn that Boccanegra is responsible for having killed Gabriele's father. Sickened and defeated by the years of endless strife and hatred Boccanegra now only seeks peace and the end of 'ancient hates'. He extends the hand of friendship to his one-time enemy who now loves and is loved by his beloved daughter (Act 3). But he has been cheated of the instant oblivion that the success of Gabriele's assassination attempt would have granted. Instead he must endure the last dregs of agony that the poison in his veins is already distilling.

But before he dies he must face and be reconciled with the image of his 'father', that is Fiesco, the father who disowned him (we know nothing of Boccanegra's biological father). The Patrician cannot believe that a Plebeian will act honourably, and can only be mollified by having his granddaughter, Maria (that is, Amelia), restored to him. Thus Boccanegra is compelled to relinquish his daughter, not once but twice. As a pirate Boccanegra was on the outside looking in, beyond the pale of respectable society. By seducing Fiesco's daughter Boccanegra became guilty of the worst sin of the *parvenu*, appearing brazenly to gatecrash the sacred citadel of the Establishment. He can only make restitution by totally prostrating himself and by acceding to the imperatives laid down by the unforgiving Patriarch. Boccanegra longs for escape, longs for rehabilitation, longs to be reconciled with eternity in the deep unconscious oblivion of the sea from which he arose (*Il mare, il mare! Perchè in suo grembo non trovai la tomba?* Act 3).

But the duties of responsibility cannot be evaded. Chaos must be faced, and in the event it is not Boccanegra who will suffer prostration but Fiesco. For if Boccanegra has suffered from pride it is as nothing to the overweening arrogance of the Patrician. The miracle is effected through the advent of Amelia. It is through the shared experiences of fatherhood, the agonies of loss and separation that they both endure, that Boccanegra and Fiesco finally succeed in transcending the purely artificial barriers birth and custom.

Boccanegra's last act is to bestow the Doge's crown onto the head of Gabriele himself. A Plebeian sanctions the election of a Patrician. But he does so in the sure knowledge that it is ultimately unimportant whether Patrician or Plebeian is in power so long as the two learn to live together in mutual respect and harmony. Peace and love – these were all Boccanegra craved.

The universality of Boccanegra's predicament in an unsafe world is the clue to the enduring success, if not widespread popularity, of this uneven, though majestic, work. The portrayal of the character of Boccanegra looks back to the anguish of Nabucco, of Rigoletto, of Filippo (*Don Carlo*) and, in certain moments, forward to the titanic rage of Otello. But of all these characters Boccanegra, with his sincere and just demands of life, is surely one of the most sympathetic.

Borsa (*Rigoletto*). A courtier at the court of the **Duke of Mantua**.
When the opera opens the Duke is conversing with Borsa. The Duke is telling Borsa his latest projected escapade: the seduction of a 'mysterious beauty' whom he has seen in church every Sunday for the last three months. Borsa is the epitome of the sycophantic courtier. He laps up everything his master tells him and clearly enters into the spirit of the Duke's amorous escapades. But he also attempts to warn the Duke of the consequences of his recklessness. The Duke dismisses recommendations of caution with his nonchalant canzone (*Questa o quella*).

Thereafter Borsa is barely distinguishable from the rest of the courtiers. See *Cortigiani*.

Briano (*Aroldo*). A holy man.
The character of Briano replaces that of **Jorg** in *Stiffelio* and fulfils an altogether more crucial function in the opera than does his predecessor. True, Jorg is on stage at the opening of *Stiffelio*, proclaiming the merits of the Holy Book and his hopes for Stiffelio's ministry. But thereafter his role is a strictly subsidiary one.

Briano, on the other hand, is the voice of **Aroldo**'s conscience, persistently calling Aroldo back to an awareness of his responsibility as a Christian. Jorg, as at the conclusion of Act 2, may prompt Stiffelio, but in that opera one feels that Stiffelio's conscience would bring him through in the end, even had he not Jorg's support.

With Aroldo it is very different. He tells **Mina**: 'Without that pious hermit you would have grieved over my death. He found me wounded at Ascalona and saved my life. Together we visited the sacred places; on the Holy Tomb we swore to live and to fight united' (Act 1). For the remainder of Act 1 and indeed the substance of Acts 2 and 3, Briano's role is almost identical to that of Jorg.

Act 4 adds a whole new dimension to the role. Aroldo has gone into retreat, principally for negative reasons; namely his misery over Mina's infidelity. Briano serves to keep reminding Aroldo of his duty to God. At the crucial moment when Aroldo appears to be about to reject Mina's plea for forgiveness he intervenes: 'the Just One said one day: "Let he who has not sinned cast the first stone". And the woman arose forgiven'. In *Stiffelio* Stiffelio finds the text for himself, while Jorg stands on the sidelines.

Briano's interjection is the deciding factor in the final Act of *Aroldo* and is almost entirely responsible for Aroldo and Mina's reconciliation.
(See also **Jorg** (*Stiffelio*).)

C

Doctor Caius (*Falstaff*).
The defining feature of Doctor Caius's personality is a ruling sense of grievance against the world, everything and everybody in it. He has an overwhelming sense of his own importance and imposes this on all who come within his orbit. The world being what it is he usually finds more than enough

justification for his chronic sense of victimization. But he also manages, as is the way with such individuals, to confirm and corroborate at every possible opportunity his expectation that he will be the victim of injustice. A man of Caius's pomposity is the ideal victim for **Falstaff**'s razor-sharp wit and the tomfoolery of his henchmen.

When the opera opens Caius is screaming for reparation (Act 1 Scene 1). He has apparently been beaten and robbed by **Bardolfo** and **Pistola** on the preceding day. The fact that the offence occurred is never in question. The question exercising Caius's mind is how he is going to be compensated for the injustice done to him? Falstaff could not make it plainer that he considers Caius deserves everything that comes to him. Thus Caius is left with an abiding sense of injustice. This is the central concern of Verdi's opera, namely the degree to which Falstaff's irresponsible and lawless way of travelling through life eventually brings down on his head a pile of retribution. Caius has on his side all the force and moral opprobrium of the bourgeois society he so paradigmatically represents. In the final scene of the opera he will have the chance to kick and stamp on Falstaff, the source of his grievance, to his heart's content. Whether it will in any way alleviate his aggravated spleen and improve his humour is a matter for conjecture.

Bardolfo and Pistola make no secret of their contempt for Caius. They are the opposite in every way to Caius, being amoral – if not immoral – and principally ruled by their physical appetites and inclinations. Caius, being a physician, has devoted himself to science and development of his intellect. In their verbal sparring (Act 1 Scene 1) Caius enjoys vaunting his superior education in the insults and epithets that he hurls at Bardolfo and Pistola, fully confounding the latter when he calls him a 'mandrake sprout'. Between the likes of Bardolfo and Pistola and Doctor Caius there will always be a deadly enmity. Each party feels threatened by, or superior to, the other party. There can be no question where Verdi's sympathies lie: Caius's vocal line is harsh and repetitive and

one can only sympathize with Falstaff and his henchmen in wanting to be rid of him as soon as possible.

What Caius cannot accept is that he allowed himself to become inebriated. He was thus deprived of that which is most important to him, his right and need to be in control of himself and to be answerable. There must inevitably be a nagging doubt in his mind: was he actually robbed, or was he persuaded to part with his money when under the influence of drink? It is the doubt in his mind that lends the almost hysterical intensity to his outbursts. He knows that finally he could not risk taking his case to court, because he was not in his right mind at the time of the offence and presumably, it all having taken place in the Garter Inn, any number of witnesses could be called against him. His only hope of redress is through his wealthy friend, the merchant **Master Ford** whom he knows to be well disposed towards him. He repeatedly warns Ford against Bardolfo and Pistola – needlessly in fact since the latter have no quarrel with Ford. Their only quarrel is with Falstaff.

Caius probably takes more exercise then he has had in years when searching Ford's house for Falstaff (Act 2 Scene 2). The fact that he knows perfectly well that it is Falstaff and not just some anonymous seducer for whom he searches adds piquancy to the endeavour. He almost matches Bardolfo and Pistola in the alacrity with which he joins in the search, snapping to attention whenever Ford barks out a new order. Aside from the exercise it is doubtful whether Caius has ever had so much fun in years, his being an essentially sedentary calling. This is particularly the case during the masquerade in Windsor Park (Act 3 Scene 2). A man like Caius would normally be tucked up in bed in his nightshirt and bed socks by midnight. Instead of which he finds himself cavorting with half the neighbourhood, dressed in a friar's cowl, and being presented with the opportunity to abuse the Knight in a way that would be unthinkable to him in the normal course of events. However his naturally fastidious nature may take exception to the physical violence. He is, in any case, distracted by the need to find **Nannetta**. Ford has given him a precise description (Act 3 Scene 1) of the way in which Nannetta will be dressed for the masquerade. Caius imagines he has found her and fondly believes by the conclusion of the scene that he has married her. In this he is sadly mistaken. He has, in fact, been wed to his arch enemy, Bardolfo. This revelation fills him with unspeakable horror, though it is no doubt safe to assume that the 'marriage' will soon be annulled.

Caius belongs to a *Commedia dell'Arte* tradition (that first entered opera with prominence in the character of Basilio in Mozart's and Rossini's operas) of the learned physician and pedant who acts as go-between betwixt the aristocracy and the ordinary man in the street. As a doctor he belongs to a distinguished profession which in social standing puts him above the merchant, but does not include him amongst the gentry. Thus Caius's grievance against Sir John Falstaff must be partially motivated by a sense of inferiority. By the end of the opera he has been deeply humiliated, but it is unlikely it will make any appreciable difference to his inordinately fussy and unattractive personality. In fact the events of the opera will almost certainly have aggravated his social unease. At least Nannetta will not have to endure his attentions between the sheets.

Il Marchese di Calatrava (*La forza del destino*). Father of **Leonora** and **Don Carlo** di Vargas.

The nature of Calatrava's role, appearing only in the first scene of the opera in which he is killed by his daughter's lover, inevitably invites comparison with the Commendatore, in Mozart's *Don Giovanni*. The Marquis's statue may not appear in the final Act, but his spirit hangs over the remaining action, particularly in the shape of his fanatically loyal son (Don Carlo) whose overriding passion is to avenge the family honour.

Calatrava cannot abide the idea of his daughter marrying a half-caste. The Incas were viewed by the Spanish as little better than savages. It makes no difference to him that **Don Alvaro** is fabulously wealthy, for his wealth is tainted by his origins. From Calatrava's viewpoint Inca blood would pollute the purity of the Calatrava lineage. He will not even discuss the matter with his daughter. He refers to Alvaro merely as 'the unworthy foreigner'.

That Calatrava loves Leonora and cares for her is beyond question. Equally beyond question is Leonora's devotion to him. This much is established in the opening pages of the opera as Calatrava bids good night to his daughter and wonders why she appears so distressed. She throws herself into his arms with such unrestrained passion as he takes his leave that Calatrava must surely suspect something is afoot. Having said which, Alvaro is hardly subtle in his approach to the house. If Leonora's maid, **Curra**, hears Alvaro's horses' hooves then presumably so does Calatrava. At any rate he has sufficient misgivings to order his servants to break down the door just at the moment that Alvaro and Leonora are about to make their escape. He is in a towering rage, principally due to offended vanity. He renounces his daughter, refusing to acknowledge her as such. When Alvaro bares his chest, inviting Calatrava to strike him, it only confirms the old man's conviction as to the baseness of Alvaro's origins.

Calatrava's death is purely accidental; Alvaro throws his pistol to the ground with too great abandon and it goes off accidentally, mortally wounding the Marquis. Calatrava does not realize it was an accident and with his dying breath he curses his daughter. The opera will show that his curse is only efficacious in the short term. Eventually Leonora will find peace in the arms of Mother Church.

Of all Verdi's father-figures Calatrava is perhaps the most purely negative, in that he never has the opportunity to demonstrate any redeeming feature. His domineering influence over his daughter has blighted her young life and renders her one chance of happiness stillborn.

Captain of the Longbowmen (Un capitano dei balestieri) (*Boccanegra*).

Like **Amelia**'s maidservant (**Ancella**) this is surely an unnecessary extravagance on Verdi's part. The Captain appears only at the opening of Act 3 when he returns **Fiesco** his sword and tells the old man that the Guelfs have been defeated, information that could have readily have been supplied by **Paolo** or **Pietro**. He then precedes **Boccanegra** into the ducal hall and, as the Doge's herald, requires that the citizens of Genoa put out their torches: 'let not the heroic dead be offended by the shouts of victory'. In other words he calls a halt to the celebrations in honour of the victory of the Plebeians over the Patricians.

Don Carlos (*Don Carlo*)

'In many ways he is intelligent but in others shows less understanding than a child of seven. He asks questions continually but without discrimination as if from habit. He shows little ambition and his only enthusiasm seems to be eating where his excesses are said to be the cause of his sickly condition. Not entirely bad-looking, his head is nondescript, his brow low, his chin extremely long and his skin pallid. He is not broadshouldered and lacks height. One shoulder is a little higher than the other and his back a little humped. His chest is narrow and his legs weak, the left one being longer that the right. His voice is thin and wheedling. He stammers and has problems with his 'l's and 'r's. Still, he manages to make himself understood. He is violent, irritable to the point of fury and many people wonder what might happen if he was out of control. Still, he is extremely pious, fond of trustworthy, honest people and is very generous. In short, Don Carlos is a frail and feeble minded prince but, on the other hand, he is the son of a powerful monarch.'

The Austrian ambassador to his sovereign Ferdinand, Philip's uncle.[16]

Historical Note. The historical Don Carlos was if anything an even more inadequate personality than the character portrayed in Verdi's opera. Nevertheless the fundamental lineaments of his relationship with his father are largely adhered to. Suffice it to say there was little love lost between them. Philip habitually humiliated his son in front of the court. Carlos became increasingly, and with some justification, paranoid, and took every opportunity to lampoon his father. Finally, out of patience, Philip had him placed under house arrest. Carlos's personality thereafter disintegrated and he died not long after.

It would be wrong to blame Don Carlos entirely for his sorry destiny. He never knew his mother, Maria of Portugal, who died only two days after he was born. Maria was the love of Philip's life. It is more than probable that Philip never forgave his son for her death which would explain his apparent detestation of him.

During Carlos's formative years, 1550–59, Philip was away in Flanders and in England and Carlos was brought up by a succession of guardians. Carlos was initially highly suspicious of the new Queen, Elisabeth di Valois, not unnaturally, since any progeny forthcoming from his father's new marriage could well threaten his own chances of succession. But he soon found an ally in Elisabeth, who seems to have gone out of her way to help the young man and worked tirelessly to achieve some sort of rapprochement between Carlos and his father. In all this Schiller was faithful to history, though emphatically not in making Elisabeth and Carlos lovers. This was an adumbration of subsequent historians relying on unsubstantiated gossip from disaffected members of Philip's court. The friendship between the two is well documented and if there had been any whiff of scandal surrounding the relationship we can be certain it would have materialized at the time.

---

[16] Quoted in *Don Carlo and Company*, Christopher Morgan, page 106 (Julia MacRae Books).

One possible explanation for Carlos's inadequate personality, apart from the inter-breeding that was rife in the Hapsburg clan, could be that when he was in his teens he suffered a serious injury to his head when he fell down a flight of stairs. His head swelled to twice its normal size and he fell into a coma. He was only saved by a miracle, worked by exposing him to the remains and shroud of a saintly Franciscan monk. In the 20th century it has been a notable feature of many cases of serious criminal offenders, notably serial killers, that they have, in early life, suffered serious head injury.

Don Carlo is the least heroic of all Verdi's title roles. **Oberto, Ernani, Macbeth, Nabucco, Otello, Rigoletto, Falstaff** are all characters who are deeply flawed human beings, yet each one has a kernel of greatness, something that raises them above the average. Meet any one of them in the street and you would take a second look. It is doubtful that you would even notice Don Carlo. This may sound unnecessarily unkind, but it should be understood that it is not Carlo's fault if he never attains to the heroic. It has been his misfortune to have a power-fully domineering father who has succeeded in permanently stunting his emotional development. With no room to manoeuvre for himself Don Carlo has grown up an entirely re-active personality. He cannot have any idea of his own without reference to someone else. Least of all can he act without the catalyst of another man's will to prompt him. That man is **Rodrigo**. Don Carlo only succeeds in relating to the world at all through his friend's passionate idealism. When Rodrigo is killed he attempts for a time – and it almost seems as though he might succeed – in taking on his friend's mantle and carrying forth Rodrigo's determination to see Flanders liberated. But fate did not decree a political future for Carlo.

Carlo's greatest need is to return to the womb from whence he came and that is precisely what Verdi and his librettists grant him at the close of the opera when he is apparently 'abducted' by the spirit of his grandfather and dragged into the cloisters from which presumably he will not emerge again. Womb imagery pervades throughout the role of Don Carlo. In Act 1 he elects to catch first sight of his bride to be in the forest of Fontainbleu. In Act 2 Scene 1 he is dis-covered in the cloisters of the monastery of San Yuste by the tomb of his grandfather. In Act 3 he is in the Queen's gardens at mid-night. The scene is so dark he cannot even see to whom he makes his declaration of love. In Act 4 he is confined in an underground prison. There is very little of the daylight world in Don Carlo's life.

When he does venture forth Carlo is self-evidently incapable of conducting himself in an appropriate manner. He has no political acumen whatsoever, as is evidenced in the *auto-da-fè* scene. His disinclination to emerge into the daylight world is not assisted by the fact that the woman he has set his heart on marrying is suddenly married to his father and becomes his stepmother. Don Carlo is an artist *manqué*. He has all the sensibilities of the artist, the receptivity to beauty and access to passion, but he has no outlet for his sensibilities, nor the discipline required to turn them to good account. To be fair to him, neither does he have the opportunity. But then one has the feeling that if the opportunity presented itself he would not know what to do with it. He is, however, capable of taking great risks. Witness the fact that he has left the Spanish Court without leave (Act 1). He knows well that his father will be furious. Nevertheless he has a mind of his own when it comes to acquiring what he wants. He is desperate to have a glimpse of the girl he is expected to marry.

When Carlo first sees **Elisabeth** she is dispensing alms to the woodcutters in the middle of the forest. The image is thus forever fixed in his mind of his bride as a nurturing mother-figure, that which has been so grievously lacking from his life in Madrid (Carlo's mother died two days after he was born – see Historical Note). He is enchanted by Elisabeth's smile: 'I saw her and at her smile the sun seemed to shine forth'. There are not many smiles around his father, who is a stern disciplinarian and prematurely aged. By the time Carlo comes to make himself known to Elisabeth they are both lost in the forest, both in actuality and metaphorically. Elisabeth has a possibility of escape – she is accompanied by her esquire, **Tebaldo**. Carlo has no possibility. His only hope is to make himself known to Elisabeth. He introduces himself as a Spanish nobleman. He seems to have great difficulty in acknowledging and presenting himself.

Elisabeth does not know at first what to make of him. She gives vent to her fears concerning the new life that awaits her in Madrid. Carlo is solicitous but he maintains the pretence of being the Infante's messenger. He has a distinct sense of the histrionic. He assures her that Carlo will want to 'live at her feet' and then gives her the ill-fated casket in which she will discover the portrait of himself (see **Synopsis**) and thereby be forced to recognize him. He thus places the onus on an appropriate reaction to the situation squarely on Elisabeth's shoulders. She must do the work. Once she has recognized him all he can do is reiterate over and over, 'I love you, I love you – you alone I long for, I will live for you – for you I will die!' Elisabeth is carried away by his ardour and declares that she returns his love in equal measure. Carlo has never known such happiness. It looks as though it could be a match made in heaven: the spirited young girl with the adoring, romantic Prince. But it is not to be.

As soon as **Count di Lerma** has announced that there has been a change of plan and Elisabeth is to marry Carlo's father, King **Philip II**, his happiness collapses. The iron fist of his father has reached across from the Escurial and snatched away Carlo's first possibility of real joy. For a temperament such as Carlo's it is a catastrophic development. His reaction is typically petulant: 'a chill pierces my heart! An abyss opens before me – and you sanction it, O heaven!'. Carlo's greatest shortcoming is his tendency to wallow in self-pity. His only consolation can be that Elisabeth is every bit as distressed as he is.

It is an indication of how out of love with life he is that he seeks solace at the tomb of his grandfather, the Emperor Charles V. It is a peculiar human tendency always to idealize the departed and imagine that if the deceased were not deceased all life's problems would be solved. Certainly there was little love between Philip and his father, although Charles undoubtedly respected his son's abilities, which is more than can be said for Philip concerning his own son. Carlo probably inherited his temperament more from his grandfather than his father, which does not mean that Charles would necessarily have been sympathetic.

The only person who can rescue Carlo from himself is Rodrigo, for Rodrigo cares about Carlo, but at the same time has concerns beyond the personal preoccupations that tend to predominate in Carlo's psyche. Rodrigo instinctively realizes that Carlo's chief problem is a poor self-image, that he needs to be taken out of himself and made to realize that he can make a positive contribution in the world beyond the four walls of the Spanish palace. Carlo would do anything for Rodrigo.[17] It is probably Rodrigo's reminder that he will one day be King that persuades him to accept unreservedly the challenge of championing the Flemish cause. For Carlo's single most pressing need is to assert his independence from his father.

By the end of Act 2 Scene 1 one has hopes that Carlo might surmount his natural disadvantages. By the conclusion of Act 2 Scene 2 one is forced to the realization that any such assumption would be premature. In his exchange with Elisabeth, *Io vengo a domandar*, he shows himself to be unstabie to the point of hysteria. He takes no account

---

[17] No doubt a case could be made among contemporary directors that their relationship is essentially homosexual. Such an implication would only confuse the opera's dramatic delineation and is unwarranted. Inspired with new hope by his friend's exhortation to him to learn to become a king Carlos swears eternal comradeship with his friend and devotion to the cause of liberty in Flanders (Act 2 Scene 1).

of the fact that Elisabeth is in an extremely difficult position herself. All that concerns him are his own unruly emotions: 'I am so unhappy! I can endure no more! I have suffered so much . . . Alas my soul is crushed, my heart is chilled'. It would be contemptible were it not so evident that he is not in control of himself. Elisabeth gently tries to remind him that she has a responsibility to her duties as Queen. Carlo's only response is to faint, collapsing at her feet which, as he has already made clear, is the only place he wants to be. When he comes round he misinterprets Elisabeth's genuine concern for him as a cue to declare his undying passion for her. Elisabeth is horrified, knowing that at any moment Philip could come in, as in fact he does. She therefore does the only thing she can do in the circumstances and violently repulses him. Carlo inevitably takes this to mean she does not love him at all and flees in desperation declaring, 'I am accursed!' Carlo suffers from what psychologists call 'the fallacy of central significance'. In other words he imagines that whatever he thinks or feels must be of critical concern to the rest of the world.

When Carlo receives **Eboli's** note of assignation (Act 3 Scene 1) he immediately assumes it is from Elisabeth. 'My heart is drunk with love', he declares. It is symptomatic of how entirely wrapped up in himself he is that he does not even stop to check that it is Elisabeth he addresses when Eboli arrives in the garden. Instead he launches into a passionate outpouring of love. It is the sort of mistake one only makes once. When he realizes that it is not the Queen he is addressing he is, not unnaturally, mortified. He immediately imagines that over his head 'heaven's thunderbolt is hovering ready to burst'. Once again it is Rodrigo who rescues him. Carlo has nothing to say for himself but repeated self-lacerations; 'I have been a fool . . . I have sullied a mother's name', while Rodrigo attempts to defend his honour and save his reputation. He does however manage to gather his wits sufficiently to prevent Rodrigo from stabbing Eboli. After Eboli has left and Rodrigo requests that Carlo hand

over to him any incriminating papers, Carlo for one panic-stricken moment wonders whether Rodrigo is going to turn against him (an inevitable side effect of Carlo's sort of solipsism is a tendency to be paranoid). He is quickly reassured, and time will prove that his faith in his friend is not misplaced.

In the meantime Carlo determines to prove to Rodrigo that he is worthy of his friend's love and, without reference to him, organizes the deputation of Flemish Deputies to make their case publicly before the King at the forthcoming *auto-da-fè*. This also gives him an excuse to plead his own case with Philip. Carlo has always been one for the grand gesture, and this is certainly his grandest gesture to date. The King is outraged and predictably refuses to pay any attention either to his son's plea to be given a mandate in Flanders or the Flemish Deputies' plea for mercy, in spite of the fact that Rodrigo and Elisabeth both encourage Philip to pay heed. This scene clearly shows Carlo's chronic inability to gauge the best way to cope with his father. A public showdown is certainly not the way. Philip simply digs his heels in feeling, rightly, that he is being bullied and blackmailed. Carlo, aware that he is making no impression on his father, loses all self-control and draws his sword. This in itself is a treasonable act. Were he capable of any degree of rationality he would realize that Rodrigo was doing him a service by intervening and demanding that Carlo surrender his sword.[18] In fact Rodrigo is merely returning the compliment Carlo paid him when he prevented him from murdering Eboli. But Carlo does not see it like that. He only sees evidence of Rodrigo's gross betrayal. His disenchantment cannot be alleviated when Philip forthwith raises Rodrigo to the rank of Duke. Carlo is no doubt convinced, thereby, that Rodrigo is conniving with Philip in order to undo him.

Carlo must now undergo the humiliation of being imprisoned. It may be that, to some

[18] It should be noted that Carlos does not draw his sword in order to attack the King but to emphasize the point that he is determined to fight for the cause of Flemish liberation.

extent, this is a relief to him, since it relieves him of the burdens and responsibilities of living in the daylight world. One wonders if Carlo would not have been happier had he never had to emerge into the daylight at all. Even now he claims that his love for Elisabeth is torturing and killing him. However during his time spent in jail he undergoes something of a sea-change. He has accepted that he is of 'no more use to the living' (Act 4 Part 2), although he does still spare a thought for the Flemish people. He hopes that Rodrigo may be able to continue the work he has started. He is dismayed to learn that Rodrigo has transferred suspicion onto himself by allowing Carlo's incriminating papers to be found in his possession. His first thought is to ensure that Rodrigo is exonerated. He will reveal all to the King, he declares. Rodrigo persuades him that he must do no such thing, but save himself in order that he may be of assistance to the Flemish.

When Rodrigo is killed Carlo is genuinely anguished. It is the single biggest loss that could have befallen him. When Philip appears Carlo violently repudiates him. 'You no longer have a son! As a ruler, my ideals lie with him!' He assumes that Philip was responsible for the assassination, whereas in fact Philip is as grief-stricken as he is, having known nothing of the Inquisition's edict on Rodrigo's life. Carlo has nothing more to say to his father.

In one sense Rodrigo's death is the best thing that could have happened to Carlo. For now he must truly stand on his own two feet. His meeting with Elisabeth (Act 5) contrasts markedly with their previous meeting. It takes but the gentlest reminder ('think of Rodrigo') to remind him where his future loyalty lies. 'I want a sublime, towering monument to be raised to him, fine and noble as no king's has ever been', he says. It is still an extreme, knee-jerk reaction, but it is legitimate. He is now haunted by the same vision of Flanders' suffering that has haunted Rodrigo. He has taken on Rodrigo's idealism and with it he gains something which matters to him greatly – Elisabeth's respect. 'Before

today, no human power would have wrenched my hand from yours! But on this great day honour has vanquished love within me.' He can embrace Elisabeth and yet not waver in his determination to answer the call of honour and duty. It is a moment of revelation to Carlo, who has never experienced the pure delight of an objective passion, knowing only the febrile promptings of his own unstable nature. He can bid Elisabeth farewell with regret but without remorse. He knows now, for the first time in his life, what he must do. He has found his destiny.

This may appear to make all the more inexplicable Verdi's decision to introduce the supernatural element at the conclusion of the opera by having Carlo dragged away by the spirit of his grandfather. In Schiller's play Carlo is simply handed over to the Inquisition by his father with the words, 'I have done my duty. Now you do yours'. This would have carried far greater dramatic eloquence. But thematically it makes eminent sense that Carlo should be returned at the end to the womb of unconsciousness from which he has never successfully released himself. It is a much debated point. At the very least, in the librettists' defence, it can be said that Carlo is doomed anyway by the Inquisition. The appearance of Charles V rescues him from an ignominious fate at the hands of the Holy Office. It also indicates that he has finally succeeded in rehabilitating himself into his heritage and the destiny which was originally laid out for him.

Carlo has achieved something his father never could, namely, with the invaluable assistance of Rodrigo, he has confronted the world and, most importantly his father and, again through the critical intervention and support of his friend, triumphed. He has realized for himself an agenda and finally abjured the lure of the womb so temptingly on offer in the love of his stepmother.

The conclusion of *Don Carlo* epitomizes a law of life which is explicated throughout the operas of Richard Strauss and in particular *Die Frau ohne Schatten*: that only through renunciation can one achieve one's true objective. For it is at the moment that

Carlo finally renounces his love for Elisabeth (Act 5) and accepts that he must embrace the ideals bequeathed him by his friend, and prevail in the world, that he is rescued from a fate for which he is so clearly unsuited. For the one thing we know about Carlo is that he cannot cope with the exigencies of the world in which he finds himself. He is by temperament a poet and a dreamer and he has been forced to become a soldier and a politician. The 'War in the heart' to which the Friar refers is not an auspicious foundation on which to build a career in the world of power politics.

Carlo's story is indeed a strange odyssey. He is, in many ways, a very modern sort of hero, or anti-hero, the apparently spineless man. In twentieth-century literature the spineless man is usually defeated. In nineteenth-century Italy such an outcome would have been unthinkable.

Don Carlo, King of Spain (*Ernani*)

Historical Note   Charles V (1500–1558), Holy Roman Emperor (1519–1558). Son of Philip I and Joanna of Spain, and grandson of Emperor Maximilian I, Charles inherited the Spanish throne in 1516. When he was elected Holy Roman Emperor in 1519 he became ruler of the largest number of territories ever united under a European sovereign. His achievements were considerable in spite of the enormous range of dominions he ruled over. Through him Spain became a leading world power. In spite of years of conflict with France, he managed to keep control over large disputed territories in Italy and the Netherlands. During the Reformation Charles was unable to stem the growing spread of Protestantism, particularly in Germany, but was able to keep the Ottoman offensive against Christian Europe at bay. By 1556 he was exhausted and abdicated, having first divided his empire between his son, Philip II (**Filippo, *Don Carlos***), and his brother, Ferdinand I of Austria. Charles retired to the monastery of San Yuste, in Spain (where much of the action of *Don Carlos* takes place) where he died two years later.

Don Carlo is first and foremost an historical figure, imbued with a strong sense of his own historicity. He aspires to transcend his own baser nature. He is thus a potentially heroic figure, though in Hugo's play and Verdi's opera, he is supplanted in the heroic stakes by the bandit, **Ernani** whom he, or rather the baser part of himself, is responsible for outlawing. According to Ernani Carlo has robbed him of all his worldly possessions and, worse, his honour. He has also been responsible for the death of Ernani's father. We are not privy to the events to which Ernani refers, but that Ernani feels that an injustice has been done him is irrefutable.

Unlike Ernani, who can see no need to emulate anybody, Carlo seeks to emulate Charlemagne (Holy Roman Emperor of the 9th century who fostered a great cultural revival). Carlo is the representative of that code of honour that Ernani most despises. For Carlo there is no ambiguity. He has never arrived at a point in his life where he has found himself obliged to declare, as does Ernani: 'I hate myself and the light of day'. He is the figure without which the light of day would have no meaning, for he is the figurehead in which all that belongs to the daylight world has its origins. Without him there would be anarchy and chaos.

Yet Carlo is besieged with anarchic longings. He is in love with a woman who is betrothed to another man, and that man happens to be the very pillar of the establishment that he, Carlo, represents. To attempt to poach this man's woman is tantamount to sabotaging the very order he seeks to uphold and without which his life would cease to have any meaning. It is a dilemma. Unlike Ernani, Carlo does not suffer existential angst; he is content to be alive. He does not need to question why God cast him adrift on the Earth, for he is not aware that he is adrift. He is alive for a purpose and that purpose is clearly defined although, through his passion for Elvira, he loses sight of it.

The opera may be named after Ernani and may belong in theatrical terms to Silva, but there can be no question that the most eloquent moment in it is when Carlo is suddenly, like Paul on the road to Damascus, struck with a blinding revelation at the tomb of Charlemagne (Act 3). This revelation is to have fundamental consequences for the lives of those who fall within his jurisdiction. He is on the point of despatching the traitors to be executed when he recalls the resolution that has guided his life to date, namely that if and when he ascends the imperial throne he will prove himself worthy of the office and of his great predecessor, Emperor Charlemagne. He will exemplify the Christian virtues of compassion, forgiveness and understanding.

At this critical moment when, within the space of a few moments, he has been confronted by a plot to undo him on the one hand and achieved his life's ambition of election to the Emperor's throne on the other, he does not forget his resolution and succumb to the pride inherent in a worldly position such as he now inhabits. Instead he recalls himself to a sense of his divinely ordained duty and dispenses forgiveness. The moment recalls a similar moment in Act 2 Scene 2 in Mozart's *La Clemenza di Tito*, though where Tito is little more than a cardboard cut-out, Verdi has made a warmly human and believable figure in his Don Carlo. The forgiveness that Carlo confers has a greater significance than that of Tito, because we are aware of his human, all-too-human failings, of his lust and vengefulness.

If *Ernani* has a central theme it is this power of human resolution carried through to its logical conclusion. During the course of the opera we see that power in both its best and worst applications; in the justice and forgiveness dispensed by Carlo and in the hideous revenge that de Silva takes upon Ernani. The principle remains the same. It is uniquely human that we can elect to pursue an ideal or a vendetta, that we can choose to remember an injustice or a moment of revelation down the years: remember it and act upon it. Thankfully there are as many Carlos in the world as de Silvas.

Don Carlo di Vargas (*La forza del destino*). Son of the **Marquis of Calatrava** and brother to **Leonora** di Vargas.

Don Carlo is above all a loyal son to his father. He sees his role in life exclusively in terms of upholding the family honour and propriety. As soon as he learns of his father's 'murder' and sister's elopement he dons the disguise of a student, **Pereda**, and sets out in hot pursuit.

At the village Inn of Hornachuelos (Act 2 Scene 1) Don Carlo describes for the benefit of the assembled company how he pursued the guilty couple as far as Cadiz, but to no avail. Everywhere he goes he hears tell how Leonora died with her father. This is purely for the benefit of his auditors and to avert suspicion from himself. He claims that Don Carlo has now sailed for America and that he, Pereda, has returned to his books. In fact, as his close questioning of **Trabucco** shows, he is well aware that he is close on the lovers' trail. Learning nothing from Trabucco and earning himself a rebuke from the **Mayor** for suggesting that they instigate a practical joke on the beardless stranger (who he is clearly more than half convinced must be Leonora), his pursuit will take him all across Spain and halfway across Italy.

Carlo is next discovered in a forest outside Velletri, a town just outside Rome (Act 3 Scene 1). He has apparently joined the Spanish campaign in Italy (under the pseudonym of Don Felice de Bornos) as adjutant to the General, presumably having discovered that **Alvaro** has joined the army. He is not prepared for the fact that Alvaro will save his life. However, when he discovers Alvaro's true identity he has no hesitation in obliterating from his mind any sense of obligation to his saviour. He refuses to accept that there might be any mitigating circumstances, so obsessed is he with his desire for vengeance. When Alvaro's life is saved by the **Surgeon** after he has been seriously wounded in battle, Carlo rejoices that Alvaro lives, thus enabling him the pleasure of himself taking Alvaro's life. The absurdity of his blood lust seems never to occur to him. Carlo's scena (M*orir, tremenda cosa*: Act 3

Scene 3) maps out an extraordinary transition in Carlo's psyche. From expressing a profound awareness of the awesomeness of death and sincere compassion for a suffering human being, Carlo is all too quickly transformed into a raging beast craving one thing only: blood for blood. When his duel with Alvaro is interrupted by the arrival of a patrol he is beside himself with frustration (Act 3 Scene 3). Alvaro makes his escape. It will be five years before Carlo again catches up with him.

Carlo can see nothing but cowardice in Alvaro's recourse to the religious life. When finally confronted with his enemy in Franciscan habit he taunts him mercilessly. When all else has failed he resorts to physical violence, slapping Alvaro in the face. Alvaro can restrain himself no longer and the two fight. Carlo is mortally wounded. As he lies dying he is suddenly confronted by the face of his sister, Leonora. This is too much for him. He does not hesitate: he plunges his dagger into Leonora's breast.

Ostensibly it is Carlo's maniacal persistence that aggravates a thousandfold all the miseries endured by Alvaro and Leonora. In fact it is only the hand of the Marquis stretching out from beyond the grave. As Alvaro and Carlo's comradeship in the early part of Act 3 demonstrates, the two have much in common. In another life they might have ended as staunch friends, like, for instance, Don Carlo and Rodrigo in Verdi's next opera, *Don Carlo*.

Carlo (*I Masnadieri*). Elder son of **Massimiliano**, the reigning Count of Moor. Carlo is one of the most fascinating of Verdi's leading tenor roles. He bears some comparison with his namesake, **Don Carlo**, from the opera of the same title (also based on Schiller). Both are emotionally unstable, guided by instincts and passions rather than by the light of reason.

Exiled by Massimiliano from his homeland on account of his dissolute lifestyle, Carlo dreams only of being reconciled with his father and reunited with his beloved **Amalia**. But his entreaties are apparently met with indifference and threats of deprivation and imprisonment should he ever return. One might wonder why Carlo never suspects his brother of treachery. Since his father is obscurely aware that **Francesco** is responsible for much of his grief, why does Carlo never entertain similar misgivings? The answer lies in Carlo's temperament. Like all Byronic heroes he is not given to thinking so much as to excesses of passion. He is above all an idealist with a head full of vague notions of what life should be but with no clear conception of how to achieve it.

Carlo's greatest desire is for freedom. But he never stops to ask himself, freedom for what? He only knows what he does not want. Principally he does not want any limitation placed on his freedom. In other words he does not want to grow beyond the blissful fecklessness of childhood. His ideals and ideas, culled from the histories of Plutarch, are based on an image of heroic endeavour in an age long antecedent to 'the age of weaklings', which he is forced to inhabit. The essence of the Romantic personality is this craving for a simplicity, where the exigencies of actually living in the world are never allowed to interfere with the fulfilment of the personal vision. This idealism is responsible for both the worst and the best aspects of humanity.

In Carlo the best is represented by his love for his father and for Amalia and his determination to see justice done. The worst manifestation of his idealism is his irrational reaction to events, exemplified in his total loss of self-control (Act 4 Scene 1) when Amalia has just been dragged before him and he suddenly realizes the futility of hoping to reconcile his life with the brigands with his desire to be rehabilitated in his former life. 'Tear her from my neck! Kill that old man! Kill her too, kill me, kill all of you! O that all the living could be destroyed at one stroke!' he rants. This outburst epitomizes what Freud meant when he said that a baby's frustrated rage, if unleashed on the world, would destroy it. Since life cannot give him what he most desires, unlimited freedom on the one hand and domestic bliss on the other, he would, if he could, destroy all that life offers (or rather withholds from him).

Carlo's justification to himself for giving himself over to criminality is that he has been rejected by the world in which he belongs. In fact when he throws his lot in with the brigands he is merely taking the path of least resistance. It never occurs to him that the reason he finds himself alienated and adrift in the world is not through anybody's fault but his own. He has chafed against the strictures of Court life, then chafed against his isolation and ostracism while forgetting that he is only reaping the inevitable result of having distanced himself from his father, his lover and society. He could, if he chose, devote himself to learning a profession, but that would be replacing one slavery with another. He prefers to beat his breast and bewail the fact that he cannot have his cake and eat it. This may seem an uncharitable judgement on a character whose principal problem is possessing a nature of unusual intensity and imagination.

Initially Carlo appears to be simply a latter-day prodigal son. As the drama unfolds it becomes clear that his case is very much more complex. Had his brother not intercepted his father's letter of forgiveness and Carlo thereby been rehabilitated in the bosom of his family, he would very quickly have become restless again. He needs to fight against his environment. He justifies his temperamental proclivities with the abstractions culled from the pages of antique writers. He is, in fact, a perfectly normal healthy young male whose aggression is aimed at the world in his efforts to find self-expression away from the domineering influence of the father. Francesco, on the other hand, has allowed his natural aggression to stagnate and become inverted so that eventually its only expression lies in bitterness and resentment directed against his own kin. The problem for both brothers is that they cannot make the break conclusively. Carlo, up until his final moment on the gallows, continues to hanker after his father's approval.

Finally it is fate that Carlo fights. Like Byron's Childe Harold he shakes his fist at a malign destiny. It never occurs to him that his energies would be better employed in confronting the problem head-on, that his passion is an absurdity. We none of us can blame our fathers or brothers for the circumstances into which we are born. We are given our temperament by heredity. Gnashing one's teeth, beating one's breast is as futile as the infant screaming because it is deprived of the mother's breast. Sooner or later it will have to stand alone and cope with all the pain and frustration of contingency. How the child responds to the challenge will determine the lineaments of its future destiny. The fundamentally infantile nature of Carlo's needs is underlined when he cons his father into giving him his blessing (Act 4 Scene 1). He does not have the courage to confront his father, even though Massimiliano has just indicated his longing to be forgiven by his son. There is no possible justification for his deception now, other than that he wants his father to suffer (that is, he wants to punish his father for having caused him so much suffering, even though Massimiliano has made it perfectly clear that he deplores the alienation from his son). It is this ego-centricity that invites comparison with Don Carlo (*Don Carlo*). In that opera there is the same titanic struggle between father and son. There too the son persists in punishing his father up until the last moment (although it could be argued that Fillippo's son has more justification than Massimiliano's). What characterizes both personalities is a total lack of focus to their *weltsmerz* and idealism.

It is this lack of focus, and inability to distance himself from his passions, that ensures Carlo's downfall, while at the same time lending to his character its colour and appeal. Having said which, the murder of Amalia in the closing pages is the unforgivable knee-jerk reaction of an hysteric. But then Carlo is the very epitome of the Romantic hero, who refuses to be constrained by anything. If life can only be endured in slavery, then it ceases to be valid. Carlo's final act constitutes an existential statement, an assertion of the right to unconditional freedom.

DON CARLO

Opera in 5 Acts. Libretto by Josephe Méry and Camille Du Locle after Schiller's drama (1787).

First performance: in French, as *Don Carlos*, 11 March 1867 at the Paris Opéra. This Paris version was considerably revised by Verdi and Antonio Ghislanzoni, reduced to 4 Acts and performed in Italian on 10 January 1884 at La Scala, Milan, since when there have been various revisions and alterations in use. The synopsis below is based on the five-Act version in which Act 1 from 1867 is joined to the four revised Acts of 1884.

Cast:

Don Carlo, Infante of Spain (tenor)
Elisabetta di Valois (Elisabeth of Valois) (soprano)
Filippo II, Re di Spagna (Philip II, King of Spain) (bass)
Rodrigo, Marquese di Posa (baritone)
La Principessa d'Eboli (Princess Eboli) (mezzo-soprano)
Il Grande Inquisitore (bass)
Tebaldo (Thibault): page to Elisabeth (soprano)
Il Conte di Lerma (tenor)
Un Frate (a Friar) (bass)
Un araldo reale (a Royal Herald) (tenor)
Voce dal Cielo (a Voice from Heaven) (soprano)

Time: 16th century
Place: France and Spain

Synopsis

Act 1 The Forest of Fontainbleu. A peace treaty is about to be signed between Spain and France by the terms of which the Spanish Infante, Don Carlo, will marry the daughter of Henry II of France, Princess Elisabeth. Don Carlo has travelled incognito to France in order to catch a glimpse of his bride before the wedding. A hunt is in progress. Foresters are busy cutting wood whilst their wives are seated round the fire. Elisabeth enters on horseback. She is escorted by her page, Tebaldo, and a party of huntsmen. She distributes alms to the woodmen before passing on with her retinue. When the clearing is deserted Don Carlo emerges from behind the trees. It is quickly clear that he has been entranced by his first sight of his future bride (*Io la vidi*). He prays to God to smile on their union.

Huntsmen are heard in the distance signalling the close of day. Carlo suddenly becomes aware that he is alone in the forest with no idea how to find his way back to the palace. Tebaldo's voice is heard offstage calling for squires and pages. Carlo hides as Tebaldo enters with Elisabeth, lamenting the fact that they are lost. Carlo steps forward, startling the young Princess and her page. He introduces himself as 'a stranger; a Spaniard', and offers to act as their escort, although we already know that Carlo is himself unsure how to find his way back to the castle. Tebaldo catches sight of the castle, however, and offers to go and fetch an escort for Elisabeth. Elisabeth is prepared to condone her page's rashness in leaving her alone with a stranger; since she is to be married to the Spanish Infante she puts her trust in Spanish honour. Tebaldo hurries away.

Elisabeth sits on a rock and, to her surprise, Carlo kneels before her. When she asks him why he is at her feet he does not answer her directly. Instead he places some branches on the dying embers of the woodcutters' fire. He then tells her that when at war soldiers have to 'beg brushwood of the earth' to make their campfires; 'when the flame glows so beautiful and bright it is a harbinger of victory or love'. Elisabeth asks if he has come from Madrid and whether the peace settlement is about to be concluded. Carlo replies that the marriage, 'with my King's son, Don Carlo' will be arranged before dawn in order to secure peace. Elisabeth longs for news of her future home, Madrid, and particularly of her husband-to-be. She confesses that she is frightened lest Carlo's love for her does not measure her own and she will be stranded, alone in a foreign country. Carlo swears passionately that Elisabeth's love will be returned. Elisabeth is taken aback and asks who it is that addresses her. The Prince's messenger, Carlo replies, and produces a jewel case which he has brought for her. (This jewel case will take on a weighty significance later in the opera.) When Carlo tells her that the jewel case contains a portrait of the Prince, Elisabeth is at first apprehensive. 'I dare not open it', she says. Her curiosity, however, gets the better of her. On being confronted with the portrait she immediately recognizes the man before her.

Carlo loses no time in declaring his love. Elisabeth is totally overcome (*Di qual amor*). It is more than she could have hoped for, that the man of whom she has dreamt so much should be so personable and so passionate in his declarations of love for her. She feels sure that their meeting must be a good omen for their future happiness.

A cannon is heard in the distance. Elisabeth interprets it as a signal for rejoicing. The windows of Fontainbleu light up in confirmation. The couple revel in their mutual happiness. Tebaldo returns with a litter and pages carrying torches. He advances, kneels and kisses the hem of Elisabeth's gown. He begs Elisabeth to keep him in her service. Elisabeth gladly consents, and then Tebaldo proclaims: 'Queen, I salute you; Wife of King Philip'. Both Elisabeth and Carlo are stunned. A crowd is heard rejoicing in the distance, gradually drawing closer. The crowd enters, led by the Spanish Ambassador, the Conte di Lerma, the Contessa D'Aremberg (Elisabeth's companion), ladies-in-waiting and pages bearing a litter. The Conte di Lerma formally demands to know if Elisabeth will accept the King's hand in marriage. Elisabeth's response is barely audible. The Court resumes its chorus of rejoicing while Carlo and Elisabeth express their suffering. Di Lerma escorts Elisabeth to her litter and the procession moves on towards the palace, leaving Carlo alone and distraught.

Act 2 Scene 1 The Cloisters of the Monastery of San Yuste. The tomb of Charles V is seen in the background. It is dawn. The monks are heard singing in the chapel. They sing of the late emperor whose 'haughty spirit now trembles at the feet of his Maker' (*Carlo il sommo Imperatore*). A solitary Friar imprecates against the overweening pride of the emperor who 'aspired to rule the world in spite of Him who guides the stars on their undeviating course across the skies'. 'Grand' è Dio sol', the Friar intones. He is echoed by the other monks. It is a solemn and awe-inspiring scene, which immediately places the whole drama of Carlo and Elisabeth's love in a far greater perspective. The ghostly presence of the solitary Friar will play a crucial role in the final denouement. Day dawns gradually and the monks begin to leave.

Don Carlo enters, pale and distracted. He has come in the hope that the tranquillity of the monastic surroundings will grant him some solace, but he cannot eradicate the image of Elisabeth from his mind. The Friar approaches him with the less than comforting words that 'War in the heart will abate only in Heaven'. Carlo is terrified, for he imagines he sees his grandfather in the Friar's habit. He has heard that the ghost of his grandfather may be encountered in the Cloister.

Rodrigo enters. Carlo greets him passionately. It is immediately clear that Rodrigo is to Carlo a pillar of strength and solidarity in an uncertain world. His confidence will be proved justified by the course of the action. Rodrigo does not know of Carlo's misfortune in love. He comes to Carlo now as ambassador for the oppressed Flemish people. He is alarmed to note how wan Carlo appears and begs him to tell him the cause of his misery. When Carlo confesses that he is in love with Elisabeth, who is now his stepmother, Rodrigo is horrified. For a brief moment Carlo fears his friend will turn against him. However Rodrigo's only concern is to ascertain that Philip remains oblivious. Reassured that this is the case he sees a way of combining the duties of friendship with political expediency. Carlo must obtain sanction from Philip to travel to Flanders and there take up the Flemish cause against Philip's tyranny. Carlo confirms his agreement just as a bell sounds, announcing the imminent entrance of Philip and

Elisabeth. The thought of seeing Elisabeth is deeply disturbing to Carlo, but Rodrigo exhorts him to 'strengthen (his) wavering spirit' (*Dio che nell'alma infondere*).

The royal entourage passes through, Philip stopping for a moment to kneel in prayer before his father's tomb. The monks are heard in the distance intoning their solemn chant. Carlo is distraught at the sight of his beloved Elisabeth on his father's arm. Rodrigo attempts to comfort him and together the pair confirm their undying friendship: ('Vivremo insiem').

Act 2 Scene 2   A garden at the gates of the cloisters of Saint Yuste. While the king and queen pay their respects at the tomb of Charles V the ladies must wait outside the monastery. They have taken shelter from the fierce midday sun under the huge dense firs that surround St Just. A page is tuning a mandolin. The princess Eboli is amongst the group. She is plainly bored. She objects to the restrictions of court etiquette. She asks the ladies if they will help her wile away the time by singing a Saracen song, the one about the veil, so conducive to love (*Nel giardin del bello*). The song tells how a Moorish dancing girl has been wooed by Mohammed, the king, who has grown tired of his wife. The king begs her to raise her veil. If she will give him her heart she shall have the throne. At this the dancing girl lifts her veil to reveal that she is herself the queen.

Elisabeth enters from the monastery. Eboli notes that 'a secret sadness weighs upon her'. As she encounters the carefree atmosphere surrounding the ladies of the court Elisabeth reflects how long it is since she felt any joy. Tebaldo announces Rodrigo. Rodrigo tells Elisabeth that her mother has entrusted him with a letter for her. As he hands over the letter he slips a note into her hand, muttering to her to read it. It is from Carlo, urging Elisabeth to put her trust in Rodrigo. Rodrigo moves over to Eboli in order to give Elisabeth a chance to read the note. Eboli is eager for news of the French Court which she knows to be very different from the austerities of the Spanish court. Rodrigo shamelessly flatters her.

Elisabeth, meanwhile, has finished reading the letter and note. She expresses her gratitude to Rodrigo and invites him to ask a favour of the Queen (thus indicating that she welcomes his assumption of role of go-between on her's and Carlo's behalf). Rodrigo, in response, asks nothing for himself, but instead requests that Carlo be allowed to see Elisabeth. Eboli, in an aside, remarks that once when she was standing near to the Queen she noticed Carlo quivering in agitation. She dares to hope that Carlo is in love with her. Rodrigo tells Elisabeth that what grieves Carlo is Philip's coldness towards him. A single loving word from Elisabeth would mean so much to him. Elisabeth can scarcely control her emotion. Rodrigo is insistent and finally Elisabeth commands Tebaldo to fetch her son. Eboli, still pursuing her own train of thought, secretly hopes that Carlo will open his heart to her. As Carlo enters all tactfully make to depart.

Carlo loses no time in begging the Queen to help him (*Io vengo a domandar*). He cannot endure the atmosphere at the court and must escape from it. He wishes the Queen to ask the King to send him to Flanders. Elisabeth's response is merely to murmur 'My son', which sends Carlo into a paroxysm of self-pity; 'Not that name, but the one you called me once!', he cries. Elisabeth, addressing him formally as 'Prince', assures Carlo that she will endeavour to ensure that Philip posts him to Flanders. Carlo is beside himself: 'Not a word, not a single word for the wretch who is being exiled?' Elisabeth points out that he should understand the reason for her silence; she is motivated by a profound sense of duty. 'I place my hope in God, in my innocence', she says. Carlo becomes increasingly agitated and passionately declares his love for her. Caught off guard Elisabeth's reserve breaks down and she acknowledges that to live beside Carlo on this earth could make her believe herself in Heaven. This is too much for Carlo who collapses at her feet.

Coming to, he finds himself cradled in her arms. He imagines himself already transported to Heaven. Elisabeth does not know what to think. She even wonders if he is dying. Carlo suddenly springs up and reiterates his declarations of love. Elisabeth recoils in horror: 'Finish your work, hurry to kill your father. Then, bespattered with his blood, you can lead your mother to the altar', she cries. Carlo rushes out in despair. Elisabeth falls to her knees, exclaiming, 'Ah! The Lord has watched over us!' (presumably she means in not allowing her to succumb to her dearest wish, to be united with Carlo).

Tebaldo enters and announces the King, who enters with Rodrigo, Eboli and others. Philip is outraged to find the Queen alone. He has decreed that Elisabeth should never be left without at least one lady-in-waiting present. He demands to know who should have been in attendance. The Contessa d'Aremberg steps forward. Philip summarily dismisses her; at daybreak she shall return to France. Everyone is shocked by the insult to the Queen and the countess bursts into tears. Elisabeth is devastated. In a soaring solo (which prefigures Desdemona's solo in Act 4 *Otello* when publicly humiliated by her husband) she consoles her friend and gives her a ring as a token of her regard. She tells the Contessa not to talk of her own unhappiness.

Philip, meanwhile, remains coldly to one side. He mutters to himself that a 'noble heart' is dissembling in his presence. As will become apparent very shortly he has his own suspicions about his wife and his son. Elisabeth and the rest of the court make to depart but Philip recalls Rodrigo with the peremptory command: 'Stay!' ('Restate!') He wishes to know why Rodrigo has not yet requested an audience: 'I know how to reward all my protectors', he says, 'you have loyally served the crown'. Rodrigo is defensive: 'What could I hope from the favours of the king? The law is my shield'. Philip is unruffled: 'I like a proud spirit', he says: 'I pardon boldness'. But, he adds menacingly, 'not always'. He finds it incomprehensible that Rodrigo, the soldier by temperament and background, should choose to remain inactive. He asks what he

can do for Rodrigo. For me, nothing, Rodrigo replies, but for others. He launches into a passionate advocacy of the Flemish cause (*O Signor, di Fiandra arrivo*). For Philip this is not a matter for discussion. He is convinced that the only way to deal with heretics and 'innovators' is to excise them with the sword. He makes the extraordinary statement: 'Death, in this hand of mine has a fecund future'. Rodrigo is appalled. Philip reminds him of the peace that pertains in Spain itself: 'The same peace I offer to Flanders'. Out of patience Rodrigo responds: 'It is the peace of the tomb. Oh king beware that history does not say of you "he was another Nero"'. For anybody other than Rodrigo such audacity would be a capital offence. Philip, however, lets him have his say.

Rodrigo proceeds to paint a vivid portrait of Philip's empire as a huge ghastly desert where 'the priest is a hangman, every soldier a bandit'. He pleads with Philip to emulate 'God the redeemer. Give freedom to the world'. Philip remains ominously silent and then retorts: 'Oh, strange dreamer! You would change your ideas if you knew the heart of man as Philip knows it'. He then issues his first warning to Rodrigo to beware the Grand Inquisitor. Philip is well aware, if Rodrigo is not, that the real power in the land rests in the hands of the Church. Rodrigo is in many ways remarkably naïve.

Now Philip turns to what is most pressing to him, his desire to have Rodrigo at his side. Rodrigo is adamant that he prefers to remain independent. Philip rebukes him: 'Sei troppo altier!' ('You are too haughty!') But it is a prelude not to a further rebuke but to an unburdening of his own innermost anguish. In a brief instant we catch a glimpse of the profound loneliness that underpins the austerity of this man, weighed down as he is by the awesome responsibilities he must carry. He tells Rodrigo to observe his royal palace: 'anxiety encircles it, an unfortunate father and yet more miserable husband!' Rodrigo is taken aback. Philip confides to him that he suspects a liaison between Elisabeth and Carlo. Rodrigo leaps to Carlo's defence but Philip implores Rodrigo to keep watch over his wife and son. He grants him free access to the Queen at all times. For the second time in the opera Rodrigo finds himself in the role of close confidante and trusted friend. First it was the renegade son and now the suspicious father.

Rodrigo is strangely exhilarated by the sudden realization that for the first time Philip has actually opened his heart. He is about to depart when Philip detains him and warns him again to beware of the Grand Inquisitor. He repeats the injunction three times, then regally extends his hand to Rodrigo who humbly kneels and kisses it as the curtain falls.

Act 3 Scene 1   The Queen's Garden. A moonlit night. Carlo is reading a note from Eboli, requesting an assignation in the Queen's gardens at midnight ('A mezza-notte, ai giardin della Regina'). Since the note has been sent anonymously, Carlo assumes it is from Elisabeth and is overjoyed, thinking all his torments at an end. Eboli enters. She is veiled. Mistaking her for Elisabeth in the darkness, Carlo pours out his love for her. Eboli is overcome, not having suspected the strength of Carlo's passion. 'Amata, amata io son' ('I am loved!') she joyfully exclaims. Suddenly Carlo realizes his mistake. Eboli is puzzled by Carlo's abrupt change of demeanour and desperately affirms her love for him. She warns him that he is in danger from his father and Rodrigo, whom she has overheard discussing Carlo. She vows that she alone can save him. Carlo is distraught to think that Rodrigo and his father are confidantes. He brushes aside Eboli's offer of love. Suddenly she realizes the truth: Carlo is in love with the Queen.

Rodrigo enters, and overhearing Eboli's accusation quickly intervenes. He assures Eboli that Carlo is raving. Eboli is not to be deflected. 'I know everything', she tells Rodrigo. She goes on to warn him that she is a formidable and powerful enemy. She is like a 'wounded tigress' who seeks only revenge. Rodrigo responds with comparable threats while Carlo laments his miserable destiny. Bitterly Eboli reflects how she used

to be in awe of the saintly Elisabeth. Now she discovers that all the while Elisabeth was brazenly indulging 'the cup of love to the last drop'. Rodrigo is out of patience. He draws his dagger and makes to strike Eboli. Carlo has sufficient wits left to restrain his friend. Eboli is not intimidated. So tormented is she by her own chaotic desires, she would welcome death. Rodrigo throws aside his dagger, commenting that his one hope is guidance from the Lord. Eboli resumes her imprecations and threats. Carlo is in despair. He realizes that Eboli knows everything and could well carry out her threat to reveal his clandestine love for the Queen. Eboli exits, determined on revenge.

Rodrigo requests that Carlo give to him any important papers, notes or secret documents that he may be concealing. At first Carlo is taken aback. Having just learnt that Rodrigo is Philip's confidante he inevitably suspects his friend's motives. But his hesitation is only fleeting and he hands over the documents that he has on him. His faith in Rodrigo at this moment will later save his life.

Act 3 Part 2   A large square before the church of our Lady of Antioch in Madrid. To the left is the Royal Palace, in the background a flight of steps leads to a lower square, where the tip of a funeral pyre is visible. A festive peal summons all to an auto-da-fé, the ritual burning of heretics. Halberdiers have difficulty in controlling the vast crowd that is pouring into the square. (Spuntato ecco il di d'esultanza).

Monks lead those condemned to death by the Inquisition across the square. They sing of the dawning of this 'terrible day' when sinners shall die. But there is still time for repentance and the condemned can at least be saved from eternal damnation, if not from losing their lives. A procession, including Elisabeth and Rodrigo, enters from the Palace and draws up before the church steps. A Herald stands before the closed doors of the church and commands that they be opened. The doors open and Philip is revealed. He reminds the people how, when he was first crowned, he swore to put the wicked to death by fire and sword. The people hail their King but are interrupted by the arrival of six Flemish deputies, led by Carlo himself. They enter slowly and kneel before the King. Elisabeth is horrified when she sees Carlo. Rodrigo is mystified. Philip demands to know who they are.

Carlo tells his father they are envoys from Brabant and Flanders. The six deputies intone their complaint. They speak on behalf of the unhappy Flemish people and have come to plead for clemency. Philip is not impressed: 'You have been false to God, traitors to your King', he says. He orders his guards to remove them. Everyone (apart from the monks who echo Philip's accusations of disloyalty to their king and to God) pleads with Philip to have mercy on the Flemish. Philip is unmoved. Then Carlo boldly asks that he should be given the mandate over Brabant and Flanders. Philip is incredulous: 'Madman!' he expostulates, 'you expect me, personally, to offer you the sword with which to murder your King?' To the horror of all present Carlo draws his sword. Philip calls on his guards to disarm Carlo. Nobody steps forward. It is the closest Philip has come to experiencing total insurrection. Incensed, he seizes a sword from the Captain of the guard. Rodrigo steps forward and demands that Carlo surrender his sword. He undoubtedly fears for Carlo's safety. He takes Carlo's sword and presents it to Philip, who immediately elevates him to the rank of Duke, before ordering the procession to proceed to the festivities. Leading Elisabeth by the hand and followed by the Court he takes up his position in the stand. The people resume their chorus of rejoicing, the monks their ominous chant, while a voice from on high is heard inviting the poor souls of the heretics to fly up to enjoy the peace of the Lord (thus effectively making a mockery of the entire proceedings).

Act 4 Scene 1 The King's study in Madrid. Dawn is gradually breaking. Eboli, true to her word, has accused Elisabeth of having an affair with Carlo and has given Philip his wife's jewel casket, containing the portrait of Carlo, as proof. So far Philip has

not been able to bring himself to open the casket. He is alone in his study in Madrid. She never loved me, he reflects sadly in his half-conscious state (*Ella giammai m'amo*). He recalls the day that Elisabeth first arrived from France and how she gazed sadly at his white hair. Coming to, he notices that daylight is breaking. Bitterly he reflects on how he can no longer find sleep. The only sleep for him will be the final sleep beneath the black vault in his tomb in the Escurial. If only the royal crown could give him the power to read men's hearts. But this will ever remain a closed book to him. 'If the Prince sleeps the King loses his crown and the husband his honour', he reflects.

The Conte di Lerma announces the Grand Inquisitor, for whom Philip has sent. The Inquisitor, who is aged ninety and blind, enters, supported by two monks. Philip needs to discuss the fate of his son. He tells the Inquisitor about Carlo's rebellion and the dilemma this causes him. The Inquisitor merely requires to know what punishment the King intends for his son. 'Let him escape, or allow the axe ...', Philip responds. He asks whether, as a Christian, he could be forgiven for killing his own son. The Inquisitor reminds him that in order to redeem Mankind God sacrificed His Son. Everything, including paternal affection, must be silenced in order to exalt the faith. Reluctantly Philip concedes.

Now the Inquisitor asks Philip whether he has anything further to ask of him. When Philip answers in the negative the Inquisitor raises the question of Rodrigo, the King's friend who, as far as the Church is concerned, is becoming troublesome (*Nell'ispano suol mai l'eresia dominò*). 'Carlo's treason which has enraged you so is as nothing in comparison with his', the Inquisitor says. Philip tries to justify his friendship for Rodrigo but the Inquisitor is not impressed: 'Why are you called King if a lesser man can be your equal?' he demands. He then accuses Philip of being influenced by a 'tainted mind'. 'Return to your duty', he warns Philip, and proceeds to demand that he surrender Rodrigo to the Inquisition. When Philip refuses the

Inquisitor threatens to summon Philip himself. The latter loses patience and dismisses him. The Inquisitor retreats but not before accusing Philip of destroying the work of years. Clearly aghast at his own audacity Philip pleads with the Priest that peace should be restored between them. 'You must forget what has passed here', he says nervously to the Inquisitor's retreating back. 'Perhaps', is the Priest's final word. 'Thus must a throne always bow before an altar', Philip bitterly reflects.

At this moment Elisabeth rushes in and throws herself at her husband's feet. She has come to demand justice (*Giustizia, giustizia, Sire!*). The casket in which she keeps her jewels has been stolen. Philip reveals the casket and coldly requests that Elisabeth open it. When she refuses he grabs the box and opens it himself. He is confronted with his worst fear – a portrait of Carlo. He may have already suspected this, but it is quite a different matter to be confronted with the hard evidence. He is devastated. 'Have you nothing to say?' he demands. Elisabeth remains calm and dignified. 'You know perfectly well that my heart was once promised to your son', she says. 'Now I belong to you, submissive to God, but I am as chaste as the lily'. She is outraged that Philip should suspect her. Angrily Philip warns her that she may think him weak, but weakness can quickly turn to fury. When Elisabeth asks him of what she is guilty he explodes: 'if she has dishonoured him, blood will flow'. To which Elisabeth responds by telling him that she pities him. 'The pity of an adulterous wife!' Philip screams. Elisabeth collapses in a faint. Philip calls for help. Eboli and Rodrigo enter.

On seeing Elisabeth unconscious on the floor Eboli is immediately overcome with remorse. Rodrigo is outraged: 'Sire, could it be that in so vast an Empire you are the only one you are unable to control?' In an aside he makes it clear that he welcomes this turn of events. There can no longer be any subterfuge. Now is the hour for action. He will if necessary die for Spain, so long as he bequeaths her a happier future. Elisabeth

revives. She poignantly expresses her grief at the barren misery of her predicament. Philip, meanwhile, is becoming convinced that he has done her an injustice, and that she has not been unfaithful to him. He curses his suspicions. Philip and Rodrigo depart, leaving Eboli alone with the Queen.

Eboli throws herself at Elisabeth's feet, begging for mercy. Elisabeth is startled out of her mournful reverie. Eboli tells her, without further ado, that it was she who stole the casket, that it was she who accused Elisabeth of infidelity. She further confesses that she herself is in love with Carlo but that he had spurned her. This is what causes her such torment and jealousy. So far Elisabeth is prepared to forgive. However, Eboli is determined to unburden herself of all her guilt. She now confesses that she has been the King's lover; 'the sin which I accused you of, I, I myself have committed'. Elisabeth is outraged. She declares that Eboli may choose between exile or the veil. She must leave at daybreak. Elisabeth exits, leaving Eboli alone and distraught.

Bitterly Eboli curses her beauty (*O don fatale, o don crudel*), the cause, as she sees it, of her downfall. All hope for her is gone and henceforth her lot will be to suffer. She has betrayed her Queen and her punishment will be to languish in a convent. Then her thoughts turn to Carlo. Tomorrow he will be executed. Her fiery temperament reasserts itself as she resolves to save him.

Act 4 Scene 2 An underground prison where Don Carlo is confined. Rodrigo enters and speaks to the jailers who retire.

Carlo expresses his gratitude to Rodrigo for visiting him. He tells Rodrigo that he has little strength left and that his love for Elisabeth 'tortures and kills' him. He himself is of no more use to the living, but Rodrigo can still save the beleaguered Flemish. Rodrigo assures Carlo of his affection and tells him they must now say farewell, for he has reached the last day of his life (*Per me giunto è il di supremo*). He tells Carlo not to weep for him because he dies gladly, knowing that Carlo will thereby be saved. Carlo is mystified by this talk of death. Rodrigo tells him that he has ensured that the papers he took from Carlo were found in his possession. The documents contain enough proof of treason for the Inquisition to have put a price on his head.

As Rodrigo speaks two men, one in the uniform of the Inquisition and the other carrying an arquebus, enter silently by the prison stairs above the cell where Carlo is imprisoned. Observing Rodrigo and Carlo they remain quietly in the background, unnoticed by the two friends. Rodrigo does not need prompting. He knows he has no time to lose. Urgently he tells Carlo to continue the work already started, to free the Flemish people from the tyranny of King Philip. Suddenly a shot rings out. Rodrigo is hit. As he falls, dying, he observes that the King has certainly lost no time in seeking revenge. But he still has important matters to communicate to Carlo. Elisabeth will be waiting for him at San Yuste on the morrow. She knows everything, he tells him. Rodrigo can now die happy in the knowledge that he has been instrumental in preserving 'a Saviour for Spain' (*Io morrò ma lieto in core*). As Carlo was destined to reign, so Rodrigo was destined to die for him. He dies and Carlo falls despairingly across his friend's body.

Philip enters, accompanied by grandees of his Court. He has come to return to Carlo his sword. Carlo is appalled at the very sight of his father, whom he believes culpable of his friend's murder. Philip is equally appalled at the sight of Rodrigo's corpse. Carlo tells his father that he no longer has a son. From now on Carlo's ideals are the same as Rodrigo's. Philip is hardly listening. Gazing at Rodrigo's body he lets out an anguished cry: 'Who will restore this man to me?'

He has no time to dwell on his grief. An alarm sounds and a commotion is heard from outside the prison. The people have come to liberate the Infante and are in an ugly mood. Philip, to the astonishment of the Grandees, commands that the gates be opened. The crowd pours in. Eboli enters, masked. She goes straight to Don Carlo, urging him to flee. Philip asks the people what they want. When they reply, 'the Infante', he offers Carlo

to them. At this moment the Inquisitor enters, to the consternation of all present. The Inquisitor commands the crowd to prostrate itself before the king. The crowd, in terror, kneels, pleading for mercy. Philip proclaims: 'Almighty God, all glory to Thee'. The crowd shouts 'Long live the King' as Philip and the Inquisitor descend among them. The people, still kneeling, plead: 'Mercy!'

Act 5 The Cloisters of San Yuste, as in Act 2. It is a moonlit night. Elisabeth enters and kneels before the tomb of Charles V. She addresses herself to the deceased Emperor, begging him to intercede for her at the throne of the Lord, to show some compassion for her suffering (*Tu che le vanità*). She reveals that she has sworn to Rodrigo to watch over Carlo. He must follow his destiny which will be enfolded in glory. As for herself she feels her day has already reached its evening. It is a sad acknowledgement for so young a girl. She thinks nostalgically of her beloved homeland, of France and Fontainbleu. Pathetically she prays that the lovely gardens of this Iberian land; 'the turf, the brooks, the fountains, the woods, the blossoms', should sing of hers and Carlo's frustrated love. She bids farewell to the golden dreams and lost illusions. Now her heart has only one desire: the peace of the grave.

Carlo enters. Elisabeth forestalls any outpourings of love. She wants Carlo to think only of his departed friend and the ideals he stood for; 'it was not for foolish ideas he sacrificed himself', she says. Carlo raises little objection. He confirms that all he wants is to raise 'a sublime, towering monument' to Rodrigo on Flemish soil. He echoes the vivid portrayal of the suffering Flemish people that Rodrigo himself painted for the King in Act 2. He will go to them and, whether he triumphs or dies, it will be of no consequence to him so long as he knows he has Elisabeth's blessing. Elisabeth is elated by Carlo's renewed determination. 'This is the sacred flame of heroism', she says. This is the love which 'kindles the strong and makes a God of a man'. Carlo, thoroughly inspired, declares that he hears the people calling him through Elisabeth's voice. If he dies for them it will be a noble death indeed. Elisabeth urges him not to delay but to go at once. Carlo reflects that previously nothing would have induced him to leave Elisabeth, but now 'honour has vanquished love'. Elisabeth is overcome with emotion and weeps. Together the ill-fated couple confirm that they will meet in a better world, where they shall attain the happiness they 'yearned for but which ever escaped them on Earth'.

As they bid each other farewell for ever Philip enters, followed by the Grand Inquisitor and officers of the Inquisition. He seizes Elisabeth's arm. 'Yes for ever!', he echoes, ' I demand a double sacrifice. I shall do my duty'. He turns to the Inquisitor and asks what he intends to do. The Inquisitor confirms that the Holy Office will also do its duty. He instructs the guards to seize the pair. Carlo, defiantly calling out that God will defend him, moves back towards the tomb of Charles V. At this moment the Cloister gates open. The 'Friar' of Act 2 appears, but now in regal robes and crown. It is Charles V. The Inquisitor recognizes the voice of Charles, as do his officers. Philip is terrified at the sudden apparition of his father who proceeds to drag Carlo into the cloister as the curtain falls, leaving everyone present, including the audience, bewildered. Is it a ghost, a mass hallucination or is it actually the Emperor who never died but secluded himself all those years in the cloister? Even Verdi, fifteen years after the opera's premiere, was writing to his librettist and enquiring after the true significance of the Emperor's appearance at the end. If the composer himself was not clear it is difficult to see how we can ever be certain. Essentially it does not matter. What matters is the fact that it is the patriarchal spirit that entirely predominates in this opera, as it does in *I Foscari* and *Simon Boccanegra*, the two closest blood relations to the opera of *Don Carlo*.

'I will make it my duty in the play to avenge prostituted humanity in depicting the Inquisition, and to pillory most fearfully the blots on its history. I wish to thrust deep into the heart of a type of man which the dagger of tragedy has so far only grazed.' Thus Schiller's stated objectives while writing his play.

Verdi's music raised what could have been simply a propagandist exercise into a great work of art with a humanitarian message that far transcends the political message, vital though it be. Human beings, like it or not, live out their lives and loves always within a political context. The lives of Philip, Eboli, Elisabeth, Don Carlo and Rodrigo are not their own because their destinies are inextricably bound up with that of the State. In the case of a historical drama such as *Don Carlo* this is accentuated by virtue of the fact that all the characters are embroiled at first hand in the politics of state. But it is not just the great and the good who are thus compromised. It is the lot of all mortals who participate in a society. The dilemmas faced by the protagonists in *Don Carlo* are our dilemmas, only writ large, which is why we can so easily empathize with them. This could, of course, be said of any one of Verdi's historical dramas, but where *Don Carlo* is different is in the complexity of the characters' interactions, and in the stark contrast between what *is* and what could, or even should be.

The presence of the Friar with his imprecations against 'war in the heart' places a huge question mark over the intrinsic value of all the searching, not to say anguish, of the main protagonists. Each of them is preoccupied with an obsession: Rodrigo with Flanders, Don Carlo with Elisabeth, Philip with his own contingency as monarch and his personal mortality, Eboli with herself, Elisabeth with fulfilling her duty. How justifiable are these obsessions? Where do they lead the characters? The Friar, the Voice from Heaven and the apparition of Charles V succeed in distancing us from each of them and in turn demand that they themselves re-evaluate their lives. Finally this is what makes *Don Carlo* one of the most stimulating and rewarding of all Verdi's operas.

Carlo VII, King of France (*Giovanna d'arco*)
Historical Note. Charles VII (1403–1461) reigned as king of France from 1429. His father, Charles VI, had been defeated by Henry V of England and forced to sign the Treaty of Troyes whereby Henry would succeed to the French throne. In 1429 Joan of Arc persuaded Charles that she had a divine mission to expel the English from Northern France. She raised the siege of Orléans, defeated the English at nearby Patay and thus secured Charles's coronation at Reims.

As portrayed in Verdi's opera Carlo hardly cuts an heroic figure. When the opera opens he is despairing and on the point of surrendering to the invading English. As the opera draws to a close he is also despairing, believing **Giovanna** to be dead. For it is Giovanna who rescues him from himself. Through her exceptional conviction and energy she succeeds in achieving what Carlo, devoid of imagination, cannot achieve. Carlo is, in the opera, totally re-active. He is a man waiting for his destiny to happen. When he has a dream in which the Virgin Mary commands him to set his helmet and sword at the foot of the Virgin's statue he unhesitatingly obliges (Prologue Scene 1). What has he to lose? Nothing. It is for this very reason that he is receptive to the prompting of his dream world. Having nothing to lose, not even his kingdom, for he believes it already lost, he is freed of the responsibility of attachment. It is a most unlikely circumstance for a king, or any head of state, for by definition the role of ruler, which makes persistent demands on the individual's levels of tolerance and detachment, cannot be lightly relinquished.

Carlo has arrived at a point where he desperately needs help. He has lost touch not only with his own people, his mission and purpose, but also with himself. But no other person can help him. Giovanna is not so much another human being as an image of transcendence that lifts him beyond what he has allowed himself to become. She is, in short, a personification of the Virgin herself,

the Holy Mother of all that is. He falls in 'love' with that which he most lacks, principally the conviction with which to prosecute an apparently hopeless cause. There comes a point in any human life where the obstacles appear so insurmountable that the only way forward is through an apparently absurd act of commitment which in itself requires relinquishing all that has previously defined the life-illusion by which that individual has sustained himself. By giving himself over to the prompting of the dream world, which is his only consolation, Carlo opens himself to a whole new world of possibilities. Giovanna is the reward.

Inevitably Carlo misinterprets Giovanna's significance for France. His rational mind cannot help seeing the image of femininity in which his saviour is cloaked. He 'falls in love' because this is what he is conditioned to by his biological and stereotypically masculine nature. The symbology of Joan of Arc (see *Giovanna d'arco* entry) is highly complex. One cannot blame Carlo for his apparent short-sightedness for it is in fact only the average short-sightedness of the moonstruck lover writ large. Joan of Arc is an archetype. She combines both the nutritive and fiercely aggressive aspects of the feminine. She cannot be owned; her role is to empower, not to be overpowered. Even at the end of the opera Carlo cannot accept the fact that it is not Giovanna herself that he needs, but what she has already given him. He does not want her to leave him and he begs her to remain. What he wants is to replace one dependency with another.

When, at the outset of the opera, Carlo renounces all hope of turning the war around he renounces the very thing that has defined his existence; in other words he renounces his ego-centred consciousness. When, at the end of the opera, he attempts to detain Giovanna it is an expression of desperation at the realization that the act of renunciation is not something which can be engaged upon once and once only. It is an ongoing necessity of human life. If he were to detain Giovanna, and make her his consort, he would be ratifying a status quo which is the total reverse of all that Giovanna has come into this life to illuminate. Her appearance in his life is nothing less than an annunciation. Her brief career represents a sudden explosion of freedom and the possibility of transcending the impossible. As king and head of state Carlo is essentially committed to preserving the status quo. This is more normally, from a sociological perspective, the province of the feminine.

Giovanna comes to Carlo in exactly the same way as a doting young male lover comes to a young girl and awakens her to herself, breaking through the barriers of her fear and her virginity and, to use a cliché, 'sweeping her off her feet'. The problem with being swept off one's feet is that in direct proportion to the intensity of the experience the fall to earth will be all the more traumatic. For what the individual has to realize is that the intensity of the experience is not something given from without but something that has been triggered within. Carlo has to learn that Giovanna has given him something inviolable that he now needs to learn to release within himself. He no longer needs Giovanna even though he thinks he does. What he needs is to remember what she has given him. Carlo's true journey only commences as the curtain falls on the action of the opera.

Cassio (*Otello*). Otello's lieutenant.
Cassio is the unwitting progenitor of the miseries that unfold in Shakespeare, Boito and Verdi's drama. His name is a cudgel which is used throughout, principally by **Desdemona** to beat from Otello's brain the last vestiges of reason. Oblivious until the final pages of the drama to **Iago's** treachery, Cassio is a pawn in the latter's obsessive desire to unseat Otello. And all because Iago resents Cassio's advancement above himself.

When the opera opens Cassio is at the forefront of the stage anxiously awaiting Otello's safe delivery from the storm in progress (Act 1). Cassio has no grudge against Otello; rather he has to thank him for his present station. Iago refers to Cassio as 'that foppish captain', but Iago is an unreliable witness.

Once Otello has stepped safely ashore Cassio accompanies him inside the castle, oblivious to the plan being hatched between Iago and **Roderigo** to discredit him. When he returns it is to be offered a drink by an apparently affable Iago. The plot is to encourage him to become inebriated and then to embroil him in a brawl. Iago knows well that Cassio, in spite of having no head for liquor, can easily be persuaded to imbibe, the more so when the toast is Desdemona.

As his increasingly extravagant eulogies make clear Cassio worships Desdemona. Has he not acted as go-between in the difficult courtship of Otello and Desdemona? However he has absolutely no erotic interest in her. He admires her in the same way as do all other inhabitants of Cyprus, as the Romans would have admired a vestal virgin. She is a paragon of purity and simplicity such as gives hope and solace in an uncertain world. (Cynically speaking, any assistance he has given Desdemona and Otello has brought him all the career advancement he could wish for.) He is, as becomes clear in Act 2, passionately involved with his own mistress, Bianca, who jilts him when Otello demotes him.

The plot succeeds all too easily. Iago has convinced Roderigo to provoke Cassio, knowing that the latter is hot-headed and will easily be provoked, as indeed is quickly proved to be the case. Roderigo accuses Cassio of being a drunkard and Cassio launches himself at him. **Montano** separates the two men. Cassio then draws his sword and engages Montano in a duel resulting in the former governor being wounded. This is more than Iago could have hoped for.

Cassio cannot be accused of lack of discrimination for failing to discern the treachery at the heart of Iago's solicitude, since every other character in the drama is similarly deceived. It is, however, noticeable that when Iago assures him he will soon be restored to the favours of his mistress he interjects 'Non lusingarmi' ('do not flatter me'). At some subliminal level he must have his doubts as to Iago's integrity. He allows himself to be persuaded to plead with

Desdemona to intercede with Otello on his behalf. This he does, unaware that Iago has ensured that Otello should witness his interview with Desdemona from afar and that Iago will deliberately encourage Otello to misconstrue the interview.

After the opening of Act 2 Cassio does not appear again until the opening of Act 3, but his presence is felt throughout. Desdemona takes her role as Otello's consort and the special favour she enjoys with the Cypriot people seriously. She likewise also takes seriously the task Cassio sets for her. In spite of Otello's increasing dementia she does not tire of pleading his case with disastrous consequences for herself, and indeed Cassio. From this point on Cassio does not exist in the opera as a character per se. He is merely a name, a collation of phonemes, with which to flagellate Otello. The character himself is oblivious to the fact that Iago is pouring poison, more vitriolic by the droplet, into Otello's all-too susceptible ears. The tale that Iago paints (*Era la notte*) (Act 2) is a total fabrication. If it was ever the case that Cassio enjoyed an erotic dream while sharing a bed with Iago then it was about Bianca that he was dreaming and not Desdemona.

When Cassio enters the great hall of the castle (Act 3) it is because he has been summoned by Iago who needs to provide the proverbial icing on the cake by giving Otello the 'ocular proof' he so desperately craves of Cassio's treachery. Cassio cannot possibly know that he carries that proof on him, namely the strange handkerchief that suddenly appeared in his rooms (planted there at Iago's behest by **Emilia**). Nor does he know that Otello is closely observing them as Iago craftily turns the conversation to Bianca and soon has Cassio laughing. Cassio is as quick to laugh as to anger, what the Elizabethans would have termed a choleric temperament. The reason for his levity is that Cassio has grown tired of his affair with Bianca, now doomed since his demotion, and has set his sights elsewhere. This plays perfectly into Iago's hands. Otello is all the time eavesdropping and, observing Cassio's mirth, is convinced that he is being mocked,

assuming Cassio speaks of his affair with Desdemona. Iago leads him out of earshot of Otello and somehow manages to turn the conversation so that Cassio shall remember the handkerchief that he has recently discovered in his lodgings. Cassio needs no persuading, first to produce it, and then to rhapsodize at great length – 'miracolo vago dell'aspo e dell'ago' ('enchanting miracle of needle and thread').

He is interrupted by the arrival of the Venetian ambassadors. Iago persuades him to withdraw. But he soon receives a summons from Otello himself who, through gritted teeth and before the assembled dignitaries, announces that Cassio has been commissioned to take Otello's place as Governor since Otello is recalled to Venice. The news must inevitably come as a surprise to Cassio. He barely has a chance to register his good fortune, however, for Otello causes universal outrage by seizing Desdemona and violently forcing her to her knees. Cassio reflects, 'What raises me to the skies is the wave of a hurricane'. He leaves speedily with the rest of the company after Otello has brutally cursed his wife. He can only be appalled by Desdemona's plight but equally he is at a loss to know what to do to assist her.

The next he knows is that he is being set upon by Roderigo in the dead of night. Cassio's quick reflexes save him from the assassination attempt and it is Roderigo who is slain. The audience is not privy to this scene but is witness to Iago persuading Roderigo that Cassio must be killed in order to ensure that Desdemona remain in Cyprus.

In Act 4 Emilia enters Desdemona's apartments with the news that Cassio has killed Roderigo. Cassio then enters with Iago and Lodvico to witness the final denouement. He is appalled at Iago's treachery, for the first time becoming aware of the extent to which the love of Otello and Desdemona has been destroyed by Iago's villainy. He desperately attempts to prevent Otello stabbing himself but it is too late.

Cassio has done nothing with which he needs to reproach himself other than to allow his natural hot-headedness and lack of self-discipline to make him such an easy prey for Iago's wiles.

Cavalieri della Morte (Knights of Death) (*La Battaglia di Legnano*). See **Knights of Death**

Count Ceprano (*Rigoletto*). Courtier at the court of the **Duke of Mantua**.
Ceprano is the representative of a long line of husbands that the Duke has attempted to cuckold. The Duke usually has his way, not just because of his superior social position but also because of his superior vitality.

There is nothing remarkable about Ceprano. His facelessness causes one to reflect that in a sense the Duke's victims deserve their fate. For the Duke understands something they do not, that above all, the women he battens upon want to be taken beyond themselves, not just flattered, but transfigured. For the brief moment that the Duke is with them he gives them a glimpse of something of which the likes of Ceprano, decent and respectable though he is, would be incapable.

Although Ceprano's grudge is against the Duke he is all too happy to fall in with the plan to humiliate **Rigoletto**. For Rigoletto has made Ceprano the special butt of his acerbic wit. The courtiers' plan is fundamentally based on cowardice. They cannot exact revenge on the Duke who is protected by his social station. Rigoletto is easy prey because he is poor and disabled. In spite of the obvious justification that they have endured much humiliation at the hands of the jester it reflects poorly on the likes of Ceprano that they take such obvious pleasure in humiliating Rigoletto who is, after all, only doing his job, and does not enjoy the immunity that their wealth and privilege confer on them.

Ceprano would never contemplate employing an assassin, although he has as much justification as Rigoletto has. But such a course of action would be an affront to his station. Even though he might desire it Ceprano would feel he was consigning himself to eternal damnation were he to assail the Duke.

In spite of his own distress Ceprano joins in with the other courtiers in deriding the distraught **Monterone** (Act 1 Scene 1). He does not have the imagination to reflect on how he would feel had his daughter been a victim of the Duke's licentious behaviour.

Once Rigoletto reveals that it is not his mistress but his daughter that the courtiers have abducted, Ceprano in common with all the others ceases to have anything to say for himself (Act 2). The courtiers, in spite of themselves, are shamed by Rigoletto's evident distress and speak only in aggregate.

Countess Ceprano (*Rigoletto*)
The Countess only appears in the opening scene of the opera. She is the first woman to be seen being wooed by the licentious **Duke of Mantua** who deplores the fact that the Countess is leaving the party. She declares that she must go with her husband to Ceprano. When the Duke fervently kisses her hand she begs him to be calm, not surprisingly since her husband is close at hand.

The scene provides a startling illustration of the brazen thoughtlessness of the Duke, who has no consideration for the embarrassment he may cause the object of his limitless desires. Later in the opera (Act 1 Scene 2) the courtiers convince **Rigoletto** that they are intending to kidnap the Countess, when in fact they are intending to kidnap Rigoletto's daughter, **Gilda** (the Ceprano palace being situated immediately opposite to Rigoletto's house).

Il Chirurgo (The Surgeon) (*La forza del destino*). See **Surgeon**

Chorus (*Aida*)
Of all Verdi's operas *Aida* is perhaps the most dependent on its chorus for its success. The opera was designed as a Spectacular along the lines of French Grand opera, and as such demands huge forces to ensure that it effectively evokes the age of the Pyramids when Egypt was a great power.
Act 1 Scene 1   Ministers, priests, officers and others have been summoned by the **King** to the great hall in the royal palace at

Memphis to learn that their country has been invaded by Ethiopia. All are enraged at the aggressor's audacity but are delighted to learn that Thebes is already preparing to trounce the invader, 'spreading war and death'. They take up the King's battle cry, 'War! War! Tremendous, pitiless war!' All concur that Radames shall be the leader and then echo the King's exhortation to go forth to the sacred banks of the Nile and there bring death to the invader. They exit with **Amneris**'s great cry, *Ritorna vincitor!* echoing in their ears.

Act 1 Scene 2. Priests and priestesses surround **Ramfis** at the altar in the Temple of Vulcan at Memphis. 'Thou, who from nothingness didst draw the seas, the earth, the heavens, we invoke thee!' Ramfis and the priests intone whilst the Priestesses call to 'Great **Phtha**!' As Radames is brought to the altar the priestesses perform a sacred dance and the priests place a silver veil over his head. Once Ramfis has raised his invocation the priests echo his words, 'May the sacred sword, tempered by the gods, become in your hand blazing terror and death for the enemy', concluding, 'Oh god, custodian and avenger of this sacred land, lift thy hand over the land of Egypt'. The priestesses then take up the chant of the single **Priestess** that inaugurated the scene, 'Mighty, mighty Phtha! Spirit of the world!' and the scene closes with all raising a great cry: 'Immenso Phtha!'

Act 2 Scene 1. Slave girls are hailing Radames's victory over the Ethiopians as they dress Amneris for the victory celebrations. Young Moorish slaves dance around the princess, waving great feather fans. As **Aida** approaches Amneris signs to the girls to withdraw. Aida and Amneris's scene is interrupted by a chorus of Egyptian soldiers from outside calling, 'War and death to the invader!' The interruption emphasizes Aida's predicament and adds poignancy to the confrontation between the princess and the slave girl by indicating the latter's utter powerlessness.

Act 2 Scene 2 This is the central scene of the opera and it is essential that each member of the chorus is clearly aware of the precise role he or she plays. The great gate has been raised in the city of Thebes to welcome the victorious Egyptian army. The King has journeyed thence, accompanied by ministers, priests, captains, standard-bearers and slaves bearing huge feather fans.

Amneris enters accompanied by Aida and other slave girls. The populace sing 'Glory to Egypt and to **Isis**, protectress of the sacred land! To the King who rules the Delta joyful hymns we sing!' Women prepare to dance the mystic dances. The priests invite all to lift their eyes to the gods, the arbiters of victory. Now the triumphal procession commences. The Egyptian troops, following the trumpeters, pass in review before the King. Then come the chariots, the ensigns, the sacred vessels and the statues of the gods. A band of dancing girls carry treasure won from the enemy. Finally Radames is borne in on a litter carried by twelve captains. All welcome the conquering hero.

Radames's first action is to request that the Ethiopian prisoners be brought before the King. The prisoners enter escorted by guards. **Amonasro**, dressed as an officer, brings up the rear. All are astounded when Aida recognizes her father among the prisoners. Amonasro immediately cautions her not to reveal his true identity as the Ethiopian King. His pleas for clemency for the prisoners are echoed by the prisoners and slave girls themselves and reiterated by the populace. But the priests are quick to declare that the gods have condemned the prisoners to die. If it were not for the intervention of Radames one can be certain that the Ethiopians would indeed have been put to death in accordance with the priests' wishes. But Radames exercises his victor's prerogative and the King, in view of the fact that the fatherland owes everything to Radames, can hardly refuse his request. The slaves are naturally overjoyed that their lives are to be spared. The priests have no alternative but to yield to the King's decree but recommend that all should sing a hymn to Isis, 'protectress of the sacred land'. The Egyptian populace dutifully sing in praise of Isis while the slaves sing in praise of 'merciful Egypt'.

Act 3   A chorus of priests is heard from within the Temple of Isis praying to the goddess for succour. Amneris and Ramfis arrive in a boat with a group of heavily veiled women and guards. They all enter the temple. At the conclusion of the Act priests and guards emerge from the temple in order to assist with the arrest of Radames. Some of the guards rush off in pursuit of Aida and Amonasro. The rest remain with Ramfis to whom Radames surrenders.

Act 4 Scene 1   In the hall of the King's palace Amneris is standing near to the gate leading to Radames's cell. She commands the guards to bring the prisoner to her. The guards duly fetch Radames and remain throughout the ensuing scene between Amneris and Radames, then escort the prisoner back to his cell. Then priests enter and descend into the prison. Their voices and that of Ramfis are heard praying to their god for enlightenment: 'Let our lips pronounce thy justice', they declare. At this moment Radames, surrounded by guards, crosses the stage and goes down into the vault. Then, as Ramfis reads out the charges against Radames, the priests echo his demand that Radames defend himself. Radames remains silent. The priests conclude that this is a tacit acknowledgement of guilt and sentence Radames to die a traitor's death. 'Beneath the altar of the offended god you, living, shall be entombed', they tell him. They ascend from the vault, reiterating to the distraught Amneris that Radames is a traitor and shall die.

Act 4 Scene 2   Once Radames's tomb has been sealed the priests and priestesses are heard from above singing hymns, invoking the gods. As the opera draws to a close the chorus is heard throughout calling on 'Mighty Phtha'.

Chorus (Alzira)

When the curtain rises on Alzira Zamoro's tribe of Indians is in the process of torturing the aged Spanish governor, Alvaro. The Indians tie Alvaro to a tree trunk and then dance around him, chanting with relish: 'Die, die, covered with insults. Let his martyrdom

be cruel but slow. Wring the cowardly sobs from him, pile torment on torment'. They work themselves into a frenzy and then, 'shouting with frantic joy, rush at the prisoner, some with darts, other with spears and burning brands' (SD). They are interrupted by the arrival of Zamoro who calls a halt to the torture and liberates Alvaro. The Indians are delighted to see their leader, whom they had believed to be dead. They are even more elated when they learn that the Indian tribes are all rising 'as one man', finally to cast off the Spanish yoke. They join Zamoro in singing a bloodthirsty chorus invoking the god of war.

Act 1 Scene 1   Officers from the Spanish army are gathering in the square of Lima. The chorus is divided into three sections. The first section is informing the other two of a message which has recently arrived from the King. Alvaro then appears and announces that he is handing over his command to his son, Gusmano. The soldiers hail Gusmano, who then addresses them and decrees peace between the Spanish and the Inca. He reveals that the peace is to be consolidated by his marriage to the Inca girl, Alzira, with whom he is already in love. The soldiers all express the hope that Alzira may return his love.

Act 1 Scene 2   Indian girls join Alzira's sister, Zuma, in reflecting on Alzira's misery and pray that their mistress may find some peace in sleep. When Alzira suddenly erupts from her couch and rushes about the stage as though demented, the girls try to calm her. Alzira has been dreaming of her true love, Zamoro, whom she believes to be dead. The girls are moved by Alzira's plight but encourage her to try and forget 'an unlucky lover whom heaven has made such war upon'. The girls retire at the behest of Alzira's father, Ataliba, who now enters.

Spanish officers and soldiers and Indian maidens accompany Gusmano and Ataliba as they surprise Zamoro and Alzira in an amorous embrace. All are astounded to see Zamoro alive. Gusmano orders the soldiers to arrest him. The soldiers are about to drag Zamoro off to his execution when Alvaro intervenes on Zamoro's behalf. When news

111

arrives that Lima is under attack from a host of Inca warriors, Gusmano decrees that he will meet Zamoro on the battlefield. Spanish and Indian warriors make off in their separate directions, brandishing swords, to prepare for battle. The women hold Alzira back as she attempts to follow.

Act 2 Scene 1 Spanish soldiers are carousing within the fortifications of Lima. They are celebrating their victory over the Incas. Meanwhile Indian prisoners in chains, guarded by Spanish soldiers, cross the stage. Gusmano enters and the soldiers sing in praise of their leader. When Alzira enters Gusmano dismisses them.

Act 2 Scene 2 The Indians greet Zamoro, who has for a second time escaped execution at the hands of the Spanish. They encourage their dispirited leader to look to the future. Zamoro becomes distraught when he learns that Alzira and Gusmano's wedding is already underway. The Indians try to comfort their leader, to no avail. They fail to prevent him from rushing off in search of 'vengeance and death'.

Act 2 Scene 3 In the Great Hall of the governor's residence Gusmano's wedding preparations are in progress. The hall is crowded with Spanish soldiers. Alzira's maidens express the hope that their mistress's marriage to Gusmano may be the signal for enduring peace in Peru. When Zamoro suddenly appears brandishing a dagger and stabs Gusmano Spanish soldiers surround him. Zamoro's life is only spared due to Gusmano's intervention. All watch, dumbfounded, as Gusmano, in his dying moments, exemplifies Christian compassion by blessing the union of Alzira and Zamoro.

Chorus (*Aroldo*)

Whereas *Stiffelio* opens with **Jorg** alone on stage, expounding on the virtues of the Holy Book, *Aroldo* opens in the midst of the banquet which in *Stiffelio* takes place later in Act 1.

The Chorus is heard offstage singing in praise of **Aroldo** who has recently returned to Kent from Palestine, covered in glory. Where the Chorus of *Stiffelio* is comprised

of his friends and members of his congregation, in *Aroldo* the Chorus consists of crusading knights and their ladies. Some of the knights have accompanied Aroldo on Crusade for they sing (Act 1 Scene 2): 'It is good to return home peacefully from the ferocious battlefield! It is enjoyable to recount dangerous adventures to the applause of one's contented dear ones!' Otherwise the outline of the Chorus's role in Acts 1–3 Scene 1 is the same as in *Stiffelio*.

Since the scene in the church which concludes *Stiffelio* was excised in order to placate the censor the Chorus in *Aroldo* are compelled to transform themselves into Scottish shepherds, women and hunters for the final Act, set on the shores of Loch Lomond.

Shepherds are joined by hunters who have apparently had a successful day's hunting; 'not a single thrust went amiss', they proudly proclaim. Having all greeted each other and joined in 'thanks and praise to the kind heavens', they disperse.

Shortly after, the bell from a nearby village tolls an *Ave* and voices are heard in the distance joining together in prayer. By now night has fallen. A storm is brewing. Mountaineers and women enter from all sides and make for the lake where a ship is in distress. It is the ship bearing **Mina** and **Egberto**. The mountaineers throw a rope to the foundering vessel. The rope is presumably taken in hand by Egberto for the mountaineers succeed in pulling the boat ashore. All join in praising God for having saved the travellers. They then encourage the strangers to knock at the door of a dwelling which apparently houses two hermits. (The hermits will shortly be revealed to be none other than Aroldo and **Briano**.)

Chorus (*Attila*)

The chorus in *Attila* plays variously Barbarians, **Ezio's** Roman soldiery, Aquilean refugees, hermits and Druid priests and priestesses.

Prologue Scene 1 When the opera opens the stage is crowded with Huns, Herulians, Ostrogoths and other Barbarians, all followers of **Attila**. They have just reduced the town of Aquilea to a heap of rubble and are revelling in the fact that, 'Shouts, pillage, groans, blood, rape, devastation, massacre and fire are Attila's sport!' They reckon they have found Valhalla (the Norse equivalent of heaven) on earth.

As Attila himself arrives they all prostrate themselves before their leader. After Attila's greeting they sing in praise of 'the king of a thousand forests, the minister and prophet of Odin'.

Odabella enters, accompanied by an entourage of 'maidens of Aquilea', all of whom have been rescued by **Uldino**. The maidens remain mute, allowing Odabella to act as their spokesperson. At the conclusion of the scene the Barbarians renew their extravagant praise of their leader: 'Long live the king who reveals to the earth with what brilliance Odin surrounds him! If he scourges he is like a torrent in flood; if he rewards valour he is like a dew'.

Ezio enters with an entourage of Roman officers. Attila shortly dismisses all attendants, Romans and Barbarians, so that he and the Roman envoy may be alone.

Prologue Scene 2   A chorus of hermits greets the dawning of a new day after a night of fierce storms. They sing in praise of the Creator who has brought them safely through the night.

They then observe and greet the arrival of **Foresto** and refugees from the sacking of Aquilea. The Aquileans praise the Creator for different reasons from the hermits; they are just thankful to have escaped with their lives. They are also grateful to Foresto for having been their 'leader ... shield and salvation'. They attempt to console Foresto for the loss of his beloved Odabella, although they must know that there can be little hope that he will ever see her again. But they cannot allow him to become dispirited. They welcome his rousing affirmation that their homeland shall rise once again like a Phoenix from the ashes.

Act 1 Scene 2   Uldino enters accompanied by Druids, captains and kings. They have come to take instructions from Attila

(whether any of them are followers of the treacherous Uldino is not made explicit). Attila exhorts them to go forth to fresh battles and the assembly acknowledges its readiness to prosecute whatever campaign Attila may see fit to embark on.

Act 1 Scene 3   Attila's camp. A chorus of maidens and children, clad in white, is heard first in the distance, singing in 'religious harmony': 'Come, imbue our minds, Spirit of Creation ... Let the treasure of life shower on us from thy forehead'. Their chorus sounds an incongruous note in the midst of Attila's bloodthirsty war-mongering. The chorus is led by the future Pope **Leo** who has come to warn Attila against attempting to sack Rome. His followers, not having been privy to the fact that Attila has already been visited by the Pope in a dream are amazed at how efficacious their mission proves. They liken it to the defeat of Goliath at the hands of the shepherd boy. For Attila prostrates himself before the deputation and ultimately withdraws.

Attila's followers, meanwhile, are perplexed by their leader's sudden capitulation. They are aware that something assails him but are at a loss to know what it is. Never before have they seen Attila prostrate on the ground and they could never have believed it would be before a Roman Priest.

Act 2 Scene 1   A party of Attila's slaves presents itself to Ezio. They are preceded by some Roman soldiers. The slaves have been sent to invite Ezio and his captain to join their master. Ezio agrees to follow them and the slaves leave.

Act 2 Scene 2   Attila's camp is prepared for a solemn feast. The Barbarians prepare themselves with alacrity to feast on 'limbs and severed heads until the morning'. While they sing Attila takes his place at the banqueting table, followed by Druids, priestesses, captains and kings.

Ezio arrives at the feast accompanied by his captains. Some Druids detach themselves from the assembly and warn Attila not to sit at the same table as the 'foreigner' for they have perceived ill omens in the skies. Attila will have none of it and the Druids withdraw, expressing the hope that Odin will protect him. Once all are seated the priestesses divide into two groups and sing a strange song which seems to assert that only the sound of the trumpet can bring relief to the human heart. As if to confirm the song's import a sudden gust of wind extinguishes all the torches. All rise in 'an instinctive movement of terror'. Silence and general gloom descend on the assembly. The Barbarians are convinced that the spirit of the mountains is responsible for the occurrence: 'Terror and mystery hold sway over our souls', they declare. The sky clears, everybody heaves a sigh of relief and the feasting resumes. Then, when Odabella dramatically prevents Attila from drinking the poisoned drink that Uldino has prepared for him, the assembly is cast into uproar. All exhort the King to 'return to blood and fire and punish the traitors ... we will be no more the sport of their gods'. They clearly feel that all Attila's misfortunes stemmed from the moment he set eyes on the Aquilean, Odabella, and they are not far wrong. However they are forced to acknowledge that Odabella has now saved Attila's life.

Act 3 A chorus of Barbarians is heard offstage welcoming Odabella as Attila's consort. 'Beauteous is your face, pure as the dawning day', they sing.

Again offstage the chorus is heard, this time in the role of Roman soldiery, shouting for vengeance as they commence an assault on Attila's camp. In the final scene the Roman soldiers burst onto the stage and declare, 'God, the people and the king are fully avenged'.

Chorus (*Un ballo in maschera*)

In the outer Acts the Chorus portrays the officers, gentlemen and their womenfolk who belong to the Governor's circle of friends and acquaintances. In Act 2 the chorus is largely committed to portraying the people of Boston, who habituate the fortune-teller, Ulrica's, cavern seeking reassurance about the future.

Act 1 It is morning. Gentlemen, deputies, townsfolk and officers are waiting in the drawing-room of the Governor's mansion for the Governor, **Riccardo**. The officers and gentlemen are reflecting that the Governor is 'shielded in this dwelling by the love of a virgin world'. They are confident that Riccardo will attend to their needs. Meanwhile **Samuel, Tom** and their henchmen are full of less charitable thoughts. They are plotting revenge for those who have died in the Governor's service.

Riccardo enters, greets everyone and gracefully accepts the petitions that the deputies deliver to him. Having gained Riccardo's reassurance that he will attend to their requests the gentlemen exit to await his judgement. Later **Renato** and **Oscar** invite them to return. Riccardo makes no reference to their petitions but instead invites them to accompany him that night to Ulrica's cavern. The conspirators see this as possibly being an ideal opportunity to carry out their assassination of Riccardo. The others welcome the idea of an adventure, 'at last a bit of folly brightens this life which heaven gave us', they reflect. They agree to meet Riccardo at 3.00 am, in disguise, at the oracle's cavern.

Act 1 Scene 2 When the curtain rises townsfolk are already present in the cavern awaiting their turn with the seeress. The women and children call for silence as Ulrica is telling the fortunes of a young couple. The people are quite certain that Ulrica obtains her insight from being in league with the Devil but appear blithely unconcerned by the fact. When Riccardo arrives, disguised as a fisherman, he pushes his way through the crowd and notices that none of his party has yet arrived. The townsfolk tell him: 'Ruffian, stay back!' They do not realize they are addressing the Governor. Suddenly the scene darkens. Ulrica announces, 'It is he!' (that is, the 'King of the Depths') and everyone exclaims, 'Hurrah for the sorceress!' Ulrica calls for silence and all watch with bated breath as she reads **Silvano's** palm. When her prophecy is almost immediately borne out, due to Riccardo's speedy intervention, all are delighted. When Amelia's **servant** asks Ulrica for a private audience for his mistress Ulrica asks the company to leave, on the pretext that she wishes to 'join with Satan (and) gaze into the face of Truth'. This strikes everyone as perfectly reasonable and they depart to await events. Eventually they become impatient with waiting and their voices can be heard from outside the room demanding to be readmitted. Ulrica duly opens the door to them and this time admits not just the townsfolk but also Riccardo's guests, who have now arrived, and the conspirators.

Impatient now, the crowd demands that Ulrica mount her tripod and chant her prophecy. Riccardo comes forward and, maintaining his disguise, asks for his future to be read. The people, clearly mesmerized by Riccardo's eloquence, echo the final words of his song (*Di tu se fedele*). They remain agog as Ulrica reads his palm, and when she indicates her unwillingness to reveal what she sees they become insistent. All are shocked by Ulrica's announcement that Riccardo can expect to die soon. Will he die by an assassin's hand, they wonder? 'The mere thought makes one's heart shudder'. Ulrica prophesies that Riccardo shall be killed by 'the first to touch (his) hand today'. When Renato arrives and is the first to shake Riccardo's hand the crowd, mostly comprised of Riccardo's friends, are incredulous.

Silvano, having spread the word that Riccardo is at Ulrica's cavern and having relayed his good fortune, enters with a large crowd of townsfolk. They all swarm into the cavern, singing in praise of Riccardo. Their chorus, 'Oh son of England, beloved of this land; rule in happiness, for health and glory smile upon you', is in stark contrast to the plotting of the conspirators and Ulrica's dark prophecy for Riccardo.

Act 2   The conspirators are lying in wait in the fields outside Boston intending to ambush Riccardo, who is engaged in his secret tryst with **Amelia**. Unfortunately for them they are rumbled by Renato who, on his way to rescue his beloved lord, overhears them discussing their plot to murder Riccardo. By the time the conspirators make their ambush Renato has already warned

Riccardo who has made his escape. They are heard first in the distance, then gradually drawing closer. When they enter Renato is ready for them with drawn sword. When they realize that it is Renato and that he has recognized them they fall upon him. Renato would surely have died had not Amelia's veil fallen off at this moment. The conspirators find it hugely amusing that Renato has unwittingly been cuckolded by his master: 'What gossiping there'll be about this. What comments we'll hear in the town!' they chuckle.

Act 3 Scene 2   Riccardo's guests are preparing to enjoy a ball at his mansion. Most are wearing masks, some are in costume, while others are in evening dress. Some are seeking friends, others are trying to escape discovery, some greeting, others pursuing. They sing in similar vein to all other revellers in Verdi's operas: 'Love and the dance go on in these joyous halls, while life is only a fleeting dream'. The guests continue in this vein throughout the scene. The conspirators enter dressed in blue dominoes and red sashes, this being the agreed dress by which they may recognize each other. They circulate in the crowd. In effect they have little to do other than act as cover for Renato, who has already been elected as the one to commit the murder. The guests are predictably appalled at Riccardo's assassination and incredulous when they discover who the murderer is. Their minds must surely revert to Ulrica's prediction. They are about to lynch Renato but are prevented by Riccardo. All are abashed by Riccardo's extraordinary magnanimity as, with this dying breath, he pardons his murderer. The curtain falls as all exclaim, 'Night of horror, night of horror!'

Chorus (*La Battaglia di Legnano*)

When the curtain rises soldiers from Piacenza are passing across the stage. They are followed by platoons from Verona, Brescia, Novaro and Vercelli. The surrounding streets are thronging with people, likewise the balconies above, from which the people shower the troops with flowers. 'Long live Italy!', they shout and continue to sing in praise of the unconquered Lombard League. After **Arrigo**'s cavatina distant voices are heard, drawing gradually nearer. It is **Rolando** with his Milanese troops. Shortly after their arrival on stage a bray of trumpets is heard announcing the **Consuls** who welcome the troops and exhort them to swear an oath to defend Milan. All present duly swear, after which the Consuls move off, followed in turn first by the troops and then the populace.

Act 1 Scene 2   A chorus of handmaidens wonders why their mistress, **Lida**, is so sad and avoids the joyous celebrations taking place in the city. Lida tells her maids of her woes and the women withdraw in order 'to allow her to give full rein to her grief'. The women notice that Lida's countenance only brightens at the mention of Arrigo's imminent arrival. When a **herald** is announced Rolando dismisses the handmaidens in front of whom it would be inappropriate to conduct affairs of state.

Act 2   The officers and magistrates of the Council of Como are assembling. The Councillors reflect on their long-standing enmity with the Milanese. When the **Mayor** announces the deputation from Milan the Councillors take their seats. In response to Rolando's plea that past animosities be put aside the Councillors join the Mayor in reminding Rolando that they already have a pact with **Federico Barbarossa**. They allow Rolando and Arrigo to have their say. They are equally surprised by Barbarossa's sudden appearance and they join the Emperor in warning the Milanese that an 'avenging thunderbolt' now threatens them. All are impressed by the prospect of Barbarossa's massed army and the scene concludes with everyone agreeing that there can be only one resolution to their difficulties; 'terrible war! To the death!'

Act 3   The **Knights of Death** descend singly and in silence into the subterranean vaults of the Basilica of San Ambroglio. They are gathering to swear an oath and welcome Arrigo into their number (see **Synopsis**). The Knights ritually demand from the eldest among them that Arrigo be admitted.

Arrigo is then required to kneel at the foot of a grave. The eldest Knight binds him with his sash, then all the Knights cross their swords over his head. They then raise Arrigo to his feet and all embrace him. Finally, when Arrigo too has unsheathed his sword, they pronounce their oath with a single voice. The oath consists of a vow to fight for Italy unto death. If any should prove cowardly in battle he shall be execrated: 'Let his vile name spell infamy to every nation, to every age'.

Act 4   Women, old men and children are on their knees outside a church in Milan listening to the psalm-singing that comes from within the church. The psalm, 'O my God, make them like unto a wheel, and as the stubble before the wind and like as the flame that consumeth the mountains', imprecates against the enemy. The Chorus prays for the safety of the men fighting in the war. Voices are heard offstage proclaiming 'Victory!' All rise to their feet. The second Consul enters with senators, followed by a great crowd of citizens. The Consul announces that the enemy has been defeated, and invites all to raise a hymn of thanks. He passes into the church with the senators. The citizens embrace one another, mingling kisses with tears of joy. Meanwhile a number of platoons are seen passing in the distance on the return from the battle. 'Let victory resound from the Alps to Charybdis!' the people shout, 'Let Adriatic reply, "Victory" to Tyrrhene! Italy rises again robed in glory!' Their exultation is tempered by the sound of funereal trumpets.

Shortly Arrigo is borne in by a squadron of the Knights of Death. Milanese captains follow. Arrigo is laid on the steps of the church and the Knights withdraw as Rolando approaches the dying man. All comment that Arrigo will soon 'reap the reward of his valour in heaven'. The second Consul enters, followed by soldiers and the triumphal chariot just as the chorus is heard from within the church praising the Lord. Arrigo notices the banner on the triumphal chariot and the Knights bring the standard within his reach so that he may kiss it before he dies. All call on the Lord to 'open the empyrean to your faithful warrior'.

Chorus (*Boccanegra*)

The action of *Simon Boccanegra* revolves around the conflict between the Patricians, whose chief representative is **Fiesco**, and the Plebeians, who successfully secure the election of their demagogic hero Simon **Boccanegra** as Doge. The people of Genoa are as much a part of the fabric of the action as is the sea, whose presence is felt so keenly throughout.

In the Prologue **Paolo**, who has his own agenda, convinces the commoners that they must vote for Boccanegra. Paolo uses the Fieschi palace as a focus for the people's discontent with the Patricians and plays on their naturally superstitious inclination. All are aware that the beautiful Maria, Fiesco's daughter, is imprisoned in the castle by her father. Paolo describes to them how a ghostly light, 'like a tormented soul', appears in the windows of the palace at night. The people comment 'it is as though it were haunted by ghosts'. At which moment a light appears and the people all flee in superstitious dread. Paolo has done a good job of convincing them that the Fieschi are to be shunned at all costs and that their vote should be for Boccanegra. By the end of the Prologue Boccanegra has been elected and the people return to celebrate the election of a commoner and local hero as Doge. The curtain falls on their cries of 'Long live Simon!'

Act 1 Scene 2   In the Council Chamber of the Doge's palace twelve Councillors of the people are seated opposite twelve Patricians. Seated to one side are four maritime consuls and their constables. The Councillors are favourable to the King of Tartary's offer of peace but are not prepared to consider peace with Venice. Boccanegra attempts to plead with them, pointing out that Adria and Ligouria have a common fatherland.

He is interrupted by the sound of trumpets from outside. A mob is pursuing **Gabriele** who has just killed Lorenzin, who was previously a popular candidate for the Doge's office. When Boccanegra hears cries of 'Death to the Doge!' he orders the doors of the palace to be thrown open that he may himself address the mob. A herald addresses the mob and shortly voices are heard proclaiming 'Long live the Doge!' Verdi had an acute perception of the volatility of mob psychology (as did Wagner in his opera *Rienzi*. The character of Rienzi has already been invoked by Boccanegra. Rienzi was himself in a very similar situation to Boccanegra, caught between opposing political factions and striving to effect a reconciliation).

The mob erupts into the Council Chamber, preceded by Gabriele, who forthwith confesses to having murdered Lorenzin for his part in the abduction of **Amelia**. The people will not hear ill spoken of Lorenzin, but when Amelia has related her abduction they conclude that the villain was rightfully executed. Patrician or no, Gabriele is forgiven, though his attempt on the life of Boccanegra is less easy to condone. The assembly is much affected by Boccanegra's passionate plea for peace between the warring factions in his speech (*Fratricidi! Plebe!*). 'He knows how to calm our anger as the caress of a soft breeze soothes the troubled sea', they reflect to themselves. All are appalled at the curse which Paolo is forced to utter against whoever is responsible for the outrage done to Amelia. While Boccanegra does not openly accuse Paolo himself of being the culprit there can be few present who do not realize that Paolo is in effect calling a curse down upon himself.

Meanwhile Gabriele and Fiesco's plot to oust Boccanegra is coming to a head. As Act 2 draws to its conclusion a chorus of Guelph supporters is heard outside the Doge's palace threatening to assault the palace of 'this crowned Devil'. No doubt tales have been told and retold with ever greater elaboration and exaggeration of the self-imposed malediction Boccanegra has extracted from Paolo. What the Guelphs do not realize is that one of the chief sources of inspiration, Gabriele, has just learnt that his beloved Amelia is none other than Boccanegra's daughter. In that instant Gabriele determines never again to take up arms against Boccanegra, and snatching his sword rushes off to fight against, rather than with, the insurgents. It is an extraordinary volte face, inexcusable from an idealistic viewpoint (see **Gabriele**). Deprived of one of their figureheads the Guelph's revolt crumbles. When Act 3 opens it is to shouts of 'Evviva il Doge!' from the ever fickle people of Genoa. A chorus is also heard in the distance singing the praises of Gabriele and Amelia: 'let then these nuptials of love be the forerunners of peace', the people pray. As the opera concludes Fiesco, from the balcony of the Doge's palace, proclaims, in accordance with Boccanegra's dying wish, Gabriele the new Doge. The people shout for Boccanegra but are told he is dead: 'Pray for the peace of his soul'. The slow sombre tolling of a bell is heard. All kneel in prayer.

The role of politics is crucial in the plot of *Simon Boccanegra*, but the most pertinent feature of the tale remains the way in which it is the personal passions of the chief protagonists that ultimately dictate the eventual outcome. To the people it is neither here nor there whether a Plebeian or Patrician occupies the throne, so long as the incumbent respects their liberties.

Chorus (*Don Carlo*)

Act 1   When the opera opens the gentlemen of the chorus arrive on the stage in the role of French huntsmen. They are in the midst of a hunt in the forest of Fontainbleau and pass through in hot pursuit of their quarry. They accompany **Elisabeth di Valois** and her page, **Tebaldo**. There is also a group of (mute) woodcutters on stage to whom Elisabeth distributes alms. The woodcutters and the royal retinue then pass on, leaving the stage clear for **Don Carlo**'s soliloquy. Later in the scene Tebaldo returns with a letter informing Elisabeth that she is to be married to the Spanish king. He is accompanied by pages carrying torches. Shortly afterwards a crowd of people, Spanish and French, arrive in the company of the Spanish

ambassador, Count **di Lerma**. They include Elisabeth's companion, Countess **d'Aramberg**, and her ladies-in-waiting. They are initially heard in the distance, singing in celebration of the accord that has just been achieved between France and Spain. When they enter they remain oblivious of the private tragedy that the new treaty represents to Carlo and Elisabeth, but continue to proclaim, 'To Spain's queen, glory and honour!' They depart singing the same.

Act 2   In the cloisters of the monastery of San Yuste monks sing at the tomb of the Emperor Charles V, who is now 'nought but silent dust. At the feet of his Heavenly Maker his haughty spirit now trembles'. They pray that God may be merciful on his soul. 'Great is God alone', they affirm. As day dawns they disperse leaving the stage free for Carlo who has been observing them the while. Towards the close of the scene the monks are heard from within, intoning the same prayer as **Philip** arrives at the tomb of his father with the Queen.

Act 2 Scene 2   The ladies of the Spanish court are outside the cloisters of San Yuste awaiting the King and Queen. They seek shelter from the fierce morning sun beneath the huge fir trees that proliferate in the gardens. They eagerly agree to allow Princess **Eboli** to entertain them with the Saracen song, 'the one about the veil, so favourable to love'. They clearly enjoy the song and join in the chorus. Immediately after Eboli has finished her song Elisabeth enters from the monastery. While the main protagonists converse the ladies occupy themselves in discreet conversation amongst themselves. Later in the scene they take the cue from Eboli and **Rodrigo**, leaving Elisabeth alone with her stepson. Later they return with Eboli and Rodrigo, but too late to be in attendance when the King enters from the monastery. Since the King has issued specific decrees that the Queen should not be left unattended this is a serious omission and one which will cost the Countess d'Aramberg her position. All the Queen's attendants are appalled by Philip's summary dismissal of Elisabeth's favoured companion and comment that he thereby insults the Queen. It is clear to everyone that the reason for Philip's decree is that he does not trust his wife. They are all moved by Elisabeth's obvious distress and join Rodrigo in trying to console her. They then follow their Queen who, having taken tearful leave of the Countess retires, supported by Eboli.

Act 3 Scene 2   The entire chorus is employed for the great *auto-da-fé* scene in the square before the church of Our Lady of Antioch in Madrid. An *auto-da-fé*, ostensibly for the salvation of heretics' souls, was the occasion for a public holiday, the general spirit being little different from that one would now experience at a funfair. The stage directions indicate that the Halbadiers have difficulty in controlling the vast crowd that throngs in the square. 'The day of rejoicing has dawned, all honour to the greatest of Kings!' the crowd choruses, 'The people have confidence in him, the world is prostrate at his feet'. Inevitably the chorus must be partly viewed as being motivated by fear as in any totalitarian state, for such was sixteenth-century Spain. The people must not only kow-tow, they must be seen to kow-tow. Not only that, but they must appear to do so with joy. The penalties for not doing so are underlined as monks lead across the square those condemned by the Inquisition to be burnt at the stake. 'The day has dawned, the day of terror, the terrible day, the fatal day', which can be expected by all who do not toe the party line.

As a procession including Elisabeth and Rodrigo emerges from the palace and makes its way to the church steps the people's declarations of 'Honour to the King!' gather in intensity. They echo the words of the herald as he stands before the closed door of the church and calls upon the door to be thrown open so that the 'venerated sanctuary' may restore the King to the people. The doors open and the King is revealed. The moment is a purely symbolic one, emphasizing that it is purely through the grace of God and God's agency on earth, the church, that the King is granted to the people to rule over them in this temporal world. Philip

announces his sworn duty to put to death the wicked by fire and by sword. The people chorus, 'Glory to Philip! Glory to heaven!'

The crowd will witness with astonishment the audacity of the Infante and the Flemish deputies, but their sympathies are with them. Since there is safety in numbers they join the deputation in pleading with Philip to show mercy. This is the first indication in the opera of the clear division that pertains between the monarchy and the church on the one hand and the general populace which includes many of the dignitaries that surround the King on the other. The monks echo Philip's words accusing the Flemish of being 'traitorous to God', while the people are joined by Elisabeth, Thibault and Rodrigo in continuing to plea for Philip to have mercy on the Flemish people's suffering. All acknowledge that Carlo must truly be out of his mind when he draws a sword in the King's presence. Nobody, however, is willing to intervene to disarm him, not even the captain of the guards. The situation has become potentially explosive and is only defused by the intervention of Rodrigo. For Rodrigo has made no secret of his advocacy of the cause of Protestantism in Flanders. Therefore, when he deliberately appears to uphold the King's authority by himself disarming Don Carlo his action forthwith undermines any possibility of open rebellion that might have been suggested by Carlo's audacity. The people resume their deferential shouts of 'Honour to the King!' and pass on to enjoy the spectacle of the *auto-da-fé*.

Act 4   The populace has stormed the prison in Madrid where Carlo is incarcerated. They are oblivious to Rodrigo's machinations that have already secured Carlo's release. As di Lerma confirms, 'the people are infuriated'. 'Let us strike!' they repeat over and over again, 'No one can stop us! ... He shall tremble and bow the head, tremble before the avenging people'. The people have found a hero, a figurehead for their discontent, in the person of the Infante. They take courage in numbers. This could not be a more stark contrast to the scene of celebrations and glorification at the auto-da-fé. If it were not for the intervention of the Inquisitor, who knows what the outcome of this insurrection might have been?[19] The Inquisitor's sudden appearance before the people represents an immediate indication of divine wrath. All rebellious instincts are instantly quelled. The people revert unthinkingly to their habitual state of submissiveness, fall to their knees and plea for mercy. The Inquisitor and King descend among them.

Act 5   At the conclusion of the opera the Inquisitor and the King, who have followed the Infante and the Queen to the cloisters of San Yuste, are accompanied by officers of the Inquisition. As the curtain falls the officers are dumbstruck by the sudden and inexplicable appearance of the Emperor Charles V.

Chorus (Il Corsaro)

The chorus in Il Corsaro is split between Corrado's pirates and the Turks (the followers of Pasha Seid), odalisques and handmaidens. The corsairs belong to that family of anarchic spirits that are never far away in Verdi's operas, ever ready to undermine the premises of the respectable world and expose the illusion of security that is humanity's first recourse, such as the robbers in I masnadieri, the Barbarians (Attila), the gypsies (La forza del destino), the followers of Urgel (Il Trovatore), the bandits (Ernani).

Act 1 takes place on the corsairs' island in the Aegean. The corsairs are heard offstage expounding their philosophy: 'Our fatherland and kingdom is the foaming wave . . . our life is one of changing fortune, now a sneer, now a welcome smile; death is an

everlasting rest, a borderland between joy and sorrow'. The corsairs enter with Giovanni, who has a letter for Corrado. They are anxious to learn the contents of the letter, but Corrado reveals nothing. However, to the corsairs' delight he announces that he himself will lead them into battle against the Turks. They disperse shouting, 'To arms, to arms!'

Act 2 Scene 1   A chorus of odalisques regale Gulnara with the joys that await her as the star of Seid's harem. Gulnara is not impressed. When a Eunuch announces that Seid requires Gulnara's presence the latter decrees that the other odalisques shall go with her. The odalisques persistently remind her that she is the only one the Pasha desires, but Gulnara is inconsolable.

Act 2 Scene 2   On the shores of the harbour of Corone a chorus of Turkish soldiers and officers imprecate against the pirates who threaten their trade routes. When Seid arrives they all prostrate themselves before their master, then echo with relish his exhortation to fight in the name of Allah. Later, when Corrado's pirates have ignited a ship in the harbour, the Turks rush off to 'meet the danger'. Then voices of the odalisques are heard, calling for help from the harem, which has caught fire. By now Corrado's pirates have overrun the scene. They rush to save the girls in the harem, while the Turks variously call on Allah and threaten death to the aggressors. The pirates are quickly surrounded and overcome by the Turks. Some of the pirates manage to escape. The Turks are ecstatic at the ease of their victory. 'The dreaded hydra's head is cut off', they chorus. The odalisques plead with Seid to have mercy on Corrado since he saved their lives. Their pleas fall on deaf ears and the Turks declare that Corrado and the pirates shall die a savage death.

Act 3 Finale   A chorus of handmaidens implores Medora not to despair. Then the pirates spy Corrado's ship. They are delighted to be reunited with their leader and join the handmaidens in expressing their gratitude to Gulnara for assisting in Corrado's escape. All are dismayed that Medora has taken her

---

[19]   Sixteenth-century Spain remained devoutly Catholic and, as is repeatedly made clear throughout the opera, the real power was wielded by the Inquisition, which was very little different in profile and function from the Secret Police and intelligence forces that proliferated in the 20th century: Gestapo, KGB, FBI, etc. All have been formed in order to safeguard an orthodoxy which sooner or later has been proved to have outlived its relevance or usefulness but, while it maintains its mandate, instils terror into all who come within its orbit.

own life just at the moment she could have been reunited with her beloved. The pirates are distraught when Corrado flings himself into the sea as the curtain falls.

Chorus (*I Due Foscari*)

Act 1 The Council of Ten and the Junta are assembling in a hall in the Doge's palace. All are asserting the importance of 'Silence!' and 'Mystery!' in the conduct of Venice's affairs. (In *I Vespri Siciliano* Act 2 **Procida** exhorts the Sicilian rebels, 'In darkness and in silence let us ripen our revenge'. Such a philosophy would seem more applicable to the conspirators in a Resistance movement than to the legitimate arbitrators of justice.) Only through caution and dissembling has Venice achieved her present pre-eminence. Only through caution and dissembling will that pre-eminence be maintained. When all are assembled they agree to follow the Doge, **Francesco Foscari**, who has preceded them into the hall of the Ten.

Act 1 Scene 2 **Lucrezia's** handmaidens attempt to comfort their mistress who fears her husband, **Jacopo Foscari**, is about to be sentenced to death. Her handmaidens encourage their mistress to put her faith in the justice meted out by merciful heaven.

Act 1 Scene 3 Members of the Council of Ten and the Junta enter from an adjoining hall. The chorus is divided into two so that a dialect is developed. The Councillors decide on Jacopo's fate. He shall be exiled to Crete. He must go alone and his departure must be public. The Councillors congratulate themselves on their impartiality: 'Here the mighty Lion (of Venice) with sword and wing overtakes and smites whatever mortal should dare to defy him in word or thought'.

Act 2 Finale In the chamber of the Council of Ten the Councillors and the Junta are gathering. They are anxious to hasten Jacopo's departure. Justice must be done: 'let it flash and like a thunderbolt strike the traitor', they declare. The Doge enters and indicates that he bows to their jurisdiction with regard to his son. The Councillors welcome his reasonable attitude. Jacopo enters and attempts to persuade his father

to influence the Council to retract the sentence against him. The Councillors are immovable: 'The law cannot be cheated; here justice is all-powerful', they state. Lucrezia's entrance with her two sons does nothing to soften their attitude and finally Jacopo is escorted out by guards.

Act 3 The old Piazzetta of San Marco gradually fills with people and maskers, entering from various directions who meet, greet each other and wander about. A carnival atmosphere prevails. The people revel in the beauties of the city they inhabit and the amusements that await them. **Loredano** invites the throng to make its way to the seashore where the gondolas await. There, waving their white handkerchiefs, they cheer on the gondoliers with a barcarole. Two trumpeters emerge from the Doge's palace and sound a fanfare. The populace recognize it as signifying the 'justice of the Lion'. They withdraw and remain at a distance. There can be no clearer indication of the dread which the Council of Ten has instilled into the general populace. The people watch sadly as Jacopo is escorted out of the palace and forced to bid farewell to his wife and children. They join **Pisana** and **Barbarigo** in reflecting, 'Who can restrain his tears at such a dreadful sight?'

After Jacopo's departure the Council of Ten demands an audience with the Doge. They solemnly enter the Doge's apartments. Loredano acts as their spokesman and demands that the Doge surrenders the ducal ring. When the Doge strenuously objects all join in urging him to accede. If he does not of his own volition he will be compelled. They reassure him that he will enjoy perfect peace among his 'dear ones'. They are deaf to the obvious objection the Doge raises that they have already deprived him of the dearest person he has in the world, namely his son. But Foscari realizes he has no option but to relinquish his office. One by one he off-loads his marks of office, the ducal ring, the ducal crown and finally he is relieved of his cloak by one of the senators. When Loredano, with unrestrained glee, announces Francesco's successor other senators upbraid him: 'He is unhappy enough. Respect his grief'. They realize that the bell of St Mark which announces his successor will be for Foscari his death-knell, as indeed it is. Foscari falls dead and all declare, somewhat unnecessarily, 'He has died of grief!'

Chorus (*Ernani*)

The chorus of *Ernani* is divided between **Ernani**'s bandits, **Carlos**'s attendants, **Elvira**'s ladies-in-waiting, **de Silva**'s knights and conspirators.

Act 1 Scene 1 When the curtain rises a gang of bandits and rebels are carousing, eating and drinking, playing cards or cleaning their weapons. They sing of the joys of their existence: 'Let's gamble, since gold is vain treasure; it goes as it comes. Let's gamble, if smiling beauty doesn't make life more pleasant ... Be happy! Let's drink! Let's drink!' Ernani appears and they remark on their leader's 'pallor of countenance'. They attempt to lift his spirits with their hedonistic philosophy. When Ernani tells them of his plans to abduct the Aragonese maid, Elvira, with whom he is in love and who is about to be married to another (de Silva), they are only too happy to agree to assist him. It is part of their credo that the 'sweets of love' are the natural reward for a bandit's bravery. They make off towards de Silva's castle to effect the abduction.

Act 1 Scene 2 Elvira's ladies-in-waiting enter their mistress's apartment bearing rich wedding gifts from de Silva. 'How many maidens of Iberia will envy you', they exclaim. Elvira cannot agree and the ladies are forced to reflect as they depart that 'she may be a bride, but she is no lover, since she shows no rejoicing'.

Later in the scene when de Silva enters Elvira's apartments to discover her in the company of two strange men he is accompanied by several of his knights who listen respectfully as de Silva pours out his grief at what he imagines to be his betrayal and then swears revenge for his dishonour. 'That noble heart cannot repress his scorn', they observe. They are aghast when they realize that one of the two men is none other than their king,

Don Carlo. They are, however, grateful to note that the presence of the king appears to restore a semblance of sanity to their master, the more so when Carlo reveals that he intends to stand for election as Emperor. As the attendant's comment, 'The king's residence has brought new honour to de Silva's castle'.

Act 2 Knights, pages and ladies-in-waiting are in attendance on de Silva. They sing a chorus of rejoicing for the impending wedding: 'Let the marriage, deserving, be blissful, and if it can be happy with offspring, as the sun is reflected in the waves, give them the parents' wisdom and beauty'. The attendants can have no inkling of the utter improbability of de Silva and Elvira's union bearing fruit. Shortly after Elvira enters in bridal dress, followed by her attendants who remain at a distance. All are, surely, astonished, at the advent of Ernani in his disguise as a pilgrim, and at de Silva's magnanimity in offering him refuge. De Silva calls on his men to guard the towers of the castle then signals to Elvira to retire with her ladies. He leaves, followed by all his attendants.

Later in the scene when Carlo enters he is attended by sundry knights, some of whom he shortly instructs to search the castle. They return from their search and describe how they have searched for Ernani in vain. But they have disarmed the sentries, as is indicated by the weapons they bear. Then Elvira rushes in, followed by her attendants. When Carlo decrees that he will take Elvira hostage against de Silva surrendering Ernani, his knights reiterate to de Silva that he has no option but to obey. Elvira's attendants are all well aware what this will mean for de Silva: 'this will hasten de Silva's death more than the ravages of age', they exclaim. Carlo departs with his knights, taking Elvira, accompanied by her attendants. A little later de Silva summons his knights who come running and confirm their readiness to fight for their lord: 'Blood, blood, revenge, revenge; if de Silva's voice urges him on, each will be more bold!'

Act 3 Gentlemen of the chorus accompany Ernani and de Silva to Charlemagne's tomb at Aix-la-Chapelle as part of the league of conspirators. They are, as yet, ignorant of the purpose of the expedition. De Silva enlightens them. Carlo is apparently awaiting election to the Imperial throne. The league are of one mind that he should not achieve that august position: 'Let him first fall, like a spent torch. He crushed the rights of Iberian lands. Every arm that is here will be armed', they declare. De Silva decrees that the duty of murdering Carlo shall fall to one man only and they draw lots. Ernani's name is drawn. The conspirators then swear an oath to ensure that Iberia will be redeemed from servitude.

A cannon shot is heard, followed by two successive shots announcing Carlo's election. At this moment Carlo himself appears from the vault, followed by pages carrying velvet cushions bearing crown, sceptre and various other imperial insignia. They are surrounded by German and Spanish ladies (see **Synopsis**). Carlo immediately reveals that he is aware of the conspirators' presence and orders his guards to separate the nobility from the commoners (see **Synopsis**). However, the conspirators are fortunate that Carlo has recently resolved to rise, 'like an eagle on the pinions of virtue'. Remembering his resolution he suddenly announces pardon to the conspirators. All raise a hymn of praise to the Emperor for his extraordinary act of clemency.

Act 4 It is the occasion of Ernani's wedding to Elvira. Ladies, gentlemen, maskers, pages and serving maids come and go, talking excitedly among themselves. They sing in praise of the happy couple, then suddenly notice a masker dressed in a black cloak. It is de Silva, awaiting his moment of revenge. The guests and attendants deplore his gloomy presence and exclaim, 'Let only joy, only festivity resound here'. They leave as Elvira and Ernani enter. The stage is left to the three main protagonists for the remainder of the opera.

Chorus (*Falstaff*)

The role of the chorus in *Falstaff* is minimal. *Falstaff* is primarily an ensemble opera and barely seems to need a chorus.

Act 2 Scene 2 **Ford** is assisted in his search of his house for the interloper, whom he already knows to be **Falstaff**, by his servants, who smugly reflect that 'if he falls he'll never escape – nobody can save him'. They then break down the screen, believing that Falstaff is behind it. All are amazed to find **Fenton** and **Nannetta** revealed instead.

Act 3 Scene 2 A chorus of little girls dressed as white and blue fairies, nymphs, elves and imps take part in the tormenting of Falstaff. They form a circle around their Queen, played by Nannetta. A second circle is formed by older spirits. The gentlemen of the chorus are grouped to one side and the women to the other. (From a purely practical point of view Verdi and Boito thus ensured that the children were safely contained.)

The small fairies pick flowers and the older ones advance towards the oak tree under which Falstaff cowers. The spirits thereafter echo the exclamations of the principals as they surround the terrified knight. Finally little boys, dressed as nymphs, come running in and jump all over Falstaff. This is the cue for the entire chorus to commence a full-scale assault on him and kick him, 'from foot to topknot! Throttle him, squeeze him', etc. They roll Falstaff over and over and eventually pull him up on all fours and make him kneel. Having him thus at their mercy they continue the assault. Once Falstaff has managed to extricate himself, **Alice, Meg** and **Quickly** organize the children for the 'wedding' (supposedly of Fenton and Nannetta, but in reality of **Caius** and **Bardolfo** (see **Synopsis**). All enjoy the joke hugely and join in the final fugue which concludes the opera: 'Tutto nel mondo è burla' ('the whole world is a jest').

Chorus (*La forza del destino*).

The chorus of *La forza del destino* must variously portray peasants, pilgrims, soldiers, monks and beggars.

Act 2 Scene 1 In the great kitchen of an inn in the village of Hornachuelos peasants greet each other as the host and hostess prepare a meal and three couples dance a *seguidilla*. All sit down to eat as the hostess places a soup tureen on the table. After the 'student' (**Don Carlo**) has said grace all attention is focused on the food. The company is delighted when the gypsy, **Preziosilla,** comes skipping in. The men hope she will tell their fortunes. Preziosilla encourages them all to join the army and fight the Germans in Italy. With her spirited song the gypsy succeeds in firing up all the peasants with thoughts of what a fine, splendid thing is war. A band of pilgrims passes slowly by on their way to Holy Week celebrations. All kneel and pray to the Lord for mercy.[20] The pilgrims having passed on, the company resumes its carousing. All entertained by the 'student's' exchange with **Trabucco** who ultimately flees the foreigner's importunate questioning. They leap at the idea of painting the beardless youth with two moustaches, but the **Mayor** intervenes to scotch the idea. They listen to Carlo's story with rapt attention and reckon that 'Pereda' has displayed a generous heart in his dealings with his beleaguered friend. The Mayor decrees it time to retire and gradually the scene empties as all disperse to their beds.

Act 2 Scene 2   From within the monastery monks can be heard chanting the matinssong. Later **Guardiano** summons the monks to assemble at the High Altar. Guardiano then tells them of the 'poor soul' who seeks asylum in the monastery and orders that noone shall approach the cave where the penitent will take refuge. The monks join Guardiano in reiterating a vigorous threat of anathema against any who disobey the Superior's decree. They then join Guardiano in uttering a benediction on the new incumbent. They do not have any inkling that the penitent is a woman, and Guardiano does not intend that they ever should, this being the purpose of his edict against any monk approaching Leonora's cave.

Act 3 Scene 1   Soldiers can be heard offstage playing at cards as **Alvaro** reflects

on the misfortunes that pursue him. The voices recede during Alvaro's aria but then return as the soldiers imprecate against Carlo, to whose aid Alvaro rushes. Later the soldiers are heard calling, 'To Arms!' Clearly the enemy has been engaged.

Act 3 Scene 2   An army **Surgeon** and some orderlies are on stage. Sounds of battle can be heard offstage and the orderlies run to a window that they may report on the action. Apparently Herreros (Alvaro) is leading the forces. They describe how Herreros falls, wounded, and how the adjutant leads the Spanish to victory. Voices are heard variously calling, 'Long live Italy!' 'Glory to Spain!' and, finally, 'Victory!'

Act 3 Scene 3   A patrol arrives at the Spanish encampment near Velletri. They contemplate exploring the camp but then, realizing that dawn is about to break, move on. Later a merry chorus is heard offstage singing of the glories of the soldier's life. Preziosilla is with them. She encourages the soldiers and the womenfolk to come to her and have their fortunes told. All gather round her. She encourages all to go 'Forward, forward!' They drink to their hero Herreros and to his worthy friend, Don Felice de Bornos (Carlo).

Trabucco, the peddler, arrives with a tray full of cheap merchandise. All gather around him and inspect his wares. Trabucco announces that he buys as well as sells and the soldiers search themselves for anything sellable and present the peddler with rings, watches, necklets, etc. They haggle over the price, Trabucco is obviously delighted with the profit he makes on the transactions. The soldiers are less happy, most of them well aware that they have been swindled. They order the peddler to move on.

Peasants enter begging for bread. Their homes and fields have been devastated by war and they are starving. They are soon joined by a group of men who have just been conscripted to the army. They lament having been torn away from their mothers and loved ones. The rest of the company goodnaturedly attempts to cheer the spirits of the new recruits, while Preziosilla points out to

---

[20] Dramatically the point of this extended prayer is that it provides a nice counterpoint to **Leonora's** desperate prayer that she be spared her brother's wrath.

them that there are plenty of pretty faces amongst the women who already follow the camp. It is not long before the recruits have been persuaded into a dance by the camp followers.

The dancing is only interrupted by the arrival of **Melitone**, who vigorously upbraids them for their revelries. The soldiers alternately mock and tease the Friar. The Italians and Spanish start squabbling. The Italians want to give Melitone a good thrashing, while the Spanish come to his defence. Finally Melitone is chased away. Preziosilla shouts to the soldiers to leave him alone and when they do not heed her, she seizes hold of a drum and, imitating its sound, *Rataplan, rataplan, rataplan!* manages to catch their attention. They crowd around her and join in the riotous chorus. Preziosilla understands a simple fact about mob psychology: all it needs is a focus for its energies in order to bring it under control.

Act 4 Scene 1 A crowd of beggars of both sexes and all ages has arrived at the monastery. They have apparently already been waiting for an hour and call for charity. Eventually Melitone, assisted by a lay brother, brings in a large cauldron of soup and starts ladling it out. The beggars jostle and squabble and Melitone becomes increasingly impatient with them. The beggars have only one thought, which is to fill their bellies. The women observe that Father Rafaele was far more charitable with them. They wish he would return. Melitone is exceptionally bad tempered. Finally he chases the beggars off.

Chorus (*Un giorno di regno*). The chorus is entirely made up of the servants and vassals of Baron **Kelbar**.

Act 1 Scene 1 Servants and vassals of the Baron are celebrating the fact that they and the house of Kelbar are about to host a double wedding. They busy themselves with preparations while the Baron and the **Treasurer** converse. Then, when Delmonte announces, 'His Majesty', they utter suitably sycophantic platitudes. Later they echo the Baron's reassurances to the King that no

recompense is required: 'So welcome a visit has been its own reward'. They marvel at 'the beautiful soul concealed within (his) august person'. This is all directed at the Cavaliere **Belfiore**, who is posing as the King.

Act 1 Scene 2 A chorus of peasants and servants bring fruit and flowers and offer them to the bride-to-be, **Giulietta**, who is alone in the gardens of the castle. They wonder why Giulietta's lovely face is 'clouded with grief'. When Giulietta makes it plain she does not want to marry the old man, they express the hope that 'Heaven may free (her) of all (her) torments'. What else can they be expected to say?

Act 1 Scene 3 The servants come running when the Treasurer shouts for assistance as the Baron lays about him. They must then concentrate their attention on attempting to restrain their apoplectic master. They are, in company with everybody else present, considerably abashed by the sudden advent of the 'King' in the midst of the fracas. By the end of the Act, however, they join all the principals in expressing confidence in the royal 'judgement' which will surely 'bring back the previous harmony ... and the previous friendships'.

Act 2 Scene 1 The Baron's servants are in a high state of dudgeon because they have just learnt that one of the two weddings is not to take place. They reflect vociferously on the capriciousness of the aristocracy: 'they change their moods as easily as they change their clothes'. They, on the other hand, are perfectly happy and content in spite of their lowly station in life (for a brief moment one wonders if the opera has a revolutionary agenda beneath the frippery. But the suspicion is quickly subsumed in the machinations of the plot as it blunders forward). **Edoardo** addresses the servants as, 'My good friends' and one has the impression that the young man has often had recourse to the servants' quarters for amusement to escape the starched rectitude of life above stairs. When Edoardo complains how cruelly fate has treated him the servants point out that the world has always been like that: 'Money, not virtue, has the power to buy love'. They are delighted, however, to learn that Edoardo has found true love.

Act 2 Scene 2   The servants are on hand to welcome the arrival of Count **Ivrea** who is supposedly to marry the **Marchioness**. They can hardly be surprised that that marriage also falls by the wayside and are delighted to bless the union of Edoardo and Giulietta, whom they know to be a well-matched couple. When the 'King' reveals that he is not the King at all but the Cavaliere Belfiore they are dumbfounded. But they soon pull themselves together and join the rest of the Company in expressing the hope that all may be 'good friends and forget the past'.

Chorus (*Giovanna d'Arco*)

The chorus in *Giovanna d'Arco* is divided between French officers and villagers, English soldiers and choruses of demons and angels.

Prologue Scene 1   Officers and villagers of Domrémy lament the defeat they have suffered at the hands of the English. They are dismayed at their King's despair and acknowledgement of defeat. Their dismay is intensified when **Carlo** first gives instructions that his troops defending Orleans should lay down their weapons and then absolves his people from their oath of allegiance, declaring; 'Let the English king sit upon my ancestral throne'. When Carlo regales his people with the dream he has had of a painted statue of the Virgin beneath an oak tree, some of the villagers immediately recall that there is such a painted statue in a similar place to that Carlo describes. But they are disturbed by the fact that they know it as a place of evil. 'When the plaintive bells greet the dying day, and the star of love, the moon, slowly sails through the silent air, in the horrible forest the storm ever rages; amid the horror of thunder and lightning there the demons assemble, there with wizards and witches, they make pacts and covens, and with poisonous potions assuage sins', they observe. Carlo, however, will not be dissuaded from his intention of visiting the shrine. In spite of their misgivings the people declare

that, 'ever loyal and silent we will follow our king'.

Scene 2   **Giovanna** is assailed, first by a chorus of demons then a chorus of angels. The demons tell her she is a beautiful girl who should be devoting herself to love and surrendering her chastity to 'delirious youth', that is, to Carlo, who longs for her. The angels, meanwhile, exhort her to be the 'Lord's herald', and thereby ensure the liberation of her homeland.

Act 1 Scene 1   English soldiers outside Reims bewail their defeat at the hands of the French, led by the mysterious girl (Giovanna). Their only thought now is to return to their homeland. They remind their commander, **Talbot**, that they have always thrown themselves into battle with a bold heart but, 'against the fury that Hell unleashes what avails intrepid valour in war?' Their courage is reawakened by the advent in their midst of **Giacomo**, Giovanna's father, with his offer of delivering his daughter to the English. For Giacomo believes, like the English soldiers, that Giovanna is in league with devil. The soldiers encourage Giacomo to make all haste in turning Giovanna over to them.

Act 1 Scene 2   Angel's voices are heard chiding Giovanna, who has just declared her love for Carlo, for having succumbed to the allure of worldly love. Shortly after the victorious French army greet their king and Giovanna. They notice that Giovanna is disturbed but can elicit no explanation. A chorus of demons assails Giovanna. The demons rejoice for they sense that Giovanna is on the verge of giving herself to them by acceding to the allure of world pomp and carnal love.

Act 2   The people of Reims are crowded in the square before the cathedral of Saint Dionysius. They are preparing for the triumphal arrival of Giovanna and sing in praise of their 'wondrous maid'. The crowd is then divided by soldiers who form up in two ranks. After the chorus the band leads the way to the accompaniment of intermittent cheering. Then follow girls, clad in white and carrying branches, heralds and halberdiers. Next come pages, robed magistrates, marshals bearing batons, nobles with swords, sceptres, orbs, coronets, cloaks and judges' staffs. Delegates and girls strew flowers, the king is borne beneath a canopy by six barons. Courtiers, servants and troops bring up the rear. The entire procession enters the cathedral.

A hymn is heard from within the cathedral giving thanks for France's good fortune. At Carlo's behest the people applaud Giovanna as their king kneels before the maid. Their joy turns to horror as Giacomo roundly denounces Giovanna and accuses her of having made a pact with the devil. They cannot fail to notice that Giacomo's accusation appears to be corroborated by Giovanna's demeanour as Carlo tries to persuade her to defend herself. When a sudden storm breaks out the people are finally convinced that the girl they have but recently been hailing as their saviour is indeed guilty of devil-worship. Such is the fickleness of crowds. Giovanna does nothing to convince them otherwise, merely bursting into tears and throwing herself into her father's arms. Now the people enjoin Giovanna to flee and take her evil arts to the English. 'What will history say of us? ... Who will restore our glory to us?' they wail, forgetting that had it not been for Giovanna they would have by now been in the hands of the English.

Act 3   From within the English encampment a chorus of English sentries is heard (offstage) announcing the incursion of the French. A chorus of French soldiers is heard claiming that the English stronghold has been captured.

In the final moments of the opera, Giovanna is borne in on a stretcher. The French people liken her to an angel: 'On her innocent face a shining aureole falls from Heavene', they declare. As Giovanna dies they perceive a halo of white light surrounding her and proclaim that she will 'live on in the heart of every Frenchman'. The opera concludes with the chorus of angels welcoming Giovanna while the chorus of demons bewail their failure to take possession of the maid's soul.

Chorus (*Jerusalem*)

Act 1   Knights and their ladies congregate in the gallery of the **Count of Toulouse's** palace in order to celebrate the conclusion of civil war (occasioned by the strife between the Count and **Gaston**, Viscount of Béarn). They are delighted that an accord has been reached between the two men; an accord symbolized by the fact that the Count has given his blessing to his daughter, **Hélène's** marriage to Gaston.

When the **Papal Legate** announces that the Count has been appointed by the Pope to lead the French Crusaders to the Holy Land, all invoke God's assistance with their enterprise and think with joy of the moment when they will take possession of Jerusalem. All adjourn to the chapel, there to raise their hymns, and incidentally leaving the stage clear for **Roger**.

All are inevitably appalled by the Count's (apparent) murder and have no doubt that Gaston is the guilty party: nobody has been convinced by the latter's desire for a reconciliation with the Count. They join in confirming the Papal Legate's execration of the murderer.

Act 2 Scene 1   A group of pilgrims is dying of thirst in the mountains of Ramla in Palestine. They are rescued by the hermit (Roger). Their entrance is quickly followed by the arrival of the Crusaders, led by the Count, to obtain the hermit's blessing. When the hermit declares his intention of joining them in battle all unite in asserting their confidence in a victorious outcome.

Act 2 Scene 2   The Crusaders are heard, from within the **Emir's** palace where Gaston and Hélène are imprisoned, summoning their compatriots to arms as the sacking of Ramla proceeds.

Act 3 Scene 1   The Crusaders burst into the Emir's harem which is the last bastion of resistance in the town of Ramla. Catching sight of Gaston they all join the Count in determining that the murderer shall be put to death.

Act 3 Scene 2   Gaston is on his way to his execution. A chorus of penitents laments Gaston's suffering and pleads for mercy on his behalf.

Act 4 Scene 1   The Crusaders are preparing in eager anticipation for their final assault on the city of Jerusalem. They make off in the direction of the Holy City.

Act 4 Scene 2. The Crusaders congregate in the Count's tent and sing to the glory of God who has assisted them in conquering Jerusalem and ensured that justice prevails.

Chorus (*I Lombardi alla prima Crociata*)
The chorus plays an extraordinary part in the unfolding of *I Lombardi*.

Act 1 Scene 1   The chorus is divided three ways between the citizens of Milan (by far the greater part), a chorus of nuns and a chorus of cut-throats.

The citizens of Milan witness the public pardoning of **Pagano**, son of Lord Folco, who sometime in the past has attempted to murder his brother, **Arvino**. The citizens welcome the reconciliation between the two brothers, but share concern with all the main protagonists as to whether Pagano is truly contrite. At the outset of the scene they recapitulate, for the benefit of each other and the audience, the events that led to Pagano's disgrace and exile. They all agree that 'in his terrible and hollow eyes still appears the fierce tempest of his soul; though possible, it is rare indeed for a wolf's fury to change to the peaceful spirit of a lamb'.

The chorus of nuns is heard praying offstage for the peace of mankind. The principal dramatic purpose is to provide a stark contrast with the vengeful thoughts that Pagano is at that very moment entertaining. Pagano comments, 'Virgins, heaven now is closed against your prayers'.

The chorus of cut-throats is comprised of the free-lance ruffians that **Pirro** has assembled in order to assist with Pagano's intended revenge on his brother.

Act 1 Scene 2   The chorus is comprised of Arvino's guards and soldiers who arrest Pagano after he has murdered his father and proceed to excoriate him.

Act 2 Scene 1   The chorus appears as ambassadors, soldiers and people reporting to the tyrant, **Acciano**, who apprises them of the imminent ingress of the Crusaders. All swear to ensure that Allah shall triumph over the infidels.

Act 2 Scene 2   The Crusaders have arrived at a plain outside the city of Antioch. Arvino, their leader, has consulted a local hermit (Pagano) who inspires the Crusaders with hope for the successful prosecution of their campaign. They join the hermit in pouring derision on 'ridiculous Allah!'

Act 2 Scene 3   The women of the chorus play the odalisques in Acciano's harem, while the men play Crusaders. The scene is the enclosure of the harem. The odalisques' attention is entirely focused on **Giselda** who has recently arrived in the harem. They are envious of Giselda who is loved by Acciano's son, **Oronte**. The odalisques taunt Giselda mercilessly. They all hurry off but come face to face with the Crusaders who have breached the castle's defences and have slain their master, Acciano. 'Who will save us from the barbarians' wrath if the Prophet has abandoned his faithful?' they cry. The Crusaders enter with Arvino. They will be amazed by Giselda's pacifist outburst and must restrain Arvino from making an attack on his daughter's life.

Act 3 Scene 1   In the valley of Jehoshaphat, near Jerusalem, crusading knights, women and children exult in the proximity of the Holy City and remember the details of Christ's Passion as they view the scene. They pass on, leaving the stage free for Oronte and Giselda. Later cries are heard from the Crusaders: 'To arms! To arms!'

Act 3 Scene 2   Crusading knights inform Arvino that his brother, Pagano, has been seen prowling around the camp. All are incensed at the thought of the parricide in their midst and determine to ensure they exact vengeance on him.

Act 4 Scene 1   A chorus of celestial spirits sing comforting words to Giselda who is asleep.

Act 4 Scene 2   The Crusaders and Pilgrims sing, *O Signore, dal tetto natio* and pray for the success of their endeavours, thinking longingly of their beloved homeland. They greet with joy the news that the fountain of Siloam is gushing forth water for they are parched with thirst. Arvino tells them to slake their thirsts and then sally forth into battle, for 'today the Holy Land shall be ours!' All anticipate victory.

Act 4 Scene 3   From outside Arvino's tent can be heard the Crusaders' shouts of 'Victory!' indicating they have taken possession of Jerusalem. The opera finishes with a rousing chorus with everyone affirming their faith in the invincible Lord.

Chorus (*Luisa Miller*)

The chorus in *Luisa Miller* is principally occupied playing villagers in the (peasant) village where **Luisa** Miller grew up in the shadow of Count **Walter**'s castle. They also double up as attendants and servants in Walter's castle.

When the curtain rises the villagers are on stage with **Laura**, Luisa's best friend. They call to Luisa to awake on the morning of her birthday for which they have gathered to celebrate (*Ti desta, Luisa, regina de' cori*). They present Luisa with posies of flowers as 'a simple pledge' of their friendship. This scene radiates pastoral simplicity. When **Rodolfo** arrives the villagers realize that Luisa's happiness is complete. 'never was seen a love more ardent and true', they observe. Then the church bells summon them and all gradually enter the church, singing as they go.

Act 1 Scene 2   The Duchess **Federica** enters with her suite of ladies-in-waiting, pages, servants and archers. The attendants pour lavish praise on Federica: 'Beauty in you is without arrogance, greatness in you is without pomp. The shy, secluded star is destined to shine radiantly'. As soon as Walter has greeted his niece the ladies-in-waiting and the rest of the attendants withdraw.

Act 1 Scene 3   A hunt is in progress. The voices of the hunters are heard in the distance as they pursue their prey. As the act reaches its climax a crowd of archers and villagers enters **Miller**'s house, just as Miller is vehemently defending his dignity. The archer's leap to their lord's defence whilst the villagers, with Laura, can only stand by and watch, dumbfounded, as Rodolfo reveals that he is Walter's son. All are concerned for Luisa as Walter shamelessly insults the girl. The villagers are astounded when Walter suddenly relents and releases Luisa, being ignorant of

the true nature of the threat with which Rodolfo blackmails his father.

Act 2 Scene 1   The villagers arrive at Luisa's house in a high state of agitation, for they have important news for her. They have witnessed her father's arrest, which they describe in vivid detail. When **Wurm** enters they all bridle. It is clear that Wurm is universally detested. Wurm orders all the villagers out, and they depart with some reluctance at leaving Luisa alone with him.

Act 2 Scene 3   Wurm, thinking himself about to die at Rodolfo's hands, fires his pistol in the air. Soldiers and servants come rushing in. They immediately notice that Rodolfo's eyes 'glitter horribly with anger'. They stand by and observe the hysterical exchange that once again takes place between Walter and his son as Act 2 draws to a conclusion.

Act 3   Luisa's friends, Laura and other villagers watch sadly as Luisa writes what is, unbeknown to them, a final letter of farewell to Rodolfo who, believing Luisa unfaithful, is to be married to Federica. The villagers plead with Luisa to 'Yield, yield to our friendship' but to no avail. Luisa's mind is made up. She asks them why the church is so brightly lit. The villagers tactfully refuse to tell her the truth, which is that the wedding of Rodolfo and Federica is imminent. The villagers leave with Laura when Luisa's father enters. As the opera draws to its tragic conclusion the villagers become aware of calamity in Miller's house and re-enter to find Rodolfo and Luisa both dying. Rodolfo's last act is to kill Wurm, a death which the villagers will not mourn. But they certainly will mourn the death of Luisa, whose birthday they were so happily celebrating at the opening of the opera.

Chorus (*Macbeth*)

The chorus in *Macbeth* must divide itself between witches, messengers, cut-throats, Thanes, ladies, refugees and soldiers. The opera opens with the three witches on stage.[21]

---

[21] 'The main roles of the opera are, and can only be, three: Macbeth, Lady Macbeth and the Chorus of Witches. (The Witches) make up a real character, and one of the greatest importance'. Verdi to Piave (1846)

In Shakespeare's play these are taken by three individual actors. Verdi divides the ladies of the chorus into three groups.

When the opera opens the second and third groups are meeting up with the third witches and reporting on their exploits. They are interrupted by the sound of a drum announcing the approach of **Macbeth** and **Banquo**. In turn they hail Macbeth: 'Thane of Glamis, Thane of Cawdor and King of Scotland'. They then turn their attention to Banquo: 'Lesser than Macbeth and greater. Not happy as he but happier than he. Though you be none, you shall father kings'.

A small chorus of messengers arrives with the news that Macbeth has just been created Thane of Cawdor, thus corroborating the second part of the witches' prophecy. The messengers are surprised by Macbeth's apparent indifference to the news, not having been witness to the witches' prophecy. When all have departed the witches again materialize and, according to the stage directions, 'circle in the air'. They declare they will await the fulfilment of the fates at the witches' Sabbath when they are confident Macbeth will return to them. This is fulfilled in Act 3 Scene 1.

Act 1 Scene 2   The inmates in Macbeth's castle are all awakened by **Macduff**'s frantic cries of 'Murder! and Treason!' The chorus includes Thanes, ladies and servants. When Banquo announces that their king has been murdered all are horrified: 'Open wide thy maw, oh Hell, and swallow all creation in thy womb; upon the unknown loathed murderer let thy consuming fire fall, oh heaven!' At this juncture they have no inkling that the murderer is none other than their host. They call on God to enlighten them: 'Great God, Almighty God, we trust in Thee!' For an opera – and of course play – where the occult influences predominate it is notable how frequently the protagonists turn to God for solace and enlightenment. From the time the witches utter their prophecies in Act 1 Scene 1 until **Malcolm** kills Macbeth in Act 4 nobody's life, from the highest noble to the lowliest servant, is entirely secure.

Act 2 Scene 2   A chorus of cut-throats is meeting to carry out its latest commission. They seem unperturbed by the fact that it is the King who commissions them and that it is one of the greatest nobles of the land they are required to slay. As is the way with any successful businessman they care not who commissions them, or whom they are required to victimize, so long as they are paid. The cut-throats clearly relish their vocation. They disappear among the trees to await their quarry. Once Banquo has been murdered one of the cut-throats is seen crossing the stage in hot pursuit of the escaping **Fleance**.

Act 2 Scene 3   All the greatest in the land are gathered at Macbeth's castle to celebrate his coronation with a massive banquet. They hail their king and settle down to enjoy themselves (incidentally expressing similar sentiments to those expressed by Violetta's guests in *La Traviata*): 'Let's drive away dull care from our breasts; let pleasure be born and melancholy die'. The cut-throats appear at one side of the stage to report to Macbeth the success of their commission, but the guests will be oblivious. However, they cannot fail to notice when Macbeth starts shouting at the ghost of Banquo. None of them can see the ghost and must assume that Macbeth is raving. **Lady Macbeth** attempts to distract them with a drinking song, but she is soon interrupted by Macbeth again ranting, apparently at the vacant air. Since Macbeth virtually admits his guilt when he demands, 'Can the tomb disgorge the murdered?' it is not surprising that the guests are considerably disquieted and reflect: 'A den of cut-throat ruffians this land has become', especially in view of the recent murder of Duncan.

Act 3   In their cave the witches are gathered round a boiling cauldron into which they are throwing a variety of choice ingredients: a poisonous toad, a tongue of viper, a finger of an infant strangled at birth, the heart of a heretic, etc. They dance around the cauldron, chanting as they go. A ballet ensues which one assumes will only employ the ladies of the chorus on the periphery. Macbeth arrives and enquires what the 'hags' are about. 'A deed without a name', they reply, which seems a fairly accurate description for their preoccupations. Macbeth has come to enquire after his fate. The witches summon various spirits to answer his queries and counsel him how best to question the apparitions. When Macbeth faints, after the vision of eight kings emanating from Banquo's succession, the witches summon spirits of the air to restore the King to consciousness. By the time Macbeth has regained consciousness they have vanished.

Act 4 Scene 1   There is often to be found in Verdi's operas a chorus of refugees (see *Attila* Chorus). This is partly an inevitability in operas which deal in patriotic wars, but what is noticeable is that Verdi often lavished on these unfortunate victims of circumstance some of his most beautiful music. Such an instance is the *Patria oppressa!* which opens Act 4. 'No one sheds a useless tear for those who suffer and those who die. Oppressed country! Down-trodden country! My country! Oh, my homeland!'

The advent of Malcolm and his army brings the refugees new hope and courage. Malcolm marshals them each to hew down a bough from Birnam forest with which to camouflage themselves as they advance to reclaim their homeland. They agree with Malcolm and Macduff that (Macbeth's) 'horrible crimes have wearied the Everlasting'.

Act 4 Scene 3   Macbeth's sad ruminations are interrupted by women's voices offstage announcing Lady Macbeth's death. Then soldiers rush in with the news that 'Birnam Wood is on the move'. This is, for Macbeth, a death-knell since he has always believed, according to the **Apparition**'s prophecy, that he would prevail until Birnam Wood uprooted itself and moved. He has naturally been comforted by the thought that this is an impossibility. However, he does not quail but calls for his sword and arms and summons his soldiers to arm themselves. 'Death...!' he declares (the soldiers presumably conclude he refers to the death of the enemy, though it is certain he acknowledges his own impending demise), 'or Victory!' the soldiers and Macbeth conclude.

Act 4 Scene 4   Malcolm is summoning his soldiers to arms. Battle is engaged and soon Malcolm's soldiers are heard calling 'Victory!' quickly echoed by the women among the refugees. Soon the stage is crowded with the triumphal soldiers and refugees calling for Macbeth. Macduff indicates the tyrant's corpse and all celebrate their liberation, and hail Malcolm as their King.

Chorus (*I Masnadieri*)

It is not often that the chorus gives the title to an opera. But this is the case in *I Masnadieri*. Having said which their role, as robbers, is relatively small.

Act 1 Scene 1   While **Carlo** is absorbed in his volume of Plutarch his friends can be heard from within the tavern proclaiming, 'With dagger and wine cup none can match the bandit!'

Several young men enter with a letter addressed to Carlo. It is from his brother warning Carlo not to return home, for if he does all that will greet him will be a solitary dungeon and a diet of bread and water. Carlo's friends realize that this is their opportunity to persuade Carlo to be their captain. As they anticipated they have no problem persuading him. They all rush out to commence their new life as a professional band of outlaws.

Act 2 Scene 1   **Amalia** is kneeling at the tomb of **Massimiliano**. From the castle can be heard a chorus of revellers expounding a hedonistic philosophy (worthy of *La Traviata*). They are not interested in mourning the (apparently) deceased Massimiliano, 'Let black hues not disturb the party', they say. They justify themselves with the philosophy, 'Future fate is the terror of the feeble... Let us rejoice, for fleeting are the hours of laughter: let pleasure guide us from wine cups to kisses'. Massimiliano's court is taking its cue from the evil **Francesco**, who imagines he has finally rid himself of both father and brother. The philosophy it expounds would sound equally fitting coming from the lips of Carlo's brigands.

Act 2 Scene 2   In the Bohemian woods. Bandits enter. Some are complaining that they have been idle all day (*Tutto quest'oggi le mani in mano*). Others relay the news that **Rolla** has been captured. Their captain (Carlo) has vowed to 'make a bonfire' of Prague in revenge. At that moment flames can be seen in the distance; 'the Captain kept his word', the bandits declare. Cries are heard in the distance and dishevelled women and children emerge from the trees. They are fleeing from the torched city. 'The end of the world has come', they cry before making off through the wood. (Note: All through his career Verdi showed a deep compassion for the plight of exiles and casualties of war. See also **Attila, Macbeth, Nabucco, Aida**, etc.) This little vignette powerfully undermines any tendency to glorify the bandits' exploits.

The bandits are amazed to find Rolla still alive. He collapses and they ply him with brandy. Since he is too exhausted to relate what has transpired he calls on the bandits who escaped with him to fill in the others with what has happened. They duly describe how they torched the city, the panic that ensued and how Carlo rescued Rolla from the hangman's noose. The other bandits congratulate them on their victory 'for might and ingenuity'. Carlo enters and tells the bandits that they will be leaving at dawn. Since Carlo is looking downcast and distressed the bandits think it best to leave him to himself and make off into the woods.

Later in the scene the bandits rush in to tell Carlo that they are apparently surrounded by a thousand soldiers. Carlo exhorts them to take courage and all join together in proclaiming their determination to put the army to rout.

Act 3 Scene 1 Amalia is wandering alone in the forest and hears the chorus of bandits singing in the distance: 'Pillage, rape, arson, killing, for us are pastimes, sheer amusement'. (See also *Attila* Scene 1 where the barbarians expound a similar philosophy.)

Act 3 Scene 2 opens with the bandits reiterating these sentiments as they stretch out on the ground, relaxing after their recent exertions (*Le rube, gli stupri, gl'incendi, le morti...*). 'We lead a life of freedom', they declare. 'Mercury is our patron and the moon our sun'. They do not allow themselves to succumb to the disabling emotion of compassion, and maintain that they have no fear of the moment when the hangman's noose finally catches up with them. Their philosophy is purely anarchic and is in striking contrast to the torturous obsession with honour that characterizes most of Verdi's chief protagonists, including Carlo himself. The real interest in *I Masnadieri* lies in the fact that it is abundantly clear throughout that Carlo himself does not share the philosophy of the men he leads.

Carlo enters and the bandits rise to greet him. Carlo tells them to sleep while he keeps watch. The bandits lie down and sleep. They are woken by Carlo firing a shot from his pistol and shouting, 'Wake up you lumps of stone!' They all rise groggily to their feet and are amazed when Carlo points out Massimiliano and declares that he is his father. Carlo calls for revenge. The bandits swear to do his bidding, namely to bring Francesco alive to him. 'Heaven's destroying wrath, today we are your sword!' they shout as they rush out.

Act 4 Scene 1 Some servants come running in with **Arminio**, whom Francesco has summoned. They leave to fetch a priest at Francesco's bidding.

Later voices and cries are heard offstage announcing that the bastion has been reduced to dust. Carlo's bandits have assailed Massimiliano's castle.

Act 4 Scene 2 Several bandits enter and come slowly towards Carlo with lowered heads. They bring the news that Francesco has evaded them. Then other bandits arrive dragging in Amalia. They are congratulating themselves on having obtained a 'splendid prize' but are nonplussed by Carlo's violent reaction. He shouts to the bandits to 'tear her from my neck! Kill that old man! Kill her too, kill me, kill all of you'. Carlo then turns to his father and Amalia and declares that he is the chief of those 'robbers and murderers'. This admission is in direct contravention of his oath of solidarity and confidentiality with the bandits. Stunned and outraged they come forward and accuse

Carlo of perjury. They bare their chests and pointing out their wounds to Carlo state: 'These wounds made you ours; look, traitor! We have them because of you'. They are appalled at Carlo's final hysterical act of stabbing Amalia and mortally wounding her. As the curtain falls the bandits surround Amalia, calling after Carlo, who rushes off shouting, 'To the gallows!'

Chorus (*Nabucco*)

Nabucco is second only to *Aida* in being primarily a chorus opera. It could be said that it is more about the destiny of an entire people than about any one individual.

Act 1 ('Jerusalem') Hebrews, Levites and Hebrew virgins bewail the fact that they have been defeated by **Nabucco**. The 'horrible howlings of barbarian legions' threaten their Holy Temple. The Levites invite the maidens to 'rend' their white veils, raise their arms in supplication and pray that the fury of the savage enemy may be rendered as naught. The virgins dutifully oblige. All beg the Lord to prevent the 'Assyrian foe' from sitting 'amongst his false idols upon the throne of David'.

Their distress is considerably alleviated when **Zaccaria** enters with **Fenena**, Nabucco's daughter, who has been captured and is being held as hostage. This gives them renewed hope and enables them to receive the news of Nabucco's advance with a degree of equanimity. They join with Zaccaria in affirming that the 'false god of Bel' shall be vanquished, 'as night before the shining sun, as dust before the wind'. They depart leaving Fenena in the charge of **Ismaele**.

Later **Abigaille** arrives with a band of Babylonian soldiers disguised as Hebrews. The soldiers remain mute while Abigaille, Fenena and Ismaele wrangle. But then Nabucco approaches and the temple starts to fill with Hebrews and Levites, all in a high state of alarm. They have been powerless to stem the advance of the Babylonians: 'Calamity! Who will now defend the temple of the Lord?' they wail. Voices of Babylonians are heard from outside the temple, hailing their King.

Soon Babylonians are flooding into the temple followed by Nabucco himself on horseback. This in itself is an unheard-of blasphemy. The Hebrews are overwhelmed by a sense of their own impotence and can only pray to God for help. The Babylonian soldiers again remain mute, leaving it to their King to confirm their ascendancy. When Ismaele prevents Zaccaria from sacrificing Fenena the Hebrews are appalled by his apparent treachery. They join Zaccaria in pronouncing anathema on him.

Act 2 ('The Wicked Man'). Scene 1 Babylonian soothsayers and nobles of the realm accompany the **High Priest of Baal** into Abigaille's presence in the royal apartments of Nabucco's palace in Babylon. They tell Abigaille how they have spread the rumour that Nabucco is dead, having fallen in battle. They describe how the people clamour for Abigaille to take the throne. They are delighted by Abigaille's acquiescence, which they must have anticipated, and reassure her that 'the vengeance of Bel will thunder alongside yours!'

Scene 2 Levites assemble outside Fenena's apartments which Zaccaria has just entered in order to initiate Fenena into the Hebrew faith. The Levites are, however, ignorant as to why they have been summoned. Ismaele enters and tells them Zaccaria requires their presence within, but the Levites recoil in horror at the sight of the traitor. They refuse to countenance Ismaele's pleas for mercy. They firmly believe him to be 'accursed of the Lord'. He therefore 'has no brethren and no man on earth will vouchsafe him a single word!' They are interrupted in their fulminations by the arrival of Zaccaria's sister, **Anna**, who implores the Levites to exercise forgiveness since Ismaele has, in fact, rescued a Hebrew girl. Fenena is now converted to their faith.

The Levites have no chance to respond since news arrives that Nabucco is 'dead' and the people are calling for Abigaille. Fenena is about to rush off, to everyone's consternation, but is waylaid by the arrival of Abigaille, and shortly after by Nabucco, who is still very much alive. When Nabucco declares, 'There is only one God ... your King!', that is, himself, the Hebrews are appalled at his blasphemy. They are then clearly gratified when Nabucco is struck down: 'See how avenging heaven has struck the presumptuous man!' they declare.

Act 3 ('The Prophecy') Nobles, sooth-sayers, people and soldiers sing smugly of the peace that now prevails in Assyria. Nabucco enters and all withdraw. When Nabucco learns that he has effectively con-demned his own daughter to execution he frantically calls for guards. Several present themselves, but Abigaille points out that they are in fact guarding him as a prisoner.

Act 3 Scene 2   The Hebrews, in chains, are sentenced to forced labour on the banks of the Euphrates and sing wistfully of their beloved homeland to which they seem to have little hope of returning (*Va, pensiero*). Zaccaria exhorts them once again to take courage for he is certain he can discern a day when their chains will be broken: 'The wrath of the Lion of Judah falls already upon the treacherous sand!' The Hebrews are inspired by his prophetic words and feel within themselves renewed courage.

Act 4 ('The Broken Idol')   Voices call for Fenena, arousing Nabucco from his stupor and alerting him to the fact that his beloved daughter is on her way to her execution. His cries for help bring Abdallo, accompanied by those Babylonian soldiers who have remained loyal to Nabucco. They all confirm that 'The traitors shall fall like locusts to the ground!' They make off with their King to save Fenena.

Act 4 Scene 2   Fenena is about to be sacrificed when voices off are heard calling, 'Long live Nabucco!' Nabucco arrives with his soldiers just in time to put a stop to the execution. All are astounded when the image of Bel falls of its own accord and smashes. When Nabucco confirms that the Jewish God 'alone is great; mighty is he alone!' all are overwhelmed and fall to their knees in praise of Jehovah, who finally has prevailed.

Chorus (*Oberto*)

Act 1 Scene 1   A chorus of knights, ladies and vassals joyfully greet the arrival of Riccardo, Count of Salinguerra at the castle of Bassano. Riccardo is to be married to Cuniza, sister to the despot Ezzelino da Romano. Ezzelino does not appear in the opera but has blessed the union of his sister to Salinguerra for the latter have always been useful allies. Such a union can only strengthen his own position and hopefully lead to the establishment of an enduring peace. It is these hopes that the lords and ladies celebrate. 'Come Riccardo! Be our tutelary genius; you can still spread happiness in this region; the whirlwinds of war rage through the cities of Italy; peace will smile on the happy marriage', they sing. Riccardo's confident bearing rein-forces their optimism for the future of the marriage, and the possibility of the peace it represents.

Act 1 Scene 2   Within a magnificent hall in Ezzelino's palace some knights and ladies sing in extravagant praise of the bride, Cuniza: 'Fortunate bride, come to us with your true love! You resemble the dawn which tints the sky with rose, adorns and brightens it. Your heart is as pure as the snowflakes on the shoulders of the Euganian hills', etc. The chorus exits as Riccardo enters.

In the interim between this scene and when the chorus reappears Oberto has made himself known to Cuniza and revealed that Riccardo was already betrothed to his daughter, Leonora. Cuniza has magnani-mously agreed to relinquish her love for Riccardo and compel the latter to behave honourably towards his first love. The knights and ladies arrive just as Cuniza forces Riccardo to confront Leonora. All comment on how the poor girl's face is 'tortured with grief'. When Oberto reveals himself all are aghast, for Oberto is known as the sworn enemy of Ezzelino and of the Salinguerra. The knights and ladies realize that this could indicate the resurgence of bitter animosity and the possibility of renewed warfare. They pray for a peaceful outcome.

Act 2 Scene 1   A chorus of ladies-in-waiting is attending Cuniza and commiser-ating with her. When Cuniza resolves to lead Riccardo to Leonora and obey the voice of 'shining rectitude' the ladies affirm that 'the traitor did not deserve so great and dear a person!'.

Act 2 Scene 2 A chorus of knights laments the events of the day and prays that the betrayed girl, 'deprived of hope', may be consoled, for 'misfortune and virtue are companions in this life'. They are heard offstage, calling on Oberto. They then arrive on stage and reassure the old man that he need have no fear of Ezzelino since Cuniza has saved Oberto and now requests that he attends her. Oberto is not interested in being saved.

It is often cited as a central weakness of the libretto of *Oberto* that the denouement (the fight between Oberto and Riccardo) occurs offstage and is merely reported by the chorus of knights. In fact the chorus does not even report the fight, but rather gives vent to general moralizing – as is frequently the case in Solera's libretti: 'And from the Cross God spoke only of peace! Deaf to that voice, man has delighted in blood. Alas, misfortune! And both are the glory of a region! Peace henceforth! Fraternal strife is cursed by the Lord!' Their ruminations are interrupted by sounds of clashing steel, indicating a duel in progress. They rush off in the direction of the sounds.

They return to report to Cuniza that they have found Oberto's corpse, bathed in blood. As Leonora enters all lament the misfortune that has overwhelmed her and, taking the lead from Cuniza, attempt to console the 'poor girl'. They reassure her that she is 'in the bosom of friendship'. A messenger enters with a note from Riccardo announcing his flight into exile and requesting pardon. Leonora is inconsolable. As the curtain falls the chorus prays: 'May her laments move heaven to pity!'

Chorus (*Otello*)

At the opening of the opera the entire chorus is on stage in the role of Cypriots (Act 1). A storm is in progress and the people have all rushed to the harbour since the ship bearing the Venetian general, **Otello**, who has recently won a great victory over the Turkish fleet, is expected any time. Undoubtedly many of the citizens have relatives and loved ones aboard the ship as well. They give a vivid portrait of the storm in progress: 'Lightning! Thunder! Whirlpools! Tempestuous storms and thunderbolts! The waves quake, the winds quake, the depths and the heights quake! A grim and blind spirit, dizzily plunging, cleaves the air. God shakes the wild heaven, dark as a pall. All is smoke! All is fire! The horrid darkness becomes a conflagration, then dies out more baleful still'. As the storm increases the women become increasingly agitated and pray to God to protect the ship that even now attempts to cast anchor in the harbour.

Suddenly it becomes clear that the ship is safe and the Cypriots raise a great shout of joy. Voices offstage are heard calling, 'Lower the boats! All hands to the ropes!' All join in helping to pull the ship ashore and those on board disembark safely. When Otello appears, his sudden apparition out of the midst of the tempest and announcement of victory has something almost Messianic about it. The Cypriots erupt in praise of their leader. As they cry, 'Long live Otello! Hurrah! Hurrah!' Otello enters the castle, accompanied by soldiers.

The Cypriots relish the thought of the Turks being defeated. 'Dispersed, destroyed, engulfed, buried in the terrible depths!' they roar. The storm subsides and some of the Cypriots begin to build a fire while the rest crowd around, 'turbulent and curious'. As the fire blazes they break into song (*Fuoco di gioia*) (this celebration of fire represents a stark contrast to the watery storm that has preceded this scene). Meanwhile tavern workers hang coloured lanterns on the branches of the arbour. Soldiers crowd round the inn tables, chatting and drinking. The whole scene is one of festivity and celebration. The fire dies down. **Iago** proposes a toast to Otello and **Desdemona** which is greeted by thunderous 'Hurrahs!' from the Cypriots.

During the colloquy which now develops between Iago, **Cassio** and **Roderigo** the Cypriots initially remain aloof. However they all join in the chorus of Iago's drinking song and are hugely amused as Carlo becomes increasingly drunk. When the scene turns ugly and Cassio and Roderigo start brawling and swords are drawn the people become restless, the women seeking to flee while the men attempt to arbitrate. Their passions are quickly ignited by the Machiavellian Iago and a riot is all set to develop when Otello appears. Furiously he upbraids the combatants. The people soon disperse to their homes.

Act 2. A chorus of women and children, together with Albanian and Cypriot sailors, sing in praise of Desdemona as they bring flowers and gifts to her. Their affection for her is so obvious and their good wishes so heartfelt it makes all the more monstrous the calumnies that Iago is instilling in Otello's mind concerning his bride's infidelity. As yet the people are unaware of the tempest soon to be unleashed in their leader. Desdemona kisses some of the children, while women kiss the hem of her gown. She bestows a purse on the sailors. Gradually the crowd disperses.

Act 3 Cypriots are heard offstage hailing the arrival of the Venetian ambassadors. 'Long live the Lion of St Mark!' they sing. As Otello prepares to greet the ambassadors dignitaries of the Venetian republic enter with ladies, gentlemen, soldiers and trumpeters. A ballet welcomes the envoys. All witness the acme of Otello's passion as he humiliates his wife. Everybody to a man is horrified. The ladies plead with Otello to have pity on Desdemona, while the gentlemen give an eloquent description of Otello's frenzy: 'That black man is deadly, and blinded by the shadow of death and terror! With nails he claws at his horrid breast! His eyes are fixed on the ground ... then he deifies heaven with his dusky fist, raising his rough countenance towards the sun's lofty rays'.

Finally Otello rouses himself and, 'terrible in his wrath', turns on the crowd and commands them to leave. Cries of 'Hurrah!' are heard from Cypriots offstage who are oblivious to the tragedy being enacted onstage. Their cries of 'Glory to the Lion of Venice' are echoed by Iago with fearful irony as he places his foot on the now prostrate form of

Otello, who has finally succumbed to a fainting fit and thus cannot hear the cries of 'Long live Otello!' It seems unlikely that Otello will live much longer.

The chorus plays no part in the final denouement of the opera.

Chorus (*Rigoletto*)

Unusually in Verdi's operas (the only other comparable instance that comes to mind is *La Traviata*) the chorus in Rigoletto is restricted to one role, that of the **Courtiers** at the court of the **Duke of Mantua**. See **Cortigiani**.

Chorus (*Stiffelio*)

Stiffelio is principally a private drama and the chorus plays only a subsidiary role.

In Act 1 the chorus acts as a company of **Stiffelio's** supporters in 'festive mood'. They have come to **Stankar's** castle to celebrate Stiffelio's return from his travels. His friends greet Stiffelio with the accolade: 'You are the glory of Germany who banishes all vice'. There is dramatic irony in this since **Raffaele** has just requested a secret assignation with Stiffelio's wife, **Lina**. Lina is distraught, while Stiffelio is at this stage blissfully unaware that his wife has been unfaithful to him. Stiffelio reminds his friends that 'to God alone you should sing praises. Then shall your song echo throughout the universe'. Stankar leads all the friends through to the banqueting hall whence the scene changes for the finale.

Stiffelio's friends are enjoying themselves hugely and sing once again in praise of their hero: 'May joy and peace reign here in harmony; may love smile in truth and constancy – the love which he would spread amongst mankind, the love which makes equal the master and the slave'. When **Federico** asks in all innocence what will be the theme of Stiffelio's forthcoming sermon Stiffelio, believing Federico to be his wife's lover, launches into a tirade against, 'the base treachery of the wicked'. He then proceeds to publicly humiliate his wife. His friends remain muted throughout the dramatic altercations, only remarking as the Act draws to its conclusion, 'Ah why ... did some demon sow suspicion in Stiffelio's heart?'

Act 2 The chorus is heard offstage as the congregation in Stiffelio's church. They sing a hymn inviting the Lord to have mercy on them, which again has heavily ironic overtones, since Stiffelio at that moment is in no mood to show mercy towards his wife. The congregation is once again heard intoning the same words, 'Have mercy!' at the opening of the final scene in the opera (Act 3 Scene 2). They must all be aware of the turmoil in which recent events have thrown their preacher. They keep reiterating their plea for mercy as Stiffelio mounts the pulpit.

They must surely be uncomfortable as Stiffelio commences to read Christ's exhortation to forgive the adulteress: 'Whoever among you is without sin, let him cast the first stone'. Lina makes her way to the pulpit and collapses at the foot of the steps. It is with enormous relief throughout the church, and not least to Lina herself, when Stiffelio concludes the text, 'And the woman rose up, forgiven'. All repeat, 'Forgiven! Forgiven!' and echo Stiffelio's pronouncement, 'God has spoken it', as the curtain falls.

Chorus (*La Traviata*)

The chorus divides its time between playing guests at **Violetta's** party in Act 1, guests at **Flora's** party in Act 2 and Parisian citizens in carnival spirit (Act 3 offstage).

Act 1 When the party opens Violetta's party is just getting under way. Some guests have already arrived, some are arriving and are being greeted by those already present. Those just arriving admit they are late because they have been playing cards at Flora's. All the guests have one philosophy only and that is, as they declare, that 'pleasure adds zest to life'. Violetta motions her guests to be seated for supper and all cheerfully oblige for now the wine will start to flow and 'Wine is a friend that puts secret sorrow to flight!' They join in the chorus of **Alfredo's** drinking song (*Libiamo ne' lieti calici*) with alacrity. They then accept Violetta's invitation to commence the dancing. The only small cloud that blights the horizon of their hedonistic enjoyment comes when Violetta shows clear signs of being unwell. At her behest they proceed to the ballroom without her, however. They return later flushed from their exertions and thank Violetta for her hospitality. It does not seem to occur to any one of them to enquire if Violetta has recovered from her dizzy spell. They depart into the dawn to return to their beds.

Act 2 Scene 2 Once again guests are arriving, this time at Flora's party. Many of the guests wear masks and gypsy costumes. The gypsy girls invite the guests to allow them to read their palms. When this leads to some home truths being revealed all decide it is safer to draw a veil over what is 'past and gone. What is done cannot be undone. Let us welcome what is to come'. **Gastone** enters with a group of guests dressed as Spanish bullfighters. They relate a tale concerning a bullfighter who killed five bulls in a single day in order to impress an Andalusian maid. They conclude the tale with the somewhat wistful observation that 'here our hearts are gentler, we make do with fun and games'. This is the cue to move towards the gaming tables.

All are surprised to see Alfredo in their midst and amused when Alfredo admits he does not know where Violetta is. 'How unimpassioned!' they comment. The guests then watch as Alfredo soundly thrashes the **Baron Douphol** at cards. They can hardly fail to be aware of the uncomfortable subtext to the contest between the two men. Finally it erupts as Alfredo invites all the guests to come to him and then brutally humiliates Violetta. They are all outraged by his behaviour. 'We've no use for you', they declare. It is not just that Violetta is a woman but that Alfredo's behaviour is unpardonable by any standards. They are the more outraged because, like their hostess, Flora, Violetta is a courtesan and therefore unable to defend herself. Alfredo's outburst undermines the entire edifice of their superficial and ultimately hypocritical existence. Thus, when they say to Violetta, 'Each one of us has shared your pain', it is no mere empty rhetoric – they truly mean it.

Act 3   A masked chorus is heard offstage from within Violetta's sickroom. It strikes a discordant note and must inevitably remind Violetta of the life she once led. The chorus hail the advent of the 'Fat Ox... the pride and boast of every butcher'. Paris is enjoying a carnival while Violetta lies dying.

Chorus (*Il Trovatore*)

The chorus in *Il Trovatore* is divided four ways between retainers and soldiers of the Count **di Luna**, gypsies, **Manrico's** soldiers, nuns and monks

Act 1 Scene 1   Di Luna's retainers and soldiers are keeping watch outside the Count's apartments. In particular they are keeping watch for the Troubadour, whom the Count fears as his rival in love for **Leonora**. It is cold and the men are bored and tired. They press their captain, **Ferrando**, to entertain them with the true story of Garcia, the Count's brother. Ferrando duly regales them with the story (see **Synopsis**). The men are clearly superstitious and become increasingly horrified as Ferrando relates how the Count's son was bewitched. Their horror turns to righteous indignation and anger when they hear of the revenge taken by the gypsy's daughter. Then Ferrando plays on their superstitious dread by telling them of the rumour that the gypsy's soul still haunts the earth and shows itself in various forms. The men all agree that she has been spied, 'on the edge of the rooftops ... Sometimes she changes into a hoopoe, or an owl! Other times, a raven; more often a civet-owl flying through the dawn like an arrow!' Ferrando adds, for good measure, that apparently one of the Count's servants died of fright when the gypsy struck him on the forehead. It happened, Ferrando tells the horror-struck men, at midnight. At that moment midnight strikes and a drum is heard summoning the soldiers to their posts. The soldiers and retainers hurriedly disperse.

Act 2   A band of gypsies is seated around a bonfire. They note that 'the endless sky casts off her sombre nightly garb, like a widow who lays aside at last the sad, black veils of mourning'. They pick up their tools,

and resolve to make off to work. The men order the women to pour them drinks since 'body and soul draw strength from wine'. The women dutifully hand out cups of wine, then all hail the sun's rays as they appear over the Biscay mountains. They are just about to depart for work when they are stopped in their tracks by **Azucena's** song (*Stride la vampa!*). They find her song sad and tell her so. Then, urged by an old gypsy they pack their tools and make off for the town, singing as they go.

Act 2 Scene 2   Some retainers accompany the Count and Ferrando to the convent where Leonora prepares to take the veil. Di Luna (who must have received word of Leonora's intention) has come with the express intention of abducting Leonora. Ferrando and the retainers hide in the shadows to await events, while di Luna accosts Leonora. The women of the chorus, meanwhile, are within the convent in the role of nuns who are heard exhorting the new aspirant. Some of the nuns enter with Leonora. They soon encounter the Count and are suitably outraged. The nuns must be aware of Leonora's plight for when Manrico arrives they comment, 'Heaven has taken pity on you'. Armed men enter with **Ruiz** to assist Manrico in his bid to prevent Leonora from entering the convent. Manrico's men should far outnumber di Luna's men to make sense of the fact that the Count's retainers accept the situation as hopeless and appear powerless to prevent Manrico from making off with Leonora, in spite of the Count's fulminations.

Act 3 Scene 1   A military camp. Di Luna's soldiers are amusing themselves, some playing cards, some polishing their weapons. They are awaiting the signal to begin the assault on Castellor. They are delighted to learn from Ferrando that there is certain to be plenty of 'booty' within the castle: 'You're inviting us to a dance!' they sing. They join Ferrando in expressing confidence that victory will be theirs. Other soldiers now drag in Azucena, who has been found wandering around the camp. They remain agog as the scene unfolds, and mute, until the moment Ferrando identifies Azucena as the original gypsy's daughter, and therefore guilty of the younger son's death all those years ago. 'She's the one!' they cry, echoing Ferrando. At a sign from di Luna the soldiers drag Azucena away.

Act 3 Scene 2. Manrico's retainers enter, having been rounded up by Ruiz under instructions from Manrico, who has just heard of Azucena's capture. They agree with enthusiasm to help Manrico in his bid to rescue his mother.

Act 4 Monks are heard from within the tower of the Aliaferia palace, where Manrico is imprisoned. They intone a *misere*, a clear indication that Manrico is shortly to be executed. The Count enters with some guards and instructs them that as soon as dawn breaks the son is to go to the scaffold and the mother to the stake. The guards withdraw.

Chorus (*I Vespri Siciliani*)

The chorus is divided between French soldiers in occupation and the Sicilian populace. When the opera opens French soldiers are sitting drinking around a table in front of the door to the barracks. Sicilian men and women cross the square, singly and in groups. They cast looks of disgust at the French soldiers. The French think nostalgically of the homeland, while the Sicilians think only of vengeance. The Sicilians respectfully greet the Duchess **Elena** as she crosses the square and heads towards her palace.

Roberto, who is completely drunk, taunts the Sicilians to sing in praise of their conquerors. He then moves threateningly towards Elena and urges her to sing. She calmly agrees and as the French take their seats the Sicilians draw protectively near to Elena. They become inflamed with her song exhorting them obliquely to take courage. They determine to avenge 'the evil shame' while the French continue, increasingly noisily, their carousing. Eventually the Sicilians become so enraged they draw their daggers and fall upon the French soldiers. They desist almost immediately, however, at the sight of **Monforte** who suddenly appears on the steps of the Governor's palace. Monforte makes

an imperious gesture and the entire crowd flees, leaving the square deserted.

From **Procida** (Act 2) we learn that the problem facing the resistance movement is that the people of Sicily seem to have lost their 'old valour' and lack the will to cast off their yoke. Procida's companions arrive soon after him, and gather around their leader. Procida despatches one to 'round up the faithful' and another to fetch **Arrigo** and Elena. He then exhorts the remaining Sicilians to 'ripen' their revenge, for the 'cruel oppressor does not fear and does not expect it'. The Sicilians all echo his words, then make off.

Later in the scene the entire populace of Palermo emerges to witness the marriage of the twelve engaged couples (see **Synopsis**).

Act 3 Scene 2 A magnificent hall in the palace (see **Synopsis**). The Sicilians and French are enjoying themselves. 'Oh splendid festivities', they sing; 'Oh nights fertile with merry dances, with rare beauties! They are a celestial ray, those vivid lights that instil in our hearts love and pleasure!' Eventually the crowd disperses in the apartments of the palace and in the gardens. Revellers come and go, gathering refreshments while the dancing continues in the hall within. Finally the Sicilians arrive. They lose no time in surrounding Monforte.

Elena is about to assassinate the Governor but is prevented by Arrigo. All are horrified by what appears to them a rank betrayal. They had assumed that Arrigo was one of their staunchest supporters. They hurl invective at the coward. Their scorn is only exacerbated when Monforte makes to embrace Arrigo. None of the Sicilians is yet aware that Monforte is Arrigo's father. At a sign from Monforte the Sicilians are arrested and dragged away.

Act 4 Some members of the chorus will act as French soldiers on guard in the courtyard of the fortress which is the scene for this Act. As Arrigo presents himself at the main gate the soldiers allow him to enter. After Arrigo and Elena's duet Procida enters, escorted by soldiers. As he approaches Elena Arrigo moves aside and signals the soldiers to leave.

Towards the conclusion of the Act the courtyard fills with a crowd who have come to witness the execution. Procida and Elena are led towards their execution in the great hall of justice where four penitents are praying and several soldiers stand bearing torches. Monks are heard from within chanting. The chanting continues throughout the preparations. A group of women enters the courtyard and kneel. They beg for mercy for the condemned. The crowd, standing behind the soldiers in the courtyard also kneels and prays. At the last minute Monforte announces a stay of execution and soldiers escort Procida and Elena down the steps from the hall towards Monforte. There is general rejoicing, increased when Monforte announces the wedding of Arrigo and Elena to take place that very day as the Vespers are heard striking. Glasses and pitchers are brought out from the guard house. French and Sicilians drink together in celebration of their newly discovered amity.

Act 5 Knights and maidens are circulating in the gardens of Monforte's palace prior to the wedding of Arrigo and Elena. They sing of the forthcoming wedding and the possibility of peace it represents. When Elena appears the maidens offer her flowers and join the Knights in singing her praises. The pastoral nature of this scene is all the more poignant in view of the blood-bath of the final denouement.

Elena dismisses the company as Arrigo arrives. Shortly after some gentlemen appear at the door of the palace then come forward looking for Arrigo who, at a sign from Elena, decides to follow them to see his father. Later Monforte comes out of the palace with French Knights and ladies. As the bells start to ring out the stage floods with Sicilians who run in from every direction carrying torches, swords and daggers. Shrieking for vengeance they hurl themselves on Monforte and the French as the curtain falls.

First Consul and Second Consul of Milan (Primo Console e Secondo Console di Milano) (*La Battaglia di Legnano*)
The consuls act as figureheads to the Lombard League, exhorting the troops to new acts of bravery and leading the oath in Act 1, where **Rolando** and the Milanese swear to defend Milan with their blood if necessary. The consuls then lead the troops off to battle.

In Act 4, when the Lombard League has successfully defeated **Federico Barbarossa** at the battle of Legnano, the consuls are again at the head of the troops on their victorious return. The Second Consul takes the lead and relays the good tidings, describing how **Arrigo** was responsible for the decisive turn in the battle. Apparently Arrigo hurled the emperor, 'slain or wounded from his saddle'. The consul then exhorts all to raise a hymn of thanks to the 'King of Kings' (God).

Corrado (*Il Corsaro*). A pirate chieftain.
Corrado is a typical, passion-driven Byronic hero, in revolt against the world, his fate and all that life attempts to give and take from him. 'I am unhappy but avenged', he announces at the opening of the opera. In other words he has fulfilled the necessity of his own inner being by refusing to compromise with a daylight world which otherwise would have reduced him to a hollow husk. He is, in the tradition of all heroes, fearless, because he acknowledges no greater authority than his own inviolable self, to which he has been fiercely true. (His beloved **Medora** can only see death and disaster hanging over his relentless dedication to the light of his own integrity.)

Corrado's calling is a criminal one but his (and the poet's) perception of it is highly romanticized. It is criminality in the mode of Robin Hood; it is the need to rectify a perceived injustice. His enterprise is misguided but ennobled by the reckless self-abandon with which it is prosecuted. Corrado belongs to that family of characters in Verdi's operas inspired by Byron and Schiller who are doomed by the intensity of their own revolt.

Corrado throws himself into the midst of the enemy camp and he and his pirates successfully rout the Turks. But instead of withdrawing while he has the advantage he allows his chivalrous instincts to get the better of him and goes to the rescue of the girls in the Pasha's harem (Act 2 Scene 2). Thus he is soon overcome and captured. **Seid** taunts him: 'You are a stealer of women; how I admire you!' Threatened with hideous torture it is Corrado's turn to deride his enemies. 'You have defeated us, but your anger has not diminished our greatness', he says. Corrado has the confidence of the man of principle, which does not, however, save him from remorse when locked away in the Pasha's dungeons awaiting his grisly fate (Act 3 Scene 2).

Confronted with his redeeming angel, **Gulnara**, Corrado for the first time in his life comes up against a moral dilemma for which he can find no immediate solution. He has saved Gulnara from her captivity; more than that he has saved her life. She is undeniably attractive but his loyalties are with Medora, whom he knows pines for him. Gulnara offers him freedom. In return for his having saved her life she will save his, but at what cost? This is what torments Corrado. Their mutual predicament is a bond potentially far stronger than the bond which ties him to Medora. Besides which Gulnara offers him a dagger with which to murder Seid in his sleep (Act 3 Scene 2). But such an act is unthinkable to a man of Corrado's temperament. Gulnara has compromised herself with 'servants, soldiers and guards' in order to ensure Corrado's release. It is a heavy load for his conscience to bear. It could never have occurred to him that the day might dawn when he would owe his life to an odalisque. His whole being revolts against the idea; 'Leave me to my fate', he implores Gulnara; 'My death is appointed in heaven. The universe wages war against me; God has fixed his seal on it'. It is the only response he can find. Gulnara has succeeded in attacking his most vulnerable place, his pride. He has always been the master of his own destiny. The woman he loves – certainly on the evidence of the opera – is entirely passive and yielding and this is what he expects of a woman.

Thus when Gulnara, invoking shades of **Lady Macbeth**, rushes off to murder Seid in

his sleep, it is a profound shock to Corrado's psyche. Women, in his experience, simply do not behave like this. How can he accede to this? How can he accept such an outrage against nature? Paradoxically it is the very fact that Gulnara kills Seid that reawakens Corrado's chivalrous instincts. How can he leave Gulnara to face the music now, since her sole motivation has ostensibly been to effect his release? 'Why, woman, did you wish to add to my remorse?' he demands of her. Then, 'Fate is too terrible, too cruel to me: if I may not love you I can at least save you'. Thus he tacitly acknowledges that he loves Gulnara, but will not allow himself to, for the sake of a love that awaits him at home. There could be no clearer exemplification of the way in which all love is founded on the exigencies of mutual need at any given time. It also illustrates the element of free will that is an essential part of all love relations. Corrado's true nobility lies in his ability to transcend the demands of necessity and of his instinctive desire to hold true to the original commitment that he has already made to Medora, even though at this moment she must appear to him light years away from the exigencies of the moment.

Reunited with Medora it is to find that, having convinced herself that her husband would not return, she has taken poison (Act 3 Scene 3). More guilt, more remorse. Corrado's only consolation is that he is able to convince her that, in spite of Gulnara's love for him, he has remained faithful to her. The true absurdity of the end of the opera lies in the fact that Medora's death opens for Corrado a possibility for the future, and yet Corrado throws that future away by flinging himself into the sea. But then that is the absurdity of human love and of opera.

IL CORSARO *(The Corsair)*

Opera in 3 Acts. Libretto by Francesco Maria Piave after Byron's poem, *The Corsair* (1813). First performance: 25 October 1848 at the Teatro Grande, Trieste.

Cast:
Corrado: pirate chieftain (tenor)

Giovanni: a pirate (bass)
Medora: Corrado's mistress (soprano)
Seid: Pasha of Corone (baritone)
Gulnara: favourite in Seid's harem (soprano)
Selimo: one of Seid's warriors (tenor)
Eunuch (tenor)
Slave (tenor)

Time: early 19th century
Place: An Aegean island and the Turkish city
of Corone

Synopsis

Act 1 Scene 1   The corsairs' island in the
Aegean. A bay surrounded by steep cliffs. In
the distance, surmounted on a high, preci-
pitous crag is a large, square Byzantine tower.
To the left, among the rocks, can be seen
huts and caves where the corsairs shelter. It
is sunset.

Corsairs are scattered here and there on
stage. Offstage a chorus expresses its delight
in the life of the pirate (*Come liberi volano i
venti*). 'Our fatherland and kingdom is the
foaming wave', they sing – 'our proud spirits
can defy danger and death'. Corrado enters
as the pirates sing of their determination to
make merry and let 'the cheer of our cups
drown the curses of the dying mariner'.
Corrado shares the sentiments of his
comrades and expresses the same hatred of
mankind that has forced him to live the life
of an outcast. Whatever he attempted in life
was apparently doomed. 'Feared and execrated' by mankind, he admits he is 'unhappy
but avenged' (*Tutto parea sorridere*).

Giovanni and other pirates enter hurriedly
and present Corrado with a letter from a
Greek spy. The pirates urge him to read the
missive and reveal the mystery he has been
concealing from them. Corrado reads the
letter and immediately determines that the
pirates shall sail forth under his command
and take up arms against their foe, the
'Mussulman' (the Turks) (*Sì: de corsari il
fulmine*). With rallying cries of 'To arms, to
arms!' all disperse. Corrado goes to the
turret.

Act 1 Scene 2   Medora's room in the old
turret with a balcony facing the sea. Medora

waits impatiently for the return of her
beloved Corrado. She takes up her harp and
expresses the hope that her lament, with the
assistance of the harp, may reach the ears of
her absent lover. Medora is full of foreboding
(*Non so le tetre immagini*). She is condemned
to 'weep forever in the shadow of a mystery'
and any ray of hope is but 'a fleeting glance
of lightning that deceives'. Better to die, she
feels; in which case all she asks of Corrado
is a loving tear on her behalf. 'Virtue will
not deny grief for one who has died of love',
she reflects.

Corrado has entered, meanwhile, and
overheard her last sentiment. He pledges his
love and pleads with her to have courage,
for he has a duty to fulfil which will take
him away from her. Medora becomes distraught and tells him of the dark imaginings
that beset her (*No, tu non sai comprendere*).
Corrado does his best to reassure her but
refuses to disclose the nature of his mission.
A cannon shot is heard offstage, this being
the signal for Corrado to depart. Medora
begs him not to go, convinced she will never
see him again. Corrado answers that he is
equally certain that he will return. A second
cannon shot is heard. Corrado can linger no
longer. He leaves as Medora falls in a swoon.

Act 2 Scene 1   A delightful room in Seid's
harem. Odalisques present embroidered veils
and jewels to Gulnara. They tell her of the
joys which await her in the arms of the Pasha,
whose 'chief delight' she is (*O qual perenne
gaudio t'aspetta*). Gulnara is not impressed.
She is, she assures her companions, the most
wretched creature on earth. The Pasha may
love her, but she loathes him. Her heart
cannot be bought with jewels and gold. Her
thoughts turn to her homeland. When she
recollects the pure air of her native skies she
can forget the chains in which her soul now
languishes (*Vola talor dal carcere*).

A Eunuch announces that the Pasha is
about to celebrate a victory and desires
Gulnara's presence. Gulnara is forced to
acknowledge her slavery. She consoles herself
with the thought that perhaps one day
heaven will take pity on her suffering and
'satisfy that longing that kindles and

destroys' her heart (*Ah conforto è sol la speme*).

Act 2 Scene 2 A magnificent pavilion on the shore of the harbour of Corone. The Turkish fleet is at anchor, brightly lit and festively decorated. On the left can be seen the spectator part of the harem, lit by torchlight. On the right is an awning with tables laid out beneath it.

A chorus of Muslim soldiers and officers sing of their determination that the 'obnoxious rabble' of pirates shall fall to their swords. Their beloved Pasha will make the seas safe for their trading. Seid enters, followed by Selimo and other followers. All prostrate themselves. Seid addresses his troops, exhorting them to victory in the forthcoming battle against the pirates, and leads a hymn to Allah, the conqueror: 'Holy in peace, terrible in war, is Allah's great name for the Osmans! ... For Osman's warriors there is no danger if they fight in his name' (*Salve, Allah!*).

A slave enters and announces that a dervish, who has recently escaped from the clutches of the pirates, begs an audience with Seid. Seid commands that he be brought in and Corrado, disguised as a dervish, is led in. He explains that he was rescued by a kindly fisherman and now comes to seek protection. Seid rails against the pirates and demands to know, do they not fear his wrath? Corrado states that he has had little dealings with them but assures the Pasha that the pirates mock him. Corrado makes to leave but Seid detains him. At this moment a dazzling light suddenly fills the sky. A ship has been set alight in the harbour and the fire is spreading through the Turkish fleet. Seid demands that arms be brought to him. His suspicions immediately fall on the dervish and he commands that the latter be taken prisoner forthwith and 'cut into pieces'. Corrado throws off his hood and cloak to reveal himself clad in helmet and armour. He calls to his comrades to take courage and to advance. Meanwhile his pirates enter and Corrado orders them to put the Turks to rout. The voices of Gulnara and the girls are heard from the harem, screaming for help. Corrado rushes to assist them.

He soon returns carrying Gulnara in his arms and followed by pirates dragging the odalisques behind them. Corrado hastens to reassure the odalisques that they shall be respected by the pirates. He then exhorts his men to take courage and make 'one mighty effort'. But the pirates are outnumbered and the Turks are gaining the upper hand. Realizing their position is hopeless some of the pirates flee. Those remaining are surrounded and overcome. Corrado himself is forced to yield, but Seid orders that he be spared from immediate execution. Seid addresses Corrado. 'Valiant indeed!' he mocks, 'You are a stealer of women'. Corrado refuses to be intimidated. Gulnara, meanwhile, admits to herself that she feels a 'flame of love' for Corrado that she has never felt for Seid. Giovanni, one of Corrado's pirates, reflects philosophically: 'What use is daring in a strong man's breast if fortune does not favour him with her smile? Corrado has challenged fate too boldly and now must bend his neck before it'. The odalisques regret Corrado's failure to save them while the Turks revel in their victory.

More pirates are dragged in in chains. Selimo reports that others have been slain but some have escaped to their caves. Seid prevents Selimo from pursuing them. He knows it would be useless trying to locate them and he is satisfied to have Corrado as his prisoner. Corrado's petulant defiance makes Seid all the more determined that he will devise horrible tortures, 'scarcely known to man or demon', for Corrado. Corrado will then suffer a slow and agonizing death, Seid promises him. Gulnara and the odalisques attempt to intervene on Corrado's behalf but Seid is not disposed to be merciful. If anything, Gulnara's intervention only exacerbates Seid's rage and strengthens his resolve. Corrado and Giovanni remain defiant; 'You have defeated us, but your anger has not diminished our greatness', they declare.

Act 3 Scene 1 Seid's apartments. Seid is revelling in the fact that he finally has Corrado at his mercy. It becomes clear that what most enrages him is the suspicion that Gulnara is in love not with him, but with his enemy. He calls on heaven to grant him thunderbolts with which to 'burn the vile wretch to ashes' should Gulnara betray his love (*Cento leggiadre vergini*). He calls Selimo and orders him to fetch Gulnara. He further orders that Corrado should be executed the next day. The thought of the torture to which Corrado will be subjected revives his spirits. As for Gulnara, 'if she harbours deceit in her soul she shall find her lover a tyrant' (*S'avvicina il tuo momento*).

Gulnara enters. Seid dissembles warmth and affection. However he tells Gulnara that Corrado will die the next day. Gulnara suggests that it might profit Seid more to let Corrado live and put a ransom on his head. This fuels Seid's suspicions. He openly accuses her of being in love with Corrado. Gulnara attempts to defend herself but Seid's ire is inflamed. He warns that it is not only the pirate's life that is in danger but her own as well (*Sia l'istante maledetto*). Seid's ranting only confirms Gulnara's determination to save the man she loves. Seid exits muttering, 'Trema, trema!' ('Tremble, tremble!') Gulnara is not intimidated.

Act 3 Scene 2   Inside a tower. At the back of the stage, in the centre, is a closed door leading to the sea and next to it a balcony with a large grille. On the left is a door with iron bars, leading to the upper galleries of the harem. To one side is a straw mattress. Corrado, in chains, is pacing up and down. He thinks of Medora and the unhappiness which the news of his fate will cause her (*Eccomi prigioniero*). Exhausted by his pacing, and realizing the futility of any hope of escape, he throws himself on the mattress and falls asleep.

Gulnara enters cautiously. She stands looking down on the sleeping form of Corrado, who soon stirs in his sleep. As he awakens he cannot conceal his delight at seeing Gulnara, although he is dubious as to how she can rescue him (*Seid la vuole*). His thoughts revert guiltily to Medora who pines for him at home. Gulnara is devastated to realize that Corrado loves another. Corrado assumes that Gulnara is in love with Seid but Gulnara disabuses him. She tells him that

she has bribed servants, soldiers and guards in order to come to him and that a ship is waiting for him. Realizing that he distrusts her, Gulnara gives Corrado a dagger to help him with his escape. Corrado, however, refuses to arm himself with a 'treacherous' dagger and urges Gulnara to leave him to his fate. 'My death is appointed in heaven', he tells her. Gulnara finally loses patience and exits, brandishing the dagger herself. A storm breaks out and Corrado prays that lightning may strike and cut short his wretched existence. Eventually the thunder stops and the sky gradually clears.

Gulnara re-enters, 'casting a horrified glance behind her'. She staggers and falls to the ground. 'The deed is accomplished!' she announces. She has apparently slain Seid. Corrado is appalled that she has made herself a murderess on his behalf. Gulnara hopes that her action will be proof of her devotion to him and that he will now at least do her the courtesy of fleeing with her (*La terra, il ciel m'abborrino*). Corrado realizes the irrefutable logic of this and the two depart.

Act 3 Scene 3   A seashore as in the first act. A ship is at anchor. Medora is confronting a band of pirates and demands from them news of her beloved. She is convinced by their demeanour that Corrado must have perished, as she had feared. She is comforted only by the fact that she knows she is dying, for she has taken poison. The pirates sight a ship approaching land and recognize it as Corrado's. 'What have I done?' Medora exclaims in horror.

As Medora and Corrado are reunited she tells him that she can now die happy. She goes on to ask who the strange woman is who weeps at his side. Corrado informs Medora that Gulnara was originally Seid's favourite but has since saved his life (*Per me infelice vedi costei*). Gulnara frankly reveals that she was motivated more by love than pity. Medora is distraught and tells Corrado that she is dying. Horrified, Corrado recollects where his true loyalties lie. He embraces Medora and pleads with her not to die. Gulnara declares, 'You shall live on in the sad beating of our hearts' and begs

Medora to take Gulnara's tears of repentance to heaven. Medora dies in Corrado's arms. Corrado in desperation throws himself into the sea, the pirates hasten to save him and Gulnara faints. The curtain falls.

Whereas it is customary to point to the libretti of *Alzira*, *Il Trovatore* and *I Vespri Siciliano* as being the weakest Verdi set, in the author's opinion the libretto of *Il Corsaro* must take the prize. There are no characters in the drama with whom one can empathize, except for Gulnara. Medora is the epitome of the 'dying swan'. One has already lost patience with her before the conclusion of her first encounter with Corrado. Her faint-heartedness is only emphasized by the presence in the drama of a woman with real spirit.

In many of Verdi's operas the presence of two female leads is to the mutual benefit of both characters, each personality gaining in colour and definition through the presence of the other. In the case of *Il Corsaro* Gulnara's feistiness is entirely to the detriment of Medora whose lack of spirit critically unbalances the work. For one is forced to wonder what on earth Corrado sees in her and why he puts himself through all the anguish he endures throughout the opera in order to be reunited with her. When he is finally reunited with her it is only to discover that she has already taken her own life. The final absurdity comes when Corrado throws himself into the sea at the end of the opera. His only reason for committing suicide at this juncture is his grief at the suicide of his beloved Medora. Undoubtedly there are some characters who would commit such an absurdity, but it does not make sense in the light of what we know about Corrado from the evidence of the drama so far. If we had some evidence of the sort of existential angst that assails Carlo (*I Masnadieri*) or the mental instability exhibited by Don Carlo (*Don Carlo*) or Otello there would be some logic to his action. But we do not. Corrado is apparently a courageous and committed man with a deep sense of loyalty and honour. His refusal to give in to his feelings for Gulnara, who so heroically rescues him, is admirable in the first place, but his willingness to throw his life away, and with it the possibility of making a new life with Gulnara, appears sheer lunacy.

One is forced to question what it is in Corrado that makes him place his entire destiny in the hands of such an unworthy object for his passion. Presumably it must be down to his own sense of worthlessness. It could be argued that an outlaw must, by definition, be besieged by a sense of worthlessness. Why else is he refusing to advance himself in the real world but devoting himself instead to swiping at it from the sidelines? Such an argument would be to undermine the entire premise on which the Romantics – Byron and Schiller in particular – base their writings, namely that the real world – the world as you and I find it and have to live it – is itself unworthy and demeaning, which is why all their greatest heroes are outlaws, corsairs, bandits, thus indicating that the real world, that of society, has no place for men of their calibre and integrity.

A hero must in some way reflect if not the author himself, then at least the author's conception of what it is to be heroic. Carlo (*I Masnadieri*), Don Carlo (*Don Carlo*), Jacopo Foscari (*I Due Foscari*) are all passion-driven. Where Descartes said, 'I think, therefore I am', they would say, 'I feel, therefore I am'. The problem with defining your existence by the way you feel is that you inevitably become subject to every little mood swing. This is clearly a problem for all the Byronic heroes in Verdi's operas. One has the feeling that if Corrado had given himself a few moments to collect himself he would have realized the absurdity of ending his life when he does. This may sound a coldly rationalistic approach to what is clearly a hot-blooded romantic drama, but what is successful in drama may not necessarily be true to life and vice versa. We may wish that Corrado had given his life one more chance, but would that be more true than the desperate option he elects to take? Corrado's suicide in all its absurdity would be more fitting in a play by Sartre or Camus than a play by Byron. Paradoxically his action is a demonstration of the hero's freedom to choose what he does with his life at any given moment. This is the true explanation of the apparently absurd acts of all the Byronic heroes: Carlo's dementia at the end of *I Masnadieri*, Ernani's suicide, etc. Having said which, one must admit that it should not be necessary intellectually to justify a drama. Either it works or it does not. In the final analysis *Il Corsaro* does not.

Cortigiani (Courtiers) (*Rigoletto*)

As is the way with courtiers anywhere, they both reflect and give form to the monarch they serve. The court of Mantua is a hotbed of gossip and intrigue, because gossip and intrigue are the lifeblood of the **Duke of Mantua**. The Duke believes that anything he desires belongs to him by divine right. The courtiers exist in a permanent stage of siege, never knowing what to expect next from their master, particularly when it comes to their womenfolk, because the Duke is no respecter of other men's wives, as is shown in the opening scene of the opera.

When the plot is hatched against **Rigoletto** it is not really Rigoletto the courtiers seek to attack but the Duke himself (Act 1 Scene 2). For Rigoletto is nothing but the embodiment of the Duke's unbridled licence. Nevertheless the depth of their sycophancy is exposed when they surrender the girl (**Gilda**) into the arms of their lovesick lord. When they learn that Gilda is Rigoletto's daughter, and not his mistress as they had assumed, they are astonished and also, if they could admit it, deeply abashed. It had never for an instant occurred to them that the hunchback could have had a wife, let alone a daughter. Suddenly they are struck by the viciousness of their action. Their grudges against the jester are forgotten as they are confronted with a pitiful spectacle of suffering humanity. Their only recourse at this moment is to the time-honoured expedient of claiming immunity (by inference) for they gather at the door to the Duke's apartments and refuse to grant Rigoletto admittance (Act 2), thus at one and the same time confirming to Rigoletto the presence of his daughter within and confirming their own inviolability as servants of their master. They have already related to the Duke the events of the previous evening with great relish. They feel self-confident in the presence of the Duke for it is from him that they take their cue for everything. They are never themselves. It is this realization that prompts Rigoletto's violent vituperation against the whole vile race of courtiers (*Cortigiani, vil razza dannata*).

As Rigoletto knows only too well, what motivates the courtiers is gold. When Rigoletto has been reunited with his daughter and imperiously dismisses the courtiers, who would never admit to being intimidated, they pretend to themselves that 'with children and with madmen it is often best to make believe'. It is they, not the hunchback, who are the children and madmen.

The Count of Toulouse (*Jerusalem*). Brother of **Roger** and father of **Hélène**.

The Count of Toulouse replaces the role of **Arvino** in *I Lombardi*. The part is nowhere near as significant as that of Arvino. In *Jerusalem* there is no longer the motive of rival brothers in love. The drama in *Jerusalem* takes on an altogether more exotic taint. It is not the Count's wife that his brother desires but his daughter. Such a blatant instance of incest may have mitigated against the work's early success (though it hardly explains why it has not found a place in the repertoire in the latter half of the 20th century). Whereas in *I Lombardi* Pagano aims to kill his brother and ends up killing his father, in *Jerusalem* Roger intends to kill **Gaston** but his hired assassin accidentally wounds, though not fatally, his brother, the Count. The Count's wounds must have been serious since at the time everybody believes him to be dead. It may well take most of the four years that elapse between Acts 1 and 2 of the opera for the Count to regain his strength sufficiently then to travel to the Holy Land on Crusade.

Thereafter the Count's role runs more or less parallel to that of Arvino, though inevitably truncated. For instance there is only one scene in the Count's tent in Palestine where in *I Lombardi* there are two. Like Arvino one of the first people the Count meets when he reaches the Holy Land is his brother, although he does not recognize him as such. Also like Arvino he has an ugly confrontation with his daughter when he denounces Hélène for consorting with Gaston, whom he still believes to be responsible for the attempt on his life. But this is a far more conventional father/daughter confrontation than the extraordinary scene in *I Lombardi* when Giselda denounces her father with, as far as Arvino is concerned, no justification other than childish hysteria. Giselda believes her father responsible for the deaths of her beloved and his father (Oronte and Acciano). Hélène only has to confront her father's disapproval which, in the circumstances, is entirely justifiable.

As in *I Lombardi* the battle for Jerusalem is won through the exceptional valour of the man the Count believes to be his mortal enemy. The final scene has an even greater significance for the Count than for Arvino. Since Arvino has always known his brother to be guilty, the duty of compassion, with which he is presented when the identity of the unknown valorous warrior is revealed to him, is clear. For the Count it is more complicated. First he is confronted by the man to whom he owes success in battle admitting to be the man whom he most detests. Then, almost immediately, he is confronted with the fact that it is not Gaston who should have been the object of his hatred all these years, but his own brother. This is the central distinction between the two operas.

Only in the final pages does the Count learn the truth about his brother and is, in the same moment, required to confer his forgiveness. There is much to forgive, not only the attempt on his life, but Roger's incestuous passion for his daughter. It is too much to assimilate in a moment. What is incontrovertible is the fact that Roger has clearly paid a heavy price for his sins and that he has repented and seeks to atone. Has not the Count sought his blessing on the Crusaders' battles? And has not Roger

proved a worthy warrior in the fight against the Muslims and ultimately saved an innocent man, Gaston, from being executed for *his* crimes? The Count's destiny is altogether more complex than that of Arvino, which ultimately is to the benefit of the opera.

Cuniza (*Oberto*). Sister of Ezzelino da Romano (who does not appear in the opera but is an ally of **Riccardo**, Count of Salinguerra).

Historical background. Cuniza da Romano appears in Dante's *Inferno*. But unlike her brother, Ezzelino (see **Synopsis**), who appears in Hell, Dante places Cuniza in Paradise (*Canto IX*) on the basis that whatever her sins were during her lifetime she repented of them. This is entirely in keeping with the spirit of the character as she appears in the opera.

Cuniza da Romano was famous for her amorous intrigues. She was married four times and indulged in many extra-marital affairs, including with the poet, Sordello, 'he who was so distinguished by his eloquence, not only in poetry but in every other form of utterance' (Dante: *De Vulgari Eloquentia.* 1.15). But she also had a reputation for charitable deeds, one of the most notable being her liberation in 1265 of all the serfs on her father's estates. She died in 1279 or 1280.

Cuniza is ostensibly the victim in the opera, far more than is **Leonora**. For Leonora is the focus of everybody's – and principally Cuniza's – desire to avenge and rehabilitate her. But Cuniza is not a victim because she does not perceive herself as such. Certainly she has moments of regret, but she genuinely does not want her happiness to be built on someone else's misery. Whereas we only witness Leonora's misery (the recollection of her former bliss in Riccardo's arms), we witness Cuniza's odyssey from a state of ecstatic euphoria on the eve of her wedding, to anger and misery on discovering her intended's guilty secret, and finally to a glowing sense of justice and rectitude as she engineers a rapprochement between the warring factions and finally declares her intention never to leave Leonora.

Cuniza's selflessness may seem a little difficult to swallow, but this very selflessness can be seen as central to the era's – and by association to the composer's – conception of the ideal woman. This conception is often counterbalanced in Verdi's later operas by the virago: viz. **Aida/Amneris, Luisa Miller/Frederica**, etc. The psychological type first explored in the character of Cuniza reaches its apogee in the character of **Desdemona** in *Otello*.

When Verdi revised *Oberto* in 1840 he supplied Cuniza with an extended cavatina to replace 'Il pensier d'un amore felice' (Act 1 Scene 2). In this new cavatina Cuniza recalls her early childhood and beloved mother: 'In those early years an angel stands close beside children. From these pure souls he chases away sorrow and weeping'. Cuniza prays that the angel may stand by her still in her married life. Dramatically this is much stronger than the original which is more straightforward, but does not establish with anything like the same precision the unfolding of Cuniza's character. It is because of her faith in a guardian angel and the untroubled nature of her childhood that Cuniza can, with impunity, renounce her own desires when she learns of Riccardo's betrayal. She has a simple trust in life, the very reverse of Leonora's angst, for Leonora carries a huge burden of guilt instilled in her by her father. Significantly it is not her father to whom Cuniza refers, but to her mother.

Cuniza does suffer a premonition of impending sorrow but she allows Riccardo to allay her anxiety. The revised 1840 edition of the duet with Riccardo is in every way superior to the earlier version and should be included in revivals. In it Cuniza confronts Riccardo with her doubts on whether she can trust him. She allows herself to be comforted by her lover, for she reckons that 'the sincerity of his feelings show in his noble visage'.

Cuniza is no mere dying swan; she has considerable pluck, as is apparent when she is confronted, in her private apartments, first by Leonora and then by **Oberto**. By the end of Act 1 she is psychologically at the same point as Leonora and Oberto remain throughout the drama, namely consumed with bitterness and anger. What is remarkable about Cuniza is that she grows beyond that anger. Cuniza has the opportunity to release her anger fully in her confrontation with Riccardo (Act 1 Scene 2) but in the event barely takes advantage of it. As soon as she realizes that Leonora's accusations against Riccardo are well founded she redirects her very real love for Riccardo onto Leonora. She identifies herself with Leonora. She allows herself to be loved and to love and ultimately to grieve through Leonora. She admits that she is guided by her conscience, for she acknowledges within herself that, albeit unwittingly, she is responsible for having stolen Leonora's love from her.

Cuniza's plans to avert bloodshed come to nothing because she has reckoned without Oberto's relentless sense of offended honour and need to see justice done. The masculine need to follow a chosen course to its logical conclusion whatever the consequences is entirely alien to her. She adapts to the dictates of necessity, however painful that may be. Years later Verdi, in the character of **Amneris**, would explore the predicament of a woman who although never actually promised love yet demands it as an inalienable right and would scorn Cuniza's magnanimity as insanity.

Curra (*La forza del destino*). Maid to **Leonora** di Vargas.
Act 1 Scene 1 Curra has obviously been apprised of Leonora's plan to elope with Don **Alvaro** and has apparently been willing to accompany her mistress in her flight. Curra is notably outspoken and upbraids her mistress for thinking of 'confessing all' to the Marquis of **Calatrava**, her father. She encourages Leonora to assist her in packing. She has confidence in Alvaro, which Leonora clearly does not share, and looks forward with excited anticipation to her new life in exile.

It is not clear from the text what happens to Curra at the conclusion of Act 1 when the Marquis, her master, has been accidentally killed. Since she does not reappear in the drama it can be assumed that she will either remain in the Calatrava employ or seek a new position. She will lament the loss of her mistress and the romance and adventure which Leonora's elopement promised her.

D

Dama (*Macbeth*). See **Attendant** to Lady Macbeth

Danieli (*I Vespri Siciliano*). Representative and spokesman for the Sicilians.
In this role Danieli epitomizes the generality of Sicilians who seethe with rage under the onus of the French occupation, and yet can never raise quite enough steam to cast off their yoke. It takes the leadership qualities of **Procida**, finally, to raise the Sicilians from their apathy. When he does he is forced to employ duplicitous means.

For Procida incites the French officers to run off with the Sicilian brides-to-be (Act 2) on the very threshold of their weddings. Danieli is betrothed to **Ninetta**, **Elena**'s maid who is one of the first brides to be abducted by the French soldier, **Roberto**. Danieli is appalled by his own cowardice in allowing such an affront to his manhood. It is this more than any other consideration that finally dispels any hesitation in Danieli and his fellow countrymen concerning a wholesale massacre of the French.

Delil (*Giovanna d'arco*). A King's officer.
Delil announces the arrival of the King, **Carlo**, at Domrémy (Prologue Scene 1); the celebrations in honour of **Giovanna** after the victory at Reims (Act 1 Scene 2); the news that the enemy is routed and that Giovanna has been killed (Act 3).

Delmonte (*Un giorno di regno*). **Belfiore**'s steward.
Delmonte's appearances frame the action of the opera. He appears at the outset, announcing His Majesty's imminent arrival (Act 1

Scene 1), and at the end of the opera, when he announces the arrival of a court courier bearing an important letter for Belfiore (Act 2 Scene 3). It is the letter relieving Belfiore of his duties. Delmonte has been assigned to serve as Belfiore's steward for the duration of the latter's 'reign', that is, for the single day that the real King is travelling back to Poland, and Belfiore is assigned to act as decoy.

Delmonte is probably, in the usual course of events, just another squire in Stanislaus's court, who has been residing in exile in France for the last twenty-four years (which fact leads one to suspect that Delmonte may be a French national).

Desdemona (*Otello*). Otello's wife.
In Shakespeare's play Desdemona's father, Brabantio, describes her (Act 1 Scene 3) as 'A maiden never bold, of spirit so still and quiet that her motion blushed at herself'. In the opera Desdemona's name is first mentioned by **Iago**, for whom she is from start to finish merely a pawn in his plot to unhinge Otello. Iago swears that he will secure Desdemona who at present subjects herself to 'the dark kisses of that thick-lipped savage' for **Roderigo** (Act 1). Later in the scene Iago initiates a brawl by convincing Roderigo that he has a rival for Desdemona's affections in **Cassio**. This is entirely fictitious. Desdemona is devoted to Otello and Cassio to his mistress, Bianca. But the audience does not know this. As far as the audience is concerned, judging from Iago's rantings, Desdemona is a common whore who can easily be secured for anybody who happens to fancy his chances.

If the role is portrayed judiciously it should be apparent on Desdemona's first entrance that Iago grossly slanders her. She has eyes only for Otello. It also quickly becomes apparent that her love for Otello has its origins in her profound compassion for the suffering endured by Otello in his early life.

The first half of Otello and Desdemona's duet (*Gia della notte*) (Act 1), is given over to nostalgic reminiscences, culminating in Desdemona's declaration: 'and I loved you for the dangers you had passed and you loved me that I did pity them'. The sensual image of their love that Iago chooses to purvey is as far from the truth as could possibly be imagined. If the motive of the first half of their duet is love, the second half is suffused with a religious connotation. Desdemona says: 'may Heaven drive away all care', to which Otello replies: 'To this your prayer let the Celestial Host answer Amen'. Desdemona echoes him: 'may it answer Amen'. Their kiss is more a consecration than a consummation. Only the morning star, Venus, summons them away to bed.

So far Desdemona has been seen only through the lenses of those around her. In Act 2, where Iago already has set to work on undermining Otello's faith in his wife, Desdemona is first seen in the distance in a vignette which only underlines the impression of her purity that has already been established. The expressions of love of the Cypriot women and children are reminiscent of Cassio's expressions of devotion when in his cups in Act 1. This is not the devotion of lovers but the worship of a symbol of womanhood, of unsullied purity that is cherished for its unique virtue. It should clarify for the audience that of all things Desdemona does not incite erotic passion. Women and children especially do not gravitate to a sensuous whore, let alone offer gifts of lilies and roses as though at a holy shrine. This scene ensures that there can be no doubt that Iago's accusations are preposterous. It thereby reveals the depth of Otello's paranoia that he can even entertain a suspicion as to their veracity. As Otello himself observes: 'if she be false then Heaven mocks itself'.

When Desdemona first presents her suit on behalf of Cassio, she has no reason to suspect that Otello may already be half convinced that Cassio is her lover (Act 2). Since Otello virtually suffers an epileptic seizure every time Cassio's name is mentioned, one is forced to wonder why Desdemona persists with such obduracy in pleading on his behalf. But then it is that same obduracy that has allowed her to fly in the face of convention

in marrying a Moor in the first place. One must try and see it from her perspective. She genuinely feels that an injustice has been done to Cassio and she cannot understand why Otello, who is normally so fair in his jurisdiction, should be so adamant in his refusal even to discuss Cassio's case with her.

Initially Desdemona must assume that Otello is not well. Very soon she assumes she has offended him in some way, but she cannot for the life of her imagine how. That it does not occur to her that it may have anything to do with Cassio becomes clear when she resumes her suit in Act 3 Scene 2. Otello is already beyond reason and before long accuses her first of being false, then of being a 'vile strumpet' and finally of being a 'cunning whore'. Desdemona can no longer be in any doubt as to what afflicts her husband: he suspects her of infidelity. But it never occurs to her that he suspects Cassio of being her lover. For she can still declare openly, and without embarrassment, in earshot of Otello, 'you know how true in the affections I bear Cassio' (Act 3). The violence of Otello's reaction to this confession must surely alert her. But she has no means of proving or disproving or in any way defending herself to her husband. She is trapped in a public scenario and in the Court of Otello's demented imagination, she is already tried and convicted. Desdemona can only crumple and weep, overwhelmed for the first time in her young life with compassion for herself and consequently, again for the first time in her life, inspiring compassion in others.

Up until now it is Desdemona who has always been the purveyor of compassion. The gratitude of the Cypriot women and children suggests that she has been prodigal with the compassion she feels for those less fortunate than herself. She has led a blameless life and now will be punished for it. It is not given to human beings to live blameless lives. This is a hubris of its own. In a metaphysical sense she is more guilty of hubris even than her husband. It is the worse for being entirely unconscious. Her naïveté is an offence in the same way as is that of Elsa in Wagner's *Lohengrin*.

Desdemona's only sin (if sin it is) to date has been to defy her father. She has thus turned her back on the one authority that she can recognize after God and before her husband. Her psyche has been formed by obeisance before this triumvirate of masculine omnipotence: God, Father and Lover. She has always been owned. In defying her father she has severed that tie. In obdurately refusing to allow the injustice perpetrated on Cassio she refuses to kow-tow to her husband's egotistical mania. In bowing before the Virgin and accepting whatever fate may send she defies God as Father and supreme arbitrator (Act 4). She refuses to acknowledge the superior will of any authority over her own. And yet the whole rebellion is carried out with supreme unconsciousness.

When Desdemona dies it is with the knowledge that whatever thoughts have traversed her young mind she is entirely innocent. She has been the victim of a cosmic joke, a monumental injustice which can only be unravelled beyond the boundaries of an indifferent universe. The supreme irony at the heart of the story of Otello lies in the fact that the combined fates of Desdemona and Otello give all too powerful credence to Iago's nihilistic philosophy as expounded in his *Credo* (Act 2). The conclusion would seem to be: it is as meaningless that we live and meaningless that we die.

A Doctor (Medico) (*Macbeth*)

Appears in Act 4 Scene 2. Lady Macbeth's **Attendant** has encouraged him for two successive nights to keep watch for the sleepwalking Queen. He questions the Attendant closely. Once confronted by **Lady Macbeth** he quickly appreciates the import of the Queen's frantic exclamations and gestures and is appalled.

Shortly after (Act 4 Scene 3), it is announced that the Queen has died. Presumably the doctor will have attended her dying moments.

Dorotea (*Stiffelio*). **Lina's** cousin.

Dorotea is on stage at the opening of the opera and tells **Stiffelio** how a boatman has been asking for him several times. Stiffelio assumes that this must be Walter, 'the good boatman', with whom he has already met.

Dorotea will be agog when Stiffelio relays the boatman's story. It clearly does not occur to Dorotea that her cousin, **Lina**, might be indulging in an illicit affair. For later she unwittingly aids and abets the exposure of Lina's affair by volunteering that she knows Lina possesses a key to the volume of Klopstock in which **Jorg** has observed a young man concealing a letter (Act 1 Scene 2).

Thereafter Dorotea remains very much in the background. She is present in the church at the conclusion of the opera when she joins with the rest of the congregation in begging for mercy for Lina. There is no malice in Dorotea; she is just young and naïve. (See also **Elena** (*Aroldo*).)

Baron Douphol (*La Traviata*). Violetta's protector.

Douphol's role in the drama is more symbolic than actual. He lurks in the background as the embodiment of Violetta's alternative existence, much as Lescaut in *Manon Lescaut* (Puccini) is the embodiment of Manon's preference for a luxurious lifestyle. The difference is that where Manon rejects Des Grieux in favour of the Marquis, Violetta does it the other way round, rejecting Douphol for **Alfredo**. In other words Violetta rejects luxury in favour of love. However, by midway into Act 2 it would seem that Douphol has the upper hand since Violetta has been forced to go crawling back and beg him to be reinstated as his mistress. She needs his 'protection', having both run out of money and run foul of public morals.

The Baron is present at both Violetta's party (Act 1) and **Flora's** (Act 2). He is immediately suspicious of Alfredo and visibly sulks at dinner when all Violetta's attention is for Alfredo (Act 1). Otherwise he contributes nothing to the scene, and this is surely part of Verdi's intention. Where Alfredo has everything to offer Violetta (above all the possibility of salvation from her illness), Douphol has nothing but his money.

However, by the time of Flora's party (Act 2) Douphol's star is in the ascendant. Having accepted back the 'prodigal daughter' he warns her against having anything more to do with Alfredo. He is aware of the presence of Alfredo's father and no doubt senses a catastrophe afoot. Enjoying his ascendancy he engages Alfredo in a duel at cards, and loses. But he can afford to lose; he has money to burn and has the far greater prize, namely the most celebrated courtesan. Alfredo's outburst and cruel humiliation of Violetta will only convince him of the young man's unreliable character.

That he does not give a jot for Violetta's feelings is evidenced by the total absence of support towards her after Alfredo's outburst. Rather it is his dignity that is offended. His response is notably correct, what society would expect of him, no more, no less. In a whispered aside to Alfredo he assures the young man that his behaviour will not go unavenged. In the duel that ensues the Baron is wounded, but according to the letter **Germont** sends to Violetta he is soon recuperating. In the meantime Violetta's condition has deteriorated and Douphol loses all interest in her.

By the opening of Act 3 Douphol is no longer supporting Violetta. No doubt he would argue that he is not a charity. Since Violetta is of no further use to him, why should he continue to support her? Such strictly mercenary thinking is characteristic of his type and distinguishes him from the supremely impractical, but ultimately superior, character of Alfredo.

I DUE FOSCARI

Opera in 3 Acts. Libretto by Francesco Maria Piave after Byron's drama, *The Two Foscari* (1821).

First performed 3 November 1844 at the Teatro Argentina, Rome.

Cast:
Francesco Foscari: Doge of Venice (baritone)
Jacopo Foscari: his son (tenor)
Lucrezia Contarini: Jacopo's wife (soprano)

Jacopo Loredano: member of the Council of Ten (bass)
Barbarigo: Senator, member of the Junta (tenor)
Pisana: friend and confidante of Lucrezia (soprano)
Officer of the Council of Ten (tenor)
Servant of the Doge (bass)

Time: mid 15th century
Place: Venice

Synopsis
Background. In 1423 Francesco Foscari became Doge of Venice, having successfully defeated his rival, Pietro Loredano. Pietro opposed Foscari's policies to such an extent that the latter declared openly that he could not consider himself truly the Doge as long as Pietro lived. A few months later Pietro and his brother, Marco, died suddenly. The rumour was that they had been poisoned. Pietro's son, Jacopo, believed this was the case and had it inscribed on the brothers' tombs. He also wrote in his private business books that the Foscari were his debtors for two lives.

Meanwhile the Doge's son, also named Jacopo, was exiled from Venice for accepting bribes from foreign rulers. His sentence had been passed by the Council of Ten, headed by one Ermalao Donato. In 1450 Donato was murdered. Jacopo and his servant had been seen in Venice the previous night and it was assumed he was guilty. He was brought back to Venice, tortured and banished to Crete.

In desperation at the thought of never seeing his beloved homeland again Jacopo wrote to the Duke of Milan, pleading with him to intercede on his behalf. The letter was intercepted and once again Jacopo was returned to Venice and tortured. It is at this point that Verdi's opera opens.

Act 1 Scene 1   A hall in the Doge's palace, Venice. There is a row of Gothic windows through which can be seen scenes of the city and lagoons in the moonlight. To the right are two doors, one leading to the Doge's private apartments, the other to the main entrance. On the left are two more doors leading respectively to the hall of the Council of Ten and the state prisons. Two wax torches on the walls light the scene.

The Council of Ten and the Junta are assembling. The assembly extols the virtues of Venice: 'May silence and mystery preserve her forever, be the guiding spirit of all who rule her and inspire them with fear and love of her' (*Silenzio, mistero*). Thus is announced a major theme of the opera, the deliberate policy of misinformation that gives to political life the unpredictability of nightmare.

Barbarigo and Loredano enter. Having ascertained that all are assembled, and most particularly the Doge himself, they lead the assembly into the hall of Ten. As they proceed the senators hail the virtue of justice, which concept is added to those of silence and mystery as being the chief arbitrators of existence. That the concepts of silence, justice and mystery are hardly compatible bedfellows does not seem to concern them.

Jacopo Foscari is led in from the dungeons by the Officer of the Council and two Comandadori and instructed to wait. Jacopo expresses great relief at being out of the dungeons and able to breathe air that is 'untainted by sighs and groans'. The officer enters the Council chamber. Left alone Jacopo goes to the window and looks out towards the sea over the roofs of his beloved Venice. He reaffirms his loyalty to his homeland and recalls the agonies of exile (*Dal più remoto esilio*).

The officer returns from the Council and tells Jacopo he will soon be summoned before it. The officer piously assures Jacopo that he can hope for mercy and pity, which only causes Jacopo to erupt in scornful derision: 'Only hatred ... is locked within their breasts' (*Odio solo, ed odio atroce*). Yet Jacopo is determined that innocence shall give him the strength to 'withstand their severity'. He enters the Council chamber with the officer.

Act 1 Scene 2   A hall in the Foscari palace. Several doors are surmounted with portraits of Procurators, Senators, etc. of the Foscari family. Along the backstage wall is a series

of Gothic arcades through which can be seen the Grand Canal and, in the distance, the Rialto bridge. The hall is lit by a large lantern hanging from the centre of the ceiling.

Lucrezia enters hurriedly from one of the rooms, followed by her handmaidens who are trying to restrain her. She is in a state of great agitation as she awaits news of the Council of Ten's sentence on her husband. She puts her trust in the Doge, Jacopo's father, to show mercy. Her handmaidens attempt to calm her and remind her that ultimately Heaven will ensure justice is done. Moved by their exhortations Lucrezia prays to Heaven for succour (*Tu al cui sguardo onnipossente*).

Pisana enters in tears. She has just heard that the Council, 'in their mercy', have sentenced Jacopo to further exile. Pisana knows that this will cause Lucrezia great grief. Lucrezia erupts in fury: how can they talk of mercy when her husband's exile only extends her separation from him? She calls on Heaven to see that justice finally is done. Pisana and the handmaidens join in assuring her that the 'Eternal One in Heaven will protect the innocent'.

Act 1 Scene 3   A hall as for Scene 1. Members of the Council of Ten and the Junta enter. They are all congratulating themselves on the even-handedness of the justice they have meted out to the younger Foscari: 'Let all the world know that here against the guilty ... the laws keep their guard with equal force. Here the mighty Lion with sword and wing overtakes and smites whatever mortal should dare to defy him in word or thought'. All depart.

Act 1 Scene 4   The Doge's private rooms. There is a large table, covered with damask, on which stands a silver candlestick, writing materials and papers. A large armchair stands nearby.

The Doge, Francesco Foscari, enters and throws himself into the chair. He is enormously relieved to be alone at last. Yet, he reflects, is he ever really alone? The 'eye' of the Ten reaches everywhere: 'I am but a crowned slave!' he bitterly laments. In the Romanza: *O vecchio cor* he wishes that his heart, which beats in his breast exactly as it did in earlier years, would become as 'cold at least as when the tomb shall receive (it)'.

A servant enters and announces Lucrezia. Francesco reminds himself that he must be to Lucrezia the Doge first and foremost, and father-in-law second. Lucrezia, weeping, rails against the 'hoary-headed tigers that call themselves the Council of Ten'. Francesco bids her to remember to whom she speaks and to show respect for her country's laws. Lucrezia is not, however, to be pacified. She insists that Francesco knows as well as any that the laws of the Council of Ten are laws of 'hatred and vengeance'. She begs him to give her back her beloved husband (*Tu pur lo sai che giudice*). Francesco confesses that his heart is stricken, 'beyond all mortal belief'. He would give all his possessions and all his remaining days to see his son once more 'guiltless and free', but he cannot deny the evidence of the Court. Lucrezia is amazed that he should doubt for an instance Jacopo's innocence.

Francesco points out that an intercepted letter from Jacopo to the Duke of Milan has given indisputable proof of Jacopo's guilt. Lucrezia retorts that the only reason Jacopo penned the letter was in order to see his beloved homeland once again. True, but it was a crime nonetheless, Francesco replies. As the Doge he is powerless to come between the accused and the accuser. Lucrezia insists that if he has no power, then the least he can do is plead as a father on his son's behalf. In spite of himself Francesco is moved to tears at the realization of his own impotence. His tears give Lucrezia some cause for hope that he may yet intercede on Jacopo's behalf.

Act 2 Scene 1 The state prisons. A dim light penetrates through a vent, high in the wall. To the left there is a narrow staircase leading up to the palace.

Jacopo is seated on a marble slab. The scene that ensues bears close comparison with the opening scene of Act 2 of Beethoven's *Fidelio*, where Florestan, also unjustly imprisoned, is similarly discovered in darkness. However, whereas Florestan is visited by a vision of Leonora, his redeeming angel, Jacopo is visited by a vision of thousands of ghosts, rising up from the ground. One is advancing on him 'of giant size and savage aspect, bearing his severed skull in his left hand. He shows it to me . . . and with his right hand flings in my face the blood that trickles from it'. Suddenly Jacopo recognizes the ghost. It is Carmagnola, a famous condottiere condemned to death by the Council of Ten. Jacopo points out to the ghost that he himself is in a similar position, awaiting his fate in a dark dungeon. Apart from the fact that Jacopo inevitably fears he himself may be sentenced to execution, his vision of Carmagnola can be seen as giving expression to the fear that his own fate is in some way retribution for the injustice done to Carmagnola. Finally, he can no longer tolerate the hideous spectre and falls to the ground in a faint (*Notte! Perpetua notte . . . Non maledirmi, o prode*).

Lucrezia enters. On seeing the body of her husband slumped to the ground she fears he may be dead. She bends over him and feels his heart. She is infinitely relieved to note that it is still beating. Jacopo, delirious, imagines himself still in the presence of the ghost of Carmagnola. When he comes to his senses and realizes it is his beloved wife who speaks to him he is overjoyed, although he assumes she must have come to bid him a final farewell. Jacopo is quite prepared for the fact that he, like Carmagnola before him, may have been sentenced to death. But Lucrezia reveals that he has been sentenced to a fate, 'more dreadful than death could ever be . . .', namely continued exile from his beloved family. If Jacopo experiences any sense of relief that he is not to be executed he does not show it. He concurs with his wife in expressing anguish at the thought of enduring separation. The sound of gondoliers singing is heard in the distance. The sound epitomizes all that Jacopo most cherishes about his homeland. Bitterly he declares: 'There all is laughter; here all is death' (*Maledetto chi mi toglie*).

Wrapped in a large black cloak the Doge enters the prison, preceded by a servant carrying a torch. The servant places the torch to one side then exits. Lucrezia and Jacopo run to meet the Doge. Ecstatically the three embrace. Francesco confirms his love for his son. 'Believe it from my tears', he says. He has only feigned severity towards his son. He declares 'Here I am not Doge'. Technically he knows the Council of Ten are perfectly justified in extending Jacopo's exile, but as a father he can only deplore the separation that must ensue. Both Francesco and Lucrezia take comfort in the fact that one day they shall all meet again, once this 'earthly exile' is over. Eventually Francesco tears himself away from Jacopo and Lucrezia's embraces. He bids farewell. They shall meet again, but then he will be the Doge. They cannot meet again as father and son.

Loredano enters, to the dismay of the other protagonists. 'Do you still mock us, cruel man?' Lucrezia demands. Coldly Loredano addresses Jacopo, telling him that the Council has already assembled in order to see him embarked for Crete. The ship awaits. He orders the guards to ensure Jacopo's swift departure. Jacopo and Lucrezia upbraid Loredano for his heartlessness. Loredano, aside, confirms his infinite contempt for the race of Foscari, and satisfaction that the hour of the vengeance he has so longed for is at last at hand. Francesco, meanwhile, urges Jacopo and Lucrezia to restrain their 'fearful wrath'. Finally Jacopo departs, escorted by guards. He is preceded by Loredano while his father follows, leaning heavily for support on Lucrezia.

Act 2 Scene 2   Chamber of the Council of Ten. The Councillors and the Junta, among whom is Barbarigo, are gathering in order to witness Jacopo's final humiliation. They all confirm their determination that he shall never escape the 'vengeance of Venice'.

Francesco enters, preceded by Loredano, the Officer of the Council and Comandadori. Pages bring up the rear. He goes solemnly to take his place on the throne. Once he is seated all follow suit. Francesco addresses the Assembly, reassuring them that although he retains 'a father's heart, his face will remain that of the Doge' and he will see that justice is done. Jacopo is escorted in by four guards.

Loredano demands that the culprit should read his own sentence. He gives the parchment to the official, who gives it to Jacopo, who reads it to himself. 'The Council in its mercy has thus saved your life', Loredano comments. Jacopo begs his father to plead with the Council on his behalf, but Francesco remains true to his earlier stated resolve to play the Doge irrespective of his paternal love: 'The Council has delivered judgement. Go, my son, be resigned to your fate'. He rises and the Assembly follows his example. Loredano commands that Jacopo leave forthwith.

The guards are about to escort him hence when Lucrezia enters with her two sons, followed by various handmaidens, including Pisana. Jacopo runs to embrace his children. The Councillors are outraged that a woman should have gained admittance to their chamber. Jacopo leads his children, both of whom are weeping, to the Doge's throne where they kneel at Francesco's feet. Jacopo then makes one final plea to his father to heed the grief his exile will cause his family (*Queste innocenti lagrime*). Francesco maintains his stoic display of indifference. Lucrezia, meanwhile, attempts once more to 'move the Councillors' hearts to mercy'. Barbarigo attempts to awaken Loredano to some sense of compassion, if not for Jacopo, then at least for the children. Loredano is scornful: 'in those tears my vengeance triumphs!' he declares. Pisana and the ladies echo their mistress's pleas, but to no avail. The Councillors remain unmoved. Finally Lucrezia pleads that she and her children may be allowed to accompany Jacopo into exile. But Loredano is implacable. He takes the children from Jacopo and hands them over to the Comandadori. Realizing that all appeals are in vain Jacopo, in desperation, begs his father to at least be a mentor and protector to his grandchildren. Francesco cannot bring himself to respond. Jacopo is escorted out while his wife falls in a faint. She is supported in the arms of her ladies as all depart and the curtain falls on Act 2.

Act 3 Scene 1   The Piazzetta di San Marco. The canal is crowded with gondolas.

At the back is a view of the island of Cipressi (now called San Giorgio). The sun is setting.

The stage, initially empty, begins to fill with people and masquers who enter from various directions, meet, recognize one another, chat and are generally noisy and cheerful. It is Carnival time and the people are on their way to the regatta. Loredano and Barbarigo, who are masked, enter. Loredano cynically observes that the people give not a jot who is the Doge. Then he calls to the crowd and exhorts them to commence the festivities with the customary song. All go down to the seashore and, waving white handkerchiefs, they cheer on the gondoliers with a typical Barcarole (*Tace il vento, è quieta l'onda*). Two trumpeters enter from the Doge's palace, followed by Messer Grande. The trumpets sound and the people withdraw and remain at a distance. Even the gondolas disappear as a galley ship appears down the canal, flying the flag of St Mark. Barbarigo is surprised by the populace's retreat, 'They have no reason to be afraid' he remarks. Loredano replies laconically, 'This rabble has no spirit'.

The police chief steps ashore and is handed a paper by Messer Grande. Then Jacopo Foscari emerges slowly from the Doge's palace, escorted by a guard with Lucrezia and Pisana following. Jacopo tells his wife that his only hope now is that the ship that bears him to his exile may be wrecked. Lucrezia is appalled, but Jacopo observes that 'far from you my life is a living death' (*All' infelice veglio*). His thoughts then turn to his children and he begs his wife to ensure that they are imbued with virtue and that they grow up in the certain knowledge of their father's innocence. He exhorts his wife not to show her grief, for this would only gladden their enemies. Loredano grows impatient. Why, he demands of the Messer Grande, do they not set sail? Jacopo and Lucrezia ask who is behind the mask. Loredano reveals himself and Jacopo recognizes his 'devilish enemy'. Sadly he bids a final farewell to his father, children and wife whilst everybody present, except Loredano, is moved by the plight of his family. Escorted by the chief of police and guards Jacopo boards the galley. Lucrezia faints in Pisana's arms. Loredano enters the Doge's palace. Barbarigo exits by another street and the people all disperse.

Act 3 Scene 2   The Doge's apartments, as in the first act. The Doge enters, clearly grief-stricken. He has lost three sons to early deaths; now the fourth and last is taken from him to a shameful exile. He lays down the crown, whose weight has become unbearable to him. He deplores the isolation he now suffers (*Oh morto fossi all'ora*).

Barbarigo enters hurriedly, carrying a paper. It is a letter he has just received from one Nicolo Erizzo, a Venetian nobleman, writing from his deathbed. In the letter Erizzo confesses that it was he who had killed Ermolao Donato and therefore Jacopo Foscari is innocent of the crime. Francesco is overwhelmed with relief that his son is thus exonerated. Lucrezia enters, distraught. She bears the news that Jacopo died on the ship bearing him to exile. Francesco's joy quickly turns to anguish. Lucrezia vows that the Foscaris shall never rest till vengeance has been wreaked for her innocent husband (*Più non vive!*). 'A son expects as much blood as the tears he has shed' she cries as she exits.

A servant enters and tells Francesco that the Ten demand to speak with him. Francesco has an immediate sense of foreboding. 'What new disgrace have they in store for me?' he wonders. The Councillors enter solemnly, led by Barbarigo. After bowing to the Doge they group themselves around him. Francesco replaces the Ducal crown on his head. Loredano steps forward and portentously announces that both the Council and the Senate are of the opinion that Francesco should, in respect of his great age and grievous sorrow, be relieved of the cares of the State. In other words he should resign his office. Francesco is astounded.

So that there should be no misunderstanding Loredano declares that they have come to take from his hands the ducal ring. Francesco's amazement turns to fury: 'No mortal strength shall ever wrest it from me!' he asserts. He recalls how twice in his thirty-five year reign he has asked leave to abdicate and twice the Council has refused him. Indeed he was actually forced to take an oath that he would die as Doge. 'I, Foscari, will never break my oath' he declares. The whole Assembly erupts in uproar. Either he must resign his power or 'the Lion will compel (him) to obey'. Francesco is outraged. Is this his reward for a lifetime of service to the State? (*Questa dunque è l'iniqua mercede*). They have torn an innocent son from a father's breast and now they are to deprive a Doge in his declining years the honour of his crown, he reflects bitterly. The Councillors tactlessly point out that he can now enjoy perfect peace among his dear ones. What dear ones remain to him, asks the Doge, now that he has been deprived of his only remaining son? In response the Councillors merely intone 'Obbedir!' (Obey!).

Defeated, Francesco calls for Lucrezia to be brought before him. Then he takes the ring from his finger and gives it to a Senator. Loredano approaches Francesco, commanding him to lay down all the other accoutrements of office. Francesco refuses to give the crown to Loredano, handing it to another Senator and then allowing another to remove his cloak. Lucrezia enters. Francesco takes her hand and is about to leave with her when suddenly the bells of St Mark start to ring, announcing the election of Francesco's successor. Loredano delightedly informs him that Malipiero is elected as the new Doge. The other Councillors, embarrassed by Loredano's triumphal gloating, are fearful that this final blow will prove too much for the old man. As Lucrezia desperately calls on her father-in-law to summon his courage and rise above the fate which has so beset him Francesco, with a cry of 'My son!', falls dead. Loredano takes a note case from his breast pocket and writes the words, 'I am paid!'

When the curtain falls on *I Due Foscari* it is not so much Jacopo but his father's tragedy that lingers in the mind. Where Jacopo appears to be always on the verge of hysterics, Francesco retains throughout stoic dignity in spite of the most grievous suffering. In truth Francesco has far more justification for bewailing his fate than does his son. For where Jacopo has wilfully contravened the rules of the 'game', Francesco has always submitted himself to the dictates of duty. He receives little enough recompense – indeed his years of service are cynically thrown back in his face. For all that he has striven to exercise total impartiality where his son's fate is concerned, his only reward is to be stripped of his office. At the end of the opera he has nothing to show for his life. The message would seem to be a despairing one, whether you adhere to the rules and play the game, like Francesco, or openly revolt against the tyranny of mediocrity, like Jacopo, you are equally likely to be confounded in the end. This is, in fact, fairly average Romantic pessimism.

The real problem for both Francesco and Jacopo is that neither has sufficient energy, either in revolt or in service, to surmount the inevitable pettiness of political contingency. It takes exceptional velocity to excel either within or without the system. Finally this explains the opera's relatively speedy eclipse in the Verdi canon. There is no single heroic figure in the drama. Father and son spend most of the opera bewailing their respective fates. The only vaguely heroic action in the opera is that of Lucrezia when she bursts into the sacred portals of the Council of Ten's chamber with her two children and demands justice. Her action may appear futile in retrospect, but it was worth the attempt and succeeds in shaming all but the most hardened hearts. It is interesting that recently there has been a revival of interest in *I Due Foscari*. It would seem that its sexual politics are more in accord with our relativistic age than with nineteenth-century chauvinism.

There is another aspect of the tale which, however, may be less easy for contemporary audiences, namely the fact that Jacopo finds exile a more terrible punishment than even execution. We for whom nationalistic sentiments have become suspect at best and downright chauvinistic at worst, must inevitably find it difficult to empathize. But one does not have to look too far back in history to find nations where the supreme good, weighed above all other considerations, was dedication to the fatherland. In any culture where nationalistic fervour and its attendant paranoia is uppermost, life divorced from the homeland becomes unthinkable. For the homeland is synonymous with the lover, father, mother, or, for that matter family (which is but the nuclear reflection of the greater matrix, that is, the State in which it has its being). In any such culture the sole role of the father, and of the husband, is to engender a dignified status for the family and thereby ensure its furtherance throughout ensuing generations. This explains not only Jacopo's and Lucrezia's anguish but also, and most especially, Francesco's, for Francesco is father, father-in-law, grandfather and head of State. The fact that he is himself impotent underlines the crisis that afflicts the whole Venetian body politic.

For in having ceded authority, ostensibly to the Senate (that is, the rule of law), the Doge has rendered his own position ineffectual. Theoretically this can only be beneficial to the State. In practice it leaves the life of the individual entirely at the mercy of political factionalism. However much Francesco may yearn to protect the interests of his family he is prevented by those who would obey not the spirit but, first and foremost, the letter of the law. The Fatherland, being deprived of a father-figure, inevitably veers towards becoming a Matriarchy. Nevertheless the morality of the Foscaris, and presumably most other Patrician families, remains rigidly Patriarchal. When the Foscari chafe against the constraints placed upon them they only give voice to a fundamental schism in the body-politic, which nothing short of long endurance and the passing of several generations will do anything to alleviate.

The Duke of Mantua (*Rigoletto*)

Historical Note The character of the Duke is based on the colourful personality of François I of France (1494–1547; King 1515–1547), known in English history chiefly by the fact that he met with and bested Henry VIII on the Field of the Cloth of Gold. On this occasion it was reported that François succeeded in 'laying out' the astonished and chronically proud English king at the conclusion of a wrestling match. François was indisputably a womanizer. In his heyday he probably did indeed resemble Verdi's Duke of Mantua. His sister wrote of her brother:

'This prince was a man somewhat enslaved to pleasure, having great delight in hunting, games and women, as his youth led him, but having a wife of peevish disposition, to whom none of her husband's contentments were pleasing' (translated Francis Hackett, Heinemann, 1934).

The Duke's wife does not appear in the opera, but she is referred to (Act 2 Scene 2) when the **Page** requests to see the Duke on the Duchess's behalf. The courtiers make it plain that they have strict instructions never to disturb the Duke on his wife's behalf – for obvious reasons.

In Verdi's opera the Duke of Mantua replaces the king, François I around whose personality and court Victor Hugo set his play, *La Roi s'amuse*. The Duke, as portrayed in Verdi's opera, has no political substance. He is simply a force of nature: a *Don Juan* of irresistible energy, charisma and attraction. All the women who come into contact with him through the course of the opera – **Gilda, Giovanna, Maddalena,** the **Countess Ceprano** – fall hopelessly under the influence of his magnetic charm. This alluring persona must be established by the interpreter from the very outset. The whole future credibility of the drama stands or falls on this point.

There is nothing subtle about the Duke's methods of conquest. The confidence – nay arrogance – his social standing affords him ensures that he meets little opposition even from the husbands of the women he seeks to take to his bed. He is careless of the consequences either for himself or for the women he seduces. He lives for the moment and lacks the imagination to empathize with people less fortunate than himself. It certainly never occurs to him that his behaviour could lead somebody – least of all his jester – to take a contract out on his life. Surrounded by beautiful women the Duke is like a child in a sweet shop. He only knows that he must possess and consume.

The intensity of the Duke's feelings when thwarted is expressed in his aria, *Parmi veder le lagrima* (Act 2). Deprived of what he wants he bursts into tears. He genuinely feels that his world has come to an end. No hint of irony should enter the interpreter's rendering. Verdi gives to the Duke one of his most alluring and pathetic (in the true sense of the word) melodies. For the Duke's whole sense of identity is bound up in what he can acquire and in what he possesses. This does not encourage him to consider the pain he causes others. He enjoys the discomfiture of those who have become the butt of his jester's barbs, for **Rigoletto** represents the unlicensed liberation of his own anarchic instincts. Rigoletto says what he himself would like to say but is prevented by the convention of social nicety.

Rigoletto is, by the nature of his calling, condemned never to be himself. There is never a moment when the Duke is not himself. It is this unbridled licence that inspires hatred and envy amongst those who serve him, but his overweening confidence renders him immune to the ill-feeling by which he is surrounded. The wealth of vibrant and sensually alluring music that Verdi lavishes on the Duke is all that is needed to define his personality. There are no depths to be plumbed. The Duke's is a sunny, extrovert temperament that experiences pain only as a passing inconvenience. His two canzoni (*Questa o quella* and *La donna è mobile*) encapsulate his philosophy of life: life is too short, either to possess or to be possessed. The world is full of an infinite variety of possibilities, all of which are there for the taking. Anybody who does not is a fool and deserves whatever misery he must endure.

Such is the Duke's hedonistic life philosophy. It would be quite possible for a stage director to decide that the Duke's libertinism stems from a chronic Oedipal complex and suppressed homosexuality. Such an interpretation has certainly been applied to Mozart's *Don Giovanni*, who is the Duke's most obvious operatic antecedent. More interesting is the moral, or rather anti-moral, philosophy implicit in the play; namely that it is an accident of fate that allows the Duke to entertain his happy-go-lucky philosophy, in the same way that it is an accident of fate that Rigoletto was born a hunchback. Had the Duke been born with the disabilities that afflict Rigoletto he might see things a little differently. Conversely, had Rigoletto been gifted with the Duke's temperament he might have coped a great deal better with his disability. It depends how much one considers temperament is formed by circumstances or heredity. One thing is certain, as surely as the Duke attracts good fortune for himself, Rigoletto attracts ill.

When the censors deplored 'the revolting immorality and obscene triviality' of the libretto their opprobrium was surely dictated by the fundamentally amoral assumptions which underpin the drama. It is not good behaviour, endurance or suffering that is rewarded in this life, but the sheer brute force of the individual will and the energy which drives it.

As the curtain falls on Verdi's opera it is the Duke who survives and prevails. Principally this is because he is unconscious; he has no moral sense. Evil is only that which deprives or fails to please him. The Duke would never lament with Hamlet that 'conscience doth make cowards of us all'. He lacks the power of introspection and consequently the curse of self-division. He has no reason to doubt his abilities. The evidence of each day reinforces his confidence. It would take nothing short of a social revolution to break that confidence or convince him that the universe was not created solely for his pleasure. The Duke may not be an admirable character, but he is certainly an enviable character. Of all the principal characters in Verdi's operas he is the least self-divided, save perhaps Iago in *Otello*.

E

Eboli (*Don Carlo*).

Historical Note Princess Eboli was born in 1540. She was an heiress of the wealthy Mendoza family and was gifted in marriage in 1553 by Philip to his favourite, Ruy Gomez, to provide the latter with wealth and status. Gomez was given the job of acting as guardian to the wayward Infante. In order to fulfil his obligations he and his wife moved into an apartment adjacent to those of the Infante. Between 1559 and 1573, when Gomez died, Eboli bore him no less than nine children. If one accounts for inevitable miscarriages there was probably rarely a time when she was not pregnant. It is reckoned by historians that at least one of her children was fathered by the King. At all events it would seem unlikely that she had much time for extra-marital affairs.

Eboli was chief Lady-in-Waiting to the Queen, in which capacity she held the keys to all Elisabeth's closets. So it was perfectly possible that she acquired the Queen's jewel case, as in the opera, although since there is no evidence that there ever was an affair between Carlo and his stepmother, let alone that Philip became insanely jealous, it is unlikely that she took advantage of her situation in this way. As far as Eboli's affair with the King is concerned, if it did occur it is more than likely that it was with her husband's full knowledge – and connivance, even. She was not a sympathetic character. After her husband's death (which happened years after that of Elisabeth's) she did attempt to enter a convent of her own volition, but caused such havoc among the nuns that she was forced to leave. She returned to court but soon became inextricably embroiled in court intrigue and was eventually banished. Even that wasn't enough. Her lifestyle in Pastrana, where she betook herself, caused such outrage thereafter that she was soon imprisoned in a room in her house from which she apparently never re-emerged.

It is entirely appropriate that at our first glimpse of Eboli she is claiming the centre of attention amidst the ladies of the Court outside the monastery of San Yuste (Act 2 Scene 2). Eboli is a lady of superior vitality who needs to be at the centre of attention. She hates nothing so much as being excluded. Her very first lines, 'Within these hallowed walls the Queen of Spain alone may enter', suggest a hint of pique. Certainly she has equivocal feelings about the young Queen. She has been the King's mistress, but she knows that she herself can never be Queen. In spite of herself it is irksome to her. For someone of her temperament there can be no stopping until the summit is reached, and she must know that she has reached about as far as it is possible for her to go. At this juncture in her life a certain ennui sets in, a sense of frustration which festers.

Born a woman into a man's world her greatest weapon is her sexuality and she has no compunction about using it. The Saracen song of the veil that she sings tells of a Moorish King who falls in love with a beautiful young almah (a Moorish dancing girl) who keeps herself always veiled. The King becomes impatient and longs for her to lift her veil so that he can look on her beauty. He tells her that he no longer desires the Queen. 'Bend down', he says, 'I want to content you'. At this moment he suddenly realizes that the girl is none other than his own wife. Eboli tells the story with obvious relish. It appeals to her sense of humour. She enjoys anything that smacks of intrigue or mystery.

Eboli senses a mystery surrounding the new young Queen but cannot work out what it is. She has noticed that 'a secret sadness seems to weigh upon her'. She has also noticed, one day when standing near to the Queen, that Carlo became considerably agitated. From this observation she adds up two and two and arrives at five; 'Could he be in love with me?' she wonders. She decides that she would like to be loved by the Infante. She decides that she is in love with him herself. She sends him a note suggesting a rendezvous at midnight in the garden.

To Eboli's great delight Carlo keeps the assignation (Act 3 Scene 1). Without any prompting he pours out his undying love to her. This is more than Eboli could have hoped for: 'I am loved! I am loved!' she exclaims. It is what she secretly wants more than anything else, to find a lover who truly loves her and desires her for herself. Underneath the veneer of cleverness and sophistication she is chronically insecure. All her life she has manipulated people and events to her own ends. The problem with always being in control, of always knowing what you want, and getting it, is that you long to be taken by surprise; you long for the unexpected; you long, if you are Eboli, to be swept off your feet. And here she is, suddenly swept off her feet. She had not expected such total capitulation and passion from Carlo. She has always been a mistress of sex and she has never found someone who has wanted her for anything other than sex. For a brief instant she imagines she has found, in Carlo, a man who loves her for herself and who in turn she can love and protect. One can surmise, as is the case with many strong-minded women, Eboli has been ineffably attracted to Carlo because he so clearly needs protecting from the exigencies of living.

Carlo realizes some time before Eboli does that it is not the Queen he addresses, which is why he suddenly becomes distracted. Eboli misinterprets his distraction. She thinks he is thinking of the 'thunderbolt' which hovers over his head. She admits that she has heard Philip and Rodrigo talking together and is thereby aware of the danger in which Carlo has placed himself through his intemperate opposition to his father (one can be certain that Eboli eavesdrops on every important conversation that transpires in the palace). She assures Carlo that she can save him, for she loves him as much as he loves her.

Suddenly the bubble bursts and she realizes that it has all been an illusion, a case of mistaken identity, just as in her song. Carlo is saved the full force of her spite by the arrival of Rodrigo. But Eboli is not a woman to be scorned lightly. She resorts to threats, and we can be sure they are not idle threats. The progress of the opera will prove how lethal she can be.

Eboli is now consumed with bitterness towards Elisabeth, 'and I used to tremble before her!' Elisabeth has always seemed to her such a plaster saint. And yet, in spite of herself, Eboli has stood in awe of her, for Elisabeth represents all that Eboli can never be. Where Eboli is self-obsessed Elisabeth is selfless. Where Eboli lusts Elisabeth loves. Where Eboli is ambitious Elisabeth is disinterested. And now she discovers Elisabeth to have been all the time seeking only 'to taste of pleasure and drain the cup of love to the last drop'. Eboli will ensure that the world will learn just what a little hypocrite Elisabeth is.

When Rodrigo pulls a dagger on her Eboli is almost glad, because now she despises her own foolishness in thinking that she might have been loved for her own sake. She invites Rodrigo to stab her. But Carlo intervenes and she is left with no option but to carry out her vengeance to the letter. She goes straight to the King and tells him (erroneously) that his wife is having an affair with his son. She also steals Elisabeth's jewel case from the Queen's apartments, feeling certain that it will be found to contain incriminating evidence. It does not take her long to realize what an injustice she has inflicted on Elisabeth. In fact the moment she enters the King's chambers and sees Elisabeth prostrate on the ground she is consumed with remorse; 'I have committed a fiendish crime', she admits to herself (Act 4 Scene 1). It is only in this moment that she realizes just how equivocal are her feelings towards Elisabeth.

The discovery of the affair, as she supposed, between Elisabeth and Carlo made her detest Elisabeth so that all she wanted was to destroy her. Now that she has almost succeeded in doing so she realizes, too late, that her problem was never with Elisabeth but with herself. Carlo's rejection of her was a severe psychological shock. It unbalanced her. In her confrontation with Elisabeth she refers to the love, anger and hate she felt for her; 'the cruel jealousy which tore my heart inflamed me against you', she confesses. She has become a victim of her own chaotic emotions. Principally Eboli does not know what she wants, or rather she did not know until Carlo declared his love for her. In spite of all the political intrigue and social whirl into which she has thrown herself ultimately this is all Verdi's Eboli ever really wanted. She is an intensely vulnerable woman, as becomes clear in her great *scena* (*O don fatale*) in which she curses the beauty which has led her to grow vain and haughty, and that has led her so far from her true objective in life. Her determination to enter a convent is no mere rhetoric; it is a sign of genuine contrition. She needs to atone, not just for her crimes against Elisabeth, but also her crimes against life. But before she does – and this is entirely typical of Eboli – she will try and rectify some of the damage she has done. It is not explicit what she intends to do. One must assume that she collaborates with Rodrigo in deflecting the blame onto him, thus securing Carlo's pardon and release from prison.

As is so often the case in Verdi's operas the mezzo role represents the shadow aspect of the soprano role (others include Maddalena [*Rigoletto*], Amneris [*Aida*], Azucena [*Il Trovatore*], Federica [*Luisa Miller*]). The two are inextricably relative to each other. Were Eboli not present in the drama to irritate and confound the objectives of the other protagonists Elisabeth could well appear a plaster saint and Philip would never have been forced to confront head-on his own insufficiency as a husband. When the curtain falls on *Don Carlo* it is Eboli's passion and devastating remorse that lingers in the imagination. She is the most flawed of all the protagonists and thereby the most sympathetic.

Edoardo (*Un Giorno di Regno*). A young officer, nephew to Gasparo Antonio della Rocca, **Treasurer** of the States of Brittany, and in love with **Giulietta**.
Edoardo is that curiously uninteresting specimen, a young man with nothing better to recommend him than the fact that he is in love. But then *Un Giorno di Regno* is a comedy and complexity of character is not

necessarily a prerequisite for successful comic drama.

Edoardo is in the unenviable position of having for a rival in love his own uncle, who in spite of being in all other ways unsuitable, from a worldly perspective is far more eligible than he. Since Giulietta's father, the Baron **Kelbar**, is only interested in worldly success, Edoardo's chances look forlorn. Edoardo has no means of his own and would be quite unable to support a wife, let alone a wife as spoilt and demanding as Giulietta will undoubtedly turn out to be.

When Edoardo first appears in the opera, he is apparently resigned to the fact that he has lost all hope of winning Giulietta. He flings himself at the feet of the 'King' (**Belfiore**), and offers to devote his 'useless life' to him (Act 1 Scene 1). He no doubt hopes that he may find death on the battlefield. Edoardo is delighted that the 'King' accedes to his request. The effect of his interview with Belfiore is to goad the latter into action, post-haste, to ensure Giulietta's proposed marriage to the Treasurer is thwarted, and that Edoardo is thus enabled to marry his true love and pursue his true destiny, which is emphatically not on the battlefield.

Giulietta attempts to console her lover (Act 1 Scene 2) with the fact that she is relying on her cousin, the **Marchioness**, to extricate her from the marriage. Edoardo does not give too much heed to this. At this particular juncture he is only happy to have some time alone with Giulietta, something which he owes entirely to the good grace of the surrogate King. While Edoardo indulges in sweet nothings with Giulietta the 'King', meanwhile, is strenuously attempting to keep the Baron and Treasurer pre-occupied (Act 1 Scene 2).

When Edoardo and Giulietta approach the Marchioness they discover that she is apparently quite uninterested in their plight. This is dispiriting for the lovers who appear oblivious (as youth usually is) to the fact that the Marchioness has problems of her own. Eventually, they do elicit a response from the Marchioness, who assures them that the old man will be 'well duped'. As it turns out the

Marchioness does precious little to assist them – it is Belfiore who ensures the Treasurer is duped. Since Belfiore and the Marchioness are not communicating one cannot suppose that he acts at her behest.

When matters come to a head, and the Baron is spluttering with rage at the Treasurer's rejection of his daughter, Edoardo keeps his head, unlike Giulietta who cannot conceal her delight (Act 1 Scene 3). He puts his faith now entirely in the 'King', who presumably by now has taken on the aspect of a fairy godfather to him.

Act 2 opens with Edoardo regaling the servants, who are considerably disgruntled at the sudden cancellation of the wedding, with the welcome change in his fortune that the cancellation represents. He addresses the servants as 'my good friends' (no doubt Edoardo has spent more of his childhood downstairs than upstairs). Giulietta is of a more practical bent than her lover, and is aware that there still remains a major obstacle to their being married, namely that Edoardo is a pauper. She knows only too well that her father will never countenance her marrying Edoardo until he acquires some means of his own. She does not appear to take seriously Edoardo's job as King's esquire, which is just as well, since it is a figment of Belfiore's imagination. In any case, the problem appears to be solved when the 'King' decrees that the Treasurer devolve onto his nephew a castle and five thousand crowns per annum. How the Treasurer will view this when he discovers the 'King' is not the King at all is a matter left well outside the purview of this opera.

When Giulietta becomes obstreperous (Act 2 Scene 2) and refuses to countenance the fact that Edoardo may have to go away in order to fulfil his role as King's esquire, Edoardo has a little foretaste of what it will be like to be married to this extremely strong-willed young woman. However, he seems quite equal to the task, holding his ground and refusing to budge. He does after all owe the King everything. As Giulietta realizes she is making little headway she shows signs of relenting, but one has the impression that this marriage will be a battleground for much of the time.

Egberto (*Aroldo*). An elderly knight and Mina's father.

The central dilemma in *Stiffelio* is that between two conflicting moralities: the requirements of the worldly, socially prescribed concept of honour on the one hand, and the Christian ethos of compassion and forgiveness on the other. Lina's father, Stankar, is the representative of the first and Stiffelio representative of the second. The same basic dichotomy prevails in *Aroldo* between the life philosophies of Egberto and Aroldo, although it is inevitably watered down since the title role is no longer a priest but a Crusading knight.

A priest, by definition, is someone who devotes himself to the pursuit of spiritual values above all else. A crusading knight is 'fighting the good fight', aiming to spread the 'good news', but his principal objectives are worldly. Concomitant with those objectives is a concern above all else with honour, even above the ultimate value of compassion. Without honour there is no possibility of prevailing in the world; the crusading knight would thereby find himself in an invidious position. Thus when Stiffelio declares: 'the wrongs against one's honour survive as long as one's soul' (Act 3), we may accept it as hyperbole appropriate to the intensity of his emotion. When Aroldo speaks these words he speaks what is, for him, a literal truth. Aroldo cannot conceive of life without honour. Stiffelio knows that his faith demands that he endure a life without honour if that is what God has decreed for him.

The purpose of introducing this discussion here is that it critically alters the balance of the opera. In *Aroldo* the character of the chief protagonist is effectively brought into almost precise alignment with that of his father-in-law, whereas in *Stiffelio* the two are perfectly distinct. Egberto's chief concern is for the honour of his family. Aroldo's chief concern is his own personal honour as a medieval knight. In a sense Egberto's concerns are the more altruistic. The lineaments of Egberto's role remain very similar to those of Stankar throughout Acts 1–3, but the addition of Act 4 (in *Aroldo*) adds considerably to the role's profile. In *Stiffelio* Stankar's role effectively comes to a close at the moment he kills **Raffaele**. There is no suggestion that society will exact retribution for the murder. In *Aroldo* Egberto is forced into exile in order to escape retribution for his crime. His daughter accompanies him. Father and daughter have both regressed, for they now take refuge in each other.

In some obscure way Aroldo has become the guilty party for had Mina never left the protective embrace of father and family in order to marry Aroldo the crisis which has befallen them would never have happened. Even if Egberto has lost all that was previously important to him, his homeland, social position and honour, he must, however, feel that he has regained something he had lost, namely the undivided attention and companionship of his daughter. Such a feeling is, however, entirely illusory, as Verdi was to explore with infinitely greater power and poignancy in the final Act of *Rigoletto*.

Mina's thoughts remain all for her husband. When suddenly, against all her expectations, she is confronted with him she knows only that she wants to be rehabilitated into her husband's affections. It is in this moment that Egberto shows his true nobility of character, something that Stankar is denied in the earlier opera. For Egberto goes on bended knee to Aroldo and begs him to forgive his daughter: 'An unhappy father whom you see in tears implores you for forgiveness and falls at your feet' (Act 4). In this moment his obsession with social position which has led him to the brink of suicide (see Act 3) has been obviated. He tacitly acknowledges that there are values which transcend what is required by the exigencies of living in society. He acknowledges that his daughter's life and happiness are more important to him even than his own dignity. Thus the odyssey travelled by Egberto is actually far more radical than that travelled by either Stankar or Aroldo himself. This is *Aroldo's* biggest gain over its predecessor.
(See also **Stankar** (*Stiffelio*).)

Elena (*Aroldo*). Cousin of **Mina**.
The role of Elena is small (one line) but crucial. **Aroldo**, having picked up the book in which he believes an illicit love letter to his wife has been concealed (Act 1 Scene 2), finds the book locked. Elena volunteers the information that **Mina** has the key. Unwittingly she thus incriminates Mina. She does not contribute significantly to the remainder of the opera.
(See also **Dorotea** (*Stiffelio*).)

Elena (*I Vespri Siciliani*). Duchess Elena, sister of Duke Federigo of Austria, in love with **Arrigo**.
When Elena first appears (Act 1 Scene 1) she is lamenting the loss of her beloved brother who was an ardent Sicilian patriot and who was executed for treason by order of the French viceroy, **Monforte**. Since Elena's would-be lover, Arrigo, was implicated in the plot for which Federigo was executed it is generally assumed that he will be executed as well. In which case Elena would have double cause to mourn. As it turns out she will not need to mourn Arrigo, in the short term at any rate (see **Arrigo**).

Elena cannot afford to allow her personal feelings to override her political role as a figurehead of the Sicilian resistance movement. The people look to her for leadership and with good reason, as is proved in the opening scene where the French soldiers deliberately provoke her. With ineffable poise Elena sings what is in effect a thinly-veiled rallying cry to the oppressed Sicilians (*In alto mare e battuto dai venti*). The French are too drunk to notice but the Sicilians hear Elena's message loud and clear, although it will be a considerable time before they act upon it. Elena's grief over her brother's execution is tempered with a fervent desire to see the crime (as she sees it) avenged. She burns with hatred for Monforte and longs to see the French ousted from her homeland.

In **Procida** Elena finds both father figure and mentor. Where she has only her febrile emotions to guide her Procida is eminently practical and uses all his native wit to engineer a scenario by which a full-scale massacre of the French can be effected. Elena is thus hugely relieved to see him return to Palermo (Act 2). For Procida speaks with the conviction and passion of long devotion to the cause of independence. He gives all those around him, including Elena, the courage to take charge of their own destinies. Thus it is Elena who first proposes that the wedding of Sicily's young couples should be used as the pretext for a massacre. As it turns out the wedding celebrations will prove to be only the first step on the road to the 'Sicilian Vespers', albeit a crucial one. For it is the stealing of their sweethearts that finally goads the Sicilian men out of their apathy. (Note: It is more than probable, though not explicit, that **Ninetta**, Elena's maid, knows of the plot, apprises the other brides and thus gives justification for their apparently speedy acquiescence when taken hostage by the French.)

Elena's relationship to Arrigo is initially complicated by the difference in their respective social stations. Once it materializes that Arrigo is Monforte's son their love appears an impossibility. Elena's anguish is compounded by the fact that she is consumed with guilt for having allowed herself to indulge in an amorous passion at all. She feels that all her attention should be devoted to avenging her brother's death. Nevertheless she finds a way in which to reconcile her conflicting needs by transferring onto Arrigo the duty of avenging her brother. It is, in fact, a test for him. If he will wreak vengeance on Monforte she will be his. At this juncture (Act 2) she does not realize what an impossible demand she is making of Arrigo (nor, for that matter, does he). Arrigo is only too happy to take on the challenge.

No sooner done than Arrigo is summarily arrested and led off to the Governor's palace by Monforte's officers, there to learn that Monforte is in fact his father. Elena can only assume that Arrigo will now suffer the same fate as her brother. However she does not allow the personal tragedy that threatens her to prevent her from assisting Procida in his task of animating the young Sicilian men after their brides have been carried off by

the French (Act 2). She joins Procida in taunting **Danieli** for having stood by and allowed **Roberto** to run off with his sweetheart.

Elena then accompanies Procida to Monforte's palace in the hope of rescuing Arrigo and avenging her brother at one and the same time. When the opportunity presents itself to slay Monforte she does not hesitate, but lunges at him with a dagger she has been concealing beneath her gown (Act 3 Scene 2). She is beyond thinking of the consequences. Her one thought is to salve the gaping wound that has been tormenting her ever since her brother's execution. Great is her astonishment when Arrigo prevents her carrying out her intention. Elena is dumbstruck. She has nothing to say to Arrigo but merely joins Procida and Danieli in lamenting Sicily's 'dark fate'. Now it would appear that the Sicilians' cause is truly lost. If Arrigo can defend the enemy and betray his countrymen, then what hope is left? 'Ah, beloved fatherland, my first love, I leave you prostrate in blood, in sorrow! May your holy breath be kindled with greater ardour, and let the sun's light shine darkly upon him!' Thus the three patriots bewail their hopeless plight.

Now Elena must languish in jail (Act 4), assuming Arrigo's love and devotion to Sicily's cause were nothing but a sham. Her only consolation can be that soon she will be reunited in death with her beloved brother. When she is summoned from her cell to see Arrigo she attempts to contain her anger. But when he begs forgiveness her sense of outrage erupts. How dare he beg forgiveness; his treachery is beyond forgiveness. Her disdain compels Arrigo to tell her the truth. The truth is a colossal relief for Elena. Knowing that Monforte is Arrigo's father solves the riddle of his apparent treachery. She wants to forgive him. She wants to believe him, although she acknowledges that Arrigo's birth sets a 'barrier of blood' between them. But at least she can die happy in the knowledge that Arrigo has not betrayed her wilfully. It never seems to occur to her that Arrigo must surely be able to influence Monforte to pardon her. Such is the generosity of her nature that it is at this moment immaterial to her whether she lives or dies. She is only happy in the knowledge that her love for Arrigo is justified. When she hears the conditions of her reprieve from the sentence of execution – that Arrigo must publicly acknowledge his father – she implores him not to. Let her rather die. It may seem strange that she does not want Arrigo publicly to recognize his father, particularly since she knows this to be the case and that such a public declaration could save her life. But for Elena it is a question of honour. As far as the Sicilians are concerned Monforte is a tyrant and enemy of their country. Arrigo's public recognition of him as his father would only compromise both him and Elena in the eyes of the Sicilians.

Arrigo refrains from intervening until Procida arrives and the executioner takes Elena in charge, at which point he can contain himself no longer and passionately calls on his father, who forthwith calls a halt to the proceedings. For Elena it is a moment of impossible self-division. She is inevitably relieved that her life is spared, and the more so that she can now be united with Arrigo. But the joy and relief on a personal level is by far outweighed by her awareness of the impossibility of any amity being achieved between the Sicilians and the French, and the rank betrayal that any rapprochement would represent to her brother's memory. Hence her stifled exclamation, 'Never!' when Monforte announces her union with Arrigo as a 'seal of friendship between rival peoples'.

By the opening of Act 5, however, Elena has so far abandoned her scruples that she can declare, 'O shores of Sicily, let a serene day shine; enough horrible vengeances lacerated your bosom! Filled with hope and forgetting how much the heart suffered, let the day of my rejoicing be the day of your glories'. The truth is that for Elena it is a relief to be liberated from the onus of guilt and anger which she has carried with her ever since her brother's execution. Now she wants to put the knives away once and for all. Unfortunately for her Procida is of quite another caste of mind. He will not be able to meet his Maker until he has seen the fulfilment of his crusade to achieve Sicily's liberation. Where

Elena is prepared to forget in order to consummate her love for Arrigo, for Procida there can be no such substitute.

When Procida tells Elena that the sound of the church bells ringing out at the conclusion of her wedding ceremony will be the signal for the massacre to commence, Elena is appalled: 'At the foot of the altar! Here! Before heaven!' she expostulates. For the second time she declares, 'Never!' All the old conflicts revive within her. Inwardly she knows she cannot betray her friends. But at the same time she is not prepared to allow her love for Arrigo to be used as the pretext for a massacre, the first victim of which will undoubtedly be Arrigo's father. In a flash she sees the only way out of the predicament. She must refuse to allow the wedding ceremony to proceed. But her refusal carries little conviction. In truth her marriage to Arrigo is all she wants and, ironically, the one person who sees this quite clearly is Monforte. Thus it is Monforte himself who initiates the final denouement, who refuses to countenance Elena withdrawing from the marriage, and who takes her hands, and those of his son's, and joins them together announcing, 'I join you, O noble couple'.

Procida gives the sign for the bells to ring out. Frantically Elena implores Monforte to flee. In that moment she finally, once and for all, turns her back on the obsessive urge to vengeance which has driven her every waking moment since her brother's death. She rediscovers her humanity. Not so Procida and the rest of the Sicilians who now swarm onto the scene brandishing their weapons and shrieking 'Vendetta! Vendetta!' ('Vengeance! Vengeance!').

Elena is one of the most interesting of Verdi's heroines. Partly this is because her predicament exemplifies the central dilemma of love versus duty which Verdi usually reserves for his male characters. Whereas in earlier operas Verdi had been inclined to present two heroines, more or less delineating contrasting aspects of the feminine (ego and id, if you like), viz. Aida/Amneris, Abigaille/Fenena, Leonora/Azucena, etc.) in *I Vespri Siciliani*,

Elena has no shadow counterpart. Rather she carries her shadow within her; indeed she almost allows the shadow to consume her. Arrigo saves her from becoming an angry raving fanatic. (The poet Yeats memorably lamented what happened to Maud Gonne after she devoted herself to the cause of Irish nationalism: '... Have I not seen the loveliest woman born/Out of the mouth of Plenty's horn/Because of her opinionated mind/Barter that horn and every good/By quiet natures understood/For an old bellows full of angry wind'. ['A Prayer for my Daughter'.] While one may deplore the incipient chauvinism in his attitude, Yeats's real lament was not that his beloved allowed politics to make her fanatical, but that she did violence to her essential self – or her essential self as he perceived it.)

Elena knows that finally it is not Sicily that she needs but a relationship that is built in spite of all that has previously defined her. What she needs is to be reborn. If she perishes in the massacre at least she will perish in the knowledge that she has achieved something few human beings achieve, namely sloughing off the detritus gathered through a lifetime, detritus that sooner or later adheres and immures us long before we are physically immured. It is for this reason, more than any other, that Elena excites our sympathy and admiration.

Elisabeth de Valois (*Don Carlo*)

Historical Note Elisabeth de Valois. Daughter of Henry II of France and Catherine de Medici, Elisabeth was a beautiful and intelligent young woman. Barely sixteen when she left France to become Philip's consort, she undoubtedly took her new role seriously. She had a remarkably open disposition and her reputation was never sullied by intrigue or scandal. She was in fact universally trusted, which is why it was possible for her to sustain an open friendship with Carlos, the King's son, while never inviting any hint of scandal.

When she first arrived in France there was much squabbling between Elisabeth's French maids and the Spanish maids until finally, as Philip became exasperated with the situation, Elisabeth sent all but three of her maids back to France. This was typical of her selflessness and desire to fulfil her new role to the best of her abilities. There is no evidence that she did not love Philip as much as he her, always of course within the context of an arranged marriage. She wrote to her mother: 'Philip is so good a husband and renders me so happy by his attentions that it would make the dullest spot in the world agreeable to me' (this may have had something to do with Philip's known prowess in the bedroom). Throughout the few remaining years of her life Elisabeth was dogged by ill-health, only exacerbated by being pregnant four times in as many years. She bore Philip two daughters and had two miscarriages. It is probable that the last of these was responsible for her early death at the age of only twenty-two. This happened only three months after Carlos's death and it was whispered at the time, and immediately after by Philip's detractors, that perhaps he had had her killed in order that he could marry Anne of Austria, which marriage suited him politically. This is not borne out by history. The French Ambassador was in attendance throughout Elisabeth's final illness and never gave any hint of foul play. Philip was grief stricken when she died and remained devoted to the two daughters she had borne him.

For most of the opera – all of it if the revised edition is employed – Elisabeth de Valois is in exile. This is the central and most important facet of her character; she is a displaced person. She dreams of her homeland and does not feel at all at home in the Spanish Court. Nor does she love the man she has married; rather she loves his son, and this is not a matter of perversity on her part. She was originally supposed to marry the son, but politically it was expedient that she should marry the father instead. It is the more difficult for her to accept because when she learns that she is to marry Philip she has already met Don Carlos and been enamoured of him. In the 16th century it was not permitted for daughters, least of all daughters of Kings, to choose their mate; they had to do what their fathers told them. Verdi, who had himself lost one daughter, had a particular fascination with father/daughter relationships (see **Oberto** conclusion). Overtly *Don Carlo* is not an opera in which this matter is addressed for Elisabeth's natural father does not appear. But implicitly the theme is strongly in evidence, for Philip, in temperament, status and bearing, is far more suited to be her father than her husband. There are occasions when such marriages can work, when the girl can bring the older man a new sense of vitality and youth, while the man confers on the young girl a sense of security and stability which she would not find in a younger man. However the marriage of Elisabeth and Philip is not such an instance because, loveless, it is rooted in fear, desperation and paranoia. It is essential, in the author's view, to perform the five Act version, not least because therein one has the opportunity to witness Elisabeth on her home territory in the forest of Fontainbleau (Act 1), the homeland after which she hankers throughout the opera. This is where Elisabeth belongs.

Carlos travels to Fontainbleau in order to make her acquaintance prior to their marriage. It is significant that when he first catches sight of her she is dispensing alms to the poor. Elisabeth is, above all, a person who cares and is compassionate. Carlos is someone who needs to be cared for, who needs reassurance and compassion. His first glimpse of Elisabeth must be enormously reassuring to him. Elisabeth is oblivious that she is being watched. When Carlos makes himself known to her it is a shock. A strange man appears suddenly from out of the forest in the middle of the night. It is a strangely archetypal situation for both of them. Each is as overwhelmed as the other. Elisabeth, however, feels safe in Carlos's company, safe enough to dispense with her page and very soon to unburden herself concerning her anxieties about her proposed marriage to the Spanish Infante. 'A secret terror besets my heart. I shall be going far away, an exile', she says. It is natural for a young girl to be

apprehensive, but Elisabeth is no dying swan. She confirms that she will 'set forth cheerfully, my heart filled with hope'. Carlos's response is so ardent that Elisabeth wonders who this man before her can be. Still Carlos does not reveal his identity to her. Instead he gives Elisabeth a jewel case in which he tells her she will find a likeness of the man she is to marry. Opening the case she is confronted by a portrait of the man who kneels before her. Carlos immediately and passionately declares his love. Elisabeth is overwhelmed but not speechless. She declares straightaway, 'with what love, what passion my soul is filled!'

There is a charming naïvety about this first encounter of the young lovers. They have only just met, yet here they are, partly by necessity, almost as though to convince themselves, swearing their undying love for each other. For Elisabeth it is as though all her young dreams have come true. 'If love has guided us', she exclaims, 'if it has led you to me it has done so because it wants us completely happy'. How wrong she will be proven to be.

The cannon which sounds from the palace at this moment inevitably, in retrospect, seems to sound the death knell of all possibility of happiness for her. And yet for the moment the two are oblivious: 'Let us renew, drunk with love, the vow which united us; our lips spoke it, heaven heard it, our hearts meant it!' Then Thibault arrives with the news that they are not to be married after all. Elisabeth is to be married to the King, Carlos's father. It is the sort of psychological shock a young girl with Elisabeth's sensibility would be entitled not to recover from. No longer is it a question of 'Praise be to Heaven' that her thoughts tend, but rather, 'towards a harsh and pitiless fate'. No wonder that when Philip recalls her arrival in Spain he remembers her as 'sad faced, gazing at (his) white hair' (Act 4 Scene 1).

Philip was only in his mid thirties when he married Elisabeth, but he was indeed prematurely aged and must have presented a daunting prospect to the young French princess. There can be little left of that cheerful hope with which she had intended to embark upon her new life. Elisabeth, however, has a strong sense of duty and once having accepted the inescapable she applies herself to the best of her abilities to fulfilling the role granted her. Above all it is her piety that determines her stoicism. She does what is expected of her, accompanying the King whenever he requires her to accompany him, whether it be to the tomb of his grandfather, or to the *auto-da-fé* (Act 3 Scene 2). It has not gone unnoticed that Elisabeth is less than ecstatic in her new life. 'A secret sadness weighs on her heart', Eboli observes (Act 2 Scene 2).

When Elisabeth receives Carlos's note requesting a meeting (Act 2 Scene 2) it causes her immense suffering. 'I can scarcely bear it', she mutters to herself. But she manages to retain her regal composure. The situation becomes even more unbearable when Rodrigo pleads on Carlos's behalf. The one thing Elisabeth dreads is having to meet with Carlos again. She has found a way of coping with the fact that she is now married to his father, but at all costs she does not want to have to play mother to the man she truly loves. Even so she agrees to see her 'son'.

Carlos initially manages to present a formal stance proper to his stepmother. Elisabeth is lost for words. All she manages to say is, 'My son'. This is the last thing Carlos wants to hear. He very quickly becomes hysterical, even to the point of collapsing at Elisabeth's feet. Elisabeth is genuinely distressed, but never for a moment does she forget that she is the Queen and Carlos her stepson. Carlos's hysteria does not make it any easier for her. In fact it makes it intolerable. Eventually she screams at him: 'Finish your work, hurry to kill your father, and then spattered with his blood, you can lead your mother to the altar'. What makes her so angry is that she could so easily lapse into hysteria herself, but will not allow herself to. Why can Carlos not control himself? It is his impulsiveness and emotional incandescence that makes him both so attractive and so impossible.

Elisabeth is thus in an extremely vulnerable state when her husband enters and summarily dismisses her favourite companion, the Contessa d'Aremberg. The Contessa bursts into tears and, in a moment of searing poignancy, Elisabeth attempts to console her friend: 'You are banished from Spain but not from my heart. With you the dawn of my life was still happy. Return to our native land; my heart will follow you'. As a farewell gift she gives the Contessa a ring, 'as a last token of my regard'. With the loss of the Contessa Elisabeth loses the last link with her beloved homeland.

At the *auto-da-fé* Elisabeth must be astonished to see Carlos leading in the Flemish deputies (Act 3 Scene 2). It is somehow so out of character, but at the same time she must sense the suicidal impulse behind Carlos's actions and feel more than a tinge of responsibility. But she is powerless. All she can do is join Rodrigo and Thibault in seconding Carlos's plea to the King.

When Elisabeth discovers that the casket Carlos gave her has gone missing from her rooms she is both fearful and very angry (Act 4 Scene 1). The casket is the only thing left which links her to Carlos. Her nerves are frayed and she is tired of the prevailing atmosphere of paranoia and suspicion in the palace. She goes straight to her husband's apartments and demands justice: '*Giustizia! Giustizia!*' she cries. 'I am cruelly treated in your Court and outraged by mysterious unknown enemies.' She is perhaps not yet aware that the treatment she receives originates with Philip himself who is insanely jealous and insecure. When Philip reveals he has the casket already in his possession Elisabeth is horrified, for she knows that it still contains the portrait of Carlos. Her only hope is that he will not be able to open it. She refuses to open it herself when Philip commands her. But she has underestimated her husband's determination. He easily breaks the clasp and is confronted by the likeness of his son. Elisabeth feels utterly powerless. She knows that nothing she can say can negate the evidence. She does, however, attempt to reason with her husband, pointing out that she was originally betrothed to Carlos. But Philip will have none of it. He is determined to believe the worst. As he rants and rails at her Elisabeth makes the fatal mistake of expressing her pity for him. Philip loses all self-control and appears about to strike her. It is too much for her outraged sensibility and she faints. When she comes round she is oblivious to her surroundings and gives vent to her sense of total desolation: 'I am a stranger in this land! I have no remaining hope on earth!' She longs only for death to release her.

Eboli's confession that it was she who stole the casket comes as no surprise to Elisabeth, but she is genuinely shocked to learn that Eboli is herself in love with Carlos. Nevertheless, this is something she cannot fail to empathize with and, in the light of this revelation, she is willing to forgive Eboli a great deal. But when Eboli further admits that she is herself guilty of the very same sin of which she has accused Elisabeth her heart hardens. For Eboli infers that she has been the King's mistress since Elisabeth's marriage to him. This is too much for even Elisabeth's generous nature. She gives Eboli a choice between exile and the veil.

In his death throes Rodrigo describes to Carlos how he has apprised Elisabeth of his plan to rescue Carlos from prison and displaced the suspicion of treason onto himself (Act 4 Scene 2). He has also told her of his determination that Carlos should take over from him in his quest to save Flanders. Finally he has implored Elisabeth to meet with Carlos once more and she, as Act 5 confirms, obliges.

Elisabeth arrives at the tomb of Carlos's grandfather and, like Carlos himself before her, finds solace in the peace of its surroundings: 'Tu che la vanità'. Her homesickness is becoming a chronic nagging pain although, as she admits, she can still appreciate the lovely gardens of 'this Iberian land'. For the first time since Act 1 we have a chance to share with Elisabeth's innermost thoughts and it is quite obvious that her love for Carlos remains as strong as his for her, which in itself proves what Herculean powers of self-discipline she has had to employ in order to contain her true feelings through the

miserable years of her marriage. She knows that there can be no let up: 'Farewell, bright golden dreams, lost illusions! The knot has been cut, the light snuffed out! Farewell yet again to the years of my youth! Yielding to cruel pain, the heart has one sole desire: the peace of the grave!'

When Carlos appears Elisabeth begs of him only that he should 'forget and live'. When he refers to their love she quickly silences him and exhorts him to think of Rodrigo: 'It was not for love-sick thoughts that he sacrificed himself'. Once again she gives no expression to her own innermost feelings. She fulfils her duty and despatches Carlos to do Rodrigo's bidding and save the Flemish people. The pressure becomes too much, however, and she breaks down in tears: 'they are tears of the soul', she tells Carlos, 'and you can see what tears women can shed for heroes'. She tells him that a day will come when they will find 'the longed-for bliss' that has always eluded them on earth. They sing together of the longed-for day. It is a far cry from the passion of their first meeting and the hysteria of their exchanges in Act 2. Carlos has grown into independent manhood. Elisabeth can now respect as well as love him. They have never been so close, and yet their union has never been more impossible as is emphasized by the intervention, firstly of her husband and the Grand Inquisitor, and then the spirit of Carlos's grandfather.

As the opera closes Elisabeth is terror-struck and bewildered. Rather like Rebecca, in Daphne du Maurier's tale, she has married into a family and history over which she has no control and in which she is more or less helpless. In how many marriages is one partner not similarly marginalized by the overpowering forces of heredity, confusions of blood and instinct? Elisabeth's predicament is not uncommon, which is why it is so easy for us to empathize and sympathize with her, and finally to admire her.

Elvira (Ernani). Niece of Don Ruy Gomez de Silva, to whom she is betrothed.
Elvira may at first glance appear to be the most faceless of all Verdi's heroines (except

Medora). This is because the opera is dominated by three very strong male characters, **Ernani**, **Carlo** and **de Silva**, and revolves principally around their obsession with Elvira. This should right away tell us something about Elvira. The fact that she commands the adoration of no less than three very strong-willed men indicates that she is no dying swan. She is an extremely spirited lady on whom Verdi lavishes some of his loveliest music. Nevertheless she cannot help appearing a mere pawn in the machinations of the men who crave her love. The central conflict for Elvira is that her temperament is not suited to the age in which she finds herself. Had she been born in the 1990s she might well have made a successful business executive or politician. She is a feisty young girl, but in sixteenth-century Spain she has no option but to restrain many of her natural instincts and urges.

Elvira knows her heart; she knows that she loves Ernani. The problem for her is that she is a victim of a rigidly hierarchical society. The story of *Ernani* could be used as a tract to illustrate the evils of a chauvinistic society where the woman is an object to be possessed. This is not to say that each of the men, in their own way, would not care for her, but Elvira does not wish to be cared for. She wants to be loved and to love passionately. Of all Verdi's heroines she speaks her mind the most fearlessly. Thus she is not in the slightest bit intimidated when wooed by the king. When Carlo tries to persuade her to elope with him she rejoins: 'God forbid!' When he tries to take her by physical force she addresses him with withering contempt: 'Where is the king? I do not recognize him'. She then snatches a dagger where it hangs at Carlo's side and threatens to stab both herself and him if he does not desist (Act 1 Scene 2).

Elvira only accedes to Silva's desire to marry her when she believes Ernani to be dead. But she has no intention of enduring a bridal bed with the old warrior. She intends stabbing herself at the altar (Act 2). As it turns out she is saved from having to follow through this desperate resolve, though the grief that awaits her is a great deal crueller. She does not realize that Ernani, in order to save his life so that he can in turn rescue Elvira, has made a pact with Silva whereby he will kill himself at any given moment should Silva choose to give the sign: a blast on the horn that Ernani has given him.

Thus when the horn call sounds on the eve of hers and Ernani's nuptials, Elvira is ignorant of its import (Act 4). Confronted with Silva so spitefully seeking to wreck her one chance of real happiness she threatens to kill him and then is appalled by her own audacity and sin. She cannot help feeling guilty. She pleads desperately with Silva, reminding him that she is herself of the family of de Silva (he is her uncle).[22] Surely the old man could summon some compassion for her? After all, Carlo has managed to take a grip on himself and his passions and has not only forfeited his claim to Elvira but also forgiven both Silva and Ernani their blatant treason. Silva, unfortunately for Elvira, is of very different mettle to the king. He can find not a shred of compassion either for her or for Ernani. Thus Ernani's oath must be honoured and he must die. It seems like the ultimate confirmation of a hostile destiny, certainly for Ernani, but also for Elvira who, having been a passive victim of the passions of the menfolk who have latched onto her, has finally found a resting place for her own erotic passion.

But there is to be no consummation. In the opera she swoons. In Hugo's play she joins Ernani in killing herself, as does de Silva. Perhaps Verdi and his librettist were concerned that such an ending would leave too many corpses on the stage and they might fall foul of the censor. For Elvira it really makes no odds. Her life, in terms of the vital woman that she so demonstrably is, is over.

It is a recurring feature of all Romantic drama that the heroine turns her back on the possibility of security and stability (represented in this opera by Carlo the King

---

22 Which begs the question of **Roger's** 'incestuous' passion in *Jerusalem*.

on the one hand and the wealthy and aged de Silva on the other) in favour of a life of risk in the arms of some outlaw or bandit. Thus the heroine, by necessity, in exactly the same way as the hero, consciously turns her back on the biological role predestined for her by Nature and ratified by society. She seeks to elude the ever-present perils of acceding to the staus quo.

Emilia (*Otello*). Iago's wife and **Desdemona's** maid.

Emilia occupies a uniquely uncomfortable position in the opera, poised as she is between the work's evil genius and his innocent victim.

Emilia is in attendance (Act 2) when **Desdemona** is receiving and dispensing alms to the Cypriot people. She enters the hall of the castle with Desdemona. When **Otello** throws aside the handkerchief with which Desdemona offers to soothe his brow, Emilia instinctively picks it up. **Iago** demands she surrender it to him. Emilia is immediately suspicious. 'What trickery are you about? I can see it in your face', she says. She clearly knows her husband and his 'wicked spite'. No doubt she has been on the receiving end of it all too often. The face a man displays to the world is usually very different from that he exhibits at home. Iago treats his wife abominably: 'You are Iago's slut of a slave', he snarls at her (Act 2). Emilia refuses to surrender the handkerchief and finally Iago physically wrests it from her. Emilia reveals that she is well aware that no good can come from whatever it is that her husband is plotting: 'God keep us always safe from danger', she prays. She leaves the scene with Desdemona, who already finds that Otello behaves strangely towards her.

In Act 3 Emilia enters the hall of the castle with Desdemona, who has been summoned by Otello. By now she cannot fail to be aware that there is something drastically wrong in her mistress's marriage. She must also be obscurely aware that her husband has something to do with it. She remarks to Desdemona on how sad she seems, to which Desdemona replies, 'Emilia, a great cloud disturbs Otello's reason and my fate'. Emilia very soon has the opportunity to confirm this with the evidence of her own eyes, for Otello snarls at Desdemona then lashes out at her, apparently with no provocation. Emilia is truly shocked, commenting, 'This innocent heart shows neither /a spasm nor a gesture of hatred /within her heart. She painfully represses her grief. /Teardrops fall mutely on her sad face. /No, he who does not weep for her /has no pity in his breast'. She flees the scene with her distraught mistress.

Act 4 Emilia tries to comfort Desdemona as her mistress prepares for bed. She brushes Desdemona's hair as the latter recalls the 'Willow Song' that a previous servant, named Barbara, used to sing. When Desdemona gives Emilia her ring and then passionately embraces her in farewell she can have little doubt as to what agitates her mistress. But she is only a maidservant and is powerless to do anything to help; or so she thinks. It may seem incredible that Emilia does not realize that her husband is behind all Desdemona's miseries, and act accordingly to prevent any further mischief. But Emilia is not gifted with great reserves of intelligence or imagination and is totally in thrall to her husband, as she is to her master, Otello. She has little room for manoeuvre being entirely subservient, if not by nature, then by circumstance and force of habit.

It might be thought that Emilia, knowing Desdemona's mood and trepidation, would remain in the vicinity of her mistress's bedroom, ready to intervene if necessary. However, since Otello enters the bedroom by a secret door she can have no way of knowing what transpires within. When she finds the door locked, however, her suspicions must be aroused.

Presumably she learns of **Roderigo's** murder either from Iago or from **Cassio** himself. At any rate she is greatly agitated by the news. But it is nothing to her distress when she discovers the dying form of Desdemona. When Otello admits to the crime and tells her to corroborate with Iago the fact that Desdemona was Cassio's 'whore', Emilia's worst fears are confirmed.

Now she loses all sense of deference before the Moor: 'Dolt! And you believed him?' she splutters. She instinctively knows that Iago is solely responsible for the tragedy. When Otello starts ranting about Desdemona's handkerchief she need doubt no longer. Both Otello and Iago are threatening and abusive towards her, but she is no longer intimidated. She refuses to be silent and reveals how Iago wrested Desdemona's handkerchief from her. When **Montano** lets it be known that Roderigo, in his dying moments, has revealed to him Iago's 'evil wiles', the case for the prosecution is complete.

All through history there have been instances of women married to monsters who have genuinely remained oblivious to the true nature of their spouse (one thinks in recent times of the case of the Yorkshire Ripper). Emilia will no longer wish to be married to a man capable of such malice. She has had her suspicions about Iago previously. She knows his temper and his capacity for deception, but she would never have believed him capable of such appalling callousness.

L'emir de Ramla (Emir of Ramla) (*Jerusalem*)
The Emir replaces the Tyrant of Antioch (Acciano in *I Lombardi*). Acciano is a far more central character than is the Emir, for the simple reason that both his wife and son also appear in the opera. His son, Oronte, in particular plays a leading role in the drama of *I Lombardi*. The Emir is simply a cardboard villain. He is referred to (Act 2 Scene 1) where **Raymond** informs **Hélène** that **Gaston** is his prisoner.

Act 2 Scene 2 takes place in the Emir's palace, where the Emir makes a brief appearance in which he learns that a Christian woman has been discovered in the town. Hélène is brought in soon after, and the Emir decides the best way of discovering her identity would be to leave her alone with Gaston. Having eavesdropped on the lovers' reunion he ensures their capture when they attempt to escape.

By the time of Act 3 Scene 1, which takes place in the Emir's harem gardens, the Crusaders have already taken possession of the town and most of the Emir's palace. He must realize he is living on borrowed time (it hardly seems the moment for him to be entertained with a ballet by his odalisques, but then the Jockey Club had to be appeased somehow).[23]

Enrico (*Aroldo*). **Mina**'s cousin.
Enrico has the misfortune to be dressed in a similar fashion to **Godvino** at the festivities celebrating **Aroldo**'s return (Act 1 Scene 2). He is thus mistaken for Godvino and is temporarily suspected of being Mina's lover. Enrico does indeed take the incriminating book from the table and inspect it, but finding it locked leaves it and continues to mingle with the other guests.

Briano, meanwhile, has told Aroldo that Enrico is the culprit. When Enrico seconds **Egberto**'s request that Aroldo relate the heroic deeds of King Richard in Palestine, Aroldo, convinced that Enrico mocks him, tells a story of a man who betrayed 'faith and honour'. As he does so he picks up the book in which he suspects Enrico to have hidden a letter.

Thus, all unwittingly, Enrico precipitates the denouement of the action. Presumably Aroldo continues to suspect Enrico, for Egberto appropriates Godvino's letter and Aroldo is none the wiser as to the identity of the culprit. He will suspect Enrico (who does not reappear in the drama) until the moment when he is confronted with the truth (Act 2 Scene 1).
(See also **Federico di Frengel** (*Stiffelio*).)

---

[23] It was to satisfy the members of the Jockey Club in Paris that every opera performed at the Paris Opera had to include a ballet if it was to have any chance of success. The tradition was to have a ballet performed at the beginning of Act 3, the ostensible reason being that the members of the Jockey Club needed time to dine. Once they had dined they liked to adjourn to the opera in time to catch their particular amour, very often a member of the *corps de ballet*, performing on stage. Verdi only grudgingly bowed to this tradition. The ballet music for *Jerusalem* was the first ballet that Verdi composed.

ERNANI

Opera in 4 Acts. Libretto by Francesco Maria Parve, after Victor Hugo's play, *Hernani* (1830).

First performance: 9 March 1844 at the Teatro la Fenice, Venice.

Cast:

Ernani: a bandit (tenor)
Don Carlo: King of Spain (baritone)
Don Ruy Gomez de Silva: Grandee of Spain (bass)
Elvira: his niece and betrothed (soprano)
Giovanna: her confidante (soprano)
Don Riccardo: the King's steward (tenor)
Iago: Silva's steward (bass)

Time: early 16th century
Place: Spain

Synopsis

Act 1 Scene 1   A mountain retreat in Aragon. In the distance is seen the Moorish castle of Don Ruy Gomez. It is nearly sunset. A band of rebel mountaineers and bandits are eating and drinking. Some are playing cards, others are cleaning their weapons.

The bandits sing of the joys and exigencies of the bandit's life (*Evviva! Beviam! Beviam! –* see **Chorus**). Ernani enters. The bandits wonder why he appears so pensive. They attempt to encourage him to join them in a drink. They confirm their solidarity with him: 'we have the same lot in life and in death. Our arms and hearts are yours'. Ernani thanks them and then reveals what troubles him. He has fallen in love with an Aragonese maid, Elvira and she with him. But she is being wooed by the elderly knight, Don Ruy Gomez de Silva who, 'tomorrow is confident of dragging her to the nuptial bed' (*Come rugiada al cespite*). Ernani proposes that they should abduct her from the castle in order to avert such a calamity. The bandits happily agree to assist him. Adventure is what they crave above all else. Ernani confirms his love for Elvira (*O tu che l'alma adora*) and they all set off for the castle.

Act 1 Scene 2   Elvira's apartments in de Silva's castle. It is night and Elvira is alone.

Elvira reflects with anguish on her situation. The more de Silva presses his suit, the more convinced she becomes that Ernani is her true love (*Ernani! Ernani, involami*). Whatever fate might throw at them she would rather have a precarious existence with Ernani than imprisonment in de Silva's castle.

Ladies-in-waiting enter bearing rich, worldly wedding gifts. They sing of the great beneficence that is being bestowed upon Elvira with de Silva's love. Elvira is gracious towards them but in an aside she reveals how deeply she despises all the trappings of affluence that they parade before her (*Tutto sprezzo che d'Ernani*). 'There is no jewel can change hatred into love', she comments. The ladies-in-waiting reflect that Elvira may be a bride but she shows no rejoicing. They all exit.

Don Carlo enters, followed by Giovanna. He tells Giovanna to fetch Elvira to him. Giovanna tells him that her mistress has for several days avoided all company. She infers that it is because de Silva is absent. She then departs to do Carlo's bidding.

Left alone Don Carlo reflects that although he loves Elvira, she cares nothing for his love, nor the power that he wields, but loves instead a bandit. For a man like himself this is incomprehensible. Elvira enters and Carlo immediately declares his love. Elvira is scornful but Carlo begs her to flee with him. Elvira is adamant. When Carlo refers to her passion for Ernani Elvira comments: 'Every heart contains a mystery'. This is the cue for Carlo to unburden his 'heart's mystery', his all-consuming love for Elvira (*Da quel di che t'ho veduta*). He reiterates his plea to her to flee with him so that he may make her his queen. For answer Elvira remarks: 'Haughty blood of Aragon flows in my veins. A crowned splendour cannot impose love on my heart'. Carlo becomes impatient. He seizes her arm and impetuously declares that he shall possess her, come what may. Elvira witheringly retorts: 'Where is the king? I do not recognize him'. When Carlo threatens to become imperious Elvira snatches a dagger that hangs at his side and commands him to leave, otherwise she will stab both of them.

At this critical impasse Ernani enters from a secret door. Confronted with Ernani all Carlo's frustration and contempt for the bandit overflow. Ernani is not afraid to respond. Reminding Don Carlo that he was responsible for killing his father and stealing all his possessions and honour, Ernani challenges Carlo to a duel. Elvira comes between them with dagger drawn and threatens to stab herself if they will not desist. Suddenly de Silva enters and launches straight into his recitative, *Che mai vegg'io*. Not surprisingly he is outraged to find not one, but two men in his betrothed's apartment. He summons his knights, who enter together with Giovanna. 'Let each bear witness to the dishonour and shame being brought upon his lord', he says. In his aria, *Infelice! E tuo credevi* he bewails to himself the dishonour that has fallen on his aged, white head. Then, rallying himself, he turns to Ernani and Carlo and challenges them to give him satisfaction. He calls on his squires to fetch his battle-axe and sword, for he craves vengeance (*Infin che un brando vindice*). He commands that the two men wait outside.

Iago, Silva's steward, enters and announces the royal equerry, Don Riccardo. De Silva welcomes this arrival: 'he shall be witness of my vengeance', he says. But then Riccardo turns to Carlo and declares: 'only loyalty and homage are due to the king'. De Silva is flabbergasted. He had no idea that one of his bride's seducers was the king himself. Everybody comments how de Silva is immediately restored to reason by this revelation (*Vedi come il buon vegliardo*). De Silva kneels before Carlo and begs forgiveness, explaining that he was confused by Carlo's disguise. Carlo is magnanimous and whispers urgently to de Silva that he desires 'a faithful man's counsel'. Death has taken his 'august ancestor', and now there is to be an election for his successor to the Imperial throne. He invites himself to stay at de Silva's castle with his company for the night. He does not wish to expose Ernani and tells de Silva, 'this trusted man will leave at once'. Ernani is unimpressed. He reflects to himself

that every remaining hour of his life he will devote to thoughts of revenge for his father, who was killed by the royal forces. Elvira implores Ernani to make good his escape.

Carlo meanwhile declares to de Silva and Riccardo his ambition to acquire for himself the imperial crown and his intention to bring 'clemency and justice' to the office. The attendants observe that de Silva's fury has been transformed into joy through the great honour that Carlo does him by taking up residence in his castle. Elvira, to the distress of her attendants, is inconsolable.

Act 2 A magnificent hall in the castle. Portraits of the de Silva family, handsomely framed, are surmounted by silver crests. Beside each painting stands equestrian armour. Knights, pages and ladies-in-waiting are in attendance upon de Silva.

The attendants all sing in praise of Elvira's great beauty and pray that the marriage may be blessed with offspring (*Esultiamo!*). De Silva enters with Iago, telling the latter to bring to him an itinerant pilgrim who has apparently just arrived at the castle. The pilgrim is ushered in. It is Ernani in disguise. De Silva, who does not recognize him, asks Ernani what he wishes. Ernani replies that he asks for hospitality. De Silva assures him that in the tradition of his family he offers unconditional hospitality to any stranger who becomes a guest in his house.

Elvira enters, emerging from her chamber in bridal dress and accompanied by attendants. De Silva proudly introduces his bride and requires to know of Elvira why she is not adorned with the ring and ducal crown. Learning that Elvira is to be wed to de Silva within the hour, Ernani cannot keep up the pretence any longer. He throws off his pilgrim's habit and declares: 'such gold as can satisfy every avid wish, I offer it all to you. Take it, the price of my blood. A thousand warriors are pursuing me like dogs and wild beasts. I am the bandit, Ernani. I hate myself and the light of day' (*Oro, quant'oro ogn'avido*). De Silva thinks, not entirely without justification, that Ernani must have lost his mind. Ernani urges de Silva to take him as his prisoner in return for the reward on his head. But, ever mindful that he has invited Ernani into his castle and is bound by the laws of hospitality, de Silva orders his men to man the battlements to ensure Ernani's safety whilst he is in the castle. He makes a sign to Elvira to retire with her ladies and then leaves, followed by Iago and attendants.

When he has gone Elvira returns. Ernani immediately upbraids her for her faithlessness. She explains that she thought him dead. She then reveals a dagger she carries under her dress with which she was intending to stab herself on the steps of the altar. Ernani begs her forgiveness and declares his love. Together they reaffirm their mutual devotion. As they embrace de Silva returns. He rushes between them, sword in hand, spluttering with rage. Before he can do anything, however, Iago hastens in with the news that Carlo has arrived at the castle gate with a squad of soldiers and is demanding to be admitted. De Silva instructs Iago to admit the king. Ernani demands that the old man grant him death forthwith. De Silva is scornful (*No, vendetta più tremenda*). He is determined that it shall fall to him alone to wreak vengeance. In the meantime he will conceal Ernani from the king. He ushers him through a secret door behind a portrait. Elvira retreats to her apartments as Carlo enters, accompanied by Riccardo and knights.

Carlo demands to know why he finds the castle armed. He is convinced that the old man is harbouring a rebellion. De Silva, head bowed, confirms his loyalty. Carlo, however, is convinced that de Silva is sheltering Ernani. He orders de Silva to surrender the bandit or he will torch the castle. De Silva invokes the laws of hospitality which prevent him from betraying a guest. When Carlo demands either his head or Ernani's, de Silva is steadfast: 'Take mine!' Carlo commands Riccardo to relieve de Silva of his sword and then search the castle. De Silva maintains that his men are loyal to him and will not betray Ernani. Carlo is incensed at the old man's audacity and warns him of dire consequences (*Lo vedremo veglio audace*). Carlo's knights return and report that they have searched

the castle in vain, at which Carlo threatens to resort to torture.

Elvira, who has been eavesdropping on the scene, can forbear no longer and rushes in. Throwing herself at Carlo's feet she pleads with him to be merciful. Carlo is taken aback. He cannot, however, ignore her pleas and tells de Silva that he will hold Elvira hostage. Either de Silva must surrender Ernani or he will leave with the girl. This is too much for de Silva. He pleads with Carlo not to take Elvira, 'the only solace on this Earth to a wretched old man'. But when Carlo demands to know Ernani's whereabouts, de Silva recovers himself and tells Carlo to take Elvira. He will not betray his trust. Carlo is overjoyed at last to have Elvira in his possession (*Vieni meco*). De Silva is distraught. His attendants all express concern for their master. Elvira is equally distraught. Only Carlo is satisfied. Carlo departs with Riccardo and the knights, taking Elvira who leans on Giovanna's arm. Her ladies follow.

Left alone de Silva declares his undying hatred for the king who has deprived him of his most precious possession. He takes two swords from his armoury and opens the secret door that conceals Ernani. He presents Ernani with one of the swords and orders him to follow him outside and fight. Ernani objects on the grounds of de Silva's advanced years. De Silva is outraged, but Ernani is so insistent that de Silva is forced to take notice. When he tells Ernani that the king has abducted Elvira Ernani is appalled. It suddenly becomes clear that de Silva does not realize that the king is his rival in love. Ernani enlightens him. De Silva immediately calls for his knights. Ernani demands to be granted a part in the vengeance. De Silva is unwilling to grant Ernani anything other than a speedy death. So Ernani proposes a compromise. Let him first participate in Silva's vengeance then de Silva may kill him. He hands de Silva his hunting horn and tells him, 'At the moment when you want Ernani dead, if he hears a blast Ernani will die at once'. De Silva demands that he swear to it. The two confirm their oath.

De Silva's knights enter and de Silva instructs them to pursue the abductor. Baying for blood the two infatuated men, accompanied by de Silva's knights, depart in pursuit of their king.

Act 3 Charlemagne's tomb at Aix-la-Chapelle. The tomb bears the inscription: 'Carlo Magno'. A staircase leads from a large door. Two dim lights hang in the centre. Carlo and Riccardo enter stealthily, wrapped in cloaks. Riccardo carries a torch. Riccardo has brought his king to witness a meeting of those who are conspiring against Carlo. Carlo determines to hide behind Charlemagne's tomb. He is in a fever of expectation, not only because of what he may witness, but also because the electors are at this very moment deliberating as to who should be elected Holy Roman Emperor. Carlo dismisses Riccardo, instructing him to fire three cannon shots should he be elected and then bring Elvira to him. Riccardo departs.

Left alone, Carlo gives way to existential ruminations. 'Sceptres! Riches! Honours! Beauties! Youth! What are you? Barks floating upon the sea of the years, which waves strike with constant troubles, until reaching the tomb's reef, your name plunges into nothingness.' He determines that should he be granted the imperial throne he will be a virtuous and great leader (*Oh, de' verd'anni miei*). He opens the gate of Charlemagne's tomb with a key and disappears within.

Conspirators enter stealthily, all wrapped in huge cloaks. Amongst the conspirators are Ernani, de Silva and Iago. Having ascertained all conspirators are present de Silva reveals to them that Carlo aspires to the Holy Roman Empire. He then decrees that they should elect by lottery one man from among them to commit the deed of murdering Carlo. Each man draws out a tablet and inscribes his name, then throws the paper into one of the tombs. De Silva goes and draws one name forth. It is Ernani's. Ernani is overjoyed. Finally he has a chance truly to avenge his father's death. De Silva begs Ernani to grant him the task. In exchange he will spare Ernani's life and give him all his worldly possessions. Ernani refuses. De Silva produces

Ernani's horn and reminds him that he could compel Ernani to kill himself forthwith at which the latter pleads to be allowed to strike first. 'Then, young man, the most horrible revenge awaits you', de Silva mutters.

The conspirators now join in a rousing chorus (*Si ridesti il Leon di Castiglia* – see **Chorus**). At this moment a cannon shot is heard outside, startling everyone present. Then another shot is heard and the door of the monument opens. As a third shot is heard Carlo appears. The terrified conspirators exclaim, 'Carlo Magno imperator!' ('Charlemagne, the Emperor!') to which Carlo dramatically strikes the bronze door three times. 'Carlo Quinto' ('Charles V!'), he corrects them.

The great gateway of the vault now opens and six electors enter, dressed in gold brocade, followed by pages carrying velvet cushions, bearing the crown and sceptre and other imperial regalia. German and Spanish ladies and gentlemen surround the Emperor. Elvira and Giovanna are amongst them. Riccardo brings up the rear of the procession, which is illuminated by torches.

Riccardo formally announces Carlo as the new Emperor. Carlo loses no time in exerting his imperial authority. He tells the electors of the conspiracy against him, and orders the guards to round up the mob and take them prisoner, but to single out any nobles amongst them and take them straight to the block. Ernani proudly advances through the nobles and addresses Carlo: if the nobles are to die then he should be amongst them for he is a Count, Duke of Cardona and Don Juan of Aragon. He has failed in his mission to avenge both his father and his country and now offers his head to Carlo. Carlo merely remarks, 'Your head shall fall with the others'. At which Elvira, for the second time in the opera, falls at Carlo's feet and begs for mercy. Carlo attempts to silence her, but when Elvira, rising, declares: 'Pity is an august virtue', Carlo is suddenly reminded of his former resolution. Staring at the tomb of Charlemagne he remembers how desperately he desires to emulate his great predecessor's virtues (*O sommo Carlo, più del tuo nome*). Turning to the conspirators he grants forgiveness to them all. Amazed at the self-control that he has suddenly found, he leads Elvira to Ernani declaring to them, 'you shall marry. Love each other always. Glory and honour to Charlemagne'. (It is hardly necessary to draw the comparison with the ending of Verdi's earlier opera, *Alzira*.) All sing their praise for the new Carlo, all, that is, except de Silva, who mutters darkly of his craving for vengeance. Carlo's sudden metamorphosis does not impress him.

Act 4   Don Juan's palace in Aragon. A terrace. At the back is a grille, through which can be seen the illuminated gardens of the palace. Ladies, gentlemen, maskers, pages and serving maids come and go, merrily talking amongst themselves.

The guests sing in praise of the bride and groom, Elvira and Ernani (*O come felici gioiscon*). They then draw attention to a masker who has appeared dressed in a black domino and who is looking impatiently about him. All notice that he hides his wrath with difficulty. As he departs, 'with threatening gestures', and other maskers appear the chorus expresses relief. (The masker is, of course, de Silva.) Elvira and Ernani emerge from the ballroom and the guests exit.

The couple sing of their newfound happiness and relief at the passing of their troubles. Their happiness is short-lived. A horn is heard in the distance. It is de Silva summoning Ernani to be true to his oath. Elvira is oblivious to the horn's significance, although she quickly becomes aware of Ernani's agitation. He has spotted an 'infernal grin' in the shadows and realizes it is de Silva. Ernani tells Elvira that an old wound is causing him trouble and despatches her to find some medicine. Ernani vainly hopes that perhaps his imagination is playing tricks on him. He is about to follow Elvira into their bridal chamber, but is forestalled by de Silva, still masked, who appears at the top of the stairs. De Silva repeats verbatim the words of Ernani's oath and then, approaching Ernani and removing his mask, demands to know if Ernani intends to keep his pledge.

Ernani tries to plead with the old man at least to let him, 'drink from the cup of love' (that is, have one night with Elvira) (*Solingo, errante e misero*). But de Silva gives Ernani a dagger and a flask of poison and offers him a clear choice between the two. Goaded by de Silva's insults Ernani takes the dagger and is about to stab himself when Elvira rushes in and restrains him. Incensed beyond reason she rails at de Silva, even threatening to kill him herself. Then, appalled at her intemperance, she breaks down weeping and begs forgiveness. De Silva is unmoved. Ernani realizes that de Silva's anger is uncompromising but Elvira continues pleading, admitting to de Silva that she loves Ernani. De Silva remains adamant. Ernani begs Elvira to stop weeping. De Silva threateningly reiterates the words of Ernani's oath and Ernani, realizing that he cannot escape his destiny, thrusts the dagger into his breast. Elvira would follow suit, but Ernani, with his dying breath, commands her to live.

Even at the last de Silva appears to feel no remorse as he exults in the satisfaction of his crazed need for vengeance. As the curtain falls Ernani dies and Elvira falls unconscious. Only de Silva remains, calling on the 'demon of revenge' to come and gloat.

Ernani explores the extraordinary and unique capacity that human beings possess for living their lives by the light of an ideal or an obsession. This capacity represents the very essence of what it is to be human. It can manifest itself in both the greatest and the very worst aspects of humanity, as evidenced in this opera and specifically in the character of de Silva. The opera might perhaps have been better titled 'Don Ruy Gomez de Silva' for it is his monolithic obsessiveness that overshadows the whole work and draws into its net the destinies of all the main protagonists. The whole is contained within the social code of honour that characterized the morality of late sixteenth-century Spain; honour before all else. The ravages that can attend a strict adherence to such a code provided grist for Verdi's mill many times over.

Concomitant with this code of honour are the laws of hospitality, laws which are embedded in the universal psyche since the birth of consciousness (Wagner has his barbarian chieftain, Hunding, invoke those same laws in his mythological opera, *Die Walküre*). Thus de Silva variously gives sanctuary to both his rivals in love. It would be unthinkable for him not to, even when he finds Ernani in the arms of his betrothed. The laws of hospitality are self-perpetuating; thus Carlo feels honour-bound not to expose Ernani. As rivals in love the two men are in equally compromising situations. Carlo only manages to escape by the simple expedient of revealing that he is the King. It would be dishonourable to take advantage of his ascendancy by having Ernani arrested.

It can be seen that such a code encourages a level of decency in human behaviour that is almost extinct in our more liberal age. Conversely the rigid adherence to the letter of the law which characterizes de Silva's maniacal pursuit of Ernani leads to untold misery for all the protagonists. In Hugo's play de Silva commits suicide along with Ernani at the conclusion (so, for that matter, does Elvira). This has the effect of underlining the personal misery which is at the root of de Silva's behaviour. In the opera he remains standing over the body of Ernani and the prostrate form of Elvira, gloating over the consummation of his revenge. This makes him an altogether less sympathetic character and critically alters the balance of the drama, for it confers on de Silva an aura of malignancy that is not present in Hugo's play. It does, however, leave the audience in no doubt as to where lies the *deus ex machina* underlying the action.

De Silva's passion is perverse and invites horror, and yet it raises him above the average. It could be argued that in that case 'better the average'. This is the paradox at the heart of all such obsessiveness, and at the heart of Verdi's opera.

Ernani (*Ernani*). A bandit.
Ernani is one of a family of outlawed Romantic heroes in Verdi's operas that include **Don Carlo** (*I Masnadieri*), **Don Alvaro** (*La Forza del destino*), **Manrico** (*La Trovatore*), **Corrado** (*Il Corsaro*). Outlawed they may be, for some mole of nature or momentary failing, but usually the outlaws far outstretch those who work within the establishment in terms of imagination and creative endeavour. They are heroes by virtue of the fact that they do not accept the status quo. They wish to transcend it in some way.

Having said which, in reviewing Ernani's career, it is difficult to see at first sight how he transcends the lives of the other protagonists. Why is he outlawed? Ostensibly because his father has been dishonoured and killed by the King, but in reality he is a bandit because if he were not a bandit he would die of suffocation within the confines of a narrow moral code that severely limits the possibility of what is permissible for one individual to do. Throughout Verdi's opera, and Hugo's play, the rigidity of the codes of honour that dictate the boundaries of all the characters' interactions are exemplified as pernicious and life-denying. The sacrifice that Ernani makes at the end of the opera is supposedly in obeisance to those same moral codes, but in reality exposes the absurdity of a rigid adherence such as is exemplified by the character of de Silva. This exposé is far more explicit in Hugo's play than in Verdi's opera, for in the former de Silva commits suicide with Ernani. The fact that in Verdi's opera de Silva merely stands amidst the devastation of the newly-weds and gloats obscures the original author's message.

Ernani loves a woman who is also loved and wooed by two other men. Inevitably the woman gives her heart to him in recognition of the far greater possibility of liberation from the constraints of her life that Ernani can offer her than either Carlo, the King, or de Silva, the aged warrior. Ernani appears never to doubt Elvira's commitment. He knows his strength. As an outsider and renegade he may be disadvantaged in social terms, but he is also very much stronger than either of his rivals. He cannot afford not to have faith. De Silva is in an unreal position from the outset because he is so clearly an unsuitable bridegroom for such a young girl, being old enough to be her grandfather. Carlo, being the King, is eminently suitable from a worldly point of view. What spirited girl in her right mind would turn down the opportunity of being married to the King? But Elvira does not need a king. For the king is figurehead of the state, of a moral order in which she is confined. She needs to be liberated. Instinctively Ernani realizes this. It is this which gives him his confidence. He is determined that in the sadness of his exile Elvira shall be his 'consoling angel'.

When, in the fever of passion, Ernani confronts de Silva he declares: 'I am the bandit Ernani. I hate myself and the light of day' (Act 2 Scene 1). He speaks only a partial truth. If he hates himself so much, if he had hated the light of day so much (synonymous with the world which operates only in the light of day) he would have killed himself long ago. Why did he not? Because he retains an image of what life *could* be for him in the arms of Elvira. He retains a vestige of hope. While his external circumstances appear so hopeless he lives in a false position; what Sartre would call 'mauvais fois', but with that unique human gift for enduring the absurd he persists with his life, expecting nothing, hoping nothing, but still waiting. He may not have hope but he is, in happier moments, consumed with expectancy, and while there remains a glimmer of expectancy there is a reason to continue enduring.

When Elvira confirms that she had intended to stab herself at the altar of her marriage to de Silva, the glimmer of light that has sustained Ernani until now becomes a joyous flood of hope, such as he has not known in years. From this moment his self-pity is confounded. He can from now on surrender himself to his destiny. When he makes the rash vow that he will kill himself at any given moment should de Silva demand it, it is clearly a means of extricating himself from an impossible predicament. He never has any intention of not honouring the vow he makes to de Silva, but subconsciously he must hope that de Silva's humanity will eventually assert itself. United in a common cause with de Silva to rescue Elvira from the arms of the king, the possibility that de Silva will hold him to his oath must surely recede to the outer limits of his mind. Certainly he attempts to avert the calamity by appealing on a purely human level to de Silva's better nature. Sadly for him, and Elvira, de Silva is uncompromising.

And yet Ernani knows, within himself, the power of a vengeful obsession. For all his life he has carried with him the determination to avenge his father's death at the hands of Carlo's forces. This has been the ruling obsession of his life. This is why he lives as an outlaw. According to him, Carlo has 'stolen my possessions, my honour'. We do not know for what reason, or whether the king was justified in his action. What we do know is that Ernani is intractable in his determination to see justice done. Where he differs from Silva is in his willingness to accept the king's clemency and utilize it as a sign for a new life with Elvira (Act 3). Did he not have Elvira it is doubtful whether he would put aside his vendetta. She is the possibility of new life and hope for the future. De Silva has no such hope. He is fatally deprived of the one thing that would give his old age meaning, and deprived at that by his long-term rival who owes his existence to the code of honour by which de Silva has lived his life.

For de Silva there can be no turning back. The penalty must be paid. When it comes to it Ernani does not shirk the inevitable but plunges the dagger into his breast (in the play he opts to take poison). Ernani's death is meaningless if we do not acknowledge the moral code that demands it. Within the strictures of that code it is entirely necessary and inevitable. For in a sense Ernani's life has reached its apex in the moment that he has found love, and with it the capacity to praise life and transcend his earlier proclamation, 'I hate myself and the light of day'. In the few moments in which he embraces Elvira in the knowledge that she gives herself to him without reservation he finds a reason to live and affirm life, such as it is given to few men to realize. So beleaguered has been his life that he can value those few moments more than most people can affirm a whole lifetime of appeasement.

Note: It is undeniable that it is Ernani himself who, when giving his horn to de Silva (Act 2), says that on hearing a blast he will die at once. This is actually quite unnecessary. What de Silva wants is the opportunity to fight with his rival on the field of honour. He does not require that Ernani should kill himself although he is quite prepared to acquiesce in Ernani's proposition. It is, however, symptomatic of Ernani's entirely typical, Romantic death-longing that he volunteers to kill himself: 'I hate my life and the light of day'. He lacks the imagination to envisage that there might come a day when his life is not such a burden to him as it is now.

Arrigo's Esquire (*La Battaglia di Legnano*)
Arrigo's esquire has no contribution of his own to make. In ensemble passages he serves to second and corroborate his master's sentiments, exactly as a good esquire should.

Eunuch (Eunuco) (*Il Corsaro*)
Gulnara, the Pasha **Seid**'s chief odalisque, is waited upon by eunuchs, symbols of the Pasha's chronic insecurity and paranoia. Looked at another way, their presence is representative of the Pasha's eminent pragmatism. The sole function in the opera of the eunuch is to communicate to the girls in the harem, and to Gulnara in particular, the Pasha's desires.

Ezio (*Attila*). Roman envoy.
When **Attila** first meets Ezio (Prologue Scene 1) he hails him as 'the mightiest warrior, a worthy adversary to Attila, the shield and boast of Rome'. This is no empty rhetoric, for Ezio has been responsible for the defeat of Attila at the battle of Châlons and Attila does not bandy words lightly. The highest praise Attila could give to any man would be to call him a worthy adversary to himself. However Attila's high opinion of Ezio quickly evaporates when the latter proposes that he will turn traitor to Rome and join forces with Attila. Ezio is disgusted with the decadence that prevails in Rome and wants to usurp the current Emperor, Valentino, whom he sees (justifiably) as being effete and ineffectual. But these reasons are repellent to Attila. How could he be expected to condone the betrayal of a despot, being one himself? Ezio quickly realizes that he is not going to persuade Attila to join him and reverts to his former role as envoy. He is about to deliver 'the will of imperial Caesar' but is cut short by Attila who is not willing to parley. Ezio is unconcerned because he knows that he commands superior forces. Having already defeated the Hun's 'rabble' he can see no reason why he should not do it again.

Ezio is not interested in diplomacy. The only language he understands is that of the sword. He is therefore disgusted when he receives a missive from Rome (Act 2 Scene 1) informing him that a truce has been signed with Attila and that he is recalled to Rome (*Dagli immortali vertici*). Ezio laments the passing of Rome's former days of glory and most of all the fact that 'a valiant veteran warrior should have to submit before a faint heart, a puny slave'. His ruminations are interrupted by a chorus of Attila's slaves sent by Attila to request the company of Ezio and his captains at a forthcoming banquet to celebrate the recently ratified peace. The slaves depart, leaving one behind. It is **Foresto**, in disguise, who has come to enlist Ezio's support, and that of the Roman troops, in ambushing the Huns on a prearranged signal once Foresto has ensured the murder of Attila. It is a well-tried tactic to remove the leader first and then assail the rank and file who, leaderless, then present little opposition. Ezio is only too happy to oblige. Since the banquet is that very evening he can after all pretend he never received the Emperor's message recalling him to Rome. It is more than probable that he does not give a thought to the consequences anyway, so disenchanted is he with the role of appeaser in which he has been cast by his masters.

In Act 2 Scene 2 Ezio arrives at the feast with his captains and also **Uldino** and Foresto. He is welcomed by Attila who obstinately ignores warnings from the Druids as to Ezio's intentions. Ezio renews his offer of an alliance with Attila but now it is purely a formality. Attila remains scornful. When Uldino's attempt to murder Attila by poison is thwarted by **Odabella's** intervention Ezio is incredulous. 'Who could have revealed the secret? Who could have trusted it to a lover's heart?' Only a weakling could have been so stupid. Nevertheless it gives him hope that now he himself may have the pleasure of destroying Attila who so scorns his repeated offers of assistance.

At the wedding of Attila and Odabella (Act 3) Ezio grows impatient but, from long experience, realizes that patience is of the essence, particularly when an ambush is planned. He encourages Foresto to restrain his 'jealous fury'. When Odabella enters, apparently fleeing the ghost of her father who has intercepted himself at the crucial moment when she was about to submit to Attila's embraces, Ezio realizes that there is no time to be lost. They must commence the ambush forthwith. He is impatient with Odabella and Foresto. This is no time for tears or jealousy. Attila enters and Ezio watches quietly while he and Odabella wrangle. Then taking his cue from Foresto, who tells Attila that his hate will only be quenched when Attila is dead, he chimes in: 'You have already exceeded your measure of crimes; heaven's wrath hangs over you'. At this point sounds offstage indicate the Romans' assault on Attila's camp has commenced. Ezio watches as Odabella stabs Attila and joins the rest of the company in claiming: 'God, the people and the king are fully avenged'.

Disaffected as he is Ezio is fair game for the first needy despot that comes his way. Ultimately he is only concerned for his own advancement, and will do whatever is necessary to achieve it. He is the very reverse of a sentimentalist.

F

FALSTAFF

Opera in 3 Acts. Libretto by Arrigo Boito after Shakespeare's comedy, *The Merry Wives*

of Windsor (1600–1601), and passages from *Henry IV* concerning Falstaff.

First performance: 9 February 1893 at La Scala, Milan.

Cast:
Sir John Falstaff (baritone)
Ford (baritone)
Fenton (tenor)
Doctor Caius (tenor)
Bardolfo: follower of Falstaff (tenor)
Pistola: follower of Falstaff (bass)
Alice Ford (soprano)
Nannetta: daughter of the Fords (soprano)
Mistress Quickly (mezzo-soprano)
Mistress Meg Page (mezzo-soprano)

Time: The reign of Henry IV
Place: Windsor

The events of Verdi's opera are principally taken from *The Merry Wives of Windsor*, though in Shakespeare the character of Falstaff is fully established through the Historical plays – Henry IV Parts I and II. It is there that Falstaff's immorality, razor wit, disreputable habits and companions, and above all his chronic inability to be answerable to anybody but himself are fully established. In *The Merry Wives* his immortality is ensured as a symbol of society's perennial need for sacrificial victims. Boito, with great skill, managed to incorporate much of the essential character painting from the historical plays into his adaptation of *The Merry Wives*.

Synopsis

Act 1 Scene 1   A room in the Garter Inn. A table, a big armchair, a bench. On the table are the remains of breakfast, several bottles and a glass, an inkstand, pens, paper and a lighted candle. A broom leans against the wall. Sir John Falstaff is busy heating the seal of two letters on the flame of the candle. He then seals them with a ring. Afterwards he puts out the light and begins to drink, comfortably stretched out in the armchair. Bardolfo, Pistola and the host are in the background.

Doctor Caius enters suddenly, screaming for Falstaff. Falstaff either does not notice, or is too inebriated to care. Ignoring Caius he calls for the host. Bardolfo, meanwhile, waylays Caius who, still shouting and drawing near to Falstaff, accuses the latter of having beaten his servants. Falstaff's response to the accusation is to order another bottle of sack. Not to be gainsaid Caius resumes his accusation: 'you've worn out my bay mare and broken into my house'. Falstaff laconically observes, 'but not your house-keeper!' Caius is in no mood for ribaldry. He demands an explanation. Falstaff gives it: 'I did precisely what you say I did'. And for good measure he adds that he did it on purpose. Caius threatens him with the Royal Council. Falstaff is not impressed.

Now Caius turns his fury onto Bardolfo and accuses him of having got him drunk on the previous day. Bardolfo, taking the hint from his master, agrees with him and then goes on to complain that he is sick. Caius is a doctor; perhaps he can help him with a prescription. He invokes his enormous rubicund nose as evidence. Caius is becoming increasingly apoplectic. Pointing to Pistola he claims that having got him drunk Bardolfo and Pistola emptied his pockets. Falstaff summons Pistola, who comes forward reluctantly, and demands to know from him if there is any substance to Caius's accusation. Caius does not give Pistola a chance to respond but dramatically empties the pockets of his robe where he claims there should be, 'two shillings from Edward's reign and six half-crowns'. Now there is not a sign of them.

Pistola has picked up a broom and announces that he wishes to fight Caius. Instead the two men proceed to indulge in violent verbal sparring, climaxing with Caius calling Pistola a 'mandrake sprout', which epithet somewhat nonplusses the far-from-literate Pistola. Then Pistola loses all self-restraint and hurls himself at the doctor. Falstaff restrains him with a gesture. He then demands that Bardolfo own up as to whether he emptied Caius's pockets. The whole scene is a charade, which the three men must have rehearsed a thousand times, aimed at

confusing and confounding the unfortunate victim, whoever he might be. Bardolfo maintains that Caius drinks heavily, before falling into a stupor, in which state he dreams. This is enough for Falstaff: 'the facts are denied', he tells Caius and dismisses him. Pistola and Bardolfo, clapping their hands, escort Caius to the door shouting an 'Amen' after him.

Once Caius has gone Falstaff upbraids his henchmen with the maxim; 'steal with politeness at the right time', adding, 'you are clumsy artists'. He then examines the bill which the host has brought with his bottle of sack. Pistola and Bardolfo start carolling again, clearly nervous that the moment of reckoning has arrived. Falstaff shuts them up and, throwing Bardolfo his purse, demands to know what is in it. Bardolfo makes a grand ceremony of producing from the purse, 'two marks and one penny', which is all that remains. Falstaff is not amused. 'You are the ruin of me', he exclaims as he rises from the table. He blames Bardolfo's nose for their predicament: 'I've been soaking that purple fungus of yours for thirty years, now – it costs too much . . .'. He breaks off from his complaint to summon the host for a bottle of wine, then resumes, 'you're eating up my substance'. If Falstaff ever grew thin he would not be himself and nobody would love him. Regarding his gargantuan belly he declares: 'In this great abdomen are the thousand tongues that proclaim my name'. Pistola and Bardolfo chorus: 'Falstaff immenso! Falstaff enorme!' After this buffoonery Falstaff calls his minions to attention: 'It's time to sharpen our wits'.

Falstaff tells them that, on his wanderings around town, he has observed two ladies whom he imagines to be enamoured of him: Alice Ford and Meg Page. Falstaff is particularly enamoured of Alice, who happens to be married to a wealthy merchant, 'who is (according to him) more generous than Croesus'.[24] He describes in graphic terms

---

24 Croesus was the last king of Lydia (560–546 BC). He was so rich and powerful that his name became proverbial for great wealth.

how Alice has turned 'her burning glance' on his massive body and seemed to say, 'I am Sir John Falstaff's'. He has decided that Meg and Alice between them will be his, 'Golconda'[25] and his 'Gold Coast'.[26] He sits down forthwith to address the letters which he has already written and was sealing at the opening of the scene. He then commands Pistola and Bardolfo to deliver them. But Pistola and Bardolfo consider it beneath their 'dignity' and 'honour' to play messenger boys so Falstaff gives the letters to the page boy, Robin, to deliver.

When Robin has departed Falstaff turns the full force of his invective onto his companions (*L'onore! Ladri!*). This is a justifiably famous passage, combining the triple geniuses of Shakespeare, Boito and Verdi. Devoted principally to refuting all the prime usages of honour, it concludes: 'can a dead man feel honour? No. Does it live only with the living? Not even, because flattery inflates it, pride corrupts it and calumny sickens it. And for me I'll have none of it. No! No! No!' He takes the broom and chases Bardolfo and Pistola, who avoid the blows by running here and there and taking refuge under the table. Finally, fearing for their hides, Bardolfo and Pistola flee. Falstaff follows Pistola out.

Act 1 Scene 2   In Ford's garden. Mistress Meg Page and Mistress Quickly enter and cross to Ford's house. On the steps they meet Mistress Alice Ford and Nannetta who are coming out. The women greet each other. Alice and Meg are all agog because they have each received a letter from Falstaff declaring his love. Nannetta and Quickly urge them to tell them the cause of their excitement. Finally Meg admits that she has received a letter. She takes it from her pocket. Not to be outdone Alice then produces her letter and gives it to Meg, telling her to read it. Meg in turn gives her letter to Alice. Quickly and Nannetta are bursting with excited anticipation.

The two women proceed to read the letters. They quickly realize that the letters are exactly the same. As one reads the other is able to complete the sentence. This is what Falstaff wrote: 'Oh splendid Alice/Meg. I offer love and love I ask for. Don't ask me why, but say to me, "I love you". You are the merry wife, I the merry companion. Between us we make a merry pair. Let us make a pair in happy love; the beautiful lady and the man of great distinction, and your face shall shine upon me like a star, like a star over immensities'. All the women fall about laughing at this last extravagance. Alice then finishes reading: 'Answer to your squire, John Falstaff, Knight'. Their merriment exhausted the women suddenly explode with indignation: 'Mostro!' ('Monster!') 'We must cheek him, make a show of him. We must make a fool of him. Oh what fun!' They each then variously expound on the particular qualities that render Sir John Falstaff so distinctive: 'the oil oozing out of his greasy hide; that man's a cannon if he goes off; you're done for', etc. (*Quell'otre! Quel tino!*). Nannetta assures her mother that if there is to be some fun she wants to be a part of it. The women leave in high spirits.

Almost immediately Ford, Caius, Fenton, Bardolfo and Pistola enter. The latter two have defected from Falstaff's employ and have run to Ford to warn him that he is in dire danger of being cuckolded. Caius is still fuming about his ill-treatment at the hands of Falstaff and his henchman: 'those two at your side are no flowers of virtue', he warns Ford. Ford is feeling distinctly beleaguered, wondering which of his companions he should listen to. Finally he demands that Pistola repeat his accusations against him. Pistola does not spare Ford's sensibilities: 'In short, that enormous Falstaff wants to get under your roof, steal your wife, break into your money box and take possession of your bed'. With barely concealed alacrity Falstaff's two ex-retainers warn Ford that he will shortly be sprouting a pair of cuckold's horns.

The four women re-enter. Nannetta and Fenton immediately catch sight of each other.

---

[25] An ancient Indian city, west of Hyderabad, renowned especially for its fabulous diamonds.
[26] Historically the west coast of Africa from Cape Three Points to the Volta river, where alluvial gold is washed down.

Alice is alarmed to see her husband and decides to keep out of his way. Meg asks if Ford is jealous and Alice confirms that he is. Alice, Meg and Quickly make off, leaving Nannetta and Fenton. Fenton begs a couple of kisses from his sweetheart. The two lovers murmur sweet nothings to each other. Then Fenton becomes too fresh with his hands and Nannetta calls a halt. Anyway she hears someone coming. It is her mother and the women returning. Fenton hides in the shrubbery and Nannetta goes to meet her mother and friends.

Alice is wondering what to do about Falstaff. Nannetta suggests sending someone to see him. All agree this is a good idea and Alice elects Quickly as the ideal candidate for the mission. She tells Quickly to 'offer him the sweet inducement of a rendezvous'. Quickly accepts with alacrity. All agree that first they'll flatter him, then they will 'turn him inside out' (Alice's scheme), 'dump him in the river' (Nannetta) and 'roast him on the fire' (Alice). 'What joy! What fun!' If anybody had any doubts about an element of sadism which always emerges in the battle of the sexes, this should allay them.

The women are just cheering Quickly on her way when the latter notices a movement in the shrubbery from Fenton, who is still hiding there. Thinking they are being spied upon the women run off quickly. Only Nannetta remains behind. Fenton emerges. He has only one thought and that is to resume his love-making. He tries to kiss Nannetta, but she covers her face with her hand. Fenton kisses her hand and makes to kiss it again, but Nannetta lifts it as high as she can in the air and Fenton is unable to reach it with his lips. She informs Fenton that 'Love is a lively tournament and its court rules that the weaker wins over the stronger'. She winds her hair around Fenton's neck and announces, 'Now you are captured'. They continue in this flirtatious vein until Nannetta calls a halt: 'Short games are the best ones', she declares and, hearing someone coming she runs off. Fenton goes away singing, 'the mouth that is kissed is never unlucky'.

The men re-enter. Ford has decided he must pay Falstaff a visit in disguise. He swears Bardolfo and Pistola to secrecy. The ladies return, chattering nineteen-to-the-dozen at the same time as Caius is trying to warn Ford off Pistola and Bardolfo. The latter offer advice to Ford on how best to undo Falstaff. Fenton can only think of his beloved Nannetta. The women meanwhile are plotting the most efficacious ways of having their revenge on 'that wineskin, that barrel'. Finally Alice calls a halt. She urges Quickly to delay no longer but to set off at once to visit Falstaff. 'I want him to mew for love like a tomcat', she says. The women are all agreed and take their farewells until Alice declares, 'You'll see that terrible, triumphant belly puffed up with pride'... 'Puffed up then popped', the others shriek. Finally, after one more reminiscence of the last sentence of Falstaff's letter they depart in high spirits and laughter.

Act 2 Scene 1   A room at the Garter Inn. Falstaff is stretched out in his armchair, in his usual place, drinking sherry. Bardolfo and Pistola are near the entrance. Beating their breasts in an exaggerated show of repentance they advance into the room and announce they are returning to Falstaff's service. Bardolfo tells Falstaff there is a woman waiting to see him. It is, of course, Mistress Quickly. Falstaff instructs Bardolfo to admit her. Bardolfo exits and returns immediately with Quickly.

Quickly makes a deep curtsey to Falstaff, who remains seated (*Reverenza! Se Vostra Grazia vuole*). She approaches with 'great respect and caution' and begs a few words with him in private. Falstaff regally agrees to grant her an audience and dismisses Bardolfo and Pistola, who exit making grimaces. With another deep curtsey Quickly advances and commences, 'Madam Alice Ford...' At the mention of Alice's name Falstaff is all ears. Quickly tells him that Alice is consumed with love for him. She has received his letter, thanks him and would like him to know that her husband always goes out from two to three o'clock in the afternoon. Falstaff can visit her quite freely at that hour. Quickly adds, 'Poor lady! Her sufferings are cruel! She has a jealous husband'. Falstaff does not appear too perturbed by this. He merely instructs Quickly to report that he will wait impatiently for that hour and will not fail her.

Now Quickly progresses to her second message, which this time is from Mistress Meg Page. Apparently Meg's husband is very seldom absent, 'poor lady! A lily of candour and faith. You bewitch them all', Quickly concludes. 'There's no witchcraft in it, only a personal fascination that I have', Falstaff assures her. But then a pertinent question occurs to him: 'Does the one know about the other?' 'Heavens, no! Women are born deceitful', Quickly promises him. On the strength of this good news Falstaff produces his purse and announces that he wishes to remunerate Quickly. 'Who sows grace reaps love', Quickly responds archly. Falstaff extracts a coin and gives it to Quickly, dismissing her as he does so. She bows deeply and exits. Left alone Falstaff is ecstatic (*Va, vecchio John*). He imagines how, 'all the mutinous women together are risking damnation for me!' He is suddenly overcome by an excess of gratitude towards his monstrous body that serves him so well in the lists of love.

Bardolfo enters and announces a certain 'Master Fontana' (Ford in disguise). Apparently he brings with him a demijohn of Cypress sherry for his Lordship's breakfast. Falstaff instructs Bardolfo to make Fontana – 'a fountain that spills out such liquor!' – most welcome. Bardolfo goes to fetch Ford, who advances and bows deeply. Pistola enters, carrying a demijohn which he places on the table. Bardolfo and Pistola remain in the background. Ford is carrying a money-bag. Falstaff returns Ford's salute. Ford announces himself as, 'a man who has great abundance of the good things in life ... who spends and scatters ... as the whim dictates'. Falstaff, overflowing with *bonhomie* goes to shake Ford's hand, assuring him that he would most definitely like to make his acquaintance.

Ford tells Falstaff that he wishes to speak to him in confidence. Meanwhile Pistola and Bardolfo are hugely enjoying the scene from the sidelines. They know Falstaff well enough to know that he will fall headlong into the trap being laid for him. Falstaff catches sight of them and peremptorily dismisses them. Then he turns to Ford and assures him he is all ears.

Ford commences with a promising proverb: 'They say that gold opens every door'. Falstaff chimes in, 'Gold is a good captain and always goes forward'. Just so that Falstaff should be in no doubt of his intentions Ford produces a bag of coins which is apparently so heavy he needs assistance to put it onto the table. Falstaff is delighted to help him. Then Ford reveals the real reason for his visit. He is desperately in love with a lady in Windsor, one Alice Ford, but she does not love him. He has done everything he can think of to woo her, but to no avail. Falstaff can barely conceal his glee and self-satisfaction as Ford bewails his lack of success. Merrily he starts to hum a little madrigal: 'Love gives no truce so long as life endures! It is like the shadow which, when you fly from, it follows you, and when you follow, it flies from you'. 'Fontana' mournfully joins in and then reflects, 'and this is the madrigal I learnt at great cost'. Falstaff is all solicitude. However, he ventures to wonder why the gentleman has chosen him to confide in. Now Ford shamelessly flatters Falstaff (to which the latter responds with a 'gesture of humility'), and then presents him with the bag of money. He tells Falstaff to, 'Spend it! Spend it and squander it!' In return all he wants is advice on how to conquer Alice. Falstaff requires further elucidation. So Ford is specific. Falstaff's task will be first to make a preliminary assault on the fortress, which will then make it that much easier for Ford to follow. Without further ado Falstaff accepts the money-bag and assures 'Fontana' that he will shortly possess Ford's wife. He informs Ford that he is himself already far advanced in the conquest of Alice; indeed within half an hour she will be in his arms. He has recently received word that she will be available between two and three o'clock, her husband being absent during that time. Ford cannot resist asking if Falstaff knows the husband. 'May the devil take him off to hell with Menelaus,[27] his ancestor!' Falstaff rejoins. 'That Master Ford is a beast! A beast!' Falstaff proclaims, then gathers up the bag and makes off, leaving Ford behind to explode with rage and indignation (*È sogno? O realtà?*).

Ford is almost incoherent with anger: 'O marriage! O hell! Woman; demon! Let blockheads have faith in their wives ... O ugly fate! ... Horns! Beast! Goat! Twisted cuckold! Ah! the horns, the horns!' His thoughts turn to the 'filthy, evil, damned Epicurian'. First he'll get them together, then 'I'll grab them. I'll explode! I'll avenge the insult', he splutters.

Falstaff re-enters wearing a new doublet, hat and cane. He invites Ford to accompany him on his way. Ford agrees and they start to leave. At the door they make complimentary gestures to each other to concede precedence. Finally they exit arm in arm.

Act 2 Scene 2   A room in Ford's house. In the centre a large window from which can be seen the garden. To the right a door, another to the left and a further one towards the back on the right, giving onto the stairway. More stairs to the rear at the left. A closed screen is leaning against the wall beside a great fireplace. Chest of drawers, small table with flowers, a seat locker, a large chair and several high-backed chairs furnish the room. On the large chair is a lute.

Alice and Meg enter laughing, followed by Quickly and then by Nannetta, who stands aside sadly. Quickly relates that Falstaff has fallen headlong into the trap. The others encourage Quickly to tell them exactly what transpired at the Inn. Quickly tells her tale with relish, concluding: 'he believes both of you to be madly in love with his charms'. She warns Alice that Falstaff will be arriving between two and three o'clock. Alice comments that it is already two o'clock and calls out of the window to her servants, Ned and Will. She tells Quickly that everything is

already prepared then returns to the window and calls out into the garden, telling the servants to bring the laundry basket.

Suddenly Alice realizes that Nannetta is looking thoroughly miserable. She goes to her daughter and asks her what troubles her. Nannetta bursts into tears and tells how her father has decreed that she should marry Doctor Caius. The women all agree that this is utterly absurd. Nannetta soon recovers her spirits when she realizes her mother will have none of it.

Ned and Will arrive carrying a basket full of dirty linen. Alice instructs them to put it to one side and then, when she gives the cue, empty it into the river. She dismisses the servants. Alice hurries to fetch a chair to put by the table, whilst Nannetta puts her lute onto it. Then, on her mother's instructions, she helps to place the screen between the laundry basket and the fireplace and open it out. Alice toasts the 'Merry Wives of Windsor',[28] and reminds Meg to play her part as planned. She tells Quickly that if anything goes amiss she will whistle. Nannetta places herself on guard. Quickly, meanwhile, has gone to the window and now spies Falstaff approaching. Alice posts Nannetta and Meg to their stations. Together with Quickly they exit. Alice seats herself at the table, takes the lute and strums a few chords.

Falstaff enters. He sees Alice playing the lute and begins to sing: 'At last I've plucked your radiant flower'. He takes Alice by the waist. She has stopped playing and risen from the table. Falstaff commences his campaign with a lamentable lack of tact by wishing that Master Ford would 'pass on to a better life' so that she could thereby become his Lady and he her Lord. Alice manages to dissemble coyness. Falstaff imagines Alice decorated with his coat of arms and laden with jewels. Alice forswears jewels: 'I despise the false god of gold', she claims, 'For me it is enough to have a veil knotted at my throat, a buckle at the waist and a flower for my hair.' She puts a flower in her hair. Falstaff is

---

[27]   Menelaus was the cuckolded husband of Helen of Troy who eloped with Paris.

[28]   Title of the Shakespeare play on which much of the action of the opera is based.

immediately inflamed and advances. Alice takes a step back. Falstaff declares his love and advances further. Alice takes another step back, warning him of the wages of sin.

Now Falstaff describes (*Quand'ero paggio*) how once upon a time he was a slender little page boy, supple and nimble; 'a vision, pretty, light, gentle and charming'. Alice decides this is the moment to introduce a little cold *douche* into the proceedings: 'You mock me. I am afraid of your deceits. I fear that you are actually in love with … Meg'. 'I cannot stand her face', is the prompt reply. Falstaff does not want to dwell on this topic. He is growing impatient. He tries to embrace Alice, who energetically resists. He again takes her by the waist.

Quickly, who has been listening from the antechamber and no doubt realizes that things are getting out of hand, calls to Alice, then enters, pretending to 'pant in haste'. She comes to report that Mistress Meg wants to talk to Alice and that she is apparently in a 'rare state'. Falstaff, initially irritated, quickly apprises that Meg's advent at this juncture would be a disaster for him. He must hide. But where? Alice directs him behind the screen. Falstaff hides. Quickly makes a sign to Meg, who enters feigning extreme agitation. Quickly exits. Meg brings news that Alice's husband is on his way, 'yelling about some man'. He says that he wants to cut the man's throat. She declaims so that there can be no possibility that Falstaff does not hear her.

Now Quickly enters, also in extreme agitation, with one difference. She is *genuinely* alarmed. She shouts to Alice to save herself. Master Ford is actually approaching, 'like a thunderstorm … yelling, blazing, thundering'. Alice quickly picks up that this is no joke. Apparently Ford has breached the garden fence and has with him a whole posse of men. As if to confirm the veracity of her statement Ford is heard offstage shouting, 'Scoundrel!' At this moment Falstaff, now thoroughly alarmed, was just emerging from behind the screen but, hearing Ford's voice, hastily disappears again. Alice rapidly closes the screen around him so that he is completely concealed.

Ford enters, shouting orders to his followers: 'Shut the doors! Bar the Staircases! … We'll flush the wild boar!' Caius and Fenton run in. Ford commands Fenton to search the corridors. Bardolfo and Pistola break into the room, shouting, as Fenton goes to do Ford's bidding. Bardolfo and Pistola are in their element. Ford orders them to cut off the interloper's escape and to search the antechamber. Bardolfo and Pistola exit brandishing cudgels. Alice confronts her husband. 'Are you out of your mind?' she asks. Ford answers her question with another: 'What is in that basket?' 'Dirty linen.' 'Dirty linen indeed!' He then thrusts a bunch of keys at Caius and orders him to 'open everything'. Caius runs out. Having yelled to the servants to bolt the gates to the park Ford turns his attention to the laundry basket. Furiously he drags the linen out of it, scattering the contents all over the floor. Finally he has to accept that Falstaff is not concealed therein (considering Falstaff's bulk one would have thought that this would have been immediately evident). Ford rushes out shouting instructions.

Alice, Meg and Quickly immediately turn their minds to the question of getting Falstaff out of the house. Meg suggests the basket, but Alice thinks he is too fat. Falstaff, who has emerged from behind the screen, reckons that anything is worth a try to escape from that raging lunatic. Meg enjoys adding to Falstaff's discomfiture by pretending to be surprised at finding him there at all. Falstaff is already half inside the basket. 'I love you, I love you alone. Save me! Save me!' he exclaims. With enormous difficulty he manages to squeeze himself inside the basket. He begs the women to cover him. They hurriedly do so. Nannetta and Fenton enter. They still only have eyes for each other and are all but oblivious to the hullabaloo around them. Nannetta leads Fenton behind the screen where they continue their love-making uninterrupted. Their voices can be heard carolling their bliss.

Meanwhile the voices of Caius and Ford are heard close at hand. They sound anything but blissful. Caius runs across the room,

followed by Ford who almost collides with
Bardolfo and Pistola. Ford is becoming increasingly desperate: 'Tear the house to
pieces', he shouts. Bardolfo and Pistola exit.
Caius looks up the chimney, then Ford hurls
himself on the cupboard, which is locked.
He cannot find the keys so he attempts to
force it with a pen. Finally he succeeds in
opening it, but Falstaff is not within. He has
by now become quite irrational. He even
looks inside the little drawer in the table. A
moment comes when the tumult subsides.
Nannetta and Fenton can be heard audibly
kissing each other behind the screen. Ford
immediately leaps to the conclusion that it
is Falstaff with his wife. Slowly and
cautiously he moves towards the screen
muttering imprecations. Bardolfo and Pistola
re-enter and loudly announce that they have
been unsuccessful. Ford, under his breath,
tells them that he has found the culprit. A
stunned silence follows in the room and Ford
dispenses his orders in a hushed whisper. He
is now a military officer in charge of a
campaign. Pistola and the servants are to be
the right-wing, Bardolfo and Caius the left
wing and the others will, 'step lively and stave
in the bulwark from behind'.

Meanwhile Meg and Quickly are hugely
enjoying themselves: 'Risk is a pleasure that
increases the fun and stimulates the spirits',
Meg comments. Falstaff sticks his face out
of the basket and Quickly pushes him back.
Falstaff's stifled cries can be heard from
within. Again he sticks his nose out, only to
be shoved back down. The women realize
they are going to have to keep a very close
watch on their prisoner. Once again Falstaff
sticks his nose out, and once again he is
shoved back down. By now all the men have
reached the screen and have their ears pressed
tight up against it. 'What pathetic laments!'
Ford comments. Finally he calls for silence
and orders: 'Together! . . . One . . . Two . . .
Three'. They overthrow the screen. General
consternation ensues. For it is not Falstaff
and Alice that confronts them, but Fenton
and Nannetta. Ford is almost as furious to
discover his daughter in Fenton's arms as he
would have been had he discovered Alice

with Falstaff. He gives Fenton his marching
orders. Nannetta, terrified, runs away.
Fenton, likewise, reckons it best to make
himself scarce. Bardolfo runs towards the
stairs, convinced Falstaff must be there. 'Cut
him to pieces', Ford commands. All the men
race to the stairs.

Alice, who has entered just at the moment
Nannetta and Fenton were discovered and
has been keeping a low profile, now calls
for her servants, Ned, Will, Tom and Isaac.
Nannetta re-enters with the servants and a
little page boy. Alice instructs them to empty
the basket out of the window into the river,
'near the bulrushes in front of the washer-
women'. Meg, Quickly and Nannetta are
delighted at the prospect. Nannetta warns
the servants that there is 'a big fish' inside
the basket.

Alice orders the page boy to find her
husband. She has resolved he should be told
the whole crazy story. 'The moment he sees
the Knight soused in water he'll be cured of
any jealous fancy', she remarks. The servants
heave the basket up to the windowsill. A
crack can be heard from the bottom of the
basket. Then basket, dirty linen and the good
Knight, Sir John Falstaff are tumbling out
of the window into the river below. As the
curtain falls on Act 2 Alice, seeing Ford come
in, takes him by the arm and leads him
rapidly to the window.

Act 3 Scene 1   Outside the Garter Inn.
The inn is to the right, with a sign bearing
the motto: *Honi soit qui mal y pense* (Evil
unto him who evil thinks). There is a bench
near the door. It is sunset. Falstaff is seated
on the bench, meditating. He arouses himself, beats his fist on the bench and turning
towards the inn calls for the host. Then he
returns to his meditations on the 'thieving,
cheating world' he inhabits (*Mondo ladro.
Mondro rubaldo!*). He asks for a glass of hot
wine. His dignity has been gravely offended.
He feels that he has only been saved from
drowning by his mighty belly. 'Virtue doesn't
exist any more. Everything is declining', he
declares, clearly having forgotten his own less
than scrupulous reasons for being at Ford's
house in the first place. He grows maudlin,

reflecting on the black day that will dawn on the world when he leaves it.

The host returns with a large glass of heated wine on a tray, puts it on the bench and retires to the inn. Falstaff sips the wine, smacking his lips. He unbuttons his waistcoat, stretches out then drinks deeply. Slowly, bit by bit his customary good spirits return. He reflects on the virtues of good wine, 'that dispels the stupid gloom of discouragement, lights up the eyes and the wits'. As he thinks about it he warms to the topic and gives a vivid description of the animating properties of wine: 'a dark vibrating thrill comes into the tipsy man, thrilling every fibre in the heart, the gay wind flickers with the thrill and the mad globe quivers with a thrilling madness! The thrill invades the world'. Falstaff is truly a visionary!

Mistress Quickly enters and curtseys, interrupting Falstaff's ruminations. She comes with a message from 'the lovely Alice'. At the mention of Alice's name Falstaff leaps up and tells Quickly that she 'and the lovely Alice can go to the devil! He vividly catalogues the miseries he endured when incarcerated with the Fords' dirty linen before being dumped into the water: 'Canaglie!!!' ('Bitches!'). At this point Alice, Meg, Nannetta, Ford, Caius and Fenton – one after the other – peek out from behind the house opposite the inn, listen, then hide again.

'She's innocent', Quickly insists. 'The fault was with those damnable menservants. Alice is miserable... praying to her saints'. She has written Falstaff a letter. Quickly takes a letter from her pocket. Falstaff begins to read it, watched with some incredulity by Alice, Ford and Nannetta. 'He'll fall for it again', Nannetta comments. Her mother caustically adds; 'Men never learn'.

The letter invites Falstaff to a rendezvous in the Windsor Royal Park at midnight. It tells Falstaff to come disguised as 'the Black Knight' and to meet under Herne's Oak. Quickly explains that the oak is reputed to be a place of witchcraft: the Black Knight hanged himself from one of its branches. His ghost has been seen to appear there.

Falstaff is not perturbed by tales of the supernatural. He is only delighted to have been granted an assignation. His good humour is now thoroughly restored. He takes Quickly by the arm and invites her to join him inside the tavern. The two disappear inside, much to the delight of the party watching, who realize that once again Falstaff has fallen, hook, line and sinker into the trap they have laid for him.

Imitating Quickly's mysterious tone, Alice recapitulates the story of the Black Knight. Then Alice dismisses it as, 'Fairy tales for children'. But she cannot resist resuming the story to the point where the fairies appear and two horns emerge from the Black Knight's forehead. The thought of this gives her ineffable joy. She warns her husband that he also deserves punishment. Ford begs her forgiveness, which is tacitly granted.

Now Alice is anxious to prosecute the latest plan for Falstaff's undoing. She sets to, casting the masquerade. Nannetta shall play the Queen of the fairies, Meg will be the 'Green Nymph of the Woods' and Quickly will play a witch. Alice will have little boys with her who will pretend to be elves, ghosts, devils, bats and imps. All will hurl themselves upon Falstaff in 'his mantle and horns' and 'raise a real tempest around him until he confesses his wickedness'. They will then unmask themselves and before daybreak 'the merry brigade will be gone'. Meg points out that evening is drawing in. All agree to meet later at Herne's Oak.

As they exit in different directions Quickly emerges from the inn. Seeing Ford and Caius talking together she remains on the threshold to listen. Ford is reassuring Caius of his determination that the Doctor shall be the one to marry his daughter. Having ascertained that Caius knows the disguise that Nannetta will be wearing at the masquerade he instructs that the pair should come to him with covered faces; she in a veil, he in a 'friar's cowl'. Ford will then bless them as man and wife. Quickly is outraged. She goes straight after Nannetta to apprise her of what she has heard.

Act 3 Scene 2   Windsor Great Park. Herne's Oak stands in the centre. The banks of a ditch can be seen in the background. The trees and shrubs are in bloom. It is night. The far-off cries of night watchmen can be heard. As the moon rises its light gradually illuminates the park.

Fenton enters. He sings rhapsodically of his love (*Dal labbro il canto estasiato vola*). At the conclusion Nannetta's voice is heard, echoing her lover from offstage. Fenton runs in the direction of Nannetta's voice. Nannetta enters and the two embrace. Alice enters with Quickly and separates the two lovebirds. She then gives Fenton a friar's black habit to wear. Alice has already decided that Ford's attempt to dupe his daughter into marrying a man she does not love is to be thwarted and turned to their advantage. When Ford marries the pair it will not be Nannetta and Caius, but two unsuspecting victims. Quickly has already decided on a suitable marriage partner for Dr Caius, namely Bardolfo. Meg runs in and relates that she has already hidden the imps along the ditch. Alice hears sounds of Falstaff approaching and calls for silence. All exit.

Falstaff enters with two stag horns on his head. He is clothed in a voluminous mantle. As he enters the town clock starts chiming midnight. Falstaff counts the chimes, then reflects on how 'love can change man into a beast'. He is undoubtedly aware of the *double entendre* – even when alone he cannot resist a witticism. Alice appears and he goes up to her, 'inflamed with love'. As soon as she is within reach he grasps her arm and pulls her to him: 'Come, I'm trembling and fervent', he declares. Alice avoids his embraces and Falstaff becomes absurd: 'I am your slave! I'm your frisky stag. Now let it rain truffles, radishes and fennel; they'll be my fodder. And love will overflow'. When Alice tells him that Meg has come with her Falstaff's joy is doubled: 'Now quarter me like a buck chamois at table!' he quips.

Suddenly Meg's voice is heard calling for help. Alice pretends to be frightened. Meg's voice is heard again: 'The witches are coming!' Falstaff becomes alarmed. Alice

rushes off and Falstaff collapses at the foot of the oak tree. Nannetta's voice can be heard calling for nymphs, elves, sylphs, dryads, sirens. She shortly arrives with her entourage. Falstaff is petrified and throws himself face down on the ground. All the main protagonists accompany Nannetta, who is Queen of the fairies: Meg as the Green Nymph, Alice as a fairy, Bardolfo in a monk's habit with the cowl pulled down but without a mask, Pistola as a satyr, Caius in a grey habit, without a mask, Fenton in a black habit with a mask, little girls dressed as white and blue fairies, nymphs, elves and imps. Falstaff remains motionless with his face to the ground.

Nannetta spies her quarry and all move forward cautiously. Having positioned the fairies, Alice makes off, leaving Falstaff at her daughter's mercy. Nannetta is impatient for the show to begin. The little fairies arrange themselves in a circle around their Queen. The older spirits form a second circle. The men form a group to the right and the women a group to the left. Nannetta calls upon the fairies to dance and the spirits to pick flowers (*Sul fil d'un soffio etesio*) which, under Nannetta's guidance, they proceed to do, all the time moving closer to the oak under which Falstaff is laid out.

Alice, masked, and Quickly, masked as a witch, enter, followed by Bardolfo who stumbles over Falstaff. Bardolfo calls out, 'Halt where you are!' Pistola comes running in. Falstaff is by now beside himself and calling for mercy. Quickly starts the fun by prodding him with a stick while Bardolfo and Pistola prod him with their feet. Then everybody joins in the fun. Bardolfo calls for an exorcism.

While all this is transpiring Caius is looking for Nannetta. Fenton and Quickly hide Nannetta from him and, with Alice and Quickly protecting her, Nannetta moves off to the back with Fenton. Quickly instructs them to return as soon as she calls.

Bardolfo's exorcism is by now well under way. It is, of course, nothing like a proper exorcism but simply consists of inciting the elves, imps *et al.* to torment Falstaff: 'Prick him and stick him with your sharp-pointed snouts!' Little boys dressed as imps come running in and commence jumping up and down on Falstaff. Alice, Quickly and Meg encourage the elves to, 'Sting him, sting him, sting, stick, pluck, pluck, prick, pinch him until he howls!' The imps duly clamber all over their victim, who rolls about, howling in anguish. By now Caius, Ford, Bardolfo and Pistola are also joining in with alacrity, hurling at Falstaff all the worst epithets they can think of. Finally they pull him up on all fours, make him kneel and then resume their bullying. Bardolfo takes a stick from Quickly and beats him. They insist he repent. Falstaff is in no position to argue and hastily repents. He is, however, not so beleaguered as to be prevented from making some pertinent observations about his tormentors. He repeatedly accuses Bardolfo, whom he does not at first recognize, of stinking. In his excitement Bardolfo allows his cowl to fall back from his face. Having identified him Falstaff lets forth a string of invective against Bardolfo, for which he is applauded by all, bar Bardolfo himself. Quickly takes advantage of the confusion to take Bardolfo aside and offer him a white veil with which to disguise himself once more. She then leads him off behind some trees. Caius, meanwhile, has recommenced his search for Nannetta.

Ford comes forward and, with an ironical bow, greets Falstaff. 'Who is it now who wears the horns?' he enquires. Falstaff for once in his life is lost for words. He still thinks of Ford as 'Master Fontana', his benefactor from the previous day. Alice puts him in the picture. Quickly comes forward now and speaks plainly: 'Did you really believe two women would be silly enough to give themselves body and soul to the devil for the sake of a "dirty, fat old man"?' Falstaff is forced to concede that she has a point. 'I'm beginning to perceive that I have been an ass', he says ruefully. Then in a flash of insight he makes a deputation for the defence: 'Every sort of common clown makes fun of me and glories in it, but without me they would not have a

pinch of salt for all their arrogance. I am the one who makes them so clever. My wit creates the wit of others'. All applaud him.

Ford now declares that he wishes the 'fine masquerade to be crowned with the betrothal of the Fairy Queen'. Caius, masked, and Bardolfo, dressed as the Fairy Queen, enter, holding hands. Each is oblivious to the identity of the other. Ford calls on the nymphs to surround the couple. Nannetta and Fenton have just reappeared. Nannetta is wearing a thick blue veil which completely covers her. Fenton is in dark habit and mask. Alice announces that another couple wants to be admitted to the 'happy betrothal'. Ford, all unsuspecting, invites the two couples to come forward. Alice encourages the elves to approach with their lanterns. Ford pronounces a blessing on the couples. Alice takes the smallest boy by the arm and places his lantern so that it illuminates the face of Bardolfo as soon as his veil is removed. Another elf, guided by Meg, is ready to illuminate the faces of Nannetta and Fenton. Ford dramatically decrees that all masks should be removed. The two couples duly do as they are bid. Everybody except Ford, Caius and Bardolfo falls about laughing. Caius is horrified when he realizes that he is married to Bardolfo. Ford is initially apoplectic but then acknowledges there is nothing he can do about it. Alice points the moral: 'Man often falls into the nets woven by his own malice'. Falstaff cannot resist teasing Ford: 'Dear good Master Ford, and now, tell me; Which one is the dupe?' Ford points to Caius: 'He!' All the men point fingers at each other: 'You', 'No', 'Yes', 'They' until Alice invites her husband to regard the 'sweet, eager love' of his daughter and her lover. Nannetta goes to her father and begs his forgiveness. Ford cannot find it in himself to be churlish and blesses anew his daughter's union.

Falstaff calls for a chorus and leads the final moral, which was Verdi's final and evergreen comment on life and the art which he had strenuously served all his life (*Tutto nel mondo è burla*):

'The whole world is a jest;
man was born a great jester,
pushed this way and that
by faith in his heart or by reason.
All are cheated! Every mortal being
laughs at every other one,
but the best laugh of all
is the one that comes last'.

All through his career Verdi set to music tales in which one or more of the characters is obsessed with the need to preserve honour. The attraction for us, and possibly for Verdi, of Shakespeare's Falstaff is that he gives not a jot for honour: 'Does honour put food in your stomach? Can it mend a broken shin? Of course not. What is it? A word. And what is a word? Hot air which is dispersed in an instant'. If only **Arrigo** (*La Battaglia di Legnano*), **Renato** (*Un ballo in maschera*), **Don Carlo** (*La Forza del Destino*), **di Silva** (*Ernani*) and a whole host of other characters in Verdi's operas had had Falstaff's attitude to honour a great deal of misery would have been avoided both for themselves and for their families (but also, it has to be admitted, a great deal of Verdi's finest inspiration). Honour is a social convention belonging to the world, relating to the individual's relationship to the world around him and the people he encounters. It has nothing to do with the individual's existential being. Place an individual in isolation and he no longer has any need to concern himself with honour. As a character in Sartre's *Huis Clos* memorably remarks: 'Hell is other people'.

Human beings cannot exist in total isolation; all lives are interdependent so it is pointless to deny that a social code is crucial. But if it becomes the be-all and end-all of existence, life ceases to be worth living. In *Stiffelio* and *La Forza del Destino* Verdi, a confirmed agnostic, had an opportunity to explore how the obsession with honour can be transcended by the virtue of Christian compassion. In *Falstaff* Verdi explored another way of dealing with the problem, if not actually transcending it, namely through the sheer physical excess and exuberance of the *bon vivant*. Blake said, 'If a fool were to persist in his folly he would attain to

wisdom'. It is certainly an adage that could be applied to Sir John Falstaff.

There is an unavoidable streak of sadism in the story of *Falstaff* which, if it was not for the charm and vivacity of Verdi's music, could well become disturbing. As with all viable comedy, the tale has a serious undertone. Beyond all the individual quirks of character, all the buffoonery and slapstick comedy, there lurks a welter of black emotion, which is the prime motivation behind the action. This only serves to illustrate the old adage: 'Heav'n has no rage, love to hatred turn'd Nor Hell a fury like a woman scorn'd'.[29] *Falstaff* could almost be entitled 'Desdemona's revenge'. If *Otello* demonstrates the appalling consequences of a man allowing himself to be corrupted by jealousy, *Falstaff* demonstrates, humorously, the potentially dire consequences to a man who fails to offer the proper deference and respect to a woman. The whole drama of *Falstaff* originates from the fact that Falstaff elected to send the identical letter to two different women. Had he just sent the one letter the matter could have been dismissed as just a huge joke. The fact that he sends duplicates indicates that he is not remotely interested in the women for themselves. He might as well have sent the same letter to every woman in Windsor.

Beneath all the hilarity in Act 1 Scene 2, when the women review Falstaff's letter, is a deep sense of humiliation. Alice and Meg must each privately think, 'so that is all I am worth, now; to be the victim of an old man's avarice and total absence of regard'. For Alice there is the double humiliation of realizing that her husband actually takes seriously the threat posed by Falstaff. How could he imagine she would even contemplate a relationship with such a 'tub of lard'? The punishment meted out to Falstaff may seem excessive, but it is no more than he deserves.

Falstaff (*Falstaff*)

The character of Sir John Falstaff is one of Verdi's greatest achievements and one of the

---

[29] Congreve, *The Mourning Bride* III, 8, 1697.

finest operatic creations in the entire repertoire. Verdi manages to instil into Shakespeare's rumbustious Knight all the experience of a lifetime suffused with great highs and terrible lows. Of a generally pessimistic disposition it took until he was nearly 80 for Verdi to allow the deep humanity which had always characterized his art to find full expression in a comic opera.

Above all *Falstaff* exudes a real sense of fun, and this is having taken into account the darker hints of sadism which prevail in the latter half of the drama. Presiding over all the imbroglios, all the absurdities and all the insanity is the gargantuan and hugely likeable figure of Falstaff himself. It is Falstaff who best sums himself up (Act 3 Scene 2): 'Every sort of common clown makes fun of me and glories in it, but, without me, they wouldn't have a pinch of salt for all their arrogance. I'm the one who makes them so clever. My wit creates the wit of others'.

Falstaff may be an unconscionable rogue, but it is he who enlivens the usually humdrum lives of the Windsor bourgeoisie. Above all Falstaff believes in excess. He does not know the meaning of the word moderation which, after all, is the very essence of the bourgeoisie that always seeks to preserve the status quo. In terms of material wealth it is the lot of the aristocracy to be given, by dint of birth, that which others must strive through long life and much toil to attain. Those that are given usually, sooner or later (usually sooner), take what they have been given for granted. Falstaff takes for granted that when he opens his purse money will fall out. When it does not he is aggrieved. But it is not something he will have a sleepless night over. For a man of wit there is always money out there to be had.

It is natural that Falstaff, at this juncture, should turn to one of the wealthiest men in town. But it is sublimely ridiculous that he should imagine that by appropriating **Ford's** wife he could thereby appropriate the man's gold. But Falstaff is not logical. When wooing **Alice** (Act 2 Scene 2) he promises her much gold and that she shall be laden

with many jewels if only she will give herself to him. This is, of course, hogwash. Falstaff has not even enough money to pay for a barrel of sack, let alone jewels for Alice. That Alice knows this perfectly well is indicated by her response which, in the best romantic tradition, suggests she has no interest in gold. For Alice and **Meg** must surely have concluded by now (it is never made explicit) that Falstaff is simply gold-digging when he writes the identical letter to both women. Either that or he is sex-starved. In fact both apply to Falstaff, but sex is not really an issue for him. All his libido goes into his stomach. All that really concerns him is safe-guarding his biggest asset, for without his stomach he would be as nought.

Falstaff vividly remembers the days when he was a lithesome young boy (*Quand'ero paggio* [Act 2 Scene 2]) and in his imagination he can still be that lithesome young boy. But if given the choice he would not want to return to those days, because with those dashing looks and nimble limbs would come responsibility, responsibility which he is more than happy to be without these days. His girth confers on him a certain status, a certain power in the world. When he loses his temper, as he does with **Pistola** and **Bardolfo** (Act 1 Scene 1), it is awe-inspiring to behold. As **Quickly** accurately comments (Act 1 Scene 2), he is like a cannon waiting to go off, and woe betide anybody who happens to be in his way when he does.

In Falstaff's stomach is his potency. He woos Alice in order not to satisfy his sex urge, but in order to acquire the means to satisfy his stomach. He accuses Bardolfo and Pistola of 'eating up' his substance. If Falstaff ever got thin he would not be himself, nobody would love him; 'in this great abdomen are the thousand tongues that proclaim my name' (Act 1 Scene 1). Pistola and Bardolfo know the routine. They chime in, 'Enorme Falstaff! Immenso Falstaff!' Indicating his paunch Falstaff proudly declares, 'This is my kingdom. I'll make it greater'.

When Falstaff rhapsodizes about Alice's many charms it is tempting to think that he is genuinely inspired with love until he relates, 'The goddess turned rays of light through a burning glass upon me, on me, my merry leg, my big thorax, my masculine foot, my healthy, erect and massive body!' (Act 1 Scene 1). It is all me, me, me. He continues, 'and her desire burned up in her so much at sight of me that it seemed to say: *I am Sir John Falstaff's!*' And it dawns on us that he is not remotely interested in anybody other than Sir John Falstaff.

Having said which Falstaff is a philosopher of some profundity, and this is what makes him so attractive. For were he only interested in eating and drinking he would be extremely uninteresting. There is nothing more tedious than another man's passion or excess in which no-one but he can participate. But all the time that Falstaff has lived and swindled his way though life he has observed that the world is ruled by humbug. It is this that causes him such outrage when Bardolfo invokes his honour as the reason he cannot deliver Falstaff's letter to Alice Ford. Falstaff's outpouring (*L'Onore! Ladri!*) is the result of a raw nerve having been twitched.[31] As a member of the aristocracy Falstaff has been surrounded all his life by people to whom honour is the highest virtue. But long ago Falstaff has had to abandon the luxury of being primarily concerned with his honour. Had he not he would have starved, and that would be unthinkable.

There is an interesting subtext in Falstaff's outpouring on honour, namely that Verdi himself had spent his entire career setting tales which revolved principally around the concept of honour and the way in which it can wreck a man's life. Don Carlo in *La Forza del Destino* and Stankar in *Stiffelio* are obvious instances. Both men are obsessed with the concept of honour and both suffer because their code is at total variance with the code of Christian compassion, which predominates in both works. For Verdi, who was agnostic and certainly did not suffer a religious crisis at the end of his life as did Wagner, Falstaff's outpouring in the opening

scene of his last opera may well be an accurate picture of how Verdi himself came to think on the subject. It also effectively gives the lie to the countless situations in which characters have been ruined by their obsession with honour. In the final analysis honour is a concept linked exclusively to an individual's ego. It is principally what motivates Master Ford in this opera, and what makes him so enraged when he hears that his wife is having an affair. For all that he appears an unconscionable egotist, Falstaff is not egotistical in the sense that Ford is. His perspective on life is too all-embracing. Referring to honour he states categorically: 'Flattery inflates it, pride corrupts it and calumny sickens it . . . and I'll have none of it!' He has some way to go before he can truly say that and mean it. Falstaff has already been seen inflated with pride and flattery, and the opera will demonstrate how he invites calumny. But before the evening is out he will be reduced to utter prostration as he is mercilessly beaten and humiliated at the hands of the 'Merry Wives' and their accomplices. An encore of the 'L'Onore' monologue would not be out of place at the opera's conclusion. For as befits a philosopher Falstaff must learn to experience the reality of that which he preaches. Having done so he can then speak with authority.

For Falstaff every day is an adventure and his greatest asset (apart from his stomach), the irreplaceable asset of which he is never short, is his razor-sharp wit. Falstaff gives the expression 'living off your wits' a new meaning. When he lays his plans to repair his dwindling fortunes he does not intend any malice. He truly considers that he confers on the Merry Wives, whose assets he seeks to appropriate (in more ways than one), an honour. And for a short time Alice and Meg, while in their separate houses and unaware that an exact replica of the letter each has received has been sent to the other, undoubtedly do feel honoured. This is Falstaff's gravest error. It is symptomatic of the problem he has with everything he undertakes, that far from being capable of doing anything by halves, he must always

---

[31] For origin of this speech see *Henry IV* Act 5 Scene 1.

do too much and thereby ultimately defeat his purposes. His girth itself is indicative of the problem. All living creatures eat and drink in order to survive. Falstaff cannot stop eating and drinking. The very act of eating and drinking confirms for him his existence, especially drinking.

At the opening of Act 3, when Falstaff is recovering from his ordeal in Act 2 Scene 2 and feeling uncharacteristically despondent, it is a large glass of mulled wine that revives his spirits and elicits from him a paean to the virtues of wine that amounts almost to a mystical vision of enlightenment: 'Drinking good wine is like the sun, wonderful thing! Good wine dispels the stupid gloom of discouragement, lights up the eye and the wits; from the lips it goes to the brain and there awakens the little maker of thrills; a dark vibrating thrill comes into the tipsy man, thrilling every fibre in the heart, the gay wind flickers with the thrill and the mad globe quivers with a thrilling madness! The thrill invades the world!'[31]

This can either be dismissed as drunken nonsense or seen as a profound expression of a discovery to which few of us happen upon, namely that the distinction between subject and object is more or less illusory and is only waiting to be transcended. The great artists and saints devote themselves to achieving this, but it is not only the artists and saints who do achieve it. It is also quite possible to happen upon that transcendence by chance. All that is required is that the ego be relinquished. For most humans this is well nigh impossible. For a man like Falstaff it is a condition that he can rediscover day in, day out, through sheer enjoyment of being, and in being able to consume. He loves food, he loves drink, he loves company, he loves women. He is in love with his own existence, which is not at all the same thing as saying he is in love with himself. **Doctor Caius** is in love with himself. He takes himself extremely seriously. He takes offence at the smallest

slight, real or imagined. He lives in a permanent state of neurotic irritation. He never relaxes because he always has something to do, some grievance to address.

Falstaff is rarely aggrieved. When he has been sorely ill-used by the 'Merry Wives' and has far more cause than Doctor Caius has ever had to be aggrieved he does not let forth a stream of vitriol against the women. Rather he contemplates the world in which such injustice can be visited upon an individual: 'O world of crime! Virtue does not exist anymore. Everything is declining'. A moralist would say he should be reflecting on why he has been so ill treated and seeking forgiveness for his sins. But that would be to miss the point. Falstaff always sees himself in the broadest possible perspective. He never forgets for a moment that he is part of a world which does not always behave according to one's expectations. Yet it is the world that nurtures him, feeds and waters him. The world has made him and he owes it to the world to grace it with his presence. This is Falstaff's moral code.

When Falstaff contemplates his own passing he laments the fact, not on his own account, but from the perspective of a world which will be a great deal the poorer without him. The hymn to wine, quoted above, comes immediately after he has momentarily lapsed from his usual philosophic lightness of being and noticed, almost as though for the first time: 'I'm getting too fat'. He gives of himself unstintingly and he expects the world to give back to him in equal measure. When it fails him it does not occur to him to blame himself. It is entirely the world's fault.

It could be argued that Falstaff simply indulges in the pathetic fallacy, transferring his own disenchantment onto the world; and in a sense that is exactly what he does. But it is that ability to identify himself and his feelings with the world and thereby feel at home in the world whether comfortable or not, that differentiates him from all the other protagonists. The other inhabitants of Windsor are all sublimely unconscious of the fact of their existence. They live for the here and now in a passive sense. They fret over

---

[31] This passage represents a brilliant distillation by Boito of Falstaff's speech in praise of Sherris: *Henry IV* Act 4 Scene 3 ll. 86–123.

this or that. They do not actively participate in the world. They only participate in that which concerns them intimately at any given moment. Falstaff has actually taken ownership of the world. He knows that the world is vast, but so is he. His gargantuan appetites reflect a gargantuan universe. The worst thing that can happen to Falstaff is that his appetites be circumscribed and the world shrink around him until it can no longer accommodate him.

This is precisely what happens to Falstaff when he is squeezed into Ford's laundry basket (Act 2 Scene 2). His cries of suffocation and the pantomimic way in which he keeps emerging only to be pushed back down are hilariously funny in the theatre, but for Falstaff it is the worst possible nightmare. For he is suddenly limited to a degree unprecedented in his life. His predicament is a vivid expression of the pass to which his life has come. Because he has made of his body his entire universe, because he has relied on his body for his identity in the world the most severe lesson he has to learn is to be without it. It is the moment to which his life has been moving, the moment of negation of that which matters to him, the ultimate chastisement of his ego. From this moment Falstaff *should* never be the same again.

Yet Falstaff's ego is remarkably resilient. In the scene where Quickly tries to keep him concealed in the basket he keeps bouncing back (Act 2 Scene 2). At the opening of Act 3 it becomes clear that Falstaff has not learnt his lesson. He still allows himself to be deceived by his own vanity. Quickly's second visit to try and entice him to Windsor Park at midnight is by way of a test. Any ordinary person, having endured what Falstaff has had to endure that afternoon, would have nothing more to do with Mistress Alice. Indeed Falstaff's first reaction is, 'You and your lovely Alice can go to the devil!' This is a sensible reaction. But Falstaff's vanity has not been sufficiently pruned. This resilience is both his potential downfall and his greatness. One quaff of wine and his customary high spirits are re-established. He has reconnected with the stars and is ready to recommence his assault on the world. But his vanity blinds him to the improbability of Alice truly pining after him. She certainly gave precious little evidence at their first rendezvous. She was in fact notably coy, quite clearly having no desire to have him slobbering all over her. So now Falstaff must don a pair of horns – the very horns that he has tried to place on Ford's forehead. This, if anything will, should alert him to the unlikelihood of a successful outcome. It is glaringly obvious that he is being 'set up'.

When the worst happens and Falstaff finds himself being beaten black and blue by what must feel like the entire population of Windsor, the light begins to dawn. He admits, 'I begin to see that I have been an ass'. He begins to perceive that his appetites cannot be satisfied at whatever cost. He must learn to be in control of his appetites. They must be at his service, not the other way round. It is a tough lesson for him to learn. But Falstaff's greatest attribute is his generosity. He bears no umbrage. At the end of the opera he can still laugh, both at himself and at the world. 'The whole world is a jest; man was born a great jester.' Falstaff certainly was.

Federico di Frengel (*Stiffelio*). Lina's cousin. Federico plays a small but crucial role in the main action of the drama. He has the misfortune to be in the wrong place at the wrong time. In Act 1, just after **Raffaele** has inserted his letter of assignation to Lina into a volume of Klopstock, Federico arrives on the scene, having decided to revisit the book about which **Stiffelio** and **Jorg** have waxed so lyrical. Federico is clearly an avid follower of Stiffelio. He is on stage at the opening of the opera to welcome Stiffelio on his return from his travels abroad and is amongst the congregation in the final scene in the church.

Unfortunately for Federico, Jorg mistakenly thinks that it is he who placed the letter in the book and tells Stiffelio of his suspicion. Thus when Federico quite innocently asks Stiffelio what will be the subject of his forthcoming sermon, he is subjected to a diatribe on the 'villain who sold his master' (Judas).

He remains oblivious to the true reason for Stiffelio's anguish, wondering with the rest of the assembly, why 'some demon did sow suspicion in Stiffelio's heart'.

By the end of the opera Federico must be clearly aware of Lina's infidelity. Stiffelio all but spells it out when he reads from the Gospel on the adulteress at the feet of Jesus, and then publicly proclaims his forgiveness of Lina. This act of apparently supreme selflessness must surely justify for Federico his unstinting admiration for the preacher. (See also **Enrico** (*Aroldo*).)

Duke Federigo of Austria (*I Vespri Siciliano*). Elena's brother.
Does not appear in the opera, having been executed as an enemy of the French State before the action commences. It would appear there was scant justification for his execution; his only crime being to have an affair with a Swabian girl. Even the French officer, **Vaudimont**, expresses unease concerning the pretext for the execution (Act 1).

Federigo's sister, Elena, has only one thought, and that is to avenge her brother's death. Her feelings are confused by her love for **Arrigo** (also an associate of Federigo's). Her conflict is temporarily ameliorated when Arrigo readily agrees to be the instrument of her revenge, but returns when it materializes that Arrigo, in spite of his association with her brother, is half French, his father being none other than the French governor, **Monforte**.

Federigo's death is finally avenged at the conclusion of the opera when the Sicilians massacre the French at the very moment that Elena is to be married to Arrigo.

Don Felice de Bornos (*La Forza del Destino*). See **Don Carlo**

Fenena (*Nabucco*). Daughter of Nabucco.
Fenena demonstrates all the positive virtues that her (adoptive) sister, **Abigaille**, so strenuously attempts to quell within herself. Fenena allows herself, without qualms, to be led by her lover and companion, **Ismaele**, exactly as Abigaille turns her back

on all imperatives beyond herself. Where Abigaille's frantic desire for political ascendancy is ultimately thwarted, Fenena's purely personal love for one man (who happens to have been born a political enemy) effects a revolution far more far-reaching than any of the agendas stemming from the short-sighted, egotistical motives initiated by her father and half-sister.

Fenena has no political ambitions. Her idealism is that of love: the love that has been awakened in her by the glamorous young Hebrew prince who suddenly appears in Babylon as the Jewish ambassador. When Ismaele is thrown into prison, presumably on some meaningless pretext (or possibly at the behest of Abigaille, wishing to distance her sister from the man she herself has fallen in love with), Fenena's passion is inflamed even more. She risks all in order to help Ismaele's escape.

When the opera opens the tables have been turned and Fenena is now a prisoner of the Hebrews, who have recently been defeated by the Babylonians. She has in fact become the Hebrews' trump card in the battle with Nabucco for, as the king's daughter, she is viewed by the high pontiff, **Zaccaria**, as the Hebrews' last chance of holding on to their liberty. Fenena is not naïve. In her first encounter with Ismaele, who loses no time in declaring his love for her, she upbraids the young man for speaking of love when his countrymen's situation is so perilous (Act 1). While she may want nothing more than that Ismaele should release her and that they should rush off into the sunset together, she is aware that this would entail Ismaele in betraying the 'sacred duty' he owes to his father and to his country. She would never ask this of him.

Fenena's final conversion to the Jewish faith is prompted by the behaviour of her sister, who breaks in upon her scene with Ismaele, and swears vengeance upon them both. In that instant she realizes that there is nothing left for her in her homeland. All her life she has had to give precedence to her older sister. Her father is engaged in vendettas of his own with which she cannot possibly feel sympathy. More than this, though, she has an opportunity to contrast the apparent selflessness of Ismaele with the fanatical bloodlust of her 'sister'. She calls upon the one God to protect her 'brother', for thus she now characterizes her lover (Act 1).

That her love for Ismaele alienates her from her father must be a source of great pain and terror for Fenena, for she loves her father in spite of the fact that his one aim is to crush the very people from whom her lover has arisen and to whom she wishes to belong. However Verdi and Solera do not portray Fenena's anguish, only her joy at being embraced into the Jewish faith. For in Jehovah and through his emissary on earth, Zaccaria, she finds the faith she has always lacked.

It is almost a relief to Fenena that she is to be sacrificed, for thus she will reconcile the irreconcilable. In death she will no longer suffer the impossibility of torn loyalties, the guilt concerning her father, her country and even her sister that must assail her in the small hours of the night. For we see enough of Fenena's nature to know that she will be susceptible to guilt. She worries on behalf of Ismaele, that he will be driven by torn loyalties. Such is her love for him that she does that which is in her power to assuage his torments, but by so doing she trebles her own susceptibility to grief.

Ultimately, however, Fenena is redeemed by the power of her faith and the power of her faith is in direct proportion to the necessity of it. For faith is not something which can be sought and found. Faith is always discovered when there is absolutely no other recourse. In every life there comes a moment when no received wisdom, no ordinary panaceas for the ordinary ills of life is enough. There comes a moment when one must either succumb to insanity or give oneself wholly and only unto faith. What definition we choose to give the object of that faith is immaterial so long as it be entirely transcendent, something that is beyond our limited understanding. Fenena's choice of Jehovah over the craven images of the Babylonians and Assyrians is so central to the whole ethos underlying the drama that it is essentially a vote for humility and a rejection of the hubris underpinning her father's and her sister's desires and egotistical drives. Fenena needs to reject their life values for the sake of her own humanity.

While the role of Fenena may be the least glamorous in the opera it is yet the most significant.

Fenton (*Falstaff*)

Fenton has very little to distinguish him as a character other than the fact that he is desperately in love with **Nannetta**, daughter of the wealthy merchant, **Master Ford**. One has the feeling that Fenton loves because he has nothing better to do, and one can sympathize a little with Ford's reluctance to see his daughter married to him. He is well aware that Ford does not favour his suit of Nannetta and would prefer the physician, **Doctor Caius**, as a prospective husband for his daughter. Luckily for the young lovers Nannetta's mother, **Alice**, is on their side, as are the other 'Merry Wives'. None of them has any time for the tedious doctor. The love affair of Fenton and Nannetta fulfils an unwritten law that there should always be a young love interest in a comedy. Puccini was to repeat the equation evidenced in *Falstaff*, albeit within different parameters, in his one comic opera, *Gianni Schicchi*.

When Fenton first appears on stage he is attempting to ingratiate himself with the man he hopes will one day be his father-in-law, by offering either his wits or his sword to assist in putting **Falstaff** in his place (Act 1 Scene 2). Since three other men are trying to talk to Ford at the same time he does not receive a notable response, which was perhaps part of his intention. Once Nannetta arrives on the scene Fenton has eyes only for her. He is truly besotted and, as is the way with young lovers, his only desire is to get his hands and lips on his sweetheart. He shows himself to be something of a poet (which certainly would not help recommend him to Ford) when wooing Nannetta. Referring to her lips he pleads: 'Let them scatter words and show their pearls, lovely to see, sweet to kiss' (Act 1 Scene 2). (In Italian this reads, 'Che spargon ciarle, che mostran perle, belle a vederle, dolci a baciarle!') As he retires to the bush, where he is forced to hide as the 'Merry Wives' arrive, he comments: 'the mouth that is kissed is never unlucky'.

Fenton no doubt enjoys the plans, that he overhears being discussed by the three women, to 'gull' Falstaff. However his only concern is to find another opportunity to be alone with Nannetta. All the shenanigans surrounding the general outrage over Falstaff's behaviour only hinder his pursuit of love. In Act 2 Scene 2 he is completely oblivious to what is transpiring in Ford's house. Nannetta is of like mind and they both wish only to find somewhere they can continue their romance without interruption. The large screen in Alice's apartment seems like an ideal hiding place until it suddenly collapses around them and they find themselves face to face with an extremely irate Master Ford. There are moments when discretion is indeed the better part of valour and Fenton reckons this is one of them. He scurries off.

Fenton appears to know nothing about Ford's plot to marry Nannetta off to Doctor Caius, nor of the Merry Wives' plans to foil the plot. For when **Quickly** gives him the black habit of a friar to don he asks: 'What does this mean?' He does, however, know of the plan to humble Falstaff, and he is present in Windsor Park at the opening of Act 3 Scene 2. His aria, *Dal labbro il canto estasiato vola*, consists of nothing more than an elaborate metaphor revolving around the various uses of lips: singing songs of ecstasy, kissing the beloved's lips, etc. When Alice makes reference to her husband's betrayal and the need to turn the tables on him Fenton tries to discover her intention, but to no avail. 'You must obey swiftly and silently. Chance flies away as quickly as it comes', Alice tells him.

Fenton will indeed have cause to celebrate Alice's willingness to snatch at the fleeting opportunity that presents itself that night to ensure her daughter's happiness, though he may justifiably be concerned when it comes to the moment of unmasking and once again coming face to face with Master Ford. Fortunately for him Ford has had a long day and is in the mood to be magnanimous. Fenton and Nannetta are unlikely to forget the day of their wedding.

Ferrando (*Il Trovatore*). Captain of **di Luna's** guard.

Ferrando's function is similar to that of the chorus in Greek tragedy. He is on stage at the outset of the opera and must grab the audience's intention, compelling them to listen to the tale he narrates for the sake of the Count's tired retainers. The subsequent action of the opera will only be comprehensible in the light of the information he divulges (*Di due figli*). The retainers are on guard against the advent of the Troubador who seeks to press his suit with **Leonora**, with whom di Luna is in love. For a summary of Ferrando's narration see the **Synopsis**. The scene establishes an atmosphere of dark foreboding which pervades throughout the opera.

Ferrando accompanies his master and various retainers to the convent where Leonora is about to take the veil (Act 2 Scene 2). Di Luna is in a high state of agitation which is only exacerbated when **Manrico** appears. Ferrando and the other retainers are forced to restrain their master who draws his sword and looks as though he would slay Leonora rather than see her depart with Manrico. Since the Count's men are hopelessly outnumbered by Manrico's forces, Ferrando realizes it is essential to restrain his master. The moment Manrico has departed with Leonora, di Luna orders a siege of Castellor, the castle where Manrico has taken refuge. Ferrando will be responsible for setting up camp below the ramparts.

On his next appearance (Act 3 Scene 1) Ferrando reports to di Luna that an old gypsy has been found wandering in the vicinity. When **Azucena** is dragged in it is Ferrando who recognizes her as the gypsy responsible for burning di Luna's baby brother. This is a very important function of Ferrando's role in the opera, for he is the only main protagonist, apart from Azucena, old enough to have been present at the events he describes at the beginning of the opera. He is thus the only person able to identify Azucena.

When Ferrando learns that Azucena is Manrico's mother he is determined, as are all the Count's retainers, that she shall die a hideous death: 'Wretch, you will see a pyre rise here in a little while. Nor will that earthly fire be your only punishment! The flames of hell for you will be an eternal stake! There your soul will be forced to suffer and to burn'. Ferrando has fulfilled his function in the drama and does not reappear.

Fiesco ('Andrea') (*Boccanegra*). A Genoese nobleman.

Fiesco is the representative of a proud Patrician family whose honour he guards with passionate assiduity. The possibility that a Plebeian might be elected as Doge is, for Fiesco, unthinkable. The fact that the Doge should have seduced and dishonoured his own beloved daughter, Maria, makes the situation intolerable for him.

When Fiesco first appears (Prologue) it is to bid adieu, not just to his dying daughter and home, but to a whole way of life over which he has exercised a monopoly. That monopoly has been rent asunder by the anarchic advent of his daughter's disobedience and the inevitable swing of history's pendulum away from the status quo. A reactionary character, he will be forced to undergo, through the course of his life and of the opera, many painful lessons. Principally he must learn to relinquish, to forego the tradition, the family, the status quo in which his fragile ego has almost become immured.

Within the first phrase of his soliloquy (*A te, l'estremo addio*), he commits the unpardonable sin of blasphemy. How could the Blessed Virgin suffer his daughter's virtue to be ravished? It never occurs to Fiesco – and nor for that matter would it occur to any fourteenth-century father – that his daughter may have desired that her virtue be ravished, that she may have found great

happiness with **Boccanegra** and that what has in fact killed her has been her father's antagonism. 'The tortured soul of a sad father was condemned to the torment of dishonour and grief', Fiesco intones. His misery stems from his own egocentredness and his inability to think beyond the concept of honour. He pleads with Maria to pray for him. Much later in the opera his granddaughter will likewise pray to Maria to intercede on her behalf and inspire her father to forgive her lover.

The confrontation with Boccanegra (*Qual cieco fato*) is painful, but necessary – a welcome catharsis for accumulated bitterness. Fiesco does not attempt to restrain himself. He is appalled at Boccanegra's melodramatic gesture of baring his chest, considering it demonstrative of a woeful lack of breeding. Nevertheless Boccanegra's obvious distress does move him to make a concession. If Boccanegra will surrender the child of his union with Maria (Fiesco's granddaughter), Fiesco will be prepared to entertain pardoning Boccanegra. When Boccanegra, however, reveals that this is impossible since he does not himself know where the girl is to be found, Fiesco reiterates his refusal to contemplate a reconciliation until his stipulation is fulfilled. He turns his back on Boccanegra and coldly refuses to discuss the matter further. He withdraws a little way off, but then remains concealed. It would seem he wants to witness the moment Boccanegra discovers that Maria is dead. This obsessive relish in seeing vengeance done is Fiesco's least attractive characteristic and also that which brings upon himself the bulk of his suffering. His triumph when Boccanegra discovers Maria's corpse is shortlived however, for almost immediately he hears the people of Genoa proclaim Boccanegra their new Doge. 'Hell burns in my breast!' he declares as the curtain falls on the Prologue.

With Boccanegra as Doge Fiesco has two options: either to go into exile, or to go underground. He chooses the latter option and assumes the disguise in which he appears throughout the remainder of the opera as Andrea. How he comes to gain the position as guardian of **Amelia** – his own grand-daughter, did he but know it – is not made explicit. What is made clear is that Fiesco knows that Amelia is an orphan and not a Grimaldi, for he makes it his business to apprise **Gabriele** of the fact when the latter asks his permission to marry Amelia. Fiesco clearly respects Gabriele and is perfectly happy for him to marry his ward (Act 1 Scene 1). After all they are already united in seeking to depose Boccanegra in favour of the Patricians. In fact Fiesco does not need to be told that Gabriele is in love with Amelia; it has been quite apparent to him. His respect for Gabriele is only confirmed by the young man's refusal to be dissuaded from his love for Amelia by the revelation that she is of lowly origins. This scene with Gabriele adds a new dimension to the character of Fiesco, who otherwise demonstrates only a fierce fanaticism and rancour, notably in his scenes with Boccanegra. Nevertheless it is significant that he concludes the interview with Gabriele with a heartfelt wish, 'Let the day of vengeance dawn soon'. Even in his friendships Fiesco is motivated by the negative forces of hate and lust for revenge.

The kidnapping of Amelia leads Fiesco to throw caution to the winds. Together with Gabriele he storms to the Doge's palace pursued by an angry mob (Act 1 Scene 2; see **Chorus**). This is the turning point in his life. For the first time he openly demonstrates his dissension at a political level. For although Fiesco does not realize that Amelia is his granddaughter she is the one person he deeply cares about. He is outraged by the traumas to which she has been subjected. When he arrives at the palace he does, however, keep his peace and leave it to the younger man – Gabriele – to voice their outrage before the Doge. Amelia, concerned to prevent her beloved guardian from publicly implicating himself, begs him to conceal his rage. It is, however, too late for such pretence. Boccanegra, unaware of 'Andrea's' true identity, has Fiesco arrested and imprisoned.

Paolo takes pleasure in telling Fiesco that the Doge has already signed Fiesco's death warrant (Act 2 Scene 1). It is unlikely this is

truly the case but merely a ruse on Paolo's part to persuade Fiesco to murder Boccanegra in his sleep. Fiesco, however, is scornful of such a cowardly crime, preferring to await his end. A Patrician through and through, honour is for Fiesco the highest duty. All his plotting against Boccanegra has been motivated by the honourable desire to see the Patricians, in his eyes the rightful inheritors of the State, restored to power. Now he accepts, if not with equanimity, with resignation his inevitable fate. Languishing in prison Fiesco is ignorant of the fact that Gabriele, having discovered that Boccanegra is Amelia's father, has turned his back on all political strife and seeks now only to support Boccanegra's fight to achieve an accord between the warring factions. Thus, as he is granted his freedom, handed back his sword and told that the Guelfs have been defeated he remarks that it is 'a sad freedom'. He may reflect that he has been let off lightly, for at the same moment that he is liberated he meets Paolo being led to his execution. Apparently Paolo has taken up arms with the rebels. Knowing himself condemned Paolo tells Fiesco with relish how he has himself condemned Boccanegra to death, having administered a slow poison. Paolo also boasts how it was he who was responsible for Amelia's abduction. Fiesco is so outraged he draws his sword and, in a rare moment of loss of self-control, nearly saves the public executioner the trouble of despatching Paolo, but he pulls himself together when he realizes that Paolo merely seeks to avoid the humiliation of a traitor's death.

Fiesco is genuinely appalled by Paolo's revelation that he has poisoned Boccanegra. Boccanegra may have been a long-standing adversary but Fiesco would never have wished such an ignominious and dishonourable death for him. The guards have barely dragged Paolo away to his execution when Fiesco sees Boccanegra approach (Act 3). He conceals himself and watches as Boccanegra, left alone, goes to the window and expresses regret that it was not given to him to find a grave in the sea which has always felt like his true home. Fiesco takes his cue from this and accosts Boccanegra: 'It would have been better for you if you had'. Oblivious to the fact that Boccanegra is overjoyed to see him, giving him a last chance as it does to effect a reconciliation, Fiesco can only reiterate with redoubled vehemence, his old cry for vengeance. Finally Boccanegra succeeds in making Fiesco listen to him when he relates that his daughter, long believed lost, has returned in the form of Amelia Grimaldi. This is a monumental shock to Fiesco. He is overcome with grief to think that all the years he has nurtured Amelia he has been tending his own granddaughter without realizing it. His grief is intensified by the bitter awareness that he is to be reconciled with his daughter's lover only in the hour of the latter's death. What truly strikes him in this anguished moment (*Piango, perchè mi parla*), so movingly evoked in Verdi's music, is the great guilt that he must shoulder for the inordinate pride that has kept him for so long alienated, not only from Boccanegra, but from his granddaughter, from the world and most of all from himself. Boccanegra's magnanimity only underlines the pain and guilt that overwhelms him. Stuttering, he reveals to Boccanegra Paolo's treachery. Boccanegra does not need to be told. He feels death working within him.

As he observes his granddaughter weeping at the feet of her dying father it is given to Fiesco to enunciate the dark philosophy that underpins the entire work: 'All mortal happiness is false enchantment. The human heart is a spring of never ending tears'. The supreme irony of Fiesco's destiny comes in the closing pages of the opera. Finally the moment he has dreamed of has arrived when he can proclaim to the people of Genoa that the Plebeian Doge has died and that the throne will pass to a Patrician. Now it can give him no pleasure. The lie of his own existence and passionate preoccupations have been revealed to him. He is too old to find the energy for rebirth. He can only lament the waste of his life. What comfort remains he will find through the love of his granddaughter and her husband. Fiesco's fate

more than a little invokes that of Shakespeare's demented old King Lear.

The real tragedy and lesson of Fiesco's life lies in the fact that for a large part of it he already possesses, without knowing it, that which he most yearns after, and which most torments him. He allows politics so to sour his life and vision that he cannot even recognize his own flesh and blood. When Boccanegra prays that the rival factions learn the arts of peace and love ('Fratracidi!'), it is Fiesco who most needs to listen. He remains until the eleventh hour blind to the grace which has always been his.

Filippo II (*Don Carlo*). See Philip II

Fleance (*Macbeth*). Son of Banquo.
Fleance is out walking with his father when Banquo is killed by the cut-throats, under orders from Macbeth (Act 2 Scene 2). His father's dying words to him are to flee to safety, which he manages to do, thus ensuring that the line of Banquo will be secured down the centuries as prophesied by the witches (Act 1 Scene 1).

Flora Bervoix (*La Traviata*). A courtesan and friend of Violetta.
Flora cares about Violetta rather as a fellow slave might have done in the galleys. They share the same lot in life. It is not a particularly happy lot but it has its compensations, principally a luxurious lifestyle such as neither she nor Violetta could otherwise have dreamed of.

Unlike Violetta Flora is a picture of health and clearly considers herself lucky. She does not contribute much to the scene of Violetta's party (Act 1), although she enjoys teasing **Baron Douphol** by observing how handsome and attractive **Alfredo** is. She probably admires Violetta's audacity in encouraging Alfredo's advances. She herself would never dare to jeopardize her own meal ticket by straying from the embraces of the **Marquis d'Obigny**, her protector.

When Violetta leaves Paris Flora clearly misses her friend and misses no opportunity to invite Violetta to her parties. But Violetta absents herself for many months. One day Flora is surprised to find Violetta has accepted her invitation and attends, not on the arm of Alfredo, as she would have expected, but escorted by her erstwhile protector, Baron Douphol. Flora does not ask the reason for the change of escort. Nevertheless she is concerned for her friend's well-being and horrified, as everybody is, by Alfredo's public denunciation of her. She is genuinely anxious about Violetta, unlike the Baron, who is more concerned for his dignity. Flora would have more reason than the Baron to be appalled for it is her party that has been wrecked by Alfredo's outburst.

She is nowhere to be seen in the final act. It is quite probable that she may have been forbidden by her protector from ever associating with Violetta again after the events which have culminated in the Baron being wounded. Flora is made of very different mettle from her friend. She would not jeopardize her livelihood and lifestyle for anybody or anything. Violetta has effectively ostracized herself from her profession by associating with such an altogether unreliable character as Alfredo would appear to be.

Flora's main importance to the opera is the letter that she writes enticing Violetta back to Paris and reminding her of her former existence.

Folco (*I Lombardi*). Father to **Arvino** and **Pagano**.

Does not appear in the opera but is slain (offstage) in his bed at the opening of Act 1 Scene 2 by Pagano who imagines he is murdering his brother. Thus Pagano, who had every intention of turning himself into a fratricide, unwittingly becomes a parricide and is 'branded with the mark of Cain'.

Another opera could be written on the reasons that Pagano so detests his brother (other than the obvious) which must inevitably stem in part from the elder Folco.

Ford (*Falstaff*)

The character of Ford cannot fail to invoke memories of Verdi's previous masterpiece,

Otello. For the single defining feature of Ford's character is his insane jealousy. But whereas *Otello* is a tragedy and must illustrate the dire effects and consequences to a man when he gives way to his baser nature, *Falstaff* is a comedy, the eventual aim of which is to show that ultimately it is possible both for the characters and the audience to laugh at even the most outrageous eventualities.

Ford is a successful merchant. He has accrued considerable wealth and is therefore a conspicuous member of the community. He cannot help but be conspicuous and inevitably he must attract attention to himself and his family. If the truth be known Ford enjoys the attention that comes his way. What point is there in achieving wealth and standing in the community if you cannot enjoy the prestige it brings? The problem is that his standing in the community breeds envy. To be fair to **Falstaff** he is not envious as such, but he certainly desires to appropriate that which Ford has gained for himself through hard work and ingenuity.

Ford first hears of Falstaff's designs on his wife, **Alice**, from Falstaff's disaffected retainers, **Bardolfo** and **Pistola**, who can themselves hardly make a favourable impression upon him. In any case, their reputations have probably preceded them (Act 1 Scene 2). They are, in other words, unreliable witnesses. But where Ford's situation is crucially different from that of Otello is that Otello is given to understand that his wife is actively engaged upon an affair, whereas Ford is only alerted to an imminent act of theft. Yet such is Ford's temperament that he makes no such distinction.

When Ford learns from Falstaff himself that Alice has agreed to a rendezvous with him (Act 2 Scene 1) he immediately assumes the worst and flies into a towering rage. His monologue (*È sogno? O realtà?*) precisely complements that of Falstaff in Act 1 Scene 1 (*L'Onore!*). For where Falstaff pours scorn and derision on the notion of honour, Ford cares only to hold on to his honour and quickly becomes obsessed with the notion that he is sprouting a pair of cuckold's horns:

'O marriage! O hell! Woman; demon! Let blockheads have faith in their wives!'

It never seems to occur to Ford that Alice may be entirely innocent. The only evidence that he has of his wife's infidelity is the word of Falstaff and his retainers. But Ford is not given to extensive reflection. He reacts to events as they happen. In business, no doubt, this stands him in good stead. In marital life it is well-nigh disastrous. By the time he arrives at his home (Act 2 Scene 2), hot on the heels of Falstaff, he is beside himself. He treats his wife as though she is little better than a whore. (One thinks of the Count in Mozart's opera *La nozze di Figaro*, who similarly leaps to all the wrong conclusions on the slenderest of evidence). Ford is a 'right' man, incapable of brooking any opposition, determined that he is always right and that at all costs he should have his own way. Again these are undoubtedly necessary qualities when chairing a board meeting, but inappropriate in the domestic sphere.

A self-made man like Ford is primarily concerned to enhance his social station. Having achieved the wherewithal, in terms of riches, to sustain a comfortable lifestyle he needs then to find ways to accredit himself in the eyes of a world still fundamentally feudal in structure and outlook. A man like **Doctor Caius** can be a great asset to a man like Ford, who has the problem of every self-made man: that he is considered by society a *parvenu*. Ford must be aware that Caius is a ludicrously unsuitable husband for his daughter on any human level, but socially he knows that a respected physician is exactly the sort of son-in-law he wants. Caius must be aware of this and never misses an opportunity to ingratiate himself with the merchant. **Fenton**, on the other hand, has nothing to recommend him, other than that he happens to be the man **Nannetta** wants to marry. However, from Ford's perspective, that is no recommendation.

Alice, therefore, has to set about re-educating her husband. Once having clarified with him the sequence of events that led up to her rendezvous with Falstaff (Act 2 Scene 2), she turns her attention, aided and abetted by her friends, to putting Ford right about his daughter's marriage. It is typical of Ford that he does not refer to anybody, least of all his wife or Nannetta herself, on the matter. Rather he intends to ensure that he gets what he wants, come hell or high water. In fact he intends cheating his own daughter into marrying a man she does not love, using the masquerade planned for Falstaff, as a convenient front. He tells Doctor Caius exactly how Nannetta will be disguised (Act 3 Scene 1) so that Caius can bring her to Ford that he may bless their union.

It is an unspeakable way for a father to treat his daughter under any circumstances. It is the more incredible in view of what has just transpired in his own marriage. One would have thought that Ford would be seeking every possibility of making amends for his unpardonable behaviour towards his wife. But Ford is not one to waste time in repairing past mistakes. Rather he ploughs on to the next one. In this respect he is very similar to Falstaff, who apparently fails to learn his lesson from his ill-treatment in Ford's house (Act 2 Scene 2) and therefore must be further chastised. Ford also must be further disciplined. Luckily for Nannetta, Mistress **Quickly** has overheard Ford arranging matters with Doctor Caius and steps in to ensure that the plot is foiled. Thus when the moment arrives for Ford to marry his daughter to Caius (as he thinks) he discovers that he has, in fact, blessed the union not of Nannetta and Caius but of Caius and **Bardolfo**. He is also duped into blessing the union of Nannetta and Fenton, who are slyly introduced, still in disguise, by Alice, as just 'another couple of languorous lovers'.

By this stage of the opera even Ford is beyond further resistance and manages to accept with good grace his wife's mild reproof that 'man often falls into the nets woven by his own malice'. When Nannetta asks for his forgiveness he embraces both her and Fenton, commenting; 'if you cannot avoid a little trouble you should take it with good humour'. He must feel by this time a certain kinship with Falstaff and readily joins the latter in the final chorus proclaiming that 'the whole world is a jest'.

Foresto (*Attila*). An Aquilean knight.

Foresto leads the Aquileans into exile after their homeland has been put to rout by **Attila** and his army of Huns. For Foresto the situation is doubly painful because he has had to leave behind his beloved **Odabella** who has been taken prisoner by Attila. The Aquileans try to boost Foresto's morale. Their intervention awakens him to an awareness of his responsibility to his fellow countrymen. He deliberately puts his own private anguish aside in order to exhort his people to new hope: 'from the seaweed of these billows, like a new phoenix arisen, thou shalt live again more proud and more lovely, the wonder of the land and sea!' (Prologue Scene 2).

As soon as an opportunity presents itself Foresto dons the disguise of a Hun and sets out to rescue Odabella. Having reached Attila's camp he spies on the enemy and is horrified to note that Odabella appears to be collaborating with Attila. When she absents herself from the camp he follows her to a nearby wood and accosts her (Act 1 Scene 1). It would appear he has not over-heard her aria, *O! Nel fuggente nuvolo* in which she sings of her great love for him. Judging only by what he has seen he assumes the worst, that Odabella has given herself to the enemy. Odabella vigorously defends herself, pleading that far from being the offender she is in fact the victim. Only when she reminds him of the story of Judith and Holophernes is Foresto pacified (see **Synopsis**). When Odabella produces Attila's sword as proof that her ultimate aim is revenge Foresto relents. He throws himself at her feet, though Odabella wryly remarks that she would prefer it if he threw himself on her breast. Together the two sing of their rapture.

Foresto is witness to Attila's rebuff at the gates of Rome (Act 1 Scene 3) and can reflect with satisfaction on the 'might of the Eternal God... Before a devout and pious assembly the king of the Barbarians now withdraws'. Foresto thereafter is emboldened, in spite of his Barbarian disguise to approach the Roman general, **Ezio**, to enlist his help in

finally putting Attila to rout (Act 2 Scene 1). But Foresto then makes the mistake of telling Odabella of the plan to murder Attila (Act 2 Scene 2). **Uldino** is to administer poison into the king's cup. Odabella, however, is not to be cheated of her private revenge and actually prevents Attila from drinking the poison. Thus she reveals that she knows of the plot and Attila demands to know the identity of the culprit. Foresto is horrified that Odabella has been deceiving him all along. It never occurs to him that she might have her own agenda. Nevertheless he steps in and claims to be the villain, thus saving Uldino from certain death. Uldino is suitably gratified. Now it is Odabella's turn to save Foresto from persecution, which she does by claiming for herself the right to punish the criminal. If Foresto had any imagination he would realize that this was tantamount to a declaration of solidarity. For were Odabella truly of the enemy's party she would gladly allow Foresto to be hung, drawn and quartered by the Huns. As it is Foresto can only mutter with suppressed rage: 'May the scourging of remorse which awaits you last forever'.

Foresto assumes that Odabella will now go through with her proposed wedding to Attila and he enlists the help of Uldino in effecting his revenge (Act 3). However he is forestalled by the arrival of Odabella herself, who has received a visitation from the ghost of her father. Attila enters in pursuit of his fugitive bride and is met by a formidable alliance of his three deadliest enemies: the Romans, represented by Ezio; the Aquileans, represented by Foresto and the Bretons, represented by Uldino. Foresto is about to effect the ultimate revenge by running Attila through with his sword but is thwarted by his fiery lover. Odabella determinedly steps into the breach and stabs Attila with his own sword, as she had always intended.

Whatever the future has in store for Foresto it will not be one of uncomplicated domestic bliss. Odabella's behaviour is entirely concordant with the Amazonian costume she sports.

LA FORZA DEL DESTINO

Opera in 4 Acts. Libretto by Francesco Maria Piave after the drama, *Don Alvaro o la fuerza del sino* (1835), by Angelo Pérez de Saavedra, Duke of Rivas, and on a scene from the play, *Wallensteins Lager* (1799), by Schiller.

First performance: 10 November 1862 at the Imperial Theatre, St Petersburg. Revised version first performed on 20 February 1869 at La Scala, Milan.

Cast:
Il Marchese di Calatrava (bass)
Donna Leonora di Vargas: his daughter (soprano)
Don Carlo di Vargas, Leonora's brother (baritone)
Don Alvaro (tenor)
Preziosilla: a gypsy girl (mezzo-soprano)
Padre Guardiano: Franciscan monk (bass)
Fra Melitone: Franciscan monk (baritone)
Curra: Leonora's maid (mezzo-soprano)
Trabucco: muleteer and vendor (tenor)
A surgeon (Il Chirugo) (baritone)
Mayor of Hornachuelos (Un Alcade) (baritone)

Time: the middle of the 18th century
Place: Spain and Italy

Synopsis
Act 1 The castle of the Marquis of Calatrava, near Seville. A room hung with damask. On the walls hang family portraits and coats-of-arms. The room is furnished in eighteenth-century style, but is in a bad state of preservation. In the rear wall are two windows; the one on the left is closed, the one on the right is open, allowing moonlight to flood the room. Each of the side walls has two doors. The first, on the right opens, onto a hallway, the second is the door to Curra's room. To the left are the Marquis' and Donna Leonora's apartments. Just left of centre there is a table covered with a damask cloth. On it are a Spanish guitar, vases of flowers and two silver candelabra with lighted candles. Near the table is an armchair and various items of furniture bearing a clock and a portrait of the Marquis. The room is surrounded by a parapet.

The Marquis of Calatrava, carrying a lamp, is bidding goodnight to his daughter, Leonora, who appears preoccupied. Curra enters from Leonora's apartments. As her father closes the balcony window Leonora, in an aside, expresses her anguish. She knows that her lover, Don Alvaro, is planning to enter from the balcony, preparatory to eloping with her. The very name of Alvaro is abhorrent to her father, not simply because he loves his daughter but because Alvaro is the sole survivor of a noble Spanish family, hated and condemned for having allied themselves to the Incas in an attempt to throw off colonial rule. Leonora knows this only too well and yet pretends to herself that she will be able to bring her father round. The Marquis is puzzled by Leonora's distress but, failing to gain any explanation for his daughter's melancholy, makes to leave. Leonora, knowing that she will not see him again, throws herself passionately into her father's arms. He kisses her tenderly, takes up his lamp and goes off to his room.

Curra closes the door after him, then comes back to Leonora who is convulsed with weeping. Curra, who is party to the planned elopement, is to accompany Leonora in the latter's self-imposed exile. She takes a bag from a wardrobe and starts packing linens and gowns. Leonora tells her that she was on the point of confessing all. Curra replies that if she had, 'tomorrow Alvaro would either be lying in his own blood, or imprisoned in Seville, where he would probably be hanged – and all this because the one he loves does not love him'. In her aria (*Me pellegrina ed orfano*), Leonora gives vent to the conflict which assails her between her love for Alvaro and her horror at leaving country, family and father. Curra tries to distract her mistress by encouraging her to help her pack. Leonora is beginning to wonder if perhaps Alvaro might not come; it is already well past midnight. She is almost relieved at the thought she might be spared the torture of exile. But the sound of horses heralds Alvaro's arrival. Leonora is distraught. Curra comforts her as Alvaro enters from the balcony and throws himself into Leonora's arms (*Ah, per sempre o mio bell'angiol*).

Alvaro is immediately aware of his lover's agitation. Leonora observes that it is almost daybreak and Alvaro explains that a thousand things have detained him, though nothing would have prevented him from keeping their rendezvous: 'a love such as ours wins over all obstacles'. He tells Curra to throw Leonora's baggage into the courtyard, but Leonora stops her. Alvaro urges her to follow him and leave her 'prison'. Horses are ready to take them to a priest, who is waiting at the altar. In ecstatic terms he describes how 'the sun, god of the Indies, lord of my royal race', will tomorrow shine on their wedding joy. It is too late, objects Leonora; she wants to put off leaving until tomorrow; she wants to see her father one more time. If Alvaro truly loves her he will not oppose her dearest wish.

Alvaro cannot help but sense Leonora's reluctance to carry through their elopement. 'Tutto comprendo... tutto, signora' ('I have understood everything'), he says bitterly. 'May God forbid that your weakness let you follow me. I release you from your promise; marriage would mean death for us'. He is interrupted by Leonora's passionate avowal of love: 'I am yours, with all my heart, and with my life', she declares. They make ready to depart.

But Leonora's prevarications have ensured that her father has been alerted. The lovers hear the sounds of a door opening and closing. They are thrown into confusion. If they left immediately, they would probably escape. But still Leonora prevaricates. After several blows on the door the Marquis de Calatrava bursts into the room, accompanied by two servants with lamps. He is in a towering rage, obviously having concluded what is afoot. Leonora flings herself at her father's feet. 'I am your father no more', Calatrava thunders. Alvaro intervenes: 'I am the guilty one'. He bares his chest and invites the Marquis to strike him. Calatrava is scornful. 'Your conduct shows the baseness of your origins', he says. He then orders the servants

to arrest Alvaro. Outraged, Alvaro threatens the two servants with his pistol and swears that anybody who moves shall die. He will yield only to Calatrava. He declares that the guilt is entirely his own and that Leonora is as pure as the angels. He throws his pistol to the ground. As it strikes the ground it goes off, mortally wounding the Marquis. With his dying breath Calatrava curses Leonora. As the servants carry the body of the Marquis to his room Alvaro drags Leonora to the balcony whence the couple make their escape.

Act 2 Scene 1   The large kitchen of an Inn in the village of Hornachuelos. To the left is the street door, to the rear a window and a table, piled with food. To the right, towards the rear, is a blazing fire. Further downstage is a stairway leading to the bedroom. A long table is laid for supper. The innkeeper and his wife are busy preparing the meal. The Mayor is seated near the fire. Muleteers, including Master Trabucco, and villagers throng the stage, some dancing. Don Carlo, Leonora's brother, disguised as a student, sits at one of the tables. He is seeking his sister and her lover, having sworn vengeance on them for the death of his father.

The chorus of villagers extols the virtues of the Inn (see **Chorus**). The hostess sets down a large soup tureen on the table and the Mayor announces supper. He requests the 'student' to say grace, which the latter does. Leonora appears in the doorway. She is disguised as a man. She recognizes her brother and quickly withdraws. Meanwhile the company eats with alacrity, full of praise for the repast. The student adds his praise in Latin, which is entirely lost on the hostess. He then starts questioning Trabucco, who remains to one side. (He keeps himself aloof, he tells the 'student', because being a Friday he is fasting.) Don Carlo questions him about his 'passenger', but Trabucco refuses to be drawn into conversation.

They are interrupted by the arrival of the gypsy, Preziosilla, who enters, skipping and calling, 'Hurrah for war!' The men all jostle to have her sit next to them. When they ask her to tell their fortunes she urges them to join the army, go to Italy and fight the Germans. 'Death to the Germans!' they all shout. In a rumbustious song Preziosilla extols the virtues of war and promises the men she will be with them (*Al suon del tamburo*). She then reads the palms of everyone present. When she arrives at Carlo her brow furrows. 'Oh, you will experience terrible miseries', she tells him. Carlo is naturally disturbed. Preziosilla whispers to Carlo that she knows he is not a student: 'No-one can make a fool of me', she says. But she promises to keep quiet about her suspicions. She rejoins the rousing calls for war with the rest of the company.

A band of pilgrims passes slowly by. All rise and respectfully remove their hats. The pilgrims are on their way to the Holy Week celebrations. All kneel and join the pilgrims in prayer. 'Extend thy hand, O Lord, save us from the sufferings of Hell', they intone. Leonora, who has reappeared and is standing unseen by the door, prays to be saved from her brother. She goes back into her room and shuts the door before the company can notice her presence. All take their places at the table and pass round a flagon of wine. Carlo resumes his inquisition of Trabucco, to no avail. Trabucco will not even say whether his passenger was male or female: 'I notice nothing about a traveller save his money', he says. Don Carlo is persistent, directing his questions also at the Mayor who refuses to divulge any information about the stranger. Finally Trabucco loses patience with Don Carlo and departs for the stable, where he intends to sleep with the mules, who 'know no Latin, nor are they Bachelors of Arts'.

Carlo has noticed that the stranger accompanying Trabucco was beardless. He suggests that they should all play a trick on 'him' by painting a moustache on his face. 'We shall have a good laugh', he says (he has an ulterior motive, for he hopes thus to discover the true identity of the stranger). The Mayor, however, declares that as Mayor he must protect all travellers and he opposes the scheme. He now turns to Don Carlo and demands to know where he is from, where he is bound and who he is.

With complete assurance Don Carlo gives a fabricated version of his background (*Son Pereda, son ricco d'onore*). Calling himself 'Pereda', he describes how he graduated from Salamanca, rich in honours, and is soon to qualify as a doctor. He pretends that he was befriended by one Carlo di Vargas, whose father had been murdered by his sister's seducer. He has assisted Vargas in pursuing the guilty pair, though he was soon given to understand that the girl had died with her father and only the seducer was still at large. (It will later be revealed [Act 3 Scene 3] that Carlo does not actually believe that Leonora has died.) Vargas is committed to tracking down the villain and has sailed for America, while Pereda has returned to his books. The company is satisfied with Carlo's fabrication – all, that is, except Preziosilla, who does not believe a word of it and makes her incredulity apparent. The Mayor breaks up the proceedings, observing that the hour is late and it is time that they all retire to bed.

Act 2 Scene 2   A clearing on the slopes of a mountain. To the right a rocky precipice. To the rear, in the centre, the facade of the Church of the Madonna of the Angels. The church door is closed but lights can be seen through the large window above the door. More mountains and the village of Hornachuelos are in the background. To the left is the entrance to the monastery. A bell rope hangs beside the door. A rough stone cross adorns the top of four steps.

Leonora enters, still disguised. She has come to seek sanctuary at the monastery. In her soliloquy she reveals the events leading up to her appearance at the inn in the previous scene. In the flight from her father's house she and Alvaro became separated and she believes he must have perished. Carlo's revelation that Alvaro has sailed for America has cut her to the quick. She believes herself totally abandoned. Up until that moment her only comfort has been the thought of being reunited with Alvaro. Now he has deserted there is no recourse but the Cloister. She falls to her knees and prays (*Madre, pietosa Vergine*). She begs forgiveness and resolves to expiate her sins in the solitude of the monastery.

An organ sounds, accompanying the chanting of the monks. It fills Leonora with hope: 'May this music bring comfort and peace to my troubled soul', she prays. She begins to walk towards the monastery, but wonders whether she dare ask for sanctuary at such an early hour. However she overcomes her scruples and rings the monastery bell. A small window opens and a lantern shines out, illuminating Leonora's face. As she draws back in fright Fra Melitone speaks from within. He is far from affable. Leonora asks to see the Father Superior, saying she has been sent by Father Cleto on 'urgent business'. Grumbling, Melitone prepares to admit her. But Leonora, knowing that it would be considered sacrilege were her identity as a woman to be discovered, insists she will wait outside. Melitone grumpily promises to announce her, but if he does not return then, 'Goodnight!' He does, however, soon return in the company of Padre Guardiano who dismisses him. He leaves, muttering imprecations.

Leonora immediately reveals that she is a woman. Guardiano is appalled, particularly in view of the compromising hour. When Leonora tells him she has been sent by Father Cleto Guardiano recalls having received a letter from Cleto and is thus able to identify her. He brushes aside his instinctive revulsion and, indicating the Cross, invites Leonora to let the voice of Heaven speak to her. Leonora kneels at the foot of Cross and kisses it. She tells Guardiano that since coming to the monastery she is no longer haunted by the 'bloodstained corpse' of her father, nor his fearful curse. Now she wishes only to emulate another woman (about whom she has heard from Father Cleto) who lived out her days as a penitent among the nearby rocks (*Ah, tranquilla l'alma sento*).

Guardiano warns Leonora not to act merely on an impulse. She is so young she could live to regret such a decision. For who can read the future? How can she know her heart will not change with time? He tries to persuade Leonora that she would do better to seek refuge in a Convent, but Leonora will not contemplate a Convent, or indeed anywhere other than where she has arrived. She has heard the voice of heaven here, at the foot of the cross. If Guardiano turns her away now she will wander the mountains on her own, seeking food from the woods and pity from wild beasts.

Finally Guardiano relents. He directs her to a cave amongst the rocks surrounding the monastery, where she can remain incognito. Only he will know who she is. Every seventh day he will leave her a frugal meal at a nearby spring. Having commanded Melitone to summon the friars so that Leonora may take communion, he gives Leonora a Franciscan habit to wear.

The great doors of the church open, revealing the high altar, illuminated by candles. To the sound of organ music two lines of monks proceed down the sides of the Choir, carrying lighted tapers. They kneel on each side of the altar. They are followed by Padre Guardiano, then Leonora in monk's habit. Leonora kneels at the foot of the altar and receives Communion from Padre Guardiano, who then leads her out of the church as the monks group themselves around her. Leonora prostrates herself before Guardiano as he solemnly extends his arms over her, chanting the while. He tells the brother monks that a 'soul' has come, repentant of its sin, to seek salvation (*Il santo nome di Dio Signore*). He tells them that this soul will dwell 'in the holy cave' and he issues an interdict against anyone attempting to visit the penitent, on pain of damnation. All the monks join in confirming a curse on anyone who disobeys the edict.

Guardiano tells Leonora to leave. She will never see another living person. She will have a bell which she can ring, should danger threaten her, or should she have reached her final hour. When this happens the monks will rally to comfort her soul before it returns to God. Leonora kisses the hand of the Abbot and walks alone towards the hermit's cave. The friars, after putting out the candles, retreat into the church. Guardiano stops at the door and, extending his arms in the direction where Leonora has retreated, blesses her.

Act 3 Scene 1 A forest near the town of Velletri, Italy. It is pitch dark. Voices of soldiers playing cards can be overhead offstage. Don Alvaro, in the uniform of a captain of the Spanish grenadiers, comes forward slowly. He is thinking with bitter regret of Seville, of Leonora and of the night when all possibility of happiness was snatched away from him (*La vita è inferno all'infelice*). He reflects on his father, who sought to free Peru from colonial rule and win back his crown through alliance with the Incas (see **Alvaro**). His thoughts turn to Leonora and the hope that she should never forget him. He believes her dead and prays that she may intercede for him (*O tu che in seno agli angeli*). Now all he dreams of is release from his anguish, an honourable death in battle.

Offstage voices are heard again. It is clear that a fight is in progress. When a voice is heard calling for help Alvaro immediately rushes off to offer assistance. Sounds of clashing steel can be heard. Officers run across the stage in confusion. Alvaro returns with Don Carlo who has apparently been involved in a quarrel over cards. Alvaro finds it hard to believe that one of so noble a bearing as Carlo should have become embroiled with such company. Carlo explains that he is now in the area because his military orders have brought him here. He asks to whom he owes his life. Alvaro replies, 'to chance'. Carlo gives his name as Don Felice de Bornos, adjutant to the Commander in Chief. Alvaro now gives his name as Don Frederico Herreros, Captain of the Grenadiers. Don Carlo recognizes the name immediately. He is the hero of the army (which is news to the audience; Alvaro has obviously cut a distinguished career for himself under his pseudonym in the army). Don Carlo claims that he has longed to make the friendship of Herreros. Shouts and the sound of a trumpet are heard offstage and the two prepare to go to battle. They rush out together.

Act 3 Scene 2 The Spanish officers' quarters near the Italian battlefield. Upstage are two doors; the one on the left leads to a bedroom, the other being the main door. It is morning. The sound of fighting is heard offstage. An army surgeon and some soldiers are watching the battle from the window.

The surgeon looks through a telescope. He reports how Herreros is heading the affray. Then in horrified tones he describes how he is fallen. But then the Spanish rally and chase the enemy into retreat. Shouts of 'Glory to Spain!' and 'Long live Italy!' are heard offstage. Then Alvaro, wounded and unconscious, is brought in on a stretcher by four Grenadiers. Don Carlo is at his side. The stretcher bearers lay Alvaro down gently. The surgeon is concerned to note that Alvaro suffers from a chest wound. Alvaro comes round and all he can say is 'Let me die!' Carlo tries to comfort him, telling him that he will be awarded the Order of Calatrava.[32] The name of Calatrava is a monumental shock to the ailing Alvaro, who exclaims, 'never!' Carlo is startled. Alvaro indicates that he wants to speak with Carlo alone and Carlo dismisses the surgeon.

Alone with the man who, in another lifetime, might have been his brother-in-law, Alvaro makes Carlo swear that he will carry out his dying wish. He tells Carlo to take a key from an inside pocket in his jacket. He points to the valise on the table and tells Carlo that he will find therein a package which, he tells Carlo, 'I trust to your honour. Within it there is a secret which must die with me. Burn it when I am dead'. Carlo swears to do his bidding. The two embrace and take leave of each other as Alvaro is borne into the bedroom to be operated on by the surgeon.

Carlo is left alone. He is suddenly overwhelmed by a sense of the awesomeness of death (*Morir! Tremenda cosa!*). He finds it difficult to conceive that a man of such

---

[32] The Order of Calatrava is not a fiction of Rivas' but an actual Spanish military order of knighthood, founded by Sancho III of Castile in 1158. The knights took a vow of poverty, obedience and conjugal chastity (presumably Leonora was conceived before di Vargas was admitted to the order). The order became an Order of Merit in 1808.

courage and daring as Herreros should die. Then he wonders why Alvaro shuddered at the name of Calatrava. He wonders if Alvaro knows of the dishonour that was brought on the house of Calatrava. Then it occurs to him: 'Heavens! What if he himself were the seducer!' He realizes that he can quickly confirm if this is indeed the case by opening the valise. He proceeds to do so and draws forth the sealed package. Then he pauses, suddenly aware of the conflict that will assail him if Herreros is indeed his sister's seducer and his father's murderer. He has sworn an oath to Alvaro to destroy the package. Above all he owes his life to him. He precipitately throws down the package. 'I came here to redeem my honour, not to blemish it with more shame', he declares. He determines never again to allow himself to entertain committing such an unworthy act.

Nevertheless he cannot avoid the fact that his curiosity is aroused. Maybe there will be something else in the valise that will afford him some clue as to whether Alvaro is indeed the man he has been searching for. Honour may prevent him from opening the package he promised to destroy, but he has made no promise with regard to the other contents of the valise. His hand alights on a portrait. It is not sealed. He opens it and is immediately confronted with a likeness of his sister. Now his old blood-lust is reawakened. The wounded man must indeed be Alvaro. His one hope now is that Alvaro may survive the surgeon's knife in order that he – Carlo – may take revenge for his family and kill him.

As if in answer to his prayer the surgeon announces that Alvaro's life is saved. Carlo is ecstatic, for now he can wreak his vengeance. His thoughts turn to Leonora. Surely she must be in the vicinity as well? 'Ah I should be entirely happy if it should be given to this sword of mine to despatch both to Hell with a single blow!' he concludes.

Act 3 Scene 3 A military encampment near Velletri. Forward and left a peddler's shop. To the right another where food, drink and fruit are sold. Nearby are tents, a tradesman's hut, etc. It is night and the scene is deserted. A patrol enters, cautiously, on reconnaissance. Having ascertained that everybody is asleep the patrol moves on. Day breaks gradually.

Alvaro enters, lost in thought. He reflects on how it would appear he is not to be granted a moment's peace. He bewails the fact that having come so close to death he has been summoned back to a life he finds onerous in the extreme. Don Carlo enters and Alvaro greets him affectionately. Carlo remains coldly aloof. Having ascertained that Alvaro is fully recovered from his wounds, he demands to know if he is strong enough to fight a duel. Alvaro is puzzled and wants to know with whom. Carlo spitefully asks if Alvaro has had any messages from 'Don Alvaro, the Indian' at which Alvaro concludes that Carlo must have broken his oath to him. Carlo disabuses him but confirms that he has found Leonora's portrait in the valise. He then reveals his true identity. Alvaro is not perturbed by Carlo's threats. Nor is he afraid of death, but it grieves him to have to fight with one who offered him his friendship. He attempts to reason with Carlo. He tells him that it was not he, but destiny that killed Don Carlo's father. 'Nor did I seduce that angel of love', he avers. He tells Carlo that he believes Leonora is dead. Carlo, however, does not believe his sister to be dead. Leonora had apparently taken refuge with one of the family. Carlo pursued her there but arrived too late; Leonora had already fled.

Alvaro is ecstatic to hear that his beloved is still alive. He hopes that Carlo will accept his joy as proof of his honourable nature and hopes that they may unite in looking for Leonora: 'I swear that a noble origin makes me your equal and that my family's crest is refulgent as the sun', he declares (*No, d'un imene il vincolo*). Carlo is incredulous. Does Alvaro really imagine that his origins make any difference to their sworn enmity? How can Carlo forget the dishonour that Alvaro has brought on his house? He confirms that his duty is to kill Alvaro first and then Leonora. Alvaro is appalled. He draws his sword and insists that before Carlo kills his sister he must fight him in mortal combat.

Their duel is interrupted by the arrival of a patrol from the camp who restrain the combatants. Carlo is incensed and shouts invective at Alvaro who, however, is suddenly overcome by a sense of total resignation. What now is left to him but to put himself into the hands of Almighty God? He decides to retire to the cloister. As he exits the rest of the company gradually follows.[33]

The sun rises, drums and bugles sound the reveille. Gradually the camp awakens to action. Spanish and Italian soldiers of all arms emerge from tents, cleaning their weapons, uniforms, etc. Vendors circulate, selling liquor, fruit and bread. Preziosilla is standing aloft on one of the huts telling fortunes. The soldiers sing of the glories of the soldier's life. Preziosilla encourages them all to come to her for a reading; the soldiers need little persuasion and eagerly surround her.

The attention of everyone is suddenly drawn to Trabucco, the peddler, who comes out from a stand to the left. He carries a box of cheap merchandise, scissors, pins and soap. He offers to 'buy and sell whatever you want', and the soldiers, presumably in order to buy drinks, crowd round him offering to sell anything they think may be of value. Trabucco strikes a deal with each of them. Peasants enter, begging for bread. The war has destroyed their homes. They are followed by new recruits, lamenting the loss of all that they love. The Vendors surround these latter, cheerfully offering wine with which to forget their miseries. Preziosilla makes her way among them, taking some by the arm and generally attempting to bolster their flagging morale. Finally all join in the chorus to the glories of war and, encouraged by Preziosilla, commence a lively dance. Very soon the racket and confusion have reached fever pitch.

Fra Melitone enters and is caught up in the whirl of the dancing. He finds himself cavorting in the arms of the Vendors. Finally he manages to extricate himself and starts

to preach at them, railing against the soldiers' lasciviousness and licence: 'Is this a Christian camp or a lot of Turks?' he rants. He brands them all heretics and 'sewers of sin'. The Italian soldiers surround him and it looks as though he is destined for a beating, but he manages to escape. The soldiers are about to make off in pursuit of Melitone when Preziosilla, sensing that the situation is getting out of hand, picks up the nearest drum and, with several other drummers following suit, commences beating it (*Rataplan, rataplan, della gloria*). The soldiers come running and gather round her, followed by the rest of the crowd. They all sing a chorus to the glories of patriotism and war and run out as the curtain falls.

Act 4 Scene 1   A courtyard inside the monastery of our Lady of the Angels in Hornachuelos. The cloister gardens with orange trees, oleander and jasmine are enclosed by a gallery to the left. A door opens to the road to the right, another door above on which is written 'Clausura'.

Guardiano is pacing up and down, reading his breviary. From the left enters a crowd of beggars, men and women of all ages carrying crude bowls, pots and plates. They cry out for charity. Melitone enters, wearing a large white apron and assisted by a lay brother, carrying a cooking pot. They put the pot down in the centre of the yard and the lay brother departs. Melitone grumpily starts to ladle out the soup. The beggars crowd round, squabbling over the size of the portions. When a woman demands four portions because she has six children Melitone is immediately censorious: 'You would not have them if like me you whipped your back with a rough scourge and spent all your nights reciting the rosary and miserere'. Guardiano tries to silence him but Melitone continues to rail against the beggars who lament the fact that they are no longer served by the affable Father Raffaele. Out of patience Melitone kicks the tureen over and evicts the rabble: 'you are beggars worse than Lazarus'.

The gate bell rings loudly. Guardiano commands Melitone to open the gate and

---

[33] The first half of Act 3 Scene 3 is often, inexcusably, omitted in performance.

exits. Melitone opens the gate and returns with Don Carlo, who is dressed in a full cloak. Carlo is in no mood for small talk and asks for Father Rafaelle. Melitone tells him there are two Father Rafaelles, one from Porcuna, 'fat and deaf as a post', the other 'lean and dark' with a piercing glance. He asks Carlo which one he wants, to which Carlo replies, 'the one from Hell'. (Presumably the fat Raffaele is the priest referred to by the beggars in the previous scene, while the lean and hungry Raffaele is, as we shall soon discover, none other than Don Alvaro.) Melitone goes off to fetch Raffaele. Left alone Carlo reflects to himself that it was useless for Alvaro to attempt to hide under the hypocritical robes of a monk. 'Now only blood can wash away the stain which outraged my honour and I shall spill it all, I swear to God' (*Invano Alvaro ti celasti al mondo*).

Alvaro enters in monk's robes, unaware at first of the identity of his visitor. Carlo reveals that it is five years since their last encounter, during which time he has been seeking out Alvaro. Now they must fight. He offers Alvaro the choice of two swords. Alvaro points out that his monk's habit shows that he is doing penance for his sins and begs Carlo to let him alone. Carlo is scornful of Alvaro's repentance and claims to sanctity. It takes all of Alvaro's five years of spiritual training to restrain himself when Carlo brands him a coward. He pleads with Carlo to have pity on him. 'Let fierce words and threats be dispelled by the winds', he says. Carlo is unmoved: 'you besmirch the very name (of pity)', he says. He demands that they fight.

Alvaro swears that Leonora was not dishonoured: 'it is a monk who gives you his oath', he says. He throws himself at Don Carlo's feet. Carlo is not impressed. Disdainfully he tells Alvaro that his abasement before him only confirms the stain on his crest. Alvaro is provoked beyond endurance. He leaps to his feet, vehemently protesting his family's honour. When Carlo compounds the offence by saying: 'it is coloured by your half-breed's blood', Alvaro can contain himself

no longer. He demands a sword. Carlo shouts triumphantly, 'finalmente!' ('at last!'). It has the effect of defusing Alvaro's passion. He drops the sword and limply implores Carlo 'not to allow the Devil to triumph'. Carlo's patience is exhausted. He goes up to Alvaro and slaps his face, determined to provoke a response. He is not disappointed. Alvaro snatches up the sword again and the two rush out to fight their duel.

Act 4 Scene 2   Outside Leonora's cave. A valley crossed by a stream and flanked by steep cliffs. To the rear a cave, closed by a door; above it a bell which can be rung from within. The sun is going down and the scene gradually darkens. The moon comes out, shining brightly as Leonora emerges from her cave, pale and distraught.

Leonora is deeply disturbed and prays for peace (*Pace, pace, mio Dio*). She will never be able to efface the image of her beloved from her mind: 'for God blessed him with such beauty and with such virtue'. She prays that she might be allowed to die, for only in death will she find peace. She goes to a rock on which the Abbot has left food for her. She deplores the fact that the bread will only prolong her suffering by prolonging her life. But then suddenly, with horror, she realizes that someone is profaning her sacred refuge and solitude. With extraordinary vehemence she curses the intruder: 'Maledizione! Maledizione!' She retreats into her cave.

From offstage can be heard the clash of swords, then Carlo's voice shouting: 'I am dying! Confession! Save my soul!' Alvaro enters with drawn sword. He throws it down with a despairing gesture. Echoing the final words of Leonora's aria he shouts: 'I am damned!' Seeing Leonora's cave he runs to the door and knocks. Leonora at first refuses to open the door but instead rings her bell and calls for help. But then, drawn by the desperation in his voice, she unwillingly answers the stranger's summons. The two lovers are suddenly face to face. But, as Alvaro only too quickly realizes, there is a bitter irony in the timing of their meeting: 'cruel destiny, how you mock at me. Leonora is alive and I must find her, only when I have killed her brother'.

Alvaro has no further time to bewail his fate for at this moment Leonora, who has gone to attend to her dying brother, re-enters. She is mortally wounded and supported by Guardiano. Carlo, confronted in his dying hour by Leonora, has kept faith with his determination to wreak vengeance and has stabbed his sister. Alvaro is beside himself: 'Oh vengeful God, are you still not satisfied?' he cries. Gently Guardiano implores him not to curse but to humble himself: 'before him who is holy and just' (*Non imprecare; umiliati*). Leonora joins Guardiano in imploring Alvaro to weep and pray. Guardiano tells Alvaro to kneel. He does so at Leonora's feet. He feels certain that he will be redeemed by Leonora's love. Leonora dies content, convinced that holiness will bless her and Alvaro's love. Alvaro bewails the fact that he is meanwhile left on Earth: 'Only the guilty one will escape punishment', he exclaims. The curtain falls as Guardiano confirms that Leonora has ascended to God.

There can be no doubt that Verdi's original ending is both dramatically and psychologically more *veristic* than the watered down revision. In the original, St Petersburg, edition the fight takes place on stage. Carlo falls mortally wounded, calls for a Father to take his confession and Alvaro runs to the cave. When Leonora appears, Carlo naturally assumes the two have taken refuge in the cloister together. (The only real absurdity in the plot is the fact that both Leonora and Alvaro end up in the same monastery without realizing it.) Leonora rushes to her lover and embraces him. While she is doing so Carlo stabs her. Carlo dies avenged. Leonora dies having forgiven Carlo and affirmed her love for Alvaro. There is a final scene in which thunder roars incessantly and lightning flashes with increasing frequency. The friars are heard chanting the *miserere*. Guardiano enters with the whole community bearing torches. All are amazed at what greets their eyes. Don Alvaro revives and runs to a high rock. When Guardiano calls to him using his assumed name, Father Rafaelle,

Alvaro answers: 'Fool to seek Father Rafaelle. I am an emissary from Hell'. Calling on the Earth to open that Hell may swallow him, he climbs higher up and then hurls himself into the ravine below. All express their horror and, falling to their knees, pray for mercy as the curtain falls. It will be seen that this ending is more in line with the ending of Verdi's earlier operas, *Il Corsaro* and *I Masnadieri*.

The central themes in *La Forza del Destino* are not original: conflicts arising from sexual love and family honour; a girl's conflict between filial loyalty and sexual love; a man's ostracization through accidents of birth and fate. But Verdi's music elevates what could have been just another Spanish tragedy into high pathos, notably in his depiction of the three main characters, Alvaro, Leonora and Don Carlo.

In the first two acts it is the fate of Leonora that occupies our attention. Thereafter the focus shifts to Don Alvaro. All the lovers' woes stem from Leonora's reluctance to leave the paternal home. If she had not prevaricated in the first instance her father would not have been shot and the lovers may well not have been hounded to an early death themselves. It is almost as though Leonora intuits the tragic outcome of their liaison before it is ever begun. Or, looked at another way, you could say that she actually engenders the tragedy.

Alvaro, on the other hand, has been an outsider, through accident of lineage, all his life. His love for Leonora must surely be partly a longing to be accepted and to belong to the society in which he lives, though this is certainly not a paramount consideration. Otherwise he would never have entertained the notion of eloping with Leonora. Like Sigmund, in Wagner's *Die Walküre*, Alvaro is pursued by misfortune. (It was a stroke of genius of the makers of the film *Jean de Florette*[34] to use Alvaro's melody from the duet with Don Carlo in Act 3 to express

---

[34] Director: Claude Berri 1986. Music Jean Claude Petit.

Jean's sense of victimization in life.) Leonora represents Alvaro's one hope of redemption from himself and from his destiny. Alvaro is a true poet, summoning some striking imagery to express the depth of his passion for Leonora, notably in Act 2 Scene 1.

It is significant that both the lovers choose to turn to the cloister when their love is thwarted, for it underlines the essentially religious nature of their search. Leonora finds the father-figure which she has lost, or rather never had, in the figure of Padre Guardiano, while Alvaro finds a sense of belonging – a home – in the cloister. The fact that they both end up in the same monastery seems to suggest that their marriage has found its true expression through their combined, though unconscious, devotion to God.

A stumbling block for them both, individually and as an item, is the fiercely vengeful nature of Leonora's brother, Don Carlo. He is totally identified with his father and all that his father represents: family honour and prestige. However in the course of the opera it becomes clear that Carlo is quite capable of warmth and generosity. He is a man living out an idea with maniacal persistence (in this he invites comparison with de Silva in **Ernani**), in spite of the fact that it contradicts his own better nature. He is genuinely grateful to Alvaro for having saved his life (Act 3 Scene 2) but will not allow that fact to prevent the fulfilment of his quest to exact vengeance for family dishonour. Alvaro's behaviour is incomprehensible to Carlo, lacking imagination as he does. He sees Alvaro's retreat to the cloister as a coward's way out. Carlo's attitude is representative of the narrow worldly standpoint against which Alvaro has been in revolt all his life.

There can be no question that Verdi was principally inspired by the fate of the three main protagonists. He also takes special relish in his portrayal of the hypocritical monk, Melitone. It has often been pointed out that Melitone represents one of the first indications that Verdi would be capable of portraying Falstaff – that is, capable of comedy. Otherwise the scenes with Preziosilla are distinctly below the level of inspiration

that elsewhere pertains. The Guardiano scenes, on the other hand, contain some of Verdi's best music for chorus and bass voice. The dichotomy could not be clearer in this opera between the common venality of the soldiers and gypsies, on the one hand, and the higher aspirations of the main protagonists and monks as represented by Father Guardiano.

It is surely significant that the commission for *La Forza del Destino* came from St Petersburg, for of all Verdi's operas this one has a distinctively Russian flavour. The fates of Leonora and Alvaro – their existential crises and search for redemption through Holy Mother Church would be perfectly apt in a novel by Tolstoy or Dostoievsky. The opera transcends its origins and must take pride of place with *Un balloin maschera* as being the most satisfying of Verdi's middle period.

Francesco Foscari (*I Due Foscari*). Doge of Venice and father of **Jacopo Foscari**.
Historical Note Francesco Foscari (c1370–1457) was Doge of Venice for 34 years (1423–1457). He assumed an aggressive stance towards the Italian mainland and thereby attained for Venice recognition of its territorial status. His undisguised nepotism was the cause of the discontent that led to his downfall. The circumstances of his death were similar to those portrayed in the opera.

Francesco wages a losing battle with the rival claims of his love for his son and his sense of duty to his political role as Doge of Venice. His is a curiously tragic fate. All his life he has chafed against the pettiness and bigotry of political life. Twice he has begged the Senators to release him from his duties and on each occasion he has been refused. So he has endured, being forced to compromise his better nature and finer instincts.

Francesco has fathered four sons. By the time of the opera three have died tragically young. Only Jacopo survives to give him hope for the future and he is repeatedly disgraced. Jacopo's exile causes Francesco particular anguish, not just because it is his son, but because he is aware of the injustice that has been done. Jacopo is innocent of the crime of which he is accused but Francesco cannot prove it. Francesco knows that it is **Loredano** who is behind the machinations that ensure Jacopo Foscari's enduring exile but can do little about it (see **Synopsis**). Only when **Barbarigo** comes to him with the death-bed confession of one Errizo, declaring responsibility for the murder of which Jacopo is accused, does Francesco believe that he has the means to confound his enemies. But the reprieve has come too late. His son has died on board the ship bearing him back to exile.

The action of the opera centres around the occasion of Jacopo's final trial for the crime of having written a letter to the Duke of Milan, imploring him to intercede on his behalf. After five years of exile Jacopo pines after his beloved Venice. He lives only to be reunited with his family and homeland. From a purely human standpoint it is entirely natural that Jacopo should do everything in his power to try and escape the sentence passed on him. But the law is the law and Francesco, as Doge, must be seen to uphold it, even though he may sympathize entirely with his son.

Francesco takes his duties seriously. He knows that the Republic exists only by virtue of the rule of law. He must not just be seen to uphold it, but must in actuality uphold it, or render his own position and life's work meaningless. The joy that he experiences when he learns from Barbarigo that his son is exonerated of the murder of which he is accused is precipitated by the realization that he can now legitimately plead his son's cause without risking being accused of allowing his feelings as a father to influence his judgement. It is typical of his destiny that it is too late. When the bells ring out for his successor before he has barely been relieved of his robes of office it is too much for his frail heart. All his life he has been a pawn of the political forces to which he has given himself.

Interestingly the story of the two Foscari emphasizes the difficulties of a head of state whose powers are severely circumscribed by democratic legislature long before the Republican ideal had reasserted itself. Francesco suffers not under the strictures of the legislature itself but under the abuse of that same legislature, and the bureaucratic mentality that insists on adhering solely to the letter of the law. 'More injustice is done within the letter of the law than without it' would seem to be the message of Byron's drama, so eloquently enhanced by Verdi's opera.

Jacopo Foscari (*I Due Foscari*). Son of **Francesco Foscari.**

Jacopo's destiny is characterized by stark dichotomies and polarities, chiefly the anguish of exile on the one hand and the bliss of reconciliation on the other. Mostly it is the former that predominates in his life. When the opera opens Jacopo has been summoned from exile and thrown into prison for a crime he did not commit. The darkness of the dungeon and the radiance and light of his beloved Venice is another central polarity. His first words are: 'Ah yes that I may feel again; that I may breathe air untainted by sighs and groans' (Act 1 Scene 1). The darkness of the dungeon and the misery of exile are almost synonymous in his consciousness. For both separate him from what gives to life its meaning; his homeland, the love of his wife and children and last, but by no means least, his father. The central trauma for Jacopo is, ostensibly at any rate, that all his miseries stem from his father who, as Doge, is ultimately responsible for his political destiny. The ambiguity of Verdi's conception of the father/son relationship is never so explicit as in this opera. That the father is both infinitely remote and also crucially immanent is irrefutable. The apparent incongruity of the two roles (an incongruity that is yet central to our cultural conception and psychological understanding of the father), father as mentor and protector on the one hand, and father as castigator on the other, is tacitly accepted by the son.

The two chief moments of repose that Jacopo enjoys in the opera come firstly when he is reunited with his wife and secondly, and most crucial to his psychological equilibrium, when he receives irrefutable confirmation of his father's love for him (later in the same scene), in spite of the fact that Francesco must nevertheless be the continued instrument of his ostracism. Jacopo knows perfectly well that his father is politically impotent. He knows that it is not Francesco *per se* that condemns. He knows that his enemies are his father's enemies and that they share a common fate. But it is one thing to know something and quite another to be able to accept it. He still cannot forgive his father for not putting his role of father above that of Doge; the mandate given to him by nature above that of his civic responsibilities. And yet herein lies a central problem for Jacopo. Through his extended exile his homeland has come to be the focus for his sense of existential meaning. Away from Venice he is at a loss, distraught. But Venice is only the sum total of its parts. It is first and foremost a community of human beings built and sustained for the mutual benefit of all its citizens. In all societies there is an unwritten contract between each and every citizen dictating the terms on which the individual may expect the succour of the society in which he has his being. In a Republic that contract is explicit. Human beings remain fallible, whatever the grandeur of their ideals and conventions. In any political relationship there will always be the possibility of a miscarriage of justice. Innocent citizens are accused and punished for heinous crimes they never committed. This is one of the inevitable penalties of being a part of the body politic. Jacopo's devotion to Venice has become indistinguishable from his devotion to life. The one without the other is unthinkable and this is in fact his Achilles heel. He is not in love with life, *per se*, with existence. His devotion is to his father, his homeland, his wife and his children: in other words all that keeps him attached and saves him from having to confront his individual destiny as a human being. One cannot help at various points in the drama becoming impatient with Jacopo's obsession.

In dramatic and musical terms a direct comparison can be drawn between the scene which opens Act 2 of Verdi's opera and the opening scene of Act 2 of Beethoven's *Fidelio*. The comparison is constructive. Jacopo is obsessed by a vision of Carmagnola, a famous condottiere, who was unjustly condemned to death by the Council of Ten. Jacopo assumes that his present predicament must be retribution for the injustice done to Carmagnola by his father in his capacity as Doge. Jacopo's vision is in fact a combination of three things: firstly his dread of being himself condemned to execution (that is, his fear); secondly his guilt over the role his father – and by association he himself – has played in propagating an injustice; thirdly his desire for atonement. In other words Jacopo is entirely obsessed with his own negative emotions. Florestan, in Beethoven's opera, is in an almost identical predicament to Jacopo. But his thoughts, far from dwelling on his own misfortunes, turn first to God and thereafter to his redeeming angel, Leonora. Because Florestan, and by association Beethoven (who would never have had the patience to write an opera about Foscari), has an enduring faith in life *per se* and in a guiding destiny. It never occurs to him to give up hope. Jacopo could never say 'Doch gerecht ist Gottes wille!' ('Yet God's Will is just!') He is too busy feeling sorry for himself.

In the moment that Jacopo takes his young sons to kneel at the feet of their grandfather in the hope that Francesco will thereby relent (Act 2 Scene 2) it becomes extremely difficult to retain any respect for him. It is a deliberate attempt to manipulate his father with no thought of the anguish he might cause Francesco. By the time he finally departs into exile one cannot help feeling that it is not a moment too soon. News of his death from a broken heart comes as no surprise. Thus he would seem to hurl at his unfortunate father the ultimate reproof. Francesco's death, likewise from a broken heart, evokes in us far greater sympathy. At least he has lived a life in which he has attempted to reconcile the conflicting demands of his political position with his personal loyalties and affections. He has endured. When he dies it is more a question of exhaustion than defeat. His son, on the other hand, appears defeated before he has started.

Francesco (*I Masnadieri*). Younger son of **Massimiliano**, Count of Moor.

The role of Francesco cannot be understood without reference to that of his brother, Carlo. For Francesco's personality has been determined by the role in which fate has cast him: second in line to inherit, second in his father's affection; a perpetual 'also-ran'. In a healthy temperament such a lot might encourage independence of spirit and determination to prove himself against all the odds. But Francesco's is not a healthy temperament. He allows a sense of grievance to fester until his psyche is entirely consumed by negative emotions: bitterness, resentment and a passion to be avenged on 'Nature's misdeed in making me the younger brother'.

Carlo plays into his brother's hands by becoming delinquent to the extent that Massimiliano is forced to send him into exile. But Francesco is impatient. He has no intention of waiting until his father dies naturally before he can inherit. He determines on murdering Massimiliano. But how to do it and get away with it? The plan to cause Massimiliano's death by reporting that Carlo has been killed at the battle of Prague is typical of Francesco's cowardly and indolent nature. He hopes to achieve his ends without having to exert himself beyond the absolute minimum. He even has the gall to fabricate Carlo's 'dying' message, bequeathing Francesco the hand in marriage of his intended bride, **Amalia**. It is not that Francesco is in love with Amalia; it is simply that it will add piquancy to his ascendancy to possess, and abuse, Carlo's beloved. He knows perfectly well that Amalia does not love him. That fact only increases his delight. Francesco would be bored by a willing and responsive love. For him love-making is only another means of giving expression to his need to be avenged on an uncomprehending world.

Francesco's spare time is taken up with day-dreaming about the day when all will see him revealed in his 'true, terrible aspect', and all will be forced to bow down before him. 'Sobs, tears, fear and suspicion shall replace all laughter and joy. All will be assailed by starvation, imprisonment, dishonour and untold suffering' (Act 1 Scene 2).

Francesco leaves it to his servant, **Arminio**, to deliver the news of Carlo's death to Massimiliano. Inevitably he overplays his expression of grief – inevitably because it is pure sham. When his father throws himself upon him, instinctively acknowledging that Francesco is at the root of his misery, Francesco is unperturbed. He is, in fact, delighted that 'grief, remorse and wrath' assail his father. 'Let his heart break and scatter his scanty breath of life' (Act 1 Scene 3), he says in an aside. When it appears his father has died he cannot dissimulate any longer. He leaps up in jubilation. 'Then I am master', he declares. It is the moment he has dreamt of.

Later, when he hears the old man's cries for help within the coffin, he may experience a moment of superstitious dread, but it is quickly superseded by determination that on no account shall his father be returned to the living. He closes the coffin and orders it to be thrown where there will be no risk of anyone hearing the old man's cries (not portrayed on stage but described by Massimiliano [Act 3 Scene 2]). Significantly it never occurs to him to finish off his father and ensure that he can never again be a plague to him. This would be totally out of character. In any case his father is of no use to him dead; he would lose any focus for his consuming need for revenge. While his father is alive he can cause him suffering. More importantly he can enjoy the thought of causing him suffering. The idea of a long, agonizing twilight is exactly the sort of punishment he would wish his father.

It is never specified whether Arminio acts on Francesco's instructions in taking meagre rations to Massimiliano. We know Arminio suffers pangs of conscience over the deception he has been forced to execute so it would be feasible that he acts behind his master's back. But it would be equally plausible to suppose that Francesco intends to keep his father alive for the reasons given above. Without an object for his frustrated rage and self-loathing his ego collapses.

While wanting nothing so much as to see his father's demise, at the same time the prospect of it terrifies him. He knows that reconciliation with his father is impossible. He could never admit to himself that what he longs for more than anything else is to be embraced by his father in the same way that his brother is embraced. The fact that Carlo is banished brings him no consolation, because he knows that Carlo's absence from Court causes Massimiliano more anguish than his presence ever did. At some subliminal level Francesco undoubtedly hopes that by announcing Carlo's death he may succeed in supplanting Carlo in the old man's affections. While his father is alive there is still that glimmer of hope, even though it is not a hope that Francesco could ever allow himself to admit to.

In Act 4 Scene 1 the torment of Francesco's deranged mind erupts in a dream, which on the surface would appear to be a conventional expression of guilt over the murder of his father. In reality it is an expression of that sense of ostracism that has besieged Francesco all his life. The Son of Man dies in order to intercede at the throne of God for the remission of our sins. Christ died for all Mankind, for all, that is, except Francesco himself, who is beyond the pale. Francesco's dream invokes the shame of Macbeth (also Wagner's Tannhauser). Unlike Macbeth, however, Francesco was never under any compulsion. He has never been goaded to his sin. It is not weakness of character, so much, as a congenital disposition toward brooding and rancour that afflicts him. He has none of Tannhauser's delight in sensuality. He has no creativity, therefore he has no hope of forgiveness, for he has no means to reconcile himself to the exigencies of life.

Finally, as he reveals his incapacity for prayer (that is for humility), it is the shade of Claudius, (in Shakespeare's *Hamlet*) that hovers over the scene. Like Claudius he has allowed his resentment to run out of control to the point where he can justify murdering his father and (even if only by inference) his brother. The murder solves nothing, as the 'resurrection' of his victim makes symbolically clear. He has no future because he cannot reconcile himself to the past or, for that matter, to the present. His destiny remains in limbo.

Un Frate (*Don Carlo*). See **Friar**

Frederica (*Luisa Miller*) Duchess of Ostheim and the Count's niece.
Frederica plays a crucial role in the drama but is given precious little substance as a dramatic character. Indirectly she causes the deaths of **Luisa** and **Rodolfo**. She might appear as a *femme fatale* par excellence, but she is nothing of the kind. Rodolfo himself refers to Frederica's generous heart and recalls how they shared together the pure joys of their early years.

When Frederica learns from Rodolfo that he does not love her but is in love with another, she becomes imperious (Act 1 Scene 2). Nevertheless, the fact that she tells him were he to kill her she would forgive him with her dying breath would seem to indicate her genuine love for him. Why else would she contemplate forgiving him? However, her pride will not allow her to forgive him the fact that he now loves another: 'Do not expect forgiveness from my jealous heart. Love scorned is a fury that cannot forgive'.

The main interest in Frederica's role exists in the scene of her confrontation with Luisa (Act 2 Scene 2) where she endures a direct conflict between her jealous fury and her common humanity. Her humanity tells her clearly that Luisa is being coerced, and that, in spite of her avowals to the contrary, she is in love with Rodolfo. To Frederica's shame she chooses to ignore the evidence of her own instincts and accepts Luisa's words at face value, because that is what she wants to believe. She believes herself to be in love with Rodolfo because she holds in her heart the image of their youthful intimacy. Frederica's life has been on hold since she allowed herself – what choice had she? – to be coerced into marrying the old Duke. If it was Schiller's intention in his play to underline the fact that, in spite of what we may wish to the contrary, the world of power politics often bests and discounts the hopes and dreams of the human heart, then Frederica is as much an illustration of that thesis as the two main protagonists. Doubtless through all the long years of her marriage to the elderly Duke she dreamt of the day when she might be reunited with her true love, Rodolfo. Unfortunately Rodolfo, not so constrained (or constrained in a different way from Frederica), has moved on.

The possibility of Frederica's marriage to Rodolfo has been propagated by Rodolfo's father, for whom Frederica's wealth and title are the principal attractions. Presumably the thought has never occurred to Rodolfo, for whom Frederica is past history. He has other agendas, not least the need to escape the domineering influence of his father.

Frederica is a truly tragic figure. She is the victim of a fate that allows her to be born into an age when daughters had no possibility of determining their own destinies. Thus, having been compelled to enter into a loveless marriage, she becomes emotionally stunted. When Rodolfo finally consents to marry her it is not because he loves her, but because he has deliberately turned his back on what he wants. He no longer cares. Had the marriage gone ahead it would have been as loveless as was Frederica's to the elderly Duke. Rodolfo at least prevents Frederica from entering upon a second sham marriage. This can be little consolation to her as she learns of her betrothed's suicide, even as she prepares to join him at the altar. Her tragedy is left to our imagination though, for she does not reappear in the opera after Act 2 Scene 2.

A Friar (*Don Carlo*)

Throughout the opera an equation is drawn between the Friar and the spirit of the deceased Emperor Charles V, **Philip**'s father and **Carlo**'s grandfather. At the conclusion of the opera Philip unequivocally identifies the Friar as being his father, while in Act 2

Scene 1 Carlo already wonders if it is not his grandfather who approaches him.

At the opening of Act 2 Scene 1 the monks are heard intoning 'Charles, the supreme Emperor, is nought but silent dust'. The Friar continues, 'He aspired to rule the world, regardless of Him who guides the stars on their constant course in the sky. His pride was immense, his error profound!' The Friar then prays that peace and forgiveness may descend upon the sinner.

Carlo has entered the cloisters and, unaware of the Friar's presence, soliloquizes: 'I seek in vain the peace which my heart so desires'. The Friar approaches him and observes, 'Earthly sorrow still pursues us in the cloister; war in the heart will abate only in heaven'. The inference is that, for Carlo, entering the cloister and withdrawing from life is no answer to the problems which assail him in the outside world. The confrontation between Carlo and the Friar establishes a link on several different levels, the temporal and the spiritual being only the most obvious. It is also a confrontation between generations. A link is established between grandfather and grandson which effectively leaves the intermediary, Philip, out in the cold. It has the vicarious effect of underscoring Philip's isolation in the drama.

With his erratic impetuosity Carlo has within him more of the spirit of his grandfather than of his father, 'il prudente'. The same instability that led Charles V to greatness in the worldly sphere on the one hand, and to total rejection of it on the other, is clearly evident in his grandson. The Friar is the mediator between the two generations. He also presents an effective antidote to the monumental and oppressive presence of the Grand Inquisitor. The Inquisitor is the personification of Blake's Old Nobodaddy, the prescriptive and unforgiving avenging Father of the Old Testament who, in contradistinction to the compassionate God of the New Testament, primarily issues decrees and punishment. The Friar may also sound prescriptive, but he is prescriptive from a quite different perspective from that of the Inquisitor. For the Inquisitor represents the worldly power of the Church. The Friar is within the Church but it remains for him but a temporary habitation, suspended between the temporal and the eternal. He represents the challenge of the cloister, where the true self, the godhead must be confronted. This is something that Philip and Carlos, locked as they are in a temporal power struggle, the perennial struggle of generations, the struggle between father and son for assertion and potency in the world, are fatally prevented from doing. Philip, in particular, is entirely isolated, both from the world and from his essential self, because all his dealings with the Church are via the Inquisition that cares nothing for the succour of the individual but only for the safeguarding of the Church's supremacy in perpetuity. This is what gives such eloquence to the conclusion of the opera which firmly establishes that the prerogative in truth rests not with the Inquisition, but with the lonely challenge of the cloister.

G

Gabriele Adorno (*Boccanegra*). Genoese nobleman, a Patrician, in love with the girl he assumes to be **Amelia** Grimaldi (in reality Boccanegra's daughter, Maria).

Gabriele detests **Boccanegra** whom he believes to be responsible for his father's death. Since we are not privy to the details of the elder Adorno's demise it is impossible to know how justifiable is Gabriele's detestation of Boccanegra. Suffice it to say Gabriele's every waking moment is devoted to thoughts of revenge. He has found a staunch ally in the person of Amelia's guardian, Andrea (**Fiesco**). Gabriele knows Andrea's true identity, although it is only in the final scene that the audience is privy to this fact. With Andrea and Lorenzin (who does not appear in the opera) Gabriele plots the overthrow of Boccanegra. He does his best to keep his treasonous activities from Amelia, but he has reckoned without the latter's perspicacity.

When Gabriele first appears in the opera (Act 1 Scene 1) he has just fulfilled an assignation with his fellow conspirators in the gardens of the Grimaldi palace, the conspirators' preferred meeting place since it is relatively immune from prying eyes and ears – all that is except those of Amelia whose habit it is to take the air on the balcony opening off her apartments. Amelia is well aware that he and her beloved guardian are plotting and she is afraid of the consequences for them both. Gabriele is not willing to discuss these matters with her, and especially not where there is a risk of them being overheard. As Amelia passionately attempts to persuade him to abandon his vendetta against Boccanegra and concentrate his energies on his love for her Gabriele responds in kind by telling her affectionately, if a trifle patronizingly, not to 'try to fathom the dark mysteries of hate' but to concentrate on love. Throughout the opera Gabriele persistently underestimates Amelia, yet repeatedly he will owe not only his political survival, but his life, to her timely intervention.

Gabriele can only be delighted when knowledge of Boccanegra's impending suit on behalf of **Paolo** convinces Amelia that she and her lover must be married forthwith. But first he must seek the permission of Amelia's guardian. This gives Gabriele no cause for concern, for he is a close friend of Andrea's and does not anticipate his opposition. When he learns from Andrea the truth about Amelia's lowly origins he is no way dissuaded from his intention to proceed with the marriage. There can be no clearer demonstration of the sincerity of his feelings for her. However the lovers will have to undergo many trials before their marriage can take place. The first of these will be the kidnapping of Amelia, at Paolo's behest, by the two-timing Lorenzin. Gabriele is so outraged, firstly by the affront to his beloved, and secondly by Lorenzin's duplicity, that he has no hesitation in summarily executing his one-time friend and ally – not, however, before gleaning that Lorenzin has been acting upon the orders of a 'man of power'. Gabriele instantly assumes this to be Boccanegra. All his actions thereafter must be understood in the light of this misapprehension. Even after Boccanegra has so dramatically exposed Paolo at the conclusion of the Council Chamber Scene (Act 1 Scene 2) a niggling doubt must remain in Gabriele's mind, a doubt that is played on, with almost fatal consequences, by the ever wily Paolo.

Gabriele's immediate reaction to Amelia's kidnapping is to make his way, together with Fiesco, to the Doge's palace, there to confront Boccanegra. In the meantime the Plebeian mob has learnt of Lorenzin's murder and are baying for blood. By the time Gabriele and Fiesco arrive at the Palace they have an angry mob on their heels (Act 1 Scene 2). Face to face with the man he now assumes to be not just responsible for the death of his father, but also the abduction of his intended bride, Gabriele cannot restrain himself from physically assaulting the old man. It is Amelia who prevents him from committing murder by intercepting herself between the two men she cares for most. Gabriele is immediately placed under arrest. Were it not for the fact that Boccanegra has recently discovered that Amelia is his long-lost daughter, and is therefore disposed to listen to her wishes and show lenience towards his assailant (if for no other reason than that Amelia wishes it), he would undoubtedly have had Gabriele executed for treason.

Amelia supplies a crucial moderating influence on both her father and her lover. It is to be regretted that she does not see fit to tell Gabriele the truth about her relationship to Boccanegra; this simple expedient could have saved both father and lover, not to mention herself, a great deal of heartache. As it is Gabriele cannot be expected to appreciate that Boccanegra's leniency towards him – not even requiring him to surrender his sword – is due to the old man's love for his recently discovered daughter. He is only half-persuaded that the real villain is Paolo, and happily lends a receptive ear to the latter's insinuations concerning Boccanegra's intentions towards Amelia (Act 2).

In his recitative and aria (*O inferno! Amelia qui!*) Gabriele gives vent to his pent-up frustration and confusion. It is far simpler for him to believe Paolo, and thus believe that the murderer of his father and his lover's seducer are one and the same person, than to have to continue in a fog of uncertainty. Gabriele needs to have a focus for his energies. Possessing no powers of self-reflection or analysis, he easily becomes prey to whatever a man like Paolo sees fit to put in his path. Because he cannot abide uncertainty he fails to observe the dictates of commonsense and suspend judgement until such time as he is in possession of all the facts. He prefers instead to take on trust, from somebody he must know to be untrustworthy, a supposition which contradicts all that he knows – and loves – in Amelia. His own unworthiness is never more evident than when he declares that 'if a dark cloud has tarnished her innocence and deprived her of her virtue may I never set eyes upon her again'. It is the oldest and vilest form of male chauvinism.

As if to upbraid him it is at this very moment that Amelia enters. And it is in the ensuing scene, as Gabriele lets forth a stream of invective against his lover, that one is forced to wonder why Amelia does not put an end to both their miseries and tell Gabriele that she is not Boccanegra's lover but his daughter. Instead of which she allows his misconception to fester on, once more with almost fatal consequences for her father. [Note: It is of critical importance for the logical unfolding of the plot that Gabriele is not seen to overhear the colloquy that transpires between Boccanegra and Amelia while he is concealed on the balcony, for Amelia here openly addresses Boccanegra as 'Father', and it is quite clear when Gabriele emerges from his hiding place that he remains oblivious to the truth.]

As he stands over the sleeping form of Boccanegra he has to goad himself into the act of murder, by reminding himself of his duty to his deceased father. For Gabriele has himself received from Boccanegra no provocation – nothing to justify his impending crime. Quite the reverse, in fact: Boccanegra has shown him only kindness, understanding and forbearance. Indeed he has publicly declared his burning desire to achieve unity and an enduring peace in the state of Genoa and an end to all factional disputes. Part of Gabriele's problem is that he does not listen. He only ever hears what he chooses to hear and whatever happens to fit in with his mood of the moment.

Once again it is Amelia who intervenes, saves her father's life and her lover from the worst consequences of his rashness. And now, finally, Gabriele learns the truth. He is instantly mortified, and begs Boccanegra's forgiveness. He is overjoyed at the opportunity to redeem himself by quelling the insurrection that threatens outside the palace. Gladly he agrees to convey Boccanegra's messages of peace to the mob. His political ambitions have become irrelevant. Forgotten is his desperate desire to avenge his father's death. Through Boccanegra's magnanimity he is at last able to put the past behind him and look solely to the future. For in the future is hope and light, while behind is only darkness and obscurity. All along it has been Amelia who has held aloft a beacon of light, who has refused to allow herself to be enmeshed in the horrors of the past (and she certainly has every bit as much to lament as does her lover).

When Gabriele returns from his mission of peace it is to find Boccanegra already in his death throes, a martyr to Paolo's poison (Act 3). He is astonished to see Fiesco at Boccanegra's side (it is only at this late stage of the opera that we learn that Gabriele has been aware all along of the true identity of 'Andrea'), but delighted also to realize that finally old enmities have been put aside and that there now exists a real chance of enduring peace. For Gabriele's political perceptions have been revolutionized from the moment that he learned that his beloved Amelia is the daughter of a Plebeian, and his erstwhile arch-enemy at that. In that moment he learns a profound truth; namely that all political 'convictions' are dictated by internal pressures of temperament and proclivity. He has travelled a long way from the arrogant young man who declared that if his beloved's virtue had been assailed by a 'dark cloud' then he never wanted to see her again.

Nevertheless he can hardly have anticipated Boccanegra's dying decree that he, Gabriele, should succeed to the office of Doge, for it turns on its head the assumption which underpinned the Plebeian mandate, that no Patrician should even be allowed within the Council Chamber, let alone succeed to the Doge's throne. But then Boccanegra's life's work has been to undermine this narrow factionalism. It is in this moment that the true nobility of Boccanegra's endeavour comes home to the young Patrician, as he kneels with Amelia beside the old man's death bed. His anguished tears confirm his genuine distress.

What sort of Doge Gabriele will make is open to question. On the evidence of the opera his is a rash and intemperate nature. He is highly impressionable and susceptible to violent mood-swings, hardly an encouraging profile for a leader of men. He will undoubtedly have to contend with the enmity of the most die-hard of the Plebeians. He will need to demonstrate every bit as much wisdom and restraint as his predecessor has had to call upon. His greatest asset will be the love and support of his bride, for Amelia has demonstrated throughout remarkable qualities of endurance and forbearance. For all his faults Gabriele is possessed of a fundamental nobility of spirit: witness his ready willingness to lay aside his political hatred when presented with the higher dictates of love and compassion. The image of his remarkable predecessor will surely haunt Gabriele, and hopefully inspire him to perpetuate Boccanegra's liberal and humanitarian policies.

Gasparo Antonio della Rocca (*Un giorno di regno*). See **Treasurer**

Gaston (*Jerusalem*). Viscount of Béarn.
The role of Gaston replaces that of **Oronte** in *I Lombardi*. Unlike Oronte Gaston does not belong to the enemy people. He is one of the Crusaders and yearns to reclaim the Holy Land for Christendom as much as anybody. Thus the motive of conversion in *I Lombardi* is now missing. However, there

is a concomitant gain, that Gaston becomes the innocent victim of the false accusation that he is responsible for the attempted assassination of the **Count of Toulouse**. Unfortunately for Gaston he is universally believed to be guilty of the crime since nobody has taken seriously his attempt at a reconciliation with the Count. His ostensible motive for the crime is a potent one, that the Count has been responsible for the death of his father. But this grievance is put aside in the very opening scene of the opera in which the Count offers peace to Gaston and his family and Gaston, in return, offers allegiance to the Count who is to lead the French Crusaders to Palestine. However he is anxious to be reconciled with the Count because otherwise there would be no possibility of his marrying **Hélène**. There is no equivalent in *I Lombardi* for the motive of persecuted innocence. Everybody is quite clear in that opera who the villain is – Pagano.

Gaston must suffer all the miseries of Pagano without having in any way warranted his ostracism. The **Papal Legate** pronounces anathema on him and Gaston finds himself an outcast and a pariah. He must wander the earth's surface for the same period as does his rival, **Roger**, who is genuinely conscience-stricken and in search of redemption. The only thing that Gaston has to sustain him in this period is his knowledge of his innocence and of the injustice that has been done to him. He does not even know if Hélène still loves him.

Arrived in Palestine Gaston is soon taken prisoner by the **Emir** of Ramla. He must expect a grisly death. He could not have arrived at a darker, more desperate pass in his life. From this moment (Act 2 Scene 2) his fortunes can only improve, although his troubles are not over yet. He does, however, enjoy a respite when, miracle of miracles, Hélène suddenly appears at the harem. Although the scene of their reunion retains the music of the lover's duet in Act 3 Scene 1 of *I Lombardi*, the scene in *Jerusalem* has a far greater poignancy. In *I Lombardi* Oronte and Giselda are both distraught,

dispossessed but at liberty. In *Jerusalem* they are both prisoners. Any plans for the future are purely speculative. They do not know if they are going to even live beyond the next day.

As it is their attempt to escape from the Emir's harem is foiled. The arrival of the Crusaders only serves to exacerbate Gaston's plight, for the Count immediately recognizes his would-be assassin and forthwith condemns him to be executed. Execution in itself does not hold too great a horror for Gaston, but the manner of it certainly does. The prospect of losing his life he can come to terms with, but not relinquishing his honour. For he knows himself to be unjustly condemned.

It may stretch credibility but there is natural justice in the fact that the one to rescue Gaston from his ill-fate is the man who inflicted it on him in the first place, Hélène's uncle Roger. Not only does Roger give Gaston his sword, but encourages him to join the Crusaders in their assault on Jerusalem. When the battle is won and the Count of Toulouse is on the point of asking some extremely awkward questions (for Gaston remains visored throughout) Roger is on hand firmly to deflect all culpability onto himself where it rightly belongs.

The only guilt Oronte, in the earlier opera, has to bear is for deserting the religion of his forefathers (although this issue is not addressed in any great depth in Solera's libretto) and for leading Giselda into a rootless existence (which matter is addressed). But these are peripheral issues and Oronte remains a peripheral character. Gaston, on the other hand, is very much the central character of *Jerusalem*. It is *his* fate around which the opera revolves. The fact that at the conclusion of the opera he prevails and that he and Hélène are granted a second chance gives *Jerusalem* an altogether a more satisfying dramatic coherence than *I Lombardi*. The final scene brings the action full circle and gives the young lovers an opportunity to resume the relationship which was so disastrously interrupted by Roger's fateful intervention.

Gastone, Viscount de Letorières (*La Traviata*)

It befalls Gastone to apprise **Violetta** of the love she has inspired in **Alfredo** Germont, who is apparently one of his most valued friends. No doubt Gastone has been forced to endure endless hours in which a lovesick Alfredo unburdens himself to him of his frustrated passion. In exasperation Gastone has finally insisted that they go where Alfredo may have a chance of confronting the object of his passion. On Gastone's part this is probably a matter of self-preservation.

At dinner (Act 1) Violetta sits between Alfredo and Gastone. Gastone has probably engineered this in advance, possibly with **Flora**'s connivance. He then takes it upon himself, since it is clear that Alfredo never will, to tell Violetta that Alfredo thinks of nobody but her. When she was ill Alfredo visited daily. Violetta suspects him of teasing her; such devotion to an ailing courtesan is unusual. But Gastone is in earnest and Violetta confronts Alfredo, who admits that it is true. Gastone becomes exasperated with Alfredo, who does not utter so much as a single word throughout the meal. Finally he insists that Alfredo should propose a toast to Violetta. It would be churlish of Alfredo to refuse, and he obliges with the famous drinking song (*Libiamo ne'lieti calici*). Having effected an introduction Gastone takes a back seat for the remainder of the scene and concentrates on enjoying the party. He and the other guests move into the next room when the dancing begins, leaving Violetta and Alfredo alone. Curiosity soon gets the better of him and he cannot resist popping his head round the door. There is some lively banter, then he withdraws again, happy to observe that his mission is accomplished.

Gastone attends **Flora**'s party (Act 2 Scene 2) in disguise as a bullfighter. He is in the company of several others, similarly accoutred. He enters fully into the party, clearly enjoying the masquerade. He does not exchange a single word with Alfredo. He is, in common with all present, surprised to see him at the party. He cuts the cards and deals at the gaming table where Alfredo sits down to play against the **Baron Douphol**. He must be keenly aware of his friend's feverish condition. He manages to whisper to Alfredo to spare Violetta's feelings, if at all possible. However sparing Violetta's feelings is the last thing on Alfredo's mind. Gastone will be pleased and relieved that Alfredo wins each of the games of cards, but then, when Alfredo loses control of himself and shrieks abuse at Violetta, he is as aghast as everyone else. He turns his attention to attempting to console the inconsolable Violetta.

Gastone plays a small but crucial role in the drama, reminding us that once upon a time Alfredo did have a normal existence before becoming maniacally obsessed by his passion for Violetta.

Germont (*La Traviata*). **Alfredo**'s father.

Germont is the catalyst for the crisis in Alfredo and **Violetta**'s lives. He is the *pater familias* par excellence. He lives for the honour, happiness and fulfilment of his family. Not personal fulfilment, let it be noted. Before the individual comes the family, before the family comes society. Germont exudes the ethic of responsibility above all. Yet as an individual he is not without genuine compassion. Yet his compassion only becomes necessary because of his own original lack of it, the deliberate blindness that he induced in himself when it came to the all-important matter of protecting the propriety of his family.

When Germont goes to visit Violetta (Act 2 Scene 1) it is with every expectation of being greeted by a woman of no moral character. Until he meets Violetta he can only assume that she is an adventuress taking advantage of his son in order to live a life of gilded luxury. When he sees the property, which is substantial and luxuriously appointed, his sense of moral outrage can only be confirmed. What is his surprise, then, when he is greeted by a lady possessing dignity and poise who immediately succeeds in shaming him for his ill-mannered breech of courtesy and abuse of her hospitality? He is momentarily at a loss. Nothing that he has prepared in his mind to say to this woman seems remotely applicable to the lady standing before him. If he has prepared a speech it deserts him and he is forced to converse with Violetta, for whom he immediately feels sympathy and admiration. But he cannot afford to forget the reason for his visit, which is the future happiness of his beloved daughter. He must persuade Violetta to renounce his son. He knows that trying to persuade Alfredo to renounce Violetta will be impossible. If he previously assumed Violetta to have some devilish hold over Alfredo the reality must convince him that Alfredo has in fact found for himself a remarkable soul-mate. Nevertheless the facts of her origins cannot be denied and neither can the purpose of his visit.

The successful interpreter of Germont will not project merely the stern father figure, but rather a combination, unique in operatic literature, of father, potential lover, friend and ultimately redeemer. He comes to admonish and condemn. He leaves having done neither. All he has achieved is replacing one misery with another: Violetta's for that of his daughter's. Inevitably his greater allegiance must be to his daughter. The parameters of his odyssey become clear when, in the final scene, he announces that he has come to visit Violetta in order to call her daughter.

But now he must tackle his son. He has promised Violetta he will do everything in his power to ameliorate Alfredo's distress. He meets with Alfredo just as the latter has read Violetta's letter announcing her intention to return to her previous life. He cannot therefore achieve any line of communication with him. Alfredo is totally distracted, his one thought being to go in pursuit of Violetta. Germont's aria (*Di Provenza il mar*) has very much the air of a prepared speech. He may as well have left it at home. Alfredo is not listening. Alfredo rushes off in pursuit of Violetta. All Germont can do is follow. Germont's handling of his son would no doubt have been very different had his worst expectations of Violetta's character been confirmed. But since he knows Violetta to be quite different from his presuppositions

– instead a woman worthy of respect and forbearance – he cannot find it in him to take a purely prescriptive stance towards Alfredo. He must also realize that it would be useless.

In Act 2 Scene 2 Alfredo is like a man possessed. Germont can only watch in horror as his son publicly humiliates Violetta. Nobody knows better than he how unjustified Violetta's humiliation is. He is appalled, as any father would be, at Alfredo's hysteria and lack of self-control. Yet he blames himself. He must reflect that in attempting to protect his daughter he has only succeeded in reducing his son. Germont is not stupid. He can understand why Alfredo behaves as he does, although naturally he cannot condone it. Nevertheless society demands that he disown his son on the spot. Alfredo's public humiliation effectively sounds the death knell for Violetta, and Germont instinctively recognizes this.

After the duel in which **Douphol** is wounded by Alfredo and the latter takes refuge abroad Germont writes to his son attempting to put the record straight, even though he must know it is too late and the damage has been done. It is nevertheless indicative of Germont's fundamentally generous nature that he does so in spite of the fact that he will be seen to condone a situation that is inimical to his social standing and probably his daughter's happiness. On the other hand a cynic could observe that Germont now knows that Violetta is dying and whatever the outcome of his letter there is no possibility of her setting up home with Alfredo again and propagating the scandal that has been so injurious to his reputation. But this would be to ignore the evidence of Verdi's score. In the final scene Germont is genuinely overwhelmed with grief by Violetta's predicament and the suffering for which he still feels responsible. Nothing about Alfredo's liaison with a courtesan could have been predicted.

Germont expects life to obey certain rules. His meeting with Violetta has forced him to throw the rule book to the winds. Violetta has influenced his life almost more than she has that of Alfredo, for Alfredo has been passionate and compassionate from the outset. He has never had to think twice about making a commitment to a 'loose' woman. But for Germont it is different. Violetta's lifestyle is the epitome of the very thing that most threatens the bourgeois respectability that is at the core of Germont's existence. The whole episode has, in fact, done him a colossal favour, for it has released the human being from behind the social mask. Not only has he been released from the bondage of his own moral code, but by association he has released his family by taking the cue from his son. If his daughter is rejected by her betrothed, then one could feel that the man in question was not worthy of her.

Germont's odyssey reflects an odyssey required of all who come into contact with Dumas' story and Verdi's opera. For in both is exposed the hypocrisy of the double standards that were such a notable feature of nineteenth-century Victorian life, whether in England or abroad. The tendency was to bifurcate existence between what may be done and what may be seen to be done. It is a tendency which has prevailed throughout history. But it is a tendency which must be undermined, and it is the purpose of the arts to do so.

Verdi's opera was greeted with howls of protest and outrage because ostensibly it outraged public morals, which is only another way of saying that it attacked people's individual consciences, just as Germont's conscience is attacked and revolutionized in the opera.

Giacomo (*Giovanna d'Arco*). Father of Giovanna.

The penitential role of the father in Verdi's dramas is never so explicit as in *Giovanna d'arco*, for Giacomo refuses to accept the fact that his daughter may be extraordinarily gifted and may have aptitudes beyond anything in his experience. In her desire to fight as a man he can see only that she denies him a father's natural prerogative and the loving devotion and acquiescence of a daughter. That he loves her beyond all else in his widower's existence, that she is as dear to

him as is Luisa to her father, Miller, in *Luisa Miller* is without doubt.

In the final analysis his condemnation and betrayal of his daughter is not the result of malice but of wilful ignorance. This becomes clear when he witnesses Giovanna at prayer near the conclusion of the opera (Act 3) and is forced to accept that he has been misguided all along. In that moment he is consumed with remorse. Confronted with the proof of her innocence Giacomo now has the justification to effect the reconciliation that he has been longing for ever since he handed her over to the enemy.

From Giacomo's viewpoint Giovanna has been in league with the devil from the moment that she demonstrated an inclination to individuate. Her behaviour by any standards is unnatural for a girl growing up in a rural setting to God-fearing parents. Anybody who prefers their own company, who prefers to remain aside from the norm, automatically invites suspicion. That she is known to frequent a forest glen, reported to be the haunt of witches and warlocks, fuels his suspicions. (It never seems to occur to him, or any of the other villagers, the incongruity of a shrine to the Virgin Mary being in a place of devil worship.) Confirmation is provided for him when he witnesses his daughter in company with no less than his King. This is not because Giacomo reckons the King to be in league with the devil but because it is completely unheard of for a peasant girl of the 15th century to conduct a liaison with a King. Giacomo assumes that the only way such an eventuality could have come about is through Giovanna having made a pact with the devil.

He goes straight to the enemy, the English, and offers to deliver Giovanna, his own daughter, into their hands. Not only that, but he expresses the wish to fight with the English against his countrymen because he now assumes that France is tainted with the devil. His action is entirely motivated by self-preservation. He needs to disassociate himself from his homeland in order to preserve his immortal soul. If he were to support Giovanna he would become guilty by association and share in what he feels sure will be his daughter's eternal damnation.

Giacomo's self-serving piety is the very thing that his daughter is incapable of recognizing, let alone identifying herself with. Giovanna's great tragedy, as George Bernard Shaw brought out so clearly in his play, *St Joan*, is that she is incapable of making herself understood, of communicating the nature and origin of her inspiration to less gifted individuals. The sanctity of her mission is, to her, self-evident. But it cannot be thus to her father, by virtue of the fact that he *is* her father. He is incapable of viewing her aspiration dispassionately and can only characterize her as the very reverse of what she actually is.

Of all Verdi's father-figures Giacomo's lot is the most impossible. Any father can expect that his daughter may run off with a lover or be seduced by a playboy philanderer. But no father could expect that his daughter would grow up to believe that her mission is to save her country by going to battle under instructions from voices in her head. The torment that Giacomo endures, when he goes to the enemy with his offer of collaboration, is given expression in a poignant speech where he reflects: 'I know that original sin/leads us along a path of thorns,/I know that to the wretched/a brighter, dearer land will appear...', concluding, '...let a father's tears/moisten the vile mud!/Weak is the flesh,/but the soul is greater than any pain' (Act 1 Scene 1). Giacomo explains his actions to himself in terms of pious observance but he cannot excuse himself.

Verdi was never so eloquent as when portraying tormented fatherhood, particularly when it is the father/daughter relation that he depicts, and the father is a widower. Perhaps that has something to do with the fact that he never had a chance to indulge a daughter himself. The death of Verdi's children in infancy along with his first wife must have left an abiding guilt.

Gilda (*Rigoletto*). Daughter of **Rigoletto**.

Gilda endures to an exceptional extent the burden of guilt attendant upon having been born to a wounded parent. It is an archetypal syndrome that every child must carry to more or less of an extent, but for Gilda it is a crushing weight that threatens to strangle her life before it has even begun. Her mother having died in her infancy, she is the sole repository for her father's tormented sense of life-frustration. He smothers her with love.

Rigoletto's greatest fear is that he will lose this one ray of light in his existence, so he keeps her, for all intents and purposes, a prisoner, closely guarded by a maid. Luckily for Gilda **Giovanna** (Gilda's nurse) is sympathetic. She knows that a young girl needs to be able to accept the attentions of admirers, and when the admirer happens to be a dashing young man, whom she herself finds enormously attractive, and who also pays handsomely for her cooperation, she can see no reason to observe to the letter her employer's draconian decrees. Thus Gilda finds an ally in Giovanna merely by virtue of the fact that her maid is a woman also and knows her needs. It is something the hunchback suspects (why else does he reiterate his decrees with such intensity?) but can neither understand nor condone.

Brought up in total seclusion from the world Gilda can have no conception of what lies beyond the confines of the parental home. She falls in love because it is natural to do so and because the **Duke of Mantua** intends that she should. He knows an easy prey when he sees it. The fact that Gilda disobeys and contravenes her father's most stringent prohibitions overwhelms her with guilt but also with the excitement of transgression. Years of thwarted energy, the very essence of youth, is released in her through the flattering attentions of the unknown young man.

Why does it matter so much to Gilda that her admirer be poor? Because all her life she has been indoctrinated by her father to believe that noblemen – courtiers especially – are not to be trusted. She wants a lover her father might approve of, even though in reality she knows he could never approve of any lover she takes. Her horror is all the greater, then, when she learns the truth about her admirer: when she is forcibly abducted and compelled to submit to his passion. For the second time in the drama she confesses to great shame (Act 2: the first time being when she admits to Giovanna that she has lied to her father [Act 1 Scene 2]).

Her father's desire for revenge is quite disproportionate, in her eyes, to the crime which, if she could but admit it (which she cannot), was not entirely unpleasant or uninvited. The real shame stems from the transgression of her father's behest and the fact that she loses her virginity in the arms of her father's employer and within the precincts of the scene of Rigoletto's own incessant shame. Shame is hereditary and cannot be assuaged, least of all by the startling absence of recrimination towards her from her father. She begs Rigoletto to exercise forgiveness of the Duke, but Rigoletto is beyond her reach.

From the moment of Gilda's surrender to the Duke, Rigoletto has his own agenda to follow and forgiveness is not part of it. In the primeval battle between father and lover Gilda must allow nature to take its course, and may the best man win (in the event, nature revelling always in inequality, the Duke will be proven the best man by virtue of the fact that through sheer charisma he eludes Rigoletto's rough justice). It is this that convinces Gilda that she must sacrifice herself in order to save him. A ray of light has entered the drabness of her customary universe and life without it no longer seems bearable. She would rather die in the service of that ray of light than continue to live in the shadows. Despite the misgivings she feels over leaving her father she instinctively realizes that it is time for her father to fend for himself and for her to exercise the right to self-determination that she has long been denied. She dies in the service not of the Duke but of her own right to live. It is for this reason that she justifies the epithet of heroine. She is no dying swan. She fights and ultimately dies for what she needs and wants.

UN GIORNO DI REGNO (King for a Day), or *Il Finto Stanislao* (The False Stanislaus) Melodramma giocoso in 2 Acts. Libretto by Felice Romani after A V Pineu-Duval's comedy, *Le Faux Stanislas* (1808).

First performance: 5 September 1840 at La Scala, Milan.

Cast:
Cavaliere Belfiore: posing as Stanislaus, King of Poland (baritone)
Il Barone de Kelbar (buffo bass)
La Marchesa di Poggio: young widow, niece of the Baron (soprano)
Giulietta, the Baron's daughter (mezzosoprano)
Gasparo Antonio della Rocca: the Treasurer of the States of Brittany (buffo bass)
Edoardo de Sanval: his nephew (tenor)
Il Conte Ivrea: Military Commander of Brest (tenor)
Delmonte: Belfiore's Steward (tenor)

Time: 18th century
Place: Baron Kelbar's castle, near Brest

Background   Romani's libretto is based on a play by Juan Pineu-Duval, entitled *Le Faux Stanislas* (The False Stanislaus). This play was loosely founded around historical events in Polish history. In 1704 Stanislas Leszczynski (1677–1766) was elected King of Poland. In 1709 he was deposed and fled to France where he was granted asylum by Louis XV. Stanislaus's daughter, Marie, eventually became the French King's wife. Louis helped his father-in-law regain his throne and in 1733 Stanislaus travelled back to Poland in secret, disguised as a coachman. While he was in transit a young French officer, Beaufleur (**Belfiore**), impersonated the King in public.

Synopsis
Act 1 Scene 1. The castle of the Baron Kelbar. A gallery. Servants and vassals sing in excited anticipation of the double wedding that is shortly due to take place: 'a fairer day never smiled upon the house of Kelbar'. It is particularly exciting because the King is to attend (*Mai non rise un più bel dì*).

The Baron and Treasurer enter. The Baron congratulates the Treasurer on having chosen his daughter, Giulietta, as bride. According to him, she is, 'a precious branch of a great tree of heroes' (presumably he includes himself in that precious tree). The Treasurer assures the Baron his marriage to Giulietta will always be 'happy and prosperous' and will soon produce a 'famed and honoured offspring that will make our two families universally respected'. Both men seem equally delighted with the prospect of the forthcoming marriage in spite of the fact, as they themselves admit, it has caused many raised eyebrows. But what matter when they have as witness the King of Poland himself? (*Tesoriere garbatissimo*).

Delmonte enters and announces that His Majesty approaches to greet his host. The servants sing in honour and excited anticipation. Belfiore enters, dressed as the King. He demands that there should be no ceremonies as he is bored and sated by 'customary rituals'. He assures the Baron that he is well pleased with his reception and will be informing the court accordingly. In an aside the 'King' wishes his Parisian companions could be present to witness the farce (*Compagnoni di Parigi*). Resuming his regal manner he reiterates that he requires no ceremonies. The assembly assure him that they all marvel at 'the beautiful soul concealed within (his) august person'.

The Baron enquires whether the King will be present at the forthcoming double wedding. When the 'King' hears that one of the marriages is to be that of the Baron's niece, the Marchioness of Poggio, he is visibly shaken, the Marchioness of Poggio being his own intended bride. The Baron cannot fail to notice the 'King's' disquiet, but the 'King' stalls further questioning by requiring to be left alone. All depart leaving the 'King' alone to consider his position. He realizes that as soon as the Marchioness arrives his true identity will be unmasked. He forthwith sits down to write a letter to the Court, requiring to be relieved of his duties, since if he continues in his role of King he risks losing his love.

Edoardo enters and throws himself at the 'King's' feet. He begs to be allowed to follow the King to Poland and to devote his 'useless life' to him. The 'King' graciously accepts this priceless gift, and Edoardo further prostrates himself in gratitude. The 'King' raises him up and informs him that henceforth he shall serve as his Esquire and remain at his side always. Edoardo is overjoyed, though less enthusiastic at the prospect of having to witness his beloved Giulietta married to another man. The 'King' makes a mental note to ensure that if nothing else he will see to it that the marriage of Giulietta and the Treasurer shall be confounded. Edoardo, meanwhile, confirms his willingness to risk the perils of death on behalf of his King. The 'King' humours him and the two men exit (*Proverò che degno io sono*).

The Marchioness enters, cautiously and unseen, and looks after the departing figure of Belfiore. She is, not surprisingly, confused. She has been led to expect that the King will be attending her wedding. Instead she is certain she has recognized the man she really hopes to marry, Belfiore. She determines to dissemble. She will pretend to go ahead with her marriage to Count Ivrea and then, hopefully, her true love will reveal his hand. Already a widow all the Marchioness now requires is 'love and youth'. But if Belfiore is untrue to her she will never love again (*Grave a core*).

Act 1 Scene 2   A garden. Giulietta is seated sadly on a bench. A chorus of peasants and servants brings her gifts of fruit and flowers (*Si festevola mattina*). 'How fortunate is the man who will soon wed this immaculate lily', they sing. Having delivered their gratuities they notice that the bride-to-be is looking far from happy. Having first expressed her undying love for Edoardo (*Non san quant'io nel petto*), Giulietta elects to unburden her soul to the servants. She is brutally frank: 'I do not want that old man. I am not such a fool. My heart throbs for another', she says. One wonders why the servants do not reclaim their recently proffered gifts. They merely express the wish that heaven may free her of all her torments and depart.

The Baron and the Treasurer enter. The Baron informs Giulietta that she is shortly to be presented to the King and that her fiancé is at hand. Giulietta lamely protests that she is inclined to melancholy. The Treasurer insinuates that he will have the remedy on their wedding night to cure her of her misery. Belfiore enters with Edoardo. Giulietta is delighted to see her true love. The Treasurer, however, is dismayed to see his nephew. He is presumably well aware that Giulietta and Edoardo are lovers. Belfiore informs the Treasurer that Edoardo is now to be his Esquire. He then, in an effort to give the young lovers some time to themselves, tells the two old men that he wishes to consult them upon a matter which requires 'deep analytical discussion'. The Baron and the Treasurer are duly flattered. Belfiore tells Edoardo he may not join them since his rank does not permit him to be party to State secrets and instructs him to keep his future aunt (Giulietta) company. Edoardo is only too happy to comply. The Treasurer is disgruntled. Belfiore seats the Treasurer on a bench in such a way that his back is towards Giulietta. He then faces the two men and concentrates their attention on a map he lays out in front of them.

The sextet which ensues (*Cara Giula alfin ti vedo!*) is initially comprised of the lovers, Giulietta and Edoardo, making the most of the opportunity afforded them to confide in each other; while Belfiore engages the Baron in earnest conversation on the lineaments of a projected battle and the Treasurer divides his attention between the map and his increasing ire at the obvious ardour his nephew is demonstrating towards Giulietta. Belfiore enjoys the latter's discomfiture hugely. Finally Belfiore rises and announces 'Enough for now', and the lovers separate. The Treasurer heaves a huge sigh of relief.

A servant enters and announces the arrival of the Marchioness. Now it is Belfiore's turn to be uncomfortable. Giulietta and the Baron announce they will go and meet her, but to Belfiore's dismay the Marchioness is already entering. The Baron and Giulietta hurry to embrace her. The Treasurer and Edoardo greet her politely. Belfiore attempts to remain apart and hide his embarrassment. The Baron commands his niece to kneel down before the 'King', indicating Belfiore who remains aside with the Treasurer and Edoardo, attempting to feign indifference. The Marchioness apologises for her unintentional affront, claiming she had no idea the King was to be present. Belfiore, assuming the most regal manner he can summon, assures her, 'It is nothing'. A doubt enters the Marchioness's mind: is this Belfiore or is it really the King? It is certainly her lover's face, but she is forced to wonder whether her frustrated love does not encourage her to see her lover's image everywhere.

The others have noticed her distraction. Belfiore's one idea is to escape as quickly as possible. He tells the men that he has need of their 'talents'. His esquire (Edoardo), meanwhile, will keep the ladies company. The Baron and the Treasurer are overjoyed at the honour the 'King' does them in requiring to consult them. Giulietta and Edoardo are delighted at any further opportunity of uninterrupted time together, while the Marchioness, still mightily confused, resolves to wait upon events. The 'King', the Baron and the Treasurer exit.

The two lovers immediately turn to the Marchioness who is pacing back and forth, lost in thought. She hardly hears their pleas to help them in their predicament, so absorbed is she in her own thoughts. All that concerns her is whether the 'King' is in fact the King or her erstwhile lover, Belfiore, whom she thinks has deserted her. Edoardo and Giulietta become increasingly frustrated at the Marchioness's lack of response to their appeals for help (*Bella speranza invero*).

The lovers agree that the Marchioness is going to be no help to them at all and are on the point of leaving when she recovers herself and detains them. She admits her mind has been elsewhere but now she will ensure that she will do everything she has promised them. The lovers are hugely relieved that they have an ally after all. The Marchioness reassures them that she knows what love is and will ensure that the old man, the

Treasurer, will be 'duped'. All three join together in affirming that, 'we're in love and we're young. We have spirit and warmth; if Fate has been against us, love is on our side; with its help, it is possible to fight even Destiny'.

Act 1 Scene 3   The gallery, as before. Belfiore enters with the Treasurer, to whom he is directing shameless flattery. Belfiore tells the Treasurer that if he (the Treasurer) were not already committed to the Baron, he, as King, would confer on him a 'Ministry, the Princess Ineska, and, with her, valuable property with large returns'. The Treasurer immediately assures Belfiore that he will rid himself of all commitments forthwith. Belfiore is making full use of the opportunity to help Edoardo and Giulietta. He exits. The Treasurer, all unsuspecting, congratulates himself on his cleverness. Thoughts of the fortune that soon might be coming his way override all other considerations.

The Baron enters carrying a document. He has brought the marriage contract to show to the Treasurer (*Diletto genero, a voi ne vengo*). The Treasurer girds himself to break the news that he will not be marrying Giulietta. As he starts to explain the Baron interrupts him impatiently and urges him to sign the document. The Treasurer is now forced to be specific: 'I will not sign'. The Baron's response is predictable: 'you must be mad!' When the Treasurer finally manages to pluck up the courage to give his reasons for refusing to marry Giulietta, namely that the King wants him as a minister and prince, the Baron is apoplectic. He takes the news as a personal affront (*Tesorier! Io creder voglio che sia questo un qualche gioco*).

The Treasurer becomes exceedingly nervous; 'Good Lord! . . . he is like gunpowder about to explode!', he mutters to himself. His fears are confirmed when the Baron demands that he draw his sword. This is too much for the Treasurer who makes to beat a hasty retreat. The Baron grabs hold of him and the Treasurer, thoroughly frightened now, shrieks for help. Giulietta, the Marchioness, Edoardo and servants come rushing in from all sides. The Treasurer begs

his nephew to save him, the Baron splutters about the insult to his family honour and Giulietta, the Marchioness and the rest of the company wonder what on earth is happening. Finally Edoardo manages to persuade the Baron to relate the cause of his rage. Giulietta is overjoyed to learn that the Treasurer does not wish to marry her. The Baron, however, is not amused; his thoughts now tend toward revenge. Now the Marchioness steps in. Surely, she says, the best revenge would be for Giulietta to be married off immediately? She knows a young man who would be most suitable. At which Giulietta chimes in, 'Yes, father, with your permission I'll marry his nephew'. However, the Baron does not take kindly to the suggestion: 'No . . . the house of Kelbar has not sunk that low'. All he wants is blood. Luckily for the Treasurer there are now enough people present to restrain the Baron.

In the midst of the imbroglio the 'King' enters. He regally demands to know what is going on. All are embarrassed. Belfiore advances slowly, studying everyone closely. The Baron is extremely chastened, aware that to quarrel in the presence of a monarch is a grave insult. The Treasurer, on the other hand, is hugely relieved at the advent of the King. He might now have some hope of escaping with his life. The Marchioness, Giulietta and Edoardo are also all relieved. Only the servants join the Baron in expressing nervous concern. Belfiore, meanwhile, has come to the conclusion that the Treasurer must have reneged on his promise.

He demands to know the cause of the dispute. Everybody tries to explain at once until Belfiore silences them and demands a rational explanation. Once again all vie for the King's attention until Belfiore loses his temper and dismisses the assembly with a dire warning of the consequences of incurring the Royal wrath. Everybody begs his forgiveness and then joins him in expressing confidence in the ultimate justice of the Royal judgement, whensoever it may be forthcoming.

Act 2 Scene 1   A gallery. The Baron's servants are chattering amongst themselves about the recent events (*Ma le nozze non si fanno?*). They reflect, philosophically, that it has ever been thus with the aristocracy: 'They change their moods as easily as they change their clothes'. They, on the other hand, pride themselves on always being the same.

Edoardo enters and regales the servants with his recent change of fortune. He is evidently on good terms with the servants who are genuinely pleased that his sorrows are over. Edoardo rhapsodizes on the joys of 'a single ray of hope' (*Pietoso al lungo pianto*). Without 'the faint pleasure that is born of hope', he continues, 'love is an agony'. The servants agree that happiness has returned for Edoardo and they exit. Belfiore, Giulietta and the Treasurer enter.

Belfiore, still in regal mode, demands to know of Giulietta and the Treasurer why the Baron so opposes the marriage of his daughter and Edoardo. Giulietta sums it up in one: 'because he is poor while the Treasurer wallows in money'. Belfiore swiftly announces a solution. In that case the Treasurer will give one of his castles and an income of five thousand crowns per year to Edoardo. The Treasurer asks for a little time to consider this proposal but the 'King' decrees that there is no time to waste and the Treasurer must decide at once. The Treasurer can hardly do otherwise than agree. All leave except the Treasurer.

It is now the Treasurer's turn to splutter with fury. But he quickly consoles himself with thoughts of the Ministry and the Princess that is soon to be his. He has little chance to bask in his anticipated good fortune for the Baron enters and without preamble demands satisfaction. The Treasurer girds himself anew. The Baron threatens to 'devour him like an egg' (*Tutte l'armi si può prendere*). The Treasurer is not impressed: or rather if he is impressed he is not going to let on. He proceeds to express the hope that the Baron has made mention in his Will where he desires to be buried, for buried he certainly will be, and in the not too distant future. The Baron is somewhat taken aback by this sudden display of bravado from the Treasurer, who is not slow to notice that even the Baron is deflected by thoughts of his own mortality. The Baron demands to know what weapons the Treasurer plans to use. Now the Treasurer's imagination runs riot: 'Imagine a barrel full of gunpowder; you and I firmly seated on it as if on horseback... With a fuse in hand we bid each other good night and ignite the barrel. Boom! A head flies here, the legs there, here an arm....'

The Baron is not impressed with talk of barrels and fuses. He is a 'brave warrior' who relies upon his sword. He demands that they fight a duel forthwith. The Treasurer is caught off guard and continues to insist that barrels and fuses are more efficacious. The Baron now accuses the Treasurer of cowardice and tells him he will have him caned by his servants. The Baron is by now in a great lather and the Treasurer congratulates himself on the success of his technique for averting the immediate threat to his life and limb.

Act 2 Scene 2 A hall with glass doors leading to the garden. The Marchioness and Belfiore are both on stage, eyeing each other from a distance and muttering to themselves. The Marchioness is perplexed, to say the least, and longs only for Belfiore to stop dissembling (*Ch'io non posso il ver comprendere?*). Belfiore realizes that the Marchioness is angry but determines to hold his own. He approaches her and addresses her formally. The Marchioness is equally reserved. Both know they are playing a charade, but neither will give any quarter. Belfiore kicks off by nonchalantly observing that it is plain to see that the Marchioness is thinking of 'il Cavaliere'. The Marchioness replies that she has decided that Belfiore is not the husband for her. She further asserts that there will be no forgiveness for the cavalier. Belfiore keeps reminding himself that she is pretending and just succeeds in holding on to his dignity.

The Baron enters hastily to announce that he has heard from the Commander (the Marchioness's betrothed, Count Ivrea) whose arrival is imminent. He exits hurriedly leaving the Marchioness the opportunity to aim a swipe in Belfiore's direction: 'I am grateful to the Count. He loves me sincerely, and I would wed him today'. She further states: 'The Cavaliere has mocked sufficiently. He abandons me as prey to his rival'. This it too much for Belfiore. He exclaims, 'You will see him fight for your hand with all the Counts of Brittany'. However, he is still addressing the Marchioness in the third person and still refuses to acknowledge that he is not the King but Cavaliere Belfiore.

The Marchioness takes the opportunity to sing an aria (*Perche dunque non vien?*) in which she rhetorically asks why her cavalier does not reveal himself 'to the one who adores him'. Even though she is angry now she would soon calm down. When she has finished Belfiore remains silent. She wonders why. 'I do not know what to say', is all Belfiore can muster. In that case the Count shall have her hand and her pledge, the Marchioness declares.

Servants of the Baron enter in a flurry. The Count is approaching. The Marchioness announces hastily that she will go to greet him and 'forget that unfaithful one'. Henceforth she will shun his presence. Belfiore is by now beside himself. But it is too late. The Marchioness has left, as have the servants. Belfiore himself exits disconsolately.

Giulietta enters. She is blissfully happy and grateful to the 'kindly King' who has aided her contentment. Edoardo enters. He has come to tell Giulietta that he must soon leave with the King who commands that he accompany him into battle (*Giurai seguirlo in campo*). Giulietta is not amused. Edoardo may be the King's Esquire, but first and foremost he is her bridegroom. Edoardo invokes his honour and tactfully recommends she should apply herself to the gentle art of reflection. Reflect? I never reflect, she announces. What would you have me do? Edoardo asks in despair. Exactly as I wish, rejoins Giulietta. But that's impossible, Edoardo objects. Oh, it will be possible, Giulietta concludes. She will go to the King and plead her case. Edoardo suggests that the King may have more on his mind than

Giulietta's demands. Much against her will Giulietta appears to be on the brink of conceding that Edoardo may have a point. We can at least hope, she says. Mollified somewhat they sing together of their love and their certainty that they will be able to reconcile the conflicting demands of love and duty.

Act 2 Scene 3   A gallery. The Baron, the Marchioness and the Treasurer have just greeted Count Ivrea. The Baron is reassuring Ivrea that the Marchioness has totally forgotten 'that madman' (Belfiore); indeed she now hates him as much as she once loved him. The Marchioness interjects that she is ready to marry the Count, but only on condition that Belfiore does not return within the hour. At that moment Belfiore enters, still in his guise as King. With him are Edoardo and Giulietta. Ivrea bows deeply. Belfiore announces that he must leave on important business. The Marchioness is dismayed. She declares that she had hoped that he would attend her wedding (*A tal colpo preparata*). Belfiore replies that, 'weighty matters will not permit it'. In that case let the marriage contract be signed at once, the Marchioness insists. But Belfiore is one step ahead. He tells the Marchioness, much to the latter's chagrin, that the Count must accompany him on a secret state mission. Everybody present is surprised. The Marchioness is at a loss, which fact is not lost on Belfiore who is beginning to enjoy the game of cat and mouse they play.

Delmonte enters and announces the arrival of a courier from the Polish court who apparently bears 'an important letter' (*Sire, venne in quest'istante*). Belfiore is impatient. He hopes that this might signal the end of the farce. He grabs the letter from Delmonte. It is indeed the news he had hoped for. The real King, Stanislaus, has safely arrived and he can stop masquerading. He announces that shortly he will reveal 'the mystery', but first he declares that Giulietta and Edoardo must be married. He knows that once he ceases to be 'King' he will have no influence over affairs. He desperately wants to ensure that Giulietta is not married to the doddery old Treasurer. He decrees that the witnesses shall be the Treasurer and the King. The Baron can do nothing to prevent it. All proclaim 'Long live the happy couple!'

Then Belfiore reads out the letter he has received in which he is informed that he may now relinquish the Crown, but has meanwhile acquired the title of 'Marshall'. The Baron asks incredulously, 'Then who are you?' To which Belfiore replies, 'The Cavaliere Belfiore'. He goes to the Marchioness, embraces her and adds, 'Faithful to my first love!' The Baron is completely nonplussed, but realizing he is utterly helpless in this new turn of events, he joins the others in hailing the real King, who is safe through Belfiore's efforts, and celebrating two very happy marriages. They conclude, 'So perhaps the joke has spared us many sighs and tears'.

Many parallels can be drawn between Verdi's two comic operas, not least the double wedding and the intended, entirely inappropriate, marriage of an elderly man to a young girl. Both are primarily ensemble operas, although by the time Verdi came to write *Falstaff* in collaboration with an infinitely superior librettist the pace accorded the action had increased enormously. In many ways *Un giorno di regno* can be seen as a rehearsal for *Falstaff* or, looked at another way, *Falstaff* was Verdi's triumphant response at the end of his life to the audiences and critics who had condemned the earlier work and almost rendered his career stillborn.

Verdi was an intensely proud man and he never forgot the humiliation of that early fiasco. He always had an equivocal attitude towards comedy. As a man he was not unduly given to levity, having a dry and often barbed sense of humour and a fundamentally pessimistic, Hardyesque outlook on life. Yet he was, above all, a man of the theatre with an ingrained sense of dramatic timing. Even in *Un giorno di regno* there are clear indications that this invaluable gift could one day be usefully put at the service of comedy.

Giovanna (*Giovanna d'Arco*)

The character of Joan of Arc is one of the great archetypes of our culture, an abiding myth that gives each successive age something to ruminate on. It could be said, with justification, that Solera's libretto is a crude affair, yet it is, frankly, no more crude than any other operatic libretto. The central facet of Giovanna's character is her existential self-division and this is preserved as faithfully in Solera's libretto as in Schiller's play. It has been said that Solera reduced the plot nonsensically by uniting the love interest with Joan's mission to save France (in Schiller's play Joan falls in love with Lionel, an English officer). Thus there is ostensibly no confusion between her mission and her human, all-too-human, love for a man. In fact it makes no difference where the man comes from. The conflict for Joan from the start is between what she craves as a woman and the dictates of her spiritual calling. It therefore makes perfect dramatic sense that her mission and her love should become embodied in one and the same man. It serves to underline the impossibility of her predicament and the fact that the two are entirely incompatible, or certainly from Joan's standpoint.

For Joan is obedient to only one authority: her own inner voices. In the opera these are graphically represented by the chorus of angels on the one hand and the chorus of demons on the other. The one incites her to heroic deeds while the other mocks her aspirations and reminds her that she is but a mortal woman with all the frailties that entails. The angels make it perfectly clear that the two are irreconcilable. She must forgo all earthly desires because these stem from the devil. In Solera's reduction of the plot Giovanna does not need to be reminded of her predicament by her voices. She only needs to look at **Carlo**. He feeds the conflict, and yet she cannot help being attracted to him.

Giovanna's conflict is underpinned by the straight role-reversal symbolized by the exchange of helmet and sword (Prologue Scene 2). Carlo has a vision of an image of the Virgin who commands him to lay down his helmet and sword at the exact spot where

Giovanna, who craves a helmet and sword with which to arm herself for battle, will find them. It does not require any great psychology or perspicacity to see that Carlo is handing over to Giovanna his own potency, both with which to empower and protect her. In that moment he unmans himself. He relinquishes his masculinity in order that Giovanna may take it unto herself and marry it to her natural instinctive femininity. Carlo becomes as helpless as the father and villagers that Giovanna leaves behind.

It is when Carlo becomes identified for Giovanna with the life of lost innocence, which she has chosen to relinquish, that she feels the first stirrings of love. For Carlo becomes the embodiment of that world from which she has distanced herself. It is always that which we deny that we must love, for better or for worse. That Giovanna makes an entirely conscious decision to turn her back on the life which she has known and to which a large part of herself – the womanly part – still belongs, is made abundantly clear as she soliloquizes: 'To you, merciful Virgin, I entrust my humble cottage, my father's grey hairs and the simple sheepfold, until I return to sing hymns of praise to you!' There is a keen sense of regret in the leave-taking. It is no Rimbaudesque revolution against bourgeois stultification.

When Giovanna sets eyes on Carlo, who predominates over the material, worldly order which still threatens to pull her back from her divine destiny, she must see a possibility of taking with her into the great unknown that sense of security and ordinariness that otherwise would be lost forever. She cannot allow herself to give way to her emotional needs, because the instant she does so she knows she invalidates her spiritual mission. This stark dichotomy between human needs and transcendent urges is the very stuff of which genius, in any form, is fashioned. How far can the human spirit surmount the biological basis of its being?

In the case of Joan of Arc the dichotomy is complicated by the simple fact that she was a woman living in a man's world long before it was admissible for a woman to wish to excel in the world of politics, commerce or even battle. (How, one wonders, did Joan gain the respect of the average infantryman under her command? It must have been unthinkable – not to say bizarre – to them to be led into battle by a woman. Did they perhaps not realize that she was a woman until after battle had been enjoined and won through her exceptional valour? How did Charles VII (Carlo) really feel about the fact that a woman, a mere peasant at that, had usurped his position and succeeded where he had failed? The answer to these questions lies in the outcome of the trial that led to the historical Joan's execution for heresy. Nobody, not the King, not the army officers and certainly nobody from the church, lifted a finger to prevent her execution. For in truth they were all hugely relieved. Joan was an assault to masculine vanity. That she assured their ascendancy in battle meant that they could not quibble in their day-to-day interactions with her, but neither could they explain or condone it. Her success was inexplicable, and that was impossible to support.)

One of the most eloquent moments in the role of Giovanna comes after her victory against the English. She escapes from the festive celebrations in the palace and expresses intense relief at finding herself: 'with the open sky/high above, where the pure air stirs' (Act 1 Scene 2). This is the essence of her craving. She does not want worldly success and honour. It only causes her anxiety. Now she only wants to return to the simplicity of her life in the country. It is immediately after this scene that she openly declares her love for Carlo. What Giovanna must seek is a release from her own self, from the stifling prison of personality. She craves more intense life. Were she to return to her father's home she would probably very quickly become restless and long for the field of battle again. Joan is not intellectual, or rational even. She cannot explain to herself her own moods and needs. She simply flows with them. But as soon as she flows in one direction she is pulled in another. The one thing of which she is incapable is being satisfied. This in itself torments her, for it proves to her that she must essentially be wicked. Her real battle is, in fact, with Original Sin. As the chorus of demons points out at the end of Act 1: 'are you not/of the line of Eve?' Whether she likes it or not this is incontrovertible.

When her father publicly accuses her (Act 2) Giovanna cannot help feeling that it is no more than she deserves. Her love for Carlo has convinced her that she is a miserable sinner. Her father's accusation merely corroborates that conviction: 'Against my stricken soul/thunders the voice of the Eternal' (Act 2), she says. Now she welcomes the prospect of martyrdom because it will save her from herself and her irremediable, as she sees it, wickedness. Confined in chains (Act 3) she knows that the only value for a human being is the freedom to act of his or her own volition. She denies her love for Carlo for she can acknowledge it for what it is, a distraction from her true purpose. The weaker part of her nature wants nothing so much as to return to the equilibrium that she enjoyed before she set out on her quest. But having rejected Carlo she can resume her dialogue with God (or her own higher self, however you like to look at it). It is this that effects her reconciliation with her father, for in that moment her father realizes how very wide of the mark he has been in suspecting his daughter of cavorting with demons. Giacomo only perceives a partial truth, for he divides reality into strict compartments of good and evil. For Giovanna it is not so simple. There is nothing simple about the lot she has chosen for herself. But the fact that she is rehabilitated in her father's affections means that she can resume her military career without guilt.

Giovanna's entire career to date has been blighted by the fact that her father has condemned her endeavour from the start. Without his support and solidarity she can only be consumed with guilt. Everything about her faith stems from the father she lacks. The voices that come to her dictate what she should do and she obeys. Because they come from above they carry the authority of a supreme mandate. They come from the father who she needs to know, the father who wishes her to become what he is. This is entirely distinct from the desires of her natural father for whom his daughter's desire for military glory is perverse and incomprehensible. Giacomo does not want a daughter who supersedes him. Like Miller (*Luisa Miller*) he wants a daughter to make his old age comfortable. That she sets quite a different agenda for herself confirms in his eyes her wickedness, for it was then an article of faith that the girl's obedience to her father was synonymous with obedience to God the Father, who is the supreme arbitrator and who has decreed that a girl's sacred duty is to obey her natural father in all things. (This is what makes so monstrous instances of father–daughter incest which can only ever be a matter of abuse since the daughter is always, by definition, a victim.)

Solera's instinct in making Giovanna's reconciliation with her father the occasion of her transfiguration is entirely sound. For in that moment the profound rift that her religious obsession has opened up in her psyche is healed. That her father condones her endeavour and actively encourages her to fulfil her destiny; that he recognizes her as an individual in her own right; that he releases her from bondage, from the stranglehold that he has had over her young life means that Giovanna can now for the first time act with impunity – without guilt. Thus liberated she can accede joyfully to death, which is always the natural and inevitable destiny of all human life. More than that she can joyfully embrace it in the certain knowledge that she has succeeded, where few human beings succeed, in realizing herself without the necessity of denying her origins. Her acceptance into the company of angels acknowledges the enormity of her achievement. The fact that in the opera she dies of wounds received in battle, rather than being burnt at the stake (as was the case historically), underlines the fact that this is no tragedy that we are witnessing, but the fulfilment of an entirely natural process.

Giovanna (*Ernani*)

Giovanna replaces the colourful character of Donna Josefa in Hugo's play. Donna Josefa has some amusing and lively exchanges in the play which are wholly lacking in the role of Giovanna, who is just another stock operatic maid. She has little imagination and cannot understand why her mistress is not overjoyed at the approach of her wedding day, even though she must surely be aware where **Elvira's** true affections lie. For a woman like Giovanna it would be happiness enough to be married into exceptional wealth and position. A girl in service cannot afford the luxury of prioritizing the dictates of sentiment and passion.

Giovanna (*Rigoletto*). Gilda's nurse.

Giovanni plays a crucial role in the drama by default. Because she sees no reason to prevent her charge's assignations with the **Duke of Mantua**; because she accepts money from the latter for her silence; and because she empathizes with Gilda's youthful passion she precipitates the crisis that overtakes **Rigoletto's** household. Even had she observed Rigoletto's strictures and refused the Duke's bribes, however, it is doubtful whether the latter would have been deflected from his intention to seduce Gilda.

Giovanna plays a similar role in Gilda's life as Magdalena does to Eva in Wagner's *Die Meistersinger von Nürnberg*. Like Magdalena Giovanna is more than just a nurse; she is friend and confidante to Gilda, who otherwise endures an entirely solitary existence. Perhaps she was Gilda's wet nurse. At any rate she is the only female companion or role model Gilda has had since her mother died in her infancy.

Giovanna flatly disobeys her employer's instructions by allowing the liaison between Gilda and the Duke to develop. But the Duke is so obviously a 'gentleman' (principally, in her eyes, because he always has ready money to dispense in her direction) that he seems to her to be an excellent and eligible suitor.

One can only imagine the wrath that Rigoletto will direct against Giovanna when he learns from his daughter how long the liaison with the Duke has been going on. Undoubtedly Giovanna will lose her job. Even had her disobedience not come to light her role in the Rigoletto household would become redundant with the death of Gilda. Gilda's abduction and subsequent demise will undoubtedly cause Giovanna intense grief and heart-searching.

GIOVANNA D'ARCO

Lyric Drama in a Prologue and three Acts. Libretto: Temistocle Solera after Schiller's tragedy *Die Jungfrau von Orleans* (1801).

First performance: 15 February 1845 at La Scala, Milan.

Cast:
Carlo VII: King of France (tenor)
Giacomo: Shepherd of Domrémy (baritone)
Giovanna: his daughter (soprano)
Delil: a king's officer (tenor)
Talbot: Commander-in-chief of the English army (bass)

Time: c1429
Place: France

Historical Note   The name of Joan of Arc has entered into popular consciousness with the force of myth. Nevertheless there is no doubt that she existed and that she played a crucial part in turning the tide in the Hundred Years War.

Joan of Arc was born to prosperous peasants. At the age of thirteen she started hearing mysterious voices.[35] She identified the voices as belonging to Saints Michael, Margaret and Catherine. The voices convinced her that her destiny was to save France by going to the aid of the Dauphin who had been disinherited at the peace of Troyes in 1420 and who was at that time (1429) attempting to ward off the English at the siege of Orleans. Joan succeeded in convincing a local commander and the Dauphin of her credentials and then justified her claims by going on to lead the French troops

---

[35] Amongst contemporary theories as to the cause include the possibility that she suffered a brain tumour.

to victory, apparently against all the odds. The Dauphin was then crowned Charles VII at Reims Cathedral. However Joan's star was soon to be eclipsed, principally through the petty rivalries and resentment caused by her success amongst the nobility and military commanders. In 1430 Joan was captured by the Burgundians who sold her to the English who put her on trial as a witch. She was burned at the stake in May 1431 at Rouen. The court's decision against her was reversed in 1455 and in 1920 she was canonized, neither of which was of much help to the unfortunate maid.

Many works of art have been stimulated by Joan's story, the most significant dramatic works being George Bernard Shaw's *St Joan*, which concentrates largely on her trial and the moral dilemmas faced by all concerned, and Tchaikovsky's opera *The Maid of Orleans*. Like Tchaikovsky's opera Verdi's is based on Schiller's play which pays scant attention to the facts of Joan's life, though it does retain the fundamental predicament Joan faced in a world ruled by superstition and dread. It is extremely unlikely that she had a love affair with the Dauphin, or with any other man for that matter. She certainly did not die in battle.

Synopsis

Prologue Scene 1 Domrémy castle. A large courtyard leads to the Royal Apartments. Ladies, magistrates, halberdiers, guards of honour, commoners and a group of King's officers fill the stage.

The King's officers report that the war is going against them. The city of Orleans will soon fall, not through any lack of courage on the part of troops, but through starvation: 'A huge horde of thieving barbarians is destroying this wretched land'. The commoners assume that the catastrophe must be retribution for France's past acquisitiveness.

Delil enters and announces the King. All comment on the King's anguished expression. Carlo addresses his officers, telling them to travel to Orleans and instruct the defending troops to surrender. He absolves all from their oath of allegiance. He relates how he

prayed to Heaven: 'that if it be the will of Heaven to punish heinous crimes, then the scourge should strike me alone'. He was then overcome by a strange, but pleasant lethargy and beheld a 'divine vision' of the Virgin who commanded him to lay down his helmet and sword at the foot of an oak in the depths of the forest where there stands a painted statue of the Virgin (*Sotto una quercia*).

The villagers comment that they know of a place in the vicinity, exactly as described by Carlo in his dream. Carlo's only desire is to see an end to the suffering and bloodshed of the French nation. He eagerly asks the villagers to describe for him where he might find the sanctuary. The villagers are reluctant to let him go for, as far as they are concerned, far from being a sanctified area it is a place haunted by demons, witches and wizards: 'woe if a man is caught unawares at their evil revels! No more will he see that light of day if he does not yield to the devil', they declare. Carlo refuses to be put off: 'Where the Madonna is, Hell cannot reside', he responds. He renounces his crown, which has become a deadly burden and torment to him, and departs, exhorting his subjects to leave him in peace. The people, however, resolve to remain with him, 'ever loyal and silent'.

Prologue Scene 2 A forest. To the right is a rock upon which rests a shrine to the Virgin, dimly lit from inside. To the left an oak tree with a stone seat beneath dominates the foreground. Towards the back is a cave. The sky is dark and stormy. A bell is tolling, summoning the faithful to prayers for the departed. Giacomo enters. In common with the villagers he is convinced that this is a place of evil. He has come to keep vigil because he is consumed with the suspicion that his daughter – Giovanna – visits the site, 'on stormy nights', and may well even have entered into a pact with the devil. Giovanna appears on the rock and kneels before the shrine, unseen by Giacomo. He hides in the cave.

Giovanna descends from the rock. Her thoughts are all for the terrible plight of her country and her frustration that she is unable to contribute to the war effort. She visits the shrine nightly to pray for a coat of mail, sword and helmet with which to equip herself for the battlefield (*Sempre all'alba*). She sits on the stone bench and, having begged the 'Queen of Heaven' to pardon her bold prayer, she falls asleep. (This scene establishes the true reason for Giovanna's nightly vigils and discredits her father's groundless fears.)

Carlo enters. He recognizes his surroundings from his dreams. He lays his sword and helmet on the ground and kneels in prayer.

Meanwhile Giovanna, in her sleep, is experiencing a vivid dialogue between choirs of demons, on the one hand, and angels on the other. The demons attempt to persuade her to forego her crazed desire to go to battle (*Tu sei bella*). She is a beautiful young girl and should be dedicating herself to love. As they finish speaking the clouds clear suddenly and the forest is flooded with brilliant moonlight. The angels urge her to rise, for 'the heavenly ones will satisfy your generous desire! . . . France shall be free through you'. The helmet and sword that she so desperately craves is awaiting her. They warn her against harbouring worldly love (that is, paying any heed to the chorus of demons). Giovanna leaps to her feet. Her eyes flash as though 'under the influence of divine inspiration'. 'I am ready', she declares.

Carlo, alerted by her voice, descends from the rock. Giovanna runs to it and returns with his helmet and sword. Then proudly she declares to the king that she is 'the warrior maid, who will lead you to glory' (*Son guerriera*). Carlo is understandably bemused, but at the same time carried away by Giovanna's radiant conviction and purpose. He gladly accepts her invitation to follow her to the battlefield.

Giacomo, meanwhile, has been watching and is astounded to see the King in company with his daughter. He is quite unable to comprehend the true reason for the King's presence. He assumes that Giovanna has given herself to the devil out of insane love for the King. His words provide an ironic counterpoint to Carlo's ecstatic outpouring that he has discovered his redeeming angel.

Naturally inhibited by the King's presence Giacomo remains aside and watches, powerless, as his daughter leads Carlo off to battle.

Act 1 Scene 1 An isolated place, strewn with rocks. Reims can be seen in the distance. English soldiers are scattered around in groups. Women weep over the dead whilst others see to the wounded. The soldiers have one thought, to return home to their native land, having been put to rout by the French. Talbot sums up the situation when he laments: 'Alas, a hundred triumphs destroyed in a single day!' He upbraids the soldiers for their cowardice, but the latter vehemently defend themselves (*O duce, noi sempre mirasti*). They are convinced that the French have made a pact with the devil. What other explanation can there be for their sudden excess of valour?

Giacomo enters. His dishevelled appearance reflects his disordered mind. He tells the English that the evil girl (his own daughter, Giovanna): 'who harasses you shall be your prisoner'. He sets one condition, namely that he may be allowed to fight with the English against the base French (*Franco son io*). Revitalized by this new turn of events, Talbot orders a 'tent of war' to be erected while the soldiers eagerly declare their intention of building a blazing pyre on which to burn the 'evil wretch'. Giacomo is suddenly overcome with the enormity of what he has done. The English are impatient to act immediately on his offer of help, and Talbot leads him and his soldiers off in search of Giovanna.

Act 1 Scene 2 A garden at the Court of Reims. Giovanna enters, wearing a helmet, cuirass and sword over her usual clothes. She is assailed by an acute sense of anxiety. For all intents and purposes her job is done now that she has ensured victory for the French. She hankers after the simplicity of her past life, after the forest where she used to pray, her father, their cottage and the simple clothes she used to wear (*O fatidica foresta*). She is not interested in the celebrations that are now in progress at the Court.

Giovanna has just made the decision to return home when Carlo enters. Realizing that Giovanna is on the point of leaving he throws himself at her feet and begs her to reconsider (*Chiede ognuno che mai fusse*). He declares that since the day she first appeared to him he has loved her with a 'supreme love'. Giovanna is moved, in spite of herself. She begs him to respect her as he has hitherto. She is no longer the Virgin's emissary but just a frail young girl with no defences against this sort of passion. Eventually she can resist no longer and she declares that she has equal love for Carlo. No sooner has she done so than the chorus of Angels reiterates its warning from the Prologue: 'Woe if you harbour worldly love in your heart!' Giovanna, who alone can hear the voices, breaks free from Carlo's embrace. She is trembling with terror. Carlo is at a loss to know what afflicts her. He tries to console her, but to no avail (*È puro l'aere*). Having only a moment ago revelled in Carlo's love, Giovanna now pleads with him to leave her. Then she imagines she hears the voice of her father crying: 'Die, you sacrilegious girl!' She becomes quite deranged. Carlo attempts to calm her.

Delil enters with standards and King's officers. They relate how the streets of Reims are crammed with people clamouring for their King who is to be crowned this day. Delil hands a standard to Giovanna who, still distracted, takes it mechanically from him. The officers wonder what ails her, but Carlo dismisses them, telling them to proceed with the celebrations. He will follow with Giovanna shortly.

Once the officers have departed Carlo pleads with Giovanna to follow him to the cathedral and be the one to place the crown on his head, 'amidst the shouts of rejoicing' (*Vieni al tempio*). Giovanna, however, is totally wrapped up in her own tortured musings. Her one thought is to take flight. 'Who will take me to a strange land where I can hide my shame?' she asks. A chorus of demons assails her inner ear, exulting in the victory they have won over the heavenly powers: 'Already you belong to us! . . . let us dance . . . as soon as Satan joins the revel the woman is ours!' they taunt (*Vittoria!*

Vittoria!). Finally Carlo seizes Giovanna's hand and leads her away.

Act 2   The cathedral square in Reims. In the foreground to the left is the cathedral of Saint Dionysius. The square is crowded with people, all singing in celebration of 'the wondrous maid' who has saved them from the English (*Da cielo a noi chi viene*). The crowd is now divided by soldiers into two columns. The band leads the way to the accompaniment of cheering. Then follow girls in white, holding branches, heralds and halberdiers. Behind them come pages, magistrates clad in robes, marshals with batons, then nobles with swords, sceptres, orbs, coronets, cloaks and judges' staffs. The path is strewn with flowers. Giovanna brings up the rear holding her standard. Then, as the bells peal out and guns fire salvoes the King enters beneath a canopy, held aloft by six barons. Behind him are courtiers, troops and servants. When the procession enters the cathedral the music stops and silence reigns.

Giacomo is alone. He reflects that now the time is ripe to 'strip myself entirely of a father's character, now I become the thunderbolt of the angry Lord'. It causes him untold anguish that he should have to turn his back on his own daughter. His one wish is that Giovanna may be saved from eternal damnation (*Speme al vecchio era un figlio*). There is a fanfare of trumpets within the cathedral, followed by a hymn. The choir is heard singing in praise of the Lord at the conclusion of the coronation. Giacomo wonders how it is that Giovanna can abide being in a holy place of worship, since he still believes that she is in league with the devil.

Giovanna hurries from the cathedral. She is clearly deeply distressed. She is followed by Carlo, crowned as King and leading the procession. Giacomo mingles with the crowd. Carlo detains Giovanna and pleads with her to accept the homage of himself and his people. He declares that henceforth France shall have two patron saints, Dionysius and Giovanna, to whom a temple will be erected. This is too much for Giacomo who cries out: 'God forbid such blasphemy!' He then proceeds to relate for all to hear (*Comparire il Ciel m'ha stretto*) how Giovanna has made a pact with the devil, 'for the sake of evil, worldly love'. The people are horrified. Carlo refuses to believe that 'an angel's form' could clothe the soul of a sinner (*No! forme d'angelo*). He prays for divine enlightenment and begs Giovanna to refute her father's accusation. Giovanna, however, has no intention of doing so. So consumed with guilt is she that she considers her father's blandishments to be the truth. For has she not succumbed to sensual longing for Carlo?

When Carlo calls on Giacomo to provide proof the latter grabs hold of Giovanna's hand and demands, 'in the name of God the avenger, are you not sacrilegious?' Giovanna cannot reply. Finally Giacomo demands that she swear on the soul of her mother. Giovanna remains silent. Suddenly the assembly is thrown into uproar by an outbreak of thunder and lightning. This seems to suggest that Heaven confirms Giovanna's guilt. The people are by now convinced she is a witch and want nothing more to do with her. When Carlo tries to console Giovanna, promising her his aid, Giacomo upbraids him: 'The only aid lies in the Lord'. Giovanna bursts into tears and throws herself into her father's arms. Giacomo invites her to accompany him to where a blazing pyre awaits to purify her soul. Giovanna gladly accepts the chance of redemption offered her by her father. Carlo, meanwhile, inveighs against the fickleness of the people who have but a few moments ago been celebrating the victory which Giovanna has ensured for them. He is forced to recognize that his power as King is circumscribed: 'What avails this royal purple, this crown, if I am defeated, chained by the vile fury of the people?' he asks bitterly. The people meanwhile call for Giovanna's immediate banishment (*Fuggi o donna maledetta*).

Act 3   Inside a fortress in the English encampment. Stairs lead to a tower overlooking the battlefield. Giovanni, in chains, is slumped on a bench. She is still in the same clothes but without helmet and sword. There is a stake nearby. She is tormented by the sounds of battle raging offstage and by the hopelessness of her situation. She longs to join the affray and lead the French once more to victory instead of which she is held captive in 'the loathsome enemy camp!'

Realizing that it is useless to struggle against her chains Giovanna gives way to lethargy. Gradually her imagination takes over as she pictures the scene of battle. Giacomo enters and stands unseen, watching her. She exhorts the troops to courage, then she imagines she sees the King, surrounded by the English. In desperation she calls out: 'O merciful God, will you abandon me now thus?' This gives Giacomo pause for thought. Surely if his daughter were in league with the devil she would not call on God? What follows serves to confirm his growing suspicion that he has been mistaken all along about his daughter. Giovanna fervently calls on God to listen to she who now has quelled all worldly desires and is once again devout and pure in her devotion to Him (*Amai ma un solo istante*).

Giacomo is overwhelmed by the enormity of his error. As Giovanna rises from her seat and implores God, 'who broke Saul's chains', to shatter hers Giacomo runs to her, weeping, and unfastens her chains himself. 'You are free!' he cries. 'Forgive your tearful father.' Giovanna is overjoyed to see her father (*Or dal padre benedetta*). She beseeches him to bless her and then to give her his sword so that she may rejoin the battle and ensure that 'not one of the invaders will ever see his homeland again!' Giacomo gives her his sword and joyfully exhorts her to lead her country to fresh victory. He prays that the truth has not dawned on him too late. As Giovanna rushes off Giacomo climbs to the top of the tower and surveys the battlefield. He relates, for the benefit of the audience, what transpires as Giovanna flings herself into the mêlée, rescues the King and swiftly sends the English into retreat.

Carlo enters with French officers. He expresses amazement that yet again he has been saved by Giovanna, even after he had abandoned her to the blind rage of the people. Giacomo advances. 'Punish me!' he exclaims. Carlo has no such intention. He tells Giacomo how, when Giovanna came to his rescue on the battlefield, she told him to return to the fortress and defend her father.

Delil enters with the news that Giovanna is dead. All are stunned into silence. Giacomo hides his head in his hands. The King gazes with great sadness at his followers and then slowly advances to address them. He implores that one of them should stab him to the heart, for he has no heart left to rule (*Quale più fido amico*). Giovanna is carried in on a stretcher. All bewail her demise, but then suddenly Giovanna rises to her feet and moves 'as if by supernatural force'. Recognizing her father and her King she asks for a French banner that she may 'restore it to Heaven as a trusty messenger!' Carlo gives her the standard. In her final moments she experiences a vision of the Virgin descending from Heaven in order to accompany her hence (*S'apre il cielo . . . Discende la Pia*). She sinks to the ground. As she does so a starry light appears in the sky. The soldiers lower their standards and all kneel before Giovanna's body. The chorus of Angels welcomes her while the Demons are heard bewailing: 'Punishment to us is the triumph of Heaven! Torment to us is the triumph of Heaven!'

If Schiller's play serves to humanize the story of Joan of Arc, Solera's reduction for Verdi's opera takes the process one step further. While Joan's battle with her human-all-too-human limitations remains, the central issues of the drama have become that much more focused: on one hand, Joan's relationship with her father; on the other hand Joan's relationship with the King. It may seem that this reduces the scope of the drama. In practice it does not. It simply renders it that much more suitable for operatic treatment, and particularly operatic treatment by Verdi, whose greatest inspirations always stemmed from the conflicts engendered by human intercourse rather than the conflicts between the human and the numinous.

Of the two relationships it is that of Giovanna and her father that is principally featured. Solera's greatest gift as a librettist was to bring forth archetypal situations. In the relationship of Giacomo and Giovanna, taking his cue from Schiller, he has delineated an interesting variation on the standard father/daughter conflict where the father cannot relinquish the daughter. Schiller's play opens with Giacomo declaring that it is time Giovanna took a husband as her sisters have already done. He would appear to be pushing her out of the nest. In reality he merely seeks to retain her by decreeing the who, the how and the when of her marriage. In other words he seeks to keep her well within his own orbit. Giovanna has different ideas which will take her away from the father and the homestead. Giovanna has a mission, and playing Daddy's little girl is not part of it.

As far as Giacomo is concerned his daughter's desire to save France from the English invader is sheer perversity, if not lunacy. When her efficacy in the battlefield is proven there can only be, in his mind, one explanation, namely that she is in league with the devil. The devil is traditionally the scapegoat for all we cannot comprehend or accept. Since Giovanna wilfully refuses to play the role ascribed to her by her father she is cast out and disowned. In fact Giacomo actively wills his own daughter's destruction. It is not until the eleventh hour that he realizes that all the perversity, or rather blindness, has been his own.

The true problem arises from the stereotypical expectations imposed by Society. A father's daughter is supposed to fulfil a certain preordained function. By refusing to fulfil that function Giovanna appears to make a full frontal attack on her father's and, by association, Society's central illusion. She has not set out to do so. She is simply responding to her voices which, if we blanch at ascribing them as she does to the archangels Catherine, Margaret and Michael, we can safely ascribe to the dictates of her own inner necessity.

The urge to go out into the world and conquer is, from the perspective of fourteenth-century society, the provenance of the son not the daughter. It is hardly surprising, therefore, that Joan of Arc has become an icon for the latter-day feminist movement.

Her urge to transcendence of herself, her origins and the expectations imposed on her is traditionally a masculine urge. There are few males who succeed in their ends as spectacularly as did Joan of Arc. The secret of her success was undoubtedly the unique balance that she exemplified between masculine aggression and feminine intuition. (In the 20th century there is ample evidence to prove what a powerful combination this can be.) For the successful politician, soldier or leader exemplifies a power that transcends the merely egocentric thrust of the male. The female leader does not merely emulate the attributes of the male, she uses her femininity, her instinctive certainties, to manipulate events in her favour. She will also employ her sexuality to exercise control in the male-dominated environment in which she finds herself.

Having said which, there is no evidence, in the case of Joan of Arc, that she ever overtly exploited her sexuality. Her strength at the head of the French army was her inviolability. Because she acted entirely at the behest of her voices she retained an aura of mystery and numinosity which mitigated against any tendency for the soldiers to be tempted into viewing her as a woman. Herein lies the absurdity of Schiller's notion that Joan engaged on a love affair with an English officer. Even more obtuse is the notion that she and the French King were lovers. This is not to say, however, that her intrinsic femininity was not an invaluable ally in her crusade. The very fact that she was acting at the behest of her voices conferred on her the authority of an oracle, a latter-day Sphinx. It was an accepted fact that such a woman was by definition virginal and a total stranger to carnal love. Since the French King and his army knew that their future destiny rested in Joan's hands it is ludicrous to suppose that they would have jeopardized that possibility by trivializing Joan's status to that of a sex or love object.

In one sense it could be said that the historical Joan never left the orbit of the father. Her fixation was merely transferred from her biological progenitor to the transcendent imperatives of her Father in Heaven. This is where Schiller critically alters the profile of Joan's story. From the standpoint of dramatic exigency he was justified. Whatever the drama of events there can be no psychological drama in the narration of a single-minded dedication. There was, of course, drama enough in the conflicts that rose between Joan's dedication and the world in which she found herself. But this was not enough for the Romantics. It certainly would not have been enough to stimulate Verdi's genius. There must also be 'War in the heart' (see also un **Frate** [*Don Carlo*]). This is what Schiller, and later Solera, contributed to Joan's story.

All Schiller's heroes could more accurately be described as anti-heroes, since they rarely prevail, viz. Carlo (*I **Masnadieri***), Carlo (***Don Carlo***), Rodolfo (***Luisa Miller***). All are torn asunder by conflicting needs. They share a burning urge to transcendence, but are eventually defeated by the apparent impossibility of sustaining any degree of intensity in a brutal and disinterested world. Joan is the exception to the rule. The war within her soul so graphically (and, it has to be admitted, so banally) portrayed in Verdi's opera by the choruses of angels and demons, causes Joan much anguish. Ultimately it is the angels that prevail. The Byronic hero that Schiller excelled in portraying as much as did the English poet is usually anima-driven, that is, he is more receptive to the promptings of the feminine within him than the masculine. He is not comfortable with his existence in the world. He would rather withdraw to a mountaintop and vent his spleen for the benefit of the elements. With Joan of Arc Schiller turned the prototype, that he himself had helped to establish, on its head. Joan is an animus-driven female and apparently thereby, according to the poet, infinitely better equipped to contend with the world.

Giovanni (*Il Corsaro*). A pirate and **Corrado**'s lieutenant.
Giovanni delivers a letter to Corrado (Act 1 Scene 1) sent from the pirate companions in Greece. The message summons the pirates

to battle against the Turks. Giovanni is captured with Corrado by the Turks after the pirates' daring raid on **Seid**'s harem (Act 2 Scene 2). He remarks, aside: 'What use is daring in a strong man's breast if fortune does not favour him with her smile? Corrado has challenged fate too boldly and now must bend his neck before it'. Apart from thus revealing a philosophical turn of mind, Giovanni does not contribute further to the drama.

Giselda (*I Lombardi*). Daughter of **Arvino** and **Viclinda**.

The role of Giselda is dramatically one of the most interesting that Verdi wrote for soprano. In his operas there are two distinct types of soprano role. On the one hand there are the powerful dramatic heroines of the early operas, Abigaille (*Nabucco*), Odabella (*Attila*), who become in the course of time the powerful leading ladies of the middle and late operas, Lady Macbeth, Leonora (*La Forza del Destino*), Aida, Elena (*I Vespri Siciliani*). On the other hand there are the 'dying swans' who first emerge with Medora (*Il Corsaro*) and develop into the doomed heroines, Gilda *(Rigoletto)*, Violetta (*La Taviata*), Elizabetta (*Don Carlo*), Desdemona (*Otello*).

Giselda occupies a place somewhere between these two polarities. She is the daughter of a domineering father and yet she possesses a powerful mind of her own, which is engendered and honed principally through force of circumstance. At the opening of the opera she is overjoyed that her uncle, **Pagano**, has finally been rehabilitated into the family (Act 1 Scene 1) but she is keenly aware that her father does not share her joy. She is soon forcibly made aware of the reasons for her father's disquiet when Pagano attempts to murder her father but instead murders her grandfather in his bed. It is a great deal for a young girl to absorb; parents, uncles and grandparents are supposed to be there to offer succour, not to murder each other in their beds. Giselda does at least manage to restrain Arvino from exacting extreme retribution on Pagano (Act 1 Scene 2).

When Giselda next appears she is prisoner in the harem of the tyrant of Antioch, **Acciano**, and being taunted by the other odalisques in the harem (Act 2 Scene 3). It is never precisely specified how Giselda came to be incarcerated in the tyrant's harem; presumably she has accompanied her father on a Crusade and then been abducted by Acciano's scouts looking for useful additions to the harem. Giselda is understandably miserable. The only consolation she has is that she is loved by and, in spite of herself, feels irresistibly attracted to, the tyrant's son **Oronte**. This fact however is not making her life in the harem any easier, for the other girls are jealous of the favours shown her by their prince.

Giselda's one thought at this moment is to escape and see the successful prosecution of her father's Crusade. However there is inevitably a conflict of interests between her sense of duty and faith on the one hand, and her love for the infidel on the other. This conflict is brought sharply into focus when she learns that her father has killed both Oronte himself and Oronte's father, Acciano. In this moment Giselda almost loses her reason. It must seem to her that all human relations, and the most intimate relations at that, are doomed to be blood-soaked. She lets forth a stream of invective against the whole bloody business of war: 'No, no! It is not God's just cause to soak the earth with human blood; it is base folly, not pious sentiment, that you should awake to the Moslem's wealth! These were not heaven's words, no, God does not will it, no, no, God does not want it!' Giselda speaks from the perspective of a suffering woman, caught up in a world apparently ruled by violence and bigotry. Why, when people should love each other, are they killing each other? And what is all this to do with Christian compassion and forgiveness? To Giselda it is pure idiocy.

Her vision of the holocaust has a ring of truth that resounds down to the 21st century, with an almost eerie prescience. 'What dark blindfold divine power tears from my eyes! The vanquished rise, and fearful vengeance lies in the shadow of the coming age! To none will it be granted to give up the ghost where he first drew breath! The impious holocaust of human bodies was always offensive to the God of mankind . . . Already I see your heads hanging, the sport of the winds; I see floods of barbarians arise to suppress the subdued peoples of Europe! For it was never the word of God for men to shed these torrents of blood. No, God does not will it, no God does not will it; He came down only to speak peace!'[36]

Giselda's outburst almost reads like a pacifist's manifesto. It is certainly a crie-de-coeur which is incomprehensible to her father, who becomes so enraged at her blasphemy and sacrilege that he pulls his dagger on her as though to give ultimate credence to his daughter's complaint. For basically Giselda's words are a direct frontal assault on her father's whole world view. If what she says is true – and we would today be far readier perhaps than the Italian patriots of the 19th century to accept the veracity of her denunciation – it renders all Arvino's life and striving futile.[37]

Giselda is to regain her beloved Oronte for, as it turns out, he was not killed at all but was just knocked to the ground. He thence determined to remain alive at all cost so that he might see his beloved again. But Giselda's faith is to be one of continuous frustration. Her time with Oronte is to be brief indeed, in fact only long enough to learn from him that he wishes, like his mother, to convert to the Christian faith and that he is passionately committed to their love to the extent that he is willing to elope with her (Act 3 Scene 1). Before they can elope however Oronte, in honour of his faith, must fight with the Crusades. In the fight he is mortally wounded and Giselda must endure his dying in her arms (Act 3 Scene 3). One can only sympathize with her when she cries out 'God of my fathers, now hear me! Thou didst take my mother from me and preserve me for days of distress . . . This love is the sole comfort for my sorrow – and Thou didst take it from me . . . How cruel!'

She is overheard by the Hermit who upbraids her for her blasphemy, but is genuinely compassionate towards her. Thus, at this critical moment of her life, she receives the living embodiment of the true Christian ethos, from the man who all her life she has been taught to revile as the basest of sinners. She is oblivious to the irony, since she does not recognize Pagano, but this fact speaks more eloquently for the values she hopes to discover in Christianity than any Crusade.

When she receives a vision in which Oronte appears to her and reassures her it is the final proof of the justice of her stance (Act 4 Scene 1). Yet Giselda is no pious prig; she wants to put her newfound enlightenment into practice, which she does when, in response to Oronte's prompting, she alerts the Crusaders to the proximity of the gushing fountain of Siloam. It would be too much to say that Giselda's happiness is complete when she witnesses the reunion of Arvino and Pagano, but at least it helps to make sense of the intense suffering that she has endured in her young life.

Il Giudice (A Judge) (*Un ballo in maschera*). See **Judge**

Giulietta (*Un giorno di regno*). Daughter of Baron **Kelbar**, in love with **Edoardo**, betrothed to Gasparo Antonio della Rocca, **Treasurer** of the States of Brittany.

The love affair of Giulietta and Edoardo invites comparisons with those of Almaviva/Rosina (*Il Barbiere di Siviglia*) and Norina/Ernesto (*Don Pasquale*), as well as Nannetta and Fenton in Verdi's last opera *Falstaff*. In

---

[36] Giselda's repeated reiterations that God does not will it are a direct reference to the cry, 'it is God's will' that went up at the Council of Claremont in 1095 when Pope Urban II summoned all Christians to the first Crusade. It became the rallying cry, thereafter, for all who would venture on Crusade.
[37] Solera was an opportunistic librettist who was always on the look out for tub-thumping sentiments to stir his audience. Verdi, however, was anything but opportunistic. He was a sincere patriot and champion of Italian independence, but he was above all a humanist who deplored violence, and while not overtly religious all his works overflow with a profound compassion for human suffering.

comedy it has always been obligatory to have a young love interest, especially young love thwarted by the procrastination of crotchety parent/guardians. Giulietta belongs squarely to this tradition, being a high spirited young lady who knows her own mind and is determined to have her own way, in spite of the fact that all the odds seem stacked against her. One thing is for sure, she will never allow the fuddy-duddy old Treasurer to take her into his bed.

On the morning of her wedding she is in despair when her attention is diverted by a chorus of peasants and servants who present her with gifts of fruits and flowers (Act 1 Scene 2). She can barely bring herself to be gracious. The peasants realize something is amiss and question her accordingly. It is all the prompting she needs to give vent to her frustration. The peasants are sympathetic but inevitably powerless to help. She is fortunate that both **Belfiore**, in his guise as the 'King', and the **Marchioness**, are aware of her predicament. Belfiore in particular makes full use of his newfound elevation in life to assist the young lovers by engaging the attention of the Baron and Treasurer so that Giulietta shall have time to converse in private with her beloved. The chance to be alone with Edoardo, even if only very briefly, is hugely appreciated by the young girl. She tells Edoardo that she is relying heavily on her cousin, the Marchioness, to extricate her from her marriage. At first the young lovers find the Marchioness somewhat preoccupied and unsympathetic to their pleas for help. However she soon pulls herself together and agrees to help in whatever way she can.

It is in fact Belfiore who comes to her rescue by ensuring that the Treasurer decides he no longer wants to marry her (see **Synopsis** Act 1 Scene 3). Giulietta can hardly contain her delight, much to the Baron's fury. When the Marchioness suggests that the best revenge on the Treasurer would be for Giulietta to marry the Treasurer's nephew, Edoardo, forthwith her joy is complete. The Baron is less happy, chiefly because Edoardo has no money. But the 'King' solves that problem as well, by insisting that the Treasurer give his nephew one of his castles and five thousand crowns per annum. With the whole universe, including the 'King', conspiring to ensure Giulietta's future, how can she fail to feel that the world is hers to command?

By Act 2 Scene 2 Giulietta is threatening to become obnoxious. She commands Edoardo to stay with her and refuses to listen to his proposal that since he is now the King's esquire he must accompany the monarch into battle. She is prepared if necessary to engage upon a collision course with the very man who has made it possible for her to be with Edoardo in the first place. It is the thoughtless arrogance of youth. Giulietta gets away with it because she manages to command with ineffable charm. She is probably just flexing her muscles; deep down she must recognize the perversity of the behaviour. For the moment all that matters to her is to be together with her beloved.

Belfiore champions the cause of Giulietta and Edoardo's love to the bitter end. Even when he has received the letter which releases him from his monarchical duties, he does not divulge the fact until he has insisted that Edoardo and Giulietta be married immediately (Act 2 Scene 3). Having ensured the Baron gives his permission to the match Belfiore cheerfully drops the charade.

It is to be hoped that the couple will live together 'happily ever after', though having seen Giulietta's behaviour at various stages of the drama, one may reserve a grain of sympathy for Edoardo.

Giuseppe (*La Traviata*). A servant employed by **Alfredo** and **Violetta** in their country retreat.

Giuseppe's very presence indicates that the lovers are making little concession to the total absence of income which characterises their idyll (money and the influence that it, or lack of it, has on people's lives is a major theme in *La Traviata*).

Act 2 Scene 1 Giuseppe enters with Violetta and **Annina**. He presents a letter to Violetta and then exits with Annina. Soon after he announces the arrival of **Germont** and then, at Violetta's bidding, ushers him in. Later he enters hurriedly to tell Alfredo that 'Madam has gone'. He is perplexed: 'What does it mean?' he mutters to himself. Violetta and Annina have clearly not apprised him of their plans. Alfredo, however, does not seem surprised by Violetta's departure, so Giuseppe must assume that all is in order. Events will prove him wrong. He will shortly be out of a job.

Godvino (*Aroldo*). A knight.

The role of Godvino is virtually unaltered from that of **Raffaele** in *Stiffelio*. Since he does not participate in the additional Act 4 no substantial alteration is made to his contribution to the main body of the opera. The reader is thus referred to the entry for **Raffaele**.

Doctor Grenvil (*La Traviata*)

The doctor is more than just a doctor to **Violetta,** he is a friend. This is evidenced by his presence at both Violetta's party (Act 1) and **Flora's** (Act 2). Indeed Violetta, during her final illness (Act 3), makes reference to what a good friend Doctor Grenvil is. When Grenvil has been summoned to the bedside of the ailing Violetta he quickly appraises the situation, namely that Violetta has very little time to live (Act 3). He tries to keep her spirits up, however, by assuring her she is well on the road to recovery. Violetta is not deceived. Grenvil tells **Annina** the truth. He is clearly devoted to Violetta and joins Annina and **Germont** in lamenting her passing in eloquent terms. It is doubtful if Grenvil would have taken any fee for his services, knowing as he does Violetta's straightened circumstances.

From a sociological point of view the doctor's presence is interesting because he is the only other 'working' person in the drama, aside from Violetta and Flora, the courtesans. All the other characters come from the moneyed upper classes and use the courtesans and doctor for their convenience. There is therefore an innate complicity between Violetta and the doctor. Both are equally helpless and unable to avert the inevitable.

Father Guardiano (*La Forza del Destino*). The Father Superior, or Abbot, of the Convent of our Lady of the Angels.

Guardiano is the representative of a reality beyond the petty blood feud that so blights the lives of the main protagonists in the opera. He provides safe haven for both **Don Alvaro** and **Leonora** from the avenging pursuit of **Don Carlo**. Guardiano receives word from Father Cleto (who does not appear in the opera) that he is sending to his convent a young woman who has been ostracized by her family and is in mortal danger. Since Guardiano presides over an assembly of monks it is a highly unusual request. Unlike **Melitone** Guardiano proves himself worthy of his calling, accepting Leonora into the convent and offering compassionate guidance.

In Act 2 Scene 1 Guardiano stipulates that Leonora should live apart from the monks in a hermit's cave. He himself will provide her with a frugal meal once a week. He calls the monks together and makes them swear an oath, on pain of excommunication, that they will never venture near the hermitage where Leonora resides.

Act 4 Scene 2 discovers Guardiano solemnly reading his breviary while Melitone grudgingly distributes alms to the poor. He has occasion to upbraid Melitone for his lack of charity. It is conceivable that Guardiano is witness to the scene between Don Alvaro and Don Carlo. It is not specified whether he knows Don Alvaro's true identity. Either way he would be curious about a visitor to the monastery.

Guardiano's appearance in the opera's final scene, supporting the mortally wounded Leonora, assures us that he has heard Leonora ringing the bell that he has left with her to ring should she be in danger or should her final hour have arrived. In the original version of the opera Guardiano can only watch with horror as Rafaele turns his back on the five years that he has devoted to the religious life and commits the heinous sin of suicide. In the revised edition he cautions Don Alvaro not to curse his fate but to humble himself. The opera closes with

Guardiano's assurance to Don Alvaro that Leonora has ascended to God.

The music with which Verdi imbues the character of Guardiano gives a depth and nobility to the character that is not otherwise evident from the text. He is no mere plaster saint but a genuinely holy man who appears as a paradigm of what a man may become if he renounces all worldly preoccupation. The alternatives, as represented by Don Carlo and Don Alvaro, Melitone and Trabucco *et al.*, each in their different ways is sufficiently pernicious to emphasize the desirability of striving after the level of detachment that Guardiano represents.

Gulnara (*Il Corsaro*). Odalisque in **Seid's** harem.

Where **Medora** is the prototype of the dying swan (with whom Byron, and by association Verdi, was evidently weary), Gulnara represents the vitality of life and energy that fights her own corner to the last, even though she faces apparently insuperable difficulties. Gulnara is the Pasha's favourite in his harem. But she cannot abide her master and dreams only of the day when she may escape. Whereas Medora is convinced that life contains nothing for her but tragedy, Gulnara allows herself to hope. Because the adversity has been thrust on her from without, rather than by the tyranny of her own emotions (as is the case with Medora) Gulnara allows herself to hope for a brighter future beyond the miseries of the present. This is the fundamental difference between the two women. Medora is trapped in the present; Gulnara lives and fights for the future.

Gulnara loves **Corrado** not so much for himself (she does not even know him) but for the fact that it is he who gives her the possibility of escaping from her plight. He puts himself at great personal peril in order to save her and the other odalisques. He endures the Pasha's derision for her sake. Most women might feel that being thrust from life in a Turkish harem into the clutches of a marauding pirate was a fairly wretched exchange. Not so Gulnara. She recognizes that Corrado, in spite of his illegal trade, is

a man of honour. He does not save her merely to enslave her further, but because he recognizes that she craves liberty from the Pasha's tyranny. Corrado's actions appear to be motivated entirely by chivalry. Naturally she cannot avoid feeling a degree of ambiguity toward him. Is he demon or god? she wonders. But she acknowledges that he has lit in her breast a 'flame of love such as Seid could never kindle' (Act 2 Scene 2).

Gulnara is not slow to see the opportunity offered to her. She pleads with Seid to spare Corrado (Act 3 Scene 1) but knows that her pleas fall on deaf ears. When Seid accuses her of loving the pirate and proceeds to threaten her with torture and death, Gulnara's natural independence of spirit asserts itself. She is enraged that Seid should treat her with such contempt and she determines on revenge. Deploying all her feminine wiles she bribes her way into the dungeons with the specific intention of effecting Corrado's release, and hopefully of securing from him some assurance of a return for her devotion (Act 3 Scene 2).

Gulnara is dismayed to learn from Corrado of his love for Medora. But it does not deflect her from her resolve. Unlike Corrado she has no qualms about wielding a 'treacherous dagger'. While Corrado bewails his fate and begs God to cut short his wretched life (in this moment he and Medora seem admirably suited to each other), Gulnara hastens to do what is necessary: despatch Seid. It is something she has been dreaming of all the interminable hours she has been the victim of his unwanted embraces. In truth this revenge is even more sweet to her than her freedom. Corrado is appalled. No woman that he has ever encountered, least of all his beloved Medora, would have even contemplated committing murder.

Gulnara is deeply disturbing to the equilibrium of Corrado's psyche. For Corrado has always tried to appease Medora, who requires only his beloved presence. She has no interest in his life or well-being except insofar as it affects herself. Their relationship is essentially passive. Gulnara, on the other hand, is a pro-active woman who knows what she wants, goes for it and gets it. It confuses Corrado that Gulnara claims she does it only for love of him. This is a burden Corrado could do without. Paradoxically Gulnara is every bit as demanding as Medora. She likewise requires Corrado's love and similarly refuses to be gainsaid. While Medora kills herself in order to bind herself to Corrado, Gulnara murders Seid in order to demonstrate her commitment.

When Gulnara is confronted with Medora herself, who is already dying, she has no hesitation in admitting her passion for Corrado (Act 3 Finale). She appears genuinely concerned for Medora, however, although one cannot help wondering if it does not secretly please her that she is to be rid of her rival. She gives no such indication, however, but instead prays that Medora shall carry to Heaven her tears of repentance.

When Corrado hurls himself into the sea she is suddenly bereft of the one person who has so far given her freedom meaning. However one need have few fears for Gulnara's future. She is eminently capable of fending for herself.

Gusmano (*Alzira*). Son of **Alvaro**, Governor of Peru.

Gusmano is the prototype of the man who will never be satisfied until he can have that which is unattainable to him. As such he epitomizes a central trait in human nature, one which Voltaire, the author of the play on which Verdi's opera is based, clearly saw could only be redeemed by the Christian ethic, not as propounded and dogmatized by the Catholic Church, but as originally propounded by Christ and reported in the Gospels. This is the central aim of Voltaire's play.

It follows that Gusmano is the central character in Verdi's opera. He is the one who, of all the characters, needs redemption. Gusmano pines after another man's betrothed. His desire has added piquancy because **Alzira** belongs to a race which, in his view, is inferior to his own. She is thus not only unattainable but unworthy. Nevertheless the pursuit of his personal desire is given political credibility by virtue of the fact that a treaty is sought with the Incas and his marriage to Alzira can thus be viewed as a political triumph. Gusmano's 'love' for Alzira belongs in the same bracket as that of Pagano for Viclinda (*I Lombardi*) and di Luna's for Leonora (*Il Trovatore*). His need originates from the same chronic sense of grievance which characterizes those stillborn affairs. Gusmano sets his sight on that which is most unattainable because only by surmounting the impossible will he assuage his need to cauterize his intrinsic sense of worthlessness. It therefore does not matter to him that Alzira remains alien to, and alienated from, him. Her antipathy only exacerbates his passion, as does the fact that she was previously betrothed to his arch enemy, **Zamoro**, whom he has but recently subjected to hideous torture before, as he thinks, condemning to execution. Gusmano does not realize – and it has to be admitted this stretches credibility – that Zamoro escapes execution. Nor does he realize that his own father owes his life to Zamoro's timely intervention when Alvaro was destined to die a miserable death. Believing Zamoro dead Gusmano assumes that all he has to contend with is Zamoro's baleful spirit.

It is one of Voltaire's central concerns in *Alzire* to show how the so-called civilized Spanish are in fact far more savage than the Savages. It is the Savage, Zamoro, who, on the first page of the libretto, introduces the motive of compassion by ordering the release of the elderly Alvaro, this in spite of the fact that he has been tortured and left for dead by the Spanish. Zamoro's action exemplifies the true challenge of the Christian ethic which, more often than not, requires that the adherent directly contravene his innermost desires and instincts. In the same way that Zamoro learns compassion, through having been on the receiving end of callous brutality, so Gusmano only learns the meaning of the concept when he has been fatally stabbed by Zamoro. In that moment he recognizes that he has truly deserved Zamoro's hatred. That Zamoro would have ideally 'turned the other cheek', renounced his desire for Alzira, and allowed the wedding to go ahead, is beside the point. Drama is not, and can never be, about Saints; for the Saint has succeeded in transcending his human, all-too-human limitations. In any case, had Zamoro 'turned the other cheek', it is doubtful whether Gusmano would have ever learnt the lesson which makes of his last moments on Earth a truly transforming experience.

Thus Voltaire succeeds in underlining, in the character of Gusmano, a central absurdity which characterizes all human existence. It is only when we are brought to crisis point that we realize our true potential. The absurdity is compounded by the fact that often what we think we most want is not actually what we really want. If it were, we should attain it. Gusmano does not really want Alzira, though he has convinced himself that he does. What he most needs is to be redeemed, in the same way that his father, Alvaro, object of Zamoro's compassionate intervention, has been redeemed from his own egotism. Gusmano's egotism is a burden to him, though he does not realize it.

In Act 1 Gusmano gives tacit acknowledgement to his unease when he says: 'whatever a man could ask for a benign heaven has offered me. It has covered me with glory, laid a world at my feet, but this does not satisfy my soul' (compare with **Monforte** [*I Vespri Siciliano*]). At this juncture in the drama he imagines that what his soul requires is Alzira. It is not. Alzira is merely an *image* of what it is that he desires. She, as an individual, is not the solution to his problems. He does not know her even to the extent that Alvaro (*La Forza del Destino*) knows Leonora or Manrico (*Il Trovatore*) his beloved. How could he?

Throughout world literature it is observable that most of the great love stories concern couples who are, more often than not, separated by an apparently insuperable divide. On a mundane level this simply emphasizes the transcendent nature of love. Psychologically, however, it underlines the fact that the love-emotion originates in a desire to conquer and assimilate that which is most alien, that which is most not the self. Only through such assimilation can the self expand beyond the narrow confines of its personal evolution and become truly a part of the universe it inhabits. The love stories of *Romeo and Juliet*, *Tristan and Isolde*, *Pelleas and Melisande* are not paradigmatic of normal human relations. This is underlined by the fact that they all – each and every one of them – inevitably result in the deaths of the two protagonists. As such they remain locked in the self-obsessed, self-defeating world of Eros. They do not realize their full potential which can only be to transcend the limitations of the personal ego. These relationships are metaphors for a psychic necessity. What Gusmano sees in Alzira is a potentiality for redemption from the sterility of his worldly self. Only when he has been fatally wounded does it come home to him that it was not Alzira for herself that he desired but what she represented.

Alzira belongs with the man for whom her need is as great as his need for her. When a man or a woman loves someone who does not in any way return that love, whose need is for something quite other than that which is offered or imposed, then the result can only be tragedy for the one who loves. For the 'love' is not love at all, but a projection of something the individual lacks within him or herself. Gusmano's soul is sick for lack of meaning content in his life. Nothing that he has done has stemmed from any inner necessity. He has always lived at the behest of his father's desires who, in his turn, has always worked at the behest of the Spanish empire and his king (synonymous with obeying the behest of his father). He has never individuated. One could say the same of Rodolfo (*Luisa Miller*), Francesco (*I Masnadieri*) and Alfredo (*La Traviata*), to mention only a few.

The death which Zamoro metes out to Gusmano is the greatest gift that he could have been given. For in the few moments remaining to him he discovers what it is he has lacked. By giving his blessing to the union of Zamoro and Alzira he tacitly acknowledges that life is not about the 'smash and grab' philosophy that has previously defined his existence, but about discovering, and then endeavouring to consolidate, a deep-rooted purpose beyond the pulling desires of the personal ego. His tragedy is easily identifiable: he only discovers that after which he searches when it is too late to integrate the revelation into his everyday life.

An Old Gypsy (Uno Zingaro) (*Il Trovatore*)
In Act 2 Scene 1 the old gypsy urges the other gypsies to make haste into town. Since the day is advancing they need to 'forage for their daily bread'.

H

Hélène (*Jerusalem*). Daughter of the **Count of Toulouse.**
The role of Hélène replaces that of **Giselda** in *I Lombardi*. The roles are, however, quite distinct from each other. Where Giselda discovers her love for **Oronte** through her captivity in **Acciano's** harem, Hélène knows where her love lies before she ever travels to Palestine, indeed before the action of the opera commences. The only cloud on her horizon is that her father may prevent her union with **Gaston**, since the Count was responsible for the death of Gaston's father. But since Gaston is willing to contemplate a rapprochement there can be no reason why her father should not relent. In the event the Count gives his blessing to the marriage and Hélène has every reason to be confident about her future. She has, however, reckoned without the perverse passion that her uncle, the Count's brother, **Roger**, harbours for her.

Once Roger's assassin has (mistakenly) tried to kill her father and Gaston has been accused of the crime all Hélène's dreams of happiness dissolve, for Gaston is outlawed and anathematized and there appears to be no possibility that she can ever be married to him.

Some time during the four years that elapse between Acts 1 and 2 Hélène is given to understand that Gaston has died. But when she arrives in Palestine with her father she is overjoyed to learn from **Raymond** that Gaston is still alive, though imprisoned by the **Emir** of Ramla. Hélène has never for a moment doubted her lover's innocence, and has nurtured her love for him during the years she has been separated from him. Her first thought is to see him somehow. It is more than probable that in order to do this she deliberately ensures that she is captured by the **Emir**.

In Act 2 Scene 2 the Emir is told that a Christian woman has been found in the town of Ramla. To have been just 'found' Hélène must have made herself conspicuous. Having been reunited with Gaston she finds a strength she has not known since last she was with her beloved. It is she that initiates their escape plan which is only foiled at the eleventh hour through bad luck.

Liberation soon arrives in the person of her father, who is leading the Crusaders' attack on Ramla. But the liberation is a two-edged sword. It only leads to further anguish for Hélène. Her father roundly denounces her for her renewed association with Gaston and sentences Gaston to be dishonoured and executed. Hélène cannot expect her father to share her conviction of Gaston's innocence. Roger's final act of revealing his guilt to his brother releases Hélène into a new possibility of life and happiness in the same way as her uncle's original perversity has blighted her young life. Unlike Giselda (*I Lombardi*), who must live out her days with only the memory of the love she enjoyed with Oronte, Hélène has a chance to live out her love with Gaston. This makes a much more satisfying conclusion to the opera, which in any case carries a redemptive message.

Herald (Un Araldo) (*La Battaglia di Legnano*)
The herald interrupts the crucial scene (Act 1 Scene 2) where **Rolando** introduces (or rather reintroduces, did he but know it) **Arrigo** to his wife, **Lida**. The herald brings news that Italian spies returning from the Alps have observed 'a mighty army of imperial troops' on the march. The **Consuls** have decreed that the captains and senators are to assemble. Rolando departs post-haste, leaving his wife at the mercy of Arrigo who is outraged that

Lida has married Rolando, when she had promised herself to him.

A Royal Herald (*Don Carlo*)

The herald appears in Act 3 Scene 2 on the steps of the church of Our Lady of Antioch in Madrid, prior to the *auto-da-fé* for which the population of Madrid has congregated in the square. The herald calls on the doors of the church to open and restore to the people their King. It is a purely ritualistic moment, underlining the fact that the King is given to the people solely through the Grace of God.

Herald (*Jerusalem*)

In Act 3 Scene 2, in the public square in Ramla where **Gaston** has been led to hear his final sentence from the **Papal Legate**, the herald is given the task of stripping Gaston of his armour, piece by piece. With each piece he calls out, for the benefit of the assembled crowd: 'Herewith the helmet – shield – sword – of a treacherous and ignoble knight'. Gaston cries out in despair, 'You lie!' but the herald has no mandate to parley with the prisoner. He merely does his job.

Herald (Araldo) (*Macbeth*)

Announces the Queen to **Macbeth** (Act 3) at the witches' cave. **Lady Macbeth** has followed her husband thence, eager to know the result of Macbeth's enquiries.

Herald (Araldo) (*Otello*)

The herald opens Act 3 of the opera by announcing the imminent arrival of the Venetian galley that is bringing the Ambassadors to Cypress. **Otello** then dismisses him.

The herald returns later in the Act, in company with **Lodovico**, **Roderigo** and other dignitaries of the Venetian Republic. He is despatched by Otello to bring **Cassio** to the Great Hall.

Don Frederico Herreros (*La Forza del Destino*). See **Don Alvaro**

High Priest of Baal (*Nabucco*)

The High Priest of Baal holds the equivalent position in the Babylonian hierarchy to

Zaccaria in that of the Hebrews. He is, however, only afforded a minimal role in comparison with that of Zaccaria. The latter has three major scenes and almost predominates over and above even the title role.

The High Priest of Baal appears in Act 2 Scenes 1 and 2 and Act 3 Scene 1. On each occasion his only thought seems to be for vengeance. It is not the vengeance of the Lord, as is the case with Zaccaria, but the petty vengeance of an egotistical man.

I

Iago (*Ernani*). De Silva's steward.

The character Iago in this opera has nothing in common with his more illustrious, or notorious, namesake in *Otello*. He is just another operatic steward, announcing the Royal Esquire, **Don Riccardo** in Act 1 and the arrival of the King in Act 2, and accompanying his master to the meeting place of the conspirators at Charlemagne's tomb in Act 3. He is noticeably vociferous in the latter scene, being obviously imbued with his master's hatred of the King. He does not accompany Silva in Act 4. One would not envy his position when Silva returns home having wreaked his vengeance, although in Hugo's play where de Silva commits suicide, Iago would have presumably been out of a job.

Iago (*Otello*). Otello's Ensign.

Iago is the epitome of the Machiavellian opportunist. Whereas in Shakespeare's play he is no more than this, Boito and Verdi, through the agency of his *credo*, elevate his iniquity to a Mefistofelien grandeur, with not just a political but also a metaphysical agenda. It is worth quoting Iago's *credo* because all his actions need to be understood in the light of his nihilistic philosophy:

'I believe in a cruel god who has created me in his image and whom, in anger, I name. From some vile germ, or base atom I am born. I am evil because I am a man and I feel the primeval slime in me. Yes!

This is my creed! I believe with a firm heart, as ever does the young widow praying before the altar, that whatever evil I think or do was decreed for me by fate. I believe that the honest man is just a jeering buffoon and both in his visage and in his heart that everything in him is a lie; tears, kisses, looks, sacrifices and honour. And I believe man to be the sport of an unjust fate from the germ of the cradle to the worm of the grave. And then? Death is nothingness. Heaven is an old wives' tale.' (Act 2)[38]

It does not take much adversity to instigate these sort of thoughts in a human being. The problem with all such thought processes is that they inevitably attract to the individual confirmation of his misanthropy. Very quickly he is convinced of the objective reality of his negative impulses. Being thus convinced, there is an immediate collapse of all sense of values and the growth of a conviction that the only real value is self-interest. Iago could be any human being who has experienced in his life some minor setback or other (was not Adolf Hitler a failed artist?). In Iago's case his lack of career advancement and his sense of being undervalued by those he serves has been the catalyst that has pushed him over the dividing line between passive misanthropy and active malevolence. His belief that 'I am evil because I am a man' is not something particular to him but a symptom of the entire human condition. His humanity is defined by his malevolence.

What makes Iago so dangerous is that he is an acute psychologist. His nerves are so stretched by the resentments that seethe within him that he can sense with almost preternatural sensitivity what motivates and afflicts those around him. Like attracts like, and Iago recognizes not the virtues of those around him, but always and only the flaws, the weakness at the core (as he would see it) of all human beings. He knows where **Otello** is most vulnerable; he knows where **Cassio** is most vulnerable; he knows where **Roderigo** is most vulnerable. And he knows he has nothing to fear from **Desdemona**'s essentially passive personality.

Iago bitterly resents Cassio's advancement over himself. His first action in the opera is to encourage a brawl between Roderigo and Cassio (Act 1). Cassio becomes so inflamed that he wounds **Montano**. Otello is so outraged that he demotes Cassio, as Iago intended he should. Having then encouraged Cassio to petition Desdemona, Iago ensures that Otello witnesses the two together and immediately commences dropping dark hints as to the nature of their relationship (Act 2). Desdemona inadvertently assists in promoting Iago's ends by incessantly pleading on Cassio's behalf. Iago insists his wife purloin a handkerchief which Otello has impatiently thrown aside when Desdemona attempts to soothe his brow with it (Act 2). The handkerchief has the same significance for Iago as would an item of personal property secured

---

[38] The best refutation of Iago's philosophy has been provided by Arnold Toynbee in his posthumous masterpiece: 'Mankind and Mother Earth'. In a chapter entitled 'The Biosphere' he writes: 'The progression of life has produced an ascending series of species only if we assess assent in terms of power. Mankind is the most potent species that has arisen so far, but mankind alone is evil. Human beings are unique in being able to be wicked, because they are unique in being conscious of what they are doing and in making deliberate choices . . . When a tiger satisfies his hunger by killing and eating his victim, he suffers no pangs of conscience. On the other hand, it would have been a purposeless and unnecessary and supremely wicked act if a god had created a tiger to prey upon the lamb and had created the human being to slay the tiger and had created the bacillus and the virus to maintain its species by killing human beings *en masse*. Thus, *at first glance* [author's italics], the progression of life looks evil – evil objectively, even if we discard the belief that this evil has been deliberately created by a god who, if he has done his work deliberately, must be more wicked than any human being has ever yet had the power to be. However, this first judgement on the consequences of the progression of life testifies that, besides the evil in the biosphere, there is a conscience in the biosphere which condemns and abhors what is evil. This conscience resides in Man'. The crucial phrase here is, 'at first glance'. Iago's philosophy is a knee-jerk response to what superficially appears to be the fact of evolution. It is the fact that he ignores the prompting of conscience that renders him ultimately ineffectual.

by a medieval witch or voodoo priest. It is an agent for the exercise of magical influence. Possession of the handkerchief is, for Iago, tantamount to having Desdemona and Cassio in his power. He probably does not realize at first what significance it holds for Otello. When this becomes apparent Iago must bless the instinct that insisted he steal it.

Knowing that Otello's ruling obsession is to obtain proof positive of Desdemona's infidelity, Iago enters upon the evidence for the prosecution at the first available opportunity. First he prepares the ground by telling Otello (*Era la notte*) how he has overheard Cassio in his sleep making love to Desdemona and sighing: 'I curse the fate that gave you to the Moor' (Act 2). According to Iago Cassio, in his sleep, imagines he is in bed with Desdemona and entwines his limbs with those of Iago ('And then sir, would he gripe and wring my hand'). By the end of Iago's narration Otello is in such an impassioned state that the mere mention of the handkerchief is enough to convince him, and leads straight into the oath of allegiance and vengeance that Otello and Iago swear together (*Si, pel ciel*). It is the moment (halfway through the drama) of supreme ascendancy for Iago. From now on he knows that, concomitant with his ascendancy, will be Otello's downfall.

Iago now arranges that Otello shall witness him in conversation with Cassio (Act 3). He will talk to Cassio about his mistress, Bianca, who has apparently jilted Cassio since he lost his captaincy. He will endeavour to convince Otello that they are talking about Desdemona. The *coup de grâce* comes when Iago persuades Cassio – which is not difficult since Cassio has no inkling of the deception being wrought by Iago – to produce the handkerchief from his doublet. This is finally the ocular proof that Otello has all along demanded. Iago can barely contain his delight. His music overflows with the insane jocularity that characterizes the finale of Verdi's *Falstaff*: (*tutto il mondo è burlo*). The same anarchic spirit pervades, though in the context of Otello's utter moral collapse, it takes on a singularly sinister overtone.

The scene with the Ambassadors from Venice, however, sees the inception of Iago's downfall (Act 3). When he learns that Otello is recalled to Venice and Cassio is to take over as governor of Cyprus he momentarily loses his self-control. But almost immediately his brain goes into overdrive. Iago knows that the only way to keep Otello in Cyprus is to kill Cassio. Otello is only too ready to agree that Cassio must die, believing as he does that Cassio is his cuckold. Iago leads him to believe that he will do the deed although he has no intention of thus exposing himself. Roderigo shall do the deed. It is not difficult to persuade Roderigo since the latter's only concern is that Desdemona shall not depart for Venice. Cassio's death will mean that Otello must remain in Cyprus. At the end of Act 3 Iago still *appears* invulnerable. As Otello, who has suffered a sort of epileptic seizure, lies prone on the ground Iago, 'with a gesture of triumph, placing his foot on the inert Otello', ironically cries: 'Ecco il Leone!' ('Here is the lion!') (Act 3). He has, however, played his last card.

Iago's undoing will be his wife who, in loyalty to her husband, has kept her silence, even in the face of overwhelming evidence that she is married to a monster. Confronted with the dying Desdemona Emilia can no longer restrain herself and reveals all (Act 4). Iago is forced to flee from **Lodovico** and his soldiers. Will he be caught? It is unlikely.

Iago would not hold up well to incarceration, inquisition and execution. Either he will escape entirely or commit suicide. He is no hero. He has made political ambition the centre of his existence. Thwarted, he has resorted, with a cynical disregard for all human feeling, to deceit and more deceit. He has consecrated himself to evil and so it is irrelevant whether or not he is brought to justice. His true punishment is the total failure of his plan for political ascendancy.

The horror at the heart of the tale of Otello – and this is undoubtedly what appealed to Verdi – is the fact that Iago proves terrifyingly efficacious. He may not achieve his own ends, but in unseating Otello and being avenged on all those above him in station (yet whom he considers his inferiors in intelligence) he could not have been more successful. The sad truth about Iago is that his perception that he is himself of superior intelligence is undoubtedly accurate. It is the fact that he has absorbed the political reality that superior intelligence is not necessarily a guarantee of upward mobility that leads him into crime. Ultimately it is a short cut which can only backfire on himself, as eventually it does.

The problem for Iago is that sixteenth-century society did not offer a man of Iago's peculiar temperament and abilities the range of opportunities on offer to his twentieth-century counterpart. Nowadays he would probably have flourished as an entrepreneur – excelling in the backroom politics of corporate finance where a relativistic moral stance is the *sine qua non* and where the qualities exhibited as vices in the drama of *Otello* would be viewed as positive virtues.

Imelda (*La Battaglia di Legnano*). Lida's maidservant.

Imelda is never far from Lida's side. She appears to be the perfect maid, and yet it is her lapse in accepting a bribe from **Marcovaldo** and surrendering to him Lida's letter that precipitates the whole ugly denouement of the opera (Act 3 Scene 3).

Imelda clearly knows of her mistress's simmering passion for **Arrigo**, for she brings the news of Arrigo's survival and imminent arrival with obvious alacrity (Act 1 Scene 2). As is the way with operatic maidservants Imelda loves nothing better than intrigue. It does, after all, alleviate the monotony of daily domestic chores. The bribe offered her by Marcovaldo must certainly have been substantial for her to consider accepting it. It is inconceivable otherwise that she would so grievously have betrayed her mistress's trust. More curious still is that she is at her mistress's side, as ever, in Act 4. Maybe she has redeemed herself by assisting her mistress in extricating herself from Arrigo's apartment, where Lida has been incarcerated by her raging husband (Act 3). Certainly Lida is grateful for the news that Arrigo survived

the leap from the balcony by which he made his escape.

Imelda is as overjoyed as any at the news of Italy's victory, but dismayed when it materializes that Arrigo has been mortally wounded. Whether Lida will retain Imelda may be open to question. **Rolando** himself may be less than happy to have his wife retain a maid who is willing to cooperate in clandestine transactions behind his back.

Imelda (*Oberto*). Confidante of **Cuniza**.

Imelda is witness to the extraordinary sea-change that overtakes her mistress, from blissful preparations for marriage to her beloved **Riccardo** to self-sacrificing protection of her rival in love, **Leonora**.

In Act 1 Scene 2 she joins Cuniza's other attendants in serenading her mistress (see **Chorus**). She may eavesdrop on the duet that ensues between Cuniza and Riccardo. She receives Leonora into the Salinguerra castle and, oblivious of the import of Leonora's visit, announces her to her mistress. She can only watch in dumb astonishment at what ensues and is forced to acknowledge that Cuniza's intended bridegroom has been guilty of dishonourable behaviour. Then, when Riccardo enters the scene she joins with the rest of the company in praying for a resolution to the imbroglio.

At the opening of Act 2 she announces Riccardo to her mistress. No doubt she behaves to Riccardo with the stiff impertinence that only a loyal handmaiden could display. She waits patiently while Cuniza gives vent to her grief then asks her mistress's instructions. She will be astounded at Cuniza's selflessness. Imelda accompanies Cuniza in the search for Riccardo and **Oberto** and the vain attempt to stop the duel. The women are too late to prevent the bloody outcome. Aware of the true compassion Cuniza feels towards Leonora, Imelda will be among those comforting the distraught woman at the close of the opera.

Ines (*Il Trovatore*). Leonora's maid.

Ines appears to be more of a companion than attendant. She is genuinely concerned about

Leonora's passion for **Manrico** (Act 1 Scene 2). 'You are nursing a dangerous flame', she says. Like **Ferrando**, in Act 1 Scene 1, Ines serves the important function of filling in the very considerable background information necessary to a comprehension of the plot. In Ines's case she is not the narrator, but the audience, as Leonora describes to her how she first became besotted with Manrico. Ines is in no way reassured by Leonora's explanation: 'a sad, but vague presentiment is stirred in me by this mysterious man', she comments. But it is useless for her to try and deflect Leonora from pursuing the fulfilment of her passion.

Ines's presentiments will prove to be justified, but not before Leonora has resolved, when convinced that Manrico has been killed, to enter a nunnery. This cause Ines no joy, as is revealed when she arrives at the convent in company with Leonora, weeping copiously (Act 2 Scene 2). She is horrified when **di Luna** appears, knowing as she does di Luna's violent passion and rage. But apparently she is content when Manrico suddenly arrives and claims Leonora for himself. She joins the nuns in commenting, 'heaven had mercy on you'. It is obvious that for all the women, including the nuns, taking the veil is considered the very last resort when all else in life has failed. Ines does not appear again in the opera.

The Grand Inquisitor (*Don Carlo*)

Theoretically the Inquisitor of Verdi's opera is Diego de Espinosa, one of two Inquisitors who held office during the period of the opera, although Espinosa was neither aged nor blind. In reality Philip was not nearly so in thrall to the Inquisitor as the opera appears to maintain, for it was he himself, not the Church, who appointed the Inquisitor and was responsible for the administration of the Inquisition. The Pope distrusted an institution with such an obviously political agenda. The Inquisitor automatically became a member of the Council of State and was thereby an important adviser to the King.

The Grand Inquisitor is referred to long before he appears in the opera. At the conclusion of Act 2 Scene 2 Philip warns Rodrigo to 'beware of the Inquisitor'. When Rodrigo questions him as to why he should beware of the Inquisitor Philip is evasive. But Rodrigo does not need to be told. He must know that his advocacy of the Flemish rebellion, which is principally fuelled by Protestant heretics, will automatically bring him to a head-on collision with the Catholic Church. It might seem strange that the Inquisitor does not appear in Act 3 Part 2 (the *auto-da-fé* scene) since the scene revolves around the impending burning of heretics. When he does appear, in Act 4 Part 1, it becomes clear why he has not appeared previously, for his confrontation with the King is the climax of the opera. Any previous appearance would have detracted from the impact of what can only be described as a clash of the Titans. Verdi's music underlines the brooding malevolence that characterizes the Inquisitor's mission to stamp out all heresy in the kingdom, and above all his determination to ensure that he always imposes his will.

Don Carlo is dominated by the dynamics of the father/son relation. Up until this moment it has been Philip whose presence has loomed ominously above the action. Suddenly, in this scene, Philip is toppled. His essential vulnerability has already been established in the preceding scene, first in his lonely soliloquy and then in his desperate confrontation with his wife. Now one is forcibly made aware that Philip, aside from his domestic difficulties, is not even autonomous in his kingdom. The Inquisitor behaves towards him exactly as he himself is prone to behave towards his son and to the members of his court, namely with thinly veiled contempt. The Inquisitor is old and blind – blinkered might be a better description. He has devoted his life to the preservation of Holy Mother Church. He is fanatical in his devotion and will not tolerate any threat to the Church's hegemony. He is therefore enraged when he learns that Philip is protecting an incipient heretic, that is Rodrigo. He is aware of Carlo's subversion but he does not take the Infante seriously.

He knows that Carlo is in thrall to Rodrigo. He takes Rodrigo very seriously indeed. Thus when Philip asks for his counsel regarding his son the Inquisitor is impatient. As far as he is concerned it is barely an issue. If Carlo is rebellious he should be expunged. After all, did God not sacrifice his Son in order to redeem the world?

When Philip attempts to indicate that, as far as he is concerned, the interview is at an end the Inquisitor is having none of it. He goes straight to the point: 'There is one who wishes to undermine the divine ediface. He is the King's friend, his constant companion, the demon of temptation, who spurs him on to ruin. Carlo's treason, which so enrages you, in comparison with his seems a futile sport'. When Philip lamely protests that he has sought out and found a friend, the Inquisitor is incredulous: 'Why have you the title of King if a lesser man can be your equal?' The Inquisitor has devoted his life to service and obedience. He has never allowed himself the luxury of a friend, let alone a wife, a son, a mistress and all the other worldly indulgences the King allows himself. Therefore he does not even attempt to conceal his contempt for Philip's specious reasoning. 'I demand of you the Marquis de Posa', he declares. When Philip refuses point blank he threatens the King with being summoned himself before the Inquisition. Kings must learn their place in the order of things. Above and beyond all Creation is God, then there is the Church, responsible for propagating and protecting God's word on earth, and only thereafter come kingdoms and powers. In the Inquisitor's eyes Philip evokes the shade of Samuel (Samuel abhorred the way in which Saul, the first King of Israel, assumed priestly prerogatives and disobeyed divine ordinances). The Inquisitor departs from the King's apartments in high dudgeon.

As it turns out he does not need to wait for Philip to hand Rodrigo over to him. Rodrigo himself ensures the Inquisition is given ample justification for warranting his assassination. Presumably alerted by the reverberations of the insurrection demanding the Infante's release (Act 4 Part 2), the Inquisitor is on hand at the prison where Philip is fighting a losing battle to assert his authority over the mob. There can be no clearer indication of the Church's easy superiority than in the mob's instant submission when the Inquisitor appears. All fall to their knees in terror.

At the conclusion of the opera (Act 5) the Inquisitor accompanies the King to the cloisters at San Yuste, there finally to take in hand the rebellious Infante. But in this he is cheated. Like it or not there is a power beyond that of Mother Church and even Inquisitors require the occasional timely reminder of their mortal status (see **Synopsis** and **Friar**).

Isaure (*Jerusalem*). Companion to **Hélène**. In *I Lombardi* Giselda does not have a companion; she has her mother, Viclinda. Isaure takes the place of Giselda's mother. Viclinda plays a crucial role in the unfolding of *I Lombardi* for it is she who is the object of Pagano's thwarted passion. Since in *Jerusalem* Hélène herself has the dubious honour of being the object of thwarted passion (her uncle, **Roger**) it became necessary, when reworking the libretto, to introduce a companion for Hélène specifically for the opening scene (Act 1 Scene 2 in *I Lombardi*) where Hélène kneels in prayer. In *I Lombardi* this is an effective scene for mother and daughter, though the motivation for kneeling in prayer is entirely different. There, mother and daughter have just been warned by Arvino of impending danger. In *Jerusalem* Hélène pleads with Isaure to join her in praying for **Gaston**, that is, for the successful outcome of Gaston's forthcoming bid to acquire Hélène's hand in marriage.

A companion is perhaps more suitable for a love-sick young girl than a mother. Hélène will need all the strength a young girl can muster to cope with the trials that the years to come have in store for her (see **Hélène**). Isaure travels to Palestine with Hélène (Act 2 Scene 1) but thereafter fades from the main action, only reappearing in the final scene where she is on hand to witness her friend's reunion with Gaston, who is finally exonerated of all guilt.

Isis (*Aida*).

Sister and bride to Osiris, daughter of Geb and Nut, and mother to Horus. Isis is the ideal wife and mother. She is also believed to be a powerful enchantress. She therefore represents a powerful symbol of the feminine archetype, especially in its nutritive aspect. For when Osiris was murdered violently by his brother, also her brother, Seth, she ensured his regeneration by piecing together the scattered remnants of his dismembered body.

There is a symmetry and logic about the Egyptian pantheon of gods which is profoundly satisfying. In a very real sense Verdi's life work could be seen as embodying the dynamics encapsulated in the pantheon, particularly in relation to the rival brothers, Osiris and Seth (see *Il Trovatore*, *I Lombardi* and *I Masnadieri*). Osiris taught humankind the arts of agriculture and civilization. He was a wise and just ruler. In psychological terms he can be equated with the ego, which must die if the self is to achieve fulfilment. His rival brother, motivated principally by jealousy, tricked and murdered Osiris and then persecuted his wife, Isis and her young son, Horus, who was to inherit his father's mantle and to become identified with the reigning Pharaohs in Egypt.

If Osiris represents ego, Seth represents alter-ego, the shadow aspect of the god. He became known as the lord of misrule and chaos, the god of storms. He also exemplified a forceful sexuality. The relation between Osiris and Seth can be equated with that of Apollo and Dionysius, in Greek legend. The Greeks in fact identified Apollo not with Osiris but with his son, Horus. It makes little difference either way. Horus represents legitimacy, by which order is maintained in the world. He also combines within himself antinomies (the sun and the moon were his eyes) thereby maintaining a balance, and equilibrium in the world. Seth's role is as crucial, and ultimately as fruitful, as the parts played by Osiris and his son. For without the destruction and havoc that he purveys there would be no possibility of regeneration or rebirth; there would only be stasis. There

would also be no possibility of generation, or regeneration, without the critical role played by Isis. Inevitably a time will come when Seth, by necessity, must prevail and it is at those moments that Isis intervenes. Through her entirely selfless devotion and intuitive wisdom she literally succeeds in piecing together the shattered remnants of civilization when war and dissent wreak havoc. At these times lover and enchantress become mother, both in her nutritive and matriarchal aspects.

Ismaele (*Nabucco*). Nephew of Sedecia, King of Jerusalem.

While Zedekiah is an historical figure – who does not appear in the opera – his nephew, Ismaele, is an invention of Solera's, as is his beloved **Fenena, Nabucco's** daughter. Solera undoubtedly created the characters in order to supply a love interest, mandatory in Italian opera at that time. But also, and more importantly from the point of view of dramatic structure, he needed a focus for the conflict of cultures and a possibility of breaching the apparently unbreachable gulf between the Babylonians and Hebrews. The only way to effect this was through a Romeo and Juliet style love relation between individuals from the opposing nations. Solera also manages to include a love triangle by having Fenena's sister, **Abigaille**, also in love with Ismaele, though her love is not returned. Abigaille's love is more an expression of her insane jealousy of, and rivalry with, her 'sister' than any intrinsic passion for Ismaele.

Before the action of the opera Ismaele has been sent to Babylon by his father as Ambassador to Judah. There he has fallen in love with Fenena and been imprisoned by Nabucco, presumably because Nabucco became aware of his daughter's infatuation. He escaped with Fenena's assistance and returned to Jerusalem. It is not long before he meets again with Fenena, but this time their roles are reversed. Fenena has been taken hostage by the Hebrews, as the Babylonians threaten to invade Jerusalem.

Ismaele earns universal contempt from his countrymen when he intervenes at the moment **Zaccaria** threatens to stab Fenena in response to Nabucco's deliberate blasphemy (Act 1). His action is seen as nothing less than blatant treachery, for Fenena was the only bargaining tool possessed by the Hebrews in their battle with Nabucco. However it should be added that had Zaccaria actually succeeded in stabbing Fenena it is more than probable that Nabucco, in his rage, would have slain all the Hebrews present, including Zaccaria. It never occurs to the anguished Hebrews that Ismaele might in fact have saved their lives.

The full venom of the Hebrews' vitriol only falls on him when Ismaele comes to summon them to witness Fenena's adoption into the Jewish faith (Act 2 Scene 2). Giving him no chance to defend himself they hurl curses at him. One senses that he is only saved from being stoned to death by the arrival of Zaccaria's sister, **Anna**, quickly followed by the pontiff himself.

No sooner is Ismaele reconciled with his people than he learns that Nabucco is 'dead'. The people call for Abigaille and hence Fenena's situation becomes ever more precarious. Ismaele's fears for her are confirmed when she is taken prisoner and condemned to death, unwittingly, by her own father who has been duped by Abigaille into signing a death warrant for all the Hebrews (Act 3 Scene 1). If Abigaille hopes that she may thus be able to blackmail Ismaele into giving himself to her in exchange for Fenena's life she is sadly mistaken. There is no indication that Ismaele even requests an audience with her. In fact nothing more is heard of Ismaele until the final pages of the opera when Fenena has been saved from her fate by Nabucco's restoration to sanity and resumption of his authority.

This curious omission provides the interpreter of the role with an interesting challenge. He must decide for himself what course of action Ismaele takes through the crucial period of his beloved's imminent execution. His demeanour at the scene of Fenena's martyrdom (Act 4 Scene 2) should give eloquent testimony to his anguish and subsequently his relief when Fenena is reprieved. In this last he has no opportunity to express himself, only joining the rest of the assembly in giving thanks to God. The assumption must be that by this stage the drama has evolved far beyond the feelings of the individual protagonists who have served as no more than a temporary focus for the far greater issues being worked out through the struggle of the two mighty belief systems: Judaism and the idol worship of the Babylonians.

Count Ivrea (*Un giorno di regno*). Military Commander of Brest, betrothed to be married to the **Marchesa di Poggio**.
The Count only appears in the very final scene of the opera, though he is referred to throughout. When he does appear he has very little to say for himself. In the true tradition of comedy, where everything is exaggerated, the Count will probably be suitably decrepit, in order to contrast with the Cavaliere **Belfiore**, who is the hero of the opera, and the Marchioness's true love.

As the Count enters (Act 2 Scene 3) he is in conversation with Baron **Kelbar** who reassures him that the Marchioness has changed completely. She 'no longer thinks of that madman; she hates him as much as she loved him'. This would seem to indicate Ivrea knows that the Marchioness's affections lie, or have lain, elsewhere. It is also possible that the Baron refers to the Marchioness's first husband. It is more than likely that the Marquis would have been known to the Count, coming as he does from the same exclusive echelon of society.

Ivrea appears to be overawed in the presence of the Marchioness, readily agreeing to accept whatever condition she may place on their marriage. 'Command me Madam', he says. Unfortunately for him the condition she places, namely that Belfiore should not return within the hour, is nullified when Belfiore returns immediately (the Marchioness has no doubt seen Belfiore coming when she places the condition). Everybody, except the Marchioness, assumes that the man that enters is the King, and for the time being the Marchioness continues the charade by proclaiming her hopes that the 'King' can be present at her wedding. But the 'King' has come to announce that he has to depart forthwith on a 'secret state mission' and the Count is to accompany him immediately.

The Count is not amused. Worse is to come. Belfiore receives a missive which at last enables him to reveal his true identity and he and the Marchioness are happily reunited. The Count has no opportunity to vent his spleen because the opera is now over, and he must join the **Treasurer** and Baron in agreeing 'let us be men of good cheer, and agree to hold our tongues'.

J

JERUSALEM

French version of *I Lombardi*. Libretto by Alphonse Royer and Gustav Vaäz, based on Solera's libretto.

First performance 26 November 1847 at the Paris Opera.

Cast:
The Count of Toulouse (baritone)
Roger: his brother (bass)
Hélène: the Count's daughter (soprano)
Isaure: her companion (soprano)
A soldier (bass)
Adhemar de Monteil: Papal Legate (bass)
Gaston: Viscount of Béarn (tenor)
Raymond: Gaston's steward (tenor)
The Emir of Ramla (bass)
The Emir's officer (tenor)
A herald (bass)

Time: 1095–1099
Place: Toulouse, Palestine

Synopsis
Act 1 A gallery connecting the Count of Toulouse's palace and his chapel. It is the early hours of the morning. Gaston, Viscount of Béarn is taking his leave of Hélène. He assures her that he will attempt to effect a reconciliation with her father, who was responsible for killing his father. Gaston will

put aside his grievances if only the Count will grant him Hélène's hand in marriage (*Adieu, mon bien aimé*). Gaston leaves and Isaure enters. Aware of Hélène's distress Isaure kneels with her in prayer (*Vierge Marie*). The women leave the stage, which now becomes gradually suffused with light as the sun rises. The gallery fills with lords and ladies, who enter variously, singing in celebration of the conclusion of civil war.

The Count enters, together with Gaston and Roger. The knights are assembling in readiness to set forth on a Crusade to the Holy Land. The Count magnanimously offers Gaston peace and furthermore confirms his blessing on Gaston and Hélène's union. All celebrate the new accord, not least the young lovers. There is only one who refrains from rejoicing and that is the Count's brother, Roger, who in spite of the fact that she is his niece, is passionately in love with Hélène. Oblivious to his brother's perverse passion the Count has thoughts only for the forthcoming Crusade. The Papal Legate announces that the Pope has decreed that the Count should be the leader of the French Crusaders. The Count's first act as leader is to invest Gaston with the white cloak which was to become a distinctive feature of the Crusading knights' apparel. A servant removes the Count's cloak and places it around Gaston's shoulders. Gaston joyously swears his allegiance. The scene concludes as all think with eager anticipation of the moment when they shall take possession of Jerusalem (*Cité du Seigneur!*). An organ sounds from the chapel, calling everyone to a recollection of their holy duty, all that is except Roger who can only think of his love for Hélène (*Oh! dans l'ombre, dans le mystère*).

Roger has employed a mercenary soldier who now appears and receives instructions to seek out 'two knights dressed in golden armour (the Count and Gaston) and to kill the one *not* wearing a white cloak (Gaston) (Roger has not been present in the previous scene and does not realize that his brother has given his cloak to Gaston). The lords, ladies and nobles continue to sing of their eager anticipation of the holy battles ahead.

Roger remains disinterested and calls, Iago-like, on the spirit of evil to assist his enterprise.

Cries of 'Murder!' are shortly heard from within the chapel. Then Gaston rushes in, thus immediately confirming that Roger's assassin has murdered the wrong man (the Count). This is immediately confirmed as the Count, wounded, descends the steps of the chapel, supported by knights who accompany him to his apartments. The soldier responsible loses no time in accusing Gaston of being responsible for the crime. Nobody questions his version of events, since the knights have in any case doubted the sincerity of Gaston's reconciliation with the Count. All join in excoriating the murderer (*Sur ton front est lancè l'anathême*).

The Papal legate sentences Gaston to exile and is then joined by the entire assembly in pronouncing anathema on him. Roger is consumed with remorse for his crime.

Act 2 Scene 1 The mountains of Ramla in Palestine. For three years Roger has wandered in search of redemption for his sins and finally he has ended up in Palestine where (like **Pagano** in *I Lombardi*) he lives as a hermit in the mountains. Also like Pagano, Roger has established a reputation for exceptional holiness. He has made a secret vow to himself that he will die only when he has assisted the Crusaders in reclaiming the Holy Sepulchre from the Muslims. Never for a moment does he cease reflecting on his crime and praying for forgiveness.

When the curtain rises Roger is kneeling in front of a Cross outside his cave (*O jour fatal! Ô crime!*). Gaston's esquire, Raymond, enters. He has been in the desert for many days without water and is dying of thirst. He tells the hermit that he is but one of many pilgrims in a similar plight. Roger rushes to the pilgrims' assistance.

Hélène enters. She has travelled to Palestine with her father who, it now materializes, was not mortally wounded by Roger's assassin as was originally thought. Hélène believes Gaston to be dead. But she now learns from Raymond that Gaston is in fact alive but has been taken prisoner by the Emir of Ramla. She is overjoyed that he still lives (*Quelle*

ivresse! Bonheur suprême!) and rushes off to search for her beloved.

The pilgrims come into view. They are weak from lack of water (*O mon Dieu! ta parole est donc vaine!*). A lively march announces the imminent arrival of the army of Crusaders, at the head of which is the Count of Toulouse. The Crusaders have come to obtain the hermit's blessing on their endeavour. Roger is naturally astounded to see his brother alive. The Count does not, however, recognize Roger. For Roger, this is the moment he has been awaiting, the moment when he can assist the Crusaders in helping to defeat the Muslims and thus atone for his crimes. He declares his intention of accompanying them into battle and joins in a triumphalist chorus which concludes the scene (*Le Seigneur nous promet la victoire*).

Act 2 Scene 2 A room in the palace of the Emir of Ramla. Gaston, a prisoner of the Emir, reflects on his great love for Hélène (*Je veux encor entendre*). The Emir appears. He has heard that a Christian girl has been found in the town of Ramla. The identity of the girl is soon revealed for Hélène is brought in. The officer is all for cutting her head off forthwith, but the Emir is curious. He decides the best way to discover for himself her identity is to leave her alone with Gaston. In spite of their desperate circumstances the pair are ecstatic at being reunited. They swear to be true to each other whatever fate may bring. Hélène suggests a means of escape. She knows that the Crusaders are about to attack the town. The Emir's officers will thus be distracted. Why not take advantage of the tumult to make their getaway? They are about to implement her plan but are forestalled by the Emir's guards who quickly surround the couple.

Act 3 Scene 1 The gardens of the Emir's harem at Ramla. The Crusaders have occupied the town and most of the palace. But the Emir is holding Hélène hostage in his harem. The odalisques dance a four-piece ballet (see **Appendix: ballets**) by the conclusion of which the Crusaders have arrived at the gates of the harem. Hélène prays for deliverance. Gaston appears at her side just as the

Crusaders come storming through the gates, with the Count at their head. Catching sight of his daughter in the company of the man he assumes to be responsible for the attempt on his life four years earlier the Count denounces his daughter. Hélène defiantly protests her lover's innocence and invokes God's vengeance on those – including her father – who unjustly accuse him (this contrasts markedly with Giselda's outpouring in *I Lombardi*, which is not in defence of her lover but a generalized condemnation of the whole Crusading enterprise) (*Non... votre rage*). Incensed, the Count drags her away.

Act 3 Scene 2 A public square in Ramla. Gaston is led in to the strains of a solemn funeral dirge. He has been condemned to death for his supposed crimes. The papal legate announces that he is to be executed under the walls of Jerusalem. But first he is to be stripped of all his honours. Gaston pleads for mercy (*O mes amis, mes frères d'armes*), but to no avail. A herald strips him of his armour, piece by piece, denouncing Gaston the while as a traitorous and disloyal knight. Gaston, despairing, protests his innocence, but the knights merely repeat their maledictions on him. Meanwhile penitents intone a Latin psalm.

The scene sustains a powerful intensity, which prefigures that of **Radames**'s trial in *Aida*. Gaston desperately demands that he be granted immediate execution, since he has no fears and is confident that he can stand proudly before God in knowledge of his innocence (*Frapper bourreaux*).

Act 4 Scene 1 On the edge of the Crusaders' camp in the valley of Jehoshoaphat. Roger is regarding with emotion the valley in which lies the city of Jerusalem, the object of his quest for atonement. The Crusaders are preparing for their final assault on the city and invoke God's assistance in their sacred endeavour. The legate requests that the hermit attend the last moments of a knight condemned to die. The knight is, of course, Roger's rival, Gaston.

The Crusaders move on. Hélène is amongst them and remains behind to take a final farewell of her beloved. Roger thus finds himself confronted with the two people who have had the most critical influence on his destiny. In spite of his trepidation he gives Gaston God's blessing. Gaston's main concern is that he appears destined to die without first having been able to fight the infidels. Roger takes pity on him and, presenting him with a sword, tells Gaston to sally forth with the Crusaders and capture the Holy Sepulchre. Gaston joyfully takes the sword and, together with the hermit, makes off towards the city, there to join with the Crusaders.

Act 4 Scene 2 The Count of Toulouse's tent. The battle for Jerusalem has been won. The Count enters, accompanied by various knights, all bearing the Muslim standards which they have captured. Amongst the knights is one who keeps his visor down, yet who has fought valiantly in the battle and was the first to raise the Crusaders' flag in the Holy City. When the Count requires to know his name Gaston responds, 'You have vilified it. Destroy the sword and lead me to my execution!' At this moment Roger enters. He is mortally wounded and has only one thought in his dying moments, to achieve reparation for his sins. He tells the Count 'You must not punish an innocent man for a crime that I committed, I, Roger, your own brother'. He implores his brother to forgive him so that he may die, shriven. The Count relents and grants Roger his forgiveness before granting the latter's final request; that the flaps of the tent should be turned back so that Roger may see the Crusaders' flag flying in the breeze over Jerusalem. Thus Roger can die at peace as the curtain falls.

As will be seen from the above, the plot of *I Lombardi* was radically altered for the French version, even though the general psychological outline was preserved. Unlike the case of *Stiffelio/Aroldo* where the revision indubitably resulted in a loss of dramatic coherence, it can be said with confidence that in the case of *Jérusalem* there is only gain in this respect. Where *I Lombardi* provides a fascinating patchwork of episodes and imbroglios, *Jérusalem* succeeds in pulling together many of the disparate threads, removing a great deal that is superfluous and generally focusing the attention with much more consistency on the two central issues, namely the love of Gaston and Hélène, and the search for spiritual redemption of the flawed, though eminently human character of Roger. In addition Verdi made several distinct improvements to the score, although it is not within the scope of this study to elaborate on this aspect (readers are referred to Osborne, Budden and Grove).

It would be too much to say that *Jérusalem* should replace *I Lombardi*, which has a charm all of its own, but certainly it should take an honoured place alongside it in the repertoire. It is incomprehensible to the author that the work is only rarely performed and virtually unobtainable in score or on disc. The only available recordings are pirate recordings (see Discography) and these come without libretto. One can only assume that the overt nature of the subject matter is considered by opera managements and record companies politically too sensitive to warrant exposure

Joan of Arc. See **Giovanna d'Arco** (*Giovanna d'arco*)

Jorg (*Aroldo*). **Aroldo**'s servant.
In *Stiffelio* the character of Jorg plays a critical part in the drama, fulfilling the role taken in *Aroldo* by **Briano**. In *Aroldo* his part is supplanted by that of Briano, Aroldo's spiritual father-confessor.

Jorg is merely Aroldo's servant and is not even afforded a singing role. He is summoned only once in the opera, Act 3 Scene 1, when Aroldo is interviewing **Godvino** and tells Jorg to fetch **Mina** to him.

Jorg (*Stiffelio*). An elderly minister.
When the opera opens it might appear that one is in the presence of an Old Testament prophet. Jorg is alone on the stage, declaiming in thunderous tones upon the merits of the Holy Book and exhorting **Stiffelio** (who is not present) to 'go forth; May your words

be a destroying tempest, a devouring wave, a blasting thunderbolt for God's enemies upon this earth!'

Jorg is Stiffelio's mentor; an elderly preacher who has devoted his life to God and considers himself blessed to have found a young man to take up his mantle and spread the Word with all the passion and fervour of youth that has now deserted him. He is at Stiffelio's side at almost every crucial moment in the drama. He is never explicit but it is probable that he could wish Stiffelio was not married. He appears to accept the grief that Stiffelio suffers because of his wife's infidelity as the inevitable price for associating with the weaker sex. He is by nature puritanical. When he attends the celebrations for Stiffelio's return (Act 1 Scene 2) he does so unwillingly and with bad grace: 'I shun the joys of this world', he says. When Stiffelio points out that the celebrations are in his, Stiffelio's, honour, Jorg's dour reply is, 'I leave them to the profane for they hold perils and snares for a man's honour'. He assuredly feels the same about women, **Lina**'s infidelity and the surrounding imbroglio can do nothing to persuade him to alter his outlook.

When Stiffelio is at his lowest ebb, having just discovered that **Raffaele** is his wife's seducer, Jorg is at hand to call him back to his 'right mind' and remind him of his responsibility to his congregation (Act 2). It is Jorg who first alerts Stiffelio to his wife's clandestine affair (Act 1). He also aggravates the situation by mistaking the identity of the co-respondent, thinking it to be **Federico di Frengel** who just happened to be in the wrong place at the wrong time. The fact that he is prepared to leap to conclusions and point an accusing finger without sufficient substance to his allegations seems to indicate that Jorg does well to be wary of commerce with other human beings. He is certainly not immune to human frailties.

It is Jorg who delivers Raffaele into Stiffelio's hands (Act 3 Scene 1). Presumably he assumes that Stiffelio wants to give Raffaele the opportunity to make an honest woman of Lina. He may well have been delighted had the divorce gone through and

Stiffelio become free to devote himself exclusively to God. As it turns out Raffaele is summarily executed by the outraged **Stankar**. It would have been better for Raffaele had Jorg not intervened.

In the concluding scene of the opera (Act 3 Scene 2) Jorg is unclear as to Stiffelio's precise intentions. Had he been in Stiffelio's shoes at the church he would no doubt have delivered a 'fire and brimstone' sermon, publicly humiliating Lina.

However, in the circumstances, he cannot fail to be moved by Stiffelio's exemplary exhibition of Christian compassion when he publicly forgives Lina. Jorg is an essential pillar of the Ahasuerian community and a bedrock of support to Stiffelio.
(See also **Briano** (*Aroldo*).)

A Judge (Il Giudice) (*Un ballo in maschera*) The Judge's sole function in the drama is to present to **Riccardo**, the Governor, the indictment against **Ulrica** (Act 1 Scene 1). He makes the mistake of telling Riccardo that Ulrica attracts the worst sort of people to her cavern and is suspected of being in league with the devil. Riccardo is immediately intrigued and refuses to heed the Judge's recommendation that Ulrica should be banished forthwith. Had the Judge's counsel been heeded the outcome of the opera might have been very different.

K

Baron Kelbar (*Un giorno di regno*). Uncle to the **Marchesa di Poggio**, father to **Giulietta**. The action of the opera takes place in Baron Kelbar's castle. The Baron has arrived at a critical crossroads in his life; he imagines he has engineered a perfect (perfect from his perspective that is) marriage for his daughter, Giulietta, to Gasparo Antonio della Rocca, the State **Treasurer**. He has also engineered what he imagines to be a perfect match between his niece, the Marchesa di Poggio, for whom he clearly feels responsible, and Count **Ivrea**. He will be confounded on both counts.

Neither his daughter nor his niece wish to marry the men he has lined up for them, and he will discover it is more than his life is worth to force them against their will. He has also reckoned without the wiles of the man his niece truly loves, **Belfiore**, who just happens to have been appointed to act as substitute for the King. The Baron however has no idea that Belfiore is not the real King (he has obviously never met either Belfiore or the King), although he does know that the Marchioness has been besotted with 'some madman'.

The Baron thinks he has the extraordinary honour of entertaining the real King, and this honour makes his happiness complete. He hopes that the 'King' will be present for the double wedding that he plans. Thus it is that when the Treasurer tells him that he will not be marrying Giulietta he is completely nonplussed, and very soon apoplectic (Act 1 Scene 3). It is an unpardonable affront to his honour, and for a man like the Baron that is tantamount to treason. He can only assume the Treasurer has lost his mind. 'Have you gone mad?' he asks him. The Baron has no patience with equivocations. He demands, 'What! you reject my daughter?' The Treasurer protests, 'I am not rejecting her'. The Baron concludes, 'then you accept her'. His mind turns to his noble ancestors, he feels the blood rushing through his head, at which point he loses all self-control and lurches at the Treasurer. Luckily for the Treasurer the whole household, including the 'King', intervene to restrain him (Act 1 Finale).

However, the Baron cannot let the matter drop. It churns in his mind and aggravates his spleen. So at the first opportunity he tackles the Treasurer again and demands satisfaction. 'I will devour you like an egg', he declares (Act 2 Scene 1). When the Treasurer starts recommending alternative ways of fighting a duel the Baron only sees evidence of the Treasurer's cowardice and dilettantism. Finally, out of patience he declares that he will venture no further 'in weapons' with him (which is exactly what the Treasurer had hoped he would say) and further declares that he will have the Treasurer chastised 'with a cane' by his servants. He thereby salves his wounded pride with the thought that the Treasurer is no better than a dog.

In any case, he must now turn his attention to the remaining wedding, that of the Marchioness and Count Ivrea, whose arrival is imminent (Act 2 Scene 3). It does not even occur to him that this marriage might go the same way as that of his daughter. When the Marchioness declares that she will marry the Count so long as Belfiore does not return within the hour he feels quite confident that there will be no hitch for, as far as he is concerned, Belfiore is safely in Paris. When the 'King' enters he sees no reason for concern, but then the 'King' announces that the wedding cannot go ahead since he needs to take the Count with him on important business. This bombshell is quickly followed by the King's decree that Giulietta should marry **Edoardo**. The Baron, being a man who knows his place in the order of things (that is, the social order, there being no other as far as he is concerned), can do nothing about this. If the King decrees it, it is as good as a divine ordinance. But the real bombshell is still to come. Having achieved, with almost indecent haste, the Baron's permission to Giulietta and Edoardo's marriage, the 'King' turns out to be not the King at all, but the Chevalier Belfiore.

It is surprising that the Baron does not run him through with his sword on the spot, but this is not a tragedy, this is comedy, and all must live happily together ever after. The Baron must shrug his shoulders, reflect 'you cannot win 'em all', and join the others in asserting 'let us be men of good cheer and agree to hold our tongues'. It would be surprising if this expression of *bonhomie* did not cost him a little effort.

King of Egypt (*Aida*)

The King of Egypt, as portrayed in Verdi's opera,[39] is little more than a figurehead,

answerable in all things to the Priesthood, headed by Ramfis. (For further discussion of the role of religion in political life in ancient Egypt see **Ramfis**.)

At the opening of the opera Ramfis tells **Radames** that he must inform the King of the Deity's decree. Ramfis is the mouthpiece of the Deity's decree and it is the King's job to see that the Deity's decree is carried out in the material world. Thus the King is, in fact, third in the pecking order of rule. First come the gods, then Ramfis as the gods' emissary and figurehead of the priesthood, and only then comes the King. (There is a precise parallel to this in *Don Carlo*, where the King is answerable to the Inquisition, which in turn is supposedly answerable to God.) What the King can and cannot do is severely circumscribed from above. (It is this fact which makes all the more extraordinary the revolution effected by the Pharaoh, Akhenaten (c1379–1362 BC), who virtually displaced the whole pantheon of Egyptian gods and their priests, setting himself up as the mouthpiece of the one divinity, Aten. It is also hardly surprising that the Pharaohs who came after and no doubt bowed to pressure from the outraged priesthood, did everything in their power to obliterate all evidence that Akhenaten had ever lived, let alone reigned over them.)

In Act 1 Scene 1 the King has summoned the people together to exhort them to take up arms against the Ethiopians and to appoint Radames Commander-in-Chief over the armies. By Act 2 he knows that the battle is won and is celebrating victory (Act 2 Scene 2). He is willing to entertain clemency towards the Ethiopian prisoners, but he comes up against the priesthood who vehemently protest that the prisoners should be executed. However, he is saved from an embarrassing climb-down when Radames (having reminded the King that he had promised Radames, should he return victorious, to ask whatever he wished for), demands that the Ethiopians

---

[39] This depiction of the King bears scant comparison with the actual Egyptian Pharaohs who, from the time of the new kingdom (c1500 BC), were themselves the chief mediators between the gods and Man, and were believed to become

gods themselves. Hence the fact that their mummies were always fashioned in the form of Osiris, with plaited beard, crook and flail.

be given their freedom. Ramfis realizes that a compromise will have to be reached and stipulates that **Aida** and her father, who nobody, least of all the King, knows to be the Ethiopian King, should remain as hostages while the rest of the prisoners are released. The King announces, 'I yield to your good counsel', though he must know that he has little option. To contradict Ramfis would be tantamount to taking issue with the gods themselves, an unthinkable affront. As it turns out the priest's caution will prove to be all too well founded.

Thereafter the King does not reappear. The trial and conviction of Radames for treason is left entirely in the jurisdiction of the priesthood. An offence against the State was an offence not just against the King but, by association, against the priests and gods they represented. The King's political impotence is nowhere better illustrated than by his absence in the second half of the opera. The one apparently autonomous act for which the King is responsible is the offering of his daughter's hand in marriage to Radames. Unfortunately this is, as far as Radames is concerned, an unwanted gift. The last thing he desires is the King's daughter. The gesture at least affords **Amneris** a few moments of joy, but precipitates the crisis which leads to Radames's downfall. In real terms the possibility of being admitted to the ruling dynasty and thus succeeding to the throne is the only worthwhile gift the King has to offer. However, even if Radames were in love with Amneris it is doubtful whether he would truly wish to exchange his eminently pro-active role as Commander-in-Chief of the armies for the merely figurehead role of Pharaoh.

Knights of Death (I Cavalieri della Morte)
(*La Battaglia di Legnano*)
Appear in Act 3 Scene 1 of the opera when, in a dark and sombre ritual, they admit **Arrigo** into their midst.

The Knights of Death are a specially formed group of fighters who have taken an oath to die in defence of their country rather than be captured. When the knights ask

Arrigo what is his wish, Arrigo replies, 'to die with you, or triumph with you'. The knights decide that Arrigo is worthy to be included amongst their number and proceed with the ceremony of initiation (see **Synopsis**).

In Act 3 Scene 3 Arrigo is imprisoned by **Rolando** in a room high up in the tower of the castle. Arrigo, knowing that if he fails to join his comrades he will be breaking his oath and branded a coward and deserter, fit only for eternal damnation, in desperation flings himself from the balcony.

The next time Arrigo appears he is being borne in on a stretcher, carried by a squadron of the Knights of Death (Act 4). Arrigo has survived his fall from the tower and rejoined his confederates in time to take part in the Battle of Legnano in which he has distinguished himself. However he has been mortally wounded. He asks the Knights to lay him down on the steps of the church, which the Knights duly do and then respectfully withdraw a short distance. Thus they are on hand to witness Arrigo's reconciliation with Rolando and the latter's forgiveness of **Lida**. (See also **Chorus**.)

L

Lady Macbeth (*Macbeth*). Wife of **Macbeth**. **Background Note** The historical Lady Macbeth (c1005–c1054), whose first name was Gruoch, was the granddaughter of Kenneth III, a Scottish king, murdered in 1005, 36 years before the play begins. Macbeth was her second husband. By her first husband she bore a son, Lulach, who succeeded briefly to the throne after Macbeth's murder but was quickly dethroned by Malcolm. Gruoch's royal lineage undoubtedly assisted Macbeth's claim to the throne, but there is no evidence that she took any part in persuading him to pursue this claim, as in the play and the opera.

If any one of Verdi's characters was to be singled out as epitomizing the destructive power of the feminine, it would be Lady

Macbeth. Of course the creation of this character was not Verdi's, nor his librettists, Piave and Maffei, but Shakespeare's. The librettists managed to retain the essential outline of the character, but in order fully to understand the character with all its rich complexities it is necessary to study the play.

Verdi effected an operatic revolution with Lady Macbeth's very first entrance by having her speak, as opposed to sing, the words of a letter she has just received from her husband. Thus he announces at the outset that this is no ordinary leading role for an operatic soprano. The part is, above all, a dramatic creation and can only be successfully projected by a singing actress. In a famous letter Verdi wrote, in a high state of alarm, to Salvatore Cammarano, who was producing *Macbeth* in Naples, concerning the casting of one Madame Tadolini in the role of Lady Macbeth:

'Madame Tadolini, I believe, is to sing Lady Macbeth, and I am astonished that she should have undertaken the part. You know how highly I regard Madame Tadolini, and so does she, but for the sake of us all I feel I must say that her qualities are too fine for this role. This may sound absurd, but Madame Tadolini is a handsome woman with a beautiful face, and I want Lady Macbeth to be ugly and evil. Madame Tadolini sings to perfection, and I don't want Lady Macbeth to sing at all. Madame Tadolini has the voice of an angel, and Lady Macbeth's should be that of a devil . . . the most important numbers in the opera are the duet between Macbeth and Lady Macbeth and the Sleep-walking scene. If these two numbers fail, then the entire opera will fail. And these two numbers definitely must not be sung. They must be acted and declaimed, with hollow, masked voices. Otherwise it will make no effect.'

Lady Macbeth is essentially a voluptuary. She revels in the joys and sensations of material wealth, power and success. She does not know the meaning of the word self-denial. In no way does she sacrifice her own happiness for her husband's career – quite the reverse. She lives only for the reflected glory that her husband's ascendancy may afford her, and woe betide him if, in any particular, he falls short. She is aware that Macbeth is possessed of an essential nobility of nature and she instinctively realizes that it falls to her to make up in ruthlessness what he lacks. For a time she is terrifyingly efficacious. She only ceases to be so when she recognizes the futility of attempting to alter the course of nature, and when the violence she does to her own nature finally takes its revenge. For Lady Macbeth attempts to outstrip her husband, and all men, in the masculine aggression that she sees as the only means of achieving worldly ascendancy. As she famously declares in Shakespeare's play she would gladly 'dash (her baby's) brains out'[40] if the fulfilment of her ambition required it. Such an image causes such instant revulsion that it is difficult, in the theatre, to empathize or sympathize with her predicament, even when she finally loses her wits at the play's conclusion. In the more generalized expression of opera there is not quite the same alienating affect, although her relentless bullying of her husband is clearly delineated.

Lady Macbeth's crime is not so much against Macbeth, Duncan and the world at large, but against herself. Macbeth and Duncan have made their choices: Macbeth by marrying such a woman, Duncan by taking kingship upon himself with all its attendant perils. It could be said that the witches' prophecy introduces an element of fatalism and inevitability into the tale which weakens the relevance of the drama to contemporary mores. For within the matrix of the fatalistic determinism which pervades, it is firmly established that neither Lady Macbeth nor anybody else in the drama ever had a chance. All the characters are merely obeying predetermined laws whereby the murders of Duncan and Banquo at the hand of Macbeth, and Macbeth's demise at the hand of Malcolm, can be seen as inevitable, but the events are only predetermined insofar

---

40 See Shakespeare's *Macbeth*, Act 2 Scene 7.

as the principal protagonists accept as legitimate the terms of reference within which the witches propound their prophecies. Were Lady Macbeth alive today it would be quite unnecessary to postulate infernal powers as the inspiration of her fiendish career. If all reference to infernal powers is removed *Macbeth* becomes a very modern drama indeed. For in the character of Lady Macbeth Shakespeare portrays the very essence of the animus-ridden woman whose intrinsic femininity finally takes revenge in madness and death.

The extent to which Lady Macbeth forces herself against her natural instincts becomes explicit in her aria *La luce langue* (Act 2 Scene 1) where Verdi's music makes it abundantly clear that she views with dread the inevitability of fresh crimes piling on crime: 'Nuovo delitto!' ('A new crime!') – the hesitation is only momentary, but unmistakable. She dismisses it immediately with the declaration: 'E necessario! E necessario!' (It is necessary! It is necessary!) Necessary to whom? The only necessity lies in her, and her husband's, continued immunity to justice. Lady Macbeth has attained what she has always dreamed of, the throne of Scotland, and what she has discovered – too late – is that it is not the panacea for all ills. The voluptuous pleasure that she so craves and anticipates eludes her. Why? Because it is something she has wilfully expropriated with barely a pretence at legitimacy. Her conscience (something on which she had not calculated), goes into overdrive. Unlike her husband she refuses to pay heed. She attempts to obliterate it. But it will not be obliterated. It erupts when she is asleep and off guard.

All her life Lady Macbeth has dissembled because all her life her aims have been illegitimate. She does not love Macbeth; she needs him. He suits the purposes of her ravening ego. Macbeth's feeling for his wife far outstretches hers for him because he is the one who acknowledges his dependency. Their marriage, like all marriages, is a mutual dependency, but because it is rooted in a fundamentally negative *Weltenschaung* the

bond which binds them is a thousand-fold stronger than that which binds the average married couple. For they are two against the world and very quickly they have only each other. However, when they have murdered Duncan and apparently evaded justice, they discover, too late, that they no longer even have each other because, inevitably, each blames the other. There is a real poignancy in the moment when Lady Macbeth asks her husband why he continuously avoids her (Act 2 Scene 1). Suddenly, at the moment when she has attained the apex of her ambitions – the Scottish throne – she is alone, more alone than she has ever been. She has never had to cope with having to be alone. Alone she is nothing. She finds that there is no longer any *raison d'être* to her life.

Where now to go? If she dreamed of mad Dionysian revels in the royal castle she is sadly mistaken. The man who has achieved her ends for her has become not just disinterested, but actively hostile. Without Macbeth to bully, who is she? All her married life her one motivation has been to activate her husband, to goad his fundamentally philosophic temperament into action. Deprived of a focus for her formidable energies, she crumples. Too late she realizes the absurdity of her existence.

Her death-knell is sounded when she hears from Macbeth how he has witnessed a vision of Banquo's descendants ascending the Scottish throne (Act 3). Not only does this emphasize the futility of their enterprise, but it makes her cruelly aware of her self-imposed sterility. From a purely biological point of view sterility is synonymous with worthlessness. For most human beings this need not mean that the individual is not capable of achieving fulfilment through other means. But for Lady Macbeth it is at the moment she ascends the Scottish throne with her husband that she achieves her dearest ambition. There is no other reason for her to exist other than to propagate the lineage of Macbeth. Since she has deliberately denied her femininity in order to obtain the throne in the first place she is in a double blind. Never has the old adage, 'You cannot have your cake and eat it', been more applicable than in the case of the Macbeths. Lady Macbeth dies, quite simply, from lack of any reason to go on living.

Laura (*Luisa Miller*). Peasant girl, friend of Luisa.

It is safe to assume that Laura has been Luisa's closest friend throughout their childhood. Her only concern throughout is for her friend's well-being and she is with Luisa at each crucial turning point in the drama.

At the opening of the opera Laura is at the forefront of the villagers who are celebrating Luisa's birthday. In Act 1 Scene 3 Laura joins with the villagers in expressing their horror when Luisa is reviled by Count **Walter**. Their relief is immense when Walter rescinds his order to put Luisa and her father in chains. It is Laura who has to bear the news to Luisa that her father has been arrested (Act 2 Scene 1). At the beginning of Act 3 Laura's distress is great as she witnesses her friend pining away, having lost all hope of betrothal to her beloved. Laura tries in vain to persuade Luisa to take some food and she does the best she can to protect Luisa, particularly when Luisa wants to know what transpires in the church (Act 3 Scene 1). Laura tells a white lie, 'The Count is inaugurating his new seignior', since she knows that the truth, namely that the wedding of **Rodolfo** and **Frederica** is in progress, would kill her friend.

The presence of Laura and the other villagers throughout the drama underlines the cultural gap between Luisa and her father on the one hand and all the other main protagonists, including Rodolfo, on the other. In typical Romantic fashion the country folk compare very favourably with the nobility, demonstrating warmth and compassion where their opposite numbers appear cold and calculating.

Leo (*Attila*). Bishop of Rome.
Historical Note Leo 1 (the Great: c390–466, Pope 440–461). One of only two Popes to be called 'the Great'. He summoned the Council of Chalcedon in 451 where he achieved acceptance of his definition of the

Incarnation. The following year, the period in which the opera is set, Leo made a treaty with Attila, thus saving Rome from devastation by the Hun. In the opera Leo appears as Bishop of Rome before he has become the Pope.

The future Pope Leo appears in a dream to **Attila** and warns him against continuing his campaign against Rome. In his aria, *Mentre gonfiarso l'anima* (Act 1 Scene 2) Attila tells **Uldino** of his fearful dream and the Prelate's precise words: 'Thou art appointed a scourge only against mankind. Withdraw! The path is barred; this is the territory of the gods'. Assuming it was but a dream Attila determines to ignore the dream's message. He is all the more appalled, therefore, when he is confronted by the very same priest who appeared in his dream and who proceeds to enunciate the very same words with the same intonation that he already has imprinted on his memory (Act 1 Scene 3). It is a moment of supernatural terror which leaves Attila aghast. For the first time he is at a loss in front of his own warriors, who are nonplussed at the sight of their usually brazen leader rendered witless.

Leo does not reappear in the opera, but this one appearance is pivotal and should be taken by a singer who can match the force of Attila's own enunciation, since the phrases he sings exactly echo those at the climax of Attila's great aria.

Donna Leonora di Vargas (*La Forza del Destino*). Daughter of the **Marchese di Calatrava**.

The action of *La Forza del Destino* is so disparate that it is useful to chart Leonora's place in the action. It may not otherwise be immediately clear how she achieves the transition from doting daughter to anguished penitent.

Act 1 Scene 1 Leonora has returned home to her father's house in order to escape the attentions of the 'unworthy foreigner', **Don Alvaro** – or so her father would like to believe. Certainly Leonora appears to be torn between her love for her father and her love for Don Alvaro. She has just overcome her scruples to elope with Don Alvaro when her father accosts the pair and is accidentally killed by Alvaro. Leonora is traumatized and flees with Don Alvaro, almost in spite of herself. In the affray accompanying their flight she becomes separated from Don Alvaro. Disguised as a man she takes refuge soon after in an Inn at Hornachuelos (Act 2 Scene 1), only to discover her brother is staying there disguised as a student and in pursuit of her. Like Don Alvaro, after his thwarted duel with Don **Carlo**, Leonora realizes that her only recourse can be to the cloister. From one Father Cleto, who does not appear in the opera, to whom she tells her whole story, she gains a letter of recommendation to the Father Superior, **Guardiano**, of the Convent of our Lady of the Angels. Guardiano offers her refuge. She is to live apart from the monks in a hermit's cave. He will ensure that she is provided with one frugal meal each week. Leonora hopes to find in Guardiano the same sense of hope and repose that Don Alvaro had hoped to find in Leonora.

The scene of Leonora's acceptance into the monastery (Act 2 Scene 2) represents for Leonora a monumental reconciliation. Rejected by her own family she is embraced by an altogether more universal family. The mid-point of the opera sees the heroine reborn.

Five years elapse and Leonora is still tormented by dreams of her lost beloved. Her great scena, *Pace, pace, mio Dio* (Act 4 Scene 2) is one of the most evocative scenes in the opera, and not only through the force of Verdi's music. When the scene opens the sun is setting and the moon emerging. Leonora should only appear on stage when the sun has entirely disappeared and the scene is illuminated purely by moonlight. Leonora does not emerge into the sunlight. The sunlight world is the world previously inhabited by her father and still inhabited by her brother. She has never found a niche for herself in this world. Indeed it has only brought her grief and guilt. She has refused any longer to participate and now inhabits only that realm which holds no terrors for her and in which she can feel perfectly at home.

An equation between Leonora and the moon is surely intentional. She has taken on a man's garb in a male fraternity, yet she remains a woman who can only reveal her true identity under cover of darkness. The fact remains that, whether comfortable or not, whether harassed in the daylight world or concealed in the womb of night, Leonora remains in an invidious position. Initially unable to make the break away from the father she has been forcibly wrenched from his purview only to find herself prevented from making a commitment to her lover. She is in limbo. She does not truly exist. How can she? She can only commune with the moon, a symbol that so exemplifies her own remoteness from the world and her self-imposed chastity. Five years is a long time to withdraw from the world but the heart does not count the minutes. It would make little difference to Leonora if it were fifty years. For her, time has stood still since that hideous night when her lover accidentally murdered her father and she became an outcast from society. She has no more made a commitment to the religious life than if she had entered herself into a brothel. If she had been prepared to offer her life to God she would have entered a Convent. Her consciousness of sin will not allow it. Even if it did her emotional stagnation would make a mockery of it. There is only one thing now that she values, and that is her solitude, the solitude in which to nurture her grief.

Leonora is oblivious to the fact that Don Alvaro has taken refuge in the same monastery as herself under the pseudonym of Father Raffaele. When he comes hammering at her door she is appalled, even though initially unaware that it is he. For five years she has not set eyes on another human being. When confronted by Don Alvaro in a monk's habit, confessing that he has just killed her brother, who seeks confession, she is initially quite unable to grasp the situation. She rushes to the stricken body of her brother. Carlo's last act on recognizing Leonora is to mortally wound her. With her dying breath Leonora promises to intercede at the throne of God on Alvaro's behalf. There in the Promised Land they will be united.

One senses that for Leonora death is indeed a blessed relief. There is no difference in this between the original and revised endings of the opera, except that in the original the duel between Carlo and Don Alvaro happens on stage so that when Leonora goes to the dying Carlo her own demise is witnessed by the audience. In the revised version she is stabbed off-stage.

Leonora's central predicament lies in her inability to sever the ties that bind her to her father. When it comes to the moment of leaving the parental home in order to be united with her beloved Alvaro she is overcome with apprehension. On the evidence of the events in Act 1 Scene 1 she is far from ready to respond to the challenge. She is thoroughly confused, torn between her need to remain in the obscure, bounded world of her childhood, under the close scrutiny and care of her father and her need to launch herself into a life of risk and insecurity. (The penalties for not taking the plunge have been immortalized in the poetry of Emily Dickinson.) The sad truth that must inevitably remain with Leonora ever after is that her prevarication cost her father his life. Certainly she is haunted by her father's curse on her. It almost seems as though she wills a confrontation between her father and her lover. It could be argued that she needs Alvaro to kill her father in order to liberate herself. More to the point she needs somebody else to make a resolution that she finds impossible to make.

Leonora lives in an excessively patriarchal society where it is taken for granted that the individual's needs are entirely subservient to the concept of family honour. Her brother clearly takes on the mantle of her father in defending the di Vargas honour. In this father and son only obey the social codes of the culture and times in which they lived. But it is, as the opera demonstrates, to the chronic detriment of the individual's personal development. The men remain locked in their narrow interpretation of events while Leonora remains tormented by what she is forced to concede is her abiding guilt.

Guardiano represents for Leonora the caring father figure she never had. But it does not prevent her from being tormented by memories of her lost love. In real terms it may seem absurd that Alvaro enters himself into the very same monastery in which Leonora has taken refuge. But thematically it makes perfect sense, for Alvaro will always be immanent within her as she in him. There is exceptional dramatic justice in the fact that she is united with Alvaro just at the very moment that both he and she herself independently have given vent to the most intense despair. Only such an excess of passion could break the stalemate that has pertained in their lives these past five years. The opera may belong to Don Alvaro, but Leonora's predicament echoes and confirms it. She is as much in exile as Don Alvaro and her route from loving daughter to social outcast to religious penitent exactly parallels that of her lover.

Leonora (*Oberto*). Oberto's daughter.
Like **Gilda (*Rigoletto*)**, Leonora is a notably passive personality. No man, in spite of her strongest desires, supplants her father in her affections. In her character Verdi endorses a prototype of the suffering heroine which he will never hereafter entirely abandon, although the precise circumstance of the woman's anguish will differ from opera to opera in terms of both degree and circumstance.[41] To this woman is revealed a possibility of both immanence and transcendence through the abandonment of self in the other. Her entire sense of meaning in life becomes focused on the commitment of the loved one.

In Verdi's operas it is usually the case that the woman is held in the stranglehold of a father's love. The love of her seducer becomes at one and the same time a consummation

---

[41] This operatic prototype was perhaps most effectively established in the character of Donna Elvira in Mozart's *Don Giovanni* about whom Kierkegaard wrote so eloquently (see Kierkegaard's *Either/Or*).

and release from that overpowering presence which she carries with her. Unable to disassociate herself from the emotional parameters of the experience she cannot fathom the true nature of the experience. She can only assume that her seducer is the sole originator of her release. She will thus either pursue him to the ends of the earth or, abandoning all hope of redemption, believe she has been guilty of cardinal sin and give herself into the protective embrace of a nunnery.

Leonora is abandoned by **Riccardo**, who then seeks out a more politically astute marriage. She goes in pursuit, ostensibly because Society – and her father – demand that she restore her lost honour, but in reality because that is all that she can do. The alternatives given to her by her father, either to compel Riccardo to make an honest woman of her or to die, are in fact the only options she herself can contemplate. When she is confronted by her father in the enemy camp of the Salinguerra family, she is at first mortally afraid (Act 1 Scene 1). This is the first time that she has been face to face with him since her disgrace. That her seducer is her father's arch enemy, who has only just defeated him in battle, confounds her anguish (and her father's fury – the parallel with **Aida**'s predicament hardly needs underlining). Once Leonora has acceded to Oberto's demand that she repair the irreparable she briefly experiences the bliss of his embrace: 'Secure in my father's embrace my strength is greater', she declares.

Leonora empathizes with **Cuniza**'s suffering for it is a mirror of her own recent suffering (Act 1 Scene 2). If at a base level it gives her any pleasure to destroy the relationship which has so blatantly usurped her own she maintains a facade of sympathetic concern. She is pitiless, however, when face to face with Riccardo. Her only concern is to shame him. In the morality which pertained for centuries prior to our own, once a woman had given herself she was not only 'possessed', but was herself in possession. Riccardo has flouted not one, but two rules of civilized behaviour between the sexes. That Cuniza is prepared to be merciful must be irksome

to her, as it certainly is to her father. Despite all her rage she has to admit that she still loves Riccardo. In other words she *needs* Riccardo. From the moment that she discovered the power conferred by Eros she cannot be without him. For Eros is an addiction as much as alcohol or drugs. Sexual passion confers a heightening of consciousness beyond anything a young girl such as Leonora could previously have experienced.

When Cuniza compels Riccardo to return to his first love, Leonora can only exult. She has won a double victory. She has both flouted the supreme hegemony of the father and at the same time won his approval through reducing her lover to a state of ignominy. If the relationship had endured its future would not have been a happy one. But it is unnecessary for us to speculate on a future which is not granted them. The wild wrath of the father will only be appeased by blood letting. Riccardo, shamed as he is by the 'tender maidens', is only too happy to submit. It is indicative of Leonora's naivety that she does not suspect the improbability of the men accepting her and Cuniza's glib manipulation of events.

When Leonora next sees her father he is lying, a corpse, in his own blood (Act 2 Scene 2). She suffers an extremity of anguish and is forced to acknowledge herself as culpable. When Riccardo's letter is read out declaring his self-imposed exile and begging forgiveness she is scornful. Confronted with the reality of the destruction she has wrought on her father Riccardo has become an irrelevance. When she first fell in love with Riccardo she no doubt convinced herself that her love was purely a matter of being attracted to a dashing young man. But can we really suppose that somewhere within her there was not a little corner that revelled in the fact that she was surrendering herself to her father's most vehement enemy? For did not her father abandon her to go and fight this man? Is it not a sweet revenge to be lying in that man's arms? But once that man has killed her father the sweetness of her revenge has evaporated and she is left only with a huge and abiding sense of guilt. Oberto decreed that she must either seek redress or die for her sin. By declaring her intention to enter a convent she is finally compelled to accept the latter option.

Leonora (*Il Trovatore*). Lady-in-Waiting to the Princess of Aragon.

On her first entrance (Act 1 Scene 2) Leonora tells her maid, **Ines**, that her love for **Manrico** took root at the moment that she awarded him the victor's wreath at a tournament. Manrico was an unknown contestant. In the young girl's imagination he is therefore the angel whose advent presents the possibility for her of escaping from the aimlessness of her life. The fact that he is the victor gives her confidence that her fate will be safe in his hands.[42]

Ines is stirred by a 'sad but vague presentiment' by Leonora's determination to prosecute her love for Manrico. Her concern is the natural concern of the conservative minded for anything that is unproven or beyond the orbit of everyday experience. Leonora cannot be dissuaded. She knows that her fate is irrevocably bound up with that of the unknown troubadour. When she descends into the garden she is as confused as Eboli in Act 3 Scene 1 in *Don Carlo*, caught in the darkness between two opposing polarities. Whereas Eboli does not know what she wants, Leonora knows precisely and is only momentarily deceived by **di Luna's** more

---

[42] The motive of the unknown knight winning the tournament and carrying off the girl is of course endemic in tales of Arthurian legend and medieval chivalry. It is enshrined in Wagner's *Die Meistersinger von Nürnberg*, although there the contest of physical prowess has become sublimated into one of artistic attainment. The aim remains the same: to find the one who is the most eligible and worthy to be granted the ultimate prize. Leonora's will to sacrifice herself bears comparison with Senta in Wagner's *Der Fliegende Holländer* and many other Romantic heroines. *Il Trovatore*, more than any other of Verdi's operas, belongs to the land of myth and archetype which partly explains its enduring fascination. Manrico and Leonora will never be united from any sense of mutual identification but rather through separation and adversity, both of which destroy any ambiguity and confirm their passion.

immediate and desperate presence. Were Leonora to choose di Luna she would have elected for the path of social respectability and inevitable stultification. There must be a small part of her that would welcome the simplicity of such a resolution, but it is only a very small part. Her true path lies in the darkness and potential for chaos represented by the Troubadour's anguished voice. Manrico's need for her is so much more intense than di Luna's. Instinctively she must recognize this.

When Leonora believes Manrico has been killed something dies inside her. For in that moment she has lost any hope of redemption from the meaningless of her existence. Because her love for Manrico is a love from afar, a love that is fuelled by an ideal, it has no object other than to worship. Retiring to a convent is therefore an entirely logical step for her to take. It is for this reason that for a young girl in fifteenth-century Spain the urge to enter a convent was almost a knee-jerk reaction to unrequited love. Leonora can have no hope that Manrico will come to her rescue at the eleventh hour. That di Luna appears is almost an inevitability. She is certainly not interested in being rescued by di Luna. But the appearance of Manrico is little short of a miracle for her. His apparent resurrection from the dead can only confirm her apprehension of him as her saviour. Manrico gains ascendancy by virtue of the fact that he is now perceived by Leonora and di Luna, who believe him dead, to be the resurrected god (in the case of Leonora) or fiend (in the case of di Luna). From this moment it is no longer necessary for Leonora to devote herself to an abstraction, for now she has before her the incarnation itself.

Leonora does not know Manrico either personally or, in the Biblical sense, physically. He is as remote from her as God the Father. Her language confirms the equation: 'Have you come down from Heaven? Or am I in Heaven with you?' Di Luna, meanwhile, has become for her a tiresome irrelevance, and only incidentally, when he draws his sword, a terrifying threat to the consummation of her love. She departs with Manrico convinced that if he has not come from Heaven she must have been transported thence.

Leonora is now to be married to the man of her dreams, yet the realization of her dreams is fraught with danger. 'What a grim light shines on our wedding', she reflects (Act 3 Scene 4). Manrico consoles her with the thought that even if he should die his last thought will be for her. It is small consolation for a young girl on the eve of her wedding. But Manrico's love and need for her is so immense that she allows herself to be comforted as the organ is heard within the chapel summoning her to 'the joys of a chaste love'. This is the distinction between the separate loves of di Luna and Manrico. Di Luna is primarily motivated by lust and anger, whereas Manrico loves her as an icon.

Paradoxically Manrico's passion is all reserved for his mother – who is not his mother at all. As word arrives that **Azucena** is in grave peril Manrico, summoning more passion than he has shown in the entire opera, rushes off to rescue her. What are Leonora's feelings when Manrico tells her that Azucena is his mother? For a gentlewoman to marry the son of a gypsy would be almost unheard of. Yet Leonora has always known that Manrico's origins were murky. It can make little difference to her at this juncture, other than the desperation that she might lose her beloved in his quest to save his mother. 'I cannot bear these grievous blows... How much better it would be to die!' she declares. Death-longings suffuse the opera. Leonora and Manrico have this in common with Tristan and Isolde. Like that other pair of doomed lovers from Chivalric Romance they are creatures of the night who long for nothing so much as the bliss of unconsciousness.

By Act 4 Scene 1, when Leonora knows that Manrico has been taken prisoner and will almost certainly be executed, she has only one wish: to give her own life on the altar of her love for Manrico. Her aria, *D'amor sull'ali rosee*, comes cheek-by-jowl with the *Miserere* of the monks within the citadel, praying for the souls of the soon-to-be departed. Leonora imagines she sees death 'hovering as on sable wings' above the tower in which Manrico is incarcerated. She swears that she will prove there is no stronger love on Earth than hers for Manrico. Either she will save his life by sacrificing hers or they will be united in eternity.

The love of Leonora and Manrico, with its united longing for the joys of chaste love ('Gioie di casto amor'), is as close to a religious passion as it is possible to come within the context of a secular story. The Italian conductor, Gianandrea Gavazzeni, referred to *Il Trovatore* as the Italian *St Matthew Passion*. On first acquaintance with Verdi's opera such an allusion may seem absurd. Close study of text and music will reveal the true justice of such a claim.

Leonora, who has been dramatically peripheral throughout, is suddenly isolated. Only her already failing powers alert Manrico to the fact that she is dying. With the supreme illogicality, and necessity, of love all is now forgiven. Leonora has become an angel. There is no time left for recrimination or even reconciliation.

Count di Lerma (*Don Carlo*). The Conte di Lerma acts as **Philip's** ambassador and herald.

Act 1 of the opera takes place in France, where Philip's court (though not Philip himself) has travelled in order to conclude a treaty with Henry, King of France, father of **Elisabeth de Valois**. Di Lerma interrupts Elisabeth and **Carlos's** first meeting and declaration of love, to announce the French King's intention to grant her hand in marriage to the Spanish King. Di Lerma may register a moment of surprise at finding Elisabeth alone in the forest with the Infante. He announces that Philip wishes to allow Elisabeth 'complete liberty' to decide whether she wishes to accept the honour. Di Lerma does not expect for a moment that Elisabeth will decline. It possibly passes him by that she sounds less than enthusiastic in her acceptance. As far as di Lerma is concerned it is a mere formality.

While Elisabeth deplores the turn of events and all sing her praises di Lerma escorts her to her litter and the procession moves off towards the palace. Di Lerma is undoubtedly present at the *auto-da-fé* (Act 3 Scene 2) but does not make any specific contribution. He next appears when he announces with portentous *gravitas* the arrival in the King's chambers of the **Grand Inquisitor** (Act 4 Scene 1). The fact that di Lerma is present at this moment, announcing what is essentially a private audience, suggests that he operates as an equerry to Philip as well as ambassador.

Di Lerma is present at the prison where Carlo is incarcerated and where Philip travels in order to pardon his son (Act 4 Scene 2). Fearful for the King's safety he warns that the people outside the gates are infuriated and demanding the release of the Infante. He will inevitably be nervous when Philip demands that the gates of the prison be thrown open to admit the populace. The Act concludes with di Lerma leading the people, who have been cowed by the Grand Inquisitor, in proclaiming: 'Evviva il Re!' ('Long live the King!')

Lida (*La Battaglia di Legnano*). **Rolando's** wife.

Lida is one of Verdi's less spirited heroines. She conceives of her life as tragedy and suffers accordingly. In her opening preamble and address to her maids-in-waiting, she reflects on how both her parents and her brothers have died serving the cause of Italian independence: 'too many are the wounds, never to be healed, that dire fate has inflicted on my heart!' Principal among these wounds is the loss of her one and only love, **Arrigo**, whom she assumes to have died like her brothers and parents before him. She prays only for death (in this she reminds us of Medora [*Il Corsaro*]). The only thing that keeps Lida from killing herself is that she has (like **Amelia** [*Un Ballo in Maschera*]) a son. She married Rolando out of a sense of duty, since it was her father's dying wish that she should do so (Act 1). Clearly she has fulfilled her marital duties to the extent of providing her husband with an heir. But she cannot truly dedicate herself to her marriage since she still hankers after Arrigo, who was her first love.

It is possible that the German prisoner, **Marcovaldo**, senses her disquiet, which motivates him to press his suit. Lida is outraged by the German's audacity. When she learns that Arrigo is alive she is overjoyed (Act 1). The intensity of her emotion at the news takes her by surprise and forces her to accept what she has refused hitherto to accept, that Arrigo is the one and only love in her life. She candidly admits that she views her life 'of sorrow' as a justifiable chastisement for her 'guilty affection'. She needs to be miserable in order to assuage her guilt. When Arrigo upbraids her for having married Rolando when she had already promised herself to him and gives her no opportunity to defend herself, Lida is mortified. In her eyes she has only done as necessity dictated. She did not want to betray her love for Arrigo, nor his for her. The fact that she has done so causes her the most intense grief. Can he not see that? Apparently not, for, having hurled abuse at her, he precipitately leaves her to her fate.

If she thought she was unhappy previously, Lida is now distraught. For a brief moment she thought, albeit irrationally, her miseries might be at an end. Now they are multiplied tenfold. For now, Arrigo having so conclusively repulsed her, there is no hope. Worse is to follow when she discovers that Arrigo has joined the 'Squadron of Death' (Act 3), for she knows this is tantamount to signing his own death warrant. She sends him a letter, begging for a meeting and tacitly admitting to her love for him. Foolishly she gives the letter to her maid, **Imelda**, who allows herself to be bribed by Marcovaldo, who promptly shows the letter to Rolando. Now Lida finds herself with considerable explaining to do. She is presented with an impossible conundrum. She knows where her love lies, and she knows where her duty is, and ne'er the twain shall meet. When Arrigo does not answer her letter, she goes to see him. She needs to confront him eyeball to eyeball. She needs to find a resolution to her predicament, and the only way she can do that is to put herself into the firing line.

When she knocks on Arrigo's door she does not realize just how fully into the firing line she will place herself. For Rolando is close behind (Act 3). Thus it is that the very essence of her predicament becomes manifest, as she can only have dreamt in her worst nightmares. The very impossibility of it is inescapable. A choice must be made and she cannot make it. As it is Rolando makes the choice for her by incarcerating her with the man of her dreams. But this is no solution, and Arrigo knows it as well as she does. Within seconds of the door being bolted he has ejected himself out of the room via the balcony. For him the solution is simple; he will go gladly to his death with the Squadron of Death. For Lida it can never be so simple, particularly in view of the fact that she has a son.

She endures hours of misery locked in Arrigo's room. It is not made clear how she extricates herself. One must assume that Imelda rescues her. At any event she is discovered, in Act 4, outside a church in Milan, praying with the rest of the Milanese for the success of the Lombard League's campaign against the Germans. Only now does she learn that Arrigo survived his leap from the balcony and has rejoined the Squadron of Death. When news comes that the League has been victorious she is as delighted as any, but when Arrigo is borne in, mortally wounded, all her joy evaporates. The depth of her love is demonstrated by the fact that at this moment all her thoughts are not for herself but for Arrigo, arrived at his final hour. She pleads with her husband to put the knives away and be reconciled with his friend. Since Arrigo is now generally perceived as the saviour of Italy, having been the one to fell **Federico Barbarossa**, it would be difficult for Rolando to refuse. He is persuaded that 'a man who dies for his country cannot be so guilty in his heart' (a dubious assertion) and one must assume that Lida herself will be reconciled with her husband. Whether she will be able to reconcile herself to the final, irreversible loss of Arrigo is another matter.

Lina (*Stiffelio*). Wife of Stiffelio.
The character of Lina anticipates in more ways than one that of Amelia in *Un Ballo in*

Maschera. Both are married to upright men, whom they betray with men who have previously had the trust of their husbands. Both are mortified by their infidelity, and both end up confronting their respective consciences in a deserted field at night.

In two crucial respects, however, they are different. Where Amelia's true love is her illicit passion for Riccardo, Lina's true love is for her husband. Where Amelia has a son by her husband Lina has none. Having no child, Lina has less cause to remain with her husband. Yet, in spite of her infidelity, there is never a moment in the opera when her commitment to Stiffelio is in question. By her own admission she was, 'taken by surprise' by **Raffaele**. She was vulnerable and Raffaele took advantage. This is what Lina means when she says she was betrayed by him. She never wanted to be unfaithful to Stiffelio, but has increasingly succumbed to the strain of being married to an idealist whose every thought is for his spiritual mission. The least part of Stiffelio and Lina's married life is their love-life. Lina is 'betrayed', in terms of the spiritual ethos she embraces through her husband, by her physical needs – no more.

When Stiffelio returns (Act 1 Scene 1) to general acclamation and rejoicing Lina is inevitably stricken with remorse. She cannot help having imbued from her husband an acute consciousness of sin. Thus although she knows her liaison with Raffaele was nothing more than a momentary lapse, and that her true devotion to Stiffelio is unaffected, she is also acutely aware that in Stiffelio's eyes she is guilty of a sin which renders her beyond the pale. This consciousness of sin is exacerbated by her father's rigid adherence to a strict code of honour, whereby it is not so much the sin itself, but the possibility that Lina's fall from grace may become common knowledge, and thus bring dishonour on the family name, that concerns him.

Lina is caught between the two extremes of the masculine need to take control: on the one hand her husband's obsessive spiritual quest, and on the other her father's fanatical devotion to the family honour. Neither the concerns of her husband nor of her father are truly meaningful to her. She respects them but cannot feel the inherent necessity of them. She certainly cannot identify with them. The only necessity she can truly recognize is to live out the deep abiding love she has for Stiffelio. Her own inner sense of betrayal and failure in having allowed herself to be seduced by Raffaele is more than enough punishment for her. This becomes clear in the opening scene of the opera when Stiffelio regales the entire household with Walter's account of how he witnessed Raffaele making a hasty retreat from her apartment. She learns, possibly for the first time, that Raffaele dropped some papers. Walter has retrieved them and given them into Stiffelio's keeping. That Stiffelio decides to destroy the papers, refusing to be party to a 'guilty secret', only accentuates Lina's sense of guilt and worthlessness. When it comes to explaining away the absence of her wedding ring Lina is at a loss. (It is never actually specified in the opera what Lina has done with her wedding ring. It would have been entirely out of character for her to have given it to Raffaele. The most likely explanation is that her conscience, hyperactive as it is, will not allow her to wear it.) She is saved from having to provide her husband with an immediate explanation since Stiffelio is called away. Instead she must contend with her father.

Stankar is appalled when he realizes that Lina intends confessing all to Stiffelio. He sees it as evidence of his daughter's ingratitude and selfishness, far worse than the actual crime she wishes to confess to. He is prepared to forgive her unfaithfulness but he cannot forgive her for bringing dishonour to the family name. Thus Lina is trapped, unable to confess on the one hand, and unable to live with the consciousness of her sin on the other.

When Stiffelio takes possession of the volume of Klopstock, in which Raffaele's letter is concealed, Lina is appalled, but at the same time probably relieved. She desperately needs to shed the burden of her guilt. Had her father not intervened this would have been the moment she would have confessed (Act 1 Scene 2). The humiliation

would have been agonizing, but better that than the moral anguish which assails her now.

It is small wonder, then, that at the opening of Act 2 Lina finds herself wandering in the cemetery, where her mother has recently been buried, for at this juncture in the opera it would seem she has little future to live for. Yet never for a moment does she contemplate suicide. Lina has absorbed enough of her husband's faith to make it unthinkable for her to consider taking her own life. Rather she prays to her mother to intercede for her in heaven. When Raffaele appears her one concern is to persuade him to leave her alone and disappear. His continued presence is a constant reminder to her of her sin. She does not love him. Since Stiffelio's return she knows this beyond any shadow of doubt. She knows that their liaison threatens to jeopardize everything that she most values in life.

When Raffaele refuses to leave, Lina determines to tell Stiffelio everything. But she has reckoned without her father. For the second time in the opera Stankar forestalls her and thus deprives her of at least achieving the catharsis of confession. Lina cannot summon the courage to disobey her father's stern command to leave, but she is afraid for Raffaele's safety, realizing that Stankar is out for blood. She may not love Raffaele but she does not want him to die on her account. Lina is not witness to the duel that her father and Raffaele start but which is interrupted by Stiffelio. When she does re-enter, alerted by the sound of clashing swords, it is to find her father and Stiffelio confronting each other. Assuming, erroneously as it turns out, that Stiffelio now knows the identity of her seducer she begs his forgiveness. This time there is nothing her father can do to prevent Stiffelio from reaching the inevitable conclusion. It is an enormous relief to Lina that finally the truth is out: 'Ah, at last the thunderbolt has broken forth to roar about my head', she exclaims. Thanks to Jorg Lina is saved from witnessing her husband and lover fighting.

Lina knows she deserves her husband's reproach. What takes her completely by surprise is Stiffelio's cold and ruthless determination to divorce her (Act 3 Scene 1). She finds his statement that, 'offences against honour last as long as life itself' difficult to accept. For in that statement she can hear her father's life-denying ethos. Such a declaration is unworthy of the man she married. She knows that he is worth a great deal more than that, which is why she has always loved him, and still does.

Lina signs the divorce document because she hopes by doing so she can banish the man she no longer recognizes and because, as far as she is concerned, it is just a piece of paper bearing no relation to her love for Stiffelio. She insists that Stiffelio now listen to her. He need no longer listen to her as a husband, for she has signed the divorce papers, but she knows his sense of duty will compel him to listen to her as a penitent supplicant. Hence her impassioned plea, 'Ministro, ministro, confessatemi!' ('Minister, minister, hear my confession!') (these words had to be excised from early performances in order to placate the censor who was not willing to contemplate a married priest, let alone a married priest turning into a raging Otello due to his wife's adultery). Lina can now make the only confession that is truly meaningful to her, that she has always loved her husband and always will. When Stiffelio asks, 'but what of him?' Lina replies 'it was a betrayal'. By this she means a betrayal in many different senses: a betrayal of Stiffelio, a betrayal by herself of herself, and a betrayal by Raffaele not just of her but also of Stiffelio. Stiffelio is in no mood for Jesuitical subtleties, however. He interprets it one way only: 'he betrayed you'. Lina does not contradict him. One might wonder why. Surely she should not allow the whole blame to fall on Raffaele? But she knows it to be the only way to regain her husband and in a sense Raffaele deserves whatever befalls him. So she lets it pass. In any case it is academic since her father has already ensured that Raffaele has paid the price for his crime by murdering him.

Jorg drags Stiffelio off to the church where his congregation has been patiently waiting. Lina follows, albeit veiling herself to avoid detection. She knows she cannot just leave Stiffelio. She knows that their conflict has to be seen through to its conclusion. Above all she needs Absolution. She enters the church incognito, either because she does not know whether she should be there at all or because she does not know how Stiffelio will react. As it is Stiffelio recognizes her and is at a loss to know what to do. On Jorg's advice he seeks wisdom from the Holy Book.

Opening the Bible Stiffelio reads how Jesus pointed to the adulteress at his feet. Lina takes the cue. Oblivious of the congregation around her she mounts the steps of the pulpit on her knees, collapsing at her husband's feet. As Stiffelio reads the words, 'and the woman rose up and was forgiven', echoed by all the congregation, Lina rises to her feet 'with hands raised' and calls on Almighty God. It is all she has wanted all along, to be reconciled with herself, her husband, her family and with her God. She needs a public expiation. She deserves forgiveness because she never sought out sin; it befell her. Her faith in Stiffelio would appear to be justified.

From a modern-day feminist perspective *Stiffelio* could be seen as an indictment of the marginalization of women's rights that for so long pertained in Western society, and especially in areas of religious fundamentalism. In fact the chief issue in the drama – and for Lina – is the apparent incompatibility of the masculine and feminine perspectives without the mediating force of a compassionate ethos.

Lina's predicament makes one think of that of Anna Karenina, in Tolstoy's novel. She is similarly confused. About midway through the novel, when Anna's husband has discovered his wife's infidelity, Anna attempts to explain to him what led her to stray:

'I wanted to stay . . . don't be surprised at me. I am just the same as I used to be, but there is another woman in me, and I am afraid of her. It was she who fell in love with him. I wanted to hate you, but could not forget myself as I was before. I am not that one. I am my real self now.'

Anna's words would sound perfectly apt on Lina's lips.

(See also **Mina** (*Aroldo*).)

Lodovico (*Otello*). Ambassador of the Venetian Republic.

Act 3 opens with a herald announcing the imminent arrival of the Venetian galley bearing the Venetian ambassador. Some time elapses before Lodovico appears (Act 3). He brings with him a message from the Doge recalling **Otello** to Venice and appointing **Cassio**, Otello's deputy, in Otello's absence. Lodovico is representative of the mundane world with which Otello has so disastrously lost touch, wallowing, as he does, in a swamp of subjectivity. The ceremonial ambience that enters with Lodovico is refreshing, even if the illusion of restoration of order and sanity is short lived.

Lodovico is not at first aware that Otello is seriously deranged. He greets **Desdemona** and then approaches Iago, asking for news. He wonders why Cassio is not present, and although he does not comment he will surely be perturbed to learn from Iago that Otello is displeased with Cassio. He is appalled when Otello, apparently unprovoked, lashes out at Desdemona. 'My mind does not dare think what I have seen to be true', he declares. All that Lodovico knows of Otello is his reputation for sublime courage and heroism in battle. It is incomprehensible to him that the hero should so far forget himself as to physically assault a woman in public; and his own newly wed wife at that. He tries to intervene on Desdemona's behalf only to be studiously ignored. Instead Otello seizes Desdemona and forces her to the ground shrieking, 'A terra!... a piangi!' ('On your knees!... and weep!') (Act 3). Lodovico assists **Emilia** in helping the distraught Desdemona to her feet and, in company with all present, expresses the most intense compassion for Desdemona. He cannot help but contrast husband and wife: 'his dark hand is shaking, he pants with fury, while weeping she lifts her ethereal face to heaven'.

When Otello peremptorily dismisses the company Lodovico attempts to draw Desdemona away with him. Desdemona breaks free from his grasp and rushes to her husband, whereupon Otello utters his demented curse. As everyone leaves in horror Lodovico leads Desdemona away. He will not glean any explanation from Desdemona herself, who is as perplexed as anybody. Whether Iago tells Lodovico that Desdemona is suspected of infidelity is left to the audience's imagination. If he does tell him we can be sure that the accusation will be received by Lodovico with utter and justifiable incredulity.

Lodovico has retired to bed when he is disturbed by sounds of Emilia calling for help (Act 4). He rushes to Desdemona's room and is met by the sight of Desdemona's prone body on the bed and Otello, clearly demented, nearby. He listens as Emilia reveals the extent of her husband's treachery and when Iago flees joins the rest in attempting to stop him.

When Otello rushes towards his scimitar Lodovico demands he surrender it. But he can only watch helplessly as Otello takes his farewell and stabs himself, dying as the curtain falls.

I LOMBARDI ALLA PRIMA CROCIATA
(The Lombards at the First Crusade)

Opera in 4 Acts. Libretto by Temistocle Solera, based on Tomasso Grossi's poem, *I Lombardi alla prima crociata* (1821–1826)

Cast:

Arvino: son of Folco, the Governor of Rhodes (tenor)
Pagano: Arvino's brother (bass)
Viclinda: Arvino's wife (soprano)
Giselda: their daughter (soprano)
Pirro: Arvino's steward (bass)
A Prior of Milan (Un Priore di Milano) (tenor)
Acciano: tyrant of Antioch (bass)
Sofia: his wife (soprano)
Oronte: their son (tenor)

Time: 1099
Place: Milan, Antioch, the country near Jerusalem

Historical Background *I Lombardi* takes place at the time of the First Crusade (1095–1099) which was called by Pope Urban II with the express purpose of reclaiming the Holy Land, and in particular the holy city of Jerusalem from the Seljuk Turks, whose rise to pre-eminence in Palestine had made it almost impossible for the faithful to make pilgrimages to the holy sites in safety. The Crusaders captured Jerusalem in 1099, as portrayed at the conclusion of Verdi's opera.

Synopsis

Act 1 'La Vendetta'. (The Revenge). The square outside the church of Sant' Ambrogio in Milan. Joyful music is heard from within the church. Citizens discuss the cause of the rejoicing, namely that Pagano has finally been pardoned for his attempted fratricide and has been allowed to return home (*Oh nobile esempio!*). Some years previously Pagano and his brother, Arvino, had both fallen in love with the same woman, Viclinda. She had chosen Arvino and Pagano, in a fit of jealous rage, had attempted to murder Arvino. Pagano was then exiled. He is now returning home, having apparently repented. However, the citizens notice Pagano's tormented appearance: 'in his terrible and hollow eyes still appears the fierce tempest of his soul; though possible, it is rare indeed for a wolf's fury to change to the peaceful spirit of a lamb'.

Pagano, Arvino, Giselda, Viclinda and Pirro enter, preceded by the Priors of the city and by servants bearing torches. Pagano kneels on the ground and, 'with contrite heart', he begs forgiveness of the world and of God. Arvino embraces his brother and declares: 'let a brother's embrace set the seal on your pardon'. All sing in praise of Arvino's magnanimity. Giselda notices that her father is considerably perturbed and wonders why he cannot share in her immense joy. Arvino does not answer his daughter, but reflects to himself that he has noticed that there is still fury in his brother's glance. He has justification for his concern since Pagano confides in Pirro that 'Heaven itself shall not protect them from my fury'. Pirro assures Pagano

that he will always be at his service. The citizens sense something of the dark undercurrents lurking beneath the surface of Arvino's and Pagano's reconciliation, and pray that this may not be like 'the kiss with which Judas betrayed the Lord'.

A Prior comes forward and declares that Arvino has been proclaimed the leader of the Lombard Crusaders. Arvino accepts the 'weighty charge' and again invites his brother to embrace him. All express determination that censure and dishonour shall fall on any 'who impiously breaches his sacred promise'. It is clear that they have Pagano particularly in mind. Arvino and Pagano in response to this call draw swords and swear blood brotherhood. A chorus of Nuns is heard offstage praying for the peace of mankind (*A te nell'ora infausta*). Pagano, in an aside, declares that 'heaven is closed' to the Nuns' prayers, for he intends that very night to wield his sword against his brother. He is still consumed with longing for Viclinda; it would seem that his enforced absence has only exacerbated his desire (*Sciagurata! hai tu creduto*). Pirro indicates that there are 'many trusty men' awaiting his orders. He points to some nearby bushes in which several men are apparently concealed. Pagano gives instructions that they should torch his father, Folco's, palace (home also to Arvino, and his family) that very night. He warns them that it will be dangerous since Arvino has many retainers. The cut-throats confirm that they are not afraid. Pagano exults in the thought that he is finally going to achieve vengeance (*O speranza di vendetta*).

Act 1 Scene 2 A gallery in Folco's Palace Arvino's quarters are on the left, and the other apartments to the right. The scene is lit by a lamp.

Viclinda has been disturbed to see Pagano again, and is convinced that 'in that wicked face appeared a cloud of anger, not repentance'. Giselda enters and Viclinda summons her daughter to pray with her. Arvino now enters hurriedly from his apartment. He tells his wife to go to her room, but not to go to bed, for although it may be the result of his over-active imagination he thinks he has heard 'the sound of many feet'. He exits. His wife and daughter pray to the Blessed Virgin, to intercede for them (*Salve Maria, di grazie il petto*). Then they retire and Pirro stealthily enters, with Pagano. He tells Pagano that he has been tipped-off by servants that Arvino has already retired to his quarters. Pagano can hardly contain his relish that the moment of vengeance has finally arrived. He cautiously enters Arvino's quarters. The light of flames is seen from within. Spying the flames Pirro rushes off with drawn sword to join the other cut-throats in the massacre that has already commenced. Giselda rushes across the stage. Pagano drags in Viclinda. He warns Viclinda that it is no good crying out as there is nobody to hear her, but then Arvino's voice behind him stops him in his tracks. Pagano is frozen to the spot. He thought he had just killed Arvino. If it was not Arvino he murdered who was it? In shocked tones Giselda and Viclinda tell him that he has just killed his own father. Pagano is horrified. All join in reviling the parricide. Arvino draws his sword and is about to avenge his father's death when Giselda intervenes imploring him not to 'add crime to crime'. Pagano, who is as horrified as any at his crime, is about to kill himself with his sword, but is prevented by the guards, and then all declare that Pagano is henceforth branded with the 'fatal mark of Caine, and wherever he roams a demon will always be at his back' (*Va! sul capo ti (mi) grava l'Eterno*).

Act 2 'L'uomo della Caverna' (The Man of the Cave). A hall in the Palace of Acciano in Antioch.[43] Giselda has accompanied her

---

[43] Founded in 300 BC, Antioch was the capital city of the Seleucids. It was an essential trade link between the East and the Mediterranean. In 64 BC it was appropriated by Rome but was captured by the Arabs between 637–638 AD. The Crusaders captured it in 1098 and it became an important centre of Christianity until 1268 when it was captured once again, this time by Egypt. *I Lombardi* takes place just at the moment that the Arabs were being superseded in Antioch by the Christians. That Christianity is already taking hold is evidenced by the fact that Pagano has chosen to reside in the hills outside the city and

father on Crusade and has been captured by Moslems and incarcerated in a harem.

Acciano is seated on his throne. Before him stand ambassadors, soldiers and citizens. Acciano has just been briefing the ambassadors on the Crusaders' incursions. 'Strong and cruel, they exult in rape and robbery', he says. Everywhere they go they leave a trail of havoc and ruin. All join together in invoking Allah's wrath on the infidels. They depart leaving the stage clear for Oronte and Sofia.

Oronte has thoughts only for the girl he loves, Giselda. He asks his mother if she has any news of Giselda. 'She sighs, she weeps and calls upon her dear ones, yet the unhappy girl loves you', Sofia replies. This is just what Oronte wants to hear. He has only one desire, to be united with Giselda (*La mia letizia infondere*). Sofia points out that before he can make her his own he will have to adopt the Christian faith. Oronte confirms that this will present no obstacle to him, for he, like his mother, has come to believe in the 'God of love' (the Christian God). Sofia has already been converted to Christianity. She is overjoyed to learn that her son shares her new faith. Oronte, however, still has some nagging doubts, and prays that he may soon be united with Giselda, who will surely comfort his doubting mind and heart (*Come poteva un angelo*).

Act 2 Scene 2 The entrance to a cave on a mountainside outside Antioch. A hermit comes out of the cave. It is Pagano who, after his attempted fratricide and successful patricide, has withdrawn from the world and is living the life of a penitent. Pagano dreams of the moment he may see the Crusaders' banners 'gleaming from the mountain peaks' (*Ma quando un suon terrible*). Part of him feels guilty that he remains aloof from the world and its battles: 'Who am I that the rainbow of peace should smile on my soul?', he reflects. He knows that when he sees the

---

has gained a great reputation for holiness. It is Pagano who leads the Crusaders to the city when they kill Acciano, the tyrant of Antioch, and thus take control of the city.

'shining Cross' (the Crusaders' flag) his 'stiff right hand will grasp the sword; then (his) soul will again be redeemed in heaven'.

Pagano sees someone in Moslem dress approaching. He makes to retire back into his cave, but the man detains him. It is Pirro, his erstwhile accomplice. Pirro does not recognize him, so changed is he through years of austerity. Pagano has gained a reputation in the vicinity as a man of exceptional holiness, and it is for this reason that Pirro has sought him out. He tells the hermit that he was a Lombard and that he helped a parricide, and then fled to Antioch and denounced his faith. Terror and grief now guide him to the hermit. Pirro's sudden appearance must be a dreadful shock to Pagano, but he gives no hint of recognizing him. He exhorts Pirro to 'Rise and have hope!' Suddenly they are interrupted by sounds in the distance; the Crusaders are spread across the plain. Pagano is overjoyed. Now a band of musicians can be heard playing military music. Pirro swears that he will make it his business to give the Crusaders admission into the city.

By now the Crusaders have arrived at the hermit's cave. Pagano is startled to realize that they are Lombards. He is even more startled when he recognizes his own brother at the head of the army, but again he gives no sign of recognition. Arvino will have no chance of recognizing him, because Pagano retrieves a helmet and sword from his cave which he dons and greets Arvino with lowered visor.

Meanwhile the crusading warriors spread out over the mountainside. Arvino announces that he has come to ask the hermit for his prayers. Like Pirro, Arvino has been guided to the hermit by the local people who all assert that he is a man of God. Arvino reports that his daughter has been abducted by Moslems and that he has sought her in vain. Having ascertained that Arvino has a strong army of followers, the hermit reassures him that he will see his daughter again. Arvino leads him to a promontory from which he can show the hermit the forces gathered on the plain below. Pagano is delighted to see such a resplendent army. He tells the Lombards

to follow him and he will lead them to the city. All the Lombards are fired by the hermit's ardour (*Già la croce per l'aure balena*).

Act 2 Scene 3 A harem in Acciano's palace. Odalisques crowd around Giselda, who lies dejectedly on a sofa. She is the most recent addition to the harem. Why is she always weeping, the other girls wonder (*La bella straniera che l'alme innamora!*)? After all, 'she alone rules in Oronte's heart'. They are jealous of the new arrival and mock her mercilessly before running off. Giselda, left alone, prays to her deceased mother to come to her assistance (*Se vano è il pregare che a me tu ritorni*). She feels quite desperate in her predicament; 'I see a weight of days of horror press upon me like a sombre spectre', she laments.

Suddenly, shouts are heard from off-stage. They come from the other women of the harem, which has been breached by the Crusaders. Turkish soldiers come rushing in pursued by Crusaders. They in turn are followed by women of the harem, including Sofia. Giselda is delighted to see the Crusaders, but horrified when she learns that they have already killed her beloved Oronte and his father, Acciano.

Arvino enters together with the hermit and more Crusaders. Realizing that her father has been responsible for the deaths of Oronte and Acciano, Giselda covers her face with her hands in horror. Arvino seeks to embrace his daughter but is violently repulsed. Giselda breaks out as if 'stricken with madness' in a passionate denunciation of the Crusade (*No! no! giusta causa non è d'Iddio*). 'It is not God's just cause to soak the earth with human blood', she cries. She becomes increasingly impassioned. It is an extraordinary outburst that dumbfounds her father and all present. (For full text see **Giselda**.) Arvino fails to silence her and becomes so enraged that he draws his dagger and actually appears about to kill his own daughter. Everyone moves to restrain him. They all reflect that Giselda must have lost her reason (although in fact nobody has spoken so much sense since the opera began).

Act 3 'La Conversione' (the Conversion). The valley of Jehoshaphat. Several hills are scattered through the landscape, the most important being the Mount of Olives. Jerusalem can be seen in the distance.

Crusading knights, women, pilgrims enter bare-headed in procession. The pilgrims are ecstatic at the sight of the walls of Jerusalem. They recall with emotion how this was the site of the Passion story; 'On that hill the Nazarene wept for the fatal city; there is the mountain where wretched mankind received salvation'. They pass on through the valley, their voices receding into the distance.

Giselda enters. She has escaped from the claustrophobia of her father's tent and is wandering alone in the desert. She has thoughts only for Oronte now. Oronte enters. The two fall into each other's arms. Giselda is overwhelmed since she had thought Oronte dead. Oronte explains that he was but thrown to the ground in the affray. His only thought being to see Giselda again he became 'a coward' and fled the city. Thereafter he has wandered from land to land, following his one desire, to see Giselda again before he dies. Giselda confirms that wherever he goes she will be with him. Oronte is overwhelmed at this proof of Giselda's love for him. He warns her that being with him will not be an easy lot: 'for bridal bed, you will have the sand of the limitless desert, for your song of love the howling of the hyena' (*Per dirupi e per foreste*). Giselda will not be discouraged, and Oronte is fired with new hope for the future. He realizes that Giselda is deserting everything that has defined her existence to date: her parents, the hills of Lombardy, her native skies (*O belle, a questa misera*). He declares that he too will forsake all for the sake of their love. Also he will now embrace the Christian religion. Calls to arms are heard from the Lombardy camp.

Act 3 Scene 2 Arvino's Tent. Arvino has just witnessed his daughter eloping with Oronte. He is outraged at his daughter's behaviour and expresses the wish that she had never been born. Some knights enter, bearing the disturbing news that Arvino's brother, Pagano, has been seen in the vicinity of the Crusaders' camp. The knights are certain that all their misfortunes stem from Pagano's crimes, and urge Arvino to 'pursue the villain'. Arvino needs little prompting (*Si! del ciel che non punisce*). 'Were he hidden in hell he could no longer escape me', he declares.

Act 3 Scene 3 The entrance of a grotto. Through an opening in the rear can be seen the banks of the Jordan.

Giselda enters supporting Oronte, who is mortally wounded. She lays him down on a boulder deploring the gravity of his wounds. Oronte senses that he is dying. Giselda tries to console him, but to no avail. She breaks out in bitter reproach against a God who so consistently brings her suffering and loss. At this moment the hermit enters and demands to know 'who accuses God?' He proclaims their love a sin and tells them that they must turn to the 'true faith'. Giselda and Oronte need no persuading. The hermit blesses their union. Oronte momentarily feels new strength, but it soon evaporates (*Qual voluttà trascorrere*). He tells the distraught Giselda that he will await her in heaven. The hermit attempts to console Giselda with the thought that 'one day among the angels (she) shall receive the mercy of joy'.

Act 4 'In Santo Sepolcro' (The Holy Sepulchre). A cave in the hills near Jerusalem. Giselda is alone and asleep. In her dreams she is visited by a vision of celestial spirits, including that of Oronte. The spirits inform her that she should rejoice, since she has assisted a soul in finding grace in Heaven. Giselda rises, still asleep, and calls on Oronte to appear to her. Oronte duly appears and tells her that she is not deceived; he has been 'granted grace' (*In cielo benedetto*). He exhorts her to 'Go, cry aloud to your people, that hope should fortify them; the fountain of Siloam will bring them fresh water'. The vision vanishes and Giselda awakens in great agitation. She feels revitalized at the realization that what she has just experienced was not just a dream but a true visitation from her beloved Oronte (*Non fu sogno! In fondo all'alma*).

Act 4 Scene 2   The Lombard camp near Rachel's tomb. The Crusaders and pilgrims are imploring the Lord not to desert them but to aid their enterprise. They think longingly of their beloved Lombard hills which contrast so markedly with their present surroundings of arid desert (*O Signore dal tetto natio*). They are parched with thirst. The voices of Giselda, Arvino and the hermit can be heard offstage urging the men to go to Siloam. They then enter. Giselda is overjoyed when she sees the fountains of Siloam gushing forth water. Arvino exhorts his men to slake their thirst and then, fortified anew, scale the walls of Jerusalem. 'Today the Holy Land shall be ours', he proclaims. With cries of 'War! War!' all confirm their determination to take up arms and fight in the name of the Almighty.

Act 4 Scene 3   Arvino's tent. After lengthy sounds of battle the hermit enters, supported by Giselda and Arvino. Having apparently been the first to scale the walls of Jerusalem he has been mortally wounded and is now semi-delirious. Suddenly he asks Arvino who he is. When Arvino gives his name the hermit becomes distraught and, looking at the blood on his hands, breaks out 'This is Arvino's blood! Oh Hell, open at my feet! It is our father's blood!' Giselda tries to comfort him. Arvino asks the hermit his name, and the latter replies, 'I am Pagano'. He begs Arvino to forgive him in his dying moments (*Un breve istante*). Encouraged by Giselda, Arvino embraces his long lost brother. Pagano then begs to see the Holy City and the tent door is drawn back to reveal the city of Jerusalem. Overcome with emotion Pagano lifts a hymn of praise to a merciful Lord who allows the assassin to die in contentment. Arvino unconditionally pardons his brother and begs him to intercede for him in Heaven, whilst Giselda bids Pagano die in peace. She reminds him that he will find her beloved Oronte and mother in Heaven. All sing in praise of the God of victory who is 'the salvation, the guide, the glory of the valiant who open their hearts to thee!'

I Lombardi has, in common with *La Battaglia di Legnano*, the fact that it was partially conceived as nationalistic propaganda. It followed hard on the heels of *Nabucco*. Verdi was acutely aware that one success did not automatically guarantee the success of his next opera. His initial success with *Oberto* had been succeeded by the disastrous failure of *Un giorno di regno*, after which he had very nearly given up composing. Verdi never made the same mistake twice.

I Lombardi was fashioned around a story which was bound to appeal to the Italians searching for metaphors with which to bolster their own search for independence and unification. But like *La Battaglia di Legnano* the story of *I Lombardi* is very much more than just nationalistic tub-thumping. Verdi always needed strong interaction of character to stimulate his creative juices. Solera's libretto has been much maligned for its inequalities and downright absurdities. But, casting logic aside (essential in any case when addressing the operatic medium), *I Lombardi* contains a wealth of fascinating psychological insight, not least into the dynamics of family relationships around which the tale unfolds. Herein will be found the mother/son relation, the father/daughter relation, father/son relation, mother/daughter relation and, most pertinently, that of two brothers and their rivalry. In fact this whole gamut of family relationships, in addition to the more customary exploration of star-crossed lovers and the relationship of the individual to God, forms a rich and complex tapestry.

If one reviews the Verdi canon one finds in addition to the more frequently cited instances of father/daughter, father/son relations, a plethora of instances of male bonds, whether they be of blood, love, hate or simple friendship. The rivalry of brothers is one of the oldest themes in world culture. The theme is immortalized in the Old Testament story of mankind's very first offspring, the sons of Adam and Eve, Cain and Abel. Cain's offering to God was rejected where Abel's was accepted. Cain murdered Abel and was then outlawed, condemned to live his days a wanderer and outcast. The significance of this story and its relevance to the story of Arvino and Pagano lies in the fact that, strictly speaking, Cain's sense of grievance was justified. His ostracization was apparently the result of mere capriciousness on the part of the Lord. In such cases there is rarely an ostensible reason for the inequality that manifests itself between siblings. It is something given, and thereby incontrovertible. Somehow it must be confronted and lived through by both parties. The only other two comparable sets of brothers in Verdi's operas are Francesco/Carlo Massimiliano (*I Masnadieri*) and Manrico/di Luna (*Il Trovatore*). In both cases there is a deadly enmity between the brothers, an enmity which, in each case, is only resolved by the death of one of the two. The scenario explored in *I Lombardi* is altogether unique in that the two are ultimately reconciled through the extraordinary will to health of the wounded party, Pagano.

At the outset it would seem that Arvino and Pagano stand in a very similar relation to each other as do Francesco and Carlo: a deadly hatred of one for the other on account of a long, festering grievance. In the case of Arvino and Pagano it is the fact that they have both been in love with the same woman who has returned Arvino's love and not Pagano's. But in the final analysis it is not material what is the cause of the grievance; it is the fact that it exists at all. It is symptomatic of a deep rooted neurosis or, in the most extreme cases such as that under review, psychosis, that has its origins in the very earliest beginnings of life. In the case of Manrico/di Luna this is explicit, though complicated by the fact that the brothers do not realize they are brothers. The other motive contained within this rivalry is that of sexual jealousy. If there was ever an indication of the element of projection that is at the foundation of all sexual relationships it resides in these instances where two brothers vie for the same woman. This is something common to the three operas under review. Manrico and di Luna are both in love with Leonora; Francesco and Carlo with Amelia, and Arvino and Pagano with Viclinda.

If it is true that all men fall in love with the image of their mothers, then it makes perfect sense that two brothers should fall in love with the same woman. But this is not really the issue. The mother can be found reflected in a thousand different women. The real issue is why both elect to find the image in the same place. In reality it is not the case that both fall for the same image; rather it is the case that one falls and the other follows. This is the meaning behind Cain's rhetorical question: 'Am I my brother's keeper?' No, he should not be, but inevitably he is for, in Cain's instance, he has turned the tables on his brother who was originally *his* keeper. Paradoxically by murdering Abel he has forced upon himself the role of his brother's keeper. It is this need to usurp the potency of one, and thereby ameliorate his own feelings of inadequacy, that is always at the root of such unfathomable complexes. Sibling relations are no different from other relations. There will always be one side that is more dominant, active, aggressive than the other. The other may not be congenitally suited to an active role, but will nevertheless always resent the passivity apparently inflicted by the other. In such instances of rivalry in love, the love is returned to one while the other looks on from the sidelines, consumed with rage and envy. The woman is not loved and needed for herself. It is the mere fact that she is possessed by the brother that creates the imbroglio.

Inevitably a contributory factor must be the attitude of the parents towards the offspring. Pagano kills his father, thinking his victim to be his brother. His mistake can easily be interpreted as a monumental Freudian slip. The very fact that the brothers' father sleeps in Arvino's bed bespeaks volumes (why, one wonders, did Arvino, sensing impending danger, allow his father to sleep in his bed?). From Pagano's point of view his father has to die, for his very existence is a reproach. The moment the deed is done, however, Pagano is consumed with remorse. Suddenly the depths of his alienation from life come home to him. It is as though he has been acting and reacting on automatic pilot for years and is now confronted with the disastrous consequences of having allowed himself to wallow in such an infantile and regressive state of unconsciousness. He realizes that he has now no option but to take responsibility for his existence.

Pagano has already been granted a second chance after his first attempt at murdering Arvino. But the failure of that attempt has only exacerbated his sense of grievance. Had he failed a second time in murdering Arvino it is probable that nothing would have changed in his psyche. But the fact that the attempt not only fails but turns him into a parricide administers just the sort of shock that his psyche has been waiting for. Consciousness of sin is not just Adam's curse, it is also mankind's greatest gift, since it forces the individual to stand above his life and take stock. This Pagano does in the time-honoured fashion by becoming a wanderer on the face of the earth. His crime has rendered him automatically an outcast. The difference this second time is that he is now conscious of why he is an outcast. He seeks to address the problem in the only way a human being can, by withdrawing himself and dedicating himself to finding the centre within himself from which he has so disastrously strayed. His reward will be that eventually he is rehabilitated not just to the society but, most importantly, to the brother, whose very existence has been at the root of his inability to function.

Time after time one finds in Verdi's operas instances of characters who are forced to the realization that ultimately the anguish they endure is self-inflicted and the only solution is to resign themselves to a greater authority. It may take many years before a degree of detachment becomes possible (one thinks of Leonora and Alvaro in *La Forza del Destino*). But if finally the result is a degree of equilibrium then the attempt will have been worthwhile. It would be possible to propound at equal length on all the other relationships in the opera, but ultimately unnecessary. *I Lombardi*, on first acquaintance, appears to lurch along in fits and starts, constantly bringing new surprises and often

at first glance appearing farcically inconsequential. Closer inspection will reveal in each case that librettist and composer were entirely cognizant of the abiding truths not just of religion but also of psychology and the social sciences. There is nothing in *I Lombardi* that is any more or less absurd than the average absurdity of human existence that we must all confront sooner or later.

Jacopo Loredano (*I Due Foscari*). Member of the Council of Ten.
Loredano has one consuming ambition: to be avenged for the deaths of his father, Pietro Loredano, and uncle, Marco, both of whom he believes to have been murdered by **Francesco Foscari** (see **Synopsis**). To this end Loredano wages an unceasing campaign against the Foscari. He is an astute politician and therefore never steps beyond the bounds of legality, or not so that anybody would know it.

It is difficult to know historically to what extent Loredano can be blamed for the series of misfortunes that accost the Foscaris. More than likely **Jacopo Foscari** did accept bribes from foreign rulers; such was standard practice. It is the fact that Jacopo was caught, tried and sentenced to exile that suggests the hand of Loredano. Normally the Doge's son would be granted tacit immunity to such punishment. It is an old story in politics; use the letter of the law to defeat your enemies, even though you may be perfectly aware that the accused has only indulged in generally accepted practice. When Jacopo was sighted in Venice on the night before Donato's murder it was no doubt a paid agent of Loredano who disclosed the fact. It is more than possible that Jacopo was never there in the first place. Finally we can be certain that Loredano is behind the interception of Jacopo's incriminating letter to the Duke of Milan. Loredano is relentless and ultimately efficacious, because he believes from the start that he has right on his side. He apparently never wavers from this conviction. Only when the curtain falls can he truly feel vindicated.

Ostensibly Loredano is the villain of the opera. In fact there is no villain, only opposing politicians. Loredano is convinced that the Foscari are responsible for the death of his kinsmen. He may be wrong but he certainly never seems to entertain any doubt. It is this conviction of his own rectitude that makes of him such a lethal opponent to the Foscari, for nothing that he does is outside the law. Never does he seem to be assailed by guilty conscience or remorse. Thus he is literally remorseless.[44]

At every stage of Jacopo's trial and sentencing Loredano takes pleasure in gloating over his enemy's discomfiture. This alone renders him detestable, not only to the Foscari but to the audience. He is never more contemptible than when informing Lucrezia that she and her children may not be permitted to join Jacopo in exile. Loredano's quarrel is not with Lucrezia. The relish with which he enjoys her distress is totally unwarrantable, other than by virtue of the fact that he thereby twists the knife in the wound of Jacopo's suffering. An Iago figure in many ways, Loredano retains in his own mind a perfectly justifiable motive for his vindictiveness.

Lucrezia Contarini (*I Due Foscari*). Wife of Jacopo Foscari.
Lucrezia describes herself on her first entrance as 'the daughter of Doges and a Doge's daughter-in-law' (Act 1 Scene 2). She is not intimidated by a Doge and believes that she can appeal to **Francesco**'s humanity. Before he was a Doge he was a father, she declares. But Francesco will prove a tougher nut to crack than she could possibly have anticipated, for he takes his role as head of state extremely seriously. He knows that legally there is nothing he can do to save his son. Lucrezia can never understand that Francesco puts his obligations as Doge above his

natural affections as a father. To her it is inexplicable that he could stand aside while his son is tortured and show no sign of using his influence to put an end to Jacopo's suffering. She attempts to cajole him but is coldly rebuffed. Later, when she pleads with him, weeping bitter tears, she has more success (Act 1 Scene 3) but when it comes to the critical moment Francesco refuses to compromise his office. Only the fact that she knows how much the old man suffers beneath his cold exterior allows her to forgive him his inflexibility.

Lucrezia is infinitely relieved to learn that her husband has been spared execution, but relief quickly turns to despair when she learns that his exile is to be indefinite, and that she may not join her husband. Her devotion to Jacopo is absolute. Throughout the opera she passionately pleads his case but to no avail. Her part is an eloquent illustration of the impossible lot of a wife and mother in the almost exclusively masculine world of fifteenth-century Italian politics. She may be a Doge's daughter but she has no political ambitions of her own. She only wants to see justice done. From her ancestry she must have gleaned a profound knowledge of the workings of the Senate. She senses that her husband is not receiving the justice due to him. She knows that Loredano is behind Jacopo's persecution, but again she is powerless to do anything about it.

Lucrezia's finest hour comes at the conclusion of the opera after her husband has died. Far from blaming the Doge for the severity which has led to his own son's death, she offers him succour and friendship in the last moments of *his* life, for she knows that he is as much a victim as is her husband and she herself. Her only feeling for the old man is one of compassion. He is being subjected to an indignity that no Doge should have to suffer. She assists him from the chamber and is still supporting him when he collapses and dies.

All her life Lucrezia has existed on the periphery of great events. She has cared unstintingly for Jacopo and cares for his father as much. Left without either she is

---

44 It would be interesting to chart the careers of criminals, both political and otherwise, and identify the precise moment when doubt, remorse, guilt kick in and render their endeavour stillborn. Failure of conviction is at the root of all failure of endeavour, whether criminal or legitimate.

bereft of all except her children. Inevitably she must fear for their safety. But that is not our concern for the opera concludes with the death of Francesco.

LUISA MILLER

Opera in 3 Acts. Libretto by Salvatore Cammarano after Schiller's tragedy, *Kabale und Liebe* (1784).

First performance: 8 December 1849 at the Teatro San Carlo, Naples.

Cast:

Luisa Miller (soprano)
Miller: her father, a retired soldier (baritone)
Count Walter (bass)
Rodolfo: his son (tenor)
Frederica, Duchess of Ostheim: the Count's niece (mezzo-soprano)
Wurm: an employee of the Count (bass)
Laura: a village girl (mezzo-soprano)
A peasant (tenor)

Time: early 17th century
Place: a village in the Tyrol

Synopsis

Act 1 **L'amore** (Love) Scene 1 A peasant village. On one side Miller's humble dwelling, on the other a little country church. In the distance, through the trees can be seen the towers of Walter's castle. It is spring and a cloudless day is dawning. The villagers are gathered to celebrate Luisa's birthday. The villagers sing of their affection for Luisa and of her purity and sweet nature (see **Chorus**). Miller expresses his great love for his daughter and also voices his concerns about her newfound lover, Carlo (Rodolfo in disguise), who has only recently arrived at the Court and is unknown to the villagers. Luisa tries to allay her father's fears, assuring him of Carlo's nobility of spirit, virtuous heart and of their great mutual love (*Lo vidi, e'l primo palpito*).

Laura and the villagers present posies of flowers to Luisa. As the latter accepts the flowers she notices a young hunter who steps forward and also presents her with flowers. It is Rodolfo. Luisa urges her father to embrace him for 'he loves (him) like a son'. Luisa and Rodolfo then confirm their great love for each other while Miller, in an aside, voices his misgivings (*T'amo d'amor ch'esprimere*). He implores God not to allow his daughter to become the victim of 'a common seducer'. The church bell rings and, with the exception of Miller, the crowd makes for the church, singing as they go.

Wurm enters. He tells Miller he has heard everything and reminds him that it is now a year since he approached Miller for his daughter's hand in marriage. At that time Miller raised no objection but now appears to favour the stranger's suit over his own, in spite of the fact that Wurm is considerably advanced at the Court. Miller retorts that he only promised his daughter's hand to Wurm if it should be Luisa's wish. He points out that the choice of a husband is sacred and that he is a father, not a tyrant (*Sacra la scelta è d'un consorte*). Wurm is not impressed. He accuses Miller of weakness and warns him of dire consequences. He now reveals Carlo's true identity, that he is, in fact, Rodolfo, the son of Count Walter, Miller's liege lord. Without waiting for a response he leaves. Miller is grief stricken. Though he does not say as much he is clearly convinced that Walter's son could not possibly have honourable intentions towards a mere peasant girl (*Ah! fu giusto il mio sospetto!*).

Act 1 Scene 2 A large room in Count Walter's castle. Walter enters, followed by Wurm. Wurm has just told of the Count of Rodolfo's wooing of Luisa. Walter is appalled, since he intends that his son should marry the wealthy duchess Frederica, who is infatuated with him. Walter demands to see his son. Wurm retires.

Alone, Walter reflects that everything in his life has turned out well with the one exception of his errant son (at this stage the audience is not aware that Walter has achieved his ascendancy by murdering his cousin and that Rodolfo knows of this). In stark contrast to Miller's sentiments concerning a father's duties (Act 1 Scene 1), Walter does not cherish the duties of paternal love: 'a resentful God has made it terrible punishment, hellish torture for me', he declares (*Il mio sangue la vita darei*).

Rodolfo enters. Walter gives no indication that he is privy to Rodolfo's wooing of Luisa and embraces his son, giving him the joyful news that Frederica will shortly be his bride. Rodolfo is naturally dismayed. Walter underlines all the benefits of marriage to Frederica, who has been left a sizeable inheritance by the Duke, her first husband. She also, apparently, has influence at the German Imperial Court. Rodolfo retorts that he is not ambitious by nature. He is about to tell his father about his true love, but Walter anticipates him and refuses to allow him his say. He insists they go forthwith to meet the Duchess. It is his duty to offer her marriage, he tells Rodolfo. 'Obey me, my wishes are laws', he declares (Ataliba uses virtually the same words when browbeating his daughter, Alzira). But before they can depart the Duchess enters with her suite of ladies-in-waiting, pages, servants and archers. The attendants sing in praise of their mistress (see **Chorus**). Walter tells Frederica that his son craves the honour of speaking with her. He maintains that he must 'expedite the arrangements for the hunt' and – not before a threatening word in his son's ear – he departs. Frederica's attendants also depart, leaving their mistress alone with Rodolfo.

Rodolfo decides the only course of action is to be honest and appeal to Frederica's generous heart. However, he makes the mistake of addressing her as 'Duchess', and Frederica immediately stops him, reminding him that they were childhood playmates. She has never ceased to be his Frederica. Rodolfo goes down on his knees and tells her he must confess a secret anguish. In stuttering phrases he confesses that 'destiny binds (him) to another'. He begs mercy and offers to plunge his sword into his breast at her feet, but Frederica is scornful of his melodramatics. She tells him that if he were to kill her with his sword she might forgive him before she dies. But he should not expect favours from her jealous heart. 'Love scorned is a fury that cannot forgive', she concludes.

Act 1 Scene 3   A room in Miller's house. Distant horn calls in the mountains and valleys indicate that there is a hunt in progress. A chorus of huntsmen is heard in the distance. Luisa is anxiously watching from the window, for Rodolfo has promised to leave the hunt in order to come and see her. Miller enters and collapses into a chair. He tells his daughter he has received confirmation of his worst fears. Luisa is betrayed. Exhaustion turns to anger as he tells his daughter the truth about her lover, that Rodolfo has lied about his name and background. Now, Miller continues, Rodolfo is about to make a 'splendid match'. He is on the point of swearing vengeance on the seducer when Rodolfo enters. Rodolfo addresses Luisa, reassuring her that although his disguise is revealed his feelings for her remain unchanged. Impetuously grasping Luisa's hand, he kneels with her before Miller and urges the old man and God to witness his vow that he is Luisa's 'husband'. Miller immediately thinks of the Count, Rodolfo's father, and the wrath which will inevitably fall on them. Rodolfo is unperturbed. He tells Luisa and her father that he is in possession of a terrible secret which would make the Count grovel at his feet.

At this moment the Count enters. Luisa and her father are horrified. Walter announces that he has come to call a halt to this 'sinful intrigue'. He pours scorn on his son's declaration of love for Luisa, calling the latter a 'venal seductress'. Outraged, Rodolfo draws his sword, while Miller reminds Walter that he was once a soldier and will not endure such insults, even from his lord. Walter calls on his retainers, who enter immediately with Laura and the villagers. The villagers are astounded to learn that Luisa's suitor is in fact the Count's son. Walter orders both Miller and Rodolfo to be put in chains. Luisa kneels in supplication at the Count's feet. For Miller this is insupportable: 'among mortals innocence is not yet so oppressed that it needs to kneel before an arrogant lord. Bow low before God, the chastiser of the wicked, not to one who has human appearance but the heart of a wild beast in his breast', he declares (*Fra i mortali ancora oppressa*).

Rodolfo meanwhile struggles with conflicting emotions, caught as he is between filial duty and his love for Luisa and last, but not least, knowledge of his father's crime. Walter pours forth invective against his ungrateful son and the girl who thrusts a 'vile love' between him and his son. Luisa prays to be saved from her oppressor (the Count). All the villagers are moved to tears by Luisa's pathetic plight. Walter reiterates his command to the retainers to arrest the couple. At this moment Rodolfo draws his sword and, standing in front of Luisa, threatens to slay anybody who dares to approach them. Outraged, Walter seizes Luisa and hands her over to the archers. He then challenges his son to strike him. Rodolfo swears to follow his betrothed to jail. Walter is unperturbed. 'Very well, follow her', he tells his son. At which Rodolfo loses all self-control and threatens to stab Luisa rather than let her be at the mercy of Walter's retainers. Walter remains unmoved. He would be only too pleased were Rodolfo to kill Luisa. (At this moment Rodolfo displays the same sort of uncontrolled emotional petulance as do both Carlo in *I Masnadieri* and Don Carlos in *Don Carlo*, two other operas based on Schiller plays.) Goaded beyond endurance Rodolfo threatens to reveal the terrible secret that he is harbouring. This is too much for Walter who immediately orders Luisa's release. The Act concludes with general rejoicing at this unexpected turn of events.

Act 2 **L'intrigo** (The intrigue). Scene 1 A room in Miller's cottage. Villagers hurry in, looking for Luisa, who comes immediately from her room, certain that they must be bringing bad news. Her father has been absent from home for some time. The villagers confirm her worst fears. They describe how, returning home, they witnessed an old man being dragged off in chains by the Count's officers to the castle. Luisa is about to leave forthwith for the castle, but is prevented by the arrival of Wurm who dismisses the villagers and insists that Luisa must hear him out.

Wurm confirms that Miller is imprisoned in the castle dungeons. Luisa demands to know his offence and is told that her father dared to make the Count the object of abuse and threats. The punishment for such a crime could be execution. Wurm, however, has come to strike a deal with Luisa. He tells her that the Count requires that she write and put her signature to a letter which Wurm will now dictate. The letter is addressed to Wurm and in it she must admit that she never loved Rodolfo but because of his social position she wanted to 'ensnare' him. She now begs forgiveness of Wurm, her 'first love', and in order to avoid Rodolfo's anger suggests that Wurm should come to her and that they should elope together. Thinking only of her duty to her father (*Tu puniscimi, o Signore*) Luisa writes and signs the letter. Once she has put her signature to the letter Wurm has a further salvo to hurl at her. She must now accompany him to the castle and there, in front of 'a noble lady' (Frederica), declare herself madly in love with Wurm. Luisa is appalled and at first refuses to cooperate. But she realizes that unless she acquiesces her father will die. Bitterly she accuses Wurm of tearing her heart to shreds (*A brani, a brani, o perfido*). She feels the 'violent shudder of death' in her whole body. All she wants now is for her own father to close her eyes. Wurm merely tells her that time is the healer of all sorrow and that he cherishes the hope of clasping her hand.

Act 2 Scene 2 A room in Count Walter's castle. Walter is railing against his son. He determines that he must hold fast to his task, to protect himself at all costs. Walter has no concern for his son's welfare, or indeed anybody else's. Wurm enters and informs him that the 'threads of the cabal' are all in place. Luisa had surrendered to threats and will come to the castle. Meanwhile a paid messenger has been despatched with the letter Luisa has signed to deliver it to Rodolfo.

Walter and Wurm now recapitulate the events which constitute the 'terrible secret' that Rodolfo has threatened to disclose. Walter had a cousin who stood to inherit the title of Count. At that time Wurm was a close confidante of Walter's cousin. The old man decided to take a young bride. More than probably this marriage would have seen the birth of children, thus depriving Walter of the inheritance he desired for himself and his son, Rodolfo. Wurm revealed these intentions to Walter, then suggested a 'horrible solution'. Walter's cousin should be despatched with. Thus they murdered him in a dense forest and spread the rumour that the old man had been murdered by robbers. Unfortunately for them Rodolfo came upon the older Count before he finally expired and heard from his dying breath the truth about his assailants. This latter fact Wurm has not appreciated. He is convinced that he will be destined for the gallows when Rodolfo divulges the truth. Walter reassures him that they need only to stand firm together.

Frederica enters and at a sign from Walter Wurm retires. Walter reassures Frederica that she need not fear on account of Rodolfo's love for Luisa, for Luisa's heart belongs to another. Frederica is incredulous, but Walter opens a secret door to admit Luisa herself who will confirm, before Frederica, the truth of what Walter says. Luisa is ushered in to the accompaniment of whispered threats from Wurm. Luisa is overwhelmed by being in the presence of the woman who will shortly win her beloved Rodolfo's hand in marriage. Frederica, in spite of herself, is affected by Luisa's obvious innocence and ingenuousness. She asks the girl straight out whether she is in love and with whom. Luisa, never for a moment forgetting her duty to her father, confirms that she is in love with Wurm. Frederica presses her on the subject of Rodolfo but Luisa reiterates that she has never loved Rodolfo. Frederica is insistent. She notices that Luisa blushes when she denies loving Rodolfo. In spite of her immense turmoil, however, and desperate desire to tell the truth, the presence of Walter and Wurm will not allow Luisa to forget her father's peril. Gathering her strength she points at Wurm and confirms: 'I foster for him alone a true, immense and ardent love'. Frederica is satisfied, as are the two men.

Only Luisa suffers unspeakable torment: 'if I remain here, I shall fall lifeless at her feet', she says in an aside.

Act 2 Scene 3 A hanging garden in the castle grounds. Rodolfo hurries in from his apartment, holding Luisa's letter. A peasant follows him. The peasant has been bribed by Wurm to deliver the letter in which Luisa has confirmed, under duress, her love for Wurm. The peasant explains that he has delivered the letter to Rodolfo rather than the letter's addressee because of 'the vague suspicion of some plot or other' and the hope of reward from Rodolfo. Having thrown him a purse Rodolfo dismisses the peasant. He then calls a servant and commands him to fetch Wurm. He is extremely agitated (*Oh! fede negar potessi*). He recognizes Luisa's handwriting and is completely at a loss to know why she has betrayed him. The letter makes a mockery of all the vows, the hopes, the joy, the tears, the anguish they have endured together. He can only conclude that she has betrayed him in the vilest manner. He recalls the moments (*Quando le sere al placido*) when Luisa had, 'in angelic tones', confirmed her love for him. Now, 'she has betrayed me', he keeps reiterating to himself.

Wurm enters. Rodolfo gives him the letter. Darkly Rodolfo tells Wurm: 'for both of us this is the hour of death'. He produces two pistols. Wurm, taken aback, makes to leave but Rodolfo thrusts one of the pistols at him. Wurm, terrified, fires his pistol in the air. Soldiers and servants hurry in, followed by Walter. Wurm disappears into the crowd. Rodolfo reflects bitterly how cowardice sprouts wings. He falls to his knees in front of his father.

Walter quickly appraises the situation and realizes that Luisa's letter has achieved exactly what he has hoped for. Deliberately misinterpreting his son's anguish he tells him that of course he must do that which will afford him happiness and offer his hand in marriage to his true love (Luisa). When Rodolfo cries out that Luisa has betrayed him Walter suggests that Rodolfo should show his contempt for Luisa by leading another bride – the Duchess Frederica – to the altar. Rodolfo precipitately concedes. He is beyond caring. 'Prepare the altar or the grave for me, I abandon myself to fate', he says. The servants all urge him to rely on his 'compliant father's wisdom', while Walter cynically promises his son that one day he will be happy.

Act 3 **Il veleno**. The poison. A room in Miller's cottage. Luisa is writing at the table. Laura and a group of villagers look sadly on. They are seriously concerned for Luisa's well-being (see **Chorus**). Laura tries to persuade her to eat, but to no avail. Luisa has resolved that she will starve herself to death. She notices that the church is all lit up and wonders what transpires. In fact it is the marriage ceremony of Rodolfo and Frederica. Laura is anxious to try to keep this from Luisa who, however, does not seem particularly interested. She resumes her writing. Miller enters. Laura and the other peasants determine that father and daughter should be left alone together.

Miller is appalled at the cost to his daughter's happiness of his release from prison. He has learned from Wurm of Luisa's sacrifice. Luisa's calmness concerns him. He realizes that his daughter is in a dangerously depressed state of mind. He asks her what she is writing and Luisa hands the letter to him, asking him to ensure that it is delivered. Miller opens the letter: 'Horrible treachery separated us, Rodolfo. An oath stops me from saying more. There is a place where neither deception nor oath can have any influence over us...'. Miller immediately suspects that his daughter refers to the grave. His suspicions are confirmed by Luisa herself. In a poignant passage she reflects that 'for two pure, trusting souls, death holds no terror. It is an angel who opens the heavens where love smiles eternally'. Her father observes that there is no forgiveness for suicide, to which Luisa rejoins: 'is love a sin?' Miller is overcome by emotion. 'The love that a father has sown, he must gather in his late years and, cruel child, can you leave me a harvest of tears and sorrow?' (*Di rughe il volto*). Luisa is immediately consumed with guilt and tears up the letter. 'For you, dear father, I will stay alive', she says. Overcome with remorse for her selfishness she falls at her father's feet. Miller lifts her up and embraces her warmly. Luisa now proposes that they should run away together since, in the Count's domains, 'cruel danger would surround us'. Miller agrees to this and the two sing of their future life together: 'roaming where our destiny lead us, begging people for bread . . . but always at her father's side will be his daughter' (*Andrem raminghi e poveri*). They determine to set forth at dawn.

The organ is heard playing from the church. Sadly Luisa kneels to pray, aware that this will be the last prayer she utters on 'the dear soil where happily I led my life and where he told (her), "I love you"'. Miller has departed. Enveloped in a long cloak Rodolfo enters, followed by a servant. Rodolfo dismisses the servant, telling him to inform his father that when the ceremony is ready he will find his son at Miller's cottage.

When the servant has departed Rodolfo takes a phial from his breast pocket and pours its contents into a jug of water. Luisa rises from her prayer and is startled to find Rodolfo watching her. He shows her the letter she wrote to Wurm (*Hai tu vergato questa foglio?*). Asked whether she wrote the letter, Luisa can only reply truthfully in the affirmative. Rodolfo now complains of a dreadful thirst and points to the jug into which he has recently poured the poison. Luisa pours him a glass of water and Rodolfo drinks. He then passes the beaker back to her and invites her to drink. Luisa drinks, unaware that they have both just consumed a deadly poison. Rodolfo tells her to fly, for another man awaits her just as another woman is waiting to follow him to the altar. Then, throwing down his sash and sword in a dramatic gesture, he declares, 'they wait in vain'. He bids farewell to his sword and Luisa, startled, asks him what is the matter. Rodolfo complains he can hardly breathe and Luisa offers him another drink from the poisoned jug. 'The vile girl seems to know what she is offering me', Rodolfo declares bitterly. Luisa is appalled at his venom. Rhetorically Rodolfo wonders how God 'can deck in such angelic form a spirit from Hell'. Luisa still feels constrained by the oath she swore to Wurm, and thus unable to reveal the truth. As the castle clock chimes Rodolfo announces: 'Woman, for us the terrible last hour has struck'. He demands to know if she was truly in love with Wurm, and warns her against lying since: 'before the lamp dies you will stand before God'. When Luisa asks him to explain himself he tells her that she has drunk poison with him. Luisa is ecstatic for, confronted by death, she at last feels able to break her oath of silence and reveal the truth. She describes how her father was taken prisoner and how she was forced to write the letter confirming her love for Wurm in order to save her father's life. Rodolfo is horrified and curses his destiny. Luisa begs him to curb his fury against God. Their cries alert her father who enters.

Rodolfo confesses that he has murdered Luisa, who is already succumbing to the effects of the poison. Luisa's only desire now is that Rodolfo should remain close to her in her death throes. Rodolfo is stricken with remorse and begs her forgiveness while Miller laments his shattered dream of a blissful old age in the company of his beloved daughter. Villagers enter with Wurm and Walter. Rodolfo, catching sight of Wurm, seizes his sword and runs him through. 'My death be your punishment, evil man', he exclaims. Then he turns to his father: 'Look on your punishment', he cries as he falls dead beside Luisa. The two fathers and the neighbours can only look on in shocked incredulity as the curtain falls.

It has been said that *Luisa Miller* is a drama demonstrating the ascendancy that worldly ambition and exigencies may often achieve over affairs of the human heart. That this thesis is illustrated in Verdi's opera as much as in the source, Schiller's play *Kabale und Liebe*, is beyond question. The real question, however, is to what extent or to what cost that ascendancy is achieved, if indeed it can be termed ascendancy at all. Since the prime instigators of the cabal, Walter and Wurm, are both severely compromised, not to say

utterly prostrate, by the conclusion of the drama, ascendancy would hardly seem to fit. More accurately one might say that the drama illustrates how affairs of the human heart may well be confounded in this life by the petty ambitions and obsessions of the politically minded. But in the end it is the nobility of human love and compassion and its ability to transcend all worldly considerations that shines through. The world may have little truck with the unworldly demands and strivings of the human heart, but it is only these strivings that make of human life something worth living. Such was undoubtedly the message enshrined in Schiller's play and enthusiastically embraced by Verdi.

Ultimately Luisa and Rodolfo's sacrifice is unnecessary. They could, had they been made of stronger metal, have followed the example of many other operatic lovers and eloped. It is possible that the relative lack of popularity of the opera has to do with this central omission. By no stretch of the imagination could Luisa and Rodolfo fall into the category of heroic lovers. Their predicament is very little different from that of Tristan and Isolde and a host of other couples caught up in wholly unpropitious circumstances.

The class barrier is a powerful obstacle and one that neither are equipped temperamentally to overcome. But this is as nought compared with the far more onerous barrier to their relationship epitomized by their inability to break away from their respective fathers. This is the nub of the matter. Neither can quite make the leap away from the cosy comfort of infancy and childhood, where all is prescribed and they are merely obliged to conform. Both make valiant efforts to escape but are ultimately incapable of making the leap into the unknown and unfriendly arena of total independence.

Rodolfo, a victim of his emotions from first to last, never stops to question the authenticity of Luisa's letter of betrayal. One might say: why should he? since the letter is so obviously in Luisa's handwriting. But that would be to miss the point. He knows that Luisa is a defenceless peasant girl. He knows that his father is a power-hungry politician.

It would not take too much imagination to put two and two together. The real problem is that Rodolfo does not want to put two and two together. In common with most of Schiller's heroes he has become too accustomed to being victimized. It is so much more comfortable to continue conforming to the role that destiny has thrust upon him. He has learnt his role in life and now he must live it. His assumptions about life are such that he expects always to be defeated. Because he expects defeat and eclipse, that is what he gets.

Similarly Luisa is conditioned to accept the passivity of her peasant existence. Her failure to individuate is more understandable. She has also always been a victim, a victim of her father's overbearing love and concern. The real subject matter of *Luisa Miller* is the ease with which human beings accept this condition of victimization, and the dire consequences of allowing this status quo to pertain.

Rodolfo and Luisa's lives could have been so different had they chosen to assert themselves and their love. This world will always aim to victimize the individual, but the victim has a choice; if he chooses suicide he has failed. Luisa and Rodolfo fail, in simplistic terms, through a chronic reluctance to grow up.

Luisa Miller (*Luisa Miller*)

As with so many of Verdi's heroines Luisa's central dilemma is the conflict between her duty to her father and her love for her lover. But of all her stable mates Luisa is the most self-sacrificing and the most incapable of breaking the bonds which tie her to her father. Most of Verdi's other heroines, when forced to make a decision, will go with their lovers rather than allow duty and filial affection to stand in the way. The consequences may be dire, but they usually manage to assert their independence (even Gilda (*Rigoletto*)).

Having been brought up without a mother in a home where the only parental authority stemmed from her father Luisa cannot recognize any authority or emotional commitment

beyond that one. When her father is taken prisoner she is presented with a clear choice. Either she can sacrifice her lover, and therefore her personal happiness, or she can sacrifice her father. Since death is the penalty for one, while simple exile from the embraces of her lover (the full joy of which she can hardly have experienced) is the other, there is really no choice for her. Very few girls faced with a similar predicament would do differently from Luisa.

The problem, however, is that Luisa is incapable of differentiating between a righteous mandate and one that is wholly unjustified and therefore unbinding. When she agrees to swear that she does not love **Rodolfo** and that her devotion is all for **Wurm** Luisa is required to swear a falsehood (Act 2 Scene 1). She does so in order to save her father's life. For her it is justifiable and she carries it through. Thereafter she contemplates suicide, for life without Rodolfo is unthinkable, particularly since she would have to live with the consciousness of having committed perjury. When her father, demonstrating that he is as selfish as Rodolfo's father, **Walter**, demands that she give him some consideration and think of the grief and anguish that her suicide will bring on him, she unquestioningly puts aside all thoughts of it. Instead she commits herself solely to her father and his happiness, wilfully sacrificing her own. From a moralistic viewpoint her behaviour is exemplary, that is, from the standpoint of a paternalistic philosophy which expects that the individual sacrifice him/herself for the greater good of the whole.

From a psychological viewpoint her decision is, however, entirely regressive. It is her very passivity and acquiescence that causes her lover's death. Had she sought him out as soon as she secured the release of her father and put him in the picture then it is possible that both of their lives could have been saved. But she is quite unable to assert her independence. She cannot even admit the importance of her feelings for her lover to the extent of sacrificing her father's purely selfish requirement that she give over her youth to his happiness. The vision they paint, the two of them wandering the Earth, is very similar to that Goethe depicts in his tale of Mignon.

Incredibly, Luisa even feels the force of her oath to Wurm binding her to silence after she has learnt her lover is in his death throes. Only when she learns that she herself is dying does she feel liberated to reveal the truth. The chains that bind her to life are inexplicably intertwined, in fact synonymous with, the chains that bind her to her father. For her, romantic love is only possible on the other side of the grave. This of course is typical of German Romanticism, enshrined in Schiller's play. Ever the two shall be irreconcilable: Eros on the one hand and duties and responsibilities of living in society on the other. Schiller's play only perpetuates the myth.

Count di Luna (*Il Trovatore*). A young nobleman from Aragon.

The title, di Luna, literally means 'of the moon'. This could conceivably also be translated as 'lunatic'.

Di Luna is certainly moon-struck, obsessed as he is by his love for **Leonora**. Robert Graves would have said he was enslaved by the White Goddess of Celtic legend.[45] If so it is all the most negative aspects of the Goddess that he encounters.

Di Luna's first appearance in the opera (Act 1 Scene 2) under the balcony of the woman he loves might suggest that he is to be the romantic hero. But his words are the words not of a romantic lover but of a man obsessed. The audience already knows from **Ferrando**'s narration (Act 1 Scene 1) that 'Jealousy's fierce serpents are writhing in his breast'. It has also been established by Leonora herself in the preceding scene that all her thoughts are for the unknown troubadour. **Manrico**'s voice breaks in just as di Luna is about to mount the steps of Leonora's apartments in order to claim her for his own (Act 1 Scene 2).

Confronted with his rival di Luna's one thought is to remove him forthwith, a resolution which is only confirmed by the

---

[45] See 'The White Goddess', Robert Graves (Faber 1961)

fact that he overhears Leonora declaring her love to Manrico. Then for a brief, blissful moment he imagines, in spite of all the evidence to the contrary, that Leonora really does return his love, for she comes rushing down into the garden and flings herself at him, declaring 'at last, merciful love leads you to my arms'. In these few moments di Luna is speechless. But then Manrico's voice comes from the trees accusing Leonora of faithlessness, and she quickly realizes that she has mistaken di Luna for her true love. Leonora immediately and unreservedly declares her love for Manrico. Di Luna can only stand aside, 'burning with fury' and impotence.

One can assume that di Luna carries within himself a burning resentment for the loss of his youth. He is no doubt also assailed by the inevitable guilt associated with having been the survivor of an unforeseen family tragedy. For did not his father's dying words command him to devote all his energies to finding his lost brother? There is no ostensible evidence in the opera that di Luna has taken this injunction to heart; rather it would seem that all his energies are devoted to attempting to evade the responsibility. And yet his loathing for the Troubadour far exceeds the rage of a lover confronting a potentially successful rival. Unconscious of the fact that he actually confronts his own brother, he yet projects his sibling hatred onto Manrico. The dispossession experienced in infancy only keeps recurring in his life. Until he becomes conscious of the mechanisms which promote this he cannot go forward. Only as the curtain falls on the last Act does di Luna have consciousness thrust upon him. By then it is too late to avert catastrophe.

Di Luna is doomed to perpetual frustration. Just when he learns that Manrico has been killed he learns that Leonora is entering a convent (Act 2 Scene 2). The thought of losing her for ever destroys all moderation in him. What he has failed to attain through patient wooing he now determines to obtain by force. It is the reaction of the spoilt child and confirms that he does not deserve to be granted Leonora's love. He is obsessed with the gratification of his own desires. His 'love' is such that it leads him to the brink of insanity. Crazed, and literally beside himself, he declares that not even God shall steal Leonora from him. The imperative of his desire is such that he would cheerfully invite damnation (as does, for instance, Don Giovanni in Mozart's opera). Di Luna's love is no more sincere than the serial lover who is incapable of denying his lust its satisfaction, and refuses to contemplate the fact that the object of his lust may have feelings of her own. His love is pure projection of his needs, needs that are paradigmatically infantile.

The nuns' invocation to Leonora, this latest 'daughter of Eve to turn away from error, desire and sin', only inflames di Luna's resolution that not even God shall come between him and the satisfaction of his desire. This is the very epitome of hubris and confirms in advance the inevitability of di Luna's nemesis. When Leonora herself declares her resolution to turn to 'Him who is the only support of the grieving', di Luna can restrain himself no longer. He advances, intending to seize Leonora. In that moment Manrico steps forth and once again the two brothers are face to face in confrontation. Thankfully for di Luna his retainers are aware that he is beside himself, and restrain him from attempting to fell Manrico. They instinctively realize that di Luna is 'fighting fate itself which is this man's (Manrico's) defender'. His retainers disarm him. Di Luna must accept: 'I have lost my mind'. He has also lost the girl. Helpless and seething with rage he watches as Manrico leaves with Leonora.

Di Luna torments himself with thoughts of Leonora in Manrico's arms. All his life his fate has been, in spite of being the elder son, to cede supremacy to his absent brother. Manrico having taken possession of Leonora is the final insult.

When di Luna discovers that **Azucena** is Manrico's mother (Act 3 Scene 1) it only confirms his belief that the gypsy is the source of all his miseries – on the one hand responsible for his guilt at the loss of his

brother, and on the other progenitor of his rival in love. Little does he know that brother and rival lover are one and the same.

Di Luna is aware that he abuses the power conferred on him by condemning both Azucena and Manrico to death. For him it is a convenient means of excising, or so he thinks, a permanent thorn in his flesh. When he is confronted by Leonora begging mercy for her beloved he is intransigent.

Leonora attempts out-and-out supplication, appealing to his better nature, although she must know this is futile. She abases herself before him, inviting di Luna to: 'stab me, drink my blood, trample upon my corpse – but save the Troubadour!' Di Luna is unmoved, inevitably, for he cares neither about Manrico nor, indeed, about Leonora. The lie of his love, his narcissism, is never more clearly revealed than in his scene. Like Azucena he has engendered and nurtured within himself so virulent a thirst for vengeance that not even Leonora's pleas can move him. The distinction between di Luna and Azucena lies in the fact that Azucena's passion is prompted, ostensibly at any rate, by the altruistic need to avenge an injustice perpetrated on her mother, while the only injustice di Luna seeks to avenge is that of his own thwarted desire. When Leonora offers herself in return for clemency towards Manrico, di Luna is all too easily persuaded. So blinded is he by his own lust that the utter implausibility of Leonora's proposal never occurs to him. As di Luna exults that at last Leonora is his ('You're mine! Mine!') Leonora is exulting in the fact that her final act on Earth has been to save her lover.

Di Luna would be shamed by the utter selflessness of Leonora's love if it were not for the fact that he is engulfed by his own passion to possess. If he had the perspective to feel shamed by Leonora he would have known that she would never, *could* never, have given herself to him.

As Leonora dies di Luna realizes that he has been duped and orders Manrico's immediate execution. Azucena is dragged to the window to watch. She reveals the truth too late for di Luna to save himself from the guilt of murdering his own brother. With her dying breath Azucena realizes that in spite of herself her mother has been avenged. Three of the four protagonists have achieved their destinies. Manrico and Leonora will be 'united in Heaven'. Azucena has seen vengeance wreaked on di Luna. Only di Luna remains. Despairing, he exclaims as the curtain falls: '*E vivo ancor!*' ('And I must still live!') That is to be his curse; the punishment for his solipsism.

M

MACBETH

Opera in 4 Acts. Libretto by Francesco Maria Piave and Andrea Maffei after Shakespeare's tragedy (1605–1606).

First performance: 14 March 1847 at the Teatro della Pergola, Florence. Revised version (by Verdi and Piave from the French translation of Nuttier and Beaumont) first performed 21 April 1865 at the Théâtre Lyrique, Paris.

Cast:

Macbeth: a General in King Duncan's army (baritone)
Banquo: another General (bass)
Lady Macbeth (soprano)
Macduff: a Scottish nobleman (tenor)
Malcolm: the King's son (tenor)
Lady Macbeth's attendant (Dama) (mezzo-soprano)
Doctor (Medico) (bass)
Servant of Macbeth (Servo) (bass)
Assassin (Sicario) (bass)
Herald (Araldo) (bass)
1st Apparition (Apparizione 1) (baritone)
2nd Apparition (Apparizione 2) (soprano)
3rd Apparition (Apparizione 3) (soprano)

Time: mid 11th century
Place: Scotland

Synopsis

Act 1 Scene 1 A blasted heath. Three covens of witches, thunder and lightning. The first coven is eager to discover from the second and third covens what they have been up to. The second coven has slit the throat of a boar while the third has been cursed by a steersman's wife and in revenge intends drowning the steersman at sea. A drum is heard in the distance. The witches realize that this signals the imminent arrival of Macbeth, who shortly enters in company with Banquo. The two men have apparently been victorious in battle (*Giorno non vidi mai*). 'So foul and fair a day I have not seen', Macbeth remarks. 'Nor so glorious', is Banquo's reply. They are startled by the witches who hail Macbeth as 'Thane of Glamis!' then 'Thane of Cawdor!' and, finally, 'King of Scotland!' Macbeth is shaken by this. Banquo, impressed by the witches' prophecies, requires that they now prophesy on his behalf. The witches are, as ever, ambiguous. The first hails him as: 'Lesser than Macbeth and greater'; the second: 'Not happy as he, but happier than he'; and the third gives the most impressive pronouncement: 'Though you be none, you shall father kings'. Having hailed the pair of them the witches vanish, leaving the two men considerably disquieted.

Messengers now arrive with the news that Macbeth, in recognition of his valour on the battlefield, has been created Thane of Cawdor. Macbeth points out that the Thane of Cawdor is still alive. But the messengers disabuse him; Cawdor has just been executed for treason. Banquo is immediately struck by the speed with which the witches' prophecy is being fulfilled. Macbeth is already thinking ahead (*Due vaticini*). Since the first two parts of the prophecy have been fulfilled presumably he can count on the third part being realized and he will shortly become king of Scotland. Already it occurs to him that he could give fate a helping hand by murdering the current incumbent, Duncan. Appalled at himself for entertaining such a thought he banishes it: 'I will not lift a grasping hand to the crown that fate offers me'. Banquo intuits Macbeth's train of thought and muses to himself that 'often the evil spirit of Hell speaks truths in order to ensnare us, and later abandons us, accursed, above the pit it has prepared for us'. The messengers, meanwhile, are surprised by Macbeth's apparent insouciance. All depart their separate ways and the witches re-materialize. They determine to adjourn and await the moment when Macbeth will seek them out for confirmation and guidance from their oracle (*S'allontanarono!*).

Act 1 Scene 2 Macbeth's castle of Dunsinane. A large hall with many rooms leading off. Lady Macbeth enters, reading a letter from her husband describing the day's events (*Nel dì della vittoria*). She is exhilarated by the news that Macbeth may very well soon become king and determines that her husband should do whatever it takes to ensure the swift realization of the witches' prophecy. She will do everything in her power to ensure Macbeth does not let this opportunity pass by (*Vieni! t'affretta!*).

A servant enters to announce that King Duncan is coming that very evening to spend the night at Dunsinane. Lady Macbeth, having ascertained that her husband is with the king, dismisses the servant, commanding him to ensure that Duncan is given a befitting welcome. She can barely contain her excitement. She calls on all the 'ministers of Hell that inspire and spur mortals on to bloody deeds' to arise and 'let not the knife see whose breast it is it smites' (*Or tutti sorgete*). She has already resolved that Duncan shall be murdered that very night. Macbeth enters. His wife loses no time in telling him her plans. Macbeth lacks his wife's conviction, but has little chance to argue with her since festive music from without announces the imminent arrival of the king. A cortege escorting the king crosses the stage. The Macbeths fall in behind the cortege, which also includes Malcolm, Banquo, Macduff and other Thanes and courtiers.

Some time later Macbeth returns with a servant. He instructs the servant to tell his wife as soon as his nightly drink has been prepared, this being the prearranged signal that Macbeth should do the deed. He is to be advised by a stroke on the bell. The servant withdraws. Macbeth is now assailed by a vision of a dagger inciting him to violence. He wrestles with his conscience over

Duncan's murder – and loses. The scene is a close paraphrase of Macbeth's speech, 'Is this a dagger I see before me?'[46] (*Mi si affaccia un pugnal?*) His ruminations are interrupted by the bell that seems like 'a knell that summons [Duncan] to heaven or to hell'. He enters the king's apartments.

Lady Macbeth enters. Macbeth's voice is heard from within expressing alarm at the sound of someone approaching. Lady Macbeth is immediately concerned that Duncan may have awakened, 'before the fatal blow'. Macbeth returns, dagger in hand, clearly overwrought. He announces that the deed is done. Examining his bloodstained hands he is appalled at the crime he has just committed (*Fatal mia donna!*). Apparently he overheard the grooms saying their nightly prayers and attempted to say his own 'Amen', but the 'intractable word froze upon my lips'. Lady Macbeth attempts to calm him, but Macbeth is inconsolable. His wife becomes disgusted at his feebleness. Finally she orders him to return the dagger whence he found it and to smear the guards with blood in order that the blame shall fall on them. Macbeth is appalled at the thought of re-entering Duncan's chamber. Out of patience Lady Macbeth snatches the dagger from him and goes into the chamber herself. At this moment there is a loud knocking at the castle gate. Macbeth starts guiltily; his hands are still covered in blood. His wife returns. Her hands are also covered in blood. 'A splash of water and they are clean', she says, and then 'The deed, too, will pass into oblivion'. Macbeth knows this will never be the case. His wife is scornful and finally succeeds in dragging him from the scene.

Day is breaking. Macduff enters with Banquo. Apparently the king has requested that he be woken early. Macduff enters the king's apartments while Banquo waits behind, overwhelmed by a sense of foreboding (*Oh qual orrenda notte!*). Macduff returns, horrified by what he has discovered. He summons the household with frantic calls while Banquo goes to see for himself what

---

[46] See Shakespeare's *Macbeth*, Act 2 Scene 1.

has transpired. When he returns Macbeth and the rest of the household have all assembled. Banquo announces, in portentous tones, the murder of their king. All, including the Macbeths, join in calling on God to assist them in revealing the murderer (*Schiudi, inferno, la bocca*). This is one of the most significant moments in the Macbeths' odyssey since although they are ostensibly dissembling innocence, they are in reality acknowledging their guilt and pleading for the possibility of atonement. The Act concludes with all placing their trust in God. In view of Lady Macbeth's recent invocations to the powers of hell, this is particularly eloquent.

Act 2 Scene 1   A room in the castle. Macbeth is now king. Duncan's son has taken flight to England and is thus assumed guilty as his father's murderer.

Macbeth, deep in gloomy thought, enters, followed by his wife. Lady Macbeth is wondering why her husband avoids her and is so sunk in despondency. 'What is done cannot be undone', she tells him. Macbeth is haunted by the fact that the witches hailed Banquo as father to a line of kings. He has convinced himself that it is now necessary to murder Banquo. Lady Macbeth is only anxious that this time her husband may prove 'firm of purpose'. Macbeth is no longer the vacillating, incipient criminal; he is already steeped in blood and aware that if Banquo succeeds to the throne his murder of Duncan will be rendered futile. However, he is not going to commit the deed himself. He rushes off to employ the services of a band of cut-throats.

Left alone Lady Macbeth is suddenly overwhelmed by an awareness that their first crime has already necessitated a fresh one. The mood of her aria (*La luce langue*) echoes Banquo's dark mood just prior to the discovery of Duncan's murder and also prefigures Banquo's sense of foreboding before his own murder. But Lady Macbeth deliberately suppresses any sense of foreboding and turns her mind to 'the voluptuous joy' of being queen.

Act 2 Scene 2   A wooded park in the castle grounds. Two bands of murderers have met. They have both been engaged by Macbeth to murder Banquo for whom they now determine to lie in wait (*Sparve il sol*). As they conceal themselves Banquo enters with his son, Fleance. Banquo is once again overwhelmed with a premonition of impending disaster. He confides his anxiety to his son (*Come dal ciel precipita*). The two move off into a cluster of trees that conceals the murderers. Shortly Banquo's anguished cries are heard, urging his son to flee. Fleance rushes across the stage with one of the murderers in hot pursuit.

Act 2 Scene 3   The Banqueting Hall in Macbeth's castle. The Macbeths are greeting their guests. Macbeth calls on all to be seated and on his wife to propose a toast. Lady Macbeth duly obliges (*Si colmi il calice*). Her drinking song, significantly, calls on all to banish hate and anger: 'Let's drive away dull care from our breasts; let pleasure be born and melancholy die'. Her refrain revolves around the word 'muoia' – 'die'. (It is a very different sort of Brindisi from that sung by Violetta in *La Traviata* (Act 1), although paradoxically the situation is very similar in that both are sung by condemned women.)

As Lady Macbeth concludes, one of the murderers presents himself at a side door. He is bespattered with blood and Macbeth is anxious that he should not be seen by his guests. He ascertains that Banquo is dead but is appalled to learn that Fleance has escaped. Returning to his guests he tells them that he has been awaiting Banquo's arrival. Since Banquo spurns their company he will himself take Banquo's seat at the feast. As he is about to sit the ghost of Banquo appears. It is only visible to Macbeth who, terror-struck, demands to know 'who has done this?' The guests are puzzled by their King's behaviour. Assuming he is unwell they announce their intention of departing, but Lady Macbeth insists they stay. She frantically attempts to pacify her distraught husband. But Macbeth is beyond her reach. He rails at the ghost: 'Can the grave give back the dead? . . . Can the tomb disgorge the murdered?' Finally his wife succeeds in calming him. However, no sooner has she resumed her drinking song than the ghost reappears and Macbeth is shouting at it, 'Hence, spirit of hell!' This time the guests are in no doubt that Macbeth is seriously deranged. They are also aware that the King's behaviour must surely indicate a guilty conscience. The Act concludes as Lady Macbeth continues her desperate attempts to pacify her husband and the guests variously express their unease.

Act 3 Scene 1   The witches' cave. In the centre is a boiling cauldron. Thunder and lightning. Three groups of witches sing as they concoct their devilish brew and invoke the infernal powers (*Tre volte miagola*). A witches' revelry ensues (Ballet: see **Appendix**).

Macbeth appears outside the cave with some attendants. He orders his retainers to wait until summoned then enters the cave. He demands that the witches reveal to him his fate. The witches summon the spirits. There is a flash of lightning and a helmeted head rises from the cauldron. The apparition warns Macbeth to 'Beware Macduff!' and then vanishes. Now there is a peal of thunder and a child covered in blood appears. This apparition announces: 'Bloody and cruel you may be – no man of woman born shall harm you'. This gives Macbeth some consolation and he almost decides to let Macduff live. There is more thunder and lightning and then a young boy appears with a crown upon his head and a tree in his hand. He tells Macbeth: 'You shall be glorious and invincible till Birnam wood you see set in motion and come against you!' This is even greater consolation to Macbeth who observes that: 'No wood was ever moved by magic power'.

Macbeth now demands to know whether Banquo's descendants will ever ascend his throne. But the witches order him not to seek the answer to this question. As Macbeth threatens them with his sword the cauldron vanishes and from beneath the ground comes a melancholy and solemn sound of bagpipes. Eight kings appear and file past. At the end comes Banquo, carrying a mirror in his hand. Macbeth is terrified. He sees in Banquo's mirror the spectres of future kings. Laughing, Banquo points out his descendants for Macbeth's benefit. Macbeth makes to lunge

at them with his sword then, realizing they are but apparitions, desperately asks the witches: 'Shall they live?' As the witches confirm that they will indeed live, Macbeth falls, senseless, to the ground. The witches summon spirits of the air to revive the King. Spirits slowly rise and begin to dance. As they finish Macbeth regains consciousness. The spirits vanish, as do the witches.

A herald enters and announces the queen. Lady Macbeth enters and Macbeth relates what he has seen and heard. When he describes the appearance of Banquo's offspring Lady Macbeth shrieks: 'Death and annihilation to the villainous breed!' As Macbeth begins to regain his fighting spirit the couple confirm that: 'The enterprise by crime must end . . . since with blood it was begun'.

Act 4 Scene 1   A deserted place on the borders of England and Scotland. Scottish refugees – men, women and children – are gathered together. Macduff stands sadly aside.

The refugees sing of their unhappy plight (*Patria oppressa!*). Macduff, meanwhile, laments the loss of his wife and children, murdered by Macbeth. He is tortured by the sense of his own helplessness, prevented by exile from doing anything to save his family or avenge their deaths (*Ah la paterno mano*). He prays to God that one day he may come face to face with Macbeth and exact his revenge. Martial music is heard. Malcolm enters at the head of a troop of English soldiers. They are lost. The refugees tell them they are at the forest of Birnam. Malcolm orders every man to cut a bough off every tree to use as camouflage. He then incites all to take up arms and follow him. The moment for vengeance has arrived. They comfort themselves with the thought that already Macbeth's star is in eclipse, plagued as he is by his conscience and by unrest in the country.

Act 4 Scene 2   A hall in Macbeth's castle. It is night. The doctor and Lady Macbeth's attendant are keeping watch, for Lady Macbeth has apparently taken to sleepwalking. The doctor is growing impatient.

For two nights they have kept watch and there has been no sign of Lady Macbeth. Suddenly she appears. She sets down a light and starts rubbing her hand. The attendant explains to the doctor that her mistress thereby imagines she is washing her hand. Lady Macbeth commences her extended soliloquy (*Una macchia è qui tuttora...*). It is quickly apparent that she is re-living the night of Duncan's murder. She has soon revealed her guilt. The doctor and attendant are horrified. Lady Macbeth continues desperately trying to wash the blood from her hand. The two observers pray to God to have mercy on her.

Act 4 Scene 3   A room in the castle. Macbeth is discovered, alone. He is now almost totally isolated. Most of his subjects have turned against him. His wife has become insane. Macbeth's only consolation is the witches' prophecy that he cannot be harmed by 'any man of woman born'. Yet he feels the life in his veins draining away (*Pietà, rispetto, amore*). Only curses will attend his passing, he reflects. Women's voices are heard and Lady Macbeth's attendant enters to announce the death of the Queen. Macbeth's only reaction is the famous expostulation: 'Life... What does it matter? It is a tale told by an idiot, full of sound and fury signifying nothing!' The attendant withdraws. Soldiers suddenly crowd into the hall. They have just noticed something impossible. Birnam wood is on the move. This is devastating news for Macbeth. He orders his breastplate, sword and dagger to be brought to him and rushes off to: 'Death... or Victory!'

Act 4 Scene 4   A wide plain. Malcolm is leading his men under cover of the foliage they have cut from Birnam wood. He orders them to throw down their branches and engage in the battle. Macduff enters in hot pursuit of Macbeth. As he catches up with the 'Butcher of my children' Macbeth desperately rejoins that he cannot be slain by any man: 'of woman born'. To which Macduff replies: 'I was not born – untimely ripped from my mother's womb was I!' They fight and Macduff deals Macbeth a fatal blow. With a cry Macbeth falls, dead. Scottish women enter hurriedly and in agitation. To their relief they realize that the tumult has ceased. Shouts of 'Victory!' are heard offstage. Malcolm enters with his men. Macduff points to the corpse of Macbeth. All join in exulting at the tyrant's death and congratulating Macduff for his heroic deed. The curtain falls.

For a man of Verdi's fundamentally dark and pessimistic disposition the story of Macbeth was a gift. It is noticeable that Verdi's halfdozen masterworks were all dour tragedies: *I Due Foscari, Macbeth, Rigoletto, La Traviata, Il Trovatore, Otello*. Perhaps what most appealed to Verdi in *Macbeth* is that the central preoccupation is with guilt and the wages paid by those riddled with it. For Verdi himself was guilt-ridden for no ostensible reason other than the obvious, namely the early death of his young wife and infant children.

Elsewhere *Macbeth* has been referred to as the first clarion call of Verdi's genius. This is no mere hyperbole, for *Macbeth* is the first opera in the Verdi canon to differentiate its composer clearly from his peers, Donizetti and Rossini, who had both written works of dark dramatic passion in addition to their comic masterpieces. Verdi himself had given hints in *I Due Foscari* and *Attila* of what he was capable of, but neither of these works occupies a psychic sound-world that is distinctly memorable in the way that *Macbeth* certainly is. Think of *Macbeth*, and the moments that immediately resonate in the mind are Lady Macbeth's Recitative and Aria (Act 1 Scene 2); Banquo's brooding prior to the murder of Duncan (*Oh qual orrenda*); Banquo's aria (*Come dal ciel precipita*); Lady Macbeth's aria (*la luce langue*) and her sleepwalking scene; Macduff's lament at the loss of his murdered wife and children (*Ah, la paterna mano*); and Macbeth's own valedictory aria. These are all moments of dark soliloquy. It is as though none of the characters are capable of relating to each other, all being trapped in a solipsistic nightmare of their own. There is something frantic and furtive about the work and its protagonists, something Verdi undeniably inherited (and embraced) from Shakespeare. The moments of dark soliloquy are only alleviated, not by moments of joyous abandon, caustic humour or even chinks of light (as for instance in Desdemona's scene with the Cypriots in *Otello* Act 2), but by scenes of supernatural horror. The banquet scene is blighted by Macbeth's hysteria and his wife's false, bright attempts to cover for him. All is dark, dark, dark.

It was in the dark that Verdi felt most at home. For in dark obscurity lies the origin of passion. The superficial talent looks outward towards fashion and contemporary trends, and attempts to propitiate that which he finds. The original creative artist knows that ultimately nothing changes. Fashions come and fashions go. Human nature remains the same. For all that Verdi was a sound businessman, who eventually achieved huge popularity and commercial success, he was first and foremost an artist who sought to plumb the depths of human experience.

It was no mere accident that Verdi worshipped Shakespeare above all other dramatists, for he sought a similarly all-embracing depiction of reality. But ultimately whether the setting was ancient Egypt, the Barbarian north, Scotland or Sicily was immaterial to him. What Verdi wanted to know was why his characters behaved in the way that they did. He was a natural dramatist, because he knew that first and foremost the illusion must be instantly accessible. In order to achieve this it was necessary to have a clear-cut scenario with strongly etched personalities, encountering clearly identifiable and recognizable predicaments. Macbeth's predicament may not be one which you or I are likely to encounter, but the price he pays for deliberately ignoring the prickings of his own conscience certainly is something to which we can relate.

Macbeth 'hath murdered sleep' and with it turned the daylight into night. He has turned the natural order of things on its head. This is the inevitable effect of ignoring the dictates of conscience. Like *Otello*, the tale of *Macbeth* is partly a cautionary tale. The two main protagonists both end up dying, one insane and the other despairing. In the meantime the Macbeths turn the lives of their subjects into nightmares. In this respect there is considerable justification for transferring the action of the opera to the bleak ambience of a twentieth-century totalitarian state. For fascist politics, whether explicit or implicit, are always founded on paranoia. Verdi understood paranoia. He also understood the banality of evil and the superstition that it breeds. Thus his opera encompasses with equal facility the darkly oppressive and tortured ruminations of the individual protagonists on the one hand, and the inanity of the witches on the other.

The story must also have appealed to Verdi's atheistic tendency, for the whole crisis originates from the moment Macbeth allows himself to be hoodwinked by supernatural intervention, or, put another way, allows his fragile ego to be flattered by the promises of greatness that are suddenly placed before him. Such supernatural interventions are always an expression of a need within the individual to whom they occur. Macbeth, as the action of the drama demonstrates, is chronically incapable of making any resolution for himself. He distrusts life and thereby makes himself fair game for any capricious prompting from the unconscious. His problem is his passivity. How often do we come across the same problem in Verdi's operas of a hero who, in spite of much 'sound and fury', ultimately cedes responsibility for his destiny to the woman in his life. It may be that the woman can lead him forward, as in the case of Elisabeth (**Don Carlo**), but more often than not this chronic dependency has disastrous results for both parties. The hero, having been released from his apathy, finds that he is unable to contend with the responsibilities of autonomy, while the heroine is unable to support the full weight of that she has undertaken.

The story of *Macbeth* exemplifies this syndrome and provided Verdi with the perfect opportunity to give vent to the savage pessimism concerning human affairs which was never far from his sensibility.

Macbeth (*Macbeth*). A general in King Duncan's army.

Background Note Verdi's Macbeth stands in a similar relation to his historical equivalent as does Boris Godunov, in Mussorgsky's opera, to the historical Tsar. Whereas in *Macbeth* the tyrant is shown in the process of moral disintegration through having committed a heinous crime, the historical facts are rather different. It was no more unusual in eleventh-century Scotland than in sixteenth-century Russia for a nobleman who aspired to the throne to do whatever was necessary to achieve his end.

By the standards of the day Macbeth (c1005–1057) had as legitimate a claim to the throne as did his predecessor, Duncan I. Like Duncan Macbeth was a grandson of Malcolm II, who had himself appropriated the throne by murdering his cousin, Kenneth III. Macbeth's claim was strengthened by his marriage, for his wife was the granddaughter of Kenneth III. Macbeth did not assassinate Duncan in his bed as portrayed in the play. However he challenged Duncan for the throne and the latter was killed in the ensuing battle. Shakespeare used an account from Holinshed's Chronicles concerning a previous royal assassination and applied it to *Macbeth*.

Macbeth was not even a tyrannical ruler. His reign saw Scotland blessed with peace and prosperity. He and his wife, Lady Macbeth, were staunch supporters of the Church and in 1050 Macbeth went on a pilgrimage to Rome. The only fact in the story which is historically correct is Malcolm's invasion at the conclusion of the drama. However Macbeth was not killed by **Macduff**. Malcolm defeated and killed Macbeth at Lumphanan, in Aberdeenshire, nowhere near Dunisane.

Macbeth is one of opera's anti-heroes, doomed by his own failings and weakness. He is intelligent, but not intelligent enough to break away from the domineering influence of his wife's all-powerful will. It is a fair assumption that it has been **Lady Macbeth**'s will that has assisted Macbeth in rising to the position of pre-eminence which he enjoys when the opera opens. So far they have made a good team: she in the driving seat and he in the passenger seat, behaving rather like a performing monkey. Macbeth is that most despised and ridiculed of all masculine types, the hen-pecked husband. Yet, as is proper to the world of myth (for the history of Macbeth has entered into our mythic consciousness), it is on a grand scale. As is the way with myth his predicament can be interpreted on many different levels. He is at one and the same time Hamlet, Claudius, Titus (Andronicus), Odysseus, Achilles and Oedipus. He is, above all, flawed and guilt-ridden. It is because he is guilt-ridden that the witches are able to assail him at the outset. They see his vulnerability.

Banquo is strong and wholesome because he is not as intelligent as Macbeth. He does not question and he is his own man. He is not 'owned' as Macbeth is owned. Macbeth can never be himself because he has never had to stand on his own two feet and be himself. He has always been pushed from behind, propelled into the limelight. Once there he does not know what to do or which way to turn. He must await instruction.

The witches never said that it was a precondition of his becoming king that he should murder Duncan. They foresee that Macbeth will murder Duncan because otherwise he will have nowhere to go. For he has a wife who is above all ambitious for him. Worldly ambition cannot be satisfied until the pinnacle has been attained. Lady Macbeth makes it quite clear that until that pinnacle is attained her husband has only one option, and that is to 'screw (his) courage to the sticking place'.[47] For Lady Macbeth, courage and ambition are synonymous. She has no transcendent sense of to what or to whom courage should be owed. There is nothing beyond the self. This is the only altar at which all masculine valour and human endeavour may be applied.

Macbeth has no strong moral concepts or precepts with which to oppose his wife's

---

[47] See Shakespeare's *Macbeth*, Act 1 Scene 7.

solipsism. He is an empty vessel, supremely fatalistic. Only a supreme fatalist would listen to the witches in the first place. Medieval Scotland may have been a haunt for witches and warlocks but, as portrayed through Shakespeare's sixteenth-century eyes, it was not primarily a superstitious land. It was a country where the Catholic Church had taken firm hold, nowhere more so than among the ruling classes. Macbeth is well aware that he listens to and invokes infernal powers. So is his wife.

Lady Macbeth is motivated principally by the primal urges of power and sex. The two are synonymous for her. Macbeth, on the other hand, is acutely ill at ease. He craves legitimacy. Unlike his wife he does not need to sleep in order for the wisdom of the unconscious to come to the surface. His subconscious and conscious minds are in fact almost perfectly aligned. It is the lack of a controlling ego that signals his downfall.

Only a mind lacking all objectivity could allow him to reveal his guilt with such awesome vividness as in the banquet scene (Act 2 Scene 3). This is not a mere Freudian slip; this is a full-scale eruption from the subconscious. His wife, for the first time in their relationship, is powerless to control him. Macbeth needs this release. For too long he has been a mere pawn in the unravelling of his wife's obsessions. If he was not so congenitally feeble, he would take the revelation of Banquo's ghost as an indication that it is time to step back. Like **Pagano** (*I Lombardi*) he needs now to take upon himself sackcloth and ashes. Instead he seeks out the witches again.

Macbeth recognizes that the witches have not merely been the agent of his downfall, but that they are the source from which he has for the first time in his life gained a true illumination. They have enabled him, for the first time, to confront his true self. All his life Macbeth has been a soldier. When faced with the prospect of murdering Duncan his problem is not that he is naturally squeamish and cannot cope with the trauma of spilling blood. Through his wife's goading he has ended up murdering his better self in order to secure a quick fix.

Macbeth would never have murdered Duncan of his own volition. In Jungian terms he has chosen to project his *anima* onto the very epitome of the destructive aspect of the feminine. Lady Macbeth makes it a principle to excise all that is most distinctly feminine in herself, most especially the mothering instinct. The Macbeths' marriage is sterile, and always will be, because Lady Macbeth is far too busy living out her own animus (her need to exteriorize the masculine side of her own psyche). Because this is so powerful it leaves virtually no room for manoeuvre to her husband, who is reduced to seeking guidance from supernatural (or subconscious) sources.

The problem with such sources, as Macbeth finds out to his cost, is that the messages can be either confusing or ambiguous. Whether he would have become king had he not murdered Duncan is an imponderable. The witches, or rather the racial unconscious that they serve, have intuited that he would murder Duncan because he is so fatally passive. When Macbeth returns to their coven for further enlightenment (Act 3) he is only shown what will be if he persists in the course that he is currently pursuing. Macbeth thinks that he has no alternative, although, in fact, there is always an alternative, particularly once Lady Macbeth has vacated the driving seat.

Unfortunately it is too late for Macbeth. His identity by now is so bound up in the warped mentality of his wife that he cannot contemplate a life without her. His notorious declaration: 'Life... What does it matter? It is a tale told by an idiot, full of sound and fury, signifying nothing!' is only an admission of the futility which has come to predominate in his own existence, principally through the fact that he chose early in life to surrender his will to the superior will of the woman he married.

The Macbeths' sins are compounded by the fact that, apart from the heinous nature of their crimes, they also sin against one of the oldest moral laws: the law of hospitality by which even an arch enemy, once invited into the home, is granted immunity from retribution. Verdi has already explored this theme in *Ernani* (see de Silva).

Macbeth's real sins are sins of omission, omitting to look behind the surface meanings of the prophecies by which he chooses to guide his life. The witches never said that Birnam wood would not move. Indeed they made it perfectly clear that a day would come when it would. Likewise, 'no man of woman born will kill you' is not the same thing as saying 'no man will kill you'. Even if he takes this at face value, he might reflect that if he is not killed by another man, he may well be killed by the exactions of his own desperate conscience.

Ultimately Macbeth's chief problem is his lack of imagination.

Macduff (*Macbeth*). A Scottish nobleman and Thane of Fife.

It is uncertain whether there was ever an historical Macduff. Shakespeare took the character from Holinshed's Chronicles, itself based on the partly legendary history of Hector Boece. If Macduff did exist he was probably a ruler of Fife, who allied himself to Malcolm Canmore (see **Malcolm**) in the latter's campaign against Macbeth. In the play Macduff turned out to be 'not of woman born', but it is extremely unlikely that Caesarean section was practised in Scotland in the 11th century. As with so much in the drama of *Macbeth* this was probably poetic licence to emphasize the extraordinary nature of Macduff's destiny.

Macduff is loyal to his king. Second only to his king is his family. He is destined to lose each and every one of these individuals who give meaning to his life. Inevitably Verdi, who had recently lost his own wife and two children in quick succession, empathized with Macduff's plight. But where Verdi lost wife and children to the arms of marauding disease, Macduff loses them to the egocentric mania of a thoughtless despot. It may be difficult for a contemporary interpreter of the role to understand the depth of passion that is engendered in Macduff by the murder of King Duncan, although we have a close historical correlative in the murder of President Kennedy in 1963. As was the case for the

American nation with the loss of Kennedy, so Duncan's murder is experienced by Macduff and the rest of the Scottish people as the calamitous loss of a benign father-figure.

Macduff's immediate reaction on discovering Duncan's corpse is to arouse the Court (Act 1 Scene 2). Nobody can find words adequate to express the depth of their emotion. Instead they all – **Malcolm** and Macduff included – revert to rhetorical invocation of the heavenly powers to assist them in discovering the identity of the murderer. Since the murderer is in their very midst it is not surprising that enlightenment proves to be a long time coming.

Unlike Duncan's son, Malcolm, Macduff does not flee immediately into exile. He attends the banquet thrown by the Macbeths to celebrate their ascendancy (Act 2 Scene 3). Macbeth's demented behaviour and the murder of **Banquo**, reported shortly after, convince him, in company with many of his countrymen, that it is not safe for him to remain in Scotland. For with the murder of Banquo, once Macbeth's closest friend, it becomes clear that Macbeth is utterly ruthless. If he murders his closest friend nobody is safe.

It seems incomprehensible, therefore, that Macduff chooses to leave his wife and children behind. It apparently never occurs to him that the tyrant might stoop so low as to threaten their lives. When he learns that they have been murdered he is inevitably distraught, not just over the loss, but because he is consumed with guilt (Act 4 Scene 1). The only consolation left him is the possibility of exacting revenge. Thus when he comes upon Malcolm he accepts with alacrity the latter's suggestion that they join forces to depose the tyrant. When he comes face to face with Macbeth (Act 4 Scene 3) he assaults Macbeth where it most hurts the tyrant (that is, his pride), before slaying him in honourable combat. He takes special relish in revealing that he was 'untimely ripped' from his mother's womb, thus confounding Macbeth's belief in his own invulnerability.

It could be said that the violent nature of Macduff's birth has been echoed throughout his life, which has proved to be a catalogue of loss – the loss of king, of homeland, of wife and of children. Only in the moment that he runs Macbeth through with his sword and then hails Malcolm as Duncan's legitimate heir can he feel that some semblance of order has been restored to a universe that hitherto has appeared all too perilous.

It is tempting to see the role of Macduff as merely a sop to the established tradition, in Italian opera, of a leading tenor role. In fact it is interesting to note how many of Verdi's operas do *not* contain a leading tenor role. Even his very first opera, *Oberto*, does not have a tenor lead. The truth is that Verdi was not particularly enamoured of the tenor voice. For his money the male voice which afforded the greatest possibilities of breadth of expression was the baritone, a voice type for which he was almost single-handedly responsible. As his career developed Verdi discovered a useful extension to the baritone range in the voice of the *tenore di forza*, culminating in the histrionics of Otello. Interestingly, in his last opera *Falstaff*, Verdi reverted to his favoured schematic of a principal baritone with subsidiary, or marginal, tenor role. Macduff is such a role. But it includes an aria of such expressive range and power (*Ah, la paterna mano*) that it is usually ascribed to a major artist.

Maddalena (*Rigoletto*). Sister of **Sparafucile**. Maddalena does not appear until Act 3 of the drama. She lives with her brother in a ramshackle inn on the outskirts of Mantua. The inn is in reality a front for Sparafucile, who is a professional assassin. Judging from the dilapidation of the inn, business in Mantua is not too brisk.

Maddalena plays a crucial part in luring her brother's victims to their doom. As Sparafucile describes to **Rigoletto**, on his first encounter with the hunchback (Act 1 Scene 2), Maddalena 'dances in the streets – she's pretty – whomever I want, she entices – and then...'. And then he murders them.

Maddalena, on her first appearance (Act 3 Scene 1), is described as 'a buxom young woman in gypsy costume' (SD). She attempts to keep some distance between herself and the **Duke**, knowing as she does his pre-destined fate, but in spite of herself she finds him irresistible. She is no fool and realizes that he is a compulsive seducer. But the sheer exuberance of his nature overwhelms her. Considering the fact that she habitually uses her charms to lure her brother's victims to their inevitable doom it is the more remarkable that she becomes so intensely involved with the Duke. It is a tribute to the Duke's charismatic personality that she does.

Maddalena represents everything that **Gilda** is not. Where Gilda is a virgin Maddalena is a whore. Where Gilda loves, Maddalena lusts. When Gilda attends Mass, Maddalena dances in the streets. As one who seduces in order to kill, Maddalena evokes the darkest, most treacherous aspects of the feminine. Yet something about the Duke redeems her from her customary self.

In one respect Maddalena and Gilda are very similar. Both are entirely answerable to the men they live with, Gilda to her father and Maddalena to her brother. Both pine for liberation from the stifling influence of their 'partner' through the anarchic will to self-enjoyment represented by the Duke. Both instinctively recognize in the Duke a capacity for pleasure which neither has been allowed to develop within themselves. In a paradoxical sense Maddalena's subservience to her brother condemns her to the same almost monastic isolation as Gilda endures at the hands of her overprotective father. Both learn love, in the true sense of the word, selflessly. Maddalena may not go to the extent of sacrificing herself, as does Gilda, but she risks her brother's wrath and is prepared to sacrifice the subsistence that her brother's trade provides in order to ensure her lover's reprieve (admittedly it is she who recommends substituting another victim).

The free spirit that the Duke embodies is too precious to sacrifice. Whether Maddalena's one night of passion with him will give her the courage to throw off the yoke of her brother's tyranny is debatable. There is much about her gypsy lifestyle she enjoys, but she can be certain that the day will come when the need to leave will overcome the need to subsist. On that day she will flee the life she has inherited to discover what she may fashion for herself.

Malcolm (*Macbeth*). King Duncan's son and heir to the Scottish throne.

Historical Background Prince Malcolm Canmore (c1031–1093). Son of Duncan I, Malcolm was only a young child when Macbeth seized the throne from his father, who was killed in battle (not murdered as in the opera). Malcolm spent most of his youth in England. In 1054 he attempted an invasion of Scotland which was largely unsuccessful, but he returned in 1057 when he prevailed, defeating and killing Macbeth.

Malcolm's reign inaugurated a crucial period in Scottish history. It was Malcolm (not the probably fictitious Banquo) who was an ancestor of the Stuart dynasty of which James I was the first king of England.

After his father's murder Malcolm cannot fail to realize that his own life is in danger. He flees across the border, thus providing the Macbeths with perfect justification for pointing the finger at him. Malcolm is in an impossible position after his father's murder. Had he stayed in Scotland to claim the throne he would assuredly have been murdered himself. But his flight to England would seem to implicate him in the murder of his father.

What Malcolm cannot know is that the Macbeths are far more concerned about **Banquo**'s offspring succeeding to the throne than they are about Malcolm's legitimate claim. In fact the witches make no mention of Malcolm in their prophecies. Insanely blinded by their ambition the Macbeths miss the most obvious potential source of their nemesis. While Scotland languishes under Macbeth's tyranny Malcolm busies himself raising an army to march into Scotland and reclaim his inheritance. What **Macbeth** does not realize is that it will be Malcolm who will effect the apparently impossible, namely that Birnam wood should uproot itself and move against him.

Malcolm and **Macduff** make a formidable alliance against the tyrant. Malcolm seeks to avenge the death of a father and Macduff seeks vengeance for the murder of his wife and children. They cannot fail, for they are full of passionate intensity where Macbeth has lost all lust for life. Macduff and Malcolm's lives have been rendered sterile by Macbeth's tyranny, but Macbeth's life has been sterile from the start.

Malcolm plays little active role in the drama, nor is his role dramatically interesting. There is no question mark hanging over it. Like Macduff, he has been the victim of gross injustice, and there is no doubt in his mind, or the audience's, what he has to do. He has moral right entirely on his side. He knows it; we know it. Thus, at the conclusion of the opera, he plays his role as saviour and redeemer with single-minded efficacy.

Manfredo (*I Vespri Siciliano*). Sicilian patriot.

The role of Manfredo is hardly distinguishable from the generality of Sicilians (see **Chorus**).

He is among the first of the Sicilians to meet **Procida** on his return from abroad at the opening of Act 2. Later in the Act he arrives with the engaged couples and takes instructions from Procida who, when the French soldiers make off with the Sicilian girls, prevents him from taking arms against the French, but instructs him rather to concentrate on ensuring **Elena**'s safety.

In his one independent line Manfredo expresses trepidation at pursuing the French to the ball which is planned at **Monforte**'s palace. They will have swords, he comments. Procida immediately rejoins, 'And we, daggers and hearts'.

This may appear a small contribution to the argument, but is, in fact, crucial. For it underlines the problem facing the leaders of the Resistance, Procida and Elena, in overcoming the Sicilians' fundamental recalcitrance when it comes to confronting the occupying army. (See also **Danieli**.)

Manrico (*Il Trovatore*). An officer in the Prince of Vizcay's forces, son of **Azucena**.

The character of Manrico has much in common with the historical Jaime de Urgel (see background to **Synopsis**). The most striking similarity is that both men had powerful mothers from whose domination they never escaped. Jaime's mother, Donna Margarita, was a heartless virago who lived only for the vicarious pleasure of seeing her son on the throne. She was undoubtedly a pernicious influence on Urgel whose chief weakness was a total inability to make a resolution and carry it through.

In *I Lombardi* Verdi had already visited the scenario of two brothers in love with the same woman. He had also touched on the theme in *La battaglio di Legnano* although there it is close friends (as in *Un Ballo in Maschera*), not brothers, who contend for the same. In *Il Trovatore* that early outline reaches fruition. The situation is different in one important respect. Neither of the two men succeeds in legitimizing their passion for the woman in marriage. Ostensibly either one could win. In reality there is no question where **Leonora**'s loyalty lies. It is Manrico she loves. If she cannot be wed to him she will enter a convent. She will certainly have none of **di Luna**. Manrico is an outsider, ostracized by Society, but also by himself. He has never known his two parents or family, but he is ignorant of that fact. He assumes that Azucena is his mother. He loves her as a mother, yet he cannot help feeling for some reason inexplicable to him, dispossessed. His very words heard offstage, '*deserto sulla terra*' ('All alone on the earth, at war with his evil fate, his only hope is in one heart, a heart for the Troubadour') (Act 1 Scene 2), underline this central facet of his persona.

The love of the Troubadour is more akin to worship than to love as it might be perceived in the 21st century. The object of the love is closely aligned with the Virgin Mary whom she evokes. For Manrico everything in his existence is far in the distance. Only his mother is immanent. But he needs to escape from his mother's orbit, for his mother has for him only one role in life, and that is to achieve the revenge she dreams of day and night; the revenge which was dictated to her by her mother in her final hours of extremity. Manrico needs to extract more out of life than ever can be the case while he remains under the overpowering influence of Azucena.

Whereas in Wagner the split *anima* is the rule, in Verdi it is the split *animus*: two suitors for the same woman. As Manrico and di Luna (brothers, did they but know it) confront each other (Act 1 Scene 2) this motive is underlined. Di Luna refuses to give Manrico the dignity of legal arrest. He demands that they fight a duel. Manrico is an imposter and must be despatched as unceremoniously as a common criminal. From Leonora's point of view it is Manrico whose very strangeness and self-sufficiency give him ascendancy over di Luna. He offers a possibility of transcending the limiting bonds of the society in which she lives.

Manrico has been taken from his mother in infancy. There can be no replacement for the true mother. This is the sole explanation for Manrico's sense of being deserted on the Earth. All his days he carries with him the awareness of an absence, though he cannot explain it. He remains unconscious.

The story of the opera is largely a process of uncovering all that he has not been able, through no fault of his own, to acknowledge in his life. When Azucena recounts how she attempted to effect her revenge on the old Count for the death of her mother (Act 2 Scene 1) and ended up killing her own son, Manrico is not slow to realize the obvious implication. 'I am not your son! Who am I? Who, then?' Azucena emphatically reassures him and refuses to discuss the matter further. Yet it must inevitably niggle in the back of Manrico's mind that he may well not be who he thinks he is. This uncertainty concerning his origins must explain the extraordinary passion with which he flings himself at every crisis that looms in his life.

Azucena attempts to reassure Manrico further by recapitulating all the reasons he has to be grateful to her as a mother. She recalls how she rescued him from the battle-fields of Pelilla where Manrico had been seriously wounded by di Luna. This in turn forces Manrico to recall a previous occasion when he had di Luna at his mercy at the conclusion of a duel and found himself unable to kill his adversary. Manrico is at a loss to explain this: 'the thrust that was to pierce him already flashed in the air, when a mysterious feeling stopped my hand as it descended. Suddenly a sharp chill ran shuddering through my being as a cry came down from heaven that said to me: Don't strike!' It was a subliminal awareness that it was his own brother he was about to kill. It remains, however, incomprehensible to Azucena who makes Manrico swear that should the opportunity re-present itself he will not fail again. Manrico swears that he will plunge his sword into 'that wicked heart' (whether Manrico has the opportunity again in the battle to which he rushes off at the conclusion to Act 3 is not revealed).

In the meantime, when news arrives that Leonora is about to enter a convent and take the veil, Manrico is distraught: 'To lose her! Oh woe! To lose that angel!' His mother notices he is beside himself. She frantically tries to restrain her son, but to no avail. Manrico knows that he must put his love for Leonora above even that for his mother. In Act 3 Scene 2 the scenario will be exactly reversed. Meanwhile he must know that if he sacrifices his love for Leonora he will remain for ever at Azucena's behest. It is interesting that in the fight to save his love for Leonora Manrico prevails (Act 2 Scene 2), whereas in the fight to protect his mother he fails (Act 3 Scene 2). There simply is not the same need within him. His need for Leonora is grounded in his desperation to be rehabilitated, if not by Society then at least by humankind. Leonora's love for him offers him that chance.

Manrico's finest hour comes when he succeeds in procuring Leonora for himself in spite of di Luna's intervention (Act 2 Scene 2). All his life he has been bested by di Luna. He may not be aware that di Luna is his brother, but as long as he can remember he has been in di Luna's shadow. For di Luna is a powerful member of the establishment, the establishment from which Manrico feels himself excluded.

While Azucena is being threatened with the very immolation that she has dreaded all her life Manrico is preparing to sever the bond that has bound him to Azucena hitherto by marrying Leonora (Act 3 Scene 2). Leonora is full of foreboding: 'What a grim light shines on our wedding!' They are outside the chapel in the castle of Castellor, which the rebels have but lately taken possession of. The castle is under siege from di Luna and his troops. In his aria, *Ah si, ben mio*, Manrico confirms that his last thought will be for Leonora – they will be united in Heaven.

When the couple's bliss is shattered by the arrival of **Ruiz** with news of Azucena's arrest Manrico is almost unmanned: 'My legs fail me, my eyes are clouding over'. The intensity with which Manrico tells Leonora that Azucena is his mother proves, superficially at any rate, his conviction that this is indeed the case; at a more profound level it indicates his refusal to acknowledge the truth of her revelation; that she cannot be his mother since she burned the wrong baby. What follows only confirms his desperation at this moment. He is almost callous towards Leonora. *Di quella pira* is a cabaletta thrown away with hectic abandon: Mother can wait no longer. It is the most dynamic aria in the opera; possibly in all Verdi. It is suffused with the masculine energy and thrust that is so distinctive a feature of Verdi's musical style. Yet there is irony in the fact that it is motivated entirely by Manrico's oedipal obsession which has only incidentally been transferred onto Leonora. In this moment all protestations of love are forgotten. Leonora has become superseded: 'Before I loved you I was yet her son. Your suffering cannot restrain me'. He leaves, desperately summoning all his retainers to arms. Leonora has ceased to exist for him. In this moment it becomes incontestable that the true focus of Manrico's *anima*-projection is his mother and not Leonora.

Manrico is defeated, captured and taken to the Aliaferia palace (Act 4 Scene 1). He is now powerless – as indeed he has always been. However, Manrico has found his true destiny. He is about to give his life on the altar of his love for his mother.

As Azucena falls asleep Leonora enters. She urges him to flee, but refuses to accompany him. Manrico quickly guesses the price that Leonora must have negotiated with di Luna. He turns the full force of his frustrated rage on her, for a few moments displaying all the egocentric pride of his rival. The illusion of the chaste, redemptive virgin, concerned only for his salvation has been momentarily shattered. Leonora has become abhorrent to him. Manrico is no more prepared to listen to reason than was di Luna in the previous scene. Azucena awakens and re-commences her fond dream of returning to the mountains with Manrico. She cannot even acknowledge Leonora's presence, let alone the ultimate sacrifice that Leonora offers her son.

Manrico, as soon as he becomes aware that Leonora is dying, is overcome with remorse. She dies in his arms, but Manrico will join her very shortly. Di Luna enters just as Leonora expires. Realizing that he has been cheated di Luna orders Manrico to be taken straight to the scaffold. The essential split in Manrico's psyche prevails right to the end, for his final words are a passionate farewell to his mother. The split will only be healed by his death, which ensues promptly.

La Marchesa di Poggio (*Un giorno di regno*). A young widow, niece of the Baron **Kelbar** and lover of **Belfiore**.

The Marchioness has one agenda throughout the opera, which she states with admirable clarity on her first appearance (Act 1 Scene 1): 'I shall pretend to give my hand to the old commander (Count **Ivrea**). We shall see then if the lover (Belfiore) will reveal himself'. It is a dangerous game to play, but then their whole relationship, as portrayed in the opera, is a charade. She knows perfectly well that the 'King' is her beloved Belfiore, but the masquerade is so inexplicable that her rational mind cannot come to terms with it. Anyway Belfiore is remarkably convincing

as the 'King'. It is not an aspect of him that she has come across before.

When she first sees Belfiore in his guise as the King she thinks it must be a prank, but when Belfiore shows no sign of recognizing her she begins to doubt herself and wonders if she has just become so besotted that she sees her lover's image everywhere (Act 1 Scene 2). In speech and manner he is that 'roguish Cavaliere', she observes. But then why does her uncle treat him like the King, and why does Belfiore behave like the King? It is an imponderable she cannot fathom.

When **Giulietta** and **Edoardo** turn to her for help in their predicament, she is too preoccupied with her own problems to be of much assistance. In a revealing aside the Marchioness comments, 'I do not know what I hope for; I cannot say what I want; I only know that I still love him and that he has deceived me' (Act 1 Scene 2). The Marchioness tells Giulietta, on their first meeting, that she has come to the castle post-haste on her account. We know that the Marchioness has been married and widowed. Presumably her husband was an elderly man so we can therefore assume that she does not wish to see Giulietta having to endure what she had to endure.

Ironically it is almost entirely Belfiore's efforts that ensure Giulietta is saved from marrying the **Treasurer**. The Marchioness lends moral support and intervenes at one crucial moment only. When the Baron regales Giulietta and Edoardo with the fact that the Treasurer refuses to marry Giulietta the Marchioness intervenes quickly, suggesting that the best revenge on the Treasurer would be to marry Giulietta to Edoardo (Act 1 Scene 3). The Baron is not receptive, but the entrance of the 'King' at this moment gives the March-ioness something else to think about, for she has already resolved to herself that she is not, under any circumstances, going to marry the elderly Count Ivrea, any more than she is going to allow Giulietta to marry the Treasurer. However she intends to make Belfiore pay for his outlandish behaviour by appearing to push forward her marriage to Ivrea, even though it is the last thing she wants.

By Act 2 Scene 2 the Marchioness is becoming desperate at Belfiore's continued masquerade. She longs for him to 'confess'. She can barely contain herself and, referring to Belfiore in the third person, she informs the 'King' that she will not be marrying him. She resorts to a powerfully expressive aria (*Perche dunque non vien?*) in which she appeals to her lover to stop playing games. Belfiore is nonplussed, but unable to do anything to relieve his lover's suffering.

The Marchioness plays her dangerous game to the last. She agrees to marry Ivrea, but only on the condition that Belfiore does not return within the hour. Belfiore enters immediately. It is more than likely that the Marchioness has already sighted Belfiore before making this stipulation, and is therefore confident that she will not have to go through with the marriage to the elderly Count. Belfiore announces that the wedding cannot go ahead because he requires the Count to accompany him on matters of urgent business. The Marchioness is mortified, in spite of the fact that Belfiore has saved her at the eleventh hour from a marriage she does not wish to embark on.

At this critical juncture Belfiore receives a letter stating that Stanislaus has reached Warsaw. He is at last able to reveal the true reason for the masquerade. The Marchioness's happiness is complete when Belfiore finally acknowledges his own name and embraces her with the words, 'Faithful to (his) first love!'

The Marchioness (*Un giorno di regno*). See La **Marchesa** di Poggio

Marcovaldo (*La Battaglia di Legnano*). German prisoner.
Marcovaldo has been taken prisoner by **Rolando** during one of his campaigns as an officer of the Lombard League against the incursions of the so-called Barbarian hordes (the Germans). Rolando has given Marcovaldo the free run of his castle. It is not clear in the action of the opera what Marcovaldo has done to deserve this special dispensation. When he first appears (Act 1) his primary

agenda is revealed to be the seduction of Rolando's wife, **Lida**. Lida will have none of it. She is appalled at the German's audacity. On this occasion Lida does not have to suffer Marcovaldo's suit for long as they are interrupted by the arrival of **Imelda** bearing the news that **Arrigo** is still alive and on his way to visit her with her husband. Marcovaldo is not slow to notice that the mention of Arrigo's name causes Lida some consternation and that a 'vivid blush' rises to her cheeks. He determines to observe her closely and discover the 'secrets of (her) heart', which he does very quickly, as soon, in fact, as he observes Lida and Arrigo together. With some justification, Marcovaldo surmises that the two are lovers.

Realizing that he has a perfect opportunity to have his revenge on the uncooperative Lida, Marcovaldo determines to find the first opportunity to apprise Rolando of the situation and expose Lida's infidelity. The moment presents itself when he realizes that Lida has given a note to Imelda to deliver (Act 3). He follows Imelda and bribes her to give him the letter. As he suspected the letter is addressed to Arrigo and its contents would appear to confirm his suspicions. He takes it straight to Rolando. He makes the mistake of telling Rolando of the affair before furnishing him with the proof. Rolando reacts immediately by reaching for his dagger. Fortunately for Marcovaldo Rolando discovers that he is unarmed. Marcovaldo can barely conceal his relish when Rolando reads aloud the letter in which Lida refers to her and Arrigo's 'ancient love'. 'The longed-for moment of my revenge has ripened', he gloats as Rolando becomes more and more enraged.

Marcovaldo is not seen again in the opera. He has proved to be the catalyst in bringing out into the daylight the dynamics of the love triangle that has, all unwittingly, developed between the three main protagonists. In this sense Marcovaldo serves a useful, and ultimately fruitful, function in the lives of Arrigo, Lida and Rolando. Without his assistance who knows how the triangle would have resolved itself? Probably only through many years of festering frustration and bitterness, in the case of Arrigo and Lida, and increasing perplexity in the case of Rolando, unable to ascertain why his wife grows increasingly distant from him. It is unlikely that Rolando will see it like this, and Marcovaldo's position in the household once husband and wife are reconciled will have become untenable. Presumably he will be repatriated.

There is surely a chauvinistic intention in portraying Marcovaldo as an undeserving, scheming, and frankly despicable scoundrel. Consciously or otherwise, Verdi and Cammarano underline the unworthy nature of the German aggressors. Combined with the tyrannical and inflated nature of Federico Barbarossa (Act 2), a generally disagreeable and stereotypical portrait is given of the enemy, who deserve every bit of the defeat that the Italians finally mete out to them.

'Maria' (*Boccanegra*). See **Amelia**

The Marquis of Calatrava (*La Forza del Destino*). See **Calatrava**

The Marquis d'Obigny (*La Traviata*). Flora's protector.
The Marquis is little more than Flora's shadow. Unlike **Baron Douphol**, Violetta's protector, he does not have a significant role to play in the unfolding of the drama. His presence merely adds symmetry and gives an air of acceptable normality to the courtesan/protector relationship which is so crucial a facet of the drama.

In Act 2 Scene 2 there is an amusing vignette between Flora and the Marquis in which they each have their palms read by the 'gypsies' and the Marquis is revealed to be unfaithful. Flora upbraids the Marquis as though he were her husband. The Marquis clearly enjoys the game. The relationship between the Marquis and Flora is a model of what such a relationship should be, a matter of mutual convenience where each party knows the rules and adheres to them. It makes a stark contrast to the endless troubles that the Baron has with Violetta, whose headstrong nature is not ideally suited to the 'game' in the way that Flora so

evidently is. The Marquis can consider himself lucky.

Marullo (*Rigoletto*). Courtier at the court of the Duke of Mantua.
Marullo's name is an Italianized version of Marot. Clement Marot was a French poet, a contemporary of Rabelais, Ronsard and Villon, who were all working in Paris during the reign of François I (1515–1547), Verdi/Piave's model for the **Duke of Mantua**.

It is Marullo who first discovers that **Rigoletto** keeps a woman in his house. He assumes she is his mistress. The idea of the hunchback keeping a mistress is hugely amusing to him. He readily falls in with **Ceprano's** plan to find some way to take revenge on the Jester. Since there is nobody at the court who has not at some time been the butt of Rigoletto's razor-sharp wit, it is hardly surprising that Marullo joins in with the plan. It is Marullo who deliberately deceives Rigoletto into thinking that he and the other nobles are in the street outside his house for the purpose of abducting Ceprano's wife, and then blindfolds the all-unsuspecting Rigoletto (Act 1 Scene 2).

After the abduction of his daughter (Act 1 Scene 2) Rigoletto pleads with Marullo for mercy. Perhaps he assumes that the poet must have a finer sensibility than the other courtiers, although there is no evidence in the opera to justify this assumption. Marullo is as heartless as the rest, although it would be a mistake entirely to blame him. He takes his lead, as do all the courtiers, from the feckless Duke. The cruelty that is manifest in their behaviour is purely the result of the thoughtlessness and lack of any sense of responsibility which characterizes the Duke's lifestyle. (See also **Cortigiani**.)

I MASNADIERI (The Robbers)
Opera in 4 Acts. Libretto: Andrea Maffei after Schiller's drama, *Die Räuber* (1781).

First performance: 22 July 1847 at His Majesty's Theatre, London

Cast:
Massimiliano: Count of Moor (bass)

Carlo: his elder son (tenor)
Francesco: his younger son (baritone)
Amalia: an orphan and niece to the Count (soprano)
Arminio: steward to the Count's family (tenor)
Moser: a priest (bass)
Rolla: companion of Carlo (baritone)

Time: early 18th century
Place: Germany

Background Note The plot for Schiller's *Die Räuber* came from an issue, in 1775, of a magazine called *Haug's Swabian Magazine*. It is possible that *Die Räuber* was partly conceived in order to avenge the injustice perpetrated on Schiller's friend, the poet Christian Friedrich Daniel Shubart (1739–1791). Schubart's imprisonment by Duke Karl Eugen for ten years without trial was an outrage against the liberalism of the times and left the poet a broken man. When the Robbers in Schiller's play reflect on Carl Moor's (Carlo in the opera) megalomania, 'He wants to risk his life just to win admiration' it probably echoes something a friend of Schiller's once said to him, to the effect that he was less concerned with poetry than with the laurels he could win for himself.

Synopsis
Act 1 Scene 1 A tavern on the borders of Saxony. Carlo is engrossed in a book. 'When I read Plutarch[48] I am impatient, disgusted with this age of weaklings'. Thus opens Verdi's opera *I Masnadieri*. It is an arresting opening. It announces straightaway that the opera has an existentialist theme, that it is not just about love or murder (both of which are inevitably part of the recipe), but about what makes a life meaningful. It also tells us

that the chief protagonist, Carlo, is a dreamer and an idealist: 'Oh if in the cold ashes of my fathers there still glowed a spark of the spirit of Arminius![49] Like him, I would set free all Germany, so that, compared with this model, Sparta and Athens would be slaves in chains'. Carlo is also an outsider; he is disgusted with the company into which he has fallen: 'my shameless companions in error', for they reflect the sorry pass that his own life has come to. He craves only one thing, his father's forgiveness that he may be rehabilitated with his family, his homeland and his beloved Amalia (*O mio castel paterno*). He has written to his father expressing his repentance and now believes that there is a real chance of gaining his father's pardon. His hopes are shortly to be dashed.

Several young men enter with a letter for Carlo. It is from his brother, Francesco, and informs him that his father wishes him to know that he should not return unless he wishes 'to fare on bread and water, a solitary prisoner in a dungeon'. Carlo is enraged that his 'passionate entreaties' have fallen on such deaf ears: 'Oh that I could raise sea and earth with a roar and unite them in war against mankind'. It is typical of his character that he should inflate personal woes to involve all of mankind. When he rhetorically demands: 'Where is the sword to bring death to such vipers', his companions immediately pledge him their solidarity and implore him to become their chief and captain. Carlo needs no persuading, for there is apparently no escape route for him. There is no way back, only on further into criminality and chaos. His sense of grievance erupts into a violent cabaletta (*Nell'argilla maledetta*) in which he pledges to sow terror and violence. The true significance of this scene only becomes apparent in the scene immediately following.

---

[48] Plutarch (c46–120 AD): Greek biographer. The book Carlo is reading is undoubtedly 'Parallel Lives' in which Plutarch gives biographies of pairs of Greek and Roman soldiers and politicians, and then proceeds to draw comparisons between the two. The book became immensely popular during the Renaissance and was a major source book for Shakespeare's Roman plays.

[49] Arminius (BC 17–21 AD): A German chieftain. Originally he served in the Roman army, but deserted to lead a campaign against Rome. He effectively saved Germany from becoming a Roman province and thereby ensured that the Empire's frontier did not extend beyond the Rhine.

Act 1 Scene 2   A room in the Castle of Count Moor. Francesco is alone and exulting at the success of his plan to undo his favoured brother. Like Edmund (Shakespeare's *King Lear*), Francesco has chafed all his life at his brother's superior place in his father's esteem (though there is no suggestion that Francesco is a bastard). 'At last I have avenged/Nature's misdeed in making me the younger/on my brother' (this makes one think of Edmund's speech: 'Thou, Nature, art my goddess . . . why bastard? wherefore base? When my dimensions are as well compact,/My mind as generous, and my shape as true,/As honest madam's issue? [Act 1 Scene 2]). Unlike Edmund Francesco plans not only to usurp but also to despatch his father. He reasons to himself, since the lamp of his father's life burns low (*La sua lampada vitale*) there is no harm in hastening the old man's inevitable and imminent demise. How best to do it? he wonders. Then, in a flash of inspiration the solution comes to him.

Arminio enters and Francesco instructs him to disguise himself and then go to Massimiliano and tell him that he has just come from the battle of Prague where he left behind Carlo's lifeless corpse. Arminio is doubtful whether Massimiliano will believe him. But Francesco convinces him that he will provide proof which will make the news incontrovertible.

Francesco is left alone to exult in the fact that soon he will be the master (*Tremate o miseri*). Like any tyrant he demands that the world reflect his own anguish: 'to laughter and joy shall succeed sobs, tears, fear, suspicions'. His world-hatred has been fashioned by deprivation, whether real or imagined, rejection and resentment.

Act 1 Scene 3   A bedroom in the Castle. Massimiliano Moor is asleep in a chair. Amalia approaches quietly and stands, looking down on the sleeping old man. Amalia has every reason to hate Massimiliano since he has banished his son, Carlo, with whom she is in love. But she cannot bring herself to hate him (Amalia knows nothing of the machinations of Francesco). Suddenly she remembers the features of the man she loves

above all others. In an intensely erotic aria (*Lo sguardo avea degli angeli*) she remembers the ecstasy of the embraces she enjoyed in the arms of her beloved Carlo. But in conclusion she sadly reflects that however sweet her memories they are nothing more than that.

Massimiliano is likewise dreaming of Carlo. He is subliminally aware that Carlo is suffering great unhappiness and that it is Francesco who keeps him separated from his elder son. Disturbed by his obvious distress Amalia awakens him. Massimiliano confesses that he was dreaming of Carlo. He is acutely aware that he has destroyed all Amalia's young hopes and begs her not to hate him for it. Amalia reassures him that she could never hate him. Massimiliano, still half asleep, reflects to himself that he is dying and is devastated that his favourite son will not be with him in his last hour, while Amalia reflects that her only wish now is to die as well so she may be reunited with Carlo in eternity.

Francesco enters with Arminio, the latter heavily disguised. Barely concealing his relish Francesco announces that he brings with him the bearer of bad tidings. Arminio claims to have been a comrade of Carlo's in the columns of King Frederick.[50] He describes how Carlo was admitted to the army as a beggar (much to Amalia's distress) and how at the battle of Prague: 'the brave young man fought until his whole body was wounded'. Francesco, in a melodramatic attempt to convince all present of his great grief, rushes on Arminio. Massimiliano signs to Arminio to continue. Arminio describes how Carlo, with his dying breath, had instructed him to take his blood-soaked sword to Massimiliano and say to him: 'Thus does the son you cast out die in despair amid battle and slaughter'. Massimiliano gives vent to his all-too genuine grief. Satisfied that he is achieving his ends, Arminio cannot resist adding: 'And the last word he uttered was "Amalia"'. Amalia breaks out with loud lamenting.

---

[50]   Frederick II ('The Great'), King of Prussia 1712–1786.

Now Francesco delivers his *coup de grâce*. Showing Amalia the sword he points at where Carlo has (supposedly) written in blood: 'Death releases you, Amalia, from our oath. Francesco, you must take Amalia to be your wife'. Amalia is devastated, taking this as proof that Carlo never loved her. Massimiliano, in an anguished aside, upbraids himself for his guilt in indirectly bringing about his own son's death. Then he throws himself upon Francesco. Francesco is not perturbed. He merely gives thanks that his ruse has worked and prays that his father's age and grief will bring about his hasty demise. Amalia's thoughts are all with her beloved Carlo. She presumably knows intuitively that Carlo did love her and would never have wished her to give herself to Francesco. Arminio, meanwhile, is appalled at the grief that his deception has caused. That he has good reason for remorse is proved when Massimiliano collapses and is immediately presumed dead by Amalia. Francesco is jubilant: 'Dead? . . . then I am master!'

Act 2 Scene 1   A precinct adjoining the chapel of the castle. To one side rise several gothic sepulchres. On the most recent one is carved the name of Massimiliano Moor. Amalia is kneeling at the Count's tomb. She has taken refuge here from the 'infamous banquet' celebrating Francesco's accession. The chorus is heard in the distance proclaiming a hedonistic philosophy (see **Chorus**). Amalia is outraged at the lack of respect Francesco shows for his father's departed spirit. Her only consolation is that the revellers cannot 'disturb in death the peace of which (they) robbed him in life'. In an elegiac aria (*Tu del mio Carlo al seno*) she consoles herself further with the thought that Massimiliano is now reunited with his son, Carlo. She bewails the fact that she is left behind on the earth to live in woe.

Arminio enters. He has come to seek Amalia's forgiveness for his part in Francesco's deception. Amalia is only persuaded to listen to him when he tells her that Carlo is alive, not only that but her uncle also still lives. Before she can question him further Arminio departs. Amalia is astounded at the news. But the urgency of Arminio's demeanour convinces her that he tells the truth. She is overwhelmed with rapture, to which she gives vent in a fierce cabaletta (*Carlo vive?*).

Francesco enters and upbraids Amalia for continuing to lament his father's death. He passionately declares his love for her and invites her to reign with him as his consort. Amalia, her suspicions about Francesco confirmed, is outraged by his declaration. Her disdain only inflames Francesco's perverted passion. He now reveals his true nature, threatening her with incarceration and calling her a whore – 'I would have everyone blush at your very name. I will drag you by your hair'. He attempts to pull her to him. Amalia momentarily disarms him by pretending contrition and begging his forgiveness. She pretends to embrace him and as she does so snatches his dagger with which to ward him off. Francesco is incensed, but is forced to acknowledge that, temporarily at least, he is defeated.

Act 2 Scene 2   The Bohemian woods. In the distance Prague can be seen, half hidden among the trees. Bandits enter. They discuss (see **Chorus**) how Rolla is in prison and how their captain (Carlo) has sworn to torch the city of Prague. At that moment a red glow is seen illuminating the sky. It is Prague on fire. The brigands realize that Carlo has been true to his word. Cries are heard, then dishevelled women and children emerge from the trees. They are convinced that the end of the world must have come, so terrible is the devastation to their city.

Rolla enters with some brigands. All on stage are amazed to see him. He has apparently been liberated just at the moment he was due to be executed. He demands brandy, which the brigands ply him with. He is too exhausted to tell his tale more fully and leaves it to the brigands. They describe how Carlo literally snatched the noose from Rolla's neck. Carlo enters, lost in thought. He announces that they will leave at the crack of dawn. The brigands depart, leaving Carlo alone to contemplate the majesty of the sunset.

Carlo is overwhelmed by the discrepancy between the beauties of nature and the hideous nature of his crimes (*Di ladroni attorniäto*). He thinks despairingly of his lost love, Amalia.

The brigands rush in. Apparently they are surrounded by a thousand soldiers. Carlo exhorts them to fight. All sing a rousing chorus of defiance to the surrounding army.

Act 3 Scene 1   A lonely place by the forest near Massimiliano's castle. Amalia gives thanks that she has escaped Francesco's clutches, but now she is lost in an un-identifiable wasteland. The voices of the brigands calling: 'Pillage! Rape! Arson!' are heard in the near distance, causing Amalia considerable alarm.

Carlo enters and recognizes Amalia. At first Amalia keeps her eyes averted, only raising them when she hears herself addressed by name. The two lovers, so long separated, are joyfully reunited. Amalia insists they must flee. Carlo's only thought is to ensure Amalia does not discover the sort of company he keeps. Amalia questions him closely. Carlo is evasive, but moved when he realizes how much Amalia has suffered in his absence. 'But now . . . a rainbow of peace has dispersed the storms. Our torments are over, our anguish is past', they declare. Amalia tells Carlo of his brother's perfidy. Carlo reassures her and they sing together of their great love (*T'abbraccio, o Carlo [Amalia]*).

Act 3 Scene 2   In the forest. In the centre are ruins of an ancient keep. It is night. The brigands are stretched out on the ground. They sing together (see **Chorus**), glorifying the virtues of pillage, arson, rape and killing and of their readiness to meet their fate when the hangman catches up with them (*Le rube, gli stupri*).

Carlo enters. The brigands rise and greet him. Carlo orders them to sleep. He will keep watch. The brigands lie down and sleep.

In an anguished soliloquy Carlo contemplates and rejects the possibility of suicide. Having taken a pistol and loaded it, he flings it away and determines to endure.

Arminio enters. He has come surreptitiously with food for the imprisoned Massimiliano.

Carlo is as yet unaware that his father is incarcerated in the ruins of the keep. Arminio takes the meagre food supplies to the grille of the keep and calls to the 'wretched inmate' that he brings his supper. Massimiliano's voice is heard from within. Arminio dare not linger. He gives the old man his food and departs. As he leaves he is heard to murmur: 'Wicked son!' Carlo has been observing this and intercepts Arminio, demanding to know his identity.

At this moment Massimiliano, hearing another voice, calls out from the dungeon. Arminio tries to prevent Carlo approaching the keep, but to no avail. He flees. Carlo shakes open the grille and is confronted with his father, who is reduced to a pitiful state of emaciation from his long ordeal. Carlo only recognizes his father by his voice. Since he believes Massimiliano to be dead he has difficulty in comprehending the fact that he is still alive. Massimiliano recounts how he came to be incarcerated (*Un ignoto, tre lune or saranno*). Apparently he had only collapsed from the shock of Arminio's revelation that Carlo had died. But Francesco lost no time in packing him into a coffin. When he came to and found himself being buried alive he called out for help, at which Francesco opened the coffin, but immediately closed it again. He had the coffin transported to the keep, where Massimiliano has languished ever since. Having finished his tale Massimiliano faints.

Carlo is appalled. For a time he remains motionless. Then, having recovered himself, he fires a pistol and shouts to the brigands to bestir themselves. Having wakened them he points to the unconscious figure of his father and cries out for vengeance. They, the brigands, shall be 'the Ministers of Heaven's divine justice'. The brigands kneel and demand to know what they should do. Placing a hand on the unconscious old man Carlo requires that each one of them swear to avenge: 'these saintly white hairs' and bring the parricide (Francesco) to Carlo, alive, so that he, Carlo, may have his personal revenge. The brigands rush out and Carlo remains, falling to his knees beside his father.

Act 4 Scene 1   A suite of several rooms in Massimiliano's castle. Francesco enters in haste; he is clearly agitated. He has awakened from a nightmare and believes himself to be 'Betrayed! . . . the dead arise. They shout at me, "Murderer!"' He calls for servants.

Arminio enters and Francesco demands that he fetch the priest. As Arminio is about to depart Francesco restrains him and tells him to send someone else for the priest. He desperately demands to know of Arminio whether the dead can arise (this scene echoes a similar scene in *Attila* (Act 1 Scene 3), where Attila tells Uldino of a dream which torments him). He describes his dream (*Pareami che sorto da lauto convito*). What he describes convinces Arminio that his master has experienced a vision of the Day of Judgement. The import of the dream is that the Son of Man may have died to save humanity from its sins, but not those guilty of the sin of parricide, of which Francesco is guilty. Arminio exits in horror.

The priest, Moser, enters. He assumes that he has been summoned so that Francesco may 'mock at God', as is apparently his wont. Francesco asks him what is the sin that most excites God's wrath and Moser replies without hesitation parricide and fratricide, at which the infuriated Francesco silences him. Moser, who no doubt suspects Francesco of being guilty of both (as indeed Francesco believes himself to be), cannot resist intoning: 'Human thought cannot conceive of them'.

Arminio enters. He is clearly terrified. He has just observed a 'furious troop of horsemen' advancing on the castle. Francesco, who is himself delirious with fear, orders everyone to the chapel: 'let everyone pray for me', he orders. He then menacingly commands Moser to give him absolution. Moser refuses, telling Francesco that only God can absolve him of his sins. Francesco, for the first time in his life, kneels and prays. Like Claudius (*Hamlet*) his thoughts 'remain below', that is, they will not ascend to Heaven. Rising in fury he declares: 'Hell shall not mock me!' But his defiance carries little conviction.

Act 4 Scene 2   The forest, as in Act 3 Scene 2. Daylight is dawning. Carlo is seated

by his father. Massimiliano has apparently not recognized his son. His thoughts are with Francesco. In spite of all he has suffered at Francesco's hands he appears to wish his son no ill and only has compassion for him. This is incomprehensible to Carlo, until Massimiliano makes it clear he does not blame Francesco for his ill-treatment but considers he has been justifiably punished for having turned his back on Carlo. When Massimiliano expresses the wish that Carlo may forgive him Carlo seizes the opportunity to gain his father's blessing, even if only unwittingly on his father's part. He begs Massimiliano: 'now give me the price of your ransom, old man, and give your deliverer your blessing'. He kneels before him. Massimiliano, kissing him, gives his benediction: 'Take this kiss, beloved stranger, like the kiss of a loving father, and let me imagine it to be the kiss of a devoted son'. Carlo is overwhelmed, even though his father remains unconscious of the true significance of the encounter.

Several brigands enter, approaching slowly and with lowered heads. They report that they have been unable to capture Francesco. Carlo is overjoyed. He no longer has any wish to perpetuate the family feud, least of all to stain his hands with his brother's blood.

More brigands arrive, dragging Amalia in with them. Massimiliano is overjoyed to see Amalia. Amalia has eyes only for Carlo. She throws her arms around his neck, imploring him to defend her. Carlo is overwhelmed by a sense of shame. In an extraordinary outburst he exhorts the brigands to kill his father, his lover, himself and themselves: 'Oh that all the living could be destroyed at one stroke!' he exclaims. The brigands assume he is delirious. Carlo addresses his father: 'Behold, that son whom you cursed. He was smitten and rejected, even by God'. He then draws his sword and rushes on the brigands, his former companions, 'menacing and ferocious'. He curses them for dragging him from Heaven into the abyss. Then he turns to Amalia and his father and proclaims the fact that he is the chief of these robbers and murderers.

All are astounded, not least the brigands, who cannot understand why Carlo feels impelled to reveal his relationship to them. Dejectedly Carlo accepts that all his dreams and hopes of happiness are fled (*Caduto è il reprobo!*). He has reckoned without Amalia who, having recovered from her astonishment, throws herself into Carlo's arms. Angel or demon, she declares, she will not leave him. Carlo is overcome with emotion. They sing of their great love while Massimiliano, who has also recovered from his astonishment, reflects on his guilt in having rejected his son. The brigands, meanwhile, have taken fright at the prospect of losing their leader. They berate Carlo, calling on him to remember his irrevocable oaths of solidarity. Carlo does not need prompting: 'It is true', he cries. 'They tear the veil from my eyes. I fall headlong from my dream of Heaven'.

Suddenly he realizes that his life is no longer his own. He belongs to the bandits. Amalia, realizing she is about to lose the lover she has for so long pined after and only so recently regained, implores Carlo to kill her since life without him will be unbearable. Carlo is by now beyond the call of reason. He knows only the dictates of his overriding passions. He calls on the bandits to witness his sacrifice as he stabs his beloved Amalia. The bandits, appalled, try to prevent him, but it is too late. Having killed the person he most cares about Carlo has only one desire, to be dragged to the gallows. He rushes off, presumably to give himself up to the authorities. The curtain falls as the brigands call on him to wait. Amalia is dying. Carlo is oblivious.

Schiller's play provided Verdi with an ideal vehicle with which to develop the themes that he had already established as of greatest significance to him: the dilemmas of fatherhood and the inevitable conflicts that arise between personal ambition and political justice. The rivalry between sons is also a theme that reappears in *Il Trovatore* and highlights the problems that can arise when two sons compete for their father's attention, affection and inheritance.

The four main characters in *I Masnadieri* provide a paradigm of the family unit in which the only anomaly is the replacement of mother by lover in the person of Amalia. In the same way that both sons compete for the affection of the father, so both compete for the affection of the same woman. Again a parallel can be drawn with *Il Trovatore*. As in *Il Trovatore* the beloved is more mother than lover. As in *Il Trovatore* one brother reveres the beloved as a symbol of perfect womanhood, representative of the Eternal Feminine; the other seeks to possess merely out of a sense of outraged masculine pride (although admittedly di Luna's love for Leonora is of a nobler nature than Francesco's lust, which seeks only to desecrate and debauch).

A central theme of the play is a re-working of the parable of the Prodigal Son. Carlo longs only to return to his father. His father longs only that his errant son should return. But both are thwarted by the outraged pride of the other son, Francesco, who, never having rebelled, expects that all should befall him as by divine right. The truth is that he is the son who has at all times attempted to love and obey and yet, in reality, has done nothing to earn the father's respect. For the father must expect that his son will rebel. Without that rebellion there can be no justifiable belief that the son may prove capable. An open rebel, such as is exemplified in the character of Carlo, is greatly to be preferred to the kind of surreptitious rebellion Francesco demonstrates, not only because in the latter case the father can have no way of knowing that his son *is* in rebellion, but because it is fundamentally the rebellion of a coward who cannot squarely face the consequences of his actions and is not willing to take the risk of being cast out. The desperate attempt at all times to please means that huge reservoirs of resentment accumulate in the depths of the psyche. Publicly Francesco can only be that which is expected of him. He keeps for the privacy of his chamber that which he truly is. In other words he becomes, in spite of himself, that most dangerous of animals, a Machiavellian politician.

All stems from the father, as Amalia intuitively recognizes. The father is punished, not because of anything that he himself has done, but because it is in the very nature of fatherhood that he should be punished by sheer virtue of the need to supersede him. Fathers must be superseded. It is the duty of the mother somehow to ensure the smooth transition from father to son and, if possible, further to ensure that there is an equitable distribution between the progeny. Since there is no mother it falls to Amalia to step into the breach. Because neither son is equipped to shoulder responsibility, Amalia is forced into an unreal position. She must ultimately side with the father. This Schiller's play and Verdi's opera make abundantly clear and it is for this reason, more than any other, that Amalia must die. While she lives there can only be stasis. Once she has been sacrificed and Carlo has handed himself over to justice in certain expectation of execution, only Massimiliano and Francesco remain. The schism in the family has been healed. Massimiliano will almost certainly pardon Francesco, who will be relieved of the rivalry and jealousy that have so poisoned his existence, and live to be a creditable successor to his father. The potency of Schiller's tale lies in the very unpredictability of the outcome and the way in which it exemplifies the centrality in human affairs of family politics.

Massimiliano (*I Masnadieri*). Reigning 'Count of Moor'.

Massimiliano is an old man by the time of the action of the opera, weary of life and of the futility of family dissension. He has always had a special affection for his elder son, **Carlo**, but has become riddled with guilt on account of his younger son, **Francesco**, for whom, justifiably, he feels very little affection. The situation is complicated by the fact that Carlo has always been a rebel and so far has done little to prove himself a worthy successor to the Count's title. He has led a dissolute life since going to university and has angered his father to the extent that the latter is all too easily persuaded by Francesco that Carlo is beyond reform. He

is oblivious to the fact that Carlo longs for nothing so much as his father's forgiveness.

Massimiliano becomes a victim of his own infirmity. There comes a point in a father's life when he desires – or should desire – to cede sovereignty to his offspring. Massimiliano no longer has the energy to unravel a situation which he knows to be wrong. He believes Francesco because it is easier to do so, even though it means being cast off from his favourite son. He will pay a heavy price for his indolence, not least by being buried alive by Francesco, a powerful metaphor for the surrender of volition, which is Massimiliano's chief sin, even if more a sin of omission than actuality. This is occasioned by his swooning fit on learning the news, manufactured by Francesco, that Carlo has died in battle. For Massimiliano it is as though he has died in himself, for Francesco has never manifested any of the characteristics that he would wish to propagate. With Carlo die his best hopes for himself. The only purpose in life for a man born into a hereditary position is to see that position enhanced by the qualities he and his children can bring to it. Carlo may have rebelled and brought shame to his father through his disreputable friends and the places he frequents, but at least he demonstrates something of the energy, fire and, above all, the integrity that Massimiliano would wish to see in a son of his. Francesco, on the other hand, exudes bitterness, resentment and political ambition.

That Massimiliano is obscurely aware that he owes his misfortunes to Francesco is made abundantly clear (Act 1 Scene 3) when **Amalia** comes upon the old man asleep, dreaming of Carlo and complaining: 'Francesco, ever in my dreams. Will you tear him from me?' Yet it is a long way from instinctively knowing something and consciously acknowledging it. Incarcerated in the ruins of a castle and left to die of starvation Massimiliano has plenty of chance to reflect on the blindness that has led him to such a sorry pass. Massimiliano is incarcerated and liberated by his offspring: incarcerated by the son who swears allegiance and obedience, liberated by the son who determinedly pursued his own agenda. The theme of brothers' rivalry for a father's affection has a time-honoured ancestry, both in myth and in history. Partly it is always representative of a war in the progenitor's psyche. On the one hand there is the aspect that demands total subservience and obedience from his offspring and on the other the side that demands the son makes the heroic endeavour to become independent of the stranglehold of the parental home and background. The first usually prevails in the short term, while the latter, which is the essential prerequisite of future growth, must prevail in the long term.

Massimiliano's destiny reaches its apogee when he begs forgiveness of his prodigal son (Act 4 Scene 2), even though he does not himself realize it is his son he addresses. It is inevitably a shock to him to discover that Carlo has been living the life of a brigand, but his only reproof is for himself: 'And did I, in my guilt, contaminate the pure soul of this son of mine? Will no chasm open up to swallow me? Has God no more whirlwinds?' His only concern is to be absolved by Heaven for his great guilt in having cast out his son and thus bearing, as he sees it, ultimate responsibility for Carlo's ostracism.

As in so many dramas which Verdi elected to set we find in the relationship of Massimiliano to his two sons one of those fatal relations in which it is impossible to apportion blame. The fact that Massimiliano does blame himself is something over which he has no control. In the service to his hereditary position he has sacrificed too much of his own independence and instinct, which have found expression in the older son's rebelliousness. A man must naturally be most attracted to that which he himself most lacks. To the younger son, who has always toed the line and for his pains been marginalized, it is excessively galling that he can never supersede Carlo's place in his father's affections. Massimiliano cannot feel any affection for Francesco for the simple reason that he sees reflected his own slavery to a set of ethics which have circumvented and stunted his own personal growth.

Mayor of Como (Il Podestà di Como) (*La Battaglia di Legnano*)

The mayor has the dubious honour of presiding over the city council that convenes to receive and summarily rebuff the envoys from Milan, **Arrigo** and **Rolando** (Act 2). The mayor is unaware that the emperor, **Federico Barbarossa**, is waiting in the wings. Federico has obviously been alerted as soon as news reached Como of the Milanese deputation and he has decided to make it the occasion for a showdown. The mayor and councillors are but pawns in the machinations of the despot.

Mayor of Hornachuelos (*La Forza del Destino*)

The Mayor only appears in Act 2 Scene 1 where he is taking supper at the Inn near Hornachuelos where **Don Carlo** and **Leonora**, separately and unbeknownst to each other, have taken refuge for the night. Don Carlo attempts to extract information from the Mayor regarding the guest who recently arrived with Master **Trabucco**. Carlo suspects the arrival may be his sister, Leonora. The Mayor is not to be drawn on the subject (one wonders whether Leonora has already taken him into her confidence as she clearly already has Trabucco).

When Carlo suggests they play a practical joke on the unknown traveller by painting a moustache on his beardless face, the Mayor remembers his official capacity as 'protector of all travellers' and makes it clear he will not tolerate any such behaviour. In response to Carlo's persistent questioning the Mayor turns on him and asks a few questions of his own: where is Carlo from, where is he going and who is he?

As representative of secular authority the Mayor bears ill-comparison with the representative in the opera of spiritual authority, **Padre Guardiano**. Nothing the Mayor can do will alter the outcome of the blood feud in the Vargas family one jot. Guardiano, on the other hand, offers a very real possibility for **Alvaro** and Leonora to understand and grow beyond the misery of their predicaments.

Medico (*Macbeth*). See **Doctor**

Medora (*Il Corsaro*). Corrado's mistress.
The role of Medora is peculiarly ungrateful
for the interpreter. For her fate, as depicted
in the opera, is almost entirely negative.
Desperately in love with the pirate, **Corrado**,
she yet must endure separation from him by
virtue of her beloved's profession. Her
opening words underline her misery: 'Oh
how eternal seem the hours when he is far
from me' (Act 1 Scene 2). Her only consolation is to play her harp. All she longs for
is a 'loving tear' from her beloved should
Corrado come to weep over her ashes . . .

Medora is the passive alter-ego of the
energetic **Gulnara,** who plays a far more pro-
active role in the drama. Yet it is Medora
whom Corrado loves, and throughout the
opera he is consumed with longing and guilt
concerning the beloved he leaves at home.
Where Gulnara is an eminently modern
heroine, Medora is typical of the languishing
maiden of medieval chivalric romance who
sits in her tower awaiting her absent lover.
Medora gives Corrado no joy, only anguish,
projecting onto him her own acute anxiety
at the necessity of his absence. Nothing
Corrado can say in their duet (Act 1 Scene
2) can assuage her misery. Her final complaint reminds him that he may return to find
her dead: 'Ah stay if you have a heart in your
breast, or I shall die of grief!' His refusal to
stay is characterized as wilful cruelty. She
refuses to be consoled. When he does leave
she swoons.

It has to be admitted that it is difficult to
see why Corrado would wish to return to
her. Her love is hardly a positive force in his
life. When he does finally return it is through
the agency of another woman who loves him,
and whom he loves in return. But Corrado's
love for Gulnara is a love he refuses to
acknowledge to himself, or to anyone else,
so consumed is he with guilt concerning the
ailing Medora.

When Medora, true to her word, dies,
having consumed poison because she is
convinced that Corrado has abandoned her,
it is the ultimate demonstration for Corrado

of his own worthlessness. He throws himself
into the sea, presumably so that he may be
reunited with his beloved in Heaven. His
action is ostensibly noble self-sacrifice, but
yet has a hollow ring to it. It is as though he
feels honour-bound through the misery he
has brought to Medora. Since there has not
been a shred of evidence in the opera that
Medora and Corrado have ever enjoyed the
raptures of love it is difficult not to feel that
Corrado would have done better to ride off
into the sunset with Gulnara. Only Medora's
self-obsession makes this an impossibility for
him.

Melitone (*La Forza del Destino*). Franciscan
friar in the Monastery of our Lady of the
Angels.
Melitone provides some comic relief in the
drama, much as the grave digger does in
Shakespeare's *Hamlet*. His function in the
drama is, however, a serious one. In his small-
mindedness and lack of charity he represents
all that Verdi saw as being pernicious in the
Church – a literal interpretation of the sacred
texts, a fundamentalism at odds with the true
spirit of Christianity. The distinction between
Melitone and **Guardiano** is the same as that
Christ made between himself and the Sadducees
and Pharisees. Melitone has no humility, no
charity and no love. He is a hollow shell
where a warm and loving heart should be.

Melitone's character is established on his
first appearance when **Leonora** arrives at the
Monastery of our Lady of the Angels in the
small hours of the morning (Act 2 Scene 2).
She is greeted by Melitone, though 'greeted'
is hardly the word to describe his lack of
charity. He is immediately suspicious of the
newcomer (he would be horrified if he knew
she was a woman) and leaves Leonora out
in the cold while he goes to check with the
Father Superior. He returns some time later
with Guardiano, who promptly dismisses
him. There is nothing that Melitone hates
more than being excluded. He has the
mentality of a village gossip. He makes off
muttering, 'always secrets and only these
Holy men must know them. We are but so
many cabbages!' Guardiano tells him to keep

his peace. The only time Melitone manages to 'keep his peace' is during the service which concludes the scene in which Guardiano commands Melitone to assemble the friars. Melitone obeys without a murmur.

Guardiano must have confidence in Melitone's abilities, for he despatches him to Italy to 'bandage the wounds and salvage the souls' of the soldiers fighting there against the German invader (Act 3 Scene 3). Melitone is hardly the ideal candidate for the task, however. He inevitably loses his temper with the high-spirited soldiers and vendors at the military encampment, and only invites further trouble for himself by delivering a sermon upbraiding all and sundry for their sins. He owes it to the gypsy girl, **Preziosilla** (though he would be pained to admit it), that he escapes with his life, for the soldiers are all for giving the ill-spirited monk a sound drubbing. It will be with great relief that Melitone returns to Spain, although his experiences in Italy will have done nothing to improve his temper.

Act 4 discovers Melitone ladling out soup to the beggars who regularly congregate outside the monastery.[51] In this scene Melitone displays a total absence of Christian charity. He ladles out the soup with extreme ill-will, making it clear that he considers the beggars a bunch of scavengers and scoundrels. His attitude earns him a rebuke from Guardiano, who hovers in the background reading his breviary. Melitone is, however, not responsive to his superior's rebuke. He clearly has much to learn, not only in terms of charity, but also in obedience, one of the first requisites of a God-fearing monk. Finally he loses patience completely, kicks the pot of soup over and drives the beggars out of the yard. Surprisingly Guardiano utters no further reproof, though one can be certain that Melitone will be required to repeat a good many 'Hail Marys' in order to atone for his behaviour.

---

[51] Begging remains to this day far more prevalent in Spain and in the Mediterranean countries generally than it does in England. It could be argued that a sun-drenched climate induces far greater apathy and also a greater inclination to generosity.

In the meantime he must admit **Carlo** to the monastery (Act 4 Scene 1). He takes an instant disliking to the stranger. Carlo's attitude is haughty and disdainful. Melitone has, in fact, met his match in Carlo, who contains within himself even more rancour than does the bad-tempered monk. He does Carlo's bidding and fetches Father Raffaele (**Alvaro**) without demur. Melitone does not reappear in the opera.

Messenger (un Messaggiero) (*Aida*)

The messenger comes fresh from the battlefield (Act 1 Scene 1) and is required by the **King** to give account of the progress of the Ethiopian invasion of Egypt. The tale he tells is not an encouraging one and leads to the King's exhortation to his people to take up arms against the invader.

Messenger (Messaggiero) (*Il Trovatore*)

The Messenger brings **Manrico** a message (Act 2 Scene 1), presumably from **Ruiz**, announcing that Manrico's followers have taken Castellor and that **Leonora**, believing Manrico to be dead, is preparing to take the veil. Manrico tells the messenger to make a horse ready for him and the messenger hurries off.

Miller (*Luisa Miller*). Luisa's father.

In Schiller's play Luisa's father is the local music teacher. In Cammarano's libretto he has become a retired soldier. Miller is the very archetype of the doting father who threatens to strangle the life of his young daughter, not through imposing excessive restraints but through excess of devotion.

In Act 3 it becomes clear what a weight of guilt Luisa carries as a result of her father's overwhelming concern for her well-being. The problem for both Luisa and Miller is that Luisa's mother is no more, and they are two against the world. As their bond develops an unnatural (not perverted, take note) intensity is only to be expected. That Luisa desperately needs to escape is also only natural. The opera charts her attempts to break the bond. In the end it is **Rodolfo** who achieves her liberation, but only at the cost of her young life.

Miller is a man who has served all his life in the army. He has had to learn servility. But he has concomitantly, out of sheer self-preservation, developed a fierce and unbending pride. Thus, in his old age, he can finally afford the luxury of being servile to none but God. He can thus acknowledge, if only at the end of his days, every human being's birthright. His speech, *Fra I mortali ancora oppressa* (Act 1 Scene 3), is nothing less than a liberal manifesto: 'Among mortals, innocence is not yet so suppressed that it must be seen kneeling in the presence of a haughty Lord. Bow low before that God, chastiser of the wicked, not to one who has human appearance, but the heart of a wild beast in his breast'.

Miller's refusal to kow-tow to **Walter** is not just a personal triumph but a triumph for humanity against tyranny. It is all the more distressing, therefore, that having displayed such fortitude he should so blatantly impose his own brand of tyranny on his daughter, requiring her to sacrifice her young life for his happiness. In this moment it would be possible to question the motives of all his actions to date. Is it really his daughter's well-being that concerns him most, or is it his own dignity and honour (Act 3)? The two are, in reality, inextricably entwined. Whatever his motives, the fact is that his emotional blackmail succeeds in persuading Luisa to desist from her intention of committing suicide. It saves her life, and this must inevitably be Miller's prime concern at this moment.

Whatever shortcomings Miller may have he compares very favourably with the other father in the opera, Rodolfo's father Count Walter. Where Walter has no interest in his son's well-being, Miller appears constantly altruistic. At first sight it may seem that this is the author's chief objective: a bland contrast of worthy and unworthy fatherhood. But this is too simplistic. What we have is far more interesting, namely a comparison between two different types of fatherhood, the father/son and the father/daughter relationships. These are archetypal relationships and it is as archetypes that they should be reviewed in *Luisa Miller*.[52]

'Fathers dote on their daughters' is a truism as much as 'Fathers expect their sons to follow in their footsteps and enhance their name and standing in the world'. Whichever is the case it is rarely a question of selfless devotion. In a daughter the father discovers the feminine side of himself cut loose into the world. Inevitably that exteriorized image is compounded by the reflection of the lover that he, the father, has transformed into Mother. From the moment that Lover becomes Mother the male loses something and the offspring become a barrier. At this stage of life many fathers take a mistress. The father of a daughter does not need to take a mistress; he now has one, and she will become the receptacle not only of his protective, nurturing instincts, but also of a fair share of his libido, which is not to suggest that abuse is necessarily involved (though that it does occur in such situations is hardly surprising, particularly where the parent lacks intelligence or imagination). It was a stroke of genius on Cammarano's part to dispense with Luisa's mother, who does not contribute significantly in Schiller's play, anyway. Her absence in the opera significantly alters the profile of the drama, contributing a far greater focus and also symmetry.

Miller has doubts about his daughter's unknown admirer from the start. He senses that Rodolfo is not what he makes himself out to be and naturally he distrusts him. His worst suspicions are confirmed when **Wurm** tells him that 'Carlo' is, in fact, Walter's son, Rodolfo (see Act 1 Scene 1). But he quickly appreciates Rodolfo's sincerity. Thereafter his only concern is for the reaction of Rodolfo's father. When Walter refers to Luisa as 'a venal seductress' (Act 1 Scene 3) Miller cannot restrain his outrage. It is more than probable that he has never dared to speak his mind in this way before. It is as though a lifetime's

---

52   It should be remembered that *Luisa Miller* may be an Italian opera but it is a setting of a German play, Schiller's *Kabale und Liebe*. While after its premiere the opera fell into relative neglect, it was in Germany where its fortunes first revived early in the 20th century. However Italianate the music, the spirit of the drama remains German.

accumulated outrage bursts its banks when Walter so insults his daughter. He nearly pays for it with his life, but in reality he has played into the enemy's hands, for he becomes a mere pawn in Walter and Wurm's machinations to secure Rodolfo's marriage to **Frederica**. Convinced by Wurm that she holds her father's life in her hands, Luisa quickly accedes to their demands, even though it means denying the one thing that is more important to her than anything else: her new-found love for Rodolfo.

When Miller returns home after being released from prison in Count Walter's dungeons, he already knows the sacrifice that Luisa has made on his account (Wurm has told him). He has not, however, expected to find his daughter contemplating suicide. His way of approaching this new trauma – difficult enough for any parent – either reveals his own Achilles heel, as we have already seen, or demonstrates admirable psychological perspicacity, however you like to look at it. If psychological perspicacity, it has to be said, it is no more than textbook common sense. He does not get angry, he does not command Luisa to pull herself together. Rather he gives her a reason to live by appealing to her sense of filial responsibility. When Luisa suggests they should run away together, Miller must realize that his tactics have paid off. If there is something to run away from, something inimical, then logically there is some reason for living. There is a sense of value of what makes life bearable or not.

Miller agrees readily and he and Luisa sing together of the new life that lies ahead of them: 'We will go roaming and poor/ where destiny takes us,/ begging people for bread/ we will go from door to door'. To Miller's devastation it never comes to that. It would not be a supportable existence for either of them, anyway. When Luisa unwittingly drinks the poison that Rodolfo has himself imbibed she fulfils the only destiny it is possible for her to fulfil, finally breaking free of the father whom she loves so dearly, but who can never be a substitute for the lover that she needs. As she is released through

death so Miller, in losing her, is cruelly returned to the realities of having to live out his days in a cold, friendless world, without the succour of his daughter who would but have been surrogate wife and mother.

Mina (*Aroldo*). Aroldo's wife and daughter of **Egberto**.

The outline of Mina's role is very much the same as that of **Lina** in the original opera, *Stiffelio*. However, in Act 1, she is not constrained to hear her husband relay the boatman's account of how he witnessed her lover's precipitate exit from the window of her apartments. In *Stiffelio* this is the first torturous step in the process of dismantling Lina's conscience. In *Aroldo* the progress of Act 1 seems altogether more arbitrary.

The chief difference between the two roles lies in the manner in which the husband forgives the errant wife. In *Stiffelio*, Stiffelio grants Lina forgiveness in front of the entire congregation to whom he has just preached a sermon based on the text from *John*, 7.53–8.11 concerning the adulterous woman. In *Aroldo* the forgiveness is an altogether less public affair; the *rapprochement* takes place on the shores of Loch Lomond where Aroldo has retreated together with his spiritual confessor, **Briano**. It is of the essence in the re-writing of *Stiffelio* that the emphasis was moved away from the religious message which is at the heart of the original opera. For *Stiffelio* can easily be seen as a morality play that enshrines the sanctity of compassion as a value transcending all others. The same is true of *Aroldo*, though here the message is implicit rather than explicit.

At the conclusion Mina still desires forgiveness from her husband above all, but it is not necessary for her publicly to abase herself. It has become a more intimate tragedy. Her sin also becomes concomitantly not so much a spiritual fall from grace as a social stigma. This is emphasized by the fact that Mina has accompanied her father into exile. For Egberto is purely concerned for the social standing of his family. Mina's disgrace has become his disgrace, and Mina's guilt is as much for the grief and social ostracism she has brought upon her father as it is about the collapse of her marriage.

Mina makes an eloquent speech to her husband in which she begs his forgiveness (Act 4): 'When the years have conquered my heart and the grief has turned my hair white, when these eyes have been stilled by tears, and at last I hear the final hour strike do not deprive me of the hope, the solitary hope that I will at least be able to die forgiven'. This speech was unnecessary in the original opera for it is understood that it is Stiffelio's duty as a minister of God to forgive his wife. The drama is not so much between husband and wife but between Stiffelio, the man, and Stiffelio the priest.

In *Stiffelio* the crisis arrives when Lina signs the divorce document proffered her by her husband and then turns to him and says: 'It is no longer your wife who supplicates, it is the sinner who stands before you' (Act 3 Scene 1). She dramatically calls on him: 'Minister, minister, hear my confession'. Since it was these very lines that were considered so scandalous by the censor of the time they were inevitably excised when it came to refashioning the opera, as was the utterly crucial fact that Lina's husband is first and foremost a man of God. Thus Lina's desperate plea for forgiveness loses its piquancy since (in *Aroldo*) there is no confusion in Mina's mind between the roles her husband fulfils. He is just her husband and she is merely an unfaithful wife. In the hands of Puccini this would undoubtedly have become a scene of unbearable poignancy. But then Puccini's peculiar genius was for evoking the purely personal. This was never Verdi's genius. Verdi's genius was always fired most by conflicts between duty and personal passion. This is what the original drama encapsulated and is almost entirely mitigated in *Aroldo*.

(See also **Mina (*Stiffelio*).**)

Guido di Monforte (*I Vespri Siciliani*)
French viceroy in Sicily.

Monforte belongs to a long line of father-figures in Verdi's operas, fathers who are tormented by their relationships to their offspring. In Monforte's case this is to his illegitimate son, **Arrigo**, a Sicilian patriot.

When the opera opens Monforte has only recently heard that he has a son by a woman with whom he had an affair many years previously. He receives a letter from the mother, written on her deathbed, in which he is informed that his son is none other than Arrigo, a Sicilian patriot, who is at that moment languishing in one of his prisons awaiting execution. His mother's intervention does indeed save Arrigo's life, for Monforte is conscience-stricken. He knows he treated Arrigo's mother abominably and deserves her hatred but he cannot tolerate the thought of being abominated by his son, let alone be responsible for his execution. He also knows it will be a well nigh impossible task to effect a reconciliation and he is compelled to exercise remarkable forbearance throughout the opera.

Monforte is no Scarpia (Puccini's *Tosca*). He may be the viceroy appointed by an enemy army in occupation, but beneath the cloak of political necessity he is above all a doting father. Thus he epitomizes that central dilemma explored in almost every one of Verdi's operas, the dichotomy between the dictates of duty and of private passion. Monforte must know he is reviled, not only by Arrigo, but by the entire Sicilian population. He has had to harden his heart to being the object of universal revulsion because it is his duty to France to do so.

When Monforte first confronts Arrigo (Act 1) it is immediately after the latter has been released from jail through his intervention. Arrigo cannot believe his luck. He assumes that the judges have pardoned him not under orders from, but in spite of, Monforte. Monforte accepts this and is not unduly troubled. He knows he cannot expect an outpouring of gratitude from the youth. Besides which he cannot help admiring Arrigo's fiery spirit, even though it be employed mostly at his expense. His invitation to Arrigo to join the French forces is an absurdity and he knows it. He would think less of his son were he to accede to the invitation. Neither can he be surprised that

Arrigo refuses to heed his injunction not to visit the house of the Duchess **Elena**. Indeed the injunction has the precise opposite effect on Arrigo who rushes off to the self-same house at the conclusion of Act 1. Monforte looks on with 'emotion but without wrath'.

Monforte's discovery of his son fills a vacuum in his life for, as is the case with all politicians, he has given himself to the pursuit of power and worldly affluence with no thought to the life he suppresses and represses within himself. Now that he has found a source of meaning in his life he has only one thought: to hold on to it. At all costs he must effect a reconciliation with his son, for in his son he sees an image of the idealistic youth he killed off in himself many years previously. To his court Monforte's obsession must seem an absurdity. Why does he suddenly demand that the Sicilian patriot, enemy of the French crown, should be treated with 'the greatest respect'? It is a tribute to the respect in which his officers hold him that they readily accede to his bizarre edict.

Typically Monforte imagines that Arrigo can be bought, as he himself has allowed himself to be bought with the incitements of wealth and fame. His vanity is affronted by Arrigo's violent rejection, but his need for Arrigo overcomes even his overweening pride. He is reduced to pleading with his son like a demented lover. The approach is infinitely more efficacious than the previous strategy. Momentarily Arrigo accedes to his embrace but then, horrified with himself, he tears himself away (Act 3 Scene 1).

For Monforte the true indication that he is gaining his son's affection comes in Act 3 Scene 2 where Arrigo pleads with him to flee for his life prior to the final massacre. Monforte appears quite untroubled by the news that his life is in danger. It is not important to him. What is important is that Arrigo cares enough to tell him. When Elena actually makes to strike Monforte Arrigo does not hesitate but flings himself between his father and Elena's dagger. This is the final proof Monforte has been waiting for. Giving no thought to the fact that Arrigo

has hopelessly compromised himself with his compatriots Monforte blithely assures him that he will defend him. Henceforth father and son can live happily together. Arrigo is horrified. He has no intention of living in his father's shadow. He has been brought up to revile him.

Monforte gives little thought to his son's anguish. All he sees is an end to the impasse which has stunted his own life for so long. To ensure his son's love he is willing to be as unscrupulous as he has always been in his political life. He does not hesitate to hold his son to ransom, threatening to execute Arrigo's erstwhile closest friends, commencing with the woman he loves, Elena, if he does not publicly proclaim his filial devotion. Once having obtained this Monforte is pleased to proclaim in public his blessing on his son's union with Elena. It is more than likely that had Arrigo not publicly declared himself his son Monforte would have allowed Elena's execution to proceed (Act 4) even though this would have for ever after compromised any possibility of retaining Arrigo's love and respect. Monforte's public self-image is more important to him in spite of all protestations to the contrary.

At the conclusion of the opera it is Monforte's love of pageantry that precipitates the 'Sicilian Vespers' for, ignoring Elena's objections, he joins her hands with those of his son, thus giving the sign for the bells of Palermo to ring out, this being the signal (though of course Monforte does not know it) to the Sicilians to launch their massacre.

Montano (*Otello*). Former Governor of Cyprus.
Montano is at the quayside, at the opening of the opera, awaiting the arrival of **Otello's** returning ship (Act 1). In spite of having been succeeded by the Moor as Governor of Cyprus, he appears to bear Otello no rancour. He acts as his deputy in Otello's absence.

Montano is appalled, when he comes to request **Cassio's** presence on the ramparts, to discover him drunk, only then to be assured by **Iago** that Cassio is often thus. It does not occur to him, any more than it does to anybody else, to suspect Iago's word. When Cassio and **Roderigo** fall to brawling he attempts to separate them, but for his pains is himself wounded by the infuriated Cassio. Otello is appalled to find Montano wounded and orders his officers to help Montano into the house.

Montano does not reappear until the final scene of the opera (Act 4). Presumably he is nursing his wounds. However he is sufficiently restored to have encountered the dying Roderigo who has revealed to him Iago's 'artful villainy'. Iago makes his escape; Montano orders his arrest and then watches helplessly with **Lodovico** and the others as Otello takes his farewell of **Desdemona** and kills himself. Having been physically wounded on account of Iago's perfidy Montano has more reason than most to feel a grievance against Iago. If Iago is caught – and this is by no means certain – he will show little mercy.

With Otello's death Montano will presumably resume the governorship of Cyprus, for an interim period at any rate.

Count Monterone (*Rigoletto*). A nobleman. Count Monterone belongs to that large operatic family of outraged fathers of which **Rigoletto** himself is a prime example. In Monterone's thunderous imprecations against the libertine **Duke of Mantua** he invites comparison with Mozart's Commendatore (*Don Giovanni*).

Monterone appears only twice in the opera, but on each occasion he has a profound effect on the chief protagonists. In Act 1 Scene 1 Rigoletto mocks Monterone's fury over his daughter's assaulted honour. Monterone then curses both the Duke and Rigoletto. The Duke is able to laugh it off but Rigoletto takes the Count's curse very much to heart. It is the specific terms in which Monterone couches his curse that strike home in Rigoletto's conscience: 'You who laugh at a father's grief . . .', for Rigoletto is a father himself and should know better than to mock Monterone.

Later (Act 2) Monterone is being dragged to the palace dungeons and, stopping before a portrait of the Duke, he bitterly reflects how his curse has been in vain and that the Duke will, presumably, live happily on. Rigoletto observes from afar and determines in that moment to avenge Monterone by proceeding with his plan to ensure that the Duke will pay with his life for his crimes.

The reason that Monterone's curse has no effect on the Duke is that the latter does not for a moment take it seriously. Rigoletto, on the other hand, cannot forget the old man's words. It is not ultimately Monterone's curse that breaks Rigoletto, but his own conscience (see **Rigoletto**). The injustice done to Monterone is only another example, in this blackest of all Verdi's operas, of the total absence of natural justice that would appear to prevail.

Moser (*I Masnadieri*). A priest.
Moser appears in Act 4 Scene 1. He has been summoned from his bed, in the middle of the night, by **Francesco**. Apparently Francesco is in the habit of calling the priest from his bed, usually in order to mock religion. However this time Francesco looks genuinely haunted. He wishes to know what crime, in Moser's opinion, most excites God's wrath. Moser answers, with perhaps a little too much relish, that the two sins most unpardonable in the eyes of God are parricide and fratricide. One senses that he must suspect the truth about Francesco, although he has no proof.

When Arminio reports that the castle is under attack and the chapel has been razed to the ground it must be confirmation to Moser that Francesco is beyond redemption. Confirming all too clearly the import of Francesco's dream (see **Francesco**), Moser's last words to Francesco are 'God denies you forgiveness. The abyss lies before you'.

Moser is one of the earliest examples in Verdi's operas of the priest who acts as the spokesman for an unforgiving and inflexible ethos, which was usually predominant in the historical eras in which most of Verdi's operas are set. Verdi made no secret of his anti-clericalism. It is clear that he was more concerned to give expression to vitality of the life-instinct in opposition to the sterile dogmas of the established Church, dogmas which were responsible, in Verdi's eyes, for more human misery than ever was caused by ordinary mortal sin.

N

NABUCCO

Opera in 4 Acts. Libretto: Temistocle Solera after the drama, *Nabucodonosor* (1836), by Anicet-Bourgeois and Francis Cornue.

First performance: 9 March 1842 at La Scala, Milan.

Cast:

Nabucco [Nebuchadnezzar]: Assyrian king and ruler of Babylon (baritone)
Abigaille [Abigail]: a slave, believed to be the eldest child of Nabucco (soprano)
Zaccaria [Zechariah]: a Hebrew prophet (bass)
Ismaele [Ishmael]: nephew of Zedekiah, King of Jerusalem (tenor)
Fenena [Phenena]: daughter of Nabucco (soprano)
Anna [Hannah]: sister of Zaccaria (soprano)
Abdallo [Abdullah]: an old retainer of Nabucco (tenor)
High Priest of Baal (bass)

Time: 586 BC
Place: Jerusalem and Babylon

Synopsis
Each part of the libretto is headed by a quotation, or a paraphrase, from the Bible.
Act 1 Jerusalem.

Thus saith the Lord: Behold I will give this city into the hands of the king of Babylon: he will burn it with fire.

Thus Solera prefaces the first part of his libretto.

The interior of the Temple of Solomon. The Hebrews are lamenting the recent overthrow of Jerusalem by the Babylonian King,

Nabucco, and his forces. Most particularly they lament the desecration of the Temple. The Levites call on the Hebrew virgins to pray for deliverance. The virgins oblige and are shortly joined by all the Jews in imploring Jehovah not to permit 'the Assyrian foe to sit among his false idols upon the throne of David'. Zaccaria, the Most High Pontiff of the Hebrews, enters, leading Fenena, Nabucco's daughter, by the hand. They are accompanied by Zaccaria's sister, Anna. Zaccaria is in triumphant mood, for Fenena is a valuable hostage for the Hebrews. He tells the assembly to take courage for they have been granted a sign that they shall be delivered. 'Which one of us trusting in Him has perished in the hour of extremity?' he asks rhetorically (*D'Egitto là sui lidi*). Ismaele, nephew of Zedekiah, King of Jerusalem, enters, followed by a band of Hebrew soldiers. He comes with the news that the Assyrian king is advancing upon Jerusalem. Zaccaria, putting his faith in the Almighty God of Abraham, refuses to be perturbed. He hands Fenena into Ismaele's care. He is confident that Fenena will prove a powerful weapon with which to browbeat the enemy. Little does he realize that Fenena and Ismaele are already lovers (*Come notte a sol fulgente*).

After the Hebrews have departed Ismaele and Fenena are left alone. Fenena is impatient with Ismaele's talk of love, but the young prince cannot but remember the courageous way in which Fenena assured his escape from prison when Ismaele was serving as Judean Ambassador in Babylon, especially in view of the fact that her sister, Abigaille, was consumed with a raging passion for him. He reassures Fenena that now the tables have turned he will likewise ensure her liberation. He is about to reveal to her a secret exit when Abigaille enters, sword in hand, followed by a band of Babylonian soldiers, disguised in Hebrew attire. She announces dramatically that the Temple is taken. She reviles Fenena and assures her that her bridal bed will also be her tomb. Aside to Ismaele she confirms her love for him, which can either bring him life or death. If he will return her love she offers to save his people from the fate that otherwise threatens. Ismaele is adamant he will give her his life but not his love. Meanwhile Fenena declares her conversion to Judaism and prays that Jehovah may show mercy on her people. The Temple now fills with Hebrews and Levites, all in uproar, for it seems that Nabucco is prevailing and drawing near to the Temple.

Zaccaria re-enters. He is outraged at the blasphemy inherent in the Assyrian king's refusal to dismount his horse within the Temple precincts. All fear calamity is finally upon them. Zaccaria demands to know who granted admittance to the Babylonians, and Ismaele points out to him that the Babylonians who entered with Abigaille are disguised as Hebrews. There is no more time for recrimination. Nabucco himself enters on horseback. Zaccaria grabs hold of Fenena and threatens her with a dagger if Nabucco will not at least dismount from his charger. Reluctantly Nabucco realizes he must concede and dismounts. Abigaille, in an aside, makes it clear she would have been delighted had Fenena perished. Fenena pleads with her father for mercy, but Nabucco is consumed only with thoughts of bringing Zion to its knees. He orders the Hebrews down on their knees, 'defeated slaves' that they are. He pours derision on the God of the Jews who has failed to answer his challenge to battle. Zaccaria again threatens Fenena with his knife. This time he appears about to carry through his threat, but is prevented by Ismaele who wrests the dagger from the priest's hand. Fenena throws herself into her father's arms. Nabucco is out of patience. He orders the Babylonians to sack the Temple. In the ensemble that concludes Act 1, Fenena, Anna and Ismaele reflect on the dilemma of Ismaele's love for Fenena. Nabucco and Abigaille confirm their resolution to sack the Temple and show no mercy to the Hebrews, while Zaccaria and the Hebrews revile Ismaele for his apparent betrayal.

Act 2   The Wicked Man.

Behold the whirlwind of the Lord goeth forth with fury; it shall fall upon the head of the wicked

Scene 1   The Royal apartments in Nabucco's palace. Abigaille enters hastily. She carries a parchment in her hand which she has apparently discovered by chance amongst her father's belongings. It proves that Abigaille is not in fact Nabucco's daughter, but the offspring of slaves. She is consumed with resentment at the way in which Fenena has been left as Queen whilst Nabucco is engaged on his mission to exterminate Judea. Meanwhile she must stand aside, powerless, with nothing better to do than 'observe the loves of others!' (that of Fenena and Ismaele). Holding now the proof that her father intends passing over her in favour of her younger sister, frustrated in love, Abigaille has thoughts only of vengeance. Suddenly overcome by remorse she remembers (*Anch'io dischiuso*) how there once had been a time when she was capable of love and compassion.

The High Priest of Baal enters, accompanied by soothsayers and nobles of the realm. He has come to report that Fenena is releasing the Hebrew prisoners. The High Priest and his entourage are so outraged by this that they have come to offer their support to Abigaille if she will usurp the throne. In order to assist her they have already spread the rumour abroad that Nabucco has fallen in battle. Abigaille is overjoyed. She delights at the thought that 'Royal princesses (Fenena) will come hither to beg favours of the humble slave' (*Salgo già del trono aurato*).

Act 2 Scene 2   A hall in the palace with many rooms leading off. It is night. The hall is dimly lit by a single lamp. Zaccaria enters, accompanied by a Levite carrying the Tables of the Law. He beseeches his God to make himself known and prevail over the Heathens, the Babylonians (*Tu sul labbro de' veggenti*). Then, together with the Levite he enters Fenena's apartment. Other Levites enter. All are perplexed as to why they have been summoned. Ismaele enters and before he can tell them why Zaccaria has summoned them the Levites, who have not forgotten and cannot forgive his intervention in the confrontation with Nabucco (Act 1 Scene 2), interrupt him with curses. In spite of

Ismaele's frantic pleas to the Levites they are implacable. They are only silenced by the arrival of Fenena, Zaccaria, Anna and the Levite carrying the Tables of the Law. Anna tells the assembly to forgive Ismaele, for he 'saved a Hebrew maid' (Fenena). Zaccaria confirms this to be the case. The Levites have no opportunity to demand further explanation since a tumult from without announces the fact that Abigaille's supporters have been successful in spreading the rumour that Nabucco has died.

Abdallo, Nabucco's faithful retainer, enters and counsels Fenena to flee while she still can, for the people are crying for Abigaille and condemning Zaccaria and his followers. Fenena will not hear of flight. She is only prevented from hurrying out and confronting the 'impious rebels' by the arrival of Abigaille herself in the company of the High Priest of Baal, nobles, soothsayers and Babylonian men and women. Abigaille goes straight up to Fenena and demands the crown from her. Fenena exclaims 'I'd rather die first!' just as Nabucco himself arrives. Interposing himself between the two women he seizes the crown and sets it upon his own head. 'Take it from off my head!' he taunts. He leads the ensemble in which all express the belief that: 'the moment of direst wrath is fast approaching . . . a day of mourning and vexation is preparing' (*S'appressan gl'istanti*). Then Nabucco, with 'haughty disdain', pours scorn on the gods of both factions, Babylonians and Hebrews, and announces that there is only one god: the King (himself). This time it is not just the Hebrews, but all present who are appalled at his blasphemy. They are even more horrified when Nabucco insists they all kneel down and worship him. Zaccaria fulminates against his 'insane pride'. Nabucco summarily orders that Zaccaria be conducted to the foot of the idol where he shall perish with his people. Fenena intervenes and announces that as she is now converted to Judaism she will die with them. Beside himself Nabucco seizes his daughter roughly by the arm and forces her to her knees, reiterating: 'I am king no more, I am god!'

At this moment there is an almighty crash of thunder and a thunderbolt bursts above Nabucco's head. The terrified king feels his crown being lifted from his head by a supernatural force. The onset of madness begins to manifest itself in his whole appearance. In a stuttering monologue he expresses the confusion that has suddenly beset him: 'Who seizes me? . . . Who is crushing me? Who lays me low? . . . Who is destroying me? Who? Who?' (*Chi mi toglie il regio scettro?*). He turns to his daughter for support, although he can hardly see her. 'Alas, I am surrounded by phantoms . . . they have flaming swords of fire!' Finally he falls unconscious to the ground. Zaccaria announces portentously, 'Heaven has punished the boaster!' Then Abigaille picks up the crown that has fallen from Nabucco's head (thus showing that she has absorbed little of the lesson exemplified by her father's sudden downfall). 'But the greatness of the people of Baal shall not be eclipsed!' she proclaims.

The final scene of Act 2 is remarkable for its forward sweep and relentless momentum. Indeed the action progresses so swiftly that full appreciation demands previous study of the libretto.

Act 3   The Prophecy.

The wild beasts of the desert shall dwell in Babylon, together with owls; and hoopoes shall dwell therein.

Scene 1   The Hanging Gardens of Babylon. Abigaille is seated on the throne with soothsayers and nobles at her feet. The High Priest, surrounded by his followers, stands near an enormous golden statue of Baal. The nobles, soothsayers, soldiers and people sing of the joys of peace, 'worthy reward of valour' (*È l'Assiria una regina*). The High Priest addresses Abigaille, demanding that the wicked children of Judah should be destroyed; 'first and foremost, that woman, whom I dare not call your sister . . .' (Fenena). Abigaille feigns surprise.

But before she has a chance to answer they are interrupted by the arrival of Nabucco. His appearance is dishevelled and his clothes in tatters. The guards, led by Abdallo, give way respectfully before him. Abigaille, however, is not inclined to show respect towards her foster father. She orders the guards to conduct 'the old man' back to his apartments. Nabucco is not so deranged that he cannot recognize an affront to his dignity. He demands to know who dares to raise his voice in the presence of Nabucco. Then, brushing Abdallo aside, he approaches the throne. He prepares to mount it, but catches sight of Abigaille. Abigaille descends from the throne and dismisses her 'loyal subjects'.

When the two are alone Nabucco demands to know whose side she is on (the parallels with King Lear's predicament in Shakespeare's play need no underlining). Abigaille seizes the opportunity to demand Nabucco's royal seal on an impeachment against the Hebrews, including Fenena. Nabucco is wary. Something troubles him but he cannot identify the source of his disquiet. Only after he has placed his royal seal to the document does Abigaille tell him that he has effectively signed his own daughter's (Fenena's) death warrant. Nabucco is distraught. He searches in the breast of his tunic for the document which proves that Abigaille was born to lowly slaves. But Abigaille has long ago purloined this document (see Act 2 Scene 1) and she now produces it from her bosom and tears it to shreds. Nabucco is suddenly overcome with a sense of his impotence. Abigaille is triumphant.

Trumpets from without announce the death knell of the Hebrews, condemned by Nabucco. The latter calls to the guards, who come running. But Abigaille is quick to point out that they have not come to do his bidding, but have come at her instigation to imprison him. Nabucco is reduced to utter prostration. He begs Abigaille to have mercy on a foolish old man and grant him at least: 'the life of his heart's delight' (*Deh, perdona, deh, perdona*). This is not an argument likely to affect or influence Abigaille who, all her life, has been resentful of Fenena's far stronger pull on her father's affections. She remains unmoved.

Act 3 Scene 2   The banks of the Euphrates. The Hebrews, in chains, are subjected to forced labour. Their thoughts dwell on their beloved homeland (*Va, pensiero*). In their enslaved condition the only recourse they have is to the prompting of memory and imagination: 'Golden harp of the prophetic seers, why dost thou hang mute upon the willow? Re-kindle our bosom's memories and speak of the times gone by! Mindful of the fate of Jerusalem, either give forth an air of sad lamentation, or else let the Lord imbue us with fortitude to bear our sufferings!'

Zaccaria attempts to lift the spirits of the Hebrews, upbraiding them for raising lamentations to the Almighty in the manner of timorous women. He declares that he can see into the future and that he foresees the inevitable downfall of Babylon (*Del futuro nel buio discerno*). The Hebrews are impressed and are soon echoing Zaccaria's conviction that their 'shameful fetters' shall soon be broken.

Act 4   The Broken Idol.

Baal is confounded: his idols are broken in pieces.

Scene 1   An apartment in the palace. Nabucco wakes distractedly from a deep sleep. He has been dreaming that he was being pursued through the woods, 'panting like a haunted beast'. It is a novel experience for the erstwhile tyrant. He has become a mere mortal with all the attendant frailties.

He hears voices, offstage, shouting, which makes him long to be reunited with his sword and his charger, 'like a young girl longs for dancing'. The voices can now clearly be heard, pronouncing the name of Fenena. Nabucco rushes to the balcony and is greeted by the sight of Fenena, her hands bound in chains and weeping. She is running between ranks of soldiers. The voices confirm that she is to be put to death.

Suddenly the true horror of his situation dawns on Nabucco. He is a prisoner in his own palace and can do nothing to prevent his daughter's execution. In his desperation he falls to his knees and begs the God of the Jews to forgive him. He declares that he will raise an altar and a temple sacred to Judah's God, if only he be rescued from the anguish and confusion which clouds his brain. As if by a miracle he can sense his mind clearing almost as he utters the words of his prayer. Hearing renewed shouting from outside he rises and begins to pound frenziedly on one of the doors. Abdallo enters, accompanied by soldiers. The old man quickly realizes that his king has regained his sanity and joyfully reunites him with his sword. Nabucco exhorts the soldiers to follow him as he reclaims his rightful position as King of Assyria.

Act 4 Scene 2   The Hanging Gardens. Zaccaria, Anna, Priests of Baal, soothsayers, Hebrews are all on stage. The High Priest of Baal stands beside a sacrificial altar. Fenena and other condemned Hebrews are brought in to the melancholy strains of a funeral march. Fenena kneels before Zaccaria as the latter exhorts her to: 'Go and win the palm of martyrdom'. Fenena confirms her readiness to leave behind: 'this mortal body that, heavy as lead, detains us here'. At which point voices, off, are heard calling: 'Long live Nabucco!' Nabucco enters, blood-stained sword in hand and followed by Abdallo and soldiers. He calls a halt to the sacrifice about to take place and commands his soldiers to shatter the idol. As he does so the idol falls of its own volition and shatters into pieces. All present fall to their knees in amazement and proclaim it a divine miracle.

Nabucco now calls on the Hebrews to return to their native land and build a temple to the one God. All join together in celebrating the might of Jehovah. They are only interrupted by the arrival of Abigaille who, consumed with remorse, has taken poison. She is supported by two soldiers. She begs to be pardoned for her crimes and tells Nabucco of the love of Fenena and Ismaele and prays that their union may be granted his blessing. With her dying breath she implicitly confirms her faith in the one God and prays that she may not be damned. The Hebrews assert that God will lift up the afflicted. She collapses and dies. The curtain falls as Zaccaria calls upon Nabucco, as servant of Jehovah, to be the King of Kings.

Inevitable comparisons may be drawn between the plot of Nabucco and those of Rossini's Mosé, Bellini's Norma and Saints-Saëns' Samson et Dalila. All attend to the plight of a besieged people searching for means of salvation from their oppressors, specifically within the context of their religious differences. All contain to some degree the Romeo and Juliet love motive: the lovers from rival camps, compromising or contributing to some sort of rapprochement. (Aida could be included in this canon, except that there the religious dissension is subsidiary to the more political agenda.)

All his life Verdi contemplated making an opera of Shakespeare's King Lear. One possible reason that it never materialized is that he had already set the play's principal theme, if not the actual plot, in the story of Nabucco. The central theme of both stories is the punishment of a man's outstanding hubris and that man's long road back towards a state of grace with all the suffering attendant thereon. There are other incidental parallels in King Lear: two brothers, one a bastard (Edmond) and one legitimate (Edgar), where the illegitimate seeks to usurp the legitimate. In Nabucco Abigaille almost succeeds in usurping Fenena only to be undone at the end by her own consuming and self-consuming passion. The confrontation between Nabucco and Abigaille (Act 3 Scene 1) evokes all too clearly the confrontation of Lear with his daughters. Like Lear Nabucco has expected too much of his progeny. He must pay the consequences of not allowing them to individuate, requiring unconditional love and loyalty as though by divine right. It is not his right – a parent should not demand what cannot be given, only that which can be given freely and without coercion.

Fenena's defection to the Hebrew faith is no different from Cordelia's desire to marry the King of France. It is not a declaration of withdrawal of love from the father, merely a declaration of the right to self-determination away from the father. When Cordelia tells her father that she can offer him just the love due to a father, no more, no less, she enunciates a simple truth; that is all that a daughter should owe. Any more and she ceases to have an identity of her own. She becomes a mere cipher for the longing (and *anima*-projection) of the father. Fenena's rebellion complements that of Abigaille in the same way that Cordelia's does that of Regan and Goneril.

But where Fenena and Cordelia's rebellions are grounded in a genuine sense of self-worth – an identity that deserves to be given the opportunity to come to fruition – Regan, Goneril and Abigaille all base their rebellion on a deep sense of insecurity and self-loathing. Through the years of domination they have allowed resentment and bitterness at the lack of self-determination imposed upon them from above, to corrupt their natures so that now they have no clear motive for revolt other than the purely negative impulse of revenge, revenge for the years of oppression. Were Lear and Nabucco to die they would continue exerting their revenge on any and all who happened to fall within their sphere regardless of the fact that the object of their resentment was no longer present. In Jungian terms the *animus* within them has become so entirely predominant that they have lost all communication with that which truly defines them, their femininity. Identified with the *animus*, synonymous with the father, they live in dread of the castration that will deprive them of identity and give them no recourse but to become that which they are, but have no appetite for.

When the father is similarly suffering from the dread of castration (in the father's case usually brought about by the fear attendant upon encroaching old age), a titanic struggle inevitably ensues. This is the central battle enshrined with equal force in Shakespeare's play and Verdi's first masterwork.

Nabucco. Assyrian king and ruler of Babylon.
Nebuchadnezzar (c630–562 BC) was one of the greatest of Babylonian kings. He was the son of Nabapolassar (who founded the New Babylonian empire) and ruled for over 40 years (605–562 BC). While he is chiefly remembered in the West for his mass deportation of the Jews from their homeland to Babylonia in 586 BC his reign yet

represented the very peak of Babylonian civilization.

The story of *Nabucco* is the story of a proud man brought low by his own overweening pride but ultimately finding redemption through the excruciating experience of nemesis. In the character of Nabucco we find fulfilment of the promise implicit in the earlier father-figure, Oberto. But it is on a much more mythic scale. Verdi did not again return to the epic proportions of *Nabucco*. Even in his final great triumvirate of operas (*Aida*, *Otello* and *Falstaff*) the passions explicated are largely personal in nature. With the possible exception of Carlo in *I Masnadieri* Verdi did not again undertake to portray a character in contention not with man or woman, but with God. *Nabucco* thus has a unique fascination.

No background is given, nor is it necessary to know anything more than that Nabucco is the heathen aggressor, threatening to undermine the religion and way of life of the Hebrews in their native land. His very entrance (Act 1) is a blasphemy, mounted as he is on his charger within the precincts of the Temple. When he dismounts from his charger it is not out of respect for the Hebrews' Temple but because, as king and politician, Nabucco is first and foremost a pragmatist. Mounted on his charger he is an easy target for any would-be assassin. If some nicety of conscience enters into his acquiescence to **Zaccaria**'s behest then it is purely unconscious. He loses no time in telling the Hebrews that he has already challenged their God to battle and their God did not come. He is only momentarily checked in his resolve by Zaccaria seizing his daughter, **Fenena**, and threatening to slay her. (There is no record of the Biblical Nebuchadnezzar having had a daughter, but in Verdi's opera Fenena is the one person who has access to her father's capacity for compassion and mercy.) That Fenena's life is saved by an infatuated Hebrew can be little solace to Nabucco. He certainly makes no special dispensation towards **Ismaele**, except in so far as the latter escapes with his life.

Nabucco remains unaware that his daughter has embraced the Jewish faith (see also Sofia and Oronte, *I Lombardi* for comparable instances of surreptitious conversion). When he does discover her betrayal it is immediately subsequent to his declaration that he is now himself to be worshipped as a god. His daughter's defection at the very moment of his outstanding hubris underlines the isolation and ostracism that he has brought upon himself. All his life Nabucco has achieved his ends by force alone. He knows nothing of the gentler arts of reason and persuasion. Thus, when confronted with his disobedient daughter, he knows no other way of compelling her submission than brute physical force. He seizes her roughly by the arm and orders her to prostrate herself before the god, that is, himself (Act 2 Scene 2). In that moment he contravenes every natural law and it is in that moment he is struck down. No longer acknowledging any authority superior to his own will he alienates himself, not only from his people and his own flesh and blood, but also from himself. For the responsibility he imposes upon himself is too great. Suddenly he is reduced to the helplessness of an infant, but with none of the insouciance. He is plagued by paranoia. 'Who is crushing me? Who lays me low? Who, who is destroying me? Who? Who?' In his supreme helplessness he turns to the one person on whom he has always relied upon for succour, his adored daughter. But she is no longer there, for he has cast her out.

Only the realization of the extreme peril in which Fenena stands (Act 3 Scene 1) will release Nabucco from the existential nightmare into which he has cast himself. For in the daughter is the image of the mother and the lover and of the natural order from which he has exiled himself. Confronted with the spectacle of Fenena, surrounded by soldiers en route to their execution (Act 4 Scene 1) Nabucco has two alternatives: either he can accede to his own apparent helplessness, incarcerated as he is, or he can once again make the leap of faith necessary to any predetermined act of will. In other words he must accept his own contingency in the same instance that he recognizes that of his daughter. At any given moment of his incarceration he could have beaten on the doors of the prison, initiated his own release and, incidentally, that of his people. But until he perceives Fenena's peril he has no motivation and consequently no effective will. He is an empty shell at the mercy of the fearfully efficacious will of the woman he has brought up as his own daughter, but who, in his heart, he has never been able to acknowledge or embrace. **Abigaille** has the most powerful motivation of all for hatred and for resentment. Nabucco, for all his faults, for all his aggression, does not hate; he is only consumed by power-lust.

Instinctively Nabucco has always been aware that in the person of Abigaille he is harbouring 'a viper to his bosom'. Why else would he carry with him the document confirming Abigaille's low-born origins? His worst fears are confirmed when Abigaille reveals that she has purloined the document and proceeds to destroy it in front of his eyes (Act 3 Scene 1). It is the end for him of any hope that he may prevail by political means. His only recourse thereafter can be to his own inner resources and, in the appropriate parlance, to God, not some exterior idol, fashioned by man in the likeness of man, but to the God of the Jews, the God who dwells omnisciently without and within and cannot be imagined. It is when he finds the pure, blind faith which is his only route back to sanity and rehabilitation in the world that he can re-access the potency that has ensnared his ascendancy thus far.

In the book of Daniel, Chapters 3 and 4, it is described how Nebuchadnezzar's conversion was effected when he witnessed the survival of the three Levites, Shadrach, Meshach and A-bed-nego, after they had been thrown into the burning fiery furnace. Thereafter Nebuchadnezzar lost his kingdom and was 'driven from men, and did eat grass as oxen, and his body was wet with the dew of heaven, till his hairs were grown like eagles' feathers, and his nails like birds' claws'. The survival of the three Levites is a demonstration of the power of faith over even the most extreme exigencies.

In the same book of Daniel we read of Daniel's survival in the lions' den, and also of the writing on the wall at Belshazzar's feast. The Old Testament is riddled with such tales and also with precognitive or visionary dreams which determine the destinies of many leading protagonists. Julian Jaynes has postulated that it was at this stage of human evolution that a split began to manifest itself not only in human consciousness, but also concomitantly in the human brain (see Julian Jaynes, *The Origin of Consciousness in the Breakdown of the Bicameral Mind*, Houghton Mifflin, 1971). Recent research into brain physiology has suggested that the right half of the brain is the home of the intuitive unconscious, while the left half of the brain houses the rationalistic mind, or ego. The left brain plots and schemes and asserts itself in the world, while the right brain lives almost entirely outside time. Jacob's dream, the visions of Nebuchadnezzar and Belshazzar, all manifestations of God's intervention, as described in the Old Testament are, according to Jaynes' theory, examples of the right brain (home presumably of Freud's unconscious and Jung's archetypes) asserting itself in order to rectify an unwonted imbalance threatened by the tyranny of the left. The advent of a strongly paternalistic, all-omnipotent God which characterized this period of Jewish culture inevitably led to a bifurcation between what is felt and what is consciously willed. In other words it led to the advent of conscience with all its attendant benefits to civilization but also potential for neurosis and psychosis. Nabucco's odyssey can be seen as the odyssey of Western consciousness at a critical stage in its evolution.

Note: It is noticeable that there is no passage of Nabucco's role that can readily be extracted from the score, unlike for instance the role of Zaccaria. It is indicative of the fact that Verdi was already, at this early stage of his career, inclined to through-compose, particularly when the character's psychological profile recommended it. This tendency was only truly to reach fruition at the end of Verdi's career with the operas *Otello* and *Falstaff.*

Nannetta (*Falstaff*). Daughter of the **Fords**. In *Un giorno di regno* Verdi brought to the operatic stage a story which revolved around a double wedding, one of which was to be that of a young girl, Giulietta, daughter of Baron Kelbar, an associate of her father, to the ageing Treasurer Gasparo della Rocca. In *Falstaff* Verdi revisits precisely the same scenario. Nannetta is to be married to her father's friend, the physician **Doctor Caius**.[53] Doctor Caius is about three times her age and a bigot. Nannetta certainly does not love him. She is already in love, and knows perfectly well who she wants to marry, namely young **Fenton**, who regularly serenades her; who makes love to her (sometimes with more ardour than she can cope with); and above all is someone with whom she can be certain of having fun. For Nannetta is a fun-loving girl. She is fortunate that her Mother, **Alice**, supports her desire to marry Fenton and not the disagreeable Caius. It is also fortuitous, from Nannetta's point of view, that Alice happens to be in the midst of a marital crisis, for it means that Alice is looking for any way to pay her husband back for his unreasonable behaviour.

Nannetta enjoys every minute of the scheming of the 'Merry Wives' to gain redress for the insult dealt them by the fat Knight. From the moment her mother receives **Falstaff**'s letter (Act 1 Scene 2) she can barely contain her excitement. She cannot bear the thought that she might miss out on something. Thus she pushes herself right to the forefront of the plans to trounce Falstaff.

---

[53] In Shakespeare's play, Anne, the equivalent character to Nannetta, is the daughter of Page, not Ford. Although Page is of a much milder disposition than Ford Anne has twice the problems of her operatic counterpart, for she has not one, but two unwelcome suitors, in addition to the lover she wants, namely Slender (favoured by the father) and Doctor Caius (favoured by her mother). Anne's comment on the prospect of being married to Doctor Caius is colourful: 'Alas, I had rather be set quick i'th'earth, and bowl'd to death with turnips' . . .

However, when Fenton appears Nannetta has eyes and ears only for him. She leads her lover behind the screen so that they can continue with their love-making and the pair remain oblivious to the shenanigans all around them (Act 2 Scene 2). Unfortunately for them they fail to hear Nannetta's father, together with his henchmen, preparing to knock down the screen. Nannetta's chagrin when she is revealed to the eyes of her father *in flagrante delicto* is such that she is, for the only time in the opera, struck dumb. She scuttles away as fast as she can.

It is, inevitably, a source of huge relief to Nannetta that her mother and friends refuse to countenance Ford's plans to marry her off to Caius that very same evening, but instead determine to assist her in marrying the man of her dreams. Nannetta's wedding day will be one to remember in the years to come.

Having first played a major part in the gulling of the unfortunate Falstaff, she is then married to Fenton by her unsuspecting father, in tandem with the bizarre coupling of Bardolf and Doctor Caius (see **Synopsis**). Her joy is complete when she begs, and obtains, forgiveness from her father and his blessing on her marriage. Nanetta has plenty of justification for the assertion 'The whole world is a jest' which concludes the opera.

Ninetta (*I Vespri Siciliani*). Sicilian girl, maid to **Duchess Elena**, in love with **Danieli**. Like her lover Ninetta serves as a spokesperson for the Sicilian folk who struggle to survive under French domination and who long to be released from their burden but can never quite summon enough focus to their resentment to effect that which they hanker after. Ninetta dotes on her mistress. She knows that Elena is under close scrutiny from the French. She is also keenly aware that Elena grievously mourns the recent death of her beloved brother, Federigo.

In Act 1 Ninetta shows herself to be extremely protective towards Elena, particularly when the latter is threatened by drunken French soldiers. Her love for Elena is indeed more noticeable than her love for **Danieli**. Beyond either of her two loves her truest devotion is to freedom. The continuous threat to her freedom, represented by the French on her native soil, stirs within her all the feelings of bitterness, anger and resentment that so patently consume the menfolk, including her sweetheart. She has probably come to know **Arrigo** since the latter became one of Duke Federigo's staunchest supporters. A fiery, idealistic nature like Arrigo's could only make a strong impression on a young girl like Ninetta. She must inevitably have become aware of the attraction between her mistress and Arrigo. She joins her mistress in attempting to dissuade Arrigo from aggravating **Monforte**, but their efforts are to no avail (Act 1). But then Ninetta does not know, any more than Elena, that Monforte is Arrigo's father.

When the day comes of her wedding to Danieli (Act 2) Ninetta must be overjoyed. But her joy is short-lived for, arriving at the scene of the wedding, she is confronted by the licentious French soldiers. She is powerless to do anything to protect herself, and before she knows where she is she is being carried off by **Roberto**. She may protest at her plight and is undoubtedly outraged at the behaviour of the French soldiers, but when we next see Ninetta she is, in company with the other Sicilian brides, being wafted along the shore aboard a splendidly decorated boat. She is elegantly dressed and is indisputably enjoying the luxury that Roberto and the other French officers are lavishing on her. It is so totally unaccustomed and quite beyond the means of a Sicilian peasant like Danieli that she cannot help being flattered. (Note: It is possible that Ninetta knows from the outset about the plan to goad the Sicilian men out of their apathy. This would explain her and the other Sicilian women's apparent acquiescence when being serenaded by the French officers.)

The roles of Ninetta and her lover are a throwback to the early Commedia dell'Arte characters, a tradition that reached its apogee in Mozart's *Don Giovanni* and *Le nozze di Figaro* with the characters of Masetto/Zerlina and Susanna/Figaro. Ninetta and

Danieli serve the same function as do Zerlina and Masetto in *Don Giovanni*, underlining the chronic effect on an average couple of the machinations of the privileged and wealthy. The fact that Ninetta is flattered by the attentions of the French soldiers does not for a moment mean that she does not love Danieli and is not sensible to the grief her abduction will cause him. While Ninetta plays no very noticeable part in the remainder of the drama, we can be certain that she will be right behind her lover when he is finally granted a pretext to take arms against the French. She wants independence for Sicily as much as he does, not only for herself but for her beloved mistress.

O

OBERTO, Conte Di San Bonifacio

Opera in 2 Acts. Libretto by Antonio Piazza, revised by Temistocle Solera.

First performance: 17 November 1839 at La Scala, Milan.

Cast:

Cuniza: sister to Ezzelino of Romano (mezzo-soprano)
Riccardo: Count of Salinguerra (tenor)
Oberto: Count of San Bonifacio (bass)
Leonora: his daughter (soprano)
Imelda: Cuniza's confidante (mezzo-soprano)

Time: 1228
Place: Ezzelino's castle, near Bassano

Historical Background The two characters that figure in the history books are Ezzelino da Romano, one of the most feared and hated tyrants in Italian history, and his sister, Cuniza (see **Cuniza**). Ezzelino does not appear in the opera, but his spirit hangs over much of it since most of the action takes place in his castle in Bassano. It is on his account that Oberto has been forced into exile and therefore has had to abandon his daughter.

Ezzelino appears in Dante's *Inferno* in the seventh circle in Hell, where violent criminals are punished (see *Inferno, Canto XII*).

Ezzelino was of German descent. His name means 'little Etzel', or Attila. The association with the notorious Hun is entirely justifiable. He was known as 'the son of a devil' and successively made himself lord of Verona, Vicenza, Padua and other cities in North East Lombardy. He became Imperial vicar under Frederick II. Eventually his atrocities were deemed beyond the pale and Pope Alexander IV called a Crusade against him. In 1259 he was defeated at Cassano, wounded and taken prisoner. He died a few days later when he wilfully tore the bandages from his wounds.

Oberto, Count of Bonifacio, having been defeated in battle, takes refuge in Mantua. While away at war his daughter, Leonora, has resided with his sister in Verona. Leonora has been seduced by Oberto's enemy Riccardo, Count of Salinguerra. Riccardo has remained incognito and, having promised Leonora marriage, has abandoned her. When the opera opens he is about to marry Cuniza, the sister of his ally, Ezzelino da Romano. Leonora has just arrived in Bassano intending to confront her seducer before his marriage to Cuniza takes place.

Synopsis

Act 1 Scene 1 A beautiful countryside scene near the castle of Bassano. A chorus of knights, ladies and vassals celebrate Riccardo's recent victory and impending wedding to his ally, Ezzelino's sister, Cuniza (*Di vermiglia, amabil, luce*). Riccardo acknowledges their greeting, and rejoices in the fact that all his arduous days at war have led to this moment of supreme happiness (*Questi plausi a me d'intorno*). He swears he will keep his enemies at bay (*Già parmi d'udire il fremito*). All move towards the castle of Bassano.

Leonora enters and sings of her betrayal (*Ah, sgombro è il loco alfin!*). She recalls the rapturous moments when she first fell in love with Riccardo (*Sotto il paterno tetto*). In spite of his betrayal she still loves him and suffers deeply because of his cruelty. She follows the bridal group towards the castle.

Oberto enters and (in a moment which prefigures Procida's arrival in *I Vespri*

Siciliani) sings of his great joy at having returned to his homeland (*Oh patria terra*). Yet it is a distressing reason that brings him home. He comes in pursuit of his 'ungrateful daughter'. He has heard from his sister how Leonora has been seduced and abandoned by his enemy, Riccardo. So enraged is he with her that he fears she may cause his early death.

Leonora arrives in the village. She is planning on entering the castle unobserved at nightfall, when the wedding is due to take place. She is dismayed when confronted by her father, clearly anticipating his wrath. Oberto is forthright: 'you have stained the honour of your father's declining years' (*Non ti bastò il periglio*). Leonora is genuinely contrite. She admits she has brought shame and disgrace on them and invokes her deceased mother who 'sees my weeping from heaven' (*Del tuo favor soccorrimi*). Oberto rejoins: 'She sees your sin and shudders!' He tells his daughter that she must either confront her seducer and expose his crime or she must die. Leonora is determined to avenge herself and again be worthy of her father's love. Reassured Oberto embraces her. This scene is one of the first of many father–daughter confrontations in Verdi's operas.

Act 1 Scene 2   A magnificent room in Ezzelino's palace. A chorus greets the bride with platitudes (see **Chorus**). The scene has parallels in many of Verdi's subsequent operas: *Un giorno di regno, Ernani, Il Corsaro, La Battaglia di Legnano, Aida*.

Riccardo enters. Cuniza thanks her attendants graciously and asks them to leave. Riccardo comments that Cuniza seems downcast. Cuniza tells her bridegroom that the joy she feels on her wedding day is yet mingled with 'a mysterious fear'. Riccardo attempts to dispel her fears for, as he tells her, if she brings 'a gloomy image' with her to the altar it will be a source of concern to him. Cuniza brushes aside her doubts as 'a dream that does not last' (*Fra il timore e la speme diviso*). Riccardo assures her that without her love he would prefer death and, as they exit, he confirms his love for her: 'our lives shall run like a limpid stream until death summons us to the grave'. It is an illusion soon to be shattered.

Leonora enters accompanied by Cuniza's confidante, Imelda. She requests an audience with Cuniza, assuring Imelda that it is a matter in which Cuniza will be interested. Imelda goes in search of Cuniza.

Left alone Leonora is overcome by apprehension. She is acutely aware of the proximity of her father, who is hiding nearby and will overhear her conversation with Cuniza. Her only concern is to be worthy of her father's forgiveness. Cuniza enters and asks Leonora how she can help her. Leonora tells Cuniza that her renowned virtue has drawn 'an unhappy girl' to her. She then reveals that she is the daughter of Oberto. Cuniza is horrified to realize that she is in the presence of the daughter of her family's arch enemy, but Leonora warns her to be discreet since Oberto has accompanied her to the castle. Cuniza has no time to compose herself before Oberto himself enters.

Oberto immediately declares that he stands before Cuniza an unhappy man, that he hopes for pity from her heart, that he is the victim of a harsh fate and that he has been dishonoured by a coward. Cuniza displays remarkable *sang froid* in her response, which is to assure Oberto that if she can, she will help him overcome the peril in which he finds himself. Leonora tells Cuniza that only she, Cuniza, can rectify the wrong suffered by herself and her father, but she warns Cuniza that she will be appalled when she hears the identity of the culprit and the nature of his crime. In spite of a grave sense of foreboding Cuniza demands that they tell her the truth. When Oberto and Leonora relate the history of Riccardo's treachery Cuniza is naturally horrified. Her grief quickly turns to anger and, inspired by Oberto's passion (*Su quella fronte impressa*), a desire for revenge. Oberto and Leonora promise their assistance in effecting Cuniza's revenge. Cuniza leads Oberto and Leonora into an adjoining room.

Riccardo, Imelda, knights and ladies enter. The scene is set for the finale. Cuniza takes a perverse pleasure in introducing Leonora to Riccardo. Riccardo realizes that his secret must be discovered. At first he tries to pretend that Leonora was faithless. Leonora is outraged: 'I was betrayed, I was deceived, and now I am slandered too', she exclaims. Oberto, who has been listening, cannot contain himself any longer and erupts with imprecations against Riccardo. The whole court is stunned. But they need little persuading of Riccardo's guilt. Leonora's distress is all too apparent and convincing (*Sentiero a te incognito*). In the final ensemble of the Act all join Oberto in affirming that Riccardo's hour of reckoning has arrived.

Act 2 Scene 1 Cuniza's private apartments. In stark contrast to the opening of Act 1 Scene 2, Cuniza's attendants are now bewailing her betrayal. Imelda enters and tells Cuniza that Riccardo wishes to speak with her. The mention of Riccardo's name prompts bitter reminiscences from Cuniza (*O, chi torna l'ardente pensiero*). She recalls how one glance from Riccardo, 'one sweet smile – to me was life, joy, paradise!' Now, she continues, 'they reach my heart in vain, like prayers on an icy tomb'. Imelda asks her mistress what she intends to do. Revealing a high-minded rectitude previously barely suspected Cuniza tells Imelda that she herself will lead Riccardo to his first sworn love, Leonora. 'Let the unhappy girl's grief find shelter in my breast', she declares. For 'friendship is a holy emotion, equal to that of love'.

Act 2 Scene 2 A remote place near the castle gardens. A chorus of knights bewails the suffering that their princess, Cuniza, endures; 'In this life virtue and misfortune keep each other company', they observe.

Meanwhile Oberto awaits the arrival of Riccardo with whom he will fight a duel. He looks forward to avenging his family's dishonour, which demands the wrongdoer's blood (*L'orror del tradimento*). The chorus of knights is heard calling for Oberto. Entering they tell him he has no need to fear Ezzelino for Cuniza has saved him. Oberto commands them to go on ahead; he will join them. He is not impressed. He does not wish to be saved; he wants only vengeance. On this day either he or Riccardo must die. If it is to be himself a war-cry shall arise from his corpse, cursing the Salinguerra clan (*Ma tu superbo giovane*).

Riccardo arrives and Oberto scornfully tells him that this is not a contest between 'tender maidens'. He invites him to draw his sword and defend himself. Riccardo at first refuses to fight in such an unequal conflict. But when Oberto calls Riccardo a coward the latter can no longer restrain himself and draws his sword.[54]

At this moment Cuniza and Leonora enter. Cuniza stops Riccardo in his tracks. Riccardo is forced to admit to himself that he feels a mixture of shame, remorse and vexation at the sight of Cuniza, whose love he has forfeited. Leonora, meanwhile, cannot help but admit that she still loves Riccardo in spite of the shame that he has brought on her. Oberto continues to rail against Riccardo's infamy.

Cuniza lays matters clearly before Riccardo. She will forgive him, she tells him, if he will give himself in marriage to Leonora. Oberto is infuriated by these procrastinations. In a fierce aside he tells Riccardo that he can accede to Cuniza's demands, but then he must wait for Oberto in a nearby wood so that they can conclude the matter honourably with swords. Riccardo agrees and offers his hand to Leonora. Cuniza selflessly blesses their union. Leonora promises to give herself wholly to Riccardo if only he will return repentant to her. Riccardo is genuinely moved by Leonora's evident sincerity, and regrets that he must wound her further by depriving her of her father. Oberto, meanwhile, is contemplating the moment when he will finally wash 'the shameful stain' from his name with his enemy's blood. Cuniza mourns the loss of her love but comforts herself with the thought that the peace she shall have no longer may 'yet smile upon that

---

[54] It is an operatic stock-in-trade from Mozart's *Don Giovanni* onwards (see Act 1 Scene 1 of *Don Giovanni*; Don Giovanni versus the Commendatore) that the anti-hero refuses combat with an older man, is goaded for cowardice and then enjoins battle, usually slaying his opponent.

unhappy girl'. Oberto goes into the wood, whilst everyone else exits.

A chorus of knights reflects that in spite of the apparent truce there is still anger between the two Counts (see **Chorus**). Their musings are interrupted by the sounds of clashing swords. They rush off into the wood.

Riccardo enters, sword in hand, as if he is being pursued. He fears he has killed Oberto and is consumed with horror at what he has done. He only desires now to flee. He hears groans which he imagines emanate from the stricken old man. He kneels in prayer and pleads for mercy (*Ciel pietoso, ciel clemente*) before rushing off.

Cuniza enters breathlessly with Imelda, followed by the whole court. Cuniza is desperate for news. She fears the worst. The chorus relay the shocking news that Oberto has been found lying in his own blood and that Leonora has collapsed with grief.

Leonora is brought in. She bewails the loss of everything she holds dear. Cuniza goes to her and attempts to console her, telling her that she will never leave her. Leonora feels that it was she herself who killed her father through succumbing to Riccardo in the first place. She is beside herself with anguish and remorse.

A messenger enters, carrying a letter for the princess. Trembling, Cuniza opens the letter. It is from Riccardo, telling her that he has flown to Italy to seek asylum abroad. He begs Leonora's pardon and confirms his undying love. Cuniza is clearly moved by Riccardo's obvious repentance and suffering. Leonora, however, does not wish to hear any more. She tells Cuniza to hide the 'blood-stained letter', which shames 'that pitiless man'. She declares her intention of entering a convent. 'May my weeping and sorrow hasten my death', she exclaims. The curtain falls as she collapses into the arms of the women who surround her.

A certain fascination must inevitably attach to the first products of burgeoning genius. It is tempting, and often possible, to discover the seeds of all that is to come in the years to follow. In Wagner's first opera, *Die Feen*, one finds a sketch containing all the major themes that were to obsess the composer throughout his career. Coincidentally the same can be said of Verdi's first opera, *Oberto*. It is incontestable that the father–daughter relationship was particularly engrossing for Verdi. An entire volume could be dedicated to the subject. It should be added that the father–son relation was hardly less engrossing for him. Either way it can be said with certainty that it is the paternal relation that preoccupied Verdi to a far greater extent than the romantic love relation (which was to become the special provenance of Puccini).

When Oberto first appears in the opera he is spluttering with rage over the dishonour his daughter has brought on his name. How many of Verdi's father-figures have cause to splutter over the misdeeds, omissions or fate of their progeny? It would be useful to list these occasions, if it were not for the fact that the list would have to include virtually every one of Verdi's 28 operas. If there is not a biological father involved then there will be a father-figure, such as de Silva (*Ernani*), Leo (*Attila*), Lodovico (*Otello*). (Seid's relation to **Gulnara** [*Il Corsaro*] could be said to be an abuse of the father–daughter relationship if one considers that the Pasha is a kind of 'father' to the inhabitants of his harem.) *Macbeth* is concerned primarily with primogeniture. The single exception where a father-figure is not prominent is *Un ballo in maschera*, though even there it could be said that **Renato** takes on the aspect of an avenging father when he learns of his wife's infidelity.

In *Oberto* there is no need to search for the father-figure. Oberto is the prototype of the father who cannot relinquish his daughter, who succeeds in instilling in her an enduring sense of guilt, and who eventually dies in the attempt to salvage the honour that his daughter's lapse has so critically compromised. Yet it is not as though Oberto is unsympathetic. There can be no doubt concerning his genuine love and affection for Leonora. Unfortunately his natural impulses are overlaid by the necessity to conform to the standards dictated by society. This is where *Oberto* lays the ground rules for Verdi's ongoing investigation of the theme.

One cannot escape the fact that Verdi lost his own children at a cruelly young age, a tragedy in the true sense of the word. No father should expect to have to bury his own children (although in the centuries before the discovery of penicillin and antibiotics infant mortality was all too common). There can be little doubt that this was a defining event in the development of Verdi's mature psychology, and that throughout his works, from *Nabucco* on, he was working out, over and over, the rage, desperation and guilt at having been deprived of the opportunity of himself being a father. *Oberto* had been written, but had not yet reached the stage, when his children died within just over a year of each other. They had barely survived their first year of life. In the light of this tragedy the tale of Oberto almost seems to map out the anguish of loss even before it had so critically occurred in the composer's life. Thereafter the theme was to be revisited repeatedly.

The father is never a happy figure. He suffers either through loss of honour, loss of love or actual loss of offspring. Verdi's greatest inspiration emerged in response to the dark desperation of these many varied tragedies. Usually the father is cast as a baritone role (the voice type that Verdi, more than any other composer, established as a *fach* entirely distinct from the extremities of bass and tenor, viz. Arvino, Francesco Foscari, Giacomo, Rigoletto, Germont, Boccanegra, Amonasro, Ford). The title role in Verdi's first opera is progenitor to them all.

Oberto (*Oberto*). Count of San Bonifacio. Oberto is the first in a long sequence of domineering father-figures in Verdi's operas: viz. Nabucco, de Silva (*Ernani*), Miller (*Luisa Miller*), Giacomo (*Giovanna d'arco*), Stankar (*Stiffelio*), Rigoletto, Germont (*La Traviata*), Fiesco (*Boccanegra*), Calatrava (*La Forza del Destino*), Filipo (*Don Carlo*), Amonasro (*Aida*), etc. These are not all

biological fathers but they all fulfil the role of father in some way. This list only touches the tip of a relationship which obsessed Verdi and elicited from him some of his most memorable music. As in Wagner's *Die Feen*, *Oberto* can in many ways be seen as an exposition for themes that were later to receive elaboration.

When Oberto first enters he greets with emotion his native country. This should be understood in the context of the time in which the opera is set (1228) when Italy consisted of many different countries. Oberto is from Bassano, has been defeated in battle by the Saliguerras and is now living in exile in Mantua. At the conclusion of his engagement in battle Oberto has learnt from his sister, who lives in Verona and has been looking after his daughter, **Leonora,** for the duration of her father's absence, that Leonora has been seduced by Oberto's arch enemy, **Riccardo,** Count of Saliguerra, and then has been deserted by the same. Leonora has gone in pursuit of Riccardo. Outraged at the dishonour to his family Oberto determines on vengeance and goes in search of his daughter, even though he knows this means entering what has now become enemy territory.

Oberto's opening soliloquy reads like a preparation for Procida's great soliloquy in *I Vespri Siciliani*, 'O patria, o cara patria' ('O fatherland, O beloved fatherland'; Act 2). Oberto is no longer young and is aware that he is placing a colossal strain on his already failing health by returning to his one-time homeland. Exile is a peculiar condition which breeds a certain resilience and self-sufficiency in those who endure it. It also tends to engender a degree of paranoia (one well-known American businessman attributes his phenomenal success to his motto, carried with him all his life since being a refugee from Nazi-occupied Hungary: 'Only the paranoid survive'). Oberto's paranoia renders him fiercely proud and implacable. Where the younger generation are prepared to be conciliatory Oberto will not be moved from his fixed purpose. He makes his daughter swear that if she does not obtain redress for the injustice done to her she must die, that is, kill herself. From our perspective, at the start of the millennium, this may appear monstrous. *Oberto* takes place in 1228, but I suspect that fathers today in similar circumstances might feel as incensed as Oberto, although Society will no longer condone such draconian measures. Were former ages less civilized, or were they just more honest? Certainly Verdi could empathize.

The ethos supporting a drama such as *Oberto* knows nothing of feminist liberation. It is set, as are most nineteenth-century operas, in a historical context where a daughter was her father's most prized possession and gift. Her honour was experienced as his own. Without an understanding of this fact, Oberto's behaviour (as Rigoletto's, Fiesco's, Calatrava's *et al.*) will appear incomprehensible. The very fierceness with which Oberto prosecutes his endeavour is evidence of his love for his daughter. Having received Leonora's unquestioning acquiescence Oberto wants nothing so much as to embrace and console her.

When Oberto enters the castle of the Salinguerra he knows that it is at great personal peril and it matters not a jot to him. He is a man with a mission. He throws himself on the mercy of **Cuniza**. Since Cuniza is immediately sympathetic he has no problem engaging her cooperation. For Riccardo he has nothing but disdain, the more so when the latter suggests that a fight between them will be unequal because of Oberto's age. Oberto sees this merely as confirmation of Riccardo's cowardice. In Oberto's recitative and aria, 'Ei tarda ancor!' 'He still delays' (Act 2 Scene 2) it becomes clear that all the talk of vengeance and honour is a means of generating the necessary courage and energy to engage his adversary. He will welcome death. Why will he welcome death? Because he is old and the responsibilities of upholding a harsh ethical code, which may well conflict with every natural inclination, have become a severe strain to live with. Not that Oberto would ever admit as much. For him it is paramount that in the eyes of Society he dies

having achieved honour for his family. It should never be forgotten that Oberto has been defeated in battle. That in itself is a dishonour. Avenging the dishonour done to his daughter is a way of avenging the humiliation he himself has endured.

When he learns from the Salinguerra knights that he has been 'saved' by Cuniza – a woman – he is scornful. His scorn turns to derision when he sees the manner in which he has been saved. He warns Riccardo that this is no contest between 'tender maidens'. Much as Riccardo may wish to disagree his own honour cannot allow him to pass up the summons to defend himself. Oberto waits in the wood in the full knowledge that he awaits his own death, which is why he keeps protesting that one thing only matters to him, 'to wash the infamy from my name with the blood of this base man'. It will be his own blood that flows, but with his death will come a blessed respite from the anguish imposed upon him by the call of duty.

Odabella (*Attila*). Daughter to the Lord of Aquilea.

In Solera's libretto the character of Odabella is a transcription of the character in Werner's play of Princess Hildegunde of Burgundy whose father had been murdered by Attila.

The woman with a grudge – which could be termed in psychological parlance the avenging *anima* – is no stranger to the operatic stage. Odabella is as powerful as any, a direct descendant of Abigaille (*Nabucco*) with whom she shares many characteristics as well as with Wagner's Brünnhilde and Ortrud. Odabella's first act in the opera is to demand that **Attila** return her sword to her. Rather than return her sword Attila gives her his own sword. It is unnecessary to underline the symbolism of this moment. Suffice it to say he signs his own death warrant, rendering himself impotent for the duration of the opera. Odabella can hardly believe her luck.

However Odabella is not entirely a virago. In Act 1 Scene 1 she weeps freely and gives vent to her longing for a life of normality, the love and succour of a father and of a lover, that has been denied her and that she has so assiduously denied herself. She is dismayed by **Foresto's** rejection of her and only manages to pacify her lover by invoking the Apocryphal story of Judith and Holophernes (see **Synopsis**). She is delighted by Attila's obvious distress at **Leo's** admonition (Act 1 Scene 3) taking comfort in the might of the eternal God who is so clearly fighting on the side of Attila's enemies. Yet she does not want to see Attila bested by any but herself. She has only one thought: to avenge her murdered father.

In common with so many of Verdi's heroines, Odabella's emotional development has apparently been stunted by her abiding love for her father. Yes, she loves Foresto, but her love for him is secondary to her need to avenge her father's death. (It does nothing for Foresto's credibility as a heroic patriot that he so unquestioningly dotes on Odabella.) Yet Odabella needs Foresto as much as he needs her; she needs his unquestioning loyalty; she needs to know that there is a possibility of his replacing her sainted father, though this is something she would never be able to articulate to herself.

The strength of Foresto's credentials is to be tried to the utmost, for Odabella gives herself to Attila, becomes his bride and submits to his embraces. Not because it gives her any pleasure to do so but because thus she is granted a chance of fulfilling her mission. That her need for vengeance is largely self-centred is proved by the fact that she has no compunction about jeopardizing another's safety when it comes to protecting her own right to fulfil her mission. It is not so much that she needs her father but that she needs to assuage the guilt she feels for his demise. She exposes **Uldino**, who is similarly motivated by purely personal needs, to great danger, apparently without remorse (Act 2 Scene 2).

Odabella's invocation of her father at the end of the opera, 'menacing and still bleeding' (Act 3), has a hollow ring about it. Why has Attila never suspected her treachery? Because Odabella succeeds in the manner of all efficacious warriors and/or politicians in

compartmentalizing her emotions. She is, in fact, mildly psychotic. Her desire for revenge has the same intensity as that of Carlo (*La Forza del Destino*) and de Silva (*Ernani*). It is the same motive force which fuels Iago (*Otello*). The only difference is that Iago has allowed his obsession to turn inward and eat away every last vestige of objectivity that might have prevented him from destroying Otello with such callous brutality. Carlo, de Silva and Odabella at least admit, either to the world or to themselves, the cause of their delirium.

What singles Odabella out from her operatic relatives is the fact that there is a part of her which clearly enjoys her quest. In this lies the secret of her ability to keep Attila oblivious as to her true agenda. She is not just playing a part, she is living out a vital need, a necessity which enables her not just to dissemble, but actually to be that which she needs to be. The avenger must develop an intimate relationship with his/her victim. A relationship based on hatred cannot be so far from one based on love; the need to consume and assimilate is very little different in either case. Odabella convinces Attila because she wants to convince him. Her task is facilitated by the fact that Attila finds her irresistibly attractive. He wants to believe that she desires him as much as Odabella wants him to believe that she desires him. For Attila is tired and haunted by premonitions of nemesis. In the moment he surrenders his sword to Odabella he actually wills his own demise. Attila would not surrender his sword unless he expected that it would be returned to him. The heroic man's greatest need is to achieve immortality by shedding his mortality. He needs his life to be a continuous game of Russian roulette. Only thus can he feel alive. The greatest horror for such a man is to have to contemplate his mortality through a long life. For in that lies the possibility of fear entering, and fear is the antithesis of the heroic. Attila is no fool. He knows what he is doing when he surrenders his sword. He embraces the inevitable risk. His entire life has been devoted to the rewards of risk. Odabella merely grants him that after which he most yearns.

Officer of the Council of Ten (Il Fante) (*I Due Foscari*)

The officer escorts **Jacopo Foscari** from the dungeons to the Hall in the Doge's palace where the Council of Ten is to meet to pronounce sentence (Act 1 Scene 1). He leaves Jacopo to wait in an antechamber which gives Jacopo the opportunity to vent his feelings in the aria '*Dal più remoto resilio*' and then returns to tell the prisoner that he will soon be apprised of his fate. 'You may hope for pity, for mercy...' he primly assures his prisoner. Jacopo erupts with fury for he knows perfectly well that the Council of Ten's idea of pity is unlikely to coincide with his.

The Emir's officer (Un Officier du Emir) (*Jerusalem*)

In Act 2 Scene 2 the officer relays to the **Emir** that a Christian woman has been discovered in the town of Ramla, a fact which is soon corroborated by **Hélène** appearing almost immediately.

The officer is at the Emir's side in the final moments before the harem is overrun by the Crusaders (Act 3 Scene 1).

Oronte (*I Lombardi*). Son of Acciano.

Oronte is the son of a despot and has therefore grown up in an atmosphere of fear and hatred. He has been entirely dominated by the presence of his all-powerful father. He no doubt has never wanted for anything, but neither has he had anything that has ever really meant anything to him. In contemporary parlance he is the eleventh-century equivalent of 'a poor little rich kid'. Since he does not need to concern himself with the problems of subsistence he must confront head on the fact of his own existence. Oronte's freedom is built on the enslavement of others and is, by definition, without foundation.

Suddenly into Oronte's life comes the young Christian girl, **Giselda**, the latest acquisition to his father's harem. Presumably Oronte has free access to the harem and, in the past, would have made full use of the privilege. But when he comes face to face with Giselda he experiences something far more than the simple desire to possess her. For Giselda is utterly foreign to him in every way. She looks different from the other girls and she clearly chafes against her lot. She has an entirely different set of values from himself or anybody else he has come across. Above all she belongs to the faith that his mother, **Sofia**, has recently adopted, the faith which is in direct contradiction to that of his father.

This is the agonizing split in Oronte's psyche: whether to embrace the faith, morality and ideals of his father and fatherland, or whether to embrace the newly discovered faith of his mother, who has deliberately turned her back on all that her husband represents. Oronte takes the cue from his mother. Sofia is living a lie, caught between two opposing value systems: her husband's despotic and egotistical reign on the one hand, and the compassionate ethos of the Christian faith on the other. The two are irreconcilable. It is, as is so often the case, given to the younger generation to reconcile the apparently irreconcilable.

The love story of Oronte and Giselda is none other than a re-telling of the Romeo and Juliet motive of star-crossed lovers struggling to achieve understanding in a world consumed with hatred. Verdi and Solera had already explored the theme in *Nabucco* (see **Fenena** and **Ishmaele**) and Verdi was to revisit the theme repeatedly. On his first appearance (Act 2 Scene 1) Oronte learns from his mother that Giselda 'sighs, weeps, and calls upon her dear ones; yet the unhappy girl loves you'. Oronte declares that there is 'no happier mortal on earth' than he. His reaction speaks volumes about his state of mind. At this stage he is still only truly concerned for his own needs, irrespective of the girl he loves. It should pain him that Giselda suffers, which is why his mother mutters to herself, 'Oh may God thus enlighten my son's mind'. Oronte tells Sofia 'Would that I could instil my happiness into her dear heart'. This is still not the same thing as wishing to address the cause of her suffering, however. Her miserable state is an inconvenience he wishes to be rid of in order that he can 'fly aloft (with her) where no mortal can go'.

Oronte's accession to the Christian faith is at this juncture perfunctory. One cannot help feeling that it is a purely pragmatic matter of wishing to make himself truly eligible to the girl he adores. He says as much: 'many a time already have I thought in my heart that the only true God must be that of that angel of love'. This makes perfect psychological sense but is a fairly slim reason for abandoning the faith into which he was born. The events of the next few hours will radically alter his perception, for shortly after this exchange with his mother Acciano's castle is invaded by the Crusaders, at the head of whom is Giselda's father, **Arvino**. Oronte's father is slain in front of him and he himself is left for dead. In fact he only dissembles death because he has no desire to die before he has had a chance to be united with Giselda. He goes into exile: 'I wandered from land to land...' (Act 3 Scene 1) and all his thoughts are for Giselda; his only desire is to see her before he dies. When he finally catches up with her he waits for the first opportunity to be alone with her. One might think he would have equivocal feelings about Giselda, since her father has been responsible for his father's death. But Oronte has already grown away from his father and in a sense his father has already died for him in the moment that he discovered Giselda and the Christian faith. He is keenly aware that he is hardly an eligible husband for Giselda: 'I have lost everything! Friends, parents, homeland, the throne', he says. He imagines any possibility of a life with Giselda to be out of the question. He is therefore overjoyed when Giselda confirms that she will stay with him always. He paints a bleak picture of what that will mean for her: 'My path is accursed. I move through crags and forests like a wandering beast; the sport of winds and tempests. I often shelter in a cave, a hovel! For bridal bed you will have the sand of the limitless desert, for your song of love the howling of the hyena'. Giselda is not deterred and Oronte's happiness is complete.

Oronte's passage in life is a classic exposition of the hero myth (see Joseph Campbell's *Hero of Many Faces*), something which Wagner spent his whole career excavating. The hero must first sever all ties. He must dispel the domination of the father and cut loose from the mother. He must learn to stand alone in a world which is alien, even hostile to him. He may find final refuge in the love of a woman, but he must ward against merely making the woman a surrogate mother (as, for instance, does Siegfried in Wagner's *Ring* drama). Finally he must learn, as the toughest lesson of all, to relinquish life itself. The hero is the one who attains because he learns to relinquish.

Oronte has undergone a critical transformation since his first appearance. He is now genuinely concerned for Giselda in and of herself. Her willingness to relinquish finally convinces him to let go once and for all of the faith that has hitherto defined him.

Oronte has hardly confirmed his allegiance to the Christian God when cries of 'To arms!' are heard from the Crusaders' camp. After years of despair and uncertainty Oronte is only too glad to put his new faith immediately to the test. 'May death alone divide our souls, neither heaven nor earth can tear me from you', the lovers declare to each other. This is no mere hyperbole. Death does indeed divide their souls. Hardly has he found Giselda than Oronte finds himself dying in her arms.

Oronte's destiny is complete when the hermit (**Pagano**) receives him into the Christian faith with the exhortation, 'May the holy waters of the Jordan be for you the fount of life!' (Act 3 Scene 3). Momentarily Oronte feels revitalized, but he cannot escape the destiny that all his young life he has rejected. Now he has finally found that which he needs to embrace and has himself in turn been embraced. He dies in the total conviction that he will one day be reunited with Giselda in Heaven.

If one takes a literal view of his transportation to Heaven then his appearance to

Giselda (Act 4 Scene 1) would seem to justify that conviction. Either way Oronte's love for Giselda gives her the strength to go forward in life even after he has departed.

Oscar (*Un ballo in maschera*). A Page.

The role of Oscar is the only travesty[55] role Verdi essayed, with the single exception of Tebaldo in *Don Carlo*. The sexual ambiguity which inevitably surrounds the page has encouraged some directors to concentrate their attention more on the relationship of **Riccardo** and Oscar than that of Riccardo and **Amelia**. There is some historical justification for this in that the character of Riccardo is based on that of Gustav III of Sweden, who was almost certainly homosexual. It does, however, make a mockery of Verdi's score.

It is incontestable that Oscar is an essential ingredient of Riccardo's life. He reminds Riccardo of his younger self; of the irresponsible gaiety that he left behind him forever when he assumed the role of Governor. He is therefore a mirror to the man and can be said to corroborate his essential narcissism. Anybody who would seek an audience with Riccardo must first propitiate Oscar. This is made clear at the outset when Oscar tells **Renato**: 'the way is open to you at last'.

At the same time Riccardo is apparently incapable of reaching any resolution without reference to Oscar. When confronted with the **Judge**'s banishment of **Ulrica**, Riccardo intuitively wants to defend the seeress, but having no logical explanation for his desire he turns to Oscar: 'What have you to say of her?' By way of reply Oscar launches into *Volta la terrea* in which he pleads for the sorceress, not on any logical grounds, but purely on the basis that she does no harm, in spite of the fact she is almost certainly in league with the devil. A moralist would say that this in itself proves the degeneracy of Riccardo's Court. In fact Oscar's advocacy is more indicative of a liberalism which

---

[55] (Italian: *travesti* – '*disguised*'). A role played by the opposite sex. Other comparable travesty roles are Cherubino (Mozart's *Le nozze di Figaro*) and Octavian (Richard Strauss's *Der Rosenkavalier*).

refuses to condemn what it cannot comprehend. The Judge's determination to see justice done only confirms Oscar's conviction that Ulrica should be allowed to continue her trade. He is naturally subversive, and besides, he wants to question her himself as to what the future holds for him. Riccardo is only too happy to comply with Oscar's desire that Ulrica should be given a chance. He is by nature a sceptic and wants nothing so much as to humour his page boy. So Riccardo decrees that his entire court should convene at Ulrica's cavern that night and judge for themselves.

The fact that Riccardo places himself above the judiciary in itself signals his own demise which, in turn, stems from the anarchic influence represented by the page boy, who is too young to comprehend the significance and importance of the rule of law.

There is an eloquent moment in Ulrica's cavern when Oscar intercepts himself when Riccardo is about to have his palm read by the sorceress and demands that he, Oscar, should be the first (Act 1 Scene 2). Riccardo imperiously requires that Oscar yield the honour to him. For the only time in the opera Oscar accedes without question. In this tiny interchange more is revealed of the relationship between Oscar and Riccardo than in all the rest of the opera. Hitherto it may have appeared that Riccardo is in thrall to Oscar. Not at all. Oscar fulfils a function ordained by Riccardo. It is convenient for Riccardo to use Oscar as an intermediary between himself and the rest of the world. Oscar knows his station and Riccardo knows precisely how to remind him of it. When necessary Oscar will defer. When required Oscar will behave like an obnoxious brat.

Oscar is absent from Riccardo's side in the meeting with Amelia (Act 2 Scene 1). It is interesting to observe Riccardo without the presence of Oscar. Up until now he has appeared witty, brilliant, brittle, incorrigible. Suddenly his soul is exposed; his insecurity and need for reassurance and need to be accredited by a woman's unconditional love. Thus one becomes keenly aware that Oscar's presence is a socio-political necessity for Riccardo; a buffer between himself and a world he does not trust. The best way to reduce an enemy is to make a mockery of him. This Oscar does superbly well, principally by virtue of his naivety.

Oscar is unaware of the machinations and complexities which motivate Riccardo and his courtiers. He does not take seriously any threat to Riccardo's life. How could Riccardo be at risk? When Oscar joins in the syco-phantic chorus in praise of Riccardo at the conclusion of Act 1 one realizes that in the young boy's consciousness Riccardo has attained the status of a deity. For Oscar he represents a benign, all-giving father-figure. It is inconceivable to Oscar that anyone should want to harm Riccardo, let alone kill him. Thus, all unsuspecting, he aids and abets the conspirators (Act 3 Scene 2) and helps ensure Riccardo's murder.

At the conclusion of the opera Oscar is entirely bereft, perhaps more than any other protagonist, including Amelia, for he must now reconstruct his identity which has hitherto become almost synonymous with that of his master.

OTELLO

Opera in 4 Acts. Libretto by Arrigo Boito after Shakespeare's tragedy (1604–1605).

First performance: 5 February 1887 at La Scala, Milan.

Cast:

Otello: a Moor, General in the Venetian army (tenor)
Iago: his Ensign (baritone)
Cassio: Otello's lieutenant (tenor)
Roderigo: a Venetian gentleman (tenor)
Lodovico: Ambassador of the Venetian Republic (bass)
Montano: Otello's predecessor in Cyprus (bass)
A Herald (bass)
Desdemona: Otello's wife (soprano)
Emilia: Iago's wife (mezzo-soprano)

Time: the end of the 15th century
Place: Cyprus

The source of Boito's libretto was Shakespeare's play, *Othello*, which in turn was based upon an Italian novella by Giovanni Batista Cinthio (1504–1573), in a collection entitled 'Hecatommithi', published in 1565.

Synopsis

Act 1   A port on the coast of Cyprus, close to the official residence of the Governor. An inn with a pergola. In the background the castle battlements and the sea. It is evening. Thunder and lightning are raging.

Iago, Roderigo, Cassio, Montano and various onlookers are gathered by the quayside anxiously looking out for the ship which returns Otello to Cyprus (*Lampi! tuoni! gorghi!*). As the storm rages all fear the ship and those on board will perish, except for Iago who, in an aside to Roderigo, expresses the hope that 'the frenzied belly of the sea may be her tomb!' The storm abates sufficiently for the ship to anchor safely and Otello disembarks. In one of the most startling entrances in the repertoire Otello exults (*Esultate!*). The Cypriots cry, 'Long live Otello! Victory! Victory!' and Otello enters the castle, followed by Cassio, Montano and soldiers. Iago and Roderigo remain behind. Roderigo is in love with Desdemona, Otello's wife but is perplexed as to how he might win her. Iago assures him that it is only a matter of time before Desdemona will tire of 'the dark kisses of that swollen-lipped savage' and that she will be won over to Roderigo. Iago promises to help Roderigo for, in spite of appearances to the contrary, he hates 'that Moor'. The reason for his anger is that Cassio has been promoted to the position of captain that Iago feels should be his by right. Iago freely admits to Roderigo that such is his nature that if he were the Moor he would not wish to have a Iago around him.

Cassio re-enters and Iago leads Roderigo upstage in order to carry on the conversation out of earshot. The Cypriots, meanwhile, have lit a huge bonfire. They gather round and begin to sing (*Fuoco di gioia*) while the tavern servants hang coloured lanterns on the branches of the arbour. Soldiers crowd round the inn tables, chatting and drinking. Iago, Roderigo and Cassio join in. Iago, knowing that Cassio cannot hold his liquor, determines to make him drunk (*Chi all'esca ha morsa*). At first Cassio demurs but in the atmosphere of rejoicing and general merriment he is easily persuaded to drink. He quickly becomes hopelessly inebriated. This is the first part of Iago's carefully orchestrated revenge for he now encourages Roderigo to pick a quarrel with Cassio.

Montano enters. He is appalled to observe Cassio's drunkenness and when Iago informs him that Cassio is thus every night determines to tell Otello. Roderigo taunts Cassio who immediately hurls himself at him. Montano separates them, accusing Cassio of being a drunkard. At which Cassio draws his sword and engages Montano in a duel. Iago half-heartedly urges the pair to desist while energetically exhorting the onlookers to raise the alarm.

Otello enters and commands the fighting to stop. He demands an explanation from Iago. Iago pretends innocence. Otello is appalled to find Montano wounded. At this moment Desdemona enters. Otello is enraged that his beloved's sleep should have been disturbed by the brawling. Angrily he demotes Cassio with immediate effect. He commands Iago to go into the 'frightened city' with a patrol and restore peace. He orders everyone else to return to their homes.

Alone again Otello and Desdemona sing of their love for each other (*Già nella notte densa*). They relive their early courtship. Otello is overawed by the intensity of his own emotions. One senses that he has a very long way to fall.

Act 2   A hall on the ground floor of the castle. A partition divides it from a large garden at the rear. Iago is consoling Cassio. He suggests that Cassio should persuade Desdemona to intercede with Otello on his behalf. He tells Cassio that Desdemona often strolls in the shade of the trees nearby with his (Iago's) wife, Emilia. He despatches Cassio to await the two ladies.

Left alone Iago reflects that Cassio's end cannot be far off. In an extended monologue he gives expression to his nihilistic philosophy (*Credo in un Dio crudel*) (for full text see **Iago**) which puts Iago's scheming onto an altogether cosmic scale.

Desdemona appears and, to Iago's delight, Cassio goes to her. Cassio and Desdemona can be seen walking up and down the garden. Iago watches them intently. Otello enters.

Iago sets to work on undermining Otello's faith in his wife by planting doubts as to Cassio's motives concerning Desdemona. Having thoroughly provoked Otello Iago now warns him against allowing himself to become a victim of jealousy.

Desdemona reappears in the palace. She is surrounded by Cypriot and Albanian sailors, women and children who come forward in turn offering flowers and other gifts. It is a purely pastoral scene which establishes Desdemona's innocence beyond all reasonable doubt and makes all the more heinous Iago's insinuations. As she dispenses alms the sense of her purity and integrity is only confirmed. Otello is as moved as any by Desdemona's all-too-apparent innocence and grace. Iago, meanwhile, mutters his intention to shatter the 'sweet accord'.

Desdemona kisses several of the children whilst several of the women kiss the hem of her gown. She gives a purse to the sailors and the islanders disperse. Desdemona, followed by Emilia, enters the hall and approaches Otello. She has come to plead with her husband on Cassio's behalf. Otello, already consumed with doubts, mutters 'not now'. But Desdemona is not to be deflected. She is perplexed by his obvious discomfiture. When he complains of a headache Desdemona attempts to soothe his forehead with her handkerchief. Otello casts it aside. Unobserved Emilia picks it up. Otello demands to be left alone. But Desdemona stays and Otello, in an aside, soliloquizes on the possible reasons his wife might have for being unfaithful: his blackness, his advancing years, his inadequacy as a lover (*Forse perchè gl'inganni d'arguto amor*). Desdemona attempts to reassure him but he remains oblivious to her.

Meanwhile a quarrel is developing between Iago and Emilia. Iago demands that Emilia give him the handkerchief she has just retrieved. Emilia, suspecting her husband's motives, at first refuses. Iago wrenches it from her. Otello insists that Desdemona leave him. As Emilia makes to depart with her mistress Iago warns her not to mention the handkerchief. Iago remains aside and unseen to observe Otello. He determines that he will conceal the handkerchief amongst Cassio's belongings.

Otello cannot believe that Desdemona could be false. As he broods on his wife's loyalty, or lack of it, Iago observes with delight that his poison is working. He approaches Otello in an open and cordial manner. Otello rounds on him. 'You have lashed me to the cross!' he fumes. No suspicion about his wife and Cassio had ever entered his thoughts until now. 'Ed ora! Ed ora!' ('And now! And now!'), he cries (*Ora e per sempre addio*); now it is farewell to sacred memories; farewell to the 'sublime delights of the mind', to troops, victories, 'tumult and songs of battle'. It is the end of 'Otello's glory'.

As Iago tries to pacify him Otello rounds on him again, demanding that he give him proof of Desdemona's guilt. He seizes Iago by the throat and throws him to the ground. Iago pretends wounded innocence. He makes to leave but Otello detains him. He is beside himself. He believes Desdemona is true, and he believes she is not. He believes that Iago is honest, and he believes he is false. He wants proof; he wants certainty. Iago again plays all innocence: 'What certainty do you need?' he asks, 'to see them embraced, perhaps?' He then proceeds to drive the knife well and truly home. He describes a dream that Cassio had one night (*Era la notte*). Cassio murmured in his sleep: 'Sweet Desdemona; we must hide our love . . . I curse the fate that gave you to the Moor'. Iago relates his tale with such conviction it never occurs to Otello this is pure fabrication. All his doubts about Iago are dispelled. With supreme cunning Iago continues to protest his own doubts: 'I only described a dream', he says.

He is ready for the kill. As if the thought has only just occurred to him he 'remembers' having seen a handkerchief belonging to Desdemona in Cassio's hand. It was the same handkerchief that Otello gave Desdemona as pledge of his love.

Otello is now beyond any rational reflection. 'The hydra entwines me in its serpent's coils', he howls, 'Oh! Blood! Blood! Blood!' He kneels and swears that by 'the marble heavens! By the forked lightning! By death and by the destructive sea!, this hand which I raise and extend shall soon blaze in a savage fit of rage!' Iago kneels beside him. 'Witness be the sun', he says, 'that to Otello I fervently dedicate heart, arm and soul if he also steels his will to bloody deeds!' Together Otello and Iago raise their hands to Heaven and swear vengeance (*Sì pel ciel*).

Act 3   The great hall of the castle. On the right a large portico leading off to a smaller room. At the rear a terrace. Otello and Iago are deep in conversation. A herald enters. The herald announces the imminent arrival of the Venetian galley which is conveying the ambassadors to Cyprus. Having acknowledged this news and dismissed the herald Otello commands Iago to continue. Iago tells Otello that he will bring Cassio to the hall and, 'with crafty enquiries', persuade him to 'gossip'. Meanwhile Otello should conceal himself nearby in order to be able to observe the encounter. Desdemona approaches and Iago makes to leave, but before he exits he turns back to Otello and, in a lowered voice and with 'much intention' says two words; 'Il fazzoletto . . .' (the handkerchief . . .').

Desdemona enters and greets her husband (*Dio ti giocondi*). Otello goes to Desdemona and takes her hand. 'Warm moisture bedews its tender beauty', he tells his wife. His words are heavily ironic throughout the ensuing scene. 'It yet knows no hint of grief or age', Desdemona replies. She then, fatally, mentions Cassio's name. Otello immediately complains of an aching brow and begs Desdemona to soothe it with her handkerchief. When she produces one he demands that she use the one he gave her. He warns her of dire consequences if she has lost it. Desdemona is increasingly apprehensive. Otello demands that she fetch the handkerchief. Desdemona is perplexed. She assumes that Otello is deflecting the conversation away from Cassio and keeps reiterating the latter's name, causing Otello ever greater convulsions. Suddenly he seizes her and commands her to look him in the face. 'What are you?' he asks her. 'Otello's faithful wife', Desdemona replies. 'Swear it!' Otello demands. 'Otello surely believes me faithful', Desdemona replies, to which Otello rages at her: 'I believe you wanton . . . swear you are chaste . . . swear it and damn yourself!' By now Desdemona is thoroughly frightened. She pleads with Otello to believe her 'honest and true'. Otello, in spite of himself, is moved. '*Ah! Desdemona! Indietro! Indietro! Indietro!*' ('Ah, Desdemona! Away! Away! Away!'), he cries. He desperately wants to believe her.

But when Desdemona frantically tries to placate him and asks 'What is my fault?' he becomes enraged again: 'The blackest of crimes is written on the white lily of your brow', he storms. 'Are you not a strumpet?' Desdemona is aghast. Changing suddenly from anger to 'the most terrible calm', Otello takes her by the hand and conducts her to the door. 'I would make amends', he says. 'I had thought you (pray pardon if in thought I wronged you) that canny whore who is Otello's wife'. The last phrase is screamed at her as he forces her through the door.

Otello reflects on the collapse of all his dreams and his happiness (*Dio, mi potevi scagliar tutti mali*). 'God! Thou mightest have rained upon me all the afflictions of poverty, of shame . . .' He could have coped with anything, anything but this. Desdemona was the ultimate reward for his heroism, the hope of a different sort of life in the future, a life which might give some meaning to the hollow pomp of his past victories. 'Dimmed is that sun, that smile, those rays by which I live and which give me joy', he reflects bitterly. He works himself into a state of near-hysteria finally resolving: 'Ah! damnation! First she shall confess her sin and then she

shall die! Confession! Confession!' Iago enters and Otello lurches towards him. 'The proof!' Otello demands with frantic intensity. Iago tells him that Cassio is nearby. 'Oh heavens! Oh joy!' Otello exclaims. Iago restrains him and makes him hide behind a pillar at the back of the balcony. He runs to meet Cassio, who is lingering uncertainly at the end of the portico.

Cassio is expecting to meet Desdemona, not for a clandestine tryst, as Otello might think, but because he hopes she has successfully obtained his pardon. Otello, meanwhile, cannot hear the whole conversation; all he catches is his wife's name. Iago now leads Cassio closer to where Otello is hiding. In jovial tones he encourages Cassio to speak of 'she whom he loves' adding, in an undertone, 'of Bianca'. As Iago and Cassio smile and laugh Otello can barely contain himself. Only too aware that Otello is listening Iago leads Cassio away. The latter starts to tell Iago of the embroidered handkerchief that has mysteriously appeared in his lodgings. Iago asks if Cassio has it with him and Cassio produces it from his doublet. Iago takes the handkerchief and holds it behind his back to ensure that Otello can see it closely. This is the confirmation of his wife's guilt that Otello has both craved and dreaded. Iago enjoys playing with the handkerchief and encouraging Cassio to admire the intricate tracery of its design. He likens it to a spider's web, 'whence your heart is caught' (*Questo e una ragna*) (it is, of course, Iago who is the spider attracting all into his web). Cries of '*Tradimento!*' ('Treachery!') are heard from behind the pillar.

A fanfare of trumpets is heard, then a cannon firing. It is the signal for the arrival of the Venetian ambassadors. Iago advises Cassio to leave, which he does.

Otello comes forward. He confirms that he has seen and understood everything and demands that Iago obtain some poison which he can administer to Desdemona that very night. Iago opines that it would be better to strangle her in her bed, 'there where she has sinned', he points out. Then Otello issues what is for Iago the justification of all his machinations: 'Iago, as from now I appoint you my captain', he announces. The ambassadors are approaching and Iago suggests that Desdemona should attend, ostensibly to avoid suspicion of anything being amiss, but in reality because he knows that now the mere sight of his wife will inflame Otello's rage beyond endurance. Iago exits to fetch Desdemona, and Otello prepares to meet the ambassadors.

Lodovico, Roderigo, the herald, dignitaries of the Venetian Republic, ladies, gentlemen, soldiers and trumpeters enter followed by Iago, Desdemona and Emilia. With cries of 'Hurrah! Hurrah! Long live the Lion of St Mark!' all greet Otello. Lodovico brings greetings from the Doge and Senate to 'the triumphant hero of Cyprus'. Meanwhile Desdemona has entered. She is oppressed. She cannot account for Otello's mood. 'A great cloud disturbs Otello's reason and my fate', she tells Emilia, voicing a presentiment of impending catastrophe. Otello appears to be reading the letter from the Venetian Doge, although his concentration is elsewhere. Lodovico asks after Cassio. Iago replies that Otello is not pleased with him. Desdemona expresses the hope that soon Cassio will return to grace. Innocently she tells Iago how 'true an affection' she has for Cassio. 'Curb your prating lips', Otello snarls at her. Then suddenly, unable to restrain himself any longer, he lashes out at her. The court is appalled. Otello, oblivious to the general consternation, demands that the herald summon Cassio. Incredulous, Lodovico questions Iago, 'Can this be the hero? Is this the warrior of glorious deeds?' Shrugging his shoulders Iago merely replies, 'He is what he is'. When Lodovico asks him to explain himself Iago says 'It is better to keep a still tongue'. He might have added, 'but only when it suits me'.

Cassio enters. Now Otello reveals that he has been summoned back to Venice and Cassio has been elected his successor. His announcement is punctuated with asides to both Iago and Desdemona. Iago is aghast at this news. Intermittently goading Desdemona Otello commands that crew and troops be ready for imminent departure for Venice. As Desdemona approaches her husband Lodovico appeals to Otello to comfort her. But Otello grabs her roughly and forces her to her knees: 'To the ground! . . . and weep!' ('A terra! . . . e piangi!') he roars. She does indeed weep for the loss of the 'Sun' (Otello's love), that 'serene and bright, gladdens sky and sea but cannot dry the bitter tears of my pain and grief'. All express their horror at Otello's inexplicable behaviour.

Meanwhile Iago exhorts Otello to pull himself together and swears to exact revenge on Otello's behalf. He will ensure that Cassio is murdered forthwith. He has no intention of bloodying his own hands, however. He tells Roderigo who, it will be remembered, truly is in love with Desdemona, to be ready to despatch his rival. (Iago has nothing but contempt for 'deluded lovers'.) Otello, rousing himself and, 'terrible in his anger', dismisses the crowd: 'Begone!' ('Fuggite!'). It is no way to speak to the Venetian dignitaries, but Otello is well beyond the niceties of etiquette. Lodovico tries to encourage Desdemona to leave with them but she breaks away and runs to her husband. Otello bellows at her 'Light of my life, I curse you!' ('Anima mia, ti maledico!'). Horrified, all leave in disarray. Desdemona is led away by Emilia and Lodovico.

Otello and Iago are alone. Otello's delirious mind returns to the moment of the inception of his misery when he overheard Iago muttering, 'I like that not' ('ciò m'accora!', Act 2 Scene 3). He remembers the handkerchief and, completely overcome, faints. Iago stands over him and gloats. From outside come the cries of 'Viva Otello!' and 'Gloria al Leon di Venezia!' as the Cypriots hail their hero. Triumphantly placing his foot on the inert form of Otello, Iago shouts 'Ecco il Leone!' ('Behold the Lion').

Act 4 Desdemona's bedchamber. A bed, prayer-desk with a picture of the Madonna above, table on which is a lighted candle, mirror and chairs. There is a door to the right. It is night. Desdemona is making ready for bed, whither she has been sent by Otello. He is apparently calmer. However,

Desdemona is quite clear about the danger she is in. She asks Emilia to lay her white bridal gown on the bed. 'If I should die before you, then shroud me in its veil', she says. Mechanically she sits down in front of her mirror. She remembers how her mother had a maid called Barbara who loved a man who forsook her. Barbara used to sing a song 'the Willow Song'. While Emilia unties her hair Desdemona sings the song with its haunting refrain (*Piangea cantando nell'erma lauda*). 'Let us sing! Let us sing!, sweet willow' ('*Cantiamo! Cantiamo!*'). The song expresses all the anguish and incomprehension Desdemona endures. She takes her wedding ring from her finger and gives it to Emilia. She imagines she hears wailing. 'Who is knocking at the door?' she wonders. Emilia reassures her that it is only the wind. The song concludes: 'He was born . . . for his glory, and I to love him and to . . .'. Desdemona is close to tears. Emilia makes to leave but Desdemona calls her back. Passionately embracing her she bids her maid farewell. Emilia exits.

Desdemona kneels to pray before the image of the Madonna (*Ave Maria, piena di grazia*). She remains kneeling for some time, resting her head on the prayer-desk, repeating the prayer of which only the first and last words are audible. Finally she rises and goes to the bed.

Otello enters by a secret door. He places a scimitar (sword) on the table then stands before the candle, undecided whether to extinguish it.[56] He looks at Desdemona then puts out the light. The room is now only illuminated by the light above the prayer-desk. He goes towards the bed and looks down on the sleeping Desdemona. He kisses her three times. On the third kiss she awakens.

Otello asks if she has prayed tonight. 'If you can think of any crime you have committed that awaits grace from heaven, ask for it now', he commands her. 'Why?',

---

[56] At this point in the play Othello soliloquizes, 'It is the cause, it is the cause, my soul': Act 5 Scene 2.

Desdemona asks. 'Make haste. I would not kill your soul', Otello retorts. 'Talk you of killing?' Desdemona asks. 'Ay, I do', is Otello's reply. 'God have mercy upon me', Desdemona says, to which Otello rejoins, 'Amen'. He tells her to think of her sins, 'My sin is love', Desdemona replies. 'For that you die', Otello retorts. 'Because I love you, you kill me?' Desdemona asks. Now Otello accuses her of loving Cassio and giving to him the handkerchief which Otello had given her. She vehemently protests her innocence. When Otello, who is becoming impassioned, demands that she confess, Desdemona asks that Cassio be brought in to speak for himself. Otello reveals that Cassio is dead. As Desdemona pleads for her life Otello's resolve hardens; 'Down! Down, strumpet!' Nothing can stop him now. He strangles her.

Emilia is heard knocking at the door. She has come to report that Cassio still lives and has murdered Roderigo. At that moment Desdemona's voice can be heard faintly from the bed, 'Unjustly . . . unjustly killed . . .'. Emilia is horrified. 'I die innocent . . . farewell . . .', Desdemona says with her dying breath. Otello owns to having killed her. 'She was Cassio's whore! Ask Iago', he says. Emilia rounds on him: 'Fool! And you believed him!' Otello grabs Emilia, who breaks free and frantically calls for help.

Lodovico, Iago and Cassio enter, followed by Montano and men-at-arms. Emilia demands to know if Iago believes Desdemona unfaithful. 'I believed so', he answers. Otello mentions the handkerchief which he believed Desdemona had given to Cassio. Ignoring Iago's command to 'hold her tongue', Emilia relates how her husband had 'torn that handkerchief from (her) hand by brute force'.

Montano has learnt from the dying Roderigo of Iago's villainy. Otello demands that Iago refute the charges. Iago will not. He runs from the room, pursued by Montano's men. Otello rushes to the table, where his scimitar lies. Lodovico demands he surrender it. Otello drops the scimitar and goes to the bed (*Niun mi tema*). Regarding the corpse of his beloved Desdemona he observes, 'How pale you are! And still and mute and beautiful'. Overwhelmed with grief he pulls from his doublet a dagger and stabs himself. With his dying breath Otello remembers how he has kissed Desdemona before she died. '*Un bacio . . . un bacio ancora . . . Ah! . . . un altro bacio!*', he murmurs as he falls dead on the bed across Desdemona's body.

The tale of *Otello* is a cautionary tale in which a single base emotion is taken and expanded on a massive scale.

At an existential level the tale represents a dire warning against the penalties of not taking responsibility for our lives. Otello is putty in Iago's hands because, once the seed is sown, he is almost entirely passive. He could, if only he had a marginally more reflective nature, at any moment have stopped himself short, and thereby have averted calamity. But he does not. He appears incapable. In reality he is disinclined, for the truth would actually render him more impotent than the sordid lie. It would invalidate his political self, the self which occupies the world and which he has striven so long to secure for himself. It is easier for him to believe Iago than to believe his wife. For if he believed his wife he would have to acknowledge that he has been guilty of a disastrous lack of judgement where Iago is concerned.

It might seem, from an outsider's perspective, incomprehensible that Otello does not dismiss his ensign, but this would be to leave him rudderless. (The degree to which Iago has made himself indispensable is confirmed in that telling moment in Act 3 when Lodovico, on his first entrance, approaches Iago before anyone else.) Otello relies absolutely on his ensign for he has no political acumen of his own. He is first and foremost a soldier. His capitulation before Iago's villainy is proof of one thing only – his chronic insecurity. He wilfully blinds himself to the true horror of what is transpiring. Why? Because it confirms his own sense of inherent worthlessness, be it in the council chamber or the bedroom, or anywhere other than on the battlefield. There must be a part

of Otello that wants to be rid of the responsibility of his marriage and of his governorship. There must be a part of him that welcomes nemesis. Otherwise he would not let it happen. He knows Desdemona is guileless. Why, then, does she persist in her suit on behalf of Cassio? In his eyes it is proof positive of her guilt. Either that or he must conclude it is evidence of congenital idiocy. The one thing he cannot recognize is the truth.

In their love duet (Act 1) it becomes clear that Otello and Desdemona have attained the acme of blessedness in their relationship. Bliss such as this cannot endure. One feels that if Iago had not come along Otello would quickly have found another means with which to destroy his happiness. *Otello* is an exploration of the nature of human freedom. The true suspense in the drama is not, will Lodovico be able to unravel the imbroglio, or will Desdemona be able to escape with her life, but will Otello at any moment succeed in distancing himself from the chaos of his aggravated emotions? Will he call a halt to the insanity he has entered upon? Sadly, only when it is too late.

Otello A Moor and a general in the Venetian army.

When Otello first suspects that **Desdemona** may have been unfaithful he goes through, in his mind, the reasons why she might have fallen out of love with him: 'Perchance because I do not understand the subtle deceits of love; perchance because I have fallen into the veil of years; perchance because I have on my face this dark hue'. If he was being really honest with himself he would reverse the order of his paranoid ruminations: firstly, his dark skin, secondly, his age, thirdly, his inadequacy as a sympathetic lover.

All his life Otello has worked to overcome disadvantages (as he and the world into which he was born perceive them) given him by fate. He succeeds beyond his wildest imaginings. He gains the love and approbation of a white nobleman's daughter. He gains the total confidence of the State and, while most of his compatriots languish in slavery, he raises himself above the enforced ignominy of his youth and becomes a General, responsible for repulsing the marauding Saracens. Then into his life comes a fiend; a fiend who is yet an acute psychologist and who quickly identifies Otello's Achilles heel, namely his sense of inferiority. The fiend is, of course, Iago who, with unerring instinct, leads Otello by the nose to his downfall.

When Otello first appears it is to arise out of the sea like some Greek god in the midst of a thunderstorm (Act 1). He is the epitome of the hero. He has vanquished the enemy. He is oblivious to the storm which rages around him. He is triumphant. He calls on the people of Cyprus to rejoice as he and his heart rejoice, for he returns to claim the bride of his desires. He has every reason to be proud. While in Boito's libretto he does not enumerate the dangers with which he has wrestled (as Othello does for the Court in Act 1 Scene 3 of Shakespeare's play), those same dangers are implicit throughout the love scene with which Act 1 of the opera concludes: 'You loved me for the dangers I had passed and I loved you that you did pity them' (Act 1). It is the danger that has united Otello and Desdemona. It will prove to be a relationship fraught with danger.

The danger besets them from the moment that Otello steps ashore. He is not a man adapted to the niceties of civilian life. He can prove himself in battle; this is a language he can understand. He can have no conception of the treachery that waits around every corner, and most especially the envy, which is the main motivation of the less heroic of his lesser countrymen. His plight is little different from that of Julius Caesar who could express himself, with the sword and in words, the language of romance, but could not comprehend the legalistic casuistry and ambition of those around him.

It is significant that Otello demotes Cassio, not because he fights but because his fighting has disturbed his beloved wife. Once in the arms of Desdemona, Otello can no longer be objective (Act 1). To this extent he deserves his downfall.

The love of Desdemona transforms Otello into a visionary. The kiss that he shares with his wife at the end of Act 1 turns his attention to the stars above, and especially the Pleiades that have just arisen. (The Pleiades in Greek mythology were the virgin companions of Artemis 'Diana, huntress, chaste and fair'.) Certainly Otello seeks to find in his wife an impossible standard of purity. Verdi's music underlines the mystical nature of his love. Such a love can only be corrupted and renders Iago's task all too simple. So fragile is Otello's ego that he will believe Iago's insinuations in spite of all contradictory evidence. Deep down he knows that Desdemona is entirely innocent of any wrongdoing, and yet he allows himself to be convinced. Not only that but he makes a conscious decision; he consciously bids farewell to all that matters most to him; all that has given his life meaning: *ora e per sempre* (Act 2).

In the true Romantic tradition Desdemona has been, for Otello, the reward for all his trials of endurance and suffering. If she is not true to him then his whole life has been a mockery. He may as well throw it away. There is something of the suffering of Job in Otello's predicament. He can only burn until he is entirely consumed, until his last vestiges of pride are cauterized. The Greeks would undoubtedly have seen his downfall as punishment for hubris. Having said which it is noticeable that in his initial entrance, *Esultate*, Otello acknowledges 'Ours and *Heaven's* is the glory'. Otello is not really guilty of hubris. The true monstrosity of his downfall lies in the fact that there is no existential justification for it. It would seem to be an example of the tyranny and eventual ascendancy of meaninglessness, which is only another word for evil (see Iago).

Only at the very end of the opera can Otello, awakening as though from a dream, acknowledge the deception that he has allowed to possess him. Only Verdi's music offers a possible redemptive value to Otello's final kiss on the lips of his dead wife (Act 4). With his own dying breath it is a sort of *liebestod* – a transfiguration, a possibility of a new beginning up amongst the Pleiades, far from the potential taint of human lust and greed.

Otello's darkest hour comes at the conclusion of Act 3 when he publicly humiliates Desdemona. For Desdemona is no Lady Macbeth or Abigail. She cannot stand up for herself. Of all Verdi's heroines she is the most womanly. It is this that makes Otello's treatment of her appear all the more atrocious, for it is clear to everybody else present, all those not locked in Otello's solipsistic nightmare of suspicion and self-hatred, that Desdemona could not possibly be guilty. That Otello is appalled in spite of himself is indicated by his sudden and total abnegation of consciousness and responsibility (Act 3). It is the moment of Iago's greatest ascendancy.

During his soliloquy, *Dio! mi potevi* (Act 3) Otello exclaims . . . 'Oh grief, oh anguish! Torn from me is the mirage wherein I blithely lull my soul. Quenched is that sun, that smile, those rays by which I live, that give me joy!' Otello applies the metaphor to his love for Desdemona. It could just as well be applied to himself. Never was Blake's dictum, 'If the Sun were to doubt it would soon go out', more applicable than it is to Otello.

Otumbo (*Alzira*). Peruvian warrior.
Otumbo appears in the Prologue and in Act 2 Scene 2. He serves the important function of throwing into relief the far more enlightened character of his compatriot, **Zamoro**.

At the outset of the opera Otumbo is discovered dancing round a tree to which the elderly Spanish Governor, **Alvaro**, has been tied. He is inciting his fellow warriors to make sure the old man's martyrdom is as slow and cruel as possible. He craves vengeance for the deaths of so many of his compatriots. His plans for Alvaro, however, are thwarted by the arrival of his chieftain, Zamoro, who orders Alvaro's release.

Otumbo is a typical example of the over-zealous henchman who genuinely believes he is serving his master's and his country's best interests, but is incapable of understanding the wider perspective which is the prerogative of the politicians. It is no doubt a matter of keen regret to Otumbo that he cannot expedite his torture of Alvaro (Prologue Scene 1). But he does not disclose his feelings. He does, however, express his joy at Zamoro's unexpected return. It gives all the Inca warriors cause for hope and diverts their attention from unworthy exploits.

Otumbo and his fellow warriors are like hyperactive children. If their energies are not channelled through the superior will of an adult they quickly turn delinquent and run amok. Fortunately an alternative channel for Zamoro's warriors' energies is imminent. Zamoro exhorts the tribe to storm Lima in revenge for his torture in the hands of **Gusmano**. 'Greedy for gold and greedy for blood', they rush off to put the Spanish to rout. But Alvaro has gone ahead of them and will prove to be a powerful advocate for peace. He is successful in convincing **Ataliba** and Gusmano, who lusts after **Alzira**, but no word reaches Zamoro and the other warriors. By the time they reach Lima Zamoro has already been discovered by Gusmano in the arms of Alzira and the old hatreds have been re-kindled. Battle is enjoined and Otumbo and the other Inca tribes are put to rout by the Spanish. Zamoro is taken prisoner. Thus once again Otumbo becomes the titular head of the tribe. Now he has an opportunity to demonstrate his true loyalty to his chief, which he does in fine style, arranging to bribe, with Inca gold, the guards who watch over Zamoro. Thus Zamoro escapes prison on what otherwise would undoubtedly have been the eve of his execution.

It is Otumbo who reveals to Zamoro the fact that Alzira is to be married to Gusmano (Act 2 Scene 2). Otumbo is not gifted with imagination. It never occurs to him that Alzira might be entering into the marriage under duress. He exhorts Zamoro to flee and to 'forget a faithless woman. She is henceforth unworthy of such affection'. Whether this is a practical move on Otumbo's part to incite Zamoro to renewed vigour is debatable. Since there is no sign of the triumphalist blood lust of the Prologue and his only concern appears to be for Zamoro's safety it

357

seems unlikely. He is dismayed at his chief's anguished gestures and exclamations and attempts to restrain him to no avail. Zamoro rushes off to seek out and kill his rival in love. Otumbo cannot begin to comprehend what assails Zamoro and does not follow. Only recently defeated in battle he has no wish to lead his warriors to a certain death. He will have to wait with the rest of the tribe to learn the outcome, which will be as unexpected and as joyful for him as it is for the other protagonists.

Ovando (*Alzira*). Spanish duke.
Ovando enters **Ataliba's** apartment (Act 1 Scene 2) with the news that a 'hostile throng' of Inca natives has crossed the Rima river and is approaching Lima. Apparently the throng is demanding the release of **Zamoro**. The news enables **Gusmano** to honour his father's wish to release Zamoro, whom he has just discovered in the arms of **Alzira**, without losing too much face. Gusmano tells Zamoro he can leave but they will meet on the battlefield. Ovando is overjoyed at the prospect of the battle ahead and of shortly witnessing a 'mountain of enemy corpses'. The battle that follows is indeed won by the Spanish. Ovando's blood lust is presumably satisfied.

At the start of Act 2 Ovando brings to Gusmano the military court's sentence on Zamoro, which only requires Gusmano's signature. Ovando is shortly after dismissed when he returns to discover that Gusmano is proposing marriage to the native girl Alzira, Zamoro's betrothed. He is dumbfounded. He is clearly not privy to his master's passion for the Inca girl. However, in the manner of an experienced courtier, he is quickly adaptable and readily agrees to spread the glad tidings through the city. To a man like Ovando marriage to a savage would be quite unthinkable and an affront to his honour. At the same time, political animal that he is, he will appreciate the diplomatic advantage of such a union.

Ovando is on stage for the concluding scene of the opera where he witnesses Zamoro's attack on Gusmano and the latter's remarkable act of forgiveness and benediction on the union of Zamoro and Alzira. All this might be thought beyond the comprehension of a man like Ovando, with his limited imagination and understanding, but – and this is more an effect of Voltaire's polemic rather than dramatic verisimilitude – he joins with **Zuma**, **Alvaro** and **Ataliba** in celebrating Gusmano's nobility of spirit in pardoning 'the man who made him bleed'.

The implication is that the virtues of compassion and forgiveness are such self-evidently universal truths that no human being can fail to be moved by them.

P

Pagano (*I Lombardi*). Brother of **Arvino**.
The character of Pagano is the focal point of Verdi's opera. He commits two of the most heinous sins known to Man: (attempted) fratricide and parricide. These sins were committed because he lusted after his brother's wife, another heinous sin. The murder of his father was accidental; he had thought he was murdering his brother, not realizing his father was staying in Arvino's apartments. However this does not change the fact of his crime any more than Oedipus's ignorance exonerates him from the murder of *his* father.

When the opera opens Pagano has already been in exile some years for having attempted to murder his brother. In the opening scene he is being rehabilitated, having apparently expressed contrition for his sin. In fact Pagano only feels rage at his exile, and now dreams of revenge. The motivating force behind his crime has been his love, or rather lust, for **Viclinda**, Arvino's wife. Apparently, even in exile he has been able to think of nothing but his frustrated love: 'As the Italian volcano draws its nourishment from the waters, so did I, far from you, increase in the force of my love' (Act 1 Scene 1). Thwarted in possessing that which he most desires, Pagano seeks only to destroy. He reflects to **Pirro**: 'yet this soul of mine was not born to crime! It was in love's power to sanctify it or turn it to evil!' In other words he blames his 'love' for his crimes. It is in reality not his love that is responsible but his own lack of self-knowledge. His 'love' is not really love at all, it is just longing for that which he cannot have.

Pagano's problems must inevitably stem from his relationship to his brother (see **Synopsis** conclusion). For some reason he has always resented the very fact of his brother's existence, and cannot bear him to have anything that he cannot have. This can be the only explanation for his ongoing desire for Viclinda, even after years of exile and absence from her. In such a case as this there comes a point when a human being's longing for something no longer has any relation to the thing itself, but is to do with some gaping wound in the individual's psyche. It is a wound that cannot be healed until identified and even then will never be totally cauterized, but at least once it has been identified it can be accepted. Pagano's nature is not reflective. He lives by his emotions, largely his hysterical and irrational need to possess that which he cannot have.

Pagano has returned to Milan specifically in order to murder his brother and claim Viclinda for his own (Act 1). In order to do this he is prepared to go through the humiliation of publicly admitting his guilt, and then embracing his brother. Even as he does so he has a band of cut-throats in the wings preparing to torch Folco's palace so that he can obtain entrance to his brother's apartments. But he cannot entirely conceal his lack of genuine contrition. The citizens of Milan all observe that 'in his terrible and hollow eyes still appears the fierce tempest of his soul' (Act 1 Scene 1).

Viclinda herself observes, 'In that wicked face appeared a cloud of anger, not repentance' (Act 1 Scene 2). When the moment comes to murder Arvino Pagano feels inexpressible joy. Having done the deed, as he thinks, he drags Viclinda out of the apartment as though she were a pile of booty that he has just claimed, not the woman he has dreamt about for so many years. He threatens her with a knife and taunts her

when she seeks to call for help. This is not the behaviour of a man who loves, but rather of a man who hates. One can be certain that had Pagano's bid to steal his brother's wife been successful the marriage would not have lasted long. His passion is little different from that of the Romantic (one thinks of Hector Berlioz for instance) who loves from afar and yet, when he succeeds in gaining the object of his passion, finds the reality quite different from the image he has carried with him for so long. However, Pagano will not have the opportunity to marry Viclinda, for suddenly he hears his brother's voice from behind him. He has not murdered his brother at all, he has murdered his father. The shock of this is too much for Pagano's fragile psyche. He seeks forthwith to put an end to his life, and is only prevented by the intervention of his brother's guards.

At face value it would seem inexplicable that Pagano should have no qualms about murdering his brother, and yet be mortified to the point of suicide at the thought of having murdered his father. Pagano's behaviour is merely an illustration of that unique human ability for abstracting from reality, and sooner or later losing touch. This ability can give rise to works of genius, or equally to deeds of atrocity. In other words anything becomes possible. Pagano's only thought for many years, to the point where it has become a total obsession, has been to wrest Viclinda from his brother. Since he cannot claim Viclinda of her free will, the only logical alternative is to remove his brother and claim her by force. His first attempt was thwarted and he has been punished by being exiled, presumably for well over a decade. These years have done nothing to lessen his longing for Viclinda which is now exacerbated a thousandfold by the inevitable accumulation of bitterness and resentment. We can assume that when Pagano returns to Milan he feels it his bounden right to exact revenge on the brother who has denied him that which he most desires.

Thus he does not equate murdering Arvino with the cardinal sin of fratricide. There is no evidence in the libretto to suggest that

Pagano harbours any resentment against his father. It has therefore never occurred to him to murder his father. When he discovers that this is exactly what he has done it is like the proverbial cold douche thrown over a drunken man. It suddenly and dramatically brings him to a realization that he has been absent from himself. He has allowed himself to become the victim of his thoughts rather than remaining in control of them.[57]

Pagano's situation provides a good definition of Original Sin. His retreat to the mountains of the Holy Land and dedication of the remainder of his days to prayer and repentance is a tacit acknowledgement of that fact. In the moment that he discovers he has been guilty of parricide he realizes that he has allowed himself to become little short of insane. Insanity is more often than not involuntary. Occasionally, though, it is purely a case of collapse of the will, a deliberate decision on the part of the individual to relinquish responsibility. For a man like Pagano a moment will come when he has a clear choice, either to let go of the past and go forward in life, or remain fixated on the demands of his chaotic emotional nature. For Pagano this moment undoubtedly came when his life was spared after his first attempt on his brother's life and he was sent into exile. The moment passed and he allowed the wound to fester within him to the point of complete imbalance. Now he knows (Act 1 Conclusion) that he has no choice but to go forward. 'On my forehead the Eternal brands the fatal mark of Cain; terror will consume my flesh more than the fire and snakes of Hell, Ah! Though I roam through glad flowers, in grottos, through forests, over mountains, my head will always be bloody; a demon will forever be at my back'.

Once ensconced in the Holy Land Pagano has only one desire, to see the Crusaders' banners 'gleaming from the mountain peaks' (Act 2 Scene 2). He hopes that by assisting

in the overthrow of the infidels he will in some way receive remission from his sins. It is interesting that Pagano still sees hope of redemption in terms of wielding his sword. It is not enough for him just to retire from the world and become a sainted hermit. He needs to restore the world. He needs to see the Christian faith, which he has so offended, prevail in the Holy Land, where, in his eyes, it rightfully belongs. When Pirro appears at his cave, it must be a shock, but it is partly a pleasant shock since it indicates to him that his brother must be in the vicinity. It is Pagano's dearest wish to be reconciled with his brother and obtain pardon for his sins.

Pirro's sudden appearance must inevitably bring back the past. Pagano is glad to be of assistance to the man who was once his accomplice (there is no indication that Pirro recognizes Pagano; some years have elapsed and Pagano will now be heavily bearded and wasted in comparison with his former appearance). He is overjoyed when he learns that the Lombard Crusaders have finally arrived. It seems barely credible that the first person to greet him is Arvino, but then this is Opera. The least that can be said is that Arvino is certainly the individual he most needs to see.

When Arvino arrives Pagano has already donned helmet and sword and lowered the visor on his helmet, so there is no danger that his brother may recognize him. It may seem strange that Pagano, who has devoted himself so assiduously to leading a holy life, should even contemplate taking up armour and weapons, but in the time of the Crusades it was considered a man's Christian duty to 'fight the good fight' and rescue the Holy Land sites from the ignominy of the 'infidels'. Arvino would see it as yet further confirmation of the hermit's holiness that he is already prepared for battle.

One can only imagine the depths of Pagano's emotion as he exhorts the Lombards to follow him into battle and reassures Arvino that he will soon see his daughter again. He forthwith leads Arvino to **Acciano's** palace, where **Giselda** is held captive. It would appear that Pagano has made it his business

---

[57] There is a Greek word which accurately describes Pagano's experience at this juncture, namely 'metanoia', which connotes a sudden, dramatic and unexpected change of mind and heart.

to keep abreast of what transpires in the world beyond his cave, even though he holds himself aloof from it. Pagano will probably empathize with Giselda's outburst, though he will fear for her safety as Arvino becomes enraged with (what he sees as) Giselda's blasphemy and sacrilege (Act 2 Scene 3). For Pagano it would be unspeakable if his brother were now to murder his own daughter.

When Pagano becomes aware that **Oronte** and Giselda are about to elope he does his best to prevent it. Arvino describes 'how the man of the cave threw himself on the fugitive being carried off on an Arab steed. In a flash all of them vanished from my sights' (Act 3 Scene 2). Exactly what transpires is not clear from the libretto, but eventually Pagano catches up with the fugitives only when Oronte has been mortally wounded and is shortly to die. Pagano is on hand to give solace to the dying man and to Giselda. It is for Pagano particularly pleasing to be able to welcome a 'heathen' into the Christian faith, and particularly since Oronte is his niece's beloved.

In his capacity as man of God Pagano speaks with almost oracular authority throughout the second half of the drama. He tells Arvino with unflinching certainty, 'you shall see your daughter again' (Act 2 Scene 2). Then he tells the Lombards 'this night you shall pitch your tents, I swear it, within the lofty city' and in Act 3 he reassures Oronte on his death bed 'one day amongst the angels you shall receive the mercy of joy'. This is not arrogance or hubris, it is the confidence of a man who has acquired total faith and wants to instil it in all who come into contact with him, particularly the Lombards towards whom he feels he owes so much reparation. His faith is the result of years of penance and suffering. It is rock solid and incontrovertible. It takes an obsessive temperament to withdraw from the world and devote itself utterly to penance and prayer. Pagano has learnt to re-channel the energies that formerly were entirely devoted to his fruitless longing to be united with his brother's wife. How many of the great saints (St Augustine and Thomas à Becket spring to mind) have started out in

life as voluptuaries or as 'sinners', and then turned their back on all that previously defined them. Conversion, in actuality, is a pragmatic matter. Whether it is Saul on the road to Damascus or a hippie in India, it is a question of suddenly recognizing that all that previously defined you is no longer applicable: your life illusion no longer works. If the pursuit of ruthlessly egotistical ends leads to nemesis then it has to be rejected as a *modus operandi*. It is necessary to start again.

In our own time rebirthing is a popular form of therapy. But in truth such therapy is of dubious worth for life itself usually dictates when, if ever, there shall be a probability of re-birth. In the case of Pagano life has certainly presented him with the necessity of rebirth. This is a theme which is particularly to be found in the libretti of Temistocle Solera. *Nabucco* is about the revolution in a tyrant's life when he is suddenly struck down and must start again from scratch. Nabucco, like Pagano, embraces the Christian faith and the ethos of compassion as the logical antidote to the senseless brutality of his former existence. There is in all this a propagandist agenda on Solera and Verdi's part, but it is not within the scope of this study to pursue this. All that we are concerned with is the motivation of an individual whose life has hit rock bottom.

The irony of Pagano's destiny is that it leads him inevitably back to bloodshed, but this time bloodshed legitimized by society and by the faith to which he adheres. For Pagano the difference now is that it is his own blood that is spilt and he is finally released from the awesome responsibility of his solitary destiny. He is also, most crucially, reunited with and pardoned by his brother. He can die content that he has paid his due.

Mistress Page (*Falstaff*)

As a personality in her own right, Mistress Page is overshadowed by her friend, **Alice Ford**, who is altogether the more proactive of the two 'Merry Wives'. Partly this is to do with the logistics of the tale, wherein Alice is the wife with the jealous and tyrannical husband, and also the mother of

Nannetta, both of whom play leading roles in the drama.

If it were not for the overpowering presence of **Falstaff** himself, the opera could almost be seen as a family drama concerning the fortunes and misfortunes of the Fords. But Meg plays a critical part in the unfolding of the action, even if she does not have quite the 'face' of either Alice or Mistress **Quickly.**

Meg's day starts, as does that of Alice, with the arrival of Falstaff's letter (Act 1 Scene 2). Her first thought is to share the news with her friends. She rushes round to Alice's house. On the way she meets Mistress Quickly. Knowing Quickly's propensity for gossip Meg decides to keep her own counsel until she has seen Alice, for Meg is by nature cautious. When Alice informs her that she has also received a letter, and a precise replica of the letter Meg has received at that, the latter is perplexed. What is she to think? If she was flattered at first she is very soon indignant. Significantly her exclamations echo closely those of Mistress Quickly, for Meg is essentially a reactive personality. She does not initiate anything, she just enjoys being one of the gang.

There is something of the schoolmistress about Meg. She tells Quickly to be sure she does her job properly, and is the first to notice that they are being observed (Act 1 Scene 2) from the bushes by **Fenton,** who is in hiding. By the end of Act 1 Meg is sounding as vitriolic about Falstaff as are her friends: 'If the pitch smears him, we'll hear him shriek, then that letch of his will soon disappear'.

One suspects that Meg may be something of an old maid in her attitude towards men. Her husband (who does not appear in the opera) could well be henpecked. Either that, or he is even more formidable than Alice's husband and is therefore kept well away from the shenanigans.[58] Whatever the case, Meg clearly enjoys the 'gulling' of Falstaff. Her role in Act 2 Scene 2 is to appear as

soon as Falstaff thinks he is making headway with Alice, and announce the 'imminent arrival' of Alice's husband. As it turns out **Ford** actually *does* arrive home, and Meg finds herself having to assist Alice in escaping her husband's wrath. Nevertheless, she manages to slip in a few well aimed volleys at the unfortunate Falstaff, as the latter tries to squeeze himself into the laundry basket.

When Ford thinks he has found his prey behind the screen, Meg assists Quickly in keeping Falstaff concealed, which task is made all the more difficult by the fact that Falstaff insists on popping his head up for air every other minute. By this time Meg has experienced a revelation which she shares with Mistress Quickly: 'danger is like a dash of pepper to a game like this, risk is a pleasure that increases the fun and stimulates the spirits and the heart'. Once having got a taste for danger and risk, Meg cannot get enough of it. She clearly enjoys the story that Alice relates of the ghostly black hunter who haunts Windsor Park (Act 3 Scene 1): 'I can feel a chill of fear', she exclaims with relish.

In the masquerade (Act 3 Scene 2) Alice assigns Meg the role of the 'Green Nymph of the Woods'. As such she is put in charge of the imps, who are to be played by children. Thus she finds herself in charge of a whole horde of Windsor's youngest and liveliest. Meg is quite equal to the task; she lines them up along the ditch in plenty of time for Falstaff's arrival. Later, as the 'show' begins, Meg's voice can be heard calling for help from the woods: 'The witches are coming!' Falstaff flings himself face down on the ground in genuinely helpless terror.

Meg joins in the final humiliation of Falstaff with alacrity, calling upon him to repent. In truth, Meg is experiencing a return to the excesses of youth, as is everybody who takes part in the masquerade. The supreme irony is that all the masqueraders owe the fun they are having at Falstaff's expense to Falstaff himself, as he himself acknowledges when he remarks, 'My wit creates the wit of others'. The events of the day have been for everybody concerned a voyage of discovery, none more so than Meg Page.

---

[58] In Shakespeare's play Meg's husband fully participates and is presented as consistently mild and cheerful. He never seems to doubt for a moment his wife's fidelity.

A Page (Un Paggio) (*Rigoletto*)

The page has a small but crucial part to play in the drama. In Act 2 Scene 2 when **Rigoletto** is desperately searching for some sign that his daughter, **Gilda**, is in the palace the page enters and announces that the Duchess wishes to speak to the **Duke** (this is the only reference made in the opera to the Duke's wife, although in the stage directions to Act 2 there is reference to portraits of the Duke and his wife). At the mention of the Duchess the courtiers close ranks. They are obviously under strict instructions not to disturb their master, who is at that moment in the arms of Gilda. **Ceprano** tells the page that the Duke is asleep. When the page reveals that he knows the Duke has only just been with the courtiers, **Borsa** claims that the Duke has gone hunting. The page expresses incredulity that the Duke has gone unescorted and unarmed. He knows the syndrome only too well. The courtiers make it plain that the Duke is unavailable and the page departs without satisfaction. Rigoletto has followed the scene carefully and is by now convinced the Duke is with his daughter.

Paolo Albiani (*Boccanegra*). Favourite courtier of the Doge.

Paolo is the archetypal self-serving courtier whose lust for power brings nemesis upon himself but also threatens at its foundation not only himself but the system he attempts to bend to his will.

When the opera opens (Prologue) Paolo is striving to ensure the election of Simone **Boccanegra** as Doge. He takes the proposal to Boccanegra himself, but is met with reluctance. Paolo overcomes Boccanegra's reluctance by convincing him that it is his best means of achieving **Fiesco's** sanction for his marriage to Fiesco's daughter, Maria. Throughout the opera Paolo demonstrates that he is a worthy disciple of Machiavelli. He knows exactly how to manipulate people and events to his own ends. This is particularly apparent in the ensuing scene in which he plays on the commoners' superstitious gullibility to convince them that they should give their vote to Boccanegra in preference

to the Patricians. The conclusion of the Prologue sees his successful bid for vicarious power, with Boccanegra hailed as the new Doge.

In **Pietro** Paolo has a worthy ally. Pietro does all Paolo's spadework, acting as *agent provocateur* amongst the people of Genoa. Paolo himself, as is the way with all who lust after power, does the absolute minimum necessary to achieve his ends. Paolo is the brains, Pietro the brawn. In return for assisting Boccanegra into the Doge's seat all Paolo asks is an occasional favour from Boccanegra, such as furthering his suit with the beautiful **Amelia** Grimaldi. He forgets that Boccanegra himself never sought power for its own sake and owes Paolo nothing.

When Boccanegra discovers that Amelia is his long-lost daughter (Act 1 Scene 2) he immediately withdraws his support of Paolo's suit. By way of explanation all he will tell Paolo is 'It is my will'. Paolo cannot be expected to understand this; all he can see is Boccanegra's ingratitude. But, as is his habit, if he cannot get his way by fair means then he will achieve it by foul. He determines to kidnap Amelia, or rather he commands Pietro to organize the abduction. He thus resorts to a 'smash-and-grab' policy, which will result in his final undoing. Oblivious to the fact that Amelia is Boccanegra's daughter – not that the knowledge would substantially affect his resolution – Paolo signs his own death warrant. He has reckoned without the pluckiness of Amelia, who, having the blood of a corsair in her veins, is not easily restrained. She easily succeeds in intimidating Lorenzin (her captor) and escaping. She loses no time in indicating to her father who was the perpetrator. Boccanegra has had enough political experience to know that Paolo cannot be tackled head-on. So he attacks Paolo where he is weakest, in his overweening pride and passionate need for anonymity (Act 1 Scene 2). Paolo's humiliation at the end of Act 1 is complete. To appreciate how complete it is necessary to understand the real power that would have been ascribed to a curse such as Boccanegra compels him to utter upon himself. Even a man like Paolo would have felt the force of such a self-imposed valediction. He is visibly terrified.

When he has recovered from the initial horror of his exposure Paolo's thoughts inevitably turn to revenge. The humiliation that Boccanegra has inflicted upon him requires only one punishment: death. Like all criminals Paolo is basically spoilt. Deprived of his dignity his mind becomes fixated on thoughts of vengeance. By the opening of Act 2 he has already thought of the means by which to effect his revenge – it is inconceivable that he would think of perpetrating the deed himself. He will incite Fiesco or Gabriele to murder Boccanegra in his sleep. Failing that he will poison Boccanegra's drink. Poisoning is traditionally the last resort of the coward. He reflects with relish on how his victim will die in slow and hideous agony. When Fiesco scorns the suggestion that he should murder Boccanegra in his sleep Paolo turns to Gabriele who, being younger and of a fiery disposition, he knows will be much easier to convince. Gabriele is given no choice in the matter. Paolo tells him that unless he murders Boccanegra he will himself be killed. He locks him in the Doge's apartments.

Gabriele would indeed have fulfilled his commission had Amelia not intervened. Paolo still has the insurance policy of the poison that he has already poured into Boccanegra's goblet. Had he simply left the poison to do its work and made off it is possible he would have escaped with his crimes, but his impetuous rage gets the better of him and he takes up arms with the other rebels in the streets of Genoa. He is caught and summarily sentenced to be executed. The only comfort left to him as he goes to the gallows is the knowledge that he has likewise condemned Boccanegra. He cannot resist boasting of the fact to Fiesco (Act 3). He also enjoys telling Fiesco that it was he who was responsible for abducting Amelia. Vainly he hopes that Fiesco may save him the indignity of execution by killing him himself. Fiesco, however, restrains himself and Paolo must meet the fate of all traitors. The character of Paolo is a convincing portrayal of the Machiavellian adventurer who usually ends up hoist with his own petard.

Papal Legate (*Jerusalem*). See Adhemar de Monteil

Peasant (un contadino) (*Luisa Miller*)
Act 2 Scene 3   The peasant has been given a letter by **Luisa** to deliver to **Wurm** (it is the letter that Wurm has compelled Luisa to write and has himself dictated). In the letter Luisa declares her love for Wurm over all others.

The peasant clearly knows of **Rodolfo's** love for Luisa and hopes for a better reward from Rodolfo than he would receive from the mean-spirited Wurm. He is not disappointed. Rodolfo throws him a purse (presumably with more money in it than the peasant would normally expect to see in a year).

Pereda (*La Forza del Destino*). See Don Carlo

Philip II (Filippo II). (*Don Carlo*). King of Spain.
Historical Note   Philip II (1527–1598), King of Spain, Naples and Sicily (1556–1598) and of Portugal (1580–1598) was the only legitimate son of the Emperor Charles V. He married four times: Mary of Portugal (1543), Mary Tudor (1544), Isabella of France (Elisabeth de Valois) (1559) and Anne of Austria (1570). The action of the opera can therefore be assumed to take place during the decade 1559–1570. The *auto-da-fé* portrayed in Act 3 Part 2 historically took place in 1559 in Valladolid as part of the celebrations to mark Philip's return after several years spent in Flanders and England. He was received as a conquering hero.

Reference by the crowd at the opening of the *auto-da-fé* scene (Act 3 Scene 2) to the 'greatest of Kings . . . who has the world prostrate at his feet' reflects the golden age which had apparently dawned in Spain at this stage of his reign (the defeat of the Spanish Armada was not to take place until 1588). The fact that after 1559 Philip did not once leave Spain gives an indication of the confidence with which he ruled and the confidence he instilled.

Carlos said of this father, with regard to the latter's reluctance to travel abroad: 'My father deems that the Emperor journeyed sufficiently for himself and his son. The King reposes now, both for the Emperor and his own pleasure'. The truth is that Philip, who had no gift in human affairs, preferred always to treat matters from a distance and in abstract.

Whereas in the opera it appears that Philip is entirely in thrall to the Church and the Inquisition, this is a distortion of the reality. Certainly Philip was a devout Catholic with a strong crusading impulse. But the various wars on which he engaged, notably against the Ottoman Empire and England, were principally motivated by his desire to expand the Spanish and his own power base. His aggrandizing policies left the country economically crippled. In reality there was little justification for his campaigns since the New World colonies had already made sixteenth-century Spain the richest country in Europe.

Philip was entrusted by his father with the regency of Spain when he was only 22 years old. He was nicknamed 'il prudente', the cautious. He was by nature conscientious and dutiful, quite unlike his father. His first marriage was to a cousin, Mary of Portugal, whom he genuinely loved. He also fathered several bastards by one Donna Isobel. He then married Mary Tudor, partly in order to bring England back into the Roman Catholic faith, but also because England would be a useful addition to the Empire. At the start of his reign Philip achieved a massive victory at St Quentin. Peace talks were called at Cateau Cambrésis. Princess Elisabeth was to be married to Philip's son, but Mary Tudor died meanwhile, leaving Philip without a consort. Philip proposed to Queen Elisabeth of England but was rejected. So he decided to marry the French Princess.

Philip is not an old man in the opera, although it is difficult to believe this when one hears him speak of himself. When the action of the opera takes place he is in his mid thirties. But he is prematurely aged. It is tempting to say that Philip was prematurely

aged from the day that he was born. His father was not enamoured of his son who was disinclined to involve himself in the outdoor pursuits and manly pastimes which Charles so favoured. Nevertheless he respected his son's abilities. Philip was studious and serious to a fault. He had no time for frivolities. He had an abiding sense of guilt and distrust of the world, bordering on the paranoid. In contrast to his young bride Elisabeth, Philip saw dissimulation as being the hallmark of kingship. It was said of him that 'his dagger follows close on his smile', and he was not trusted. This aspect of Philip's character is brought out clearly in the opera by Verdi and his librettists but is only comprehensible in the light of his relationship to his father (see **Friar**).

Philip was never popular with the public. He was a disastrous father, humiliating Carlos regularly in front of the Court. Carlos's insufficiencies were clear for all to see but Philip's inability to cope with his son must be ascribed in part to the lack in his own life of a compassionate father-figure.

Philip makes an unsympathetic impression on his first appearance (Act 2 Scene 2), when he enters the garden of the San Yuste Monastery to find **Elisabeth** alone. He has given express orders that Elisabeth should not be left alone for (as will become clear in his interview with **Rodrigo** later in the same scene) he already fears that she is having an affair with his son, **Don Carlo**. Philip is not cruel by nature, but he will not tolerate disobedience or slackness. He is a disciplinarian, born and bred. He himself has a keen sense of the duties which have befallen him and he sees no reason why others should not have the same sense of responsibility. When he banishes the Contessa d'Aremberg to France he merely exercises a king's prerogative. He must also suspect that the Countess has been aiding and abetting Elisabeth's clandestine meetings with her stepson. Philip needs to be in control. His young wife does not love him. There is no love or joy in his life. Therefore he cannot abide anybody else experiencing either love or joy. All must bow down before the same, miserable God that he himself is compelled to worship.

Philip hardly notices his wife's tearful farewell to the Countess. His mind and eyes are elsewhere, trained on the person of Rodrigo di Posa. He has always valued Rodrigo as a friend, yet the Marquis is now in grave danger of incurring his and, more critically, the Inquisition's displeasure. 'How in my presence a noble heart dissembles', he mutters to himself. When Rodrigo is about to leave Philip calls him back and demands to know why since his return to court Rodrigo has not asked to be admitted to the Royal presence. Rodrigo's response is frankly insulting: 'What could I hope for from the favour of Kings?' But Philip chooses to let it pass. He admires Rodrigo's spirit. He may see in him the man his own father, Charles, would have preferred for a son: the brilliant extrovert, soldier and courtier, well-practised in all the liberal arts and the idealist that he himself could never be. He genuinely would like to help Rodrigo and yet at the same time knows that there is nothing he can do for him. His hands are tied more completely than if he were the Pope himself ('Thus the Crown must always bow before the Church', he exclaims bitterly after his altercation with the Inquisitor, Act 4 Scene 1; Rodrigo does not even bow to his king). When Philip tells him, 'I love a proud spirit', he means it. He is one himself but can find no outlet for his spirit other than in acts of petty tyranny such as we have just witnessed. But these are no outlets. These are compromise solutions which leave behind only anger and bitterness, not only in the victim but within himself. Thus he tolerates Rodrigo's passionate outpourings on behalf of the suffering Flemish. Rodrigo's passion is as dear to him as his pride. Passion is the gift of the young and Philip has never been young. He may describe Rodrigo as a 'strange dreamer', but he comprehends more than he lets on. Comprehending is one thing, embracing quite another and Philip would never embrace that which he should not embrace. 'You would change your ideas if you knew the heart of man as Philip knows', he tells Rodrigo. If it

is not decreed by divine ordinance as passed down to him by the Inquisitor, it is not to be countenanced because it would upset the equilibrium by which the world keeps turning and he retains his throne.

It pains Philip that Rodrigo remains haughty and aloof from him. He craves this man's friendship and longs to be able to unburden himself to him. For Philip has nobody in whom he can truly confide. He would never dream of confiding in a woman – either his wife or his mistresses – and all the men around him are his subordinates. Maintaining a regal aloofness he manages to gain Rodrigo's attention: 'Your gaze has dared to penetrate to my throne. Learn the anguish and grief within my head weighed down by the crown! Look now at my royal palace. Anxiety enfolds it – an unfortunate father, husband more miserable still!' This takes Rodrigo by surprise. Philip will not elaborate other than to say in stuttering tones: 'The Queen . . . a suspicion troubles me . . . my son . . .'. When Rodrigo leaps to Carlo's defence Philip's rage and impotence boil to the surface: 'Nothing beneath heaven is so precious as what he has taken from me!' he cries. Restraining himself again he tells Rodrigo that he is relying on him to 'search their hearts'. Knowing that he can trust him implicitly he grants Rodrigo free access to the Queen at all times. He does not realize that he has thus played straight into Rodrigo's hands by assisting the latter's agenda for Flanders. While Rodrigo exults in the unexpected 'dawn' that lights up the sky, Philip is only content that he has succeeded in unburdening himself of the fearful oppression that has been weighing on his soul. So that Rodrigo should have no illusions and because he is first and foremost the King he extends his hand that Rodrigo may kneel and kiss it. It has cost Philip much to unburden himself. This scene, which follows hard on the heels of Philip's peremptory dismissal of Elisabeth's companion, presents us with a contradictory picture of the monarch. It succeeds in establishing Philip not just as an arrogant despot but as a suffering human being, as vulnerable as any in the drama.

When Philip next appears (Act 3 Scene 2) he has regained his public persona: 'When I first placed the crown on my head, oh my people, I swore to heaven that bestowed it on me, to put the wicked to death by fire and sword'. Philip, for all that he chafes against the Inquisition, remains a devout Catholic. (Putting the wicked to death by fire and sword was viewed by the Church as assisting in the redemption of eternal souls.) He is taken totally by surprise by the sudden appearance of the Flemish deputies with his son at their head. He is outraged. Were he another sort of man he would realize that he is in an impossible position. If he refuses to give the deputies a sympathetic hearing he is declaring to the world that there is a total rift between himself and the heir to the throne. Don Carlo has pushed him into a corner in which there is little room for manoeuvre or escape. Philip's response is predictable; he loses his temper. Blithely ignoring the fact that he has thousands of witnesses, most of whom support Carlos and sympathize with the plight of the Flemish, he rants at the deputies: 'You have been false to God and traitorous to your king'. Carlos now speaks out for all the world to hear, more boldly maybe than he has ever dared to speak to his father, demanding that he be given responsibility for Brabant and Flanders. Philip's reaction is immediate and unambiguous: 'Madman! You dare make such a demand? You expect me to offer you the sword with which one day you would sacrifice the King!' Carlos draws his sword, to the horror of all present, and Philip, enraged, summons the guards to remove Carlos from his presence. The guards ignore his summons and finally Philip seizes a sword from the captain of the guard and is on the point of engaging his son in combat when Rodrigo intervenes. This is extremely gratifying to him, for it confirms that he has one champion on whom he can rely. Not only that but it confounds the suspicion of treason that surrounds Rodrigo. He forthwith elevates Rodrigo to the rank of Duke while Carlos and the deputies are led away under arrest.

When the curtain rises on Act 4 we are confronted with the sad truth that underpins all Philip's rage and bitterness, the fact that he is a broken man who seeks, like every other human, to find love. He is in his study, half asleep and reflecting (*Ella giammai m'amo!*). He recalls the day when Elisabeth arrived from France and gazed sadly at his white hair.[59]

Gradually Philip becomes aware that it is dawn. The dawning of another day is no cause for joy for him. He is tired of his life, tired of watching it slip by with nothing but ever new responsibilities and pain to show for it. Dismally he thinks of the day when he will finally be able to sleep 'beneath the black vault there, in my tomb in the Escurial'. Philip resists any tendency to self-pity either in himself or in others. His emotion at this point is dictated by resignation and an over-riding sense of fatality. There is, however, real desperation in his plea: 'If the royal crown could but give me the power to read human hearts which God alone can see!' He knows that his greatest shortcoming is his inability to put himself in another person's position. Other people's feelings are a mystery to him. Locked in his own private nightmare he has no capacity to empathize and cannot begin to comprehend how others might have a quite different perception from his own. When he complains that Elisabeth's heart is closed to him he must know that it is largely his own fault. Even if she wanted to open her heart to him he is too unapproachable.

Philip's musings are interrupted by the arrival of the Grand Inquisitor. Philip must gird himself afresh at this moment. He knows that he must propitiate the Inquisitor and it is irksome to him. However it is he who has taken the initiative and summoned the Inquisitor to him. He has been meditating on the problem of his rebellious son. He is at his wit's end and wondering whether it

---

[59] This has its basis in history. For it is recorded that when Philip and Elisabeth first met Elisabeth could find nothing to say to her new husband. Philip irritably exploded: 'What are you staring at? To see if I have grey hairs?'

might not be possible to be rid of Carlos once and for all. The fact that he is more or less convinced that Carlos and Elisabeth are engaged in an affair does nothing to soften his attitude. But if he condones his own son's execution how will it stand with his eternal soul? This is what concerns him. For Philip is a God-fearing man – fear being the operative word.

Philip opens the interview by asking the Inquisitor if, as a Christian, he can sacrifice his son for the world. The Inquisitor has no hesitation in reminding Philip that in order to redeem mankind God sacrificed his own Son. As far as the Inquisitor is concerned there is nothing to discuss. Philip quickly realizes this and hopes to call an end to the interview. But the Inquisitor will not leave until he has had his say with regard to Rodrigo. He tells Philip unequivocally that Carlos's 'treason' pales into insignificance by comparison with Rodrigo's. Philip must surely have anticipated this line of attack, but it makes it no easier to contend with. Lamely he argues that he has finally found in Rodrigo a 'loyal heart' in whom he can put his trust. The Inquisitor is not impressed: 'Why have you the title of King, Sire, if a lesser man can be your equal?' he demands. Philip has no answer. It is his fate that wherever he turns he can never escape that which he most dreads: himself. Indeed it is because he dreads it that he is repeatedly forced into situations where he has no option but to confront himself. There is no hope that he can make the Inquisitor understand this. He probably could not articulate even it to himself.

In any case the Inquisitor moves the conversation swiftly from the subject of Philip, for whom he has nothing but contempt, to the matter of Rodrigo's advocacy of heresy. When he demands that Philip hands Rodrigo over to the Inquisition, Philip is adamant. The Inquisitor proceeds to threaten him with being summoned himself before the Inquisition. At this point Philip loses his temper and calls a halt to the interview. As the Inquisitor retreats Philip becomes nervous. Has he gone too far? He asks the old priest that there should be peace between them.

The Inquisitor's response is not encouraging: 'Perhaps', he says as he withdraws. Philip erupts in irritation: 'thus the throne must always bow to the altar!'

At this moment Elisabeth bursts into his chambers and demands redress for the injustice she suffers (*Giustizia! Giustizia!*). Philip is not in a receptive mood. Her tirade so soon after the Inquisitor's is more than he can tolerate. Something inside him goes cold. He has had enough of being harangued. Is not he, after all, the King? And is it not he who is being betrayed? He thrusts the casket at Elisabeth with no explanation and demands that she open it. When she refuses he forces the lock himself. He has a fair idea of what to expect, but it does not make the actuality any easier to contend with. What husband would want to be confronted with unimpeachable evidence that his wife is having an affair with his son? He demands an explanation. Elisabeth remains dignified, which only increases Philip's ire. She reminds him that she was once betrothed to Carlos. She expresses dismay that he should doubt her. Philip is not listening. He only hears the rush of his own blood and his utter helplessness: 'You think me weak and seem to defy me; weakness in me can turn to fury'. There is no going back now. He warns Elisabeth that if she has betrayed him then blood will flow. Elisabeth then has the unmitigated effrontery to tell him that she pities him. Now Philip loses all self-control. He makes to strike her. Elisabeth faints. Immediately remorseful Philip rushes to the door and calls for help.

Philip tolerates Rodrigo upbraiding him for his loss of self-control because he knows it is justified: 'oh, cursed be the fatal suspicion, the work of a demon from hell!' he reflects. He knows deep down that Elisabeth is innocent and he knows that his behaviour has been unforgivable. His misery knows no limits. He is beleaguered on all fronts and in the midst of it he is confronted by the fact of his own utter inadequacy as a husband and as a man.

Philip's life is not going to grow any easier in the short term, for Rodrigo now ensures that Carlos's incriminating papers are found in his (Rodrigo's) possession. The Inquisitor thereby has irrefutable evidence of Rodrigo's guilt and can no longer be gainsaid. A writ is put out on Rodrigo's life. This is far more painful to Philip than if he had had to condemn his own son. Instead he must go to the dungeons where Carlos is confined and restore to his son his liberty and his sword. When Carlos tells him that Rodrigo has deliberately deflected the guilt onto himself, Philip is appalled (although part of him must be glad to learn that his most trusted adviser has not turned traitor). Such generosity epitomizes all that Philip most values in Rodrigo. Confronted now with Rodrigo's corpse he lets out what can only be described as an anguished howl: 'Who can ever restore this man to me?'

However he has no time to grieve since the prison is being assailed by a mob demanding the Infante's release. He orders that the prison gates be thrown open so that he may confront the mob. Since they demand the Infante, whom he has just released, he hopes he will have no problem appeasing them. But he cannot be certain. He has always remained aloof from the people. It must be deeply alarming now for him to be confronted with such a large crowd. Luckily the Inquisitor arrives and subdues the crowd. It is an eloquent moment, heavily underscoring the fact of Philip's own impotence. The very sight of the Inquisitor instils terror into the mob, which immediately becomes acquiescent. Philip proclaims, 'Almighty God, all glory to Thee', thus tacitly acknowledging the Inquisitor's sovereignty. In return, all call out, 'Long live the King!' and beg for mercy. The Inquisitor has gained the life of Philip's closest friend, as he had demanded, and now gives a demonstration to Philip of the advantages to the King of submitting himself before the supremacy of the Church.

Now the Inquisitor demands that Carlos be sacrificed. It is undoubtedly the Inquisitor who has discovered that Elisabeth and Carlos will be meeting at San Yuste. When Philip sees his son and wife together it is almost a vindication of his earlier loss of self-control.

'I shall do my duty', he tells the Inquisitor, 'I demand a double sacrifice'. There will be no double sacrifice, however, for at the end of the opera it is Philip's own father, Charles V, in whose shadow Philip has always walked and whose spirit hangs over the entire drama, who prevails, rescuing Don Carlo and dumbfounding all present, including the audience.

All Philip's problems stem from the lack of accrediting from his own father and his sense of his own worthlessness. When Elisabeth declares, '*Pietà me fate . . .*' ('I pity you') she means it. Philip is certainly deserving of compassion, though so starved of all warmth and love is he that he appears beyond all attempts to assist him. The drama of *Don Carlo* delineates for Philip an unravelling of all that he most cares for. It is a catalogue of loss that can only befall someone who has no intrinsic self-esteem.

Philip's recognition of his father at the conclusion of the opera is a revelatory moment for him, for Philip has never been able to reconcile himself with the father, either in real or in spiritual terms. In his role as father he confronts only failure. In his role as son he confronts only failure. He can appease neither the father nor the son within himself, for he has never found the essential core to his own being. He loves Carlos, his son, but is rejected by him. In Rodrigo he finds the son he does not have, but ultimately Philip is rejected by him also. Why is it that his only experience is of rejection? Partly it must be because of the rejection that he himself suffered at the outset of his life. Inevitably, therefore, he can only perpetuate the cycle of rejection, himself rejecting those who come to him for love. Were he to reflect upon it he would never be able to perceive the syndrome because he would always find perfect justification for his actions. How can he not reject Carlos, since he so blatantly sets himself up in rebellion against him? In reality Carlos only does what he, Philip, personally was never able to do; and this is what makes it all the more insupportable to him. He was never able to make for himself a separate, clearly defined identity. He does not know who he is. How, therefore, can he be expected to recognize the separate identity of others?

Yet the rebellion of the son against the father is a psychological necessity. It cannot be avoided. Philip's rebellion thus continues long after his father has apparently departed. He rebels vicariously through his tacit alliance with the forces of rebellion as epitomized by Rodrigo's advocacy of the cause of Flemish independence. When he cries, with such heart-rending poignancy, 'Who can restore this man to me?' (Act 4 Scene 2) it is a cry of desperation from his own deepest self, acknowledging that he is now forever bereft of any possibility of redemption.

In Carlos Philip quite simply confronts his own insufficiency as a son. But in the Inquisitor he finds a father against whom he can himself attempt to rebel. Yet something in him always prevents him from running the full mile. It was Verdi's genius to perceive that the confrontation between Philip and the Inquisitor is the central confrontation in the whole drama (Act 4 Scene 1), for it is essentially a confrontation between father and son. It is a pitched battle of wills, as it must always be, and it will, if the life-force is to be in any way properly served, inevitably result in the ascendancy of the son. For the father must by definition represent the forces of stasis and retrogression, while the son by definition represents hope and possibility for the future. The tragedy of this scene is that it results not in Philip's ascendancy, but in that of the Inquisitor. When, at the conclusion of the scene, Philip cries, 'Thus must the throne always bow before the altar' we can justifiably translate: 'thus must the son always bow before the father'.

Philip accedes with utter desperation to the necessity of his fate. Carlos, meanwhile, continues to work out his rebellion. For Philip the most painful thing about his son's rebellion is the way in which Carlos apparently appropriates his closest friend, Rodrigo. For in this appropriation the true nature of his regard for Rodrigo, previously unvoiced and unacknowledged, becomes explicit, that Rodrigo represents all that he himself wishes

Carlos could be and yet paradoxically most dreads him becoming. This is an active threat to his paternal authority. Rodrigo represents something that neither he nor Carlos can ever aspire to: the single-minded and incontrovertible dedication to a single ideal. Philip and Carlos must both by virtue of their worldly elevation – never sought for but thrust upon them – bow before the exigencies of *Realpolitik*. They must compromise. Rodrigo represents the purity of the single flame that neither of them can ever hope to attain to. Presumably when Charles V abjured the world he sought a possibility of discovering within himself, within the womb of the cloister, that single flame and discovered that, after a lifetime's dedication to compromise, it was all but impossible; 'War in the heart only abates in heaven'.

Pietro (*Boccanegra*). A courtier.
Pietro serves principally as **Paolo's** henchman. He does not himself initiate any significant events but responds to the will of Paolo's more forceful personality. At the opening of the opera (Prologue) he is being persuaded by Paolo to support the nomination of **Boccanegra** as Doge in exchange for 'gold, power and honour'. 'For such a price I will achieve the people's trust', Pietro says. He exits and returns shortly with sailors and workmen who express their intention of supporting Lorenzin. Pietro tells them that Lorenzin has sold himself to the Fieschi but he has someone else in mind, a hero and a commoner. At this moment Paolo steps forward and names the man in question, Boccanegra, a pirate, who has brought much wealth to Genoa and is a popular local hero. The people readily accept him as their choice of candidate. By the end of the scene Pietro is relegated to cheerleader. He departs with the rest of the crowd only returning at the conclusion of the Prologue to celebrate the *fait accompli* of Boccanegra's election.

After Paolo has been snubbed in his attempt to woo **Amelia** he instructs Pietro to arrange for the girl to be kidnapped (Act 1 Scene 1). Pietro dutifully complies but the abduction goes awry and Amelia manages to escape. Pietro, however, is not present for the débâcle. He has left Amelia with Lorenzin and is present in the Council Chamber at the opening of Act 1 Scene 2. When **Gabriele** is sighted at the head of a mob advancing on the Doge's palace Pietro quickly surmises that Amelia's abduction must have been discovered. He warns Paolo to flee. When Gabriele relates to the assembly how Lorenzin had, with his dying words, implicated 'a man of power', Pietro is convinced that Paolo will be unmasked. But in fact Gabriele assumes that the villain is Boccanegra himself. Boccanegra, however, knows perfectly well who the perpetrator is. When Boccanegra so publicly and spectacularly humiliates Paolo at the end of Act 1 Pietro must inevitably fear for his own safety.

However he does nothing to distance himself from Paolo for, at the opening of Act 2, he is still obediently serving Paolo's every whim. Here he is being commanded to fetch the prisoners (Gabriele and **Fiesco**) from the dungeons. Whether or not Pietro knows Paolo's intention to murder Boccanegra is not explicit. He does not appear again in the opera and there is no suggestion that he will share Paolo's fate. Presumably he sensibly makes himself scarce after his mentor's demise.

Pirro (*I Lombardi*)

Pirro is listed in the cast list as Esquire to **Arvino**.[60] But when first encountered in the opera he is conspiring with **Pagano** to assist in the murder of Arvino. He is thus the Judas figure in the drama. He must have reasons for his discontent and have retained an old loyalty to Pagano for he appears to assist Pagano with alacrity.

Pirro assures Pagano that 'your smallest sign shall be my command' (Act 1 Scene 1). He has already gathered a formidable gang of cut-throats to storm the Folco palace that very evening. It must be he who admits the cut-throats to the palace. When they have set it alight Pirro becomes exultant: 'let us

---

[60] Some sources list Pirro as Pagano's Esquire which, however, greatly reduces the interest and logic of the role.

join in the savage game. I well know how to change face', he says. There is no more dangerous adversary than a discontented servant. Whatever the reason for Pirro's discontent it causes him no advancement or joy once Pagano is revealed as a parricide and is cast out, 'branded with the mark of Cain'.

When Pirro next appears (Act 2 Scene 2) several years have passed and he has been tormented by guilt over his crimes. Word has reached him of the great holiness of the hermit who resides in the hills outside Antioch, but he has no idea that the hermit is, in fact, Pagano. Nor does he appear to recognize Pagano when face to face with him. Pagano cannot fail to recognize Pirro because the latter introduces himself: 'My name is Pirro, and I was a Lombard. I lent my hand to a parricide. Fleeing here like a coward I have renounced my faith. Terror and grief now guide me to your feet in supplication'. All Pagano manages to say to him is 'Rise and have hope', at which point the Crusaders arrive.

Pirro is determined to redeem himself by assisting the Crusaders in breaching the walls of Antioch. That he is successful is proved by the fact that the Crusaders, led by him, appear in the harem of **Acciano**'s palace having already killed the tyrant (Act 2 Scene 2). Pirro probably perishes in one of the affrays but at least he will feel he has atoned for his sins.

Pisana (*I Due Foscari*). Friend and confidante of **Lucrezia**.

On the whole Pisana is never far from her mistress's side. In Act 1 Scene 3 she rushes in and tearfully tells Lucrezia of **Jacopo**'s further banishment. She knows this will grieve Lucrezia and must anticipate many tears and lamentations. She does not accompany Lucrezia into the dungeons when Lucrezia goes to visit her husband (Act 2 Scene 1) but does so when her mistress goes to plead with the Doge (Act 2 Scene 2) and again when Lucrezia goes to see her husband off on his last journey into exile (Act 3 Scene 1). At all times she seeks to support her mistress's cause, pleading with the Councillors for mercy.

She is notably absent from Lucrezia's two final appearances; first when she apprises **Francesco** of Jacopo's death and then to give support to Francesco when the old man is deprived of office (Act 3 Scene 2). By this stage of the drama Lucrezia is too distracted with grief to turn even to her most trusted confidante.

Pistola (*Falstaff*). Follower of **Falstaff**.

A pistol was in Elizabethan times, as it is now, a small firearm. It was often used in Elizabethan ribaldry as a metaphor for the penis.

'I did never know so full a voice issue from so empty a heart' (*Henry V* Act 4 Scene 4), the Boy remarks after encountering Pistol. Verdi and Boito knew their Shakespeare, and it is conceivable that Verdi had this quote in mind when he wrote the part of Pistola. For Pistola is explosive and brainless at the same time. His role thereby affords the actor considerable opportunities for comedy.

Shakespeare's intention with the character of Pistol was partly to satirize the grandiosity of much Elizabethan drama and literature, especially that of Christopher Marlowe. Pistola is therefore a caricature of all the worst masculine traits, being loud-mouthed, insensitive, self-centred, self-opinionated and vulgar. He lives from the neck down, having little or no native wit. In this he stands in total contrast to Falstaff, who, in spite of his boorishness and enormous physical bulk, is possessed of a razor-sharp wit. Pistola only excels in bad rhetoric. In Shakespeare he constantly asserts his prowess as a great hero on the battlefield, but then when it comes to going into battle (see *Henry V* Act 3 Scene 2) he proves to be a total coward. In the case of the smaller characters there is relatively little in Boito's libretto to go on, though a great deal in Verdi's music.[61]

---

[61] There is some evidence that Shakespeare may originally have intended to include Falstaff in *Henry V*, but then for some reason replaced him with Pistol. For in that play Pistol displays an uncharacteristic degree of wit which would have sounded far more suitable coming from Falstaff's lips.

Pistola is on stage at the opening of the opera, but remains in the background. Both he and **Bardolfo** are feeling somewhat sheepish since the previous night, having first plied him with liquor, they have robbed **Doctor Caius**. As the curtain rises, Caius is making a vigorous complaint to their employer (Sir John Falstaff) about their behaviour. Pistola has nothing but contempt for a 'book-learned gentleman' like Doctor Caius. The only language Pistola understands is that of physical extravagance. His temperament is choleric. In this he contrasts with Bardolfo, who is fundamentally sanguine, if not bone idle. Pistola is not exactly industrious, but he does need to be up and doing. **Quickly**'s description of Falstaff might be more appropriate to Pistola: 'That man is a cannon; if he goes off you're done for'. If Pistola is inactive for too long he likewise is liable to explode. Thus when Falstaff invites him to defend himself before the good Doctor, Pistola's reaction is to grab a broom and demand to be allowed to fight Caius. He then engages in a vigorous bout of verbal sparring which comes to a halt when Caius calls him a 'mandrake sprout'. Having no idea what or who a 'mandrake sprout' may be, Pistola is momentarily lost for words, and when that happens there is only one recourse: physical violence. He hurls himself at the unfortunate Caius. However, when Falstaff reminds him to restrain himself he meekly obliges, thus indicating the degree to which he is in thrall to Falstaff. In spite of himself he cannot help acknowledging the latter's superior wit.

Shortly after this pantomime Falstaff dismisses Caius, and Pistola joins Bardolfo in ceremoniously escorting the Doctor out. The two clap their hands and carol an 'amen' the while. When Falstaff turns his attention to his current lack of funds, Bardolfo and Pistola become restive and hope to deflect attention from the unwelcome subject by joining their master in celebrating the enormity of his girth. Pistola understands and celebrates enormity, just as he despises little people (such as Doctor Caius). However, it cannot fail to register with him that Falstaff is broke, and therefore will not be able to pay his wages. When Falstaff requires him to deliver a letter, he declares 'I wear a sword through my belt' and refuses point blank to oblige, as also does Bardolfo. It is all the occasion Falstaff needs to sack the pair of them.

After the first scene Pistola acts almost entirely in tandem with Bardolfo. Having sold to **Ford** the information that Falstaff is shortly going in pursuit of his wife, Pistola plays little proactive part in the gulling of Falstaff, only taking the opportunity to exert physical force or malice when called for. It is, after all, a farrago dreamt up by women, and as far as Pistola is concerned, women are for one thing only . . .

Pistola joins Bardolfo in returning to the Garter Inn in time to introduce Mistress Quickly (Act 2 Scene 1). Falstaff dismisses the pair of them, but they return with Ford who is disguised as 'Master Fortuna'. They then hover in the background, agog as to whether Falstaff will take the bait proffered him, which to their huge satisfaction he does. Thereafter they stick close to Master Ford and assist the latter in searching his house for the interloper (a fact surely not lost on Falstaff from within his basket) (Act 2 Scene 2). Pistola's contribution is inevitably clumsy and noisome.

In the final scene (Act 3 Scene 2) Pistola is on hand to join in the drubbing meted out to Falstaff by virtually the entire community of Windsor.

The conclusion to the opera will be rather lost on Pistola since he would infinitely prefer a good fight to cheerful moralizing.

Il Podesta di Como (*La Battaglia di Legnano*). See **Mayor of Como**

Preziosilla (*La Forza del Destino*). Young gypsy girl.

Preziosilla's lively presence in the central acts of the opera provides an essential relief from the surrounding tragedy. The light-hearted fatalism of her fortune-telling provides a slick contrast to the death-obsessed passion of the three main protagonists. Superficially Preziosilla provides the justification for the opera's title, for the destiny which she reads in **Carlo**'s palm, and in those of the soldiers going to war, is fixed and immutable. In the original version of the opera (and Rivas's play) **Alvaro**'s suicide would seem to corroborate Preziosilla's fatalism. However in the revised edition the message would seem to be that destiny can be side-stepped through the power of Christian love, compassion and humility.

Preziosilla is unfailingly cheerful. She may be the mouthpiece of doom for some, but she is not herself affected. She remains objective and stands aside from the prevailing obsessions. She can be amused by the way the main protagonists lacerate themselves. Her calling and background also contrast dramatically with the solemnity and idealistic passion of Padre **Guardiano** and his monks. It is almost as though Verdi and his librettists are saying, 'Look, there is another way. Life does not have to be so miserable. It is only human beings that make it thus. If you would renounce all attachments and wander the Earth's surface as I do, living off my wits, you might be a lot happier for it'. But nobody is listening.

In Act 2 Scene 1 Preziosilla sees straight through Carlo's disguise. This is typical of her; she sees the truth and is not afraid of voicing it. She knows that the majority of human beings are consumed solely with cares concerning the morrow. Because she lives somewhere suspended between present, past and future she has no fears for her own morrow and, not being locked in the negative feedback of care and anxiety, she can intuit other people's needs and fears. Thus when the new recruits to the army are lamenting their lot she succeeds in taking them out of themselves. When the soldiers look like lynching **Melitone** she averts a riot by exercising a little psychology. She defuses the situation by diverting the soldiers' energies into concentrating on their common aim, the successful prosecution of the war (Act 3 Scene 3). That by so doing she succeeds in altering the destinies of some of the soldiers, who undoubtedly would have been court-martialled and shot had they succeeded in lynching Melitone, is just another illustration of the way in which Preziosilla influences people's lives.

Preziosilla acts as a tonic for all who come into contact with her. She is always cheerful and optimistic. She may well be employed by the army to recruit but there is nothing sinister in this. She is above all a gypsy and a wanderer who refuses to align herself with any specific cause, other than the cause of freedom within the constraints that fate, as she knows only too well, always places on freedom.

Priestess (una Sacerdotessa) (*Aida*)
Appears in Act 1 Scene 2, when she leads the invocation to mighty **Phtha** to hearken to the Egyptians' plea for succour in the forthcoming battle with the Ethiopians. The solo voice of the Priestess is the only solo soprano voice to be heard in the opera apart from that of **Aida**. It fills a similar function to the 'Voice from Above' at the conclusion of the *auto-da-fé* scene in **Don Carlo**, moving the focus away from the here and now towards the numinous. Since the entire Egyptian way of life was suffused with a sense of the immanence of the deity this is especially apposite at this juncture of the opera.

A Prior of Milan (Un Priore di Milano) (*I Lombardi*)
The Prior of Milan proclaims **Arvino** leader of the Lombard Crusades in the opening scene of the opera.

Giovanni da Procida (*I Vespri Siciliano*). Sicilian patriot.
Procida is the figurehead for the Sicilian resistance movement against the French occupation. When the opera opens he is abroad scouring Byzantine and Spain in search of assistance and funds for the resistance. But his search is in vain and he returns home with the sole intention of exhorting the Sicilians to help themselves.

Act 2 of the opera opens at the moment Procida returns to his homeland (his greeting to his beloved fatherland, O *patria, o cara patria* is reminiscent of **Oberto's** return from exile in Verdi's first opera). The aria *O tu Palermo* is justly famous, being one of Verdi's finest cantalenas, combining Procida's twin emotions of tender love for his homeland and passion to ensure its resurgence. He knows that his first job will be to activate the apathetic Sicilians: '*Siciliani, ov'è il prisco valor?*' ('Sicilians, where is your former valour? Up, rise up to victory and honour'). Procida's voice is a rallying cry to the people of Sicily who gather around their hero.

Procida immediately despatches one of his companions to announce his return, another to summon **Arrigo** and the Duchess **Elena** to him. 'In darkness and in silence let us ripen our revenge. The cruel oppressor does not fear and does not expect', he exhorts his compatriots, 'the great hour has struck at last. You will only be able to die content if Sicily is redeemed'. Procida's first entrance establishes him as a formidable adversary to the French viceroy, **Monforte**. The rest of the drama will resolve into a battle of wills between the two leaders.

Procida loses no time in organizing an insurrection. He readily falls in with Elena's suggestion that the wedding ceremony of Palermo's engaged couples should be the occasion for a denouement. Procida is in his way every bit as unscrupulous as is Monforte. He is adept at lofty rhetoric but at base concerned only to see the fulfilment of his chosen objectives. He takes on the mantle of *agent provocateur* and wilfully encourages the French officers **Roberto** and **Tebaldo** not to hesitate to take their chances with the Sicilian girls. The officers are easily persuaded that they are only exercising a victor's prerogative. The Sicilian men are inevitably enraged when the French make off with their brides-to-be. Procida is not slow to take advantage of the situation, taunting the men for their lack of courage in allowing their sweethearts to be so easily poached from them. In this he is aided and abetted by Elena, whose desire for vengeance is no less intense and who looks upon Procida as a father-figure.

When Arrigo is taken prisoner by the French Procida naturally assumes that Arrigo is in mortal danger. It is consequently a monumental shock to Procida when Arrigo dramatically prevents Elena's attempt to assassinate Monforte (Act 3 Scene 2). He can only assume that Arrigo has gone over to the enemy (which in a sense he has). Procida's immediate reaction is to excoriate the young man. He pays no heed to his pleas for mercy. All the Sicilians join him in denouncing Arrigo as a traitor.

Procida is forthwith imprisoned, as is Elena. He must assume that his crusade to save Sicily is finally at an end. Incarcerated in the castle dungeons he is powerless to do any more to further the cause of Sicilian independence. For Procida to be deprived of his liberty is the greatest calamity imaginable. All his life he has devoted himself to the cause of liberty; indeed he has enslaved himself to it. But it has been an enslavement he has willingly undertaken. He longs for 'a day, an hour', to be at liberty again in order to effect his life's mission. It is at this nadir of his career that he receives word that assistance is at hand. A ship from Aragon is on its way, 'laden with gold and arms'. But Procida is powerless. It is just one of many moments that Verdi seems particularly to relish, where fate appears to be hopelessly stacked against the chief protagonists. It is also exactly in these moments of extremity that Verdi's true genius shines (in this he bears comparison with the English novelist, Thomas Hardy, whose tales exude a similarly doom-laden atmosphere).

In spite of his desperation Procida scorns Arrigo's attempts to plead for his life (Act 4). When he learns that Arrigo is, in fact, Monforte's son it only confirms his sense of the utter hopelessness of his – and the Sicilians' – predicament. As the moment of his execution draws near he calls on Elena to join him in prostrating themselves before God. It is in this moment that Procida is rescued from being just another egotistical chauvinist such as de Silva (*Ernani*), di Luna (*Il Trovatore*) or Don Carlo (*La Forza del Destino*). Faced with death he has the humility to seek redress from a higher authority. As it turns out he is pardoned at the eleventh

hour. It is a scene of immense power which invokes the scene in Dostoevsky's *The Idiot* where the author so vividly describes through the character of Prince Myshkin his own experience of mock execution. However where Dostoevsky was changed for life by the experience Procida appears unrepentant. He does not truly learn from the experience, does not learn the lesson so patently waiting to be learnt, namely, that there is a greater reality than that of nationalistic chauvinism.

As soon as Procida is released he sets about organizing the massacre he has so long dreamt of. Arrigo and Elena's wedding ceremony shall be the occasion for the massacre. Procida makes the mistake of telling Elena: 'just as soon as you have spoken your ardent yes, and when the sacred bells give the announcement of the performed wedding, at that instant in Palermo and everywhere let the massacre begin!' It never occurs to Procida, so blinkered is he, that Elena may have another agenda now and that the thought of her wedding being the occasion of a massacre may be deeply repugnant to her. If it does occur to him the thought probably gives him a grim satisfaction, since he will find it well-nigh impossible to forgive Elena for so blithely accepting the fact that Arrigo actually belongs to the enemy's camp. When Elena remonstrates with him Procida's only response is derisory: 'Holier to you than the fatherland's soil? (that is, her marital vows). Ah, I would give everything'. Even his honour.

It is incomprehensible to Procida that Elena should even contemplate marrying an enemy. When Elena defends Arrigo (Act 5) Procida dares her to go to the French and denounce him. He displays no hint of compassion for Elena's predicament; indeed he is now as remorseless as de Silva (*Ernani*). He piles on the emotional blackmail. 'Think of your brother. He pointed out to you the path of honour'. His blandishments do not have the effect he hoped for.

Suddenly Elena refuses to proceed with the marriage ceremony. Once again Procida sees himself thwarted. He could not possibly have predicted who will redeem the situation for him. It is his arch enemy Monforte who refuses to countenance Elena's refusal to marry Arrigo, who joins the young couple's hands together and thus precipitates the denouement. At the end of the opera Procida's calls for vengeance are echoed by the Sicilians as they hurl themselves on Monforte and the French. As it was for de Silva, in the earlier opera, it is the moment to which Procida's entire life has been leading. We can only be certain that it will bring him no happiness.

Q

Mistress Quickly (*Falstaff*)

Mistress Quickly is one of the most down-to-earth and warmly recognizable roles in the entire repertoire (she would have found an ideal interpreter in the legendary Ernestine Schumann Heink, with her enormous girth and multitude of children).

Quickly is a generation (or two generations in **Nannetta**'s case) older than the other women in the opera, and has 'seen it all before'. She has learnt that a degree of cynicism is advisable in this world, and can be comfortably equated with realism, particularly when it comes to dealing with the opposite sex. She acts as a sort of catalyst to the younger women, goading them into action when necessary but also restraining them. She loves to gossip, because through gossiping she finds a window onto the 'human comedy'. She is always, to an extent, on the periphery, commenting on the antics of the chief protagonists. Thus she makes the perfect go-between, having no agenda of her own other than to enjoy herself.

Quickly has nothing but contempt for **Falstaff**, whom she sees as epitomizing all that is worst in the male sex: vanity; self-indulgence and egotism. In Act 1 Scene 2 she comments 'Falstaff deserves no consideration'. She therefore relishes every moment of her interviews with him at the Garter Inn (Act 2 Scene 1 and Act 3 Scene 1). She is entirely ingratiating, and he never for one moment suspects her of irony. In the normal course of events it is unlikely that she would

ever give Falstaff the time of day. She has no problem with the gentry *per se* – it is part of Quickly's charm that she is by nature egalitarian – but she strenuously objects to a member of the gentry taking advantage of those less exalted.

Quickly knows how to lead Falstaff into the trap the 'Merry Wives' lay for him; it is simply a matter of flattery. Tell him he is the world's greatest lover and he will believe it. She has no problem in convincing him that his love is returned in equal measure by both **Alice** and **Meg**. When Falstaff wonders if the two women know about each other, Quickly reassures him, 'Heavens, no! Women are born deceitful' (Act 2 Scene 1). Again the irony is lost upon Falstaff. Similarly, Quickly's response to Falstaff's offer of remuneration – 'Who sows grace reaps love' – is a masterpiece of ingenious irony. Falstaff refers to her as 'Mercurio femina' ('Mercury woman'). He does not realize the half of it. If he would but reflect he would remember that Mercury, aside from being the winged messenger, was notoriously two-faced, his alter-ego being the 'Trickster'.

Mistress Quickly describes, for the benefit of Alice and Meg, her interview with the good knight, with 'uninhibited relish' (Act 2 Scene 1) and then joins with alacrity in the preparations for Falstaff's arrival. Placed on guard she is the first to see **Ford** arriving home, just as Alice's interview with Falstaff is getting under way. She is genuinely frightened, not of Ford himself, but on Alice's behalf.

That Quickly is not truly intimidated by Ford is proven by the fact that she does not hesitate to scotch his plans for his daughter to marry **Doctor Caius**. She knows perfectly well that this is the last thing that Nannetta wants, and resents the way in which Ford high-handedly signs away his daughter's happiness. (Who knows if Quickly herself did not have to endure an unwanted husband in her youth? Such an assumption would certainly assist the interpreter of the role.) Once having taken on Nannetta's cause she determines to see it through, and while everybody else is enjoying beating up the unfortunate Falstaff, Quickly devotes herself to plans to ensure that the marriage of Doctor Caius and Nannetta is scotched. She must have considerable fun dressing up **Bardolfo** in the unlikely guise of the fairy queen, and will have ineffable satisfaction in witnessing Ford's dismay when he realizes that his daughter has sprouted a huge rubicund nose (see **Synopsis**). In the event Caius is horrified, which will only intensify Quickly's enjoyment, for she must surely class Doctor Caius, along with Falstaff, as a puffed-up nincompoop.

The true irony in the role of Quickly is that she has more in common with Falstaff than anyone else in the opera. She remains always apart; she has a very clear philosophy of life, culled from many years of having to live it. She is beyond the age when she has to endure the earthquakes of passion that convulse youth, but she retains a huge capacity for enjoying life. She is in fact the one woman Falstaff *should* have wooed. She would have made a home for him and looked after him whilst at the same time standing no nonsense from him. And together they could reflect, by the fireside, that 'every mortal being laughs at every other, and that the best laugh of all is the one that comes last' (*Tutto nel mondo*).

R

Radames (*Aida*). Captain of the guards.
Radames's first utterance in the opera is to enquire of **Ramfis** whether the priest has consulted holy **Isis**. In truth he is not concerned about the goddess's decree. His sole interest is in the prosecution of his love for the slave girl, **Aida**.

In that he is ultimately united with, and dies in the arms of, Aida, Radames's destiny cannot be viewed as tragic. He achieves what he wants, which is not to say that he does not endure much anguish as he is forced to sacrifice his youth, his career and ultimately his life. But since youth, career and life mean nothing to him without Aida, the sacrifice must be seen as integral to his life's mission.

The celebrated aria *Celeste Aida* (Act 1 Scene 1), in which Radames declares his devotion to the slave girl, is a paradigmatic manifestation of Romantic love; an heroic man dedicates himself to an heroic endeavour in order to win the bride of his desires. All other considerations are secondary. This must never be forgotten when reviewing Radames's career. He is a lover first and a warrior second, although the two appear inextricably entwined. In order to win the bride he must prove himself worthy.

The two women who battle for his affections are both princesses and require that their man should be worthy of the affection they offer. Having said which Radames does not realize that Aida is a princess. In fact he loves her partly because she is not a princess. But he knows that the only way he could have any hope of marrying an Ethiopian slave in preference to the King's daughter, who pines after him, is by proving his prowess to be so indispensable to the **King** that the latter can have no alternative but to grant his dearest wish, however preposterous. That serving the needs of his country happens to offer Radames the prospect of a successful prosecution of his love is entirely coincidental, but means that he need not endure anything like the anguish that Aida is forced to endure. For, by praying for Radames's safe return, Aida is, by definition, indulging in thoughts traitorous to her country.

When Radames finds himself betraying *his* country, it is by default (Act 3). He had no way of knowing that Aida was the Ethiopian King's daughter. True, he should never have divulged such sensitive information to an Ethiopian, of whatever station, but then his faith in Aida is total. His faith only turns out to be misplaced because Aida succumbs to her father's blandishments.

The real dilemma for Radames is how to circumvent **Amneris**'s passion for him. This is by no means an easy matter. For while there is nothing in Radames's role to indicate that he has ever returned Amneris's love, Amneris does say that she longs for her love to 'come . . . give new life to me, *once more*, with words of love!' (Act 2 Scene 1). This may be delusion on her part or may indicate that there was a time when Radames did indeed return her love. By rights Radames should be overjoyed that Amneris offers him her love. To choose her slave in preference is a gross insult to the princess. It is unlikely that Radames would ever have managed to get away with such an affront had **Amonasro** not intervened and saved him the necessity of putting it to the test. Because he is consumed with erotic passion Radames never stops to consider the true impossibility of what he intends. Even if the King were to grant him Aida's hand in marriage, Amneris would, sooner or later, have found occasion to effect her revenge. Aida herself points this out to him (Act 3).

Radames is appalled when he realizes that he has betrayed Egypt to Amonasro and immediately surrenders himself in the full expectation that he will be executed. At this moment he does not know whether Aida has just used him in order to assist the Ethiopian cause. Yet he is quite clear that he has nothing to be ashamed of.

The role of Radames has the rare distinction of being one of Verdi's very few truly heroic leading tenor roles. His heroic status is ensured by virtue of his utterly single-minded devotion to his doomed love. When he surrenders himself at the end of Act 3 he has never been so alone.

The traitor has always been, and will always be, abhorred by all. Yet Radames does not deserve to be abhorred. His only sin is that he loves where he should not. (A psychologist might point out that this in itself is significant. Radames has a need to transgress the weight of his responsibilities to the State which place too great an onus on his young shoulders; he needs to feel there is a way out for him and consequently his eyes alight on the one girl most unobtainable and most clearly destined to compromise him.) When he declares to Amneris (Act 4 Scene 1) immediately subsequent to having been caught in the act of committing high treason: 'Before the gods and man I feel myself neither traitorous nor guilty. My incautious words revealed the secret – it is true – but both my

thought and my honour remain unstained by guilt', he enunciates a simple truth. This is no mere special pleading, although it would be undoubtedly be taken as such by the priests.

At the same time Radames still has no guarantee that he has not simply been Aida's dupe. It would be all too easy for him to wash his hands of her and take Amneris's offer of life and love. The fact that he does not represents a considerable moral victory for him. For at this juncture he is totally bereft of any certainties. All he knows is that he loves Aida and that he does not love Amneris. Deprived of Aida he has no reason to endure. When he learns that she is still alive (Act 4 Scene 1) his resolve is enormously reinforced, in spite of the fact that he can have no hope of seeing her again. The very fact that she is alive reminds him of the light which has guided him to date and to which he must remain faithful to the end.

Radames's reward is to discover that Aida's love was no illusion, that she feels as passionately for him as he for her. The poignancy of the final scene lies in the fact that they die not for each other but in spite of a world which has made of their love an impossibility.

Raffaele von Leuthold (*Stiffelio*). A nobleman.
Raffaele sums himself up when, witnessing **Stiffelio**'s magnanimity (Act 1), he remarks to himself 'such goodness should arouse in me feelings of remorse, but first I will taste the cup of pleasure'. There is no malice in Raffaele. He is simply a voluptuary ruled first and foremost by his appetites, giving little thought to the consequences to himself or to others. Having said which it would be a mistake to think of him as simply a happy-go-lucky philanderer *à la* Duke of Mantua (*Rigoletto*). Were he that he would simply absent himself from the court at the first signs of trouble and give not another thought to **Lina**. As it is he allows himself to become increasingly embroiled, until finally he pays for his thoughtlessness with his life. Initially his main concern is to avoid a scandal – he is after all a member of the nobility – and, if

Stankar is to be believed, a rather dubious member at that (see Act 2 where Stankar describes Raffaele as 'an adventurer who wraps his life in mystery' and then addresses him 'noble count Raffaele you are nothing but a foundling').

Raffaele's first concern is to prevent Lina blurting out the truth about their affair. He cannot have failed to be aware that Lina suffers acutely from pangs of conscience over her infidelity to Stiffelio. Both Lina and her father firmly lay the blame for her fall from marital constancy at Raffaele's feet. 'I was taken by surprise', is Lina's sole defence 'I do not love you in my heart'. The turning point for Raffaele comes when Lina declares she does not love him and implores him to leave the castle. Raffaele is wounded where it most hurts: in his vanity. From this moment he is determined to stand by her. She has suddenly become as inaccessible to him as when he first succeeded in seducing her, and it is the challenge of the inaccessible that gets Raffaele out of bed in the morning.

When Stankar challenges Raffaele to a duel he is at first reluctant. His justification for his reluctance can be taken at face value, namely that he considers the contest too unequal in view of Stankar's advanced years. Again, it is his vanity that speaks. He reckons without the passion that fuels Stankar's determination. As it is Raffaele is never given an opportunity to defend himself. Stiffelio's advent outside the church puts a stop to his duel with the old man and once he has fled the scene of his crime (after the conclusion of Act 2) Stankar is not disposed to offer him a second chance. Raffaele cannot accept that he has been bested in the contest with Lina's husband. He must at all costs win. If he really cared about Lina he would accept her explanation that she does not really love him and, realizing the intense anguish he causes her, would leave, but, as is the way with all casual seducers, Raffaele is fundamentally narcissistic, his only reality being what confronts him when he looks in the mirror.

His ignominious flight from Stankar's castle deals a fatal (literally, as it turns out) blow to his self-image. He cannot allow himself to be bested. He sends a letter to Lina imploring her to follow him. The letter is intercepted by Stankar and in any case his flight is thwarted by **Jorg** who, presumably acting on instructions from Stiffelio, persuades him to return to the castle. Confronted with the man that he has so shamelessly cuckolded, Raffaele remains dignified. When Stiffelio demands what he would do if Lina were free, he answers by saying 'what you suppose is impossible', by which he infers that he would do the honourable thing; marry her and take care of her. Stankar recognizes that this is an impossibility. On no account is he going to allow his beloved daughter to be married to such a man, and besides, he is not going to live with the scandal that such a conclusion would inevitably cause.

Raffaele becomes a victim of his own vanity. Had he not returned to the castle, had he accepted Lina's plea to be left to her fate, he could have continued his lifetime's 'dedication to pleasure' . . . until the next catastrophe.

(See also **Godvino**.)

Ramfis (*Aida*). Chief of the priests. The patriarchal figure of Ramfis harks back to the character of Zaccaria in *Nabucco*, though Ramfis is afforded little of the lyricism which alleviates the predominantly exhortatory nature of his predecessor's role. Ramfis, as is the way with pontiffs of all denominations, is humourless. He knows his role is to act as intermediary between the gods and men, and he plays it to the hilt. It is made abundantly clear from the outset that true power in the land belongs to the priesthood, not to the **King**, who is represented as little more than a puppet. When Radames is discovered to have betrayed his country he surrenders himself not to the guards, but to the priests (Act 3). It is the priests who put him on trial and immure him.

Ramfis is on stage at the opening of the opera (Act 1 Scene 1), apprising **Radames** of the progress of the war. This might seem a curious occupation for the chief priest; certainly it is unaccustomed in our Western culture that rigidly bifurcates the world into the secular sphere on the one hand and the religious on the other. But in terms of the theocratic society of the Egyptians, as in most pre-Christian societies, nothing could be done in the secular sphere without reference to the spiritual. It is not up to the King to name the supreme commander of the armies, but to holy Isis to whom the State must turn for enlightenment. This is established right at the outset when Ramfis tells Radames that he will inform the King of the Deity's decree.

While ostensibly a theocracy ensures that no human being can achieve absolute power, in practice it gives to the priesthood – and Ramfis in particular – extraordinary influence (in this respect see also **Inquisitor** and *Don Carlo* conclusion/**Friar**). Nothing can be done without reference to him. To what extent he believes that his judgement comes directly from the gods, or goddesses, is immaterial. Ultimately all prescriptions, secular or otherwise, will be filtered through his personality. 'Glory to the gods! Let all remember it is they who rule our destinies! Only the power of the gods can dictate the warrior's fate', Ramfis declares immediately after the King's exhortation to his armies to go forth 'unto war and death' (Act 1 Scene 1). Ramfis is always at hand to remind the King and his people that they are as nothing without the consent and endorsement of the gods.

Before Radames can go to war he must go to the temple and invoke mighty **Phtha**, life-giving spirit of the world who, 'from nothingness didst draw the seas, the earth, the heavens', to protect him and ensure the defeat of the enemy (Act 1 Scene 2). 'May the sacred sword, tempered by the gods, become in your hand blazing terror and death for the enemy', Ramfis solemnly proclaims. This scene is one of the most impressive in the score, culminating in Ramfis joining Radames in the almighty invocation *'Immenso Phtha!'* ('Great Phtha!'). The scene successfully places the human drama in a numinous perspective. This is a rare occurrence in Verdi's output, which by and large is exclusively humanistic in emphasis. But it would have been impossible to write an opera set in ancient Egypt without giving a central position to the role

of religion in society. Religion was a part of the everyday fabric of existence in a way that we today find impossible to conceive.[62]

Verdi's attitude to priesthood of any denomination was ambiguous at best and downright hostile at worst. By the end of the opera when **Amneris** is hurling abuse at the priesthood for their pitiless condemnation of Radames, the audience's sympathy has been manipulated round to viewing Ramfis and his entourage purely from a negative perspective. Yet this is entirely due to the fact that the audience's sympathy is by now not only with the lovers but also with the dispossessed Amneris. We know that Radames's treachery was inadvertent. Yet it was no more inadvertent than, for instance, was John Profumo's in the scandal which rocked the British establishment in the 1960s. Profumo was disgraced because of his failure of responsibility appropriate to a minister of state. A theme that recurs repeatedly in Verdi's operas is the inescapable obligation placed upon the individual once he commits himself in any capacity to the political arena (see *I Due Foscari*, *Boccanegra*, etc.). By the penultimate scene of the opera Ramfis and his priests may be viewed as the villains (in the same way as the Council of Ten appear in *I Due Foscari*). But they are only attempting to see justice done as prescribed in their statute books. Radames is given the opportunity to justify himself but remains obdurately silent. He knows that from the priest's point of view there is no justification for his crime.

---

[62] Edward T. Hall, writing about the Hopi Indians in his book, *The Dance of Life* (1983), has perfectly encapsulated the way in which life was ordered in so-called primitive cultures: 'Religion is the central core of Hopi life. Religious ceremonies perform many functions which, in American and European cultures, are treated as separate and distinctive entities, quite apart from the sacred: disciplining children, for example; encouraging rain and fertility; staying in sync with nature; helping the life-giving crops to be fertile and grow; relating to each other; and initiating the young into adulthood. In fact religion is at the centre, not only of social organisation, but also of government which is part and parcel of Hopi ceremonial life'. Precisely the same could be said of life in ancient Egypt.

In the triumphal scene (Act 2 Scene 2) where **Amonasro** pleads with the Egyptian King for mercy Ramfis is not inclined to countenance leniency: 'let the will of the gods be done! Destroy, O King these ferocious slaves, the gods have condemned them to die'. From his perspective the Ethiopians do not deserve mercy. They have risen against the Egyptian people and, by association, the Egyptian gods. And they have been defeated. Now they have been given into the Egyptians' hands and should be exterminated, not only because they are the enemy, but because they have blasphemed. For Westerners, accustomed to a monotheistic religion, it is best to conceive of the Egyptian gods in the same way as the old Teutonic tribes viewed Odin and his clan. The gods take a personal and very human interest in all that transpires below. They are personally aggrieved if affronted, and must be appropriately appeased.

When Ramfis observes that the Ethiopians are the enemy and are 'brave, with hearts eager for revenge' (Act 2 Scene 2) he is enunciating a simple truth. Realizing that the general consensus is against him he proposes a compromise that once again is simple common sense. If the Ethiopians are to be released, on the understanding that their King, Amonasro, is supposedly dead (which he is not) and will no longer pose a threat, the Egyptians should keep **Aida** and her father as hostage (Act 2 Scene 2). The wisdom of this advice will shortly become all too apparent.

Ramfis fulfils the role ascribed in astrological law to Saturn: Old Father Time who acts always as a restraining influence on the more chaotic forces of Mars (War), Venus (love) and Mercury (communication) *et al.* Without that restraining influence the body politic would be severely compromised by the passions of its individual members.

Ramfis and his priests may appear hateful in the eyes of Amneris but they constitute a necessary evil without which anarchy would prevail. The life of the emotions, of personal passions, is by definition anarchic. The opera, *Aida*, can be seen, in one light, as a moral fable illustrating how easily society may be undermined by such anarchic forces. Without the presence of the likes of Ramfis society would fall apart. Rigidly hierarchical priesthoods within absolutist regimes (the Spanish Inquisition was a prime example) came to fulfil something of the function of a secret police force. The only difference between the Egyptian priesthood and the FBI or the KGB in the 21st century AD is that the Egyptians still acknowledged a power beyond their own particular mandate. Their powers were thus circumscribed. Modern history has made all too clear the desirability of ensuring such circumscription. Without it the exercise of power recedes even further. It becomes a licence to give free rein to every unscrupulous or malicious instinct, in other words to exemplify the worst of which human beings are capable.

Ramfis appears never to lose sight of the fact that he is but an agent for forces greater than himself. Whether such forces exist is, in the last analysis, of no consequence. It is the fact that he believes that they do that matters and provides an automatic brake on him allowing his own personal passions to dictate the nature and extent of the proscriptions he imposes.

Raymond (*Jerusalem*). Gaston's steward.

Raymond plays a small but crucial role in the action of *Jerusalem*. He follows his master into exile after the latter has been excommunicated and outlawed for the attempted murder of the **Count of Toulouse**.

At the opening of Act 2 Raymond arrives at the hermit's home (**Roger**'s cave) in the mountains of Ramla. He has been in the desert for many days and is dying of thirst. He informs the hermit that there are many others in a similar plight and Roger rushes off to their rescue. Raymond is then accosted by **Hélène**, who has also recently arrived in Palestine. Hélène recognizes Raymond and is overjoyed to learn from him that Gaston is still alive, though imprisoned by the **Emir** in Ramla.

There is no equivalent to Raymond's role in *I Lombardi*, where the equivalent role to that of Gaston (Oronte) has a different profile (see **Oronte**). Symmetrically the role of Raymond replaces that of **Pirro** (Pagano's treacherous ally in crime). Pirro, like his master, is guilt-ridden and, also like his master devotes his remaining days to repentance and the search for atonement. Since Gaston is innocent of the crimes of which he is accused and Raymond is in no way implicated, the interest in the role is correspondingly less. He nevertheless plays a crucial role by alerting Hélène to Gaston's presence in Palestine.

Renato (*Un ballo in maschera*). Riccardo's secretary.
Historical Note Renato's historical counterpart, Johan Jakob Anckarström, was never, as in the opera, an ardent friend and supporter of the king. He was an army officer who belonged to a group of Swedish nobles disillusioned by the autocratic rule of King Gustave III. In 1792 Anckarström murdered Gustave at a masked ball. Unlike Renato in the opera he was not granted forgiveness but was seized and shortly after executed.

The destiny of Renato is inextricably intertwined with that of his master, Riccardo. Our perception of Riccardo is influenced throughout by the way in which he is perceived by those around him. To a certain extent this is true of anyone in the theatre and in life. But in the case of Renato it is amplified by the violence of his transformation. Principally this occurs when he discovers that it is his own wife that he escorts to safety from the embraces of Riccardo (Act 2). Up until this moment Riccardo has held centre stage. From this moment it is Renato that takes over. His perception of Riccardo is fatally coloured by his jealous fury. As with Shakespeare Verdi is never so potent as when exploring the ravages wreaked by the emotion of jealousy, whether justified or not. On the whole it is only in comedy that the jealousy is justified. In tragedy it is almost always unjustified, the example *par excellence* being *Otello*. Renato is no exception.

In the opening scenes of the opera Renato is portrayed as being just another sycophant courtier. He is concerned only for his master's safety. He genuinely believes that the well-being of his world depends on the well-being of the Governor. He assiduously pursues rumours of a conspiracy (as is evidenced by his producing an incriminating document in his confrontation with **Samuel** and **Tom** [Act 3 Scene 1]). Renato tries vainly to prevent Riccardo visiting **Ulrica**. Why? Because he knows the escapade will present him with a security nightmare. When he arrives at Ulrica's cavern and is greeted by Riccardo himself it is to be told by the seeress and her gullible followers that he will be the one to kill Riccardo. Such an eventuality is unthinkable to him. He dismisses it with hardly a second thought. However he does reflect to himself: 'Evil fortune forever hovers even over the greatest triumph in which a hypocritical Fate conceals an evil end'. It is as though even in spite of himself he has a premonition of catastrophe.

Renato's devotion to Riccardo is absolute. Where Riccardo is feckless, Renato is stalwart, where Riccardo loves, Renato obeys. He plays the part of the loyal servant as though his life depended upon it, as indeed it does. The life that he deems possible is at stake; the life where all is ordered and he can know his place and fill it to the best of his abilities. That place is bolstered by a wife whom he loves and who loves him, a son whom he loves and who loves him; and above all a boss who is ensuring that the natural order of things pertains. Riccardo, as figurehead, is a symbol of stability and reassurance that the world is a safe and stable place to be in. If Riccardo's life is threatened, so is Renato's whole universe, because he has never looked beyond the exigencies of the present.

It is thus profoundly shocking to discover that there is a plot against Riccardo's life. It is all the more shocking for Renato to learn that Riccardo has betrayed him with his own wife. In the moment that **Amelia**'s veil falls off (Act 2) Renato's universe crumbles. Suddenly, where everything before was well-ordered and predictable, all is now chaos and contingency. If Riccardo and Amelia can both betray him then there is nothing in the world to be relied upon. He must accept the utter meaninglessness of life. He must accept, as he has always at some deep subliminal level believed, that the world is ruled by a hypocritical fate. Once he has incontestable proof that this is in fact the case, that there is nowhere to turn, it is almost a relief.

Renato can now give vent to all the rage and madness that he has for so long refused to acknowledge (Act 3 Scene 1). Having all his life evaded the shadow part of himself it now takes centre stage with a vengeance. At first his anger is directed at his wife, the mother of his son, who has been the still point in a changing world, to whom he has always turned to for solace and who has now pulled the house down around his ears. Now she has become a whore who sells herself to the highest bidder. She is not worthy of his love, let alone his respect, nor the love of their son. She must die before he has time to feel remorse. Only some vestige of what has sustained them for so many years restrains him now. Her plea to him: *Morrò, ma prima in grazia* (Act 3 Scene 1) bids him, for the first time since the thunderbolt struck, to listen and to reflect. And in that moment of reflection he is forced to concede that the true object of his wrath should not be Amelia, but Riccardo himself.

Amelia is the personification of weakness, of all that he knows himself to be. He knows that he cannot sustain his anger towards Amelia, for she has been the victim as much as he has. It is his recognition of this fact that prompts the aria *Eri tu*. Riccardo's betrayal is doubly painful because Renato was in the very act of risking his own life in order to protect him at the very moment that Riccardo was making love to his wife. It is small consolation to him to humiliate Amelia by forcing her to be the one to choose who shall exact revenge on Riccardo. It is, however, enormous consolation that it is he who is chosen (Act 3 Scene 1). He is now fatally blinded. It never seems to occur to him that he may be doing Riccardo and Amelia an injustice. Blood must flow, because that is the only way Renato knows how to make recompense. He plunges the dagger in at the

very moment that Riccardo is taking his last farewell of Amelia. He actually hears Riccardo saying farewell, but it does not stop him in his resolve. The moment he has done the deed, however, he must know that he has made a fatal mistake. Such violence can never be a solution. He has paid the price for placing his whole life-illusion in the custody of another human being. (See also **Amelia**.)

Riccardo (*Un ballo in maschera*). Governor of Boston.

Historical Note The character of Riccardo is based on Gustave III (1746–1792), King of Sweden (1771–1792). Gustave, in common with Francis I of France (the model for the Duke of Mantua [*Rigoletto*]), was one of the most colourful monarchs to grace the pages of European history. He was a highly intelligent and gifted man who combined his artistic sensibilities with a considerable political acumen. Gustave was much impressed by the court and philosophy of Frederick the Great of Prussia (who at one point employed at his court the French philosopher, Voltaire). Gustave thereafter carried with him the Enlightenment ideal of the philosopher king.

As his reign progressed Gustave became more and more autocratic and thus found himself at the centre of much disaffection amongst the nobility. In 1792 he was shot and mortally wounded by Johan Jakob Anckarström at a masked ball at the Royal Opera House in Stockholm. Although he was probably homosexual Gustave was, unlike his operatic counterpart, married and his son, Gustave IV, succeeded him as King.

In the first half of the opera it might seem that Riccardo is a reincarnation of the Duke of Mantua (*Rigoletto*). Certainly there are many points of similarity with the feckless Duke. Riccardo's tossed away remark to **Oscar** at the opening of the opera with regard to the ball planned for the following evening: 'You have not forgotten any beauty?' could have come from the lips of the Duke himself. Yet it quickly becomes apparent that Riccardo is in fact only concerned that one particular beauty, namely **Amelia,** should not have been omitted from the list.

It is well known that the historical inspiration for the character of Riccardo, Gustavus III of Sweden, had homosexual tendencies. Some Directors have been inclined to infer a homosexual relationship between Riccardo and his page boy, Oscar. There is some justification for this, yet it would confuse the drama's central dilemma if portrayed in the opera house. That Riccardo harbours a genuine passion for Amelia and is torn asunder by guilt because of it cannot be denied. He knows that he should not love his best friend's wife, but he cannot help himself. Once having acknowledged it he knows that he has to relinquish it. In this lies the true nobility of his character. It could be argued that he merely wants to ship **Renato** and Amelia off to England at the end of the opera in order to be rid of a troublesome problem, and perhaps resume his preference for homosexual *amours*. Such an interpretation is not borne out, either by the text or Verdi's music.

Riccardo's life is lived principally for the external pomp of courtly responsibility and duty. He is not a free agent. His soul yearns for something richer and deeper than the aridity of his daily existence and he believes he has found it in Amelia, even though he knows that their relationship is an impossibility. There are some men who only choose relationships which they recognize from the start to be an impossibility. It is as though they know that for them it is not a long-term solution to their life needs. It is often a feature of men whose psyches are Oedipal – mother-obsessed – men who have great difficulty in making their own way in the world. A court is like a womb in which the psyche can feel itself comfortably cocooned from the world, so that even if the duties of office are onerous, there is always someone to turn to for each and every eventuality. It is notable that Riccardo appears throughout the opera to be incapable of making any resolution without reference to Oscar. He may not act upon all Oscar's recommendations (although he certainly does in the opera), but he needs a

sounding board for his ideas and projections. He is, in fact, chronically insecure.

Riccardo knows what a Governor should be, but does not know if he can live up to the expectations of the role life has thrust upon him. The trust which he places in Oscar lies in the fact that he projects his own younger self onto him. Oscar can see things clearly in a way that Riccardo never can, because Oscar has a freshness of perception that he, by necessity, has lost. Riccardo visits **Ulrica's** cavern, not because he deems it necessary in order to reach a judgement concerning Ulrica's fate, but primarily because Oscar tells him to. Riccardo cannot afford to shoulder the responsibility of every petty judgement presented to him. He does not want the responsibility. He does, however, want to be loved. He needs to feel that he is universally approved of. He needs to know that his fame into the future is assured. It gives him pleasure to be magnanimous, and because it gives him pleasure he prefers to be magnanimous.

Twice in the opera Riccardo saves one of his subjects from a desperate predicament: Ulrica, the seeress, in Act 1 Scene 2, and Renato at the conclusion of the opera when he makes it known that his final command as ruler is that Renato shall not be prosecuted. In Act 2 Riccardo attempts to save Amelia from humiliation, but in this he is unsuccessful. Cynically it could be said that he is only concerned to save his own skin, but that would be to ignore the central trait in Riccardo's character, by which he always manages to transcend the pettiness of his personal desires, his need to be loved. The turning point in his feelings for Amelia comes when he witnesses, quite unexpectedly, the stress that their liaison is causing her. When she appears at Ulrica's cavern seeking means of obliterating from her mind the love that she feels for Riccardo, the incongruity of Amelia's presence at such a place suddenly alerts Riccardo to his own selfishness in allowing the affair to linger. It propels him into action. Either the affair must be consummated or concluded. He determines to follow Amelia to the gallows hill, whither she has been sent by Ulrica in search of an ameliorative herb.

The thought of Amelia in such a place at midnight arouses Riccardo's most protective instincts. This is the crucial distinction between Riccardo and the Duke of Mantua. The Duke is a satyr; his only concern is his own pleasure, with no reference to the other's well-being or happiness. He is entirely outer directed. Riccardo, on the other hand, is, if not inverted, certainly introvert. He also is only concerned for his own gratification, but for him gratification involves the approval of others. The Duke cares nothing for the approval of others. He is an island unto himself. His courtiers are little better than dogs, squabbling for scraps around his feet. If they were all to vanish overnight he would barely notice their absence the next morning. For Riccardo his courtiers are the essential bolster for his fragile ego. In reality he needs Renato's friendship and support far more than he needs Amelia's love. Even more does he need Oscar, because Oscar is on hand almost, it would seem, around the clock. Because Oscar is young and ingenuous he both confirms Riccardo's own sense of maturity and substance, and also keeps his responses spontaneous and ensures he never loses sight of a wider perspective.

Why does Riccardo need Amelia? The answer only becomes clear in the latter part of the opera when it is suddenly revealed that Amelia has a son (Act 3 Scene 1). Up until this point we have only been made aware that Amelia is another man's wife, but not that she is a mother. This suddenly puts a whole new perspective on the situation. It does in fact save Amelia's life. Riccardo must be aware that Amelia is a mother, though he makes no reference to it. It is, however, probably a central factor in his need to see her as redeeming angel. She represents everything which he most lacks: solidity, affection, stability.

As is the case with all such affairs, that of Riccardo and Amelia takes wing on a mutual recognition of reciprocal needs. Amelia chafes against the constraints of motherhood and marriage to a respectable pillar of the community. Riccardo longs above all to be validated, which for him is synonymous with being needed. He picks up on Amelia's need probably long before she does his. Because Riccardo is essentially re-active. He waits for events to move him along. He does not initiate. If he did not happen to be at Ulrica's cavern on the night that Amelia decided to consult the seeress, who knows how the affair might have evolved? It is Amelia who initiates the crisis by determining to have done with it.

The sudden realization that he is about to lose her galvanizes Riccardo. His desperation in his scene with Amelia (*Teco io sto*) is very real. Repeatedly he implores her to shine the light of her love on him. He needs to be convinced that he is loveable, not just as figurehead and ruler, but as a man. He also needs to be mothered, nurtured and reassured. At the same time he dreads it. Why, otherwise, would he turn to Amelia? In purely pragmatic terms the support he gains from Renato is far more essential to him than what he seeks from Amelia. But he cannot have both. The two are mutually exclusive. He must choose. He cannot choose so he resolves to rid himself of the problem. His decision to post Renato to England can be viewed in the same light as Claudius's decision to send Hamlet to England. There may be no evidence to suggest that he plans on having Renato and Amelia murdered en route, but he certainly wants rid of a conundrum he cannot solve.

There is more than a whiff of the martyr about Riccardo. He needs to cast himself as the lonely isolated figure who can never find the ultimate appeasement that he so desperately seeks. He must conceive of life as tragedy, otherwise he has no sustainable role to play in it. The death which befalls him is in reality self-inflicted. He is repeatedly warned throughout the opera, first by Renato, then by Ulrica and finally by Amelia that his life is in danger and he takes no preventive measures. Life itself is a burden to him of which he wishes to be relieved. Also he needs to feel that he can live life on his own terms, answerable to no-one but himself – and

Oscar. Such a thing is an impossibility for anyone in a position of authority. The boss is always answerable to those over whom he has jurisdiction. Riccardo knows this but he cannot live it. He acknowledges freely that he has lost all right of jurisdiction the moment he deceived his best friend.

In Act 2, when Renato implores him to flee from the encroaching conspirators, Riccardo reflects to himself: 'Traitors, conspirators, these men who threaten my life? Ah, I too am a traitor to my friend – It is I who have wounded his heart. Were I innocent, I should challenge them. Now, guilty of love, I must flee'. Ultimately Riccardo is dogged by a sense of Original Sin, a sense that whatever he turns his hand to it is doomed, by simple virtue of the fact that it is he who initiates it. His death is inevitable because he has no confidence in his ability to contend with life.

Don Riccardo (*Ernani*). King **Carlo**'s equerry.

Riccardo is responsible for a total *volte face* in the events of Act 1. He enters at the moment that **de Silva** has just discovered **Carlo** and **Ernani** in **Elvira**'s apartments and is challenging both to defend themselves in single combat with him (Act 1 Scene 2). When **Iago** announces the Royal Equerry de Silva splutters: 'He is welcome witness to my vengeance'. To which Riccardo pompously replies: 'Only loyalty and homage are due the king'. These words have a dramatic effect on de Silva but not for the reason Riccardo might expect. For de Silva had not realized that Carlo is the king. Now alerted to the fact he immediately assumes he is mistaken in assuming Carlo guilty of lascivious thoughts towards his betrothed and humbly begs forgiveness for his audacity. Riccardo is gratified to observe 'the fires of jealousy flare up more ferociously in de Silva's breast, but respect for his king takes the place of wrath'. Riccardo is mistaken. De Silva's jealousy is not inflamed; it is totally assuaged. So powerful is his sense of duty and honour he cannot even conceive that his king might have designs on another man's betrothed. De Silva's conviction is confirmed when Carlo confides his ambition to show himself worthy of the imperial crown. De Silva joins Riccardo in reassuring Carlo of his certainty that he will rise to the challenge. On Riccardo's part this is mere sycophantic verbiage, whereas for de Silva it is almost an article of faith (as becomes clear later when he allows Elvira to go with Carlo, totally unsuspecting that Carlo is eloping with her).

In Act 2 Riccardo accompanies Carlo in pursuit of Ernani and participates in the search of de Silva's castle, but does not contribute to the argument otherwise. In Act 3 he accompanies his master to the tomb of Charlemagne, having received information that the conspirators against Carlo's life are to meet there. He is instructed by Carlo to sound the castle cannon three times should Carlo be elected Emperor while he is holding his vigil. When Riccardo gives the sign that Carlo is indeed elected the new Emperor is so overjoyed that, after initially thundering at the conspirators, he makes his first act as Emperor to grant them clemency. Riccardo takes great pleasure in officially announcing Carlo's election. He joins all the assembly in praising Carlo for his clemency.

Riccardo (*Oberto*). Count of Salinguerra.

Riccardo is a pale imitation of a hero. He is in fact more an anti-hero, in the mould of his namesake in *Un Ballo in Maschera* and of the Duke of Mantua in *Rigoletto*. Unlike them, however, Riccardo is not self-determining. He becomes a pawn in the manipulations of the women that he has recklessly taken into his life and ultimately pays the penalty for his arrogant thoughtlessness. It never occurs to him that **Leonora**, having been deserted, would pursue him. His is the type of nature that grabs whatever it wants, whenever it wants, heedless to others' misery, or simple inconvenience. He has the arrogance of inherited wealth and position. There is, however, no malice in his nature. It is more a question of lack of intelligence (compare with Raffaele in *Stiffelio*).

Riccardo's opening words to **Cuniza**'s attendants, 'Here I am among you! The day hastened by my desires has now arrived', confirms at the outset that his desires are the determining feature in his destiny. He revels in the hedonistic company of women. He requires that his desires be propitiated. It is his natural right. He has no doubt that the 'roaring of envious foes' are entirely unwarranted and deserve to be summarily silenced (Act 1 Scene 1). He takes great pride in the conquering might of the Salinguerra. He is cavalier in his regard to his bride-to-be's obscure misgivings. He tells her, 'if one sad memory remains with you it will be a sore grief for me' (Act 1 Scene 2). Cuniza dutifully asks his forgiveness. Interestingly Riccardo joins her in expressing the sentiment, 'torn between hope and fear my heart knows not what to say'.

Riccardo is supremely unconscious. He has never taken responsibility for his life or his actions. At a deep subconscious level he no doubt senses trouble, but he is never still within himself long enough to hear the premonitions that may emerge from below the brittle life of the ego.

Cuniza is an altogether stronger personality. Riccardo has found a bride who can effectively take care of his emotional life for him, leaving him free to rampage through the world. Presumably Leonora carried a similar attraction for him. But Leonora happened to be the daughter of his enemy. No doubt the seduction of Leonora started as a prank, a means of humiliating further an irritating foe. If there is any sincerity in Riccardo's later protestations of genuine love for Leonora, it is because in the process of seduction he has discovered something in himself that actually responds to Leonora, on a level beyond his usual philosophy of 'smash and grab'. However, a man like Riccardo could never allow himself to become sentimental in an affair which was initially motivated by lust.

As it turns out he has no option but to take Leonora seriously. Confronted with his guilt Riccardo's immediate, panic-stricken reaction is publicly to accuse the accuser. He left Leonora because she was faithless, he tells Cuniza (Act 1 Scene 2). Nobody believes him and thereafter he can only bluster, impotent to change a situation where the odds are hopelessly stacked against him. The righteous indignation that the entire court directs against Riccardo is reminiscent of the opprobrium poured on the head of Don Giovanni in Mozart's opera. The message is the same: Society will not tolerate the mockery of its injunctions and conventions. The miscreant must pay the penalty of social outrage.

Riccardo's cause is lost when his bride refuses to marry him and insists that he must marry Leonora. On the evidence of Solera's libretto it would seem that Riccardo cares little either way. Like the innkeeper in Sartre's *La Nausée*, he appears to be capable only of feeling an emotion when confronted. In other words when alone he feels nothing. His emotions have to be activated by the catalyst of someone else's emotions.

Thus when confronted by Cuniza and Leonora (Act 2 Scene 2) he is suddenly struck with remorse. He becomes entirely passive, delighted that Cuniza forgives him. He demands that she command him ('*Imponi!*'). He is amazed that Cuniza should require him to give himself to Leonora. Such selflessness is quite beyond the range of his comprehension. He is shamed by her and when she becomes insistent he dutifully offers his hand to Leonora, saying, 'my hand alone can make answer for me'. In this one moment he achieves a degree of self-appraisal and sense of responsibility that has hitherto been absent. He is suddenly aware that he is only going to cause Leonora further grief since he has committed himself to fighting her father. The only way to make sense of Riccardo's *volte face* at this juncture is to assume that he is suddenly moved by a sense of compassion. Cuniza's sacrifice has awakened his own better nature. In his newly awakened state the demands of honour have become inexorable.

Riccardo goes to the woods to fight **Oberto** and, as he knew would be the case, slays the old man. Now suddenly the whole edifice of his former personality collapses. He is consumed with remorse and shame. He realizes that he has just lost any possibility of a relationship with Leonora. Has he not been responsible for causing her untold grief? The sound of prolonged groans from the dying Oberto only confirms his resolution to flee. He falls to his knees and prays for mercy.

The last we hear from Riccardo are the words of the letter that he sends to Leonora, read out by Cuniza, begging for Leonora's forgiveness and confirming his devotion as in the first days of their love. Riccardo is no doubt aware when he writes the letter that it will not be received well. Nor indeed is it. Leonora wants to hear no more of him. One may hope that Riccardo will not go on to repeat the mistakes that have brought upon himself and those around him so much suffering. But one cannot have much confidence.

RIGOLETTO

Opera in 3 Acts. Libretto by Francesco Maria Piave, after Hugo's drama, *Le Roi s'amuse* (1832).

First performance: 11 March 1851 at the Teatro la Fenice, Venice.

Cast:

The Duke of Mantua (tenor)
Rigoletto: his jester, a hunchback (baritone)
Sparafucile: a professional assassin (bass)
Count Monterone (baritone)
Marullo (baritone)
Borsa: a courtier (tenor)
Count Ceprano (bass)
An Usher (bass)
Gilda: Rigoletto's daughter (soprano)
Giovanna: her nurse (mezzo-soprano)
Maddalena: Sparafucile's sister (contralto)
Countess Ceprano (mezzo-soprano)
A page (mezzo-soprano)

Time: 16th century
Place: Mantua

Synopsis

Act 1 Scene 1   A magnificent hall in the Ducal palace, Mantua. At the rear, doors opening on to brilliantly lit rooms. A cheerful crowd of courtiers and ladies, elegantly dressed. Pages wander through the throng. The festivities are at their height. Sounds of music come from within.

The Duke and Borsa enter from a room on the right. The Duke tells Borsa how he has observed a 'beauty' every Sunday at church over the past three months. Borsa wonders if the girl knows who her admirer is. The Duke confirms that she does not. Where does she live, Borsa wonders. In a remote street, a mysterious man goes there every night, the Duke replies. It will soon be revealed that the mysterious man is the Duke's court jester, Rigoletto.

A group of ladies cross the room, attended by their knights. Borsa comments on the number of beautiful women. The Duke remarks that Ceprano's wife takes the prize. Borsa is nervous that Ceprano might overhear the Duke. 'What do I care!' says the Duke and then expounds his happy-go-lucky philosophy of life (*Questa o quella*). He laughs at the fury of jealous husbands: 'Fidelity – that tyrant of the heart – we shun like a bad disease'. Meanwhile Ceprano is keeping a close eye on his wife who is escorted by another man. More courtiers arrive.

Ceprano has decided it is time to depart. The Duke fervently kisses the Countess's hand and, to the lady's embarrassment, declares his passionate love. He offers her his arm and goes out with her. Rigoletto, having observed this performance, goes up to Ceprano and goads him, commenting that he already has a pair of cuckold's horns growing on his forehead. Ceprano impatiently shrugs off the jibe and follows his wife. Rigoletto and the courtiers laugh at the Count's receding back. At this juncture there is no hint of the animosity that pertains between Rigoletto and the courtiers.

Marullo enters excitedly. He has some gossip to impart, namely the Rigoletto has a mistress (he has obviously seen Rigoletto together with Gilda and misconstrued their relationship). The Duke returns, complaining about that 'bore', Ceprano, but extolling the virtues of his wife. Rigoletto blithely suggests the Duke abduct Ceprano's wife. When the

Duke replies, 'And what about the husband?' Rigoletto suggests some alternatives: imprison him, exile him or behead him! The Duke and Rigoletto continue to banter at Ceprano's expense, but the latter, who has returned, is outraged and draws his sword. In the melée which follows Ceprano calls on the courtiers to assist him in avenging himself on the jester, while the Duke warns Rigoletto that he may become the victim of the fury he provokes. Rigoletto, with fatal hubris, refuses to be intimidated. He imagines his role as court jester gives him immunity.

The party is now disrupted by the sudden arrival of Count Monterone, the father of one of the Duke's conquests. Rigoletto mocks the old man's indignation. Infuriated, Monterone rails against the Duke and his 'orgies'. Even if the Duke were to have him executed he will return, 'a horrid ghost, carrying my skull in my hands, crying to God and man for vengeance!' The Duke orders his arrest, to the consternation of all present. Monterone haughtily curses the Duke and his jester. So that Rigoletto should be in no doubt that he is included in the curse Monterone turns to him and says, 'and you, serpent, who laugh at a father's grief, my curse upon you!' Rigoletto is horrified. Monterone exits, escorted by two halberdiers and reiterating his curse. All assure him that 'his hour of doom is nigh' before adjourning to another room.

Act 1 Scene 2   The end of a cul-de-sac. Rigoletto's modest house is on the left. There is a small courtyard, enclosed by a wall, containing a large tree with a marble bench beside. A door in the wall opens onto the street. Above the wall a terrace over a loggia. From the second storey a door opens onto the terrace, which can also be reached by a staircase in the front. To the right of the road there is a much higher wall, beyond which can be seen one side of the Ceprano palace. (These details are all pertinent to the scene which is to unfold.)

It is night. Rigoletto enters from the right, his cloak tightly wrapped around him. He is followed by Sparafucile who carries a sword beneath his cape.

Rigoletto is haunted by Monterone's curse. Sparafucile accosts him. Assuming he is a robber Rigoletto assures him he has nothing to give him. Sparafucile assures him, in return, that he does not want anything. He is there to offer his services. For a slight fee he will rid Rigoletto of a rival – 'and you have one', he adds. He reveals that he knows Rigoletto keeps a woman in the house. Like the courtiers Sparafucile is under the misapprehension that Gilda is Rigoletto's mistress. Presumably Sparafucile also knows that the Duke is conducting an affair with the girl. Rigoletto is alarmed by the fact that Sparafucile knows he keeps a woman in the house. He demands to know the man's terms. Sparafucile tells Rigoletto his *modus operandi*, how he uses his attractive sister to lure his unsuspecting victims. Rigoletto balks at the idea of employing the assassin, but wants to know where to find him should he so wish. Sparafucile tells him he will be in the same place each night. He disappears into the night.

Left alone Rigoletto reflects on how similar his and the assassin's vocations are (*Pari siamo!*). Sparafucile kills with his sword, he with his tongue. His mind reverts to the curse placed upon him. Suddenly he is overcome with self-pity and fury at the lot fate has meted out to him. He rails against the insolence of the courtiers. Once again his mind reverts to Monterone's curse. He wonders pathetically if some disaster may not befall him, then he dismisses the notion and enters the courtyard of his house. He is met by a young girl who flies into his arms. '*Figlia!*' ('Daughter!') he greets her. '*Mio padre!*' ('My father!') she responds. For the first time in the opera the audience learns the true identity of the woman in Rigoletto's life, his beloved daughter.

After the initial rapture of their reunion Gilda notices that Rigoletto is distracted. She urges him to unburden himself to her: 'Tell your poor daughter. If there is any mystery – tell it freely to her. Let her know who her family are', she says. 'You have no family', is Rigoletto's curt reply. Gilda is insistent: 'What is your name?' but Rigoletto is not paying attention. He is still brooding on Monterone's curse and Sparafucile's proposition. It has surely occurred to him that if Sparafucile knows there is a woman in his house there is no reason why others should not know, including his enemies at court. Gilda assures him that she goes out only to church, which helps to reassure Rigoletto. She resumes her questioning. She wants to know who her mother was. Mention of his lost love induces in Rigoletto a softening of mood. He tells Gilda how her mother took pity on him when he was alone, deformed and poor, and how she loved him, which was nothing short of a miracle for the cripple. He tells Gilda how her mother died and how Gilda is now all that remains to him. '*Dio, sii ringraziato!*' ('God be thanked for this'), he concludes. Gilda is overcome with grief and compassion for her father's pitiful lot in life. She begs him again to tell her his name. Rigoletto will not. His mind reverts again to Monterone's curse, a doting father himself, whose daughter has been dishonoured. Never will Rigoletto allow a similar fate to befall his beloved Gilda.

Gilda begs that she at least be allowed to see the town. They have apparently been living in Mantua for three months and for all that time Gilda has remained incarcerated in the house. Rigoletto is adamant; she is never to go out. He calls to the house and Giovanna emerges. Rigoletto demands to know if he is ever observed when returning home. Giovanna reassures him and confirms that the outside gate always remains locked. His tone softening, Rigoletto begs Giovanna to watch over 'this pure flower' (*Ah! veglia, o donna, questo fiore*), and never to let anything sully his daughter's virtue. Gilda tries to comfort him, reminding him that they both have a guardian angel in Heaven, namely Gilda's mother.

Rigoletto is distracted by a noise from the street. He opens the gate and goes out. As he does so the Duke, disguised as a student, quickly passes into the courtyard and hides behind the tree. He throws a purse to Giovanna to ensure her silence. When Rigoletto returns and asks if anyone has ever

followed them back from church she glibly replies, 'Never!' Astonished exclamations are heard from the shadows as the Duke recognizes Rigoletto. Rigoletto reiterates his instructions to Giovanna not to admit anyone into the house. When she asks, 'Not even the Duke?' Rigoletto barks, 'Especially not him' and bids his daughter 'good-night'. The Duke is even more astonished to realize that Gilda, far from being Rigoletto's mistress is, in fact, his daughter. Rigoletto recapitulates his plea to Giovanna to watch over his daughter, embraces Gilda and departs, closing the gate behind him.

The moment the two women are left alone Gilda cries out: 'Giovanna, I am ashamed'. 'Why?' Giovanna asks. Because, Gilda replies, she has not told her father about the young man who has followed them to church and who inspires her with thoughts of love. Giovanna sees no harm in it. As far as she is concerned the young man seems a 'fine man and a real gentleman'. Gilda declares impetuously that she does not want a gentleman or a prince. She would love her admirer more if he were poor. This is the Duke's cue to come forward from his hiding place. He signs Giovanna to leave, then he kneels before Gilda and, echoing her own words, declares his passionate love for her. Gilda, finding herself alone with the object of her erotic dreams, is panic stricken and begs him to leave. The Duke, who has vast experience of this sort of situation, pours out a wealth of ecstatic praise of their mutual love (*É il sol dell'anima*). Gilda has no defence against such an assault. 'Ah these are the tender, beloved words which have haunted my virgin dreams', she comments softly in an aside. She is completely overwhelmed by the strength of the Duke's ardour. She asks his name and the Duke, who has overheard Gilda's declaration that she would rather her lover were poor, tells her that his name is Walter Maldè and that he is a poor student.

Giovanna enters in a flurry. She has heard footsteps from outside, suggesting the imminent arrival of someone. It is in fact Ceprano and Borsa, come to have their revenge on Rigoletto by abducting the girl they imagine to be Rigoletto's mistress. Giovanna, on Gilda's instructions, ushers the Duke out of the garden gate from where he can make his getaway undetected. Before he departs the Duke and Gilda sing a rapturous farewell (*Addio, speranza ed anima!*). The Duke exits, escorted by Giovanna. Gilda remains behind, watching the gate through which her paramour has left. In her aria (*Caro nome*) she dwells lovingly on the name of her beloved, Walter Maldè. Taking up a light she ascends by the stairs to the terrace. Marullo, Ceprano, Borsa and courtiers, armed and masked, are in the street, to the right. As Gilda disappears into the house they enter the garden. Their voices are heard during the concluding bars of Gilda's aria extolling her beauty and expressing amazement that the hunchback should be keeping such a beautiful mistress.

Rigoletto returns. His mind is revolving incessantly around Monterone's curse. Ceprano, on seeing the jester, is all for killing him, but the others restrain him. The commotion alerts Rigoletto to their presence. However, it is so dark that he is unable to see them. Marullo explains that they have come to kidnap Ceprano's wife as a prank. Rigoletto, ever suspicious, demands to know how they intend gaining admittance to Ceprano's palace, which is immediately opposite. Surreptitiously Ceprano gives Marullo his key which the latter then passes to Rigoletto (it should be remembered that throughout this scene Rigoletto does not realize Ceprano is present). Rigoletto can feel the Ceprano crest on the key and is mollified. Reassured that they are not after his daughter he offers to wear a mask and join in the prank. Marullo puts a mask on Rigoletto, at the same time blindfolding him with a handkerchief so that now Rigoletto can see nothing at all. Marullo then orders Rigoletto to hold the ladder which the others have already put up against Rigoletto's terrace. Rigoletto does not realize, until it is too late, that he has in fact been blindfolded; thus he unwittingly aids and abets the abduction of his own daughter.

Marullo points out to his confederates that Rigoletto can neither see nor hear for his

blindfold. The courtiers excitedly whisper to each other that, 'At last this tireless mocker of men will be made a laughing stock'. Some of the group climb up to the terrace. They break open the door, then descend to open the gate for the others, who enter from the street. Then they come out, dragging Gilda behind them. She is gagged. As she is pulled across the scene she loses her scarf. She is heard calling on her father to help her. Rigoletto does not hear her. However when he touches his eyes and realizes that he is blindfolded his thoughts immediately turn to his daughter. He tears off the blindfold and mask. By the light of a lantern, left by one of Marullo's men, he sees Gilda's scarf, then the open gate. As he enters the courtyard Giovanna emerges, in a state of terror. Rigoletto stares at her, speechless. Then he tears at his hair and, with a huge effort, manages to cry out: '*Ah! La maledizione!*' ('Ah! the curse!'), before falling unconscious to the ground.

Act 2   The salon of the Ducal Palace. Two doors, one on each side wall, a larger one on the back wall. Full-length portraits of the Duke and his wife hang on the walls, flanking the great door. A huge table covered with velvet, beside it an armchair.

The Duke enters. He is obviously upset: *Ella mi fu rapita!* he bewails. It is a new experience for the effete and lustful Duke, who has been used all his life to having what he wants when he wants, regardless of whether the object of his desire belongs to someone else. Having made his getaway from Rigoletto's house some instinct apparently prompted him to return, only to find the house deserted and no sign of Gilda. He has now convinced himself that Gilda, 'alone among women has been able to inspire (him) to a faithful love' (*Parmi veder le lagrime*). In due course it will become apparent how the Duke deceives himself, but for the moment he is firmly convinced of the sincerity of his emotions.

Marullo, Ceprano, Borsa and other courtiers enter. They inform the Duke that they have abducted Rigoletto's mistress, much to the Duke's amusement and delight.

They then describe the events in graphic detail (*Scorrendo uniti remota via*). When he asks the conspirators where they have taken the girl they reply that they have brought her to the palace. The Duke is overjoyed to have Gilda so close and rushes off to complete his seduction.

Rigoletto enters. Although he pretends indifference he is distraught. The courtiers gleefully observe his distress. Rigoletto instantly realizes that they must all have been in on the conspiracy. However, he continues his pretended buffoonery while surreptitiously searching for clues. He spies a handkerchief on a table. Thinking it might be Gilda's he picks it up and examines the monogram. It is not Gilda's. He asks if the Duke is sleeping and is told he is.

A page enters with a message that the Duchess (who does not appear in the opera) wishes to speak with her husband. The page knows that the Duke has just been with his courtiers and refuses to believe that he is asleep. Borsa then tells him that the Duke has gone hunting. Again the page refuses to believe it. The courtiers, who are clearly used to covering for the Duke, lose patience and flatly tell the page that the Duke can see no-one at present. Rigoletto has been following this conversation and is by now convinced that the Duke is closeted with his beloved daughter. He flings himself among them, demanding that they surrender his daughter. The courtiers are aghast, having believed up until now that the woman they have abducted was Rigoletto's mistress. Nevertheless when Rigoletto leaps towards the main door leading to the Duke's apartments they bar his way. All the pent-up rage and frustration at years of humiliation now erupt from Rigoletto (*Cortigiani, vil razza dannata*). He tells them that while everything can be bought if the price is right his daughter is beyond any price. Nothing will prevent him from protecting his daughter. Again he makes for the door, and again he is stopped by the courtiers. Rage and indignation turn to desperation as he orders them to open the door to him. He struggles with them for a moment, then draws back, defeated. Overcome with

self-pity he tells them bitterly: 'You are all against me'. Weeping, he begs Marullo to tell him where they have hidden his daughter. The courtiers remain silent and intransigent.

Suddenly a door from a room to the left flies open and Gilda comes rushing out. She flings herself into her father's arms. Pathetically Rigoletto exonerates the courtiers: 'It was only a joke, wasn't it? I who wept before, now I laugh', he says. His daughter is weeping. She asks to speak to her father alone. Imperiously Rigoletto dismisses the courtiers: 'Off with you, all of you – and if your Duke should dare to come, tell him not to enter, for I am here'. It is an unpardonable way for a court jester to address his master's courtiers, but Rigoletto is past caring. As far as he is concerned the Duke, in dishonouring his daughter, has abandoned all right to respect. The courtiers are unruffled; 'With children and with madmen it is often best to make believe', they murmur as they depart. Rigoletto has fallen into a chair, overcome with emotion.

Alone with his daughter at last Rigoletto tells her to relate her story. He is wearily resigned as to the inevitability of what will unfold. Gilda relates how she was first approached by a handsome young man at church (*Tutte le feste al tempio*), how he came to the house and told her he was a poor student, and how she was abducted. Rigoletto is beside himself: 'I asked infamy, O God, only for myself so that her rise in life might be as great as my fall'. In a devastating image which sums up his life's pathos he exclaims: 'Ah, beside the gallows one must build an altar! But all now is lost, the altar has fallen into ruin'. He tells Gilda to give her tears free rein. What more is there for the two of them to hope for? He tells her darkly that there is something he yet must do, but then they will leave 'this house of doom' forever.

At this moment Monterone is escorted in by halberdiers. He is being led to the dungeons. He stops by the portrait of the Duke and reflects bitterly how his curse seems to have been totally ineffectual, and the seducer of his daughter will live on blithely, perpetrating the misery he leaves always in his wake. Rigoletto, who has been haunted by Monterone's curse, now feels nothing but compassion for the old man and swears that both he and Monterone shall be avenged. He addresses the portrait himself: 'Silvano, vendetta, tremenda vendetta di ques'anima è solo desio . . .' ('Yes, a terrible revenge is my sole desire'). (In reality this soliloquy is more reflection than enunciation; Gilda notices only 'fierce joy' flashing in her father's eyes.) Rigoletto utters one word: 'Vendetta!' ('Revenge!'), but Gilda does not want to hear of revenge. She pleads with her father to forgive the Duke, reflecting to herself that even though he betrayed her she still loves her seducer. Rigoletto will not now be dissuaded from his purpose. He has not forgotten the offer made to him by Sparafucile.

Act 3   The right bank of the Mincio river. To the left, a dilapidated two-storey house on the ground floor of which is a rustic wine shop. A rough stone staircase leads to a loft above, with a balcony. The outer wall facing the audience has no shutters and a bed inside is clearly visible. Downstairs in the wall of the house facing the road is a door which opens inwards. The wall is full of cracks and holes so that the interior can easily be observed. The rest of the stage represents the deserted fields along the river which runs behind a ruined parapet in the background. Mantua is in the distance. It is night.

Gilda is in the road on the right with her father, who is obviously tense. Sparafucile is seated at a table in the wine shop and is cleaning his sword-belt. He remains unaware of what is transpiring outside.

Rigoletto asks his daughter in incredulous tones: 'And you still love him?' He confirms his determination to be avenged. Gilda reiterates her plea to him to forgive the Duke. She fondly believes that the Duke adores her. Rigoletto has brought her to the inn to disabuse her. He leads her to an opening in the wall of Sparafucile's tavern from which she can see what transpires within. The Duke has just entered, wearing the uniform of a cavalry officer. Gilda is distraught. The Duke demands a room and some wine. Rigoletto

assures his daughter that these are the Duke's habits. As though to prove the fact the Duke launches into his aria (La donna è mobile) in which he unblushingly expounds his philosophy that women are not to be trusted; they will all betray you sooner or later. The man who gives himself to a woman is a fool.

Sparafucile has returned with a bottle of wine and two glasses which he places on the table. Then, with the butt of his sword, he strikes twice against the ceiling. At the signal a buxom young woman in gypsy dress comes running down the stairs. The Duke tries to greet her with a kiss but the girl, Sparafucile's sister Maddelena, eludes him. Meanwhile Sparafucile has gone out into the road. He speaks softly to Rigoletto, requiring to know if the Duke is Rigoletto's intended victim and whether he is to live or to die. Rigoletto merely remarks that he will return later to conclude their business, thus tacitly confirming that he wishes Sparafucile to carry through the assassination. Sparafucile moves off, around the house in the direction of the river. Gilda and Rigoletto stay in the road.

The Duke is now alone with Maddelena and commences his seduction (Un dì, se ben rammentomi). Shamelessly he tells Maddalena that ever since he first set eyes on her he has adored her. Maddalena knows his type and is not deceived. She mocks his empty flattery and makes it clear that she can look after herself. Nevertheless she finds him undeniably attractive (Bella figlia dell'amore). Gilda, watching from outside, is devastated and becomes convulsed with weeping. Rigoletto makes little attempt to console her. His only concern is that Gilda should realize the true nature of the man she adores and give her consent to Rigoletto wreaking vengeance for them both. Principally he seeks to salve his conscience. There is nothing Gilda can do or say to stop the assassination that Rigoletto has arranged. The very fact that the Duke has been lured to the inn by Maddalena's charms is proof that Rigoletto has instructed Sparafucile to exercise his trade. For Maddalena is the assassin's chief means of surprising his victims when they lie defenceless in the arms of his sister.

Satisfied that he has secured Gilda's acquiescence Rigoletto orders her to return home. 'Take a horse and some money, then dressed as a man in the clothes you find there, leave at once for Verona', he commands her. He tells her he will meet her there the next day. Gilda begs her father to leave with her. Rigoletto refuses. He has no other excuse than 'it is impossible'. Gilda leaves. The Duke and Maddalena, meanwhile, are comfortably ensconced at the tavern table, laughing and talking together as they drink. As soon as Gilda has left Rigoletto disappears behind the house. Then he returns with Sparafucile, counting out money into the cut-throat's hands. Having given Sparafucile half his fee Rigoletto tells him he will receive the other half on completion of the job. He will return at midnight. He will himself throw the body into the river. When Sparafucile asks his victim's name Rigoletto merely replies, 'He is "Crime" and I am "Punishment"'. He leaves.

The sky darkens. A storm is brewing. The Duke is attempting to prosecute his seduction of Maddalena but the latter is distracted by the sound of thunder and also her awareness of her brother's murderous intentions towards the stranger. In spite of herself Maddalena is attracted to him and does not want to see him murdered. Her brother enters. The Duke curtly tells Sparafucile he can sleep in the stables, 'or in hell', that is, anywhere where he will not disturb his conquest of Maddalena. Maddalena attempts to persuade the Duke to leave. Sparafucile reminds her of the twenty scudi he is to be paid for the job and gallantly tells the Duke he will gladly offer him his room for the night. He leads the Duke forthwith upstairs to view the accommodation. After caustically commenting on the fact that the room is open to the elements the Duke declares himself satisfied, lays down his hat and sword and stretches out on the bed, sleepily reiterating the refrain from his melody, *La donna é mobile*. He is shortly sound asleep.

Sparafucile returns downstairs where Maddalena is seated at the table, deep in thought. Sparafucile drinks from the bottle of wine the Duke has left unfinished. Maddalena attempts to persuade her brother to forget the murder – it is only twenty scudi after all. Sparafucile ignores her and commands her to fetch the young man's sword. She goes upstairs and stands looking at the Duke as he sleeps. She retrieves the sword and then, having closed the balcony, descends again.

Meanwhile Gilda has been home and donned the man's clothing as her father bade her. But instead of journeying on to Verona she has returned to the inn, determined at all costs to save her lover. She now appears in the street wearing boots and spurs and walks slowly towards the inn. She looks in through the crack in the wall. Sparafucile is still drinking the wine. Gilda's worst fears are confirmed when Maddalena enters with the sword and pleads with her brother not to kill the young man. Sparafucile obdurately ignores her. He throws her a sack, telling her to mend it. 'Once I have cut his throat, your Apollo will wear it when I throw him into the river', he says. Maddalena, who is growing desperate, suggests an alternative plan whereby she can keep her lover and he can gain his twenty scudi: murder the hunchback when he returns. Sparafucile is appalled at the suggestion. What would that do for his reputation? He is a man of honour. His client has bought his loyalty. Seeing the uselessness of pursuing this course of argument Maddalena determines to wake the Duke and help him escape. Gilda, in spite of the fact that she is watching a rival, is touched by the girl's devotion. Sparafucile will hear none of it. They need the money. However he does concede that if someone else comes to the inn before midnight then he shall die in the Duke's place. Maddalena is well aware of the unlikelihood of such an eventuality.

Gilda realizes that she has been presented with an opportunity to die for her lover, the 'ingrate', as she refers to him. A thousand thoughts rush through her mind; what about her father? How will he survive without her? From a bell tower half-past eleven strikes. Sparafucile realizes he must do the deed. Maddalena threatens to become hysterical and Gilda realizes there is no time to lose. If a woman like Maddalena can weep for him, how can she stand by and do nothing? She resolves that even if the Duke has betrayed her love she shall die for him. She knocks at the door. Maddalena and Sparafucile can hardly believe their ears. They think at first it must be the wind, but then they hear Gilda's voice announcing herself as 'a beggar seeking shelter for the night'. A long night it will be, Maddalena observes darkly. Sparafucile sees a perfect opportunity to silence his sister and gain his scudi. He seems to have forgotten about his honour as a professional assassin. He goes to the cupboard to fetch a dagger. Sparafucile conceals himself with his dagger behind the door which Maddalena opens to admit Gilda. Sparafucile closes the door. All is dark and silent.

Rigoletto is seen advancing down the road towards the inn. He is wrapped in a cloak. The violence of the storm has abated. At last the moment of vengeance is at hand, he reflects, almost joyously; 'For thirty days I have waited, weeping tears of blood behind my fool's mask'. Seeing the door to the tavern closed he assumes it is not yet time. Midnight strikes. Sparafucile emerges from the tavern demanding to know who is there. Rigoletto comes forward. Sparafucile tells him to wait where he is, and goes inside returning almost immediately with a sack containing, if Rigoletto did but know it, his dying daughter. Sparafucile is anxious to throw the sack forthwith into the river, but Rigoletto is insistent he wishes to do it himself. He presumably wants time to gloat over the corpse of his tormentor. Sparafucile can do nothing to dissuade the hunchback so, having received his payment, bids Rigoletto to make sure he disposes of the body where the river is deepest, wishes him a curt goodnight and disappears inside.

Left alone Rigoletto can barely contain himself. Prefiguring the moment when Iago stands over the prostrate body of Otello, *Ecco il Leone*, at the conclusion of Act 3 (*Otello*), Rigoletto exults in having his master at his feet. 'Here is a buffoon and here is a mighty prince! He lies at my feet! It

is he! Oh joy!' His exultation is short lived, for as he drags the sack towards the river he hears the voice of the Duke singing in the distance. In panic he turns back towards the inn. Then he cuts open the sack. To his utmost horror he discovers the dying form of his daughter. At first he cannot believe what he sees; it must be a nightmare. His Gilda is supposed to be in Verona. He knocks desperately at the door of the inn, but there is no response. Then he hears Gilda's voice. For a moment Rigoletto knows only relief and gratitude that Gilda is still alive. He begs her to tell him what happened. Gilda points to her heart where the dagger has wounded her. 'I deceived you – I was guilty – I loved him too much – now I die for him', she says. Rigoletto, realizes too late, that his frantic craving for vengeance has come back to strike him. 'She has been struck by the arrow of my righteous vengeance!' he laments bitterly. With her dying breath Gilda craves forgiveness for herself and for her lover. She tells her father she will pray for him in Heaven, where she will be reunited with her mother. Nothing Rigoletto can do or say will save her. She dies in his arms. The curtain falls as Rigoletto realizes the awful truth that Monterone's curse, as he feared all along, has been fulfilled.

Rigoletto is the bleakest of Verdi's operas, yet it is also one of the greatest. Something in the predicament of the central protagonist touched a nerve in Verdi. He wrote to Piave, his librettist: 'In my view the idea of this character, outwardly ridiculous and deformed, inwardly filled with passion and love is superb'.

Rigoletto is, throughout, a work of stark contrasts: the hedonism of the Duke versus the misery of the hunchback; the sordid lifestyle of Sparafucile and his sister versus the churchgoing propriety of Rigoletto's household; the Courtiers' callous insensitivity and brutality versus the acute sensitivity demonstrated by all the main characters, including the Duke himself; the Duke's native lust versus Gilda's purely romantic passion. These dichotomies are only the most obvious. But beyond the contrasts – the very stuff out of which great drama is fashioned – is the central figure of Rigoletto himself, the very embodiment of the human predicament: a finely tuned and sensitive soul contained within a malformed body, forced to fight for subsistence by persistently demeaning himself, struggling against all the odds to salvage a small corner of decency and self-respect, but ultimately being forced to concede defeat. So consumed with fear and paranoia is he that he cannot forestall the inevitable tragic outcome that he has for so long fought to elude. (The fate of the impresario, Serge Diaghelev, comes to mind. All his life Diaghelev had a morbid fear of drowning. How did he die? Through drowning.) Nowhere in Verdi's oeuvre is his sense of tragic fatality so explicit as in *Rigoletto*.

One does not have to search very far in order to discover how Rigoletto has succeeded in engineering his own fate. The abduction of Gilda would never have happened had Rigoletto not antagonized the courtiers. Rigoletto must inevitably blame himself for his daughter's downfall. He might excuse himself with the thought that he was only doing his job when he mercilessly mocked the courtiers for the Duke's amusement. But if that was all it was, the courtiers would never have taken his barbs to heart. It is because Rigoletto so consistently exceeds his brief that he inspires such resentment in those around him. His mockery of Ceprano (Act 1 Scene 1) is entirely uncalled for and needlessly cruel. He will pay a heavy price.

Had Gilda not been abducted it is conceivable that Rigoletto would not have known of his daughter's liaison with the Duke until, that is, his daughter had surrendered her virginity. The outcome would doubtless have been the same; Gilda would still have come running to her father. It is possible that in the course of her one night of passion with the Duke she has become pregnant; in which case it is a merciful letout that she is killed. The only option for a girl like Gilda would have been premature incarceration in a nunnery and a lifetime's repentance for a single moment of weakness.

The story of *Rigoletto* is possibly the darkest of all those Verdi set. *Macbeth* and *Otello* are cautionary tales where there is clearly explicable explanation for the tragedies. Rigoletto's ill fate is apparently inexplicable. It is the more horrific for it. The only blame that can be apportioned is to the apparent indifference of a God that allows such tragedies to enumerate.

Rigoletto (*Rigoletto*). Court jester at the court of the **Duke of Mantua**, father to **Gilda**.

'The jester, on the other hand, every time he opens his mouth, between a gibe and a prank, sows doubts, denigrating rumours, anxieties, alarms: for him the great mechanism is driven by infernal beasts, and the black wings that sprout beneath the cup-city suggest a snare that threatens it from within. The King has to play along: does he not give the Fool a salary, deliberately to have himself contradicted and teased? It is an ancient and wise custom at courts for the Fool or Jest or Poet to perform his task of upsetting and deriding the values on which the sovereign bases his own rule, to show him that every straight line conceals a crooked obverse, every finished product a jumble of ill-fitting parts, every logical discourse a blah-blah-blah. And yet from time to time these cranks, wiles, quips, jests arouse a vague uneasiness in the King: this too is surely foreseen, actually guaranteed in the contract between King and Jester, and yet it is a little disturbing all the same, and not only because the only way to make the most of an uneasiness is to be uneasy, but precisely because the King really does become ill at ease.'

(*The Castle of Crossed Destinies*:
Italo Calvino. Picador)

In a letter to Piave (1850) Verdi described Rigoletto as follows: 'outwardly ridiculous and deformed, inwardly filled with passion and love'. It is well known that Verdi and Piave caused a scandal by having the temerity to put a hunchback on the operatic stage, not just as part of the *Commedia dell'arte* interlude within a classic drama, but as the central dramatic figure possessing a complex psychological profile and demanding attention and ultimately respect as a profoundly tragic protagonist. The opera is aptly named, for Rigoletto is the only true protagonist, the other chief characters inviting scant scrutiny by comparison. It is Rigoletto and his fight with a malign destiny that takes centre stage from his first entrance and remains there until the conclusion of the drama.

Rigoletto feels himself exiled by man and by nature. He has no difficulty in identifying himself with the paid assassin, **Sparafucile**: 'I am he who laughs, he the one who despatches' (Act 1 Scene 2). Born a cripple there was never any possibility that Rigoletto might pursue any normal profession. The only options for him would have been in a circus or in the position of court jester. It was probably down to his wife that Rigoletto found himself able to select the second option for, as he tells his daughter (Act 1 Scene 2), he owes any shred of self-respect that he possesses to the love of this remarkable woman.

The role of court jester provides Rigoletto with the perfect means of giving expression to the accumulation of bitterness and resentment that his early years must inevitably have imprinted on his psyche. For as court jester he has carte blanche to give vent to all the vitriol at his disposal, with the simple proviso that he must make his master laugh. Since the **Duke of Mantua** is essentially ego-centred and cruel by temperament Rigoletto possesses virtually unlimited licence. The Duke and Rigoletto are ego and id. Rigoletto is able to say all the things that etiquette forbids in normal social intercourse.

Yet it gives Rigoletto no joy. He is merely earning a living to support himself and his beloved daughter. The centre of Rigoletto's universe is his daughter, **Gilda**. He dotes on her. He is determined to protect her from an evil and dangerous world. As is often the case with such frantic over-protectiveness it ends up throttling the very thing it seeks most to preserve. Had Rigoletto not been so determined to keep the existence of his daughter

a closely guarded secret then the courtiers would never have assumed that Gilda was Rigoletto's mistress. It is extremely unlikely they would have contemplated abducting Rigoletto's daughter and the whole tragic turn of events might have been averted (see **Synopsis**).

Because Rigoletto devotes all his mental energy (in his professional capacity as jester) to derision and mockery he inevitably inspires hatred in those who are the butt of his razor-sharp wit. Worse, Rigoletto clearly relishes the discomfiture of others. This is inevitably because he has had to endure so much misery himself and feels he inhabits a universe inhabited solely by people more fortunate than himself. He allows his all too fragile ego to become inflated so that when all the courtiers are muttering imprecations against him he can reflect, 'Who can harm me? I am not afraid of them' (Act 1 Scene 1).

Nevertheless **Monterone**'s curse affects Rigoletto deeply because he recognizes that Monterone is similarly vulnerable. Monterone also has a daughter and lives in constant dread that she will be discovered and ravished by a hostile and concupiscent world. Thus it is not so much the fact that Monterone curses him, but the words that the old man employs that afflict him: 'And you, serpent, you who laugh at a father's grief, my curse upon you'. It is the reminder that the man he mocks is, like himself, a father, and curses him from a father's perspective, that so appalls Rigoletto and fatally impresses itself on his conscience.

When Sparafucile approaches him (Act 1 Scene 2) Rigoletto as yet has no reason to suspect that the Duke will abduct his daughter. But the assassin gives concrete form to Rigoletto's own worst fears. Knowing his master's predilections and appetite for conquest Rigoletto must realize that it is only a matter of time before his secret is discovered. He is probably instinctively aware that Gilda is already embroiled, although he has no direct knowledge of the burgeoning romance.

Gilda is, for Rigoletto, the one pure and noble thing that he possesses in his tormented life. In the first place there was the miracle of Gilda's mother – a woman who saw beneath the damaged exterior and gave her-self freely to him. Then she died. But she left him with a daughter who thankfully bears none of the marks of her father's deformity and who is in all probability the very image of her mother. This daughter becomes, for Rigoletto, mother, lover and infant. His greatest fear is that the world which has made such a misery of his own life will eventually deprive him of this one haven of tranquillity that life affords him. It is not an uncommon syndrome in the father/daughter relation; the loser is, of course, the daughter whose lifeblood is sucked from her by the father's need. It is also not uncommon that when the child does make a bid for freedom the result tends to bear out the worst fears of the parent. For the child is completely unprepared for the rigours of a world from which she has been so painstakingly pro-tected. Her very naivety will invite the atten-tions of the most debauched and will prevent her from differentiating between the sincere and the brazenly dishonest.

Rigoletto's destiny would seem to bear out that unspoken law which dictates that that which is most feared is that which is granted. For the fear itself attracts nemesis. The fear can only be overcome by confronting it head on. Rigoletto must confront the fact that he must relinquish his daughter unto her own life or, if necessity demands it, death.

The nadir of Rigoletto's life arrives, not when he has actually lost his daughter, either after her abduction or her death, but when he unwittingly aids and abets her abduction outside his own house (Act 1 Scene 2). With fearful symbolic irony he allows himself to be blindfolded and does not even realize it until it is too late. In later years it will not be the moment of Gilda's death that haunts him, but this moment of supreme recklessness when, with unbridled alacrity, he enters into the spirit of the courtiers' avowed intention of abducting Ceprano's wife (the Countess Ceprano). He gives not a thought to the grief this might cause Ceprano. He is only relieved that he need no longer, as he thinks, fear for his daughter's safety. He himself demands a mask; he demands to be granted immunity

for the crime he colludes in. When the courtiers have made their getaway with his daughter he cries out: 'Sono bendato!' ('I am blindfolded!') – literally true but also a profound acknowledgement of his own lack of foresight.

Perversely Rigoletto expects sympathy from the courtiers (Act 2), but the courtiers cannot afford to allow themselves the luxury of extending compassion towards the cripple. For, as Rigoletto acknowledges, all that truly motivates them is gold. Thus even when he weeps, which must be a horrifying prospect for their jaundiced sensibilities, the courtiers remain immovable.

When Gilda rushes in Rigoletto tries to pretend to himself that it was only a joke on the part of the courtiers. Now he can laugh once more. But it never was a joke; it was a deadly serious attempt to exercise retribution on the jester. Reunited with his daughter Rigoletto feels empowered again. Only with Gilda can he truly be himself. Now he is answerable to nobody. Imperiously he commands the courtiers: 'Off with you, all of you. And if your Duke should dare to come, tell him not to dare to enter for I am here' (Act 2). If the conclusion to Act 1 represents the nadir of Rigoletto's life, this is the moment of Rigoletto's greatest self-realization and fulfilment, the moment when he tacitly acknowledges that social station is nothing and common humanity every-thing. This revelation is perpetuated in the ensuing scene when he acts solely as com-forter to his daughter, no longer requiring anything of her other than that she allow him to console her.

Rigoletto's second encounter with Monterone at this crucial moment brings into focus the true import of the old man's curse on him. He now swears revenge not just for himself and his daughter, but also for Monterone who is at this moment being consigned to the dungeons. It is this which makes Rigoletto seek out Sparafucile and take advantage of the latter's offer to be of service (Act 3). If he resented his employer previously Rigoletto is now consumed with a burning hatred. He is also determined to convince his daughter that the object of her affections is not worthy of her love. This is no easy task and – as the conclusion of the opera gives witness – a futile one. It may be easy to demonstrate that the Duke is a 'philandering ingrate' (Gilda's own words) but it is impossible to obliterate from the girl's heart the depths of emotion which have been awakened by the Duke's attentions. This is something that Rigoletto cannot fathom, although the illogicality of passion is by no means foreign to him. It never occurs to him – how could it? – that Gilda might return to the inn and sacrifice her life for her lover after he has proved to her the Duke's duplicity.

The words of the Duke's song (*La donna è mobile*) take on an entirely new and hideous complexion when Rigoletto hears the irreverent refrain, *after* Sparafucile has handed over the sack that supposedly contains the Duke's corpse. For the Duke's philosophy would seem to be corroborated. There is, however, no recrimination. When Rigoletto learns the truth from his dying daughter he exclaims in a moment of superb realization: 'Almighty God! She has been struck by the arrow of my righteous vengeance'. 'Vengeance is mine; I will repay, saith the Lord' (Romans Chapter 12, 19). Righteous or not it is not given to human beings to take it upon themselves. This would seem to be the stern moral of Victor Hugo's tale as translated by Piave and Verdi. Indeed the lesson of Rigoletto's tragic fate would seem to be that human beings have no control over their own destinies. However one may deplore Rigoletto's many failings, these very failings are the result not of malicious intent, but of a fate which, from the outset, placed him 'up against it'. A bleak fatalism underpins the drama. There is no hint of a benign or redeeming justice, only the heavy-handed punishment meted out by Blake's 'old Nobodaddy'.

At the end of the opera Rigoletto has lost all that is dear to him and that helped redeem him from the misery of his existence. It is futile to speculate what happens to Rigoletto after the curtain has fallen. The events which overtake fictional characters always represent a fulcrum moment of a life's span, which moment can go only one of two ways: upward towards fulfilment and self-actualization, or downward into despair and ignominy. Which path Rigoletto follows is up to the audience to decide. So imbued is he with a sense of victimization by a malign fate (Thomas Hardy would have been proud of such a character) there can be little hope that Rigoletto will survive the catastrophe that has overtaken him.

Roberto and Tebaldo (*I Vespri Siciliani*). French soldiers.

Roberto and Tebaldo are opportunists of the lowest order. They enjoy the illusion of power that belonging to a conquering army confers on them. On the evidence of the opera they spend all their spare time drinking, carousing and ogling the Sicilian girls. They are entirely without imagination and give not a thought to the fact that the Sicilians may be harbouring intense resentments towards them. They are easy prey when **Procida** turns *agent provocateur* (Act 2) for, having no gifts for reflection and being concerned only about satisfying their own brutish desires, they are all too easily duped. They are not only unimaginative but stupid. How they suppose they will escape without retribution for running off with **Ninetta** and the other girls on the eve of their weddings defies belief.

They will certainly be among the first to die in the massacre that commences as the curtain falls at the conclusion of the opera.

Roderigo (*Otello*). A Venetian gentleman. All the time that **Otello** is working himself into a lather over **Cassio** the true object of his painful obsession should be Roderigo who, unlike Cassio, is truly in love with **Desdemona** and, again unlike Cassio, actually does despise the Moor and is willing to plot with **Iago** Otello's downfall.

Roderigo harbours a consuming passion for Desdemona. What is this passion? Is it no more than a resentment against the black man with a white wife? Is it no more than a veiled racism? How much does he actually know of Desdemona that he can truly say that he loves her? Is not his love merely an adolescent infatuation, the lusting after an icon, the screen idol, the ultimately unattainable? Because Roderigo is supremely unconscious and because it is not political ambition but thwarted libido that motivates him, he invites exploitation. He allows himself to be victimized. He becomes a hopeless pawn in the political ambitions of another, infinitely stronger will and wilier intelligence.

At the opening of the opera Roderigo is watching, with the rest of the Cypriots, the return of Otello's ship in the midst of a storm (Act 1). He remarks how the ship is rushing headlong onto a rock. Iago takes his cue and lets it be known that he, Iago, would welcome such an eventuality. After Otello has come ashore Iago approaches Roderigo. What is Roderigo thinking? 'Of drowning myself' is the reply. 'Fool is he who drowns himself for love of a woman', responds Iago. The ensign now goes to work. He promises to secure Desdemona for Roderigo for 'although I feign to love him I hate the Moor'.

Where Cassio has a moment's apprehension before trusting Iago, Roderigo has none. He is silent. He allows Iago to vent his spleen. He never questions Iago's sincerity. He is only happy to have found a superior will who offers him salvation from himself. Because he is offered salvation from himself Roderigo is willing to abandon all moral scruples. He wants only to drown in his love for Desdemona. He falls in easily with Iago's plan for undoing Cassio and then Otello. He is spurred on by the thought, instilled in him by Iago, of disrupting Otello's night of love, reunited as the general will be that evening with his beloved wife. He duly encourages Cassio to drink and then provokes him into a brawl.

When they are interrupted by **Montano**, Roderigo is only too happy to accept Iago's suggestion that he run to the harbour to raise the alarm: 'Go spread confusion and horror', Iago instructs him. He has no hesitation in acceding to this anarchic plan. The anarchy only reflects the chaos within himself. That Roderigo performs his task with alacrity is clear from the turmoil that ensues, climaxing with the arrival of Otello.

Roderigo does not appear again until Act 3, when he accompanies the Venetian ambassador, **Lodovico**, into the Great Hall of the castle. He will be anxious as to the reason for the ambassador's visit. When he discovers that Otello is recalled to Venice he is distraught, for this will mean the departure of Desdemona as well. He will presumably be aghast at Otello's treatment of Desdemona. If he really loved her he would intervene, but Roderigo is only in love with himself and with the idea of being in love. He appears not to be aware of Desdemona's suffering. All he can think of is the fact that 'the sweet and fair angel is to soon disappear from my path'. When Iago suggests that the situation may be saved if only Cassio were to suffer some accident, Roderigo, in a moment of prescience, seems to foresee his own death: 'Love spurs me on, but a covetous fearful star of death haunts my path'. Yet it does not deter him. His love for Desdemona is everything. It is as unworldly and adolescent as the love of Tristan, Romeo or Pelleas, and as doomed. Like the love of those mythic lovers it feeds not on any deep acquaintance with the beloved but on an image; in psychological parlance, a projection from within. Unlike his mythic predecessors his love is not returned and is therefore doubly futile.

Roderigo meets his death at Cassio's hand because that is what he deserves. He has turned his back on life from the moment that he consecrates his life to depriving another man of the woman he loves. We do not witness Cassio slaying Roderigo in a 'dark secluded alley', but we sense that the match was never an equal one. Cassio has a vital interest in surviving. Roderigo's cause was futile from the start.

Rodolfo (*Luisa Miller*). Son of Count **Walter**. The primary fact about Rodolfo is that he is in rebellion against his father. The love that he bears the peasant girl, **Luisa**, is principally the love of a rebellious son for that which will most offend his progenitor. This is not to say that he is not genuinely devoted to Luisa in the way of any average German Romantic hero. She represents for him not only lover but also Mother – motherless as he apparently is – an image of femininity so utterly removed from the aggressively masculine power-struggles of Court life that he can only capitulate before her mystery. For Luisa offers fulfilment to a whole facet of his personality that has been rendered derelict by the overweening arrogance and narcissism of his father.

Rodolfo loves because he must. It is a question of survival for him as an individual. When he first sets eyes on Luisa he sees redemption and salvation. His passion has nothing to do with interpersonal connectedness. He is not interested in Luisa as an individual any more, in fact, than Luisa is interested in him as an individual (this is a truism applicable to almost any pair of operatic lovers). The lineaments of Rodolfo and Luisa's attachment is closer to that of Tristan and Isolde or Romeo and Juliet than, for instance, Will and Anna Bryant in D.H. Lawrence's *The Rainbow*. They do not interact. They exist totally locked within their own narcissistic dreams.

Thus, in *Luisa Miller* there is no love duet, as such. Indeed the only real confrontation between the lovers comes in Act 3 when Rodolfo accuses Luisa of betrayal. Since Luisa is confined by the oath she was forced to take by **Wurm** in order to save her father, she cannot defend herself and the scene therefore becomes more of a tirade from Rodolfo, with anguished soliloquizing asides from Luisa. The metaphysical nature of Rodolfo and Luisa's love is nowhere better illustrated. It is inconceivable that their love should ever achieve physical consummation for it is first and foremost a love raised in the spite of the world, an act of rebellion against their respective fathers who at the end of the opera are left gaping in wide-eyed astonishment over their children's corpses.

Rodolfo's faith in life has been critically undermined by his having learnt from the dying lips of the elder Count, his father's cousin, that his father was responsible for the old man's murder. A father, who should be a son's first role model, has thus become number one enemy, and also a source of cruel temptation to his beleaguered son. How often, one wonders, has Rodolfo contemplated emulating his own father in ridding himself of *his* father? For, while the elder Count was not actually Walter's father, he was a father-figure, and Walter's action in murdering him was tantamount to parricide. The elder Count lost his life because he threatened, through a second marriage, to come between Walter and his inheritance. Walter, a dutiful son himself, does everything in his power to thwart his own son's attempt at individuation, in the process giving Rodolfo far more direct motivation for parricide than he himself ever had. He killed the elder Count on the mere supposition that he might be disinherited. Rodolfo does not kill his father. He kills himself in order, one suspects, to prevent himself emulating his father. Never have the sins of the fathers been so vividly visited on the sons as in this opera.

That Rodolfo knows the power he holds is beyond question. He waits until the last possible moment before wielding it. Having done so he has publicly declared himself his father's enemy. Either he can, like Don Carlo in another Schiller play (*Don Carlo*), await the inevitable thunderbolt of his father's justifiable paranoia to fall, or he can remove himself and demonstrate his utter refusal to compromise. Rodolfo chooses the latter option because the first is unthinkable. Luisa is merely a weapon with which to flagellate his father, in the same way that Elisabeth is in *Don Carlo*.

Much has been talked about the father–daughter relationships in Verdi's operas. In fact the incidence of complicated father–daughter relationships is no greater than father–son relationships. Apart from the above-mentioned one thinks of *I Due Foscari*, *La Traviata*, *I Masnadieri*. In truth it is the father-figure that most obsesses and inspires Verdi, as it was the mother-figure – Erda in all her multifold aspects – that obsessed Wagner. The two composers are complementary: one turns inwards to the world of mythic archetype ruled by the Mother; the other looks out to the world of material and political fact and interpersonal relations (none of Wagner's characters really relate), overseen by the Father.

Rodolfo's refusal to toe the line and become a mere cipher for his father's thwarted ambitions is formed by precisely the same motivation which drives Siegfried and Parsifal out of the womb-like embrace of the forest into the unknown world beyond. It is the desperate search to achieve an individual identity – to grow up. It is Rodolfo's tragedy that he fails.

Rodolfo Müller (*Stiffelio*). See Stiffelio

Rodrigo (*Don Carlo*)
Historical Note The historical Marquis de Posa is a shadowy figure and it is unlikely that the character as portrayed in Verdi's opera bears much resemblance to the historical character. It is probable that Schiller based his character partly on that of Don John of Austria, an illegitimate son of Charles V. Don John persuaded Philip to make him Governor of Flanders. It is possible, even likely, that Don John sympathized with the Flemish heretics, for he died soon afterwards in mysterious circumstances.

The only achievement recorded in history of the historical Posa was the seduction of one of Elisabeth's maids of honour. He was caught climbing out of her window. In some accounts it is related that he paid for his rashness with his life, being assassinated one night in the street. But this is in variance with the fact that he is on record as being a pall bearer at Elisabeth's funeral.

Rodrigo is one of the noblest of Verdi's baritone roles. He exemplifies qualities of passionate idealism, loyalty and sincerity without a hint of the priggishness which afflicts, for instance, Tito in Mozart's *La Clemenza da Tito*. (A close operatic equivalent of Rodrigo's character would be Wolfram, in Wagner's *Tannhaüser*.) Rodrigo is above all a humanitarian. He is inextricably caught up in a political maelstrom

where humanitarian values are not uppermost and he must contend with Philip's reactionary and imperialist politics on the one hand and the die-hard fundamentalism of the Inquisition on the other.

When the opera opens Rodrigo has recently returned from Flanders where he has been horrified by what he has witnessed. His description (Act 2 Scene 2) invokes memories of **Giselda's** 'Torrents of blood' outburst in *I Lombardi*. 'Deprived of all light, it inspires horror and seems a silent grave! The homeless orphan roams the streets, weeping; steel and fire destroy everything, pity is banished! The ruddy waters of the river seem to run red with blood. The air is filled with the cry of a mother whose children have perished'. Rodrigo gives thanks that he has been allowed to relay his experiences to the King. Philip is notably unresponsive. As far as he is concerned the Flemish people have deserved their miseries for having been disloyal to their King.

Rodrigo has not only to contend with the King but also with the all-powerful Grand Inquisitor. The Inquisitor will not abide the 'innovations' of the Protestants in Flanders. Philip is answerable at all times and in all things to the Inquisition and he will prove to be inflexible. To Rodrigo it must seem incomprehensible (as the blood shed by the Crusaders is to Giselda in *I Lombardi*). 'What! You think by sowing death, to plant for eternity?' he challenges Philip. He appeals to him: 'Like God the Redeemer remake the world anew, soar to sublime heights above any other king!' In this Rodrigo displays extraordinary naivety. He must know that Philip's policies are at all times circumscribed by the reality of day-to-day state politics. Playing 'God the redeemer' is only for poets and dreamers. However Rodrigo is not stupid; he must be aware of the risk he runs in challenging the King. But he is also aware that he enjoys a unique position by virtue of the fact that he retains Philip's confidence. He feels it his duty to speak out. His nature is such that he almost oversteps the mark, likening Philip to Nero who was then, as now, a byword for despotic cruelty.

It is a tribute to the depth of the King's respect for, and devotion to, Rodrigo that even after the latter's outburst Philip is willing to confide in him with regard to his own personal anguish concerning his wife and son. Indeed he describes Rodrigo as being the 'only true man among the entire throng'. The fact that Philip puts his trust in him despite his outspoken attack gives Rodrigo hope that he may yet be able to turn the situation to the advantage of the Flemish people. Rodrigo never for a second wavers from making this his single most pressing priority. He is quite clear that the principal agent for the necessary reforms must be the Infante. He clearly has great affection for Carlos, but he cannot fail to see that Carlos needs challenging. He already knows of Carlos's passion for Elisabeth and is keenly aware of how dangerous this is. Carlos must be removed from court, both for his own and for the Queen's sake. Rodrigo's awareness of this necessity is only confirmed by his interview with Philip. He knows that Carlos shares his ideals, if only by virtue of his need to oppose his father's will. By installing Carlos in Flanders he could effectively ensure that Flanders is restored to peace and the persecution of heretics brought to an end. Quite how he imagines he will contend with the Inquisition is another matter. (As will be revealed (Act 4 Scene 2) the Inquisitor is well aware that Rodrigo is a potential traitor.)

Rodrigo's love for Carlos stems from that same need in him that champions the plight of the Flemish people. It is a desire to nurture the underdog. Carlos has so clearly allowed himself to be victimized and, equally clearly, will never be able to realize his true potential until he is removed from the overpowering domination of his father. Rodrigo's delight at the close of his interview with Philip ('Oh divine dream of mine, glorious hope') stems from the realization that he has a real possibility of achieving salvation for the two causes closest to his heart: Carlos and the suffering Flemish. But from this moment onwards everything goes wrong for him. It is almost as though the gods feel impelled to prove to him that there is no room in the world of *Real-politik* for his sort of idealism.

First there is Eboli to contend with. Rodrigo knows well the sort of person Eboli is, as is evidenced when he shamelessly flatters and amuses her (Act 2 Scene 2). He knows how lethal she could be if crossed, which is why when he realizes that Carlos has witlessly betrayed his love for Elisabeth and, by the same token, spurned Eboli, he is appalled (Act 3 Scene 1). His first ploy is to discount Carlos's action by appealing to the latter's well-known instability: 'He is raving, do not believe him, he is mad!' Eboli is not to be deflected so easily. She is a 'tigress, wounded in the heart' and Rodrigo knows how dangerous that can be. Unfortunately, as we already know from his interview with the King, Rodrigo lacks self-restraint. Now, once again, he loses control of himself. Realizing that Eboli threatens everything he has planned for himself, for Carlos, for Flanders and for Spain, he produces a dagger and is about to stab her when Carlos does him the inestimable service of preventing him. He can only, on reflection, be grateful to Carlos. But his mind remains in overdrive. At all costs he has to ensure that Carlos must be immune to Eboli's inevitable spite. He therefore demands that Carlos hand over to him any incriminating papers he may possess. He knows that he himself is dispensable, whereas the Infante is not. If Carlos were to be removed from the political arena all Rodrigo's campaigning would have been for nought. Carlos hands over his papers and thereby signs Rodrigo's death warrant.

Rodrigo has no prior knowledge of Carlos's plan to force a showdown with the King at the *auto-da-fé* (Act 3 Scene 2). He can hardly welcome the development for he knows Philip well enough to know that this is not the way to tackle him. Confronted in public and pushed into a corner the King will prove inflexible, as is indeed proved to be the case. Knowing that nothing can be gained from allowing the confrontation to be prolonged, and anxious to avert the indignity of King and Infante fighting a duel before the entire population of Madrid, Rodrigo steps in to defuse the situation, by disarming Carlos and presenting the latter's sword to the King. He knows that Carlos will view this as a betrayal, but then Carlos has never known what is good for him. In the meantime Rodrigo has strengthened his own position with the King who raises him from the rank of Marquis to that of Duke. This in itself will probably mean little to Rodrigo. He is the last person to be concerned about his own advancement.

In Act 4 Scene 1 Rodrigo enters the King's apartments in company with Eboli. This is partly dramatic expediency, but also might suggest that Eboli, already remorseful, may have come to him to confess what she has perpetrated and to alert him to the fact that there is a violent argument transpiring between the King and the Queen. Rodrigo has no qualms about voicing his outrage when he sees how things stand. Elisabeth is prostrate on the floor and Philip is beside himself. Rodrigo's initial sally is to the point: 'Sire, half the world is in your power; could it be you are the only one in so vast an empire you are unable to control?' In fact Rodrigo is secretly pleased that a crisis has finally been achieved, a crisis from which there can be no turning back. Philip is now in an extremely vulnerable position. Consequently Carlos's position is strengthened. Rodrigo knows now what he must do. He must make certain Carlos's papers are found in his own possession so that Carlos may be exonerated and thereby released from jail. He must confer his mantle on Carlos who must, as only he can, carry forward the Flemish cause. Rodrigo clearly knows that time is short. His proximity to the King's chamber prior to his entrance into the King's apartments suggests that he may have eavesdropped on the King's private interview with the Grand Inquisitor. In which case he would know that he is top of the Inquisitor's 'hit list'.

Whether or not this is the case he takes the first available opportunity to apprise Elisabeth of his dreams for Carlos's future and then bids her meet Carlos at San Yuste on the morrow (this is not portrayed in the opera but can be inferred from Rodrigo's final words to Carlos in Act 4 Scene 2).

Rodrigo now has only one thing left to do, and that is take his farewell of Carlos. When he reveals to Carlos what he has done (*Per me giunto è il di supremo*) the latter's reaction is predictable; he will go straight to the King and acknowledge that the culpability is entirely his. Rodrigo will hear none of it, for that would be to make a mockery of all his endeavours. Carlos must now learn to stand on his own two feet: 'Save yourself for Flanders, keep yourself for the great task. You must complete it; you will bring the rebirth of a new golden age; you were destined to reign as I to die for you'. And at that very moment a shot rings out and Rodrigo falls, mortally wounded. With his dying breath he tells Carlos to meet his mother at the San Yuste monastery. She knows everything, he tells him. He takes his leave of Carlos in the justly famed and elegiac *Io morrò ma lieto in core*. His last words to Carlos are to remind him of his duty now to 'save Flanders'.

Rodrigo is an essential mediator in the opera between Philip and his rebellious son. He gives focus both to Carlos's rebellion and Philip's recalcitrance.

Roger (*Jerusalem*)

Roger's role replaces that of **Pagano** in *I Lombardi*. Where Pagano is unquestionably the central role in the Italian opera, Roger is supplanted in the French version by **Gaston**, whose predicament more nearly invites our sympathies. For Gaston is the epitome of injured innocence. Roger's sufferings are the direct result of his own perversity.

There are several distinctions between the roles of Roger and Pagano. Pagano's resentment is that of an underprivileged brother for his more favoured sibling. There are no indications that Roger holds any grudge against his brother, other than the impossibility of being united with his niece. Roger does not set out to murder his brother, because his brother is not his rival. It could be argued that his brother could prove to be every bit as much, if not more, an impediment to his consummating his passion for **Hélène** but Roger – and in this he precisely resembles Pagano – is a man beside himself. He is not rational. Having said which he is far more practical than Pagano. He manages to deflect any blame from himself until the very last page of the opera. Then it is only because he confesses his guilt in his dying moments. Roger never has any intention of incriminating himself. He employs a professional assassin. That he has chosen his assassin wisely is proven by the fact that when he is discovered the soldier convincingly lays the blame at Gaston's feet, and thus averts suspicion from himself and Roger.

Where Pagano and Roger bear closest comparison is in the fact that both are equally appalled by the (apparently, in the case of Roger) tragic outcome of their machinations. Roger may not have wielded the dagger himself but he never intended that his brother should be killed. The fact that the **Count** is not actually dead is neither here nor there. Roger assumes him to be dead and for four years carries with him the consciousness of having been guilty of fratricide. It administers exactly the same kind of psychological shock to him as does Pagano's unwitting patricide. It cures him of his perverse passion for Hélène in the same way that Pagano was cured of his passion for **Viclinda.**

Roger's passion is more perverse in that Hélène is more inaccessible to him than Viclinda ever was to Pagano. If Viclinda had desired him there is no reason why she should not have chosen Pagano above Arvino. But she does not will it, never has and never will. It is nevertheless the decision and proclivity of a mature woman who knows her mind. Pagano, if he were not so emotionally retarded, would be forced to accept her decision. Viclinda is probably aware, in any case, that Pagano 'loves' her, not for herself, but because she belongs to his brother. Hélène, on the other hand has barely achieved adulthood. There is no indication that she has ever given her uncle any reason to desire her as a lover, other, probably, than the natural high spirits and vivacity of a young girl. There is no possibility for Roger that he can ever pursue his passion. He must know that his

brother would never countenance it. In a sense one could say that Roger's assassin hit the mark when his knife attacks the Count rather than Gaston. In the same way one could say the true origin of Pagano's dementia is his father, not his brother. The incestuous nature of Roger's passion is a far greater obstacle to its consummation than Hélène's love for another man.

Roger has four years of wandering in despair in which to reflect upon his sins. Inevitably the moment when he is confronted with his brother in Palestine has greater significance than it does for Pagano in the Italian opera. For in that moment he suddenly receives confirmation that at least he has not been guilty of fratricide. It is one weight off his conscience.

Whereas in *I Lombardi* it is through Oronte's supernatural intervention that the Crusaders are guided to 'the gushing fountain of Siloam', in *Jerusalem* the motive is introduced in an altogether more prosaic fashion. The fact that it is conferred upon the role of Roger immeasurably enhances the character's profile. For where Pagano appears principally to be concerned with donning his armour anew in order to engage in battle, Roger has the opportunity early in Act 2 to demonstrate the total revolution that has occurred in his psyche. What greater proof could there be than in his eagerness to rescue the pilgrims dying of thirst in the desert? For has he not himself been there, stranded in a metaphorical desert, where there was no spiritual nourishment other than the insane promptings of his libido? It is from this moment that the audience can be certain that Roger is deserving of the redemption that is eventually granted him (Act 4 Scene 1).

This is only confirmed when, confronted by Gaston whose life has been so blighted because of Roger's self-obsession, he has no hesitation in jeopardizing his own safety by releasing Gaston (who is awaiting execution) and then launching with him into the affray against the Moslems.

It can be no accident that Roger is severely wounded while Gaston escapes unscathed. One can assume that Roger devotes much of his energy to guarding Gaston's back, thus finally expiating his guilt. His death is not a tragedy. It is a final release for a man who has confronted demons and ultimately triumphed over them.

Rolando (*La Battaglia di Legnano*). Milanese leader.

Rolando belongs to that extensive family of outraged operatic husbands. Like **Renato** (*Un Ballo in Maschera*) he trusts his wife implicitly (which admittedly could be just another way of saying he takes her for granted). Thus the fall into chronic jealousy and outrage is all the greater than it would have been had he ever entertained the possibility that **Lida** could stray. It is made worse for Rolando that she betrays him with one of his closest friends and colleagues.

Like **Arrigo** Rolando is first and foremost a patriot. But unlike Arrigo he is a man's man. He has long since made the break from the mother; or rather he has successfully made the transition from dutiful son to dutiful husband, father and lover. Probably his worst fault is his complacency. He dotes on his wife, most particularly as the mother of his son. For in his son he sees justification for his own existence. He can die, if that is what duty demands, content in the knowledge that he has secured the future. His only concern is that his wife and son should be protected should they be deprived of husband and father. Quite naturally he turns to his closest friend to fill the gap that his absence would inevitably leave, never suspecting that he will shortly discover that this very friend has long since captured the heart of the woman he married.

Rolando is overjoyed when he discovers that Arrigo is still alive (Act 1) for he has assumed, like everyone else, that Arrigo died of wounds received in 'the flames of Susa'. He tells Arrigo that not even his marriage and the gift of a son could have assuaged his grief over Arrigo's death. He sings an ecstatic paean of welcome to his friend and then joins him, the **Consuls** and the other Lombard soldiers in swearing an oath to defend Italy to the last if need be. Thus, at our first encounter of Rolando there is no hint of dissension between the two friends, only the firmest solidarity (so far Arrigo is oblivious to the identity of his friend's wife). Compare this, for instance, with Renato and Riccardo (*Un Ballo in Maschera*) where it is all too clear that Renato in some way has subjugated himself to Riccardo in a manner that is sooner or later going to rebound on him.

This sense of solidarity between the two men is only confirmed when they travel together to Como (Act 2) as envoys for the Lombard League in order to ask for aid from the city of Como in preventing any further incursions from the Barbarian hordes. That their mission is thwarted by the sudden advent of **Federico Barbarossa** himself only strengthens the profound allegiance that grows from being confronted by adversity.

The tenuous nature of Rolando's grounds for complacency become all too clear in Act 1 Scene 2 where Lida unburdens herself to her maids concerning her perennial disquiet and unhappiness. When Rolando first introduces Arrigo to his wife (Act 1) the evidence of an erstwhile connection between them is clear to behold to all, it seems, except Rolando. At this critical moment Rolando is called away on business, leaving his wife alone with Arrigo.

Rolando's chief preoccupation is with his mission to save Italy. Whereas Arrigo fights to carve a way in the world in order to win the bride of his desires, Rolando has already won his. His motivation is quite different. He seeks to preserve and propagate that which he has obtained. It is the fundamental distinction between the artistic (introvert) temperament – Arrigo – and the worldly (extrovert) temperament – Rolando. The artist serves the muse in order to appease something that is foreign and potentially unobtainable. The worldly extrovert does not need to appease – or thinks he does not need to. He has already made attainable that which may have initially appeared unattainable (in Jungian terms he has assimilated and reconciled himself with the *anima*).

Henceforth Rolando's endeavour is based on fear – the fear of loss. It is the very opposite of the heroic as represented by the artist, which in this opera Arrigo epitomizes. But the problem for Rolando is that he is supremely unconscious. He is not aware of what motivates him until the moment of potential loss presents itself, when he is preparing to go to battle and knows he may lose his life. Then he knows what is most important to him, his wife and his son. Then it is that he turns to Arrigo and requests with passionate entreaty that his friend take care of them should he not return (Act 3).

Rolando's universe crumbles at the moment that **Marcovaldo** brings to him the letter in which Lida confirms her and Arrigo's former love. The blow is all the worse for being totally unanticipated. Thus when he confronts the 'guilty' pair (as he sees them) he is entirely irrational and without compassion, although his wife's distress is all too evident. He refuses to listen to any explanations; he refuses even to countenance the possibility that the reality of the situation may be very far from what at first sight it appears to be. His sense of betrayal is so acute that he determines that only the most extreme punishment is suitable. He projects onto Arrigo what would for him be the worst punishment – dishonour. By Rolando's code of conduct there is no worse. He locks the pair in Arrigo's room, thus hoping to ensure that Arrigo can be prevented from joining his squadron and thereby be unable to go into battle. It does not seem to occur to him that were his wife to be discovered closeted with Arrigo by some third party the dishonour to himself, as the cuckolded husband, would be exacerbated a thousandfold. Nor does it occur to him that Arrigo might make a desperate bid for freedom, as indeed he does by leaping from the balcony. Rolando, being an altogether less impulsive character than Arrigo, would have sized up the distance of the fall into the moat below, weighed up the odds of survival and discounted such a reckless action. Arrigo, careless of his own existence, does not stop to think. He leaps first, and thereby survives to fight another day.

It is to Rolando's benefit that he does, for thus he is ultimately reconciled with his friend, even though it is on the latter's death-bed. For to Rolando the logic of Arrigo's argument, 'he who dies for his country cannot be so guilty in his heart', is incontestable. He knows that Arrigo in his dying moments has nothing to lose by confirming Lida's purity of heart. Ultimately he cannot deny that Arrigo's priority is exactly the same as his own, namely the sanctity of Italian independence. Once he has overcome the grief attendant on his friend's death, he will no doubt obtain from Lida a full and satisfactory explanation for the whole sorry course of events. He may still experience jealousy – he cannot fail to be aware that his wife suffers grievously over the loss of the man she first loved – but we must hope that time will reconcile the couple and that they will ultimately be reunited through their shared loss.

Rolla (*I Masnadieri*). A brigand and companion of **Carlo**.

In Act 1 Scene 1 Rolla reads aloud, for the benefit of the audience, the letter **Francesco** has written to Carlo telling the latter that their father, **Massimiliano**, threatens to imprison Carlo in solitary confinement with a diet of bread and water should he dare to return. 'By my faith, a pleasant letter', Rolla comments ironically.

The esteem in which Carlo holds Rolla is demonstrated by the fact that Carlo risks his own life to rescue Rolla from a public execution, only succeeding in liberating him at the very moment that the noose was placed around his friend's neck (related by the bandits in Act 2 Scene 2: see **Chorus**).

It is unlikely that Carlo has ever, in his previous life at his father's court, known such a friendship, bounded as it is by the shared experiences of danger and social ostracism.

Ruiz (*Il Trovatore*). A soldier in **Manrico's** service.

Di Luna describes Manrico as being a follower of Urgel and sentenced to death. All who associate with Manrico, like his soldier, Ruiz, are thereby similarly outlawed.

The character of Ruiz is strongly contrasted to that of **Ferrando**, di Luna's captain of the guard. Whereas Ferrando is elderly, stately and verbose Ruiz is a young man of few words. He first appears at the head of a band of Manrico's followers when he arrives at the convent, presumably on Manrico's instructions, in order to assist the latter in preventing **Leonora** from taking the veil (Act 2 Scene 2). When di Luna draws his sword Ruiz is quick to disarm him. He and his fellow retainers appear quite unperturbed by the presence of the Count's retainers.

In Act 3 Scene 2 Ruiz brings Manrico the news that **Azucena** has been taken prisoner by di Luna's men. Manrico dismisses him to gather a squadron of soldiers. He achieves this with remarkable promptness, returning with the soldiers very shortly, just giving Manrico time to toss off *Di quella pira*. He then joins with the other soldiers in declaring their readiness to fight with Manrico. Unlike Manrico Ruiz escapes capture and, at the opening of Act 4, he leads Leonora to the tower where Manrico is imprisoned. He is clearly distressed by Manrico's plight. He must know it is extremely unlikely that Manrico will leave the castle alive.

S

Una Sacerdotessa (a Priestess) (*Aida*). See Priestess

Samuel and Tom (*Un Ballo in Maschera*). Conspirators.
Historical Note The characters of Samuel and Tom are based on two young conspirators, Counts Horn and Ribbing, who in common with many of the Swedish nobility were becoming increasingly disenchanted with Gustave III's autocratic behaviour. On his accession Gustave had immediately reduced the power of the nobility by removing many of their privileges.

Samuel and Tom must be considered as an entity as they rarely express themselves independently of each other. Initially they appear as stock conspirators, similar to the cut-throats in **Macbeth**. They bear a grudge against **Riccardo**, the precise nature of which only becomes clear in Act 3 Scene 1 where it is revealed that Samuel's ancestral home has been confiscated from him by Riccardo, while Tom's brother was apparently killed by the Governor. Cogent reasons, it would seem, but Riccardo is never given the opportunity to defend his actions in either case.

Samuel and Tom dream of the day when they may be avenged. They believe they have found an ideal opportunity when Riccardo resolves (Act 1 Scene 1) to attend **Ulrica's** cavern in the small hours of the night. When it comes to the moment, however, they are thwarted by the fact that the sorceress tells Riccardo that his life is in danger. Ulrica then intimates that she knows the secret Samuel and Tom conceal in their hearts (Act 1 Scene 2). When her prophecy points to **Renato** being the one who will murder Riccardo, Samuel and Tom are noticeably relieved. Momentarily alarmed when Ulrica attempts to alert Riccardo to the fact that Renato is not the only source of danger, their fears are again allayed when Riccardo refuses to pay any further heed to the sorceress's warnings. They determine to follow Riccardo and await their opportunity.

They are again frustrated (Act 2) by the ever vigilant Renato, who also follows Riccardo and warns him of imminent danger. However, when it is revealed that Riccardo has been keeping a rendezvous with none other than Renato's own wife, Samuel and Tom find themselves with an unexpected ally. At first they revel in Renato's discomfiture over his wife's adultery, but when they realize that he is in deadly earnest in requiring that they admit him into their conspiracy, of which he has full cognizance, they readily agree to meet Renato rather than risk him turning over to the judiciary incriminating evidence that he already possesses.

Samuel and Tom undoubtedly enjoy the charade played out at the masked ball where the conspirators all don disguise and use the highly emotive word '*Morte!*' ('Death!') as their password (Act 3 Scene 2). Initially when Riccardo does not appear at the ball they assume their efforts have been in vain. When Riccardo finally emerges Samuel and Tom are nowhere to be seen, leaving it to Renato to exact the ultimate revenge.

Uno schiavo (Slave) (*Il Corsaro*). See **Slave**

Seid (*Il Corsaro*). Pasha of Corone.

The sadistic Turkish Pasha is a stereotype much beloved of opera (though transcended by Mozart in *Il Seraglio*, where the sadistic streak is passed to the Pasha's henchman, Osmin, and the Pasha himself almost matches Tito (*La Clemnza di Tito*) in benevolence). Seid is no doubt a fine and noble warrior and is seen at his best when exhorting his troops to go into battle for Allah on his first appearance (Act 2 Scene 2). Thereafter we see principally the negative aspects of his personality: his determination at all costs to impose his will, and his persistent return to threats against life and limb of those who dare to oppose him, or threaten his image of himself as the centre of the universe.

When confronted by **Corrado**, before even realizing that it is Corrado, Seid immediately erupts into gleeful gloating at the expense of his enemies. 'Do they know what fearful vengeance awaits them? Do they know that I shall make dust and debris of their dens?' he rhetorically demands (Act 2 Scene 2). When Corrado reveals himself Seid's reaction is predictable: 'Let him be cut to pieces!' That Corrado has the effrontery to break into his harem is a personal insult; that he dares to steal his favourite odalisque is insupportable. He has convinced himself that he loves **Gulnara** above all the other girls. This is undoubtedly because Gulnara shows a great deal more spirit than the other girls. He loves her for the very reason that takes her away from him.

The precise nature of this 'love' is all too clearly illustrated in his confrontation with Gulnara at the opening of Act 3. In his scene and aria (*Cento leggiadre vergini*) Seid exults in the fact that he has his enemy at his mercy.

He cannot help marvelling at Corrado's audacity, particularly in having attempted, as he sees it, to steal Gulnara from him. Corrado has, in fact, done nothing of the kind. He has merely succeeded in saving Gulnara's life – which admittedly he himself had put at risk. It is doubtful if Seid would have risked his own life in order to save Gulnara. His love most certainly does not extend to self-sacrifice. It is a purely sensual love, or rather lust. What strikes Seid to the quick is his awareness that Gulnara has in all probability fallen in love with Corrado. It is this above all which inflames his rage and reminds him of the passion that he harbours for Gulnara. He recalls how all the other girls paled into insignificance when he first set eyes on her. Now, if she should betray his love, he invokes heaven to grant him the thunderbolts to 'burn the vile wretch to ashes'.

When Gulnara enters (Act 3 Scene 1) he pretends insouciance, but cannot sustain the masquerade for long. When Gulnara suggests, albeit in a matter-of-fact manner, that it might be better to allow Corrado to live, Seid is convinced that she has now given him proof that she loves the pirate. (This scene could be seen as a rehearsal for the confrontation of Aida and Amneris in *Aida* Act 2 Scene 1.) From then on he can only splutter imprecations and threats. Inevitably his behaviour inspires contempt in Gulnara, who has a far nobler model of manhood with which to compare the blustering Seid in the person of Corrado. Gulnara has never had anything but contempt for Seid because her favours have always been extracted from her under compulsion. Seid's 'love' is not love at all, but a favour which, in the minuscule world of the Pasha's harem, is no doubt something for which she should be supremely grateful. But because Gulnara never for one moment loses sight of the fact that there is a world beyond the harem – a world from which she has been snatched and after which she pines – she cannot take Seid's 'love' seriously. She sees it for what it is; the love of a spoilt child for the prize jewel in his collection. Seid represents for her only one thing: imprisonment. This, to a strong spirited girl, is intolerable.

When Gulnara murders Seid she does it for the love of a man she views as her liberator, even though he has already indicated that he is not free to return her love. Seid has no time to prepare for death. Had he the time to reflect he could not begin to understand Gulnara's motives for he lacks any imagination. It has never occurred to him that a girl from the harem, however abused, might arm herself against him. He has always lived exclusively for the here and now. He has never needed imagination. Every whim has always been catered for and, because of this, he has nothing to wish or hope for. He is propitiated.

In a paradoxical sense Seid's love for Gulnara can be seen as the love of a man who, if he did but know it, needs above all to be released from the nightmare of his own solipsism.

Selimo (*Il Corsaro*). Aga and one of **Seid's** warriors. ('Aga' is a title of nobility in Turkey, usually given to military commanders.)

The function of Selimo is similar to that of Spoletta in Puccini's *Tosca*; in other words he is required to do the Pasha's dirty work for him. In Verdi's opera this amounts principally to the torture and execution of the Pasha's arch enemy, **Corrado**.

In Act 2 Scene 2, after the Turks have overcome Corrado and some of his pirates, Selimo comes to Seid to inform him that many of the pirates who escaped are slain but that others are fleeing to their caves. He offers to go after them with his men. Seid, realizing that it would be impossible to find the pirates, orders Selim not to go. He is happy to have Corrado in captivity.

Act 3 Scene 1   Seid commands Selim to bring **Gulnara** to him and then tells him, 'Tomorrow the last sun shines for that villain (Corrado). Let him die in agony. Do you hear?' Selim hears and understands perfectly well. But he has no chance to put his orders into practice for Gulnara kills Seid and then rescues Corrado. The two flee before anyone can catch up with them.

Servant to Amelia (Un Servo d'Amelia) (*Un ballo in maschera*)

Amelia's servant accompanies his mistress to **Ulrica's** cavern (Act 1 Scene 2) and apprises the sorceress of his mistress's presence and desire for a private audience. He is despatched to bring Amelia into the cavern. Thereafter he makes himself notably scarce.

A Servant of the Doge (Un servo) (*I Due Foscari*)

The Doge's Servant announces 'the noble Lady Foscari' (**Lucrezia**) in Act 1 Scene 3. He precedes his master into the dungeon where **Jacopo Foscari** is incarcerated in Act 2. But on this occasion he has nothing to say for himself. But in Act 3 he reports to his master that the Council of Ten require to speak with him.

Servant (Servo) (*Un giorno di regno*)

The servant in Baron **Kelbar's** castle announces the arrival of the **Marchioness** (Act 1 Scene 2), much to the discomfiture of **Belfiore**, to whom the Marchioness is betrothed (see **Synopsis**).

Servant (Servo) (*Macbeth*)

Appears Act 1 Scene 2 and relays to **Lady Macbeth** the crucial information that King Duncan is to visit the Macbeths' castle that very night. This is all Lady Macbeth needs to convince her that Duncan must be murdered in order that her husband may take the throne.

Servo. See **Servant**

Sicario (*Macbeth*). See **Assassin**

Don Ruy Gomez de Silva (*Ernani*).

'For Brutus is an honourable man' (*Julius Caesar* Act 3 Scene 2). As in Shakespeare's play the question is, how do we interpret that word honourable? De Silva is indeed an honourable man in that he serves his code of honour with a religious observance. Whether that makes him an honourable man is a matter for debate. Would a truly honourable man expect a man to kill himself on his wedding night in observance of an oath given in the heat of a moment of passion and despair? It is not a nicety which de Silva is capable of fathoming. He knows only that he has been robbed of the one thing that promised to bring happiness to his old age. It never occurs to him that in fact he never did actually possess **Elvira**'s love, so he cannot actually be robbed of it.

All three men who desire Elvira think of her and discuss her as if she were an ornament, to be owned and displayed like a Fabergé egg. What singles out **Ernani**'s suit is that Elvira undoubtedly returns his love and desires to be with him as much as he with her. The egos of the other two prevent them from thinking of anything other than the gratification of their own thwarted desires. De Silva imagines that he is on the point of achieving gratification for his desires when he discovers two strange men closeted with his betrothed in her apartment. What is he to think?

De Silva is never so sympathetic as at that moment where his vanity most hurts. He gives vent to his sense of outrage and then collapses into soliloquy: *Infelice! E tuo credevi* (Act 1 Scene 2) (this, one of Verdi's most plangent melodies for bass, underlines the very real pathos of this man's predicament. His sentiments and their elegiac expression prefigure the lament of **Philip**, *Ella giammai m'amò* (**Don Carlo**), the difference being that de Silva is justified in lamenting his age, whereas Philip is still in his early thirties. It is, in fact, precisely the opposite dilemma. Where Philip has an aged heart in a young body, de Silva laments still having a youthful heart beating in his aged breast). However, his self-pity is short-lived. It quickly turns to rage, followed swiftly by determination to exact revenge: *L'offeso onor, signori*. From this moment de Silva is a man obsessed. He is only temporarily checked in his quest for revenge by the realization that one of the men in his betrothed's apartment is no less than the King. He appears to discount any thought that **Carlo** may be a rival for Elvira's affection, until, that is, Ernani enlightens him.

From that moment de Silva has no concern other than to be avenged, King or no King. Carlo has transgressed the code of honour which is sacred to him. De Silva will not be deflected. It is the only thing which keeps life burning in his old bones and prevents him from lapsing back into that self-pity that took hold at his first entrance. Thus his mania, as all such manias in essence are, is a self-protective device. If he lets go of it he will have to face the utter aloneness of his circumstances and the horror of encroaching death.

It is given to de Silva to demonstrate both the most positive and the most negative aspects of the moral code by which he rules his life so rigidly. When he grants Ernani sanctuary (Act 2) in spite of the fact that he is his rival and enemy, he obeys the laws of hospitality that say a householder should never turn away a needy guest. He does so without any hesitation and with good grace. However, his moral fibre is tried to the utmost when he finds his guest abusing his hospitality by embracing his betrothed. When the King has departed and he releases Ernani from his hiding place he wishes to go forthwith to the field of honour to fight Ernani to the death. But he is frustrated in this by the realization that the King is himself enamoured of Elvira. He therefore accepts Ernani's proposition that they should unite against their common adversary, Carlo.

De Silva learns nothing from the clemency that is shown him by Carlo when he is caught red-handed in league with the conspirators against the King's life (Act 3). Initially Carlo decrees that the commoners should be imprisoned forthwith while the nobles should be taken straight to a place of execution. One might suppose that faced with imminent execution, de Silva might reflect a little on the value of life, the more so when the sentence is reprieved. (One thinks in this instance of how the novelist, Dostoevsky, was condemned to be executed and reprieved at the last moment, an experience that changed him for life. He later incorporated a vivid description of the incident in his novel, *The Idiot*.) But de Silva is not a character given to philosophical reflection. He inhabits a solipsistic universe where only that which immediately impinges on his being is considered worthy of his attention. The moment he is reprieved he rejoices for one reason only, that he is thus enabled to wreak revenge on Ernani. In this he invites comparison with Don Carlo in *La Forza del Destino*, who exalts that Don Alvaro's life has been saved by the surgeon, thus enabling him to take revenge by killing him. The supreme illogicality, not to say absurdity, of this reasoning never seems to occur to Don Carlo any more than it does to de Silva.

De Silva is deaf to Ernani's pleas for reprieve from his oath (Act 4). When Ernani plunges the dagger into his own breast it is for de Silva, as portrayed in Verdi's opera, the fulfilment of his destiny. In Hugo's play de Silva commits suicide himself, thereby tacitly acknowledging the misery of his own existence. As is the way of opera, which has always been better suited to rhetoric than to simple poetry, it makes for a grander finale to have de Silva exulting over the stricken bodies of Ernani and Elvira.

Whether de Silva in his last remaining days will be any happier for the successful prosecution of his vendetta is debatable. Since Elvira still lives (in the opera, not the play) it is conceivable that he would take her back to be his wife, though this is unlikely in view of Elvira's fiery and independent nature. She is more likely to enter a convent, leaving de Silva to contemplate alone the wreck of his hopes for happiness.

Silvano (*Un Ballo in Maschera*). A sailor.
Silvano just happens to attend **Ulrica's** cavern on the same night that the Governor of Boston, **Riccardo**, attends and for this lucky coincidence is rewarded with promotion to the rank of officer. Silvano receives the elevation because Ulrica has predicted it and Riccardo, having overheard the prediction, determines the sailor shall not be disappointed, so hurriedly scribbles a Commission on a piece of paper and slips it into Silvano's pocket. Silvano quickly discovers the documents and inevitably assumes Ulrica is indeed susceptible to supernatural inspiration.

This little episode raises the whole question of the nature of precognition, in the same way as do the predictions of the witches in **Macbeth** (see **Ulrica**). Are the predictions fulfilled because the witnesses set about ensuring that they are fulfilled? Or would they have been fulfilled regardless? Are they truly evidence of supernatural prescience? It is a question which could be debated indefinitely. Those of a rational disposition will inevitably choose the former explanation, while those of poetic inclination will choose the latter. The sensible course undoubtedly is to keep an open mind.

Silvano is so overjoyed that he immediately rushes off to the town to apprise his friends of his good fortune. Since, when they return, they are hailing Riccardo and appear to be aware of his presence at Ulrica's cavern, one must assume that Silvano has penetrated Riccardo's disguise.

Slave (Uno schiavo) (*Il Corsaro*)
In Act 2 Scene 2 the slave announces to **Seid** that a dervish has arrived in their midst. He has escaped from the 'wicked' pirates and begs an audience with Seid. The 'dervish' is **Corrado** in disguise.

Sofia[63] (*I Lombardi*). Wife of **Acciano** and mother of **Oronte**.
Sofia is an Arab woman, married to a tyrant. She has become disenchanted with the faith of her forefathers and has secretly converted to Christianity. If her husband were to find out she would probably be tortured and

---

[63] It is interesting that Solera called Oronte's mother Sofia. In Gnostic mysticism Sofia is the wife and companion of God. It is Sofia who decides whether the soul is to live in the light or return for re-incarnation. She is thus a sort of arbitrator, motivated above all by compassion for fallen souls. Her compassion, however, brings on her great suffering. She will only rise to Heaven after struggles which will bring all the forces of Creation into play. In a sense Sofia, in *I Lombardi* echoes this conception. She is caught between entirely opposing forces and seeks to reconcile them. Ultimately she is successful, although her tragedy is that she can never know she has been successful.

killed. She seems to manage to keep her conversion a well guarded secret. When her son falls in love with a Christian girl, **Giselda,** whom her husband has recently captured and added to his harem, the conflict between her faith and that of her husband and the society she inhabits comes sharply into focus. She prays nightly that her son may see the light and be converted to Christianity. His affection for Giselda lends her hope.

When Oronte confirms that he has indeed come to the conclusion that 'the only true God must be that of that angel of love' Sofia is overjoyed (Act 2 Scene 1). This is exactly what she had hoped for. 'My son! Love has sent you an angel for your salvation!' she exclaims. But her joy will be short lived. She may have a different faith from her husband, but she still loves him as the father of her son. As for her son she has, as is the way with most mothers, made him the centre of her universe. She is thus truly horrified when she is forced to witness the deaths of Acciano and Oronte (in fact Oronte is not killed at this stage, only wounded [Act 2 Scene 3]). It is the sort of shock that very few women would ever recover from. What makes it so appalling is that her husband's murder is the result of adherence to the very faith that she has secretly adopted. She must inevitably blame herself. She may not have actually committed the deed herself but she might as well have, for she has turned her back on everything that defined Acciano's existence. Besides, has she not befriended Giselda, Arvino's daughter and encouraged the liaison between her and her son? It can be little comfort that Giselda deplores her father's actions and lets forth a tirade against the whole Crusading enterprise, nearly getting herself killed in the process. Sofia is forced to restrain her husband's murderer from killing his own daughter.

Sofia does not reappear in the opera. Believing Oronte dead she has little to live for. Maybe she will embrace her faith in totality and enter a nunnery. Her faith is a most unusual one. In the whole operatic canon there are few instances of characters who so blatantly live out a lie, not out of

malicious impulse but out of a desire to act honourably on all fronts, in Sofia's case, to her husband, her son, her son's lover, and above all her God.

A soldier (un Soldat) (*Jerusalem*)

The soldier appears only in Act 1 of the opera, but he plays a crucial role. He is a mercenary hired by **Roger** to murder Roger's rival in love, **Gaston.** He is told by Roger that he will find two knights apparelled in golden armour in the chapel, one of whom will be wearing a white cloak. The soldier is to murder the one *not* wearing a white cloak.

What Roger does not realize is that his brother has conferred his cloak on Gaston, thereby unwittingly making himself the assassin's target. Thus, through no fault of his own, the soldier attacks the Count, leaving him for dead, and in the process alerting all present to the crime. Cries of 'Murder! Murder!' are heard from the chapel. The soldier is quick-witted enough to divert suspicion from himself onto Gaston. Nobody has any problem believing him, principally because few of the knights have taken Gaston's reconciliation with the Count seriously.

Sparafucile (*Rigoletto*). A professional assassin.

Sparafucile earns his living by being in the know. He makes it his business to know who might need to employ his services. Thus when he accosts **Rigoletto** (Act 1 Scene 2) it is clear that Sparafucile knows perfectly well that Rigoletto could use his services. The fact that he accosts Rigoletto outside his own home must alert the latter to the fact that Sparafucile knows something he does not, a suspicion that is confirmed when Sparafucile baldly states that he can assist in removing a rival – 'and you have one'. Maybe Sparafucile has spoken with **Giovanna.** Whatever the source of his information he clearly knows of **Gilda's** secret assignations with the **Duke of Mantua.**

Sparafucile is under the same misapprehension as the courtiers in thinking that Gilda is Rigoletto's mistress. This is not so surprising since Rigoletto behaves towards his daughter as though she were his mistress. In common with fortune tellers and quack doctors it is part of the stock-in-trade of an assassin touting for business to create a necessity, even if no necessity actually exists. This is precisely what Sparafucile does with Rigoletto.

Before his encounter with Sparafucile Rigoletto is oblivious to his daughter's transgressions. Thereafter he is riddled with suspicions, soon to be proven all too well-founded. Like the witches in *Macbeth* Sparafucile plants the seed of discontent (in Macbeth it is ambition; in Rigoletto suspicion). Knowing that Rigoletto will find a use for him, sooner rather than later, Sparafucile tells him that he will wait every night for him in the same place. He is sublimely confident of employment.

Having gained the assignment Sparafucile's confidence seems to evaporate. He is consumed with anxiety over the successful prosecution of the Duke's murder. His sister, **Maddalena**, suddenly develops a passion for their intended victim – precisely the sort of exigency a professional assassin dreads. However, had the beggar (the disguised Gilda) not turned up in the nick of time there is no question that Sparafucile would have completed the contract, regardless of Maddalena's feelings on the matter. He agrees to the alternative plan with little thought that a substitute might actually present itself. Since it does, he has no compunction in grabbing the opportunity to pacify his sister while maintaining his professional credibility. It never seems to occur to him that Rigoletto may look in the sack to check the identity of the corpse with which he has been presented. Imagination is not Sparafucile's strongest attribute – how could it be?

The fact that Sparafucile is forced to seek out his custom would suggest that he does not enjoy a great reputation as an assassin. Professional assassins are, after all, some of the most highly rewarded members of the criminal fraternity. Either Sparafucile sees his inn as a front for his criminal activities or, more likely, he has turned to being a professional assassin to eke out the meagre returns on the tavern which, judging by the stage directions for Act 3, is inappropriately positioned for a hostelry, being well outside Mantua but not apparently accessible to any main thoroughfare.

When Sparafucile gives his name to Rigoletto the latter comments suspiciously, 'a foreigner?' (Act 1 Scene 2). Sparafucile reveals that he is from Bourgogne. This begs the question why Sparafucile has moved to Mantua. Presumably he is an exile from his native country, having fulfilled one too many contracts, which might explain his obviously straitened circumstances.

Stankar (*Stiffelio*). **Lina**'s father, an elderly colonel and Imperial Count.

Stankar has had suspicions that his daughter is having an affair long before **Stiffelio** returns home. He is concerned for only one thing, the honour of his family. As Stiffelio has devoted his life to the spiritual, so Stankar has devoted himself to the worldly. From apparently divergent standpoints, the action of the opera brings the two men remarkably close together (at the height of his passion Stiffelio actually begins to sound like Stankar; 'may all creation be unleashed against me, if I have been dishonoured'). In Stankar's case the sense of dishonour and fear of its repercussions leads him to the brink of suicide.

The concept of honour is central to a society which knows no values beyond achieving mutual respect though adherence to a code that has been formulated primarily to ensure that the individual constituents of society cohere. In this respect the Christian religion effected a remarkable social revolution, by supplanting the primacy of honour with that of compassion and forgiveness, which qualities may go against all the natural instincts, and involve a degree of self-effacement unthinkable to a man like Stankar. It is incumbent upon Stiffelio to ensure that his father-in-law's limited morality is transcended. Eventually he is triumphantly successful.

When Stankar knows for certain that his daughter has been unfaithful to Stiffelio he is appalled, not only on behalf of Stiffelio as a suffering and cuckolded husband, but on his own behalf as an upstanding pillar of the community, who relies upon his family's unblemished reputation to retain the station he has obtained in society, and ergo, the validity of his own self-image. He is consequently determined that his daughter's crime shall at all cost be concealed.

When he discovers Lina writing a letter confessing all to her husband (Act 1 Scene 1), he does not hesitate, but forbids her to send the letter. He accuses her of cowardice (for a military man the most heinous of all failings). He sees her desire to confess as purely selfish. It may ease her conscience but it will only cause Stiffelio intense suffering and the ruination of his career. Stankar will not condescend even to discuss the issue. There is nothing to discuss; his daughter will on no account confess her crime, rather she will let her sin be hidden 'as in the grave'. He is immune to his daughter's tears and to her attempts to soften his resolve.

Stankar's endeavours to keep his daughter's indiscretions a secret (Act 1 Scene 2) will ultimately be thwarted. He does succeed in preventing Stiffelio reading the note of assignation which **Raffaele** has left for Lina in the volume of Klopstock, although this involves him in snatching it from under Stiffelio's nose and tearing it up in front of the entire gathering. But in this he takes his cue from Stiffelio himself, who earlier in the opera has refused to open the notecase that the boatman Walter retrieved from the castle grounds. At that time Stiffelio threw the notecase in the fire, declaring that he did not wish to become a party to another man's guilty secrets. Stankar must assume that Stiffelio has his suspicions concerning Lina's faithfulness and feels justified in similarly destroying the crucial evidence that Stiffelio is about to be confronted with.

On this occasion, however, Stiffelio is furious with his father-in-law for interfering. Lina intervenes, pleading with Stiffelio on account of her father's advanced age. Stankar is undeterred; he is now more determined than ever to wreak revenge on his wife's

seducer, and demands the opportunity to fight a duel with Raffaele. For the second time in the opera Stankar is refused satisfaction on account of his age (Act 2), but this time he is having none of it. He deliberately goads Raffaele into taking up a sword by casting aspersions on the young man's parentage. Their fight, however, is interrupted by the arrival of Stiffelio himself.

Finally it is Stankar who ultimately gives Stiffelio confirmation of Lina's affair. For when Stiffelio, aiming to draw a halt to the duel between Raffaele and Stankar, disarms Raffaele and takes his hand to shake it, Stankar blurts out to Raffaele 'Oh, unheard of excess to take the hand of him whom you have betrayed'. He immediately realizes his mistake ('what have I said?') and then refuses to respond to Stiffelio's searching questions. Unfortunately for Stankar Lina arrives at this crucial moment and, assuming her husband knows all, begs Stiffelio's forgiveness. Now there is no turning back and Stankar's one thought is to exact reparation from Raffaele.

The scene which opens Act 3 portrays Stankar at the very nadir of his life. He has intercepted a letter in which Raffaele tells Lina that he has taken flight and invites her to join him. This is the proverbial last straw for Stankar. His only hope of retrieving his lost honour had been to see Raffaele dead. Now that possibility has gone and he is merely left with the consciousness of impotence and shame. 'I am dishonoured! Dishonoured! And what is life without honour? Shame ... . well then . . . Let it be taken from me'. He grabs his pistol intending to put an end to himself. But for a man like Stankar suicide is a form of dishonour in itself, in some ways far worse than that wrought by his daughter's seducer. And in the moment when he is about to pull the trigger, he realizes something which has eluded him all along, namely that the dishonour is but a symptom of something far greater than anything he has so far made the basis of his existence. It is his love for his daughter, his need for her and sense of having been betrayed by that which he most cherishes, that causes him the most anguish. For Lina brought 'a ray of purest love to warm the frost of my declining years'. He has built an image of her that is entirely idealized. When Lina proves herself to be an ordinary frail human being, Stankar's life illusion crumbles. This scene (Act 3 Scene 1) elucidates all the excesses of his behaviour to date. Now that Lina has failed him he has nothing to live for. Now that he has no possibility of reacquiring his honour and now that his social standing is hopelessly compromised it is a matter of honour to take his own life. For the second time he takes up his pistol and is about to fulfil his intention when **Jorg** enters looking for Stiffelio.

Jorg brings news that he has caught up with Raffaele, who will shortly be arriving at the castle. The exhilaration that Stankar displays at this moment may seem quite out of proportion, taken in isolation, but is in fact an entirely realistic reaction to Jorg's news. For Stankar this represents not just the possibility of being avenged on his wife's seducer, but more crucially the possibility of reclaiming his own life and honour. Confrontation with death in any form is always bound to be a life-defining moment (it is such an experience that convinces Elena in *I Vespri Siciliani* that it is far more important to her to see the fulfilment of her love for Arrigo than it is to see the success of Procida's crusade for Sicilian independence). Stankar has, in fact, endured what William James called, 'a vastation' where all that has previously defined his existence has crumbled. He no longer has any thought for the future. If he previously possessed faith, he has now irrevocably lost it. Now he can think of only one thing, and that is to relieve the unbearable pressure that has accumulated within him.

Stankar undoubtedly remains in earshot throughout Stiffelio's interview with Raffaele, and is on hand when Stiffelio leads Raffaele into an adjoining room there to wait while he (Stiffelio) talks to his wife. When Stankar realizes that Stiffelio is deadly serious in his determination to divorce Lina and give her to Raffaele, he knows immediately what he must do and he does it, summarily executing Raffaele. Ironically, it is the first truly

dishonourable thing to have occurred in the opera. Stankar repairs straight to church to beg forgiveness of the Lord (as presumably has been his habit throughout his life). He is as overjoyed as any that Stiffelio finds it in his heart to forgive Lina, although he will always have difficulty in assimilating the way in which Stiffelio seeks to introduce the Christian ethos into public and sectarian life. (See also **Egberto** (*Aroldo*).)

STIFFELIO

Opera in 3 Acts. Libretto by Francesco Maria Piave after the play, *Le Pasteur, ou L'Évangile et le foyer* (1849), by Émile Souvestre and Eugène Bourgeois.

First performance: 16 November 1850 at the Teatro Grande, Trieste.

Cast:
Stiffelio: evangelical minister (tenor)
Lina: his wife (soprano)
Stankar: Lina's father and an elderly colonel and Imperial Count (baritone)
Raffaele: a nobleman (tenor)
Jorg: an elderly minister (bass)
Federico di Frengel (tenor)
Dorotea: Lina's cousin (mezzo-soprano)

Time: early 19th century
Place: Germany

Act 1 Scene 1   A hall on the ground floor of Count Stankar's castle. At the rear centre a door, to the left a window. To the right a lighted hearth. In front of the window is a large table with various books – including a large, richly-bound volume with a clasp and lock – and writing materials.

Jorg is seated at the table reading the Bible and expostulating on the wisdom contained therein. He closes the book and rises from the table, expressing the hope that Stiffelio, who is expected home at any moment, 'may go forth' and spread the Word. His only concern is that perhaps Stiffelio's love for his wife, Lina, may get in the way of his ministry. Stiffelio enters with Lina on his arm. They are followed by Dorotea, Federico, Raffaele and Stankar. All greet Stiffelio joyfully.

Dorotea reports that a boatman has called repeatedly at the castle asking for Stiffelio. Stiffelio realizes that this must be Walter, a boatman who has already consulted him about a 'strange event'. Everyone urges Stiffelio to relate Walter's story. Stiffelio obliges (*Di qua varcando*).

Apparently Walter had been leaving the castle one morning when he observed an open window at which a young man appeared. (Lina and Raffaele immediately appreciate the significance of Stiffelio's narrative and are aghast.) Stiffelio continues by describing how a young woman was at the young man's side and that both seemed to be consumed with terror. The young man suddenly leapt into the river beneath the window. Clearly Walter has witnessed the hasty conclusion of an illicit night of passion.

Raffaele and Lina are both terrified that they may have been recognized. Their apprehension is in no way allayed when they learn that Walter recovered a notecase which fell from Raffaele's pocket as he jumped. Stiffelio now produces the notecase which he has with him. Everybody present is eager to know what the papers contain. Stiffelio reasons to himself that in order to return them he would have to read them, and that would only be to uncover someone's guilty secret. Rather than that he would prefer to destroy the papers (perhaps he has some inkling of the truth contained therein). He forthwith throws the notecase into the fire (*Colla cenere disperso*). All applaud his restraint. By way of explanation Stiffelio invokes the teachings that underpin his faith: 'Let brother be merciful to brother'. In an aside Raffaele murmurs to Lina the necessity of dissembling and asks to have an opportunity to talk with her. He tells her he will leave a note concealed in a volume of Klopstock[64] apprising her where and when

they should meet. He is observed by Stankar who observes darkly that if Raffaele has in any way stained his family's honour then his, Raffaele's, blood shall 'wipe it clean'. Lina affirms to herself that she has learned her lesson and will never again allow herself to lapse into sin.

Suddenly, from behind the stage, a crowd is heard declaring, 'Long live Stiffelio!' It is a gathering of friends and followers of the Minister come to welcome him home (*A te Stiffelio un canto*). They sing in praise of his goodness: 'You spread justice and brotherly love throughout the land. For holy and eternal truth you wage a fierce war'. At this reminder of her husband's exceptional vocation Lina is torn with remorse. Even Raffaele reflects to himself that he knows that such goodness should arouse in him feelings of remorse, but he admits that he cannot deny himself, 'the cup of pleasure'. Stankar, meanwhile, reflects that if Lina is truly remorseful as she appears to be, then he will stand by her and aim to assist her. Lina sinks onto a chair by the table. All the others, except for Stiffelio, follow Stankar into the room on the right.

Stiffelio has noticed that Lina has had nothing to say to him all evening, 'not even a glance'. Lina commences by addressing her husband as Rodolfo, but then stops herself and apologizes. (Rodolfo Müller was a pseudonym that Stiffelio employed when they were first introduced at the castle.) Stiffelio is not really interested in what his wife wants to call him; all he knows is that he has missed her while away on his ministry and is glad to be reunited with her. He increases Lina's torment a thousandfold by itemizing the instances of sin that he has been forced to countenance during his absence (*Vidi dovunque gemere*), including those wives who have 'broken the bonds of conjugal affection'. But now that he is with Lina again he knows that 'wifely virtue still

---

[64]   Friedrich Gottlieb Klopstock [1724–1803]; an epic and lyric poet whose overriding ambition was to create a German equivalent of Milton's 'Paradise Lost'. The book around which so much of the action in *Stiffelio* revolves is undoubtedly a copy of Klopstock's 'Der Messias', an epic, pietistic poem in twenty cantos, composed entirely in hexameters. It became a surrogate Bible for poets and artists and helped to effect a resurgence of nationalistic pride in the German language and eloquence – a pride which was then immeasurably confirmed by the work of Goethe.

exists'. Lina's conscience causes her to imagine a note of irony in her husband's voice. Her confidence is not increased when Stiffelio suddenly utters a blatant warning: 'Woe betide if I am deceived! Woe betide!' Lina becomes more and more confused. 'Your soul is great and would have forgiven', she rejoins. But Stiffelio begs to differ. 'Within every soul there lies concealed infinite treasure on which none can lay hands with impunity'. He implores Lina to confide in him, without success.

Stiffelio has not forgotten that today is their wedding anniversary and his mind reverts to his beloved mother whose ring he gave Lina on their wedding day. He takes Lina's hand and is confronted with the fact that the ring is missing from her finger. He demands to know to whom she has given it. Lina bursts into tears. By now Stiffelio is convinced that she hides a guilty secret. Lina has never seen him so beside himself: 'May I be struck down by lightning; may the earth yawn beneath my feet, may all creation be unleashed against me if I have been dishonoured!' Stiffelio fulminates. These are not the sort of sentiments one would expect from a man who has dedicated himself to a doctrine of brotherly love. Suddenly Stankar enters with the news that Stiffelio's friends await him. Stiffelio, still beside himself, erupts, 'Shall I never have a moment to myself?' He immediately regrets his outburst and leaves with Stankar, promising Lina that he will return shortly.

Alone, Lina is left to reflect on the impossible situation she has brought upon herself. She kneels and prays to God that she may be forgiven (*A te ascenda o Dio clemente*). She rises and goes to the table, having resolved to write to Stiffelio confessing her adultery. Stankar returns. He quietly approaches her and places his hand on the sheet of paper on which she is writing. He takes it up and, reading the opening sentence, immediately perceives the letter's import. He proceeds to upbraid his daughter not only for her sin but for the selfishness which, he considers, motivates her act of confession. For Stankar knows that the revelation of Lina's adultery will destroy Stiffelio. He commands her to save her husband by submitting to the love he offers her, a love she does not deserve. When Lina vehemently refuses Stankar loses his temper. She has brought dishonour on him and he despises her for it. He will not let her destroy Stiffelio (or himself). Ignoring her protestations he tells her to dry her tears (*Or meco venite*). The honour of her family and of her husband depends on her concealing her guilt. Lina is overcome with remorse but tacitly submits to her father's will. The two leave.

Raffaele enters. In spite of the fact that everyone is avoiding him (which suggests that his affair with Lina is common knowledge) he is determined to obtain a meeting with Lina. He takes a letter from his pocket and inserts it in the volume of Klopstock to which he has his own key. He does not realize that he is being observed by Jorg. Federico appears. He has come specifically to collect the volume of Klopstock (though he is ignorant of its illicit contents). He picks it up and leaves followed by Raffaele, who is naturally agitated.

Act 1 Scene 2   A reception hall in the castle. It is decked and lit up for a party. Friends of Stiffelio and the Count, together with their wives, are introduced by servants. They sing in praise of Stiffelio (*Plaudiam! Di Stiffelio*). The words of their chorus sound ironic in view of what is transpiring in Stiffelio's life (see **Chorus**). The love they refer to is, inevitably, the very opposite of carnal love on which marriage is based. Stiffelio may be adept at dispensing brotherly love but he is far from being able to extend it to his unfaithful wife. The friends retire to the back of the hall as Jorg enters. Stiffelio upbraids him for being late and Jorg tells Stiffelio darkly that he 'shuns the joys of the world . . . for they hold perils and snares for a man's honour'. He then tells Stiffelio how he has observed a man insert a note of assignation into the volume of Klopstock. But Jorg is mistaken about the man's identity. He thinks it was Federico di Frengel whom he observed making off with the book. The fact that Federico is at this moment talking to Lina with the book under his arm would seem to corroborate his supposition. Stiffelio is dumbfounded and ponders on how he can uncover the mystery.

At this moment Lina, Dorotea, Raffaele and Federico enter. Federico still carries the volume of Klopstock. Dorotea enquires whether Stiffelio is thinking about his sermon and Federico asks what the theme will be. 'An old one; the base treachery of the wicked', is Stiffelio's reply. He then elaborates (*Non solo all'iniquo*) how his curse will fall on all those who follow in the footsteps of Judas and are guilty of betrayal or who, 'defile the sacred ties of hearth and home . . . His anathema shall be merely to read aloud the inspired verse of the great poet'. As he says this Stiffelio takes the book from Federico and attempts to open it but finds it locked. Dorotea volunteers that Lina has the key. Stiffelio demands that Lina opens it. Lina is inevitably terrified. Stiffelio is overcome by foreboding of what might be revealed within the pages of the book. His thoughts are echoed by all present.

Realizing that Lina is not going to obey his order, Stiffelio breaks open the clasp himself. Raffaele's letter falls out. Stankar leaps into the breach. Snatching up the letter he declares that it is not for Stiffelio to read; he shall not know who wrote it or to whom. Stiffelio demands that Stankar give it to him, to no avail. Stankar tears the letter to shreds. Stiffelio's accumulated frustration erupts in a diatribe against the old man. Lina comes to her father's defence. It is she, not her father, who should be the object of Stiffelio's wrath, she claims. While Stiffelio continues to splutter with rage Stankar, in an undertone, demands of Raffaele that he meet him shortly in the graveyard. There he will find a weapon of his choice. The rest of the company wonders why Stiffelio has suddenly been assailed by the 'demon' of suspicion and the Act closes to general perplexity.

Act 2   An ancient graveyard. In the centre a cross with steps leading up to it. To the left is a church, lighted within. An imposing stairway leads up to the entrance. To the right, towards the rear of the stage, can be

seen Stankar's castle. The moon is out, illuminating scattered tombs over which cypresses cast their shade. One of the tombs has been erected recently.

Lina enters in great agitation. She knows not why she has ended up in the cemetery where 'all is horror!' She is drawn to the tomb of her mother who has recently died: 'She so pure!' Lina feels defiled and knows that she herself is the only person she can blame. She begs her mother to intercede for her in Heaven (*Ah, dagli scanni eterei*): 'For your sake God will not withhold His forgiveness from me'. She prays. Raffaele enters. Lina begs him to speak softly for she knows her father will be following her every move. But Raffaele knows that Stiffelio suspects Federico and that Stankar has destroyed the only evidence linking Lina to him. Lina confesses she does not love him. She was, she claims, 'taken by surprise'. To which Raffaele reposts, 'Cruel woman! Yet I will love you always'. 'Then prove it', Lina demands, 'give back my letters and my ring'. Raffaele, ignoring Lina's passionate plea to him not to destroy her life any further (*Perder dunque voi volete*), insists he will stay.

Raffaele is just reiterating his determination to stay when Stankar suddenly appears, carrying two swords. Lina tells Raffaele that Rodolfo (that is, Stiffelio) 'shall know all'. Stankar, overhearing his daughter's words, curtly tells her 'he shall know nothing'. He then demands that Lina leave. Lina, realizing that her father will brook no opposition, departs. Stankar throws off his cloak and commands Raffaele to choose one of the swords he now proffers him. Raffaele initially refuses to contemplate a duel on account of Stankar's age. Stankar is incensed and proceeds to taunt him. When Raffaele appears immovable Stankar reveals that he knows Raffaele to be an 'adventurer', whose origins are very far from being within the nobility, as he likes to claim they are. He knows that Raffaele is in fact a foundling. This forces Raffaele's hand. He demands a sword. Stankar presents the two swords and Raffaele takes one. They proceed to fight fiercely.

Stiffelio emerges from the church. Catching sight of the duel in progress he orders the two men to put up their swords, sternly admonishing them for fighting on holy ground. Stankar invites Raffaele to accompany him elsewhere. 'God will be there also', Stiffelio interjects. When Stankar attempts to pull rank Stiffelio reminds him that in this place he, Stiffelio, has the authority as God's emissary. Now it is the duty of Stankar and Raffaele to listen to him: 'Lay down your arms . . . let brother forgive brother', he decrees. 'Never!' Stankar retorts. At which Stiffelio turns to Raffaele, as the younger of the two, disarms him and then shakes his hand. Stankar is outraged: 'How dare you take the hand of him whom you have betrayed!' he exclaims to Raffaele. Thus he gives Stiffelio the first inkling as to the identity of his wife's lover. Stiffelio will no longer be gainsaid. He demands that his father-in-law reveal all. Lina, who has been alerted by the sound of clashing weapons, enters. Seeing her husband and lover opposite each other she pre-empts the situation, assuming Stiffelio knows everything. She begs Stiffelio to forgive her. If Stiffelio needed confirmation he now has it. Pathetically he begs Lina to deny it, but she remains silent. Now his misery turns to cold, bitter rage. 'You shall be crushed beneath my feet', he tells his wife. Stankar tells Raffaele that he had better pray to God, for 'with these tears (his) fate is sealed'. Stiffelio again begs Lina to justify herself, again to no avail. While Lina prays for mercy Stankar continues to threaten Raffaele who reacts in similar vein. Stiffelio acknowledges that now all doubt is removed.

Stankar observes that it is not Lina whom Stiffelio should punish. Stiffelio does not need to be told. He snatches the sword from Stankar and orders Raffaele to defend himself. Raffaele refuses. At this critical moment the congregation is heard from within the church intoning a hymn: 'Do not punish me, O Lord, in Thine anger . . . Have mercy . . . have pity, Lord'. It serves as a direct reminder to Stiffelio of a text he has forgotten; namely 'Vengeance is mine, saith the Lord' (Romans Chapter 12 verses 16–19). Jorg appears on the steps of the church. Stiffelio lets his sword fall. Jorg tells Stiffelio that his congregation await him. They require comfort from him. He appeals to Stiffelio to return to 'his right mind'. Stiffelio erupts; 'Anger and hellish fury consume my desperate being' (*Me disperato abbrucciano*). He begs to be left alone. The congregation can still be heard. 'Lift up your thoughts. Remember who you are!' Jorg urges. It is a seminal moment in Stiffelio's life, and in the opera. He kneels and prays to God to inspire him with words with which to address his congregation. All present express the hope that Stiffelio's words may be 'of peace and of pardon'. But Stiffelio exclaims, 'Of pardon, never!' As he rises to his feet he continues, 'Let the faithless woman be accursed'. Lina falls prostrate at Stiffelio's feet. Jorg ascends the steps to the cross and portentously proclaims, 'Through this cross the All-Righteous has forgiven mankind'. Stiffelio moves with faltering steps towards the cross. As he reaches it the prospect of it overwhelms him. He faints at the foot of the cross as the curtain falls on Act 2.

Act 3 Scene 1 An antechamber with doors leading off. On a table are two pistols and writing materials. Stankar enters, reading a letter. He is evidently agitated. The letter is from Raffaele and is addressed to Lina, informing her that he has fled and inviting her to follow him. Stankar is beside himself with rage. He takes up his sword and flings it from him: 'I am dishonoured! And what is life without honour?' He then takes up a pistol. He cannot tolerate the fact that he has been cheated of the possibility of redeeming his honour by slaying Raffaele. He is about to put the pistol to his head, but stops short, reflecting that he cannot leave his beloved, though erring, daughter and her noble husband. In spite of himself tears start to flow from his eyes: 'A tear dims a soldier's eyes!' he laments. His love for Lina means more to him than anything in the world, in spite of the fact that she has brought dishonour on him to the point of suicide (*Lina, pensai che un angelo*). He sits down and writes a farewell note. He seals the letter then once again takes up his pistol. At this moment Jorg enters, lost in thought. Stankar hastily conceals the pistol. Jorg is in search of Stiffelio. He brings news that he has succeeded in overtaking Raffaele. Ignoring Stankar's protests that Stiffelio will see nobody Jorg enters the latter's room. Stankar is as though reborn. If Raffaele has returned he once again has an opportunity to redeem his honour. His rapturous cabaletta (*Oh gioia inesprimibile*) affirms his delight at the possibility of being avenged. He exits.

Stiffelio emerges from his room, followed by Jorg. He tells Jorg to tell the brethren that he will shortly join them in the church. Jorg departs and Raffaele enters. Stiffelio has one question for him: What would he do if Lina were free? Raffaele answers obscurely: 'What you suppose is impossible'. Stiffelio calls for his servant, Fritz, and tells him to advise Lina that he awaits her. In response to Raffaele's question as to his intentions Stiffelio replies, 'To find which is dearer to you, a guilty freedom or the future of the woman whom you have destroyed'. He leads Raffaele into a side room and then returns. Lina enters.

Stiffelio tells her he is going away and that from henceforth they shall lead separate lives. He intends to lead his life in resignation, with his gaze fixed upon God, while she can lead hers with the man of her heart (*Opposto è il calle*). He reveals that when they married he withheld his true name because of the persecution he was suffering at the time. Thus there is no impediment to their marriage being dissolved. He hands her a sheet of paper which he has already signed and which he now requires her to sign. Lina, weeping copiously, pleads with him but her tears only seem to harden his resolve. Sounding remarkably like his father-in-law, Stiffelio declares, 'offences against honour last as long as life itself'. Realizing there is nothing to discuss Lina snatches the document from him and takes it to the table where she signs it.

Stiffelio is astounded. As Lina rightly surmises he had imagined her tears to be crocodile tears. She gives him back the paper declaring that all is now over between them. Stiffelio makes to leave but Lina detains him. She now demands that he hear her out, not as a husband but in his capacity as a man of 'holy zeal', as a confessor: '*Ministro, ministro, confessatemi!*' ('Minister, minister, hear my confession!'), she cries as she throws herself at his feet. (This line was cut out from the early performances in order to placate the censor but it is absolutely critical to the drama, for it is the first time in the opera that Lina really speaks for herself to her husband.) Stiffelio responds formally: '*Voi! Voi! che udrò?*' ('You! You! What am I to hear?'). All that Müller (Stiffelio's pseudonym) would not hear, Lina replies. If Stiffelio can propose that she can go with another, then he has no understanding of the very real love she bears him. Without him she could never find peace. She speaks with such conviction that Stiffelio is dumbfounded. 'I have always loved you', she keeps reiterating. 'But what of him?' Stiffelio demands. 'It was a betrayal'. 'He betrayed you?' 'Yes'. 'Then let him be killed', Stiffelio concludes. But he is too late. His father-in-law has already done the deed. As Stiffelio is indicating to Lina the side room where Raffaele is concealed, Stankar emerges holding a bloody sword. Jorg enters from another door.

Stankar, when questioned, will only say he has fulfilled an expiation: 'He who could have revealed my dishonour is dead'. He exits abruptly. Jorg invites Stiffelio to accompany him to 'the temple of the Lord', where he will find new strength. Stiffelio's only thought now is to flee 'these evil portals on which man has left the stamp of crime and death!' (*Ah sì, voliamo al tempio*). Lina is distraught. Never on this earth will she discover any consolation, she declares. Jorg drags Stiffelio from the room and Lina rushes out.

Act 3 Scene 2 The interior of a Gothic church supported with huge arches. No altar can be seen, only a pulpit mounted on a column, to which two flights of stairs give access. People gradually enter, Federico and Dorotea follow on. Then Lina, wearing a veil, approaches to the right of the pulpit and finally Stankar to the left. All kneel.

The congregation reiterate the hymn sung in Act 2, 'Do not punish me, Lord, in Thine anger or I shall dissolve like mist before the sun. Have mercy! Have pity!' Stankar begs forgiveness if he has usurped his authority in killing Raffaele. Lina also prays for forgiveness. Stiffelio, lost in thought, and Jorg cross the church. They are wearing long black cloaks. Stiffelio carries a large book.

As Stiffelio passes close to Lina he turns to Jorg and asks, 'What woman is that?', for Lina's face is covered by a veil. Then Lina lifts her veil and Stiffelio is overcome with confusion. Jorg urges him to open the Bible; 'The Lord will inspire you', he says. Together they mount the steps of the pulpit. Stiffelio opens the Bible and reads in a trembling voice: 'Then Jesus, turning to the assembled people, pointed to the adulteress at his feet . . .' Lina collapses in the aisle and Stiffelio continues: 'Whichever among you is without sin, let him cast the first stone . . . and the woman . . . the woman . . . rose up forgiven'.[65] Lina mounts the steps to the pulpit on her knees, falling on the last step at Stiffelio's feet. Stiffelio reiterates, 'Forgiven . . . forgiven . . . forgiven', and then, placing his hand on the Bible concludes, 'God has spoken it'. All present, except Lina, echo his words. Lina rises to her feet and with both hands raised, exclaims, 'Almighty God!' The curtain falls.

As was the case many times in Verdi's oeuvre *Stiffelio* is about the conflicting demands of passion on the one hand, and duty to family, society and the homeland on the other. It is here complicated and ennobled by the fact that Stiffelio feels his first duty is to God, and specifically to the Christian ethos which sets brotherly love above all other considerations. Confronted by his wife's seducer Stiffelio's faith is tested to the limit. It is a testament to the depths of his conviction that at the end, against all the odds and the cruellest suffering, he succeeds in surmounting his personal feelings and is able to forgive his

wife. It is a most unusual thesis for Verdi to follow. Normally in his operas the protagonists are passion-ruled and take the consequences, the apogee of this tendency, of course, being Otello.

Stiffelio represents one of three occasions when Verdi elevated Christian compassion above the dictates of human passion, the only other instances being *La Forza del Destino* (in the revised edition) and *Alzira*. It is significant that the opera came not at the end of his career, but mid-career, when he had a welter of experience behind him, while the best was yet to come. For in truth it was not the moral pointed at the conclusion of the opera that inspired Verdi but the conflict within the central character between what he knows he should do and what he is, in fact, able to do. This elicited from Verdi some of his finest inspiration and gives a first hint of the heights to which he will attain in subsequent heroic tenor roles, notably **Alvaro** (*La Forza del Destino*) and **Otello**.

Stiffelio (*Stiffelio*). An Ahasuerian preacher. The Ahasuerians are followers of **Ahasuerus**, the Wandering Jew. The very name, Ahasuerus, has connotations of poetry (Shelley and Yeats were both intrigued), agnostic mysticism and myth. By definition a follower of Ahasuerus must be a heretic in terms of the Christian church.

Thus when Stiffelio first applied to **Stankar** for his daughter's hand in marriage he used a pseudonym by which he is still known: Rodolfo Müller. It was under that pseudonym that he married **Lina**. Technically speaking therefore, his marriage has never been legally valid. Stiffelio invokes this anomaly when seeking to annul his marriage (Act 3). But the use of the pseudonym has a far greater significance than just its legal implications. For it points to a crucial split in Stiffelio's psyche, a split which must be healed before he can go forward in life. It is the split between himself, the ordinary mortal and carnal human being, and his vocation as a servant of God.

As a preacher the platitudes fall from Stiffelio's lips all too easily, as is evidenced

---

[65] See the Gospel according to St John, Chapter 8, verses 3–11.

at the opening of the opera; 'God has spoken it . . . God has written . . . Let brother be merciful to brother' (Act 1 Scene 1). It is one thing to say it, even though it be said with the greatest conviction. It is quite another to enact it. Rodolfo Müller has married into a noble family and has a loving and devoted wife who is forced to endure long separations from her husband when he is away on his numerous and arduous journeys abroad in pursuit of his ministry. Everywhere Stiffelio goes he sees injustice, misery and sin: 'Women, those simple guardians of virtue (who have) broken the bonds of conjugal affection'. This is almost the worst sin that Stiffelio witnesses, because his entire life-illusion is supported by the devotion of his wife and he takes her totally for granted. Because he spends his life purveying a gospel of high-minded seriousness he takes it for granted that those around him share and participate in those same moral tenets. It never occurs to him the enormity of the demand he makes. It never occurs to him that his wife might have needs of her own, needs which are simply not satisfied by being married to a would-be saint.

In a marriage like that of Stiffelio and Lina what is really in question is the co-existence of two entirely separate life-philosophies. This, to a certain extent, must be the case in any human relationship, but it is accentuated a thousandfold when the man is an idealist like Stiffelio. Stiffelio's idealism is the quintessence of the masculine urge to conquer and control. It is diametrically opposed to the living-in-the-moment for the here-and-now, and preservation of the status quo, which is the essence of the feminine in its nutritive aspect. Stiffelio's idealism epitomizes the intellectual quest of mankind to take control of its destiny. It is a necessary and commendable quest but it inevitably accentuates the fundamental differentiation between man and woman. Stiffelio does not comprehend this.

One half of Stiffelio sees his wife's adultery from the social perspective epitomized by his father-in-law, that is, as a matter of gross dishonour, while the other half sees it as evidence that his wife does not love him. Thus it comes as a very real shock when Lina, after she has signed the divorce documents, declares that she has always loved him. Lina's only defence for her adultery has been, 'I was taken by surprise' (Act 2), as she was, by her own needs which were totally unsatisfied in her marriage to Stiffelio. Lina did not set out to be unfaithful, she was overtaken by a ruthless adventurer whose first principle in life is to seek gratification for his appetites. Her sin, if sin it is, is one of omission. She deserves forgiveness because she has been a victim not only of **Raffaele**'s lasciviousness but, more critically, of her own human frailty, the sort of frailty that is everyone's birthright, including Stiffelio.

It is to Stiffelio's credit that he recognizes this, but only once the tidal wave of his own passion, a manifestation of his own frailty, has died down. Stiffelio's passions are all the greater because for years they have been suppressed. In taking his domestic life – his wife – for granted he has opened a chasm within himself that has been waiting to swallow him ever since he first set out on his ministry. There is a clear parallel with Otello in the way that Stiffelio's suspicions about his wife's adultery initially become fixated on the wedding ring that he gave her. With Otello it is a handkerchief. It is significant that the ring belonged originally to his mother, for emotionally Stiffelio is still in thrall to his mother. He has transferred onto Lina the role of mother, the woman who will metaphorically, if not in actuality, wash his dirty linen and make a home for him to return to. It is not an uncommon syndrome but sooner or later there is a price to pay. Stiffelio has to learn that Lina is not his mother but an independent woman with agendas quite distinct from his own. Lina effectively forces his hand. Had she not strayed he would have inevitably continued to take her for granted and treat her merely as a convenience.

It is only after Lina has signed the divorce document that she is able, for the first time, to speak her mind to Stiffelio (Act 3 Scene 1). Ostensibly she does this by appealing to him in his professional role as father-confessor. Thereby she turns the tables on him. He is quite unprepared for such a revolution. He is only saved by the faithful **Jorg** inviting him to the church. He accepts the invitation with alacrity, for at least in church there is none of the emotional uncertainty which threatens to consume him in the presence of his wife.

The faithful Jorg is the crucial bolster to Stiffelio's fragile ego. He could never have sustained the years of ministry he has already undergone without such a bolster. So much is clear from the action of the opera alone. Jorg is Stiffelio's father-confessor and mentor. Jorg is elderly and well past the age when the passions are spent and the complexities attendant upon such passions no longer pertain. For Jorg the demands and exigencies of fate are clearly defined. There are no grey areas. Whenever Stiffelio has been assailed by doubt – that greatest enemy of all faith – Jorg has been there to clarify matters and lead him back onto the straight and thorny path of rectitude. At each critical stage in Stiffelio's odyssey – his return home (Act 1 Scene 2) (where Stiffelio's interrogation of Jorg, 'Are you not late?' is highly revealing); the discovery of Stankar and Raffaele fighting (Act 2); Lina's confrontation with her husband (Act 3 Scene 1); and finally in the church for the scene of Lina's rehabilitation (Act 3 Scene 2) – Jorg is on hand.

The forgiveness meted out to Lina is meted out from on high and in public for Stiffelio's life is lived out almost exclusively in public. It is a source of real exasperation to him. When Stankar interrupts Stiffelio's first confrontation with his wife (Act 1 Scene 1) Stiffelio, in exasperation, demands, 'shall I never have a moment to myself?' It is a crie de coeur that goes unheeded.

What Stiffelio lacks is not time for himself but time to be with his wife. It is a penalty that any public figure must endure, but for a sincere man of God it is an impossibility. For the preacher must, by definition, be someone who knows how to do that which human beings find most impossible of all: commune with himself and with his Maker. Lina is, as

he comes to realize on the very threshold of losing her, the one person with whom he can commune and discover himself. If he were to lose her it would be a catastrophe for him, and he knows it. But until he can publicly acknowledge that Lina had every right to stray as she has and still be forgiven, he does not deserve her companionship.

It is the peculiar gift of characters like Stiffelio to attract to themselves individuals on whom they can project all the aspects of themselves that they cannot live out. Thus Jorg represents the true single-mindedness and devotion of the monk whose every living moment is given to communing with God; Stankar represents the outraged man of honour; Raffaele the irresponsible man who is ruled primarily by his appetites. As a preacher Stiffelio's chief mandate is to disseminate and communicate. Disseminators and communicators cannot afford to be one-sided. He must apprehend all things but never relinquish the distance that allows him to discriminate. This he comes perilously close to doing. But in the end he is saved, as he always will be, by Jorg, whose age and experience means that he can comprehend Stiffelio's predicament without himself becoming entrapped.

If, at the opening of opera, Stiffelio could be forgiven for being prone to complacency, by the end of the opera he must know that he can no longer serve his public function without addressing his private needs. It is certain that he will have a staunch ally in the person of his wife who, did he but know it, has never been far away and will, if recognized for herself, give herself unstintingly to assist him.

(See also **Aroldo**.)

The Surgeon (Il Chirurgo) (*La Forza del Destino*)

The surgeon plays a crucial role in effecting the final denouement of the opera, for he saves **Don Alvaro's** life at a critical juncture, just as **Don Carlo** has discovered that Herreros is none other than Alvaro, the murderer of his father and seducer of his sister, **Leonora** (Act 3 Scene 2). Carlo celebrates the fact that since Alvaro still lives he will be able to wreak vengeance for his dishonoured family.

T

Talbot (*Giovanna d'Arco*). Commander-in-chief of the English army.

Talbot has the unenviable lot of having to sustain a total reversal of fortunes in the war with France, principally due to the inter-vention of **Giovanna d'Arco**. His soldiers have become convinced that they are the victims of devilry and Talbot is powerless to revitalize them; 'Alas, a hundred triumphs destroyed in a single day!' he laments (Act 1 Scene 1). He upbraids his men for cowardice but must know the futility of such remonstration.

He takes on trust **Giacomo**'s assurance that he will deliver to the English the cause of their woes, his own daughter Giovanna. This is in spite of the fact that the stage directions indicate that Giacomo's 'dishevelled hair and manner betray a disordered mind' (Act 1 Scene 1). The English, however, are so demoralized that Talbot must be glad of any possibility of reviving morale. It would have been better for Talbot had he treated Giacomo's offer with more circumspection, for although the old man's offer is in perfectly good faith it signals the final crushing reverse for the English. It is only when Giovanna is in chains awaiting execution that Giacomo succeeds in clearing his mind of the mania that has led him to betray his own daughter. The reunion with her father empowers Giovanna to greater heights of audacity on the battlefield, ensuring the final defeat of the English. Talbot, if he survives the battle, will return to England a beaten man.

Tebaldo (*Don Carlo*). Elisabeth's page.

Tebaldo accompanies Elisabeth in her exile to Spain. He is first heard offstage, calling to the squires, foresters and pages (Act 1) for his mistress and he are lost in the forest of Fontainbleau. Tebaldo is frightened. He knows it is his responsibility to make sure his mistress, soon to be married to the Spanish Infante **Don Carlo**, is safe at all times. He offers Elisabeth his arm and urges her to move on, but Elisabeth is tired and wants to rest. They sit down. At this moment **Don Carlo** steps forward.

Now Tebaldo is really alarmed: 'Who is this stranger?' Having ascertained that Carlos is a Spaniard and in the suite of the Spanish Ambassador, he turns his attention to seeing if he can find them a way out of the forest. To his infinite relief he catches sight of the lighted hall of the palace of Fontainbleau from afar. He tells Elisabeth that he will hurry back and arrange for an entourage to conduct Elisabeth back to the palace (this is not really credible – Tebaldo would surely not leave Elisabeth alone with a stranger, especially a foreigner. But this omission does at least allow the dramatist time for Carlos and Elisabeth to become acquainted, unencumbered by the page's presence).

Tebaldo returns, as promised, with a litter and other pages carrying torches. He approaches Elisabeth, kneels and kisses the hem of her gown, for he has learnt, while at the palace, that Elisabeth is not to be married to the Infante but to the Spanish King, **Filippo** (Philip) II. He may be worried that soon he could be out of a job. He begs Elisabeth to deign to keep him in her service. Elisabeth agrees and motions him to rise. Tebaldo then dramatically announces: 'Queen, I salute you; wife of King Philip'. Elisabeth is dumbfounded and Tebaldo confirms that her father, Henry II of France, has pledged her hand to the Spanish King. Tebaldo cannot help but be aware that the news is not welcome to Elisabeth. He remains mute for the remainder of the scene. He is no doubt impatient to return to the pageantry that will attend the celebrations of the new détente at the palace.

In Act 2 Tebaldo has travelled with the court to the monastery of San Yuste. He awaits the Queen in the gardens outside the monastery with the ladies of the court, who are not permitted to enter. He sings with the ladies of the beauty of the gardens and the boon of the shade afforded by the pines after a long, hot day in the sun. He then joins **Eboli** in the chorus of her Song of the Veil. This scene, and Tebaldo's contribution, provides light relief after the dark preoccupations of the previous scene (Act 2 Scene 1). Once Elisabeth has entered the monastery Tebaldo fulfils his official function, announcing the arrival of **Rodrigo**. Later he is despatched by Elisabeth to fetch 'her son' (Carlos) to her. Tebaldo knows better than anybody the true relationship between Elisabeth and Carlos that was engendered by their meeting in the forest of Fontainbleau. He departs with the ladies, leaving Carlos and Elisabeth alone together.

Tebaldo, with a child's perspicacity, is no doubt aware that Elisabeth's passion is for Carlos. He will therefore be aware of the dangers inherent in Philip's intrusion on Elisabeth and Carlos's meeting. He hastens to announce the King. He will be grieved by his mistress's sorrow over the **Countess d'Aramberg**'s dismissal, but grateful that it is not he who is being dismissed.

In the *auto-da-fé* scene (Act 3 Scene 2) Tebaldo joins the populace in begging Philip to show mercy towards the Flemish Deputies. He probably feels there is safety in numbers. Thereafter he does not appear in the opera, since Acts 4 and 5 are devoted primarily to private scenes between the main protagonists.

Tebaldo (*I Vespri Siciliani*). French soldier in the occupying army in Palermo, Sicily.
Tebaldo is a mere cipher for **Roberto**. See **Roberto**.

Thibault (*Don Carlo*). See **Tebaldo**

Tom (*Un Ballo in Maschera*). Conspirator. See **Samuel**

Master Trabucco (*La Forza del Destino*). Muleteer and peddler.
Trabucco plays a small but crucial role in the drama. He gives **Leonora** safe passage on his mule when she is in flight from the wrath of her family, disguised as a man and

separated from her lover. In the Inn (Act 2 Scene 1) where they rest and where **Don Carlo** is also staying, Trabucco keeps himself very much to himself and ignores the importunate questioning of Don Carlo as to the identity of his customer. Presumably Leonora has paid him to keep silent. Trabucco observes that a traveller's money is 'all I ever notice'. Exasperated by Carlo's persistence, Trabucco finally retires to the stables to 'sleep with my mule who knows no Latin and is no bachelor of arts' (this is a direct reference to Don Carlo himself, who has just admitted, or rather boasted, to being a bachelor of arts).

In Act 3 Scene 3 Trabucco is very much in evidence, selling his trinkets and inviting the soldiers to sell him anything they have. He is clearly an astute businessman. The soldiers are well aware that they are being swindled by Trabucco's valuation of their collectibles, but they need money for drink, as Trabucco well knows. He is clearly delighted with the day's business. His mercenary ways make a stark contrast with the idealistic passions of the main protagonists. This scene obliquely highlights that idealistic passions can only be indulged in by those who can afford the luxury. Most of human life consists of grubbing around for a living.

LA TRAVIATA
Opera in 3 Acts. Libretto by Francesco Maria Piave, after the drama, *La Dame aux camélias* (1852), by Alexandre Dumas *fils*, after his novel (1848) based on his own experiences.

First performance: 6 March 1853 at the Teatro la Fenice, Venice.

Cast:
Violetta Valéry (soprano)
Flora Bervoix (mezzo-soprano)
Annina: Violetta's maid (soprano)
Alfredo Germont (tenor)
Giorgio Germont: Alfredo's father (baritone)
Gastone: Viscount de Letorières (tenor)
Baron Douphol: Violetta's protector (baritone)
Marquis d'Obigny: Flora's protector (bass)
Doctor Grenvil (bass)
Giuseppe: a servant (tenor)

Time: Around 1850
Place: Paris and surroundings

Background *La Traviata* (lit. 'the one who is led astray'). The character of Marguerite Gautier in Dumas *fils'* novel (Violetta in Verdi's opera) was based on the life of one Alphonsine Rose Plessis (b. 13 January 1824, d. 3 February 1847 at the age of barely 23), with whom Dumas had a passionate affair. When she entered society Alphonsine assumed the name of Marie Duplessis. Asked once why she chose the name, Marie, Alphonsine answered 'because it is the name of the Virgin'.

Verdi could undoubtedly identify with the story since at the time he first saw Dumas' play he was engaged on an affair with the singer, Giuseppina Strepponi, who became his lifelong companion and eventually his wife.

Synopsis
Act 1   A room in Violetta's house. A party is in progress. Violetta is seated on a sofa, talking to the doctor and other friends who come and go. Some of the guests turn to meet a group of new arrivals, amongst whom are the Baron and Flora. They upbraid the new arrivals for their tardiness. Violetta greets them all personally. Flora and the Marquis marvel that Violetta appears so happy, for they know the malady that afflicts her. Gastone, Viscount de Letorières, enters with Alfredo. The servants prepare the table. Gastone introduces Alfredo to Violetta as a great admirer of hers and one of his most valued friends. Alfredo gallantly kisses Violetta's hand as the latter thanks Gastone for 'sharing such a gift'.

The servants, meanwhile, have laid the supper table. Violetta invites everybody to be seated. All take their places, Violetta between Alfredo and Gastone, and prepare to enjoy their meal. Gastone whispers to Violetta that Alfredo thinks of nobody but her and describes how, when Violetta was ill, Alfredo visited daily. Violetta is incredulous. She confronts Alfredo, who admits it is true. Violetta observes that the Baron never

did as much for her. The Baron is incensed and remarks to Flora that the young man – Alfredo – irritates him. Violetta, meanwhile, pours Alfredo a glass of wine and Gastone suggests to the Baron that he should propose a toast. The Baron refuses and turns to Alfredo who obliges with the famous Brindisi (*Libiamo ne'lieti calici*), extolling a hedonistic philosophy; 'let's drink for pleasure, etc'. Violetta returns his toast in like kind: '*Tra voi saprò dividere*' – 'With you I would share my days of happiness'. All join in the toast. Music is heard from the other room and Violetta invites her guests to dance. All move towards the centre doors.

Suddenly Violetta turns pale and staggers. She tries to pull herself together but is compelled to sit down, as she is overcome by the deleterious effects of her condition. Alfredo is immediately at her side. Violetta tells her guests to proceed without her; she will follow soon. All except Alfredo go into the ballroom. Initially oblivious to Alfredo's presence Violetta rises and looks at herself in the mirror. She remarks on how pallid she has become. Noticing Alfredo in the mirror she starts. Alfredo launches into remonstrations about her lifestyle. If she continues as she does she will kill herself. Gallantly Alfredo declares that if only he were able he would be the most vigilant guardian to her. He declares his love. Violetta laughs at him but Alfredo is not deceived: 'You laugh, but all the same you have a heart'. He declares his great passion (*Un di felice*), while Violetta gently tells him she can only offer friendship. She would not know how to feel such a great emotion as he declares for her. She tells him to look for someone else more suitable.

The pair are interrupted by the arrival of Gastone who has come to see what delays them. Violetta resumes her habitual coquetry. Alfredo, wounded, makes to leave. Violetta presses on him a flower from her corsage and tells him to return it to her: 'when it has withered'. Alfredo takes this to mean on the morrow and is overjoyed. Impetuously he reiterates his love for her and takes his leave.

The guests all return from the ballroom, flushed from their dancing. They now take

427

their leave of Violetta. Left alone Violetta is consumed with thoughts of Alfredo (*E strano, è strano*). 'No man before kindled a flame like this', she remarks. Could she be experiencing for the first time true love? She gives vent to her sense that love is a great mystery, something quite foreign to her, in spite of the fact that she trades in its semblance in her daily profession. It attracts her, in spite of herself. But then she quickly dismisses her ruminations as folly. What does she want with moonstruck romance? Rather she would fling herself into the 'vortex of pleasure' (*Sempre libera degg'io*). Enjoyment alone shall be the recipe for whatever life is left to her. Her false gaiety is interrupted by the sound of Alfredo's voice extolling love as the 'pulse of the whole world, mysterious, unattainable'. Momentarily struck where she is most vulnerable, Violetta once again flings herself into her gospel of pleasure for the sake of pleasure as the curtain falls on Act 1.

Act 2 Scene 1   A ground floor room in a country house near Paris. Alfredo has successfully persuaded Violetta to leave her life in Paris and they have moved to a house in the country where Alfredo hopes Violetta may recover her health. He is blissful in the knowledge that Violetta has declared to him: 'I want to live faithful to you alone'.

Alfredo enters wearing hunting clothes. He puts down his gun. In his aria (*Lunge da lei per me non v'ha diletto!*) he gives expression to his love for Violetta and joy in the fact that she has finally committed herself to him (*De' miei bollenti spiriti*).

Annina enters in great agitation. She is dressed for travelling. Alfredo demands to know where she has been. To Paris on Violetta's instructions, Annina replies, to sell all Violetta's possessions. Apparently they have fallen into debt. Alfredo, in his bliss, has lost sight of the dreary realities of life. As Annina points out, living in the country, removed from the world, is very costly. When Alfredo asks why he has not been told, Annina reveals that Violetta had instructed her to conceal their plight from Alfredo. The situation is this: they need a thousand louis to pay their creditors. Alfredo is overcome

with remorse at his thoughtlessness. He dismisses Annina and, determined to set things right himself, he leaves forthwith for Paris.

Violetta enters. She is holding a sheath of papers and talking to Annina. Giuseppe follows from behind. Violetta asks where Alfredo is. She is told he has gone to Paris but will be returning before dark. Violetta is puzzled. Giuseppe presents her with a letter. Violetta takes the letter and tells her servants that a man will shortly be arriving on business and is to be shown in at once. Annina and Giuseppe exit. Violetta opens the letter. It is from Flora, inviting her to a ball that very evening. Violetta is surprised that Flora has discovered her hideaway. She throws the letter onto the table and sits down. 'She'll wait for me in vain', she says. Giuseppe returns and announces a gentleman to see her. Violetta signs to him to show the gentleman in.

Germont enters and forthwith introduces himself as the father of Alfredo, 'that headstrong boy who is rushing to his ruin because of his infatuation for you'. Violetta rises indignantly and makes to leave, reminding Germont that he is a guest in her house. Germont is surprised by her hauteur. Realizing that she should hear the old man out she returns to her seat. There must be some mistake, she says. When Germont reveals that Alfredo is about to hand over all his worldly goods to Violetta, Violetta is outraged and declares that she would never allow such a thing. Germont observes that they live luxuriously, to which Violetta replies by showing him the documents which confirm her intention to sell all her worldly goods. Germont is startled. 'Is this how the past reproaches you?' he asks. Violetta passionately confirms that she has turned her back on the past. All her love is for Alfredo now. Germont's attitude softens, but still he must reveal the true reason for his visit, to request that she relinquish Alfredo for the sake of his family's happiness and honour. He tells Violetta that Alfredo has a sister who is engaged to be married. If Alfredo refuses to return to the bosom of his family, if he persists in his feckless passion for a courtesan, the man his sister intends to marry will sever all connections with her (*Pura siccome un angelo*). Violetta at first assumes it will be sufficient for her to leave Alfredo for a short spell. But Germont is insistent. She must leave him for ever.

Violetta is frantic. She has no friends, no family. Alfredo is her entire life, aside from which she is desperately ill. She would rather die than relinquish Alfredo. Germont, in spite of the undoubted sympathy he feels for her plight, is adamant. He tells her that she is young and beautiful, now. But what when her charms have faded? Alfredo may well become bored, especially since: 'the threads that bind them together have not been blessed by Heaven', that is, they are living together out of wedlock. Violetta is all too easily persuaded and falls into a paroxysm of grief: 'Ah, for the wretched woman who has fallen once, the hope of rising is gone forever' (*Dite alla giovine, si bella e pura*). Pathetically she asks Germont what she should do. Tell him she does not love him, he tells her. He would not believe me, Violetta replies. In truth there is no easy way and she knows it. She embraces Germont and begs him to give her strength and to comfort Alfredo, whom she knows will be devastated. She goes to her writing table to write to Alfredo. Suddenly, in an excess of grief, she turns to Germont and begs him to make it clear that she has not renounced his love lightly, and to tell him how much she has suffered. 'I shall soon die', she tells Germont: 'Let him know the sacrifice I made of the love that will be his till I draw my last breath'. She says she hears someone coming and begs Germont to leave. They embrace and bid farewell. Violetta's tears stifle her final farewell. Germont exits into the garden.

Violetta sits down to write. She rings a bell, Annina enters and Violetta gives her the note with instructions to deliver it personally at once. The letter is addressed to the Baron Douphol, her protector of old. She is begging him to take her back. When Annina has departed Violetta returns to her desk to write to Alfredo. She has just sealed the note when Alfredo enters. Seeing her confusion he demands to know to whom she is writing. Violetta owns to the fact that the letter is to him, but refuses to show it to him. Alfredo lets the matter pass. He is devastated by the fact that he has received an angry letter from his father, announcing his imminent arrival. Violetta refrains from telling Alfredo that she has already endured an interview with his father. [Note: Throughout this Act there is an almost total absence of communication between the two lovers. Neither appears to know what the other is doing.] Violetta becomes greatly agitated and begs some reassurance from Alfredo of his love for her. Alfredo is bewildered. Why is she crying? Containing her pent-up emotions Violetta forces a smile and laughs off her hysterical outburst. She runs out into the garden. Alfredo reflects to himself: 'Her love for me is her whole life'. He sits down, picks up a book and reads for a moment, then gets up and looks at a clock above the fireplace.

Giuseppe enters hurriedly and announces that Violetta has just departed for Paris. Annina has gone on ahead. Alfredo is unperturbed, assuming that Annina will prevent Violetta from disbursing her estate. Then he sees the figure of his father in the garden. He turns to go out, but is met at the door by a messenger bearing the note from Violetta. Alfredo tips the messenger, who exits. He is immediately overcome with apprehension. He opens the letter and reads: 'Alfredo, when you receive this note . . .' (see **Alfredo** for full text). He lets out a shocked exclamation, just as his father enters. He falls straight into his father's arms. Germont tries to console his son (*Di Provenza il mar*), but Alfredo is hardly listening. He collapses in despair at the table and buries his face in his hands. His father, meanwhile, tries to remind him how happy he was in the family home in Provence, and of the pain his absence has caused his family, his father in particular. When he has concluded Alfredo rudely repulses him. His only thoughts are for revenge. He is convinced that Violetta has allowed herself to be lured back to the luxurious lifestyle offered by Douphol. He remains deaf to his father's pleas. He spies Flora's letter inviting Violetta to a party that very night and immediately resolves to confront Violetta there. He rushes out. Germont, who by now is utterly bewildered, hurries after him.

Act 2 Scene 2 A brilliantly lit, richly furnished room in Flora's house. There is a door at the back and one to each side. Downstage to the left is a card table; to the right a table decked with flowers, where refreshments are set out. Chairs and a sofa furnish the room.

Flora, the Marquis, the doctor and other guests enter from the left. The doctor and Flora are astounded to learn from the Marquis that Violetta and Alfredo have separated and that Violetta will be attending the party, escorted by the Baron. A crowd of guests wearing masks and gypsy costumes enter. The 'gypsies' boast of their fortune-telling skills. One of them takes Flora's hands and announces that she has several rivals. Another takes the Marquis' hand and announces that he is no model of faithfulness. Flora pretends outrage, but it is all part of the fun. The other guests encourage them not to take themselves too seriously.

Gastone enters with a lively band of guests in masks, dressed as Spanish bullfighters and picadors. The 'bullfighters' sing of the heroics of a young picador who was required to stretch out five bulls in a single day in order to prove himself worthy of his lover. All comment on the tale then declare that it is time to get down to the serious business of gambling. The men remove their masks and many make straight for the gaming tables. Alfredo enters. All greet him. It is a long time since he has been seen at such a party. Flora is just asking where Violetta is when the latter arrives on the arm of the Baron. The Baron instantly notices Alfredo's presence and warns Violetta against exchanging a single word with him. Violetta realizes that she has been extremely rash in coming at all. Flora makes her sit beside her on a sofa. The doctor joins them, while the Marquis engages the Baron in conversation.

Gastone cuts the cards. Alfredo has already taken a seat and now stakes his money. His first bet is successful. He stakes again and wins again. Alfredo darkly reiterates the old adage: 'Lucky at cards, unlucky in love'. He declares that he intends returning to the country to spend his winnings, not alone, as they might think but in company with 'she who was with me there until she ran away from me'. Violetta is becoming increasingly uneasy. The Baron has joined the table. Violetta warns him to hold his peace, or she will leave him. The Baron places a large stake which Alfredo immediately matches. Alfredo wins. The Baron invites him to double up and Alfredo agrees. Again Alfredo wins. He invites the Baron to continue the game but a servant announces that supper is served. The Baron declines to continue but promises that he 'will have his revenge later'. All leave for the supper table.

The stage is empty for a few moments. Then Violetta returns in great agitation, followed by Alfredo. She begs Alfredo to leave for, she tells him, he is in grave danger. She fears the Baron's temper. Alfredo merely observes: 'It is a question of life and death between us. If I kill him, you will lose lover and protector at a single blow'. Does not such a prospect terrify her? Violetta rejoins that her only concern is that Alfredo might be the victim. Alfredo tells her that he will leave, but only if she comes with him. Violetta's response: 'No! No! Never!' has such vehemence that Alfredo is taken aback. She tells him that she has given a solemn vow to refrain from ever seeing him again. Alfredo wants to know to whom she has made this vow. Was it to Douphol? Violetta will never reveal that it was Alfredo's own father who has destroyed their happiness. She therefore leaps at his suggestion: 'Yes, it is Douphol'. She finds it less easy to confirm her love for Douphol, but she is sufficiently convincing for Alfredo to run to the doors and summon all the guests to come as witnesses.

The company rushes in. Pointing at Violetta, who leans weakly against a table, Alfredo rhetorically demands whether they 'know' this lady? Then, ignoring Violetta's protests, he tells the assembly how, on his behalf, Violetta lost all that she possessed (in order to finance their lifestyle in the country). But now he will repay the debt. Contemptuously he throws his winnings from the gaming table at Violetta's feet. She faints in Flora's arms. Suddenly, at this critical moment, Alfredo's father arrives. Horrified at his son's behaviour he commands Alfredo to leave. The guests are equally shocked by Alfredo's conduct. Alfredo, the extremity of his passion spent, is consumed with remorse. The guests try to console Violetta. Germont reflects to himself that he alone knows the true extent of Violetta's devotion and sacrifice. The baron murmurs to Alfredo that the insult to Violetta shall not pass unavenged. Meanwhile Violetta revives and sadly reflects that Alfredo cannot possibly know the depths of her love for him, nor the reason for her renouncing it. She prays that when he does come to know it he may be saved from remorse, for even beyond the grave she will still love him.

Act 3 Violetta's bedroom. Violetta is now in the final stages of her illness. She is asleep on the bed. Annina, seated near the fireplace, is dozing. Suddenly Violetta wakes up. She asks for a sip of water, and when Annina has brought her a glass asks her to see if it is daylight. Annina draws the curtains and, looking out, sees Doctor Grenvil approaching. 'What a good friend he is', Violetta remarks. She resolves to get up, rises, but falls back. Then, with Annina's help, she moves slowly over to the couch. The doctor arrives in time to help. He feels Violetta's pulse and asks her how she feels. 'Weak in body but tranquil in soul', Violetta replies. She has apparently been seeing a priest: 'Religion is a great comfort to the dying', she remarks. The doctor tries to reassure her that convalescence is at hand. Violetta is not deceived. Grenvil takes his leave. As he departs he confides to Annina that Violetta has now only a few hours to live.

Annina cannot allow herself to be overwhelmed by the news. She returns into the room. Violetta asks if it is a holiday. Annina confirms that it is the carnival. All Paris is running wild: 'God knows how many poor souls are suffering while the people enjoy themselves', Violetta comments. She asks how much money is left in the drawer. Annina counts out 20 louis.[66] Violetta tells Annina to take half the money and give it to the poor. Annina remarks that very little would be left (she may well be thinking of her own wages, let alone the inevitable funeral expenses). Violetta simply remarks: 'It is more than I shall need' and despatches Annina to see if there has been any post delivered. Annina goes out.

Violetta draws a letter from her breast and reads it in a low voice. The letter is from Germont. He tells Violetta how, conscience-stricken, he has sent a letter to his son telling him the truth about Violetta's sacrifice. Alfredo is apparently returning from abroad, where he has taken refuge after wounding the Baron in a duel, to beg Violetta's pardon. Violetta reflects sadly that it is too late. She rises and looks at herself in a mirror. She comments on how changed she is. The roses have faded from her cheeks, and Alfredo's love 'is lacking to comfort and uphold my weary spirit' (*Addio del passato*). She prays that God may pardon and make her His own, for she knows that all is over for her in this life: '*Tutto finì, Or tutto finì*' (All is finished). A masked chorus is heard from the street below, singing in the same hedonistic fashion as was the wont of the revellers at all the parties over which Violetta presided in her heyday.

Annina hurries back. She is anxious to know whether Violetta is strong enough for the news she bears. It is joyous news; Alfredo is on his way. Violetta is indeed overjoyed. She staggers to the door as Annina opens it to admit Alfredo. The lovers fall into each other's arms. Their reunion after so much anguish and misunderstanding is ecstatic. Alfredo declares that they must leave Paris at once and return to the country where Violetta can regain her health (*Parigi, o cara, noi lasceremo*). Violetta, although she

---

[66] Puccini surely must have thought of this moment when he exactly duplicated it in *Madam Butterfly*, Act 2, where Suzuki is required to check how much money is left in the purse.

realizes the futility of such a plan, is happy to play along with Alfredo's dreams. The excess of emotion and excitement has already taken its toll. Violetta is just suggesting that they should go to church together and give thanks for Alfredo's return when she staggers and falls exhausted into a chair. Alfredo is suddenly alerted to the true gravity of Violetta's condition. Violetta tries to laugh it off and calls Annina to help her dress. Annina, although she realizes this is madness, brings Violetta's clothes. When she tries to put them on Violetta is forced to concede defeat. She falls back in her chair. Alfredo is aghast and tells Annina to fetch the doctor. Annina obediently departs. Violetta remarks: 'If you have not saved me by coming back, then no-one on earth can do it'. Suddenly she is overcome with a sense of the injustice of her position: 'To die so near the dawn, after the long night of tears', she cries out (*Ah! Gran Dio!*). Alfredo begs her not to give up. He needs all her devotion.

Germont enters with Annina and the doctor. Germont has come in order to be reconciled and 'embrace Violetta as a daughter'. Violetta willingly embraces him, though she knows she will not live to be his daughter-in-law. She turns to the doctor and says: 'You see, Doctor Grenvil, I die in the arms of those I hold dearest in the world'. In that moment the full weight of his guilt comes home to Germont. He is consumed with remorse, much as his son was at the conclusion of Act 2. Violetta's thoughts, as her final breath approaches, are now only for Alfredo. She opens a drawer and takes from it a medallion which she gives to him. It contains a likeness of her. Alfredo pleads with her to live on for the sake of their love. Germont begs Violetta's forgiveness, but Violetta is only aware of Alfredo's presence. She tells him that if he should find a new love he must give her not only his heart, but also her picture. He must tell her that she will be praying for them both. Annina, Germont and the doctor are all overwhelmed by this final evidence of Violetta's generosity of spirit. Suddenly Violetta feels as though she is reviving. The pain has abated and she imagines that she has returned to full strength. She rises from the sofa, and then falls back. The doctor feels her pulse and pronounces her dead as the curtain falls.

The central dramatic motive of *La Traviata* is, surprisingly but unmistakably, the hegemony within societal living of money. It is lack of money which leads Violetta to become a courtesan. Nothing in her make-up, as evidenced in the libretto, inclines one to see her as being any more promiscuous than her companions in the Parisian *bel monde*. It is lack of money that leads Violetta back to her former existence after she has found true fulfilment living with Alfredo in the country. It is Alfredo's guilt about his financial ineptitude which leads to his outrageous behaviour in Act 2. Finally, as Violetta's disease takes its terrible toll, a clear equation is made between her impecuniousness and impending death. As life runs out, so does the money and vice versa.

All the miseries of Violetta's existence stem from her need to make money through prostituting herself. She does not love Douphol and never has. But she needs his financial support. When she spurns it she becomes reliant on Alfredo. Alfredo cannot adequately support her because his family deplore his having taken up with a courtesan. The means may be there but they are not available, as becomes all too clear when Germont pays his visit in Act 2. Money has to be earned by propriety. When money and sex have been linked there is no propriety, therefore no money. Violetta's decision to return to her former existence is a purely pragmatic decision. It is about her and Alfredo's survival, not sexual appetite. She loves Alfredo but knows that if they continue their relationship it will lead to his social ruin.

Alfredo is basically a spoilt, rich kid who has never had to think about earning a living. Violetta's behaviour is therefore incomprehensible to him. All he can think of is his honour, or rather his masculine pride, which is wounded to the quick by the realization that Violetta is selling everything in order to support them. That Alfredo and Violetta truly love each other is beyond question. But equally beyond question is the fact that their relationship is doomed from the outset because of their disparate backgrounds and their flagrant disregard for the social mores of the age in which they live. The tragic outcome of their relationship is an inevitability. Their redeeming angel, in the end, is the very source of their greatest misery, Alfredo's father.

Germont must first and foremost act from the standpoint of head of a respectable family. Yet in spite of himself he recognizes in Violetta a woman of rare qualities and by the conclusion of his interview with her does not wish to see her wounded. But he has no choice, as he sees it – any more than Alfredo feels that he has a choice when he publicly humiliates Violetta. Like father, like son; in the aftermath of his draconian action, Alfredo is immediately stricken with remorse. He challenges Douphol to a duel. Germont attempts to effect a reunion of the lovers. But it is too late. It has always been and will always be too late for Violetta and Alfredo, for they are living and loving against the tenor of the times in which they live.

The opera also enshrines the supreme authority of the father, whose influence radically controls the destinies of the younger generation. As is more often than not the case in Verdi's operas this is not a purely negative force. Germont is portrayed sympathetically. He does not issue his prescriptions lightly. He tries to do what is right by his own lights. It may be that his intervention leads to disastrous consequences but then nobody suffers more than Germont. In a sense the father is only representative of the ethic enshrined in the society of the time. His prescriptive powers are those which society demands of him. If the father had not intervened society would have ensured the regressive actions of the new generation were compromised; because society will always be first and foremost structured around economic realities. The destiny of couples like Violetta and Alfredo must, by necessity, be fraught with difficulty. Their relationship is already under grave threat before Germont intervenes. It

is more than likely that the outcome would have been little different had Germont refrained. The debts would still have accrued and Violetta's illness would indubitably have run its course. Germont's intervention only accelerates a process that is already beyond recall.

Gasparo Antonio della Rocca (*Un giorno di regno*). Treasurer of the States of Brittany and uncle of **Edoardo**.

The Treasurer is the principal loser in the opera because he seeks to possess that which is not rightfully his to possess. By no stretch of the imagination is an ageing Treasurer a suitable husband for a spirited young girl like **Giulietta**. The Treasurer does not give a thought to the fact that he may be robbing a young girl of her youth. He is only concerned for his own gratification and advancement. That he does not love Giulietta in any sense of the word (unless you include naked lust – see Act 1 Scene 2 when he declares that he 'knows well the remedy for the sadness of a beautiful innocent girl') becomes clear when he immediately throws away all thoughts of marrying her as soon as a better opportunity comes his way. The marriage to Giulietta is a business arrangement with Baron **Kelbar**. Both men see it as a means of enhancing their respective families. They know perfectly well that the arrangement has caused 'many raised eyebrows' (Act 1 Scene 1) but it is of no concern to them. Their only concern is to feather their nests as they see fit. Both will pay dearly for their complacency.

The Treasurer is inevitably jealous of his young bride to be. He appears to know of **Edoardo**'s affair with Giulietta, for he is 'dismayed' (Act 1 Scene 2) when **Belfiore** engineers matters so that Edoardo keeps Giulietta company while he, the Baron and the 'King' discuss battle plans. His agitation only increases when he notices the intimacy that pertains between the two young people.

Once the Treasurer has accepted with alacrity Belfiore's promise of a ministerial position and a wealthy bride his only problem is how to break the news to the Baron. He does not give a thought to the fact that he might offend Giulietta's sensibilities, but he knows very well that the Baron will be outraged, as indeed he is. Nevertheless the Treasurer can hardly be prepared for the vehemence of the Baron's reaction to the news (Act 1 Scene 3). In fact he is convinced he is going to lose his life. Luckily his shouts for help bring everybody running, and the Baron is forced to restrain himself. He attempts to plead his case with the 'King' but the latter is disinclined to become partisan in a dispute between the Treasurer and the Baron. As it turns out, the Baron will not let the matter drop. He demands 'satisfaction' (Act 2 Scene 1). But now the Treasurer is forearmed; he knows what to expect. He uses his superior intelligence (and it must be admitted that there is not much to choose between the two in terms of IQ) to forestall the raging Baron by recommending a means of duelling, unheard of before or since, and certainly unfamiliar to the traditionalist Baron, namely that the two combatants should sit on a barrel of gunpowder 'proud as two Romans' with a fuse in hand thence igniting the barrel. It does not seem to occur to the Treasurer that this would rather defeat the point of the exercise since both combatants would inevitably expire. The Baron heaps abuse on him, but the Treasurer holds firm, finally concluding 'my method has worked well'.

The Treasurer may not be a courageous man and he may not be particularly intelligent, but he is wily. The problem with this sort of guile is that it usually backfires. He may end up with pots of money, but he will find fulfilment tends always to recede into the distance, because he is always too busy being wily. Verdi's opera does not relate the Treasurer's reaction to the fact that Belfiore, in his role as 'King', has settled on his nephew one of the Treasurer's castles, plus five thousand crowns per annum, in order that the Baron may have no objection to marrying Giulietta. Considering the Treasurer ends up with nothing he thought he was going to have at the outset (first of all Giulietta, then the Princess Ineska and a ministerial post) it would be surprising if he did not make some

objection, having discovered that Belfiore has no true authority to make such a decree.

It is part of the art of comedy to turn things on their head. The Treasurer has devoted all his life to hoarding money, so throughout the drama he is shown only losing it. Being a comedy he must ultimately learn to do it with a good grace, and join the rest of the cast at the conclusion in proclaiming 'let us all be good friends and forget the past'. For the Treasurer who, by definition, suffers from a chronic inability to let go and live for the moment, it is a lesson well learnt.

IL TROVATORE (The Troubadour)

Opera in 4 Acts. Libretto by Salvatore Cammarano, based on *El Trovador*, a drama by Gutiérrez.

First performance: 19 January 1853 at the Teatro Apollo, Rome.

Cast:

Conte di Luna: a young nobleman of Aragon (baritone)
Ferrando: Captain of di Luna's guard (bass)
Manrico: an officer in the Prince of Vizcay's forces, reputed son of Azucena (tenor)
Leonora: lady-in-waiting to the Princess of Aragon (soprano)
Ines: Leonora's confidante (soprano)
Azucena: a Vizcayan gypsy woman (mezzo-soprano)
Ruiz: a soldier under Manrico's command (tenor)
A Messenger (tenor)
An old gypsy (bass)

Time: the beginning of the 15th century
Place: the provinces of Vizcaya (Biscay) and Aragon, in Northern Spain.

Historical Note At the background of the action is the uprising of Count Jaime de Urgel, which took place in the kingdom of Aragon from 1410–1413. Jaime had a legitimate claim to the throne but was outmanoeuvred by Don Fernando de Antequera who, unlike Jaime, was a proven leader and soldier. The Aliaferia palace in Aragon, where Acts 1 and 4 are set, can still be visited today. It was once the stronghold of the Moorish kings of

Zaragoza. Originally it faced the castle of Castellár across the river Ebro, but Castellár had fallen into ruin even before Jaime's uprising.

Synopsis

In the opera Aragon is in a state of civil war, the Court being harassed by the followers of Urgel, Prince of Vizcaya, of whom **Manrico** is an adherent.

Act 1 *Il duello* – The duel Scene 1 A hall in the Aliaferia palace outside di Luna's apartments. It is dead of night. Ferrando and di Luna's retainers are standing guard at the door to di Luna's apartments. In order to ward off their fatigue the soldiers request that Ferrando narrate the true story of di Luna's missing brother (*Abbietta zingara*).

The old Count di Luna had two sons. One day the younger boy's nurse woke to find a 'dark, despicable gypsy crone' by the cradle of the child. The gypsy claimed only to want to cast the boy's horoscope. But the boy sickened from that day forward. Di Luna's court was convinced that the baby had been bewitched and the gypsy was arrested and burnt at the stake. Her daughter, Azucena, returned to the palace and stole the child from its cradle in an act of revenge. When the bones of a small child were discovered in the ashes of the gypsy's pyre it was assumed that the boy had been murdered. However, the elder di Luna believed his son to be still alive and on his death-bed he commanded his elder son (di Luna) not to rest until he had found him. But no trace could be found of Azucena, nor the boy.

Meanwhile it was commonly believed that the damned soul of the gypsy lived on in the world, appearing in various different forms, sometimes an owl, sometimes a raven, sometimes a hoopoe. One of the Count's men had died of fear because 'he had struck the gypsy's forehead'. She appeared to him in the form of an owl and 'looked at the sky, sorrowing, with a bestial cry!' as midnight was striking. Just as Ferrando is relating this the chimes of midnight are heard and all cry out in terror. The soldiers run to the back of the stage and servants gather at the door.

Act 1 Scene 2 The gardens of the Aliaferia palace outside Leonora's apartments. To the right a marble stair leads to the apartments. The moon is concealed by thick clouds. Leonora and Ines are taking a stroll.

Leonora describes how she first set eyes on Manrico. He was taking part in a tournament, dressed in black armour and black helmet with a black shield which had no crest on it. He won the games and she placed the victor's crown on his head. Thereafter civil war raged and Leonora saw her unknown warrior no more until one moonlit night she heard the sounds of a troubadour serenading her beneath her window (*Tacea la notte placida*). Her heart was immediately captivated. Ines expresses her concern; she has a 'vague presentiment' about this man and she urges Leonora to forget him. But Leonora is adamant that this 'mysterious man' is her true love. 'If I can't live for him, then for him I'll die' (*Di tale amor che dirsi*). The two women withdraw to Leonora's apartments.

Di Luna arrives to press his suit but is interrupted by the sound of Manrico's serenade (*Deserto sulla terra*). The two brothers – and rival suitors – confront each other. Manrico is under sentence of death as a follower of the renegade, Urgel, but di Luna refuses to arrest him, preferring, in spite of Leonora's protestations, to challenge him to a duel. Leonora descends into the grounds and momentarily mistakes di Luna for Manrico. Realizing her mistake she is prompted to make a full declaration of her love to Manrico. Outraged di Luna swears Manrico must die. The two men make off, swords in hand, as Leonora falls senseless.

Act 2 *La gitana* – The Gypsy Scene 1 On the slopes of a mountain in Vizcaya (Biscay). A gypsy camp. Azucena is seated near a fire and Manrico lies beside her, wrapped in his cloak. His helmet is at his feet. He is staring gloomily at his sword, which he holds in his hands.

The gypsies herald the break of day and set to work at their anvils (see **Chorus**). Azucena remembers the day her mother was burned at the stake (*Stride la vampa*) and describes in vivid detail the crackling flames and shouts of joy from the onlookers.

Meanwhile, one of the gypsies points out that it is now daybreak and time to 'forage for (their) daily bread'. The gypsies exit, singing. Manrico asks his mother to tell him the whole 'terrible' story. Azucena expresses surprise that he is ignorant of the events leading up to his grandmother's 'bitter end'. She then recounts how the elder di Luna had accused her mother of witchcraft, believing her to have bewitched his son. He ordered her to be burnt at the stake. On the day her mother was to be burned Azucena followed her, carrying her baby in her arms (*Condotta ell'era in ceppi*). As her mother was being dragged to the stake she cried out to Azucena: 'Mi vendica!' ('Avenge me!'). Azucena managed to steal the Count's son and she took him back to the spot where her mother had been burned. Overcome by the horrible spectacle of the flames, still burning, and the vision of her mother's torment, Azucena impetuously threw the baby onto the fire. But then she realized, to her horror, that she had confused the Count's baby with hers and had, in fact, thrown her own baby into the flames. Manrico is shocked thus to learn that he is not Azucena's son. Azucena quickly reassures him that he is indeed her son and reminds him of all the loving care she has lavished on him.

She then recalls how she heard that Manrico had been killed on the battlefield and how she journeyed to the battlefield to bury him. But she found him still alive and nursed him back to health. Discovering that it was di Luna who was responsible for wounding Manrico Azucena was outraged, for she knows that her 'son' has previously spared di Luna's life when the latter was entirely at Manrico's mercy at the conclusion of a duel. She now demands to know what 'strange pity' overcame Manrico on that occasion. Manrico describes how he had been about to slay di Luna when he heard a cry 'from Heaven that said to me: Don't strike!' Azucena makes him promise not to hesitate if he ever has di Luna at his mercy again.

A messenger arrives with a letter from Manrico's lieutenant, Ruiz. Castellor has fallen to the rebel army and Manrico is ordered to proceed there immediately to supervise its defence. Ruiz adds that Leonora, thinking Manrico dead, is entering a convent. Ignoring Azucena's protestations that he is still not fit, Manrico rushes off to prevent Leonora from taking the veil.

Act 2 Scene 2   The cloister in a convent in the neighbourhood of Castellor. It is night. Di Luna, Ferrando and some retainers enter cautiously, wrapped in their cloaks. Di Luna is determined to prevent Leonora from entering the convent. He reflects at length on his great love for Leonora (*Il balen del suo sorrisso*). Having confirmed his determination that not even God shall come between him and his love di Luna and his followers hide. Nuns are heard chanting within the cloisters.

Leonora enters with Ines and a train of women. Ines is weeping at the thought of losing her mistress to the cloister. Leonora tells her that she has no heart any more for the sorrows of this earth and bids her confidantes to dry their eyes and lead her to the altar. At this moment di Luna bursts in and tells Leonora that the only altar for her is the nuptial one. There is hardly time for everyone to recover from the shock of di Luna's sudden appearance when Manrico enters, accompanied by a sizeable force of his retainers. Leonora is overjoyed, and di Luna thunderstruck, for both believe Manrico to be dead. Ruiz and the retainers shout 'Long live Urgel!' and fighting breaks out between the rival factions. Di Luna attempts to prevent the lovers leaving but is driven back. Manrico makes off with Leonora and the nuns flee into the convent.

Act 3   *Il figlio della zingara* – The Gypsy's Son. Scene 1   A military camp. On the right is di Luna's tent. There are soldiers everywhere, some playing at dice, some strolling around. Ferrando emerges from di Luna's tent. The soldiers are awaiting the summons to battle. More reinforcements arrive. Ferrando tells the soldiers that an attack on Castellor is planned for the following morning. The soldiers welcome the call to arms (*Squilli, echeggi la tromba*) and disperse. Di Luna comes out of his tent. He is obsessed with the thought of Leonora in Manrico's arms, but his spirits are buoyed up by the thought of the imminent battle and his determination to separate the lovers.

Ferrando reports to di Luna that a gypsy has been found near the camp. Azucena is brought in. Di Luna demands to know her purpose. All Azucena will say is that 'It is the gypsy's custom to move her wandering steps without any plan'. But when di Luna asks her where she has come from she replies: 'From Biscay', which revelation startles both di Luna and Ferrando. As Azucena relates how she wanders about searching for her lost son who 'left and forgot (her)' and for whom she feels a love such as no other mother on earth could feel, Ferrando begins to suspect that he knows her identity.

Di Luna questions her further, asking if she remembers the abduction of the elder Count's child fifteen years ago from the di Luna castle. Azucena, bewildered, asks di Luna who he is, to which the latter replies: 'The stolen boy's brother!' Ferrando has by now recognized her as the gypsy who stole the Count's younger son: 'She's the one who burned the child', he tells di Luna, who is delighted finally to have the gypsy in his power. He commands his soldiers to seize her. Azucena, beside herself with terror, calls on Manrico to come to her aid, but Manrico is far away and oblivious to her predicament. Di Luna and his retainers are astounded to learn that Manrico is Azucena's son. Di Luna celebrates a double victory.

Act 3 Scene 2 A hall at Castellor with a balcony at the back. Leonora and Manrico are about to be married. Manrico tells Leonora that they are in great danger, for on the morrow the castle will be attacked. But he consoles her with a fervent expression of his undying love (*Ah sì, ben mio*). The chapel organ is heard, but as the couple are about to depart for the wedding ceremony Ruiz enters with news that Azucena has been taken prisoner. She is about to be burned at the stake. Manrico does not hesitate. He

gives Ruiz instructions to summon his men and then rushes off to assist his mother (*Di quella pira l'orrendo foco*).

Act 4 *Il supplizio* – **The Punishment.** Scene 1 Outside a wing of the Aliaferia palace. There is a tower in one corner. Ruiz and Leonora enter, shrouded in cloaks. Ruiz points out the tower where Manrico is imprisoned, then exits.

Leonora prays that her loving thoughts may find their way to her beloved in his hour of need (*D'amor sull'ali rosee*). Monks intone the *Miserere* within the palace. Manrico's voice is heard from within bidding Leonora farewell. Leonora swears to be everlastingly faithful before concealing herself (*Tu vedrai che amore in terra*).

Di Luna enters and forthwith gives orders for Manrico to be beheaded and Azucena burned at the stake at dawn. Aware that he is abusing his powers he yet blames Leonora for his intemperance: 'That's what you drive me to, O fatal woman', he exclaims. Leonora appears and desperately pleads for Manrico's life. The intensity of her pleas only exacerbates di Luna's desire for revenge. Finally, realizing she has no further option, Leonora offers herself to him, if only he will release Manrico. Triumphantly di Luna accepts. But when he turns away to give orders to a guard Leonora surreptitiously swallows poison concealed in her ring. Careless of her own life, Leonora is only ecstatic that thus she has saved Manrico from execution. Di Luna, equally ecstatic for his own reasons, leads Leonora into the tower.

Act 4 Scene 2 A dungeon in the Aliaferia palace. In one corner there is a barred window. Azucena is lying on a rough blanket. Manrico sits beside her. They are awaiting their respective ends. Azucena is delirious and clearly close to death. She is still possessed by hallucinations of the day her mother was burned. Manrico tries to comfort her. They sing of their longing to return to the mountains (*Ai nostri monti*). Azucena falls asleep.

Leonora enters and urges Manrico to flee. Manrico is overjoyed to see her, but when Leonora reveals that she cannot flee with him he quickly appreciates that she must have struck a deal with di Luna. He knows only too well that the only recompense di Luna would accept would be Leonora herself. He is appalled and fiercely reviles her. Even when she collapses at his feet, already subject to the effect of the poison she has taken, he still repudiates her pleas for mercy. Only when she tells him that she is dying, and why, does he realize his error and her great sacrifice.

Di Luna enters and quickly appreciates that he has been duped. He orders Manrico's immediate execution. He drags Azucena to the window to watch. As Manrico dies Azucena tells di Luna he has killed his own brother: '*Sei vendicata o madre!*' ('You are avenged, oh mother!') she cries with her dying breath. Horrified di Luna exclaims: '*E vivo ancor!*' ('And I still live!') as the curtain falls.

Il Trovatore is above all a tale about a mother's love both for her own mother and for her son. The work proceeds through a series of encounters in which this love is examined from many different angles, not least of these being the potential for transcendence inherent in any love relation which is built neither on interpersonal communication, nor on erotic infatuation. Such a relation may only exist in the pages of fairy tales and romantic operas. But the very fact of its insistent recurrence suggests that it makes a powerful claim on our attention. In such instances it is more often than not the case that consummation is only envisaged as being possible in death. The paradigm for this was encapsulated by Wagner in his opera *Tristan und Isolde*. Here the fundamental dualism of Eros and Thanatos has been transcended to evoke an all-inclusive transcendence that it is much closer to a religious than a romantic passion.

The love celebrated by the medieval Troubadours, as by the German Minnesingers, was essentially of a transcendent nature, where the beloved was perceived as the image and reflection of the Virgin Mary. The beloved was not worshipped for herself, but as an ideal of womanhood: Goethe's *Ewige Weibliche* of which the individual was but a single representative. In the last analysis the beloved primarily served the function of Muse for the Troubadour's artistry, which is not to say that the emotions engendered were not genuine; they most certainly were. But their highest expression was to be attained only by each lover sacrificing his life for the other and not in domestic connubial bliss. It is in this light that the conductor Gianandrea Gavazzeni's assertion that *Il Trovatore* is the Italian *St Matthew Passion* becomes comprehensible.

U

Uldino (*Attila*). A Breton patriot, retained by **Attila**.

Uldino serves Attila and bides his time, awaiting the moment when he may be avenged on behalf of his beloved homeland, previously overrun by Attila and the Huns. Uldino has in fact managed to become Attila's closest confidante, as is eloquently illustrated (Act 1 Scene 2) when Attila awakens from his nightmare vision of the Bishop of Rome, **Leo**, warning him of his impending doom. Uldino plays his part to the hilt; he appears genuinely concerned for his master.

Nevertheless it is Uldino who has ensured that **Odabella** and her companions are rescued from the sacking of Aquilea at the outset of the opera. It is also Uldino who administers poison into Attila's drinking horn at the latter's wedding feast (Act 2 Scene 2). He endures a moment of horror when Odabella reveals to Attila that the drink is poisoned, then huge relief when **Foresto** steps into the breach and confesses to the crime. Uldino naturally transfers his allegiance to Foresto and finally has the vicarious satisfaction of watching Odabella stab Attila to death.

Ulrica (*Un Ballo in Maschera*). A fortune-teller.

Vocally the role of Ulrica invites comparison with that of Azucena in *Il Trovatore*. It is more often than not given to the same singer: a dramatic mezzo with considerable histrionic powers. Dramatically there is little comparison, other than that both characters epitomize a woman possessed of strength of character and almost demoniac obsessiveness. But there the comparison ends.

As is the way with psychics and mediums the world over Ulrica's whole life is devoted to the service of her gift. Her gift is no more nor less genuine than that enjoyed by the three witches in *Macbeth*. She predicts the future and her predictions are fulfilled. A sceptic would assume that she initiates the events she predicts, and no doubt to some extent she does. But the fact remains that those who patronize her are not disappointed. It is significant that **Riccardo** has refused to countenance Ulrica's banishment (Act 1). Had he heeded the advice of the **Judge** his own fate might have been very different. It is almost as though, refusing to be ruled by the rationalistic prescripts of the judiciary, he wilfully throws himself into the arms of fate. Riccardo needs to feel that his life is ruled by a superior power. Otherwise he himself becomes the sole arbiter of the fates of all those over whom he rules. This is a weight of responsibility he is not willing to countenance. Thus Ulrica is allowed to continue in pursuance of her trade and play a critical part in determining the destinies of the main protagonists.

Whatever one's stance towards the supernatural it is impossible to deny that Ulrica, whatever her credentials, believes in the reality of her own visions. She summons her deity with the same passionate conviction as would an Indian medicine man or, for that matter, a Catholic priest. Once possessed she enjoys what can only be described as an erotic ecstasy: 'the tremendous thrill of his embrace' (Act 1 Scene 2). In this 'transport' she is able to speak with total assurance. The sceptic would say that she convinces by the sheer force of her own conviction, for the one thing that those who come to her lack most in life is conviction. The very fact that they attend a fortune-teller means that they do not believe themselves to be in charge of

their destinies. They are putty in Ulrica's hands. She only has to pronounce on their futures and they will believe her. And because they believe her they will ensure that her prophecies are fulfilled. Which does not, of course explain Riccardo's intervention in the fate of **Silvano**, unless one is sufficiently sceptical to believe that Ulrica has been forewarned of Riccardo's presence in her cavern and, knowing the Governor's character, anticipates his reaction to her prediction of advancement for the young sailor. Herein lies an alternative explanation for Ulrica's powers, namely that she is an acute psychologist. Certainly her prescriptions for **Amelia**'s lovesickness would support such an argument. But then it only exemplifies a characteristic common to all magical ritual. The practitioner is inevitably put through extensive, often arduous, trials before being allowed even so much as a glimpse of the Philosopher's Stone.

Thus Amelia must search for the herb that will cure her in a field, beneath a gallows, haunted by ghosts and death. Inevitably, the only efficacious time to pick the herb is at midnight. Amelia is terrified at the very thought, as Ulrica knows well she would be. The purpose is to prime her subconscious by administering a severe shock to her customary habit patterns. Ulrica knows instinctively what psychologists are only now beginning to fathom: that human love is a question of transference of needs, and these needs are entirely dictated by the environment in which the individual is permitted to evolve. Amelia has self-evidently lived a sheltered existence, relatively untouched by hardship or danger. Her impossible love for Riccardo, which causes her such anguish, is equally self-evidently an expression of her soul's need to find release from the fetters which confine her. The only way she is going to quell the 'love' is to confront head-on the danger which she has hitherto evaded and sublimated in the form of an illicit and hopeless passion.

Confronted with the mildly deranged and mocking expostulations of Riccardo himself, Ulrica is immediately aware that she stands before a man who challenges fate and invites his own demise, 'for he who violates the hidden realm must wash away his guilt with tears, and he who insolently challenges his fate must pay for his sin in his fate itself'. Riccardo presents a latter-day embodiment of the Prometheus myth. He is also Icarus who, sublimely indifferent to the warnings of the father (in Riccardo's case, **Renato**, his over-protective friend), wilfully flies close to the Sun and crashes to the Earth. He is guilty of the primal Greek sin of hubris, over-reaching himself and thereby offending the gods. Whether or not Riccardo's imminent death is actually written in the palm of his hand, the possibility of impending doom is implicit in his demeanour. For Riccardo is not, like the Duke in *Rigoletto*, oblivious to the tightrope he walks in life; he is only too aware that he invites disaster. He seeks it out because the routine of Court life wearies him. It chafes perpetually against his superabundant nature. Why else is he in Ulrica's cavern at 3 am?

Ulrica appears genuinely surprised when Riccardo reveals his true identity. She is also shocked that she has been condemned to banishment. This could be said to be the clearest indication that she is possessed of genuine powers, relying on her intuitive gifts which, when genuine, will always be directed outside the personal ego. She can discern the deepest secrets of those who come to her, yet remain oblivious to what touches her own personal destiny. For her gift is something quite separate from her own personal self. It is something she taps into. Jung would have identified it as the racial unconscious. The Christian mystic would say she was partaking of the Holy Spirit, while the superstitious, who largely constitute her clientele, claim that she is in league with the Devil. Ulrica herself does not need to place a label on her gift. It is just that which defines her life and being.

When Riccardo throws her a purse, thus indicating that she is reprieved from the sentence issued by the judiciary, her worst fears for Riccardo are confirmed. It is his very magnanimity, the essential trust with which he confronts the world, which convinces her that he is in mortal danger. But Riccardo will not heed her warnings; he prefers to listen to the sycophantic flattery of the sailors and townsfolk. He is beyond her help.

An usher (Usciere) (*Rigoletto*)
Soon after **Gilda** has been reunited with her father (Act 2) the usher leads **Monterone** across the stage. He is leading Monterone to the dungeons and demands of the guards that they let them pass.

V

Count Vaudimont (*I Vespri Siciliano*). A French officer, in occupation of Sicily.
Vaudimont is largely overshadowed by his superior, **Bethune**. At the opening of the opera he makes clear his discontent at the way **Monforte** has handled the trial and execution of **Elena's** brother, Duke Federigo: 'Our leader was too cruel', he comments (Act 1 Scene 1). Thereafter he barely makes an appearance (see **Bethune**).

I VESPRI SICILIANI
Opera in 5 Acts. Libretto Eugène Scribe and Charles Duveyrier.
First performance: 13 June 1855 at the Paris Opéra.

Cast:
Guido di Monforte: Governor of Sicily (baritone)
Bethune: French official (bass)
Count Vaudimont: French official (bass)
Arrigo: a young Sicilian (tenor)
Giovanni da Procida: Sicilian physician (bass)
Duchess Elena: sister of Duke Federigo of Austria (soprano)
Ninetta: her Lady-in-Waiting (contralto)
Danieli: a Sicilian (tenor)
Tebaldo: French soldier (tenor)
Roberto: French soldier (bass)
Manfredo: a Sicilian (tenor)

Time: late 13th century
Place: Palermo

Historical Note   On 30 March 1282 (Easter Monday) a riot started in a church near

Palermo at vespers (evensong) which turned into a full-scale massacre of the occupying French by the native Sicilians. The massacre was triggered by one of the occupying French molesting a woman whose husband forthwith murdered him. Sicily had a history of constant occupation and foreign rulership which was to continue until 1861 when the kingdom was finally incorporated into the rest of Italy.

Synopsis

Act 1 The great square in Palermo. At the rear are streets and buildings. To the right is Elena's palace, to the left the barracks with mounds of weapons, and the governor's palace, reached by a stairway. Tebaldo, Roberto and other French soldiers are sitting at a table in front of the barracks, drinking. Sicilian men and women cross the square. They form scattered groups and observe the soldiers bleakly.

The French soldiers sing nostalgically of their beloved native skies. The Sicilians are chafing against the presence of the soldiers. Their thoughts are for vengeance (*A te, ciel natio*). Tebaldo proposes a toast to their great captain and is seconded by Roberto. Bethune and Count Vaudimont emerge from the barracks. Roberto rises and staggers drunkenly over to Bethune. He tells Bethune he is drunk with love. Bethune warns him that Sicilian men are notoriously jealous and their women are exceedingly proud. Roberto is not deterred.

The Duchess Elena, dressed in mourning and leaning on Ninetta's arm, with Danieli following on behind, crosses the square and heads towards her palace. She has a prayer book in her hands. She is greeted respectfully by the Sicilians and stops to converse with them.

Vaudimont comments on Elena's great beauty while Bethune observes that she is dressed in mourning. He proceeds to fill in some essential background information, that Elena's brother, Duke Federigo of Austria, was beheaded and she is now a hostage of the French. She is in mourning for her beloved brother. Vaudimont feels compassion for

Elena. He considers her brother's execution was unjustified. Bethune will not hear such talk, however, and having respectfully greeted Elena leads Vaudimont back into the barracks. Danieli laments the fatal day when, 'the enemy's sword deprived our maternal land of her best sons!' Elena, meanwhile, prays for the soul of her beloved brother and swears vengeance on his killers.

Roberto, who by now is completely drunk, rises from the table and urges the Sicilians to sing in praise of their conquerors. He staggers towards Elena and invites her to lead the song. Ninetta, her maid, is immediately concerned for her mistress's safety. Elena remains impassive. Roberto becomes increasingly obnoxious. Finally Elena calmly agrees to sing. Roberto, Tebaldo and the other Frenchmen sit at the table. The Sicilians draw near and Elena sings. By the time she has finished her song the Sicilians have surrounded the French officers. Elena's song (*Deh! Tu calma, o Dio*) is provocative. Using the analogy of a shipwreck she describes how the sailors call for guidance and how God answers that Heaven smiles on him who trusts himself and exhorts the sailors to take courage: 'Your destiny is in your hands . . . let dangers be scorned'. The significance of her song is not lost on the Sicilians who decide that the moment has now come when they should avenge 'the evil shame, let us despise servitude, and God will be with us'. The French are so busy carousing they fail to realize that they are about to be attacked by the Sicilians. With daggers drawn the Sicilians fall upon the French soldiers.

Suddenly a man appears on the steps of the governor's palace. He is alone, without guards. It is Monforte, the French viceroy. He surveys the scene calmly and makes an imperious gesture. All flee, except for Elena, Ninetta and Danieli. The three express to themselves their hatred of Monforte, who in turn expresses his contempt for them (*D'ira fremo*). Their individual ruminations are interrupted by the arrival of Arrigo. On seeing Elena he runs to her. Arrigo does not notice Monforte, who now comes slowly down the steps.

Arrigo has come with the good news that he has been acquitted of the crime of which he has been accused. In spite of their fear of Monforte the judges have issued a 'just sentence'. Elena and Ninetta are overjoyed. Monforte advances, smiling, and ironically suggests that Arrigo should give thanks to the one 'who is so merciful'. Arrigo, unaware that it is not the judge but Monforte himself who has ordered his acquittal, and also not realizing that it is Monforte whom he now addresses, is belligerent. Elena and Ninetta try to restrain him. But Arrigo is not in the mood to be appeased. Brazenly he declares that he is only waiting for the chance to be avenged on Monforte. Monforte then reveals his identity. Arrigo is speechless. Monforte commands Elena and Ninetta to withdraw. Arrigo makes to follow them but Monforte restrains him. He demands to know Arrigo's name and family. Arrigo informs him that his father ended his days a fugitive while his mother died ten months ago. Monforte reveals that he knows that Arrigo has been a guest of the Duke Federigo (Elena's brother). Arrigo is emboldened by the mention of Federigo and proudly refuses to be intimidated by the governor. Monforte admits in an aside that in spite of himself he admires Arrigo's spirit.

Monforte offers Arrigo the chance of obtaining a pardon for himself by joining the French. Arrigo scornfully refuses to countenance such a suggestion. Monforte dismisses him, but not before telling him to heed a piece of advice. Pointing at Elena's palace he tells Arrigo he must never cross its threshold. When challenged as to why Monforte will only say in a mysterious tone: 'Fear: for your heart burns with ill-omened love!' These are prophetic words, as the action of the opera will prove. Monforte will say no more, other than to reiterate his injunction to Arrigo to avoid Elena. Arrigo refuses to be browbeaten; Monforte threatens to lose his temper, but Arrigo has all the rashness of youth. He rushes to the palace, knocks on the door and is admitted. Monforte watches him, 'with emotion but without wrath'.

Act 2   A bright valley near Palermo. To the right are hills covered in flowering citrus trees. To the left the chapel of St Rosalia. To the rear is the sea. A small boat arrives at the shore. Procida steps out and the fisherman who is steering it takes it away.

Procida greets his fatherland with emotion (*O tu Palermo*). He has been living in exile for many years. He has apparently been searching the world for aid to no avail. Everywhere he turned he was met with the question: 'Sicilians, where is your old valour? Come, rise to victory, to honour!' Manfredo and various other companions of Procida land on the shore and surround him. Procida commands one of them to make known his arrival and commissions another to find Arrigo and Elena and bring them to him as soon as possible. Once the two messengers have left Procida declares his intention with his fellow Sicilians, 'In darkness and in silence to ripen our revenge'. Procida's only desire before he dies is to see his beloved homeland free of the French yoke. Manfredo and the others leave.

Elena and Arrigo arrive almost immediately, emerging from the little church. Elena greets Procida with enthusiasm and begs to know whether he has been successful in gaining assistance from abroad. Procida reports that Peter of Aragon is willing to come to their assistance, but only when the Sicilians have risen up on their own behalf. Arrigo reports that the Sicilians are consumed with rage, but hesitant to take action. Procida declares that in that case they must prepare a bold, pre-emptive strike. Elena suggests that the pretext should be the occasion of the weddings of the engaged couples who will shortly be married in a mass ceremony. There is bound to be a great number of Sicilians present who will need little encouragement to take up arms should their compatriots be threatened. Procida tells Arrigo that he must be the one to incite the Sicilians' hearts to valour, then exits.

Elena, left alone with Arrigo, asks what reward he would consider adequate for the courage that is now expected of him. 'My reward is in the homage that I lay at your feet', is Arrigo's reply. It is a prelude to a declaration of love (*Ah! da tue luci angeliche*) that Elena welcomes because she returns his love. She is, however, riven with guilt, feeling as she does that her heart should be dedicated to avenging her brother's death. Arrigo, overhearing Elena wrestling with her conscience in an aside, is delighted to learn that his love is returned. He had feared that his lowly station in life and lack of means would render him an unworthy suitor for the Duchess. 'Avenge my brother and for me you will be nobler than a king', Elena reassures him. She extracts an oath from him which is willingly given.

Bethune arrives with an escort of soldiers. He presents Arrigo with an invitation from Monforte to a forthcoming ball. Arrigo scorns the invitation at which Bethune commands him to follow him forthwith to the viceroy's palace. Arrigo draws his sword but is quickly disarmed by Bethune's soldiers and led off under arrest. Elena is appalled, as is Procida who now enters and learns from Elena what has transpired. Procida is convinced that Arrigo's arrest sounds the death knell of their plans. Elena is determined Arrigo shall be freed, but is prevented from doing anything about it for the moment as a crowd of Sicilians is approaching.

Young men and girls, dressed in festive costumes and escorting twelve engaged girls, descend the hills. Ninetta is among them. From the other side Danieli advances with the engaged men. Manfredo and some friends approach Procida. Ninetta and Danieli kneel before Elena, asking for her blessing. Dancing begins but is interrupted by the arrival of Roberto and Tebaldo at the head of a column of French soldiers. Roberto motions to the dancers to continue and orders his men to break ranks and rest. They join in the dancing, which is growing more lively and animated by the minute. Standing near to Procida, Roberto and Tebaldo watch the proceedings commenting the while on the charms of the brides. Procida deliberately encourages the French soldiers to try their luck with the Sicilian brides. His aim is to goad the French, thus providing the Sicilians with a pretext for instigating a massacre.

The dancing grows more frenzied. Roberto and Tebaldo go to join their compatriots who are making ever more pressing advances to the young girls. Suddenly, at a signal from Roberto, each of the dancing men carries his partner off, whilst the remaining soldiers seize other young girls. Roberto snatches Ninetta. Danieli and the young men make to rescue their girls, but the soldiers reach for their swords. Danieli and his companions fall back. Manfredo also makes to draw his sword, but Procida stops him, signalling him to help defend Elena who is caught between the French and Sicilians. The Sicilians are outraged at the unpardonable behaviour of the French. Ninetta unsuccessfully attempts to escape from Roberto. The latter instructs his soldiers that they are to respect the Duchess Elena who is to be reserved for Procida who 'gave us such happy advice!' Tebaldo, Roberto and the soldiers leave, taking Ninetta and the other girls with them. Danieli and the other young Sicilian men stand around dejectedly, with Elena, Procida and Manfredo.

The Sicilian young men are overwhelmed with shame at not having prevented the abduction of their brides. Elena and Procida have succeeded in their aim to arouse their wrath. Elena pointedly observes that she owes the fact that she was not molested to Procida's intervention (the Sicilians do not realize that Procida was acting as *agent provocateur*). She then upbraids Danieli for having allowed his bride to be stolen. She joins Manfredo and Procida in observing with satisfaction the Sicilians' mounting rage and resolution. 'Let cowardice now be silent!' they declare – 'I feel already in my heart a lion's fury stir'.

In the midst of this tumult music is suddenly heard from the direction of the sea. The Sicilians rush to the shore. A dazzlingly decorated boat is approaching with Vaudimont, French officers and noblemen, and Sicilian girls, elegantly dressed, aboard. The boatmen are dressed in rich livery. Refreshments are being served. Some of the ladies recline on soft pillows, others hold guitars. All sing of the pleasures to come. Procida asks whither the boat is bound and Elena replies it is en route to the palace for the forthcoming ball. Procida, seeing an opportunity presenting itself for revenge, declares they must follow. Elena, Manfredo, Danieli and the rest of the Sicilians wonder how Procida means to take his revenge. Procida answers that he will go to the ball in disguise and, 'like a rapid thunderbolt', he will fall on the tyrant. Manfredo nervously reminds Procida that the French soldiers will be armed with their swords, to which Procida replies that they in turn will have their 'daggers and their hearts'. As the occupants of the boat continue singing their joyful anticipation of the pleasures to come the Sicilians clamour for vengeance. The boat moves on and Procida, Elena, Manfredo, Danieli and the Sicilians stand disconsolately in groups, watching.

Act 3 Scene 1   A study in Monforte's palace. Monforte is seated at a table and brooding on past events. He recalls how he seduced Arrigo's mother (a Sicilian) and how she had hated and despised him for his 'wicked' treatment of her. She fled, taking their son with her. 'For three lustrums (fifteen years) she hid the son from the paternal embrace and reared him in horror of his father.' Just before she died she dictated a letter, which Monforte now takes out and reads. In it she begs that 'if the bloody axe threatens the hero Arrigo, the honour of the fatherland's soil, spare at least that innocent head! It is that of your son!'

Bethune enters and reports that Arrigo has refused to come of his own free will, so has been brought by force. Monforte instructs Bethune that Arrigo is to be treated with respect and brought into his presence. Bethune exits. Left alone Monforte reflects that all the worldly honour and riches he has achieved in his life are meaningless to him (*In braccio alle dovizie*). The only happiness left to him would be if he could live near to his son. Then the hatred Arrigo feels for the French could be overcome by the immense love of Monforte's 'paternal heart'.

Arrigo enters. He is oblivious to the fact that he is in the presence of his father. He is perplexed, however, by the fact that he has, as Monforte has instructed, been treated with the greatest respect by the French officers. He is convinced that it must be some new game on the part of the viceroy. Monforte informs Arrigo that he is free to do as he pleases. When Arrigo proudly declares, 'I fight a tyrant', Monforte replies 'you fight as a coward', pointing out that he is unarmed and defenceless. He chides Arrigo for returning his clemency with such defiance and pleads for some response. Arrigo is becoming increasingly bemused. Finally Monforte gives his son the letter to read. Arrigo is at first delighted to see his mother's handwriting, but then appalled at the import of what he reads. His principal thought is that this will render his marriage to Elena impossible. 'O lady! I have lost you!' he keeps repeating.

Monforte tells him to ask for whatever he wishes and it shall be granted. 'Possession, titles, honours, riches, as much as ambition desires I can give to you', he tells Arrigo. But Arrigo only wants to be left to his fate. Monforte points out 'magnificent fame' surrounds him, that his name is 'glorious', to which Arrigo replies: 'It is an execrated name!' This is too much for Monforte. He is angered and saddened by the insult and nearly loses control of himself. Arrigo realizes that he has gone too far, but still Monforte would prefer to be reconciled with rather than alienated from his son. Arrigo makes to leave. Frantically Monforte tries to restrain him. In spite of himself Arrigo admits that he would like to yield to his father's embrace but, as he points out, the image of his mother comes between them. Monforte, he declares, was her executioner. Monforte puts an arm around his son, and Arrigo's resistance threatens to crumble. He calls on his mother for help and succour. Then he impetuously tears himself away and rushes from the room.

Act 3 Scene 2   A magnificent hall in the palace. The room is arranged for a ball and is filled with ladies and gentlemen, some of whom are in masks. Elena, Procida and

Arrigo are among the crowd. Monforte enters, preceded by his pages and palace officials. He takes his place on a raised seat and motions for all to be seated. The master of ceremonies gives the signal for the festivities to commence.

A ballet, entitled 'The Four Seasons', ensues. The Sicilians and French join in the celebration of the 'splendid festivities' and the 'rare beauties . . . that instil in our hearts love, pleasure! (see **Chorus**).

The company disperses in the apartments and gardens of the palace. For a few moments the stage remains deserted. Then Arrigo returns, followed by Procida and Elena, both masked. Procida and Elena tell Arrigo that he is amongst friends. They remove their disguises. Arrigo is dumbfounded and asks why they are here. Elena tells him she has come to save him, while Procida announces his intention to avenge 'every oppressed one'. Arrigo points to some Frenchmen who have entered the hall and urges Elena and Procida to keep their voices down. He is consumed with fear. More party guests return to the room. Sounds of dance music filter through. Elena attaches a ribbon to Arrigo's chest so that he will be easily recognized in the crowd. Procida confirms his resolve to kill Monforte. This brings into sharp focus for Arrigo his divided loyalties. Procida notices his confusion but is prevented from discovering the cause by the entrance of Monforte himself. Procida tells Arrigo to meet him in a few moments in the same place and he and Elena move on. The two disappear into the throng as dancing couples stroll in the halls and refreshments are handed round.

Monforte comes over to Arrigo who obliquely tries to warn his father of impending danger. Monforte is not perturbed. Rather he is delighted at this evidence of his son's concern for his welfare. He makes to embrace Arrigo but the latter shrinks back. Arrigo becomes increasingly agitated and finally indicates the ribbon on his chest as being a sign of the oath of vengeance he has sworn with the Sicilians. Monforte tears the ribbon off Arrigo's tunic, declaring it to be a sign of dishonour. As Arrigo makes an angry gesture

Monforte tells him he can see Arrigo is torn asunder by divided loyalties. 'French blood still courses in your bosom!' he declares. Arrigo maintains there is no dishonour in one who serves his fatherland. He continues to insist his father must flee. He has noticed Danieli and other Sicilians approaching. But it is too late.

Suddenly Monforte is surrounded. Procida and Elena are among the assailants. Elena is the first to hurl herself at Monforte, dagger drawn. Procida calls on his compatriots to defeat the French once and for all. But Arrigo flings himself in front of Monforte, shielding him with his own body. Elena drops her dagger. Monforte calls on his French officers for protection. Bethune, Vaudimont and other officers quickly surround Monforte, drawing their swords. Monforte orders them to arrest and execute everyone who wears ribbons. Only Arrigo is to be exempt for he was a 'loyal enemy'. The Sicilians are outraged by Arrigo's apparent betrayal. Arrigo is overwhelmed with shame, while the French give thanks to almighty God that their leader is saved. Monforte and Bethune implore Arrigo to give his allegiance henceforth to France. But Arrigo is not listening. He is too appalled at the predicament he finds himself in. He tries to appeal to his compatriots but is scornfully repulsed. Monforte attempts to console his son with the thought that Arrigo will from now on live under his protection, but this fills Arrigo with horror. Procida assures Arrigo since now he enjoys the protection of the French governor he can consider himself an outcast as far as the Sicilians are concerned. He turns to his compatriots and defiantly calls, 'For us, the glory; death for me!' to which the Sicilians respond with, 'Yes, for us the glory!' and, to Arrigo: 'Infamy for you!'

At a sign from Monforte, Procida, Elena and the Sicilians are dragged away. Arrigo makes to run after them but is restrained by Monforte. In desperation Arrigo stretches out his hand to his compatriots. The Sicilians contemptuously reject his advance and Arrigo collapses in his father's arms as the curtain falls.

Act 4   The courtyard of a fortress. To the left is a room leading to the prisoners' cells; to the right a gate leading into the fortress. At the rear the battlements and the main gate, guarded by soldiers. Arrigo arrives at the gate and is allowed to enter by the guards.

Arrigo informs one of the officers that it is Monforte who has instructed that he should be allowed to visit the prisoners. He shows the order to the officer and commands him to bring the prisoners to him. The officer goes off. Left alone Arrigo looks towards the prison and laments his predicament. The people he most cares about believe him to be a traitor (*Giorno di pianto, di fier dolore!*). Most painful to him is the fact that he has forfeited Elena's love.

His reflections are interrupted by the sounds of someone approaching. It is Elena herself, being led from her prison cell. Arrigo is consumed with apprehension. He knows he can only expect Elena to revile him. The prison officer withdraws and Arrigo and Elena are alone. Elena wonders if the traitor is preparing some new torment for her. Arrigo pleads for forgiveness (*Ah! volgi il guardo a me sereno*). Elena replies that since he offers no justification for his treachery he must know it is futile to ask her for forgiveness. Pathetically he declares he is not guilty, to which Elena replies: 'Was is not your hand which disarmed my arm when it was striking the dagger into the wicked tyrant's heart?' Realizing there is no way around this Arrigo now reveals the truth. The 'wicked tyrant' is none other than his father. He tells Elena that he has now paid in kind the debt he owes his father for having spared his life and he is now ready to rejoin the Sicilian cause. He claims that all he desires of his father now is to be allowed to live on or die with the woman he loves. Elena is moved, in spite of herself. She cannot deny the fact that she loves Arrigo and that it has caused her intolerable suffering to have to despise him (*Arrigo! Ah parla a un core*). She begs Arrigo to keep faith with her, even though she knows that shortly she must go to her death. Arrigo is overjoyed that Elena can find it in herself to forgive him. Ecstatically they sing of their reaffirmed solidarity.

Procida is escorted in. He approaches Elena while Arrigo moves off. The latter, displaying the order with which he has been supplied, signals the soldiers to leave and then remains aside, unseen by Procida. Procida reveals to Elena that he has received a letter informing him that an Aragonese ship is already nearing Palermo harbour. It is laden with gold and arms, which means that the Sicilians are finally achieving the foreign aid for which they have waited so long. Procida gives vent to his frustration at being confined in chains at this moment. He catches a glimpse of Arrigo and demands to know what Elena is doing in the traitor's company. As Elena is trying to persuade Procida of Arrigo's repentance Monforte enters, in company with Bethune and other officers. Monforte orders the Sicilians' execution forthwith, and commands Bethune to fetch a priest. Bethune reminds Monforte that the populace is threatening revolt. Monforte is well aware of this and instructs that the French troops should be at the ready: 'let the rebels' first cry be the signal for massacre!' he commands. Bethune leaves to implement the orders.

Arrigo demands to know why Monforte has given these orders whilst Procida, in an aside, laments the fact that he is to die just at the moment that his country needs him most. Arrigo begs for mercy on the prisoners' behalf – either that or let him die with them. Elena seizes on this plea to justify to Procida Arrigo's presence there, but Procida will have none of it. He tells Elena that Arrigo does indeed deserve to die, but not with them. He bids Arrigo go, telling him that he is 'unworthy of such honour'. Bitterly Monforte tells Arrigo that this insult is only what is due to him: 'You, my blood!' This is news to Procida who now assumes that all is lost for Sicily. The Sicilians express their grief at Sicily's apparently hopeless fate. Meanwhile monks are heard offstage chanting the *Dies Irae*. Procida invites Elena to kneel in prayer with him. Arrigo pleads again with his father to be merciful. Monforte's reply is simple: if Arrigo will openly acknowledge him as his father he will show the rebels mercy. Elena forbids Arrigo to be thus blackmailed. Even though she will go to her death she will not blame him.

The gate to the right opens and the grand hall of justice can be seen, up several steps. In the hall are four Penitents praying, and several soldiers with torches in their hands. On the first step stands the executioner, leaning on his axe. Arrigo, realizing that his father intends to carry out his threats, is horrified. Two of the Penitents come down the steps. One takes Procida, the other Elena. A group of women come into the courtyard, kneel and beg for mercy. The rest of the populace follows suit. The monks continue their *Misere*. Procida and Elena, preceded by the Penitents, move toward the steps. Arrigo tries to follow but is restrained by Monforte, who places himself between them. The executioner takes hold of Elena and it seems as though all is lost. As Elena reaches the threshold of the hall of justice Arrigo cries out, 'O Father! O father!' Overjoyed Monforte orders the executions to be aborted and announces a pardon for the prisoners. Procida and Elena, surrounded by soldiers, come down the steps and are led towards Monforte who now issues his *coup de grâce*. Not only does he pardon them but, as a seal of friendship between rival peoples, he blesses the union of Arrigo and Elena. Elena is about to protest (the last thing she ever wanted was her love for Arrigo to be used as a tool for appeasement with the French) but Procida silences her: 'You must do it! The fatherland, your brother . . . wish it!' Turning to the crowd Monforte announces, 'Peace and pardon to all!' Then, embracing Arrigo he declares: 'I find a son again'. All except Procida express their happiness and relief at the unexpected turn of events. Procida mutters darkly to himself, 'the carefree rejoicing will be turned into sorrow'. Nobody listens. Arrigo asks that he be allowed to celebrate his wedding to Elena the next day. Monforte decrees that the couple shall be married that very day when the vespers are heard. From the guardhouse glasses and pitchers are brought out. French soldiers drink with Sicilians. Monforte leads

Elena and Arrigo out. As the curtain falls Procida remains behind, surrounded by his friends.

Act 5   The gardens of Monforte's palace. To the rear some steps leading to the chapel whose dome can be seen above the trees. To the right is the entrance to the palace. Knights and young girls are in the gardens. They are celebrating the cessation of hostilities and the forthcoming union of Elena and Arrigo. Elena, in bridal dress, comes down the steps from the palace. The girls move towards her, offering her flowers. Elena thanks them (*Mercè dilette amiche*) and then expresses the hope that her wedding may truly see the end of the 'horrible vengeance' that has cursed Sicily's recent history. Clearly all reservations about the circumstances of her betrothal to Arrigo have been swept aside by the ecstasy of love.

Elena dismisses the company as Arrigo enters, pensively, from the rear. He welcomes the sudden love and happiness that have erupted into his life (*La brezza aleggia intorno*). Elena approaches and declares she will love him forever. This is all Arrigo wants to hear. He wants at all costs to forget the 'atrocious suffering' that has made his life a misery for so long. Together they sing of their love. Some gentlemen appear at the door of the palace then come out. They are looking for Arrigo. At a sign from Elena Arrigo decides to follow. He asks Elena leave to go to his father. Elena's only request is that he returns quickly. Arrigo rushes off to the palace.

Procida enters from the rear. He tells Elena that Sicily is grateful to her for at her wedding celebrations all the towers and fortresses of the land will be abandoned. The French will thus render themselves virtually defenceless. Elena assumes an enemy must be threatening. Procida loses no time in correcting her misapprehension. He tells her that just after she has said 'yes!' to Arrigo and the wedding bells ring out the massacre will begin in Palermo and throughout Sicily. Elena is appalled. So overwhelmed has she been by her love for Arrigo she never dreamt that Procida might still be plotting revenge.

Procida upbraids her for acceding to the love of a Frenchman. Elena furiously defends her love.

At this moment Arrigo emerges from the palace. Procida goads Elena to denounce him to the French. Suddenly Elena realizes that she is in the same predicament that Arrigo has been in throughout the opera: torn between patriotic loyalty and love. Arrigo approaches and tells Elena that the French banner is flying and jubilant trumpet blasts are ringing around the land. She does not hear him. Her mind is revolving round Procida's revelation that her marriage will be the signal for a massacre. What side shall I take? she wonders desperately. Arrigo notices her distraction and insists she tells him what ails her. Procida urges her to speak, if she dare. Finally Elena tells Arrigo that her brother's spirit has appeared to her and stands before her now. She can no longer marry Arrigo.

Arrigo is aghast. Procida is furious. Elena has destroyed his planned insurrection. Arrigo becomes abusive, calling her a traitress and perjurer. Eventually Elena determines that Arrigo shall know what prevents her from marrying him but then cannot find it in herself to betray her compatriots. She confirms her love for Arrigo but reiterates the impossibility of their ever being married.

Monforte enters from the palace, accompanied by French knights and ladies. Rushing to his father Arrigo tells him the marriage is off. Monforte refuses to believe it. He can clearly see how much the couple love each other. He takes both their right hands and, joining them together, proclaims them man and wife. Procida stands on the steps to the rear and calls to the bells to ring out in celebration of the marriage. Elena's frantic objections are in vain. The bells begin to ring. Elena, realizing that nothing now can avert the massacre, urges Monforte to flee. It is too late. From every direction Sicilians run in, brandishing swords and daggers, screaming for vengeance. Led by Procida they hurl themselves on Monforte and the French. The curtain falls as the massacre proceeds.

Above and beyond the obvious political message inherent in its action *I Vespri Siciliano* outlines the familiar Romeo and Juliet love motif, the lovers in body and spirit who are hopelessly separated by the mundane realities of the world in which they live. The crucial twist in the tail of this particular story lies in the fact that at the outset of their relationship neither Arrigo nor Elena are aware of how cruelly divided they really are. They believe themselves to be fighting for the same cause and that the only obstacle to their union is their disparate social background: Elena is an aristocrat whereas Arrigo is a common soldier.

It is in the nature of fighting for a cause, whether it be political or religious, that a bond is forged which transcends all normal boundaries. Particularly is this the case where the cause is one of resistance against tyranny. In the traditional manner of fairy tales, the hero must first prove himself worthy of the princess's love by fulfilling an assignation; in this case Arrigo must avenge the death of Elena's brother. This appears to present no problem for Arrigo since it is in total accord with the agenda he has already set for himself as a Sicilian patriot. As it turns out it will involve him in the murder of his own father. Because our sympathies are engaged as much, if not more, for Monforte as for his son the dilemma becomes excruciating for all concerned. It is only resolved by the fact that Arrigo, at the crucial moment when Elena is about to be executed, relinquishes his pride and publicly declares the truth about his parentage. Thus he places himself in a totally invidious position with his compatriots.

All relationships will sooner or later undergo a moment of choice, a moment when a commitment needs to be made one way or the other. Arrigo could have allowed Elena to be executed and thus for all time condemned himself in his own eyes. When it comes to it there is no option. For Arrigo does not possess an old man's fanaticism as does Procida. The fanatic will allow nothing, but nothing to get in his way, least of all love. For the fanatic everything must be sacrificed to the greater ideal that transcends all transitory needs. For an occupied country there can be only one transcendent ideal, and that is liberation. As Jean Paul Sartre discovered, living through occupied Paris in the latter half of World War II, nothing focuses more clearly a sense of values than the loss of liberty through occupation.[67]

Arrigo, as is the case with so many of Verdi's heroes, is more of an existential anti-hero than conventional hero. Verdi's heroes are, almost without exception, re-active rather than pro-active. The only two truly heroic male character in all Verdi are Stiffelio and Radames. Arrigo commits no central act of heroism (such as slaying the dragon, retrieving the Holy Relic, rescuing the damsel in distress) by which we can remember him. His public declaration that he is Monforte's son is a moral victory for him, but it is under coercion and not freely volunteered. It is in fact no more heroic than if he had stood by and allowed Elena to be executed. Had he sprung Elena from jail and then together with her led the Sicilians in their massacre of the French this might have given him a stronger profile. But even had this been so, parricide can never carry anything but an Oedipal connotation. In truth myths are, more often than not, monolithic. They present one dilemma which has only one resolution. Life is rarely like that. Verdi, the composer, was above all a humanist. His inspiration was stimulated by complex moral dilemmas which are not susceptible to any one solution. With Shakespeare Verdi shared the ability to empathize with a myriad different points of view.

The Sicilian people need to be liberated from the French yoke and will be liberated, but it cannot possibly be through the intervention of Arrigo who is himself half French. As is the case in so many of Verdi's operas the true heroism is displayed by the female rather than the male – in this case

---

[67]   See also Nikos Kazantzakis' *Freedom or Death* for a brilliant exposition of the moral dilemmas that can arise on a personal level for the victims of occupation.

Elena – and it is through the ethics of renunciation that the definitive act is achieved. (This definition would include Leonora (*La Forza del Destino*), Desdemona (*Otello*), Aida, Violetta (*La Traviata*), all of whom bow before a pre-determined fate.) The ability to embrace the dictates of necessity with magnanimity becomes a *sine qua non*. Thus Elena is prepared to go to her death rather than allow the Sicilian cause to be compromised, not to say blighted, by Arrigo's acknowledgement of his father. But Elena's love for Arrigo transcends even her love for Sicily. It is a necessity she recognizes with the same intensity with which Procida pursues the cause of Sicilian independence. Thus in Act 5 we have two conflicting necessities, addressed simultaneously with predictably disastrous results. This is the stuff of which all drama is made. The resolution will be either tragic or comic. Verdi's temperament was such that invariably the resolution, if any, is tragic, as in *I Vespri Siciliano*.

Viclinda (*I Lombardi*). Arvino's wife.

Viclinda marries into a family apparently blighted by a malign fate. Whether she should bear any responsibility for **Pagano's** passion for her is not made explicit. It is unlikely. She does not welcome his attentions and is devoted to her husband and daughter, **Giselda**. Pagano's passion for her is his problem, not hers.

Initially she is delighted (Act 1 Scene 1) when Pagano is reconciled with his brother and rehabilitated into the family. But she soon realizes that all is not well, that Pagano still harbours rancorous thoughts: 'in that wicked face appeared a cloud of anger, not repentance' (Act 1 Scene 2). When her husband sends her to her room (Act 1 Scene 2) but warns her not to go to bed her worst fears are confirmed. She kneels in prayer with her daughter – Viclinda is God-fearing in a way quite distinct from her menfolk. One feels that she does not welcome the slaughter that the Crusaders' missions entail, anymore than does her daughter. But unlike her daughter she is not willing to voice her distaste. Having said which she does not have the provocation that Giselda has.

Viclinda's shouts for help when Pagano attempts to drag her away undoubtedly save her from being kidnapped, for her husband, who is already alert to imminent danger, comes running immediately. She is naturally appalled that Pagano has murdered her father-in-law, though hugely relieved that it was not her husband who was killed.

Viclinda does not reappear in the opera after Act 1. When Giselda next appears (Act 2 Scene 2) she is praying to the spirit of her deceased mother. So presumably the strain of living with a family rent asunder by dissension has taken its toll and she has died prematurely.

Violetta (*La Traviata*)

Backgound Note In many of his operas Verdi alludes to, or actually portrays, historical events. But never did he come so close to depicting in drama real-life events with such naturalistic verisimilitude as in his transcription of Dumas' novel. To read the story of Marie Duplessis is almost to read the synopsis of the opera, from the opening dialogue between Violetta and **Alfredo** to her desire to dress in her favourite gown only minutes before she dies.

Marie Duplessis arrived in Paris at the age of fifteen and was dead by the age of twenty-three from consumption. In the interim she was courted by some of the most remarkable men of her age, including Alexander Dumas, who fashioned his novel – and later his play – *La Dame aux camélias*, around her personality. It was an invention of Dumas to claim that Duplessis had a particular passion for camellias. But it is well attested that she loved flowers. The anteroom of her apartment on Boulevard Madeline in Paris was apparently devoted exclusively to flowers. Dumas' inspiration no doubt originated in a rumour that circulated in Paris (possibly encouraged by Duplessis herself, who had a lively sense of humour) that she carried white camellias when 'available', and red ones when incommoded by her monthly period.

The story of Violetta is one of extraordinary sacrifice. First she abandons her wealth and position in Society, and then she abandons her love in order to propitiate the morals of that same Society. Whether Marie Duplessis herself would have been capable of such self-sacrifice is open to question; indeed it seems unlikely that any woman would abandon both security and love. The character of Violetta can very easily be dismissed as a male wish fulfilment fantasy, particularly on the part of Dumas, whose affair with Duplessis was not a happy one.

The figure of Violetta is one of the enduring feminine archetypes in the operatic repertoire. She could be described as the 'whore with a heart of gold' (Duplessis once told a friend, 'It is a mistake to have a heart if you are a courtesan'). Violetta is, of course, a great deal more than that. She is an acutely sensitive and innately distinguished young woman. Franz Liszt described Marie Duplessis as 'of truly exquisite nature, for, what is generally, and perhaps rightly, described as corruption, never touched her'.

It is in the nature of the courtesan's profession that she transgresses the normal conception of love. There is no possibility of faithfulness; she will, by definition, be faithless. Yet the courtesan, as opposed to the prostitute who hawks her wares on the street corner, must give the semblance of love. The prostitute may issue prohibition against this or that intimacy to ensure that the transaction remains strictly physical with no possibility of interpersonal communication. Not so the courtesan. She requires to be kept and nurtured. She needs protecting from an unkind world, for she is the very essence of femininity. She may be supported but never owned. She cannot be captured. She may gravitate towards the highest bidder, but she will have the final decision as to under whose wing she elects to take cover. She maintains her freedom by virtue of the fact that she cannot be possessed. Thus her life is a constant struggle to consolidate her freedom by delineating her uniqueness. This Violetta

(Duplessis) achieves to perfection so that she is in reality accepted, wherever and to whomever she chooses to turn. Her social mobility is the measure of her success. But she is not happy. Why? Because she is not truly cared for. She is displayed as an ornament and paraded as a jewel in this or that crown. But she is not wanted for herself, for what she conceals beneath the professional veneer. She must be the mistress of deception. She becomes all too quickly, like all great divas, the victim of her own success. She cannot afford not to be the diva, though if she does succeed in relinquishing the mask she will eventually expire from spiritual malnutrition.

When Alfredo first comes across Violetta this is precisely what is happening to her. The consumption, so aptly named, is a symptom of her malaise. Yet it is, as all disease is in essence, a liberation for her. Knowing that she is dying Violetta is relieved from the crippling fear of consequences that renders most human destinies stillborn. What she needs is to be loved for herself, that which she has chosen not to display until now. Nature has its way and the illness to which she succumbs is eloquent testimony to this hidden self which is daily suffering suffocation at the hands of the society she inhabits. The body has its own wisdom. Her condition excites Alfredo's compassion. He sees the truth of Violetta's predicament, so eloquently emblemized by the camellias that are her signature. A flower cut from its stem is already dying. Violetta has been dying from the moment she entered society and resolved to earn her living from exploiting it, and allowing herself to be exploited. Ostensibly Violetta's reason for being a courtesan is her need to earn a living. Paradoxically it is her very choice of calling that so fatally undermines her health, so that the living she earns quickly becomes an irrelevance. Once health has fled there is no living to be concerned with, there is only death. Her choice of profession is not really about earning a living, though. It is more a studied assertion of independence. The attractive young girl of no background, even in the early years of the 19th century, could have found a man to

make an 'honest woman of her'. Her living would thus have been assured. But the living, although it becomes the central issue in her life, is peripheral once she has gained a taste for the excitement of romance.

Violetta is young. She is largely unconscious. She knows nothing of what stirs within the recesses of her soul. All she knows is that she has a gift and that she is adored. Some of the most distinguished men in society desire and worship at her feet. She is a goddess in her own right. Beside the power that she wields her personal needs seem irrelevant. It is a cliché that every great talent or genius comes with a price tag. Genius is always an indication of disassociation. Only through disassociation of the psyche can the individual gain access to the great cosmic storehouse of possibility. Violetta has pursued a hedonistic philosophy of living for the moment, because anything else seems a kind of insanity. She is young, so is Alfredo. Young is naïve. Two naiveties do not make wisdom and Violetta must wait for her death chamber to attain to wisdom. In the meantime Alfredo offers her security, the like of which she has never known, that is, emotional security. Whether or not he has the means to support her becomes immaterial. She finds in the country with Alfredo the possibility of dropping the mask. She no longer needs to perform. So grateful to him is she for the salvation he offers her that it becomes as nothing to her to squander her by now considerable fortune in order to support their continued idyll.

She has reckoned without the full force of bourgeois rectitude in the form of Alfredo's family. The appeal that **Germont** makes to her is unimpeachable (Act 2 Scene 1). If he had required that she sacrifice her love for the sake of Germont's good name, Violetta would have been fully justified in ignoring his demands. Indeed she probably would have. But since it is another girl's happiness at stake, a girl who has her whole life before her, who is untainted by sexual scandal and who has a destiny mapped out for her, such as Violetta could only ever dream of, she is at a loss. There is not a hint of viciousness in Violetta's nature. If her happiness is at the expense of another's, and that other is more worthy than her, she will not hesitate. For is not she, Violetta, worthless? What rights does she have by comparison with a respectable young girl from a good family? She throws away her happiness, not out of any sense of martyrdom, but because she has no choice. She is consumed with guilt for the happiness that has befallen her, in spite of herself or anything that she might have done to deserve it. She knows that Alfredo will suffer but she cannot make that an over-riding consideration. He is too good for her anyway. Her return to Paris, and the mean-ingless life that she leads there, is an inevitability that she cannot avoid. Ever since she moved to the country she has known that it was only a matter of time. Idylls do not last.

She hurls herself back into the inanity of **Flora**'s parties (Act 2 Scene 2). She abases herself before **Douphol**. In order to survive Violetta has learnt to compartmentalize herself and her feelings. Once in Paris she does not think about Alfredo. He remains only as a dull ache in the recesses of her consciousness. The shock when Alfredo arrives at Flora's party is consequently all the greater. This is not meant to happen. Alfredo belongs to the past. The two worlds, that of the mask she has developed in order to survive, and that of her deep self, cannot be allowed to confront each other. She is consumed with panic. She knows that the two men on whom she has projected her disparate selves cannot co-exist. One of them must be destroyed. It is the moment that her whole life has been moving towards.

When Alfredo flings the money at her in full sight of all the guests at Flora's party he only corroborates the sense of worthlessness and hopelessness that has pursued her. From that moment she has no reason to live. Alfredo wounds Douphol in a duel and flees abroad. Thus she loses protector and lover in one fell swoop. There is a real poignancy in the moment on her death bed when she asks **Annina** how much money they have left in the drawer (Act 3). The twenty louis remaining is quite possibly the only remaining remnants of Alfredo's winnings.

Violetta has never been able to afford the luxury of pride. She would give half of her money to the poor because there can never be anyone less deserving than herself.

The true tragedy of Violetta is the way in which all her sacrifices lead to nothing, nothing but the death bed. She is only redeemed by Alfredo's enduring compassion which, having recognized her, can never leave her.

A Voice from Heaven (Una voce dal Cielo) (*Don Carlo*)

At the conclusion of the *auto-da-fé* scene (Act 3 Scene 2) a voice is heard from on high greeting the souls of the heretics who are about to be put to death at the stake: 'Soar towards heaven, fly, poor souls, fly up to enjoy the peace of the Lord!' It is a reassurance from on high of redemption for the victims of the Inquisition. In one sense it could be said to add credibility to the whole ethos of the Inquisition whereby heretics were burned in order to purify them in preparation for redemption in the after life. But since it is unlikely that the heretics recanted at the stake – if they had anything to recant – and are certainly not shown to do so this can safely be discounted as part of the intention of Verdi and his librettists. 'A Voice from on high' is a stock-in-trade of the Romantic operatic tradition. Its import here, coming at the end of a massive ensemble scene, is not only to give promise of eventual salvation for the persecuted heretics, but to place the entire drama in a larger perspective than any of the purely political or humanistic concerns of the main protagonists have hitherto allowed. It also foreshadows the sudden and dramatic appearance of the spirit of Carlo V at the conclusion of the opera, and, in giving promise of eventual salvation, a parallel can be drawn with the end of Act 1 of Wagner's *Parsifal*.

W

Count Walter (*Luisa Miller*)

Walter is one of the two father-figures whose presence dominate the opera. Walter epitomizes the problems of fathering a son, where **Miller** epitomizes the problems attendant upon fathering a daughter. But where Miller is benign Walter is all aggression. The father always wishes, consciously or subconsciously, for his son to achieve all that he has achieved, and more.

On Walter's first appearance (Act 1 Scene 2) he expresses his exasperation with his son, **Rodolfo**, who does not appear to share his father's ambitions for him. Walter views Rodolfo's behaviour as rank ingratitude. He only wants, he claims, to see Rodolfo happy and powerful. The two are synonymous for Walter. Without power there can be no happiness. He himself has resorted to murder in order to acquire power. It would seem such a little thing to expect Rodolfo to make a suitable marriage. He wants Rodolfo to marry **Frederica** because the latter has formerly been married to a Duke with powerful affiliations at the German Court. She is also extremely wealthy. Since the two were childhood sweethearts it is beyond Walter's comprehension that Rodolfo opposes the marriage. The desires of the human heart are the least of Walter's priorities. A man must first of all survive and thrive in the world. Later he may indulge his desires, but only having first propitiated the survival needs.

Walter takes a diametrically opposed view on marriage to Miller. Miller declares that it is a girl's sacred right to choose the husband of her desires. Walter would agree with his henchman, **Wurm**, that such a view is sentimental codswallop. A woman should be told who she will marry, while a man should choose his bride with a dispassionate eye to business. How will the marriage profit me? should be the primary concern. If pressed on the subject Walter would say that he loves his son dearly and only wants what is best for him. He will undoubtedly be distraught at Rodolfo's suicide. Indeed he may even suffer a total breakdown. It would not be untypical of such a man (one thinks of the millionaire, Aristotle Onassis, who seemed to lose all will to live after his playboy son was killed in an air crash; also the twelfth-century English

king, Henry II, who devoted his whole life to trying to bequeath his three sons a vast empire, only to have all three turn and take up arms against him. He, likewise, lost all will to live and died in his mid fifties).

Walter epitomizes the negative aspects of the father archetype. He has no concern other than to engender a glorious future for his family. That it goes so disastrously wrong is entirely down to his lack of imagination.

The cynical way in which he uses **Luisa** in his ongoing attempt to lure Rodolfo into marriage with Frederica, unpleasant to witness as it is, is but a tiny part of the Machavellian obsession which fuels this man's need to bolster his self-esteem. The fact that he has murdered his cousin in order to protect his inheritance (see **Synopsis**) demonstrates the extent to which he has passed beyond the constraints of ordinary morality in the all-consuming imperative to achieve his ends. Murder is the ultimate outpost which very few will actually pass, whatever the provocation. Untypically of his type, Walter has actually committed the deed himself. It pains him to remember it, but he can always justify it as having been committed in answer to the dictates of necessity. The very intensity with which he craves Rodolfo's advancement is, however, indicative of his need to keep reinforcing the justification to himself. For in his heart of hearts he must know it is no justification. If Rodolfo does not accede to his plans for him his whole endeavour will be rendered as nought and he will only have in his old age the fearful consciousness of guilt to accompany him. Add to this his son's suicide and the heartbreak he has brought on Miller and his family and the prospects for Walter retaining his sanity look bleak. His whole life's endeavour has been rendered a futility, worse than that, a crime against humanity, most especially his own.

Walter (*Stiffelio*). A boatman.

Does not appear in the opera but is referred to by **Stiffelio** (Act 1 Scene 1). For it is Walter who has witnessed **Raffaele**'s precipitate exit from a window of the castle, early one morning, subsequent to a night of passion with Stiffelio's wife, **Lina**. Walter did not identify Raffaele nor, apparently, the window from which he jumped.

However, he has retrieved a notecase which apparently fell from Raffaele's pocket as he made his escape. Walter has given the notecase to Stiffelio, who has overcome the temptation to open it and thus discover the identity of the intruder. Stiffelio throws the notecase into the fire instead.

Wurm (*Luisa Miller*). An employee of **Count Walter**.
Wurm is well named, although the significance of the name would be lost on an Italian audience with no knowledge of German. Wurm means worm, or snake. It also has connotations of serpent, as in the serpent that tempted Eve in the Garden of Eden.

Wurm was the instigator of the plan to murder Walter's cousin, the elder Count. He is entirely self-serving and has no concerns for the suffering he may cause others in his relentless quest to satisfy his own insatiable appetites. When he sees **Luisa** he wants her, to possess her and use her as he sees fit. His appetite for her is increased tenfold by the knowledge that **Rodolfo** is in love with her. For while Wurm owes his own advancement to Rodolfo's father, Walter, he is not himself a noble. He could be likened to a combination of Iago (*Otello*) and Spoletto (Puccini's *Tosca*); the epitome of a courtier who has achieved advancement through his own quick wittedness and cunning, yet will never quite belong and is considerably irked by his position; always just at the periphery, always, in the last analysis, in service. Thus the man is riddled with resentments. These find expression in barely concealed sadism, which erupts at any given opportunity, most notably when coercing Luisa into writing a love letter addressed to himself. There can be no clearer illustration of his complete lack of regard, let alone love, for Luisa.

It is incomprehensible to Wurm that Luisa's father should not favour him as a son-in-law, particularly as he has achieved considerable advancement at Court since he first applied to **Miller** for Luisa's hand a year

before. Miller's argument that Luisa has a right to choose her own husband seems to Wurm nothing less than feebleness. A father's job is to command his offspring, as Walter attempts to command Rodolfo. Because Wurm's personality is identified with his need to feed his own self-esteem through political advancement, with no regard to the reality of what he may or may not have to perpetrate in order to achieve it, he can never comprehend why he falls short of success. Like his master he fatally lacks imagination.

The extent of Wurm's failure to prevail is indicated in the opera by the fact that he does not utter a single word in the third Act, which is almost entirely devoted to the two main protagonists attempting to unravel the web of deception that he, Wurm, has ensnared them in. Wurm is on stage at the conclusion of the opera, which is regrettable for him, since Rodolfo's final act before expiring is to run him through with his sword. Does it occur to Wurm, in his death throes, that he has been responsible for the deaths not only of Walter's cousin, but also of Rodolfo and Luisa? That even had he lived he is further than he has ever been from acquiring what he most desires?

Wurm's central problem is that he does not know what he wants. He thinks he wants power, a beautiful wife and all the trappings of material success. A true student of Machiavelli, he will do whatever he has to do to achieve these ends. But he will never be able truly to grasp what he seeks. It will always elude him. Only when he wakes up to the fact that it is chimeras that he chases will he have a chance of redemption. Now, however, time has run out for him. With death will come absolution from responsibility which, in this world at any rate, he passes to his master, Rodolfo's father.

Z

Zaccaria (*Nabucco*). A Hebrew prophet.
The character of Zaccaria is one of the strongest evocations in opera of a biblical prophet. The biblical Zaccaria actually lived

later than in the action of the opera, being a post-exile prophet. In the Bible it is the prophet Ezekiel who goes to Babylon. The quotations which preface each of the four Acts of Solera's libretto are based on excerpts from the book of the prophet Jeremiah, who was alive at the time of Nebuchadnezzar's assault on Jerusalem (588 and 589 BC).

The strength of Zaccaria's presence in the opera ensures a fine counterbalance to the demented, demonic presence of **Nabucco**. Indeed the opera can be seen as an evocation of the battle for supremacy between these two egotists and the ideologies they represent (on another level they can be seen as the early precursors of **Philip** and the **Inquisitor** in *Don Carlo*. Certainly the same titanic struggle between the secular and the spiritual pertains). Zaccaria's egotism prevails because it is constructed on a far more secure foundation than is Nabucco's. From a narrow, moralistic perspective egotism is always pernicious, but as so often, when scrutinized more closely, the concepts of egotism, and its supposed opposite, contrition or humility, are very much more nebulous than at first would appear. Nabucco's egotism fails in its objectives because his ends are strictly limited to the advancement of his own incalculable need for self-aggrandisement. Zaccaria's egotism is placed at the service of a transcendent ethos. The egotism itself may be barely distinguishable but the ends it serves are radically different

Nabucco is only struck down at the moment he ceases to serve a superior authority, at the moment he chooses to take upon himself the mantle of supreme deity, at which moment he betrays the very essence of his humanity. Such a betrayal would be unthinkable to Zaccaria, as indeed would be resorting to the expedient of spreading a lie in order to secure political ascendancy, as does his opposite number among the Babylonians, the **High Priest of Baal**. The essence of Zaccaria's mandate is the unquestioning faith and obeisance before the numinous, so powerfully exemplified in the scene where he accepts the Babylonian **Fenena** into the Jewish faith (Act 2 Scene 2: '*Vieni, o Levita!*'). 'The Lord

wishes me to be agent of a new miracle', he announces. Zaccaria never loses sight of the fact that he is first and foremost an agent and servant.

In Act 3 Scene 2 Zaccaria takes on the true mantle of the prophet as he peers into the obscurity of the future and sees that the 'shameful chains of the Hebrews are broken! The wrath of the Lion of Judah falls upon the treacherous sand!' Then, in a direct paraphrase of lines from the book of Jeremiah (Chapter 50 verse 39) which also happen to be the basis for the lines which preface Act 3, Zaccaria envisages the day when: 'once proud Babylon shall become as a desert inhabited only by hyenas and snakes, haunted by the call of owls and hoopoes'. Thus he tries to instil fresh courage and resilience in the beleaguered Hebrew slaves. But it is in notable contrast to the exhortatory triumphalism of his speech in Act 1. For then there was still hope at a mundane, political level; now there is ostensibly no hope. The Hebrews can only rely on divine intervention, or a miracle. Zaccaria's role as intermediary between God and man has become of even more crucial importance. When Fenena is about to be put to death at **Abigaille**'s order (Act 4 Scene 2) Zaccaria seeks to transform what is a banal political execution into a noble sacrifice. He exhorts Fenena to: 'Go, win the palm of martyrdom'.

The ending of the opera, in which Zaccaria has the satisfaction of witnessing Nabucco convert to the 'true faith', is historically apocryphal, but yet has some justification in that the book of Jeremiah concludes with a description of how the Babylonian king, Evil-Merodach, released the Judean king, Jehoiachin, from prison and allowed him to dine at his table. Thereafter the Judean was pensioned by the Babylonians for life, in stark contrast to the fate of his predecessor, King Zedekiah, whose eyes were put out and who was imprisoned until the day he died. Thus an indication is given that perhaps the Babylonians realized the error of their ways and adopted a more humanitarian approach to their enemies, if not actually choosing to embrace the Jewish faith. (See also **Nabucco**.)

Zamoro (*Alzira*). Inca Prince.

Zamoro is ostensibly the hero of *Alzira* (not least by virtue of the fact that he is assigned the tenor part). But Zamoro is not the true focus of interest. That privilege belongs to the role of **Gusmano**. Gusmano is more compelling than Zamoro because he is a self-divided character. Zamoro knows all along his objective, namely the re-instatement of the Inca heritage and his betrothal to the beautiful **Alzira**.

Zamoro realizes that in order to achieve his ends and bring an end to the stalemate that pertains between the invading Spanish and the native Incas it only needs one man to relinquish his pride and break the futile circle of violence and revenge. This means an act of forgiveness and/or compassion from one party or another. Zamoro must realize that this is never going to come from the blood-thirsty Spanish. Hence it must come from him. He must instigate an about-turn through an apparently absurd act.

Zamoro has been taken prisoner by Gusmano and tortured unbearably by the Spanish. At the time he returns to his home nobody could have stronger motivation for instigating a vendetta against the Spanish. But when Zamoro discovers his compatriots subjecting the elderly **Alvaro** to torture (Prologue Scene 1), his thoughts must surely return to the agonies he himself has suffered but recently at the hands of the Spanish. His empathy for Alvaro's suffering is the very essence of the Christian ethic. Thus Zamoro breaks the perpetual cycle of violence and opens up a possibility of reconciliation. One must assume that his treatment at the hands of the Spanish has taught him to overcome the instinctive sense of inferiority that a native race must feel towards a conquering race. Zamoro has realized that the Spanish are no different – in fact they are a great deal worse – than the Incas themselves. This realization has restored his pride and made him determined to give the Spanish a lesson in common humanity. 'Return to your people', he tells Alvaro, 'and relate to them who call us savages how a savage gave you your life'.

It would be a mistake to conclude that Zamoro is thereby first and foremost a moralist, a religious leader with a mission. Far from it. He is first and foremost a warrior, a man of honour and a lover. Aside from the preservation of Inca dignity his principal agenda in the opera is to be united with his beloved Alzira and wreak vengeance on his persecutors. Later (Act 1 Scene 2), when Gusmano has Zamoro in his power and is ordering his immediate execution, Zamoro is merciless in his appraisal of the Spaniard: 'I hoped to fight you, but in vain I called you to combat. They flung me in prison at your order, Gusmano. You spoke then of fetters and of the gallows. Now you speak again, of axes and of the block and you call yourself a warrior? A hangman you are, not a warrior'. Rash words from a man who is entirely defenceless and at his enemy's mercy. But then Zamoro at this moment believes he has nothing to lose. Luckily for him Alvaro enters and, recognizing the man who saved him from torture and death, pleads passionately on his behalf. Gusmano cannot ignore his father's entreaties. Besides news arrives that Zamoro's countrymen are assembling outside Lima and demanding his release. Gusmano is forced to accept that he will have to meet Zamoro on the battlefield.

There Zamoro must endure defeat at the hands of the Spanish and once again he is captured and condemned to death by Gusmano. But still he carries with him the certain knowledge that Alzira loves him and him alone. However when he hears from **Otumbo** (Act 2 Scene 2), who has ensured his escape from imprisonment, that Alzira is to be married to Gusmano Zamoro loses his sense of perspective. All along the one thing that has sustained him has been the belief that Alzira is waiting for him. Her loss renders all his noble ideals and fierce will to endure futile. A cynic would say that Zamoro's noble ideals and desire for an honourable resolution with the Spanish have only been motivated from the start by the knowledge that Alzira is held captive. Cynicism is usually based on more than a grain of truth and this would be no exception, but it would be unfair to thus suspect Zamoro's motives all along. His warrior's sense of honour is a crucial part of his makeup, as is his romantic attachment to Alzira. Now, however, he has only one thought and that is blood.

Believing himself betrayed by Alzira and dishonoured once too often (by Gusmano) he resorts to the same sort of cowardly tactics of which he has so witheringly accused Gusmano. Uninvited and disguised in Spanish uniform he will attend the wedding feast of Gusmano and Alzira (Act 2 Scene 3). True to his word he stabs Gusmano in the midst of the wedding ceremony. Welcoming the death which he expects to befall him forthwith he invites Alzira to drink his blood and Gusmano to learn from him 'how to die'. But death does not come to him because Gusmano finally, in his dying moments, learns the lesson that Zamoro has been hoping to teach him from the start: that honour comes before all else, and most especially above self-interest, the sort of purely selfish obsession that Gusmano has persistently demonstrated. Zamoro's action in finally casting aside all scruples and resorting to the behaviour which he has deplored in Gusmano is very human. From a purely dramatic point of view it is the most believable, truly motivated action in the whole opera. That it affects the very result that Zamoro has most sought after is also entirely believable. It is the law of reverse effort. Only when Zamoro totally turns his back on that which up until now has mattered most to him – his life and honour – does he achieve what he truly wants; fulfilment through marriage to Alzira. This is the 'author's message', in Verdi's most polemical of operas.[68]

Uno Zingaro (An Old Gypsy) (*Il Trovatore*). See **Gypsy**

Zuma (*Alzira*). Alzira's sister.
Although Zuma is the heroine's sister her role is more that of Alzira's handmaiden. As is the way with such characters (see **Laura** in *Luisa Miller*) she merely reflects her sister's moods, suffering with her when she is unhappy and overjoyed when things work out as she would wish. See **Alzira**.

---

[68] This may seem a strange assertion in view of the welter of nationalistic operas that poured from Verdi's pen throughout the 'Galley' years: *I Lombardi, Nabucco, La Battaglia di Legnano, Attila*, etc. But in all those operas the message is implicit in the plots themselves. In *Alzira* the message is superimposed. Voltaire was a philosopher first and a dramatist second. The drama is constructed purely as a vehicle for his ideas.

Glossary

Aida

Act 1 Scene 1
Celeste Aida, forma divina
Celestial Aida, divine form
Mistico serto di luce e fior
mystical garland of light and flowers

Radames sings of his love for Aida and of his hopes that he may achieve a victory in his forthcoming battle with Aida's people, the Ethiopians, effect a peace between the two nations and thus be enabled to make Aida his bride.

Ritorna vincitor! E dal mio labbro
Return victorious! And from my lips
uscì l'empia parola!
issued the impious words!

Aida is dismayed at the realization of how her love for Radames has automatically rendered her a traitor to her homeland.

Act 1 Scene 2
Mortal, diletto ai Numi, a te fidate
Mortal, beloved of the gods, to you is confided
son d'Egitto le sorti
the destiny of Egypt

Ramfis invests Radames with the sacred sword with which to instigate 'terror and death' against the enemy.

Act 2 Scene 1
Fu la sorte dell'armi a'tuoi funesta
The fortunes of war have gone against you
Povera Aida!
Poor Aida!

Amneris deliberately provokes Aida to reveal her love for Radames.

Act 3
O patria mai, ma più, mai più ti rivedrò!
Oh my country, never more, never more shall I see you!

Aida laments her hopeless predicament – her father in chains, her country defeated, and her lover destined to be married to another woman.

A te grave cagion m'adduce, Aida
Grave reasons bring me to you, Aida
nulla sfugge al mio sguardo
nothing escapes my eyes.

Amonasro, realizing that Aida and Radames are lovers, determines to turn the liaison to the benefit of the Ethiopian cause.

Pur ti riveggo, mia dolce Aida . . .
At last I am with you, my sweet Aida . . .

Radames reaffirms his love for Aida and determination that she shall be his bride.

Tu, Amonasro! Tu, il Re?
You, Amonasro! You, the King?

Radames is appalled to realize that he has unwittingly betrayed his country.

Act 4 Scene 1
L'abborrita rivale a me sfuggia
My hated rival has escaped me

Amneris deplores Aida's escape and the imminent trial and execution of her beloved Radames.

Act 4 Scene 2
La fatal pietra sovra me si chiuse
The fatal stone has closed over me.

Radames, unaware that Aida has concealed herself in his tomb, bewails the fact that he will never see her again.

Alzira

Prologue
Muoia, muoia coverto d'insulti
Die, die covered with insults

Otumbo and other Indians prepare to torture and execrate the Spanish governor, Alvaro.

Un Inca . . . eccesso orriblile!
An Inca . . . Horrible deed!

Zamoro describes his ordeal at the hands of the Spanish.

Dio della guerra, i tuoi furori
God of war, inspire
Spira trasfondi ne' petti nostri
Our hearts with your righteous anger

Zamoro and the Indians prepare to go to war against the Spanish.

Act 1 Scene 1
Eterna la memoria
The lasting memory
D'un folle amor l'ingombra
of an insane love oppresses her

Gusmano reflects on his love for the Inca girl, Alzira.

Quanto un mortal può chiedere
Whatever a mortal could ask for
Benigno il ciel m'offerse
a benign heaven has offered me

Gusmano confirms that nothing means anything to him if he cannot win Alzira's heart.

Act 1 Scene 2
Da Gusman, su fragil barca
From Gusmano I fled on a
Io fuggia, dell'onde in grembo
fragile bark in the midst of the waves

Alzira describes the dream that has so perturbed her.

Nell'astro che più fulgido
On that star that shines
La notte in ciel sfavilla
brightest in the night sky
Ivi è Zamoro, e palpita
There Zamoro lives and pulsates

Alzira dreams of being reunited with her beloved Zamoro.

Risorge ne' tuoi lumi
In your eyes the star
L'astro de' giorni miei!
of my days rises again!

Alzira and Zamoro confirm their love for each other.

Teco sperai combattere
I hoped to fight you
Ma nella pugna invano
But in vain I called you
Io ti chiamai
to battle

Zamoro reviles Gusmano for cowardice.

Nella polve genuflesso
Kneeling in the dust
Ecco il padre innanzi al figlio
Behold the father before his son

Alvaro pleads with his son to exercise mercy on his enemy.

Trema, trema . . . a ritorti fra l'armi
Tremble, tremble . . . amidst arms
Vengo il dono, rivale aborrito
I will come to you, hated rival

Gusmano swears to be avenged on Zamoro.

Act 2 Scene 1
Il pianto . . . l'angoscia . . .
The tears . . . the anguish . . .
Di lena mi priva!
Deprive me of breath!

Alzira pleads with Gusmano to be merciful towards Zamoro.

Colma di gioia ho l'anima
My spirit overflows with joy
Più non domando, o bramo
I do not ask nor desire anything more

Gusmano expresses his exhilaration at having finally gained a promise of
marriage from Alzira in exchange for Zamoro's life.

Act 2 Scene 2
Irne lungi ancor dovrei
Must I once more travel far away
Carco d'onta e fuggitivo
burdened with shame and a fugitive

Zamoro laments his recent defeat and, most of all, the loss of his beloved Alzira.

461

Non di codarde lagrime
This is not the time for cowardly tears
Di sangue l'ora è questa!
But for blood!

Zamoro shrugs off his self-pity and determines to be avenged both on Gusmano and Alzira.

Act 3 Scene 1
Tergi del pianto, America
Dry your tears, America
Tergi le meste ciglia
Dry your sad eyes

Alzira's maids sing in celebration of their mistress's forthcoming marriage to Gusmano and the new accord it represents between Incas and Spanish.

È dolce la tromba che suona vittoria
The trumpet that sounds victory is sweet

Gusmano exults in his forthcoming marriage to Alzira.

I numi tuoi, vendetta atroce . . .
Your gods exact terrible revenge . . .
Misfallo orribile
Hideous misdeed

Gusmano in his dying moments gives his blessing to the union of Zamoro and Alzira.

Aroldo

Act 1 Scene 1
Tocchiamo! A gaudio insolito
Let's drink! Let each heart be
dischiudasi ogni cor!
receptive to unaccustomed joy!

The guests at Egberto's castle toast the return of Aroldo from his triumphs in Palestine.

Salvami tu, gran Dio
Save me, great God
tu che mi leggi in core
you who can read my heart

Weighed down by conscience, Mina prays for guidance.

Sotto il sol di Siria ardente
Under the fierce sun of Syria
ricoperto d'aspre maglie
recovered from harsh wounds
il mio cor nelle battaglie
while in battle
non tremava che per te
my heart only trembled for you

Aroldo unwittingly exacerbates Mina's guilt.

Dite che il fallo a tergere
Say that your heart has not
la forza non ha il core
the strength to wipe away the sin

Egberto remonstrates with his daughter over her intention to reveal to Aroldo
her faithlessness in the latter's absence.

Act 1 Scene 2
Per te della croce possente guerriero
For you, mighty warrior of the Cross
che tanto di Kenth crescevi l'onor
who has so greatly increased the honour of Kent

Egberto's guests sing in praise of Aroldo.

Vi fu in Palestina tal uomo che indegno
There was in Palestine a man so deceitful
l'onor d'un amico d'insidia fe' segno
that he laid a trap to ruin the honour of a friend

Act 2
Ah, dagli scanni eterei
Ah from the ethereal seat
dove beata siedi
where you sit in blessedness
alla tua figlia volgiti
turn towards your daughter

Mina prays to the spirit of her mother to intercede for her in Heaven.

Act 3
Mina pensai che un angelo
Mina, I thought that in you

in te mi desse il cielo
Heaven had granted me an angel

Egberto bewails the dishonour that his beloved daughter has brought upon him.

Oh, gioia inesprimibile
Oh the inexpressible joy
che questo cor innondi
that inundates this heart

Egberto exults in the knowledge that Godvino is returning and he will thus be able to avenge his family's tainted honour.

Ah, si, voliamo al tempio
Ah yes, let us hasten to the church
fuggiam le inique porte
let us flee these iniquitous portals

Aroldo readily accedes to Briano's suggestion that they leave the scene of Egberto's murder of Godvino and repair to the church.

Act 4
Angiol di Dio, Custode mio
Angel of God, my Custodian
prega per me
pray for me

Aroldo and Briano, having arrived at their place of exile, pray for divine assistance and protection.

Ah, da me fuggi, involati
Ah, flee from me, go away
nè t'appressar più mai
do not approach any closer

Unexpectedly confronted by his wife Aroldo vehemently repulses her.

Allora che gli anni avran domo il core
When the years have conquered my heart
e bianco il mio crine sarà pel dolore
and my hair has turned white on account of my grief

Mina pleads with Aroldo to grant her his forgiveness.

Attila

Prologue Scene 1
Urli, rapine, gemiti, sangue, stupri, rovine
Shouts, pillage, groans, blood, rape, devastation

Atilla's Huns, Herulians and Ostrogoths celebrate the delights of their marauding existence.

Allor che i forti corrono
While your warriors run
come leoni al brando
to their swords like lions
stan le tue donne o barbaro
your women remain, oh barbarians
sui carri lagrimando
in the carriages weeping

Odabella pours scorn on the feebleness of the Hun women.

Da te questo or m'è concesso
This is now granted to me by thee
O giustizia alta, divina!
Oh sublime, divine jusitce!

Odabella revels in the fact that Attila has just given her his sword for, with it, she intends to wreak vengeance upon him for her murdered father.

Tardo per gli anni e tremulo
Advanced in years and feeble
È il regnator d'Oriente
is the ruler of the East

Ezio offers to turn traitor to Rome and support Attila.

Vanitosi! Che abbietti e dormenti
Vain boaster! who abjectly and negligently
pur nel mondo tenere la possa
yet monopolises worldly power

Attila upbraids Ezio and warns him of his forthcoming vengeance.

Prologue Scene 2
Ella in poter del barbaro!
She in the barbarian's power!
fra la sue schiave avvinta!
imprisoned as one of his slaves!

Foresto torments himself with thoughts of Odabella's fate in captivity.

Cara patria, già madre e reina
Dear homeland, at one and the same time mother and queen
di possenti magnanimi figli
of powerful, generous sons

Foresto swears to the Aquilean people who have accompanied him into exile
that their country shall rise 'like a phoenix from the ashes'.

Act 1 Scene 1
Oh! nel fuggente nuvolo
Oh father
non sei tu padre impresso?
Is it not your image imprinted on the fleeting clouds?

Odabella has managed to snatch some time alone away from her captors. She
fondly remembers her beloved father and lover.

Si, quell'io son, ravvisami
Yes, I am that one – look on me again
che tu tradisti, infida
whom you betrayed, faithless one

Foresto confronts Odabella.

Oh t'inebria nell'amplesso
Oh enfolding you in the embrace
gioia immensa, indefinita
what immense, ineffable joy!

Foresto and Odabella exult in their reunion.

Act 1 Scene 2
Mentre gonfiarsi l'anima
As my soul seemed to
parea dinanzi a Roma
swell with pride before Rome

Attila recalls a dream he has had in which Pope Leo has cautioned him for
usurping God's prerogative.

Act 1 Scene 3
No! ... non è sogno ch'or l'alma invade!
No! ... this is not a dream that now invades my soul!

Confronted with the real Pope Leo Attila is genuinely terror-struck.

Act 2 Scene 1
Dagli immortali vertici
From the immortal peaks
belli di gloria, un giorno
resplendent with former glory
l'ombre degli avi, ah, sorgano
may the shades of our ancestors rise
solo un istante intorno!
but for an instant around us!

Ezio determines to ensure the regeneration of Rome.

Act 3
Che non avrebbe il misero
What would that wretched man
per Odabella offerto
not have offered for Odabella

Foresto, believing Odabella about to wed Attila, rails against his faithless
beloved.

Te sol, te sol quest'anima
You alone, my soul loves you alone
ama d'immenso amore!
with an immense love!

Odabella reassures her anguished beloved.

Un Ballo in Maschera

Act 1 Scene 1
La rivedrà nell'estasi
When I see her there, radiant and pale
raggiante di pallore
I shall be in ecstasy

Riccardo anticipates the joy of seeing Amelia at the forthcoming ball.

Te perduto, ov'è la patria
If you are lost, where will our country
col suo splendido avvenir?
be with its splendid future?

Renato attempts to bring Riccardo to an awareness of the responsibility he has
to his country and people.

Volta la terrea fronte alle stelle
When she turns her dark forehead to the stars
come sfavilla la sua pupilla
how her eyes flash, like lightning.

Act 1 Scene 2
Re dell'abisso, affrettati
King of the abyss, make haste
precipita per l'etra
hurtle down through the ether

Ulrica summons Satan to inspire her that she may be able to foresee the future.

Di' tu se fedele, il flutto m'aspetta
Tell me if faithfully the waves await me
se molle di pianto la donna diletta
if my beloved, having tearfully
dicendomi addio tradì l'amor mio
bid me farewell, betrayed my love

Riccardo, maintaining his disguise as a fisherman, teasingly demands that Ulrica tell him his fortune.

È scherzo od è follia
Such a prophecy is either a
siffatta profezia
joke or madness

Riccards shrugs off Ulrica's prediction that he will soon die.

Act 2
Ecco l'orrido campo ove s'accoppia
Here is the nightmarish field where
al delitto la morte!
crime and death are coupled!

Amelia, following Ulrica's instructions, has arrived at the gallows field at midnight where she hopes to find a herb that will cure her of her love for Riccardo.

Teco io sto
I am with you

Riccardo, having followed Amelia, announces himself to her.

Non sai tu che se l'anima mia
You do not know how remorse

il rimorso dilacera e rode
corrodes and cuts my soul

Riccardo describes the agonies of conscience he endures because of his love for Amelia.

O, qual soave brivido
Oh, what sweet pangs
l'acceso petto irrora!
are awakened in my breast!

Riccardo celebrates the confirmation he has just received from Amelia of her love for him.

Act 3 Scene 1
Morrò, ma prima in grazia
I shall die, but first I beg of you
Deh! mi consenti almeno
please allow me, at least
l'unico figlio mio
my only son
avvincere al mio seno
to clasp to my breast

Amelia, believing Renato is about to kill her, pleads with him for one final concession.

Eri tu che macchiavi quell'anima
It was you who stained that soul
la delizia dell'anima mia
which was the delight of my soul

Renato reflects bitterly on the loss of Amelia's love and his misplaced loyalty to Riccardo.

Act 3 Scene 2
Ma se m'è forza perderti
But if I must lose you
per sempre, o luce mia
forever, light of my life

Riccardo prepares to take a last farewell of his beloved Amelia.

Saper vorreste di che si veste
You want to know how he is attired
quando l'è cosa ch'ei vuol nascosa
while that is the one thing he wishes to conceal

Oscar initially refuses to disclose to Renato how Riccardo is to be disguised for the masked ball.

La Battaglia di Legnano

Act 1 Scene 1
La pia materna mano
A mother's kindly hand
chiuse la mia ferita
closed up my wound

Arrigo looks forward to being reunited with his beloved Lida.

Ah! m'abbraccia, d'esultanza
Ah! embrace me, my soul
tutta ho l'anima compresa
is filled with exultation

Rolando is overjoyed to be reunited with Arrigo whom he believed to have died in battle.

Act 1 Scene 2
Quante volte come un dono
How many times have I prayed
al Signor la morte ho chiesta
to the Lord to grant me death

Lida gives expression to her intense misery and reflects that only the fact that she is a mother encourages her to endure.

A frenarti, o cor, nel petto
Oh my heart, I can no longer find
più potere in me non trovo
within me the power to restrain your beating in my breast

Lida is overjoyed at the news that she is shortly to see her beloved Arrigo.

È ver? Sei d'altri
Is it true? You are another's
ed essere per sempre mia giurasti!
And you swore to be mine forever!

Arrigo bitterly upbraids Lida for her faithlessness.

Act 3 Scene 1
Giuriam d'Italia por fine ai danni
We swear to put an end to Italy's ills

cacciando oltr'Alpe i suoi tiranni
pursuing her tyrants beyond the Alps

Arrigo joins the Knights of Death in swearing a solemn oath to dedicate his life
to the cause of Italian independence.

Act 3 Scene 2
Se al nuovo di pugnando
If at the recommencement of battles
al giorno io chiudo il ciglio
on the morrow I should close my eyes forever

Rolando implores Arrigo to act as guardian to his wife and son should he die in
battle.

Ahi scellerate alme d'inferno
Ah! wicked, infernal souls
sposa ed amico tradir così!
thus to betray a husband and a friend

Rolando, having just learnt of Lida's love for Arrigo swears to be avenged on
the 'accursed pair'.

Act 3 Scene 3
Ah! d'un consorte, o perfidi
Ah wretches! you have made
scempio faceste orrendo!
a fearful mockery of a husband!

Rolando confronts Lida and Arrigo.

Vendetta d'un momento
To cut you down would be
sarebbe il trucidarti . . .
but the vengeance of a moment

Rolando swears to be avenged not through inflicting bloodshed but through
bringing about Arrigo's dishonour.

Boccanegra – see **Simon Boccanegra**

Don Carlo

Act 1
Io la vidi, al suo sorriso
I saw her, and at her smile

scintillar mi parve il sole
the sun seemed to shine forth

Don Carlo has just caught sight of Elisabeth for the first time and is immediately entranced.

Di qual amor, di quanto ardor quest'alma è piena!
My soul is filled with so much love and passion

Elisabeth, overwhelmed by Carlo's ardour, reciprocates his declaration of love.

Act 2 Scene 1
Carlo il sommo Imperatore
Carlo the supreme Emperor
non è piu che muta polve
is now nothing more than silent dust

The monks of the monastery of San Yuste reflect on the way of all flesh.

Dio, che nell'alma infondere
God, who wished to instil
amor volesti e speme
love and hope into our souls
desio nel cor accendere
may You now kindle
tu dêi di libertà
in our hearts a desire for liberty

Carlo and Rodrigo swear solidarity and dedication to the cause of liberty, specifically for the people of Flanders.

Act 2 Scene 2
Nel giardin del bello
In the garden of a beautiful
saracin ostello
saracen palace

Eboli entertains the ladies of the Court with the Song of the Veil (see **Synopsis**).

Io vengo a domandar
I come to beg a
grazia alla mia Regina
favour of my Queen

Carlo, tormented by his thwarted love for Elisabeth, begs her to persuade Philip to send him to Flanders.

472

O Signor, di Fiandra arrivo
Oh Sire, I have just returned from Flanders
quel paese un di si bel
that land once so beautiful
d'ogni luce or fatto privo
now deprived of all light

Rodrigo launches into a passionate advocacy of the Flemish cause and condemnation of Philip's aggressive policy towards Flanders.

Act 3 Scene 1
A mezza-notte, ai giardin della Regina
At midnight in the Queen's garden
sotto gli allôr della fonte vicina
beneath the laurels near to the fountain

Carlo reads a letter of assignation which he assumes to be from Elisabeth but which is in fact from Eboli.

Act 3 Scene 2
Spuntato ecco il di d'esultanza
The day of rejoicing has dawned
onore, onor al più grande dei Regi!
Honour, all honour to the greatest of Kings!

The people of Madrid hail their King, who has recently returned home from abroad and look forward with eager anticipation to the forthcoming *auto-da-fé*.

Act 4 Scene 1
Ella giammai m'amo!
She never loved me!

In an anguished soliloquy Philip gives vent to his ennui, and in particular his bitterness concerning his loveless marriage.

Nell'ispano suol mai l'eresia dominò
On Spanish soil heresy has never prevailed

The Grand Inquisitor attempts to prevail upon Philip to surrender Rodrigo to the Inquisition.

Giustizia, giustizia, Sire!
Justice, justice, Sir!
Ho fè nella lealtà del Re
I have faith in the integrity of the King

Elisabeth complains bitterly to her husband of the way in which she is treated at the Court, the latest outrage being the disappearance from her apartments of her jewel casket.

O don fatale, o don crudel
Oh fatal gift, oh cruel gift
che in suo furor mi feci il cielo!
which Heaven in its rage bestowed on me!

Eboli, who has just been banished to a monastery by the outraged Queen, curses the beauty which has led her to become vain and haughty. She determines to save Carlo from execution.

Act 4 Scene 2
Per me giunto è il di supremo
For me my final day has arrived

Rodrigo, knowing that he will shortly be executed, takes a last farewell of Carlo.

Io morrò ma lieto in core
I shall die but happy in my heart
chè potei cosi serbar
for thus I shall have been able to
alla Spagna un salvatore!
preserve a saviour for Spain!

With his dying breath Rodrigo implores Carlo not to forget the Flemish cause.

Act 5
Tu che le vanità
You who knew the vanities
conoscesti del mondo
of the world

Elisabeth, alone at the tomb of Charles V, reflects on her difficult destiny.

Il Corsaro

Act 1 Scene 1
Come liberi volano i venti
As the winds fly freely
per le immensi pianure de mari
over the immensities of the sea

The corsairs sing in celebration of their roving lifestyle.

Tutto parea sorridere
Everything seemed to smile
all'amor mio premiero
on my first lover

Corrado laments the loss of his youth and innocence; in particular he laments
the loss of his first love.

Si: de corsari il fulmine
Yes: the corsair's thunderbolt
vibrar disegno io stesso
I myself intend to wield

Corrado exhorts his companions to join him in waging war on the Turks.

Act 1 Scene 2
Non so le tetre immagini
I do not know how to make the dark imaginings
fugar del mio pensiero
flee from my thoughts

Medora laments the absence of her beloved Corrado.

No, tu non sai comprendere
No, you cannot understand
l'ambascia del mio core
the anguish of my heart

Medora attempts to prevent Corrado from leaving her again, but to no avail.

Act 2 Scene 1
O qual perenne gaudio t'aspetta
O what perennial joys await you
tu prima gioia sei del Pascia
you who are the Pasha's first delight

The odalisques in the Pasha's harem sing enviously of Gulnara's privileged status.

Vola talor dal carcere
Sometimes my thoughts
libero il pensier mio
fly from this prison
al sospirato e limpido
to the limpid air of
aere del ciel natio
the native skies I long for

Gulnara laments her servitude and longs to return to her homeland.

Ah conforto è sol la speme
Ah my only comfort is the hope
per quest'anima smarrita
that for this afflicted soul
il sentier della mia vita
life's path
non fia tutto di dolor
will not be entirely sorrowful

Gulnara prays that Heaven may eventually take pity on her misery.

Act 2 Scene 2
Salve Allah! Tutta quanta la terra
Hail Allah! May the whole earth
del suo nome possente tisuonò
resound with his mighty name

Seid exhorts his warriors to fresh triumphs by raising a hymn to Allah.

Act 3 Scene 1
Cento leggiadre vergini
A hundred charming virgins
da me chiedano amore
used to clamour for my love

Seid reflects on his love for Gulnara.

S'avvicina il tuo momento
Your moment is approaching

Seid relishes the thought of Corrado's forthcoming torture and execution.

Vieni, mia cara!
Come, my love!
mio primo ed ultimo dolce pensiero
my first and last sweetest joy

Seid seeks to confirm his suspicion that Gulnara is in love with Corrado. To his great wrath his suspicion is confirmed.

Sia l'istante maledetto
Cursed be the moment
che dal foco ei ti salvava
when he saved you from the flames

Seid rails against Gulnara.

Act 3 Scene 2
Eccomi prigioniero!
Here I am, a prisoner!

Corrado reflects on his desperate plight.

Seid la vuole:
Seid wishes it:
inutili i preghi miei ti furo
my prayers on your behalf were futile

Gulnara reveals to Corrado her love for him and her desire to rescue him.

La terra, il ciel m'abborrino
The earth, the heavens abhor me
tu sol nol dêi
you alone should not

Gulnara tells Corrado she has committed murder for love of him.

Act 3 Scene 3
Per me infelice vedi costei
You see her miserable on my account
rischiò suoi giorni
she risked her life
pei giorni miei
in order to save my life

Corrado explains to Medora Gulnara's presence at his side.

I Due Foscari

Act 1 Scene 1
Silenzio, mistero
Silence and mystery protected
Venezia fanciulla
the infant Venice
nel sen di quest'onde protessero in culla
in the bosom of these waters

The Council of Ten and the Junta extol the virtues of silence and mystery in the government of Venice.

Dal più remoto esilio
From the most remote exile

sull'ali del desìo
on the wings of desire

Jacopo Foscari expresses his great love for Venice.

Odio solo, ed odio atroce
Hatred alone, cruel hatred
in quell'anime si serra
is locked within their spirits

Jacopo expresses his determination to achieve justice for himself.

Act 1 Scene 2
Tu al cui sguardo onnipossente
Thou before whose almighty glance
tutta esulta, o tutto geme
all exult or all groan

Lucrezia prays for divine assistance in exonerating her husband.

Act 1 Scene 4
O vecchio cor, che batti
Oh ancient heart that beats
come ai prim'anni in seno
still as in former years in my breast

Francesco Foscari laments the torn loyalties which assail his heart.

Tu pur lo sai che giudice
You who have
in mezzo a lor sedesti
sat as judge amongst them know it

Lucrezia pleads with Francesco to exert his influence on the Council of Ten to give her back her husband.

Act 2 Scene 1
Notte! Perpetua notte che qui regni!
Night! Perpetual night that reigns here! ...
Non maledirmi, o prode
Do not curse me, oh warrior
se son del Doge il figlio
if I am the Doge's son

Jacopo is assailed by a vision of Carmagnola with whose plight he can identify.

Maledetto chi mi toglie
Accursed be he who snatches me
a' miei cari, al suol natio
from my dear ones and from my Lucrezia

In the midst of their troubles Jacopo takes consolation in their mutual love.

Act 2 Scene 2
Queste innocenti lagrime
These innocent tears
ti chiedono perdono
plead with you for pardon

Jacopo makes one last attempt to persuade the Council of Ten to relent.

Act 3 Scene 1
Tace il vento, è queta l'onda
The wind is silent, and still the waves
mite un'aura l'accarezza
a gentle breeze caresses the water

The people of Venice, in holiday mood, sing the gondolas on their way.

All' infelice veglio
Comfort the sorrow
conforta tu il dolore
of an unhappy old man

Jacopo begs his wife to look after his father in his absence and to instil their children with virtue before finally bidding farewell to homeland and country.

Act 3 Scene 2
Oh morto fossi allora
Oh I had rather died
che quest'inutil peso
than that this useless weight
sul capo mio posava!
should rest upon my head!

Francesco Foscari laments the loss of his fourth and only remaining son.

Più non vive! l'innocente
He is no longer alive! Innocent
s'involava a' suoi tiranni
he has fled his tyrants

Lucrezia tells Francesco of Jacopo's death on board the ship that carried him to exile and cries out for vengeance.

Questa dunque è l'iniqua mercede
This, then, is the iniquitous reward
che serbaste al canuto guerriero?
That you have reserved for the hoary old warrior.

Francesco bitterly reproves the Council of Ten for their treatment of him after long years of service.

Ernani

Act 1 Scene 1
Evviva! Beviam! Beviam!
Hurrah! Let's drink! Let's drink!
Nel vino cerchiam almeno un piacer!
Let's at least seek some pleasure in wine!

Ernani's companions revel in the pleasures of drink.

Come rugiada al cespite
Like dew to the blossom
d'un appassito fiore
of a withered flower

Ernani remembers his great love for Elvira and grief at her impending marriage to de Silva.

O tu che l'alma adora
Oh you whom my soul adores
vien, la mia vita infiora
come, revitalize my life

Ernani dreams of the day when Elvira may be his 'consoling angel'.

Act 1 Scene 2
Ernani! Ernani, involami
Ernani! Ernani! Carry me away
all'abborrito amplesso
from that abhorred embrace

Elvira longs for Ernani to rescue her from her forthcoming marriage to 'this despised old man', that is, de Silva.

Tutto sprezzo che d'Ernani
I scorn everything that does not

non favella a questo core
speak to this heart of Ernani

Da quel dì che t'ho veduta
Since that day when I saw you
bella come un primo amore
beautiful as a first love

Carlo declares his love for Elvira.

Infelice! E tuo credevi
Unhappy man! And you believed
si bel giglio immacolato
her (to be) such a beautiful, immaculate lily

Outraged at discovering two interlopers cloistered with his betrothed in her
private apartment de Silva gives vent to his disappointment and grief.

Infin che un brando vindice
As long as a vengeful sword
resta al vegliardo ancora
still remains for an old man

De Silva expresses his determination to wipe out all dishonour to his name.

Vedi come il buon vegliardo
See how the good old man
or del cor l'ira depone
now sets aside his heart's wrath

Carlo and de Silva's court are thankful to observe the way in which the
revelation that Carlo is the King causes de Silva's wrath to abate.

Act 2
Esultiamo! Letizia ne inondi!
Let us rejoice! Let us be inundated with happiness

De Silva's attendants rejoice at the forthcoming wedding of their master to Elvira.

Oro, quant'oro ogn'avido
Gold, such gold as can
puote saziar desio
satisfy every avid wish
a tutti v'offro
I offer it all to you

Ernani attempts to buy off de Silva.

No, vendetta più tremenda
No, I wish to reserve a more terrible vengeance
vo' serbata alla mia mano
for my hand

De Silva scorns Ernani's suggestion that he should kill him forthwith.

Lo vedremo veglio audace
We shall see, bold old man
se resistermi potrai
if you can resist me

Carlo warns de Silva of dire consequences if he does not surrender Ernani.

Vieni meco, sol di rose
Come with me, I want to entwine
intrecciar ti vo' la vita
your life with roses.

Carlo rejoices at finally having Elvira to himself.

Act 3
Oh, de' verd'anni miei
Oh dreams and lying forms
sogni e bugiarde larve
of my youthful years

Carlo declares his intention, should he be elected Emperor, to rise, 'like an eagle on the pinions of virtue'.

Si ridesti il Leon di Castiglia
Let the lion of Castille reawaken
e d'Iberia ogni monte, ogni lito
and every mountain and every region of Iberia
eco formi al tremendo ruggito
form an echo to its terrible roar

The conspirators at the tomb of Charlemagne resolve to fight to the death for Spanish independence.

O sommo Carlo, più del tuo nome
Oh great Charles, more that your name
le tue virtudi aver vogl'io
I want to have your virtues

Remembering his earlier resolution to 'rise on the pinions of virtue', Carlo puts aside his outrage and pardons the conspirators against his life.

Act 4
O come felici gioiscon gli'sposi
Oh how happily the bride and groom rejoice

Guests at the wedding of Ernani and Elvira rejoice at the forthcoming wedding
and deplore the presence of an unknown black masker (de Silva).

Solingo, errante e misero
Alone, wandering and wretched
fin da prim'anni miei
since my earliest days

Ernani frantically and vainly pleads with de Silva not to carry through his
vengeful hatred.

Falstaff

Act 1 Scene 1
L'onore! Ladri
Honour! Thieves!
Voi state ligi all'onor vostro, voi!
You're pledged to your honour, you!

Falstaff lectures Bardolfo and Pistola who have had the temerity to invoke their
honour as the reason they can no longer do Falstaff's bidding.

Act 1 Scene 2
Quell'otre! Quel tino!
That wineskin! That barrel!
Quel re delle pancie
That king of all paunches

Alice and her friends reel off a catalogue of invective against the libidinous
Knight.

Act 2 Scene 1
Reverenza! Se Vostra Grazia vuole
Your Honour! If Your Grace pleases

Mistress Quickly addresses Falstaff with excessive deference. She has come in
response to Falstaff's letter to invite him to a rendezvous with Alice.

Va, vecchio John, va, va per la tua via
Go, old John, go on your way

Mightily pleased with himself Falstaff looks forward to his rendezvous with Alice.

È sogno? O realtà?
Is it a dream? Or reality?

Ford has just learnt that his wife (Alice) is – apparently willingly – giving herself
to the fat Knight. He swears revenge on the pair of them.

Act 2 Scene 2
Quand'ero paggio
When I was a page
del Duca di Norfolk ero sottile
to the Duke of Norfolk I was slender

Falstaff remembers, for Alice's benefit, the days of his more supple youth.

Act 3 Scene 1
Mondo ladro. Mondo rubaldo!
Thieving world. Cheating world!
Reo mondo!
Evil world!

Falstaff, having been subjected to painful humiliation in Act 2, takes stock.

Act 3 Scene 2
Dal labbro il canto estasiato vola
The ecstatic song flies from my lips.

Fenton rhapsodically remembers the joys of kissing his sweetheart, Nanetta.

Sul fil d'un soffio etesio
On the breath of the seasonal wind
scorrete agili larve
run about, you agile spectres

Nanetta instructs the children of Windsor in their roles of fairies and spirits.

Tutto nel mondo è burla
All in the world is a jest
l'uom è nato burlone
Man is born a jester

Falstaff leads the ensemble which concludes the opera.

La Forza del Destino

Act 1
Me, pellegrina ed orfano

A wanderer and an orphan
lungi dal patrio nido
far from my native land

Leonora deplores the self-imposed exile from her family and homeland that she
is contemplating due to her intention to elope with Don Alvaro.

Ah, per sempre o mio bell'angiol
Ah, for ever, oh my sweet angel
ne congiunge il cielo adesso!
Heaven has joined us!

Don Alvaro arrives in Leonora's apartment to take her into exile with him.

Act 2 Scene 1
Al suon del tamburo
To the sound of the drum
al brio del corsiero
to the dash of the steed

Preziosilla exhorts the villagers of Hornachuelos to join the war effort in Italy.

Son Pereda, son ricco d'onore
I am Pereda, I am rich in honours
Baccelliere mi fe' Salamanca
Salamanca (University) made me a Bachelor

Don Carlo, in his disguise as a student, gives a fabricated version of his
background for the benefit of the villagers of Hornachuelos.

Act 2 Scene 2
Madre, pietosa Vergine, perdona al mio peccato
Mother, merciful Virgin, forgive my sin
m'aita quel ingrato dal core a cancellar . . .
assist me in expurgating from my heart all memory of that ingrate . . .

Leonora, believing herself abandoned by Don Alvaro, has resolved to take
refuge in a monastery and prays to the Virgin for peace.

Ah, tranquilla l'alma sento
Ah, my soul now feels at peace
Dacchè premo questa terra
Since setting foot on this soil.

Leonora pleads with Padre Guardiano to grant her refuge.

Il santo nome di Dio, Signore
May the sacred name of the Lord God
sia benedetto
be blessed

Padre Guardiano introduces the penitent (Leonora) to the monks and issues a severe interdict against any monk approaching the cave where Leonora will be sheltered.

Act 3 Scene 1
La vita è inferno all'infelice
Life is hell for the unfortunate one
O tu che in seno agli angeli
Oh you who dwell amongst the angels
eternamente pura
forever pure

Don Alvaro, believing his beloved Leonora to be dead, reflects on his sorrowful life and prays to Leonora's soul to take pity on (his) anguish.

Act 3 Scene 2
Morir! Tremenda cosa!
To die! What a tremendous thing!
sì intrepido, sì prode
so intrepid, so courageous
ei pur morrà!
And yet he will die!

Don Carlo, oblivious at first to Alvaro's identity, then discovers that the man he has befriended is none other than his father's murderer and his sister's seducer. He resolves to be avenged.

Act 3 Scene 3
No, d'un imene il vincolo
No, let the hope of a marriage
stringe fra noi la speme
seal the bond between us

Alvaro, having just learnt that Leonora is still alive, pleads with Carlo to countenance a rapprochement between them.

Rataplan, rataplan, della gloria
Rataplan, rataplan, the love of glory
nel soldato ritempra l'ardor
burns brighter in the soldier

Preziosilla reminds the soldiers who have been on the point of lynching
Melitone of their true purpose; namely to achieve victory in war.

Act 4 Scene 1
Invano Alvaro ti celasti al mondo
It was in vain, Alvaro, that you hid from the world
e d'ipocrita veste scudo facesti alla viltà
and made these hypocritical robes a shield for your villainy

After five years of searching for Alvaro, Carlo tracks him down at the
monastery where he hopes finally to be avenged for his family's dishonour.

Act 4 Scene 2
Pace, pace, mio Dio! Cruda sventura
Peace, peace, oh my God! Cruel misfortune
M'astringe ahimè, a languir
compels me, alas, to languish

In spite of all the years of solitude in the hermitage Leonora still pines after
Alvaro.

Non imprecare; umiliati
Do not curse; humble yourself
a Lui ch'è giusto e santo
before Him who is Just and Holy

Guardiano gently remonstrates with the distraught Alvaro.

Un Giorno di Regno

Act 1 Scene 1
Mai non rise un più bel dì
Never smiled a more beautiful day
per la Casa di Kelbar
on the house of Kelbar

Servants and vassals of the Baron chatter excitedly about the forthcoming
double wedding.

Tesoriere garbatissimo
Most esteemed Treasurer
una perla or tocca a voi
you are acquiring a rare pearl

The Baron and the Treasurer congratulate themselves on the wedding they have
arranged to their mutual benefit.

Compagnoni di Parigi
My Parisian companions
che si matto mi tenete
you who consider me crazy

Belfiore revels in his newfound powers as the King.

Proverò che degno io sono
I will prove that I am worthy
del favor che vi domando
of the favour that I ask of you

Edoardo offers to place his 'useless life' at the 'King's' service.

Grave a core innamorato
It is hard for an infatuated heart
È frenar l'ardente affetto
to restrain its ardent passion

The Marchioness, having recognized her lover, Belfiore in disguise as the King, confirms her undying love for him.

Act 1 Scene 2
Sì festevola mattina
So festive a morning
È di gaudio ad ogni cor
brings joy to every heart

Peasants and servants bring offerings of fruit and flowers as wedding gifts for Giulietta.

Non san quant'io nel petto
They do not know how in my breast
soffra mortal dolor!
I suffer grievous sorrow

Giulietta bewails her predicament and longs for her beloved Edoardo.

Cara Giulia, alfin ti vedo!
Dear Giulia, at last I see you!
Di parlarti è a me concesso!
I can speak with you!

Edoardo commences a quintet (later a sextet) in which he and Giulietta revel in the opportunity afforded them to be together while Belfiore keeps the Treasurer and the Baron preoccupied.

488

Bella speranza invero
A fine hope indeed
un bel sostegno abbiamo
a fine ally we have!

Giulietta and Edoardo are dismayed at the Marchioness's apparent lack of
interest in their predicament.

Act 1 Scene 3
Diletto genero, a voi ne vengo
Beloved son-in-law, I come to you
contento ed ilare io vi prevengo
in joyful anticipation to show you
che la minuta del matrimonio
the draft of the marriage contract

The Baron presents the Treasurer with the contract for the latter's marriage to
Giulietta but is almost immediately told by the Treasurer that he no longer
wishes to proceed with the marriage.

Tesorier! io creder voglio che
Treasurer! I want to believe
sia questo un qualche gioco
that this is some sort of joke

The Baron becomes threatening towards the Treasurer who succeeds in calling
his bluff.

Act 2 Scene 1
Ma le nozze non si fanno?
So the wedding will not take place?

The Baron's servants chatter amongst themselves about the strange ways of the
aristocracy they serve.

Pietoso al lungo pianto
At last love, taking pity on my
Alfin m'arride amore
long weeping, smiles on me

Edoardo confides in the servants his great happiness at his forthcoming marriage.

Tutte l'armi si può prendere
You are welcome to take up arms
de' due mondi e vecchio e nuovo
of both worlds the old and the new

The Baron attempts vainly to intimidate the Treasurer.

Act 2 Scene 2
Ch'io non posso il ver comprendere?
Why can I not apprehend the truth?
Ch'io mi lasci corbellar?
Why should I allow myself to be ridiculed?

The Marchioness prepares to confront Belfiore.

Perchè dunque non vien? Che fa? Che spera?
Then why doesn't he come? What is he doing? What does he hope?

The Marchioness pleads with Belfiore to drop his masquerade.

Giurai seguirlo in campo
I swore to follow him into battle
pugnar per lui giurai
I swore to fight for him

Edoardo attempts to·justify to Giulietta his desire to serve the 'King'.

A tal colpo preparata
I was not prepared,
Io non era, o Cavaliere
oh Cavalier for such a blow

The Marchioness is thrown into confusion by Belfiore's announcement that
Count Ivrea must accompany him on a secret mission just as she was to be
married to him.

Sire, venne in quest'istante
Sire, a court courier has
un corriere della Corte
just arrived

Delmonte delivers a letter from the Court to Belfiore relieving the latter of his
duties and thus precipitating the finale.

Giovanna d'Arco

Prologue Scene 1
Sotto una quercia parvemi
Beneath an oak tree I seemed
Posar la fronte mesta
sadly to lay my head

Carlo describes the dream he has had inviting him to lay down his helmet and
sword at the foot of a statue of the Virgin.

Prologue Scene 2
Sempre all'alba ed alla sera
Always at dawn and in the evening
Quivi innalzo a te preghiera
Here I offer my prayers to you

Giovanna prays that she my only be granted a helmet and sword with which to fight for 'oppressed France'.

Tu sei bella. Tu sei bella
You are lovely. You are lovely

A chorus of demons attempts to distract Giovanna from her true purpose.

Son guerriera che a gloria t'invita
I am the warrior who invites you to glory

Giovanna introduces herself to Carlo who is overcome with emotion by the revelation.

Act 1 Scene 1
O duce, noi sempre mirasti sui campi
Oh leader, you always saw us on the battlefield
Volar combattendo con animo ardito
fly into combat with ardent spirit

The English soldiers defend themselves against Talbot's accusation of cowardice.

Franco son io, ma in core
I am French, but in my heart
M'è prima patria, onore
first comes my country and its honour

Giacomo justifies to the English his decision to betray his daughter.

Act 1 Scene 2
O fatidica foresta,
Oh prophetic forest
O mio padre, o mia capanna
Oh my father, oh my cottage

Giovanna thinks with longing of the home she has left for so long and resolves to return home.

Chiede ognuno che mai fusse
Everyone is asking what has happened

Te la Corte attende e brama
The court awaits you and longs for you

Carlo desperately pleads with Giovanna not to desert the French cause.

È puro l'aere, limpido il cielo
The air is pure, the sky is clear

Carlo tries to console Giovanna who has just been assailed by the Angels' voices reminding her of her spiritual mission.

Vieni al tempio, e ti consola
Come to the church and be consoled
Fra il clamor de' gridi lieti
amidst the clamour of joyous shouts

Carlo makes one final attempt to persuade Giovanna to accompany him to Reims Cathedral.

Vittoria! Vittoria!
Victory! Victory!

The chorus of demons exults in its apparent victory over the Angels in the battle for Giovanna's soul.

Act 2
Da cielo a noi chi viene
Who has come to us from Heaven
frangendo le catene?
To break our chains?

The people of Reims greet Giovanna as she arrives at the cathedral.

Speme al vecchio era un figlia . . .
An old man's hope was a daughter . . .

Giacomo laments the fact that he has been compelled to sacrifice his own daughter.

Comparire il Ciel m'ha stretto
Heaven has compelled me to appear
Qui del popolo al cospetto
here in the sight of the people

Giacomo justifies, for the people of Reims, his accusations against his daughter.

No! forme d'angelo –
No! an angel's form
non son la vesta
does not clothe
d'un' alma rèproba
clothe the soul of a reprobate
che Dio detesta!
whom God detests!

Carlo refuses to believe Giacomo's accusations against Giovanna.

Fuggi o donna maledetta
Flee, oh accursed woman

The people of Reims, convinced that she must be in league with the devil, vehemently reject Giovanna.

Amai, ma un solo istante
I loved but only for a single instant
ma pura ancor son io
but I am again pure

Giovanna, to her father's amazement, confirms her purity.

Or dal padre benedetta
Now, blessed by my father
appurata dai dolori
released from all sorrow
sono ancor d'Iddio l'eletta
I am once again (one of) God's elect

Giovanna implores her father to give her his sword so that she can rejoin the battle.

Quale più fido amico
Which of my most faithful friends
me col pugnai ferisce?
will stab me with the weapon?

Carlo laments the death of Giovanna.

S'apre il cielo . . . Discende la Pia
The heavens are opening . . . the Virgin descends.

Giovanna bids farewell to Earth as she is welcomed by the Virgin into Heaven.

Jerusalem

Act 1
Adieu, mon bien-aimé, va, fuis
Farewell my beloved, go, flee
voici l'aurore!
Here is the dawn!

The lovers, Hélène and Gaston, take leave of each other, the latter reassuring Hélène that he will – for the sake of their love – strive for a reconciliation with Hélène's father, the Count of Toulouse.

Vierge Marie, ma voix te prie
Virgin Mary, my voice pleads with you
taris mes pleurs!
Heed my tears!

Hélène prays with her maid, Isaure, for a happy outcome to her love for Gaston.

Cité du Seigneur! Saint sépulcre!
City of the Lord! Holy Sepulchre!
Calvaire!
Cavalry!

The Crusaders sing in excited anticipation of the forthcoming Crusade.

Oh! dans l'ombre, dans le mystère
Oh guilty passion that I had quelled
Feu coupable que j'ai su taire
remain undisclosed in the shadows
reste encor et cache à la terre
and hide from the world
Mes angoisses, mon remord
my anguish, my remorse

Roger reflects on his incestuous passion for Hélène and determines to kill his rival, Gaston.

Sur ton front est lancè l'anathême!
On your brow was hurled Anathema!

The Count's knights and soldiers join the Papal Legate in confirming anathema on Gaston, who they believe to be guilty of the Count's murder.

Act 2 Scene 1
O jour fatal! o crime!
Oh fatal day! Oh crime!

Tombeau de ma victime
tomb of my victim
du fond de cet abime
from the depths of the abyss
toujours je te revoir
always I see you again

Roger gives expression to the intense remorse he feels for his crime and the false blame that has been attached to Gaston.

Quelle ivresse! Bonheur suprême!
What joy! Supreme blessing!
Tu m'attends ô toi que j'aime!
You await me, oh you whom I love!

Hélène celebrates the news she has just received that Gaston is not only still alive, but is near at hand in Palestine.

O mon Dieu!
Oh my God!
ta parole est
your word was
donc vaine!
then in vain!

Pilgrims, dying from hunger and thirst, fear God has deserted them and pray to be allowed to return to their beloved homeland – France.

Le Seigneur nous promet la victoire
The Lord has promised us victory

Roger joins the Legate, the Count and the Crusaders in anticipating victory for the Crusaders against the pagan hordes.

Act 2 Scene 2
Je veux encor entendre
I want to hear again
ta voix, ta voix si tendre
your voice, your voice so tender

Gaston, imprisoned by the Emir of Ramlah, dreams of his beloved Hélène.

Act 3 Scene 1
Non . . . votre rage
No . . . your rage
indigne outrage
unworthy outrage

n'est pas l'ouvrage
is not the work
d'un Dieu clément
of a merciful God

Hélène vehemently protests Gaston's innocence and invokes God's vengeance on
his accusers, including her father.

Act 3 Scene 2
O mes amis, mes frères d'armes
Oh my friends, my brothers in arms
mon coeur se fend, voyez mes larmes!
My heart is breaking, see my tears!

Gaston frantically pleads with the Papal Legate and Crusading knights to spare
him the dishonour of being branded a traitor and stripped of his nobility and
knighthood.

Frapper bourreaux!
Strike, you executioners!
Je reprends ma fierté
I reclaim my pride

Gaston proudly declares his innocence as the Papal Legate pronounces his
imminent execution.

I Lombardi

Act 1 Scene 1
Oh nobile esempio!
Oh noble example!

The citizens of Milan recapitulate the reasons for Pagano's exile and rejoice in
his rehabilitation while at the same time expressing unease as to Pagano's true
contrition.

A te nell'ora infausta
To thee in this dread hour
de'mali e del riposo
of ills and of repose

A chorus of nuns is heard praying to God to 'thwart perfidious plots and
confound impious men'.

Sciagurata! hai tu creduto
Wretched woman! Do you believe

che obliarti avrei potuto
that I would have forgotten you

Pagano broods on the fact that his love for Viclinda has only increased through being thwarted.

O speranza di vendetta
Oh hope of revenge
Già sfavilli sul mio volto
already you shine in my face

Pagano exults in his imminent revenge on Arvino.

Act 1 Scene 2
Salve Maria, di grazie il petto
Hail Mary, may the Lord
tempie il Signor che in te si posa
whom you bore within you fill your breast with grace

Giselda, fearful of imminent assault, prays with her mother for divine mercy.

Va! sul capo ti (mi) grava l'Eterno
Go! On your (my) head may the Eternal
la condanna fatal di Caino
engrave the fatal mark of Cain

Pagano joins Folco's court in invoking on his head the mark of Cain after he has murdered his father.

Act 2 Scene 1
La mia letizia infondere
Would that I could instil in her heart
vorrei nel suo bel core!
My own profound joy!

Oronte gives expression to his great love for Giselda.

Come poteva un angelo
How could heaven create
crear Stiffelio puro il cielo
so pure an angel

Oronte continues to rhapsodize about his beloved Giselda.

Act 2 Scene 2
Ma quando un suon terrible
But when a terrible sound

497

dirà che 'Dio lo vuole'
proclaims that 'God wills it thus'

Pagano, in his new role as Holy Man of God, dreams of the day when he may assist the Crusaders in reclaiming Jerusalem for Christendom.

Già la croce per l'aure balena
Already the Cross flashes in the air
d'una luce sanguigna, tremenda
with a tremendous and sanguine light

The Crusaders, fired by the Hermit's ardour, look forward to recapturing Jerusalem.

Act 2 Scene 3
La bella straniera che l'alme innamora!
The beautiful stranger with whom all are enamoured!

Odalisques in Acciano's harem dance around Giselda and taunt her.

Se vano è il pregare che a me tu ritorni
If in vain is my prayer that you return to me
pregare mi valga d'ascendere a te
let my prayer be answered that I should ascend to you

Giselda laments her predicament and prays to be reunited in Heaven with her mother.

No! no! giusta causa non è d'Iddio
No! No! it is not God's just cause
la terra spargere di sangue umano
to soak the earth with human blood

Giselda violently repulses her father and rails against the Crusaders' endeavour.

Act 3 Scene 1
Per dirupi e per foreste
Through crags and through forests
come belva errante io movo
like an itinerant wild beast I wander

Oronte points out to Giselda that being united with him will not be an easy lot.

O belle, a questa misera
Oh beautiful appear the Lombard tents
tende lombarde, addio!
to this unhappy girl: farewell!

Act 3 Scene 2
Si! del ciel che non punisce
Yes! I shall know how to emend
emendar saprò l'errore
Heaven's error in not punishing him

Arvino swears vengeance on his brother. He is as yet oblivious to the fact that
Pagano and the Hermit are one and the same.

Act 3 Scene 3
Qual voluttà trascorrere
What great joy I feel coursing
sento di vena in vena
through my veins

Oronte rejoices in his acceptance into the Christian faith.

Act 4 Scene 1
In cielo benedetto
I am blessed in heaven
Giselda, per te sono!
Through you, Giselda!

The spirit of Oronte appears to Giselda in her sleep, reassures her and tells her
to lead the Crusaders to the fountains of Siloam where they will find fresh water
to slake their thirst.

Non fu sogno! In fondo all'alma
It was not a dream! In the depths of my soul
suona ancor l'amata voce
that beloved voice still sounds

Giselda exults in the reassurance she has just received from Oronte's spirit.

Act 4 Scene 2
O Signore dal tetto natio
Oh Lord from our native homes
ci chiamasti con santa promessa
thou didst summon us with sacred promise.

The Lombard Crusaders dream nostalgically of their beloved homeland as they
suffer the cruel ravages of the desert.

Act 4 Scene 3
Un breve istante
A brief instant of life

solo resta a me di vita
only remains to me

Pagano, in his dying moments, pleads with his brother to forgive him and be
reconciled with him.

Luisa Miller

Act 1 Scene 1
Lo vidi, e'l primo palpito
I saw him, and my heart felt
il cor sentì d'amore
the first thrill of love

Luisa attempts to reassure her father concerning her love for Rodolfo.

T'amo d'amor ch'esprimere
I love you with a love that words
mal tenterebbe il detto!
Cannot express!

Sacra la scelta è d'un consorte
The choice of a husband is sacred
esser appieno libera deve
she must be completely free

Miller defends his daughter's inalienable right to choose the man she shall marry.

Ah! fu giusto il mio sospetto!
Ah! my suspicion was justified!

Miller has just learnt that his daughter's lover is the Count's son and, assuming
that Luisa has been the victim of a cynical seducer, gives vent to his anger and
grief.

Act 1 Scene 2
Il mio sangue, la vita darei
My blood, life itself I would give
per vederlo felice, possente!
to see him happy, powerful!

Walter gives vent to his frustration concerning his rebellious son.

Act 1 Scene 3
Fra i mortali ancora oppressa
Among mortals innocence is not

non è tanto l'innocenza
yet so oppressed
che si vegga genuflessa
that it must be seen genuflecting
d'un superbo alla presenza
in the presence of a haughty lord

Miller expresses his outrage as Luisa kneels before Walter who has but recently grossly insulted her.

Act 2 Scene 1
Tu puniscimi, o Signore
Punish me, oh Lord
se t'offesi e paga io sono
if I offended you and I am content

Luisa prays to God as Wurm attempts to blackmail her with her father's life into giving herself to him.

A brani, a brani, o perfido
To shreds, to shreds, wretch
il cor tu m'hai squarciato!
you have torn my heart to shreds!

Luisa has finally acceded to Wurm's demands and only prays now that her father be restored to her.

Act 2 Scene 3
Oh! fede negar potessi agl'occhi miei!
Oh! If only I could deny faith in my own eyes!

Rodolfo, having intercepted Luisa's letter to Wurm in which she confirms her love for Wurm alone, rails against her apparent perfidy.

Quando le sere al placido
When at evening time in the
chiaror d'un ciel stellato
placid radiance of a starry sky
meco figgea nell'etere
with me she gazed lovingly
lo sguardo innamorato
on the firmament

Rodolfo is incredulous at the realization that Luisa would appear to have betrayed him.

Act 3
Di rughe il volto, mira, ho solcato
See, my face is furrowed with wrinkles
il crin m'imbianca l'età più grave
the ravages of age have blanched my hair

Miller upbraids his daughter for her intended suicide.

Andrem, raminghi e poveri
We will go, wandering and poor
ove il destin ci porta
wherever fate may lead us.

Miller and Luisa dream of a new life together, far from the Count's domains and all their troubles.

Hai tu vergato questa foglio?
Did you write this letter?

Rodolfo confronts Luisa with her letter to Wurm before poisoning both himself and Luisa.

Macbeth

Act 1 Scene 1
Giorno non vidi mai sì fiero e bello!
I have never seen a day so foul and fair!

Banquo and Macbeth arrive at the blasted heath where they will be accosted by the witches.

Due vaticini compiuti or sono . . .
Two of the predictions now are fulfilled

Macbeth looks forward to the fulfilment of the witches' third prediction; namely that he will become King of Scotland.

S'allontanarono!
They have gone off!

The witches agree to foregather once the fates have fulfilled their predictions.

Act 1 Scene 2
'Nel dì della vittoria io le incontrai'
'On the day of victory I encountered them'

Lady Macbeth reads a letter in which her husband describes his encounter with the witches.

Vieni! t'affretta! accendere
Come! Hurry! I want to
ti vo' quel freddo core!
set alight your cold heart!

Lady Macbeth determines that Macbeth shall not shrink from ensuring the fulfilment of the witches' prophecy.

Or tutti sorgete, ministri infernali
Now arise, all you infernal ministers
che al sangue incorate, spingete i mortali
that inspire and spur mortals on to bloody deeds

Lady Macbeth, having just heard that Duncan is to stay at the castle that very night, calls on the infernal powers to assist her and her husband in the King's murder.

Mi si affaccia un pugnal?
Is this a dagger I see before me?

Macbeth experiences a vision of a dagger inciting him to murder Duncan.

Fatal mia donna! un murmure
My fatal lady! Did you not
com'io, non intendesti?
hear a murmur as I did?

Macbeth returns from having murdered Duncan. He is appalled by what he has done.

Oh qual orrenda notte!
Oh what an horrendous night!

Banquo is overwhelmed by a sense of foreboding just prior to learning of Duncan's murder.

Schiudi, inferno, la bocca, ed inghiotti
Open wide, oh Hell, thy mouth and swallow
nel tuo grembo l'intero creato
all Creation in thy womb

The Macbeths join their Court and the King's retinue in deploring Duncan's murder and excoriating the murderers.

Act 2 Scene 1
La luce langue, il faro spegnesi
Light thickens, the torch that
ch'eterno scorre per gli ampi cieli!
eternally flits through the far-flung heavens is extinguished!

Lady Macbeth views the prospect of engaging on a new murder with some
trepidation.

Act 2 Scene 2
Sparve il sol, la notte or regni
The sun has set, night now reigns
scellerata, insanguinata
fell and bloody

A chorus of cut-throats prepares to murder Banquo.

Come dal ciel precipita
How the darkness falls from
l'ombra più sempre oscura!
Heaven ever more impenetrable!

Banquo confides his sense of foreboding to his son Fleance.

Act 2 Scene 3
Si colmi il calice di vino eletto
Fill up the cup with the finest wine

Lady Macbeth invites her guests to drink and be merry.

Act 3 Scene 1
Tre volte miagola
Thrice the cat
la gatta in fregola
mews on heat

The witches go about their business.

Act 4 Scene 1
Patria oppressa! Patria oppressa!
Oppressed Country! Oppressed Country!

The refugees from the Macbeths' tyranny lament the lot of their beloved homeland.

Ah, la paterna mano
Ah, a father's hand

non vi fu scudo, o cari
did not protect you, dear ones
dai perfidi sicari
from the perfidious cut-throats
che a morte vi ferir!
that put you to death!

Macduff grieves over his inability to protect his beloved wife and children who have been murdered at Macbeth's behest.

Act 4 Scene 2
Una macchia è qui tuttora . . .
Yet here's a spot . . .

Lady Macbeth, sleepwalking, reveals the ravages of a guilty conscience.

Act 4 Scene 3
Pietà, rispetto, amore
Pity, respect, love
conforto a'di cadenti
the comforts of advancing age
ah! non spargeran d'un fiore
ah! will not strew a single flower
la tua canuta età
on your declining days

Macbeth is overwhelmed by an awareness of the penalty he must pay for his crimes.

I Masnadieri

Act 1 Scene 1
O mio castel paterno
Oh castle of my fathers
colli di verde eterno
hills of eternal green

Carlo thinks with longing of his homeland and of his beloved Amalia.

Nell'argilla maledetta
Into the accursed clay
l'ira mia que' ferri immerga!
Let my rage plunge these swords!

Carlo, having learnt of his continued ostracization, declares his solidarity with his disreputable companions whom he agrees to lead as their captain.

505

Act 1 Scene 2
La sua lampada vitale
The lamp of his life is already
langue, è ver, ma troppo dura
guttering, it is true, but it endures too long

Francesco resolves to find a way to murder his father (Massimiliano) while ensuring that he avoids detection.

Tremate, o miseri, voi mi vedrete
Tremble, miserable wretches, for you shall
nel mio terribile verace aspetto
see me in my true terrible aspect

Francesco relishes the thought of his forthcoming revenge on his detested family.

Act 1 Scene 3
Lo sguardo avea degli angeli
His face had the smile of the angels
che Dio creò d'un riso . . .
that God created . . .

Amalia reflects on her intense love for Carlo and grief at his exile.

Act 2 Scene 1
Tu del mio Carlo al seno
You, blessed spirit, who have flown
volasti, alma beata
to the bosom of my Carlo

Amalia laments the (apparent) death from a broken heart of Carlo's father, Massimiliano.

Carlo vive? O caro accento
Carlo lives? Oh sweet words
melodia di paradiso!
Melody from paradise!

Amalia exults at the news she has just received from Arminio that Carlo is still alive.

Act 2 Scene 2
Di ladroni attornïato
Surrounded by robbers
al delitto incatenato
enchained by crime

Carlo reflects despairingly on his predicament and thinks longingly of his beloved Amalia.

Act 3 Scene 1
T'abbraccio, o Carlo (Amalia) . . .
I embrace you, oh Carlo (Amalia) . . .
abbracciami!
Embrace me!

Amalia and Carlo are joyfully reunited and re-affirm their mutual love.

Act 3 Scene 2
Le rube, gli stupri, gl'incendi, le morti
Pillage, rape, arson, murder
per noi son balocchi, son meri diporti
are for us but pastimes, sheer amusements

Carlo's band of brigands celebrate their savage lifestyle.

Un ignoto, tre lune or saranno
It is now three months since an unknown man
mi narrò che il mio Carlo era spento
told me that my Carlo had perished

Massimiliano tells Carlo how he was buried alive by Francesco and how he has since languished in the 'terrible den' where Carlo has just discovered him.

Act 4 Scene 1
Pareami che sorto da lauto convito
It seemed to me that, having departed from a sumptuous banquet
dormissi fra l'ombre di lieto giardino
I was sleeping in the shade of a pleasant garden

Francesco relates to Arminio the vision he has had of the Day of Judgement at which he will stand accursed.

Caduto è il reprobo! l'ha côlto Iddio
The reprobate has fallen! God has smitten him

Carlo, having just revealed his true relationship to the brigands, accepts that all his dreams of happiness have fled.

Nabucco

Act 1
D'Egitto là sui lidi
There, on the shores of Egypt

egli a Mosè diè vita
He granted Moses life

Zaccaria exhorts the Hebrews to keep faith as Nabucco advances on the Holy City.

Come notte a sol fulgente
As night before the refulgent sun
come polve in preda al vento
as dust before the wind

Zaccaria calls upon the God of Abraham to assist the Hebrews in their hour of need.

Act 2 Scene 1
Anch'io dischiuso un giorno
I also once opened
ebbi alla gioia il core
my heart to joy

Abigaille laments the bitterness that now consumes her and which has eradicated the compassionate feelings of which she was once capable.

Salgo già del trono aurato
Already I ascend the bloodstained
lo sgabello insanguinato
seat of the golden throne

Having learnt from the High Priest of Bel that the priesthood supports her cause Abigaille exults in a vision of her forthcoming ascendancy.

Act 2 Scene 2
Tu sul labbro de' veggenti
On the lips of the prophets thou
fulminasti, o sommo Iddio!
hast fulminated, oh almighty God!

Zaccaria prepares to initiate Fenena into the Jewish faith.

S'appressan gl'istanti d'un'ira fatale
The moment of fatal wrath is approaching

Nabucco leads an ensemble in which all anticipate the approaching calamity.

Chi mi toglie il regio scettro?
Who takes from me the Royal Sceptre?

508

Nabucco, struck down at the height of his hubris, succumbs to madness and paranoia.

Act 3 Scene 1
È l'Assiria una regina
Assyria is a queen
pari a Bel potente in terra
as powerful as Bel upon earth

The Babylonian soothsayers and nobles celebrate Assyria's ascendancy.

Deh, perdona, deh, perdona
Oh, pardon, oh, pardon
ad un padre che delira!
A father who is delirious!

Nabucco pleads with Abigaille for Fenena's life.

Act 3 Scene 2
Va, pensiero, sull'ali dorate
Go, thought, on wings of gold
va, ti posa sui clivi, sui colli
go, repose on the slopes of the hills
ove olezzano tepide e molli
where waft, soft and mild,
l'aure dolci del suolo natal!
The sweet airs of our native land!

The enslaved Hebrew people think nostalgically of their beloved homeland, 'the banks of the Jordan and Zion's toppled towers'.

Del futuro nel buio discerno . . .
In the obscurity of the future I discern . . .
Ecco rotta l'indegna catena!
Behold the shameful chains are broken!

Zaccaria upbraids the Hebrews for their lamentations and foresees the day when Babylon shall be subject to 'the wrath of the Lion of Judah'.

Oberto

Act 1 Scene 1
Di vermiglia, amabil, luce
On the waves appears a shimmering
appar tremula sull'onda
orb of beautiful vermilion light

Knights and vassals welcome home Riccardo, Count of Saliguerra, recently victorious in battle.

Questi plausi a me d'intorno
These greetings that surround me
questi voti io devi a lei
these good wishes I owe to her

Riccardo acknowledges the greeting of his knights and vassals and attributes his triumph to his love for Cuniza.

Già parmi d'udire il fremito
Already I seem to hear the howls
degl'invidi nemici!
of envious foes!

Ah, sgombro è il loco alfin!
Ah, at last the place is deserted!

Leonora, arrives at the Salinguerra castle where she has pursued her seducer, Riccardo.

Sotto il paterno tetto
Beneath my father's roof
un angiol m'apparia
an angel appeared to me

Leonora remembers how she was seduced and betrayed by Riccardo.

O patria terra, alfine io ti rivedo
Oh my native land, at last I see you again

Oberto has returned from exile in pursuit of his daughter, Leonora.

Non ti bastò il periglio
Was not your unhappy father's danger
d'un padre sventurato
enough for you?

Oberto upbraids his daughter.

Del tuo favor soccorrimi
Save me with your grace
ciel, che agli oppressi arridi!
Heaven, that smiles on the sorrowful

In the face of her father's blandishments Leonora prays for grace.

Act 1 Scene 2
Fra il timore e la speme diviso
Torn between hope and fear

Riccardo and Cuniza contemplate their forthcoming marriage.

Su quella fronte impressa
Stamped upon that forehead
la verità tu vedi
you see the truth

Oberto impresses upon Cuniza the sincerity of his daughter's complaint against Riccardo.

Sentiero a te incognito è quel del gagliardo!
The path of the valiant man is unknown to you!

Leonora upbraids Riccardo for his treachery.

Act 2 Scene 1
O, chi torna l'ardente pensiero
Oh, who can turn my fevered thoughts
a' bei sogni del tempo primiero!
back to the beautiful dreams of that former time!

Cuniza laments the loss of her happiness.

Act 2 Scene 2
L'orror del tradimento
The horror of his betrayal
chiede dell'empio il sangue
demands the impious man's blood

Oberto confirms his determination to be avenged for his daughter's and his own dishonour.

Ma tu superbo giovane
But you, proud youth
me non vedrai fiaccato!
Shall not find me weak!

Oberto has just learned that Cuniza has renounced her love for Riccardo but this in no way mitigates against his lust for vengeance.

Ciel pietoso, ciel clemente
Piteous Heaven, merciful Heaven

Riccardo, having killed Oberto, prays to Heaven for forgiveness.

Otello

Act 1

Lampi! tuoni! gorghi!
Lightning! Thunder! Whirlpools!
turbi tempestosi e fulmini!
Tempestuous storms and thunderbolts!

The Cypriot people, gathered anxiously on the quayside, pray for the safe return of Otello's ship which is caught in the midst of a tempest.

Esultate! L'orgoglio musulmano
Exult! The Musulman's pride
sepolto è in mar
is buried in the sea
nostra e del cielo è gloria!
ours and heaven's is the glory!

Otello rejoices in his recent triumph over the Musulman.

Fuoco di gioia, l'ilare vampa
Joyful fire, the leaping blaze
fuga la notte col suo splendor
dispels the night with its splendour

The Cypriots crowd round the bonfire they have built in celebration of Otello's safe return and his victory over the Musulman.

Chi all'esca ha morsa
Whoever has tasted the nectar
del ditirambo spavaldo e strambo
of Dionysus bold and wild
beva con me
come drink with me

Iago encourages the Cypriots to drink, especially Cassio who he knows cannot hold his drink and whom he seeks to disgrace.

Già nella notte densa
Already in the dark night
s'estingue ogni clamor
every noise is extinguished

Otello declares his 'infinite' love for Desdemona at the commencement of their love duet.

Act 2
Credo in un Dio crudel che m'ha creato
I believe in a cruel God who has created me
simile a sè e che nell'ira io nomo
in his image and whom in hate I name

Iago declares his nihilistic philosophy of life (for full text see **Iago**).

Forse perchè gl'inganni
Perhaps because the subtle
d'arguto amor non tendo
deceits of love I do not understand

Otello ruminates on the reasons Desdemona might have to betray him.

Ora e per sempre addio sante memorie
Now and for ever farewell sacred memories

Otello, now convinced of Desdemona's infidelity, bids farewell to all that has previously been of value to him.

Era la notte, Cassio dormia
It was night, Cassio was asleep
gli stavo accanto
I lay beside him

Iago tells Otello of a (fictitious) occasion when he caught Cassio enjoying an erotic dream in which he made love to Desdemona.

Si, pel ciel marmoreo giuro
Yes, I swear by the marble heaven
per le attorte folgori!
By the forked lightning!

Otello and Iago swear together to be avenged for Desdemona's supposed infidelity.

Act 3
Dio ti giocondi, o sposo dell'alma
God be with you, my soul's husband
mia sovrano
my sovereign lord

Desdemona, still oblivious to the machinations against her, comes to press her suit with Otello on behalf of Cassio.

513

Dio! mi potevi scagliar tutti i mali
God! Thou might'st have tried me with all afflictions
della miseria, della vergogna
of misery, of shame

Alone, Otello reflects on his misery since he learned that Desdemona has been
unfaithful to him.

Questa è una ragna
This is a spider's web
dove il tuo cuor . . .
where your heart . . .
. . . casca, si lagna
is caught, cries out
s'impiglia e muor
is entangled and dies

Iago refers to Desdemona's handkerchief which has entranced Cassio and which
is the lynch pin of Iago's plot to unhinge Otello's mind.

A terra! . . . sì . . . nel livido fango
Stricken! . . . yes . . . in the leaden dust

Desdemona bewails the loss of Otello's love subsequent to his having forced her
to her knees in front of his entire court, including the Venetian ambassadors.

Act 4
Piangea cantando
Singing she wept
nell'erma lauda
on the lonely heath
piangea la mesta
the sad girl wept

Desdemona remembers a song of disprized love (the Song of the Willow) that
one of her mother's maids used to sing.

Ave Maria, piena di grazia
Hail Mary full of grace
eletta fra le spose e le vergini sei tu
you are the elect among wives and virgins

Desdemona prays to the Virgin Mary to have mercy on all who suffer, most
especially herself.

Niun me tema s'anco armato
Let no-one fear me even though you see

mi vede
me armed

Otello refuses to allow himself to be arrested and takes a last farewell of his
beloved Desdemona before killing himself.

Rigoletto

Act 1 Scene 1
Questa o quella per me pari sono
This one or that one, for me all are the same
a quant'altre d'intorno mi vedo
each like all the others I see around me

The Duke expounds his hedonistic philosophy of life.

Act 1 Scene 2
Pari siamo! io la lingua
We are alike! I with my tongue
egli ha il pugnale
he with his dagger

Alone for the first time in the opera Rigoletto gives vent to his intense
frustration with his lot in life.

Ah! veglia, o donna, questo fiore
Ah, woman, watch over this
che a te puro confidai
pure flower which I have confided to you

Rigoletto implores Giovanna to take vigilant care of his beloved daughter.

É il sol dell'anima, la vita è amore
Love is the sun that kindles the soul, it is life itself
sua voce è il palpito del nostro core
its voice is the beating of our hearts

The Duke woos Gilda with an intensely romantic declaration of love.

Addio, speranza ed anima!
Farewell my hope and soul!
sol tu sarai per me!
you are the only one for me!

Gilda and the Duke take passionate leave of each other.

Caro nome che il mio cor
Dear name that first made
festi primo palpitar
my heart leap

Gilda dwells lovingly on the name of her newly-found beloved.

Act 2
Ella mi fu rapita!
She has been stolen from me!

The Duke has discovered that Gilda has been abducted.

Parmi veder le lagrime
I seem to see the tears
scorrenti da quel ciglio
running from those eyes

The Duke bewails the fact that he was not at hand to protect Gilda from her abductors.

Scorrendo uniti remota via
Together we went through an obscure street
brev'ora dopo caduto il di
as soon as night had fallen

The Courtiers tell the Duke how they abducted Rigoletto's 'paramour'.

Cortigiani, vil razza dannata
Courtiers, vile damnable race
per qual presso vendeste il mio bene?
for what price did you sell my only treasure?

Rigoletto, desperately searching for his daughter, vents his spleen at the courtiers whom he knows to be responsible for her abduction.

Tutte le feste al tempio
Each holy day at church
mentre pregava Iddio
as I was praying to God

Gilda describes to her father how she came to be wooed and ultimately seduced by the Duke.

Act 3
La donna è mobile
Woman is fickle

qual piuma al vento
as a feather in the wind

The Duke expounds the philosophy behind his incessant philandering.

Un dì, se ben rammentomi
One day, if I remember aright
o bella, t'incontrai . . .
my beauty, I met you . . .

The Duke commences his seduction of Maddalena.

Bella figlia dell'amore
Beautiful daughter of love
schiavo son de'vezzi tuoi
I am a slave to your charms

The Duke effortlessly continues his seduction of Maddalena.

Simon Boccanegra

Prologue
A te l'estremo addio, palagio altero
To you a last farewell, haughty palace
freddo sepolcro dell'angiolo mio
the cold tomb of my angel

Fiesco bids farewell to the Fiesco's ancestral home where his daughter has just died.

Il lacerato spirito
The tortured spirit
del mesto genitore
of a sad father

Fiesco reflects on his own torment and prays that his daughter may intercede for him in Heaven.

Suona ogni labbro il mio nome
My name sounds upon everybody's lips

Boccanegra reflecting upon his political ascendancy is suddenly accosted by Fiesco with whom he pleads, unsuccessfully, for amity.

Act 1 Scene 1
Come in quest'ora bruna
How in this half light

sorridon gli astri e il mare
smile the stars and the sea

Amelia reflects on her troubled past and looks forward to the arrival of her beloved Gabriele.

Vieni a mirar la cerula
Come and look at the azure
Marina tremolante
shimmering sea

Amelia attempts to persuade her lover to give up his dangerous political aspirations and concentrate his energies on his love for her.

Vieni a me, ti benedico
Come to me that I may bless you
nella pace di quest'ora
in the peace of this hour

Fiesco gives his blessing to Gabriele's intention to wed Amelia.

Dinne, perchè in quest'eremo
Tell me, why do you hide
tanta beltà chiudesti?
such beauty away in this cloistered dwelling?

Boccanegra attempts to elicit more information about herself from Amelia who, it soon materializes, is his own daughter.

Figlia! A tal nome palpito
Daughter! At that name I tremble
Qual se m'aprisse i cieli
As if the heavens had opened themselves to me

Boccanegra and Amelia are reunited as father and daughter.

Act 1 Scene 2
Fratricidi!
Fratricides!
Plebe! Patrizi! Popolo
Plebeians! Patriarchs! People
Dalla feroce storia!
possessed of a fierce history!

Boccanegra pleads with the representatives of the warring Genoese factions to put aside their differences for the sake of peace and love.

Act 2
Me stesso ho maledetto!
I have damned myself!

Paolo reflects on his downfall and prepares to poison Boccanegra.

Cielo, pietoso, rendila
Merciful Heaven, restore her
Rendila a questo core
Restore her to this heart

Gabriele, believing Amelia to be engaged in an affair with Boccanegra, prays that she soon may be restored to him.

Parla, in tuo cor virgineo
Speak, let your innocent heart
Fede al diletto rendi
Restore your beloved's trust

Gabriele pleads with Amelia to put his mind at rest concerning her relationship with Boccanegra.

Ah, quel padre tu ben vendicasti
Ah, you have avenged well your father
che da me contristato già fu
who once I vanquished

Boccanegra tries to reason with Gabriele and finally reveals that he is Amelia's father.

Act 3
M'ardon le tempia!
My temples are feverish!
Un'atra vampa sento
I feel another fire
Serpeggiar per le vene
coursing through my veins

Boccanegra, feeling the first effects of Paolo's poison, revels in the fresh sea breezes.

Delle faci festanti al barlume
By the light of the festive torches
Cifre arcane, funebri vedrai
you will see strange funereal signs

Fiesco greets Boccanegra and eventually apprises the latter of his impending death.

Gran Dio, li benedici
Great God, bless them
Pietoso dall'empiro
mercifully from Heaven

Boccanegra, in his dying moments, blesses the union of Gabriele and Amelia.

Stiffelio

Act 1 Scene 1
Di qua varcando sul primo albore
As he set out from here at break of dawn
una finestra ei vide aprire
he saw a window open

Stiffelio describes how the boatman, Walter, has witnessed a young man making a precipitate exit from a castle window early one morning.

Colla cenere disperso
With the ashes may both
sia quel nome e quel delitto
the name and the crime be dispersed

Stiffelio, wittingly or not, burns the evidence of his wife's infidelity.

A te Stiffelio un canto
To you Stiffelio a song
s'innalza da ogni core
rises up from every heart

Stiffelio's friends and followers sing in praise of their leader.

Vidi dovunque gemere
I saw everywhere virtue
opressa la virtude
oppressed and groaning

Stiffelio describes, for Lina's benefit, the horrors he has witnessed during his journeys abroad.

A te ascenda o Dio clemente
To Thou, oh merciful God may

il sospiro, il pianto mio
my sighs, my tears ascend

Lina, fearful lest her husband discovers her infidelity, prays for mercy.

Or meco venite
Now come with me
il pianto non vale
tears are of no avail

Stankar refuses to countenance his daughter's intention of confessing her infidelity to Stiffelio.

Act 1 Scene 2
Plaudiam! Di Stiffelio
Let us cheer! Let us gladden
s'allegri il soggiorno
Stiffelio's sojourn

Stiffelio's friends sing in celebration of their leader.

Non solo all'iniquo
Not alone against the villain
ch'ha il Maestro venduto
who sold his Master
ma a quanti tradiscon
but against all traitors
m'udrete imprecare
you will hear me imprecate

Stiffelio, by now convinced that his wife has been unfaithful, imprecates against all who 'defile the sacred ties of hearth and home'.

Act 2
Ah, dagli scanni eterei
Ah from among the ethereal thrones
dove beata siedi
where in blessedness you sit
alla tua figlia volgiti
turn to your daughter
l'affano suo deh vedi!
Look upon her affliction!

Lina prays to her deceased mother to intercede for her in Heaven.

Perder dunque voi volete
Then you wish to destroy

questa misera tradita
this miserable betrayed wretch

Lina pleads with Raffaele to leave the castle once and for all.

Me disperato abbrucciano
In my desperation I am consumed
ira, infernal furore
with anger, hellish fury

Stiffelio, 'as though delirious', gives vent to the chaos of his emotions, pulled as he is between the conflicting demands of personal passion and his religious vocation.

Act 3 Scene 1
Lina, pensai che un angelo
Lina, I thought that in you
in te mi desse il cielo
heaven had given me an angel

Stankar laments the loss of his honour through his daughter's transgression.

Oh gioia inesprimibile
Oh inexpressible joy
che questo core inondi
that inundates my heart

Stankar celebrates the news that Raffaele is returning to the castle, thus affording Stankar the opportunity of wreaking vengeance.

Opposto è il calle che in avvenire
Opposite are the paths that in future
la nostra vita dovrà seguire
our lives must follow

Stiffelio tells Lina of his intention to divorce her.

Ah sì, voliamo al tempio
Ah yes, let us flee to the church
fuggiam le inique porte
let us flee these iniquitous portals

Stiffelio welcomes Jorg's suggestion that he should search for new strength in the 'Lord's Temple'.

La Traviata

Act 1
Libiamo ne' lieti calici
We'll drink from the happy chalice
che la bellezza infiora
in which beauty blossoms

Alfredo proposes a toast to love and wine. His love is particularly directed at Violetta.

Un dì felice, eterea
One happy day, ethereal
mi balenaste innante
you flashed like lightning into my life

Alfredo declares his passionate love for Violetta.

È strano, è strano!
It's strange, it's strange!
In core scolpiti ho quegli accenti!
Those words are engraved upon my heart!

Violetta muses on the unaccustomed emotions stirred in her by Alfredo's recent declaration.

Sempre libera degg'io
Ever free I must
folleggiare di gioia in gioia
flutter from pleasure to pleasure

Violetta, dismissing her inclination to romance, reaffirms the hedonistic philosophy which has hitherto defined her life.

Act 2 Scene 1
Lunge da lei per me non v'ha diletto!
Far away from her there is for me no joy in life!

Alfredo reflects on the great joy Violetta has brought into his life by sacrificing her previous hedonistic philosophy and committing herself to him.

De' miei bollenti spiriti
My passionate spirit
il giovanile ardore
and youthful ardour
ella temprò col placido
she has tempered with the gentle

sorriso dell'amor
smile of love

Alfredo continues to rejoice in his love for Violetta.

Pura siccome un angelo
As pure as an angel
Iddio mi diè una figlia
is the daughter God gave me

Germont tells Violetta that if his son does not forthwith discontinue his liaison
with her, his daughter's chance of happiness will be severely compromised.

Dite alla giovine, si bella e pura
Tell the young girl so beautiful and pure

Violetta, weeping, accedes to Germont's wish and tells him to tell his daughter
of the sacrifice she makes.

Di Provenza il mar, il suol
What is it that has banished from your
chi dal cor ti cancellò?
heart the beloved Provençal sea?

Germont pleads with his son to relinquish his passion for Violetta for the sake
of their family.

Act 3
Addio del passato bei sogni ridenti
Farewell beautiful smiling dreams of the past
le rose del volto gia sono pallenti
the rose from my face has already faded

Violetta, realizing she is dying, grieves over her young life that has so soon
reached its conclusion.

Parigi, o cara, noi lasceremo
Paris, my dearest, we shall leave
la vita uniti trascorreremo
united we shall go through life

Alfredo attempts to reassure both Violetta and himself as to their future together.

Ah! Gran Dio! Morir si giovine
Ah! great God! To die so young

Violetta despairingly cries out against the injustice of her predicament.

Il Trovatore

Act 1 Scene 1
Abbietta zingara, fosca vegliarda!
An old dark and abject gypsy!
Cingeva i simboli di maliarda!
Wearing the symbol of a sorceress!

Ferrando tells the Count's retainers how the Count's younger son was bewitched and apparently murdered by Azucena's mother.

Act 1 Scene 2
Tacea la notte placida
The serene night was silent
e bella in ciel sereno
and beautiful in the calm sky

Leonora describes for the benefit of her attendant how she first came to fall in love with the unknown troubadour (Manrico).

Di tale amor che dirsi
With such a love that words
mal può dalla parola
can scarcely tell

Leonora rhapsodically affirms her love for Manrico.

Deserto sulla terra
Adrift on the earth
col rio destin in guerra
at war with his evil destiny
È sola speme un cor
his only hope is in one heart
un cor al Trovator
a heart for the Troubadour

The words of Manrico's serenade.

Act 2 Scene 1
Strida la vampa!
The flame crackles
la folla indomita
the indomitable crowd
corre a quel foco
runs to that fire
lieta in sembianza!
With happy faces!

Azucena remembers the day when her mother was burned at the stake for witchcraft.

Condotta ell'era in ceppi
She was led in irons
al suo destin tremendo
to her terrible fate

Azucena describes in graphic detail how her mother perished and how with her dying breath she exhorted Azucena to avenge her.

Act 2 Scene 2
Il balen del suo sorriso
The flashing of her smile
d'una stella vince il raggio
outshines even a star's ray

Di Luna gives expression to his all-consuming passion for Leonora.

Act 3 Scene 1
Squilli, echeggi la tromba guerriera
Let the warlike trumpet sound and echo
chiami all'armi, alla pugna, all'assalto
the call to arms, to the battle, to the assault

Count di Luna's retainers look forward to commencing the assault on Castellor where Manrico and his followers are encamped.

Act 3 Scene 2
Ah sì, ben mio, coll'essere
Ah yes, my love, when I'll be
Io tuo, tu mia consorte
yours, and you'll be my wife
avrò più l'alma intrepida
I shall have even more fearless spirit

Manrico expresses his love for Leonora as they prepare to be wed.

Di quella pira l'orrendo foco
The horrible blaze of the fire
tutte le fibre m'arse, avvampò!
sets alight all the fibres of my being!

Manrico prepares to go to the rescue of his mother.

Act 4 Scene 1
D'amor sull'ali rosee
On the roseate wings of love

vanne, sospir dolente
fly, oh sorrowing sigh

Leonora, standing beneath the castle where Manrico is incarcerated, prays for her beloved's redemption.

Tu vedrai che amore in terra
You will see that there never existed
mai del mio non fu più forte
on earth a stronger love than mine

Leonora confirms her determination to save Manrico's life or, if necessary, go to her death with him.

Act 4 Scene 2
Ai nostri monti ritorneremo
We shall return to our mountains
l'antica pace ivi godremo!
There to enjoy our former peace!

As she awaits her execution Azucena dreams of returning to her home, there to live peacefully with her beloved son.

I Vespri Siciliani

Act 1
A te, ciel natio
To you, my native skies
con dolce desio
with sweet longing
torni il mio pensier
my thoughts turn

The French soldiers think nostalgically of their native land while the Sicilians chafe against the French occupation of Sicily.

Deh! tu calma O Dio possente
Oh mighty God, calm with your smile
col tuo riso e cielo e mar
both sky and sea

Elena responds to the French soldiers' incitement that she should sing for them, but uses the opportunity to incite the apathetic Sicilians to rebellion.

D'ira fremo all'aspetto tremendo
I tremble with wrath at the awful sight

Elena joins Ninetta and Danieli in expressing horror at the advent of Monforte, something which is not lost on the French Governor.

Act 2
O tu Palermo terra adorata
Oh Thou, Palermo, beloved land
a me si caro riso d'amor
smile of love, so dear to me

Procida, returned from his travels abroad, greets his beloved homeland.

Ah! da tue luci angeliche
Ah! from your angelic eyes
scenda di speme un raggio
may a ray of hope descend

Arrigo declares his love to Elena.

Act 3 Scene 1
In braccio alle dovizie
In the arms of riches
nel seno degli onor
embraced by honour
un vuoto immenso orrible
an immense horrible void yet
regnava nel mio cor
reigned in my heart

Monforte reflects how the only thing which matters to him now is to be reunited with his estranged son.

Act 4
Giorno di pianto, di fier dolore!
Day of weeping, of fierce sorrow!

Arrigo laments the circumstances that have led him to betray the Sicilian compatriots, his erstwhile friends, who now languish in prison.

Ah! volgi il guardo a me sereno
Ah! turn your gaze on me serene
per pietà del mio pregar
out of pity for my pleading

Arrigo pleads with Elena to forgive him his apparent betrayal and finally reveals the true reason, namely that Monforte is his father.

Arrigo! Ah parla a un core
Arrigo! Ah you speak to a heart
già pronto a perdonare
already prepared to forgive

Elena rejoices in the knowledge that Arrigo had good reasons for his apparent betrayal; she confesses her abiding love for him.

Act 5
Mercè, dilette amiche
Thank you, dear friends
di quel leggiadri fior
for those pretty flowers

Elena rejoices in her forthcoming wedding to Arrigo and accepts gifts from a chorus of knights and maidens.

La brezza aleggia intorno
The breeze hovers around
a carezzarmi il viso
and caresses my face

Arrigo likewise rejoices in his forthcoming marriage.

Appendix A: Verdi Editions

It is outside the scope of this volume to discuss in great detail the differences in the various editions of Verdi's operas. For clear and concise explication of this topic the reader is referred to the entries on each of the operas in the *New Grove Dictionary of Opera*. The texts used as the basis for commentary in this book are those of the most frequently performed editions of the operas. Where there are outstanding differences between editions as, for example, in the case of *Don Carlo* and *Boccanegra*, these have been mentioned in the various character studies. The following notes are a brief summary of the most outstanding revisions and/or additions that Verdi made.

Oberto

There is some confusion over the exact origins of Verdi's first opera. What seems clear from correspondence between Verdi and Pietro Massini, the director of the Teatro Filodrammatico in Milan, is that in 1836 Verdi wrote an opera titled 'Rocester' with a libretto by Antonio Piazza. There is some debate as to whether this opera was then revised and performed as *Oberto*, the main problem being that the score of *Rocester* is lost. Whatever the origins of *Oberto* it received its successful premiere in 1839 at La Scala. During the next three years Verdi added various numbers to the score. In 1840 *Oberto* was performed again in Milan. To accommodate the new exponent of the role of Cuniza Verdi wrote a new Cavatina (*O fedeli! a me diletto*) and duet for Cuniza and Riccardo. In 1841 a new duet was written for Leonora and Oberto (for performance in Genoa) and a number for Chorus (*Fidanzata avventurosa*). In the same year Verdi added an aria for *Oberto* (for performance in Barcelona). The cabaletta (*Ma fin che un brando vindice*) later became associated with *Ernani* where it is sung by de Silva subsequent to his aria, *Infelice*.

Un Giorno di Regno

Verdi's second opera was written at great speed, possibly in only three months. The original libretto by Felice Romani was probably revised and updated by Temistocle Solera, who had assisted Verdi with revisions of *Oberto*. The first performance took place in 1840 and was a complete disaster, being taken off after the first night. Verdi never forgot the humiliation of this and was not to attempt another comic opera until the very end of his life. *Falstaff* was, of course, a resounding success.

Nabucco

After the fiasco of *Un giorno di regno*, Verdi almost gave up composing. However in the winter of 1840 Bartolomeo Merelli, impresario at La Scala, managed to persuade Verdi to set Solera's libretto of *Nabucco* (which had recently been rejected by Otto Nicolai). Premiered in March 1842 *Nabucco* was a great success and in the autumn of that year it received a further 57 performances. Verdi made some small changes for the new exponents of the roles of Abigaille and Fenena. For the Venice performance the following year further changes were made to Fenena's part; a new Romanza being included in Act 4. Verdi wrote some ballet music for a revival in Brussels in 1848, but this music has not survived.

I Lombardi/Jérusalem

There are no records of negotiations between Verdi and La Scala over *I Lombardi*, nor has any correspondence between the composer and his librettist, Solera, survived. There were some initial problems with the censors regarding the religious content of the opera and Verdi made a few minor alterations. For a revival in 1843 Verdi composed a new cabaletta for Oronte.

In 1847 Verdi signed a contract with the Paris Opera to write a new opera. The result was a revival of *I Lombardi*, refashioned to suit French requirements. The librettists (Alphonse Royer and Gustave Vaëz) changed the plot considerably, although maintaining the setting as a Crusade. A ballet was added at the opening of Act 3 (traditional in French opera) and much new music was written. In spite of the fact that *Jérusalem* was well received at its first performance it failed to make a permanent mark on the repertoire and eventually disappeared. The same happened with the Italian version, *Gerusalemme*, which never managed to supersede the more popular *I Lombardi*. (See entries for *Jérusalem* for further explication.)

Ernani

Ernani was commissioned by the Teatro la Fenice, Venice. The original subject was to be a tale attributed to Sir Walter Scott and entitled *Cromvello*. Verdi, however, became enthused with Victor Hugo's *Hernani* and persuaded his librettist, Francesco Piave, to set that instead. As usual Verdi took a proactive interest in the writing of the libretto; one of the changes he insisted on was to cast Ernani as a tenor rather than contralto, as originally planned. The first performance was a great success and the opera became very popular. Verdi resisted any changes being made for subsequent performances, although he did write an aria with chorus for Ernani as an alternative finale to Act 2 which was premiered in Parma in 1844. An additional cabaletta for de Silva (*Ma fin che un brando vindice*) was inserted into performances of *Ernani* by the bass, Marini, in the same year. This piece had originally been part of an additional aria in *Oberto* and it is not clear whether Verdi sanctioned its inclusion in *Ernani*.

I Due Foscari

Not long after the premiere of *Ernani* Verdi agreed to write a new opera with Piave for the Teatro Argentina in Rome. The first choice of subject was *Lorenzin de'Medici* which, however, did not receive approval from the Roman censors and eventually Byron's *The Two Foscari* was agreed upon. Verdi and Piave corresponded frequently and it is clear that Verdi took an extremely active interest in the progress of the libretto, intervening often and forcefully. The first performance had only lukewarm success – not surprisingly perhaps after the enormous success of its predecessor. In 1846 Verdi added a replacement cabaletta for Jacopo (Act 1), which was first performed in Paris in that year.

Giovanna d'Arco

The first performances of *Giovanna d'Arco* were a great success, but Verdi was so displeased with falling standards at La Scala that he refused to allow another premiere of his works to take place there until *Otello*, some 40 years later. Verdi seems to have allowed Solera's libretto to remain more or less unchanged. Based on Schiller's play, *Die Jungfrau von Orleans*, the libretto bears little resemblance to historical facts about Joan of Arc.

Alzira

Alzira was the first opera Verdi wrote for the Teatro San Carlo of Naples and his first collaboration with Salvatore Cammarano, who was resident at the Naples theatre. Cammarano was the most distinguished librettist working in Italy at that time and had had several successes in partnership with Donizetti. Verdi took little active part in the creation of the libretto, being content to accept the work of the highly experienced and professional Cammarano. However, the opera was not a great success and it quickly disappeared. Although occasionally revived in modern times it is one of the least performed of Verdi's operas.

Attila

Although Verdi initially discussed setting Werner's play, *Attila, König der Hunnen*, with Piave, he turned to Solera to write the libretto. However Solera left Italy to live in Madrid before he had finished working on the text and Verdi called in Piave to complete the final act. Solera had planned a large-scale chorus for the finale which Piave, under instructions from the composer, abandoned for a more intimate concentration on the main characters. Initially coolly received, *Attila* was to become one of Verdi's most popular operas of the 1850s. After the premiere Verdi twice rewrote Foresto's Romanza (*Che, non avrebbe il misero*) in Act 3.

Macbeth

Verdi's first Shakespeare opera was written for the Teatro della Pergola of Florence. When the cast became known to him he and Piave worked closely together on the text to the extent that Verdi allowed nothing to pass that did not satisfy him. When it came to rehearsing the work Verdi oversaw the proceedings with meticulous attention to all aspects of the production. The first performance was a great success and Verdi continued to oversee all subsequent productions. In 1864 Verdi was asked to provide ballet music for a revival of *Macbeth* at the Théâtre Lyrique in Paris. In addition to the ballet music Verdi substantially amended the score, adding a new aria for Lady Macbeth in Act 2 (*La luce langue*), extensive alterations to Act 3, including a new duet for Macbeth and Lady Macbeth (*Ora di morte*), a new chorus at the opening of Act 4 (*Patria oppressa*), and the replacement of Macbeth's death scene with a final *Inno di vittoria*. Although the Paris version did not have the success of the original, which continued to be performed in Italy for some time, it is the version generally heard today. There are occasional airings of the 1847 version.

I Masnadieri

Verdi wrote *I Masnadieri* in fulfilment of a contract to compose an opera for Her Majesty's Theatre, London. Although the first performance was an unqualified success there had been many problems on the way. Verdi was able to write for some of the most distinguished singers of the day (including Jenny Lind and Luigi Lablache) and the librettist was his friend, Andrea Maffei, a celebrated man of letters. However, Maffei had little experience of the theatre and Verdi quarrelled with the publisher, Francesco Lucca. There were some breaks with tradition in the score; Verdi dispensed with an opening chorus, for example. After the first performance the work sank into obscurity, achieving little success in Italy and being only occasionally revived in modern times. This neglect is entirely unwarranted for the work is one of the finest of Verdi's early period.

Il Corsaro

The idea of setting Bryon's poem, *The Corsair*, had been gestating for some time in Verdi's mind. In 1845 he signed a contract with the publisher, Francesco Lucca (chief rival of Riccordi), to write three operas, one which was to be produced at Her Majesty's Theatre in London. (The idea of a publisher commissioning a work and then taking on the responsibility of finding a suitable venue was probably initiated by Lucca.) It was not until the winter of 1847–1848 that Verdi worked seriously on the score, having meanwhile completed *Macbeth*, *Jerusalem* and *I Masnadieri*. By this time his interest in *Il Corsaro* was waning. Verdi delivered the completed work to Lucca who arranged the first performances in Trieste in October 1848. Unusually, Verdi took little active interest in the preparations for his opera, not even attending the first performance. It was not a success and after a handful of revivals soon disappeared. It is only occasionally performed today.

La Battaglia di Legnano

The year 1848 saw revolutions throughout much of Europe. In Italy the revolt was against the occupying Austrians and Papal domination. In February five days of fighting on the streets of Milan concluded with the expulsion of the Austrian military and sparked a nationalistic fervour which swept across all Italy. Verdi resolved to compose a patriotic opera, in collaboration with Cammarano, to mark the prevailing euphoric mood. Cammarano suggested as a text Joseph Méry's play, *La bataille de Toulouse* and changing the action to the Lombard League's defeat of the German Emperor Frederick Barbarossa in 1176. By the time the opera was finished, however, Milan and other cities were back in Austrian hands. The premiere took place in Rome shortly before the city was officially declared a republic and received a rapturous reception, the last act being encored in its entirety. However in the next decade it inevitably suffered a decline with the Austrians still in occupation. Verdi expressed his intention to revise the libretto to appease the censors but in the meantime Cammarano died and nothing came of it. Apart from a brief revival in 1861, when the state of Italy was created, the opera sank into oblivion and in spite of the prevailing interest in Verdi's entire canon it is now only occasionally performed.

Luisa Miller

Written for the Teatro San Carlo in Naples. The librettist was Cammarano. Verdi originally thought of setting Francesco Guerrazzi's historical novel, *L'assedio di Firenze* ('The Siege of Florence'), a large-scale work which Verdi felt would suit the grandeur of the Naples theatre. However the censors rejected the idea as being politically too controversial. Cammarano suggested Schiller's play, *Kabale und Liebe*. Verdi, who had considered the play previously, agreed. Cammarano reduced Schiller's five-act play to three, giving each act a subtitle: 'L'amore' (Love), 'L'intrigo' (Intrigue), 'Il veleno' (Poison). Verdi carried out initial negotiations from Paris and then returned to Italy to work on the score, arriving in Naples in time to supervise rehearsals. The opera was initially successful but failed to attain the popularity of *Nabucco* or *Ernani*, disappearing from the main repertoire until the 1920s when it became popular in Germany. Today it has become firmly established as a favourite amongst the early operas.

Stiffelio /Aroldo

It was Piave who proposed to Verdi the recently written play, *Le Pasteur, ou L'Evangile et le foyer*, as a suitable text for Verdi's next opera. The play had been premiered in Paris in 1849 and by 1850 had already been translated into Italian. From the start there were problems with the censors. Objections included the portrayal of a married priest whose wife commits adultery and the final scene in the Church in which Stiffelio quotes the New Testament. This last was not allowed; the scene was drastically altered and in some performances the final act was omitted altogether. Lina's plea, *Ministro, ministro confessatemi!* ('Minister, minister, hear my confession!') in Act 3 had to be excised. During the following few years the opera was performed not as *Stiffelio* but as *Gugliemo Wellingrode*, the leading character being changed into a German minister of state. Verdi, unhappy with all of this, refused to allow *Stiffelio* to be performed at La Scala in Milan in 1851. In a letter to his publisher, Riccordi, he stated that it would be better to wait until he could redo the last scene without the church. Over the next few years Verdi sporadically discussed re-writing *Stiffelio* with Piave, whose idea it was to set the work in medieval times and turn Stiffelio into an English Crusader. Thus in 1857 *Aroldo* was first produced at Rimini. The opera was not so well received as its progenitor, but nevertheless survived where *Stiffelio* did not. It was not until the 1960s that *Stiffelio* was revived and it was 1993 before the original, uncensored version was given its world premiere at the Royal Opera House, London, with Edward Downes conducting.

Rigoletto

In September 1849 Verdi suggested to Cammarano setting Victor Hugo's 'Le Roi s'amuse' as an operatic subject. However Verdi was due to compose an opera for La Fenice Theatre in Venice, with the resident poet Piave as librettist, and Hugo's play was chosen. Verdi was inspired by the character of Tribolet, whom he called a creation worthy of Shakespeare and who was to become Rigoletto. 'Le Roi s'amuse', set in the sixteenth-century court of Francois I, had been banned in Paris after its first performance in November 1832. The objections were mainly concerned with the depiction of a licentious monarch on stage, although Hugo vigorously protested, stating that the real reasons for the ban were political rather than moral or artistic. Verdi was understandably concerned about setting a play with such a controversial history, but was persuaded by Piave that the Venetian authorities would not object to the choice of subject. Piave proceeded to work on the libretto, under the title of *La maledizione*. However, just three months before the first performance was due the Military Governor of Venice, having inspected the libretto, issued a ban on the work being performed, calling the plot 'revoltingly immoral' and 'obscenely trivial'. Verdi was outraged, and furious with Piave who was prepared to make the necessary changes to the libretto in order to appease the censors. Verdi, however, refused to countenance any such changes. Finally a compromise was reached and a document setting out the changes was drawn up. The action was moved from the French court to Italy and the names of the characters were changed. In particular Francois I became the Duke of Mantua and Tribolet was renamed Rigoletto. The first performance was a resounding success and the Duke's aria, *La donna è mobile*, became an instant 'hit'.

Il Trovatore

In 1851 Verdi wrote to Cammarano to suggest that Garcia Gutiérrez's *El Trovador* would be a suitable subject for operatic treatment. *Rigoletto* was enjoying great success and Verdi saw some similarities between the two tales. Both Rigoletto and Azucena were consumed by their obsessive paternal/maternal love and an overriding need for vengeance on Society. Cammarano died during work on the libretto, leaving Verdi greatly saddened. The young poet Bardare was called in to complete the text and *Il Trovatore* was finally and successfully launched in January 1853 in

Rome. At the end of the following year, whilst Verdi was engaged in overseeing rehearsals for *Les Vêpres Siciliennes* at the Paris Opéra, *Il Trovatore* was being staged at the Théâtre Italien. Its success prompted the management of the Paris Opéra to suggest putting on a French version of *Il Trovatore*. Entitled *Le Trouvère*, it was translated into French by Emilien Pacini and included ballet music (in Act 3) specially written by Verdi to conform with French tradition. *Le Trouvère* omitted Leonora's cabaletta, *Tu vedrai che amore in terra* (Act 4 Scene 1) and expanded the conclusion to the opera by re-introducing the chorus in a reprise of the *Miserere* before a short duet between Manrique and Azucena. Today *Le Trouvère* is rarely performed outside France.

La Traviata

Alexandre Dumas's novel, *La Dame aux camélias*, was published in 1848 and the play first produced in Paris in 1852. Verdi saw a performance and when he was commissioned to produce a new opera for the Teatro Fenice Theatre in Venice for the Carnival of 1853 he and his librettist, Francesco Maria Piave, decided to adapt Dumas's play. It was the first time that Verdi had used a contemporary novel as the basis for an opera. To adhere to operatic customs of the time *La Traviata* could not be set in 'modern' dress so the action was transferred back to the previous century. Verdi composed *La Traviata* in record time, juxtaposing its composition with his work on the still unfinished score of *Il Trovatore*. The first performance was a fiasco (probably as much to do with the unsuitability of the singers in the main roles as with the audience's response to Verdi's music) and it was over a year before Verdi would allow his opera to be performed again. After Verdi had made some alterations to the score – chiefly to the great scene between Violetta and Germont (Act 2) – the second production took place in the San Benedetto Theatre in Venice with a different cast, although still set in the early 18th century. This time *La Traviata* was an unqualified success and very soon achieved fame throughout Italy and other European countries, becoming one of Verdi's most lastingly popular operas.

I Vespri Siciliani

Les Vêpres Siciliennes was written to fulfil a contract for the Paris Opéra in which Verdi agreed to compose a full-scale five-act opera in the French 'Grand Opera' style. His librettist, Eugéne Scribe, was an experienced and masterful writer of the genre and took his text from his own libretto previously written with Charles Duveyrier and entitled *Le duc d'Able*. However, Verdi was dissatisfied with the text that Scribe produced and the partnership was not an amicable one. Verdi was also out of sympathy with the requirements of French Operatic traditions and at one stage asked to be released from his contract. However the Opéra refused and Verdi had no choice but to proceed. The opera was successfully premiered in 1855 and became instantly popular. It was translated into Italian by Eugenio Caimi but for censorship reasons was not given its Italian title of *I Vespri Siciliani* until six years later when Italy achieved independence. The French version is rarely performed today.

Simon Boccanegra

In early 1856 Verdi was invited to write a new opera for the Teatro la Fenice in Venice with Francesco Piave. Antonio Garcia Gutiérrez's *Simón Bocanegra* was the chosen subject. Verdi took an active interest in the progress of the libretto, even providing his own outline for submission to the censors. Later that year Verdi was in Paris and employed the services of the exiled Giuseppe Montanelli who drafted several scenes for the opera. The premiere of *Boccanegra* in 1857 was not a public success, although it received some favourable reviews. Over twenty years later, in 1880, Verdi decided to make drastic revisions both to the score and the libretto, which task he entrusted to Arrigo Boito, who was already working on *Otello*. The result was an almost complete rewriting of the work, the most important addition being the new 'Council Chamber' scene (Act 1 Scene 2). This scene was to become the central dramatic movement of the opera and it greatly enhanced a work which had previously seemed somewhat monochrome. The revised version of *Boccanegra* was first performed at La Scala in 1881 and has remained in the repertoire. There are occasional airings of the 1857 version.

Un Ballo in Maschera

Verdi had been planning for some time to write an opera based on *King Lear* and when he was commissioned by the Teatro San Carlo in Naples to produce a new opera for the 1857–1858 Carnival season he decided to proceed with this idea. However Verdi realized that the singers at the San Carlo theatre would not be up to the project and he abandoned *King Lear*. Instead he proposed to his librettist, the playwright Antonio Somma, that they should set an old libretto, *Gustave III, ou Le Bal Masque*. However when a synopsis was submitted to the authorities the subject matter – the assassination of the Swedish King Gustavus III – was deemed unsuitable to be performed in the theatre. Verdi changed the King into a Duke and reset the opera in an earlier period but still the censors would not accept the work and eventually all negotiations broke down. Finally Verdi offered the opera to the Teatro Apollo in Rome. After more lengthy negotiations it was agreed that the opera could be produced in Rome providing that the setting was not in Europe and the identity of the main character was changed. In spite of the endless reworking of the libretto and score *Un Ballo in Maschera* achieved enormous success at its premiere and has continued to be one of Verdi's most popular and renowned operas. It is occasionally performed with the original characters (Riccardo becoming Gustavus III, Renato Captain Anckarstroem, etc.) restored to their eighteenth-century setting.

La Forza del Destino

In 1860 – well over a year after the premiere of *Un ballo* – Verdi received a commission to write an opera for the Imperial Theatre in St Petersburg. After toying with the idea of setting Victor Hugo's *Ruy Blas* – a choice not entirely approved of by the St Petersburg authorities – Verdi finally settled for a Spanish play, *Don Alvaro o La Fuerza del Sino*. The premiere was only moderately successful and Verdi became dissatisfied with many aspects of the work. But it was to be some years before he made alterations by which time his original librettist, Piave, had suffered a stoke. Antonio Ghislanzoni was brought in to revise and add to the libretto for a performance at La Scala in 1869. The Prelude was replaced with the renowned Overture, parts of Act 3 were revised and the final scene rewritten (see the Synopsis to *La Forza del Destino* for a comparison of the two versions).

Don Carlo

As with *I Vespri Siciliani*, the original text of *Don Carlo* was in French and the Italian version, which is more usually performed today, is merely a translation from the French rather than a rewriting into Italian. *Don Carlos* was written for the Paris Opéra and first produced there in 1867. During the preceding rehearsal period it became obvious that the opera (in 5 Acts) was far too long and Verdi made several substantial cuts; notably the Prelude and Introduction to Act 1, part of the duet between Philip and Posa (Act 2) and the Elisabeth/Eboli and Carlos/Philip duets (Act 4). The premiere was not a success and after 1869 *Don Carlos* was withdrawn from the Opéra repertoire. During the next few years Verdi made some revisions for performance in Italy but it was not until 1882 that he proceeded to make considerable revisions to the score. Chief amongst these were the removal of the whole of Act 1 (Carlo's aria, *Io la vidi, al suo sorriso*, being inserted into the new Act 1), the ballet and preceding scene from Act 3 and the chorus of Inquisitors from Act 5. In 1884 this new version in 4 Acts, in the Italian translation, was staged at La Scala. A few years later *Don Carlo* was further performed and published with the excised Act 1 restored and it is this version which is most usually performed today and which forms the basis for discussion in the main text of this book.

Aida

In 1870 Camille du Locle – with whom Verdi had collaborated on *Don Carlo* – sent Verdi a suggestion for an opera based on a text by the Egyptologist, Auguste Mariette. The fictional story was set in ancient Egypt and as such had been deemed a suitable subject for an opera to celebrate the opening of the Suez Canal in 1870. However by the time Verdi received the synopsis the Suez Canal was already open. Eventually *Aida* was to be premiered at the new Cairo Opera House in 1871. Du Locle collaborated with Verdi on the libretto which was then translated into Italian by Antonio Ghislanzoni. The opera was an immediate success, both in Cairo and at its first performance in Italy (at La Scala) six weeks later, and has remained a firm favourite ever since.

Otello

After *Aida* Verdi virtually stopped composing (his Requiem Mass was written in 1874) and he showed no inclination to write any more operas. It was Giulio Riccordi who, in 1879, introduced Verdi to Arrigo Boito; poet, librettist and composer (his opera, *Mefistofele*, remains a firm favourite in the repertoire to this day). Riccordi and Boito suggested Shakespeare's *Othello* as a subject but although Verdi was interested in the idea he was reluctant to proceed until Boito provided a fully drafted libretto and then dragged his heels for some years before commencing composition of the score. Meanwhile Boito was employed to effect the drastic revisions to *Boccanegra* (see above) and Verdi also worked on changes to the score of *Don Carlo*. Eventually, however, work on *Otello* proceeded, Verdi composing in intensive bouts of activity interspersed with longer periods of inactivity. The opera was premiered at La Scala in 1887. Seven years later Verdi added a ballet score for the Paris premiere. He also made some revisions to the finale of Act 3, but these were not included in the Italian score and are rarely heard today.

Falstaff

Since the débâcle of *Un Giorno di Regno* in 1840 Verdi had not attempted another comic opera, although he had toyed with the idea in the latter part of his career. When Boito presented him with a draft scenario based on Shakespeare's *The Merry Wives of Windsor* Verdi was enthusiastic and immediately set to work. He and Boito collaborated closely on the text which was completed relatively quickly. As with *Otello*, however, Verdi composed the score in intensive bursts of activity with unproductive periods in between. The premiere was hugely successful and *Falstaff* quickly became established in the world's major Opera Houses.

Appendix B: Verdi's Ballets

Verdi wrote, or revised, six operas specifically for performance in Paris. These operas (*Jérusalem*, *Les Vêpres Siciliennes*, *Le Trouvère*, *Macbeth*, *Don Carlos* and *Otello*) were all given in French and included the obligatory ballet in Act 3. *Les Vêpres Siciliennes* and *Don Carlos* were written specifically to fulfil contracts with the Paris Opéra; the others were adaptations from the original Italian.

Jérusalem

The ballet for *Jérusalem* was the first ballet music that Verdi ever composed. Like the ballet for *Le Trouvère* it is non-programmatic – being simply a succession of dances inserted at an inappropriate moment in the drama (Act 3 Scene 1). The scene is the gardens of the Emir of Ramla's palace which is under siege from the Christian Crusaders. Nothing daunted, the Emir prepares to be entertained by his odalisques who proceed to dance the requisite ballet. By the conclusion of the entertainment the Crusaders are literally hammering at the gates, which are shortly to be breached.

The ballet in *Jérusalem* provides an outstanding example of how a hard-pressed composer could find himself obliged to conform to the absurdities of an archaic tradition.

Les Vêpres Siciliennes

This was Verdi's first attempt at writing the kind of Meyebeerian Grand Opera so loved by Parisian audiences. Whereas the ballets for those of his works composed initially in Italian were added to an existing scenario and could not therefore be considered strictly necessary, that of *Les Vêpres Siciliennes* (as in the case of *Don Carlos*) was designed as an integral part of the action – being the central entertainment at the ball thrown by the French governor, Monforte, in his palace.

The ballet is entitled *The Four Seasons* and proceeds as follows. Janus,[1] the two-faced Roman god, makes a grand entrance. He has come to preside over the unveiling of the New Year and opens the Earth with a golden key in order to give new life to the Seasons. A huge basket, made from evergreen winter plants covered in ice and snow, rises from the ground. A young girl, who represents winter, emerges from the basket and kicks aside the brazier that the other girls had lighted. She

---

1 Janus was the gatekeeper of Heaven. He was always represented with two faces, one in front and one behind, thus enabling him both to guard against unwarranted incursions and to protect the incumbents. He is also, in keeping with his dual aspect, associated with war. The doors of his temple in Rome were thrown open in times of war and closed in peacetime. The significance of his introduction at the opening of the ballet will not be lost on Monforte's guest.

dances to warm herself. The ice melts as the warmth of the Spring breezes penetrate the air. Another young girl, representing Spring, rises from a basket of flowers, followed shortly by Summer, who emerges from a basket surrounded by sheaves of golden corn. The Summer maiden is oppressed by the heat and she asks the Naiads if she can bathe in their cool springs. A faun jumps out, startling the bathing girls who flee. Autumn has arrived. Drums announce Satyrs and Bacchantes, whose lively dancing end the ballet.

Le Trouvère

Il Trovatore was first performed in Paris, on 23 December 1854, at the Théâtre des Italien. The success of the performances encouraged the Director to commission from Verdi a French edition, to include the traditional ballet. Verdi revised the score in its entirety, making numerous emendations to accommodate the changes of mood and sonority that were the inevitable effect of the translation from Italian into French. The soldiers' Chorus at the opening of Act 3 was altered so as to lead directly into a ballet, danced by the gypsies for the entertainment of di Luna's troops immediately prior to Azucena's capture. The ballet consists of six Spanish-style dances as follows:

1. Pas de bohemiens
2. Gitanilla
3. Ensemble
4. Sevillana
5. La Bohémienne
6. Galop

The ballet for *Le Trouvère* is the only ballet Verdi wrote for his operas in which he actually quotes music from the opera, in this case the ever popular 'Anvil Chorus'.

Macbeth

The Macbeth ballet was written for the 1865 Paris edition. The ballet occurs at the opening of Act 3 in the witches cavern and falls into three distinct sections.

In the first part a hideous orgy is in progress in which spirits and devils dance a wild *allegro vivacissimo* while the witches sit around their cauldron muttering spells and tending to their magical brew. The orgy is interrupted by the arrival of Hecate, traditionally the goddess of witchcraft.[2] All bow respectfully and contemplate the goddess in terror. The goddess looks carefully over the assembly and then informs the witches that Macbeth will shortly arrive at the cavern to discover more of his destiny (Verdi was specific that Hecate's address should be

---

[2] In Greek mythology Hecate was the daughter of the Titan Perses and of Asteria. Hecate's powers extended over all creation, Heaven and Hell, Earth and the Sea. She was sometimes represented with three heads, one of a horse, one of a dog and one of a boar, this being symbolic of her threefold nature.

conducted in mime, not in dance). Hecate tells the witches that they must give Macbeth satisfaction. She adds that should the ghostly visions which he will experience cloud Macbeth's senses overmuch, then the Spirits of the Air should be summoned to revive him. Nevertheless, under no circumstances are the witches to reveal to Macbeth the true nature of his final demise. The witches acknowledge the goddess's instructions, and Hecate vanishes as she arrived; amidst much thunder and lightning.

The third section of the ballet now commences: a sinister waltz, during which devils and spirits dance around the witches' cauldron.

Don Carlos

In the original French edition of the opera the ballet occurs at the opening of Act 3, at which point festivities celebrating the forthcoming coronation of Philip II are in progress (in the revisions of 1884 this scene was entirely expurgated, the Act opening with the arrival of Don Carlos to keep his assignation with – as he thinks – the Queen).

Elisabeth appears in company with Eboli. She is weary of the celebrations and wishes to retire in order to seek solace in religious devotion. In an eloquent moment which adds poetic justice to the opera's denouement Elisabeth and Eboli exchange their festive masks. Elisabeth retires and Eboli, left alone, reflects that thus Elisabeth has made her Queen for one night. She determines to make the most of the opportunity thus afforded her to arrange an assignation with Don Carlos. (This exchange of identities renders it far more explicable that Carlos should mistake Eboli for the Queen in the ensuing scene.)

The ballet now takes centre stage and is entitled 'Le Ballet de la Reine – La Pérégrina' and centres on the figure of a fisherman who has been despatched by the King of Spain to discover the most beautiful pearl in the ocean. In pursuit of his quest the fisherman finally arrives at a magical grotto, where the most fabulous pearls dwell, presided over by the 'Queen of the Waters'. Suspicious of the fisherman's intentions the Queen of the Waters determines that he shall be destroyed by drowning. Fortunately for the fisherman an emissary of the Spanish King arrives in time to explain to the Queen the fisherman's mission. The very mention of Philip's name fills all present with awe, and the fisherman is thereafter granted carte blanche to pursue his search. He duly decrees that none of the pearls present is fine enough to present to his master and he proposes a novel solution. The white, the pink and the black pearls shall be joined together to form an outstanding jewel worthy of the Spanish King. The three dancers depicting the pearls duly oblige by climbing into a golden shell from which shortly emerges the 'Pérégrina', an amalgamation of the three pearls that takes on the aspect of none other than the Queen of Spain herself.

The ballet thus presents not only a tribute to Philip but also to his young bride, so recently arrived from France. Princess Eboli underlines the homage by placing herself at the head of a procession of glittering chariots. The Spanish anthem is sounded and the entire company bows in awe before the spectacle.

Otello

After the triumphant premiere of *Otello* at La Scala, Verdi was given the opportunity by the then Director of the Paris Opera, Pedro Gailhard, to stage the work in Italian. Strangely Verdi refused to countenance such a suggestion and insisted that it be presented, as had all previous Parisian productions of his operas, in French. The ballet music gave Verdi a great deal of trouble, not least because he insisted on basing the music on original themes: 'something Turkish, something Cypriot-Greek, and something Venetian'. The librarian of the Florence Conservatory to whom Verdi applied for assistance could not supply anything to inspire the composer, and eventually Verdi made his own arrangements, as he was to relate in a letter to Giulio Riccordi accompanying the completed manuscript. The letter also expounds on the details of the ballet so is worth quoting at length:

'Your Doctors of Music were unable to find anything . . . but I found a Greek chant from 5000 BC! . . . If the world did not yet exist at that time, then too bad for the world! Then I found a Muranese composed two thousand years ago for a war between Venice and Murano . . . It does not matter that Venice did not yet exist. With these discoveries I have composed my good ballet, imagining how it must be performed'.

Describing the *mise en scène* Verdi writes:

'Bearing in mind the splendid scene with columns in Act 3 I have thought of writing the music in the following way: immediately at the beginning of the attack of the trumpets a group of Turkish slaves should appear. They dance unwillingly and ill-humouredly (because they are slaves). However, as this first episode ends and they hear the "Arabian Song" they become more and more animated and finish by dancing frenetically. At the "Invocation to Allah" all prostrate themselves . . . At this moment a group of beautiful Greek youths appears through the columns, and after four bars another group. They advance and at bar 13 interweave a tranquil, aristocratic classical dance. There follows at once the *Muranese* – *Allegro Vivace* in 6/8. A group of Venetian men and women advance through the columns . . . after eight bars another group. At the *fortissimo* bar 18 they meet and dance at the front of the stage. After this *fortissimo* there is some extremely light music in F# which should be more loudly orchestrated and then all the Venetians join in and dance together. The first theme, 6/8, reappears and I'd like to see another group of Venetians appear from the rear. The dancing on the "Warrior's chant" should only be performed by men. The first theme returns and all the Venetians can dance. Then at the *piu mosso* everybody can dance, including the Venetians, Greeks and everybody . . . Amen'.

Discography

Oberto

- Dimitrova/Panerai/Bergonzi/Baldani/Browner; Munich Radio Orchestra; Bavarian Radio Chorus / Lamberto Gardelli. Orfeo C105842H (2CDs)

- Ramey/Gulegina/Neill/Urmana/Fulgoni; London Voices; Academy of St Martin in the Fields / Sir Neville Marriner. Philips 454 472-2PH2 (2CDs)

Un Giorno di Regno

- Wixell/Cossotto/Jessye Norman/Carreras/Ganzarolli/Sardinero/Elvin/Cassinelli; Ambrosian Singers; Royal Philharmonic Orchestra / Lamberto Gardelli. Philips 422 429-2PM2 (2CDs)

Nabucco

- Gobbi/Prevedi/Cava/Suliotis/Carral/d'Auria/Foiani/Krautler; Vienna Opera Orchestra; Vienna State Opera Chorus / Lamberto Gardelli. Decca 417 407-2DH2 (2CDs)

- Cappuccilli/Domingo/Nesterenko/Dimitrova/Valentini-Terrani/Popp/Rydl/Horn; Berlin Opera Chorus and Orchestra / Giuseppe Sinopoli. DG 410 512-2 (2CDs)

- Manuguerra/Scotto/Obraztsova/Luchetti/Ghiaurov/Lloyd/Collins/Edwards; Philharmonia Orchestra; Ambrosian Opera Chorus / Riccardo Muti. EMI CDS7 47488-8 (2CDs)

- Gavanelli/Pick-Hieronimi/Maffezzoni/Schiatti/Burchuladze/Federici/Casertano/Blum; Chorus and Orchestra of the Verona Arena / Anton Guadagno. Koch Schwann 364272 (2CDs)

- Guelfi/Raimondi/Ghiaurov/Suliotis. La Scala 7.12.66/Gavazzeni. Armando Curcio Edition OPI 04 (Live)

I Lombardi

- Anderson/Pavarotti/Ramey/Leech/d'Arcangelo/Yannissis/Shaulis/Dean Griffey/Racette; Chorus and Orchestra of the Metropolitan Opera, New York / James Levine. Decca 455 287-2DHO2 (2CDs)

- di Cesare/Kovats/Sass/Misura/Gregor/Jasz/Lamberti/Janosi/Gerdesits; Hungarian State Opera Orchestra; Hungarian Radio and Television Chorus / Lamberto Gardelli. Hungaroton HCD12498/500 (3CDs)

- Deutekom/Domingo/Raimondi/Lo Monaco/Dean/Grant/Aparici/Erwen/Malvisi; Ambrosian Singers; Royal Philharmonic Orchestra / Lamberto Gardelli. Philips 422 420-2PM2 (2CDs)

- Carreras/Sass/Ghiuselev. 1976/Gardelli. SRO 829-2 (Live)

Jerusalem
- Ricciarelli/Carreras/Nimsgern. RAI Torino 20.12.75/Gavazzeni. Bella Voce BLV 107 213 (Live)

Ernani
- Pavarotti/Sutherland/Nucci/Burchuladze/McLeod/Morton/Miles; Welsh National Opera Chorus and Orchestra / Richard Bonynge. Decca 421 412-2DHO2 (2CDs)

- Domingo/Bruson/Ghiaurov/Freni/Michieli/Manganotti/Giacomotti; La Scala Chorus and Orchestra, Milan / Riccardo Muti. Recorded at performances in La Scala, Milan during December 1982. EMI CDS7 47083-8 (3CDs)

- Lamberti/Miller/Kovats/Sass/Takacs/Molnar/Kovacs; Hungarian State Opera Chorus and Orchestra; Male chorus of the Hungarian People's Army / Lamberto Gardelli. Hungaroton HCD12259/61-2 (3CDs)

- Lamberti/Sass/Miller/Kovats/Takacs/Molnar/Kovacs; Hungarian Army Chorus; Hungarian State Opera Chorus and Orchestra / Lamberto Gardelli. Philips 446 669-2PM2 (2CDs)

- Bergonzi/Leontyne Price/Sereni/Flagello/Hamari/Iacopucci/Mueller; RCA Italiana Opera Chorus and Orchestra / Thomas Schippers. RCA Victor GD86503 (2CDs)

- Bergonzi/Cappuccilli/Raimondi/Gencer/Catania. 1972/Gavazzeni. Arkadi HP 621 2 (Live)

- Domingo/Kabaivanska/Ghiaurov/Meliciani. Milan 1969. Armando Curcio Edition OPI 09 (Live)

- Prevedi/Glossop/Christoff. Milan RAI 25.3.63/Gavazzeni. Frequenz 043 018 (Live)

I Due Foscari
- Guelfi/Bergonzi/Vitale/Lombardo/Bersieri/Pellegrino/Bertocci/Barbieri; Milan RAI Chorus and Symphony Orchestra / Carlo Maria Giulini. Recording of a broadcast transmission in 1951. Nuova Era mono 2278/9 (2CDs)

- Cappuccilil/Carreras/Ricclarelli/Ramey/Bello/Connell/Antoniak/Handlos; Austrian Radio Chorus and Symphony Orchestra / Lamberto Gardelli. Philips 422 426-2PM2 (2CDs)

Giovanna d'Arco
- Caballe/Domingo/Milnes/Erwen/Lloyd; Ambrosian Opera Chorus; London Symphony Orchestra / James Levine. EMI CMS7 63226-2 (2CDs)

- Tebaldi/Penno/Savarese. 1951/Santini. LCD 193-2 (Live)

Alzira
- Cotrubas/Araiza/Bruson/George//Lis/Ionita; Munich Radio Orchestra; Bavarian Radio Chorus / Lamberto Gardelli. Orfeo C057832H (2CDs)

Attila

- Ramey/Studer/Zancanaro/Shicoff/Gavazzi/Surian; Chorus and Orchestra of La Scala, Milan / Riccardo Muti. EMI CDS7 49952-2 (2CDs)

- Nesterenko/Sass/Miller/Nagy/Kallay/Kovats; Hungarian State Radio and Television Chorus; Hungarian State Orchestra / Lamberto Gardelli. Hungaroton HCD12934/5 (2CDs)

- Raimondi/Deutekom/Milnes/Bergonzi/Cassinelli/Bastin; Ambrosian Singers; Royal Philharmonic Orchestra; Finchley Children's Music Group / Lamberto Gardelli. Philips 412 875-2PH2 (2CDs)

Macbeth

- Cappuccilli/Sass/Kovats/Kelen/Pitti/Bandi/Gati/Toth/Bator; Budapest Symphony Orchestra; Hungarian Radio and Television Chorus / Lamberto Gardelli. Hungaroton HCD12738/40 (3CDs)

- Nucci/Verrett/Ramey/Luchetti/Antonacci/Barasorda/Fontana/Casarini/Morresi; Chorus and Orchestra of Teatro Comunale, Bologna / Riccardo Chailly. Decca 417 525-2DH2 (2CDs)

- Taddei/Nilsson/Foiani/Prevedi/De Palma/Morresi/Carbonari/Maionica/Carral; Chorus and Orchestra of the Santa Cecilia Academy, Rome / Thomas Schippers. Decca Grand Opera 433 039-2DM2 (2CDs)

- Cappuccilli/Verrett/Ghiaurov/Domingo/Malagu/Savastano/Zardo/Foiani/ Mariotti/Fontana; Chorus and Orchestra of La Scala, Milan / Claudio Abbado. DG 415 688-2GH3 (3CDs)

- Milnes/Cossotto/Raimondi/Carreras/Borgato/Bernardi/del Bosco/Fyson/Noble/ Taylor; New Philharmonia Orchestra; Ambrosian Opera Chorus / Riccardo Muti. EMI CMS7 64339-2 (2CDs)

- Mascherini/Callas/Tajo/Penno/della Pergola/Caselli/Barbesi/Vinco/Tommasini/ Vercelli; Chorus and Orchestra of La Scala, Milan / Victor de Sabata. Recorded at a performance in La Scala, Milan on December 7th, 1952. EMI mono CMS7 64944-2 (2CDs)

- Zampieri/Bruson/Lloyd/Schicoff/Aliberti/Ahnsjo/Salomaa/Nikolic/Schmidt/ Neubert; Berlin German Opera Chorus and Orchestra / Giuseppe Sinopoli. Philips digital 412 133-2PH3 (3CDs)

- Warren/Rysanek/Hines/Bergonzi/Olvis/Pechner/Sternberg/Hawkins; Metropolitan Opera Chorus and Orchestra / Erich Leinsdorf. RCA Victor GD84516 (2CDs)

- Gobbi/Shuard. Covent Garden 1960. Bella Voce BLV 107 203 (Live)

- Mödl/Metternicn/Weber. 10.9.1950/Keilberth. MCD 974.166 (Live)

- Varnay/Metternich/Weber/Geisler (in German). Chor & Orch WDR Cologne 1954/R Kraus. Myto 2MCD 952 128 (Live)

I Masnadieri

- Bonisolli/Harris/Manuguerra/Davies/Sutherland/Ramey/Alaimo; Welsh National Opera Chorus and Orchestra / Richard Bonynge. Decca Grand Opera 433 854-2DMO2 (2CDs)

- Caballe/Bergonzi/Cappuccilli/Raimondi/Sandor/Mazzieri/Elvin; Ambrosian Singers; New Philharmonia Orchestra / Lamberto Gardelli. Philips 422 423-2PM2 (2CDs)

- Raimondi/Bruson/Ligabue/Christoff. Rome 25.11.72/Gavazzeni. GAO 135/6 (Live)

Il Corsaro

- Carreras/Norman/Caballe/Mastromei/Noble/Grant/Oliver; New Philharmonia Orchestra; Ambrosian Singers / Lamberto Gardelli. Philips 426 118-2PM2 (2CDs)

La Battaglia di Legnano

- Ricciarelli/Carreras/Manuguerra/Ghiuselev/Lichtenberger/Kavrakos/Summers/Handlos/Murray/Antoniak; Austrian Radio Chorus and Symphony Orchestra / Lamberto Gardelli. Philips 422 435-2PM2 (2CDs)

Luisa Miller

- Caballe/Pavarotti/Milnes/Gaiotti/Reynolds/van Allen/Celine/Fernando Pavarotti; London Opera Chorus; National Philharmonic Orchestra / Peter Maag. Decca 417 420-2DH2 (2CDs)

- Ricciarelli/Domingo/Obraztsova/Bruson/Howell/Ganzarolli/Michael/di Corato; Chorus and Orchestra of the Royal Opera House, Covent Garden / Lorin Maazel. DG 423 144-2GH2 (2CDs)

- Moffo/Bergonzi/MacNeil/Tozzi/Verrett/Flagello/Carturan/De Palma; RCA Italiana Opera Chorus and Orchestra / Fausto Cleva. RCA GD86646 (2CDs)

- Millo/Domingo/Chernov/Rootering/Quivar/Plishka/Wendy White/Bills; Metropolitan Opera Chorus and Orchestra / James Levine. Sony Classical CD48073 (2CDs)

- Ricciarelli/Pavarotti/Tonrangean/Quilico. San Francisco 1974/Not credited. Bella Voce BLV 107 215 (Live)

- Stella/di Stefano/Dominguez/MacNeill. Palermo 1963/Sanzogno. GDS 21033 (Live)

- Ricciarelli/Carreras/Bruson/Rinaudo. 1976/Prevatali LCD 180-2 (Live)

- Caballé/Pavarotti/Cappuccilli. Milan 1976/Gavazzeni. MCD 972 156 (Live)

Stiffelio

- Carreras/Sass/Manuguerra/Ganzarolli/di Cesare/Venuti/Moser; Austrian Radio Chorus and Symphony Orchestra / Lamberto Gardelli. Philips 422 432-2PM2 (2CDs)

Aroldo

- Caballe/Cecchele/Lebherz/Pons/Manno/Rogera/Busching; New York Oratorio Society; Westchester Choral Society; New York Opera Orchestra / Eve Queler. Recorded at a performance in Carnegie Hall, New York on April 8th, 1979. CBS Masterworks CD79328 (2CDs)

Rigoletto

- Hasslo/Hallin/Gedda/Tyren/Svedenbrant/Meyer/Ericson/Sivall/Naslund/ Kjellgren/Wixell/Nordin; Stockholm Royal Opera Chorus and Orchestra / Sixten Ehrling. Recorded at a performance in the Royal Theatre, Stockholm, Sweden on January 18th, 1959. BIS mono CD296 (2CDs)

- Milnes/Pavarotti/Sutherland/Talvela/Tourangeau/Knight/Grant/du Plessis/ Cassinelli/Gibbs/Te Kanawa/Clement; London Symphony Orchestra; Ambrosian Opera Chorus / Richard Bonynge. Decca 414 269-2DH2 (2CDs)

- Nucci/Anderson/Pavarotti/Ghiaurov/Verrett/de Carolis/Mosca/de Palma/ Scaltriti/Caterina/de Bortoli/Laurenza; Chorus and Orchestra of the Teatro Comunale, Bologna / Riccardo Chailly. Decca 425 864-2DH2 (2CDs)

- Protti/Gueden/del Monaco/Siepi/Simionato/Corena/Ribacchi/De Palma/Castelli/ Caselli/Rossi/Poldi; Chorus and Orchestra of the Santa Cecilia Academy, Rome / Alberto Erede. Decca mono 440 242-2LF2 (2CDs)

- Cappuccilli/Domingo/Cotrubas/Ghiaurov/Obraztsova/Schwarz/Moll/de Corato/ Gullino/Sagemuller/Fredricks; Vienna Philharmonic Orchestra; Vienna State Opera Chorus / Carlo Maria Giulini. DG 415 288-2GH2 (2CDs)

- Chernov/Studer/Pavarotti/Scandiuzzi/Graves/d'Arcangelo/Shaulis/Croft/Groves/ Yannissis/Grant Murphy/Maher/Lindner; Metropolitan Opera Chorus and Orchestra, New York / James Levine. DG 447 064-2GH2 (2CDs)

- Zancanaro/Dessi/La Scola/Burchuladze/Senn/Surian/Franci/Gavazzi/Gallo/ Curiel/Pertusi/Esposito/Panariello; Chorus and Orchestra of La Scala, Milan / Riccardo Muti. EMI CDS7 49605-2 (2CDs)

- Rawnsley/Davies/Field/Tomlinson/Rigby/Bailey/Squires/Opie/Jenkins/ Richardson/McLeod; English National Opera Chorus and Orchestra / Mark Elder (sung in English). EMI CMS7 69369-2 (2CDs)

- Gobbi/di Stefano/Callas/Zaccaria/Lazzarini/Gerbino/Clabassi/Dickie/Ercolani/ Forti/Galassi; Chorus and Orchestra of La Scala, Milan / Tullio Serafin. EMI mono CDS7 47469-8 (2CDs)

- Weikl/Popp/Aragall/Rootering/Takacs/Malta/Jungwirth/Ionita/Riener/Freyer/ Auer/Hautermann; Munich Radio Chorus and Orchestra / Lamberto Gardelli. Eurodisc/RCA 610 115 (2CDs)

- Tumagian/Ferrarini/Ramiro/Spacek/Saparova/Neshyba/Michalkova/Abel/ Subert/Neshybova/Szucs; Slovak Philharmonic Chorus; Czecho-Slovak Radio Symphony Orchestra / Alexander Rahbari. Naxos 8 660013/14 (2CDs)

- Bruson/Shicoff/Gruberova/Lloyd/Fassbaender/Rydl/Gabba/Matteuzzi/Moses/ Pittavini; Chorus and Orchestra of the Santa Cecilia Academy / Giuseppe Sinopoli. Philips 412 592-2PH2

- Weikl/Popp/Aragall/Rootering/Takacs/Malta/Jungwirth/Ionita/Riener/Freyer/ Auer/Hautermann; Bavarian Radio Chorus; Munich Radio Orchestra / Lamberto Gardelli. RCA Victor 74321 25286-2 (2CDs)

- Merrill/Moffo/Kraus/Flagello/Elias/Ward/di Stasio/De Palma/Kerns/Vozza/ Rinaudo/Toscano; RCA Italiana Chorus and Orchestra / Sir Georg Solti. RCA Victor GD86506 (2CDs)

- Bruson/Rost/Alagna/Kavrakos/Pentcheva/Giuseppini/Trevisan/Gavazzi/ Sammaritano/Zanini/de Gobbi/Laurenza/Panariello; Chorus and Orchestra of La Scala, Milan / Riccardo Muti. Recorded at performances in La Scala, Milan between May 13th and 21st, 1994. Sony Classical S2K66314 (2CDs)

- Agache/Vaduva/Leech/Ramey/Larmore/Miles/Bardon/Banks/Sidhom/Evans/ Moses/Bradbury/Visenti; Welsh National Opera Chorus and Orchestra / Carlo Rizzi. Teldec 4509-90851-2 (2CDs)

- Piazza/Pagliughi/Folgar/Baccaloni/de Cristoff/Baracchi/Brambilla/Nessi/Menni; Chorus and Orchestra of La Scala, Milan / Carlo Sabajno. VAI Audio mono VAIA1097 (2CDs)

- MacNeill/Scotto/Tucker/Souza. 1967/Prevatali. LCD 198-2 (Live)

- Kozlovsky/Maslennikova/Ivanov/I Petrov. Moscow 1949/Samosnd. MCD 973 161 (Live)

- Carreras/Wise/Quilico/Marsee. 1973/Rudel. SRO 843-2 (Live)

Il Trovatore
- Wilson/Bisatt/Quinn/Grevelle//Shaw/Rahme; Tallis Chamber Choir; European Chamber Opera Chorus and Orchestra / Duncan Hinnells. ASV CDDCS225 (2CDs)

- Tebaldi/del Monaco/Savarese/Simionato/Tozzi/Maragliano/Cesarini/Balbi; Chorus of the Maggio Musicale Fiorentino; Orchestra of the Grand Theatre, Geneva / Alberto Erede. Decca 411 874-2DM2 (2CDs)

- Pavarotti/Wixell/Horne/Ghiaurov/Burrowes/Clark/Knapp/Evans; National Philharmonic Orchestra; London Opera Chorus / Richard Bonynge. Decca 417 137-2DH2 (2CDs)

- Pavarotti/Banaudi/Nucci/Verrett/d'Artegna/Frittoli/de Palma/Scaltriti/Facini; Chorus and Orchestra of the Maggio Musicale Fiorentino / Zubin Mehta. Decca 430 694-2DHO2 (2CDs)

- Bergonzi/Stella/Bastianini/Cossotto/Vinco/Bonato/Ricciardi/Morresi/Mercuriali; Chorus and Orchestra of La Scala, Milan / Tullio Serafin. DG 445 451-2GX2 (2CDs)

- Corelli/Leontyne Price/Bastianini/Simionato/Zaccaria/Dutoit/Frese/Zimmer/ Equiluz; Salzburg Festival Chamber Choir; Vienna State Opera Chorus; Vienna Philharmonic Orchestra / Herbert von Karajan. Recorded at a performance in the Grosser Festspielhaus, Salzburg on July 31st, 1962. DG 447 659-2GX2 (2CDs)

- Callas/di Stefano/Panerai/Barbieri/Zaccaria/Villa//Ercolani/Mauri; Chorus and Orchestra of La Scala, Milan / Herbert von Karajan. EMI CDS7 49347-2 (2CDs)

- Bonisolli/Leontyne Price/Cappuccilli/Obraztsova/Raimondi/Venuti/Nitsche/Egel/ Nitsche; Chorus of the Deutsche Oper, Berlin; Berlin Philharmonic Orchestra / Herbert von Karajan. EMI CMS7 69311-2 (2CDs)

- Frusoni/Longhi/Servile/Tschistiakova/de Grandis/Csonka/Mukk/Pasztor/ Tandari; Budapest Festival Chorus; Hungarian State Opera Orchestra / Will Humburg. Naxos 8 660023/4 (2CDs)

- Tucker/Caballe/Zanasi/Mattiucci/Vinco/Matteini/Natali/Rigiri/Falaschi; Chorus and Orchestra of the Maggio Musicale Fiorentino / Thomas Schippers. Text included. Recorded at a performance in the Teatro Communale, Florence in December 1968. Nuova Era 2280/81 (2CDs)

- Carreras/Ricciarelli/Masurok/Toczyska/Lloyd/Cannan/Leggate/Earle/Treleaven; Chorus and Orchestra of the Royal Opera House, Covent Garden / Sir Colin Davis. Philips 426 557-2PM2 (2CDs)

- Domingo/Kabaivanska/Cappuccilli/Cossotto/Van Dam/Venuti/Zednik/ Caslavsky/Aichberger; Vienna State Opera Chorus and Orchestra / Herbert von Karajan. Recorded at a performance in the Staatsoper, Vienna on May 1st, 1978. Includes an interview with Herbert von Karajan by Marcel Prawny. RCA Red Seal 74321 61951-2 (2CDs)

- Leontyne Price/Domingo/Milnes/Cossotto/Giaiotti/Bainbridge/Ryland Davies/ Riley/Taylor; Ambrosian Opera Chorus; New Philharmonia Orchestra / Zubin Mehta. RCA Red Seal RD86194 (2CDs)

- Milanov/Bjorling/Warren/Barbieri/Moscona/Roggero/Franke/Cehanovsky/ Sprinzena; Robert Shaw Chorale; RCA Victor Orchestra / Renato Cellini. RCA Victor mono GD86643 (2CDs)

- Tucker/Leontyne Price/Warren/Elias/Tozzi/Londi/Carlin/Monreale/Frascati; Rome Opera Chorus and Orchestra / Arturo Basile. RCA Victor Opera Series GD60560 (2CDs)

- Pertile/Carena/Granforte/Minghini-Cattaneo/Carmassi/De Franco/Callegari/ Gelli; Chorus and Orchestra of La Scala, Milan / Gino Nastrucci, Carlo Sabajno. Romophone Opera Magna mono 890032 (2CDs)

- Domingo/Millo/Chernov/Zajick/Morris/Kelly/Laciura/Bater/Willson; New York Metropolitan Opera Chorus and Orchestra / James Levine. Sony Classical S2K48070 (2CDs)

- Sutherland/Pavarotti. San Francisco 3.10.75/Bonynge. Bella Voce BLV 107 216 (Live)

- Björling/Cigna/Wettergren/Basiola. Covent Garden 1939/Gui. GOP 801 (Live)

La Traviata
- Mariella Devia/Aronica/Zancanaro; Genoa Teatro Carlo Felice Chor and Orch / Daniele Callegari. Bongiovanni GB2530/31 (2CDs)

- Aliberti/Dvorsky/Bruson/Mochiki/Sawa/Mochiki/Okayama/Shikano/ Yanagisawa/Ichikawa/Ishii; Fujiwara Opera Chorus; Tokyo Philharmonic Orchestra / Roberto Paternostro. Recorded at a performance in Suntory Hall, Tokyo during 1988. Capriccio 10 274/5 (2CDs)

- Masterson/Brecknock/du Plessis/Jones/Squires/Pogson/Gibbs/Dowling/Earle/ Byles/Kitchiner; Chorus and Orchestra of English National Opera / Sir Charles Mackerras (sung in English). Chandos Opera in English Series CHAN3023 (2CDs)

- Sutherland/Pavarotti/Manuguerra/Jones/Lambriks/Oliver/Summers/Tomlinson/ Tadio/Gardini; National Philharmonic Orchestra; London Opera Chorus / Richard Bonynge. Decca 410 154-2DH2 (3CDs)

- Gheorghiu/Lopardo/Nucci/Leah-Marian Jones/Knight/Leggate/Van Allan/Earle/ Beesley/Griffiths/Secombe/Gibson; Chorus and Orchestra of the Royal Opera House, Covent Garden / Sir Georg Solti. Recorded at performances in the Royal Opera House, Covent Garden during December 1994. Decca 448 119-2DHO2 (2CDs)

- Sutherland/Bergonzi/Merrill/Pace/Carral/De Palma/Pedani/Maionica/Foiani/ Mercuriali/Frosini; Maggio Musicale Fiorentino Chorus and Orchestra / Sir John Pritchard. Decca Grand Opera 411 877-2DM2 (2CDs)

- Cotrubas/Domingo/Milnes/Gullino/Malagu/Jungwirth/Grella/Giacometti/ Foiani/Gullino; Bavarian State Opera Chorus and Orchestra / Carlos Kleiber. DG 415 132-2GH2 (2CDs)

- Studer/Pavarotti/Pons/White/Kelly/Laciura/Pola/Wells/Robbins/Hanriot/ Sendrowitz/Crolius; Metropolitan Opera Chorus and Orchestra / James Levine. DG 435 797-2GH2 (2CDs)

- Caniglia/Gigli/Basiola/Huder/Palmer/Zagonara/Baracchi/Hitchin/Walker/Dua; Royal Opera House Chorus, Covent Garden; London Philharmonic Orchestra / Vittorio Gui. Recorded at a performance in the Royal Opera House, Covent Garden on May 22nd, 1939. Eclipse Records ECRCD2 (2CDs)

- Scotto/Kraus/Bruson/Walker/Buchan/Mariategui/Newman/Van Allan/Kennedy/ Cosotti/Keyte; Ambrosian Opera Chorus; Philharmonia Orchestra; Band of HM Royal Marines / Riccardo Muti. EMI CDS7 47059-8 (3CDs)

- Scotto/Kraus/Bruson/Walker/Mariategui/Newman/Buchan/Kennedy/Van Allan/ Cosotti; Ambrosian Opera Chorus; Philharmonia Orchestra; Band of HM Royal Marines / Riccardo Muti. EMI CDS7 47538-8 (2CDs)

- Callas/Kraus/Sereni/Zanini/De Palma/Malta/de Castro/Maddalena/Susca/Leitao; Chorus and Orchestra of the Teatro Nacional de San Carlos, Lisbon / Franco Ghione. Recorded at a performance in the Teatro Nacional de San Carlos, Lisbon on March 27th, 1958. EMI CDS7 49187-8 (2CDs)

- de los Angeles/del Monte/Sereni/Chissari/Bertona/Tedesco/Polotto/Maionica/Giaiotti/Ercolani; Rome Opera Chorus and Orchestra / Tullio Serafin. EMI CDS7 49578-2 (2CDs)

- Callas/di Stefano/Bastianini/Zanolli/Mandelli/Zampieri/la Porta/Zerbini/Maionica/Ricciardi; Chorus and Orchestra of La Scala, Milan / Carlo Maria Giulini. Recorded at a performance in La Scala, Milan on May 28th, 1955. EMI CMS7 63628-2 (2CDs)

- Callas/Albanese/Savarese/Gandolfo/Marietti/Mariano Caruso/Albertini/Zorgniotti/Soley; Chorus and Turin RAI Orchestra / Gabriele Santini. Fonitcetra Classic Collection CDO9 (2CDs)

- Te Kanawa/Kraus/Hvorostovsky/Mazzoni/Borodina/Banks/Scaltriti/Gatti/Donato Di Stefano/La Guardia/Calamai; Maggio Musicale Fiorentino Chorus and Orchestra / Zubin Mehta. Philips 438 238-2PH2 (2CDs)

- Albanese/Peerce/Merrill/Stellman/Moreland/Garris/Cehanovsky/Dennis/Newman; NBC Symphony Chorus and Orchestra / Arturo Toscanini. RCA Gold Seal GD60303 (2CDs)

- Caballe/Bergonzi/Milnes/Krebill/Stokes/Iacopucci/Boucher/Jamerson/Enns/Sforza/Ruta/Tasin; RCA Italiana Opera Chorus and Orchestra / Georges Pretre. RCA Red Seal RD86180 (2CDs)

- Fabbriccini/Alagna/Coni/Curiel/Trevisan/Cossutta/Mori/Capuano/Musinu/Gavazzi/Panariello/Sammaritano; Chorus and Orchestra of La Scala, Milan / Riccardo Muti. Recorded at performances at La Scala, Milan in March and April 1992. Sony Classical S2K52486 (2CDs)

- Gruberova/Shicoff/Zancanaro/Spence/Bacelli/Begley/Sidhom/Barrell/Miles/Bronder/Folwell/Visentin; Ambrosian Singers; London Symphony Orchestra / Carlo Rizzi. Teldec 9031-76348-2 (2CDs)

- Rozsa/Ziliani/Borgonovo/de Franco/Callegari/Lenzi/Gelli; Chorus and Orchestra of La Scala, Milan / Carlo Sabajno. VAI Audio VAIA1108 (2CDs)

- Sutherland/Pavarotti. Met 22.10 70/Bonynge. Bella Voce BLV 107 217 (Live)

- Caniglia/Gigli/Basiola/Huder. Covent Garden 12.5.39/Gui. GOP 801 (Live)

- Callas/di Stefano/Campolonghi. Mexico 3.6.52/Mugnai. Melodram MEL 26021 (Live)

I Vespri Siciliani
- Studer/Merritt/Zancanaro/Furlanetto/Banditelli/Capuano/Musinu/Gavazzi/Barbacini/Chingari/Poggi; Chorus and Orchestra of La Scala, Milan / Riccardo

Muti. Recorded at performances in La Scala, Milan during December 1989 and January 1990. EMI CDS7 54043-2 (3CDs)

- Arroyo/Domingo/Milnes/Raimondi/Ewing/Sharp/Van Allan/Goeke/Collins/ Morris/Byers; John Alldis Choir; New Philharmonia Orchestra / James Levine. RCA Red Seal RD80370 (3CDs)

- Callas/Christoff/Giorgio K Bardi. Florence 1951/E Kleiber. Melodram GM 2005 (Live)

- Caballé/Domingo/Bordoni/Diaz. 1974/Queler. SRO 837-2 (Live)

Simon Boccanegra
- Nucci/Te Kanawa/Aragall/Burchuladze/Coni/Colombara/Gavazzi/Zoroberto; Chorus and Orchestra of La Scala, Milan / Sir Georg Solti. Decca 425 628-2DH2 (2CDs)

- Freni/Cappuccilli/Ghiaurov/van Dam/Carreras; Chorus and Orchestra of La Scala, Milan / Claudio Abbado. DG 415 692-2GH2 (2CDs)

- Cappuccilli/Freni/Carreras/Ghiaurov/van Dam/Foiani/Savastano/Gallamini; Chorus and Orchestra of La Scala, Milan / Claudio Abbado. DG The Originals 449 752-2GOR2 (2CDs)

- Tumagian/Gauci/Aragall/Mikulas/Sardinero/de Kanel/Tomckowiack/Pieck; Brussels Belgian Radio and TV Philharmonic Chorus and Orchestra / Alexander Rahbari. Discover International DICD920225/6 (2CDs)

- Gobbi/de los Angeles/Campora/ Christoff/Monachesi/Dari/Caroli/Bertona; Chorus and Orchestra of the Rome Opera House / Gabriele Santini. EMI CMS7 63513-2 (2CDs)

- Miller/Kincses/Gregor/Gati/Nagy; Chorus and Orchestra of the Hungarian State Opera / Giuseppe Patane. Hungaroton HCD12611/2

- Cappuccilli/Ricciarelli/Domingo/Raimondi/Mastromei; RCA Chorus and Orchestra / Gianandrea Gavazzeni. RCA Red Seal RD70729 (2CDs)

- van Dam/Gustafson/Cupido/Pittsinger/Stone/Krause/Gregoire; Chorus and Orchestra of the Theatre Royal de la Monnaie, Brussels / Sylvain Cambreling. Recorded at performances in the Theatre Royal de la Monnaie, Brussels in September 1990. Ricercar Secondo RIS093070/71 (2CDs)

- MacNeill/Tebaldi/Tucker/Flagello 1970/Levine. LCD 189-2 (Live)

- (abridged) Warren (complete role)/GarciaFilippeschi/Silva. 1950/Cellini. LCD 185-1 (Live)

Un Ballo in Maschera
- Arroyo/Domingo/Cappuccilli/Grist/Cossotto/Howell/Van Allan/Giorgetti/ Collins; Haberdashers' Aske's School Girls' Choir; Medici Quartet; Royal Opera House Chorus, Covent Garden; New Philharmonia Orchestra / Riccardo Muti. EMI 8 CMS7 69576-2 (2CDs)

- Barstow/Domingo/Nucci/Sumi Jo/Quivar/Rydl/Simic/Chaignaud/Witte/ Tomaschek; Vienna State Opera Concert Choir; Vienna Philharmonic Orchestra / Herbert von Karajan. DG 449 588-2GX2 (2CDs)

- Barstow/Domingo/Nucci/Sumi Jo/Quivar/Rydl/Simic/Chaignaud; Vienna State Opera Chorus; Vienna Philharmonic Orchestra / Herbert von Karajan. DG 427 635-2GH2 (2CDs)

- Caballe/Carreras/Wixell/Ghazarian/Payne/Lloyd/Howell/Summers/Leggate/ Elvin; Chorus and Orchestra of the Royal Opera House, Covent Garden / Sir Colin Davis. Philips Duo 456 316-2PM2 (2CDs)

- Crider/Leech/Chernov/Bayo//Rose/Howell/Scaltriti/Bronder/Banks; Welsh National Opera Chorus and Orchestra / Carlo Rizzi. Teldec 4509-98408-2 (2CDs)

- di Stefano/Gobbi/Callas/Barbieri/Ratti/Giordano/Maionica/Zaccaria/Ercolani; Chorus and Orchestra of La Scala, Milan / Antonino Votto. EMI mono CDS7 47498-8 (2CDs)

- Domingo/Bruson/Ricciarelli/Obraztsova/Gruberova/De Corato/Raimondi/ Foiani/Savastano/Manganotti. Chorus and Orchestra of La Scala, Milan / Claudio Abbado. DG 415 685-2GH2 (2CDs)

- Leontyne Price/Bergonzi/Merrill/Grist/Verrett/Flagello/Mazzoli/Basiola Jr/De Palma; RCA Italian Opera Chorus and Orchestra / Erich Leinsdorf. RCA Victor 8 GD86645 (2CDs)

- Nelli/Peerce/Merrill/Haskins/Turner/Moscona/Scott/Cehanovsky/Rossi; Robert Shaw Chorale; NBC Symphony Orchestra / Arturo Toscanini. Recorded at NBC broadcasts from Carnegie Hall, New York on January 17th and 24th, 1954. RCA Victor Gold Seal GD60301 (2CDs)

- Nilsson/Bergonzi/MacNeil/Stahlmann/Simionato/Corena/Arbace/Krause//de Palma/Pandano; Chorus and Orchestra of Santa Cecilia Academy, Rome / Sir Georg Solti. Decca Grand Opera. 425 655-2DM2 (2CDs)

- Pavarotti/Bruson/Margaret Price/Ludwig/Battle/Peter Weber/Lloyd/King/Oliver/ Peter Hall. London Opera Chorus; National Philharmonic Orchestra; Junior Chorus of the Royal College of Music / Sir Georg Solti. Decca digital 410 210-2DH2 (2CDs)

- Stella Roman/Martinelli/Bonelli/Antoine/Castagna/Cordon/Moscona/ Cehanovsky/Carter/Oliviero; Metropolitan Opera Chorus and Orchestra / Ettore Panizza. From a broadcast performance from the Metropolitan Opera House, New York on February 28th, 1942. Eklipse EKRCD12 (2CDs)

- Tebaldi/Pavarotti/Milnes/Donath/Resnik/Monreale/Nicolai Christov/van/Poli/ Alessandrini; Chorus and Orchestra of the Santa Cecilia Academy, Rome / Bruno Bartoletti. Decca Grand Opera 440 042-2DMO2 (2CDs)

- di Stefano/Roberti/Dominguez/Ansensi Mexico 2.8.60/Cellini GDS 21039 (Live)

- Welitsch/Picchi/Silveri/Noni/Watson. Edinburgh 1949/Gui O/S 4705 (Live)

- Cerquetti/Poggi/Bastianini/Stignani/Manni-Jottini. 1957/Tieri. SRO 804-2 (Live)

- Callas/di Stefano/Bastianini/Simionato/Ratti. La Scala 7.12.57/Gavazzeni. Virtuoso 2697412 (Live)

La Forza del Destino
- Arroyo/Bergonzi/Cappuccilli/Raimondo/Casoni/Geraint Evans/Zerbini/ Andreolli/Cova/Carbonari/Hammond-Stroud; Ambrosian Opera Chorus; Royal Philharmonic Orchestra / Lamberto Gardelli. EMI Opera CMS7 64646-2 (3CDs)

- Callas/Tucker/Tagliabue/Nicolai/Rossi-Lemeni/Capecchi/del Signore/Cavallari; Chorus and Orchestra of La Scala, Milan / Tullio Serafin. EMI mono CDS7 47581-8 (3CDs)

- Freni/Domingo/Zancanaro/Zajic/Plishka/Bruscantini/Gavazzi/Garbi; Chorus and Orchestra of La Scala, Milan / Riccardo Muti. EMI digital CDS7 47485-8

- Gorchakova/Grigorian/Putilin/Kit/Borodina/Zastavny/Abdrazakov/Shevtzova/ Gassiev/Bezzubenkov/Laptev; Kirov Theatre Chorus and Orchestra / Valery Gergiev. Philips 446 951-2PH3 (3CDs)

- Leontyne Price/Domingo/Milnes/Cossotto/Giaiotti/Bacquier/Senechal/Knight; London Symphony Orchestra; John Alldis Choir / James Levine. RCA RD81864 (3CDs)

- Leontyne Price/Tucker/Merrill/Tozzi/Verrett/Flagello/Foiani/De Palma/Vozza/ Bottcher/Rinaudo; RCA Italiana Opera Chorus and Orchestra / Thomas Schippers. RCA Victor GD87971 (3CDs)

- Plowright/Carreras/Bruson/Baltsa/Burchuladze/Pons/Curtis/Rigby; Philharmonia Orchestra; Ambrosian Opera Chorus / Giuseppe Sinopoli. DG digital 419 203-2GH3 (3CDs)

- Roman/Jagel/Tibbett/Pinza/Petina/Baccaloni/d'Angelo/Votipka/de Paolis/Alvary/ Gurney; Metropolitan Opera Chorus and Orchestra, New York / Bruno Walter. Recorded at a broadcast performance in the Metropolitan Opera House, New York on January 23rd, 1943. Naxos Historical mono 8 110038/40 (3CDs)

- Tebaldi/del Monaco/Bastianini/Siepi/Simionato/Corena/Maionica/De Palma/ Carturan/Giordano/Coda; Santa Cecilia Chorus and Orchestra, Rome / Francesco Molinari-Pradelli. Decca Grand Opera 421 598-2DM3 (3CDs)

- Gencer/Protti/di Stefano/Siepi. La Scala Orch & Chorus Cologne 5.7.57/Votto. Frequenz 043015 (Live)

- Stella/di Stefano/Simionato/Bastianini. Vienna 23.9.60/Mitropoulos. GDS 31022 (Live)

- Tucker/Taddei/Cavalli/Dominguez/Clabassi. Buenos Aires 1961/Prevatali. MCD 975 174 (Live)

- Milanov/Tucker/Warren. Music & Arts CD 693 (Live)

- Farrell/Corelli/Colzani/Flagello/Pechner. 1965/Guadagno. SRO 826-2 (Live)

Don Carlos

- Domingo/Ricciarelli/Valentini Terrani/Nucci/Raimondi/Ghiaurov/Murray/ Storojev/Auger; Chorus and Orchestra of La Scala, Milan / Claudio Abbado (in French). DG 415 316-2GH4 (4CDs)

- Alagna/Mattila/Meier/Hampson/van Dam/Halfvarson/Airizer/Efraty/Weir/ Donna Brown; Chorus of the Theatre du Chatelet; Orchestre de Paris / Antonio Pappano. Recorded at performances in the Theatre du Chatelet, Paris on March 10th, 13th and 16th, 1996. EMI CDS5 56152-2 (3CDs)

- Bergonz/Tebaldi//Fischer-Dieskau/Ghiaurov/Talvela/Sinclair//Franc/Wakefield; Chorus and Orchestra of the Royal Opera House, Covent Garden / Sir Georg Solti. Decca 421 114-2DH3 (3CDs)

- Fernandi/Jurinac/Bastianini/Siepi/Stefanoni/Zaccaria/Balatsch/Schmidt/Foster/ Rothenberger; Vienna State Opera Chorus; Vienna Philharmonic Orchestra / Herbert von Karajan. Recorded at a performance in the Grosser Festspielhaus, Salzburg on July 26th, 1958. DG mono 447 655-2GX2 (2CDs)

- Filippeschi/Stella/Nicolai/Gobbi/Christoff/Neri/Clabassi/di Lelio/Caroli/ Moscucci; Rome Opera Chorus and Orchestra / Gabriele Santini. EMI Opera mono CMS7 64642-2 (3CDs)

- Margison/Gorchakova/Borodina/Hvorostovsky/Scandiuzzi/Lloyd/d'Arcangelo/ Norberg-Schulz/Leggate/Roderick Williams/McNair; Chorus and Orchestra of the Royal Opera House, Covent Garden / Bernard Haitink. Philips 454 463-2PH3 (3CDs)

- Pavarotti/Dessi/d'Intino/Coni/Ramey/Anisimov/Silvestrelli/Laurenza/Zanetti/ Bolognesi/Focile; Chorus and Orchestra of La Scala, Milan / Riccardo Muti. Recorded at performances in the Teatro alla Scala, Milan during December 1992. EMI CDS7 54867-2 (3CDs)

- Sylvester/Millo/Zajick/Chernov/Furlanetto/Ramey/Plishka/Bunnell/Croft/ Horton Murray/Battle; Metropolitan Opera Chorus and Orchestra / James Levine. Sony Classical CD52500 (3CDs)

- Ghiaurov/Domingo/Cappuccilli/Malaspina/Verrett/Talvela. La Scala 19.4.70/ Abbado. Arkadia CDHP 5823 (Live)

- Domingo/Jurinac/Cossotto/Sereni/Siepi/Vinco. 1968/Varviso SRO 850-2 (Live)

Aida

- Raimondi/Obraztsova/Ricciarelli/Domingo/Nucci/Ghiaurov/De Palma/ Valentini-Terrani; La Scala Chorus and Orchestra, Milan / Claudio Abbado. DG 410 092-2GH3 (3CDs)

- Arangi-Lombardi/Capuana/Lindi/Borgioli/Pasero/Baccaloni/Nessi; Chorus of La

Scala, Milan; Milan Symphony Orchestra / Lorenzo Molajoli. VAI Audio VAIA1083 (2CDs)

- Caballe/Domingo/Cossotto/Cappuccilli/Ghiaurov/Roni/Casas/Martinucci; Chorus of the Royal Opera House, Covent Garden; New Philharmonia Orchestra; Trumpeters of the Royal Military School of Music, Kneller Hall / Riccardo Muti. EMI CDS7 47271-8 (3CDs)

- Callas/Tucker/Barbieri/Gobbi/Modesti/Zaccaria/Galassi/Ricciardi; Chorus and Orchestra of La Scala, Milan / Tullio Serafin. Digitally remastered from Columbia 33CX1318/20 (1/56). EMI CDS7 49030-8 (3CDs)

- Chiara/Dimitrova/Pavarotti/Nucci/Burchuladze/Roni/Gavazzi/Renee; Chorus and Orchestra of La Scala, Milan / Lorin Maazel. Decca 417 439-2DH3 (3CDs)

- Dragoni/Dever/Johannsson/Rucker/d'Artegna/Ferrari/Marceno/Trini; RTE Philharmonic Choir; RTE Chamber Choir; Culwick Choral Society; Bray Choral Society; Dublin County Choir; Dun Laoghaire Choral Society; Cantabile Singers; Goethe Institut Choir; Musica Sacra Singers; Phoenix Singers; Irish Army Band; Ireland National Symphony Orchestra / Rico Saccani. Naxos 8 660033/4 (2CDs)

- Leontyne Price/Domingo/Bumbry/Milnes/Raimondi/Sotin/Mathis/Brewer; John Alldis Choir; London Symphony Orchestra / Erich Leinsdorf. RCA Red Seal RD86198 (3CDs)

- Milanov/Bjorling/Barbieri/Warren/Christoff/Clabassi/Rizzoli/Carlin; Rome Opera Chorus and Orchestra / Jonel Perlea. RCA Victor GD86652 (3CDs)

- Millo/Zajick/Domingo/Morris/Ramey/Cook/Anthony/Hei-Kyung Hong; Metropolitan Opera Chorus and Orchestra / James Levine. Sony Classical CD45973 (3CDs)

- Nilsson/Bumbry/Corelli/Sereni/Giaiotti/Mazzoli/De Palma/Fiorentini; Rome Opera House Chorus and Orchestra / Zubin Mehta. EMI CMS7 63229-2 (2CDs)

- Tebaldi/Simionato/Bergonzi/Macneil/van Mill/Corena/De Palma/Ratti; Vienna Singverein; Vienna Philharmonic Orchestra / Herbert von Karajan. Decca Grand Opera 414 087-2DM3 (3CDs)

- Viner-Chenisheva/Milcheva/Nikolov/Smochevski/Ghiuselev/Tsiganchev/Vrachovski/Dimchewska; Sofia National Opera Chorus and Orchestra / Ivan Marinov. AVM Classics AVMCD1008/9 (2CDs)

- Wiener-Chenisheva/Milcheva/Nikolov/Smochevski/Ghiuselev; Sofia National Opera and Orch / Ivan Marinov. LaserLight Classics 24 421 (2CDs)

- Jones/Domingo/Cortez Vienna Staatsoper 1973/Muti. BLV 107 209 (Live)

- Callas/Baum/Simionato/Walters/Neri/Sutherland. 1953/Barbirolli LCD 187-2 (Live)

- Stella/di Stefano/Simionato/Guelfi/Zaccaria. 1956/Votto LCD 204-2 (Live)

- Lorenz/Kupper/Klose/Gonzsar/Von Rohr/Ludwig Hess RSO/Schröder. Myto 2 MCD 962 146 (Live)

- Norman/Cossotto/Lavirgen 1973/ORTF Orch/Sazogno PX 507 2 (Live)

- Callas/del Monaco/Ruffino/Dominguez/Taddei Mexico 3.7.51/de Fabritiis Virtuoso 2699222 (Live)

Otello

- Craig/Plowright/Howlett/Bottone/Kale/Squires/Rea/Rivers/Traynor; English National Opera Chorus and Orchestra / Mark Elder. Recorded at performances at the London Coliseum during January 1983 (sung in English). EMI CMS7 63012-2 (2CDs)

- Cossutta/Margaret Price/Bacquier/Dvorsky/Equiluz/Berbie/Moll/Dean/Helm; Vienna Boys' Choir; Vienna State Opera Chorus; Vienna Philharmonic Orchestra / Sir Georg Solti. Decca Grand Opera 440 045-2DMO2 (2CDs)

- del Monaco/Tebaldi/Protti/De Palma/Mercuriali/Ribacchi/Corena/Luigi/Caselli; Chorus and Orchestra of the Santa Cecilia Academy, Rome / Alberto Erede. Decca 440 245-2LF2 (2CDs)

- del Monaco/Tebaldi/Protti/Romanato/Cesarini/Corena/Satre/Krause/Arbace; Vienna State Opera Chorus; Vienna Philharmonic Orchestra; Vienna Children's Choir / Herbert von Karajan. Decca 411 618-2DH2 (2CDs)

- Domingo/Ricciarelli/Diaz/di Cesare/Zaharia/Macurdy/Malakova/Toumajian/ Pigliucci; Chorus and Orchestra of La Scala, Milan / Lorin Maazel. EMI CDS7 47450-8 (2CDs)

- Domingo/Scotto/Milnes/Little/Crook/Plishka/Kraft/King; National Philharmonic Orchestra; Ambrosian Opera Chorus / James Levine. RCA Gold Seal GD82951.

- Domingo/Studer/Leiferkus/Vargas/Schade/Graves/d'Arcangelo/Prestia/Duminy/ Hauts-de-Seine Maitrise; Chorus and Orchestra of the Opera-Bastille, Paris / Myung-Whun Chung. DG 439 805-2GH2 (2CDs)

- Giacomini/Margaret Price/Manuguerra/di Domenico/Gabriel/Mahe/Roni/le Texier/Kurnava; Slovak Philharmonic Chorus; Les Petits Chanteurs de Bordeaux; Orchestre National de Bordeaux Aquitaine / Alain Lombard. Recorded at performances in the Palais des sports, Bordeaux during March 1991. Forlane 216774 (2CDs)

- Martinelli/Rethberg/Tibbett/Massue/Paltrinieri/Votipka/Moscona/Cehanovsky; Metropolitan Opera Chorus and Orchestra / Ettore Panizza. Recorded at a performance in the Metropolitan Opera House, New York on February 12th, 1938. Music and Arts mono CD645 (2CDs)

- Martinucci/Gauci/Tumagian/Septien/Ruiz/Perelstein/Rosca/Serra; Musica Badalona Municipal Conservatory Chorus; Chorus of the Teatro Liceo, Barcelona; Barcelona Symphony Orchestra / Alexander Rahbari. Discover International DICD920435/6 (2CDs)

- Murgu/Guleghina/Bruson/Saltarin/Yoshida/Pasino/Pertusi/de Angelis; Tokyo Little Singers; Fujiwara Opera Chorus; Tokyo Philharmonic Orchestra / Gustav Kuhn. Recorded at performances in Suntory Hall, Tokyo on May 1st and 4th, 1991. Koch-Schwann 314074 (2CDs)

- Pavarotti/Te Kanawa/Nucci/Rolfe Johnson/Keyes/Ardam/Kavrakos/Opie/Cohn; Metropolitan Opera Children's Chorus; Chicago Symphony Chorus and Orchestra / Sir Georg Solti. Recorded at performances in Orchestra Hall, Chicago and Carnegie Hall, New York in April 1991. Decca 433 669-2DH2 (2CDs)

- Vickers/Rysanek/Gobbi/Andreolli/Carlin/Pirazzini/Mazzoli/Calabrese/Kerns; Rome Opera Chorus and Orchestra / Tullio Serafin. RCA Victor 8 GD81969 (2CDs)

- Vinay/Martinis/Schoeffler/Dermota/Jaresch/Wagner/Greindl/Monthy/Bierbach; Vienna State Opera Chorus; Vienna Philharmonic Orchestra / Wilhelm Furtwangler. Recorded at a performance in the Festspielhaus, Salzburg on August 7th, 1951. EMI Salzburg Festival Edition CHS5 65751-2 (2CDs)

- Vinay/Nelli/Valdengo/Assandri/Chasby/Merriman/Moscona/Newman; NBC Chorus and Symphony Orchestra / Arturo Toscanini. RCA Victor Gold Seal GD60302 (2CDs)

- Domingo/Freni/Cappuccilli. La Scala 1976/C Kleiber. 2 MCD 971 150 (Live)

- Vinay/Martinis/Schöffler/Dermota. Salzburg 7.8.51/Furtwängler. Foyer 2-CF 2002 (Live)

- Vickers/Freni/Glossop. Salzburg 10.8.70/VPO/Karajan. Foyer 2-CF 2034 (Live)

- Martinelli/Rethberg/Tibbett/Moscona. Met 12.2.38/Panizza. Music & Arts CD 645 (Live)

Falstaff

- Bruson/Nucci/Gonzalez/Sells/Egerton/Wildermann/Ricciarelli/Hendricks/ Terrani/Boozer; Los Angeles Master Chorale and Philharmonic Orchestra / Carlo Maria Giulini. Recorded at performances in the Music Center, Los Angeles on 13th–27th April, 1982. DG 410 503-2 (2CDs)

- Evans/Merrill/Ligabue/Freni/Kraus/Simionato/Elias/Lanigan/de Palma/Foiani; RCA Italiana Opera Chorus and Orchestra / Sir Georg Solti. Decca Grand Opera 417 168-2DM2 (2CDs)

- Gobbi/Panerai/Schwarzkopf/Moffo/Alva/Barbieri/Merriman/Spataro/Ercolani/ Zaccaria; Philharmonia Orchestra and Chorus / Herbert von Karajan. EMI Great Recordings of the Century CMS5 67083-2 (2CDs)

- Panerai/Titus/Sweet/Kaufmann/Lopardo/Horne/Quittmeyer/de Palma/ d'Artegna/Ress; Bavarian Radio Chorus and Symphony Orchestra / Sir Colin Davis. RCA Victor Red Seal 09026 60705-2 (2CDs)

- Pons/Frontali/Dessi/O'Flynn/Vargas/di Nissa/Ziegler/Gavazzi/Barbacini/Roni; Chorus and Orchestra of La Scala, Milan / Riccardo Muti. Recorded at performances in the Teatro alla Scala, Milan between 21st–30th June, 1993. Sony Classical S2K58961 (2CDs)

- Rimini/Ghirardini/Tassinari/Tellini/d'Alessio/Buades/Monticone/Venturini/ Nessi/Baccaloni; Chorus of La Scala, Milan; Milan Symphony Orchestra / Lorenzo Molajoli. VAI Audio VAIA1098 (2CDs)

- Taddei/Panerai/Araiza/Kabaivanska/Perry/Ludwig/Zednik/Davia/De Palma/ Schmidt; Vienna Philharmonic Orchestra; Vienna State Opera Chorus / Herbert von Karajan. Philips 412 263-2PH2 (2CDs)

- Trimarchi/Servile/Faulkner/Dilber/Comencini/di Micco/Bonitatibus/Facini/ Cosentino/de Grandis; Chorus and Orchestra of Hungarian State Opera / Will Humburg. Naxos 8660050/1 (2CDs)

- van Dam/Coni/Serra/Norberg-Schulz/Canonici/Lipovsek/Graham/Begley/ Lefebvre/Luperi; Berlin Radio Chorus; Berlin Philharmonic Orchestra / Sir Georg Solti. Recorded at concert performances in the Philharmonie, Berlin on March 6th and 8th, 1993. Decca 440 650-2DHO2 (2CDs)

- Warren/Valdengo/Resnik/Elmo/Albanese/di Stefano. NY 26.2.1949/Reiner. ARLA 85-A86 (Live)

- Gobbi/Tebaldi/Moffo/Simionato/Misciano/MacNeill. 1958/Serafin. LCD 206-2 (Live)

- Stabile/Silveri/Valletti/Tebaldi/Elmo. La Scala 26.5.51/de Sabata. Memories HR 4500/01 (Live)